Dry Borders

Dry Borders

Great Natural Reserves of the Sonoran Desert

Richard Stephen Felger and Bill Broyles, editors

 SAN DIEGO
NATURAL
HISTORY
MUSEUM

 Fondo Mexicano para
la Conservación de la
Naturaleza, A.C.

 ine
Instituto Nacional de Ecología

 ARIZONA-SONORA
DESERT
MUSEUM

 THE UNIVERSITY OF UTAH PRESS
Salt Lake City

© 2007 by The University of Utah Press. All rights reserved.

 The Defiance House Man colophon is a registered trademark of the University of Utah Press. It is based upon a four-foot-tall, Ancient Puebloan pictograph (late PIII) near Glen Canyon, Utah.

10 09 08 07 06 05   5 4 3 2 1

LIBRARY OF CONGRESS CATALOGING-IN-PUBLICATION DATA

Dry borders : great natural reserves of the Sonoran Desert / Richard Stephen Felger and Bill Broyles, editors.
    p. cm.
  Includes bibliographical references and index.
  ISBN-13: 978-0-87480-818-6 (cloth : alk. paper)
  ISBN-10: 0-87480-818-9 (cloth : alk. paper)
  ISBN-13: 978-0-87480-819-3 (pbk. : alk. paper)
  ISBN-10: 0-87480-819-7 (pbk. : alk. paper)
  1. Natural history—Sonoran Desert Region. 2. Sonoran Desert. 3. Marine animals—Mexico—California, Gulf of. I. Felger, Richard Stephen. II. Broyles, Bill.
  QH104.5.S58D79 2006
  508.72'17—dc22

                    2005028165

To

Anita Alvarez Williams,

Exequiel Ezcurra,

and

Julian D. Hayden

scholars, mentors, friends

Contents

Cinder cone halved by ocotillo, El Pinacate Lava Flow (© 2006 by Michael Berman)

The Desert Inside Us

I came for the first time to the Sierra del Pinacate in August 1980, following an invitation from Dr. Samuel Ocaña, at that time governor of the state of Sonora, to the Natural History Museum of Mexico City, where I worked as a researcher. Dr. Ocaña wanted the museum to prepare a proposal to protect the region under the designation of biosphere reserve.

It was a hot, dry, unwelcoming summer. Daytime temperatures were above 50°C (122°F). A few weeks before, a group of nineteen Salvadorans had died of dehydration and heat exhaustion trying to cross into the United States along the burning-hot Sonoyta Valley. The visit was, for me, a confrontational encounter: I did not like the place. I found it to be a dry, dusty, unfriendly, and dangerous desert, and I returned to Mexico City as soon as I could.

My spirit, however, was burning, not from the heat of the August sun but from the fire of nostalgia for the wide, open wilderness. Like a moth subdued by the dangerous light of a glowing fire, a month later I was back in the great desert, El Gran Desierto de Altar. Since then, I have never ceased to return. Swearing and mumbling against heat and drought, I was unwittingly seduced by this wonderful land. A passionate fascination grew in my heart. Slowly, gradually, the desert won my affections.

The Pinacate is an immense volcanic shield, two thousand square kilometers in size, in the heart of the Gran Desierto de Altar. It has hundreds of craters and volcanic cones. Some say six hundred, others say over a thousand. I have never counted them, and never will. I prefer to see them as they are, in their collective multitude, their throng, their sheer mass. They are definitely more than I can, or I am willing to, count.

The sierra is a true museum of vulcanology. It has colossal craters known as *calderas*, produced by immense explosions and ensuing collapse of the overlying lava layers. The largest of them are almost two kilometers wide and three hundred meters deep. Juan Mateo Manje, Father Francisco Eusebio Kino's lieutenant, described them as "immense cavities" whose sheer depth inspired "terror and awe."

In the Pinacate slopes the gigantic lava flows hang like frozen rivers of black, brittle rocks. In the deep basalt caverns thousands of bats seek refuge. They are the cupids of the desert, little gods of love that consume the sweet sticky nectar of the saguaros and carry the pollen kilometers away across the harsh Gran Desierto, so that the giant cacti can have carnal knowledge—so to speak—of other solitary plants that are patiently waiting for these winged messengers of sex to bring in the sperm of distant mates.

The flatter parts of the range show some curious formations of rocks that seem to have been laid carefully on the ground, side by side, by the skillful hand of an invisible artisan. Known as *pavements*, these surfaces are the result of the slow wind erosion of the finer soil particles. As the particles are blown away, the larger stones remain, arranging themselves on a single, neatly laid layer. Thousands of years of winds and drought have slowly built this strange and spectacular landscape.

Basalt, the black rock that forms lava, here seems to have been varnished by some prehistoric hand with a thick coating of lacquer. Known as *desert varnish*, this dark patina forms only in extreme environments—like very dry deserts or high mountains—where the lack of microorganisms and water allows the accumulation of amorphous silicates and manganese oxides. Thanks to this natural sheen we can date artifacts and rocks that have been used by ancient dwellers.

Many thousands of years ago some of the first human settlers in the sierra built large human figures with aligned stones that are discernible only from the air, like the famous Nazca figures of Peru. Based on varnish and rock alignments, we can locate the old campfires of prehistoric inhabitants. What rare calling led some of the first immigrants into the American continent to settle here, where no one dares to live today? How did they survive the extreme heat and drought? Every time I visit the Gran Desierto, these questions stay floating in my head, like a mirage in the desert's hot, turbulent midday air.

Some days the heat here is so great that the rocks fracture like brittle crystal glass. Walking in the sierra, sometimes you can hear the sounds they emit: first they utter a high-pitched screech, and then—*crack!*—they break into smaller pieces. Geologists call this phenomenon *thermoclastism*—when the rocks break as a consequence of elevated temperatures. Each time I hear one of those *cracks!* in the hot summer days, I feel the Earth is a little bit older, a little bit more experienced. A new scar has appeared on the old weather-beaten face of the desert. A new story has been recorded on the landscape, waiting for some devoted scientist to interpret it in the future.

West of the sierra, the basalt shield ends abruptly in a sea of dunes: four thousand square kilometers of sand of continental origin. Ronald Ives, an Arizona explorer who devoted his life to investigate and discover this region, was the first to realize that these sands derive from the sediments of the Lower Colorado Valley, which dried up at the end of the last glaciation, some fifteen thousand years ago, and started to move eastward, blown by the Pacific westerlies, until they hit the basalt of the Pinacate. The hypothesis has been confirmed by research on the sediments of the Upper Sea of Cortés and the Lower Colorado River Valley, where the residues produced by the erosion of the Grand Canyon have accumulated, forming a thick deposit thousands of meters deep. From this immense sedimentary mantle the dunes started blowing east. It seems almost magical to think that these gently moving dunes of soft, rounded forms are, in part, rocks of the Grand Canyon, eroded by water, transported by the river, silted, dried up, then lifted by the winds, sifted into sand, and finally deposited in the Gran Desierto. A long way indeed.

Rainfall here is scanty and unpredictable. When it rains, a pulse of life makes the arid landscape truly vibrate with activity. Some organisms are well adapted to these short-lived cycles of abundance. The annual plants survive years as seed, but when it rains they carpet the desert like a garden of flowers. Other organisms instead store water to survive times of drought. Saguaros and barrel cacti have large succulent stems, where they store last year's rainwater like a memory. To defend their watery tissues from thirsty herbivores such as bighorn sheep, mule deer, hares, or rodents, cacti have developed formidable spines and toxic compounds. The flowers, in contrast, produce abundant nectar to bribe their pollinators into their role of sexual mediators.

As annual plants—such as the evening primrose (*Oenothera deltoides*), the dune spurge (*Euphorbia platysperma*), and the sand verbena (*Abronia vilosa*)—produce so much seed, and as the perennial plants—such as cacti, creosotebushes (*Larrea divaricata*), and elephant trees (*Bursera microphylla*)—are formidably defended by spines or toxic compounds, the trophic chain of the desert is chiefly based on the consumption of seeds, which are nontoxic, easily stored, and by far the most abundant resource in times of drought. Granivory, and not herbivory, is at the base of the desert's food chain. Kangaroo rats, pack rats, ants, and birds such as the desert quail all depend on the consumption of seeds for their survival. These granivores, in turn, make primary prey for predators such as coyotes, owls, and rattlesnakes, which eat birds and rodents, or horned lizards, which consume ants.

Other, larger herbivores, like the pronghorn antelope, the bighorn sheep, or the desert gopher tortoise, consume green foliage during wet periods but can evade the effects of prolonged drought. When the plants dry up, pronghorns migrate in search of moisture pockets, bighorns ascend into the higher slopes searching for elevations where moisture has accumulated, while the tortoises enter into a state of torpor, lowering their metabolic rates until the next pulse of rain brings again a boom of growth and production to the desert.

These cycles of rainfall and drought, and the landscape mosaic of lava and sand, are what make the Gran Desierto one of the most rapidly changing and extraordinary places on earth. The beauty of this desert is rough and difficult to understand. It gets under our skin very slowly, as we unveil and understand the mysteries of these changes, the deep causes of the region's heterogeneity, the roots of its diversity.

In the Gran Desierto I developed a new view of life. The biology I studied at school had taught me that evolution was about competition, about supremacy, about killing or being killed, about nature red in tooth and claw. But here I learned, for example, about the mesquite, that wonderfully lush desert tree that taps water from deep aquifers. It would not survive if it did not have bacteria attached to its roots, fixing from the atmosphere all the nitrogen that the plant needs. And I learned here about those wasps, and butterflies, and bumblebees, and beetles that consume the honey-like nectar of the mesquite and carry the pollen across miles and miles of dunes.

I also learned about the saguaro, the gentle giant cactus that establishes under the fertile shade of the mesquite, which protects it from the harsh desert sun and feeds it with the nutrients derived from its root bacteria. And the bats that feed on cactus nectar and for months follow a botanical orgy of columnar cacti in flower, all the way from southern Mexico into Arizona.

In the desert I understood the profound meaning of all those signs of nature, like the odors of the brittlebush, the burro bush, the creosotebush, the desert lavender. A single rain in the Gran Desierto is enough to unleash the volatile fractions of all kinds of aliphatic compounds, resins, steroids, pheromones, and sweet scents; small molecules that send out signals by binding to the sensory receptors of myriad animals and attract dispersers to fruits, lure pollenizers to flowers, or charm lustful males to solitary, receptive females.

In the Gran Desierto I learned to listen to sounds of all types, like mournful songs and clicks and ultrasounds and howls and voices, which bind doves together in courtship, or keep ants on their narrow paths, or help bats to navigate in the dark, or inspire coyotes to sing to the starry dome of the night, or allow us to read aloud the field notes of Father Kino. And I learned to distinguish true colors—reds and yellows and oranges and bright blues—that signal dire warnings or offer rewards and bribes to helpful animals. After a rain, the Gran Desierto in its entirety seems to be vibrating with millions of communication signals that form a worldwide web of its own kind.

My work in the Gran Desierto changed my stereotyped image of a competitive nature, where killing and conquering was the rule for the survival of selfish genes, into a different and somewhat opposing view: Life is driven not by contest but by symbiosis and a drive for reproduction. It is not so much about supremacy as it is about cooperation between organisms and passion of the senses.

In this unique desert, a day is reached when resting under the immense mantle of stars we realize that our imagination flies there as in no other place on earth. We think of the hundreds of kilometers of solitude that surround us, and we realize with surprise that feeling so small does not produce anguish in our hearts. On the contrary, it makes us feel valuable; it gives a meaning to our connection with this great wilderness. The scale of our own smallness makes us feel part of a greater nature. When this apparent contradiction finds its nest in our emotions, we know the desert has taken hold of our hearts and of our minds. The Gran Desierto is inside us, forever. There is no way back.

—Exequiel Ezcurra

Twisted dune, Gran Desierto (© 2006 by Michael Berman)

In late afternoon a desert bighorn ram stands along the shoulder of the busy two-lane highway through the Gran Desierto in northwestern Mexico. He is waiting to cross. The flow of traffic is incessant and the noise unending. The ram is stranded, at least for this spring afternoon, cut off from others of his kind. His home range has been slashed by fence wire and a blade of asphalt, and the road is scheduled to be widened to four lanes so even more travelers can rush through this stretch, like commuters racing through a neighborhood where they neither dare nor care to stop.

We too can see them coming. The cars. The factories. The homes and trailer parks. The malls. The resorts. The people. They clamor for sun, for space, for recreation, for jobs. Residents already here aren't sure the Southwest is big enough for all comers. We live around the edges of the Sonoran Desert. Few people live in the great heart, an immense *despoblado* known as El Gran Desierto—the Grand Desert. It may be sparsely populated, but it is alluring, dynamic, important, and vivacious, alive with plants and animals that have adapted or learned to live in this sometimes harsh and frequently beautiful landscape.

By accident this heart remains a viable eco-system, largely unchanged by us humans, the ones poet e. e. cummings called "this busy monster manunkind." It has not yet been trampled or bulldozed or pumped or poisoned. What has kept the heart beating? The dearth of freshwater, the poverty of minerals, clashes of cultures, a political borderline, a bombing range, sparse forage, and a torrid climate. Our protection of this region from ourselves has too seldom been conscious.

Now, in the first years of a new millennium, we have an unprecedented opportunity—and urgency—to preserve a linked system of great natural areas and to restore much of the Colorado River delta. Governments of Mexico, the United States, and the Tohono O'odham Nation profess to care; a number of national agencies are interested in conservation; people who live here want their lifestyles and lands protected; a conservation framework has begun, but it needs completion. However, the opportunity won't last. The Colorado and its delta have been plumbed into an enormous irrigation system for fields, factories, and home faucets. The river has been wrung nearly dry before it reaches the Gulf of California, so the delta's once lush and prolific wetlands and estuaries are near death. Plants and animals have been reduced to a few surviving pockets of hope in spots like Ciénega de Santa Clara, and they wait for us to negotiate renewing flows of water. We're losing natural habitat in the Southwest at the rate of acres per hour. Scores of square miles of desert each year are forever changed, going the way of our oceans, prairies, forests, and jungles.

We have values to balance. For some people, this desert is just a void, a deserted place to plop down or set up shop; for others, it is their homeland, the source of all they have, all they know, and all they believe. The land has many values: ecological, scenic, recreational, educational, economic, spiritual, social, and scientific. Some of these values are complementary; some clash. Some renew, some deplete. Decisions must be made. Our story of the Gran Desierto and the Southwest has conflicts and crises, but it awaits resolution. We all are its authors and will write its denouement. We invite you to share its vision and help compose a story not of squander but of conservation, not of failure but of success.

We can have our desert and live here, too—but only if we inventory what we have now and work to save it from needless fragmentation, alteration, and degradation. Designations such as *biosphere, wildlife refuge, national monument,* and *wilderness* are insurance policies. But their premiums must be paid. The theme of this book is the magnificence and richness of our desert homeland—our inheritance and our legacy. With challenge comes opportunity; with understanding comes passion. This special volume is for you who live here and those who will.

We began this project with the encouragement of Joseph C. Wilder, director of the University of Arizona's Southwest Center. Joe is a visionary who makes good things happen, including the first edition of *Dry Borders* in 1997. Then we had the privilege of working with Jeffrey L. Grathwohl, director and senior editor of the University of Utah Press. Jeff was a bright lighthouse for our treasure-laden boat. We deeply appreciate the help of the rest of the Utah staff, especially production manager Jinni Fontana and managing editor Glenda Cotter, as well as freelance copyeditor Kimberley Vivier, indexer Nancy C. Ford, and marketing manager Sarah Hoffman. Our contributors, each an expert, stepped forward with their best work. Their enthusiasm was contagious; contributors and editors alike learned from this writing experience. It was genuinely exciting. For example, we cannot recount the number of late-night e-mails and early-morning phone calls made to share some new nugget of information or to ask a question. This process brought out better work from all of us. We could tell story after story—Kevin Horstman volunteering to make world-class satellite-imagery maps, Peggy Turk Boyer and Ray Turner penning their personal histories and lucid insights, Steve Nelson and Diane Boyer plotting obscure places on maps for us, and Rick Brusca, Phil Hastings, and Lloyd Findley printing out up-to-the-minute species lists. We were honored to work with our contributors, one and all, and we deeply appreciate the results. We hope this volume meets their expectations; they certainly exceeded ours.

We sincerely thank Exequiel Ezcurra for negotiating support of this book from Fondo Mexicano para la Conservación de la Naturaleza, Instituto Nacional de Ecología, and the San Diego Natural History Museum (supported, in turn, by a grant from the David and Lucile Packard Foundation). The book's dedication was in place long before we discussed funding and was not revealed until immediately prior to publication. We also acknowledge with deep gratitude support from the Arizona-Sonora Desert Museum with the help of Richard C. Brusca. These sponsors made production of this book possible. Dr. Ezcurra, Dr. Brusca, and their esteemed institutions are at the forefront of science and conservation for the Dry Borders region, and we salute their leadership.

Richard Felger's work leading to this book results from support by the Wallace Research Foundation to Drylands Institute. In fact, Linda Gray Wallace provided seed money for a project that eventually led to the first *Dry Borders* edition. We thank Joseph C. Wilder of the University of Arizona Southwest Center for making the first edition a reality. Bill Broyles is a research associate at the University of Arizona Southwest Center and gratefully appreciates its encouragement and support.

Part One

THE PLACE

One

Six Grand Reserves, One Grand Desert

Richard Stephen Felger, Bill Broyles, Michael F. Wilson, Gary Paul Nabhan, and Dale S. Turner

In the southwestern corner of the continent are the renowned Grand Canyon, Rio Grande, Great Basin, and a lesser known but equally fascinating landscape, a sun-drenched desert known locally as el gran desierto del Altar: The Grand Desert. It is a subregion at the heart of the Sonoran Desert biological zone and forms a dry borderland with the United States and Mexico. Some teasingly call it the Stinking Hot Desert and the Cactus Coast; others have seen and appreciated—or feared—parts of it and left names like the Forty Mile Desert, Tule Desert, the Malpais, Lechuguilla Desert, El Pinacate, Yuma Desert, Dry Borders, El Gran Despoblado, G—D—— Desert, and the Devil's Highway.... It deserves respect and a name to match its grandeur: the Grand Desert.

—Bill Broyles (Sunshot, 2006)

Despite its forbidding reputation as North America's fiercest desert, people have long valued the unique character of the Sonoran Desert and have worked to protect it. In 1937 a tract of this desert in southwestern Arizona was established as Organ Pipe Cactus National Monument, the first formally recognized natural area in a series of diverse, regional protected places. Other reserves followed, including the Cabeza Prieta National Wildlife Refuge in 1939 and at the outset of World War II the designation of the properties that today comprise the Goldwater Range, a military training area. In 1993 Mexico created two spectacular national biosphere reserves neighboring the protected areas in Arizona. And in 2001 the Sonoran Desert National Monument was established east of Gila Bend in Arizona (Figure 1.1).

Today we have five major protected areas and a sixth de facto area in the heart of the Sonoran Desert: Organ Pipe Cactus National Monument, Cabeza Prieta National Wildlife Refuge, and Sonoran Desert National Monument in Arizona, and Reserva de la Biosfera El Pinacate y Gran Desierto de Altar in Sonora and Reserva de la Biosfera Alto Golfo de California y Delta del Río Colorado in Sonora and Baja California. The Barry M. Goldwater Range in Arizona is not a protected area per se but generally is managed as one.

Spanning 210 miles (338 km) from San Felipe, Baja California, to just southwest of Phoenix, Arizona, these preserves cover 7,515,221 acres (3,041,410 ha), or 11.7 percent of the Sonoran Desert, making them the largest zone of contiguous protected desert anywhere in the Americas (Table 1.1). This bio-network supports a flora of at least 854 vascular plant taxa (species, subspecies, and varieties) in 447 genera and 106 families, including 91 non-native species (Felger et al., this volume, Chapter 17). This is more than one-third of the total flora of the entire Sonoran Desert—a region covering 100,000 mi^2 (310,000 km^2) in five states in Mexico and the United States (Dimmitt 2000; Shreve 1951) (Figure 1.2). We chose the name *Dry Borders* for this book because it covers about 160 of the 260 miles where the Sonoran Desert overlaps the border of the United States and Mexico.

The Environment

Soil moisture and evaporation are powerful factors influencing the distribution of plants and consequently animals in this desert region. High temperatures rival records set elsewhere in North America, and frequent winds intensify the aridity. Rainfall is largely biseasonal. Winter-spring storms originating in the Pacific Ocean can deliver widespread precipitation. Sporadic El Niño years bring exceptional amounts of winter-spring rains, which can result in spectacular displays of spring wildflowers. Monsoon summer rains are southern and tropical in origin. Often highly localized and violent, summer thunderstorms can bring heavy, brief rainfall but are sporadic and undependable.

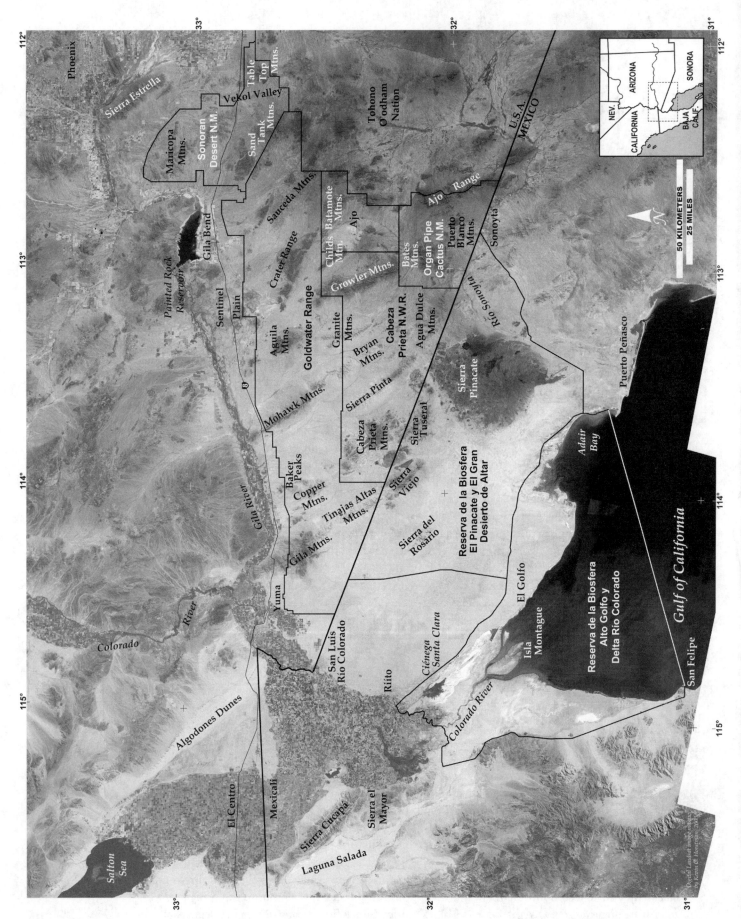

Figure 1.1. The Dry Borders region. (Digital Landsat image mosaic, © 2003 by Kevin C. Horstman)

TABLE 1.1. *Areas of the six bio-reserves (in acres).*

Alto Golfo Biosphere Reserve	2,328,349
Pinacate Biosphere Reserve	1,765,915
Goldwater Range	1,733,921
(GR-West = 691,758, GR-East = 1,042,163)	
Cabeza Prieta N.W.R.	860,010
Sonoran Desert N.M.	496,337
Organ Pipe Cactus N.M.	330,689
TOTAL	7,515,221

Occasionally, hurricane-fringe storms in late summer and fall bring deluges that produce spectacular surges in plant life.

Within the region the gradient of total annual rainfall declines from east to west and from higher to lower elevations. Annual average rainfall is less than 2 inches (50 mm) at the lower (western) elevations and at least 12 inches (300 mm) at the highest (eastern) elevations. The intensity, duration, and distribution of rainfall from one season or year to the next are highly variable and unpredictable (Comrie & Broyles 2001; Ezcurra & Rodrígues 1986; Shreve 1951). In many respects the unreliability of rainfall may have greater significance for plant life than yearly averages.

Detailed weather information for the six reserves is sketchy, but Charles Conner, who works for the National Park Service and has monitored a set of remote-sensing weather stations in Organ Pipe since the mid-1990s, reports the following readings for 2003 (personal communication). The coldest day of the year was December 28, with several low valley sites getting down to 19°F and the coldest being the Salsola site, two miles east of Blankenship Well, which recorded 11°F. Alamo Canyon, above the wash bottom, fell to 32°F, and Bull Pasture, higher up the mountain, never got below freezing. The Bull Pasture low was 33°F, typical for that site. The hottest two days of the year were July 13 and August 10. The winner was Aguajita Wash, just on the other side of the hills and east of Quitobaquito, at 122°F on August 10. Next was the Salsola site, which topped out at 116°F the same day. On July 13 two other hot sites were Growler Valley, four miles west of Bates Well, and Valley Floor, one mile west of Armenta Ranch. At both sites the temperature reached 115°F.

As for rain, Conner reports that the wettest sites in 2003 were Arch Canyon with 16.34 inches and Alamo Canyon with 15.85 inches. The driest was Growler Valley with 8.82 inches. The average of all gauges in Organ Pipe (except the Visitors' Center and the NADP site) was 11.44 inches. The maximum one-hour rain was 1.55 inches at Senita Basin on September 5. The maximum one-day rain was 3.50 inches on September 24 at Alamo Canyon. The previous day it rained 2.08 inches there, thanks to tropical depression Marty, which was easily the most significant rain event of the year. At many sites it rained continuously for 30 hours! During those same two days of Marty it rained almost 6 inches at Red Cone in the Pinacate, a site that averages little more than 3 inches annually. The maximum wind gust was 75 mph on September 1 at the Growler Valley site during a monsoon thunderstorm. Most other stations reported yearly wind maximums in the range of 40–50 mph. Publication of Conner's complete data set and the addition of more stations will boost our understanding of this region.

Plant distributions and growth are delimited here by heat, drought, and freezing. The hot weather and seasonal drought of late spring and early summer severely limit the survival and distribution of Sonoran Desert plants. Summers are long and very hot, although temperatures are generally slightly lower near the coast and at peak elevations. Maximum daily temperatures commonly exceed 100–113°F (38–45°C) from late April to early October. The highest temperature recorded for the Sonoran Desert is 134°F (56.7°C), taken in the Sierra Blanca in late June 1971 (May 1973). Winter daytime temperatures often range between 60 and 75°F (15.5–24°C), but on a few nights during each of the colder months, temperatures commonly dip several degrees below freezing. Although many species in the region are frost-sensitive, certain habitats or microhabitats can be nearly or entirely frost-free, permitting a number of species with subtropical affinities to thrive in the region.

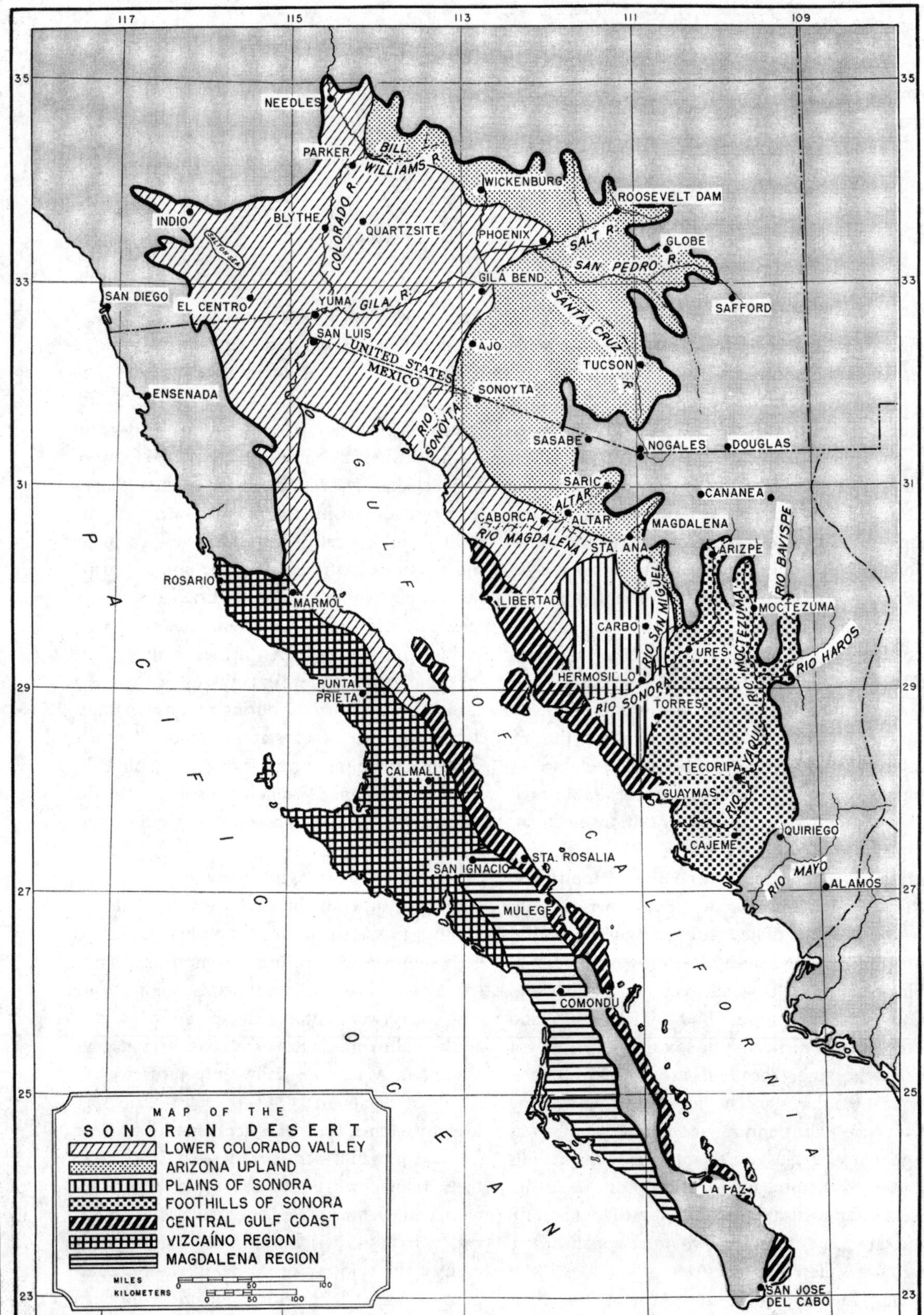
MAP OF THE
SONORAN DESERT
LOWER COLORADO VALLEY
ARIZONA UPLAND
PLAINS OF SONORA
FOOTHILLS OF SONORA
CENTRAL GULF COAST
VIZCAÍNO REGION
MAGDALENA REGION
MILES
KILOMETERS
NEEDLES
PARKER
BILL WILLIAMS R.
WICKENBURG
ROOSEVELT DAM
INDIO
BLYTHE
COLORADO R.
QUARTZSITE
PHOENIX
SALT R.
GLOBE
SAN PEDRO R.
SALTON SEA
GILA BEND
SAN DIEGO
EL CENTRO
YUMA
GILA R.
SAFFORD
SANTA CRUZ R.
SAN LUIS
AJO
UNITED STATES
MEXICO
TUCSON
ENSENADA
SONOYTA
RIO SONOYTA
SASABE
NOGALES
DOUGLAS
SARIC
CANANEA
ALTAR
CABORCA
RIO MAGDALENA
MAGDALENA
STA. ANA
ARIZPE
RIO BAVISPE
ROSARIO
MARMOL
LIBERTAD
MOCTEZUMA
CARBO
RIO SAN MIGUEL
URES
RIO MOCTEZUMA
RIO HAROS
HERMOSILLO
RIO SONORA
TORRES
PUNTA PRIETA
RIO YAQUI
TECORIPA
CALMALLI
GUAYMAS
QUIRIEGO
CAJEME
STA. ROSALIA
SAN IGNACIO
RIO MAYO
ALAMOS
MULEGE
COMONDU
LA PAZ
SAN JOSE DEL CABO
PACIFIC OCEAN
GULF OF CALIFORNIA

Figure 1.2. The Sonoran Desert. (Map from Shreve 1951)

Topography and habitats are highly varied. The area is Basin and Range terrain with northwest-southeast-trending granitic ranges and many younger mountains of volcanic origin. There are tidal wetlands, maritime strands, expansive dune fields, desert plains, desert oases, a once-great river and its delta, rugged mountains, an enormous black and red volcanic field with lava flows, cinder cones, and formidable craters (Hartmann 1989; Lumholtz 1912). The two Mexican biosphere reserves, the Cabeza Prieta Refuge, the lower elevations and approximately the western four-fifths of the Goldwater Range, and the western margin of Organ Pipe Cactus Monument are within Shreve's (1951) Lower Colorado River Valley subdivision of the Sonoran Desert—the most arid portion of this desert. Most of Organ Pipe Cactus National Monument and Sonoran Desert National Monument and approximately the eastern one-fifth of the Goldwater Range are in the Arizona Upland subdivision of the Sonoran Desert (Brown 1982; Shreve 1951). The entire region falls within the Sonoran Warm Desertscrub vegetation type identified by Barbour and Christensen (1993) and the Sonoran Biotic Province in use by biogeographers and zoologists (Ramamoorthy et al. 1993).

The desert's carrying capacity is highly variable. Except for larger mammals and migratory birds, desert animals tend toward r-selection reproductive strategies, as opposed to K-selection. These r-selection, or boom-or-bust, populations respond to feast-or-famine surges in resources. R-selection is consistent with "an unstable environment with unpredictable resources, catastrophic mortality, highly variable population size, rapid development, a short life span, small body size and high productivity" (Louw & Seely 1982:89). Prey populations drive predator populations. On the other hand, larger, K-selected mammals such as desert bighorn sheep undergo steadier population cycles with individuals growing more slowly and living longer. Although a number of external factors influence their populations, "density-dependent mechanisms have evolved within individual [bighorn] animals to regulate growth and to curtail it short of destruction of habitat" (Krausman et al. 1999:180). The food chain is complex, and even larger animals such as coyotes are omnivorous. By individual numbers and combined mass, termites and ants are the largest animal group per unit of area and have enormous though incompletely understood effects on the ecosystem (Jones & Nutting 1989; MacKay 1991). Desert ecology is intricate and mysterious, with much research ongoing (Cartron et al. 2005; Moreno 1992; Polis 1991; Robichaux 1999; Schmidt 1989; Sowell 2001).

Growth of perennial plants generally may be slow, and recruitment may occur sporadically instead of regularly or annually. Saguaro populations, for example, are maintained by surges in recruitment that may occur decades apart under natural conditions here in northern parts of the species' range. They need the right combination of summer rains and moderate winters, coupled with enough nurse plants to protect tender young plants through their most vulnerable years (Pierson & Turner 1998; Steenbergh & Lowe 1977; Turner 1990). Bursages, among the ubiquitous and essential desert species, may live more than a century but may require 30 to 100 years to revegetate areas heavily impacted by humans (Artz 1989). Prehistoric trails and campsites remain visible after millennia; modern dirt roads and runways remain largely barren compared with neighboring ground, except for sporadic ephemeral growth. Plant biomass per unit of desert area is low compared with other regions. Production of dry mass vegetation in a desert ranges from 0 to 250 grams per square meter per year, whereas grasslands range from 200 to 1,500 grams and rain forests range from 1,000 to 3,500 grams (Ludwig 1987; Sowell 2001). Restoration of larger areas disturbed by humans to a state resembling the previous mature, balanced plant community is neither economically feasible nor biologically probable within a human lifetime. It is far easier, cheaper, and more effective to protect areas from such disturbance.

We acknowledge the practical difficulties of governing and managing an arid international borderland. Although it has become commonplace to say that nature does not recognize political boundaries, the reality of the twenty-first century is that conservation efforts and administrative policies often begin or end at political or agency boundaries, as do sound land management decisions and environmental protections.

Regional Conservation History

The Dry Borders region, with its vast tracts of once-remote federal land on both sides of the international border, has experienced a series of historic attempts at protective land-management.

In the early 1930s the U.S. Congress, Interior Department, and Government Land Office were working on plans to assign and administer about eighty million acres of public lands, primarily in the West. The Taylor Grazing Act of 1934 grew out of this process, for example. In Arizona, west of the Tohono O'odham Reservation and State Highway 85 between Ajo and Buckeye, sat over five million acres of public land that seemed to have little economic value for grazing, mining, homesteading, or settlement. The mines at Fortuna and Castle Dome had played out; the few brave homesteaders had gone broke and fled the area; grazing was seasonal and unprofitable. The Grazing Service, Biological Survey, and National Park Service were already players in southwestern Arizona.

A number of citizens and professional conservationists began thinking ahead: how can we best protect, conserve, and feature the region's interesting scenery, plants and animals, and history and archaeology? In a memo to his boss on April 18, 1931, National Park Service naturalist Edwin D. McKee outlined five worthy candidates for new monuments: the organ pipe cactus, saguaro cactus, and Joshua tree, as well as Tinajas Altas and California's Picacho Peak (Eden 1956). The desert bighorn sheep and native palm were also recommended for protection.

In February 1932 Yellowstone National Park superintendent Roger Toll made a trip to southwestern Arizona to evaluate a prospective national monument to save the organ pipes and a game refuge to save the bighorn; he filed his favorable report with the National Park Service director on March 31, 1932. A group of supporters formed, including Congresswoman Isabella Greenway (who lived in Ajo and was the wife of Col. John C. Greenway, head of Phelps Dodge Mining Company); Frank H. Hitchcock (former postmaster general in President Taft's cabinet, controlling partner of the *Tucson Citizen* newspaper, and a major proponent of the highway from Tucson to Mount Lemmon); University of Arizona professors Charles T. Vorhies, Homer L. Shantz, and John J. Thornber; U.S. Biological Survey researcher Walter P. Taylor; and Carnegie Desert Laboratory ecologists Forrest Shreve and Dwight Mallory. A number of these individuals were active in the influential Tucson Natural History Society.

Early in 1933 Toll made a second reconnaissance. His report of March 7, 1933, recommended establishment of both Organ Pipe and Saguaro national monuments. In the spring of 1934 members of the Tucson Natural History Society conducted an outing to the proposed Organ Pipe monument (see Tad Nichols, this volume). Their enthusiasm for the monument generated resolutions of support from the Natural History Society and the Pima County Board of Supervisors (which, with the University of Arizona, was a catalyst in creation of Saguaro National Monument east of Tucson in 1933). Isabella Greenway agreed: "You have no idea how directly to my heart this proposal goes as for many years I have been driving between our home [in Ajo] and Tucson, and felt that this should be done" (Greenway 1934).

Buoyed by Toll's report, in 1934 the group of supporters expanded to include Frank Pinkley (director of Southwestern National Monuments and father of a number of Arizona's historic and archaeological monuments), Arno B. Cammerer (director of the National Park Service), and Harold L. Ickes (secretary of the interior). On November 19, 1934, Ickes hosted a meeting of Park Service superintendents, leaders, and staff in Washington, D.C., and issued them a challenge: "I want as much wilderness, as much nature preserved and maintained as possible" (Watkins 1990:550). Ickes had been appointed secretary in 1933, but his appetite for "crown jewels," as he called them, was whetted in 1933 with White Sands National Monument, New Mexico; Death Valley National Monument, California; Black Canyon of the Gunnison National Monument, Colorado; and Saguaro National Monument; and in 1934 with Florida's Everglades National Park and the Thomas Jefferson Memorial in Washington, D.C., among others.

The first plan for southwestern Arizona was to use the Antiquities Act of 1906 to create an enormous desert national monument four to five million acres in size. It would have encompassed most of the public land between Highway 85 and the Colorado River and south from what is now Interstate 10 to the Mexican border, and it would incorporate four of the five feature species: desert bighorn, saguaro cactus, organ pipe cactus, and desert fan palm *(Washingtonia filifera)*, as well as McKee's selection, Tinajas Altas. Early resistance came from Arizona's governor, W. P. Hunt, who called it an attempt to create "a damned billy goat pasture." The Arizona Small Mine Owners Association, Arizona Wool Growers Association, and

Arizona Cattle Growers Association, as well as the Yuma County Board of Supervisors, Yuma Valley Rod and Gun Club, and the Soil Conservation Service, also railed against the plan (Demaray 1936; Hayden 1936). Some political leaders were afraid that the monument or refuge would somehow jeopardize proposed irrigation projects along the Colorado and Gila rivers, though no clear threat or connection was made. In response, the Interior Department whittled down the proposal. The Yuma Chamber of Commerce, however, did support creation of the Kofa Wildlife Refuge (Dunbar 1935), while the Tucson Chamber of Commerce backed Organ Pipe Cactus National Monument (Mackenzie 1935).

One of the proponents, ecologist W. B. Mc-Dougall, reported, "We especially commend for favorable consideration steps of international cooperation in the creation of an international monument, or possibly an international park, in connection with the proposed organ-pipe national monument in Arizona and international refuges along . . . [the Arizona] portions of the international border" (1935). A June 1935 report by a team from Southwest National Monuments summarized the opportunity and the threats: "There is sufficient desert growth in addition to organ pipe and saguaro to give a rather typical cross section of Arizona desert vegetation. This desert growth with its setting of reddish burnt looking mountains is well worth the time of the traveler who appreciates the desert. It is desirable that the area be reserved as a national monument in order to be properly controlled. Without control haphazard blazing of desert roads, fruitless mining ventures, wholesale removal of interesting cacti and other desert plants and the unrestricted slaughter of Mountain Sheep will be the rule" (Eden 1956:16; see Davis 1957). They could have added the enormous loss of archaeological artifacts to pot hunters, who have blurred our potential understanding of prehistoric people in the region. Other reports also supported new monuments and refuges (Pinkley 1935b; Taylor 1935a, b).

Organ Pipe Cactus National Monument was established by Franklin D. Roosevelt by declaration on April 13, 1937. It was 330,000 acres (133,551 ha) in size, not the larger monument whose boundaries were beyond Organ Pipe and Cabeza Prieta combined. The King of Arizona (Kofa) National Monument, also known as the Castle Dome refuge,

was not established. It would have included the Kofa, Castle Dome, Eagle Tail, Dome Rock, and Trigo mountains in an "opportunity to preserve one of the great ranges of the Bighorn sheep," as well as desert fan palms (Pinkley 1935a:12).

The Interior Department then suggested two wildlife refuges, one west of Organ Pipe and encompassing an area of about two million acres (roughly today's Cabeza Prieta plus the Goldwater Range west of Highway 85), the other centered in the Kofa Mountains and covering at least one and a half million acres from the Eagletail Mountains nearly to the Colorado River (Figure 1.3). A jurisdictional dispute between the U.S. Biological Survey and the Grazing Service complicated the discussion. And again, opposition from sheep and cattle growers, small miners, and citizens in the Yuma area threatened to derail plans for the Cabeza Prieta and Kofa game ranges. Opposition rhetoric of that time echoes objections still heard today from some sectors: "I protest against the proposed withdrawal from entry . . . of two large areas of land in Southwestern Arizona comprising 3,400,000 acres for use and propagation of mountain sheep and goats [sic] and as game refuge. . . . Even hilly land adjacent to farming areas should be left open to entry for settlers thereon for grazing stock. Suitable rougher areas can be found for game, but game protection gets out of its natural and integrated sphere and is ruinous to conservation of water and soil resources and economy and social values and rights if used as a pretext to destroy Arizona and proper watershed development and nation's agriculture on which people fundamentally subsist" (Gibbons 1937; see also Arizona Colorado River Commission 1937).

It was suggested at a meeting of the Arizona Wildlife Federation that supporters mount a public campaign and involve the Boy Scouts of America. Frederick R. Burnham, who was born in Minnesota, grew up in California, fought in the Boer War in South Africa, and made a fortune in mining stock and properties, had a keen interest in saving big game species such as the desert bighorn (see Burnham 1928). While in South Africa, Burnham became close friends with General Robert Baden-Powell, founder of the Boy Scout movement, and continued his affiliation with scouting when he returned to the United States. To rally public support, Burnham asked George F. Miller, Scout executive in Phoenix, to adopt the refuge proposal as

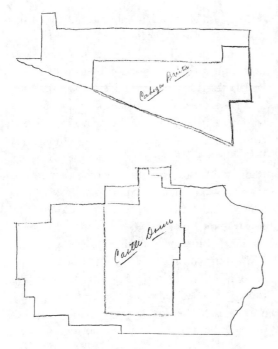

Figure 1.3a, b. Proposals for larger Cabeza Prieta and Kofa wildlife refuges, 1935 (Taylor 1935a). In both cases the smaller areas eventually were adopted (see Figure 1.1).

a conservation project. The organizational meeting was held February 3, 1938 (Simms 1938). After a year and the effort of ten thousand Boy Scouts, public opinion aligned with the refuges. Despite continued opposition of small miners and cattlemen, Arizona's congressional delegation, led by Senator Carl Hayden, encouraged the Interior Department and the Roosevelt administration to establish the refuges (Saxton 1978), although a few concessions were included to placate the opposition. The Kofa was proclaimed on January 18, 1939, and the Cabeza Prieta followed on January 25. Burnham attended the dedication ceremonies at both the Cabeza Prieta and the Kofa. John C. Phillips, who had accompanied the Carnegie Expedition to the Pinacate in 1907 (Hornaday 1908) and served as chairman of the American Game Association, also worked assiduously for creation of the two game refuges (e.g., Phillips 1931; see also Hornaday 1906, 1913, 1931).

By 1943 most of the land had been parceled. Instead of a four- or five-million-acre national monument with comparable land set aside in Mexico, U.S. officials established Organ Pipe Cactus National Monument (1937), Cabeza Prieta National Wildlife Refuge (1939), Kofa National Wildlife Refuge (1939), Goldwater Range (1940), and U.S. Army Yuma Proving Ground (1943). The Kofa National Wildlife Refuge encompasses 665,400 acres (269,287 ha); Yuma Proving Ground is 838,174 acres (335,269 ha). Mexico set aside Sierra Pinacate as a

protected forestry zone (*parque nacional*) in 1979 and then trumped it with the two biosphere reserves in 1993 (Búrquez & Martínez-Yrízar, this volume).

Small mining claims and grazing rights issues in each of these areas continued to bedevil land managers until at least the mid-1970s, though neither activity was profitable. In 1940 both the Ajo Chamber of Commerce and the Gila Bend Lions Club sensed the importance of tourism to the region and dismissed the arguments in favor of mining and grazing. Instead, they passed resolutions promoting the refuge and monument and even suggested changing the status of Organ Pipe to Arizona Desert National Park, where both mining and grazing would be excluded (Eden 1956). In 1949 Arizona congressman Harold Patten introduced legislation, H.R. 6234, to establish this national park, but it died in committee (Davis 1957).

The debate ended in a stalemate, but grazing and mining eventually were phased out anyway. Ironically for the hunters who opposed the larger monument that would have fostered desert bighorn, prospectors and small miners took a number of bighorn as camp meat, and local livestock spread diseases, both activities contributing significantly to bighorn declines (Carmony & Brown 1993; Russo 1956). Also, the Goldwater Range and Yuma Proving Grounds have seldom been open to public visitation; even today visitors must obtain permits, many or most portions are off limits, and any or all of the areas may be closed at the discretion of the base commanders. With further irony, all the areas are now closed to mining and grazing, except for a few limited grazing permits in Sonoran Desert National Monument. One wonders what the landscape and biotic community would look like today if visionary conservationists had not pushed for creation of the early monuments and refuges.

Some places within the Goldwater, Cabeza, and Organ Pipe subsequently received added layers of protection. The Cabeza Prieta Refuge gained "natural areas," which received additional shielding with a wilderness designation. Organ Pipe was declared a biosphere reserve, and much of it was designated wilderness. Parts of the Pinacate and Alto Golfo are national biosphere reserve core areas that exclude commercial activities or development. The Goldwater Range added "areas of critical environmental concern" and "habitat management areas," but those became moot after the Department of Defense assumed range management in 2001.

There have been several attempts to restore that large, integral tract of land that was available in 1935 by redrawing management boundaries and combining lands under one agency. During the Kennedy and Johnson administrations, efforts arose to create an international park using Organ Pipe Cactus National Monument as a core area. In 1965 congressional legislation (H.R. 11695) and a Department of Interior proposal were put forward to create a Sonoran Desert National Park, which would have combined Organ Pipe Cactus National Monument, Cabeza Prieta National Wildlife Refuge, and 80,000 acres (32,376 ha) of the Tinajas Altas area. Support came from a number of directions, including scientifically based, sound ecosystem management. One advocate, Frederick Gehlbach, asserted: "Above all, I support a Gran Desierto International Park, connecting Organ Pipe Cactus and Cabeza Prieta preserves with the Gila and Tinajas Altas ranges in Arizona and the extraordinary wilderness southward, the Desierto de Altar, Sonora. This oft-mentioned but untried wildland could be North America's greatest desert museum, at least twelve thousand square miles in extent, matched only by the Sierra Madre in its vastness" (1981:277). The proposal has not yet been fulfilled (see Udall, this volume), but it resurfaced in 1993 (Broyles 1993; Davis 1999; Sonoran Desert National Park Friends 1999; Yetman 1994).

The Six Major Reserves
Reserva de la Biosfera El Pinacate y Gran Desierto de Altar

This reserve, protecting El Pinacate and El Gran Desierto, was created by presidential proclamation in 1993 (Búrquez 1998). It covers 714,656 ha of the Gran Desierto in northwestern Sonora. There are two designated *zonas nucleas*, or protected (core) areas: Zona Sierra El Pinacate, covering 228,113 ha, and Zona Sierra del Rosario, covering 41,392 ha. Surrounding the two nuclear areas are 445,151 ha of managed-use and buffer area *(zona de amortiguamiento)*. Management is vested in Mexico's Ministry of Environment and Natural Resources (SEMARNAT), through the National Commission of Natural Protected Areas (CONANP), with headquarters in Mexico City and locally at the reserve office north of Puerto Peñasco, Sonora. Búrquez and Castillo (1994) describe the reserve.

The larger core area, Sierra El Pinacate, is dominated by a volcanic shield formed by a series of eruptions spanning the past two to three million years (Lynch 1981), with some major flows and cones as young as 12,000 years B.P. ± 4,000 years (Gutmann et al. 2000). This volcanic field is mostly in Sonora, but there are a few cones and flows on the Arizona side of the border. The field includes Volcán Santa Clara, also known as Sierra Pinacate or Sierra Santa Clara, numerous cinder cones, extensive lava flows, and some of the world's most spectacular steam-blast (maar) craters. Also included are granitic sawtooth ranges, such as the Sierra Blanca and the Sierra Hornaday, straddled by the more recent volcanic field. Perennial water can be found in a few rock basin catchments called *tinajas* (Broyles 1996).

The area is rugged, with sandy plains to about 100 m and then basalt layers and flows rising to Pinacate Peak at 1,206 m (about 3,957 ft). The entire reserve including the buffer areas supports a flora of 427 species, varieties, and subspecies (Ezcurra et al. 1987; Felger 2000; Felger et al., this volume, Chapter 17). Somewhat cooler and moister than the surrounding lowland desert, the mountaintop is a biological sky island. The smaller core area, Sierra del Rosario, includes most of the granitic Sierra del Rosario and extensive surrounding dune fields (Felger 1980, 2000). No perennial or even intermittent surface water exists in this extremely arid zone.

The buffer area incorporates major sections of eolian dunes, which form the largest sand sea, or erg, in North America. Mexico Highway 2 runs through the northern edge of the buffer area. The highway weaves through a series of steep, northwest-trending granitic ranges. These pre-Tertiary ranges continue northward into the Cabeza Prieta Refuge and the Goldwater Range.

Small-scale cattle grazing and associated human activities, mostly at the northern margins of the region, have damaged local areas, especially some of the waterholes, such as Tinajas de los Pápagos. Limited recreation, ranching, and cinder mining are allowed in the region. These activities are significant threats to the natural environment, as are wood cutting, off-road vehicle traffic, chemical pollution from agriculture, proposed industrial plants, and groundwater pumping to supply the growing urban areas of Sonoyta, Puerto Peñasco, and San Luis Río Colorado. At one time an illegal road from Campo Rojo to the saddle between Pinacate and Carnegie peaks exposed the area to introduction of exotic plants and poaching and harassment of wildlife. A planned coast highway, probably near the existing railroad along the boundary with the Alto Golfo Reserve, will have devastating environmental consequences.

Opportunities exist to expand the biosphere and add protections. As Exequiel Ezcurra noted, "The core areas of both the Pinacate and the Alto Golfo Biosphere Reserves might be enhanced. A more strict regime to protect the fisheries of the Upper Gulf could be established. The remainder of the Gran Desierto dunes could be also included in the protected area. The Mesa de Santa Clara, one of the richest fossil grounds in the region, could be also protected. The oases and wetlands of the Adair Bay could be included under a permanent protection regime, as wetland sanctuaries" (personal communication, 2003).

Reserva de la Biosfera Alto Golfo de California y Delta del Río Colorado

The Alto Golfo de California y Delta del Río Colorado Biosphere Reserve was created by presidential proclamation in 1993 (Figure 1.4; Morales-Abril 1994). Management is vested in Mexico's Ministry of Environment and Natural Resources (SEMARNAT), through the National Commission of Natural Protected Areas (CONANP), with headquarters in Mexico City and locally at the reserve office in San Luis R.C., Sonora. The 942,270-ha reserve overlies the delta of the Río Colorado, the uppermost reaches of the Gulf of California, and adjacent Sonoran Desert coastal areas of northwestern Sonora and northeastern Baja California. About 60 percent of the reserve area is ocean, spanning the gulf north of a line between San Felipe, Baja California, and Puerto Peñasco, Sonora. The *zona nucleo*, or core area, covers 160,620 ha and includes the delta, with Islas Montague and Gore, the Ciénega de Santa Clara, and the associated El Doctor wetlands. The surrounding buffer zone *(zona de amortiguamiento)* includes the saline mud flats and extreme desert north of San Felipe, extensive areas of the Mesa de Sonora, the La Salina *pozos* (pools), tidal wetlands of Adair Bay, and the desert between the Pinacate reserve and Adair Bay.

The delta shores rise to extremely arid mesas, badlands, sandbar islands, and dunes. The highest elevations are about 50 m on bluffs above the shore east of El Golfo, with a few peripheral hills of about 200 m. These areas, most of which remain in relatively pristine condition, support sparse perennial vegetation and a relatively small but specialized flora (Felger 2000). Rainfall is scant, but maritime dew is frequently heavy, and during winter and spring the coastal plants are often wet at dawn from condensation.

Upwellings of freshwater near the coast form widely scattered pools called *pozos*. These small freshwater oases often occur in the midst of highly saline flats—thick salt crusts devoid of vegetation. The pozos are biologically rich, especially those at La Salina and near the El Doctor wetlands (Felger 2000). The pozo plants represent remnant populations of the original delta flora (Ezcurra et al. 1988). However, as demands for urban freshwater grow, the threat to these pozos grows as well. Puerto Peñasco, for example, relies on well water from marginal aquifers piped some distance. As resorts, condominiums, golf courses, de facto American expatriate communities, and commercial enterprises multiply around the Gulf of California, the supply of freshwater will become increasingly problematic and unsustainable. American development brings welcome income to Mexican communities, but it also poses predictable consequences for ecosystems. Some Mexican citizens see it as an Americanization of Mexico and a mixed economic blessing (Weiner 2003). This American explosion also threatens to subvert Mexican local culture and politics.

Daily tidal fluctuations are extreme, reaching 9 m at the delta. During the 1850s and 1860s steamboats regularly plied the river from the delta to Yuma (Lingenfelter 1978; Sykes 1937), although thundering tidal bores and devastating tides wreaked havoc on the light steamers and other boats (Nelson, this volume). The delta, nourished by annual floods, was the fountain of life for the entire region: marine, freshwater, and terrestrial (Brusca, this volume; Glenn & Nagler, this volume).

"About 45 species of marine algae, also known as seaweeds, flourish on the surfaces of rocks and carpet the bottoms and pools in the Northern Gulf of California" (Woo et al. 2004:133), and most of these species are covered in Brusca et al. 2004, a seashore guidebook. The diverse seaweeds of the northern gulf are elegantly illustrated and discussed by Norris (1975), and more recent taxonomic and ecological studies include works by Aguilar-Rosas et al. (2002), Espinoza Avalos (1993), and McCourt (1983).

Twentieth-century dams and diversions as far north as Wyoming and Colorado have reduced the once-mighty Colorado River to a memory. The vanquished delta has almost entirely withered to dried mud and sterile, saline flats. Prolific fisheries have declined, and shrimping and fishing have been restricted. Of special concern are the endangered fish *totoaba (Totoaba macdonaldi)*; the Gulf of California harbor porpoise, or *vaquita (Phocoena sinus)*; and large populations of pupfish *(Cyprinodon macularius)* in the Ciénega de Santa Clara (Hastings & Findley, this volume; Navarro, this volume; Varela-Romero et al. 2002). Salinized water, pollution, overfishing, and agriculture continue to threaten the remaining delta ecosystem (e.g., Varady et al. 2003).

The documented vascular flora of the reserve includes at least 174 species, varieties, and subspecies (Felger 2000; Felger et al., this volume, Chapter 17). The original delta flora may have included 200 to 400 species (Ezcurra et al. 1988), but only a small fraction was recorded. Riverside riparian forests survived until upriver diversions and dams decimated the river. Cottonwoods and willows survive only as scattered trees along irrigation ditches in agricultural areas or as cultivated trees. The associated plants and animals are gone or barely hanging on. Despite the tremendous damage, remnants of a rich ecosystem persist, such as the great Ciénega de Santa Clara and associated El Doctor wetlands (see Felger 2000; Glenn at al. 1992; Glenn & Nagler, this volume).

Current investigations indicate there is considerable subsurface and some surface water flowing into the delta (see Glenn & Nagler, this volume). Restoration might be accomplished through organic agriculture, wise use of both urban and agricultural wastewater, improved quality of water discharged by upriver users, and leasing water as well as securing temporary rights to groundwater (Pitt et al. 2002). Maintaining a minimum flow of 4×10^7 m³, with occasional floods of 3.2×10^8 m³ about every four years, representing less than 1 percent of the river's annual average flow, could revive and sustain substantial parts of the delta wetlands (Glenn et al. 1996; Pitt 2001).

Figure 1.4. Dedication of Pinacate Biosphere Reserve, 1993, by President Carlos Salinas. (Photo courtesy CEDO)

Cabeza Prieta National Wildlife Refuge

The Cabeza Prieta National Wildlife Refuge was established as a game range by the U.S. government in 1939. In 1976 sole jurisdiction was transferred to the Fish and Wildlife Service of the Department of the Interior. The refuge comprises 860,010 acres (348,046 ha) in western Pima and eastern Yuma counties, Arizona. Congress designated 803,416 acres (325,142 ha) of the refuge a wilderness area in the Arizona Desert Wilderness Act of 1990. At one time four designated "natural areas" gave added protection and biological focus to the Sierra Pinta (5,120 acres; 2,072 ha), Pinacate (5,120 acres; 2,072 ha), Kearney sumac area of the Cabeza Prieta Mountains (23,040 acres; 9,324 ha), and Antelope Flat (57 acres; 23 ha; Arizona State Parks Board 1985), but their administrative meaning today is unclear. The refuge's total acreage includes ten acres in Ajo at the headquarters. Thirty acres of state land adjacent to the headquarters could be added to the visitors' center and developed with self-guided nature trails, a botanical garden, and native plant nursery (FWS 1998). A visitors' overlook and nature trail were developed near the summit of Childs Mountain in 2000.

Five major valleys interlie the main mountain ranges on a northwest orientation. Granite, gneiss, and basalt constitute the common rock types and form the valley sediment. Major washes also trend northwest, except for three internally draining playas around the south end of Sierra Pinta. The summit of the refuge is in the Growler Mountains at 3,293 feet (1,004 m), and the low point is 680 feet (207 m) on San Cristobal Wash. Special habitats include the Pinta Sands, the northern arm of the Pinacate Lava Flow, and the playas.

Perennial water can be found in several tinajas and one spring (Broyles 1996). As in the remaining part of the Goldwater Range, most of the natural waterholes have been artificially enlarged and several *represos* (stock ponds) have been built by game managers. Although the "improved" waterholes provide habitat for migratory birds, they also increase the feral honeybee population, which harms the diverse and unique native pollinator bees (Buchmann & Nabhan 1996), and they are of questionable value for target animal species (Broyles 1995; Broyles & Cutler 1999).

The flora includes 418 species, varieties, and subspecies of vascular plants (see Simmons 1966 and Felger et al., this volume, Chapter 17). Most of the refuge remains exceptionally natural and undisturbed. Endangered animals include the Sonoran pronghorn *(Antilocapra americana sonoriensis)* and the lesser long-nosed bat *(Leptonycteris curasoae yerbabuenae),* which also inhabit the Pinacate, Organ Pipe, and Goldwater Range reserves.

Recreational use consists largely of camping, hiking, and vehicular travel, primarily on the Tacna Road and El Camino del Diablo. Grazing and mining are prohibited. The military makes extensive use of low-level airspace over most of the refuge. Except for a few isolated locations where telemetry equipment for monitoring aircraft is installed, there are no authorized ground-based uses of the refuge by the military. The Air Force now restricts most gunnery training to locations north of the refuge. Frequent noise, including sonic booms from training flights over the refuge, can be annoying, but the precise environmental effects, if any, are unknown. A communications and radar center atop Childs Mountain (FAA 1998) may adversely affect the mountain's bighorn herd and the visual appeal of the refuge and surrounding area.

The major problem on the refuge is the enormous amount of illegal foot and vehicular traffic: both drug smugglers and undocumented aliens attempt to slip across the border here. These uninvited visitors have blazed miles of new roads, have abandoned vehicles, and in places have radically disturbed the character of the land and the wilderness. This environmental disaster is aggravated by the efforts of motorized law officers to search for and apprehend or rescue the offenders,

some of whom die of thirst (see Annerino 1999). A similar dire situation exists in Organ Pipe Cactus National Monument and the Goldwater Range.

Barry M. Goldwater Range

The Goldwater Range is a 1,733,921-acre (701,718 ha) Air Force and Marine Corps aerial training range established early in 1941. At one time known as Luke Air Force Range, it was renamed in 1986 in honor of Arizona's long-time senator, Barry Goldwater (1909–98) (Figure 1.5). In 1941 Goldwater, then an officer in the Army Air Corps under the command of Lt. Col. Ennis C. Whitehead, served there and helped establish the range's boundaries. The range was inactive between 1946 and 1952 (Homburg et al. 1994), which explains a surge of attempts during those years to prospect and ranch this land for commercial use (e.g., Papago Indian Chief Mine, Monreal Well). Legal boundary descriptions are in Federal Register Document 87–9191 (April 17, 1987) and the Defense Authorization Act of 1999. Resources and environmental issues are covered in Tunnicliff et al. (1986) and Hall et al. (2001).

Until the Defense Authorization Act of 1999, the land surface of this area was jointly managed by the Air Force, Marine Corps, and Bureau of Land Management (BLM). As of 2001 the eastern range (1,042,163 acres; 421,763 ha) is managed by the Air Force, with headquarters at Luke Air Force Base, west of Phoenix. It is referred to as BMGR-East. The western range (691,758 acres; 279,954 ha) is managed by the Marines from their air station in Yuma and is known as BMGR-West.

The northeastern portion of the range is in Maricopa County, the western portion lies in Yuma County, and a segment north of the Cabeza Prieta Refuge is in Pima County. The Goldwater Range lies south of Interstate Highway 8, and approximately one-third of it is east of Highway 85. The range is an important training facility because of its open airspace and its proximity to bases in Yuma, Phoenix, Tucson, and San Diego.

Six major valleys with large washes separate seven main mountains oriented northwest. As in the Cabeza Prieta Refuge, granite, gneiss, and basalt constitute the common rock types. The Mohawk Dunes occupy the eastern part of the Mohawk Valley, and other eolian dune fields occupy the southwestern part of the range. The highest elevation is 4,021 feet (1,226 m) in the Sand Tank

Mountains, and the low point is 186 feet (57 m) at the range's southwestern corner. The northeastern portion of the Sand Tank Mountains was released from the range in 1999 and formed the impetus for creation of Sonoran Desert National Monument.

The flora includes 510 species, varieties, and subspecies of vascular plants (Felger et al., this volume, Chapter 17). There is considerable change in vegetation and flora across the range's broad span. At its southwestern margin, along the international border, the climate is arid in the extreme. In contrast, the northeastern part of the range, lying at higher elevations, has more rainfall and supports a number of species not found at lower elevations farther west, such as crucifixion thorn (*Canotia holacantha*), *Hybanthus verticillatus*, white four o'clock (*Mirabilis albida*), and Arizona scarlet-bugler (*Penstemon subulatus*).

Although the Goldwater Range was established to provide an area for aerial bombing and gunnery training, destruction from those activities has been limited, with the result that vast tracts of desert have been saved from disruptive activities such as highways, mining, livestock grazing, and intensive recreation, which have altered other desert areas. Military land use includes aerial bombing and gunnery target complexes, vehicle use on approved roads, and off-road vehicle use in limited designated zones. Although these uses are distributed throughout patches of the range, the total surface area that has been notably degraded by military activities is estimated to be between 5 and 10 percent (INRMP 2003; Tunnicliff et al. 1986). However, illegal immigration and smuggling from Mexico, poorly controlled civilian off-road vehicle traffic, an excess of access roads, overuse of popular recreational areas such as Tinajas Altas, and the potential for new military training activities pose major threats to a fragile ecosystem.

The Goldwater Range, according to a 2003 environmental impact statement, "harbors a relatively unfragmented and undisturbed ecosystem that is recognized for the continuing predominance of natural processes and its rich biodiversity. The BMGR landscape is unfragmented in terms of both land use and management, and with the exception of State Route 85, is free of developed structures that may disrupt ecological connectivity across its entire span" (INRMP Community Report 2003:26). Because the range spans

Figure 1.5. Barry Morris Goldwater. (Undated photo courtesy Arizona Historical Society, Tucson, portrait file number 55906)

so much ground, links Sonoran Desert National Monument with the Cabeza Prieta and by extension the other three Dry Borders reserves, and encompasses so much habitat and so many species, it may be the single most important property of the entire region. It has crucial linkages and corridors with the Kofa National Wildlife Refuge, Eagletail Wilderness, Tohono O'odham Nation, and other lands to the north and east. Its ecological health has enormous consequences for each of the other five reserves.

Because the range is withdrawn from the general public land laws, the future of the land is uncertain and less secure than the other protected areas if Congress terminates or does not extend the withdrawal. The range could open to a full list of uses and alternative management structures, ranging from a protective national preserve or national wildlife refuge to disposal or sale to private parties or other government entities. It could become subject to residential, urban, or commercial development; new utility and travel corridors; renewed grazing and mining; or high-intensity recreation. Even if military management continues, the range is vulnerable to increased ground maneuvers with armor or artillery, light-arms ground fire, wider and more intense use of air-to-ground munitions, and louder aircraft. It remains to be seen if the military has the administrative willpower and budgetary wherewithal to adequately manage public visitors, military units, and natural resources.

Within the range three "areas of critical environmental concern" (ACECs) had been established by the BLM for special management and protection of unique or significant habitats: the Gran Desierto ACEC (25,000 acres; 10,118 ha), the Tinajas Altas Mountain ACEC (53,000 acres; 21,449 ha), and the Mohawk Mountains and Sand Dunes ACEC (113,000 acres; 45,731 ha). The Gran Desierto ACEC, along the international border in the southwestern part of the Goldwater Range, consisted of sand flats and moving dunes that are the northernmost extension of the more extensive Gran Desierto sand sea in Sonora. This ACEC was overlain by the Yuma Dunes Habitat Management Area. The Tinajas Altas Mountain ACEC included the famous Tinajas Altas waterholes. The extremely arid Butler Mountains and Valley lie at the southwestern margin of the Tinajas Altas ACEC. The Mohawk Dunes support a rich but slightly isolated dune flora similar to that of the Gran Desierto dunes (Felger et al. 2003). Even under continuing military overflights, these areas were logical for consideration as biosphere reserve core areas.

The Department of Defense made strong commitments to ecosystem management (DoD Instruction 4715.3 1996; Ecosystem Approach Memorandum 1995; Goodman 1994; Leslie et al. 1996; Notice of Intent 2000), especially during the range renewal process of 1995–2000. The military's policy on ecosystem management includes guidance for designation of "special natural areas" with appropriate management for the protection of each area. In particular,

> Portions of installation real property that have significant ecological, cultural, scenic, recreational, or educational value may be set aside for conservation of those resources, where such conservation is consistent with the military mission. (DoD Instruction 4715.3 1996:F.1.j)
>
> Areas of DoD installations that contain natural resources that warrant special conservation efforts, after appropriate study and coordination, may be designated as *special natural areas* [emphasis added]. The integrated natural resources management plan for the installation shall address special management provisions necessary for the protection of each area. Special natural areas include botanical areas, ecological reserve areas, geological areas, natural resources areas, riparian areas, scenic areas, zoological areas, "watchable wildlife" areas, and traditional cultural places having officially recognized special qualities or attributes. (DoD Instruction 4715.3 1996:F.2.e)

A detailed analysis of biodiversity management potential on the Goldwater Range identified several such areas and offered suggestions for their management (Hall et al. 2001), but they have not yet been incorporated into resource management planning. We strongly recommend special protections for these areas, including former ACEC areas, and others as "special natural areas." Other areas merit special protection because of their ecological values and because of the needs to protect the military mission from civilian intrusions, dust, and vandalism.

Earlier environmental protection of the Goldwater Range was largely by default, or an accident of circumstance. In addition to potential biosphere reserve core areas, certain regions of the range might be considered managed-use or buffer zones. We believe that military use in conjunction with enhanced environmental stewardship can be consistent with the concepts of sound ecosystem management and the proposed biosphere network (Leslie et al. 1996), but serious threats are posed by changing military policies and missions, inconsistent budgetary and command commitment, and outside users who disregard the value of the range's landscape or biotic communities. The military calls the Goldwater "nationally significant as a critical component in the largest remaining tract of relatively unfragmented Sonoran Desert in the United States" (INRMP 2003:S-1), but in the span of a few careless years the range could become an ecological and environmental disaster zone.

Organ Pipe Cactus National Monument

Organ Pipe Cactus National Monument covers 330,689 acres (133,830 ha) in southwestern Pima County, Arizona. It was set aside by the federal government in 1937 and is managed by the National Park Service, a branch of the Department of the Interior. In 1976 it was designated a UNESCO Man and the Biosphere Reserve. Approximately 95 percent of the monument received a third level of protection in 1978 when 312,600 acres (126,509 ha) were officially designated Organ Pipe Cactus Wilderness.

The total flora of the monument includes at least 643 species, varieties, and subspecies (Felger et al., this volume, Chapter 17). Reports on the flora include Bowers 1980, Felger 1990, and Felger et al. 1992 and this volume (Chapter 17). The majority of the monument falls within Shreve's (1951) Arizona Uplands subdivision of the Sonoran Desert. The Ajo Mountains, rising to 4,808 feet (1,465 m), form the eastern boundary. These mountains support at least 140 "sky island" plant species—such as oak and juniper—that do not occur elsewhere in the region or occur only in the Sand Tank and Table Top mountains in the Sonoran Desert National Monument. Most of the monument remains environmentally pristine. The Bates Mountains, Puerto Blanco Mountains, and three smaller ranges are separated by four main alluvial valleys. Most of the mountains are volcanic in origin. Perennial water can be found in some tinajas and a few springs, such as the well-known oasis of Quitobaquito (Bennett & Kunzman 1989; Brown & Johnson 1983; Felger et al. 1992).

Arizona Highway 85, which bisects the monument, is an international thoroughfare. The highway serves as an invasion corridor for non-native plants (Felger 1990) and takes a heavy toll on wildlife (Rosen & Lowe 1994). Grazing and mining are prohibited. Most other legal use is recreational and is controlled but escalating. Hunting is prohibited within the monument. Groundwater drawdown and pesticide drift from outside the monument, increasing vehicle and foot traffic by illegal entrants, and invasion and spread of non-native species from adjacent disturbed areas present significant threats to both the natural resources and visitors' experiences. Protected areas are strongly affected by matters and events outside their boundaries: agricultural pesticide and herbicide drift directly affect natural processes such as herbivory and pollination, and groundwater drawdown lowers water tables within protected areas, leaving native trees and shrubs to die.

The Park Service manages uses under the Park Service Organic Act and the monument's General Management Plan, which gives the monument a mandate "to conserve the scenery and the natural and historic objects and the wild life therein and to provide for the enjoyment of the same in such manner and by such means as will leave them unimpaired for the enjoyment of future generations" (16 U.S. Code Section 1). Organ Pipe is the most closely managed and best protected of the six areas but also the smallest and most visited.

Sonoran Desert National Monument

This newest of Arizona's national monuments was designated on January 17, 2001, by President William J. Clinton in Presidential Proclamation 7397. Its 496,337 acres (200,868 ha) incorporate the Maricopa Mountains, the Table Top Mountains, the northeastern section of the Sand Tank Mountains, the southern Vekol Valley, and adjacent areas. Preliminary resource inventories and reports include Felger et al., this volume, Chapter 17; Gunn 2000; Shumaker 2000; and Turner et al. 2000. The monument is part of the National Landscape Conservation System, which works "to protect some of the nation's most remarkable and rugged landscapes" (BLM 2001).

At least four species with current state or federal special status are present: desert tortoise, cactus ferruginous pygmy-owl, Swainson's thrush, and lesser long-nosed bat. In addition to large, well-recognized species such as desert bighorn sheep, the area contains a number of unprotected species endemic to the Sonoran Desert which have relatively limited distributions in the United States, including the Sonoran green toad, lowland burrowing treefrog, and Abert's towhee. To date, 442 plant species, varieties, and subspecies have been documented (Felger et al., this volume, Chapter 17).

The monument is vast, diverse, awesomely magnificent, and of great cultural, aesthetic, and biological significance. It ranges in elevation from about 800 feet (244 m) to 4,373 feet (1,333 m) and lies on the edge of the Arizona Uplands subdivision of the Sonoran Desert. To the west and northward, its lower elevations are in the Lower Colorado River Valley subdivision. Sonoran Desert National Monument includes three impressive mountain ranges: the Maricopa Mountains, Sand Tank Mountains, and Table Top Mountains, as well as the Booth Hills and the White Hills. Mountains in the monument harbor important populations of desert tortoises and desert bighorn sheep.

The Sand Tank Mountains are a long and complex series of mountains and hills. Javelina Mountain is a huge, eastern outlier of the Sand Tank Mountains and has its own small foothills. The Maricopa Mountains contain the site of an ongoing study of desert tortoise mortality and reproduction, which may have significance for tortoise management throughout the Sonoran Desert (Wirt & Holm 1997). The BLM has classified 24,880 acres (10,069 ha) in the Maricopa Mountains as crucial desert tortoise habitat (BLM 1985). The Maricopa Mountains support a robust population of desert bighorn sheep, estimated in 1994 to be two hundred animals (BLM 1995), and have been used as a source of bighorns to transplant to other areas. Table Top is the highest and most massive mountain in the region. Its expansive summit is best known for its isolated grassland on the 107-acre (43 ha) mesa top. The range also supports populations of desert bighorn sheep and desert tortoise and was proposed as a protected natural area by the Arizona Academy of Science (Smith 1976). Espanto Mountain, though small, provides what may be a vital refugium for desert tortoises (Wirt & Holm 1997). The Sonoran green toad apparently persists as a breeding population in the monument about five miles west of Mobile, Arizona (Sullivan et al. 1996).

The monument's mountain ranges are separated—but biologically linked—by intervening valleys and desert plains such as the Vekol Valley and the outlying Rainbow Valley, Sauceda Valley, and Gila Plain. These valleys support unique assemblages of desert amphibians and form important corridors between naturally isolated populations of montane mammals such as bighorn sheep and mountain lions. The alluvial plain of Little Rainbow Valley, east of the Maricopa Mountains, and the inselbergs (small bedrock outcrops) in it, such as Espanto Mountain, have significant biological values and provide corridors for movement between mountain ranges by desert bighorn, deer, mountain lions, and other wildlife. Such "stepping-stones" within migration corridors for movement of desert bighorn sheep (Bleich et al. 1990) may be critical to maintaining a viable bighorn population in the Sierra Estrella, which is otherwise isolated by spreading urbanization from Phoenix.

In the southern reaches of the Vekol Valley is a dense grassland. Such grasslands may have once stretched along the forty-mile length of Vekol Wash to its confluence with the Santa Cruz River, but they currently occupy primarily a 300-acre (121 ha) remnant that is now within the area of the monument (BLM 1988). Seasonal wetlands in the Vekol Valley provide vital breeding habitat for a unique assemblage of seven desert toad and frog species (Enderson & Bezy, this volume). The area

was designated a BLM area of critical environmental concern to protect these biological values (BLM 1988). Historically, Sonoran pronghorn occupied the Vekol Valley (Thompson-Olais 1994), so it may be important for recovery of the species. Vekol Wash, a ghost tributary of the Gila River, is a broad, gravel-floored channel strung down the center of the valley. The Vekol bosque is a dense tangle of mesquite, foothill and blue palo verde, ironwood, and desert willow.

The monument is managed by the Phoenix Field Office of the Bureau of Land Management. Creation of the monument grew out of concern over the disposition of about 75,000 acres (30,353 ha) of land known as "Area A," controlled and managed by the U.S. Air Force as part of the Goldwater Range. This rather unromantic label was hung on the northern and most massive part of the Sand Tank Mountains. By early 1997 the military was discussing relinquishment of Area A as part of a deal to transfer more than 100,000 acres (40,470 ha) from Desert National Wildlife Refuge to Nellis Air Force Base, Nevada; and because commercial airline corridors crossed Area A airspace, it was not exclusive for military flights. In this trade-off there were immediate concerns for its future conservation and management because Area A included some of the Sonoran Desert's most magnificent landscapes and natural habitats.

At a June 1997 meeting of the "Goldwater Group" in Tucson hosted by the Keystone Center, Gayle H. Hartmann and Bill Broyles presented a proposal to manage the entire Goldwater Range as a national conservation area, patterned after the successful San Pedro River National Conservation Area in southeastern Arizona. The San Pedro NCA was established by Public Law 100-696 in 1988. The Goldwater NCA would have continued co-management between the Defense Department and the Interior Department. The proposal was not adopted, but it did expand the discussion. Arizona senator John S. McCain introduced legislation (Senate Bill 1963) to study alternative management strategies, including a Sonoran Desert National Park and Preserve overlay of the Goldwater Range, with the military continuing to be a co-manager, but that provision did not pass. The Military Lands Withdrawal Act of 1999 turned range management solely over to the Defense Department and returned Area A and three smaller parcels to the BLM.

Much of Area A was identified in April 2000 by the Nature Conservancy as a key site for protecting biological diversity in the Sonoran Desert (Marshall et al. 2000; Morrison et al. 2003). Also, the Air Force wished to retain its rights to fly over the area and called for land management featuring "dispersed recreation" and precluding development that might someday interfere with air operations. Col. Gerald "Fred" Pease, U.S. Air Force Division of Ranges and Airspace at the Pentagon, played a key role in negotiations.

Mike Taylor, then manager of the BLM's Phoenix Field Office and now deputy state director for resources, reports:

> Our part of the Sonoran Desert National Monument started in 1996–1997, about a year after we had the first meeting at the Phoenix Field Office about the Goldwater Range issues. These meetings eventually turned into "Partners Meetings" and then the Barry Goldwater Executive Committee (BEC). We were dealing with the Range re-authorization efforts and, in one of many discussions (probably in 1998), it first came up that maybe the military did not need Area A any longer. There were a lot of give-and-take discussions going on.
>
> Gene Dahlem, now manager of the monument, and I discussed the possibility of a National Conservation Area for Area A and drew up several renditions of a potential boundary. At one time our proposed boundary included parts of the Sauceda and Batamote mountains. We worked with Henri Bisson in the Washington office—he was the Assistant Director for Resources at that time. Henri had been the BLM Phoenix District Manager, and he knew and loved the area, so he was very supportive of the idea. Col. Fred Pease seemed supportive as well, but some of the local Luke Air Force Base folks did not like the NCA boundary going past Area A into the rest of the Range. We pulled back to what is now the boundary of the monument, but unfortunately the momentum was gone and we just ended up with Area A coming back to us through the reauthorization.
>
> You may ask why. We recognized that the area is special and felt that we could justify the status an NCA would confer on it. We felt that if we were able to get some Congressional support for the idea and it came to be, then we would possibly be able to get more funding for protecting the basic needs of the area, and then we could develop detailed planning to address how the land would be managed to enhance the public's opportunity

> to see it and to provide a framework to ensure its place in the future. And, we proposed it because it's a wonderful, special place! There were lots of folks at the Phoenix Field Office who made maps for us and did write-ups and so on—they all feel the place is special, too. (Personal communication, 2004)

Many people and organizations contributed to the formation of the new national monument. The concept of a national monument instead of a national conservation area was championed by D. Dean Bibles, former BLM state director in Arizona, and Bill Broyles, working with BLM director Thomas A. "Tom" Fry III and Henri Bisson, BLM assistant director for planning and renewable resources, as well as chief of staff Ann Shields and deputy chief of staff Ken Smith of the Department of Interior. Secretary of the Interior Bruce Babbitt, who had invited President Clinton to establish other national monuments, liked the concept, and the stage was set. Babbitt, governor of Arizona from 1978 to 1987, appreciated the beauty of the Sonoran Desert and was actively recommending establishment of other monuments around the country. A number of Interior Department staff, such as Kim Harb, and former staff, such as Geoff Webb, also favored the idea. A number of people and decisions behind the scenes remain unrecognized, and we hope that eventually the full story will be pieced together and told.

A diverse array of conservation organizations championed the popular concept of the monument and rallied public support for it: Arizona Archaeological Society, Arizona League of Conservation Voters, Center for Biological Diversity, Defenders of Wildlife, Drylands Institute, Friends of Cabeza Prieta, Hia-ced O'odham Alliance, Land & Water Fund of the Rockies, National Parks Conservation Association, the Nature Conservancy of Arizona, Sierra Club—Grand Canyon (Arizona) Chapter, Sky Island Alliance, Society for American Archaeology, Sonoran Desert National Park Friends, Sonoran Institute, Southwest Forest Alliance, Tucson Audubon Society, Tucson Herpetological Society, and the Wilderness Society. Edward B. "Ted" Zukoski served as campaign manager for the groups.

Several of those groups produced detailed reports on the biological and cultural resources of the area, providing Secretary Babbitt's office with additional technical justification for a presidential proclamation (Gunn 2000; Shumaker

Figure 1.6. *U.S. Secretary of the Interior Bruce Babbitt visits the proposed Sonoran Desert National Monument, 2000. (Photo by Bill Broyles)*

2000; Turner et al. 2000). Officials from the town of Gila Bend, the Pinal County Board of Supervisors, other communities, and the state of Arizona were involved in the discussions. Following public hearings, Babbitt set into motion the creation of the Sonoran Desert National Monument, embracing an area of almost half a million acres, nearly all of which was already held by the BLM.

The executive order creating the monument was among President Clinton's final official acts (Figure 1.6). Along with several other newly designated monuments, it promptly faced legal challenges, but the monument and the Antiquities Act of 1906 were upheld by the Supreme Court in 2003.

The new monument's southern boundary arbitrarily stair-steps across Area A, leaving about half of the Sand Tank region with the military. It is hoped that there will be some minor realignment of this boundary to include crucial habitat and populations of animals and plants now just barely excluded, especially at Bender Spring. Also, the monument includes several thousand acres of Arizona State Trust Lands and private lands that should be purchased and fully incorporated into the monument in order to safeguard its future integrity.

The Sentinel Plain, covering about 25,000 acres to the west of the present monument, was proposed for inclusion but omitted from the final declaration. The Sentinel Plain possesses scant potential economic value (one person proposes making it an interstate landfill) but remains an important buffer for training activities on the Goldwater Range, has strong archaeological values, is historic Sonoran pronghorn habitat, and has wilderness character.

National monuments can be established by congressional legislation or by presidential proclamation under the 1906 Antiquities Act. Generally, national monuments are established to preserve nationally significant biological, cultural, recreational, scenic, geological, educational, and scientific values for present and future generations to experience and enjoy.

The rationale for legislative creation of Santa Rosa and San Jacinto Mountains National Monument near Palm Springs, California, in 2000 (Public Law 106-351) also acknowledged broader reasons, including to "provide the prestige of Congressional recognition," to "support tourism," to "enhance cooperative management," to "enhance funding opportunities," and to "provide additional protection for the area's natural resources" (BLM 2002). The proponents of this national monument, including Congresswoman Mary Bono, recognized the actual and potential effects that the region's dense and growing population has and will have on natural and cultural values. A similar rationale could beneficially lead to additional protections of areas in southern Arizona, including expanded or new national monuments, wildlife refuges, or parks; national conservation areas; wilderness areas; special-use areas; and special natural areas on military lands.

Sonoran Desert National Monument is adjacent to large, rapidly expanding urban areas, and threats will likely increase as Arizona's population grows. Currently, about four million people live within a ninety-minute drive of the monument, and that population may double by 2025. The obscurity of much of the monument as well as wilderness area designations are positive factors for habitat protection. Major threats include border violations, livestock grazing, off-highway vehicle use, utility corridors, increased road traffic or new roads, power plants, waste facilities, and invasive non-native species. There exists a wide variety of factors that may damage the health and integrity of natural communities and native species in the Sonoran Desert (Nabhan & Holdsworth 1998).

The ecological effects of roads are well studied and have been found to damage the biotic integrity of landscapes in many parts of the world. The monument is traversed by two paved roads: Interstate Highway 8 and Maricopa Road. Negative effects include animal mortality from collision with vehicles, modification of animal behavior, alteration of the physical environment, spread of exotic species, and overuse by humans (Trombulak & Frissell 2000). Wilderness reserves have particular value because they restrict roads, which would otherwise extend edge effects into the interior of a reserve. In addition, many animal species—some of them rare—have little tolerance for human disturbance and thus are best protected by maximizing the area without easy human access. The inclusion of already-designated or de facto wilderness land into a larger monument increases the likelihood of maintaining healthy biotic communities and a full complement of native species.

Cattle grazing in arid regions can damage a wide array of biological resources (Fleischner 1994). These impacts may include disturbance of soil crusts and stone pavement that help stabilize soil, as well as direct impacts on vegetation. Within the Sonoran Desert cattle have caused long-term population declines in the saguaro *(Carnegiea gigantea)* by removing or damaging nurse plants and inhibiting or trampling small saguaros (Abouhaidar 1992; Steenbergh & Lowe 1977). After the removal of cattle from Saguaro National Park, it took more than two decades for saguaro recruitment to make a measurable recovery (Turner & Funicelli 2004).

Cattle grazing has not been permitted in the Sand Tank Mountains for more than fifty years but continues throughout the remainder of the monument. Portions of the Sand Tank Mountains have an abundance of annual and perennial grasses that is notable when compared with other Sonoran desertscrub areas in Arizona, and the saguaro stand there is remarkable for its density. In contrast, parts of the Vekol Valley have suffered severe erosion and loss of vegetation caused by obvious overgrazing (Marshall et al. 2000). The presidential declaration creating the monument phases out grazing in part of the monument and calls for study to phase it out in the remainder.

The environmental impacts of off-highway vehicles (OHV) in arid landscapes have been well documented, showing severe consequences to plant, wildlife, and soil resources (Artz 1989; Belnap 1995 and this volume; Berry 1980; Sheridan 1979; Webb & Wilshire 1983). Although three large portions of the monument have been designated wilderness areas and the former military lands in Area A have had OHV restrictions, the lowlands remain largely unprotected. The monument declaration prohibits "vehicle travel off-road." However, it remains to be seen whether the BLM will adopt a management plan (now being written) that identifies such an extensive network of "roads" as to render this prohibition without real effect. Off-road vehicles could be controlled under the aegis of President Richard M. Nixon's Executive Order 11,644 (Nixon 1972). Smuggling of drugs and undocumented aliens, illegal dumping, and looting of archaeological sites are growing problems.

Human recreation destroys cacti and the biological soil crust, turning productive soil to moon dust (Cox 1998; Belnap, this volume) and prompting such slogans as "Don't Bust the Crust" and "Tip-toe Through the Crypto" (Cox 1998). A town or mine next to a wilderness area threatens wildlife, and weedy exotic plants outcompete native species and irrevocably change the nature of the landscape. Highways serve as invasion corridors for exotics and consume wildlife (Forman et al. 2003). Therefore, new levels and strategies of protection are being sought to meet these expanding problems and threats. One such idea, proposed in 2000 during the monument's creation process, called for establishment of a national conservation area on BLM lands running west from Sonoran Desert National Monument to the Kofa National Wildlife Refuge and including the Sentinel Plain and Sierra Estrella.

Triple Threats: Fire, Drought, and People

"One expects little rain in the desert. Indeed, proclaiming a 'drought in the desert' might sound nonsensical" (McAuliffe et al. 2003:6). In fact, it is the very unpredictable nature of rainfall that characterizes deserts (Ezcurra & Rodrígues 1986). Even in a desert, however, a series of years with substantially less than average rain can cause changes in vegetation that are visible even to the untrained eye. After a period of seven years during which most years had below-average rainfall, the extreme drought of 2002 brought about extensive death of long-lived trees and shrubs. A substantial number of oak and canyon hackberry trees perished from the desert edge in Alamo Canyon, and on the extremely arid Davis Plain a major portion of the palo verde and ironwood trees died (Felger, field notes). In Organ Pipe, Joe McAuliffe and his associates "were amazed to find whole hillsides where nearly all triangleleaf bursage plants were dead" (McAuliffe et al. 2003:6). During severe drought even creosotebushes, which face drought "head-on," can be severely affected. For example, "by spring, 2004, half of all creosotebush plants were dead" in Joshua Tree National Park in the Mojave Desert. "The widespread mortality of long-lived desert plants . . . could affect . . . desert plant communities for many decades or even a century or more. . . . At some sites . . . there was a surge in the abundance of non-native ephemerals" such as Arabian grass, which "could inhibit re-establishment of some native perennial plants" (McAuliffe et al. 2003:9). And for the most part it was these non-natives that carried the devastating wildfires the following year.

Historically, wildfires in the Dry Borders region have been uncommon and so little anticipated that several land management agencies lacked fire plans for the fires of 2005. Wildfires have the potential to alter the desert as we know it, from the smallest bee to the desert bighorn, from the smallest cactus to saguaros and palo verdes. Although there have been some notable fires in the Dry Borders region during previous years, such as the 1993 blaze across the north side of Javelina Mountain, the frequency, coincidence, and magnitude of Sonoran Desert wildfires during recent years are unprecedented. Fires in 2005 destroyed extensive tracts of prime habitat for animals such as the desert tortoise and the endangered Sonoran pronghorn. In early spring 2005 the Sheep Peak Fire consumed 250 acres in Cabeza Prieta and was followed in rapid succession by others including the Camino Fire (2,000 acres), the Growler Fire (3,000 acres in the Goldwater Range and 1,300 in the Cabeza Prieta), a Vekol Valley Fire (6,100 acres), a Goldwater Fire (13,000 acres), the Tule Fire (1,300 aces), and the Theba Fire (6,000 acres adjacent to the Goldwater Range). In June 2005 another Goldwater Fire raged across 85,000 acres, making it the single largest wildfire in the Dry Borders region in recorded history.

In the Sonoran Desert, relatively low fuel loads and usually extensive patches of nearly bare ground prevent the spread of wildfires. Yet it appears there is a steady trend toward more and more serious fires in the Dry Borders region. Why? Contributing factors include increased diversity and densities of invasive species producing high fuel loads, and increased human activity including intentional setting of fires. Smugglers sometimes start fires to distract law officers; in winter undocumented immigrants set fires to keep warm and in summer to attract law officers to rescue them from death by thirst. Lightning can start fires but was not responsible for springtime wildfires in the Dry Borders region during 2005. Some fires on the Goldwater Range have been caused by military ordnance during live-fire exercises, and lingering unexploded ordnance presents dangers to firefighters. There are other potential causes needing further study. Selected studies of interest include Brooks 1999; Brown & Minnich 1986; D'Antonio & Vitousek 1992; Esque & Schwalbe 2002; Esque et al. 2002; McAuliffe 1995; McLaughlin & Bowers 1982; O'Leary & Minnich 1981; Rogers & Vint 1987; Rutman 1995; and Swetnam 1990.

Dense, wall-to-wall stands of dead winter-spring annuals that follow higher than usual rainfall during El Niño years can carry fires. Back-to-back El Niño years can further heighten fire danger, and late summer or fall rains can produce increased growth that adds to fuel loads. The winter-spring 2004–2005 rainy season started early, ended late, and resulted in great wildflower displays as well as generating extreme fuel loads. Fire danger can start in spring and intensify as the weather becomes hot and dry in early summer. Sonoran Desert fine-fuel loads are boosted by invasive Old World annuals. Culprits include Sahara mustard (*Brassica tournefortii*), red brome (*Bromus rubens*), and buffelgrass (*Penniseteum ciliare*). Even the little but abundant Arabian and Mediterranean grasses (*Schismus* spp.) fuel fires. The Tule Fire was carried by heavy winds and ample fuel loads of Arabian grass (*Schismus arabicus*) and the native wooly plantain (*Plantago ovata*). This fire jumped from one creosotebush to another (Curtis McCasland, personal communication 2005).

While creosotebushes often resprout after a fire, cacti and most Sonoran Desert trees and shrubs are not at all fire-adapted. "These long-lived plants take decades to mature and centuries to reach their full grandeur" (Esque & Schwalbe 2002:165). After fire sweeps through brushy, densely wooded xeroriparian galleries, the legume trinity (mesquite, ironwood, palo verde) and their associated species are reduced to ashes. The spring 2005 Tule Fire that swept through West Pass and Tenmile Wash killed a swath of palo verdes, ironwoods, and 20-foot-tall desert willows along the corridor.

Fire changes the physical and chemical characteristics of the soil, affecting soil productivity, erosion, and soil organisms. Fire increases the water repellency of some already hydrophobic soils beneath trees. Intense fires can destroy biological soil crusts (see Belnap, this volume). Although as yet poorly understood, pulses of available nitrogen followed by drops in this nutrient after fires appear to favor non-native species (Sue Rutman, personal communication 2005). Estimates of historical intervals between fires in the Mojave Desert range from 30 to more than 100 years. The invasion of exotic grasses has shortened this interval to an average of 5 years in some areas, resulting in significant changes in plant communities and threats to animals such as the desert tortoise (Esque et al. 2002). Fires in the Dry Borders region were so unusual that the natural fire interval is unknown (see Rutman 1995). The slow regeneration of natural plant communities and interim loss of wildlife habitat means that the present-day larger and more frequent fires are irrevocably changing the Sonoran Desert as we know it.

Other significant changes are forecast even within the protected areas of the Sonoran Desert. Mexico has announced construction of the long-proposed highway along the coast of Sonora, including the Alto Golfo Biosphere Reserve. We can expect new communities and resorts along the route. A U.S. corporation is considering installation of a fuel refinery at Tacna, east of Yuma, and proposes construction of a pipeline to Puerto Libertad, Sonora, running through the biosphere reserves and Goldwater Range. These developments will have numerous direct and indirect effects on the wildlife, vegetation, and scenic values. With foresight, planning, and strong regulations, the negative aspects of these projects could be reduced or overcome, but there is little indication or history that the moneyed players recognize the region's natural values or care about them. With everything at stake, we all must raise expectations and promote a long-term, sustainable vision for this wild and beautiful land.

Future Conservation

The discipline of conservation biology offers several insights for conservation and protection of the six protected areas (see Meffe et al. 1997). Large reserves are required to maintain viable populations of some species (Newmark 1995, 1996). For mammal communities, at least, there appear to be strong correlations between reserve size and species diversity within reserves (Brown 1971; Dunstan & Fox 1996; Newmark 1996). Although small reserves may suffice to protect individual species with small area requirements, bigger is better for most community protection needs and natural processes. Large areas of intact, native vegetation provide migratory birds with food resources and nesting habitat where this availability may be diminished in human-dominated or disturbed settings, particularly where creatures are heavily reliant on temporally restricted resources (see Griffin, this volume; Hinojosa-Huerta, this volume; Martinez del Rio, this volume; Wolf & Martinez del Rio 2000). Large areas can also help buffer the effects of variability of resources. In general, bigger reserves suffer less from "edge effects" such as invasive non-native species and the impacts of human activities (Bierregaard et al. 1992; Foreman 2004; Newmark 1995).

Work to protect these bio-reserves must continue. Additional management frameworks, funding, support, and layers of protection could be added, and the conservation areas could be expanded. A number of agreements and treaties are in place to allow and encourage cooperation among agencies and countries (see also Nagel 1988); the major ones are shown in Table 1.2.

U.S., Mexican, and Native American conservationists have long recognized the need to link these reserves along their shared international and national boundaries (Chester, 2006; Nabhan et al. 1995). Candidate designations include biosphere reserve, World Heritage site, national wildlife refuge, national preserve, national park, and international peace park.

Nabhan et al. (1995) proposed establishment of a binational Sonoran Desert Biosphere Reserve network to include the Pinacate, Alto Golfo,

TABLE 1.2. *Selected Treaties, Conventions, and Memoranda of Understanding Concerning the Six Bio-Reserves.*

1936	Convention Between United States and Mexico for Protection of Migratory Birds and Game Mammals. February 7. Updated March 10, 1972.
1940	Convention on Nature Protection and Wildlife Preservation in the Western Hemisphere. October 12.
1945	United States and Mexico Treaty for Utilization of the Colorado and Tijuana Rivers and of the Rio Grande. Effective November 8.
1972	Convention Concerning the Protection of World Cultural and Natural Heritage, World Heritage Convention, UNESCO. November 16.
1973	United States and Mexico Agreement Confirming Minute Number 242 of the International Boundary Water Commission, "Permanent and Definitive Solution to the International Problem of the Salinity of the Colorado River." August 30.
1976	Designation of Organ Pipe Cactus National Monument as a Biosphere Reserve.
1978	United States and Mexico Memorandum of Understanding for Cooperation on Environmental Programs and Transboundary Problems. June 19.
1983	United States and Mexico Agreement on Cooperation for the Protection and Improvement of the Environment in the Border Area. August 14.
1984	United States and Mexico Agreement for Cooperation in the Conservation of Wildlife. December 5.
1984	United States and Mexico Agreement on Scientific and Technical Cooperation in Forestry. November 16.
1988–89	United States and Mexico Memorandum of Understanding on Cooperation in Management and Protection of National Parks and Other Protected Natural and Cultural Heritage Sites. November 30 and January 24.
1993	Creation of Pinacate Biosphere Reserve and Alto Golfo Biosphere Reserve.
1994	North American Free Trade Agreement.
1995	United States and Mexico Memorandum of Understanding Concerning Scientific and Technical Cooperation on Biological Data and Information. May 16.
1996	Memorandum of Understanding Establishing the United States/Canada/Mexico Trilateral Committee for Wildlife and Ecosystem and Conservation Management. April 9.
1996	Arizona-Sonora Cooperative Resource Management of Bi-national Network of Protected Places. November 27.
1997	Letter of Intent for Joint Work in Natural Protected Areas on the Border: United States–Mexico Sonoran and Chihuahuan Desert Initiatives. May 5.
1999	United States and Mexico Agreement Between the Parties for Joint Work in Natural Protected Areas on the Border. May 5.
2000	Declaration to Enhance Cooperation in the Colorado River Delta. May 18.
2000	United States and Mexico Memorandum of Understanding to Work Jointly in Matters Related to the Protection and Conservation of the Environment. May 18.

Organ Pipe, and Cabeza Prieta reserves and parts of the Goldwater Range. It should also include Sonoran Desert National Monument. Although the Mexican "Ley General del equilibrio ecológico..." defines reserve categories, including biosphere reserves, the designation *biosphere reserve* presents a unique category of protection developed by UNESCO in 1971 (Székely et al. 2005). These protected regions conserve cultural heritage as well as natural resources and feature sustainable development based on indigenous traditions of the region. Organ Pipe Cactus National Monument has been ratified as a conventional biosphere reserve by UNESCO. This region has potential for an expanded biosphere reserve designation on the U.S. side of the border and linkage with the two recently protected contiguous biosphere reserves in Mexico. Together they could in turn add the involvement of indigenous Tohono O'odham, Hia-ced O'odham, Cocopah, Quechan, and other Native American residents of the region.

World Heritage sites are sanctioned under the World Heritage Convention of UNESCO, signed by the United States and Mexico in 1972. The goal is to identify cultural and natural resources of "outstanding universal value." Designation affords no new protections per se, but it generates greater recognition from the public and from governmental funders. The Dry Borders region likely would qualify by virtue of its exemplary archaeological and ethnological value, its biological and geological formations, its habitats of threatened species of animals and plants, and its scientific, aesthetic, and conservation values. World Heritage sites bring prestige, raise awareness for preservation, generally raise the levels of protection, and may bring financial assistance and expert advice. Member nations, numbering 176 as of August 1, 2003, work to protect and cherish the world's cultural and natural heritage for future generations.

During the 1999 renewal of the Goldwater Range, some public groups suggested that it be co-managed by the Departments of Interior and Defense as a national preserve, national wildlife refuge, or national conservation area. For example, a national preserve designation would allow continued use of the range by the military and sport hunters while affording management as a national park in other respects. These proposals, which were not acted on, would have placed management of cultural and natural resources and public visitors in the hands of the Interior Department and management of military training and the military mission in the hands of the Defense Department, as well as preparing for the eventual day when the military relinquishes its uses of the Goldwater and the land reverts to public uses. The military's lease is up for renewal in 2025, or sooner if Congress so wishes.

In 1932 Canada and the United States inaugurated Waterton-Glacier International Peace Park, and it has had a long, successful history. We have a similar opportunity here along the U.S. border with Mexico with these six bio-reserves (Broyles

2004; Broyles et al. 2001). Waterton-Glacier also carries World Heritage designation.

In 2003 U.S. Interior secretary Gale Norton and Mexico's SEMARNAT secretary Alberto Cárdenas-Jimenez signed a letter to pursue a sister-park concept. To date, these sister-park pairings are informal, "letterhead" agreements to exchange information, visits, and assistance (NPS-OIA 2004). In the United States they incorporate only units of the National Park Service, but Secretary Norton would like to explore inclusion of other Department of Interior lands managed by BLM or the Fish and Wildlife Service (Karen Clark, personal communication 2004). Organ Pipe Cactus National Monument currently is a sister to the Pinacate and the Alto Golfo biosphere reserves. This relationship could be extended to include an alliance of Organ Pipe, Cabeza Prieta, and Sonoran Desert National Monument as sister parks and, with Mexico's concurrence, the Pinacate and Alto Golfo biosphere reserves. An appropriate name might be Sonoran Desert Sister Parks or Sonoran Desert Peace Parks.

We encourage formal implementation of sister parks by legislation or presidential proclamation, accompanied by appropriate funding, legal framework, and policies. Formal establishment would (a) offer visible worldwide recognition and advancement of the long-standing friendship and mutual interests of two great neighboring nations, the United States and Mexico, (b) provide an umbrella designation and regional protection for conservation but allow each unit to continue under its current mandates, policies, administration, and name, (c) advance the sister-park concept, (d) enhance local economies and promotion of tourism, (e) solidify and enhance biological, cultural, social, ecological, and environmental values of the land, and (f) provide a permanent, legal, and funded mandate for the sister-park concept.

The land management discussions of 1931 foreshadowed continuing debates. We walk a tightrope trying to balance immediate uses with long-term sustainability, single-species versus ecosystem management, consumption versus stewardship, intense hands-on management versus natural processes and reduction of human impacts, the needs of people versus the needs of wildlife, game farms versus wilderness, and customary uses by local citizens versus national good for all citizens. We must protect, defend, and care for public lands at least as vigorously as we would our own private properties. The tragedy of the commons applies here (Hardin 1968). Public lands, since they belong to all citizens, should be treated according to higher, not lower, standards of protection, care, and sustainability for common public good.

Most of these Dry Borders lands are still in near-pristine ecological condition. No other desert region in the world can match this ecological wealth, but once degraded, these lands cannot recover even in our lifetimes. We need vision, strong congressional funding and laws, agency willpower, and altruistic, far-sighted public support. What do we want these lands to be in ten, twenty, fifty, or one hundred years? The choices are ours.

Acknowledgments

Many people generously assisted us with this chapter. We especially thank Dean Bibles, Peggy Turk Boyer, Alberto Búrquez, Carlos Castillo, Dale C. Cavin, José Campoy, Gene Dahlem, Roger DiRosa, Lorraine Eiler, Pat Etter, Luke Evans, John Hall, Gayle Hartmann, Kathryn Mauz, Joseph R. McAuliffe, Curtis McCasland, Peggy Miller, Fred Pease, Ron Pearce, Adrianne Rankin, Sue Rutman, Jon Shumaker, Harold Smith, Mike Taylor, Brock Tunnicliff, Bill Wellman, Ted Zukoski, and the staff at Smithsonian Institution Archive.

Two

Remote Sensing of the Arid Borderland

Kevin C. Horstman

The American Southwest was one of the first regions to be seen from the perspective of space. In the early years of aerospace research, unmanned Viking rockets launched from White Sands, New Mexico, photographed much of the Sonoran Desert, taking low-resolution photographs that showed the region as far as the Pacific Ocean. Since the time of those early experiments the science of remote sensing has progressed along with the civilian space program. Today satellites orbit the Earth at uniform times, taking pictures at uniform scales. Space-borne scanners record pictures in several portions of the visible through infrared spectrum, plus microwave. Some of those spectral areas correspond to the colors that we see naturally, such as blue, green, and red, whereas others record infrared light and infrared heat. We can see the images recorded in these infrared light bands by displaying them in colors visible to the human eye. These new-generation satellite pictures are not photographs; rather, they are scanned images that are digitally recorded, transmitted, archived, and sold in digital form. The images can be likened to the pictures taken by digital cameras or seen on high-definition televisions, and computer processing enhances the images so that each is adjusted to fit the human visual range.

A valuable use of these digital images is geologic research of the Earth's surface, and this is especially true of the Sonoran Desert. Arizona and northwestern Sonora have a rich geologic history that is revealed in the tremendous geological diversity of the region. The rocks range in age from ancient metamorphic rocks, schists, which are more than 1.7 billion years old, to some of the youngest on Earth: lavas of the San Francisco volcanic field and the Pinacate volcanic field (Donnelly 1975).

The environments in which these rocks were deposited through time were as diverse as the rocks are. As much as 570 million years ago warm oceans, rich in marine life, left thick layers of fossiliferous limestone. Vast deserts of sand "seas" more than 250 million years ago deposited crossbedded sandstone (now often used as high-quality flagstone), and that sandstone bears footprints of reptiles that lived before the dinosaurs (McKee 1974). Volcanoes were diverse and extensive both geographically and throughout much of geologic time. Massive volcanic activity tens of millions of years ago produced lava flows that can be seen today as mesas and mountaintops throughout the region. The mountains themselves show the history of crustal deformation in the province. Thrust faults 65 million years ago built mountains by pushing rocks eastward. This crustal compression was followed by extensional faulting that formed the Basin and Range terrain that characterizes the region.

The border area of southwestern Arizona and northwestern Sonora today is a grand mixture of present-day geologic environments. In a sense, we can think of the modern geologic setting as a contemporary microcosm of the rich geologic history that formed the Sonoran Desert. The northern Gulf of California is the product of tectonic plates sliding apart and past one another, forming the San Andreas fault. Locally, the deformation along the fault produced metamorphic rocks similar to the ancient schists but at lower temperatures and pressures than before. The ocean is depositing porous limestone composed of shell fragments, essentially modern fossils. Extensive sand deserts are here again in the form of the Gran Desierto and the Algodones dune fields. Volcanoes, too, are significant features of the border region: the Pinacate volcanic field of northwestern Sonora is a broad region of diverse volcanism that is comparatively young geologically. These areas can clearly be seen from the vantage point of space, and the images shown here were digitally processed to display the regional geology and geography with added clarity.

Southwestern North America

Figure C2.1 is a satellite image of southwestern North America acquired on July 8, 1987, by the Advanced Very High Resolution Radiometer (AVHRR) orbital scanner from an altitude of 833 km (517 mi) above the Earth. The image began as a digital data file with two spectral bands (color channels): panchromatic and infrared. Two bands cannot provide an easily viewable color picture because full-color images are composed of three distinct colors (blue, green, and red). The picture as seen here contains a third, synthetic, color channel added to the original two in order to improve the image's interpretability. The new synthetic channel was created using the data of another image channel, separately processed, and this unique color image is the result.

This false-color infrared satellite image has colors that are artificially assigned: blue and green tones represent light that is visible to the human eye, but orange and red tones represent near-infrared light (not heat). The blue component represents picture data that have been computer processed to show land and shallow-water details. Red areas (representing reflected infrared light) show healthy vegetation such as forests, crops, and grasslands.

The image encompasses the entire state of Arizona, with adjoining parts of California, Colorado, New Mexico, Utah, and Nevada. Much of northern and western Sonora, Mexico, is also visible, as well as the entire Baja California peninsula. Large blue areas in the central and western parts of the image are, respectively, the Gulf of California and Pacific Ocean. Desert regions appear as broad regions of tan. Mountains are brown, with many showing areas of red, which are high forests. Other areas having the red signs of vegetation are farming regions such as the lower Gila River valley of Arizona, the Imperial Valley of California, the Colorado River delta region, and coastal areas of Sonora, Mexico.

Major geologic features also are recognizable at this scale. The light region surrounded by dark red in the upper right corner is the Colorado Plateau. Lake Powell is identifiable as a long Y-shaped feature. The Grand Canyon is visible to the west of Lake Powell, and the San Francisco volcanic field near Flagstaff is visible as dark groups of mountains south of the Grand Canyon. The mountainous Transition Zone of central Arizona is seen as an arcuate, brown to red border west and south of the Colorado Plateau. The black, roughly circular form in the upper central part of the image is the Pinacate volcanic field of Sonora. The light zone to the west is the Gran Desierto; north of that desert are agricultural fields along the lower Colorado River, and the Salton Sea is north of those fields. East and southeast of the Salton Sea is the Algodones dune field, visible as a light tan area stretching to the northwest. East of the Algodones dune field and paralleling the mountain front is the surface trace of the San Andreas fault zone. The Basin and Range province is visible throughout the Sonoran Desert to the east and Mojave Desert to the north as dark mountains dispersed among light tan valleys.

Southwestern Arizona and Adjacent Regions

The image of southwestern Arizona and neighboring regions (Figure C2.2) yields much sharper detail of a smaller area than can be seen in the regional image (Figure C2.1). The picture is actually a mosaic of three distinct satellite images, each acquired on a different orbit approximately 700 km (440 mi) above the Earth. This visible-color image was created by digitally combining parts of three Landsat Thematic Mapper images into a single, comprehensive view of southwestern Arizona and neighboring regions of California, Sonora, and the Baja California peninsula. The brightness and contrast of the individual images were independently adjusted by computer to match one another. Computer-mapping programs ensure a seamless fit along nearly undetectable boundaries. The result is a uniform picture that has been used for mapping and scientific research. The image mosaic, in the form shown here, has been specifically enhanced to make the Earth's surface look as natural as possible from the vast distance of space.

The city of Yuma, Arizona, is the gray, green, and tan zone in the upper left part of the image. Roads, railroads, and airports are visible around

Yuma, as are numerous agricultural fields. The Gila River transects the northern part of the mosaic in a west-southwesterly direction and merges into the Colorado River, visible in the top left corner of the mosaic. The Colorado flows from there to the southwest, south, and southeast into the northern Gulf of California, which can be seen in the southwestern part of the mosaic. The Colorado River has deposited a large delta, the lower parts of which are visible in the southwest corner of the mosaic as tan, silty areas adjacent to white deposits of alkaline minerals. Green (active) and tan (fallow) agricultural fields are clearly visible along both the Gila and Colorado river systems, particularly in the western margin of the mosaic.

Desert basins appear as light tan, and mountains are brown, dark brown, or gray. The ranges contain small amounts of green, which indicate locally vegetated areas. The Pinacate volcanic field of Sonora is the large dark brown and black region in the lower center of the mosaic. Extremely dark colors are characteristic of the young basaltic lava flows and volcanoes that cover the field. The vast, light tan area west of the volcanic field is the Gran Desierto. The light colors of that desert derive from the nearly complete sand dune cover in that region. South of the Pinacate volcanic field lie Cholla Bay and Puerto Peñasco, on the northern coast of the Gulf of California. Tan plumes are visible in the blue gulf waters; tides are strong in this region of the gulf, and the tan streaks are areas where currents have suspended bottom sediments at shallow water depths.

Pinacate Volcanic Field

The Pinacate volcanic field is the large dark region in Figure C2.3, a false-color infrared image acquired in 1999 by the Landsat 7 Enhanced Thematic Mapper scanner. The spectral composition of this particular image differs from that of the false-color image described above because this image uses one visible band and two different infrared bands to achieve the three bands necessary for a full-color image. Band 1 (blue light) is displayed in the blue color channel, band 4 (near-infrared light) is shown in the green channel, and band 7 (middle-infrared light) is shown in the red channel. This configuration of bands was chosen because it offers the best contrast and, therefore, the best interpretability of Thematic Mapper bands in the Sonoran Desert region. A minor disadvantage is

that features in the image do not necessarily have the same color that a viewer would normally recognize. The advantage for research is that geologic features are most clearly recognizable on images of this type, as can readily be seen by comparing this image with the visible-color image of southwestern Arizona in Figure C2.2.

The visible-color image in Figure C2.2 also shows the Pinacate volcanic field as a dark region in the east-central part of the picture, surrounded by lighter-toned regions of desert alluvium and sand dunes. The false-color Pinacate image in Figure C2.3 shows the volcanic field and the surroundings in a more vivid range of colors that is characteristic of this kind of false-color infrared image. The low desert regions and sand dunes are recognizable in shades of tan or yellow. Chlorophyll is highly reflective in the near-infrared spectrum (which is shown here as green), so the rich green areas in the volcanic field indicate plant growth that has been sustained by alluvial or ponded water. Other regions identifiable as being vegetated include bright green rectangles southeast of the volcanic field and pale green areas east of the Pinacates that indicate diffuse vegetation.

Another notable benefit of the infrared image is the ease in distinguishing different volcanic rocks within the field. Young eruptions appear dark in both images, with little color differentiation in the visible-spectrum image. The infrared image, however, shows the volcanic features in more detail because the range of colors is greater: notice that the crests of some young volcanoes actually appear as bright red tones, indicating relatively greater reflectance in band 7 (shown here as red tones). The cause of this bright red appearance, or "signature," in the Pinacate volcanic field largely corresponds to cinder cones, which also exhibit a dark, brick-red color when viewed in visible light. The red color may be the result of iron oxides that may have formed from the local oxidation of lavas late in the eruptive history of the field. Volcanic gases can convert porous, iron-rich volcanic rocks into iron oxides or hydrous iron oxides that have a visible red color. Spectral response curves (Hunt et al. 1971) indicate that the middle-infrared reflectance of those iron compounds is notably greater than the near-infrared or visible reflectance. That relatively greater reflectance would appear as a bright red area on this image.

Mexico Highway 8 can be seen as a thin, sharp line that transects the area east of the Pinacate volcanic field, and Mexico Highway 2 crosses the northernmost part of the field.

Lower Colorado River Delta

A significant feature of this region, important to both nations, is the Colorado River. The vast geographic embrace of the Colorado is visible in Figure C2.1. The river reaches the ocean at the northernmost part of the Gulf of California, where it has deposited a delta from river-transported sediments. This region generally is of low topographic relief, with broad wetlands formed among the branching and meandering streams.

The Landsat image of the Colorado River delta (Figure C2.4) comprises the same spectral bands and color assignments as those used in the image of the Pinacate volcanic field in Figure C2.3. Green areas indicate healthy vegetation. Light blue areas indicate delta regions of shallow water that are rich in salts or carbonates, and dark blue areas show areas of freshwater and marine water. Streaks of medium blue can be seen in the dark blue water of the Gulf of California, indicating sediments that are being suspended by streams and strong tidal currents and carried into the gulf.

The upper right corner of Figure C2.4 shows part of northwestern Sonora. Dunes of the Gran Desierto can be seen as lines of mottled patterns inland from the gulf. The mottled pattern shows where groups of star dunes have formed in a strong, multidirectional wind regime (Bagnold 1941). Sand and sediments brought to the delta by the Colorado River are thought to be the source of this extensive dune field.

Mountain ranges and pediments are present in the left side of this image. The brightly colored areas show the diverse rock types in these coastal mountains of the northeastern Baja California peninsula.

Summary

New kinds of sensors and the view from space offer fresh ways to see the deserts and to reveal new aspects of the geologic and human histories. The use of remote sensing, including aerial photography, has revolutionized scientific mapping. Images of the kinds shown here have indicated the presence and locations of previously unknown faults, have revealed the locations of ancient canals from the Hohokam culture, and are being investigated for evaluating the distribution of water in deserts. Such applications require complex levels of digital image processing, beyond the scope of this discussion. Intensive research of this kind means that discoveries are constantly made with these advanced techniques, contributing to an increasingly detailed understanding of this region and other arid regions of the world.

Three

A Geologic Tour of the Dry Borders Region

PETER L. KRESAN

The lower Colorado River is a region of mud and salt-encrusted tidal flats at the head of the Gulf of California; desolate sand dunes and barren plains of dust in the Gran Desierto that occasionally burst forth with a spring bloom of wildflowers; dark lavas, cinder cones, and craters in the Pinacates; linear mountains of stark white granite, mantled with remnants of ancient dark lavas in the Cabeza Prieta National Wildlife Refuge; and a sublimely lush Sonoran Desert, rich with organ pipe cactus, along the western flank of the Ajo Mountains. It is a landscape that speaks of a long series of superimposed geologic events that acted both to build up and to rip apart the land.

Because this is a visual tour using satellite imagery and aerial and ground photographs, I focus the geologic story on what we can see and what the rocks that form the landscape tell us about the events in the geologic past. We start not at the beginning but in the Mesozoic, about 200 million years ago (Figure 3.1). During the Mesozoic through the middle Cenozoic (200 to 15 million years ago) the Pacific Ocean crust plunged (subducted) beneath the southwestern margin of the North American plate. Volcanism and crustal movements associated with this subduction piled the crust into high-standing mountains, much like the active volcanoes in Oregon and Washington today. Volcanic activity appears to have been episodic, with especially active periods during the Jurassic, late Cretaceous to early Tertiary, and mid-Tertiary. Then, about 15 million years ago, the configuration of the huge crustal plates changed; subduction beneath southwestern North America ceased; and the large, explosive volcanic centers died.

Now the Pacific plate slides laterally to the northwest relative to the North American plate along the San Andreas fault and Gulf of California transform and rift system. In contrast to the ear-lier period of subduction, when the crustal plates converged, today the crust is being pulled apart; relief is being generated more by the dropping of thinner and weaker blocks of crust than by uplift; and volcanism is localized to areas where the crust is highly fractured, allowing molten rock to rise quickly to the surface from the Earth's mantle. Where the crust has literally split and dropped below sea level, basaltic lavas are actively forming new ocean crust and a new ocean basin, called the Gulf of California.

Across this dramatically active stage of bedrock plays an amazing story of changing and varied environments that have been recently influenced by the presence of humans, our thirst for Colorado River water, and our taste for gulf sea life.

Colorado River Delta and Imperial Valley

The Colorado River delta encompasses more than 7,770 km^2 (3,000 mi^2) of coastal mud flats. The delta is the major source of windblown sand and dust (loess) for the Gran Desierto and Cabeza Prieta region. At first glance, the brilliant white, salt-encrusted mud flats look like an unchanging relic landscape from the primordial Earth. The constant rhythm of the tides and the equilibrium between erosion and deposition seem to hold this flat expanse in a steady state. A closer look reveals a land undergoing dramatic and rapid change. Tectonic forces, manifested by frequent earthquake activity, are continually remodeling the foundations of the Gulf of California and delta region. Meanwhile, on the surface, human diversion of the entire Colorado River for intense agriculture and municipal use has literally halted the growth and renewal of the delta.

Actually, there are two deltas. The Colorado River (and Gila River) dumps into the actively subsiding Imperial Valley, so a completely landlocked delta fans out across the eastern flank of

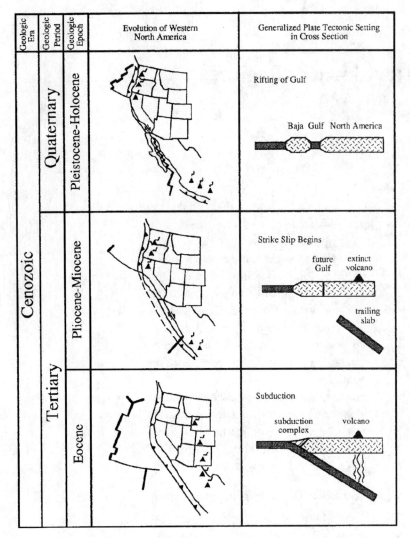

Geologic Era	Geologic Period	Geologic Epoch	Evolution of Western North America	Generalized Plate Tectonic Setting in Cross Section
Cenozoic	Quaternary	Pleistocene-Holocene		Rifting of Gulf Baja Gulf North America
Cenozoic	Tertiary	Pliocene-Miocene		Strike Slip Begins future Gulf / extinct volcano trailing slab
Cenozoic	Tertiary	Eocene		Subduction subduction complex / volcano

Figure 3.1. *Cenozoic time line for the geologic evolution of the Gulf of California region, southwestern North America. (Figure by Peter L. Kresan)*

the Imperial Valley (Salton Trough) north of the head of the gulf. This primary delta is intensively cultivated and irrigated (more on its geology later). Sediments are then carried for a short distance south along the Imperial Valley and deposited at the head of the Gulf of California. The coastal delta is entirely within the country of Mexico and is divided between the Mexican states of Baja California and Sonora.

The geologic history of the Colorado River delta is closely tied to plate tectonic processes associated with the San Andreas fault and evolution of the Gulf of California and Baja California peninsula (Figure 3.2). As recently as 15 or 20 million years ago, Baja California was part of western Sonora; a chain of composite volcanoes was explosively erupting along this ancient Sonoran coastline; and the Pacific Ocean crust was being subducted beneath the western edge of North America,

analogous to the geologic circumstances in northwestern North America today. Subduction and explosive volcanism ceased along the Sonoran and southern California coast about 10 or 15 million years ago as the boundary between the Pacific and North American crustal plates evolved into a rift and transform-fault system. Chambers of molten rock had solidified beneath the volcanoes in western Sonora, impregnating the fractured crust and stitching it together. In this way the roots of these volcanoes served to strengthen a long, narrow section of crust, which was soon to become the Baja California peninsula. As forces associated with this rifting and transform faulting were applied, the North American crust to the east of the now-dead chain of volcanoes broke to become the new plate boundary, which is now beneath the Gulf of California and represented by the San Andreas fault. Baja California and southern California are now part of the Pacific plate, which continues to move northwestward with respect to the North American plate. In fact, Baja California has moved northwestward about 300 km from its original position (Schmidt 1990).

As tectonism ripped Baja California away from mainland Mexico about 10 million years ago, the area that is now the Gulf of California subsided. For a time, sections of the gulf region may have looked much like today's Death Valley. Then, between 6 and 4 million years ago, the region was inundated by the Pacific Ocean to become the Gulf of California (Sea of Cortez). The gulf is a new and growing ocean basin. As new ocean crust forms at the sea-floor spreading centers, Baja California and southern California slip obliquely northwest at a rate of about 5 cm per year (2 in/yr). Bathymetry, seismic studies, and actual sea-floor exploration show a series of deep basins (short, segmented spreading centers)—for example, Pescadero Basin, Farallon Basin, Carmen Basin, Guaymas Basin, and San Pedro Mártir Basin—separated by long, offset transform-fault segments (Figure 3.3; Lonsdale 1989). Spreading centers are thought to exist at the head of the gulf and beneath the Salton Sea, but they are being buried by sediment from the Colorado River and other drainages in the Imperial Valley. The many geothermal areas within Imperial Valley are a manifestation of the subterranean magmatic processes typical of these spreading centers. Cerro Prieta Geothermal Area in northeastern Baja California produces brines at 400–600°C and generates close to 400 megawatts of electricity annually.

The northernmost spreading center segment probably lies beneath the Salton Sea. Geophysical evidence suggests that a small amount of ocean crust actually exists beneath the Salton Sea but is buried by a thick layer of sediments. In 1905 the main flow of the Colorado River was accidentally diverted by way of irrigation canals into the Salton Trough. Flow down the normal Colorado River channel was restored in 1907. The new lake created by this diversion was nearly 24.4 m (80 ft) deep and covered 1,036 km^2 (400 mi^2). Its shoreline was at an elevation of minus 60 m (−195 ft). The lake quickly began to shrink because of high evaporation rates (about 1.8 m, or 6 ft, per year) and became saltier than ocean water. By 1925 the Salton Sea shoreline had stabilized at minus 76 m (−250 ft). The Salton Trough has held naturally formed lakes at least four times in the past 2,000 years. In fact, the reason the Imperial Valley is so flat and also very fertile is that it is an ancient lake bed (Sharp 1994). With the drainage divide only about 12 m (40 ft) above sea level, delta sediments act as a dam to the gulf and prevent ocean water from flooding the Imperial Valley.

The Salton Trough is the largest area (approximately 2,000 mi^2) of dry land below sea level in the Western Hemisphere. The trough has impressive vertical dimensions. Torro Peak, just west of Mecca at the north end of the Salton Sea, rises to 2,658 m (8,720 ft) above sea level. The depth of unconsolidated basin-fill sediments exceeds 6 km (20,000 ft), so the relief in the basement rock is comparable to that of Mount Everest! The basin fill is largely land-laid with some marine sediments. The San Andreas, San Jacinto, and Elsinore right-lateral, strike-slip faults slice across the Salton Trough. The San Andreas trace is along the west side of the Salton Sea to the Algodones Dunes. The San Jacinto fault splits into a complex of faults, including the Imperial fault in the Borrego Desert. Earthquakes occurred along the Imperial fault in 1915, 1940, and 1979. More than twenty moderate to large earthquakes have occurred in the Imperial Valley since 1900. Branches of the Elsinore fault help define the western border of the Salton Trough and continue into Mexico (Sharp 1994).

In Mexico the Sierra Cucupá borders the west

Figure 3.2. Colorado River delta, with a portion of Isla Montague, Isla Gore, and the Sonoran shoreline. (Photo by Peter L. Kresan)

side of the Mexicali Valley. West of the Sierra Cucupá is Laguna Salada, and along the west flank of the Sierra Cucupá is the Laguna Salada fault. Geologists have suggested that a magnitude 7+ earthquake occurred in 1892 along this fault (Mueller & Rockwell 1995).

Within fifty years of the first landing by Columbus, Captain Francisco de Ulloa sailed into the estuary at the head of the "Vermilion Sea," the Gulf of California. Jesuits Padre Kino and Padre Consag journeyed across the delta flats in the early 1700s. These early explorers were impressed with the height of the tides, the strong currents, the great expanse of mud and salt flats, and the distant high mountains. Godfrey Sykes (1937), a researcher and explorer with the Carnegie Institute of Washington, recounts the history of Colorado River exploration from the Spanish to paddle-wheel steamboat navigation. Sykes's personal observations, maps, and photographs characterize the delta during the initial impact of human activities (Figure 3.4). In the early 1900s people got lost on the delta because they could not see beyond the expansive forest of trees. In stark contrast to the barren delta of today, Sykes documents the forested delta with distributary channels lined with cottonwoods, willow, and mesquites (see Boyer, this volume).

The Colorado River is one of the most thoroughly used rivers in the world. Diversions from the lower Colorado began in 1905 for agriculture

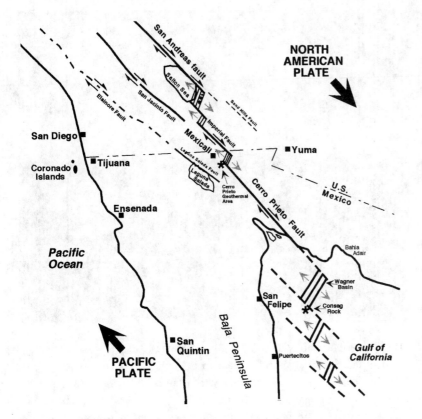

delta the coarser sediment is mostly shell debris. The most recent period of chenier formation began after the completion of Hoover Dam in the 1930s. Since that time, Lake Mead, and later Lake Powell, served to trap the sediments that were once delivered to the Colorado River's delta. Subsequent diversions of water for the agriculture and cities of the Southwest eliminated the remaining supply of water and sediment to the delta. Waves and tidal currents reworked preexisting sediments, removed the fine material, and piled up a concentration of coarser particles (mostly shells) into cheniers (Kowalewski et al. 1994; Thompson 1968).

Geoscientists, oceanographers, and ecologists at the University of Arizona, the Universidad Autónoma de Baja California, and the Centro de Investigación Científica y de Educación Superior de Ensenada are examining how the diversion of Colorado River water and sediments have affected the delta and upper Gulf of California (e.g., Aragón-Noriega & Calderón-Aguilera 2000; Carriquiry & Sanchez 1999; Flessa 2002; Galindo-Bect et al. 2000; Glenn et al. 2001; Kowalewski et al. 2000; Lavín & Sanchez 1999; Rodriguez et al 2001). Their studies demonstrate the enormity and dynamic nature of the changes that continue to occur in this great desert delta.

The Colorado River delta has changed dramatically over the last one hundred years. Although plate tectonic forces, floods, hurricanes, and tremendous tidal currents continue to alter the face of the delta and course of the river, the most recent agent of change—humans—has had the most profound effect. The Colorado River delta has essentially become a huge tidal mudflat rather than an expanding and renewing river delta.

Northern Sonoran Coast and Bahía Adair

Uplift has exposed nearly continuous beach cliffs between El Golfo de Santa Clara and the northern shore of Bahía Adair, just southwest of the Pinacate Volcanic Field (Figures 3.5 and 3.6). An occasional brackish spring occurs along this coastline. The springs appear to be located either along faults or at stratigraphic contacts between sedimentary layers. Peat mounds at the springs yield ^{14}C dates of 3,000 years old. Early Pleistocene vertebrate fossils occur in the badland cliffs of Mesa de Sonora near El Golfo (Lindsay 1984). Mesa de Sonora consists of Pleistocene sediments deposited in river-

Figure 3.3. *General tectonic map of the lower Imperial Valley and upper Gulf of California. (Adapted by Peter Kresan from Stock et al. 1991 and Lonsdale 1989)*

in the Imperial Valley. Imperial Valley used to be called the Colorado Desert, but that name did not sound inviting to land developers, so it was changed. The first major dam, Hoover Dam, was completed in the 1930s. In contrast to the lower gulf, where productivity is driven mostly by nutrient-rich upwellings, the upper gulf marine and estuarine ecosystems rely on the Colorado River. This supply of nutrients and freshwater is now cut off because the Colorado River seldom flows into the gulf. With minor exceptions, the river is diverted into canals and agricultural fields in both the United States and Mexico (Glenn et al. 1992). Whatever water eventually makes it to the coast is laden with salts, fertilizers, and pesticides (García Hernández et al. 2001).

The 10-m (33-ft) tidal range in the northern Gulf of California, one of the highest in the world, combines with winds to produce a strong littoral current and active sediment-transport system (Carriquiry & Sánchez 1999). The large tidal range and gentle offshore slope produce extensive tidal flats and meandering tidal sloughs. Long, low ridges, or cheniers, cross parts of the mud flats. Cheniers are lag deposits formed when waves wash away finer sediments and concentrate the coarser materials near the high tide line. In the Colorado River channel and delta environments. The active Cerro Prieto fault system cuts across the mesa. There is evidence for recent subsidence, perhaps due to trans-extension around the margins of Bahía Adair (Owen Davis, personal communication 1997). A series of supratidal salinas, also called *sabkhas,* rims the coastline of Bahía Adair (Ezcurra et al. 1988). Algal mats cover portions of the sabkha floors. Active transport of sand from Bahía Adair to the Gran Desierto seems to be occurring presently (Davis 1990).

Gran Desierto

The Gran Desierto is a landscape of dramatic starkness and beautiful desolation. The sand sea covers 5,698 km^2 (2,200 mi^2) and is the largest area of active dunes in North America. Discrete areas of large dunes are separated by an extensive sand sheet. Towering as high as 180 m (600 ft) above the desert floor, the dunes around the Sierra del Rosario are some of the highest. The depth of sand is unknown, but the principal source for the eolian sediments is most likely the delta of the Colorado River. Indeed, the Gran Desierto is the Namib Desert of North America.

Freezing temperatures occur occasionally during the winter months and are a significant limiting factor for various frost-sensitive plants (Felger 2000). In February 1971 snow covered the upper 300 m (1,000 ft) of the Pinacate Peaks (May 1973). The summers are long and extremely hot, with temperatures in excess of 40°C. Toward the Sea of Cortez—for example, at Bahía Adair and Puerto Peñasco—temperature extremes are ameliorated.

Pollen from packrat middens and cores of mud from Salina Grande in the Gran Desierto show that during the last glaciation the foothills east and north of the Gran Desierto were covered with desert vegetation similar to that found about 250 km north on the upper bajadas of the Mojave Desert today (Davis 1990; Van Devender et al. 1990).

The Gran Desierto is one of the most arid regions in North America. Wind accentuates the aridity. Long-term quantitative weather observations are lacking, but rainfall varies from less than 50 mm (1.97 in) per year in the west to more than 100 mm (3.94 in) per year in the Pinacate Mountains to the east. No measurable precipitation was recorded for a thirty-four-month period from 1969 to 1972, and during the remainder of 1972

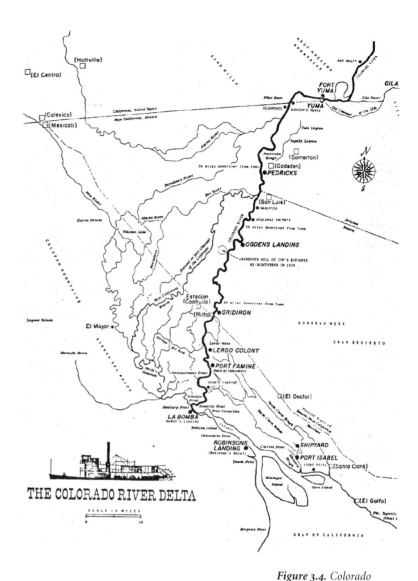

Figure 3.4. Colorado River delta in the steamboat era (1852–1916). (Courtesy Don Bufkin, 1978)

about 94 mm (3.70 in) of rainfall was recorded (May 1973). Winds in this region are variable. During the summer and winter months, wind directions are primarily from the west and south. Winds from the north have been observed in late fall. Some of the precipitation that does fall on the Gran Desierto percolates into the sands and emerges in springs *(pozos)* along the Gulf of California coastline. The pozos are probably located along faults and driven by artesian flow (Ezcurra et al. 1988).

Granitic basement rocks form abrupt mountain peaks, which in the Sierra del Rosario rise to 610 m (2,000 ft) (Figure 3.7). Some of the lower bedrock outcrops, called *inselbergs,* are partially buried by sand. Located along the southern extension of the San Andreas fault, the Gran Desierto is a tectonically active region. Earthquakes frequently shake the land. Some uplift is evident along the

Figure 3.5. Bahía Adair, oblique aerial view looking northeast to the Pinacates. (Photo by Peter L. Kresan)

Figure 3.6. Santa Clara Slough and Puerto Isabel, looking south. (Photo by Peter L. Kresan)

Figure 3.7. Sierra del Rosario and Gran Desierto dunes, oblique aerial view looking southwest. (Photo by Peter L. Kresan)

tion of the star dunes. Variable wind directions pile up the sand into a mountainous dune with little, if any, net lateral movement. Star dunes probably evolve from crescentic dunes that migrate into areas of opposing winds and become reversing dunes. The multiple arms of the star dune develop because of secondary airflow (Figure 3.10 and Lancaster 1989). In fact, complex crescentic and reversing dunes are also common dune types in the Gran Desierto.

Certainly the sand sea owes its existence to the Colorado River delta. The delta and extensive tidal flats are a plausible source for much of the blown sand. Other sources include the beaches along the gulf coast and alluvial fan plus ephemeral stream sediments that originate off the Pinacates and the granitic mountains along the Arizona-Sonora border. Climate and sea level greatly influence the supply of sand to this region. Because the bottom slope of the upper Gulf of California is so gentle, the sea level during the last glaciation would have placed the shoreline about 31 mi (50 km) farther offshore than today (Davis 1990). With the exposure of a more extensive coastal plain and higher-velocity winds typical of glacial periods, sand transport and supply were probably significantly greater during glacial periods. In fact, there is debate as to whether the Gran Desierto today is in a period of relative geomorphic stability with little net transport of sand. Perhaps significant sand transport occurs across this region only during glacial periods, when sea level is lower and conditions are generally windier.

Algodones Dunes

Just northwest of Yuma is a long (about 72 km, or 45 mi) and narrow (3–6 km, or 4–8 mi) band of sand dunes called the Algodones Dunes. The dunes are classified as barchan and transverse megadunes. The sand sheet is estimated to be about 400 ft thick. Dominant wind directions from the north and west deposit the sand along the eastern edge of the Imperial Valley (Breed et al. 1984). A series of subequally spaced interdune flats are a distinctive feature of this dune field. A segment of the San Andreas fault is buried beneath these dunes.

Pinacate Volcanic Field

The Pinacate Volcanic Field is one of the youngest and most spectacular lava fields in North America.

coast, where nearly continuous beach cliffs occur from El Golfo de Santa Clara to the north shore of Bahía Adair. Up to 150 m (492 ft) of uplift of the Mesa Arenosa has taken place along the Cerro Prieto and Punta Gorda faults, which are southern extensions of the San Andreas fault.

Giant star dunes are the most distinctive feature of the Gran Desierto (Figures 3.8 and 3.9). The star dunes occur as single, complex, or compound dunes and typically join to form parallel ridges 9 to 48 km (6–30 mi) long. Seasonal changes in wind direction play a major role in the forma-

The volcanic complex consists of a small shield-type volcano with some five hundred eruptive centers, including cinder cones and fissure eruptions, along its flanks. Although it is dormant at present, volcanic activity has been continuous but episodic during the last 1.7 million years. There have been two distinct periods. First, the shield volcano, often referred to as Volcán Santa Clara, was built by successive eruptions from a central summit vent complex, active from 1.7 to 1.1 million years ago. Then smaller, individual basaltic cones and lava flows erupted on the slopes of Santa Clara and extended out onto the desert surrounding the central vent complex. I anxiously await the next eruption.

The Pinacates sit on the western edge of the North American continental crust, immediately east of the crustal plate boundary defined by the gulf rift-spreading centers and the San Andreas transform-fault system. Given the proximity of the Pinacates to sea-floor volcanic centers, a genetic link between the two would seem reasonable. However, geochemical studies suggest that Pinacate volcanism is due to a mantle plume—a hot spot, similar to but smaller than the one that is generating the Hawaiian Islands. It appears that Pinacate volcanism is not directly related to the sea-floor volcanism in the Gulf of California.

Geochemical evidence also indicates that the Santa Clara shield volcano originated from a large batch of basaltic magma that episodically erupted to form a relatively steep-flanked volcano that is the core of the shield. As the molten rock in this large magma chamber cooled, its chemical composition changed, so that successive eruptions siphoned from it have somewhat different characteristics. Generally, as large magma bodies cool, the eruptions from them become progressively enriched with silica, which makes the lava more viscous. A more viscous lava will tend to flow more slowly and to solidify into thicker flows that can maintain a steeper slope. In contrast, the many dark lava flows and cinder cones that mantle the slopes of the Santa Clara shield are thought to be derived from much smaller batches of basaltic magma that erupted over a short enough period of time so that no change in the composition of the lavas occurred. Since the flows and cinder cones are deposited on top of the Santa Clara shield and represent individual and probably unrelated events, they are younger eruptions (1.2

Figure 3.8. *Star dune ridges, oblique aerial view, Gran Desierto. (Photo by Peter L. Kresan)*

Figure 3.9. *Star dune crest, Gran Desierto. (Photo by Peter L. Kresan)*

million years old to recent) and are referred to by some as the Pinacate monogenetic volcanoes.

The Pinacate rocks typically exhibit a porphyritic texture, characterized by conspicuously large crystals surrounded by a dark, fine-grained, and often bubbly (vesicular) matrix. The large crystals are either labradorite (clear), augite (shiny black), or olivine (green/yellow). Labradorite crystals the size of a human fist have been found, but they are always highly fractured and glassy in appearance owing to the rapid cooling of the

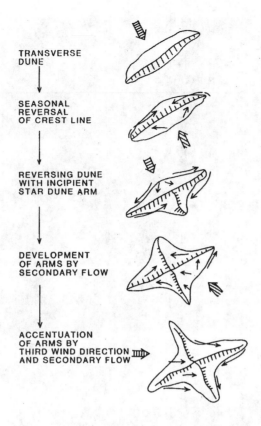

TRANSVERSE
DUNE

SEASONAL
REVERSAL
OF CREST LINE

REVERSING DUNE
WITH INCIPIENT
STAR DUNE ARM

DEVELOPMENT
OF ARMS BY
SECONDARY FLOW

ACCENTUATION
OF ARMS BY
THIRD WIND DIRECTION
AND SECONDARY FLOW

crystals during their ascent to the Earth's surface. Close inspection of the labradorite, a type of plagioclase feldspar, sometimes reveals bubble trains within the crystals. The bubbles frozen within the crystals provide clues about the pressure and temperature at which these crystals grew within the magma chamber before erupting onto the surface. The large crystals were carried from depth by the rising magma and erupted with the remaining liquid, which cooled quickly to form the black basalt. These crystals are analogous to chocolate chips in a cookie batter. If you could have withstood the heat, you could have reached into the erupting flow and collected the large, solid crystals (the chips) as they came out of the ground with the molten lava (the batter).

The size of some of the Pinacate lava flows is notable (Figure 3.11). A single flow, called the Ives flow by some, covers more than 75 km^2 (29 mi^2) of the south flank. This is 5 percent of the area of the whole volcanic field. Even though basaltic lavas are relatively fluid due to their high temperatures and chemical composition (lower silica content), as they cool, their viscosity increases rapidly. Apparently, the Ives flow erupted much like many lavas in Hawaii, where lavas can flow surprisingly large distances owing to containment within self-

forming and insulating lava tubes. Dissolved gas content is another factor that may have contributed to the fluidity of the Ives flow. Water and carbon dioxide are the most common volatile gases dissolved in the magma. There may be as much as a few percent water in a basaltic magma. Often when the magma reaches the Earth's surface, the gases exit explosively, propelling the magma out of the vent. As the gas-rich spray of lava falls to the ground, it cools into blobs of bubbly cinders that pile up to form a cinder cone. However, sometimes the gases remain dissolved in the lava, significantly decreasing the viscosity of the lava and allowing it to flow greater distances. Both lava tubes and greater fluidity due to slow escape of dissolved gases probably helped some Pinacate lavas cover great distances.

Cinder cones are essentially self-made smokestacks of volcanic cinder that pile up, while still hot and sticky, around the eruption vent. There are hundreds of cinder cones in the Pinacates. Based on the freshness of the flow surface, the youngest eruption, perhaps only a few thousand years ago, formed a cinder cone (now flattened by cinder mining) and flow in the northeastern section of the field. Cinder cones typically form during the initial phase of an eruption event when the magma contains more volatile gases. Once gases have escaped during the initial eruption, the magma often pours out of the vent at the base of the cinder cone as a flow. Even as a fluid, lava is very viscous and capable of lifting up and rafting away part of the cinder cone's slope. A cinder cone may remain active for weeks to a few years and then is not likely to erupt again.

The slopes of a new cinder cone are very porous and permeable, that is, rainfall will quickly soak into the slope of the cinder cone and not run off. With no water flowing off the cinder slope, there is little or no erosion initially. As the cinders chemically weather, clay minerals are created and slowly accumulate. Eventually, there is enough clay to plug up the pore spaces between the cinders so that rain can no longer quickly seep into the slope. Then the water can collect into gullies, which quickly enlarge and incise the slope. Eventually, a gully will breach the crater and cut deep enough to expose the internal structure of the cinder cone.

The craters are the most striking features in the Pinacates (Figure 3.12). There are ten major craters—Elegante, MacDougal, Cerro Colorado,

Sykes (Grande), Molina (Cloverleaf), Moon, Kino, Celaya, Badilla, and Díaz—of which the first six are perhaps the most distinctive. To a geologist, most of these craters represent a hybrid between a maar volcano and a caldera (Figure 3.13). A crater formed by collapse is called a *caldera*. A *maar* is a coneless volcanic crater formed by a single explosive eruption. Maar volcanoes often occur when magma interacts with a source of water—for example, in or near a lake—and becomes supercharged with water vapor. Eventually, steam pressure builds up enough to generate a very explosive eruption. The light tan, fine-grain rim of volcanic tuff with inclusions of large basaltic fragments surrounding most of these craters is good evidence for an explosive eruption, typical of a maar. However, there is more to the story, for the Pinacate craters are surprisingly circular, large, and deep, too much so to be solely the result of an explosion. Subsequent collapse of the underlying magma chamber is thought to have enlarged many of these craters.

The Pinacate Volcanic Field is located next to the Gran Desierto, now the driest region of the Sonoran Desert. This is not a region noted for freestanding water, such as lakes, in which magma could explosively erupt to form a maar volcano. Basaltic magmas are typically relatively dry and do not usually erupt explosively to form a tuff. So where did the water come from to generate these maar craters with basaltic tuff rims? No one really knows. The craters do not line up on any obvious trends, but in some cases, especially Cerro Colorado, the location of the crater coincides with a paleo stream channel or place where runoff may have concentrated enough to produce water-rich sediments in the subsurface. One can envision the magma rising to meet the shallow, water-rich sediments, where, perhaps because of a capping basalt flow or clay-rich layer, pressure builds until an explosive eruption blasts through to the surface.

Elegante Crater (1,200 m, or 3,940 ft, in diameter and 250 m, or 820 ft, deep) is the largest and most likely was formed by an explosive eruption followed by collapse (Figure 3.14). The cross section of a cinder cone and alternating lava flows and paleosols is well exposed in the steep crater walls. The oldest lava flow exposed in the crater wall is radiometrically dated at 0.5 ± 0.1 million years old. The topmost lava flow, immediately below and possibly deformed by the tuff layer, radio-

Figure 3.11. *Sierra Blanca and Ives Flow. (Photo by Peter L. Kresan)*

Figure 3.12. *MacDougal Crater, looking from Hornaday Mountains to Pinacate Peak. (Photo by Peter L. Kresan)*

metrically dates at 0.15 ± 0.02 million years old and probably represents the approximate time the crater formed. Tuff deposits exposed today account for only 33 percent of the volume of the crater. Certainly some of the soft tuff has been washed and blown away, but probably not much, given the youth of this crater. It is likely that a significant portion of the ejecta fell back into the crater during collapse, and more has subsequently been washed in. Around the bottom of Elegante Crater is a "bathtub rim" that is interpreted to be

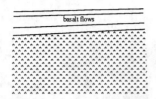

1. Stack of basalt flows on top of sands and gravels containing ground water.

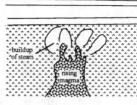

2. Injection of hot magma into gravels plus resulting buildup of steam.

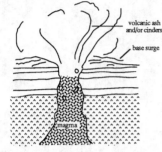

3. Very explosive eruption with ejection of volcanic ash.

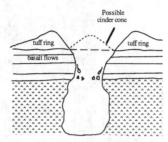

4. Possible formation of lava lake and/or cinder cone.

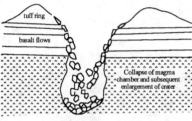

5. Collapse of roof and magma chamber and crater walls, resulting in the enlargement of the crater.

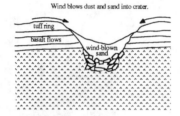

6. Wind-blown sand and dust collect in enlarged crater.

Figure 3.13. Evolution of the Pinacate craters. (Peter L. Kresan)

Figure 3.14. Elegante Crater. (Photo by Peter L. Kresan)

lake sediments. These deposits are rich in clays and carbonates; contain graded-bedding, cross-bedding, and evaporite deposits; and hold small, delicate, freshwater snail fossils that would be difficult to preserve with any transport. During the last glacial period, perhaps as recently as about 20,000 years ago, Elegante Crater apparently had a small lake at its bottom.

Cerro Colorado, with its striking basaltic tuff ring, may be the youngest crater in the field. This crater is much more a maar volcano than a caldera and looks to be a composite of a few overlapping craters. Low in the crater walls is exposed the original desert surface on which the pyroclastic surge was deposited. Just north of Cerro Colorado is a playa; to the south, the drainage flows south. Cerro Colorado apparently erupted in the middle of an old stream drainage, which it now blocks. Perhaps the water-saturated sediments within this drainage contributed the volatiles that generated the blast of foamy lava (tuff), broken rock (breccia), and steam that formed Cerro Colorado Crater and its high-standing rim.

Sykes (Grande) Crater (700 m, or 2,300 ft, in diameter and 220 m, or 722 ft, deep) and MacDougal Crater (1,100 m, or 3,610 ft, in diameter and 130 m, or 430 ft, deep) are both northwest of the central peaks. The location and steepness of Sykes Crater are striking (Figure 3.15).

Located in the remote southwestern part of the field and on the very edge of the Gran Desierto, Moon (Luna) Crater is the most unusual. It is a cinder cone surrounded by a tuff ring (Figure 3.16). A reasonable scenario for its formation starts with an explosion that forms the tuff ring. The initial explosion reduces the gas content of the magma enough that the subsequent eruption is less violent and forms the cinder cone, which fills in much if not all of the crater created during the initial blast. Blown sand from the adjacent Gran Desierto may also have helped fill in the crater. Perhaps there were cinder cones in some of the other Pinacate craters, but they subsequently disappeared with the collapse of the crater floor.

The tuff rings around the craters are littered with basaltic fragments blasted out of the crater. The larger fragments tend to collect and get concentrated as a lag deposit on the rims. Various other interesting inclusions and nodules are also found in the tuff rims. They include (1) granitic and gneissic rocks, representing basement rock from the crust beneath the volcanic field; (2) sand-stone, perhaps representing sand dunes buried by Pinacate lavas; (3) gabbro nodules with a granular mix of calcium plagioclase (white) and pyroxene (black) crystals (these nodules are interpreted to be culminates of crystals that formed from basaltic magma, perhaps as magma chambers cooled and solidified beneath volcanic vents they once fed with lava); and (4) peridotite nodules, lacking plagioclase crystals but containing olivine (green), pyroxene (black), and spinel (black). Peridotite represents upper mantle rock that is the solid residue left after partial melting generates the basaltic magma.

Holocene vegetation from ten packrat middens in the Hornaday Mountains near MacDougal Crater includes ninety-four plant taxa and provides an excellent history of vegetation and climate for the last 10,000 years (Van Devender, this volume; Van Devender et al. 1990).

Cabeza Prieta National Wildlife Refuge and Vicinity

The Cabeza Prieta Wildlife Refuge is home to the desert bighorn sheep and endangered Sonoran pronghorn. In this remote part of the Sonoran Desert jagged and naked mountains alternate with broad open valleys. Partially exhumed granitic peaks contrast with the dark covering of ancient lava flows. In places, islands of white granitic rock jut out of the remnant cover of volcanic rock, making us wonder what must still lie entombed beneath these old lava flows. In fact, an ancient desert surface, predating the 15-million-year-old blanket of lavas, is being ever so slowly uncovered and rejuvenated (Shafiqullah et al. 1980).

The landscape of the Cabeza Prieta region is a classic example of the Basin and Range Geological Province of western North America (Figure 3.17). In fact, geologic relationships exposed in the Cabeza Prieta provide evidence for when the Basin and Range began to form. Basaltic volcanism generally began about 23 million years ago in this region but is especially characteristic after about 10 million years ago. Basaltic magmas originate in the mantle and must rise to the Earth's surface relatively quickly in order to remain basaltic in composition. Andesitic volcanism, typically associated with subduction-zone volcanoes, stopped in the Basin and Range region by about 12 million years ago. The oldest lava flows in the Cabeza Pri-

Figure 3.15. Sykes Crater, with Pinacate Peak in background. (Photo by Peter L. Kresan)

Figure 3.16. Moon Crater. (Photo by Peter L. Kresan)

eta Mountains are tilted, dark brown, andesitic lavas that radiometrically date at 17–16 million years old (Figure 3.18). It is an andesitic lava cap to a granitic peak that gives this region its name, Cabeza Prieta, meaning "black or dark head" in Spanish. The high angle of tilting indicates that these andesitic lavas erupted before the Basin and Range landscape was formed and were then tilted by movements of the crust associated with the formation of the Basin and Range. Interestingly, Mesa del Malpais in the southern Lechuguilla Valley is capped by a flat-lying, 10-million-year-old basaltic lava. Raven Butte, along the east flank of the Tinajas Altas Mountains, is capped by a series of thin, flat-lying, 11-million-year-old basalt flows. In fact, most lava flows in southern Arizona younger than 11 million years are flat-lying. This

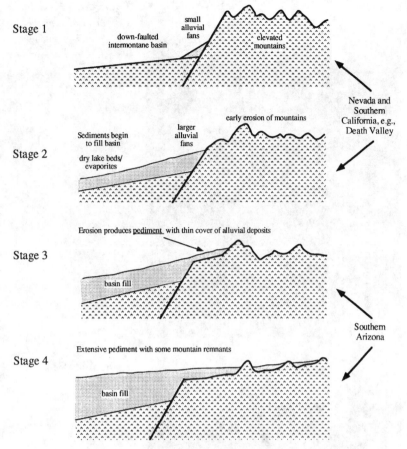

Stage 1

down-faulted
intermontane basin

small
alluvial
fans

elevated
mountains

Nevada and
Southern
California, e.g.,
Death Valley

Stage 2

Sediments begin
to fill basin

dry lake beds/
evaporites

larger
alluvial
fans

early erosion of mountains

Stage 3

Erosion produces pediment with thin cover of alluvial deposits

basin fill

Southern
Arizona

Stage 4

Extensive pediment with some mountain remnants

basin fill

Figure 3.17. *Stages in the geomorphic evolution of a Basin and Range mountain front. (Drawing by Peter L. Kresan)*

years ago). The magmas were generated within a subduction zone at a time when the Pacific Ocean crust was plunging under the southwestern edge of North America (Figure 3.1). Subsequent uplift, and erosion of the rocks once on top, led to this extensive exposure of granite at the surface.

As mentioned previously, about 25 to 15 million years ago andesite lava flows buried a desert surface analogous to the one developed today on this granite. The Gunnery Range granite is a coarse, crystalline rock made predominantly of quartz, feldspars, and mica. Physical and, to a lesser degree, chemical weathering causes the granite to crumble into a coarse sand, called *grus.* The grus collects in ephemeral stream channels, which distribute the sediment into the valleys. Fine-grained, tan, windblown dust, called *loess,* is also an abundant sedimentary deposit mantling the floor of these desert basins. Physical and chemical weathering processes also produce the rounded granite boulders and elaborately chambered cliff faces called *tafoni.* Such cavernous weathering produces a honeycomb of natural cavities and is well exhibited in the Tinajas Altas Mountains, where the chambers are large enough to crawl into. Animals often occupy these cavities.

The mountain slopes are steep, and they meet the valley floor abruptly. Even though rainfall is very ephemeral, intermittent stream flow has carved relatively steep, deep canyons into the mountains. Excavated by water, bedrock depressions called *tinajas,* or tanks, in some of these canyons trap and store storm water, sometimes for an entire year. West from the oasis at Quitobaquito Springs in Organ Pipe Cactus National Monument across the Growler Valley, Tule Desert, Lechuguilla Desert, and the blistering Yuma Desert is a series of these tinajas, some of which are dry for much of the year. The trail of these water sources defines a route known as El Camino del Diablo, or the Devil's Highway. The Camino was a southern trade route for Native Americans traveling from Arizona and Sonora to the Colorado River and southern California. Many sleeping circles, bedrock metates, and petroglyphs are found along this ancient trail. In 1540 Melchior Díaz, one of Coronado's lieutenants, ventured across. Eventually, pioneers crossed the Camino by wagon to bypass the absolutely dry, active sand desert to the south and, perhaps, to avoid rougher terrain and contact with native peoples to the north.

constrains the interval of time for the especially active rotational movements along Basin and Range faults. Apparently, the Basin and Range landscape began to form about 15 million years ago. During its initial development a greater degree of crustal block rotation occurred, tilting the preexisting lava flows, most of which were andesitic. Over about the last 10 million years high-angle normal faulting became more pervasive and resulted in significantly less rotation and tilting of the crustal blocks. In summary, southwestern Arizona began to evolve into the landscape we see today about 15 million years ago.

Beneath the dark layers of tilted and flatlying lavas is a bedrock of light-colored late Cretaceous granite, which intrudes into somewhat darker Proterozoic crystalline rocks, exposed, for example, in the southern end of the Sierra Pinta in the Cabeza Prieta National Wildlife Refuge. The extensive exposures of granite are interpreted to be part of the Gunnery Range Batholith, which is presumed to be either the roots of ancient volcanoes or magma chambers that never vented but solidified in the late Cretaceous (about 70 million

Along with Quitobaquito Springs, the most dependable water source between Sonoyta and the Colorado River is the Tinajas Altas (High Tanks) (Figure 3.19). Tinajas Altas is a series of nine natural depressions in the southern Tinajas Altas Mountains. Travelers and their animals sometimes died by the dried-up lower pools because they were too weak to climb to the upper tanks. More than fifty graves have been found at the mouth of the canyon to Tinajas Altas. Hurrying on to the Colorado River, early travelers often headed west from the Tinajas Altas into the parched and sandy Yuma Desert, only to die in the effort. Later, when the Gila River route to the north became better known, wiser travelers stayed east of the Tinajas Altas Range and journeyed north to the Gila and then along its channel to its confluence with the Colorado River. Today El Camino del Diablo is the principal four-wheel-drive route across the sublime desert of this wildlife refuge.

Gila River Trough

The Gila River valley, a prominent linear feature, is defined to the northwest by the southern edge of the Kofa and Castle Dome volcanic field. Some geologists have suggested that the lower Gila River follows an ancient zone of continental rifting. Others think it is simply a geomorphic feature defined by the regional slope of the southwestern Arizona landscape.

Organ Pipe Cactus National Monument, Ajo, and Vicinity

South from Gila Bend through Organ Pipe Cactus National Monument and into northern Sonora is a classic Basin and Range landscape mantled by Sonoran Desert vegetation. Mesozoic and Cenozoic volcanic and plutonic rocks, plus sedimentary deposits derived from these igneous rocks, are extensively exposed in the mountain blocks throughout this region (Haxel et al. 1984; Spencer et al. 1995; Tosdal et al. 1989).

The west flank of the Ajo Mountains in Organ Pipe Cactus National Monument is an especially lush desert due to the orographic effect of the relatively long and high Ajo Mountains. The Ajo Mountains are the first sizable topographic barrier to the flow of air sweeping off the Gulf of California. Rainfall is more likely to occur where moist air is first forced upward, along the west

Figure 3.18. Cabeza Prieta Mountains. (Photo by Peter L. Kresan)

Figure 3.19. Tinajas Altas (upper tanks) and El Camino del Diablo, Goldwater Range. (Photo by Peter L. Kresan)

flank of the Ajo Mountains. These mountains and this landscape evolved over the last 15 million years because of the jostling of crustal blocks and earthquake activity associated with Basin and Range crustal extension. However, the rock layers exposed in the Ajo and surrounding mountains are older and tell a variety of geologic stories.

This region was probably on the southern continental margin of North America about 600 million years ago. Paleozoic sedimentary rocks, such as limestone, sandstone, and shale, are a

Figure 3.20. Cherioni Wash, Organ Pipe Cactus National Monument. (Photo by Peter L. Kresan)

record of these ancient coastal and offshore environments but are exposed only outside the national monument. The oldest rocks in the national monument are early Jurassic rhyodacite ash and andesite lava flows. In fact, explosive volcanism is an important story here for much of the last 200 million years (Mesozoic and Cenozoic). During the Mesozoic and for most of the Cenozoic the Pacific Ocean crust subducted beneath the western edge of North America. A long chain of large volcanoes was active to the east of the subduction zone and cut right through western Arizona. This was also a period of crustal compression due to the convergence between the Pacific and North America plates. So along with the volcanism, thrust and strike-slip faulting contributed to the formation of a landscape with relatively high relief—a landscape probably analogous to the present-day volcanic Cascade Mountains in northwestern North America.

During an interval of geologic time called the Middle Tertiary, from about 25 to 15 million years ago, all hell broke loose in southwestern Arizona. Evidence for this especially active and explosive volcanic episode is recorded by the layers of lava (usually black to brown), ash flows (usually brown, red, or tan), air-fall ash (light tan to cream), and breccia exposed in the Ajo Mountains and vicinity. Montezuma's Head, a prominent spire in the northern Ajo Mountains, is a remnant of a 17–16-million-year-old rhyolite flow. Tremendous

amounts of lava and ash erupted from composite volcanoes and calderas. Recall that a caldera results from the collapse of the magma chamber roof in an explosive eruption. Although the rock layers in the Ajo Mountains clearly tell a story of explosive volcanism for the mid-Tertiary, subsequent movements of the crust along faults during earthquake activity and sculpting by weathering and erosion over the last 15 million years have essentially erased the volcanoes and calderas. Today active volcanism is restricted to localized areas such as the Pinacates and is a result of very different geologic circumstances.

The shape and aspect of landforms are closely related to the rock types that underlie them. For example, in Organ Pipe Cactus National Monument, rounded hills are likely to be made out of Mesozoic granite and metamorphic rocks associated with the uplifted and exposed roots of ancient volcanoes (Figure 3.20). The tilted layers of mid-Tertiary andesite and rhyolite lava and ash flows form the rugged and deeply incised canyons, slopes, and spires along the flanks of the Ajo Mountains. Flat-topped mesas are capped by more recent basaltic lava flows, as in the Cabeza Prieta refuge.

Quitobaquito Oasis

Quitobaquito Springs emerges from a highly fractured and foliated granite that composes the surrounding hills (Figure 3.21). Radiocarbon analysis of the spring water system suggests that the water is of local origin and less than 2,000 years old. Spring discharge is not highly correlated with local precipitation, indicating that local annual recharge may be small relative to the amount of water in the aquifer supplying the spring. Groundwater in the sands and gravels beneath La Abra Plain to the north of the Quitobaquito Hills moves south toward the Sonoyta River. Some groundwater also moves through the highly fractured granitic rocks and is discharged from springs on the southwest side of the Quitobaquito Hills and at Aquajita Spring (Carruth 1993). Felger and colleagues (1992) discuss the history, flora, and ethnobotany of Quitobaquito.

Ajo Mine

As early as 1750, Spanish prospectors worked the high-grade veins of the New Cornelia porphyry copper deposit in Ajo, Arizona. By 1930 the carbonate ore was mined out. In 1950 a new smelter was completed at Ajo to process the copper concentrates from the open-pit mine (Dixon 1966). This copper deposit formed during an interval of geologic time called the Laramide (80–55 million years ago). During this period copper, sulfur, and other metals were concentrated by hot water circulating through fractures in the shallow (1–4 km deep) roots of larger, explosive volcanoes throughout southwestern North America. Associated with the subduction of the Pacific Ocean plate beneath western North America, this volcanic activity has long ceased. The copper deposits are now exposed at or near the surface due to uplift and erosion. Weathering processes play an important role in further concentrating the ore minerals, adding to their economic value (Titley 1981).

Acknowledgments

I have had the privilege of exploring the lower Colorado River region of Arizona and Sonora with many friends and natural scientists, from whom I have learned much of what I share in this chapter. For all those great field trips to this very special region, I especially thank Yar Petryszyn, Dan Lynch, Bill Bull, Norman Meader, Joanna Coleman, Tad and Mary Jane Nichols, Jack and Georgie Boyer, Robert Scarborough, Nick Lancaster, Bill Dickinson, Bill Hartmann, Hank Oona, and the many students who have joined trips over the years. Thank you to Kevin Horstman for his spectacular

Figure 3.21. Quitobaquito oasis, Organ Pipe Cactus National Monument. (Photo by Peter L. Kresan)

satellite imagery; to Norman Meader, who produced many of the illustrations; to Nick Lancaster, who supplied the illustration on star dune formation; to Paul Damon, who has long provided me with inspiration and information on this region. This chapter is dedicated to all who love and respect the Sonoran Desert.

Four

Airing Out the Desert Basement:

The Physical Geography of the Sonoran Desert National Monument

Kathryn Mauz

The Sonoran Desert National Monument encompasses three prominent mountain ranges, their inselbergs (bedrock hills isolated from the main range by alluvial fan deposits), and parts of three major intervening basins. In an insightful if simplistic assessment, Kirk Bryan offered the following scenario for the superposition and topographic relations of rocks to one another in the Maricopa Mountains: "In addition to numerous outliers of crystalline rock, there is a hill capped by a lava flow overlying gravel. The gravel rests on an erosion surface only a few feet above the present pediment, but the lava is tilted to the east. The mountains were therefore elevated after the extrusion of the lava. In contrast to the east side, the west side of the mountains seems to be deeply buried in alluvium" (1925:221).

This description could easily serve as a generic account of the geologic sequence represented in the monument as a whole. The rock record encompasses more than 2 billion years, but much of the middle portion (representing several hundred million years) had been lost to erosion by the time the Cenozoic gravels to which Bryan referred came along. Episodes of violent volcanism, intervals of dramatic tectonic activity, and long periods of relatively quiescent alluviation intervened to create the physical landscapes we admire today.

Landforms and Landscape History

Ranges

The ranges that exist today once formed a single erosional surface of Proterozoic bedrock on which Cenozoic sediments and volcanic rocks were deposited from 53 to 13 million years ago (see Figure 4.1). Regional block-faulting in the middle Miocene broke apart this surface and created the series of roughly parallel, high-standing ranges and low-lying valleys that characterize the Basin and Range geologic province (Eberly & Stanley 1978). Pediments and piedmonts flanking these ranges today reflect surficial processes and landform evolution of the last 2 million years, from latest Tertiary through Quaternary time (Demsey 1989). Modern summits range from about 2,700 to 2,900 ft above sea level in the Maricopa Mountains, to just over 4,085 ft in the Sand Tank Mountains (Maricopa Peak on Javelina Mountain), and to 4,373 ft on Table Top in the Table Top Mountains. Mountain fronts tend to be highly sinuous and deeply embayed.

Basins and Drainage

Alluvial basins and piedmonts comprise the majority of the land area of the monument, as with the Basin and Range region generally. Valley fill deposits in this area began accumulating in the late Cenozoic following late Miocene block faulting. The rapidly subsiding basins were initially internally drained, gradually filling with sediment that in places exceeds 3,000 m in depth. By 10.5 to 6 million years ago the filled basins had coalesced and a system of external drainage had developed (Eberly & Stanley 1978). The Gila River, immediately west of the monument, has been the main collector in this tributary system for at least 3.3 million years (Morrison 1985). Thick deposits of basin-fill gravels form the modern aquifers underlying the Sand Tank Wash, Waterman Wash, and Vekol Wash systems adjoining or within the monument (Matlock 1983).

An extensive tributary system in the Vekol Valley drains the west and north slopes of the Table Top Mountains and the east slope of the Sand Tank Mountains. Bryan described a Vekol Wash that "after passing through extensive flats covered with 'galleta' grass where deposition is going on, enters . . . a shallow trench. . . . This arrangement of slightly dissected alluvial slopes, low bluffs flanking a floodplain, and a channel trench continues northward for about 10 miles and then fades out, so that at Mobile . . . 18 miles farther north, the stream has several channels, none of which are well marked" (1922:80–81). The channel he documented was much as it exists at present, although a dike system begun in the 1930s now interrupts the upper portion of the wash in the vicinity of the "galleta" (actually tobosa grass, *Hilaria mutica*) flats. Rather than continue north to join the Waterman Wash in the Rainbow Valley, as Bryan implies, the Vekol Wash in fact turns east into Pinal County at the Haley Hills and joins the Santa Cruz wash network near its confluence with the Gila River, east of the Sierra Estrella. The east side of the Table Top Mountains drains to the Santa Rosa Wash, which occupies the broad Maricopa-Stanfield Basin and (with some imagination) joins the Greene Wash and Santa Cruz wash network in a confusion of agricultural fields and canals.

North of the Vekol Valley, tributaries of the Waterman Wash drain the eastern slopes of the Maricopa Mountains. The axial drainage continues northwest through the Rainbow Valley to join the Gila River just east of the Buckeye Hills. More or less parallel major drainages, including the Bender Wash, Sand Tank Wash, and Sauceda Wash, drain the northern and western sides of the Sand Tanks and the west side of the Maricopa Mountains, crossing the Gila Plain to the Gila River west of the communities of Bosque and Gila Bend. A large, unnamed wash exits the north Maricopa Mountains south of Margies Peak and crosses the Gila River floodplain north of Cotton Center.

Bedrock Geology

Lower Proterozoic metasedimentary rocks (principally the Pinal Schist) occur throughout the Table Top Mountains, in the central Sand Tank Mountains (including Javelina Mountain and the White Hills in the western Vekol Valley), and in the southern Maricopa Mountains. These rocks are generally fine-grained, composed predominantly of muscovite and quartz with minor other and accessory minerals (Peterson et al. 1987). Exposures can range from very steep ridges to rounded hilltops, and slopes generally appear grayish or even silvery from a distance. The schist typically weathers along foliation, producing lozenge-shaped clasts and glinting gravels in alluvial settings.

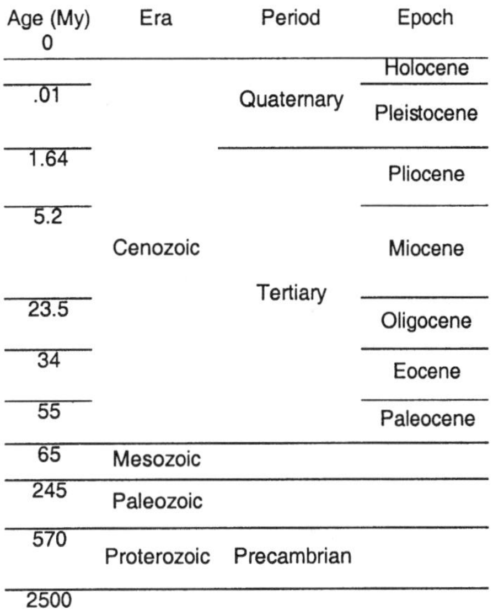

Age (My)	Era	Period	Epoch
0			
			Holocene
.01		Quaternary	Pleistocene
1.64			
			Pliocene
5.2			
	Cenozoic		Miocene
23.5		Tertiary	
			Oligocene
34			Eocene
55			
			Paleocene
65	Mesozoic		
245	Paleozoic		
570	Proterozoic	Precambrian	
2500			

Figure 4.1. Geologic time scale (ages in millions of years; after Behrensmeyer et al. 1992:543).

Intrusive rocks of similar (lower Proterozoic) age, including porphyritic (texturally, bearing large feldspar crystals within a finer-grained matrix) and leucocratic (compositionally, containing a relatively low percentage of dark minerals) granites, constitute the majority of the Maricopa Mountains. These rocks form the Margies Peak and Sheep Mountain summits, neighboring Espanto Mountain, and can be seen in the vicinity of Butterfield Pass (Cunningham et al. 1987; Reynolds & Skotnicki 1993). The middle Proterozoic-age Oracle Granite (1.4 billion years old; Shakel et al. 1977) occurs in limited exposures in the Table Top Mountains and in the Sand Tank Mountains (see Figure 4.2). This rock, a pinkish-to-whitish quartz monzonite, varies in texture from fine-grained, uniformly textured, and relatively coherent to coarse-grained and porphyritic (Peterson et al. 1987). Exposures of the latter expression disintegrate readily to grus-strewn slopes and coarse alluvium, whereas fragments of the more compact form may persist in alluvial settings as cobble-sized clasts. Regardless of exposure, slopes underlain by this lithology seem more xeric than those underlain by the Pinal Schist in similar topographic settings. Small to extensive quartz pegmatites (outcrops of massive quartz) occur within the Oracle Granite in the Table Top Mountains and have contributed to quartz-dominated pebble pavement on some of the piedmonts of this range.

Tertiary-age volcanic rocks of predominantly mafic composition occur in the southern Maricopa Mountains, the Sand Tank Mountains, and the Table Top Mountains. Only in the Sand Tank

Figure 4.2. *Intrusive contact between the Precambrian Pinal Schist (darker, upper left)—oldest rock type in the Sonoran Desert National Monument—and the intruding Oracle Granite (lighter, lower right), about 1 billion years the schist's junior. Specimen is a polished hand-sample from the Table Top Mountains. Field of view is 5.5 cm across. (Photo by Kathryn Mauz)*

Mountains are these exposures aerially extensive. Rocks of basaltic composition occur with younger, tuffaceous rocks in the Maricopa Mountains (Cunningham et al. 1987). Discontinuous, small outcrops of Miocene basaltic andesite occur in the northern Table Top Mountains (Peterson et al. 1987). The conspicuous dark caprock of the prominent peaks in the Table Top Mountains—Table Top, Antelope Peak ("a sharp nubbin of rock" in Bryan 1925:223), Black Mountain—is a Miocene-age olivine basalt (23 million years old; Eberly & Stanley 1978) that is typically fine-grained and locally riddled with vesicles (Peterson et al. 1987). Boulders of this rock cover the middle slopes of Table Top and form a lag on one of the oldest piedmont surfaces in the range, referred to by Pendall (1994) as Prospect Fan.

Sedimentary rocks are uncommon in the monument. The Pioneer Shale, a unit in the Precambrian Apache Group (between 1.42 and 1.15 billion years old; McConnell 1972) best known from the Mogollon Rim 100 miles to the northeast, is exposed very locally beneath the north summit of Table Top, where it overlies the Pinal Schist (Peterson et al. 1987; Shride 1967). Middle to upper Tertiary-age conglomerates occur in the southeastern Maricopa Mountains with volcanic rocks of similar age (Cunningham et al. 1987). A thin, poorly consolidated, Tertiary-age conglomerate (older than 23 million years) underlies the basalt caprock on Table Top and Antelope Peak. This conglomerate contains fragments of both the Pinal Schist and Oracle Granite, among other rocks (Peterson et al. 1987). Small boulders of a fine-grained, compact, dark-gray limestone have been observed on the south slope of Table Top and embedded within the thick caliche layer of a high-standing piedmont surface in the northeast part of the range. Pendall (1994) reports an outcrop of this rock, possibly of middle Paleozoic age, in the northeast Table Top Mountains. Although rocks of similar origin and age to this limestone are common in the Vekol Mountains to the south of the Table Top Mountains (Dokter & Keith 1978), the Paleozoic and Mesozoic eras are largely invisible in the rock record that can be observed within the monument.

Alluvial Geology

Surficial geology has been mapped in detail in the northern Maricopa Mountains and in the Table Top Mountains. Delineating surfaces and attributing relative ages to them incorporates a combination of the following observations of landforms and soil profiles: height above active channels, morphology and incision of drainage networks developed on the landform's surface, degree of development of the petrocalcic (caliche, or calcium carbonate–dominated) soil horizon, development of varnish on surface particles, and development of pavement or lags of larger particles on the soil surface (Christenson & Purcell 1985). Based on these criteria, particularly development of the petrocalcic horizon and qualitative correlation with absolute-dated surfaces elsewhere in the southwestern United States, geomorphic surfaces of alluvial origin in the monument have been assigned ages ranging from most recent (late Holocene) to an estimated 2 million years old (late Pliocene or latest Tertiary) (Demsey 1989; Pendall 1994). Others who have worked in this region have noted difficulties in correlating discontinuous surfaces across space, either within or between ranges, owing to differences in aspect, topographic position, vegetation and microbiota, and lithology between deposits, and to slow rates of pedogenesis regionally (Christenson & Purcell 1985; Huckleberry 1997).

In the northern Maricopa Mountains the majority of the piedmont area is occupied by surfaces of middle to late Pleistocene age (250,000 to 10,000 years old). Remnants of older (middle Pleistocene age, 790,000 to 250,000 years old) surfaces are present within the range, particularly immediately adjacent to and adjoining the mountain front. Isolated fan remnants of this age are also present on the west side of the northern Maricopa Mountains between the mountain front and the Gila River. The Rainbow Valley and the Gila Plain are occupied by Holocene-age deposits (Demsey 1989). A similar pattern is apparent for the Table Top Mountains. In the northeastern area a few large remnants of Pliocene-age (more than 1.8 million years old) surfaces are preserved, with thin upper soil underlying a thick petrocalcic horizon, and planar bedrock pediment beneath. Early Pleistocene surfaces occur both adjacent to bedrock and as isolated fan remnants (ballenas) on all sides of the range. Pleistocene-age surfaces

form the majority of the piedmont area around the Table Top Mountains, extending nearly to the Vekol Wash where they intergrade with deposits of Holocene age (Pendall 1994).

There are no significant playa surfaces or areas of internal drainage in the monument. Likewise, eolian sand is quite uncommon (there are limited dune exposures to the east of the monument in the Santa Rosa valley). On the south face of Table Top, fine-grained sediment, possibly of eolian origin, has accumulated in the interstices of the basalt boulders and appears to favor plant establishment. Cryptobiotic "crusts" of various sorts thoroughly cover the fine soil intervening among varnished boulders on Prospect Fan, and are common on granite gravel-paved surfaces throughout the Maricopa Mountains.

Confessions of a Repeat Photographer

RAYMOND M. TURNER

It all started in March 1959 on a trip to the Sierra Pinacate volcanic region. The excursion was supported by funds from the Rockefeller Foundation's Arid Lands Project at the University of Arizona and was aimed, in part, at recapturing on film desert scenes that had first been photographed in 1907 during an expedition originating in Tucson. Three members of the party—Charles Lowe, herpetologist and university professor; Rod Hastings, graduate student in history and mayor of Hayden, Arizona; and I—were active participants in the university's Arid Lands Project. Robert DuBois, geologist and university professor, and Tad Nichols, photographer, were the other members of the group (see Nichols, this volume). This band of adventurers is shown in Figure 5.1b, perched on the same rocks as the members of the 1907 expedition (Figure 5.1a).

During the previous year, Nichols and Lowe had visited the area to try their hands at matching some of the photographs taken on the 1907 Hornaday expedition to the Pinacate region. For the rest of us, this was exposure to a new and powerful addiction. As it later turned out, all that was required to feed this compulsion was a source of old photographs, a medium- or large-format camera, access to a darkroom, and a penchant for tromping around the countryside.

Repeat photography as a tool for documenting landscape change was first focused on alpine glaciers, features that undergo relatively rapid change (Hattersley-Smith 1966). As the new technology of photography matured, open landscape scenes accumulated and the potential for documenting vegetation change through time became apparent. One of its earliest uses for studying vegetation change was in Africa, where Homer Leroy Shantz (president of the University of Arizona from 1928 to 1937) traversed the full length of that continent in 1956–57, matching many photographs

that he had first taken there less than forty years before (Shantz & Turner 1958).

Many of the early travelers to the Dry Borders country carried cameras. The scenes they recorded were often used to illustrate published accounts written for readers unfamiliar with North America's most arid region. The earliest photographs were taken by D. T. MacDougal, W. T. Hornaday, J. M. Phillips, and Godfrey Sykes, who were members of the group that Hornaday assembled for the historic visit to this region in 1907. Their photographs illustrate Hornaday's *Camp-Fires on Desert and Lava* (Hornaday 1908). A mere three years later the Norwegian Carl Lumholtz, camera in hand, traveled throughout this region, taking many pictures as he went. Some of them appeared in his *New Trails in Mexico* (Lumholtz 1912). Then followed such adventurer-photographers as Forrest Shreve, Norman Wallace, Homer Shantz, and Tad Nichols. As the first third of the twentieth century drew to a close, this fascinating landscape had been captured on film scores of times, leaving a rich treasure for the repeat-photography addict to tap. A sampling of these matched photographs is presented in this chapter.

The photographic sequence of "The Outfit Coming Through MacDougal Pass" demonstrates the power of the matched-photograph technique (Figure 5.2a, b, c). The first photograph, taken by Hornaday in 1907, was matched by Tad Nichols in 1958; I matched it in 1997. Careful scrutiny of the earliest scene (Figure 5.2a) shows one half-grown saguaro and three smaller ones that are partially hidden by the nurse plant, big galleta grass. The plain shown here was described by Hornaday as "a fine meadow of galleta grass… untouched by cattle, horse, or burro," and because no large saguaros were seen, he also remarked that the saguaros were of "dwarf stature" (Hornaday 1908:162–163). By the time of the 1958 photograph

Figure 5.1a. Members of the Hornaday expedition on porous rock near Papago Tanks, 1907. From left: *Godfrey Sykes, Jesse D. Jenkins, Charlie Foster, Jeff Milton, George Saunders, John Phillips, Frank Coles, and William Hornaday.* (Photo by Daniel T. MacDougal)

(Figure 5.2b), taken during one of the region's most prolonged droughts, the grass had begun to wane, the saguaros had sprung up from beneath their protective shrub or grass cover, and more desert trees spotted the landscape. In the third photograph (Figure 5.2c), taken ninety years after the first, several of the "dwarf" saguaros of that early era had reached maturity, and the half-grown one at right foreground in the original photograph had fallen, with only its skeleton remaining; another, nearby, was dead but still standing. The extensive galleta prairie was a thing of the past, and desert trees were more conspicuous than ever. The loss of the grass is probably due in part to the presence of a cattle ranch within about one mile of this site. The ranch was built sometime during the 1960s.

This series of photographs gives rise to several interesting questions, the most intriguing being: What reset the saguaros' biologic clock at the time of the 1907 scene? Had all of the large saguaros been destroyed simultaneously in the past and was the population just beginning a comeback from that local extinction? Was the destructive force perhaps a fire burning across the galleta meadow sometime in the 1800s? We'll never know

Figure 5.1b. Members of the author's first trip to Papago Tanks, 1959. From left: *Tad Nichols, Robert DuBois, Rod Hastings* (standing), *Charles Lowe, and Raymond Turner.* (Photo by Tad Nichols, using his self-timer)

the answers to these intriguing questions, but the subject of fire was emphasized for us when in 1974 we found that a small area of the galleta meadow nearby had burned and the saguaros encompassed by the fire were scarred. By this time the galleta grass was confined to scattered patches, saving the saguaro stand from more extensive damage. As a final expression of repeat photography's ability to

THE PLACE *CONFESSIONS OF A REPEAT PHOTOGRAPHER* 51

Figure 5.2a. *The Hornaday expedition coming through MacDougal Pass, 1907. (Photo by John Phillips, from Hornaday 1908: opposite p. 164)*

Figure 5.2b. *The Nichols-Lowe expedition at MacDougal Pass, 1958. (Photo by Tad Nichols)*

Figure 5.2c. *The same MacDougal Pass location in 1997. The old road is no longer used. (Photo by Raymond Turner)*

promote speculation, one must ask whether the cattle had enhanced saguaro establishment through the animals' consumption of the grass, thereby resulting in reduced fire frequency and intensity as well as reduced competition. What about the saguaros' need for nurse-plant protection during early stages of growth? Both grass, which has been declining through time, and desert trees, which have been increasing through time, serve as nurse plants but also as competitors for scarce habitat resources such as water. The effect on saguaros of drought, grass (as fuel, competitor, and nurse plant), fire, desert trees (as nurse plants and competitors), and cattle must all be given some weight in any ecological equation designed to solve the complex mystery revealed by the MacDougal Pass photographs. This case illustrates some fundamental properties of repeat photography: it documents change but does not necessarily reveal the reasons for the change.

Of the many attractions in the Pinacate region—now a biosphere reserve—the area's deepest crater, known as Elegante since its christening by Lumholtz, is perhaps the most frequently visited landmark. In 1927, Norman Wallace, an engineer from Phoenix, visited this crater and took a series of photographs as he traversed its circular rim. In one of his photographs, one can see the crater floor, the light-colored center of which is home to many plants (primarily creosotebush and mesquite) (Figure 5.3a). I matched Wallace's photographs in 1987 and, as with other craters in the area, found the vegetation at the crater's center much sparser than before (Figure 5.3b). The loss of these plants probably was the result of a prolonged drought that had reached its peak at about the time of the visits in 1958 and 1959 (Turner 1990); or in the case of Elegante, the opposite extreme, excessive flooding, may have caused some of the loss (Bull 1974).

A hike to the crater's floor in 1987 revealed that a new exotic plant, salt cedar *(Tamarix ramosissima),* had become established at the crater's lowest point. Primarily a plant of watercourses and known in this region only since shortly before the mid-twentieth century, its presence in this xeriscape was unexpected. Further reflection, however, suggested the sequence of events that probably succeeded in bringing the plant here. Two intense rainfall events visited the region in the early 1970s: tropical storms Norma in September

1970 and Joanne in October 1972. During the downpours associated with Norma and Joanne, ponding of water occurred at the bottom of this crater to a depth of 7.2 ft and 4.9 ft, respectively (Bull 1974). By the years of those storms, salt cedar had worked its way along the Río Sonoyta to a point a mere nine or ten miles away, and the windborne, umbrella-like seeds of this plant were being deposited far and wide throughout the region. Because abundant moisture is required for seed germination and subsequent seedling establishment, a successful roothold was not possible until Norma and Joanne provided the necessary conditions. Once ensconced, this plant survives alongside the hardiest of desert shrubs. The salt cedar now growing on the crater floor may remain there for decades, but it is unlikely that new plants will become established in the absence of another tropical storm. An event causing ponding equaling or exceeding Norma's 7.2-ft depth had not occurred for at least twenty years prior to the 1970 storm (Bull 1974).

One of the main attractions of the repeat-photography process is the element of mystery that surrounds each new search for some old camera position. Although latitude-longitude coordinates are useful in roughly locating a camera site, most old photographs are not accompanied by such information, and thus (unless the relief is completely flat) the old photograph is invariably used to reoccupy the original camera position. In regions where topographic relief is at least moderate, the presence of recognizable hills or other topographic features allows the photographer to quickly approach the approximate position of the original camera. For final refinement, one first locates, on the left or right side of the old photograph, persistent features such as large rocks, peaks, or long-lived plants that lie at varying distances toward the horizon. After finding them in real life, one moves to the left or right until the closer feature is correctly lined up with the one behind it exactly as seen in the photograph. This accomplished, one is able to identify an imaginary vertical plane that extends from the distant features through the position now occupied by the observer. That plane marks an imaginary pathway along the ground that is followed unswervingly backward or forward as features identified on the other side of the photographic print are brought into proper alignment. Once a plane is identified

Figure 5.3a. *Elegante Crater as seen from the southwest, 1927. Large trees at the crater's low point are probably mesquites. (Photo by Norman Wallace, Arizona Historical Society)*

Figure 5.3b. *The same view in 1987. The camera should be forward and to the right for an exact match. The creosotebush behind the rock at right foreground persists; ocotillos are fewer in 1987. (Photo by Raymond Turner)*

from the second group of features, the imaginary vertical line representing the intersection of the two planes is located. All that remains, besides checking other parts of the lineup, is to determine the correct camera elevation, usually by comparing foreground to background features. Once located, this third plane intersects the other two at the point of the old camera position. The indispensable tripod is then erected at (one hopes) the original camera station. However, with chin on tripod head, it pays to double check the newly found

Figure 5.4. Ray Turner, near Cholla Pass, Cabeza Prieta National Wildlife Refuge, 1991. (Photo by Bill Broyles)

position by looking for proper alignment of objects near the photograph's center. The technique just employed involves parallax, which my dictionary defines as "the apparent displacement of an observed object due to the changed position of the observer."

The camera, which should be a single-lens view or press type, is now mounted on the tripod and carefully aimed at the center of the original photograph (Figure 5.4). The center can be located by drawing diagonal lines from opposite corners of the rectangular image (assuming one carries a disposable "field" copy) or by measuring with a scale the photograph's midpoint from left to right and from top to bottom. The camera is then aimed so that the ground-glass viewing screen, with center clearly marked, is positioned so that the midpoint on the screen lies on the identified midpoint of the image. At this stage it is a good idea to verify that the camera body is level from left to right, even though most historical photographers never bothered to level their cameras. Observing this step is important, in part because it gives the next addict who wants to match the photograph a better chance to get it right.

Now that the camera site has been located, the camera aimed, and the proper lens selected, the question of original camera height must be addressed. Exact height duplication is often unimportant if only distant features appear in the view, but if there are foreground features such as rocks or small plants that persist, then attention should be given this detail. Again, parallax is involved, but here measurements on the viewing screen or on a Polaroid print are useful. First, on the original print, measure the distance between two distant features such as peaks; and then, on the same print, measure the distance from some foreground object to a feature on the distant horizon above it. Repeat these two measurements on the camera's viewing screen or on a new Polaroid print. Next calculate ratios from the two pairs of measurements. If they are not equal, then adjust the camera height accordingly.

With the image now clearly focused and correctly framed on the viewing screen, lens angle can be evaluated. The focal length of the original lens is usually unknown, but contrary to the belief held by many, the two lenses need not have the same focal length to produce the same photographic scene. If the original image is wider than the image seen on the viewing screen, install a lens with shorter focal length. If that lens is unavailable, take the photograph using the lens with narrower field. Appropriate scale adjustments and cropping can be made later in the darkroom. Thus, use of the darkroom invalidates the "focal-length fallacy."

Using the Elegante Crater photographs as examples (Figures 5.3a and 5.3b), one can quickly see that the camera placement in 1987 was too far back and too far to the left. The rock at right foreground provides the anchor needed for orientation on the right side of the scene while alignment of persistent desert trees on the crater floor with features on the crater rim provides control at the left. Improper camera placement has resulted in loss of ability to interpret some foreground changes (such as the status of the ocotillo at left) but has not reduced ability to interpret distant changes.

A recent photo-matching trip to the Camino del Diablo country produced two matches that illustrate the importance of carefully following the steps given above. About two miles east of the boundary between the Goldwater Range and the Cabeza Prieta National Wildlife Refuge grows a

Figure 5.5a. Large ironwood tree growing along the Camino del Diablo, 1910. (From Lumholtz 1912: opposite p. 222)

Figure 5.5b. The large ironwood about ninety years later, 2001. The creosotebush at left foreground persists. The gray plants at midground are desert saltbush and appear to have expanded toward the camera. The old camino is no longer used. (Photo by Raymond Turner)

lone ironwood tree, or *palo fierro (Olneya tesota)*. In 1910 Lumholtz took a photograph of this tree, his camera set up beside the old Camino del Diablo (Lumholtz 1912). My wife, Jeanne, and I found this tree in November 2001, using precise directions from Luke Evans (Figure 5.5a).

Once the tree was located, exactly matching the 1910 photograph proved a challenge. First, the tree itself had changed shape because of the death of old branches and growth of new ones. In addition, only at left foreground did a creosotebush provide an anchor for establishing a plane by parallax; on the right, no foreground objects persisted, so the critical second plane could not be established. However, once the creosotebush and the ironwood tree were properly aligned with the background hills, a camera position could be selected and the film exposed. As seen in Figure 5.5b, the results were acceptable. The creosotebush has changed little; the desert club cholla (*Grusonia*

kunzei) behind it is new; the desert saltbush growing about the ironwood tree is more abundant now than before.

We measured the diameter of the tree's trunk at ground level and found it to be 2.6 feet. Using average annual diameter growth values for five ironwood trees in the vicinity of Tucson during 1956 and 1957 (Turner 1963), we arrived at an age of 405 years. The calculations were as follows: tree diameter in inches/average diameter growth per year = 31.2 inches/0.077 inches per year = 405 years. This tree, because it grows in a minor runnel, has available to it somewhat more than the four to six inches of annual rainfall that falls around it. Thus, its actual growth rate may be rather close to that of trees growing near Tucson (with long-term average rainfall of 12 inches) during dry years, such as 1956–57. At any rate, the tree was probably already several hundred years old when originally photographed by Lumholtz.

Figure 5.6a. *Small valley below Tinajas Altas, 1933. Photo taken by Tad Nichols during a trip with Ira Wiggins, Forrest Shreve, and Dwight Mallery. The automobile at left, draped with canvas, belonged to Edith Shreve; the one at right belonged to Nichols.*

Figure 5.6b. *The same valley in 2001. The camera is too far forward yet contains useful information about plant longevity. (Photo by Raymond Turner)*

began making the necessary measurements and adjustments. The sky had become fully overcast since the earlier visit to the ironwood tree, and the prospect for a flat, featureless photographic match was almost assured. As the line on the left side of the scene in Nichols's photograph was identified by parallax, an opening appeared in the clouds and a slowly moving area of bright light traveled across the landscape. With a position along the first imaginary plane at left now occupied by the camera, it was hastily moved along that plane, using the foreground rock at right and background hills as parallax objects, until the presumed intersection of the two planes was occupied. The scene was framed and the film exposed.

Darkroom matching having been completed, the results of this camera placement (Figure 5.6b) reveal that the patch of sunlight was captured on film just where intended but the camera's position was too close by one or two feet. A return trip in the near future to improve the camera's position is a gnawing possibility for this obsessive-compulsive repeat photographer.

Despite the improper camera placement, the matched photographs proved useful in documenting some vegetation changes. The catclaw acacias in the arroyo at midground are larger in 2001 than in 1933 and have overgrown the old road. Automobiles are no longer permitted in this area, which now supports a denser growth of creosotebush than before. Several brittlebush plants are visible in both photographs, but none persists from 1933 to the present. These observations are in keeping with previous findings that show that longevity for creosotebush and catclaw acacia may exceed one hundred years and that brittlebush longevity is much shorter (Bowers et al. 1995; Goldberg & Turner 1986).

In some instances, poorly matched photographs may be just as useful as closely matched ones, but for the real addict, the ultimate high can be attained only by precisely recapturing an old scene. The disappointment felt when the camera misses its mark is best described as a downer. The camera station at Tinajas Altas is high on my list of camera sites to revisit. Next time, with more care and patience, the closely matched result might be more useful for evaluating landscape change and will certainly satisfy the aesthetic sense of one who has become addicted to the photograph-matching habit.

A few miles to the west along the Camino del Diablo the traveler arrives at Tinajas Altas. This famous natural water source was visited by the Shreve-Wiggins-Mallery-Nichols party in 1933. In a photograph taken by Tad Nichols on that trip, the vehicles that appear in Figure 9.2 (this volume) are seen again parked at the mouth of the arroyo that extends down from the natural water tanks (Figure 5.6a). With plentiful background and foreground details available, I set up my Horseman 4×5 camera with Nikkor W 135 lens and

Acknowledgments

I thank Robert Webb and Terry Hadley for their reviews of early versions of this chapter, and Diane Boyer for her help with photos. The companionship of my wife, Jeanne, and that of numerous unnamed travelers on many excursions has provided diversions that have mostly kept the urge to match photographs within manageable bounds.

The repeat-photograph archive that arose following the 1959 Pinacate "expedition" now includes photographs from more than five thousand matched-photograph camera sites throughout western North America and east Africa. Among those who have become seriously afflicted with the photograph-matching syndrome are Robert Webb, Dominic Oldershaw, Tom Brownold, Tom Wise, Ted Melis, Liz Hymans, Steve Tharnstrom, Steve Young, Steve Bullock, Nora Martijena, and Sam Walton. All have contributed significantly to the archive's holdings of matched photographs. To Rod Hastings goes the credit for starting this collection, but Bob Webb deserves special recognition for expanding this remarkable archive during the last two decades. My apologies go out to all of you for whatever role I had in instilling this affliction, along with the wish that your camera's aim is always true.

Ice Ages in the Sonoran Desert:

Pinyon Pines and Joshua Trees in the Dry Borders Region

Thomas R. Van Devender

Nineteen sixty-two was the Year of the Tiger in the Chinese calendar. For ecology, it was the Year of the Packrat. At that time, two young biologists were surveying the biological resources of the Nevada Test Site. Phil Wells, a plant ecologist, and Clive Jorgenson, a mammalogist, climbed the Spotted Range, an isolated, desolate mountain, in hopes of finding relictual plants or animals on its summit—perhaps junipers or oaks. The summit proved to be as sparsely vegetated with Mojave desertscrub as the slopes. On the way down, they entered a rockshelter to eat lunch, where they found a dark organic mass full of twigs and little oval fecal pellets that Jorgenson knew to be of *Neotoma*. These medium-sized rodents are called woodrats by residents of the eastern half of the United States but have been called packrats in the desert Southwest for more than a century (Hornaday 1908). Such dark deposits were well known by miners and cave explorers, who called them *amberrat*. On examination, Wells and Jorgenson were excited and amazed to find mats of juniper twigs and seeds—the elusive junipers had lived in the Spotted Range sometime in the past!

Wells was then a student at the University of California at Los Angeles. When he returned to school, he took a piece of the Spotted Range deposit to Willard Libby, the geochemist who, more than a decade earlier, had pioneered the radiocarbon dating method. Libby reluctantly agreed to date the modern-looking sample. To his surprise, the ^{14}C content of the organic material in the sample was relatively low, indicating an age of more than 10,000 years!

Deserts are notoriously difficult places to find fossils. Most fossils are formed when they fall into water and are buried quickly and often mineral replaced. Wells had discovered a fortuitous new source of fossils in the driest portions of the North American deserts. He dubbed the sample a packrat "midden"—a term used by archaeologists and mammalogists to describe a debris pile at the edge of a village or den. The midden was cemented together with rat urine and had a rich conifer aroma. The plant remains in the midden proved to be remarkably well preserved, easily identified to species, and ideal for radiocarbon dating (Figure 6.1). Wells immediately seized the opportunity presented him, but the potential for new knowledge in these desert time capsules would take decades to appreciate. The Year of the Packrat would change how ecologists viewed the North American deserts forever.

A Time of Discovery

The next 15 years were a time of discovery—the Amber Rush to record ice-age woodlands in the modern deserts. Wells promptly published articles in the prestigious *Science* magazine with tantalizing accounts of juniper or pinyon-juniper woodlands in the Mojave (Wells & Jorgenson 1964; Wells & Berger 1967) and Chihuahuan (Wells 1964) deserts. Radiocarbon ages ranged from about 10,000 yr B.P. (radiocarbon years before 1950) to about 35,000 yr B.P. (the limits of the radiocarbon dating method at that time), covering the first part of the present interglacial (the Holocene) and the last part of the Wisconsin glacial period, which ended at 11,000 yr B.P.

As Wells's discoveries were unfolding, Paul S. Martin was a new faculty member in the fledgling Department of Geochronology at the University of Arizona, Tucson. He began his career at the University of Michigan, where his interest in biogeography led to a study of the amphibians and reptiles of Gómez Farías, Tamaulipas, in the Sierra Madre Oriental of northeastern Mexico. Modern distribution patterns in animals stimulated his interest in past vegetation changes, and the study of pollen in radiocarbon-dated sediments proved to be a way to study the history of vegetation change. In 1963 he published *The Last 10,000 Years*, summarizing the results of his pollen studies from sites in Arizona, many associated with archaeological sites (Martin 1963).

And then, like Alfred Wallace, the codiscoverer of the theory of evolution, a century before him, Paul became interested in the giant ice-age mammals and the intriguing possibility that Paleoindian immigrants were the cause of their sudden extinction 12,000 years ago (Martin 1984). He would stimulate worldwide debates on his Pleistocene overkill theory, debates that still go on today. This interest also led him to study the massive dung deposits of the Shasta ground sloth *(Nothrotheriops shastense)* in Ramparts Cave in the Grand Canyon in the northeastern Mojave Desert. He concluded from his pollen and microhistological analyses of the plant fragments in dung balls that relatively modern deserts had formed a thousand years or so before the sloths ate their last Mormon tea *(Ephedra* sp.; Hansen 1980; Long et al. 1974) (Figure 6.2). Unfortunately, in the mid-1970s the priceless Ramparts Cave dung deposits were set on fire by a tourist's torch and mostly destroyed.

In 1970 Paul challenged the students in his Paleoecology and Man class to find the first packrat middens in the Sonoran Desert. I was then an energetic red-haired herpetologist-turned-vertebrate-paleontologist of twenty-four years and had moved to Arizona only two years earlier. Kevin Moodie, another red-haired anthropologist-turned-vertebrate-paleontologist, and I headed off in my Volkswagen to the Artillery Mountains in search of ice-age fossils. With little difficulty we found shiny, dark, aromatic samples full of single-leaf pinyon *(Pinus monophylla)* needles, shrub live oak *(Quercus turbinella)* leaves and acorns, and juniper *(Juniperus* spp.) twigs. Dates of 18,320 and 30,000 yr B.P. documented a pinyon-juniper-oak woodland in a Sonoran Desert area that now supports saguaro *(Carnegiea gigantea)* and foothill palo verde *(Parkinsonia microphylla;* Van Devender 1990b).

These samples led to my conversion from vertebrate paleontology to paleoecology and began the Amber Rush in the Desert Laboratory on Tumamoc Hill in Tucson. The Desert Laboratory, founded by the Carnegie Foundation in 1905, was

Figure 6.1. Packrat. (Drawing by Helen Wilson)

the place where the ecologist Forrest Shreve conducted his pioneering studies on Sonoran desert ecology. In the 1970s Paul Martin's graduate students led a frontal assault on the ice-age secrets of the deserts of the arid regions of North America. I worked in the Chihuahuan and Sonoran deserts while Geoff Spaulding tackled the Mojave Desert and Bob Thompson the Great Basin Desert. Julio Betancourt worked on the Colorado Plateau, and Art Phillips, Ken Cole, and Jim Mead were lured into the remote grandeur of the Grand Canyon. All experienced the thrill of finding fossils of woodland or forest trees in modern deserts. The Tumamoc Amber Rushers were bright, energetic, and very individualistic, bringing with them diverse backgrounds in anthropology, botany, geology, palynology, and zoology. They developed new semi-quantitative methodologies and became midden paleoecologists, a new breed of desert ecologist and geoscientist. They documented the ice-age vegetation of arid North America in dazzling detail unavailable anywhere else in the world. These studies were summarized in *Packrat Middens: The Last 40,000 Years of Biotic Change* (Betancourt et al. 1990). Subsequent midden studies in the Dry Borders and surrounding areas included sites in Arizona: Eagle Eye Mountain northwest of Phoenix (McAuliffe & Van Devender 1998), Picacho Peak north of Tucson (Van Devender, Mead & Rea 1991), Organ Pipe Cactus National Monument (Van Devender, Rea & Hall 1991), Waterman Mountains west of Tucson (Anderson & Van Devender 1991); in Sonora: the Hornaday Mountains in the Pinacate Region (Van Devender et al. 1990) and the Sierra Bacha on the coast of the Gulf of California (Anderson & Van Devender 1995; Van Devender & Hall 1994; Van Devender et al. 1994); in Baja California: Cataviña (Lanner & Van Devender 1998; Peñalba & Van Devender 1998; Sankey et

Figure 6.2. Paul Martin and amberrat, 1976. (Photo courtesy Paul Martin)

al. 2001); and in Baja California Sur: Sierra San Francisco (Rhode 2002).

The Amber Revolution

One of the important advances in packrat midden analysis (as the new discipline was named) that Martin's Midden Marauders made over Wells's pioneering efforts was to analyze all the samples discovered, including the younger ones. Longer midden sequences from the late Wisconsin through the Holocene provided great insight into the history of the present vegetation. The richness of the midden assemblages (25–60 plant taxa per sample), the ability to identify the midden fossils to species, and to accurately age and place the assemblages in chronological sequences, proved to be relevant to many ecological and evolutionary processes, answering numerous related ecologically important topics.

Martin's own conclusion about the timing of the formation of the modern deserts was rapidly disproved. Juniper woodlands persisted in the western Grand Canyon and in most of the southwestern deserts until 8,000 to 11,000 yr B.P. in the early Holocene. In various areas, desertscrub formed either at the end of the early Holocene or at the beginning of the late Holocene, about 4,500 yr B.P. (see Betancourt et al. 1990). Middens could not shed light on the behavior or efficiency of the Clovis peoples, but the shift to more modern vegetation and climates was 3,000 to 7,000 years after the Paleoindians last hunted the Pleistocene megafauna.

The Nature of Plant Communities

Although the dynamic nature of biotic communities is now well established, debates on organismic versus individualistic concepts of plant communities were deeply rooted in the literature and were still quite heated in the 1960s and 1970s. Frederic Clements was an influential vegetation ecologist who thought communities were groups of species that evolved in tandem, responding together to environmental changes in a series of successional stages until they reached a climax that was in equilibrium with the environment (Clements 1936). Forrest Shreve (1937) and H. A. Gleason (1939) viewed plant communities as loosely knit assemblages of individual species with different evolutionary histories and thus different physiological tolerances and responses to fluctuating climates. Packrat archivists in the Dry Borders region provided the final overwhelming evidence that community composition in Sonoran desertscrub has changed continuously for the last 11,000 years, reflecting the arrivals of key species, such as saguaro, foothill palo verde, and organ pipe cactus (*Stenocereus thurberi*), and climate fluctuations on various scales (Van Devender 1990b). Isotopic evidence from deep-sea cores of fifteen to twenty glacial/interglacial cycles in the Pleistocene (Porter 1989; Winograd et al. 1997) suggests that the Dry Borders desertscrub communities and the geographic ranges of individual species have been dynamic since the formation of the Sonoran Desert 8–15 million years ago in the Miocene (Van Devender 2001).

Many Sonoran Desert plants probably evolved in tropical deciduous forest or thornscrub before the Sonoran Desert formed. Modern palo verde–saguaro or organ pipe communities in any one location are mixtures of long-lived trees, shrubs, and succulents that immigrated from ice-age refugia at various times in the Holocene and short-lived herbs that were less affected by global climate changes and have been in situ for very long time periods. *Neotoma* won the debate for Shreve and Gleason.

Ice-Age Climates in the Dry Borders

As with the nature of plant communities, the interpretation of late Pleistocene climates was polarized into two camps. Ever since a young Louis Agassiz correctly interpreted stranded boulders in the Swiss Alps as evidence of massive glaciers in the past, the Pleistocene, the only geologic period defined by climate, has been referred to as the "ice age with glacial climates." In western North America the massive dry lake beds in the Great Basin with shoreline deposits high on the mountainsides were impressive evidence for wetter climates in the past. The term *pluvial* for Pleistocene climates became widely used in this region. Even here, interpreting past climates was controversial as geoscientists applied hydrological water budget equations to the Pleistocene lakes, equations that could be satisfied either with a colder, drier climate with reduced evaporation or with actual increases in rainfall (Brakenridge 1978; Snyder & Langbein 1962).

Again, the well-preserved plant remains in the ancient packrat middens were pivotal in resolving the controversy. The ability to identify the midden fossils to species allowed the individual physiological tolerances and responses to seasonal rainfall and temperatures to be used in interpreting ice-age climates. Shreve (1915) had discussed the role of climate in controlling the elevational distributions of plants on mountains, where cold and competition often set the upper limits and heat and drought the lower limits. In the biseasonal rainfall regime of the Dry Borders region, completely different sets of annuals respond to winter-spring and summer monsoonal rainfall. Their presence and abundance in midden assemblages are excellent indicators of the seasonal distribution of rainfall in the past.

Packrat middens older than 9,000 yr B.P. consistently contained remains of plants now found at higher elevations in woodland or chaparral or at higher latitudes in the present Mojave Desert. The annual plants identified in these late Wisconsin and early Holocene assemblages were almost entirely species that grow in response to winter-spring rains. Most of the modern Sonoran Desert dominants, which are so tied to summer rainfall, and greater percentages of summer annuals did not appear in the assemblages until the middle or late Holocene. These changes in plant distributions indicated paleoclimates with much cooler summers than today and a major shift in the seasonal distribution of rainfall. Winter rainfall from Pacific fronts was much greater than today, and summer monsoonal rainfall from the warm tropical oceans

was greatly reduced (Van Devender 1990b; Van Devender et al. 1994).

Moreover, the fussy packrats had soundly refuted the cold-dry model of ice-age climates. The lowering of vegetation zones by about 600 m recorded in the middens was far less than the 1,250–1,750-m depressions of vegetation zones needed to support the paleoclimatic inferences from high-elevation glacier studies in New Mexico (Galloway 1983). In addition, Playa San Bartolo, just north of Bahía de Kino on the Gulf of California, supported a freshwater Pleistocene lake. At such a low elevation (ca. 20 m) the summer cooling necessary to fill the lake by reduced evaporation alone would have been huge.

The ice-age climates of the Dry Borders region and elsewhere differed from those of the present in ways that allowed associations of plants and animals not seen today. Counterintuitively, ice-age winters were probably on average warmer than today. Bryson and Wendland (1967) point out that massive continental glaciers would have blocked Arctic air masses from moving south and would have physically warmed frigid air descending the massive ice front. Today Arctic air masses import the coldest temperatures to the Chihuahuan Desert and the Mexican Plateau in the midcontinent and to the Sonoran Desert through the Intermountain Great Basin. Eliminating these "blue norther" cold fronts would have important consequences for the upper and northern range limits of many plants. Milder winters coupled with cooler summers created a more equable climate regime with much greater overlap of upper and lower ranges of species. Some animals, such as the chuckwalla *(Sauromalus obesus)*, desert tortoise *(Gopherus agassizii)*, and Gila monster *(Heloderma suspectum)*, which are primarily desert animals today, were living in ice-age woodlands in the Sonoran Desert (Van Devender 1990b).

Examples of "anomalous" associations in the late Wisconsin in the Dry Borders region include singleleaf pinyon, Rocky Mountain juniper, big sagebrush *(Artemisia tridentata*-type), shadscale *(Atriplex confertifolia)*, and Joshua tree *(Yucca brevifolia)* in various associations with scrub oak *(Quercus turbinella)* and desert agave *(Agave deserti)* in the Ajo Mountains (Van Devender 1990b). In the Tinajas Altas Mountains remains of hollyleaf bursage *(Ambrosia ilicifolia)*, a regional desert endemic, were found in late Wisconsin and early Holocene assemblages with singleleaf pinyon, California juniper *(Juniperus californica)*, Joshua tree, Mojave sage *(Salvia mohavensis)*, and skunkbush *(Rhus aromatica)*.

The late Holocene desertscrub communities and climates likely resemble those of the original late Miocene Sonoran Desert 5–8 million years ago. However, relatively modern communities were developed for about only 5–10 percent of the 2.4 million years of the Pleistocene (Porter 1989; Winograd et al. 1997). Thus the modern interglacial climate and ecological setting found in the Dry Borders region today is unusual, and woodland/chaparral communities with singleleaf pinyon, juniper, and Joshua tree in desert lowlands and unusual biotic mixtures were the norm for about 90 percent of the Pleistocene.

Evolutionary Implications for the Dry Borders Region

Middens have yielded abundant well-preserved macrofossils from ancient middens that were radiocarbon-dated from 11,000 to 51,000 yr B.P. Identifications of hundreds of modern species of plants and animals in the late and middle Wisconsin glacial age have important evolutionary implications. Species can respond to major climate changes through extinction, speciation, or range adjustments. Unlike the megafauna extinction (Martin 1984), virtually no extinctions of plants, invertebrates, or small vertebrates were recorded at the Wisconsin-Holocene climatic change. A spider beetle *(Ptinus priminidi)* described from three Wisconsin samples (12,330 yr. B.P., 13,400 yr B.P., and >30,000 yr B.P.; Spilman 1976) was a likely candidate for an extinct species; however, it was later reported in a late Holocene (990 yr B.P.) sample from the Puerto Blanco Mountains in Organ Pipe Cactus National Park (Hall et al. 1990) and is likely still extant in the Sonoran Desert.

Although regional endemic species such as the Ajo rock daisy *(Perityle ajoensis)* and the Pinacate groundsel *(Senecio pinacatensis)* probably reflect speciation of ice-age populations isolated during the Holocene or an earlier interglacial, the majority of the ice-age plant species in the Dry Borders region were indistinguishable from their modern descendants. Midden fossils did not record a major speciation event at the Wisconsin-Holocene climatic change 11,000 years ago. Thus species are

robust and can maintain genetic integrity through multiple glacial/interglacial climatic fluctuations.

According to the midden fossil record, species made many and varied changes in range, however. Long-lived trees and succulents including pinyons, junipers, oaks, Joshua trees, and others spread into desert lowlands while summer-rainfall plants such as saguaro and foothill palo verde were restricted to small refugia, probably in central Sonora. Winter-rainfall Baja California plants expanded their ranges on the mainland in Sonora during the Wisconsin and contracted to local relictual populations in the middle Holocene (Van Devender et al. 1994). Similarly, the desert tortoise *(Gopherus agassizii)* expanded into now inhospitable areas in southwestern Arizona and across the broad valleys that now isolate desert mountain populations in the Sonoran Desert (Van Devender 2002). Bigelow beargrass *(Nolina bigelovii)*, bladder sage *(Salazaria mexicana)*, crucifixion thorn *(Canotia holacantha)*, desert needlegrass *(Stipa speciosa)*, Mojave sage, red barberry *(Berberis haematocarpa)*, silver dollar cactus *(Opuntia chlorotica)*, skunkbush *(Rhus aromatica)*, Spanish bayonet *(Hesperoyucca whipplei)*, and many others expanded their ranges under winter-rainfall ice-age climates but are now present in Sonora only in isolated relictual populations (Felger 2000; Turner et al. 1995).

One of the more remarkable plants in the warm deserts of North America is the creosotebush *(Larrea divaricata* subsp. *tridentata)*. Unlike many Sonoran Desert dominants that likely evolved in the middle Miocene from south-central Mexican tropical ancestors after the uplift of the Sierra Madre Occidental (Van Devender 2001), creosotebush evolved in South America and immigrated to North America at some unknown time in the Pleistocene (Van Devender 1990a; Wells & Hunziker 1976). Although there are four very distinct species of *Larrea* in South America, the North American creosotebush has evolved into only three chromosomal races and one subspecies. The original diploid immigrant dispersed from the Chihuahuan Desert west and developed tetraploid populations in the Sonoran Desert and hexaploid populations in the Mojave Desert (Yang 1970). The dune creosotebush *(L. d.* var. *arenaria)*, which is restricted to the Algodones Dunes of southeastern California and the Gran Desierto of northwestern Sonora, is the most divergent North

American population (Felger 2000). Midden fossils have shown that the range of creosotebush contracted during the Wisconsin glacial period (and likely others) to the Big Bend of Texas or southward in the Chihuahuan Desert (Van Devender 1990a) and to below about 370 m elevation in the Lower Colorado River Valley and around the head of the Gulf of California in the Sonoran Desert (Van Devender 1990b). The modern distribution in most of the warm desert of North America was not established until the middle Holocene, 4,000–4,500 years ago. Analyses of stomatal guard cells in modern and fossil creosotebush leaves has shown that the biogeographical patterns are more complex (Hunter et al. 2001). The diploid populations are not restricted to the Chihuahuan Desert but also occur in Arizona and Baja California. The Wisconsin-aged populations in the Lower Colorado River Valley were the Sonoran Desert tetraploid, and the Mojave Desert hexaploid was first recorded only 8,500 years ago, suggesting the possibility of a Holocene ploidy event. The hexaploids reached their northern limits in California and Nevada between 5,600 and 3,900 years ago. It is difficult to envision the Sonoran Desert lowlands without this magnificent, tenacious South American immigrant.

Fossil Records of Desert Animals

Deserts are notoriously bad places for fossilization, considering that most preservation occurs in aquatic environments or tar pits. Deadman Cave, Arizona (Mead et al. 1984), and El Golfo de Santa Clara (Lindsay 1984; Shaw & McDonald 1987) and Rancho La Brisca (Van Devender et al. 1985), Sonora, provided important vertebrate faunas from sedimentary deposits in the Sonoran Desert region. Although animal remains are not as common as plant remains in packrat middens, they are directly associated with a paleoflora and radiocarbon date and come from dry sites well within the desert. Paleoecological interpretations need to consider that animal remains can be transported to the midden rockshelter from distant habitats. In two decades of packrat midden analysis the fossil records of small desert animals went from negligible to substantial.

Snail shells have rarely been found in packrat middens. Mead and Van Devender (1991) reported shells of *Chaenaxis tuba* (Pupillidae) in ten samples from the limestone Waterman Mountains ranging in age from 11,470 yr B.P. to 1,320 yr B.P. Interestingly, this tiny snail persisted in the area through transitions from late Wisconsin pinyon-juniper woodland to early Holocene juniper woodland to several types of Sonoran desertscrub.

Arthropods

In the 1980s Gene Hall, with the able guidance of Carl Olson, learned the art of identifying arthropod remains in Sonoran Desert middens. The specimens are usually tiny and often fragmentary, and they are heavily biased toward ground dwellers. The result was an explosion of fossil records for diverse arthropods ranging from pseudoscorpions to millipedes and insects. The most common fossil arthropods were beetles and ants. The most complete specimens were intact bodies of small beetles, especially the spider beetles (Ptinidae) and ants. Increased humidity during rains hydrates the midden surfaces inside the rockshelters, turning them into sticky amberrat traps. Midden arthropod assemblages have been reported in several Sonoran Desert areas (Hall et al. 1988), as well as the Ajo (Hall et al. 1989) and Puerto Blanco mountains (Hall et al. 1990) in Organ Pipe Cactus National Monument and the Sierra Bacha in west-central Sonora (Van Devender & Hall 1994). In general, the arthropods identified to species in the middens still live near the sites and have made few major range changes.

Deadman Cave

A cave on the north side of the Santa Catalina Mountains near Tucson yielded a rich assemblage (64 taxa) of vertebrate fossils of late Pleistocene and early Holocene age (Mead et al. 1984). Large mammals included the brush ox *(Euceratherium collinum)*, a horse *(Equus* sp.), and the Shasta ground sloth. Only the Woodhouse toad *(Bufo woodhousei)*, round-tailed horned lizard *(Phrynosoma modestum)*, zebra-tailed lizard *(Callisaurus draconoides)*, and western hook-nosed snake *(Gyalopion canum)* have been extirpated from the Catalinas, although all still occur in southern Arizona.

El Golfo de Santa Clara

The first fossil record of the giant anteater *(Myrmecophaga tridactyla)* in North America was in early Pleistocene (Irvingtonian Land Mammal Age, beginning 1.8 mya) sediments from El Golfo de

Santa Clara in northwestern Sonora (Lindsay 1984; Shaw & McDonald 1987). The nearest populations of this large tropical mammal are 3,000 km to the southeast in the humid, tropical lowlands of Central America! The El Golfo fauna included many extinct large mammals: antelope, a bear, camels, cats, horses, proboscidians, and a tapir (*Tapirus* sp.), among others. Extant species in the fauna included Sonoran Desert toad (*Bufo alvarius*), slider (*Trachemys scripta*), boa constrictor (*Constrictor constrictor*), and jaguar (*Panthera* cf. *P. onca*). The Sonoran Desert toad is a regional endemic, while the slider and boa constrictor occur today in Sonora in wetter, more tropical areas to the southeast. El Golfo is at the head of the Gulf of California in the Lower Colorado River Valley subdivision of the Sonoran Desert (Turner and Brown 1982). Today this hyper-arid desert is too dry to support any of these animals, although historically the delta of the Colorado River was a very wet area with abundant beaver (*Castor canadensis*) and extensive cottonwood (*Populus fremontii*) gallery forests (Felger 2000; Mellink, this volume; Navarro, this volume). This fauna is significant because it reflects an early Pleistocene interglacial with the climate much more tropical than today: that is, almost frost free, with much greater rainfall in the warm season, and with higher humidity.

Rancho La Brisca

The late Pleistocene (Rancholabrean Land Mammal Age) Rancho La Brisca fossil locality is located in a riparian canyon north of Cucurpe, north-central Sonora (Van Devender et al. 1985). The fauna was dominated by the Sonoran mud turtle (*Kinosternon sonoriense*) and fish, reflecting a wet ciénega paleoenvironment. The presence of the sabinal frog (*Leptodactylus melanonotus*) 240 km north of its northernmost population on the Río Yaqui indicates that the climates were more tropical than today. The presence in the fauna of a large extinct *Bison*, which immigrated to North America from Siberia only in the late Pleistocene, between about 170,000 and 150,000 years ago (C. A. Repenning, personal communication 1984), limits the age of the deposit. The coexistence of bison and tropical species helped establish that sediments near Rancho La Brisca in north-central Sonora were deposited about 80,000 years ago in the last interglacial (the Sangamon), which was considerably more tropical than the Holocene.

Midden Vertebrates

Most vertebrate remains from packrat middens are isolated elements from small animals that are transported to the rockshelters in fecal pellets of mammalian predators such as the ringtail (*Bassariscus astutus;* Mead and Van Devender 1981) or in regurgitated raptor pellets. In many cases, midden bones appear to have been partially digested. Occasionally, packrats pick up remains of larger mammals. Examples include the saber-like canine tooth of a camel (*Camelus* sp.) in a juniper midden from Vulture Cave in the Grand Canyon (Mead and Phillips 1981) and mammoth (*Mammuthus* sp.) tooth fragments in a pinyon-juniper-oak midden from the Hueco Mountains east of El Paso (Van Devender & Bradley 1990).

Van Devender and Mead (1978) reported fossil amphibians and reptiles from various Sonoran Desert midden sites. Reptiles such as the banded gecko (*Coleonyx virgatus*), chuckwalla (*Sauromalus obesus*), leopard lizard (*Gambelia wislizeni*), rosy boa (*Lichanura trivirgata*), sidewinder (*Crotalus cerastes*), and western shovel-nosed snake (*Chionactis occipitalis*), which are now mostly restricted to desertscrub habitats, were living in late Wisconsin or early Holocene woodlands. One explanation for the observed differences in habitats is that ice-age woodlands had more equable climates than today with cooler summers and milder winters (Van Devender 1990b).

Van Devender et al. (1983) reported small mammals from Sonoran Desert packrat middens. Most of them represented species still in the same areas. Range expansions were reported for a chipmunk (*Eutamias* sp.) in the Tucson Mountains and porcupine (*Erethizon dorsatum*) in the Castle Mountains and on Wolcott Peak. Small vertebrates in middens were reported from Picacho Peak north of Tucson (Van Devender, Mead & Rea 1991) and Organ Pipe Cactus National Monument (Van Devender, Rea & Hall 1991). One interesting animal in Picacho Peak midden fauna was the elf owl (*Micrathene whitneyi*). It was living in a pinyon-juniper woodland 11,100 years ago but now typically lives in palo verde–saguaro desertscrub in the area. The desert shrew was identified from a 1,510 yr B.P. sample from Alamo Canyon in the

Ajo Mountains but has been collected only twice in the history of Organ Pipe Cactus National Monument.

Ice-Age Vegetation of the Dry Borders Region

Fossil plants in packrat middens (Van Devender 1990b) provide remarkable insight into the vegetation history of the Sonoran Desert in Arizona and northwestern Sonora.

Arizona Upland

The ice-age vegetation in the elevations that today support the Arizona Upland subdivision of the Sonoran Desert was a pinyon-juniper-oak woodland (Turner & Brown 1982). In the 1970s Hal Coss, a naturalist at Organ Pipe Cactus National Monument, discovered a pinyon-juniper midden in a cave at 975 m elevation on the south side of Montezuma's Head, a prominent peak in the Ajo Mountains. He led Paul Martin, Art Phillips, Jim Mead, and me to the remote site, now designated a roadless wilderness area. From the cave entrance one has a spectacular view of the Dry Borders region with a solitary roseberry juniper (*Juniperus coahuilensis*) nearby and organ pipe cacti below. Four separate samples were dated from 13,500 to 21,840 yr B.P. (Van Devender 1990b) in an apparently gravity-defying order with the oldest layer on top. The midden assemblages record a remarkable mesic woodland vegetation with singleleaf pinyon, Rocky Mountain and Utah junipers (*J. scopulorum, J. osteosperma*), scrub oak (*Quercus turbinella*), Joshua tree, big sagebrush, shadscale, and snowberry (*Symphoricarpos* sp.). The nearest populations of Rocky Mountain juniper are below the Mogollon Rim about 270 km to the northeast. The tridentate big sagebrushes are dominants in Great Basin desertscrub communities 390 to 440 km to the north-northeast above the rim. The nearest living Joshua trees, the arborescent yucca that characterizes large areas of the modern Mojave Desert, are near Aguila, Arizona, 225 km to the north-northwest. The organ pipe cactus and other Arizona Upland dominants visible from the cave were not in the samples. Additional Wisconsin-aged midden samples from 915 m elevation in Alamo Canyon in the Ajo Mountains dated at 14,500 and 32,000 yr B.P. contained similar woodland assemblages.

Ice-age woodlands were in the Ajo Mountains for at least 18,500 years of the Wisconsin glacial. About 11,000 years ago the singleleaf pinyon, Rocky Mountain juniper, and big sagebrush disappeared from the Ajo Mountains, leaving other woodland species in a transitional early Holocene vegetation. The modern vegetation of the Ajos with a few relictual woodland plants and a broad skirt of Arizona Upland desertscrub only formed perhaps 8,000 years ago. Repeated interglacial isolations of the range likely stimulated the speciation of the endemic Ajo Mountains rock daisy.

Lower Colorado River Valley

The ice-age vegetation in the elevations that today support creosotebush desertscrub in the Lower Colorado River Valley subdivision was a xeric juniper woodland (Turner & Brown 1982). Plant remains in a series of 21 middens from lower elevations (535 to 600 m) in Organ Pipe Cactus National Monument allowed the reconstruction of vegetation in the Puerto Blanco Mountains for the last 14,000 years (Van Devender 1990b). The late Wisconsin ice-age woodland was a more xeric woodland than in the Ajo Mountains and was dominated by California juniper, Joshua tree, and Mojave sage—very similar to modern areas in Joshua Tree National Monument in California! Saguaro and brittlebush (*Encelia farinosa*) returned to the Puerto Blanco Mountains by 10,500 yr B.P. but were living in a transitional community with California juniper. Desertscrub formed by 8,900 yr B.P. but was wetter with now-riparian plants including catclaw acacia (*Acacia greggii*) and blue palo verde (*Parkinsonia florida*) living on exposed slopes. Relatively modern desertscrub formed with the arrival of modern dominants, including foothill palo verde, ironwood (*Olneya tesota*), and organ pipe cactus. The modern desertscrub communities are dominated by plants that arrived in the Twin Peaks area at various times in the last 11,000 years. Very young midden assemblages contained more species than now live at the sites, suggesting that the modern communities are still recovering from some recent climatic event. Sonoran Desert plant communities have probably never been in equilibrium.

Farther west a series of 21 middens from 330 to 580 m in the Tinajas Altas Mountains records changes in the vegetation from >43,200 to 1,230 yr

B.P. In the middle and late Wisconsin woodlands, California juniper, singleleaf pinyon, Mojave sage, and Bigelow beargrass (Nolina bigelovii) were present. A sample dated at 11,040 yr B.P. at 460 m is the lowest ice-age elevational record for single-leaf pinyon. As in the Puerto Blanco Mountains, desertscrub formed by 8,910 yr B.P. but with cat-claw acacia and blue palo verde living on exposed slopes. Elephant tree appeared in the middens by 5,820 yr B.P. Between 4,010 and 1,230 yr B.P. rela-tively modern desertscrub communities formed with the arrival of foothill palo verde.

A sample from 330 m elevation on the west side of the Tinajas Altas Mountains and nine samples at 240 to 245 m in the nearby Butler Moun-tains provide additional insight into the ice-age vegetation of the lower elevations in the modern Sonoran Desert (Figure 6.3; Van Devender 1990b). The late Wisconsin was a xeric woodland with California juniper (Tinajas Altas Mountains), Mojave sage, creosotebush, brittlebush, and holly-leaf and white bursages (Ambrosia ilicifolia and A. dumosa). The modern tetraploid race of creo-sotebush was identified in a Tinajas Altas midden dominated by California juniper and Joshua tree, radiocarbon dated at 18,700 yr B.P. (Hunter et al. 2001; Van Devender 1990b). This midden record at the height of the Wisconsin glacial maximum suggests that relatively modern creosotebush–white bursage desertscrub could have been pre-sent in the Lower Colorado River Valley for most of the 1.8 million years of the Pleistocene—after the immigration of creosotebush from South America into North America. Considering that the ice-age vegetation in all the higher-elevation areas in the Sonoran Desert supported ice-age woodlands, desertscrub in the Lower Colorado River Valley may have been more stable with a minimum of fluctuations.

A series of ten midden samples from the Hornaday Mountains in the Pinacate Region of northwestern Sonora recorded the vegetation at 240 to 260 m elevation for the last 10,000 years (Van Devender et al. 1990). Woodland species such as California juniper and Mojave sage were not found in the early Holocene, and creosotebush, brittlebush, and saguaro were desertscrub domi-nates throughout the Holocene. It seems very unlikely that common Baja California Sonoran Desert plants such as the boojum tree (Fouquieria columnaris), which have isolated populations on the Sonoran coast, dispersed around the head of the Gulf of California during interglacial periods. Blue palo verde, catclaw acacia, desert lavender (Hyptis albida), and mesquite (Prosopis sp.) in middle Holocene samples were displaced by such modern dominants as foothill palo verde, iron-wood, and ocotillo (Fouquieria splendens) by 4,430 yr B.P.

Central Gulf Coast

The Sierra Bacha near Puerto Libertad on the Gulf of California is a unique granite range that supports many disjunct populations of Baja Cali-fornia plants, including the only mainland popu-lations of boojum tree, or cirio (F. columnaris). A series of 11 midden samples from the Sierra Bacha recorded the Sonoran desertscrub with creosote-bush, brittlebush, foothill palo verde, teddybear cholla (Cylindropuntia bigelovii), California bar-rel cactus (Ferocactus cylindraceus), and cliff spurge (Euphorbia misera) at 200 to 260 m eleva-tion for the last 10,000 years (Van Devender et al. 1994). In the early Holocene (9,270–9,970 yr B.P.), boojum tree and San Diego goldeneye (Viguiera laciniata) were growing on an easterly slope fac-ing away from the ocean. This suggests that cli-matic conditions more like boojum tree areas in Baja California were more widespread on the mainland in the early Holocene, and likely during most of the glacial periods of the Pleistocene. Baja plants may have been restricted to small mainland relictual areas as they are today for as little as 10 to 20 percent of the 1.8 million years of the Pleis-tocene (Porter 1989; Winograd et al. 1997). Inter-estingly, Mormon tea (Ephedra aspera/nevadensis) was present in the Sierra Bacha from 9,970 to 2,330 yr B.P. Today the southernmost population in Sonora is in the Sierra del Viejo, about 70 km to the north (Felger 2000). By 5,340 yr B.P., modern communities developed with the appearance of desert lavender, desert nightshade (Solanum hind-sianum), ocotillo, sangrengado (Jatropha cuneata), and yellow felt plant (Horsfordia newberryi).

Vizcaino

In contrast, the late Wisconsin vegetation in the modern boojum tree–cardón desertscrub in the Vizcaino subdivision of the Sonoran Desert in central Baja California was a pinyon-juniper wood-land with many chaparral species of California (Lanner and Van Devender 1998). The five-needled

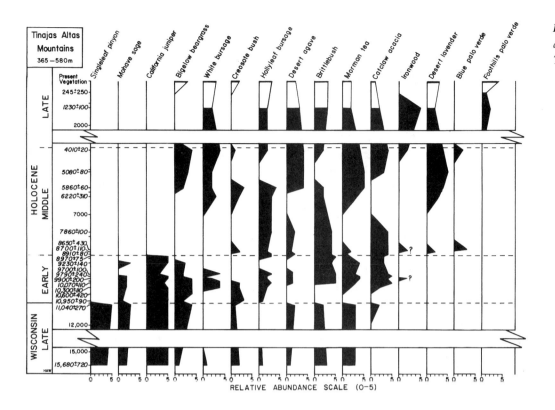

Figure 6.3. Record of ice-age flora and vegetation at Tinajas Altas.

Sierra Juárez pinyon *(Pinus juarezensis)* occurred on granite at 640 m elevation at Cataviña, and the singleleaf pinyon was on limestone at 700 m elevation at Misión San Fernando Velicata. The modern desertscrub formed in the late Holocene.

Rhode (2002) documented the southerly extent (27°32'30") of ice-age woodland vegetation on the Baja California peninsula in a report on an early Holocene (10,200 yr B.P.) midden at 780 m elevation in the Sierra San Francisco. The sample was dominated by California juniper, laurel sumac *(Rhus laurina),* and manzanita *(Arctostaphylos peninsularis).*

Summary

Analyses of plant and animal fossils preserved in packrat middens and sediments have provided remarkable insight into the history and development of desert communities in the Dry Borders region in the southwestern United States and northwestern Mexico. Many characteristic species could well have evolved in thornscrub or tropical deciduous forest in the Miocene 8 to 15 million years ago, before the formation of the Sonoran Desert. In the 1960–70s students of Paul Martin used macrofossils in packrat middens to reconstruct late Pleistocene glacial and interglacial vegetation and climates in all four major deserts of

North America. Hundreds of well-preserved fossils identified to extant species demonstrated that there was virtually no extinction or speciation in plants, invertebrates, and small vertebrates at the Wisconsin-Holocene glacial/interglacial climatic change but simply range adjustments. Fluctuating geographic ranges are normal on time scales ranging from decades to millennia, and geographic ranges should not be used as taxonomic characters. Midden assemblages definitively demonstrated that plant communities are strongly individualistic with each species responding independently to climate changes. In the late Wisconsin glacial, anomalous associations of species not found today were typical in ice-age equable climates with milder winters, much cooler summers, and a shift to winter rainfall dominance.

Fossil records of small animals from sediments and packrat middens in the Dry Borders region have provided relatively few records of range changes, reflecting more indirect relationships to climate. Sedimentary deposits at El Golfo de Santa Clara and Rancho La Brisca, Sonora, and Deadman Cave in the Santa Catalina Mountains, Arizona, yielded abundant vertebrate fossils. Packrat middens yielded snails, insects, and other arthropods, amphibians, reptiles, and small mammals from areas within the Sonoran Desert. The most dramatic fossil record from the Dry Borders region was the giant anteater from El Golfo de Santa Clara 1.8 million years ago, 3,000 km to the northwest of its modern range in the humid, tropical lowlands of Central America.

Plant remains in ancient middens documented singleleaf pinyon-juniper-oak woodland/chaparral with few to none of the modern long-lived trees, shrubs, or succulents at 550 to 1,525 m elevation in the modern Arizona Upland of the Sonoran Desert prior to 11,000 years ago in the Wisconsin glacial age. At lower elevations in the modern Lower Colorado River Valley subdivision (240 to 550 m), ice-age woodlands were dominated by California juniper and Joshua tree. Away from the mountains simple desertscrub dominated by creosotebush, white bursage, and big galleta grass was likely present for most of the Pleistocene. The tetraploid Sonoran Desert chromosomal race of creosotebush was present at 330 m elevation on the west side of the Tinajas Altas Mountains 18,700 years ago in the Wisconsin full glacial. Early Holocene (the present interglacial) samples from the Hornaday Mountains of north-western Sonora were dominated by creosotebush and brittlebush without juniper or other woodland plants. Middens from the Sierra Bacha on the coast of the Gulf of California in west-central Sonora recorded expanded ranges of boojum tree 9,500 years ago, suggesting that it and other Baja California plants on the Sonoran coast are now isolated relictual populations that were more widespread under ice-age climates.

Desert vegetation developed in the Dry Borders region in the Holocene with the final disappearance of ice-age woodland plants. Desertscrub with saguaros and brittlebush formed 8,000 to 9,000 years ago in association with catclaw acacia and blue palo verde, species now restricted to desert washes. About 4,500 years ago modern Sonoran Desert communities formed with the arrival of foothill palo verde, organ pipe cactus, and desert ironwood. Even though the climatic regime of the late Holocene was relatively modern, desertscrub communities never reached equilibrium as individual species continually responded to climatic fluctuations.

Part Two

PEOPLE OF THE PLACE

Seven

Growing Up at the Big Horn

Anita Bender McGee and Letty Bender Hofstra

Sonoran Desert National Monument southwest of Phoenix was created in January 2001. Anita Bender McGee, Letty Bender Hofstra, and their two brothers were raised within the monument's area on a ranch and gas station along what was then Highway 84. This is their story.

—*Bill Broyles*

During the 1920s our grandparents and our father and mother moved to where the remains of the Big Horn service station now stand, weary and crumbling from years of neglect and vandalism. This old service station is located on Interstate Highway 8 twenty miles east of Gila Bend, Arizona. Our family—O. A. Bender, wife Thursia, older daughters Lora and Mae, son Henry, and younger daughters Thursia and Georgia—came by train to Arizona from the Oklahoma Panhandle in 1913 and first settled in Sasco, Arizona. Sons Les and Sam stayed with relatives in Oklahoma to finish high school. After our father, O. L. "Les" Bender, returned from World War I, he homesteaded at the Big Horn. He drilled a good deep-water well and built our home and the service station. Dad, who volunteered in World War I, was injured by mustard gas in France, and the effects bothered him the rest of his life.

Dad and his father, O. A. Bender, ran cattle on open range as well as developing the gasoline station and a garage at the Big Horn. Les was also employed by the General Petroleum Corporation and had the franchise to deliver Mobilgas from the Gila Bend bulk plant to neighboring ranches and to the surrounding communities such as Ajo, Theba, Sentinel, and Casa Grande.

At the Big Horn, Dad and our mother, Laura, sold gasoline, motor oil, and auto parts, did some automobile repair, and provided water, especially during the very hot Arizona summers, to thirsty tourists and their overheated cars. During the first few years Laura was the station attendant. Especially during the 1930s she had to deal with a few "Bonnie and Clyde" characters, so she always had her loaded six-shooter nearby. While pumping gas, she had the situation under control. Also, she furnished the weary traveler with lunch if necessary. She sold sandwiches, cold drinks, and "sweet" milk, as advertised on a sign out front.

At times Les and Laura hired help from the hobos and cowboys who passed through. It would be the same men season after season who would come by the station. They would stop, stay a while, and work for our dad at the station or on the range punching cattle before leaving to follow their wanderlust until the next year. They were good, hardworking souls, just without roots. We still remember them fondly sixty years later.

During those years Big Horn had the first water well in the area. It was a hand-dug well, but later a drilling rig was brought in and the well was deepened, providing better water and more of it. In the 1930s many people in the East had developed tuberculosis, and doctors would tell them to go West. They had nothing, no place to go, and no place to live, but they always had hope. At times some would camp in the desert nearby the Big Horn station. Dad would always see to it that they had plenty of water and many times furnished them with fresh beef when the need was there. He was very good to those people.

This old structure is a good example of a building using adobe along with saguaro ribs, which was used by the earlier settlers in the Southwest desert. Part of the yard had a living ocotillo fence—some years it flowered and was beautiful. Other years it didn't do anything—it looked just like a dead ocotillo fence! The Big Horn station opened for service in the mid-1920s after a gravel-graded road connected Casa Grande to Gila Bend, then on to California.

Figure 7.1. O. L. Bender, 1919. (Courtesy the Bender family)

Figure 7.2. Big Horn station, about 1935. (Courtesy the Bender family)

Dad installed a large galvanized water storage tank near the well and beneath it built a shower for family convenience. Of course, there wasn't a hot water tank, but as we remember, no one seemed to mind. For laundry Mother had a gasoline-powered wringer washer. That was one noisy machine! She used one tub of water for four loads of laundry: towels first, underwear next, then colored items, and the "Levi's" last of all. In those days all "reputable" blue jeans were made by Levi Strauss.

Also at our Big Horn home Dad built a swimming pool with, of course, no filtration system. Once a year it would be pumped full with fresh water. That was a beautiful sight for us kids! We'd

swim all summer in that pool. By the end of the summer algae would be growing and tadpoles flourishing, but it was a swimming pool and we loved it! We also used to swim in all the dirt stock tanks that were spread across the range. In the summer any pool, stock tank, cattle trough, storage tank, or container with water in it, we swam in it.

We learned early in life while living at the Big Horn not to waste water. Mother and Dad were both very firm about this subject. When Mother would wash dishes, she'd not put much water in the pan and certainly wouldn't let water run while rinsing. She might put a few inches in the bottom of the dishpan. Waste water from the sink ran outside, watering a large mesquite tree near the house. Mother lived the last eight years of her life in Phoenix with Anita—big sinks and full-size bathtubs, not dishpans, buckets, and galvanized tubs—but Mother still only put a few inches of water in the sink to do her dishes or the tub to take a bath.

The Vekol Valley school opened in 1932, and we attended there in a one-room schoolhouse—grades 1–8—with an attendance of eight children. Dad went to Phoenix to see if we could get a teacher out in Vekol Valley. There was one other girl, Jacky Kirian, living in the Vekol Valley at that time, and a boy whose parents lived in an old car and went from ranch to ranch doing part-time labor. Dad went to Phoenix and found a teacher who had four children. For eight children, the Department of Education would hire and pay for a teacher if we provided a building and housing for her. So families all gathered together and built the Vekol Valley school, which was about ten miles east of the Big Horn station. The site was about one mile north of Interstate 8 and on the west side of Vekol Road.

A deserted house and well about a quarter mile from the school was fixed up, and the teacher and family lived there. We spent the next four school years attending the little Vekol Valley school. Mother drove us to school the ten miles each morning and returned to pick us up in the afternoon. There was a large wood-burning stove in the middle of the schoolroom used for heating and at times to prepare a stew for lunch. Our parents would provide the beef, and the hot stew for lunch was delicious. Sometimes it was a pot of beans with corn bread to go with it.

The school closed after four years because we lost our teacher and four of the students. So, starting in 1935, we rode with Bill Kirian and his daughter to Gila Bend for the fifth grade. Bill had homesteaded ten miles east of our home and was working for the WPA [Works Progress Administration] in Gila Bend. On his way to work each morning he would stop at the Big Horn and pick us up for school, and then return us home each evening. Later Dad bought a house in Casa Grande, and Mother would take us into town on Monday morning and we stayed there until noon Friday. Anita and Letty graduated from Casa Grande Union High School in 1945. 'Nita got married, and Letty went to work for the Valley National Bank in Casa Grande.

There was a mascot for the Big Horn station, and it was mounted high out front under the canopy. The mascot was a large, beautiful set of horns from an Arizona desert bighorn sheep. Dad found this set of horns in the desert. He would never shoot a bighorn. He cherished the times when they were sighted high upon the mountain or near some of the desert's natural watering places. He loved them and all wildlife. Les Bender was a natural environmentalist even back when being an environmentalist wasn't "cool."

Along with the Big Horn station there was the Bender Ranch, which took in a large area consisting of many townships—quite a spread! The Buzzard X brand was Grandfather's (O. A. Bender). Vekol Well, owned by Les Bender, was part of the Bender Ranch. They ran Herefords, Hereford crosses, Mexican steers, and mixed breeds. After O. A. Bender died, Les Bender introduced registered Brahmas—two bulls and about eight cows—from Texas. Eventually he used the Brahma bulls for Hereford crosses. Year in, year out, they kept about one hundred to three hundred head of cows, calves, and a few bulls, but they ran as many as a thousand steers when the rains permitted.

Waterholes included Lower Well, South Well, Vekol Well, Paradise Tank, Bender Spring, Rhine (Ryan) Tank, Hog Tank, and Jake's Tank (in the Table Top foothills). Dad and our grandfather used different brands to distinguish their own cattle. Grandfather used the old Buzzard X brand, and Dad used the NAI, VKO, and vee-up-vee-down.

Dad attended mainly to the petroleum business in Gila Bend and Casa Grande, and his father, O. A. Bender, mostly did the cowboy work, keeping gasoline-powered pumps and windmill water wells in good shape. Providing water for the cattle

Figure 7.3. Drilling first well at Big Horn, after World War I. (Courtesy the Bender family)

Figure 7.4. Anita and Letty Bender at Big Horn, 1933. (Courtesy the Bender family)

Figure 7.5. Laura Bender, with daughters Letty and Anita and son O. L. Jr, at the Big Horn cattle trough, 1935. (Courtesy the Bender family)

Figure 7.6. Letty and Anita Bender at Big Horn station, 1935. Note the ranch brands above namesake bighorn skull: NAI Bar and Flying XA Bar, affectionately known as Buzzard X. (Courtesy the Bender family)

Figure 7.7. Letty, Anita, and their mother, Laura, Big Horn station. (Courtesy the Bender family)

In 1939 during one such roundup on the Gila River near the old Gillespie Dam, our grandfather was riding after a cow. His horse bolted down a wash and came out under a mesquite tree. One of the branches struck the rider and killed him instantly. It was a tremendous shock to our family. After his death the range was divided, and some of it was sold. Dad took the area south of the Big Horn, encompassing the old Johnson Well along with the original Vekol Well, which our father had drilled in the early 1920s, and all this land made up his cattle ranch.

Before Grandfather met his untimely death down there on the Gila River, he and Grandma lived about a quarter mile south of the Big Horn. There was a good well, many corrals, and lots of cattle coming in for water. My sister and I could easily walk from the Big Horn down to their place even as very small children. Mother would always admonish us, "Watch for snakes!" Grandma had a wonderful pantry, and in it always was a large sack of brown sugar, invariably hard as a rock. When we visited she would give us a chunk of that brown sugar for a treat. We will never forget the trouble she had trying to break off a couple of chunks for us. That sack of brown sugar would always become very hard! Nothing was more delicious than a chunk of that brown sugar.

Grandma had many night-blooming cereus cactuses in the yard brought to her by Grandpa. They would open their blooms late in the evening, beautiful and very fragrant. One night there were thirty-six blossoms that opened. He brought her one night-bloomer that always produced a pink blossom. Normally all blossoms are a creamy white. Many years later Letty was talking to a group about these night-blooming cactuses and mentioned the pink one. An employee of the Arizona Game & Fish refused to believe there could ever be a pink blossom on a night-blooming cereus. She told him this particular one had come from an area near Gila Bend. Come to find out later this was the only known place in the world where the pink ones grow.

Our home seemed plenty large to us, but regardless winter or summer we always slept outside. The only time one would have to go inside was when it rained, and that wasn't often. We loved sleeping under the stars, and you can't believe the beauty of it—the loveliness of the Evening Star, learning the phases of the moon, finding the Milky

in dry times was a grave necessity! He also had to keep the cattle within certain borders, as in those days there were mighty few fences. However, when roundup time came, "all hands and the cook" were called into action.

Way, the Big Dipper, a falling star. We've made many a "wish upon a star" while lying on our beds at night. All of this while listening to the "love of our lives," the horses munching hay out in the corral. We can hear it and see it all now, so many years later. What a life it was!

Every summer during melon season Dad would go to Gila Bend or Phoenix and bring back a truckload of watermelons. He would have a cool, prepared place at home to store the melons, and would give us the job of keeping gunny sacks wet for their covering. The damp cool sacks would preserve their freshness for weeks at a time. Mother had a small garden that produced other good vegetables. This little garden had to be protected at all times from the birds, deer, rabbits, skunks, and other little desert denizens. We also had a flock of chickens. We lost many a chicken to coyotes and chicken hawks, and one time Mother found a mountain lion in the chicken coop helping himself to a few fat laying hens.

We had a hired cowboy who one day while out riding found two baby hawks fallen from their nest. He brought them home, and our family raised them. The hawks loved fresh meat, and frequently Dad would shoot a jackrabbit for them. They loved this and would grab it, and some way both would have their share very quickly. Dad never clipped their wings, but they still remained at our home permanently, on welfare! Many times we would go riding with hawks flying along with us. Whenever strangers arrived, the hawks would set off a big ruckus, screaming, squawking, diving, and carrying on to warn us. Both of them died the same way. The first sat on the wind charger, wind came up, and the blade knocked it in the head. Six months later the same thing happened to the other hawk. They were the best watchdogs we ever had.

After the hawk experience, Dad found two abandoned baby javelinas. The mother had been killed by a predator or by a hunter's bullet. Coyotes were already nearby when dad found them. After capturing the vicious little rascals, he wrapped them in his jacket and brought them home. We fed and cared for them, and as they grew they became very protective of all family members. Strangers driving up stayed in their vehicles as the javelinas would charge, and bite! They would be at the gate waiting as soon as a stranger drove up. Even the family was in trouble if perchance the

Figure 7.8. Corral at Johnson Well, 1940. The Vee Kay OK brand was for Vekol Well. (*Courtesy the Bender family*)

Figure 7.9. Dad ran the bulk plant for Mobil in Gila Bend until 1939. (*Courtesy the Bender family*)

javelinas didn't recognize or remember right off who you were. If you didn't smell as the pig remembered you, it would bite you. We'd sit around at night, and the pigs checked us all out by smelling of our legs. The minute they smelled a strange leg, they would bite! Javelinas are a bit nearsighted.

We also had a little white-tail fawn as a pet that dad had rescued after finding the mother dead. We raised Bambi until she reached adulthood. She would sleep in the daytime on the canvas tarpaulin that covered Dad's and Mother's outside bed. While Bambi was yet small, a cowboy from nearby Jack Clem's ranch brought in a mule deer, a fawn orphaned by a hunter's bullet probably. We named this one Pancha. So Pancha and Bambi grew up together with our family. Mother would get so vexed at them. She would hang clothes on the clothesline, and Pancha and Bambi had a good time standing on their hind legs beating at

Figure 7.10. Dad with pet deer. (Courtesy the Bender family)

and tearing up the towels and sheets. Also, Dad would let them go into the kitchen, and boy did they love the beautiful, green sweet-potato vine Mother had growing in a large glass jar. These vines make a nice inside plant. However, the deer finally demolished Mother's kitchen plant. Both of our little pet deer disappeared during a hunting season.

Our parents made a trip to Phoenix two or three times a year for supplies. We would get to go to Gila Bend quite often, but for Phoenix or Casa Grande trips Dad and Mother generally left us home. By this time we were living south of the Big Horn at Johnson Well. We didn't mind staying home alone. It didn't make any difference, for we kids were self-reliant and tough. One time they were delayed in returning, and after a few days we ran out of food. Pinto beans and a can or two of

vegetables were all we could find. We didn't seem to be concerned about it, nor did we feel neglected, and we don't remember being lonesome or feeling abused. We just handled things as they were. Nowadays our parents would have been arrested for child abuse.

A Mexican couple, Nellie and Ray Mendoza, lived on Jack Clem's ranch, a few miles to the east and about nine miles north of our place. Nellie was a beautiful woman, with red hair and brown eyes, and could she ever make tortillas. She patted out the little round chunk of dough a little bit and then hiked up her dress and patted them flat on her thighs. Whoop, whoop, whoop. That was a sight to behold! And then she flipped them onto the red-hot top of the wood stove. They were delicious served with Nellie's spicy hot chili con carne.

When Nellie visited us, she always brought her used magazines. She read *Ranch Romances* and *True Confessions,* and after she would finish, we would get the magazines. We loved this, and believe me, we learned a few things! It was very interesting reading for a couple of greenhorn girls. We would read anything we could get our hands on, and we still do. To this day we consider reading as one of the best forms of recreation.

By late 1941 World War II was raging, and we had just entered high school. To solve this school problem for the weekdays, our parents found room and board for us in Casa Grande. Weekends they would come get us for return to the ranch. We went to the USO club in Casa Grande when we could manage that! We met a few soldiers this way—did we think we were grown up, yep! Also,

Figure 7.11. Ranch house at Johnson Well, about 1945. (Courtesy the Bender family)

we had boyfriends from Casa Grande Union High School. At times they would manage to visit us at the ranch. One time our high school boyfriends rode out on their motorcycles. We would always take them horseback riding. Later Dad would put their motorcycles in the horse trailer and take the trailer out to the highway so he would be certain they could return safely to town.

Our "war effort" was spent dancing with the soldiers at the USO in Casa Grande and at Marana Army Air Force Base. The USO ambulance would come and pick up girls, and we'd all go to the dance. We'd meet soldiers, and every once in a while we'd meet a couple we liked pretty well. The first thing they knew, we'd have them out at the ranch with us. One time a couple of soldiers came out in a little old convertible called Lindy Lou. We didn't waste any time in getting them on horseback and taking them riding. Poor things! They had probably never been on a horse before. We'd go seven or eight miles before stopping. We were used to riding, and we would be dragging them along, usually with them hanging onto their saddle horn for support. Regardless, time and time again they would return to the ranch for more "fun."

One day we took them on a ride to Bender Spring. We were coming down the hill, and we kept telling them, "Don't let the horses start running when reaching the bottom of the hill. You'll be sorry!" As we headed home for the ranch, the horses always loved to run if allowed. We were coming off that hill, and this one fellow didn't follow our instructions. He let his reins go. That horse took off like a bullet. The chollas at the end of the path were very dense, and he went right

through them. The spines plastered his pants to his legs. It was an awful sight. He got back to the ranch still in the saddle, and believe me, we spent the rest of the day removing cholla stickers. We should be ashamed of ourselves. We had more fun usually after they had returned to town. They provided lots of laughter. However, when a "real cowboy" would appear from one of the other nearby ranches and come riding to our house, we'd go into a swoon. If the cowboy had boots, a Stetson hat, Levi's, and straddled a horse, we knew for certain he was a real cowboy. We got very disappointed later on in life when we would meet some that were cowboys, but lacking the courtesy, integrity, and honor of the old-fashioned real cowboys.

John Pate, a cowboy from a neighboring ranch, used to come visit our family with his violin slung across his back, riding his horse up the trail to have supper and then entertain us with his music. We all loved it! We would have violin music all evening, many times requesting songs we knew, and he would play them. Maybe he played in the same key all the time, for most songs ended up sounding much like the song played previously. We didn't care—we loved it and the musician. Now, J. D. Andrews was a handsome cowboy, a drifter, I think, who showed up at the ranch now and then, and when he did, my sister and I would go into a dreamy tailspin. He wouldn't even look at us! He didn't pay any attention to us, maybe a greeting, that's all! He was a real old-time cowboy. One didn't see many of them. To this day we are still in love with J. D. Andrews.

When we rode horseback on our own, we always carried a couple of canteens of water. On all-day trips there would be a couple of canteens strapped to our saddles. A little jerky and a can of peaches stored in the saddlebag would be lunch. Dad said this would provide sustenance and a little moisture. Other times saddlebag items could be canned tomatoes, pork and beans, Vienna

Figure 7.12. Barn and corral at Johnson Well, about 1945. (Courtesy the Bender family)

Figure 7.13. *B-10 training plane on Vekol Flat after emergency landing, 1945. (Courtesy the Bender family)*

Figure 7.14. *Prescott Rodeo, 1947. Letty* (right), *Anita* (center), *with friend. (Courtesy the Bender family)*

sausage, or even cheese and crackers. Any of these items make up good provisions for the trail.

On occasion we would ride horseback the thirty-nine-mile trip into Casa Grande for the annual rodeo. We loved to ride our horses in the Grand Parade, which took place the morning of the rodeo. Being teenagers at this point, we needed

a little social life, and our boyfriends would manage to get out to the ranch one way or another. Dad had fashioned a small, rather crude airstrip along the ridge of a hill, and once or twice a couple of our high school friends flew a small two-seater airplane into our place, landed, and departed on this airstrip. Quite a tricky experience! Other times we would ride horseback north through the east pass of the Javelina Mountains and visit our old Big Horn home—these were some of the best rides to remember, bringing back the warmest, loving family memories. To this day those wonderful memories are still in our minds and our hearts.

Several miles south of the Big Horn near Johnson Well, Dad built, in conjunction with Soil Conservation Service, a number of spreader dams, including several dams south of the Vekol Well. These dirt dams were constructed to slow run-off and allow rainwater to sink into the ground. Grasses, especially the galleta grass [tobosa], which is very good cattle feed, then would grow in abundance. At one point the Soil Conservation Service insisted on building a dam to hold water west of the house at Johnson Well. During one very hard downpour of rain originating in the Sand Tank Mountains west of the place, our father became a little agitated and said, "I think I'll walk up to the top of the dam and see if the water is rising behind the dam." He came back running and yelled, "Get Grandma! Get the baby! Get in the car! All of you get in the car!" He came racing down off that dam, made sure we were all in the car, and drove to the top of the little hilltop airport. We sat up there for a little while, and all of a sudden water broke through the dirt dam. The spillways were not adequate—water and mud poured through the ranch house. We were fortunate to survive that flood!

Table Top Mountain was the east border of Bender Ranch, and cattle wouldn't go over the mountaintop. We had drift fences at the passes and in all the canyons. The first trail up the mountain was made by Les Bender about 1939 or '40. We know he was running cattle up there, because Dad and a hired hand were up there in 1945, and the hired hand accidentally shot Letty's horse, Poncho, in the knee, and they had to kill the horse right there! It broke her heart! She loved Poncho almost as much as her dad. Dad made the poor man carry the saddle all the way down the mountain. We remember that Dad used an old Indian trail the first time we put cattle up there.

Dad sold the ranch in 1952, and the family moved to Prescott. O. L. (Les) Bender died in 1966. Whenever the opportunity arises, our families return to camp, visit, and enjoy the beloved areas of our childhood. Now this land is included in the Sonoran Desert National Monument. Perhaps the monument could be centered at the old Big Horn station with the Bureau of Land Management involved in the restoration and protection of the old station and ranch headquarters. We can help them with the area's history. We were part of it.

Acknowledgments

This essay was prompted by the Bender sisters' conversations, correspondence, and interviews with Bill Broyles, Adrianne G. Rankin (Luke Air Force Base archaeologist), and Matt Bischoff, Teresita Majewski, and Matt Sterner (Statistical Research, Inc.). Peter Hofstra also contributed. SRI was under contract to the Corps of Engineers, Los Angeles District, to record information about historic and prehistoric "historic properties" on the Barry M. Goldwater Range as part of the oral-history project of the range, initiated by W. Bruce Masse and Adrianne G. Rankin.

Eight

A Trip to Laguna Prieta

Julian D. Hayden

If a guide is someone who helps others venture farther into a place or an understanding, then Alberto Celaya ranks among the best ever. Born February 20, 1885, in Sonoyta, Sonora (Ezell 1991), Celaya worked and played in the Pinacate and Gran Desierto. Although academically untutored (or academically unencumbered, some would say), he was exceptionally observant, curious, and reliable.

He also owned a wagon and could wrangle horses and harness mules. When Norwegian explorer and naturalist Carl Lumholtz arrived in Sonoyta to hire a couple of the best local men to travel with him into terra incognita, he picked Celaya and a Papago interpreter. The year was 1909, and Celaya, at age twenty-four, had already ridden and walked to many of the places Lumholtz wanted to study.

In his classic book *New Trails in Mexico* (1912), Lumholtz wrote of Celaya, "A wagon was engaged, which was to be driven by its owner, Alberto Celaya, an intelligent Mexican who knew the country" (149), having been born at Sonoyta and raised at Quitovac. Celaya ably served Lumholtz on his extensive exploration of the region, from Caborca west to the Colorado River, from the jaggedest lava flow to the highest billowing sand dunes, and all waterholes in between.

The region was still very much a frontier—arid, unmapped, and wild. As a small boy in the early 1890s Celaya remembered his father putting food and a cigarette on a Hia C'ed O'odham (Sand Papago) trail shrine near an ironwood tree three miles from his Quitovac home. Alberto had a childhood playmate, a blind Hia C'ed O'odham girl, who had been captured by a posse that pursued and killed several Sand Papagos accused of murdering two Mexicans near Quitobaquito. Most of the Hia C'ed O'odham had recently been driven from their homeland by Mexicans trying to stop Indian raids on travelers.

In 1908 Celaya had driven cattle across El Gran Desierto. He later told Julian D. Hayden that a Sr. Sandoval, founder of the first bank in Nogales, and a Sr. Gavilondo, from Hermosillo, bought six thousand steers in Chihuahua and moved them to Sonoyta, where the cattle wintered along the river bottom. Then Celaya helped trail the herd westward to Laguna Prieta, where they rested three days, and on to the Colorado River. Celaya said they corralled the cattle on Isla Montague in the river delta before driving them to the growing town of Mexicali (see also Lumholtz 1912:245). The only people living along the route were three Hia C'ed O'odham families at Quitobaquito and two Mexican families in the delta. Much of this route was repeated with Lumholtz.

About 1928 another scholar of the Pinacate arrived to enlist Celaya's sage advice and hospitality. This visitor was Ronald Lorenz Ives, fueled by Lumholtz's book and William T. Hornaday's *Camp-Fires on Desert and Lava* (1908). Ives wrote numerous publications on this region, including *The Pinacate Region, Sonora, Mexico* and the essays in *Land of Lava, Ash, and Sand*.

In November 1953 Celaya also helped introduce two young archaeologists to the area. Paul Ezell was studying the region, but he didn't yet know the Pinacate or Gran Desierto. He and a friend, Julian Hayden, sought out Celaya to guide them, just as Lumholtz and Ives had done.

Ezell and Hayden returned together in 1958. Hayden recalled, "It was nearly five years between the first and second trips to the Laguna, due to workloads and such, and we might not have gone then had Paul's wife, Greta, not blown her top and said, 'Why don't you two damned fools either GO or SHUT UP about going!' So we went, and lost our way down in the dunes. Paul insisted on going past the halfway mark on his gas gauge. I assured him that I was not dumb enough to walk out of those dunes, and if he was so damned macho, he could start walking right there and I'd take the Jeep back. I meant it, and he knew it. So we drove back to Sonoyta, spent the night with Celaya, and with his directions drove to Papago Tanks in the Pinacate." They spent two richly rewarding days there discovering artifacts.

Ezell would publish "An Archaeological Survey of Northwestern Papaguería" (1954), a fundamental report on the area's ancient peoples, and go on to a distinguished career in archaeology. Hayden operated an excavation company, but *por la bolsa* (at his own expense) he conducted an extensive study of the Pinacate, producing a lengthy list of seminal publications on the region. Celaya, Ives, Ezell, and Hayden remained lifelong mutual friends.

Around Sonoyta, Celaya was renowned for his public service, charity, and family devotion; he earned his living by working at small mines, ranches, and civic jobs. But foremost he was a rich source of human and natural history, an inspiration to those who dared to know the vast and enigmatic desert. Celaya himself was a bit enigmatic. His father, Jesús Celaya Ortega, was born in San Gabriel, California, so Alberto not only had dual U.S.-Mexican citizenship (Ezell 1991) but spoke English, unbeknownst to most of his English-speaking friends. His mother was the sister of Cipriano Ortega, reputed bandit, full-time entrepreneur, and sometime hero who owned the hacienda at Santo Domingo. Don Alberto died in 1962; his last trip into the heart of the Pinacate was in April 1961 with Hayden. There's no telling how many students and scholars Celaya influenced through Lumholtz, Hayden, Ives, and Ezell.

One place Celaya visited with Lumholtz and then forty-three years later with Ezell and Hayden was Laguna Prieta, a lake in the western dunes. Lumholtz journeyed there in January 1910. The trio of Celaya, Ezell, and Hayden made a similar trip by Jeep in 1953. Here are accounts of those ventures.

—*Bill Broyles*

Figure 8.1. Alberto Celaya at marker 193 on the United States–Mexico boundary, 1953. In 1910 he had crossed at neighboring marker 194 while guiding Carl Lumholtz. (Photo by Julian D. Hayden)

Carl Lumholtz's Account

To reach Laguna Prieta was a more laborious task than we had expected. It seemed a long distance, and as the guide and I rode along behind the rest of the party, I expressed my astonishment at his feat of having taken cattle over this route and successfully arriving at the Colorado River. No tracks were to be seen any more except at one place, as the wind soon obliterates them....

For the last three miles before reaching Laguna Prieta we crossed the western extremity of

Figure 8.2. The Jeep for the 1953 trip to Laguna Prieta: Alberto Celaya (left) *and Paul Ezell. (Photo by Julian D. Hayden)*

the sand dunes, which attain their greatest height here, two or three of the hills being at least two hundred feet high. The lake is at the edge of the big dunes on their southern side, and the comparatively large sheet of water made a pleasing impression. Just as we descended toward it a white coyote was observed running away from the shore. At first sight, we took it for a pelican; my unruly mule prevented me from getting my field-glass

Figure 8.3. *A camp in the Gran Desierto dunes, the largest sea of sand in North America, 1953. These dunes are somewhat stabilized by vegetation, especially the pictured creosotebush (Larrea divaricata), as well as mesquite (Prosopis glandulosa), giant dune-buckwheat (Eriogonum deserticola), and joint-fir (Ephedra trifurca). (Photo by Julian D. Hayden)*

Figure 8.4. *The larger, shifting dunes en route to Laguna Prieta, 1953. Judging from the ruts, the Jeep had gotten stuck and the tarp had been laid under the wheels for traction. (Photo by Julian D. Hayden)*

quickly enough, but the Mexican who rode behind me saw distinctly that the apparition had four legs. An albino coyote, which was very shy, was once seen near Caborca.

Camp was made on a slightly elevated ground near the shore at the south-west end of the lake. Two large mezquite trees [*Prosopis glandulosa*] were growing there; they were rather abject looking as they had no leaves, but the guide had seen them with beautiful foliage in the month of May. Laguna Prieta is a salt water lake, but on the marshy shore an abundance of fresh water may be found by digging in the extensive growth of *Typha*

latipholia [undoubtedly *Typha domingensis*], popularly called bulrushes, which are thriving here; the Mexicans call them *tule*. At three places the earth had been dug away so as to make troughs two feet deep, twelve feet long and six feet wide, which were full of clear water. Many years ago, I understand, attempts at cattle raising were made by people from the Colorado River with this water as base for operations. The water, though slightly brackish, does not taste bad, but among the Mexicans of Colonia Lerdo it is reputed to have an ill effect on horses, as some of them when thirsty have been known to die from drinking it.

The lake is half a mile long and slightly less than that distance wide, running from south-west to north-east. Birds from the sea were swimming in the water which, according to the guide, becomes very low in May. The shores are soft and along the south-western part overgrown with bulrushes and reeds, while on the northern part arrowbush is found. Our mules had had no water to drink for seventy-six hours, so I remained here a day [January 28, 1910] in order to give them a rest.

Julian Hayden's Account

On that 1953 Pinacate trip, Alberto Celaya, Paul Ezell, and I went over to Laguna Prieta, southeast of San Luis Río Colorado. Don Alberto sat with Paul on the front seat of the Jeep, and I sat on the hood to hold the front end down. We took off from the highway at the boundary-line milepost [marker 193]. We got a picture of Don Alberto standing at that milepost.

We headed west toward the right (north) side of the highest dune in the Gran Desierto. Don Alberto had not been there since 1910, and he made one slight error that threw us off maybe a few hundred yards. We cut back south and damn near fell into the bloody Laguna Prieta, the most beautiful thing you ever saw in your life, a lake right there in the middle of all those sand dunes.

The dunes were standing all around it. And here was a basin with a lake in the bottom, the most beautiful cobalt blue lake you ever saw. It had oxblood-red water on the east side from the alkalis. It was astonishing. And on the far side were some mesquite trees. I got involved in collecting pottery, Yuman pottery from around the camps in the dunes, while Don Alberto and Paul walked around the lake to trace its rim.

Don Alberto pointed to a hole under a tree and said, "I dug that in 1910. Dr. Lumholtz and I drank of the water from it." And he and Paul both drank from it. Later I felt bad that I hadn't been there for that drink. It was fall and blowing and cold. Quite the experience. We had a wonderful time.

Don Alberto told his stories, of course, about Lumholtz. Paul at that time was a young professor, barely two years on the San Diego State University faculty and still a bit solemn, as young Ph.D.'s usually are. I'll never forget this because I resented it a little bit at the time. Don Alberto and I got along fine; we were talking about rockets, philosophy, and all kinds of things in my very best Spanish, which I'd picked up from my friends in the dirt trenches and construction sites of California.

Paul, however, was fluent in Spanish—he spoke Chihuahuense—and he took me aside and said, "Look, you shouldn't talk to the old man like that . . . in your Spanish. If you want to talk to him, you can translate through me."

I asked, "Why?"

He said, "You know, you don't speak Spanish very well."

"No, I reckon I don't."

And he said, "Every time you use that darned Spanish you insult the old gentleman. Why don't you talk to me and I'll tell him what you want to say?"

Figure 8.5. Laguna Prieta, a freshwater lake fed by semi-artesian springs and surrounded by sand dunes (see Ezcurra et al. 1988; Felger 2000). In drier times it shrinks to a pond or pool. Compare this vista from 1953 with Lumholtz 1912:244. (Photo by Julian D. Hayden)

Figure 8.6. The main pool at Laguna Prieta in 1953. (Photo by Julian D. Hayden)

So I got mad and cursed him, I think, but that was the end of it. Paul "knew" darned well that Don Alberto didn't understand a word of English.

Years later, after Don Alberto died, I found out that he spoke better English than either of us. He used to come home and tell his daughters what we'd said, and he'd laugh and laugh and laugh. The old joker. He knew everything we said! Hell, yes.

Don Alberto had worked in Los Angeles as a construction foreman when his children were small, because he wanted them to go to American schools. He was a boss on a big building in downtown Los Angeles and excavated an elevator shaft. It filled with water in a heavy rain, so he called together his gang and started a bucket brigade. The superintendent came by: "What are you doing that for? Put a siphon in it!"

Figure 8.7. Alberto Celaya, 1953, reflecting on a life of travel and adventure in this region: been there, done that... and would do it all again. (Photo by Julian D. Hayden)

"But, sir, how can you siphon from down below to an upper level? I thought you were an engineer." And Don Alberto told that story till he died. He was just an old boy from Sonoyta, but he knew how to get water out of a hole.

Acknowledgments

Photos reprinted courtesy of the Arizona State Museum, Tucson, and the Hayden family. The Lumholtz segment is from *New Trails in Mexico* (pages 244–246), most recently reprinted by the University of Arizona Press, Tucson, 1990. The Hayden section is from interviews with Mr. Hayden by Diane Boyer and Bill Broyles, 1990–95, transcribed by Boyer. Special thanks to Kathy Hubenschmidt and Laurie Webster, archivists at the Arizona State Museum, Tucson.

Nine

Afield with Desert Scientists

Tad Nichols

When freshman Tad Nichols arrived in Tucson to attend the University of Arizona (class of 1936), he fell in with an elite crew of natural scientists bent on describing and explaining the entire Sonoran Desert. Tad was invited to join them on a field trip, and sixty years later, with camera in hand, he was still accompanying scientists afield.

In the early 1930s the U of A had a strong and diverse staff of scholars that included Gurdon M. Butler, B. S. Butler, William G. McGinnies, Andrew A. Nichol, Robert H. Forbes, Homer L. Shantz, Walter P. Taylor, John J. Thornber, and Charles T. Vorhies.

Also in town was the Carnegie Desert Laboratory atop Tumamoc Hill, just two and one-half miles west of the campus. Its illustrious and seminal staff and associates during the 1930s included Forrest Shreve, Frederic E. Clements, Robert Humphrey, T. Dwight Mallery, Edith B. Shreve, Herman Spoehr, Godfrey Sykes, William V. Turnage, and Ira L. Wiggins (Bowers 1988; McGinnies 1981). Its founder, Daniel T. MacDougal, had initiated and overseen a number of studies and expeditions, including one popularized in William T. Hornaday's 1908 classic *Camp-Fires on Desert and Lava.* "The Hill" bustled with researchers probing the why's and how's of desert plants and animals. The roster then, as today, reads like a who's who of botany, climatology, and ecology.

Forrest Shreve would author more than sixty studies and articles on botany and biogeography. Wiggins wrote extensively on plant classification and biogeography. Together they produced the seminal and nonpareil *Vegetation and Flora of the Sonoran Desert,* a treasure that defined the Sonoran Desert.

Mallery studied meteorology and climatology and how they affected plants. He published several important articles (see McGinnies 1981) and was president of the Tucson Natural History Society, which pushed for the founding of Organ Pipe Cactus National Monument. The first reconnaissance trip to study a site for the monument, initiated by Roger Toll, was conducted early in 1932. The second trip, to Alamo Canyon of the Ajo Mountains in the fall of 1932, included scientists from the University of Arizona and the Desert Lab, who added their stamp of approval. Not only did they encourage the National Park Service to designate Organ Pipe a monument, they lobbied local politicians to support the grand idea. Tad Nichols was on that second trip.

Later he occasionally accompanied Mallery and Shreve across the Old Yuma-Sonoyta Trail, a pioneer trail that had earned the infamous appellation El Camino del Diablo. The road was a foot and wagon trail along the international border between Sonoyta, Sonora, and Yuma, Arizona. The first auto trip wasn't made until 1915, and twenty years later the road was still primitive and treacherous. Shreve collected plants, and Mallery checked his string of rain gauges, which stretched southwest from Tucson nearly to Yuma. Each foray was an adventure that tested one's courage, savvy, and perseverance.

Later Nichols traveled with ecologists Ray Turner and Rod Hastings, biologists Gale Monson and Charles Lowe, ornithologists Alan Phillips and Steve Russell, botanists Bob Darrow and Bob Humphrey, Arizona-Sonora Desert Museum director Bill Woodin, and geologists Edwin McKee, John Sumner, and Peter Kresan, among others.

Despite spending much of his life camping and traveling with field scientists, Nichols didn't follow his mentors and friends into the science lab or classroom; instead, he became a photographer. Nevertheless, what he saw through the lens frequently filled the pages of scientific texts and journals. Throughout his career he took photos for the U.S. Geological Survey, scientific publications, and even the ever-popular *Arizona Highways.* He was also a cinematographer, shooting for Walt Disney, the U.S. Indian Service, and numerous research projects. His assignments took him from the exploding Paricutín volcano in Mexico to the High Sierra of California and to the "sand seas" of the Sahara, the Namib, Saudi Arabia, and Mexico's Gran Desierto. Until his death in 2000 Nichols was still associated with the Desert Lab and the University of Arizona.

His favorite trips were along El Camino del Diablo. Here he takes us on one of his first.

—*Bill Broyles*

Figure 9.1. *Camping in Growler Valley, November 1932, on a trip with Dwight Mallery and Ira Wiggins in what is now the Cabeza Prieta National Wildlife Refuge. When he revisited the site in 1991 to match this photo, Nichols sheepishly admitted that several now-rusted tin cans may have been left there by this party. The roadster was Nichols's 1930 Model A Ford, which "could go about anywhere." (Photo by Tad Nichols)*

My first trip across the Camino del Diablo came by accident. But I had come to the University of Arizona sort of by accident, too. I went to school in Mesa [Arizona] before I came to the university. I had come out from Cambridge, Massachusetts. God bless it. It's a pretty good place, really. My folks lived there. However, I attended quite a few schools—I think two years was the longest I stayed at any one before I was requested to go look for another that might do me better.

Mainly, I was not interested. I couldn't see any reason whatsoever that I should learn all the kings and queens of England. So I didn't study. But you know, funny thing, I was interested in science. The last school I attended before coming west was New Preparatory School, a tutoring school that occupied some offices in Harvard Square. It had a good, old-fashioned scientist there who was a botanist. I took his class in botany, and I did well in that; and my drawings were so good that he later used them in lantern slides for his scientific illustration classes. Of course, I got a good grade on that and then somebody showed me a book on geology. I looked through it, and later on the exam I could answer every question, except one on glaciation. I could have passed the exam without ever taking the class. I found that natural science was where my interests lie.

So the fall of 1930 my mom sent me out West to Boys Ranch School, a campus for kids from the East who were not successful in school or else had health problems, of which I was both. She'd heard about it through friends. It was a pretty primitive place. Each guy had a little cabin, his own horse, and all that stuff. Besides school, we learned to pack a mule, ride western, and camp out. Coming to Arizona was the beginning of my life. Before that I was frequently ill with asthma and merely existed without much interest in the world in general.

The headmaster was Lionel F. Brady, known affectionately and commonly as "Major." He was headmaster of the Mesa Ranch School, which for-

Figure 9.2. *El Camino del Diablo east of Tule Well, 1933. (Photo by Tad Nichols)*

merly was the Evans School, but Brady and Evans split up. Evans came down to Tucson and established the Evans School here, while Brady kept the Ranch School in Mesa.

Brady and I became friends, and he got me interested in life again. He was a geologist and amateur archaeologist, so when I graduated and went off to college at the University of Arizona, he recommended me to Dean [Emil Richert] Riesen, head of the College of Liberal Arts and Sciences and an old friend of his. So I went to the university so to speak through the back door without taking any exams. I wouldn't have been able to pass them anyway.

Then when I was a freshman at the University of Arizona in 1932–33, I got a note from Brady saying he was going to attend a meeting down near the Gray Ranch, north of Sonoyta, with a group of scientists from Tucson, including the Tucson Natural History Society and others. Quite a few university people went: all the Botany Department, Homer Shantz, Charlie Thornber, Dr. Shreve, Ira Wiggins, and other old-timers. So I followed along in my little Model A Ford.

The group went out to Alamo Canyon in what would become Organ Pipe Cactus National Monument in 1937. We went to survey it as a possible monument, evaluate it. Some of the cowboys from the Gray Ranch were there. I remember we had quite a big group, and we camped there for two nights. There was a big discussion about the monument prospect. I cannot remember anything about the discussions, but we talked around the campfire about Organ Pipe as a monument.

We walked around the canyon, looked at the plants, and generally inspected as much as we could in two days. I don't remember very much about it, except I wish now I had taken a good set of pictures, but I didn't. Brady and I walked off by ourselves once or twice to look at some of the rock. There's a big split boulder down there that we decided had been split by the frost action. We took a photograph of that, and it may be the only photo I took there.

There I visited with Mallery, whom I had met before, and I met Dr. Shreve, who was a friend of Brady's. They told me they were about to go along El Camino del Diablo to read rain gauges [see McGinnies 1981:101–116].

I said, "Gee, that should be a great experience." I'd wanted to go since I'd heard about it earlier.

"Why don't you come along? We could use another car to help push us out."

So that's how I got on the trip. I went in my Model A roadster. I was alone, skipping some classes to go, but it was worth it.

We—Shreve, Mallery, and I—proceeded on one of their regular biennial (it was fall and spring) rain gauge readings. Wiggins joined us, too; he was working at the Desert Lab then. The regular route we took was from Ajo, only the present-day route is a little different from the old one we followed. Eventually we arrived at Tinajas Altas and then went north to Wellton and circled back to Tucson on the highway. At that time I didn't realize what they were doing, but I got interested and took pictures.

On the way Dwight Mallery had a pretty good-sized notebook in which he kept the rain gauge locations and readings. And in case he forgot, the book had the details of where the gauges were located. They weren't very far from the road. These were the old Godfrey Sykes gauges, which he had designed. They were fashioned from brass and then charged with a dose of machine oil so that the rainfall wouldn't evaporate before he got out there to read them. Mallery would pour out the rainwater into a graduated cylinder, and then, because he knew the diameter of the cup opening, he would read the level of water underneath the oil to calculate the amount of rainfall. He got his reading that way. Then he rinsed out the gauge with kerosene or turpentine, put an inch or two of machine oil back in, and reburied the gauge where no one would see it or the animals wouldn't knock it over. They left just the cup sticking up, preferably on a little mound, and oftentimes they put rocks around it so the rain wouldn't splash in.

Some of them were right on flat ground with only the top two or three inches sticking out. One had more water in it than we thought it should have, so he joked that a coyote may have come along and peed in it. He had seen that happen before. And there was quite a variation in the rainfall due to thunderstorms. It rains in one place but not half a mile away. They found that fairly interesting.

Mallery had one rain gauge atop the store at Sells, one at the Growler Pass Mine, and another at Papago Well. One was in the Pinacate lava. One rain gauge was on the side of the mountain above Tule Tank, not far up in a little pass.

Figure 9.4. Dwight Mallery near the crest of the Tinajas Altas Mountains servicing one of his rain gauges, ca. 1933. View is looking northwest toward Buck Peak. This gauge was part of an elevation study in which Mallery showed that in low, desert mountain ranges, precipitation differs little between the base and the summit (Turnage & Mallery 1941:13). (Photo by Tad Nichols)

storms and blowing sand. We were there in the fall of the year, probably October, and there had been no tracks there before us. I mean, nobody had been there all summer, and we were the first vehicles through. The roads had very little travel then.

Mallery often went by himself. He knew the road well. In some cases it was obliterated so we walked ahead, in one case about half a mile, to see where the road came out on top of the Pinacate lava. In general, it was well marked. Once it was overgrown—we had to cut some bushes to go through. There were times when it must have been six months between travelers in the early 1930s. Nobody had any business to go out there, and they knew there was sand.

Since nobody had driven across the washes, some of them were a little rough. Shreve's car was a newer one. He had a Willys-Knight, which had a split glass front windshield that you could open to get the breeze. It was actually his wife's car and she didn't especially want him to take it, so along both sides of the car Shreve would hang strips of canvas so that the roadside brush wouldn't scratch the paint. It was the better of his two cars, at least then, and it had a good deal of clearance. It would chug right along.

When we got stuck, Shreve would take one of those pieces of canvas off the side of his car and lay it down in front of the car so the car could roll onto it. When he got to the edge of that piece, he would put a second piece in front and repeat the process. I made a run for it, but got stuck and had to lay out my own canvas.

It was very leisurely. We traveled very slowly. We didn't go more than fifteen miles an hour, and we'd make frequent stops. We couldn't go very far before we'd stop again at something to look at. Shreve frequently would get out his big 6½" by 8½" plate camera, set it up on the tripod, and take pictures. He taught me something about photography. The whole trip was about five or six nights, with two nights at Tinajas Altas.

On the first trip there in 1932, the remains were still at Papago Well of the old sand pump and the big wheel that ran it, plus a lot of machinery, a forge, and stuff. As I understand it, a sand pump was a big metal tube with holes in the side of it used to get water from damp or wet sand. It went down into the well, and water would filter into the casing but sand was excluded. Then it

At Tinajas Altas he had several gauges, two north and south of Tinajas Altas and one on the east side of the Lechuguilla Valley. We'd leave Tinajas Altas and drive north. Then he had one at Raven Butte stuck up in the lava somewhere. We always wanted to visit Raven Butte Tank, but we never had enough time. He had another gauge just south of Wellton. The going was very slow because we were crossing the drainages. It was bumpity-bumpity-bump until finally coming out at Wellton.

The roads were just tracks—they'd never been graded. Sometimes there wasn't *any* road ahead of us. It had just been obliterated by summer was brought back up and the water poured into buckets.

Shreve and Wiggins had plant presses, and always in the evening they would open the presses and change the layers of cardboard. Every night they'd lay those presses on the ground and carefully transfer the plants onto other sheets, so that the damp sheets would dry. There was quite a bit of work to it, but Shreve and Wiggins were very conscientious about doing that [see Shreve & Wiggins 1964]. Wiggins was always rather formal, military-like in his stance at times. He was very businesslike and precise in everything.

If only I had taken more pictures! When you're that age, you don't realize. It was a privilege, you know, and I didn't realize how valuable the pictures would be. Shreve made lots of notes when he was in the field. He'd make notes each time he took a photograph. He kept a book recording the photos taken.

I got interested in photography back East. Another fellow there, one of the teachers, was interested and helped me get started. Several years before, I had gone to a boys' camp someplace, and at the end of summer I got a cup for the best photography, although the pictures were God-awful—the rest of the entries must have been even worse. I remember clearly that the fellow taught me how to develop a print using the light from outside through a red-glass filter. The films were not panchromatic, so they were not sensitive to red. Much later Forrest Davis at the University of Arizona Tree-Ring Lab taught me a lot about photography, too.

I had a small German camera, which I had purchased in Europe in the summer of 1930 when I went to Europe with my sister and her girlfriend. Don't ever travel through Europe with two girls! I saw these beautiful cameras that the Germans made and bought one. It was a Zeiss camera. In those days Zeiss was the best lens made. That camera got me interested in photography. Finally I began to get some really good pictures.

Shreve wasn't on the trips all the time. Dwight Mallery was the man who usually did the route. He was so nice to me. I made about five trips with him. I told Dwight, "Anytime you want to go, let me know if you want another car." I would get out into that country anytime I could. I always thought about it and dreamed about that Camino trip.

I always carried a .22 pistol or rifle with me.

Figure 9.5. *Tinajas Altas, April 1933.* From left to right: *Dwight Mallery, Ira Wiggins, Forrest Shreve, and Tad Nichols. Note canvas skirts on the car (compare with Figure 5.6a).(Photo by Tad Nichols)*

Figure 9.6. Tad Nichols and three friends at international boundary marker 190 south of Tinajas Altas in 1935 or 1938. This photo may have been taken by Howard Gentry. From left to right: Dwight Mallery, Marie Gentry, Mary Jane Hayden Nichols, and Edward Tattnall Nichols IV ("Father was called Tattnall, so my mother called me Tad").

I loved to shoot. One trip my wife, Mary Jane, came along. Mallery set up a bottle quite some distance from camp. He said to Mary Jane, "See if you can hit that one." Damned if she didn't break it on the first shot. Mallery never forgot that. He was a great guy, very friendly. He let me go along; I guess he liked the company, but he'd go alone if he had to.

I wish I could remember more what the camps were like, what we ate, and what was said. I know that Mallery's wife would fix him baked cornmeal. We'd eat sliced cold cornmeal mush.

Figure 9.7. *Tinajas Altas from Mesa of the Dead, 1933. (Photo by Tad Nichols)*

Shreve loved that. They put that in the skillet with a couple of eggs in place of bacon—cornmeal mush and eggs.

We had iceboxes, but they weren't as good as today. We'd take a block of ice. The Tucson ice plant was the only place you could get blocks of ice. Shreve had an ice chest made for the back of his car. It was insulated and probably lined with galvanized tin so it wouldn't leak. He kept a blanket over it. The ones they had at that time were too small; he wanted a larger one. If it was really hot, he kept some of his photographic plates in there.

They used to carry water on the running board—gallon cans of water. We got some water at Tule Well when we could, and Shreve showed me a wash—Coyote Wash, I think—where we dug into the sand about two feet down and water appeared. And Shreve said water is always there. You let it settle and it was very clear.

Mallery usually did the cooking. Shreve was always busy with something else around the camp, either with his plants or his notes. Mallery collected few plants, not nearly as many as Shreve, so he let Shreve do his pressing chores while Mallery got the dinner. Shreve didn't bubble over, but he was always interested in something. And he was always pointing out to me different things. He gave me something of the history of this place.

Just before the road drops down on the west end of the lava, there's a sort of flat place on the south side. I went out there about twenty or thirty yards and put my initials down with little rocks:

"TN" with the date of 1932. Each time I've been along there since, I've added to it. I've been there more than seven times (at least 1932, 1933, 1935, 1937, 1938, 1983, 1991). There were other piles of stones that other people made with dates. Some have been disturbed by wind and rain, or maybe by animals and people. Someday I'll go with you and look at it. On the old road where you cross the Pinacate lava, we saw antelope, the first antelope I'd ever seen.

At Tinajas Altas we were able to get up past the first tank and up about midway to the top. Then Wiggins saw some leaves growing in another catchment above that—cattails and things. He spent about half an hour looking for a way up there, just like a terrier or something, going around this way and that way. And finally he got up there—I think I must have leaned against the rock and he stood on my shoulders. I boosted him up so he could get those grasses and reeds. When he saw something, he'd go after it. Shreve did not go up there. Wiggins and I climbed around the right-hand side and got up to the top of the tank. I took some pictures at the same time from up there. Wiggins was pretty spry. Shreve sort of ambled along; he wasn't fast moving. He sort of took things easy, but he got his work done and he took his time.

At the base of Tinajas Altas there were the remains of many graves. Most have been dug up, with many holes there. People had dug the graves out. There were also some marked with rocks.

One time I climbed with Mallery to the top of the first hill where you look out over the Lechuguilla Valley, and then we went beyond to the top of the ridge so we could look out to the west and see the grand dunes. From the top we could easily see the road coming from Tule Tank. It was defined by the vegetation on both sides of the road, because where you have a road, you have water collecting. I remember I was quite impressed with the view from the top, because it showed the beautiful herringbone pattern of the drainage typical of the desert. It was very distinct. It was something I had been told about in geology class. We achieved the summit, and I took a photograph; I've tried since to get back to that same place, but couldn't. I want to repeat the photograph.

Now for some unknown reason in recent years, maybe 1983, somebody sent a bulldozer through there just to the south of the old road. I never saw any need for that at all. There was nothing wrong with the old road. It was sandy and smooth.

I made at least six rain-gauge trips. I made about five with Mallery and one with Howard Gentry and his wife, Marie. One trip we drove down to the Mexican border south of Tinajas Altas and took a picture at the monument there.

I also made trips with Gale Monson, Alan Phillips, and Chuck Lowe. They were collecting birds and lizards. We'd make camp every day and skin the birds and prepare the lizards. I particularly remember one camp down near Las Playas, where the road went through quite a thicket of brush and mesquite. It was perfectly dry that year, but when that silty playa bottom gets wet, there are big ruts and people get quite stuck.

On another trip I went with Glenton Sykes and Peter Kresan. It was a beautiful spring, and lots of brandegea vine was growing over the saguaros and trees. Steve and Ruth Russell were on that trip, too. The desert was blooming greatly. We went through Tinajas Altas Pass, and it was like a garden with flowers. I've also camped with Bob Darrow, Bob Humphrey, Ray Turner, Rod Hastings, Bill Woodin, Steve Russell, John Sumner, George Bratt, Alberto Celaya, and many other fine people.

The trips were all fun. That's why I went along. And the country's fascinating. It's a lonely country—you don't find that very many places anymore. I consider all of these trips fun. We always had something interesting happen. I've had a lot of wonderful trips over the years. I've been very lucky.

Acknowledgments

This edited memoir combines material from two interviews with Tad Nichols: by Jan Bowers on April 18, 1988, and by Bill Broyles on June 20, 1996. Photos courtesy of Tad Nichols. Thanks also to Jan Bowers and Jan Price of the USGS research station atop Tumamoc Hill, Tucson.

Figure 9.8. A camp along El Camino del Diablo, April 1956. From left to right: *Alan Phillips, Gale Monson, Charles Lowe, and Tad Nichols. (Photo by Tad Nichols)*

Figure 9.9. Tad and Mary Jane Nichols, with Joseph Wilder, Tucson, 1997. "Mary Jane and I have been married sixty years. We're not doing badly for being eighty-six years old." (Photo by David Burckhalter)

Ten

El Viento Negro

A Saga of the Sonora–Baja California Railroad

GUILLERMO MUNRO PALACIO

It might seem incredible to younger generations that before 1940 and the inauguration of the Mexicali–Puerto Peñasco railroad, the Baja California peninsula had no road connections with the rest of Mexico. But that was the reality. Even the pavement of Highway 2 from Mexicali to Sonoyta wasn't finished until 1957.

Before then, traveling the stretch between Sonoyta and Mexicali was an odyssey full of difficulties and perils. One had to cross an arid region covered by sand dunes and volcanic lava and go around hills and arroyos to finally reach the town of San Luis Río Colorado. From there travelers had to board a ferry pulled by ropes to cross the Colorado River, since there were no bridges across it until 1952.

Before those days only a few risked crossing this desert. And just a few tough cowboys on horseback, such the Lópezes, the Ortegas, the Parras, the Celayas, the Jaques, and other locals from Sonoyta, Caborca, and Trincheras had the nerve to guide herds of cattle from ranches in Sonora to buyers in Baja California.

When the farming rush started in the Mexicali Valley at the beginning of the twentieth century, the demand for labor to work the cotton fields and to harvest the wheat crops forced the companies and the owners of agricultural fields to travel south of Sonora, to Sinaloa and Nayarit, to hire farmworkers, just as they had done during the establishment of the farmlands south of San Luis Río Colorado in a place known as Colonia Lerdo.

Those farmers who in the 1920s hired these seasonal field workers (or *enganchados,* as they were called then) signed agreements with ship captains to bring farmworkers to the primitive ports situated along the then mighty Colorado River. Those places, with names such as La Bomba, La Bolsa, and principally El Mayor, were disembarking zones located on the Baja California side of the river, but nowadays they are only reference points buried deep in the desert, next to the highway from Mexicali to San Felipe, Baja California. Only a few people still remember the once mighty red river that ran downstream, overflowing with water from melted snow and ice from the Rocky Mountains all the way down to the delta.

Before assuming the presidency of the Mexican republic, Gen. Lázaro Cárdenas dared to take a journey through the Sonoran Desert to personally assess routes to the farms across the desert, trackless routes where many men, women, and children had died. Some fishermen from those years, such as Germán Sánchez Valenzuela and Abelardo Pino, remember the day when the general's elegant party appeared before shirtless, long-haired fishermen at the fish camp known in those days by the name Rocky Point. It had been named by Lt. William Hale Hardy of the Royal Navy in 1826 and appeared on the marine charts with this name for nearly one hundred years. According to desert driver Juan Contreras Delgadillo, the general's entourage had five automobiles, called *diligencias* [coaches], and a truck loaded with food and radio communication devices. An airplane flew over them for the whole trip and landed several times to bring them food and ice. Wherever they camped, they set up a radio to communicate with both Hermosillo and Mexicali. The local drivers included "Fili" Fernández, "El Mocho" Araiza, Pancho Verdugo, and Beto Salazar.

With that picturesque group also came Gen. Francisco Múgica, who would later serve as secretary of communications during Cárdenas's administration. The group went all over the place. Eighty or more fishermen lived at Rocky Point in houses made of stone layered on stone, without cement or mud in between them, and with roofs made of cardboard, boards, metal sheets, or pieces of wood. Some of them lived in caves or tents. They guided the dignitaries to the hotel made of stone that the infamous John Stone burned to the ground when he was deported, and they told the delegation that the American had dynamited the only well when he left (Verdugo 1985).

The fishermen also report that Gen. Cárdenas then asked them what the place was called and they responded "Rocky Point," as specified in the marine charts. It was then decided that since they were in Mexico, the name of the place should be officially changed to the Spanish equivalent, Punta Peñasco. Later a port was built and became known as Puerto Peñasco. The group climbed to the top of the hill, took some notes, and then returned to Sonoyta. From there they crossed El Gran Desierto to Mexicali.

The government of Baja California petitioned Gen. Cárdenas to build a railroad to connect the peninsula to the rest of the country once he took over the presidency. In 1923 they had tried unsuccessfully to build a railroad from Mexicali to San Felipe, Baja California, in order to transfer cargo off the ships and transport it to the interior of the country. Only seventeen kilometers of the railroad was completed.

On May 19, 1936, almost two years after his visit Cárdenas signed a decree directing the secretary of communications and public services to start working on the survey, layout, and construction of the first section of the railroad from Mexicali to Puerto Peñasco.

In June 1936 a crew led by engineer Carlos Franco began working from the place called Fuentes Brotantes (a large artesian spring at Rancho la Pastoría). From there they continued establishing work camps and stations, such as Pascualitos (about 15 km southeast of Mexicali), Lobo, Alamitos, Cerro Prieto, Laguna, Delta, Pescaderos, Victoria, Río Colorado, Mezquital, and Coahuila, all in Baja California. Once in Sonora they established the Riito (Km 62) and Medanos camps and, deep in the sand dunes, El Doctor, toward El Golfo de Santa Clara.

The construction settlement at Medanos later became Ejido Mesa Rica. The most difficult work started here: surveying and laying the rail line over the immense dunes and interminable sand in the most inhospitable region of El Gran Desierto. Temperatures in July and August reached 120°F in the shade, and the sweltering humidity was stifling. To the south lay the Sea of Cortés with its bottomless mudflats. This railroad presented enormous challenges for the engineers and workers.

Meanwhile, a camp was established in Puerto Peñasco for the engineers and a crew of workers. For the headquarters, engineer Franco made arrangements with Sra. Tecla de Bustamante to use the stone hotel. He made a commitment to re-roof and refurbish it and also to rebuild the well that had been dynamited by John Stone. A truck loaded with poles, wood, and metal sheeting arrived on September 28 or 29, 1936.

The idea was to have a crew leave from this settlement and meet another one coming from Fuentes Brotantes. Another team would build a big wooden dock to access the railroad. The engineers also received orders to survey the city around the railroad camp. The survey crew from Puerto Peñasco was under the leadership of civil engineer Ramón Martínez. Engineer Jorge López Collada was the planner. Assistant engineer José Osio was in charge of instruments, and assistant engineer José Plata was the surveyor. There was also a team of drivers and workers.

In November 1937 the two surveying and planning crews met in the heart of the desert. They were so happy that they embraced each other and toasted in celebration. Engineer Carlos Franco had satisfactorily finished the route to Puerto Peñasco. Now they had to start the most difficult part of the project: actual construction of the railroad.

On March 20, 1937, at 11:30 in the morning, a dedication ceremony was held. It was attended by such dignitaries as engineer Melquiades Angulo Gallardo, chief of construction; Rodolfo Sánchez Toboada, lieutenant colonel and governor of Baja California; journalist José Armando I. Levelier; and engineer Carlos Castro Padilla. The honor of placing the first spike went to Sra. María de Jesús Yrigoyen, a distinguished lady in her seventies whose husband, Ulises Yrigoyen, had represented President Cárdenas at the initial meeting to establish the line. She was assisted by José Castañedo, editor of *Minerva* magazine and correspondent for *La Opinión* in Los Angeles, California.

Afterward Castro Padilla and Angulo Gallardo asked for hammers and, laughing in jubilation, put the spikes in the first railroad tie,

Figure 10.1. Route of the Sonora–Baja California Railroad. (Map by Guillermo Munro Colosio)

Calexico
Mexicali
Pascualitos 0 km
Alamitos 15 km
San Luis
Lobo 10 km
Cerro Prieto 19 km
San Luis R.C.
Laguna 25 km
Delta 32 km
Pescaderos 39 km
Victoria 43 km
50
Coahuila 57 km
Riito 62 km
Medanos 69 km
El Doctor 93 km
United States of America
México
EL GRAN DESIERTO
Sonoyta
100
Lopez Collada 174 km
El Golfo
de Santa Clara
Torres
142 km
160
Gustavo Sotelo 208 km
200
BAHIA ADAIR
Puerto Peñasco 242 km
BAHIA SAN JORGE
Detail
shown
San Felipe
N
GOLFO DE CALIFORNIA

launching the conquest of El Gran Desierto. In this hostile and burning climate the titanic struggle to reach Kilometer 242 at the Puerto Peñasco station began, and it would last three long-suffering years.

José Antonio Santana, who started as a driver in 1936, recalled that he built embankments and beds for the laying of the railroad. He says the crews worked valiantly in intensely hot and cold weather because jobs were hard to find anywhere in Mexico. "Under that heat from hell, vehicle tires blew up almost daily, radiators exploded, and engines overheated and broke down," he remembered, adding that little by little they overcame the desert. "At the beginning we lived in twelve-by-twelve-foot tents, with sometimes as many as a dozen individuals crowded together to sleep. Later they built wider little wooden houses in a place known as El Álamo at Kilometer 108."

The red-hot rails and the wood ties covered with creosote burned and tore the shoulders and

hands of the workers as they struggled to lay the railroad over that desolate landscape of mountains of sand. The vehicles would get so hot that the steering wheels burned the drivers' hands.

Santana searched through his memories:

We were making dirt mounds for others to lay the rail. At the beginning, they brought drivers from Mexico City, who were elegant and wore fancy boots, riding trousers, and explorer's hats, but they were useless on the sand. They constantly got stuck and broke the engines. Carlos Franco sent them back to Mexico City and hired drivers from San Luis, who were accustomed to the desert sand. We established a campsite at Kilometer 132, but we had to stop work there for a while. Those were days of shortages, years of poverty around the world, and the iron for the railroad tracks was very costly. It was then decided to make a detour through the sand from Kilometer 132 to Kilometer 175 in order to cut off twenty-one or more kilometers instead of following the coastline. Because of the shortage of materials, that meant a lot of money saved. Engineer Raúl Castro Padilla, who had replaced Carlos Franco, figured out a new route.

Meanwhile, in 1937 engineer Jorge López Collada was in the town of Sonoyta, making studies for a project "requested by the Americans to build a railroad section to Ajo, Arizona, which would then be connected to another one from the border through Sonoyta and to the railroad in Puerto Peñasco" (Verdugo 1985:15). This assignment to extend the railroad took him three months, but it was never constructed. He was interrupted when driver Gilberto Villascusa gave him a message to report to the encampment at El Álamo.

When López Collada showed up at Kilometer 132 on July 1, 1937, engineer Castro Padilla, chief of the division, scolded him and told him to leave at dawn the next day to assess the terrain and make the necessary surveys for the shortcut. At dawn the crew—composed of López Collada; José Sánchez Islas and Jesús Torres Burciaga, who were in charge of the chains; and driver Gustavo Sotelo—left the campsite. Engineer Arturo Acosta Escobar told López Collada, "Take Nabor Flores just in case." Nabor Flores Camargo, who knew the rugged region intimately, was known as "the guide of the desert." López Collada smiled and answered that it wasn't necessary. "Look," he said, "I have all the instruments to keep us from getting lost, but if I don't come back in three days, that would be Wednesday, then send Nabor to look for me."

"That was the mistake. Leaving without a guide and alone with only one vehicle was against what we used to do. We always traveled with two vehicles. López Collada's crew went in a Ford station wagon, taking food for two days and sixty liters of water," continued Santana.

After two days the crew had not returned, and the people from El Álamo started to worry. Thursday morning, July 4, a rescue squad left; it came back that evening without finding even tire tracks or footprints. At dawn on Thursday the camp cook had spotted a light high on a sand dune; he calculated a distance of fifteen kilometers to the east, but he thought it was "the *carbunco*" (a mythological bird with a light on its forehead that most people from the region swear they have seen on dark nights in the desert). The cook didn't say a word, thinking they would laugh at him—he would regret this decision for the rest of

Figure 10.2. Gustavo Sotelo (second from left) and his vehicle. (*Courtesy Guillermo Munro Palacio*)

his long life. On Friday, July 5, a second squad left led by engineer Acosta and came back late that night with no results. By then everybody at camp was very alarmed.

The next morning two more crews were organized with five people in each vehicle. Both vehicles were pickup trucks—a GMC and a Ford—guided by Nabor Flores and Miguel Corrales. Among the searchers were José Plata, Anastasio Arenas, José Osio, Castro Padilla, Enrique Villegas, Oscar Corrales, and the retired army general Miguel Santacruz.

Another crew left with another two vehicles led by engineer Arturo Acosta Escobar, with Raúl Quiroz Morando as one of the drivers. Pedro Robles drove the other vehicle, and it carried another ten or more men. Among them were Miguel Saucedo, Secundino Meza, Reyes Vega Santana, and José Antonio Santana. Construction was at a standstill. All hands were searching for the lost men.

The region of the enormous sand dunes is vast, and some of the dunes reach heights of one hundred meters, which makes driving very difficult. In July, temperatures can reach over 120°F in the shade. This area is only a few kilometers from the coast, and in some places the searchers drove across large mudflats encrusted with salt deposits. The sticky humidity made the sand cling to their bodies, and muddy salt coated the tires and fenders. Unsuccessful, they returned with the idea of asking for aerial assistance. Engineer Castro Padilla personally left for Mexicali, Baja California, to ask for help.

Figure 10.3. *Refueling one of the planes that searched for the missing men. (Courtesy Guillermo Munro Palacio)*

On Sunday evening, seven days after engineer López Collada's crew had disappeared, Castro Padilla returned in a small aircraft rented in Brawley, California. Another plane, a six-seat Bellanca from the Department of Communications and Public Services, was already flying the search area. It was piloted by Capt. Antonio Cárdenas Rodríguez. Two additional planes, Corsairs from the Mexican Air Force, arrived from Hermosillo to reinforce the search.

Santana recalled that Castro Padilla and Nicolás Matus boarded the plane while he stayed on the ground with the airplane fuel and emergency spare parts, ready for anything. They had agreed that the searchers in the planes would communicate with the ground crew by dropping messages tied to rail spikes.

The truck led by Castro Padilla arrived in Puerto Peñasco with its crew, hoping that the lost crew had already arrived there, too. They were disappointed. So they organized other rescue teams led by engineer Ramón Martínez that left by ground for the large sand dunes. In Puerto Peñasco several fishermen got organized and sailed their *pangas* and canoes around Bahía Adair.

Abelardo Pino, a retired fisherman remembered:

> I participated on the search together with the Yaqui Jesús 'Largo' and Joaquín Matus, another Yaqui who owned a small boat called *El Cajeme.* We entered the San Judas estuary and disembarked where we thought we could find them. We would search for them all day long. Two airplanes were flying low, and they would throw us messages wrapped around lead balls, rail spikes, or rocks. Jesús 'Largo' didn't know how to read, and Joaquín Matus had stayed on the boat, so I would read them. They read, 'If you have found tracks or vultures or dead bodies, please lie down on your backs with your arms spread.' They would also throw us pieces of ice wrapped in canvas. They also dropped oranges, bananas, apples, and vegetables as well as fresh meat and chicken that we would take to the boat. They also threw water in canvas bags.

Finally, near dusk on Sunday, Castro and his pilot spotted the lost truck about thirty kilometers north of the coastline, but oddly, when they turned around, they couldn't find it again. Searching for people in the dunes was like looking for sailors lost at sea.

During the first hours of Monday, July 9, the station wagon that was following the tracks located the lost truck and saw that the crew had abandoned it. They tried to follow the footprints, but the wind had erased them. That evening found them still looking and marking the route with flags to continue the next day. They went back to camp.

Next day, they agreed that two people should walk from the place marked by the flag with two vehicles following them. It was an extremely hot day, and the sand reflected the burning temperature even more.

About thirty kilometers from the flag they found the lifeless body of López Collada. He was lying on his belly, very close to a creosotebush. He had dug under this plant in a futile search for the moisture that he needed so much. His head rested on his left arm; his lips were chapped and dehydrated, and his body swollen and decomposing. Around him they found several letters from his family. Santana said, "His last thought was for them, and perhaps he also imagined better places and climates, like Mexico City, where he was from."

About two kilometers beyond the body of López Collada, the plane located two more bodies and dropped messages to the squads, who left immediately for the marked location. There, sadly, they found the bodies of José Sánchez Islas and Jesús Torres Burciaga. Next to them were the ashes of a fire. Nabor Flores was later told that somebody had mentioned the rare light that the cook had "hallucinated" days before. The victims were still alive then, but now they were beyond help and had died a terrible death.

Sánchez Islas and Torres Burciaga were holding hands as if they were encouraging each other to continue or perhaps as a fraternal farewell between them. Their faces showed the agony and the desperate suffering caused by thirst; it can dull the mind and cause insanity. They probably felt the suffocating feeling of their tongues swelling and lost consciousness in the enervating dream of death.

The searchers had one more victim to find. They found the footprints of the driver, Gustavo Sotelo. They located him three hundred meters beyond. By the tracks they realized he had fallen several times. Stumbling, he continued for some time. He fell several more times. His last movements were on all fours, and then he crawled, dragging his body for a final stretch, until he remained totally immobilized on those immense dunes of El Gran Desierto.

"Because those were days of shortage, they intended to save twenty kilometers of rails with this detour. In the attempt to save money, four human lives and months of work were lost when they already had the original route surveyed," emphasized Gilberto Villascusa, one of the drivers. Villascusa, who worked on the railroad until 1948, was first contracted by Nabor Flores in San Luis Río Colorado when the Mexico City drivers were fired. He explained, "We had our tricks for driving on sand. We were very careful. We would deflate the tires, being careful not to overheat the engine or ruin the connecting rods." During the laying of the railroad he brought equipment, fuel, and people through the dunes from Mexicali to Puerto Peñasco.

Villascusa was the one who marked with crosses the sites where the bodies of the doomed expedition were found. With the candor of one who knows the risks of the desert, Villascusa said simply, "They ran out of gas, and then they died of thirst."

Two weeks after that tragedy another, even bigger, misfortune occurred. After the day's labors the workers were transported by rail to their campsites. On the fateful evening of July 20, instead of pulling the convoy, somebody decided to push it with the locomotive, at such a high speed that the cars derailed. The first car took out the next and then the next. The desperate screams of victims followed. This accident took the lives of eleven railroad workers and left dozens injured.

Figure 10.4. Workers and searchers erect a memorial cross at the site where López Collada died. (Courtesy Guillermo Munro Palacio)

Figure 10.5. A stone obelisk at Kilometer 150 stands in tribute to the fallen railroad workers. Four wooden crosses, each as tall as a person, front the monument, which rises about 55 feet above the sand. (Photo by Bill Broyles)

In the months preceding World War II the laying of the railroad was halted for economic reasons. President Lázaro Cárdenas traveled to Baja California to supervise the work. He had a meeting with American government officials who were concerned because Japanese fishermen, carrying powerful radios, had been spotted in the Sea of

Figure 10.6. *Puerto Peñasco about 1940. The railroad offices are to the right of the boxcars. A wye brought freight cars from the mainline to the pier. (Courtesy Guillermo Munro Palacio)*

Cortés and there were reports of foreign submarines. One result of the meeting was a mutual commitment to build a highway from Puerto Peñasco to the U.S. border. It would be constructed by the Mexican government. At the same time, the American government would build a road from Ajo, Arizona, to the border with Mexico. Those who remember this event also say that the officials even agreed to establish an American military base in Puerto Peñasco. For such an important occasion they planned a meeting of the two presidents, Roosevelt and Cárdenas, at the port. President Cárdenas ordered the construction of a luxurious hotel to host the event.

On May 5, 1940, the town of Puerto Peñasco enthusiastically welcomed the party that would inaugurate the railroad from Sonora to Baja California, the Mexicali–Puerto Peñasco section, at Kilometer 242. Present at this event were Lt. Col. Rodolfo Sánchez Taboada, governor of Baja California; Gen. Anselmo Macías Valenzuela, gover-

nor of Sonora as well as secretary of communications and public services; engineer Melquiades Angulo Gallardo; and other celebrities from both Mexican states and Arizona.

Ironically, this event almost ended in tragedy when the governor of Sonora, Anselmo Macías, claimed that during the surveying of the railroad, Baja California had taken a portion of the territory that belonged to Sonora at Kilometer 57, at a town called Luis B. Sánchez. The governor of Sonora pulled a gun, and the governor of Baja California, Lt. Col. Sánchez Taboada, had to flee abruptly back to his home state.

The construction of an elegant hotel in Puerto Peñasco was completed in 1940 and the highway in 1942. The meeting between the two presidents never took place, but a year later, in 1943, Mexican president Avila Camacho and U.S. president Franklin D. Roosevelt met in El Paso, Texas.

A novel, *El Muro y la Trocha*, by Niño Martini Yanco, was published in 1964 about the lost railroad engineers. And in the same year, a movie, *El Viento Negro*, based on the novel, was filmed at the place where the tragedy occurred. Directed by Servando González, it is considered a classic of Mexican cinematography, ranking eighty-eighth on a list of the one hundred best Mexican films. Both the novel and the movie are tributes to the fallen workers, who now live on as heroes in Mexican lore.

Acknowledgments

The author thanks Abelardo Pino, José Antonio Santana, and Gilberto Villascusa for describing their experiences in interviews.

Isabel Granillo graciously helped translate this essay from Spanish. The author's son, Guillermo Munro Colosio, drew the map.

Eleven

Sing the River

ANITA ALVAREZ WILLIAMS

Thai healers celebrated a traditional life-lengthening ceremony a few years ago in Indochina to heal their River Nan. In Nevada Shoshonean singers recorded their salt songs, inherited songlines describing and defining their traditional homeland on either side of the middle Colorado River. Chemehuevi Mathew Leivas sings to defend and restore the Colorado. Friends of the River invites volunteers to celebrate with music and poetry during their annual festival.

Hear! Hear! Earth's mighty rivers begin to receive the respect they deserve. People are learning and caring, pulling down inefficient dams, digging out invasive plants, and funding restoration of riverflow.

For the original river people the Colorado was, and for some still is, their life. For thousands of years, the great Colorado River of the southwestern United States and northwestern Mexico transported Native Americans, providing them with materials for hunting, fishing, gathering, and shelter. River floods enriched their gardens and farms and fed the long, narrow gulf.

New people came, and with their new ideas they gradually dammed, detoured, disputed, and contaminated the Colorado along her entire course. The generous flow of rich fresh waters, which had nurtured gulf tides and supported a priceless system of interdependent riparian and sea life, dwindled to almost nothing. The ever-increasing new human populations, making other use of the river, hardly noticed. "What river?" they might say. "What sea life?" The native people knew, and a few others.

Spanish explorers, guided by Native Americans, wrote with awe of this powerful river in the 1500s, as did others across the years. Major John Wesley Powell rode the wild waters of the Grand Canyon more than a hundred years ago, understanding and explaining watershed. Godfrey Sykes, who rode down the river in boats he built himself, made brilliant maps and wrote what is still the definitive book on the Colorado River delta.

Some brave the full course of the river, as did Smokey Knowland and his sons by boat in the 1970s. Colin Fletcher rafted the entire river alone in 1990, finding that the Colorado had dried up below the Mexican border. He took his walking staff in hand and followed the dry riverbed on foot to the drainage waters now comprising the Hardy River. From there he rafted between barren mud-banks, passing grass-covered Gore and Montague islands as he entered the gulf, remembering Aldo Leopold's 1922 description of the entire delta as luxuriant, teeming with life.

Wild whitewater trips thrill and spill rafters through the magnificent canyons of the upper river. Among the adventurers come the contemplatives, giving us the beautiful watercolors of Balduin Molhousen, the exquisite books of poet-photographer Eliot Porter, and the amazing detailed descriptions and drawings of Ann Zwinger, seeking and sharing understanding of the river canyons.

Fishermen and boaters head for the river at every opportunity, crowding campgrounds on weekends and holidays. We see these water enthusiasts on Interstate Highway 8, recreational vehicles trailering boats to the river on Fridays and Saturdays. On Sunday evenings a steady stream of them head west, home, their headlights bright ribbons of light across the desert.

Anyone can visit the river. My husband, Charlie, and I saw a Yuma, Arizona, television ad offering a river cruise with "the Knowland family: four generations on the Colorado River." Curious, one Sunday we drove with friends from Mexicali, Baja California, to Martinez Lake, Arizona, thirty-five miles upriver from Yuma. At one time this land, now between the Quechan and Mohave people,

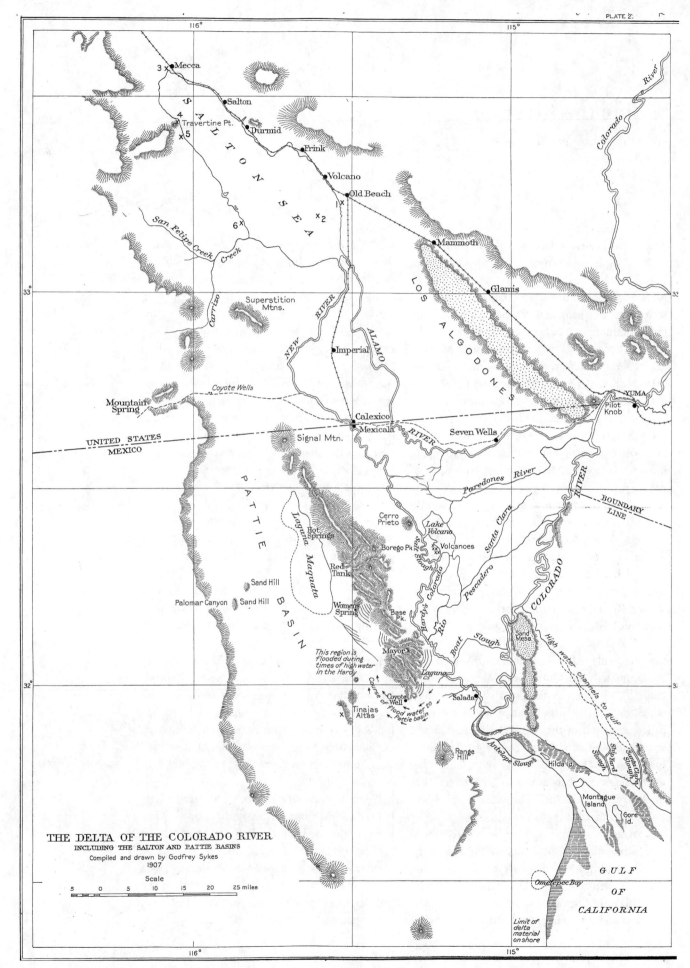

Figure 11.1. Godfrey Sykes's map of the Colorado delta, 1907. (Courtesy the Boyer family, Tucson)

probably belonged to the Cocomaricopa, Halchidoma, or Western Maricopa people.

At the Martinez Lake store we sat and waited under a ramada overlooking river docks. We could see a small post office and a few tidy mobile homes. On the cliff across the river an elaborate pueblo-style home was under construction. Upriver, high on the opposite bank, another house, disguised as a riverboat, sits permanently moored in a terraced desert garden.

The roar of a large V-8 automobile gas engine turned our heads, and around the bend of the river came Smokey Knowland, jetting toward us in an open-sided, flat-bottom boat. He settled the boat by the dock, cut the engine, and tied up to the dock. Decked out in weathered denims, an old leather vest, and a battered, bead-banded Australian Outback hat, Smokey greeted us and began wiping the night's moisture off the ten seats and the underside of the roof. He spread out plaid blankets for us to sit on and cover up with on that cool, overcast day.

In 1976 Smokey and his two sons boated the full 1,450 miles of the Colorado River. They later published a lively book about their adventures (Knowland 1985).

As we pulled out onto the river, Smokey explained that there was a fishing tournament going on that day. He said that some fishermen travel the country seeking the prizes won for the biggest bass caught in the best condition. The fish are returned to the river for future catch.

We motored up the river into the Imperial National Wildlife Refuge, the boat taking long, slow curves through deeper channels as Smokey related the long history of the Indians of the area, described the steamboats that plied the river between 1852 and 1910, and told us about the miners and farmers along the river. Native American farms and gardens mentioned by early travelers on the river were no longer to be seen.

Then Smokey steered his flat-bottom boat through a narrow opening in some tules and landed with a dull thud on the muddy bank. We clambered off, hiking up a narrow reed-walled trail to a primitive mining cabin, inhabited only by reclusive Matt the Rat, to whom Smokey delivers groceries.

Upriver we hauled onto the riverbank again and explored an abandoned century-old farm still equipped with its own ancient steam engine. A

Figure 11.2. Riverboat Cochan, *lower Colorado River, circa 1900. Note firewood stacked on deck. (Sherman Foundation, Collection, Corona del Mar)*

little ways more and we stopped again to climb up to an abandoned mine, and upriver from there we saw a campground where a flash flood had recently washed away a ramada, outhouses, and picnic tables.

At yet another landing we followed a stony path up a cliff to see ancient petroglyphs carved into desert-varnished stone. These lively figures dominate a handsome view up and down the river. One cheerful stick figure stands with raised hand, as if saluting travelers or someone across the river. Some of these petroglyphs are so old that desert varnish has begun to grow back over them, proving their antiquity. Were these carvings made by the ancestors of the Cocomaricopas, Halchidomas, Quechans, or Mohaves?

The sun came out for a while, and we rumbled tranquilly upriver, parting silvery-chocolate waters, framed on both banks by thick stands of mesquite, willow, and tules.

I remembered reading army wife Martha Summerhayes's description of a steamboat trip up this part of the river in the 1870s: "Sometimes the low trees and brushwood on the banks parted, and a young squaw would peer out at us...they wore very short skirts made of stripped bark, and as they held back the branches of the low willows, and looked at us with curiosity, they made pictures so pretty that I have never forgotten them...the fine copper color of those bare shoulders and arms, the soft wood colors of the short bark skirts, the gleam of the sun upon their blue-black hair, and the turquoise color of the wide bead-bands which encircled their arms" (Summerhayes 1979:41).

Figure 11.3. *Cottonwood forest in the delta of the lower Colorado River, circa 1900. (Sherman Foundation, Collection, Corona del Mar)*

We stopped for a picnic where Roy Morgan used to camp with his faithful dog, Lonesome, who now lies buried on that hill overlooking the river. Roy had stacked a few rocks over Lonesome and left a note in a can telling others about him and inviting them to add rocks to the cairn. Visitors started contributing rocks, and some, including children, left notes about their own dogs. Friends of the River sent the notes on to Roy for as long as he lived. The large U-shaped cairn continues to grow, its stony arms protecting a small flag-crowned plaque honoring Lonesome. We added a few rocks, remembering our own family pets.

At each stop along the river Smokey collected trash and tended paths. He and some of his "friends of the river" (no dues, no formal meetings) get together once in a while to repair or clean up as needed along the river, a fellowship of caring.

Many birds attended the edges of the river. A masked killdeer darted fast and low in and out of the reeds; great herons stalked elegantly in the deeper shallows. A few snowy egrets flashed their bright yellow legs, luring fish in waters closer to shore. Bright chestnut ruddy ducks, black caps above their white faces and blue bills, bobbed near yellow-beaked gray and brown moorhens, their very long greenish toes efficiently treading water. High across the river soared two red-tailed hawks. Later, downriver, we saw a bald eagle spiraling above us. Smokey cut the motor so we could watch the birds; hear their calls, peeps, squawks, and mutterings; and listen to the river flowing, sensing the soft wind rustling the *carrizo* and the willow fragrance along the banks.

Beaver caves appeared as large dark holes chewed into the lower bank greenery. Twice we saw a pair of young, lustrous coyotes trotting along the riverbank, stopping to look at us, trotting on, halting to look again, partly screened by the tules. Swallow nests, like clusters of small Indian ollas, clung to huge rock cliffs, and we saw other nests, big ones, carelessly stacked in tall trees.

Our trip took us twenty-three slow miles upriver. When it was time to go home, Smokey turned up the power and we zoomed back downriver, following the channel curves at speed, until he spotted that soaring eagle and stopped. Breathtaking.

I like this river. During the Cretaceous and the Cenozoic the Colorado flowed east and then north. Then, according to geologists, somewhere between 2.6 and 10.6 million years ago the Earth shifted and tilted, causing the river to change direction and wander west and southwest.

In the late 1970s and early 1980s the Colorado River surprised everyone in northern Baja California by flooding the Laguna Salada between the Sierra de Juárez and the Sierra Cucapá. That dry old lake bed, also known through time as Laguna Maquata and Pattie Lake, came to life and filled with fish.

During that flood time I drove south from Mexicali to visit my Cucapá friend Inocencia González Saiz, a talented beadworker and crafter of willow-bark skirts. She lives at El Mayor Indígena on the Río Hardy, a westerly branch of the Colorado now carrying agricultural drainage. Floodwaters had carried away most of the Cucapá homes, but with government help they had built new houses on higher ground.

"Not home," Inocencia's neighbors told me that morning, "gone fishing." Curious, I followed their directions, taking the highway south again, then off-road west along the southern edge of the Sierra Cucapá to Pozo Coyote. From where I parked under a venerable tamarisk tree beside the corral of an old ranch house, I could see small fishing boats and people moving about near the end of what appeared to be part of an old levee. Inocencia saw me and walked toward me, smiling. No time to visit, she said. She was about to go out fishing. Did I want to go along?

Of course! I ran and grabbed the necessaries, then joined Inocencia, her daughter Tonia, and her son Muñeco in their aluminum boat, settling myself among the monofilament fishing nets, orange plastic floats, and empty, capped milk bottles. Accompanied by another Cucapá family in their boat, we pushed off with a grumble, then the roar of Japanese motors. First Muñeco steered south, entering remnants of the old canal, and along that channel west and then north into the open waters of the Laguna Salada. It was an astonishing experience for me because most of my life I had known the Laguna Salada as a barren, dry salt flat.

There I was, boating along on cloud-reflecting gray-brown water between the Sierra Cucapá and the Sierra de Juárez, and in the company of friends whose ancestors had probably been fishing river and lake here for a couple of thousand years. During earlier incarnations of this lake the Cucapá would have moved quietly in reed canoes or rafts, paddling or poling directly from one of their camps on the western side of the Sierra Cucapá rather than motoring noisily as we did from the Río Hardy and around the southern point of the mountains.

Canal bank remnants formed a few narrow islands. Inocencia pointed out a family of coyotes that had been stranded on one of them by the floods. Restricted but comfortable, the coyotes looked well fed. Cucapá fishermen, said Inocencia, regularly shared their day's catch with them.

Well north of the coyotes, Muñeco cut the motor and coasted toward some tules. He paddled the boat slowly along as his mother and sister fed first one then another fishnet over the side, forming wide semicircles. Once the float-supported nets were in place, there was nothing to do but wait quietly. Inocencia lit a cigarette, and we sat rocking gently, lake water softly slapping the sides of the boat.

I thought about how the Cucapá used to spear fish, or catch them in agave or milkweed fiber nets, or hook them on lines hung with biznaga-thorn hooks. In shallows they caught fish with their hands. Near their homes they also caught fish in tubular or oval stick traps fitted with funnel-shaped openings in one end. One of these old fish traps hangs as part of the decor in the ramada restaurant of Campo Mosqueda, just northeast of the Cucapá community on the Hardy. Originally constructed of willow and arrowweed sticks or roots, these fish traps are now made of galvanized wire screen. I remembered photographing one tied to

Figure 11.4. Martín Rodríguez González manning the boat. (Photo by Anita Alvarez Williams)

a mesquite tree on a riverbank in front of my friend Adelaida's house on the Hardy and seeing another at Capitán Miguel's house at Yurimuri.

As we sat comfortably rocking in the boat, our eyes wandered along the peaks and canyons of the easterly Cucapá Mountains and across the lake to the Sierra de Juárez. The Cucapá people tell of adventures and conversations that took place when mountains and animals were people. To the west we could see the peak marking Guadalupe Canyon. During dry times the Cucapá traveled across the Salada to bathe in Guadalupe's healing, sulfurous hot springs, near which they gathered dates and roasted agave hearts in stone-lined pits shaded by blue fan palms.

As we floated quietly, waiting, Inocencia pointed out across the water to old family campsites along the eastern base of the Cucapá Mountains. Near our boat ducks dawdled complacently, and beyond them other birds busied themselves fishing.

When Inocencia said it was time, she and her family began hauling in the nets, filling the bottom of the boat with gasping carp, catfish, bass, and mullet. Fish flopped about my feet. Also caught in the net was a northern shoveler duck, lovely green head, snowy neck and breast, chestnut flanks, and white-accented black tail. Inocencia went to a

Figure 11.5. *Cucapá Adelaida Saiz Dominguez, 1972, Río Hardy. (Photo by Anita Alvarez Williams)*

Figure 11.6. *Fish covering the bottom of the boat, Laguna Salada fishing trip. (Photo by Anita Alvarez Williams)*

lot of trouble to untangle him, a rare one in these waters. She offered him to me for a pet. I admired him mightily, but when he had rested, we released him back to the lake.

My friends were pleased, saying it was a good haul that day. They would have plenty to eat and to sell to the Mexicali merchant who regularly trucked fish to Mexicali.

The Cucapá were very sad when the Laguna Salada dried up again.

A family custom of ours is to stay home New Year's Eve and then spend the first day of the year out somewhere exploring the nearby desert.

On the first day of 1989 our daughter Ila and her husband, Jorge, took their children, Jorge Luis and Adriana Luz, in their family's four-wheel-drive. Charlie and I drove ours out on the road to Tijuana and then south along the sandy western edges of the Sierra Cucapá, the eastern side of the Laguna Salada, which was again a dusty salt flat.

We were looking for some ancient rock circles and a slot in the Sierra Cucapá that we had visited years before. Following a well-traveled trail south for about forty miles, down along the Salada, we began to see the white skeletons of tall bushes, flood remnants. Approaching them, we could see that their thin branches were covered with something that from a distance resembled popcorn. Close up, we saw that they were thousands of tiny dry white barnacles, flood heritage (see Brusca, this volume).

Then the road curved inward toward the mountains, and Charlie noticed that we could save some time by cutting directly across the bare, white, cracked-earth salt flat. With Jorge following, we rolled out onto the flat and immediately sank all four wheels straight down through the saltpan crust and into mucky, wet clay. Charlie quickly honked to warn Jorge, but too late. Both vehicles had sunk to the floorboards.

We disembarked, and Charlie and Jorge got out shovels and started digging the wheels out of slurpy mud in hopes of placing a board under the bumper jack for support. Ila, the children, and I went off looking for vegetation to break off and put under the wheels for traction. All vegetation was far away, but we set off walking anyway, crunching along, leaving dark footprints through the salty crust. About halfway to the bushes we came upon a seemingly endless curving windrow of desiccated fish, hundreds of them. This had to have been where the Laguna Salada finally dried up, and these fish must have been the last to go. They were so perfectly dried that they didn't stink. Lightly dusted with glistening sand, their forms and even their scales intact, these fish were preparing to become fossils. They were beautiful.

But Ila and I looked at one another, looked at those far-off bushes, shrugged, and gave Adriana Luz and Jorge Luis their instructions. The four of us started prying up and carrying stacks of stiff, dried fish back to put under the wheels of the vehicles. The muck shovelers were surprised but were worried enough about getting out of there before darkness and the cold night that they weren't particular about what we put on the mirey clay under those wheels.

And it worked. It took hours of digging, and endless trotting back and forth to get enough fish under the wheels, but we did get out before dark and headed for a well-earned Chinese meal and home. That night, back on the edge of the Laguna Salada, near some compacted fish in a thoroughly torn-up bit of dry lake, the remaining windrow of untouched fish continued turning quietly into fossils, their iridescent scales finely coated with sand glistening faintly in the moonlight.

The Laguna Salada remains dry, but in 1992 I went fishing again with the Cucapá, this time toward the mouth of the river with Matías Saiz Portillo and his family, accompanied by other Cucapá and a second boat. I was translating for Patti Logan and Eric Keck, who were filming the Colorado River for CNN. Towing the boats, we drove south from the Río Hardy Cucapá community on the San Felipe highway, turned east onto the Laguna Salada, and headed toward the river across miles of cracked bare dry salt flat. Eric stopped to film the beat-up Cucapá vehicles seemingly headed straight for nowhere. Then the desert air dampened a little, mirages turned into scrubby halophytic vegetation, mostly pickleweed, and, at last, the river. Too shallow here for the boats, so we continued south along the river's edge.

Just before we reached our destination, Matías's son-in-law Rosendo and his wife and kids peeled their blue van off toward a narrow arm of the river and stopped. They had no boat, so they were going to wade out into the shallow water and put a net out by hand. The rest of us followed the other Cucapá a little farther south along the main river channel.

We stopped, got out of our vehicles, and looked down the steep muddy riverbank, maybe ten, fifteen feet. I wondered how we were going to get the boats into the river, and us into the boats. The Cucapá were nonchalantly getting out tarps,

Figure 11.7. Channel to the Laguna Salada, drying up. (Photo by Anita Alvarez Williams)

bed sheets, and poles, staking them out from their vehicles to provide shade on the salt flat. This was in June and well over a hundred degrees in the noonday sun. No trees, just a little saltgrass, *Distichlis palmeri*, and more pickleweed, *Salicornia*. Onesimo pointed out that the tide was coming in and that when the water was high enough we could lower the boats. Since the Cucapá can no longer fish in the contaminated Río Hardy, they have obtained permission to fish away from their community in the river's tidal zone.

When the tide had risen sufficiently, the Cucapá slid their small wood and aluminum boats down the mudbank and into the water. Matías and two of his sons, one of them with the traditional long hair of the Cucapá, jumped agilely down the wet clay bank into one of the boats, which had been preloaded with a long fishing net strung with yellow floats along one side. Eric filmed them and then filmed Patti and me slipping and sliding down the embankment into the other boat. Eric wrestled his tripod, camera, and self into Matías's boat, and they took off. Onesimo followed. The rest of the Cucapá remained behind in the day camp, watching from the shade, visiting, and drinking sodas. Normally, Juana goes fishing with her husband, Matías, but apparently they decided that the men were more appropriate for filming. Matías, hardworking, thin, and darkly weathered, is one of the few Cucapá who have continued fishing since the contamination of the Río Hardy. The tidal waters of the Colorado River where they now fish are a long way from their homes, costly for them in travel time and fuel.

Figure 11.8. *Cucapás Matías Saiz Portillo and Susana going fishing. (Photo by Anita Alvarez Williams)*

Figure 11.9. *Cucapá Juan Portillo Laguna mending a fishing net. (Photo by Anita Alvarez Williams)*

What was an average catch?

From nothing to a boatful.

Where did they buy their boat motors?

Secondhand places.

When we were quiet, the only noise was that of the river, gently, rhythmically slapping the boat.

A sudden unfamiliar sound startled us: a loud deep slithering and then a sonorous splash. A large chunk of a nearby mud cliff had calved into the river, radiating ripples toward us. "Happens often," Matías said. He and his sons began pulling in the net. In all that thirty-foot-long net there was one very small fish and a few sky-blue crabs. These were thrown to the pelican, which explained its attentiveness.

We boated farther down into the tidal waters, past a great blue heron and a few egrets, past a small crowd of white pelicans. Cumulus clouds billowed up, sheltering us from the sun. Over a period of two hours Matías and his sons put their nets out seven times, feeding the long net out, waiting, dragging it back in. Something hidden underwater snagged the net, and Onesimo had to cut it for retrieval. For all their efforts they caught a total of three corbina, each one about a foot long. The men threw several smaller fish and a few crabs back into the river.

Responding to Patti's question of why so few fish, Onesimo answered that nowadays the only way to ensure a good catch was to fish within three days of the full moon or the new moon. And when asked how he preferred to earn his living, Onesimo just smiled and said that there was nothing comparable to fishing as a way of life. Peaceful out there, no one telling you what to do, good air to breathe, and of course if he had a choice, he would choose fishing. And if there were no fish this time, next time maybe there would be. Asked about what the river meant to him, Matías responded that it was his life, that by the river he supported his family. Patti asked this question several times of several different Cucapá during that day, and each time heard similar answers.

As we returned to the day camp, we heard juvenile shouts and laughter. Seven Cucapá boys, ages maybe five to thirteen, had formed a steep, curved mudslide down the riverbank and were taking turns careening down into the water, arms and legs flung out in all directions. Their denim cutoffs and slim, dark bodies gleamed with mud by the time they hit the water, where they vigor-

Onesimo and Matías fired up their motors and headed downriver on the still-incoming tide, broad swirling silt-laden salty waters pale metallic brown. At first we were closely attended by some large brown pelicans. One of them was very friendly and bobbed right up to our boat and eyed us. A welcome breeze came up, cooled us, ruffled the pelican's head feathers.

Matías and his son fed their net out across the river and then cut their motor. Eric filmed. While we waited I translated questions and answers for Patti and Matías:

How often did they come fishing?

As often as they had gasoline for their cars and boats-—especially during the full moon.

ously splashed and swam themselves clean, only to scramble out and scamper back up to the top of the mudbank and slide wildly down again, whooping, into the water.

And another surprise. When Matías said something to his daughter's family back in camp about our poor luck in fishing, Rosendo mentioned with a modest smile that he and his boys had caught fish enough to fill two ice chests. Unbelieving, we walked over to the blue van. Rosendo flipped open the two lids, and sure enough the chests were packed with corbina. Rosendo had simply waded out across "his" small branch of the river, spreading the net when he thought the tide was right. Then his kids ran along beside and downriver from the net, splashing and herding the fish into the net. A marine rodeo. This reminded me of Newton H. Chittenden's 1902 description of "Cocopah" fishing:

> After a great fire had been built, the young men, taking long poles, sprang naked into the narrow lagoon, and began to beat the water vigorously as they advanced towards the net, which was buoyed on the surface with wild cane. They were so successful that by the time the bed of hot coals was in readiness, a pile of fish of several varieties, including carp and mullet, were floundering alongside. After being cut upon and cleaned, they were filled with, laid upon and covered with red hot coals, and in less than twenty minutes were so thoroughly roasted that skin, scales and fins pealed [sic] off, leaving the flesh as clean and palatable as if cooked by the most skillful modern caterer. (Chittenden 1901:202)

The modern differences: nobody was naked, there was only one kind of fish, and Rosendo's net was buoyed by capped plastic milk bottles instead of wild cane.

Nobody said much. Rosendo offered to repeat his performance for the camera man, but Eric was satisfied with what he had filmed. And hungry. No comment from Matías.

Eric had intended to film Juana preparing fish for her family dinner back in the community, but the Cucapá counterproposed a fish dinner right there by the river. Within moments Rosendo had dug a shallow pit in the desert floor by the river and his kids had found some dry branches and propped up a rectangular board as a windbreak. A grill and a frying pan appeared, and Juana and her daughter Roshana began filleting

fish. Normally they would just roast the whole fish on the fire, but they thought we would prefer fillets.

Roshana shook some flour and seasonings into a paper bag, added the fillets, and rattled them around inside until coated. Then she fried the fish in the pan until golden brown. When the fish were cooked, Juana produced flour tortillas and salsa, and we were invited to feast. Delicious!

In the late afternoon sun Eric continued filming Roshana, her denim skirt and fuchsia tank top a spark of color against a vast, pale desert. She remained kneeling by the small fire, frying fish until everyone was fed.

Patti interviewed Raquel and Onesimo and invited them to comment on the fish fry in their native language, which they did. The young reporters seemed surprised at the sound of the Cucapá language, saying that they expected it to sound more like Spanish, which of course it doesn't. The Hokan/Yuman/Cocopah language is ancient, and of entirely different origins than Spanish.

Later, back in the Cucapá community, Patti asked me what I would like for the Cucapá.

I said I wished they could have their river back.

Perhaps then they could fish again in the Hardy, and plant corn, beans, and squash in their gardens. Maybe then they could enjoy again their homeland, rich in flora and fauna.

And maybe then *ny'pa*, or *nipa*, their unique wild grain, *Distichlis palmeri*, which Edward Palmer saw the Cucapá gathering in 1885, could again flourish. When Palmer collected specimens of *Distichlis* near the mouth of the river, he noted that it covered forty to fifty thousand acres. Now it's almost gone, a mere fringe along the mouth of the river and on its islands.

A traditional spring food for the Cucapá, this wild grain is born of the river and irrigated by gulf tidewaters. Biologist Nicholas Yensen and his wife, Susana Bojórquez de Yensen, came looking for it in the late 1970s. Over time Nicholas found more than ninety different forms of the plant, and he hybridized some species for their seed, others as forage, and yet others for turf. In 1889 George Vasey doubted that *Distichlis* "might be cultivated outside the reach of the tides" (Vasey 1889:402). He would be amazed to learn that selected varieties of Colorado River delta *Distichlis palmeri* are now flourishing salt-water crops in the United States, Asia, Australia, and the Middle East.

Figure 11.10. *Susana and Nicholas Yensen with Distichlis palmeri. (Photo by Anita Alvarez Williams)*

Susana Yensen (1984) completed both a master's and a doctoral thesis on the nutritional values of *Distichlis* spp., and Nicholas continues traveling the world working with halophytic plants.

To germinate, *Distichlis* needs twenty-four hours of freshwater—water historically supplied by river flooding—but from then on it is nourished by the tidal waters of the gulf. The plant absorbs salts and exudes them through its stems and leaves—you can see the little salt crystals on the greenery. But the grain itself contains no more salt than domestic wheat.

The Colorado River delta already enjoys official recognition by Mexico as part of a biosphere reserve, a protected valuable place. Intending to acquaint people better with the delta in general and specifically the Colorado River in Mexico, the Museum of the Autonomous University of Baja California produced a major river exhibit in Mexicali. In November 1996, as part of the information-gathering team for this exhibit, museum director Gina Walther, exhibit director Claudia Schroeder, and three of the museum's design and installation team, plus three writers—farmer and historian Oscar Sánchez, hunter and ecologist Alberto Tapia Landeros, and I—drove down into the delta looking for remnants of the Colorado River.

We crossed the river just south of the railroad bridge, stopping to look and photograph. Three months earlier I had seen this same area of the river choked with tules, tamarisk, and other growth. Since then dredges and bulldozers had been at work digging out the growth, heaping dirt and green debris on both sides of the riverbed. The workers said they were expecting water soon.

Continuing to Colonia Coahuila (Kilometer 57), we arrived in time for breakfast. In a small restaurant we variously enjoyed rich menudo, spicy huevos rancheros, hearty *machaca con verdura,* and quesadillas made with homemade flour tortillas and *requesón,* all for research purposes, of course.

Thus reinforced, we rode the short distance to Riito and then left the pavement, driving south, down and off the Andrade Mesa, rooster-tailing dust along canal banks and dikes and crossing bare dry alkali flats until we began to see hardy pickleweed bushes. The day was lovely and clear, neither hot nor cold, with just a few high clouds.

At last, with the Sierra Pinta in view far across the Laguna Salada to the west, we came to the eastern edge of the river, tide already pushing slowly upstream, river water along the edges flowing muddily downriver. Some fair-sized patches of *Distichlis palmeri* survive there. The only seed we found was among the high-tide deposits.

I wandered through the *Distichlis* patches, looking for the little blue crabs that like to keep it company, and found many of their tiny mudhills but no live crabs, just remnants of a few empty shells or claws.

I first noticed those crabs and their affinity for *Distichlis* in 1987 when Charlie and I drove down to a nearby area with naturalist Steve Nelson to see the tidal bore (see Nelson, this volume). Steve, a U.S. Bureau of Land Management man, likes rivers and from 1984 to 1987 mapped the backcutting of the Colorado River in the lower delta. His guess then was that El Mayor would remain on the Hardy but that the water level would be much lower, maybe not enough to boat on much of the time since it would consist mainly of agricultural drainwater. Whatever comes down the Colorado, he said, would likely follow the eastern channel.

There we were—Charlie and Steve and I—sitting in a patch of *Distichlis* waiting for the mighty tidal bore, which arrived not in a roar but as a traveling ruffle. Where we sat, I noticed all these tiny blue crabs clicking and snapping around us, very busy at the base of the *Distichlis* stems. They behaved fiercely, threatening us with their tiny claws. I've noticed that whither the *ny'pa*, there the little blue crabs.

So on the museum excursion deep into the delta, I was looking for those crabs. We had wandered about half a kilometer from our van, confidently leaving it open, keys in the ignition, cameras and purses on the seats, when suddenly we noticed a white pickup appear out of nowhere, slowly approach our vehicle, and park in front of it. Someone got out of the pickup and sauntered over to our van. Suddenly alert to the possibility of a very long walk home, the swifter of us began to run back to our van.

Needlessly. Our visitor was Bernabé Rico Olguera, an ecologist working for the new Alto Golfo Biosphere Reserve covering the delta. One of the *ejidos* we had driven through had alerted him to our passing, and he had come to see what we were up to.

We introduced ourselves and described plans for the university museum river exhibit, mentioning that we hadn't found any of the little blue crabs. "Oh," he said, "you mean the señoritas. They're here, all right." He walked down to the muddy riverflat and began to dig with his hand in one of the mud-mound holes. About elbow deep, he pulled out a beautiful sky-blue crab a few inches across, one big pincer waving furiously. We were enchanted with the señorita, everyone taking pictures. I looked closely at her face, and I'm sure she was scowling. She didn't ask to be a star.

Back in the delta, Bernabé invited us to visit La Laguna del Indio. These Santa Clara wetlands shelter desert pupfish and migratory birds, including the endangered Yuma clapper rail. Following Bernabé along the river and canal banks, we came upon lovely lagoons edged with grasses, cattail, arrowweed, mesquite, and willow. Ducks, egrets, moorhens, herons, and others cruised water and sky, resting and nesting in the greenery—a birdwatcher's paradise. In the maze that comprises

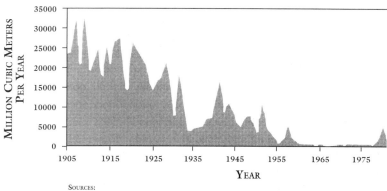

SOURCES:
1905-49, FLOW AT YUMA, ARIZONA: U.S. GEOLOGICAL SURVEY.
1950-92, FLOW AT SOUTHERLY INTERNATIONAL BOUNDARY: INTERNATIONAL BOUNDARY AND WATER COMMISSIO

Figure 11.11. Flow of Colorado River below all major dams and diversions, 1905–92. (Courtesy Sandra Postel, "Where Have All the Rivers Gone?" World Watch, May/June 1995)

the delta, we would never have found these fascinating lagoons without Bernabé.

On the way back to the highway we first heard, and then saw, some heavy equipment working, a large crane lifting huge cement pipe segments into place in a dry, powdery silt streambed. The workers said that river water was expected after the first of the year.

As we drove along, Oscar told us stories about his ranch on the lower river where his family protects a small beaver colony, and Alberto described his adventures photographing bighorn sheep and searching for information on cardón cactus.

We turned off the highway south for a look at the Río Hardy. At Campo Mosqueda the water looked healthy, but just downstream where the Cucapá live, the river was still, nearly stagnant, almost completely covered with vegetation, an exaggeration of Steve Nelson's prediction.

The name *Mohave* means "People of the River." For them and for other river tribes, the Colorado is, was, and always will be life itself. Mohave elder Priscilla Eswonia avers, "Our creator put the river down for us to live. That's how all our songs begin" (Magagnini 2003).

Sing the river.

Twelve

Campfires and Field Notes

NORMAN M. SIMMONS AND HILAH SIMMONS

The feeling was frightening, overwhelming. Alone on the western lip of the Growler Mountains, high above the valley, I suddenly felt small and vulnerable, an unimportant fleck baking in the afternoon sun. Totally alone. I felt an urge to float off the cliff, on the edge of which I was perched. Fear easily overpowered common sense, and I grabbed my canteen and headed down to my camp north of Charlie Bell Pass.

There my horse was tethered by one foot to a palo verde, standing in its shade. Feeling weak and shaky, I bedded down on my cot in the shade of the old Dodge Power Wagon, emulating the wiser bighorn sheep in the shade of rock overhangs above me.

Finally my brain kicked in, chiding me, a research scientist, for being so silly and yielding to senseless fright. As the sun dipped behind the ridge of the Growlers and the day cooled, I got up and saddled my Morgan mare, Moxie. Maybe I suffered from heat, known to make one hallucinate. Good thing I was alone—no need to explain my foolish behavior to anyone. Now, thinking back on that day in 1963, I realize that when I am alone on a mountain, I am especially susceptible to the feeling of insignificance, of being in the presence of overwhelming power. Do we build cathedrals to achieve the same end, to make the faithful humble before a symbol of power they will never attain?

It was nearly dark when I returned on Moxie, so I quickly fed her and gave her water in a canvas bucket from the fifty-gallon tank built into the back of the truck. I had camped on purpose near a dead ironwood. A few blows with my sledge on a wedge, and soon I had perfect coals for the thick steak I would cook on my grill. Time to sit and ruminate over the day as I formed some biscuits for my Dutch oven. I thought about how rarely I go to church. To those who chide me, I say that my church is a desert pinnacle or the slope of a subarctic mountain. And I am serious. There, in overpowering beauty, it is easy to feel close to God and to feel as insignificant as a speck of dust in my eye.

I had been sleeping soundly on my cot by the palo verde, but in the predawn darkness loud, raucous laughter rudely awakened me. *Ha! Ha! Ha! Haaa! ¿Que tal, señor?* Heart thumping, I grabbed my flashlight and played the light over the creosotebushes, cat's claw, and brittlebush. A dream? So real! I automatically checked under the cot for a rattler, jammed my bare feet into my boots, and carefully crept around the back of the truck. There, about ten yards away, illuminated by my flashlight, was a group of four javelina, jostling over an open barrel cactus. I had never heard javelina cry out before.

My years on the Cabeza Prieta National Wildlife Refuge in the early 1960s were spiced by "incidents," many amusing and harmless like my encounter with the javelina, some amusing only in retrospect. An aerial sheep survey suddenly ended as our Air Force Kaman Turbojet helicopter, engine aflame, auto-rotated out of the sky over the Davidson Canyon road. The pilots were calmly professional, but once we had landed safely, they clowned around as a way to release tension while we waited for the rescue helicopter. Their commander was in the helicopter that came to pick us up, and he was not amused by the colored smoke signals we had playfully set off on seeing the chopper and by one of us standing by the smoke, reading the survival manual, with flare pistol to temple.

When water roaring down a wash just after a rainstorm began to roll my truck over, it was hard for me to laugh, as it was the expensive result of my faulty judgment. The engine was a silty write-off. We were anxious to get home that day, and I had foolishly entered the normally dry wash without checking for holes hidden by the running water. As soon as the engine fan picked up water, the engine died and would not restart. Luckily, we had held the second vehicle back while I crossed in mine. By the time I gave up trying to restart my truck, the water was coming through the windows, and it was dangerous to try to make it unaided to the shore. My laughing comrades tossed me a lariat with a chain hooked to it. After fastening the chain to the trailer hitch, I tied the rope on myself, and my companions pulled me, and then the truck, out of the water.

Once, on horseback at the north end of the Sierra Pinta, I picked up some tracks of a family of sheep heading west into the Tule Desert. Their tracks showed that they were nervous, sprinting in short spurts as they proceeded without pause to the nearest hills of the Cabeza Prieta Mountains. Not much was known about valley crossings by sheep at the time, so I returned to my truck after the long ride flushed with pleasure at this discovery. It was late in the day as I headed south, so I made camp west of the south end of the Sierra Pinta. As was my custom, I tied my horse to a drag, a dry ironwood log, so it could move about as I slept. However, something frightened my horse in the wee hours of the morning, and it took off with a loud fart, awakening me as it galloped downslope, its ironwood drag digging big holes in the Tule Desert silt. I curled into a ball in my sleeping bag as the drag bounded by. Funny now, but life-threatening at the time. I went back to sleep, knowing the horse wouldn't go far with the drag. In the morning the horse was out of sight but easy to follow by the holes and drag marks made by the log.

Once I was called upon to guide famous architect Walter Kilham of Connecticut. His hobby was traveling the world to photograph wild sheep. Our first experience together began successfully, as I talked him into position for some nice photos on the Kofa Game Range. But it ended painfully. He slept that first night on one of those low-to-the-ground canvas cots held up with bent metal rods. It was a hot night so we slept under sheets. His bare feet stuck out from under his sheet and dangled close to the ground. I don't know what that giant desert centipede was thinking, but when it bit Walter's toe, he yelped and hurled his flashlight at the beast. I awoke with a start in time to see the centipede scurrying away. In short order I had his foot packed in ice and up on the dash of my truck as I headed for Yuma and the hospital.

Figure 12.1. Norman Simmons and Moxie near Cabeza Prieta Tanks, 1964. (Courtesy Norman Simmons)

My horse never broke down, but occasionally my truck did. Midday one November, as I was nosing along the base of the Sierra Pinta looking for sheep, the truck battery shifted and shorted out. Nothing I could do. No radio. Nearest civilization: Los Vidrios in Sonora, a little store on the highway run by Juan Bermúdez. Well, if I was going to walk out, I may as well be prepared for anything. So I loaded up my Kelty pack with supplies for a couple of days and headed south. Six and a half hours later, after dark, I startled the people in the store by walking in, thumping my pack on the floor, and asking for a *refresco.*

When they heard my story, they immediately offered me food and a bed. As graciously as I could, I declined and hauled out a canned chicken and some biscuits. When Julian Hayden heard the story from his friends at Los Vidrios, he made sure it got wide distribution—about this crazy gringo who appeared one night out of nowhere, carrying a houseful of stuff in his pack, including a whole chicken. I wonder if the story has been embellished since I left the desert.

Hitchhiking, I did make it home, by one in the morning. My wife had instructions not to call for help unless I was three days overdue; it is mortifying to be the object of a search. She was surprised at the hour of my arrival, but otherwise she regarded my adventure as routine. And indeed, when I looked up this story in my journal to refresh my memory, the entry was crisp and impersonal about the incident, but my notes waxed relatively poetic when describing what I saw on my hike out. "Especially impressive were the vast stands

Figure 12.2. *Norman Simmons and Moxie, Cabeza Prieta National Wildlife Refuge headquarters, Ajo, 1964. (Courtesy Norman Simmons)*

of *Bouteloua* and *Aristida* (mostly the latter, *A. adscenionis*) on the Pinta Sands, all dried; and the lush annual (some dry) and perennial vegetation along the east edge of the lava flow. There the annuals were so dense they tangled my feet. A covey of 25 quail was seen at S13/S18 in the Pinta Sands near the lava. Saw 35 lark buntings in the Pinta Sands in a group. Tracks of four antelope three miles south of USBM Pinta and the Tule Desert Road, going north."

I was not paid to have adventures, however. My job was to manage the refuge. The Fish and Wildlife Service also agreed to support my research into the social organization, behavior, and limiting effects of the environment on the desert bighorn sheep. It was pioneer work in this harsh, southwestern corner of Arizona. I had picked the Agua Dulce Mountains and the Sierra Pinta as my main study areas. Both were isolated by wide, alluvial valleys. My wife, Hilah, and refuge manager Gale Monson were enthusiastic companions during much of my fieldwork. Gale Monson was, and still is, an avid birdwatcher, and he added much to the knowledge of the birds of southwestern Arizona. Hilah was (and is) also a birdwatcher and amateur geologist. Both of them complemented my work and published their own work on birds and geology. There was much to learn about that area of the Sonoran Desert, and we frequently shared the joys of discovery.

To help me study the movements of family units of sheep, J. "Bud" Philips, our maintenance man with a love for sheep work, invented a dye spray unit that we used in the summer to mark the rumps of sheep entering waterholes in the Sierra Pinta. These color markings, along with body and horn scars, enabled us to follow individuals and family groups. Those data showed us that family groups were smaller in the refuge than in sheep populations in the rest of the United States and Canada: an average of two to three, year-long.

Most of my observations of sheep were made during the hot summer months, when the greatest stress on the sheep occurred. I lived with the sheep, bedding when they bedded, on light-colored surfaces or in caves, and alert when they were moving about. At the time, rumors circulated about how often sheep needed water. From the marked sheep, I found that ewes would go without water for up to six days during the hottest, driest time of the summer and that rams drank at least as often as ewes. They preferred to drink where there were unrestricted views and abundant escape routes. They sometimes watered at night, but only when the moon was full, or nearly so. As one would expect, avoiding heat gain in the summer was the main goal of much of their behavior, as it was mine.

My love of the desert grew with my understanding. I was fortunate enough to have the help and inspiration offered by old desert rats like Julian Hayden, Gale Monson, and Juan Xavier. They showed me how to live with the desert, to read the desert like a book. It calls for thought: why does a wagon wheel of wildlife trails lead to this place at the foot of the ridge? Why did the fox dig here in the dry granite sand? Gale had told me about "sand tanks." Some brawn applied to a shovel soon revealed the first sand tank I had ever seen, sand-filtered water pooling up cool and delicious to the lips. At Heart Tank, Juan showed me how to make a rich, nutritious cake from mesquite bean pods, using the ancient granite mortars and pestles found below the tank. Julian showed me how to find the sand root and night-blooming cereus, sources of moisture and food known well to the Sand Papago. He told me about the walnut-flavored *chia* seed, which makes the cooling *pinole* drink.

Gale was my inspiration to get to know the vegetation of the refuge. He began the first comprehensive collection of plants in the area in the 1950s, and soon I was following in his footsteps.

But I was more interested in ethnobotany than tax-onomy, and I pumped old-timers like Ed Ketchum, retired from the Border Patrol; Jim McGrady, a retired pugilist; and Juan Bermúdez about the human uses of plants. Agave, or *lechuguilla*, pro-vided juicy, sweet young stalks like sugar cane and a caudex edible when baked. Pigweed makes a delicious spinach when cooked. And many people know about jojoba nuts and oil and the delicious fruits of the saguaro, organ pipe, fishhook, and prickly pear cacti. But I also learned about poisons from plants like sapium and the fact that even the lowly creosotebush can be used for varnish, mend-ing pots, and retarding rancidity of fats and oils.

As I learned that day on the rim of the Growlers, the Sonoran Desert has a way of over-whelming your senses and making all else seem relatively trivial. Well, except for the birth of our first child. I first learned of Hilah's pregnancy on April 15, 1962, when we were prowling for signs of ancient human activity near Sheep Tank in the Growlers. We had driven the Dodge out from Ajo to the east edge of the range and hiked in. Quite a story was written on the rocks and on cave floors there, and I was soon lost in reading it. But drink-ing water was getting low, and Hilah was drinking a lot. Also, she seemed tired. I strained water from Sheep Tank, an unappealing stew of algae-laden liquid spiced with the bodies of countless insects and a deer mouse or two, through my sweaty undershirt into my gallon canteen. It was amaz-ing how good the water tasted that hot day. It extended our stay, but prudence, and Hilah's calm statement that she was pregnant, soon dictated a retreat to the truck to take her home.

Then, on October 2, 1962, Sam Miller and I were sitting on the east slope of the Agua Dulce Mountains. We had stopped searching for sheep to have a sandwich. We noticed that way to the north a helicopter was zigzagging back and forth, low over the desert floor, obviously searching for something or somebody. After a while it angled toward us. I hauled out my signal mirror and flashed it, and it soon settled onto a saddle near us. As we walked up to it through the swirling dust, out stepped Judge Gene Tally, looking seri-ous. "Your wife's in trouble. Better come with us." Leaving Sam to bring the truck home, I piled in the chopper and, heart in throat, flew toward Ajo. We landed right in the hospital yard, kicking up quite a dust storm. I got out, grubby and grizzled

Figure 12.3. Hilah and Norman Simmons cook-ing over coals near Tuseral Tank, 1961. (Courtesy Norman Simmons)

from days in the field, carrying my scruffy pack, and clomped into the hospital, drawing stares from all who saw me.

Well, I had arrived too late. Daughter Debo-rah had been born. It had been a normal delivery. The "trouble" was that in the pain of birth, my normally unexcitable wife, who would never utter even the mildest swear word, had turned the air blue with language that even the tough, worldly nurses were shocked to hear.

Thanks to anthropologist Bernard ("Bunny") Fontana, I occasionally traveled in the Cabeza Pri-eta with Juan Xavier, a Papago who was knowl-edgeable about the art and science of anthropol-ogy and was Bunny's valued sidekick. Juan Xavier, whose family name was sometimes Anglicized to "Harvey" or "Havier," was born and raised on the southern part of the Papago Indian Reservation at the village of Choulic. He grew up knowing the intricacies of cattle ranching and was an accom-plished cowboy. Like many other Papagos in this part of the reservation, Juan grew up under Pres-byterian—rather than Catholic—influence. In 1932 the Presbyterians organized a four-man Ex-ecutive Committee of the Papago People as a kind of incipient tribal council, and Juan Xavier was one of the four. Later, in 1936, he was one of a dozen or so men who worked on framing the constitution and bylaws that were adopted by the Papago Tribe of Arizona in 1937. After the first tribal elections he became the first tribal secretary.

It was through his second wife, anthropolo-gist Gwyneth Harrington, a non-indigenous per-son, that he became friends with such people as anthropologist Edward Spicer, archaeologist Emil

Haury, and artists Edith Hamlin, Maynard Dixon, and Ted De Grazia, among others. He excavated in Ventana Cave on Haury's project, working directly under the supervision of Julian Hayden. Juan and Julian became close friends, and Julian wrote briefly about him in "Talking with the Animals," published in the *Journal of the Southwest* (summer 1987, 29:226). Juan accompanied De Grazia on the latter's infamous trek into the Superstition Mountains in a futile search for the Lost Dutchman Mine. By the time I met him, Juan was living alone in a little adobe house across the street from the Spicers' home in the Old Fort Lowell district of Tucson. He did odd jobs and was more or less looked after by friends such as the Spicers and De Grazia.

One day, on our way to see a cave drawing in the Sierra Pinta that I had discovered, Juan, Bunny Fontana, and I came upon a small group of feral burros. I had been ordered by headquarters to kill burros on sight, as they were reputed to compete with wildlife and to foul waterholes. I had balked at killing burros unless we were short of meat. Well, we were, so without a word I got my rifle and dropped one. That was okay with my companions—until I began to skin it and butcher it, that is. Bunny was merely amazed, as he knew I was weird. But Xavier had a look of disgust on his face that I did not understand.

That night, we were camped at Tule Well with some surveyors. I prepared some nice, medium-rare, broiled loin steaks from the burro meat in my ice box—a special treat. Later, as I collected the plates from everyone for washing, I asked how they liked the meat. There were grunts and comments of satisfaction. When I got to Juan, he replied by smiling and showing me his empty plate. It wasn't until early the next morning that I saw an untouched steak in the sand well behind where Juan had sat. Bunny later explained that the horse was Juan's totem, and the burro was too close to the horse for him to eat.

I often reflect on my time on the Cabeza Prieta and realize that I had the ideal job. I was actually paid to wander this desert by horse, foot, and truck and to study its mysteries and admire its beauty. When fellow desert rat Gale Monson and I dropped into the new, fancy, air-conditioned refuge office in Ajo some years ago, we naturally wanted to know how our sheep and pronghorn were doing. What we discovered was unsettling.

An office had to be staffed. Trained wildlifers could no longer take off on a whim to check Sheep Tank or enjoy the hummingbird displays over the wonderful flower garden of the Pinta Sands, or spend weeks camped in the Sierra Pinta or the Cabeza Prietas, keeping fingers on the pulse of the Sonoran Desert. They didn't have a clue what was happening with the sheep in the Sierra Pinta. No one had been out there in months. We climbed back into Gale's four-by-four, mumbling agreement that we were refuge managers during an ideal time in the history of the Refuge Branch.

But was this unique to the refuge? I went from the Sonoran Desert to the Mackenzie Mountains, Northwest Territories, Canada, still on the trail of sheep, this time the white thinhorn. When I arrived in Fort Smith to take up my post as Canadian Wildlife Service (CWS) biologist, I described my past work and how I planned sheep research in the northern mountains to my fellow biologist, whooping crane expert Ernie Kuyt. His only comment, "I thought pencil and notebook biologists were a thing of the past."

I soon discovered that he may have been right; pencil and notebook field men were apparently a dying breed. CWS researchers were soon doing surveys in comfortable aircraft and staying nights in hotels in nearby villages like Norman Wells and Inuvik, much to the disgust of the old guard. These new biologists would comment to me about how most moose tracks were seen on the treed islands, away from the meadows where they often hung out. But when I asked about snow conditions—depth, thickness of crust—I drew a blank. These biologists never set foot on the snow except in a village.

With the relatively new philosophy of holistic research and management generating buzzwords, I have been handed a bigger stick with which to beat my drum: if you want to understand the whole of nature as a researcher or manager, then you must get out of the office, out of the airplane, and live with nature. Bed down in the shade of a smoke tree when the sheep bed. Get up when they do, and watch them water in the moonlight. Want to know why sheep at Eagle Tank bed on light-colored rocks in the early morning while I hug the shade? Walk over and measure the temperature of the night-cooled granite, compare it with the temperature of the sand and gravel, and see for yourself how relatively cool it is.

Figure 12.4. J. C. Page
and Norman Simmons
looking for bighorn, Sierra
Tuseral, 1961. (Courtesy
Norman Simmons)

Such is the life of a field man, the continuous enjoyment and surprises the desert has to offer when you let it titillate your senses, building your store of knowledge so you become an even better student. That siren call is incentive to get out of the air-conditioned office and truck to greet the desert on its own terms.

Hilah Simmons, Norman's wife, affectionately reminds us what it is like to be the spouse of a field researcher and land manager. What was once primarily men's work is now enjoyed and done well by women and men alike.

The Wild Life of a Wildlifer's Wife (or How to Live with a Wildlife Manager)

HILAH SIMMONS

It's up in the morning at 3, 5, or 9.
You wonder, "Will he be here or gone for a time?"
Perhaps today he says, "For a spell I'll be home."
And I say to you, by all means don't groan.
If you can get away fast enough he might baby-sit;
Of course the extra errands for him are worth it.
Back to three meals a day and coffee breaks two,
Not to mention the tourists and cohorts passing
    through;
It's strange, but they all seem to know when he's
    home.

The telephone rings and there's no time alone.
Then there are times when he leaves you for days,
At least so you think, till the receiver you raise,
And you hear him say, "Hi! I walked out 19 miles,"
Or, "I'll be back for a minute; I forgot my files."
When he says, "I'm going to Charlie Bell Well,"
If he's been home a week you think, "That's swell.
I can start on my mending and get to that letter,
Go to the meeting, and what's even better
Maybe practice the piano and sing a song . . ."
Then he says, "Why don't you come on along?"
So pack up the groceries, four slices of cheese,
And would you mind filling the water tank, please?
Grab your camera, binocs, and kids,
Bird book and bedrolls, pots, pans, and lids.
Despite bounces and jolts you must be full of shame
When your husband reminds you, "Keep watching
    for game."
And if you get groggy keep your head on the level;
If he notices you dozing he'll give you the devil.
Always be ready to stop and hop out
And pick up some tin can or trash that's about,
To stop and investigate some old mine.
But look at a dickey-bird?—we haven't time.
When nature calls take your binocs along;
It may be your only chance to follow a birdsong.
You'll feel like a queen as he cooks to your wishes
Until it is time to do up the dishes!
Maybe you would like to stargaze,
But you'll hit the sack early to make use of the days.

PEOPLE OF THE PLACE *CAMPFIRES AND FIELD NOTES*   115

Fully expect to be in his truck
The one time in a hundred when it gets stuck.
Believe it or not, each time you roam
He'll be the first to wish he was home.
Whether you went for two days or ten,
You'll always be ready to try it again.
Whether his name is Tom, Dick, or Harry,
If there's one thing for sure when a game man you
    marry:
You'll never know where he'll be when

Or when he'll be coming back home again.
But one thing's even surer than that:
You can never predict where you'll be at!
When he is home for weeks on end,
Try to remember he's still your friend.
Make use of each moment when he leaves you
    home
So you can be ready when he wants you to roam.
But here is the hottest of all my tips,
Never pass up a chance to go on his trips.

Thirteen

Godfrey Sykes and the *Hilda*

Diane Boyer

With one voice several of us demanded to know all about the burning of the *Hilda* and its consequences—which the Doctor always gently spoke of as "a might-tee close call for Sykes!" The Geographer was in the right mood, and forthwith told us this story, word for word, as here set down. (Hornaday 1908:293)

The narrator was William T. Hornaday, the book his classic work on the Pinacate region, *Camp-Fires on Desert and Lava*. The "Doctor" was botanist Daniel Trembly MacDougal, and the "Geographer" was Godfrey Glenton Sykes.

Few travelers and researchers covered as much ground in the Dry Borders region as Godfrey Sykes. Born and raised in England, he came to the United States in 1879—the same year in which he turned eighteen, completed his formal education, and lost his mother (his father had died in 1866). After tramping about both America and the world, he decided to call Flagstaff, Arizona Territory, his home base in 1886. At his nearby cow camp he met and befriended MacDougal, whom he guided through the Colorado delta for the first time in 1902. In 1906, at MacDougal's invitation, Sykes joined the staff of the Carnegie Desert Botanical Laboratory as building superintendent and moved to Tucson. He accompanied Hornaday's Pinacate expedition in 1907. He ran a string of rain gauges along El Camino del Diablo in the mid-1920s. On a 1923 trip to Puerto Libertad with dendrochronologist, astronomer, and great friend Andrew E. Douglass, he hung the moniker "boojum" on *Fouquieria columnaris*. Less well known are his early delta trips, those that planted the seeds of what would become both his passion and his profession.

The delta trips were larks, adventures for the sake of adventure. They usually began with shipping locally milled lumber by rail from Flagstaff to the Colorado River at Topock (also called Mellen), building a boat on the beach below the bridge, and then sailing, rowing, poling, and lining the craft to the Gulf of California. Sykes made numerous such journeys, sometimes with his younger brother (and only sibling), Stanley, other times with a friend or two, and later with his wife, Emma, and two sons, Glenton and Gilbert. That he made more than one of these jaunts is rather remarkable given that the first trip quite literally went up in flames. Here I reconstruct the tale of the burning of the *Hilda,* quoting, primarily, three sources: Sykes's original diary, contemporary newspaper articles, and the account Sykes wrote for Hornaday's *Camp-Fires on Desert and Lava.* In his landmark publication *The Colorado Delta*, Sykes mentions the journey only insofar as it was his first to the region. He also recorded the yarn in his 1944 autobiography, *A Westerly Trend,* but it was penned when he was in his eighties and under the cloud of a fading memory. The details are vastly different from those in the earlier accounts and give the impression of a compilation of adventures, spun and respun countless times into one rollicking, crowd-pleasing tale.

"Around The World: Two Arizona Cowboys Will Make The Journey. Result of a Plan Made in an Arizona Cattle Camp—The Little Craft is Fully Complete, but is Only Twenty Two Feet Long—The Coast To Be Skirted all the Way if Possible." Thus trumpeted the *Arizona Enterprise* on page 3 of its November 22, 1890, edition. The article continued:

> A Needles telegram of November 16th says: The two daring navigators, Godfrey Sykes and Charles McLean, who propose coasting around the world in a small boat, are now making final preparations for the commencement of their perilous

undertaking. They will launch their little craft on the Colorado River about the 23d instant and pull down the river light to Yuma, where they will ballast and provision her and then make for the world below.

Their trip, as roughly and briefly mapped out will be as follows: Reaching the Gulf of California at the mouth of the Colorado river, they will follow the Mexican and Central America coasts to South America, down to Magellan straits, thence up the east coast as far as Cape St. Roque, they will cross the Atlantic and go to Sierra Leone on the African coast, thence east along the European coast to the British islands. They will then return through the Bay of Biscay into the Mediterranean sea through Suez canal and Red sea to the Indian ocean, along the coast of China and Japan, passing by Singapore, Hongkong and Yokohama, up the Russian coast. Leaving the Russian coast at Hetropolofsky, they will cross the Pacific ocean at the Aleutian islands, and thence come down the coast of Alaska and Oregon to San Francisco.

They calculate that the trip, provided no unusual amount of bad luck overtakes them, will occupy the best part of two and a half years, and they hope to be back in time to attend the World's Fair at Chicago.

A Cherished Plan

The hazardous undertaking is not the result of a moment's thought. On the contrary, both men have cherished the idea for years, and each only awaited meeting a man who would take the same view of the matter as he did. In a "cow camp" in Arizona the two men met more than a year ago, and there and then the journey was agreed to.

Charles McLean, the elder of the two men, is a native of Paisley, Scotland, and is between thirty and thirty-one years of age. He has had seven years' experience before the mast in whaling and coasting vessels, and is an expert in sailing a small boat. He is a very quiet, unobtrusive young man, and though retiring and unassuming in conversation, has an air of decision and determination about him. He says and knows and appreciates the hardships which he will have to undergo, but he is confident of success.

"For years," said he, "I was planning a trip of this kind, and I had it all laid out ready to be put into execution, but could find no one whom I thought was just exactly the man to accompany me. Finally I drifted into Arizona and went into the cattle business, where I met 'Red' Sykes.

"One night, after a hard day's round up, we lay in camp smoking and talking, when I casually referred to my pet scheme.

"'What's that Charlie?' said Red, 'do you want to coast it around the world, too?'

"'Yes, I have dreamed of it, and thought of it for years.'

"'Then, my boy, we'll put the scheme through, for I, too, have long desired to make such a trip, and you are the very man to go with me.'"

Thus was the compact entered into, and from that day until this they have worked and look forward to the day of sailing.

The Other Man

Godfred [*sic*] Sykes, familiarly called "Red" Sykes because of the auburn hue of his locks and the ruddy, rosy glow of his face, is a native of "Merrie England," having been born in London twenty-seven [actually twenty-nine] years ago. He is a genius, and not unlike many geniuses, he is eccentric. His parents attempted to give him a thorough classical and literary education, and though, through impatience he did not remain at college long enough to obtain his degree, he is a thorough scholar, being well put up in philosophy, astronomy, mathematics, and Latin and Greek. Some years ago he took quite a fancy to navigation, and after studying it and learning all he could of it theoretically, he made four voyages around the world. In order to take advantage of his surroundings, he did not ship before the mast, but would pay his passage in vessels which did not carry passengers, and when out at sea would assist the officers in navigating their vessel, thus putting into practice the theory which he had learned.

Both men are decidedly in earnest, and determined to succeed, if success lies in their power. Both are handy at any kind of work and both are good navigators. They begin their journey with a full realization of the many dangers and privations before them, but they are confident of succeeding. Should their little vessel be capsized, she is so constructed that by removing the masts she will right herself again, and though she should be filled with water she will not sink, and when bailed out is as good as before.

From every port which the voyagers put into they will write back to their friends, and inform them in detail of their journey. Considerable interest is being taken in the enterprise here and in western Arizona, and a great crowd will assemble at Needles on the day of their departure to bid the intrepid sailors adieu and wish them godspeed.

On December 6, 1890, the *Arizona Enterprise* published a *Yuma Times* report, "Daring Navigators: The Young Men who Left Needles to Sail Round the World":

On Thursday, November 20, Godfrey Sykes and Chares [*sic*] McLean left Needles in a sail boat for a trip around the world. Their craft is 24 feet long, 7 feet 6 inches wide, draws 18 inches of water, and is schooner rigged. Their point of embarkation was about five miles south of Needles, where they were taken by a special train furnished by the Atlantic & Pacific Railroad. A large number of Needles people, with a band, went to see them off. Sail was successfully made at 5 o'clock. The boat has been expected at Yuma any time for several days, but nothing has been seen of it at this writing. Tuesday evening. There was a report that the navigators were stuck somewhere up the river. It is the opinion of those here who know the river that the boat can hardly get down safely at this stage of water. The Colorado is a very treacherous and perilous stream to navigate just now. If the young men had made a start just after the last rise in the river they might have been successful in getting to the gulf, but the depth of water now is such that navigation by any except old hands is extremely precarious.

Sykes's original diary is a worn, clothbound volume with chipped leather corners. Appropriately, it is water stained. "G Sykes, Sch *Hilda*" is carefully written in his hand on the gray fabric; the boat may have been named in honor of one of Sykes's young English cousins. The language of

the diary indicates it may have been written after the fact, possibly while the men waited in Yuma for customs papers before crossing into Mexico. Sykes describes the trip from Needles to Yuma:

The river scenery below the Needles is singularly beautiful. The Needles Canon [Cañon] itself which is about 9 miles long is very fine. Dropping down a river with the current is the best way to enjoy scenery. There is a whirlpool in this Canon which is considered rather dangerous. It is caused by a projecting point of rock at the lower extremity of a very sharp horse-shoe bend in the river. Of course the scenery in this part of the river is not so imposing & awfully grand as is that in the Grand Canon. Big blue cranes [great blue herons] are seen standing like solitary sentinels on the edge of sand bars. They will squawk as one passes by. On getting through the canon our troubles commenced again & we were constantly aground. The next day we saw a solitary house on the California side, with signs of life around it. We pulled ashore & visited the inmates, two oldish men who were living as so many men do live in this part of the world, by doing a little work in their mine for a few days, washing up & taking the gold to the settlements, bring stores with the proceeds & living on them till they are about exhausted, then repeating the process. Rather an unsatisfactory way of spending one's life. We met with several of such outfits on our trip down the river. All through the Colorado Indian reservation the river was very bad. The channel was uncertain & dodging from one side to the other in a most bewildering way. We saw lots of beaver & coon sign along the banks & Charley who is a very enthusiastic trapper was very much interested therein. Erinberg [Ehrenberg] is an old point for ferrying over the river in the early days when a trail ran from Prescott to Los Angeles, is a town very similar to some of those which one runs across occasionally in New Mexico on the old Santa Fe trail. A deserted town is at any time a melancholy sight, but a deserted adobe town is the saddest looking spectacle imaginable. After leaving Erinberg we travelled for several miles through a narrow channel or "slew" between a long island of the California shore. It reminded one of an English river, running between banks of willow & alder. Then we got out into the main river again & had more trouble with getting ashore. We hailed the sight of rocks or rocky bluffs with delight as it was a sign of a more confined river bed & presaged good river for a mile or two. On some of the most prominent points on these rocky hill sides there grow immense cacti which look like gigantic posts

Figure 13.2. Sketch of a saguaro cactus by Godfrey Sykes, from his Hilda *diary. (Courtesy Diane Boyer)*

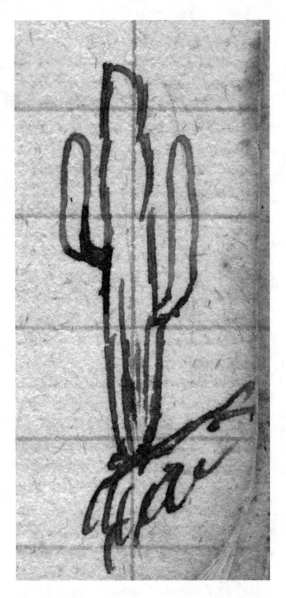

or monuments. We longed to climb up to some of them & topple them over into the river. The hills & ranges of mountains both in Arizona & California are very desolate looking, being very abrupt & abounding in sharp needle-like peaks & having their flanks utterly devoid of vegetation. We sighted a very singular looking mountain on the (third?) day after passing Erinberg. It is called Picacho which signifies point or peak in Spanish. It is also known as the Chimney rock. It was soon after sighting this peak that we got shipwrecked for the first time. We had just entered a canon, & were congratulating ourselves on an easy time for a few miles, when we saw the ripple over a sunken rock just ahead. Charley, who was steering, tried to steer the boat to one side, but the current was too much for him & we struck on it just as the boat was almost athwart the stream, breaking a hole through our starboard quarter & shaking the boat up a good

deal. She began to make water very fast, so we beached her, & unloaded all our freight of provisions, etc. It took us two days to repair damages. As the weather looked somewhat threatening we took one of our sails & erected a shelter tent ashore in the ship-wrecked mariner style. It was very snug. Just before we got ready to leave camp & get started again a man passed us on one of the singular constructions called tule rafts, which are quite common on the river. The tules of which they are constructed, are tall reeds or rushes growing to a height of 10 or 12 feet. These are cut down & tied into bundles & these bundles are then lashed together till they form a raft about 6 or 8 feet broad. The one which passed us was navigated by a solitary Mexican who civily wished us buenos dias, & was freighted with a gigantic bale of hay, some enormous squashes & a pile of watermelons. The Mexican seemed to be taking life very easily, having a long pole which he kept dragging astern till he wanted to change his course, when he would make dabs at sand bars, snags, or the bank with it so slew his raft around. We overtook him again towards evening at Norton's landing, where he was selling his melons.

A man who understands the river thoroughly can make very fair time on one of these rafts, but they are very unwieldly craft to get aground with as they will get imbedded in the sand & have to be taken apart & hauled over the obstruction a bundle at a time. After passing Norton's landing, the weather began to change & it got showery & cold.

On reaching Yuma we found the town's people looking out for us as our departure from the Needles had been reported & all were anxious to see the craft which was going to try to go around the world. Yuma is the point at which the S.P.R.R. [Southern Pacific Railroad] crosses the Colorado river & is also the location of the Territorial prison. On the California side is the old Government post of Fort Yuma which is now occupied as an Indian School for the Yuma Indians. These Indians are very similar to the Mojaves, being fine able bodied fellows, frequently over six feet in height & muscular in proportion. They seem to pass a very happy life, working when they please but putting in most of their time playing a game somewhat similar to the old school boy game of "shinney." They have in common with the Mojaves & other river Indians a curious mode of dressing their hair. They go down to the river bank & standing up to their knees in water gather up handfulls of the soft oozey mud with which they daub their sable tresses, working & kneading it well in. This is then allowed to dry for an hour or two & it is then carefully washed out. It is supposed to give the hair a glossy appearance & I give the receipt [recipe] for what it is worth to some of our civilized ladies.

Yuma is an adobe town & is reported to be one of the hottest places on earth. We found it however during our stay which was somewhat protracted, owing to the necessity of procuring our clearance papers & to the lack of the necessary blank forms which had to be forwarded from Washington. We made friends with everybody in town, including the Chinamen, one of whom gave us a letter of introduction to relatives of his in Hong Kong, & received many valuable hints as to the navigation of the lower river & head of the Gulf of California. The Yuma Indians cremate their dead (a custom which is common to most of the river tribes). During the cremation ceremony, the relatives & friends of the deceased will kill their ponies & make paupers of themselves generally, by throwing their personal property into the flames. Another custom is that if a medicine man in the tribe shall lose too many of his patients he shall die. One of them had lost 9 patients & was consequently slaughtered while we were here. Last winter the Cocopahs (who observe the same custom) killed one of their medicine men, who had been more than usually unlucky, & then not content with this sacrifice, they started in on his relations. They bagged several, but the rest escaped to the Yumas, where they lived in exile for several months.

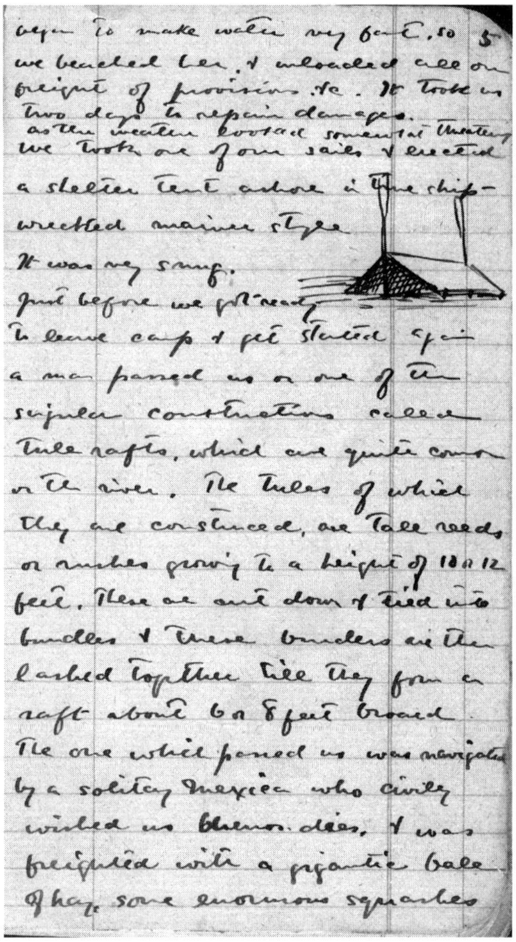

The *Hilda* diary account ends abruptly, with the next page given to a trip later in 1891. There are but two references in the diary to the rest of the *Hilda* journey. The first is a tantalizingly brief penciled note on the front free endpaper of the book: "*Hilda* lies in 114°.42′ W, 30°.47′ N." The second is buried deep within the ruled pages, marked by a faint red pencil star, in notes apparently extracted from *Sailing Directions to West Coast of Mexico & Central America from the boundary line between the United States & Mexico to Panama, including the Gulf of California* (which he further noted was number 84 from the U.S. Hydrographic Office, 1887; "Dillon's price 50 cents"): "When bound down the coast from San Felipe look out for sand banks & spits in the neighborhood of & to the south of Diggs Point. There is a good inlet which can be entered at high tide by boats, some three miles south of the point & another & much larger one about two miles further again. This slough or inlet is nearly at the outer end of a sandy point & if a look out is kept for the bars around

Figure 13.3. Page from the Hilda diary, including sketch of sail shelter. (Courtesy Diane Boyer)

Figure 13.4. Yuma Indian washing hair, from the Hilda diary. (Courtesy Diane Boyer)

its mouth is a very good refuge for boats. (The *Hilda* was burned in here)."

The only known contemporary accounts of the remainder of the voyage are from the newspapers. On February 14, 1891, the *Yuma Sentinel* reported simply: "Sykes and McLean made a bad

Figure 13.5. *Sketch of Native American woman from one of the river tribes, from Sykes's* Hilda *diary, date unknown. (Courtesy Diane Boyer)*

go. They only went to San Felipe and not around the world. By some hocus focus their little ship caught fire and was burned. They came back to Yuma on foot, at least most of the way." On February 21, 1891, the *Arizona Enterprise* printed the epic in far greater detail on the front page, in a dispatch from the *Yuma Times:*

Sykes And Mclean Disastrous Ending Of Their Voyage

Their Boat Damaged by Fire

They Return to Yuma After Numerous Ships [sic].

Godfrey Sykes and Charles McLean, the two young men who started from here six weeks ago to go around the world in a boat, returned to Yuma last Saturday and relate a thrilling story of disaster and hardship.

The voyage down the Colorado river to Yuma took over two weeks. A stay here of three weeks was necessary to procure clearance papers from the custom house. They finally set out for the gulf on Tuesday, December 30th. Two weeks elapsed before they arrived at the shipyard [Port Isabel, by then abandoned] near the head of the gulf. Here a

good wind came up and sail was set. The wind rose to a gale but the boat behaved splendidly. At the end of 18 hours they were 30 miles south of Point San Felipe, Lower California. The men thought it best to wait until the gale had subsided, so they went into a little cove, beached the boat and made camp on January 17th. The camp was some distance from the beach and most of the provisions and supplies were left in the boat. The evening of the 19th Sykes went to the boat to fill a lantern and after doing so tried to light it. The wind blew his matches out and as each match went out he threw it down in the bottom of the boat. He finally succeeded in lighting the lantern and started back to camp. A light was soon noticed in the direction of the boat. Flames ran to the top of the masts, leaving no doubt that the boat was on fire. Both men ran to the spot, hoping to at least save some provisions, but the oil can had exploded and scattered the flames. The fire was finally put out by a liberal use of wet sand. An examination revealed the fact that all the contents of the boat were destroyed. The flour was so badly soaked with oil as to be unfit for use. A barrel of water was practically all that was saved, and a few ship biscuit at the camp were all the provisions left. The boat itself was found to be unseaworthy.

After a consultation the men decided to start for San Quintin, about 75 miles distant on the Pacific coast. The tin locker lining was torn out and a couple of canteens made with some tinner's tools they were fortunate enough to save. An oyster bed was discovered near by, and with the ship biscuit, some fresh oysters and canteens of water they started. A tiresome tramp of 15 miles, consuming two days, took them into a wild, mountainous country, difficult to penetrate and utterly barren. Their provisions were about gone and they were compelled to return to their former camp. After a rest of a day they secured some more oysters refilled their canteens and again started out afoot, hoping to reach the Lerdo colony, distant 130 miles northward. Each man carried a pack weighing about sixty pounds. Days of hardship ensued. Sometimes miles of salt marsh had to be crossed, the men having to bind their shoes with strips of canvass to keep from losing them in the mud. One day they made only seven miles. After eight days, their water and food all gone, and having been compelled to throw away everything but clothes, the two men found their progress blocked by a solid wall of brush. In vain they tried to penetrate it. Two days had now elapsed since their provisions gave out. They were many miles north of the gulf and near the river. Desperation lent energy to their exhausted strength and they swam the Colorado to the eastern side. A small raft was made out of poles on which their clothing was placed and kept dry while swimming over. The river was about 500 yards wide, the current swift and the water cold. The crossing was safely made. They were now on the lands of the Lerdo colony in Sonora and about three miles from the settlement. They arrived there in the afternoon on Tuesday, February 3d. Their wants were soon supplied and to use McLean's language, "beans never looked so good." They remained at Lerdo all day Wednesday, and started for Yuma Thursday, on foot. When a few miles from town they were overtaken by a wagon and arrived here by that conveyance Saturday evening. Both men saved what money they had with them.

Near their camp below San Felipe, the wreck of a schooner was found. From papers posted in the cabin it was learned to have cleared from San Diego over two years ago. Nothing movable remained in the vessel, everything had been taken that could be carried away.

Mr. Sykes left for Flagstaff Sunday morning. Mr. McLean says they may undertake the voyage again, but probably not before a year and from some port on the Pacific coast. Both men have had enough of adventure for the present. Mr. McLean left for California Monday.

Sykes's account for Hornaday (1908:292–301), written down seventeen years after the event, is generally consistent with that in the newspapers. The embellishments are grander, possibly more or less accurate than the newspaper story, perhaps polished in the telling of the tale through the years. Hornaday may well have altered the text, too.

Well, gentlemen, it is now about seventeen years ago that I joined in with a husky Scotchman named Charlie McLean. At Yuma [Flagstaff, as noted above] we built ourselves a very good little sea boat, twenty-seven feet long, half decked over and schooner rigged. We decided to sail down the Colorado to the Gulf of California, then on down to the west coast of Central America and after that to wherever the Fates might direct us. We took in plenty of provisions, and as we ran out of the mouth of the Colorado, into the head of the Gulf, the world looked very much like our oyster.

The tides in the head of the Gulf are very heavy, and we put in a week or so playing with them, before heading down the Gulf. Finally we decided to go down on the Peninsula side, and cross the Gulf lower down.

Figure 13.6. *"The* Weary Willie *after she had been sold and rechristened the* Freda.*" Sykes built this yawl-rigged boat in 1902. The rigging is different from that of the schooner* Hilda, *the aft mast of which would have been placed forward of the rudder and would have been as tall as or taller than the fore mast. (Courtesy Diane Boyer; quotation from back of photo)*

Figure 13.7. *The sloop* Striplex *at San Felipe in February 1904. Sykes built this boat in Yuma for one of the delta trips with MacDougal. The rigging (one mast instead of two) is different from that of the more versatile schooner* Hilda, *of which there are no known photographs. (Courtesy Diane Boyer)*

One evening we ran into a little inlet near Fermin Point, and camped on shore behind a low ridge of sand that had blown up parallel with the shore. It was a rough, windy evening, with the wind blowing half a gale; and with a piece of canvas we rigged up a small shelter-tent to keep the sand out of our eyes, and out of the bean-pot.

As it began to grow dark, I went down to the boat to light our lantern. It was one of those old-fashioned railroad lanterns, that can't be trimmed without pulling out the whole bottom. I fiddled and fussed with it for quite a while, under the forrad deck of the *Hilda*, out of the wind, striking a number of matches; and, as I now suppose, I dropped some of the burning ends while struggling to get the light to suit me.

The tide was out, and the boat lay high and dry on the sand. I suppose one of my burning match-ends fell upon something burnable. But I didn't know it at the time, and went back to our camp-fire.

Half an hour later, as we chanced to look seaward over the top of the sand ridge, we saw a glare of light, and heard the popping of cartridges. We rushed for the boat, but found very little left of it, and none of our provisions. Our can of kerosene had melted open, and all that was left of the boat was pretty well covered with the best fire-maker in the world, and burning fiercely. Our water-cask, however, was still safe, and we threw wet sand upon it until the fire around it was smothered. It was absolutely *the only thing* that we saved from that boat!

Well, it didn't take much reflection for us to see that we were in a first-class fix. We knew that southward the nearest settlement was at least two hundred miles away, and no water between. Northward, the nearest settlement was about one hundred and fifty miles away, on the Colorado River; but between it and us lay a great alluvial desert plain, cut up by numerous creeks and arms of the river, some of which would be very difficult to cross.

We took an account of stock, and found that we had, of provisions, a pot of beans, thirteen hard-tack biscuits and one go of coffee in the coffee-pot. That was absolutely all!

Our guns and cartridges had all been burned up, with the exception of a little sawed-off 20-gauge muzzle-loading shotgun. This grand weapon was one that somebody had given to Charlie to use in killing small birds, and for it we had exactly two loads. We also had some blankets, my sextant, a chart, a boat compass, field-glasses and some tools. Among the tools was a soldering-iron and some solder; and so in the morning, when we had looked things over, I took the tin lining out of our water-tight locker and made a couple of canteens. They were pretty rough, but they held water, and afterward served us mighty well. I don't see how by any possibility we could have pulled through without them.

After long and careful figuring, and calculating our chances, we decided to cross the Peninsula, and make our way to the west coast, where we knew there were some settlements. Back of us lay a strip of low country about six or eight miles wide, and then the high mountains began. We filled our canteens with water, took the compass, chart, sextant, the blankets, beans and hard-tack, and started westward for the mountains.

We reached the foot of the range, and spent a whole day in trying to make our way up the face of it; but I tell you those are the most straight-up-and-down mountains that you ever saw. It was nearly, if not quite, impossible to climb up that fearful eastern wall at least where we were. At last we decided that rather than use up our time and strength in such a fearful struggle as that was, with mighty doubtful results, we had better go back to our water-cask, fill our canteens again and try for the settlements on the Colorado. We therefore ate up the remnant of our beans, hung the empty pot on a dead ironwood tree—where I have no doubt it is to-night—and the next morning went back to the remains of the *Hilda*. It was then quite clear that our only chance lay in reaching a settlement on the lower Colorado.

That night we made some small cakes out of a small handful of flour—soaked in kerosene—that we found under some wet sand in a corner of the burned boat.

On the third morning we set out northward along the coast. We had seven hard-tack each, with one hundred and sixty miles of foot travel ahead of us before we could reach the Colonia Lerdo, above the head of tide water on the Colorado River. That was the nearest prospect of another dip into a bean-pot; and it seemed a mighty long way off!

The water question was our chief worry. We thought we might make between twenty and twenty-five miles a day over the sandy country that we would have to cross, and get on fairly well on one hard-tack apiece each day; but a gallon of water per man each day seemed a mighty slim allowance. However, things turned out better than we had expected. On the morning of the third day out from our boat, when we were rounding the bottom of San Felipe Bay, we saw a coyote trail running into a small, brushy flat. Believing that it led to water, we followed it, and found a small well, or spring, of good, wholesome water. This watering-place had been known to the seal-hunters and others for a long time, and we had heard of it in Yuma, but no one had been able to give us definite information about it.

We remained there all that day. On the rocks along the shore we found lots of oysters and I tell you they were *might-tee good!* I really doubt whether we could have pulled through without them. Charlie had a fish-hook in an outlying pocket, and with it he tried to catch a fish; but it was no go.

That night as we lay in our blankets, near the spring, I felt something tugging at my toe, and looked out. It was bright moonlight, almost as light as day; and there was a coyote trying to steal my blanket.

That was his undoing. I roused Charlie, who still carried his little shotgun with its two loads. Up to that time we had not seen a single living thing sufficiently near that it could be shot. The coyote didn't seem to mind in the least our speaking or rustling around, but just stood and looked at us, much as a dog might do. After a little trouble with a damp cap, and a hunt in his pockets for another, Charlie finally made out to shoot that coyote; and as it was nearly daylight we got up, skinned him and cooked a hind leg over the coals of the camp-fire.

That was positively the rankest thing in the shape of meat that I ever tackled. Even with oyster sauce it was almost uneatable. Apparently our dead friend had lived exclusively upon a fish diet, and spoiled fish at that. Although we ate all that leg, burned the other one almost to a crisp, took it along to gnaw upon, and tried to make the best of it, I am bound to say that from that day to this I never have enjoyed broiled coyote as an article of diet.

In the lower part of San Felipe Bay we found the wreck of a little schooner, lying on the beach, and near it we also found the remains of two rusty tin cans. Those we filled with oysters and started on northward.

For thirty miles below the mouth of the Colorado River the western coast is very flat, soft and muddy. The heavy tides flood the country for miles back from the shore of the Gulf. This we had discovered on our way down. We now were compelled to steer a course toward the westward mountains, and keep close to the foot-hills until sufficiently far north to strike across eastward for Hardy's Colorado, the nearest fresh water that we were sure about.

It took us four days of pretty hard pegging to make that stretch. Our rule was to march fifty minutes of every hour and rest ten minutes, and we adhered to it quite closely. I think it was very wise. I used the chart and compass to steer by, sighting on the mountain peaks. The low country was so obscured by haze and mirage that it was very difficult to navigate without mistakes. When at last I decided that it was time to turn east toward Hardy, our canteens were about dry. With our knives we punched a little hole in the lower corner of each, drained out the last drops of water into the particular parts of our throats that seemed to be dryest, then laid down the canteens for the next wayfarer in those flats who might need them.

We reached the Hardy about on schedule time, and we took two of the longest and wettest drinks on record. It seemed as if we had never before known what it was to be thirsty. After that we began to cast about for something that we could eat, but there really seemed to be nothing doing in that line. Charlie dug up his fish-hook once more, and with a piece of twine we set a night-line. We baited it with a big, fat and most edible-looking grasshopper. It seemed a pity to gamble the hopper on the remote chance of winning a fish, but like real sports we decided to risk it.

The result justified our sportiness; for the next morning, when we looked over the edge of the bank, we saw a fine, large mullet—lying on the mud, waiting for us. Now, as far as I know, the mullet is a fish that don't take a hook at all; but that one had managed to get himself hooked in the gills, and the tide had gone out and left him high and dry.

Charlie made a dive for him over the edge of the bank, and I always accused him of trying to catch that fish in his teeth, for he came up with his face covered with mud. We rolled the mullet on the grass, gloated over him, daubed clay on him, warmed him for a few minutes over our camp-fire, then being utterly unable to wait any longer, we fell to and had a very fine fish breakfast.

We crossed the Hardy, and headed into the tule and wild-flax brakes toward the Colonia Lerdo. It took us two days to make the river, for we were then getting weak, and it was mighty hard work pushing through those marshes. At last, however, we reached the west bank of the Colorado, at a point a few miles below the colony, but on the wrong side of the river; and it was a case of swim or starve. The river was wide, and the currents were mighty uncertain. We were afraid to tackle it with our clothes on, and without a raft.

We burned off some small dead willow trees, then burned them into lengths, and with our fish twine, some bark and osiers we made a little raft, large enough to carry our clothes and blankets, and other plunder.

The water seemed awfully cold, but we had to stand it. Fortunately, we were both of us fairly good swimmers, and we pushed the little raft ahead of us very successfully. After a long pull we reached the other side and landed on a comfortable sand-bar. After that our troubles soon came to an end. We soon found an old cattle-trail, and after following it about three miles we reached the colony.

In the camp of a couple of Americans who were down in that country hunting wild hogs we found a pot of freshly cooked beans. I don't like to think how many we ate; but I know that in the middle of the night I got up to have a few more. Before

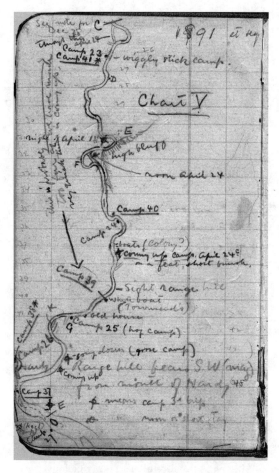

Figure 13.8. *Sketch map from Sykes's 1891–92 trip from Needles to San Felipe,* Hilda *diary. (Courtesy Diane Boyer)*

I knew it I had finished the pot, and was wishing for more. Talk about hunger! It took us a whole week to get enough!

We rested one day at the colony, then headed up for Yuma, which was about seventy-five miles away. The road was fair, and there were several watering-places, so we got on finely, and soon reached the metropolis of the Colorado desert.

McLean and Sykes's slog back to Yuma—after their abortive twenty-mile attempt to cross Baja—covered nearly one hundred eighty grueling miles in the skin-blasting wind, chill, and sun that constitute desert winters. Sykes later told his family that they had hiked mostly at night, resting under the scant shade afforded by shrubs during the day. Coyote was apparently featured twice on the menu: once as detailed in *Camp-Fires on Desert and Lava,* and again when they found a dead coyote in a water hole. They sampled water and meat, both were awful, but they had no choice. The men were exhausted and emaciated by the time they reached Yuma; Sykes lost sixty pounds from his five-foot-eleven-inch frame during the trek, much of it from dehydration. They were ravenous but

had to temper their desire to gorge. Eating watermelons helped them rejuvenate.

The two men had survived with their sense of adventure not only intact but strengthened. According to *The Colorado Delta* (1937:39–40) and *A Westerly Trend* (1944:225–228), Sykes was back for more in just a month's time. In February 1891, flood water charging down the lower Colorado River, much of it originating along the Gila River, began to overtop channel banks downstream of Yuma. The errant flow largely followed distributaries heading northwest. Sykes and a partner, identified as "Beer-Keg Tex," departed Yuma in mid-March. Their voyage took them by light boat to the Salton Sink via the Alamo drainage system, years before the famous engineering error that resulted in the creation of the Salton Sea proper. The men ultimately abandoned their boat in a mud flat and walked to the railroad siding of Volcano. Still, the sirens of the delta refused to leave Sykes alone. Come November, he was back again, this time with his brother and a friend named Will Hussey, in two boats named *Boojum* and *Snark*—names quite familiar to readers of British author Lewis Carroll. They boated from Needles to San Felipe and back to Yuma. Sykes kept a series of detailed sketch maps in the same memorandum book that contains the *Hilda* diary, along with a list of Mohave vocabulary words and a number of sketches. He returned on at least four more occasions before the nineteenth century turned over. By the time *The Colorado Delta* was published, in 1937, he had spent countless days trying to cure the "wanderlust bacillus" (as he called it) the delta induced in him.

In *A Westerly Trend* Sykes wrote that on his return to Yuma, "a newspaper was handed to me containing an account of the drowning of my brother," who had been placer-mining three miles below the Walnut Grove Dam on the Hassayampa River when the poorly constructed dam failed in the middle of the night, killing dozens of people downstream. "I was, of course, greatly distressed at the news but I was quickly relieved by receiving a letter from him in which he stated that although his drowning had undoubtedly taken place, the condition had been only temporary" (1944:224–225). Stanley and his two partners had narrowly escaped the outburst torrent, scrambling out of their tent and up a cactus-covered slope in their underwear as the debris-choked waters ripped toward their camp. It's a nice twist to the story, but it didn't happen that way: the dam had failed on February 22, 1890, a full ten months before Sykes and McLean embarked on their journey.

After the *Hilda* trip McLean and Sykes eventually returned to Flagstaff. Little is known about McLean's life other than occasional details disclosed in the local gossip columns. He and Sykes remained close friends, and McLean sometimes worked with both Godfrey and Stanley, who, by 1896, had started a fix-it shop on Aspen Street modestly called "Makers and Menders of Anything." The brothers each had married and fathered children; McLean evidently remained single. They took whatever work was available in territorial Flagstaff, which for the Sykeses meant everything from fixing bicycles to designing a portable wooden astronomical dome for Percival Lowell's 1896 Mars-viewing expedition to Mexico. (The dome was shipped back to Flagstaff and reassembled on the grounds of the Lowell Observatory, where it is still in use today.)

In 1903 McLean was hired to replace Peter McGonigle as the head of the Grand Canyon Electric Company's Bright Angel Camp, located at the bottom of the Grand Canyon. The company, incorporated by local pioneer David Babbitt, intended to dam Bright Angel Creek in order to produce power for Flagstaff. On July 27 McLean and McGonigle, on a training mission, hiked down the Bright Angel Trail to the scow kept for Colorado River crossings to the camp. They never made it across the river. Sykes, who had also worked for the Grand Canyon Electric Company, was busy celebrating his son Glenton's seventh birthday that same day with a tea party and a new tricycle, and preparing for a next-day departure for a family holiday in Oak Creek Canyon. When he learned of the disappearance of McLean and McGonigle a week later, he and fellow adventurer Will Hussey hiked into the Grand Canyon, built a boat, and joined the exhaustive but fruitless search for the men's bodies. The August 8, 1903, *Coconino Sun* listed McLean's age as forty-four and noted that he was believed to have relatives in New York. Sykes wrote of his friend in *A Westerly Trend* that "he had learned the trade of an iron-moulder, but had also been at times a cook, a fireman aboard ocean liners, and a whaler. There were obviously blank periods in his career, but, as was the custom in the West in

those days, these were not unduly enquired into. How, or why he had drifted so far West was one of these enigmas which, as far as I know, was never cleared up" (1944:210). Sykes weathered dozens of additional adventures before succumbing to death at the age of eighty-seven in 1948.

I inherited a chronic case of the wanderlust bacillus through my mother, Georgiana Sykes Boyer, daughter of Glenton, and have attempted to reduce the titer by visiting the area where the *Hilda* burned. In the fall of 2000 I sea-kayaked with two friends from the Río Hardy down the Baja Coast some two hundred miles, to San Luis Gonzaga. I had forgotten about the tiny note in my great-grandfather's diary that gave the latitude-longitude of the *Hilda's* carcass and had never even noticed the reference within the *Sailing Directions* extract. Coincidentally, we camped there anyway, among rolling sand dunes near the entrance to Estero Percebu. We deliberately camped the following night thirty miles south of San Felipe, which the *Arizona Enterprise* had listed as the site of the conflagration, at a place now called Santa Catarina on the topographic map. I vaguely hoped to find a few nuggets of suspicious charcoal or perhaps have a vision of some sort, neither of which happened. I did find beds of oysters, however, and reveled in the thought that maybe their distant ancestors helped sustain Sykes and McLean on their voyage. But it was earlier in the trip that I obtained my greatest insights into the *Hilda* epic: specifically, when slogging through thick, tenacious mud. It took over an hour to carry dunnage and kayaks up ten feet of bank as we sank thigh-deep into the muck. I had always wondered about the veracity of Great-Grandfather's proclaimed sixty-pound weight loss on the hike back to Yuma. The figure seemed entirely believable after I experienced both the volume and character of Colorado delta mud.

Acknowledgments

Special thanks to my grandfather for telling me stories when he was alive and leaving his friends to me when he died; to Bill Broyles for his kind assistance in preparing this chapter; to Steve Nelson for knowing that I would be crazy enough to join him on a delta sea-kayak trip; and to Steve Hayden for his encouragement and support, both on the sea kayak and while writing.

Fourteen

Native Peoples of the Dry Borders Region

BILL BROYLES, ADRIANNE G. RANKIN, AND RICHARD STEPHEN FELGER

Few of us modern people can stand on the edge of this grand dry borders desert and not wonder what daily life would be like out there. Surviving off the land for a few days in an emergency is one thing; living there for generations is quite another matter. Yet people have lived in the Dry Borders region for 13,000 years, maybe more. The earliest people were nomadic hunters and gatherers who found food, medicine, and materials in a broad spectrum of scattered natural resources, gathering wild plants, hunting animals, catching fish, and traveling long distances to collect salt, seashells, and obsidian. Like the Aborigines of Australia or Bushmen (San) of the Kalahari, these people made do with materials at hand; slept under rock overhangs, in brush huts, or in the open; and sometimes warmed themselves beside a fire or under animal pelts. They cracked rocks for hand tools, flaked chert and obsidian for knives and points, and rubbed stone on stone to grind seeds. They may have arrived from Asia with spear points and at some time gained the use of atlatls (Ferg & Peachey 1998) and bows with arrows. Like others in the Americas before contact with Europeans, they had fire but no metal tools or written language, and they traveled overland by foot. They lacked riding or draft animals until well after Europeans came to the region in 1540. Nevertheless, judging by the artifacts they left behind, these people were highly mobile and keenly attuned to their homeland.

At some point, in the few wet places and times, they began harvesting crops they had planted (see Felger, this volume, Chapter 15). A few localities with perennial water—such as waterholes at Tinajas Altas (Hartmann & Thurtle 2001), springs at Quitobaquito (Felger et al. 1992), and a man-made reservoir on Kuakatch Wash (Bayman & Palacios 2002)—allowed semi-permanent settlements. With the building materials they had at hand—trees, shrubs, reeds, and grasses—they constructed small shelters and one-room dwellings, some of them partly subterranean. Adobe and rock-walled buildings are known from north and east of the Dry Borders region but not within it. Along the seacoast, people drank freshwater from small artesian pools, and along the Gila and Colorado rivers they planted gardens and fields as well as caught fish and hunted game.

At some time they began making baskets. By A.D. 200 they had pottery for cookware and storage vessels for grain, seeds, fruit, dried meat, and water. They painted pictographs, pecked petroglyphs on rock faces, and "wrote" story sticks, records that require a living interpreter to mnemonically decode the symbols (Southworth 1914; Underhill 1938b).

In the last seven centuries (roughly thirty-five generations), two major events redirected human destiny. The first was the increasingly variable climatic pattern of drought and flood beginning in the fourteenth century A.D. This pattern, presumably a response to the onset of the Little Ice Age, pervaded the greater Southwest from New Mexico's Chaco Canyon to southern California's Salton Sea and northwestern Sonora (Fagan 2000). During 1381–84, large-scale flooding caused the collapse of irrigation in the Salt River valley, followed by a ten-year period of low water flow, according to stream-flow reconstructions of the Salt and Gila rivers. A severe drought in the Southwest occurred from about 1550 to 1600 (Graybill et al. in press).

The second event was the arrival in 1540 of Europeans, who brought with them new technologies, languages, social structure, diseases, crops, livestock, and lifeways that disrupted or supplanted indigenous cultures. These events radically redistributed native people and shook social structures, as well as changed technology and food production.

Nevertheless, despite harsh and variable conditions, the past peoples throughout the region lived rich, full lives, both before and after the arrival of Europeans. For example, perishable pre-European items such as blankets, clothing, baskets, and wooden objects found in caves and other contexts exhibit vibrant use of color and symbolic imagery. Likewise, ethnographic studies of the twentieth century have captured glimpses of the richness of the cosmology, mythology, songs, and performance ritual that pervaded the earlier cultures, and only recently are we beginning to appreciate the strongly historical character of traditional oral narrative (e.g., Masse in press; Masse & Espenak in press; Teague 1993; Whitely 2002). Clearly, the past peoples of the Dry Borders region were gifted observers of their natural environment and had knowledge of lands and peoples hundreds of miles from their home villages or seasonal settlements.

Original Settlers

The Paleoindian Period

Archaeologists debate the identity and arrival time of the earliest residents in the New World (Table 14.1). Conventional theory holds that the original inhabitants crossed the Bering Strait during the late Pleistocene when lower sea levels created a land bridge between Siberia and Alaska (see Madsen 2004). From here theories diverge. In the traditional model (Haury 1975), the first people to reach the continental United States were the Clovis people—big-game hunters who tipped their spears with distinctively fluted points. Clovis hunters arrived in North America about 11,000 B.C. and spread rapidly southward, their descendants soon reaching the southern tip of South America. According to this model, the American Southwest was first occupied during this southward expansion.

In this model the preceramic period (the time before pottery was made) has two segments. The first, characterized by several distinctive types of large spear points, is the Paleoindian period, extending from about 11,000 to 7,500 B.C. The second segment, called the Archaic, extends from about 7,500 B.C. to the appearance of pottery about A.D. 200. The Archaic period is characterized by smaller projectile points and an abundance of grinding stones used for processing foods. Accounts of these sequences can be found in Ahl-

Figure 14.1. Campsite artifacts: obsidian, seashell, bone, sherds. (Photo by Paul Ezell)

strom 1998 and 2001, Altschul and Rankin in press, Hayden 1998, McGuire & Schiffer 1982, McLellan & Vogler 1977, Rankin 1995, Whittlesey 1994, and Whittlesey et al. 1994.

Clovis points are best known from southeastern Arizona, where they have been found at several mammoth-butchering sites. In the Dry Borders area Paleoindian points are known from isolated surface finds. For example, Ezell (1954) discovered a Clovis point during his survey of Organ Pipe Cactus National Monument and Cabeza Prieta National Wildlife Refuge. Another Paleoindian point was collected from a gravel terrace adjacent to a wash in the northern Gila Mountains. Paleoindian artifacts have been found scattered on the surface in the vicinity of the Crater Range as well. Mammoth remains have been found in ciénega deposits at Quitovac, Sonora, and in a gravel pit at Growler near the Gila River (Ahlstrom 1998). Before the end of the Paleoindian period the mammoths and other Pleistocene megafaunal species were extinct, arguably as the result of overhunting (Martin & Klein 1984).

The main competing model agrees that the first Americans came from Siberia either by way of the Bering Strait land bridge or by seacraft, but it maintains that the first migration took place earlier—possibly *much* earlier—than Clovis (Dillehay 2000). According to this view, people were already living in the Dry Borders region when the Clovis hunters appeared. Some archaeologists subdivide the Preceramic period into the Malpais culture followed by the San Dieguito culture and Amargosa phases I and II (Hayden 1976, 1998; McGuire & Schiffer 1982). Another model divides

TABLE 14.1. *Time Frames*

Preceramic: first people to A.D. 200			
	Paleoindian: 12,000 B.C.–7,500 B.C.		
	Huckell 1984: Early Middle Late	Rogers 1939, Hayden 1976: Malpais San Dieguito I, II, III	Haury 1975: Clovis
	Archaic: 7500 B.C.–A.D 200		
	Huckell 1984: Early Middle Late	Rogers 1939, Hayden 1976: Amargosan	Haury 1950: Cochise
Ceramic: A.D 200–A.D 1540 (Formative period)			
	Hohokam Patayan Trincheras		
Early Historic: A.D 1540–A.D 1848 (Spanish/Mexican period)			
Late Historic: A.D 1848–present (American period and Mexican period)			

the Paleoindian periods into Early, Middle, and Late (Huckell 1984). All models agree, however, that for several thousand years the earliest people in the region would have found the climate, habitat, plants, animals, and surface water supply far more hospitable to human life than they are today (see Van Devender 1990, this volume).

Archaic Period

In the Archaic period (7500 B.C. to A.D. 200) a changing climate caused plants and animals to shift their geographic and elevational ranges, and the Dry Borders region evolved into the modern Sonoran Desert (see Van Devender, this volume). Archaic peoples in the area based their economy on gathering wild plant foods and hunting smaller game animals such as deer, antelope, and rabbits. For southeastern Arizona, many archaeologists refer to the Archaic period by the name Cochise culture and divide it into three stages called Sulphur Springs, Chiricahua, and San Pedro. For southwestern Arizona, some archaeologists who favor the Mojave–Great Basin model for the preceramic period refer to these times as Amargosa phases I and II (Hayden 1967, 1976; Rogers 1939). More recently, Huckell (1984) has divided the

Archaic into three stages: Early (7500–5000 B.C.), Middle (5000–2000/1000 B.C.), and Late (2000/1000 B.C.–A.D. 300). Both pottery and cultivated plants make their initial appearance toward the end of this period.

Ceramic Period

The Ceramic period begins about A.D. 200, when pottery in the Southwest first was produced in large quantities and became regionally differentiated. Many archaeologists have begun to call this the Formative period because research shows that agricultural canals go back to 1200–800 B.C. and ceramics began about 800–400 B.C. (Altschul 1995; Ezzo & Deaver 1998; Masse 1980, Masse 1991; McGuire & Villalpando 1993; Whittlesey et al. 1994). In the Dry Borders region three main cultures produced ceramics: Hohokam, Patayan, and Trincheras. Hohokam ceramics generally are plain, red, red-on-brown, red-on-buff, and polychromes with a variety of decorations (Andrews & Bostwick 2000; Barstad 1999; Haury 1976; Schiffer 1982). Patayan ceramics may show a "stucco" finish, recurved rims, and distinctive shoulders (Waters 1982, 1992). Most Patayan pottery found in the Dry Borders region is known as Colorado River

Buff Ware. The Trincheras culture left distinctive terraced hillsides, rock enclosures, and purple-on-red and polychrome pottery with sites ranging into southern Arizona (Gifford 1946; Hoover 1941; Johnson 1963; McGuire & Schiffer 1982). However, clearly distinguishing these three cultures, especially by relying on ceramic traits, is the subject of much debate.

Sorting and interpreting artifacts and then drawing cultural boundaries over time is an elusive and difficult enterprise confused by changing technologies, moving and mingling populations, trade, and an incomplete, imperfectly dated record of material cultures (e.g., McGuire & Schiffer 1982; Reid & Whittlesey 1997). Where Hohokam, Anasazi, and Mogollon are concerned, "traditional concepts of archaeological cultures . . . are proving too static to capture the dynamic culture history of past peoples" (Ferguson et al. 2004:2). And by extension, the ethnogenesis of Tohono O'odham, Hopi, and Zuni as well as other cultures displays a "complex interplay of migration, intermarriage, and linguistic exchange," an interplay that the Hopis, for example, call *Hisatsinom,* or Our Ancient People (Ferguson et al. 2004:13).

Early Historic Period (A.D. 1540–1848)

When Europeans began arriving in the Dry Borders region in 1540, they attempted to distinguish and identify the peoples they encountered. Explorers, soldiers, missionaries, travelers, and researchers lumped together various people who seemed to share territory, language, physical characteristics, and culture. They recorded "Sand Papago" in the Pinacate and Cabeza Prieta, "Papago" in the eastern Goldwater and Organ Pipe; "Cocopah," "Pai Pai," and "Yuma" along the lower Colorado; "Pima" in Sonoran Desert National Monument, and "Maricopa" along the Gila River. Other, smaller groups also were given tribal names. A group might have a name for itself, names applied by neighboring tribes, and names applied by Europeans. However, for several reasons, neither the names nor the territories assigned by the Europeans had strong basis in social or geographical reality as recognized by the Indians themselves: (1) Tribes overlapped, mingled, and intermarried. For example, between 1833 and 1838 the Halchidhomas moved in with their neighbors the Maricopas (Forbes 1965), but the name *Maricopa* itself did not appear in print until 1846 (Kroeber & Fontana

1986). Blurring even tribal distinctions themselves, social units sometimes were based on family, leadership, lineage, or dialect and language. "The actual aboriginal organization of southwestern Arizona was much more fluid than the model the conquering Europeans tried to force it into" (McGuire 1982b:61).

(2) The archaeological and ethnographic records are incomplete. Some information is skewed toward spoken accounts, and no clear model has been developed for southwestern Arizona (McGuire 1982b, 1982c). (3) Tribes were highly mobile. For example, it is surmised that the Cocopahs came downriver from the north, perhaps the Great Basin, two thousand to three thousand years ago and settled along the Colorado River between Yuma and Blythe. But starting about A.D. 1450, when the Salton Sea entered one of its drying cycles, the Quechans moved from their homes around the Salton Sea to the river lands occupied by the Cocopahs, who in turn moved into the lower Colorado and its delta (Williams 1983). And (4) indigenous people did not define their territory in modern, platted terms. Robert K. Thomas comments on the difficulty of getting Hia C'ed O'odham to generalize their geography: "Papagos do not, for instance, name ranges of mountains. They name peaks. It is difficult to pin Papagos down as to what a range of mountains is. Also, they will not put a boundary between their country and the country of other tribes. They will say, 'We traveled here, and we gathered here, and the country of the Yuma is farther down the river.' But they will not say that the Gila Mountains were the boundary between the Papago and the Yuma. It is easy to get them to say this is the original country of the Aliquippa people, but if you ask them where their country is, they will invariably give you their fields" (1991:293). Or as Vinito Garcia succinctly puts it, "Anglos gave us all these present [tribal] names, but we call ourselves O'odham people" (quoted in Bell et al. 1980:75).

Archaeologists today face similar problems as they try to match historically known peoples with prehistoric cultures known only from archaeological remains. Although it has been inferred that the modern speakers of Yuman languages—Cocopahs, Quechans, Pai Pai, and others—are descendants of the archaeologically defined Patayan culture, and that modern speakers of Piman dialects—Tohono O'odham, Hia C'ed O'odham,

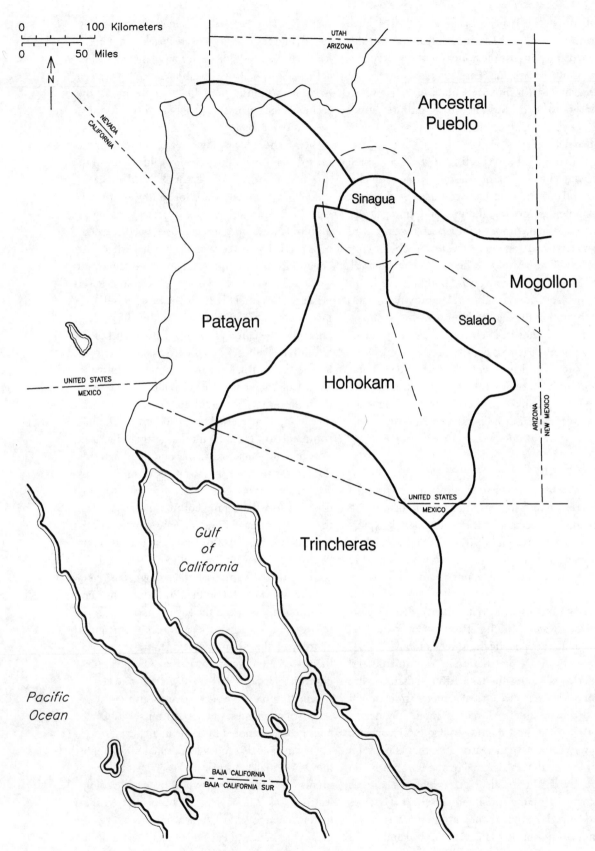

Figure 14.2. *Major ceramic groups of the Southwest, A.D. 200–1540. These generalized boundaries, based on artifact sites, may overlap and changed over time. Some types of pottery were exchanged widely. From Reid & Whittlesey 1997 and Walker & Bufkin 1986. (Map by Ron Beckwith)*

Akimel O'odham—are descendants of the prehistoric Hohokam (see Hale & Harris 1979), the connections are tenuous. The identity of the descendants of the Trincheras culture, if any, is not known.

Late Historic Period (1848–present)

With the end of the war in 1848 between the United States and Mexico, the California gold rush of 1849, and the Gadsden Purchase of 1854, much of the Dry Borders region became U.S. territory. The influx of settlers in southwestern Arizona and demographic changes in northwestern Sonora affected the ranges and resources of native peoples living on the land. Most tribes were forced into smaller territories or onto reservations; they lost access to traditional resources, and for better or worse, they increasingly adopted American and Mexican economies and lifestyles.

Historic Tribes

Residents

At least a score of Native American tribes claim a piece of the Dry Borders region as part of their homeland or history. Many tribes blend their history with religious stories and legends and are reticent to discuss sacred matters outside the tribe (Masse in press). Also, at least some traditional knowledge has been lost. Consequently, much important information is lightly documented in public literature.

The Hia C'ed O'odham had the fewest members but lived in the largest territory with the sparsest resources and driest land, although some resources were rich and concentrated. They ranged over what is today western Organ Pipe Cactus National Monument and the Goldwater Range, Cabeza Prieta National Wildlife Refuge, and the Pinacate and Alto Golfo biosphere reserves east of the Colorado delta. Outsiders labeled groups of them Sand Papago, Areneño, and Pinacateño. Variant spellings of their own name for themselves include Hiatit Ootam, HiaCed O'odham, Hia-ced O'odham, and Hia C-ed O'odham. They are closely related to the Tohono O'odham and the Akimel O'odham. Historically, their traditional desert homeland was called "western Papaguería" and the people, "Papagos." Western Papaguería extends from south of the Gila River to the Gulf of California and from the Colorado River east to the

Figure 14.3. Painted pottery, sherd. (Photo by Bill Broyles)

western edge of the modern Tohono O'odham Reservation.

Small families and groups of Hia C'ed O'odham were mobile, specializing in hunting and gathering. Some tended a few small fields of maize, squashes, and tepary beans (Lumholtz 1912). Some visited the delta and lower Colorado River to obtain materials such as willow and arrowweed for bows and arrows (Felger this volume, Chapter 15). Though the Hia C'ed were semi-nomadic in the sense of being mobile in their opportunistic quest for resources, they were not aimless wanderers. As Crosswhite (1981:51) noted of O'odham in general, "A great deal of planning and hard work were required to exploit a combination of plants and environmental resources which were available for only short periods of time during the changing seasons of the year." The Hia C'ed did have a few permanent settlements, such as Quitobaquito and Ajo, and they farmed at Suvuk and Jose Juan temporal, among other places (Doyel & Eiler 2003; Hill & Bruder 2000; Lumholtz 1912). Their expansive homeland of ocean shore and desert probably supported a few hundred people at most (Fontana 1974; Ives 1965; Lumholtz 1912). Firsthand accounts of their lifestyle include Bell et al. 1980, Childs 1954, and Zepeda 1985, but there are few primary sources documenting them (McGuire 1982b). Hia C'ed O'odham creation stories are set in Sierra Pinacate. Historically, they traveled as far as the Kofa Mountains (which they called Ge Huduj Do'ag, or the Big Middle Mountains) in Arizona, and Caborca (Kawulk, or Little Hill) and Hermosillo (To:ta Waippia, or White Wells) in Sonora.

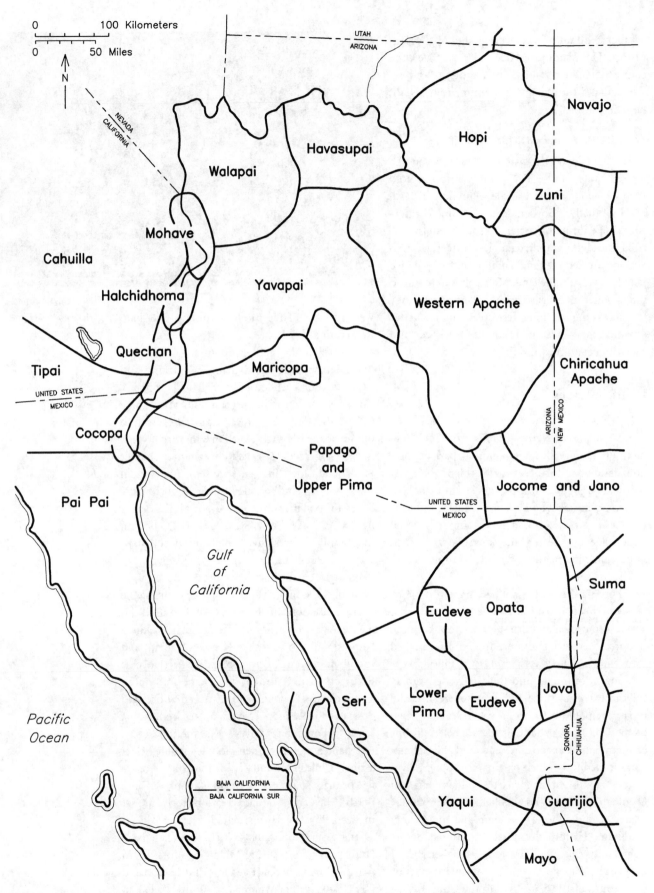

Figure 14.4. *Tribes of the Southwest, eighteenth century. These boundary lines arbitrarily suggest tribal areas that changed over time. In many cases tribes shared lands, lands were not occupied by anyone, or tribes moved seasonally or permanently to other areas. (From larger depictions in* Handbook of North American Indians, *vols. 8 and 9 [Washington, D.C.: Smithsonian Institution], courtesy the Smithsonian Institution)*

Today the Hia C'ed O'odham live in communities around the Dry Borders, in such towns as Caborca, Gila Bend, Ajo, and Phoenix. The Hia C'ed O'odham have no reservation of their own because in the Papago Land Claims Settlement of 1968 the group was included within the Tohono O'odham Nation, and some administrators believed the Hia C'ed O'odham were extinct. As a group they own land at the Darby Well cemetery and continue to work for their own reservation lands near Ajo (Allen 1996; Eiler & Doyel in press); in 2005 the Tohono O'odham Nation purchased 640 acres of private land for them south of Why, Arizona (Medrano 2005). This acquisition may become a tribal district (*Ajo Copper News* 2005). The Hia C'ed O'odham who have persevered—and there are perhaps more than a thousand living descendants—have done so by moving out of the heart of their aboriginal homeland. They also dropped their native subsistence based on hunting, gathering, and small-scale farming in favor of a cash economy.

The Tohono O'odham (formerly called Papagos) generally live east of the Dry Borders region, but they used parts of Sonoran Desert National Monument and Organ Pipe as homelands and resource areas and traveled through the Goldwater, Pinacate, and Alto Golfo to reach the Gulf of California. Such extended trips to the ocean were partly ceremonial and included purification rites as well as gathering salt, which symbolically brought rain from the ocean back to the desert (Underhill 1938a, 1946). Only a few villages, now abandoned, are known to have stood within what is now the Goldwater Range, where the people also traditionally hunted, gathered, and traveled. No historic villages are known within Organ Pipe, Cabeza Prieta, or Sonoran Desert National Monument. Like the Cocopahs and Quechans, the Tohono O'odham operated under a "minimax strategy" of subsistence, enlisting a wide variety of resources and wide range of economic alternatives instead of focusing all their effort on a few resources; this strategy met their minimum needs and guaranteed productivity with less detriment to their environment. A key to understanding their acculturation is that new plants and animals were added to their range of options, not substituted for traditional options (Hackenberg 1983).

The modern Tohono O'odham Reservation is south of Sonoran Desert National Monument

Figure 14.5. *Early Historic period ground figure. (Photo by Bill Broyles)*

and east of Organ Pipe. Created in 1916, the reservation covers 2,774,536 acres (see Erickson 2003; Fontana 1983a, 1989, 1999).

The Akimel O'odham (River Pimas) lived and still live along the middle Gila River near Maricopa, Arizona. They hunted and gathered in what is now Sonoran Desert National Monument (Rea 1998). They traded with and occasionally fought with the Quechans. They were closely allied with the Tohono O'odham in culture, trade, and language (Ezell 1983). Some are affiliated with the Ak Chin Indian Community ten miles east of the monument, and many live on the Gila River Indian Reservation south of Phoenix.

All the O'odham—Hia C'ed O'odham (Sand People), Tohono O'Odham (Desert People), and Akimel O'odham (River People)—constructed villages. The semi-nomadic Hia C'ed O'odham built ramadas at Quitobaquito and other perennial encampments. The Tohono O'odham, who moved from winter homes in the foothills to summer homes near their farms, were called the Two-Village People (Fontana 1974). The sedentary Akimel O'odham, known as the One-Village People (Fontana 1983a, b), farmed year-round and resided along the Gila River or intermittent arroyos where they could plant crops on the floodplains and divert runoff into the fields (Rea 1997, 1998).

The Cocopahs lived in the lower Colorado River valley and delta. In Mexico, *Cucapá* is the preferred spelling; American members of the tribe voted for *Cocopah* as the name of the tribe and reservation in 1974. Ancestors of the Cocopahs, it

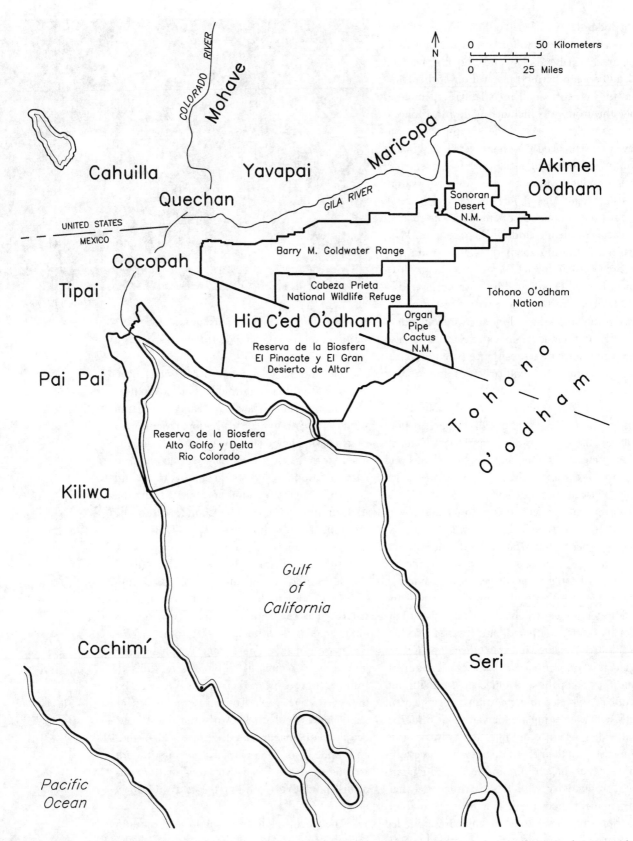

Figure 14.6. *Tribes of the Dry Borders region, about 1850, overlain on the six bio-reserves. Territorial boundaries were dynamic, changing with seasons and migrations. Some areas were uninhabited. (Map by Ron Beckwith)*

is believed, migrated from the north two thousand to three thousand years ago and settled along the Colorado and Gila rivers. About A.D. 1400–1500 they were displaced farther southward into the delta by Quechans and Mohaves (Williams 1983). When Francisco de Ulloa, the first European to visit the delta, arrived in 1539, he saw no people, for none lived at the river's mouth (Martí 1995), but a year later Hernando de Alarcón and the Cocopahs made contact along the lower Colorado River (Flint & Flint 2005). Owing to the river's flooding harvest cycles, the Cocopahs remained relatively mobile. In 1776 Franciscan friar Francisco Garcés estimated the Cocopah population at about 3,000 (Coues 1900:2:443), but by 1905 the population was about 1,500 (Kelly 1977). The decrease may be due to migration to better farmlands, intertribal warfare, introduced diseases, or the lure of modern amenities in towns, or the higher number may be an overestimate (Kelly 1977; Stone 1991). Four autonomous Cocopah bands lived in the delta in 1900: Wi Ahwir, Kwakwarsh, Mat Skrui, and Hwanyak (Kelly 1977; Williams 1983).

The Cocopahs traditionally constructed enclosed winter houses and open-sided summer houses. They used the river extensively for transportation, traveling on tule balsas and log rafts. They were good swimmers and ferried goods and children in large ollas or baskets. Their hunting and gathering grounds extended throughout the Colorado delta and, via a system of trails connecting waterholes, westward into the oak and pine-oak slopes of Sierra Cucapá, Sierra Juárez, and Sierra El Mayor (Castetter & Bell 1951:56–58; MacDougal 1907; Williams 2004). The Cocopahs and their neighbors the Quechans were quick to trade with Europeans and to adopt a cash economy. They sold melons and grain to early Spanish travelers, and by the 1850s they were employed to provide wood for steamboats and to work as deckhands. In 1870 a number of Cocopahs left the delta to help construct the railroad heading east from Yuma (John Laird, personal communication 2004).

Mexican Cucapás still live in what has been designated the Alto Golfo Biosphere Reserve, where they practice fishing as well as farming. Many American Cocopahs run modern farms. The Cocopah Indian Reservation, established in 1917, includes three areas south of Yuma totaling about 8,000 acres. As of 2002 the population was 1,088. In Mexico the main settlement is at El Mayor Cucapá, Baja California. Castetter & Bell (1951:37) note that because of warfare and relocations since first European contact, of all the peoples along the Colorado "only the uppermost and lowest, namely the Mohave and Cocopah, have retained their identity and approximately the same habitats for more than three hundred years." Cocopah history is recounted in Williams 1983.

The Quechan tribe (Yuma Indians) lived along the Colorado River near Yuma. Their stories and legends tell of trips to the Gila and Tinajas Altas mountains. Their war stories recount battles in the Maricopa Mountains and a raid through the present-day Sonoran Desert National Monument as far east as Maricopa (Kroeber & Fontana 1986). Members of the Quechan and the O'odham tribes occasionally lived together and intermarried, and early Europeans noted bilingual speakers along the Colorado River. The Quechans gathered limberbush *(Jatropha cuneata)* in the Mohawk Mountains to use in basketry. Quechan messengers and guides ranged across the Pinacate, Goldwater, Organ Pipe, and Cabeza Prieta protected areas as far east as Sonoyta and Tubutama, Sonora (Forbes 1965). Their history and lifeways are recounted in Bee 1983, Castetter & Bell 1951, Forbes 1965, and Spier 1933. The Quechan Reservation is at Yuma.

The Pai Pai presently claim 400 tribal members. They once lived from the western Colorado River delta to the Pacific shore but now are centered in a *zona indígena* near Santa Catarina, Baja California, and another at San Isidoro, Baja California. They were at one time known as Akwa'ala, one of several Yuman-speaking groups (Owen 1969; Williams 2004).

The Maricopas and Cocomaricopas largely moved away from the Colorado River to the middle Gila River between 1838 and 1852 (Harwell et al. 1983), settling near Laveen, Gila Bend, and Agua Caliente, Arizona. Their history, remembered in song and story, includes battles with the Quechans in the Mohawk Mountains and trips through the present-day Sonoran Desert National Monument from Gila Bend to Maricopa (see Spier 1933). Another name for Maricopa is Xalychidom Piipaash ('people who live toward the water'). Today the Maricopas share two reservations. One, established in 1879 and shared with Salt River Pimas, covers 53,600 acres sixty miles northeast of Sonoran Desert National Monument. Together they call themselves the Salt River Pima–Maricopa Indian

Community. The second is the Ak Chin Reservation, covering 21,840 acres east of Sonoran Desert National Monument.

Kroeber and Fontana (1986:34) remind us that "the Maricopa were not originally a 'tribe' in the formal sense of the word." Instead, they were an amalgam of at least five groups of Yumans, including the Kohuana, Halchidhoma, Kaveltcadom, and Halyikwamai (Castetter & Bell 1951). (The Kohuana were also called Kawhan, Coana, Cohuana, and Cajuenche. The Halchidhoma were labeled Alchedomas and Jalshedun. The Halyikwamai appear in the historic literature as Quicama, Tlalliquamallas, Quiquimas, and Jalliquamay. The Cocomaricopa were Kaveltcadom or Opa. From the swirl of duplicate names, it is easy to see how Europeans were a bit confused about tribal identities [see Ezell 1963b].)

The Tipai and Ipai lived on the banks of the Colorado River, as far south as the delta, and migrated seasonally into the mountains west of the delta (Castetter & Bell 1951; Gifford 1931; Kelly 1977). They also visited the Tinajas Altas Mountains, perhaps to hunt desert bighorn sheep. Tipai and Ipai have also been known by many names, particularly Diegueño, Kamia, and Kumeyaay (Luomala 1978). Today some Kamia live in Baja California and some in southern California.

The Kiliwa once inhabited the western Colorado delta as far south as San Felipe, which was their fishing center, but more recently they moved westward into the mountains, where their main village is Arroyo León, Baja California (Meigs 1939; Owen 1969).

Visitors

Other tribes had or claim to have had some relation with the Dry Borders region but do not, and did not, live within one of the six protected areas. For example, Apaches, Mohaves, and Seris used the area for passage, trade, or resources. They may have crossed the area to explore, harvest salt and a variety of seashells from the gulf, practice ceremonies and rites, trade, visit friends or relatives, talk politics, make war, form alliances, or relocate. Or they may have traded only indirectly with those living in the area. Inter-Indian trade of materials and ideas was far more widespread than most modern people imagine. For example, in 1539, about two months after the vanguard of the Coronado expedition reached Cibola, New Mexico, "linguis-tically unrelated peoples more than 350 miles away already had detailed and quite accurate descriptions of Eurupeans. And at least one individual from the lower Gila River had been to Cibola recently and had personally seen the foreigners" (Flint & Flint 2005:186). "Below Yuma, Arizona," Ford (1983:712) notes, "Spaniards interviewed well-traveled Indians who were familiar with the Zuni. They saw Hopi cotton textiles worn by lower Colorado River Yuman farmers and the ubiquitous buffalo-skin robes available throughout the area." Cotton from southern Arizona was traded to residents of the Colorado Plateau. Seashells, obsidian, pottery, and baskets were exchanged throughout the Southwest by A.D. 1000.

A wide network of trails crossed the Dry Borders region and the Southwest. Heizer (1978:692) reports that some California Indians, and we can assume others, had precise knowledge of geography beyond their territories, as "shown by their ability to make 'sand maps' that were crude topographic renderings." Traders sometimes traveled long distances; at other times goods passed along a succession of middlemen (see Flint & Flint 2005; Felger, this volume, Chapter 15). Ford mentions that "Hopi blankets reached the Quechan through exchange from the Havasupai, Walapai, and Mohave. Sea shells . . . reached Hopi through the Chumash, Mohave, Walapai, and Havasupai. Coming from the east, Comanche buffalo robes passed from Eastern Pueblo traders to Zuni, Hopi, Navajo, and then along the old shell trade networks to the Colorado River Yuman tribes and into Mexico" (1983:718). According to Heizer, "grooved stone axes of Puebloan origin are found widely throughout California," as were decorated pottery and cotton blankets (1978:691), the cotton having originated in fields along the lower Colorado River.

The Seris (Comcáac) may have traveled by foot or reed boat as far north as the Colorado delta, but lands within the Alto Golfo biosphere were not considered traditional territory for them (Bowen 1976, 2000; Felger & Moser 1985). The Seris have a name for the Colorado River and names for "campsites as far north as the mouth of the Colorado River" (Felger & Moser 1985:96, Mary Beck Moser, personal communication 2003). Williams (1974) reports that the Cocopahs had contact and occasional trade with the Seris. Today the Seris inhabit the Sonora coast from Punta Chueca to El Desemboque San Ignacio.

The Apaches, who arrived in the Southwest about A.D. 1400 from Canada (Opler 1983), raided for food, livestock, and slaves as far west as Puerto Peñasco, Ajo, and Gila Bend. One of Lumholtz's (1912:291) sources reported that Apaches formerly raided as far west as Sierra Blanca, near Puerto Peñasco, where Sand Papagos "often camped in the winter-time." Bell et al. (1980) recount the capture of two Hia C'ed O'odham girls near Sonoyta by Apaches and tell of encounters with Apaches near Quitobaquito. Thomas (1991) also records raiding. In southwestern Arizona, Apaches took slaves from at least the Pimas, Maricopas, and Tohono O'odham (Bailey 1973; Basso 1971; Goodwin 1942) and had alliances with Yavapais north of the lower Gila River. They likely were Tonto or San Carlos Apaches, both of which groups now reside primarily on reservations in eastern Arizona. The term *Apache del desierto* came to be applied to other marauders in northwestern Sonora, such as the Hia C'ed O'odham who attacked forty-niners (Childs 1954).

The Zunis (A:shiwi) live on the Zuni Reservation in northwestern New Mexico; however, tribal representatives recognize rock art symbols found on the Goldwater Range (Adrianne Rankin, personal observation). Stone (1986) notes that the Colorado River Yuman tribes traded marine shell to the Zunis. At least two Zuni clans claim to have descended from desert people, possibly the Hohokam.

The Hopis, too, may have traveled into the Goldwater Range. Tribal elders recognize rock art symbols found on the Goldwater Range (Adrianne Rankin, personal observation). Hopi religious stories recall trips to the lower Colorado River, perhaps as far as the ocean. The Colorado River Yumans traded cotton to the Hopis and in return received woven cotton cloth (Stone 1986). Ferguson (1997) notes that Hopi cultural advisers might consider Palatkwapi (lands south of the Hopi mesas) to include portions of Western Papaguería. Lyons (2003) places Hopi connections as far south as the San Pedro River of southern Arizona.

The Navajos (Diné), like the Apaches, are relative newcomers to the Southwest, having migrated from Canada five hundred to a thousand years ago (Brugge 1983). Williams (1974) reports that the Cocopahs had contact and occasional trade with the Navajos.

The Mohaves, members of the Yuman linguistic group, may have left the Mojave Desert as early as A.D. 1150 to live along the Colorado River (Stewart 1983). Williams (1974) reports that the Cocopahs had contact and at least occasional trade with the Mohaves. Some Mohaves were superb endurance runners able to cover as many as one hundred miles in a day; they also swam and floated the Colorado River (Stewart 1983). They traveled through the Sand Tank and Sauceda mountains of the Goldwater Range and Sonoran Desert National Monument to obtain obsidian (Mitchell & Shackley 1995; Shackley & Tucker 2001; Shackley 2005) and to the Gulf of California for seashells and salt to be used for ceremony and seasoning. Salt and shell trips would have taken them through the Goldwater, Cabeza, Pinacate, and Alto Golfo reserves and possibly Organ Pipe. Traditional Mohave lands extend along the Colorado River from below the Bill Williams River to north of Lake Mojave and include the Colorado River Indian Reservation and Fort Mojave Reservation.

The Yavapais at one time roamed over much of western Arizona—ten million acres by one estimate (Khera & Mariella 1983). A southern group named Tolkapaya lived north of the Gila River and Goldwater Range (Gifford 1936) but occasionally hunted or traveled south of the river and into the Goldwater. The Haka-Whatapa, another group of Western Yavapais, lived in the Kofa and Castle Dome region (Stone 1986) and likely visited the Goldwater Range. Tribal elders from the Prescott and Camp Verde Yavapai reservations recognized petroglyph symbols—particularly rattlesnake motifs—that they saw in the Goldwater Range (Adrianne Rankin, personal observation). Elders also report traveling by foot to the Gulf of California in times past, presumably through the Goldwater, Cabeza Prieta, Pinacate, and Alto Golfo reserves. The Yavapai creation story is set in the Gila Mountains.

The Walapai (Hualapai) and Havasupai tribes speak Yuman languages and so may share stories and history with other Yuman speakers, but it is not known if these groups visited the Dry Borders region. Gifford (1933) and Williams (1974) report that the Cocopahs had contact and occasional trade with the Walapais. The Walapai reservation is in northwestern Arizona; the Havasupai reservation is between the Walapai Reservation and Grand Canyon National Park.

The Colorado River Yuman tribes also traded with Pacific coast tribes, receiving abalone shell from them (Ives 1961; see Felger, this volume, Chapter 15). Gabrielinos of the Los Angeles basin and Channel Islands traded seashells, steatite, and other items as far east as central Arizona, generally by way of middlemen (Bean & Smith 1978). The Kitanemuk of the western Mojave Desert traded with the Quechans along the lower Colorado River (Blackburn & Bean 1978). The Cahuillas lived northwest of the Salton Sea, and some of them were specialized traders who traveled as far east as the Gila River to obtain goods (Bean 1978). Further research is needed on prehistoric and historic intertribal trade and travel.

In the twentieth century most of the Dry Borders region was a *despoblado*, nearly devoid of people dwelling on the land. The José Juan Orozco family lived at Quitobaquito until 1955, Abraham Armenta lived at Armenta Well in Organ Pipe, and the Chico Suni family lived west of Darby Well at Chico Shunie Well in the Cabeza Prieta until the last member, Tulpo Suni, died in 1999. In 1920 Kirk Bryan (1925) reported no one living between Quitobaquito and Yuma except an anonymous caretaker at the Fortuna Mine. In what became Organ Pipe a string of American settlers—Lon Blankenship, Rube Daniels, the Gray family, the Millers, and others—tried to ranch, with poor results. In the Cabeza Prieta Jim Havins, Alton Netherlin, Angel Monreal, and Dan Drift tried to ranch or mine. In the Goldwater Range the Smith family dug prospect tunnels, and several ranchers grazed cattle in the eastern Goldwater. In Sonoran Desert National Monument Tom Farley built a rock cabin and the Bender family ran a gas station and cattle ranch (see McGee & Hofstra, this volume). In the Pinacate the Juan Bermúdez family operated a truck stop and drilled a well for cattle at what became the Grijalva Ranch, a man lived in an abandoned car at a spot now known as El Solito, and several groups of *ejiditeros* dreamed of prosperity by raising crops or livestock.

Today, because of agency restrictions, no one except National Park Service employees resides within Organ Pipe, no one lives in Cabeza Prieta, and the only settlement within the Goldwater Range is the auxiliary base south of Gila Bend. A few people live on private ranchland inside Sonoran Desert National Monument. In the Pinacate Biosphere some people live in *ejidos* or ranchitos. Only in the Alto Golfo Biosphere Reserve, such as at El Golfo and Ejido Johnson, are there communities of homes, small stores, and active farming or fishing. Many of the fishermen who ply the open water of the upper gulf reside in Mexicali, Puerto Peñasco, San Felipe, or other communities outside the bio-reserve.

Subsistence: Human Ecology and Resources

Indigenous people of this region developed a sophisticated knowledge of plant and animal resources and may have used some in ways we modern observers can't even imagine. Details of their reliance on plant and animal species are covered in many sources, including Castetter & Bell 1942, 1951; Ezell 1961, 1994; Felger, this volume, Chapter 15; Fontana 1974; Kelly 1977; McGuire 1982a; Nabhan et al. 1989; and Rea 1997, 1998.

Today's desert environment in the Dry Borders region is harsh by most human standards, and in historical times humans struggled to make a living off the land. It is too hot (summer temperatures occasionally topping 120°F), too dry (erratic rainfall varying from one to twelve inches per year), too rocky (volcanic rocks covered in places with shallow loess soil), too sandy (a sea of sand dunes or valleys deep with porous, sandy soil), too perilous (scorpions, cactus spines, and eight kinds of rattlesnakes), and too poor (few valuable minerals, no forests, unreliable forage). In fact, the vegetation is now as sparse and the climate as hot and dry as at any time during the last two millennia. Except along the Colorado and Gila rivers, the lack of surface water ultimately limited the number and range of people here.

People must have known the location of every source of water. If we assume that a person could carry a gallon of water in skin or gourd canteens, there is no part of the region that was outside the reach of humans afoot in cooler seasons (Broyles 1996). In the early twentieth century the neighboring Seris thought little of camping several miles from the nearest waterhole, preferring to carry water daily if they could camp near food or in a comfortable place (Felger & Moser 1985; Sheldon 1993). But water is a basic requirement for all peoples. Modern studies indicate that people may require two gallons or more of water per person per day to survive the heat of summer (Adolph 1947; Schmidt-Nielsen 1964).

Native peoples undoubtedly tuned their activities to effectively use microhabitats, much like the wildlife in this region. Birds and lizards rest in shade during midday. Foxes and rodents feed at night. Bighorn sheep bed against warm rock in winter and in the shadow of boulders and cliffs in summer, seeking breezes and cooler rock (Simmons 1969). A person sitting under the shade of a tree instead of exposed to direct sun may avoid heat stress and certainly conserves water otherwise lost as sweat. Wind caves, such as the tafoni at Tinajas Altas, provide natural, relatively comfortable shelters against sun, wind, and rain. Jorgensen (1983) discusses economic and ecological adaptations. Fontana (1974:522) reminds us that "man is part of the living fauna, and as such he interacts with other fauna, with plants, with climate, and with physiography in ways that are indispensable to his life."

So, considering all the resources available to them and their successful adaptations to the environment, why did native people leave the land during historic times?

Arguably, the Hia C'ed O'odham had the toughest landscape to live in. In the 1850s they were raiding travelers on El Camino del Diablo, but by 1870 virtually all had resettled and taken jobs outside their traditional territory. Enclaves of Hia C'ed O'odham settled in Caborca and Sonoyta, Sonora, and in Dome, Adonde, and Ajo, Arizona. Juan Caravajales, reportedly the last of his tribe, lived in the Pinacate in 1909 and then reportedly disappeared (Lumholtz 1912). Actually, he moved to Wellton, Arizona, to live with others of his family who had left the desert to work on the railroad or in mines at the Castle Dome Mountains (Bell et al. 1980).

Many Cocopahs also left their land, despite having enormous water resources, fertile soil, and a long history of subsistence agriculture. Living along the Colorado River, the Cocopahs tied their livelihood to the cycles of the river, producing an abundance of food when the river ran high and chancing famine when the river failed to flood its banks and nourish crops (see Castetter & Bell 1951: 145; Kelly 1977:24). For the Cocopahs, as Kelly notes,

> the worst period of the year, and the time of famine if it was to strike, came just before the wild rice [nipa, *Distichlis palmeri*] harvest in mid-May. In bad years, anything and everything was eaten in late spring, and most families left their homes to wander over the delta in search of whatever food they could find. At this time every animal, with the exception of the coyote and the snake, was eaten, and many wild plant products that were never consumed when other food was available were gathered and eaten. The chief of these, and the food all Cocopah fell back on when everything else was gone, was tule [cattail, *Typha domingensis*] roots. Some families, living where the tule was abundant, ate little else for a month or more in the most difficult years. (1977:25–26; see also Castetter & Bell 1951; Spier 1933; Williams 1983)

Some outsiders saw ample water and fertile soil in the delta and wondered why the Cocopahs and Quechans didn't farm more extensively, both for fuller sustenance and for trade (Browne 1950; see Castetter & Bell 1951; Stone 1991). The Cocopahs and their neighbors produced less than other farming groups, such as the Gila River Pimas, who, when provided sufficient water rights, produced as much if not more than their non-Indian competitors (Ezell 1994). According to several Cocopah accounts, in the late-1800s "cultivated crops represented about one-third of the total food supply; fish about 20 per cent; rabbits, wood rats, quail, and doves about 15 per cent; and wild plants about 20 to 25 per cent" (Castetter & Bell 1951:77). Stone (1991) considers this estimate of cultivated crops too high.

At least three factors limited Yuman farming capability: the river itself, labor and production, and transportation. These were the same dilemmas faced later by corporate developers who envisioned green gold in delta fields but who first had to figure out a system of dams and dikes, railroads, highways, and ports. Corporate entrepreneurs in Mexico and the United States eventually solved these problems, but only after fifty years of high-stakes politics, venture financing, and difficult engineering did farming begin along the lower Colorado on any grand scale (Bowen 2000; Hendricks 1967, 1971).

Until the Colorado River was dammed, the river was wild and unpredictable. Some years it overflowed fields situated in oxbows or side channels that the Cocopahs had worked hard to clear, and other years it never reached them; some years the overflow came too early and some years too late. Without canals, dikes, dams, and pumps, the Cocopahs could not control the volume, timing, or location of water from the meandering river channel. And even if the Cocopahs had surplus production, they could not reside long-term at the fields because of flooding, and having no draft animals, they could not transport more harvest than they could use locally. Not only did they lack sufficient labor, but the planting season clashed with other food-procurement activities at an already lean and busy time of the year (Stone 1991). Planting season followed several months when few native plants were available and when game was scarce. The Cocopahs could plant, hunt and fish, or gather wild plants, but they couldn't risk investing their labor in only one venture. Between 1850 and 1900 fewer than half of the Mohave and Quechan harvests were successful (Castetter & Bell 1951; Stone 1991). Finally, the Cocopahs and others could not foster or sustain large families that, in the absence of draft animals and machinery, were required for extensive agriculture. In short, it was difficult to be simultaneously a mobile hunter-gatherer-fisher and a sedentary farmer (see Diamond 1999). Modern agribusiness solved the problem by importing low-paid laborers from as far away as Japan and China and feeding them food grown elsewhere (Hendricks 1967, 1971).

Away from the rivers, in the desert, the Tohono O'odham also had a calendar tied to annual food cycles (see Castetter & Bell 1942:142, 1951:145; Kelly 1977:24; Lumholtz 1912:76). These were not calendars in the modern sense of telling dates; instead, they were sequential seasons of subsistence activities and resources. Keyed to harvests of both cultivated and native plants, they also indicated times of feast and famine. Unlike the Cocopahs, the Tohono O'odham—encouraged by Spanish missionaries (Erickson 2003)—adopted draft and food animals introduced by Europeans, but they were less accepting of mechanized farm implements and they lacked the capital resources to pump groundwater into fields on any large scale. Detailed accounts of foods gathered, hunted, and cultivated by the Tohono O'odham and Pimas can be found in Castetter & Bell 1942; Felger, this volume, Chapter 15; Fontana 1974; and Rea 1997, 1998.

By the 1870s many Tohono O'odham had left their homelands to help build the railroad through southern Arizona. Eventually, many left the reservation to pick cotton, enlist in the military, or work in the mines, defense industry, or construction industry, primarily in the Phoenix and Tucson areas. They preferred to rely less on reservation social and relief programs and more on participation in the American industrial cash economy.

"The desert, which had for generations controlled them, had lost much of its power over them" (Erickson 2003:154).

In an exception to this trend, the Gila River Pimas living in the vicinity of Maricopa, Arizona, successfully competed with neighboring Anglo farmers with draft-drawn implements until farmers upstream appropriated and dammed the flow of the Gila (Ezell 1994). A government bureaucracy that favored Anglos, too little surface water, and lack of development capital stifled their efforts. When they attempted to shift to rainfall-supported crops, they could not compete. Modern Akimel O'odham farm effectively on the reservation and lease some lands to outsiders.

When the allure of mechanical farming, store-bought goods, and jobs in service and manufacturing industries was balanced against the difficulty of life on the land, many indigenous people left their traditional territories and ways. They had spent their lives looking for the best niches in the homelands, so it is small wonder that they readily sought and settled into new niches that opened to them. This migration preceded changes in Dry Borders land management by federal agencies, which did not begin until 1937. The Cocopahs and Quechans coped with the expansion of corporate agribusiness and new settlers who brought small herds of livestock. Today habitation and farming are not allowed in the U.S. bio-reserves and Goldwater Range, but visits and traditional harvests by Native Americans, as well as visitation by the public, are encouraged.

The Evidence of Peoples Past

Although the Dry Borders region lacks glamorous major structures—cliff dwellings, cities, pyramids, temples—the evidence left by ancient people can be labeled, studied, arranged into interpretations, and forged into understanding and conclusions. Native people left a network of trails that connect camps, villages, waterholes, and hunting grounds. The trails are best seen along bajadas, across cinder flats, and through mountain passes. They differ from game or cattle trails by having a width that "fits" modern hikers, who can spot occasional pottery sherds, seashells, stone tools, or campsites nearby. Modern hikers wanting to walk cross-country from "here to there" frequently find themselves following the path of some ancient traveler who had the same goal. Native people sometimes established piles of stones at junctions, passes, and waterholes to mark their passing or bless their trip. These trail shrines may stand up to four feet tall. Small clusters of rocks may have been used to hold saguaro-rib wands to mark routes, indicate directions, or designate boundaries. Rocks also were used to build hunting blinds in some mountain passes and near waterholes.

Intaglios—large human, animal, or geometric figures on the ground—are made either by outlining the figure with stones and rocks or by scraping the soil and piling the stones into windrows (Ezzo & Altschul 1993; Hayden 1982). Some figures are several hundred feet long. They may be found on desert pavements, cinder flats, or silt flats. Some are so old that they blend into the surface unless seen at certain angles of the sun. All are vulnerable to erosion and defacement by vehicles (Kockelman 1983). Indigenous people also left petroglyphs, pecked into boulders, and pictographs, painted on sheltered rock walls (Hartmann & Thurtle 2001; Hayden 1972). The figures may represent clan identities, mythological beings, personal inspirations, travel directions, visions, or records of memorable events.

Clay was fashioned into pottery vessels for cooking, storage of water and food, and ceremony. A few intact ollas, holding such items as seeds, dried saguaro syrup, dried meat, beads, and paint pigment, have been found cached in rock crevices, in caves, and on dunes. Although much of the pottery found in the Dry Borders region was made elsewhere, at least some was made here. Sources of good clay can be found near Yuma and in the Salt River valley of Phoenix (e.g., Van Keuren et al. 1997).

Stone tools were used for hammering, skinning, grinding, and chopping. Obsidian was flaked into knives, arrowheads, and spear points (see Brott 1966 for samples). In some places, such as Tinajas Altas, table-sized granite boulders hold dozens of grinding surfaces. Hand-sized stones were used as manos for grinding seeds and legume pods; pestles were made from hard-wood limbs or wine bottle–sized stones. Larger rocks of basalt and sandstone were employed as metates and gyratory crushers; though heavy (20–50 pounds), some of them were carried dozens of miles to sources of such foods as pods, grains, and seeds. Gyratory crushers are doughnut-shaped metates with a central hole that held a hard-wood pestle

Figure 14.7. Trail. *(Photo by Bill Broyles)*

Figure 14.8. Trail shrine. *(Photo by Bill Broyles)*

Figure 14.9. Intaglio. *(Photo by Bill Broyles)*

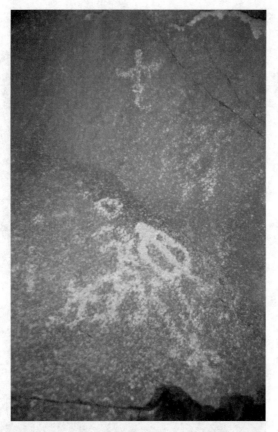

Figure 14.10. *Petroglyph.*
(Photo by Bill Broyles)

Figure 14.11. *Pictograph.*
(Photo by Bill Broyles)

Borders to use as utensils and jewelry (see Felger, this volume, Chapter 15; Tower 1945).

Ancient campsites may be indicated by "sleeping circles" where someone cleared the ground of rocks in a circle five to eight feet in diameter and perhaps erected a temporary shelter made of ocotillo wands, hides, or brush. Rock rings also are common campsite features. Sometimes sherds, chipped rock, metates, seashells, burned animal bones, or piles of horns are found at campsites (Hayden 1985). Fields, canals, hand-dug wells and reservoirs, and check dams are important records of agriculture. These features may be accompanied by villages, though few sites show evidence of walls. North of the Goldwater Range near Gila Bend are the ruins of a walled community at the Fortified Hill site and a ball court at the Gatlin site. Other human activities are indicated by agave roasting pits, pit houses, human burials, fire hearths, trash mounds, middens, quarries, and rock-flaking sites. Stone (1991) reviews the research values and investigative procedures of various types of material resources.

Many artifacts, however—hides, baskets, cordage, wooden spear shafts, clothes, reed boats, bows and arrows, brush dams—were organic and perished. Seldom were camps used long enough to have layers of artifacts beneath today's ground. Hayden (1965) labeled the region a "fragile-pattern area," where virtually all the story lies on the surface and is vulnerable to disruption (see Waters 1992).

Despite the fact that descendants of the original inhabitants no longer live on most of the protected areas in the Dry Borders region, the land remains integral to their identity and heritage, and many return to maintain contact with their religions and family histories and to seek personal and spiritual renewal. For them, this is a landscape replete with plants and animals that are sacred, salt flats where rain began, caves where a creator lived, rocks where shamans meditated, canyons where people were delivered from death, hillsides where ancestors are buried, and trails that took people on journeys of renewal, trade, and reunion. They think of themselves as coming from not just land but *this* land, *this* desert and *this* river.

What's Next?

The challenge is to protect artifacts and sites from disturbance, incidental and intended (see Masse in press; Masse & Rankin in press). Artifacts are

(Felger 1977; Hayden 1969). A quarry at Antelope Hill provided metate slabs for several of the region's tribes (Schneider 1993; Schneider & Altschul 2000).

Along the coast seashell middens indicate where people camped over time and ate countless shellfish. Occasionally, stone tools, pottery sherds, and other artifacts can be found intermixed with the shells. Some shell genera, especially *Glycymeris*, *Laevicardium*, *Turritella*, *Olivella*, and *Conus*, were harvested and then carried throughout the Dry puzzle pieces for archaeologists and the legacy of people long dead. "Preserving historical and prehistoric resources for future study and for future enjoyment . . . is vitally important, for the past belongs to all of us" (Reid & Whittlesey 1997:275).

Only a small percentage of the Dry Borders region has been surveyed archaeologically, and some surveys have been cursory. One major site, known throughout history, was not thoroughly surveyed until 2000. Critical areas to both survey and protect include tinajas, desert pavements, rock shelters and caves, mountain passes and peaks, upper bajadas, and coastal dunes (see Altschul & Jones 1989). Visitors to the desert may neither see nor appreciate the importance of scattered pottery, seashell fragments, faint marks on boulders, or small rock piles. For example, nearly 65 historic graves dating from the 1849 gold rush were obliterated by modern campers at Tinajas Altas (W. Hartmann 1989; G. Hartmann & Thurtle 2001) and along El Camino del Diablo. The imminent construction of a coastal highway from Mexicali to Guaymas will radically alter the area by allowing construction of resorts on private lands and *ejido* tracts within the Alto Golfo biosphere. Few surveys or studies have been done on coastal archaeological sites, sites that may hold key evidence regarding the arrival of the first humans in North America, especially if they came by boats or dispersed along coastlines.

Big questions remain (see Altschul & Rankin in press; McGuire 1982d). Archaeologists are still trying to answer basic questions: who lived here? when did they live here? and what was their material culture? Some questions may never be answered, but as the pace of research accelerates, many will be.

Archaeological answers, if they can be found, lie in artifacts already analyzed, in artifacts still hidden throughout Dry Borders, and in peoples whose ancestors lived here before 1540. This is a fascinating time to be a student of deep human history. There is much to suspect and surmise; there is much less known, but archaeologists are working diligently to add up the pieces to tell a fuller story, which is a compelling reason to preserve sites and artifacts still in the field. Progress depends ultimately on the depth of our resolve to protect sites. Archaeology is a dynamic scholarly enterprise. New information, new interpretations, and new theories make for exciting and enlight-

Figure 14.12. Pottery sherds. (Photo by Bill Broyles)

Figure 14.13. Bedrock metates and mortars at tinaja. (Photo by Bill Broyles)

Figure 14.14. Portable metate. (Photo by Bill Broyles)

Figure 14.15. *Rock circle. (Photo by Bill Broyles)*

Figure 14.16. *Rock shelter. (Photo by Bill Broyles)*

ening discussion, and the latest timelines are subject to tomorrow morning's discoveries in the field or laboratory. Much fascinating work has been done. More remains.

Acknowledgments

For their information, advice, encouragement, and patient instruction, we especially thank Thomas Bowen, Lorraine Marquez Eiler, Bernard L. Fontana, Gayle H. Hartmann, Julian D. Hayden, W. Bruce Masse, David N. Siegel, Sharon Urban, and Anita Alvarez Williams.

Fifteen

Living Resources at the Center of the Sonoran Desert

Regional Uses of Plants and Animals by Native Americans

RICHARD STEPHEN FELGER

Plant and animal resources across the Dry Borders were as varied and rich as the peoples who occupied the land. I think of vanquished rivers and a wealth of seafood the world may never again know. I think of giant minnows and mud turtles, and sandfood and sweet cactus fruit. I think of earlier people who lived here.

I started to make a simple list of the animals and plants used by Dry Borders people. I first turned to the classic works of Lumholtz and then Castetter and Bell. I then looked at the more recent and innovative writings of Gary Nabhan, Amadeo Rea's inspiring and detailed scholarship, the encyclopedic work of Wendy Hodgson, and some of my own work. These later authors had the advantage of deep biological knowledge, allowing meaningful interpretation of an ever more fleeting body of traditional information. There are, of course, many others, but these authors provide the cornerstones of the regional ethnobiology. I quickly found that a simple tabular listing added little to an extensive but fragmentary knowledge and that I would be able to offer interpretations and integration that would further an understanding of the arid core of the Sonoran Desert, the Alto Golfo coast, the Río Colorado delta, and the people who made these places their home.

The accounts presented here are selective summaries and interpretations of the plant and animal resources of the Dry Borders region. In cases where there are multiple references, I cited only a few prominent ones, especially those that are accessible and contain further references therein. The information presented here is necessarily brief, and more details can be found by referring to my sources and those of others too. In some cases the information is fragmentary because it is all that is available. I have emphasized food uses but also include selected medicinal uses and material culture when the information was accessible.

I have concentrated on wild plants and provide only cursory coverage of cultivated crops and some of the animals for the sake of space and because that information is covered in detail by Castetter and Bell, Nabhan, Rea, and in some cases Kelly and others. Sometimes I have kept the original, now often politically incorrect, names for some cultural groups rather than chance inaccurate interpretation. For consistency I am using the name *Cocopah*, the official name in the United States, to include tribal members on both sides of the border, even though in Mexico the preferred spelling is *Cucapá* (see Chapter 14). For the sake of accuracy, I often use direct quotes rather than attempt to paraphrase. The Hia C'ed O'odham oral history recorded by Bell et al. (1980) and Zepeda (1985) provides a tantalizing glimpse into a wealth of knowledge. It should be noted that Betty "Melvin" (Zepeda 1985) is obviously the same person as Betty "Melvion" (Bell et al. 1980).

Many of the most well-rounded regional ethnobiological works are not in the Dry Borders region itself but in adjacent or relatively nearby regions. Rea's (1974, 1997, 1998, in press) work on the Gila River Pimas and other O'odham groups is the most all-encompassing for plants, birds, and mammals. Work on the Seris (Felger & Moser 1985) covers many plants and some of the animals that also occur in the Dry Borders. The work of Bean and Saubel (1972) on the Cahuillas likewise includes many plants found in the region. Although today we do not have the luxury of witnessing much in the way of traditional animal and plant usage, we have knowledge to sometimes make better interpretations of the existing information.

Information and goods flowed between neighboring and even distant peoples (Ford 1983). People traveled and traded, talked to each other, and sometimes intermarried; they fought and took captives and adopted them into their societies.

Thus I have amalgamated some regional information. Cocopahs traveled to Baja California mountains and traded and spent time with the Pai Pais and even traded with the Diguéños in California (Gifford 1933; Jöel 1976; Kelly 1977). There are records of Seris living among the Hia C'ed O'odham (Childs 1954; Ezell in McGuire 1982:84; Thomas 1991). O'odham captives of Apaches sometimes were rescued or escaped back to their homelands (e.g., Childs 1954). Along the lower Río Colorado in 1540, the Spanish explorer Alarcón reported, "[I learned from him] further that he customarily traveled from that place along a trail that followed the river, [and] it consumed forty days. The reason that moved him to go there had been just to see Cíbola, because it was an extraordinary thing" (Flint & Flint 2005:197).

Many aspects of the ethnobiological accounts are necessarily incomplete. About 18 percent of the total Sonoran Desert flora, native and non-native, was used for food, and a similar number was probably used for medicinal purposes (Felger & Nabhan 1978). Hence, across the entire Sonoran Desert (defined by Shreve 1951 and Wiggins 1964) about 375 species of plants have been used for food. The Dry Borders has a total flora of at least 847 species (Chapter 17, this volume). Roughly 160 species of food plants and 63 species of medicinal plants are listed here. Not all the 160 species of food plants, however, are included in the floristic listing (the 847 species)—17 species are cultivated plants or species found outside the boundaries of the Dry Borders such as oaks and palms in Baja California. Thus there are about 142 species of edible plants, native and non-native, within the boundaries of the Dry Borders, or 17 percent of the total flora. It should be noted that not all these 142 species are documented as being used within the Dry Borders boundaries. Nevertheless, the number of edible plants listed here approximates the expected number, but the low number of medicinal plant species (7.6 percent of the total flora) indicates highly incomplete information.

Both plant and animal foods were prepared fresh and very often also dried and stored for future use. A wide variety of vegetables, greens, fruits, and seeds were dried whole, sliced, ground, or made into cakes and stored, as were many kinds of animal foods, including caterpillars, shrimp, fishes, deer, and bighorn. Most kinds of seeds and many other plant foods such as mesquite pods were parched, toasted, or dried and ground into flour, then boiled or steeped in water to be consumed as *atole.* No really satisfactory term for *atole* seems to be available in English, the nearest approximation being gruel, mush, or porridge. It is nearly impossible to avoid sand and gravel when preparing food on a metate that rests on the ground or on a dirt floor. Once we made bread from flour prepared on a metate (Felger 2002). It tasted good, but the sand was not pleasant. If we had consumed the flour as *atole,* the sand would have been left at the bottom of the pot.

Although a cornucopia of resources is listed in the species accounts, do not forget that this is desert country. Drought could mean hardship (Clotts 1917; McGuire & Schiffer 1982). No matter how rich the resources, drinking water was of absolute necessity. Camps and settlements or villages had to have access to waterholes and oases or the few rivers. The desert people moved seasonal residences and camps for a number of reasons, as for instance to follow their favorite harvests, when meager water supplies were threatened, or perhaps just to take advantage of more pleasant conditions or when a place became polluted with waste. Drought in the distant upper reaches of the Colorado River could spell trouble for the Cocopahs and other downriver peoples (Castetter & Bell 1951). There certainly must have been major changes for the lower Río Colorado people when the river changed course to empty into Lake Cahuilla (Salton Sea) and the delta went dry or the flow was greatly reduced. Apart from the partial filling in the early twentieth century, the last time the river flowed into Lake Cahuilla was during the first part of the seventeenth century, when the lake partially filled (Cleland et al. 2000; Schaefer 1994). It is estimated that it would take seventeen and a half years to fully fill the lake after the river changes course to empty into the dry lakebed, which is below sea level (Cleland et al. 2000).

Rich agricultural traditions existed along the Río Colorado as well as in the interior desert but on a greatly reduced scale. The prehistoric trio— beans, squash, and corn *(Phaseolus acutifolius, Cucurbita argyrosperma* var. *callicarpa,* and *Zea mays)*—were the mainstays. Dogs were the only domesticated animals. Hawks and eagles were sometimes kept in captivity for their feathers. To the north and east, people kept and raised macaws. Old World domesticated animals and plants were first brought to the Southwest with the Coronado *entrada* to New Mexico in 1540, and in the same year to the lower Colorado and Gila River region by Alarcón (Flint & Flint 2005). Apparently, few if any of Alarcón's introductions survived, and few of the New Mexico introductions reached, or survived in, the Dry Borders region. Padre Kino was the first and most important agricultural extension agent for what is now southern Arizona and northern Sonora. He brought cattle, goats, horses, and sheep, as well as wheat and many other Old World plants in the late seventeenth century. Juan Mateo Manje, soldier and close associate of Kino, reports that in 1696 at the Dolores Mission in Sonora there were "fruit trees of Castile, grapevines, peaches, pomegranates, fig trees, pear trees, and all kinds of garden produce"—all brought by Kino (Burrus 1971:95). Other Spanish colonial introductions include cowpeas, muskmelons, pumpkins, various squashes, and watermelons. Some of these, however, preceded Kino into the region.

Use of present or past tense can be a problem in presenting ethnobiological information. Although most indigenous uses and knowledge of plants and animals have disappeared from the Dry Borders region, local people are still knowledgeable about the natural world (see the various works of Gary Nabhan). Nevertheless, because most of the indigenous uses are no longer practiced, I generally use the past tense.

The plants and animals are listed in the species accounts alphabetically within major categories. The plants are arranged by family, genus, and species, with the few cone-bearing plants presented first, followed by the flowering plants; this is the same order as in the floristic listing for the region in Chapter 17. The scientific name and the English common name when known are given, and some synonyms and Spanish or indigenous names are included. The Dry Borders floristic listing (Chapter 17, this volume) provides authors of scientific names; pertinent synonyms as well as English, Spanish, and some O'odham names; and very brief descriptions and references to botanical works; these items therefore are generally not repeated here. Additional information for animals is in pertinent chapters in this volume. Occurrence in each of the six major protected areas is given at the end of each entry: AG = Reserva de la Biosfera Alto Golfo de California y Delta del Río Colorado, PI = Reserva de la Biosfera El Pinacate y

Gran Desierto de Altar, CP = Cabeza Prieta National Wildlife Refuge, OP = Organ Pipe Cactus National Monument, GR = Goldwater Military Range, and SD = Sonoran Desert National Monument. Non-native plants and animals are identified with an asterisk (*).

Acknowledgments

I thank the Wallace Research Foundation for financial support. I am indebted to many people who provided assistance, and I especially thank Tom Bowen, Bill Broyles, Kathryn Mauz, Amadeo M. Rea, and Michael F. Wilson, as well as Richard Brusca, Stephen Buchmann, Richard Cudney-Bueno, Kevin Dahl, Mark A. Dimmitt, Lloyd Findley, Richard Flint, Shirley Flint, Bernard "Bunny" Fontana, Michael S. Foster, Phil Hastings, Cathy Moser Marlett, Joseph McShane, Carlos Navarro, Tom Oberbauer, Adrianne Rankin, Ana Lilia Reina, Phil Rosen, Susan Rutman, Jeffrey Seminoff, Don A. Thomson, Tom Van Devender, Richard S. White, and Mary Wilkins.

Species Accounts
Plants
CONE-BEARING PLANTS – GYMNOSPERMS
EPHEDRACEAE – EPHEDRA FAMILY

Ephedra spp. Ephedras have an extensive medicinal history, most notably the Chinese species *E. sinica,* the original source of ephedrine. In southern Arizona a stimulating tonic tea was made from the stems (Kearney & Peebles 1960). This tea has been used to treat rheumatism, arthritis, renal and vesicle disorders, gonorrhea, and syphilis, and as a diuretic, a blood purifier, and for prevention of thirst (Curtin 1949; Moerman 1998; Owen 1963).

Ephedra aspera. BOUNDARY EPHEDRA, MORMON TEA. In northeastern Baja California the seeds, ripe in spring, were roasted, ground into flour, and consumed as *pinole.* It is reported to be bitter (Aschmann 1959; Meigs 1939). Rocky slopes. PI, CP, GR, OP, SD.

Ephedra trifurca. LONGLEAF JOINT FIR, MORMON TEA. A poultice of pulverized stems was used by Cocopahs as a treatment for sores (Gifford 1933:268). Seeds of the closely related *E. californica* were a minor food resource for Kiliwas in Baja California (Meigs 1939). Dunes and sand flats. PI, AG, GR.

PINACEAE – PINE FAMILY

Pinus monophylla. PINYON; PIÑÓN. Cocopahs and lowland Pai Pais made annual summertime trips from the torrid Colorado River lowlands to Baja California mountains to harvest pinyon nuts. Sometimes they also obtained them by trade. The nuts, variously prepared, transported, and stored, were a significant food resource (Castetter & Bell 1951; Kelly 1977). Pinyons are abundant in the Sierra Juárez, and the nuts are still collected (Tom Oberbauer, personal communication 2004).

FLOWERING PLANTS – ANGIOSPERMS

ACANTHACEAE – ACANTHUS FAMILY

Justicia californica [*Beloperone californica*]. DESERT HUMMINGBIRD-BUSH. Sweet nectar was sucked from the flower base, mostly in spring, as a minor snack food (Bean & Saubel 1972; Felger & Moser 1985). PI, CP, GR, OP, SD.

AGAVACEAE – CENTURY PLANT FAMILY

Agave deserti. DESERT AGAVE. Agaves served as a major food and provided one of the few significant sweets (Bell et al. 1980; Castetter et al. 1938; Felger & Moser 1985; Hodgson 2001; Rea 1997; Betty Melvin in Zepeda 1985:54). Plants showing signs of initiating a flowering stalk were selected, harvested, and trimmed to leave the centers—"hearts," or "*cabezas*"—which were baked in coals in pit ovens. Emerging flower stalks were also pit-baked or cooked in coals. Cooked agave hearts were sliced and eaten or formed into cakes or other products that were dried and stored. The flowers and seeds are also edible but probably had only minor importance. Cocopahs traveled to Baja California mountains to harvest agaves (Kelly 1977). People living too far away to harvest agaves themselves obtained them (as dried cakes?) by trade (Castetter & Underhill 1935; Gifford 1931). Agaves occur in nearly all Dry Borders mountains except the volcanic Sierra Pinacate (Felger 2000).

Agave leaf fiber was widely used to make cordage, burden basket nets, and sandals (Castetter et al. 1938; Betty Melvin in Zepeda 1985:54). Chittenden (1901:204) tells of Cocopahs having "noiseless sandals for deer hunting." Meigs reports that the Kiliwas made excellent sandals and nets of agave fiber. The "nets are used for many purposes. The longest ones, about 40 feet long and 3 feet wide, are used for catching rabbits" (Meigs 1939:38). PI, AG, CP, GR, OP, SD.

Agave schottii. SHIN DAGGER; AMOLILLO. Seris made arrow shafts from the flowering stalks, and the leaves were mashed for shampoo and soap (Felger & Moser 1985; Gentry 1982). It is common at higher elevations in the Ajo Mountains. OP.

Hesperoyucca whipplei [*Yucca whipplei*]. SPANISH BAYONET. This agave-like yucca was widespread across the Dry Borders region in the ice ages (Van Devender, this volume). Perhaps it was extirpated across most of the Sonoran Desert by overharvesting in deep history. The only known present-day Sonoran Desert population occurs on the north side of Sierra del Viejo west of the Pinacates (Felger 2000; Turner et al. 1995). In other regions, such as in California west of the Sonoran Desert and the Grand Canyon region, the hearts and the young emerging flowering stalks were pit-baked like those of agaves, and the flowers and seeds were also eaten (Barrows 1900; Hodgson 2001; Meigs 1939). PI.

Yucca baccata. BANANA YUCCA. This large yucca provided significant food resources in the Tohono O'odham and Pima regions. It presumably was also important in the eastern part of the Dry Borders, where it is common on mountaintops including in the Ajo, Sand Tank, and Table Top mountains. Flowering occurs in late April and May, and the fruits ripen in midsummer, but flowering and especially fruit production can be highly variable (Hodgson 2001; Turner et al. 1995). Castetter and Underhill (1935) report that O'odham made expeditions to the mountains to collect the large, fleshy fruits. The fruits were often pit-baked. Young flower stalks, flowers, and seeds were variously cooked, and the seeds were often stored. The fruit pulp was eaten fresh or cooked, was commonly made into cakes and stored for future use, and was sometimes traded with neighboring people (Bell & Castetter 1941; Hodgson 2001; Rea 1997). The dried plants, especially the roots, were made into soap and shampoo, and the leaves yielded cordage (Bell & Castetter 1941). GR, OP, SD.

Yucca elata. SOAPTREE YUCCA. This tall yucca is rare in the Dry Borders. Young flower stalks, flowers, and sometimes the seeds served as food resources. The leaves have been used as cordage, and the roots for soap and shampoo (Bell & Castetter 1941). The leaves are used in modern Tohono O'odham artistic basketry. SD.

ALISMATACEAE – WATER-PLANTAIN FAMILY

Sagittaria longiloba. ARROWHEAD. The corms (tuberous roots) were an important food resource for the Cocopahs, especially during summertime shortages. Harvesting was hard work, and it was not considered very tasty (Kelly 1977). It was perishable and not stored. In 1899 Edward Palmer recorded that "the bulbs of this plant are much used by the Cocopa Indians either raw or roasted" (Vasey & Rose 1890:28), and Kelly (1977) reports that it was one of the half-dozen most important Cocopah food plants. It is now extirpated (or rare?) in the lower Colorado River area (Felger 2000). AG.

AMARANTHACEAE – AMARANTH FAMILY

Amaranthus fimbriatus. FRINGED PIGWEED. Cahuillas cooked the young plants as greens and parched and ground the seeds, which were consumed as *atole* (Bean & Saubel 1972). It is widespread, including on dunes and in sandy places such as the Alto Golfo coast, where *A. palmeri* is generally absent. PI, AG, CP, GR, OP, SD.

Amaranthus palmeri. CARELESS WEED. This abundant, often robust summer annual was a major food plant across much of the Dry Borders region (Figure 15.1). Young or half-grown plants were consumed as greens (Betty Melvin in Zepeda 1985:56), and the small, black seeds of mature plants were parched and ground. Fresh plants were sometimes baked in coals or cooked and rolled "into a ball and baked on hot coals; this could be stored for future use" (Castetter & Bell 1951:201). The seeds, seed-bearing branches, or entire plants were often stored. *Amaranthus* was ranked next to nipa *(Distichlis palmeri)* "in importance in the list of edible wild plants" of the Cocopahs (Castetter & Bell 1951:201). Kelly (1977) provides a detailed description of the harvest and preparation. Nabhan et al. (1982) call it "desert spinach." Kelly (1977) lists *A. caudatus* as a wild-harvested *quelite,* but I question the identification. *A. palmeri* is likely the only significant wild amaranth harvested in the lower Río Colorado region. PI, AG, CP, GR, OP, SD.

Amaranthus hypochondriacus. GRAIN AMARANTH. It was formerly grown by Gila River Pimas (Rea 1997). Amaranths went out of cultivation regionally in early historic times and as a summer crop would not have been seen at other seasons. Areas of potential former cultivation include the Río Colorado and Río Sonoyta. Grain amaranths usually have whitish seeds; wild species have black seeds.

ANACARDIACEAE – SUMAC FAMILY

Rhus aromatica. SKUNKBUSH. The fleshy part of the fruit is edible (Kirk 1970). It occurs at higher elevations in some Dry Borders mountains but is not common in the region. PI, GR, OP.

Rhus kearneyi. DESERT SUMAC. The acidic fruits of related species were made into a refreshing drink (Hodgson 2001), and this species has similar, pleasantly flavored fruits. PI, CP, GR.

ARECACEAE – PALM FAMILY. Cocopahs traveling to Baja California mountains in the summer made use of the two native palms, which provided significant food resources (Palmer 1878). The fruits (the fleshy pericarp) were eaten fresh or sun-dried and stored, and the seeds were ground into flour. The bases of the young leaves (central leaf bud) were eaten as "palm hearts." Cutting the central leaf bud kills the plant, and people probably harvested young plants, which are generally abundant in palm canyon oases (Felger & Joyal 1999; Gifford 1933; Hodgson 2001).

Brahea armata [*Erythea armata*]. BLUE HESPER PALM. When I was at El Mayor with Anita Williams and Amadeo Rea in 1977, Juan García Aldama, an elderly Cocopah, told me that seeds of the "*palma azul*" were pit-baked.

Figure 15.1. Amaranthus palmeri. *(Drawing by Lucretia Brezeale Hamilton)*

Washingtonia filifera. DESERT FAN PALM. The small, date-flavored fruits were made into a beverage (Palmer 1878). The fruits were harvested using a long willow pole with a crossbar at the end like a cactus fruit-harvesting pole (Castetter & Bell 1951).

APOCYNACEAE – DOGBANE FAMILY

Apocynum cannabinum. INDIAN HEMP. The stems provided a high-quality fiber widely used in Arizona (Palmer 1878) and by Cahuillas in California (Bean & Saubel 1972; Drucker 1937). The plant was probably once common in the lower Río Colorado but is now scarce in the region (Felger 2000). The many references to hemp fiber used for fishing nets, lines, and bowstrings in the Río Colorado region may refer to this plant and/or *Sesbania.* AG.

ARISTOLOCHIACEAE – BIRTHWORT FAMILY

Aristolochia watsonii. INDIAN-ROOT. The roots were used medicinally (Felger et al. 1992). CP, GR, OP, SD.

ASCLEPIADACEAE – MILKWEED FAMILY. Probably all the local species have edible fruits. The young fruits were usually baked and served as minor food resources (Felger & Moser 1985; Gentry 1963).

Funastrum cynanchoides [*Sarcostemma cynanchoides*]. CLIMBING MILKWEED. The fresh flowers have a mild onion-like flavor and were eaten as snacks by Seris (Felger & Moser 1985). Chewing gum, made from the milky sap, was especially relished by Hia C'ed O'odham and Gila River Pima children (Curtin 1949; Philip Salcido &

Delores Lewis in Felger et al. 1992; Nabhan et al. 1982; Rea 1997:244–245 gives details of the preparation; Betty Melvin in Zepeda 1985:48, 76). PI, CP, GR, OP, SD.

ASTERACEAE (COMPOSITAE) – DAISY OR COMPOSITE FAMILY.

Dozens of Sonoran Desert species were used medicinally, especially those with aromatic and glandular or glandular-pubescent herbage, which can be especially aromatic when heated. A few examples are listed here.

Ambrosia ambrosioides. CANYON RAGWEED. This plant was used by Hia C'ed O'odham to treat arthritis (Philip Salcido & Delores Lewis in Felger et al. 1992). The roots were made into teas or infusions taken by Seri women for problems associated with childbirth and menstruation (Felger & Moser 1985) and in the Caborca region as an abortive (Eric Mellink, personal communication 1991). PI, CP, GR, OP, SD.

Ambrosia confertiflora [*Franseria tenuifolia*]. SLIM-LEAF RAGWEED. For the Tohono O'odham, Castetter and Underhill (1935:14) report that the "stalks" were eaten as greens and Castetter and Bell (1942:60) report that roots of this ragweed were one of the "staple root crops." PI, CP, GR, OP, SD.

Ambrosia deltoidea. TRIANGLELEAF BURSAGE. The branches were fashioned into a utility brush (Philip Salcido in Felger et al. 1992). PI, CP, GR, OP, SD.

Baccharis salicifolia [*B. glutinosa, B. viminea*]. SEEP-WILLOW. Yumans cooked the young shoots as an emergency food (Castetter & Bell 1951). The plant was used for many medicinal purposes by different peoples including for treating baldness and eye ailments, and for women's hygiene (Bean & Saubel 1972; Felger & Moser 1985; Moerman 1998). Gila River Pimas used seepwillow for house walls if arrowweed (*Pluchea sericea*) was not available (the pithy stems of seepwillow were less desirable than those of arrowweed, which are solid wood; Rea 1997). PI, CP, OP, SD.

Baccharis sarothroides. DESERT BROOM. The branches were made into brooms by Gila River Pimas (Rea 1997). The Tohono O'odham made arrow foreshafts from the straight stems although creosotebush was preferred (Castetter & Underhill 1935; also see *Sapindus*). Tea made from the leaves was taken by Seris as a remedy for colds, to help one lose weight, and as a contraceptive (Felger & Moser 1985). CP, GR, OP, SD.

Dicoria canescens. BUGSEED. The seeds were eaten in substantial quantities by people living along the shores of the ancient Lake Cahuilla (in a reduced phase now the Salton Sea), as shown by analysis of coprolites from prehistoric lakeshore campsites (Wilke 1978; Wilke et al. 1979), and were also a food resource in northern Arizona (Hodgson 2001). *Dicoria* is often seasonally abun-

dant in the Gran Desierto and Mohawk Dunes (Felger 2000; Felger et al. 2003). PI, AG, GR.

Encelia farinosa. BRITTLEBUSH. The yellowish resin that oozes from wounds in the stems becomes hard when dry and plastic when heated. It was used as glue or sealant for hafting arrows and waterproofing vessels (Felger & Moser 1985; Uphof 1968). Hia C'ed O'odham used it as chewing gum when soft and as bow rosin for fiddles when hard (Philip Salcido in Felger et al. 1992; Betty Melvin in Zepeda 1985:76). The resin was also used for medicinal purposes and burned as incense (Felger & Moser 1985; Uphof 1968). PI, CP, GR, OP, SD.

Hymenoclea monogyra. SLENDER BURROBUSH. Teas made from this tall, slender plant were used by the Seris to reduce swellings and pain in the lungs, and mixed with *Anemopsis* it was used to treat rheumatism (Felger & Moser 1985). The branches served Gila River Pimas for roofing and for shelter walls (Rea 1997). CP, GR, OP.

Isocoma acradenia [*Haplopappus acradenius*]. ALKALI GOLDENBUSH. It was used medicinally by many groups, including by the Cahuillas for "curing colds and sore throats" (Bean & Saubel 1972:75) and by the Gila River Pimas as a disinfectant to treat sores (Rea 1997:135), for inflammation, for "cleansing the blood" (Hrdlièka 1908: 246), and as a deodorant (Rea 1997). AG, GR, OP, SD.

Palafoxia arida. SPANISH NEEDLES. The ground plant was used by Seris to kill insect larvae infecting dogs (Felger & Moser 1985) and by Cahuillas as a source of yellow dye (Bean & Saubel 1972). PI, AG, CP, GR, OP.

Pectis papposa. DESERT CHINCHWEED. River Pimas drank tea made from the green or dry plant as a laxative (Curtin 1949). PI, CP, GR, OP, SD.

Pluchea sericea. ARROWWEED. This shrub was one of the most important and ever-present elements in the culture of the lower Colorado and Gila River people (Figure 15.2). Honeydew gathered from arrowweed foliage in early summer was a likely food resource in the Colorado delta region (Heizer 1945). According to Bean and Saubel (1972:105), "the roots of the young plants were gathered for roasting and eaten." Arrowweed was widely used medicinally (Curtin 1949; Rea 1997; Russell 1908).

The long, straight stems were extensively used by Cocopahs for traditional houses and the wattle-and-daub houses of later times. The leafy branches were often incorporated into house and shelter walls and roofing as well as quickly erected walls and screens to protect against wintertime cold and scorching summer sun (Gifford 1933; Kniffen 1931). As the common name indicates, this shrub was used extensively for arrows, such as a sharp-ended "deer arrow" and toy arrows (Gifford 1933:273). Black and red identification markings and decorations on arrows were made with "juice of arrowweed bark and pitch mixed with red or black pigment" (Gifford 1933:274). Hia C'ed O'odham likewise used arrowweed to make arrows (Childs 1954). Cocopahs used a seine-like "fence of willow twigs and arrowweed" to catch fish (Gifford 1933:268; see *Salix gooddingii*). Arrowweed was sometimes used as a cooking fuel; for example, Castetter and Bell (1951:201) state that fresh amaranth plants were "baked on a bed of arrowweed coals."

Cocopahs used the pliable stems for large, coarse storage baskets and granaries (Gifford 1933; also see *Prosopis glandulosa* and *Salix gooddingii*). Rea (1997) points out that the aromatic quality of the plant repelled insects and rodents and was a significant reason for its use in basketry granaries of the Gila River Pimas. Cocopahs and Gila River Pimas used arrowweed for firedrills (Curtin 1949; Gifford 1933; also see *Carnegiea*). Cocopahs used arrowweed scarecrows to ward off birds in cornfields and burned a "smudge of arrowweed torch" to keep mosquitoes at bay while working in the fields (Gifford 1933:263). They also used a "smudge of green arrowweed around [the] house" to repel mosquitoes (Gifford 1933:270). A prized lac, yellow to dark red-brown, collected from the stems, served as an all-purpose plastic adhesive and sealant (Euler & Jones 1956; Gifford 1933:273). This lac is especially common on the extensive stands of arrowweed along the margins of the lower Río Colorado (Felger 2000). PI, AG, OP.

Porophyllum gracile. ODORA. This aromatic plant was used by the Seris to aid childbirth and as a remedy for colds, toothache, and diarrhea—one woman said "the thing it is not good for does not exist" (Felger & Moser 1985:286). The Pai Pais used it to treat colds and cough (Owen 1963). PI, AG, CP, GR, OP, SD.

*Sonchus asper and **S. oleraceus.** SOWTHISTLE. Young plants were eaten as greens by the Gila River Pimas (Rea 1997). PI, CP, GR, OP, SD.

Thymophylla concinna. DOGWEED; MANZANILLA DEL COYOTE. Tea made by Hia C'ed O'odham from these small, aromatic plants was taken as a remedy for colds and by women after childbirth (Betty Melvin in Zepeda 1985:54). CP, OP.

Trixis californica. CALIFORNIA THREEFOLD. The Seris drank an infusion of this plant to hasten birthing, and they smoked the leaves like tobacco (Felger & Moser 1985). PI, CP, GR, OP, SD.

Viguiera parishii. PARISH'S GOLDENEYE. A decoction of the mashed roots was used by Seris as a contraceptive (Felger & Moser 1985). PI, CP, GR, OP, SD.

BATACEAE – SALTWORT FAMILY

Batis maritima. SALTWORT. The roots were used as a sweetener by Seris (Felger & Moser 1985). The young herbage is eaten as a fresh vegetable in different parts of world (Uphof 1968). AG.

Figure 15.2. Pluchea sericea. *(Drawing by Lucretia Brezeale Hamilton)*

BIGNONIACEAE – BIGNONIA FAMILY

Chilopsis linearis. DESERT WILLOW. According to Bean and Saubel (1972) the flowers and slender fruits were eaten as a minor food by the Cahuillas. They also used the strong and flexible wood for bow making and house construction. CP, GR, OP, SD.

BORAGINACEAE – BORAGE FAMILY

Amsinckia intermedia & **A. tessellata.** FIDDLENECK. There are reports of young plants eaten as greens, cooked or even fresh (Hrdlička 1908 and Russell 1908, as interpreted by Rea 1997), although I agree with Amadeo Rea that these unpleasant, rough-haired plants hardly seem palatable if not cooked. These winter-spring annuals are often abundant across a wide range of habitats. PI, CP, GR, OP, SD.

Heliotropium curassavicum. ALKALI HELIOTROPE. It was used medicinally by the Hia C'ed O'odham (Nabhan et al. 1982) as a remedy for coughs and sore throat (Felger et al. 1992); by the Gila River Pimas to treat sore eyes, sores, and wounds (Russell 1908; Rea 1997); and by Seris to treat colds and stomachache (Felger & Moser 1985). AG, CP, GR, OP.

Tiquilia palmeri. PALMER'S CRINKLEMAT. Seris made a tea from the large, thick root to alleviate stomachache or a cold (Felger and Moser 1985). PI, AG, CP, GR.

Figure 15.3. Descurainia pinnata. *(Drawing by Lucretia Brezeale Hamilton)*

BRASSICACEAE – MUSTARD FAMILY. The young plants of more than a dozen local species are potentially edible as greens, and the seeds are likewise potentially edible. These plants are available during the cooler seasons.

Descurainia pinnata. TANSY MUSTARD. The seeds were widely used for food (Bean & Saubel 1972; Felger et al. 1992; Rea 1997) (Figure 15.3). Castetter and Underhill (1935:24) say that it was "the most common [wild] seed crop" of the Tohono O'odham, but "it was not an important Cocopa food" (Castetter & Bell 1951:192). Young plants were sometimes boiled as greens or pit-baked by the Quechans (Castetter & Bell 1951). Substantial quantities of the seeds have been found in Hohokam sites, which led Bohrer (1986 in Hodgson 2001) to speculate that it was cultivated. It can be a common weed in cultivated fields, and this may have been a source for the Hohokam. The seeds, which become mucilaginous when wet, were widely esteemed for medicinal purposes (Bean & Saubel 1972; Hodgson 2001). Among the Hia C'ed O'odham the "seeds [were] used as food and eye medicine (Delores Lewis) or put in water and drunk for stomach trouble (Philip Salcido)" (Felger et al. 1992:22–23). PI, CP, GR, OP, SD.

Lepidium lasiocarpum. SAND PEPPERGRASS. The herbage of this and other species in the genus has been used in many places as a spicy condiment and as cooked greens or for salads (Hodgson 2001; Uphof 1968). The

Seris used it for the chile-like flavor (Felger & Moser 1985). PI, CP, GR, OP, SD.

Lepidium thurberi. ARIZONA PEPPERGRASS. The seeds were eaten in the Tohono O'odham region (Castetter & Underhill 1935). OP.

BURSERACEAE – FRANKINCENSE FAMILY

Bursera microphylla. ELEPHANT TREE; TOROTE. The aromatic foliage and sap were used for medicinal and ritual purposes, at least among the Cahuillas and Seris (Bean & Saubel 1972; Felger & Moser 1985), and the Gila River Pimas boiled the leaves as an emetic (Rea 1977). Lumholtz (1912:331) reports that "the root of the torote tree, crushed and left in water, furnished necessary material for the tanning" of mule deer, pronghorn, or bighorn sheep hides. *Jatropha cuneata* is also called "torote," but he probably is referring to *B. microphylla* since he calls it a "tree" and burseras are used for tanning elsewhere whereas jatrophas are not. PI, CP, GR, OP, SD.

CACTACEAE – CACTUS FAMILY

Carnegiea gigantea. SAGUARO. This well-known Sonoran Desert icon is one of the most culturally important and revered plants in the region (Bell et al. 1980; Castetter & Bell 1937; Castetter & Underhill 1935; Crosswhite 1980; Felger et al. 1992; Hodgson 2001; Lumholtz 1912; Nabhan 1982, 1985; Nabhan et al. 1982; Rea 1997; Betty Melvin in Zepeda 1985:73). The fruit, ripe in early summer, served as a major food resource, and people seasonally moved their residence for the harvest. Important saguaro fruit-gathering camps for the Hia C'ed O'odham included Ajo, Bates Well, the Quijotoa Mountains, Quitovac, and Santa Rosa (Bell 1980), and some of these camps were probably used for harvesting organ pipe fruit as well (Hodgson 2001).

The juicy, sweet pulp was eaten fresh, dried for later use (see organ pipe, *Stenocereus thurberi*), or made into syrup and wine. The protein- and oil-rich seeds were ground and consumed, either freshly harvested or stored. The seeds are digestible when the seed coat is broken, such as when ground on a grinding stone (metate). Saguaro and organ pipe wine was ceremonially important among O'odham groups and provided the only significant alcoholic beverages in the Dry Borders region. Wine was generally made from fresh fruit but could also be made from saguaro fruit syrup (Crosswhite 1980). Haury (1975) and Ezell (1937) deduced that the Hohokam used vinegar from saguaro wine to etch designs on seashells that are so abundant in the archaeological record.

The dry, woody, stem "ribs" were made into slats for house frames, walls, shelves, saguaro fruit-gathering poles, light tools, tongs for picking cholla buds and joints, cradleboards, bird cages, traps for quail, and firedrill boards (see *Larrea* and *Pluchea*). Cactus "boots" (the woody calluses formed around woodpecker holes) were fashioned into various containers or vessels, including drinking bottles, dishes, and tobacco pouches. PI, CP, GR, OP, SD.

The term *pitahaya* was used by Spaniards and others until sometime in the second half of the nineteenth century to refer to columnar cacti in general, including the saguaro and organ pipe (Castetter & Underhill 1935; Crosswhite 1980; Mitch 1972). Kino and Manje's frequent references to pitahaya fruit as a major food for the people of Pimería Alta (Burrus 1971) can include both saguaro and organ pipe. Kino and his captain make frequent mention of being given "pitahaya" fruits during their travels in Pimería Alta. Since they rarely traveled during summertime, they must have been given dried or rehydrated cactus fruits—for example, they were given "pitahayas" at Quitovac on March 12, 1701, a time when the fresh fruits would have been unavailable (Burrus 1971:265).

Cylindropuntia spp. CHOLLAS. Flower buds and young cladodes ("joints," or stem segments) were harvested in spring and cooked as vegetables. The fruits of the fleshy or succulent-fruited species were eaten fresh or cooked (some cholla species have inedible fruits because they are dry at maturity). The large "seeds" were discarded (each seed is embedded in a bony, aril-like structure). The spines, including the glochids, of chollas and prickly pear fruits were removed by several methods including vigorously brushing them in sand or gravel or soaking in water (Childs 1954; Felger & Moser 1985; Hodgson 2001; Rea 1997). Chollas were extensively used by most O'odham groups. Chollas are scarce in the lower Colorado River valley (Felger 2000). Cocopahs had access to several cholla species, especially *C. acanthocarpa* and *C. bigelovii*.

Cylindropuntia acanthocarpa. BUCKHORN CHOLLA. The flower buds and young cladodes, harvested in spring and often pit-baked (see *Suaeda nigra*), have been significant food resources for O'odham people from prehistoric to present times (Greenhouse et al. 1981; Hodgson 2001; Betty Melvin in Zepeda 1985:55). Cahuillas ate the fruits fresh or dried and stored them; ashes of the stems were applied to cuts and burns to facilitate healing (Bean & Saubel 1972). PI, CP, GR, OP, SD.

Cylindropuntia arbuscula. PENCIL CHOLLA. The fleshy fruits were eaten fresh by the Seris (Felger & Moser 1985). Gila River Pimas cooked the buds and fruit in the same manner as those of *C. acanthocarpa,* but they were said to taste different, the fruit being a bit more sour. They were harvested later in the season, and both the buds and fruits were often dried for future use (Rea 1997). It was probably a minor resource except where locally common. PI, OP, SD.

Cylindropuntia bigelovii. TEDDYBEAR CHOLLA. The Cahuillas pit-baked the buds (Bean & Saubel 1972). Seris pit-baked young stem segments and made a diuretic tea from the roots (Felger & Moser 1985). O'odham and Seri graves were often covered with brush and chollas, often this species, to discourage animals such as coyotes from digging (Felger & Moser 1985; Rea 1997). Gila River Pimas used pieces of this cholla as barricades against marauding animals in their fields (Felger & Moser 1985; Rea 1997). PI, AG, CP, GR, OP, SD.

Cylindropuntia echinocarpa. SILVER CHOLLA. The flower buds and young cladodes were prepared in a similar manner as those of *C. acanthocarpa* and often constituted a staple food in spring (Castetter & Bell 1942; Castetter & Underhill 1935). *C. echinocarpa* is primarily a Lower Colorado Valley species at lower elevations while *C. acanthocarpa* in the Dry Borders mostly occurs at slightly higher elevations (Felger 2000). PI, CP, GR.

Cylindropuntia fulgida. JUMPING CHOLLA. The fleshy fruits are available all year and were often a significant food resource. They were consumed fresh or cooked and could be dried and stored (Castetter & Bell 1942; Castetter & Underhill 1935; Felger & Moser 1985; Nabhan et al. 1982). Dried, black gum that accumulates on the stem from injuries is edible and was much appreciated by Seris and Yaquis (Felger & Moser 1985; Felger & F. Molina, unpublished field notes). This dried gum was ground, cleaned, and cooked, often in animal fat, or eaten uncooked with water added. The stems, gum, fruits, and roots have been used medicinally (Felger & Moser 1985). PI, CP, GR, OP, SD.

Cylindropuntia leptocaulis. DESERT CHRISTMAS CHOLLA. The small, fleshy fruits, red when ripe, were eaten fresh (Chico Suni in Felger et al. 1992; Rea 1997). The fruits ripen mostly in midwinter and spring. PI, CP, GR, OP, SD.

Cylindropuntia ramosissima. DIAMOND CHOLLA. Bean & Saubel (1972) report that the fruits were eaten fresh or dried for later use. The stems, with the spines removed, were boiled into a soup or dried for future use. The fruits very quickly become dry on maturing (Felger 2000) and hardly seem edible. PI, CP, GR, OP.

Cylindropuntia spinosior. CANE CHOLLA. The fleshy fruits are edible, but it is not a common species in the Dry Borders area. CP, OP, SD.

Cylindropuntia versicolor. STAGHORN CHOLLA. Flower buds and young stems were cooked (Castetter & Underhill 1935), and the fleshy fruits were eaten fresh. This species is rare in the Dry Borders area. OP.

Echinocactus polycephalus. MANY-HEADED BARREL CACTUS. Sliced pieces of the stems were eaten, often boiled or pit-baked, by Hia C'ed O'odham and others.

In "modern" times (probably during the first half of the twentieth century) the stems were made into cactus candy (Bean & Saubel 1972; Hodgson 2001; Zepeda 1985). The flower buds and seeds were eaten by the Cahuillas and others (Barrows 1900; Coville 1892). PI, CP, GR.

Echinocereus engelmannii. STRAWBERRY HEDGEHOG CACTUS. The fruits, ripe in spring, are delicious and were eaten fresh together with the small seeds (Felger & Moser 1985; Nabhan et al. 1982; Rea 1997). The cooked stems were also eaten. "They ate the meat of the hedgehog cactus...like potatoes.... Shave them and then you cut them...and put salt on them" (Betty Melvin in Zepeda 1985:61). Considerable quantities of seeds were found at a Hohokam site near Phoenix, suggesting cultivation and use as a trade item (Gasser 1982; Gasser & Kwiatkowski 1991). PI, CP, GR, OP, SD.

Echinocereus nicholii. GOLDEN HEDGEHOG CACTUS. The fruits, ripe in spring, were eaten together with the seeds by Hia C'ed O'odham (Nabhan in Hodgson 2001), probably as a minor food resource in late spring. Hodgson (2001) found the fruits to be even sweeter and better-tasting than other hedgehog cactus fruits. CP, OP.

Ferocactus cylindraceus, F. emoryi, and **F. wislizeni.** BARREL CACTUS. People across the Sonoran Desert made use of these large cacti. The flower buds and flowers were cooked and sometimes dried and stored. Sometimes the buds were eaten fresh, although they are bitter unless cooked. The seeds were ground into an oily paste. The fresh fruits are edible but very acidic or sour (Bean & Saubel 1972; Felger & Moser 1985). Barrel cactus stems were baked in a pit, and the "meat" sliced and eaten or the "pulp" otherwise cooked (Castetter & Underhill 1935; Rea 1997; Melvin in Zepeda 1985:49); in "modern" times (probably during the first half of the twentieth century) the stems were made into cactus candy (Hodgson 2001). Palmer (1871) reported that Tohono O'odham boiled pieces of the pulp in saguaro or organ pipe fruit syrup. Emergency liquid could be extracted from *F. cylindraceus* and *F. wislizeni* stems, but *F. emoryi* is apparently toxic (Felger & Moser 1985; Hodgson 2001). The stout spines, heated and bent, were fashioned into fishhooks by the Mohaves and Quechans (Castetter & Bell 1951; Palmer 1870). "When it [the plant] is not hard yet, you put it on the sore. If the plant is hard, you boil it and then wash the sore with it. The sore will get better quickly" (Melvin in Zepeda 1985:80). PI, CP, GR, OP, SD.

Mammillaria grahamii and **Mammillaria** spp. FISH-HOOK CACTUS. Fresh fruits are rather tasty and were eaten by children and probably by all ages as trail snacks (Felger & Moser 1985; Hodgson 2001). Ear drops prepared from the stems served as a treatment for earache for Gila River Pimas and Seris (Curtin 1949; Felger & Moser 1985). Gila River Pimas rubbed the red fruits "on arrowshafts to color them" (Curtin 1949:57). Fruits of *M. tetrancistra* are not edible owing to the corky base on the seeds (Felger 2000). An account of emergency liquid ("water") obtained from *Mammillaria* stems is provided by Rea 1997. PI, CP, GR, OP, SD.

Opuntia. PRICKLY PEARS. Young stem segments, cladodes or "pads" (sometimes erroneously called "leaves"), were cooked and eaten, as were the fleshy fruits—after the spines and glochids were removed, of course. As with the chollas (*Cylindropuntia*), the large "seeds" (actually each seed is embedded in a bony, aril-like structure) were usually discarded (*O. basilaris* is an exception).

Opuntia basilaris. BEAVERTAIL CACTUS. Cahuillas ate the fruits fresh. The flower buds were pit-baked or sometimes dried and stored. The pads were boiled as a vegetable and the "seeds ground into an edible mush" (Bean & Saubel 1972:95). This is one of few references to *Opuntia* "seeds" being eaten. This small prickly pear occurs in dry mountains in the western parts of the Dry Borders area but is not very common (Felger 2000). PI, CP, GR.

Opuntia chlorotica. PANCAKE PRICKLY PEAR. The fruits, comparatively smaller and drier than other prickly pears, were probably seldom eaten in the Dry Borders region, although Gifford (1936) reports that the Yavapais ate them. Castetter and Underhill (1935:16) report "an upright species of prickly pear...is utilized by washing the large waxy flowers to remove their sticky secretion then frying them in grease, formerly deer fat, now lard." This is probably *O. chlorotica*, which indeed has an upright habit. PI, CP, GR, OP, SD.

Opuntia engelmannii var. **engelmannii.** DESERT PRICKLY PEAR. The large, juicy, purplish-red fruits, which ripen in summer, were eaten fresh or dried or made into juice, jam, syrup (Betty Melvin in Zepeda 1985:63, 82–83). The young "pads" were harvested in late spring and summer and cooked as a vegetable (Castetter & Underhill 1935; Melvin in Zepeda 1985:63). This species occurs in the eastern part of the Dry Borders region, where it was undoubtedly a significant food resource. CP, GR, OP, SD.

Opuntia engelmannii var. **flavispina.** YELLOW-SPINE DESERT PRICKLY PEAR. This cactus is highly localized and in the Dry Borders occurs at former villages or places of occupation such as Agua Dulce Pass, Alamo Canyon, and Quitobaquito. I believe this prickly pear was selected and transplanted (Felger 2000; Felger et al. 1992). The plants are more robust and attractive and the fruits somewhat larger than those of var. *engelmannii*, and the spines are yellow rather than dull-colored. The uses would be the same as for var. *engelmannii*. CP, OP.

Opuntia phaeacantha. BROWN-SPINE PRICKLY PEAR. The fruits of this species are smaller, less juicy, and much less desirable for eating than *O. engelmannii* fruits (see Pinkava 2003). The "Papago distinguish two kinds of edible prickly pears (*Opuntia* sp.), one of which produces chills and nausea in susceptible people" (Castetter & Underhill 1935:22); this statement likely refers to *O. phaeacantha*, which occurs at the eastern margin of the Dry Borders, or perhaps *O. chlorotica* (the "other" kind is undoubtedly *O. engelmannii*). GR, OP, SD.

Pachycereus schottii [*Lophocereus schottii*]. SENITA. The rather small, fleshy fruits were eaten fresh by the Hia C'ed O'odham and Seris but are not as sweet as organ pipe or saguaro fruits (Felger & Moser 1985; Nabhan et al. 1982; Betty Melvin in Zepeda 1985:55). The fruits are available during warmer times of the year, especially in summer, but were not a major resource. Rea (1997) reports that the fruits were sometimes made into syrup and preserves. The stems continue to be medicinally important for a wide range of remedies (Felger 2000; Paredes et al. 2000). PI, CP (rare), OP.

Peniocereus greggii. DESERT NIGHT-BLOOMING CEREUS. The plants are everywhere scarce. The fruits ripen in summer and early fall; the pulp is sweet and juicy and eaten fresh. The large tuberous root was widely used medicinally, to treat diabetes and digestive and respiratory ailments, for example (Curtin 1949; Felger et al. 1992; Hodgson 2001). It was "chewed raw for thirst or...baked whole in ashes, peeled and eaten" (Castetter & Underhill 1935:18). These writers also claim that the "stalks" were eaten, but this seems improbable. The root was also used for shampoo (Betty Melvin in Zepeda 1985:78–79). PI, CP, GR, OP, SD.

Peniocereus striatus. SACAMATRACA. The sweet and juicy red fruits ripen in summer and are edible (Felger & Moser 1985). The tuberous roots were used medicinally (Felger & Moser 1985; Hodgson 2001). It is very rare at the southeastern corner of the Dry Borders region but is more common farther south in Sonora. OP.

Stenocereus thurberi. ORGAN PIPE; PITAHAYA; PITAHAYA DULCE. The fresh fruits are juicy, sweet, and delicious and were a major summertime harvest (Figure 15.4). The fruit pulp was eaten fresh and also dried, was made into syrup and jam, and was especially relished for wine (Childs 1954; Felger & Moser 1985; Hodgson 2001; Betty Melvin in Zepeda 1985:55). People at Quitovac sometimes harvest the fruit commercially (Felger et al. 1992). Where numerous enough, organ pipe replaced saguaro fruit for ceremonial wine since it is sweeter, juicier, and tastes better. Just as they did for the saguaro fruit harvest, the Hia C'ed O'odham seasonally moved their residence for the harvest. Lumholtz (1912:331) reports that they "used to come as far as Quitovaquito and Santo Domingo to gather mesquite beans...

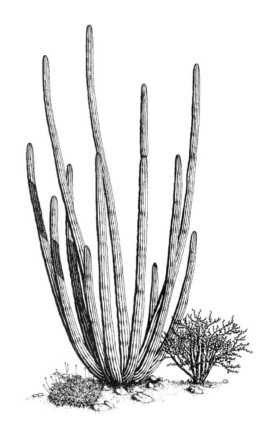

Figure 15.4. Stenocereus thurberi. *(Drawing by Matthew B. Johnson)*

and eat sahuaro and pitahaya." In northwestern Mexico the woody stem ribs served for house construction and fences, utensils, and many other utilitarian purposes. During Spanish colonial times the term *pitahaya* could mean saguaro or organ pipe (see *Carnegiea gigantea*). It is common and widespread in OP but occurs only locally in PI, CP, GR, and SD.

CAPPARACEAE – CAPER FAMILY

Isomeris arborea. BLADDERPOD BUSH. This shrub is scarce in the Dry Borders. The young fruits were eaten by the Cahuillas (Barrows 1900), and the leaves were prepared as greens (Weiss 1994). PI (higher elevations).

Wislizenia refracta. JACKASS CLOVER. According to Kirk (1970), the leaves can be cooked as greens. AG, PI, CP, OP.

CAPRIFOLIACEAE – HONEYSUCKLE FAMILY

Sambucus nigra. ELDERBERRY. The berries served Hia C'ed O'odham people "as a medicine and sometimes for food" (Betty Melvin in Zepeda 1985:65).

CHENOPODIACEAE – GOOSEFOOT FAMILY

Allenrolfea occidentalis. IODINE BUSH. The seeds, toasted and ground into flour, were made into *atole* or a drink by the Cahuillas, Gila River Pimas, Quechans, and Seris (Bean & Saubel 1972; Castetter & Bell 1951; Felger & Moser 1985; Rea 1997) (Figure 15.5). The Quechans harvested it in December after frost. Rea says it was an emergency food for the Gila River Pimas. It is especially

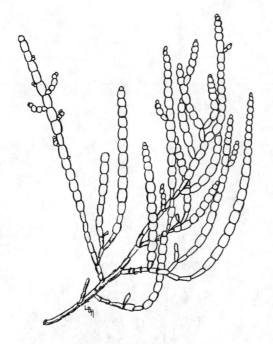

Figure 15.5. Allenrolfea occidentalis. *(Drawing by Lucretia Brezeale Hamilton)*

common at the Colorado delta and near the coast and can produce substantial quantities of seeds. AG.

Atriplex spp. SALTBUSH. Seeds of most species were parched or cooked with other foods but generally served as emergency food (Hodgson 2001). Young plants of herbaceous species or young shoots of shrubs were cooked as greens or with other foods for the salty flavor (Rea 1997).

Atriplex canescens. FOUR-WING SALTBUSH. Tea made from the leaves was taken as an emetic by the Seris (Felger & Moser 1985). PI, AG, CP, GR, OP, SD.

Atriplex elegans. WHEELSCALE. The young plants were eaten as greens or seasoning by the Gila River Pimas (Rea 1997; Russell 1908). PI, CP, GR, OP, SD.

Atriplex lentiformis. QUAIL BUSH. The cooked and prepared seeds were eaten by people of the lower Río Colorado, where this large shrub is abundant (Castetter & Bell 1951). Cahuillas crushed and steamed the herbage and "flowers" and inhaled the steam for nasal congestion; they chewed fresh leaves or smoked the dry leaves as a remedy for head colds (Bean & Saubel 1972). PI, AG, OP.

Atriplex polycarpa. DESERT SALTBUSH. The seeds were eaten (Castetter & Bell 1951) and perhaps used as a famine food by the Hohokam around Phoenix (Bohrer 1985 in Hodgson 2001). An infusion of mashed young shoots was used by the Seris as shampoo and laundry detergent (Felger & Moser 1985). PI, CP, GR, OP.

Atriplex wrightii. ANNUAL SALTBUSH. The leafy shoots were prepared as greens in summer, especially for seasoning (Castetter & Underhill 1935). The young shoots are soft and tender, making it one of the more desirable

Sonoran Desert atriplexes, but in the Dry Borders it is known only from disturbed habitats near Sonoyta.

Chenopodium spp. (including *C. watsonii*). GOOSE-FOOT. Young plants were sometimes eaten as greens, and the seeds were parched and ground as flour. These plants are generally not common in the Dry Borders region and, except for *C. murale,* are often unpleasantly stinky. CP, GR, OP, SD.

*Chenopodium murale. NETLEAF GOOSEFOOT. Young plants were eaten as greens (Castetter & Bell 1951; Castetter & Underhill 1935). The seeds, toasted and ground into flour, are apparently the only ones in the region that open like popcorn when heated (Felger & Moser 1985). It is reportedly not native in the New World, although it has a long history of use in the region (Castetter & Underhill 1935; Felger & Moser 1985; Nabhan et al. 1982). PI, AG, CP, GR, OP, SD.

Monolepis nuttalliana. POVERTY WEED. The plants of this spring annual were widely used as greens (Betty Melvin in Zepeda 1985:73). The seeds are also edible (Hodgson 2001). CP, GR, OP, SD.

Suaeda nigra. SEEPWEED. It was cooked by Gila River Pimas as greens, used for flavoring in cooking other foods, or added to cactus fruit for flavor. It was also used to line a pit for baking cholla buds of *Cylindropuntia acanthocarpa* (Curtin 1949; Rea 1997; Russell 1908). Young tender plants of this or a very similar species, called *romerillo,* are a well-known vegetable in southern Mexican cuisine. AG, CP, OP.

CRASSULACEAE – STONECROP FAMILY

Dudleya arizonica. ARIZONA LIVEFOREVER. The fresh leaves and young flowering stems of California species, including the closely related *D. pulverulenta,* were eaten in spring (Bean & Saubel 1972; Meigs 1939; Palmer 1878; Weiss 1994). PI, CP, GR, OP.

CUCURBITACEAE – GOURD FAMILY

Brandegea bigelovii. DESERT STARVINE. Seris used the roots to make a cleansing shampoo. A bitter infusion was drunk during vision quests to induce an altered state of consciousness (Felger & Moser 1985). PI, CP, GR, OP, SD.

*Citrullus lanatus. WATERMELON. This is one of the earliest Old World crops to be grown in the region (Rea 1997). Kino found fields of watermelons near the mouth of the Gila River in 1700 (Bolton 1919), and Francisco Garcés saw them at the Colorado delta on December 16, 1775 (Coues 1900), as did Lt. Hardy (1829:343, 346) in July 1826. These were relatively small watermelons of several varieties, mostly round or sometimes elongated, and of different colors. Green as well as ripe melons were stored, often for many months, in waist-deep pits in a dry place. The bottom of the pit was lined with bean vines, and the pit was covered with earth if the owners went away (Gifford 1933).

*Cucumis melo. MUSKMELONS. Different cultivars of this Old World melon have been grown in the region since Spanish colonial times. Melons were eaten fresh or sliced and sun-dried, were often made into cakes, and were stored. The cooked seeds were eaten whole or mashed (Gifford 1933).

Cucurbita argyrosperma subsp. argyrosperma var. callicarpa. CUSHAW SQUASH. This rank-growing squash was a major indigenous cultivated crop in the Colorado delta and elsewhere in the Dry Borders region and across most of the Sonoran Desert region. It has been found in Hohokam archaeological sites and is still cultivated regionally. The large, green and white mottled and striped squash and the thick, corky pedicel (fruiting stalk) are unmistakable. The fleshy part was eaten freshly cooked (baked or boiled) or was cut into long thin strips, dried, and stored "all year" (Castetter & Bell 1951:113; Betty Melvin in Zepeda 1985:57, 58, 78). The seeds were parched and eaten, ground or not, and also stored. Like all cultivated squashes, the flowers are edible, and it is a common practice in Mexico to cook the male flowers as a vegetable. Colorado River people stored the squashes "in pits like [those for] watermelons" (Gifford 1933:266). Alarcón provides several references to squash along the lower Río Colorado in August 1540: "an elder came with…some small squash," and "they have…pots in which they cook the squash" (Flint & Flint 2005:194, 196). Kino and Manje encountered squash cultivated wherever agriculture was practiced (Burrus 1971).

Cucurbita mixta, described as a distinct species in the 1940s, was previously included as a kind of C. moschata, leading to confusion in earlier literature. Merrick and Bates (1989), however, found that the name C. mixta is a synonym and should be considered part of the C. argyrosperma complex, consisting of two subspecies and four varieties that are native and wild or cultivated from the southwestern United States to Central America. The large, cultivated cushaw squash of the southwestern United States and Mexico is var. callicarpa.

Cucurbita digitata, C. palmata. COYOTE GOURD. The seeds are reported to be edible after being toasted or boiled and ground into flour (see Hodgson 2001). The roots were used to treat dandruff and were mashed in water for use as soap and bleach for fabrics (Betty Melvion in Bell et al. 1980; Betty Melvin in Zepeda 1985: 49, 54). River Pimas used juice from the root, extracted by pounding in a mortar and boiling, as ear drops to alleviate earache (Russell 1908). PI, CP, GR, OP, SD.

*Cucurbita maxima, C. moschata, and C. pepo. PUMPKINS AND SQUASHES. A number of varieties, introduced during historic times, have been grown in the

region, especially by people living along the rivers. Whole pumpkins or squashes were baked in ashes, or the fleshy part was cooked or cut into strips and sun-dried. The seeds were also eaten after parching. C. maxima was domesticated in South America, and C. moschata and C. pepo were domesticated in North America; they apparently were not grown in the prehistoric Southwest. It is not possible to distinguish the species based on the casual references to the common names. Most southwestern authors have confusingly used the terms pumpkin and squash for cultivars of any of these three species or the indigenous C. argyrosperma var. callicarpa (e.g., Castetter and Bell 1942, 1951; Gifford 1933).

Lagenaria siceraria subsp. siceraria [L. vulgaris]. BOTTLE GOURD. These gourds were grown in summertime gardens by the Cocopahs, Gila River Pimas, Tohono O'odham, and other agricultural people. Nonagricultural people obtained bottle gourds by trade (Gifford 1933; Rea 1997). The various kinds of cultivars differ in seed shape and color as well as shape and size of the gourds. All cucurbits are frost-sensitive, and since the fruits mature late in the season, the landraces grown in northern Sonora and southern Arizona were developed to produce mature fruits before the onset of frost (Rea 1997). Different sizes and shapes were fashioned into bowls, canteens, cups, dishes, ladles, storage and seed containers, and musical instruments, including rattles (Fillman Bell in Bell et al. 1980; Castetter & Bell 1942, 1951; Castetter & Underhill 1935; Rea 1997). Gourd canteens were especially valued. The small, elegant, and abstractly painted O'odham masks used in Viigida (Vikita) ceremonies (Hayden 1987; Lumholtz 1912) were made from bottle gourds, as were various Piman masks (Rea 1997). A different Hia C'ed O'odham gourd mask described by Childs (1954:38) "had long horse or cow hair for whiskers" and seems to have been used for a Pascola-style dance. Bottle gourds are represented in the prehistoric archaeological record of southwestern North America, but as with other cucurbits, there are few specimens from the Dry Borders and adjacent regions (Bohrer 1970; Gasser 1982).

Tumamoca macdougalii. TUMAMOC GLOBE-BERRY. The small red fruits, ripe in late summer and fall, were eaten fresh by the Seris (Felger & Moser 1985). The small vines are occasionally seen in the eastern part of the Dry Borders region during the summer rainy season. OP, SD.

CYPERACEAE – SEDGE FAMILY

Cyperus esculentus. YELLOW NUTGRASS. The small, tuberous roots are edible. Castetter and Bell (1951) report that the seeds were eaten by the Cocopahs. It was especially common in the lower Río Colorado. The Gila River Pimas chewed fresh or dry tubers as a remedy for coughs or colds. To alleviate the effects of snakebite the tuberous roots were chewed and repeatedly applied to the wound (Curtin 1949). PI, AG, CP, SD.

Scirpus americanus. THREE-SQUARE BULRUSH; TULE. The rhizomes were sometimes chewed (Palmer 1871). Although it seems an unlikely major food resource, it is so abundant in the Colorado delta that it may have been significant. Some general references to use of tules or rushes may refer to this large bulrush. Also see *Juncus, Phragmites,* and *Typha.* PI, AG, OP.

EUPHORBIACEAE – SPURGE FAMILY

Croton wigginsii. DUNE CROTON. The closely related *C. californicus* was used for fuel to steam shellfish and as a fish poison (Felger & Moser 1985:293). Castetter and Bell (1951:222), however, say "the use of true fish poisons was not employed by any of the lower Colorado tribes." The Cahuillas used *C. californicus* to treat earache and to relieve congestion from colds, but the plant is toxic and was used in small doses (Bean & Saubel 1972). PI, AG, CP, GR.

Euphorbia spp., including *E. albomarginata, E. melanadenia, E. pedicilifera,* and *E. polycarpa.* SPURGE. Herbaceous species in the subgenus *Chamaesyce,* including more than a dozen species in the Dry Borders, have widespread pharmacological use. A few regional examples are given here. The Cahuillas made a decoction of the plant as a febrifuge and to treat chicken pox and smallpox. An infusion was drunk to treat sores of the mouth. To treat rattlesnake bites, a decoction was taken or, more commonly, a poultice of the plant was applied to the wound (Bean & Saubel 1972). Use of euphorbia for rattlesnake bite seems widespread. Describing the site of Fort Yuma in 1854, Lt. Nathaniel Michler (1987:101) wrote that "euphorbia, a rank poison . . . [was] used by the Indians as an antidote against the bite of the rattlesnake."

Euphorbias were also used to treat cuts, earaches, infections, sores, wounds, the bites of black widow and other spiders, and the stings of carpenter bees and honey bees (Bean & Saubel 1972; Cruz Matus in Felger, unpublished notes of 1985 interview in Guaymas; Train et al. 1957; Zigmond 1981). Among the Gila River Pimas the plants were chewed as a laxative, but using too much would make one sick. It was used in the same manner to eliminate intestinal worms (Rea 1997). The Seris mashed fresh herbage (mostly from *E. polycarpa*) with salt and oil and applied it as a poultice to swollen areas. They also used the plant to treat toothache or heart pain (Felger & Moser 1985). Cruz Matus (interview, 1985), in Guaymas, Sonora, explained that the Yaquis stored the dried plant for future use or chopped it up green if needed immediately. PI, AG, CP, GR, OP, SD.

Jatropha cardiophylla. LIMBERBUSH; SANGRENGADO. The flexible stems were sometimes used for basketry by

Tohono O'odham (Castetter & Bell 1935:57). The clear sap was applied to wounds to stop the flow of blood (Kearney & Peebles 1960). OP, GR, SD.

Jatropha cinerea. ASHY LIMBERBUSH. Hia C'ed O'odham used the plant as a remedy for toothache and sores (Felger et al. 1992). This species is rare in the Dry Borders, where it reaches its northernmost limit (Felger 2000). We reported that stems were used for baskets around Quitobaquito (Felger et al. 1992), but it is likely that *J. cuneata* was used instead. PI, OP.

Jatropha cuneata. LIMBERBUSH; SANGRENGADO. The flexible stems were widely used for basketry (e.g., Felger & Moser 1985; Lumholtz 1912:331; Betty Melvin in Zepeda 1985:61), and a reddish dye was made from the roots (Felger et al. 1992) (Figure 15.6). The tender split stems were used in baskets for coiling around cattail stalks *(Typha)* or beargrass leaves (*Nolina microcarpa,* which occurs farther east in southern Arizona and northern Sonora) (Philip Salcido & Delores Lewis in Felger et al. 1992; see *Jatropha cinerea*). Childs (1954:36) reports red dye for women's buckskin dresses made from a "bush which we call Leather Weed—the Mexicans call it *Sangre en Grande.*" See *Bursera.* PI, CP, GR, OP.

Sebastiania bilocularis [*Sapium biloculare*]. HIERBA DE LA FLECHA; 'INA HITÁ. The poisonous sap was famous as arrow poison and widely feared (Felger & Moser 1985); for example, Chico Suni said it is "poison, it will kill you" (Felger et al. 1992:27). Medicinal uses include treating sores (Nabhan et al. 1982). This shrub is the host plant for a large native silkmoth (see *Eupackardia calleta*). The cocoons of this moth were used by O'odham groups for Yaqui-style pascola leg rattles, and the O'odham name for the plant refers to a pascola dance step (Chico Suni in Felger et al. 1992). PI, CP, GR, OP, SD.

FABACEAE (LEGUMINOSAE) – LEGUME FAMILY

Acacia constricta. WHITE-THORN ACACIA. The Seris drank a decoction of the mashed seeds and leaves to treat upset stomach and diarrhea (Felger & Moser 1985). CP, GR, OP, SD.

Acacia greggii. CATCLAW ACACIA. The seeds were parched and ground, or the pods pounded, and the flour consumed as *atole* or made into cakes (Castetter 1935; Russell 1908). These foods, however, were sometimes bitter and not esteemed (Bean & Saubel 1972). The Gila River Pimas drank tea from the root for stomach ulcers and more recently to alleviate kidney problems caused by alcohol consumption (Rea 1997). The hard, reddish wood served many purposes, including bows, crosspieces of saguaro fruit-gathering poles, firewood, prayer sticks (see *Aquila chrysaetos,* golden eagle), and firewood, and the flexible branches were used for cradleboard frames (Bean & Saubel 1972; Castetter &

Underhill 1935; Felger & Moser 1985; Rea 1997). PI, CP, GR, OP, SD.

Dalea mollis. SILKY DALEA. The Seris applied a poultice of the heated plant to swellings (Felger & Moser 1985). PI, AG, CP, GR, OP, SD.

Hoffmannseggia glauca. HOG POTATO. This plant is sometimes locally abundant in playas or dry lake beds and bottomlands. The tuberous "potato-like" roots were cooked and eaten by the Quechans (Yumas) and Gila River Pimas (Castetter & Bell 1951; Forde 1931). "Wild potatoes" used by the Cocopahs (Chittenden 1901; Gifford 1933) are probably this plant (Castetter & Bell 1951: 211). The Gila River Pimas sometimes got the tuberous roots from a gopher's cache during plowing (Rea 1997). PI, AG, CP, GR.

Olneya tesota. IRONWOOD. The seeds, harvested in early summer, were probably a significant resource for many groups. It is one of the few Sonoran Desert foods that was cooked in changes of water, or water-leached (Castetter & Bell 1951; Felger & Moser 1985). The seeds "were toasted, ground, and consumed as pinole" by people in the Dry Borders region (Lumholtz 1912:331). An infusion of the sapwood was drunk by the Seris as an emetic, to prevent breathing hard when running, and to obtain power or visions during the vision quest (Felger & Moser 1985). The extremely hard wood was used in many ways, including as digging sticks with a fire-hardened point, fences, firewood, house posts, musical rasps, utensils, and war clubs (Castetter & Bell 1942; Castetter & Underhill 1935; Gifford 1933; Rea 1997). PI, CP, GR, OP, SD.

***Parkinsonia aculeata.** MEXICAN PALO VERDE. The seeds (probably the seed coats) are bitter and probably toxic (Hodgson 2001; Nabhan et al. 1979). Reports of the seeds being eaten (e.g., Castetter & Bell 1942:60) should be viewed with caution. Gentry (1942), however, reports that in southeastern Sonora the fresh, green seeds were eaten raw after peeling off the seed coat. It is rare in natural areas of the Dry Borders but common around settlements. PI.

Parkinsonia florida [*Cercidium floridum*]. BLUE PALO VERDE. The seeds, available in early summer, were generally considered less desirable and less important than those of *P. microphylla*, although prepared in essentially the same manner (Felger & Moser 1985; Hodgson 2001). Nevertheless, the seeds and sometimes the flowers and green pods were eaten by the Cahuillas, Gila River Pimas, Hia C'ed O'odham, and Seris (Bean & Saubel 1972; Felger & Moser 1985; Felger et al. 1992; Rea 1997). Compared with *P. microphylla*, the immature seeds are bitter (Rea 1997). The wood is soft and was used for utensils and sometimes for fuel (Felger & Moser 1985). PI, CP, GR, OP, SD.

Figure 15.6. Jatropha cuneata. *Leafless in dry season and leafy following rains. (Drawing by Lucretia Brezeale Hamilton)*

2 cm

Parkinsonia microphylla [*Cercidium microphyllum*]. FOOTHILL PALO VERDE. The seeds, harvested in early summer, provided an important food resource for the Cahuillas, Cocopahs, Gila River Pimas, Hia C'ed O'odham, Seris, Tohono O'odham, and other Sonoran Desert people (Bean & Saubel 1972; Bell et al. 1980; Castetter & Bell 1935; Felger & Moser 1985; Felger et al. 1992; Hodgson 2001; Rea 1997; Betty Melvin in Zepeda 1985:47, 61–62). The seeds were parched, ground, and generally consumed as *atole*, and were often stored. Hia C'ed O'odham baked the flour with deer fat and water to make a bread-like mass (Fernando Flores in Bell et al. 1980). The flour was also sometimes mixed with ironwood or mesquite flour (Nabhan et al. 1979; Russell 1908). The Cocopahs gathered the seeds in mountains west of the Colorado River (Castetter & Bell 1951). The Seris ate the flowers fresh or cooked, cooked the young green pods with meat, and often got the seeds by robbing packrat nests (Felger & Moser 1985). Fresh green seeds were eaten as snacks (Felger & Moser 1985; Hodgson 2001). The wood is soft and was used for utensils, digging tools and pry bars, small sculptures, and sometimes fuel (Castetter & Bell 1942; Felger & Moser 1985). PI, CP, GR, OP, SD.

Phaseolus acutifolius. TEPARY (wild). The seeds were eaten, but the plant is scarce in the Dry Borders, where it known only from the Ajo Mountains (Nabhan & Felger 1978). OP.

Phaseolus acutifolius. TEPARY (cultivated). Teparies, the traditional cultivated beans in the region, were grown wherever agriculture was practiced, especially along the Colorado and Gila rivers and at oases such as Quitobaquito (Burrus 1971; Castetter & Bell 1951; Felger et al. 1992; Gifford 1933; Kelly 1977; Nabhan & Felger 1978; Rea 1997; Betty Melvin in Zepeda 1985:65) (Figure 15.7). Alarcón reported that in the Colorado delta in August 1540, "among other things, [they gave me] many beans" (Flint & Flint 2005:199). Kino and Manje obtained beans at Sonoyta on February 16, 1699, and in February 1702 Kino found corn, beans, and squash grown at numerous rancherías north of the Colorado delta (Burrus 1971). Colorado delta people made fishing nets from the stem fiber (Castetter & Bell 1951; Heintzelman 1857; Hodgson 2001).

Phaseolus filiformis. DESERT BEAN. Nabhan (1985) reports that the immature pods were eaten fresh and the dry seeds were boiled and eaten like lentils. PI, CP, GR, OP, SD.

Prosopis glandulosa, HONEY MESQUITE, and **P. velutina,** VELVET MESQUITE. From early prehistoric until modern times mesquite served native peoples across the arid lands of North and South America as a primary resource (D'Antoni & Solbrig 1977; Felger 1977) (Figure 15.8). It was the single most useful plant in the Sonoran Desert (Bell & Castetter 1937; Felger & Moser 1985; Hodgson 2001; Rea 1997; Betty Melvin in Zepeda 1985:49, 77). Every part of the tree was used (see Rea 1997 for a wonderful, detailed account of mesquite use and knowledge). Mesquite was the common denomi-

nator among the diverse peoples of the region, agriculturalists as well as hunters and gatherers. It was part of everyday life from cradle to grave and featured prominently in oral literature. Two very similar species occur in the Dry Borders region, *P. glandulosa* in the Lower Colorado Valley and *P. velutina* in the Arizona Upland, and I have not detected any difference in their usage (Felger 2000; Felger et al. 2001). Mesquite was one of the first food plants encountered by Europeans in the American Southwest, beginning with Álvar Núñez Cabeza de Vaca in 1535 (Adorno & Pautz 1999) and the Francisco Coronado expedition in 1540 (Flint & Flint 2005). Hernando Alarcón, associated with the Coronado expedition, was given "un pane di Mizquiqui" (a bread made from mesquite) at the Colorado delta in August 1540 (Flint & Flint 2005:208). The Nahuatl-derived term *mizquiqui* undoubtedly resulted from Alarcón's knowledge of the tree in southern Mexico.

The largest mesquite groves grow along major washes and watercourses, providing ample shade and pleasant places to camp. Mesquite pods are large and easy to pick, either from the tree when ripe or from the ground soon after they fall. The Cocopahs used a pole with a short crosspiece lashed with mesquite bark at an acute angle to serve as a hook for bending down spinescent branches to harvest the pods (Gifford 1933:267). The pod is indehiscent (does not split apart), and thus the contents do not fall out. People generally knew the location of trees or groves that produced sweeter pods and superior yields. Ripe pods would be broken open and tasted for sweetness and ripeness. In addition, mesquite pods and screwbeans were obtained from packrat nests, which allowed an extension of the harvest season (see *Neotoma;* Felger & Moser 1985; Kelly 1977).

Harvested pods would be sun-dried or fire-parched and laboriously crushed or ground into flour, often in a bedrock or stone mortar using a large pestle, which itself was likely to be fashioned from mesquite wood or from stone. There were numerous variations in the preparation of the pods and flour, for mesquite "was a versatile staple" (Rea 1997:187). In the Colorado delta region and elsewhere such as along the lower and middle Gila River, the pods were crushed in large wooden mortars made from a cottonwood or mesquite log. Mesquite and screwbean food products generally were prepared without cooking. The flour was most often steeped in water and consumed as *atole* or made into cakes. Pods were also crushed and boiled or steeped in water to make a beverage. Whole mesquite pods or cakes were stored; the flour was not stored because it is hygroscopic and soon becomes hard and undesirable. Mesquite flowers were also eaten, gently mashed in water and the sweet liquid drunk.

Mesquite pods were generally a dependable crop,

but in certain areas extreme freezing weather or extended drought might reduce or cancel the usually copious crop. Although these were rare events, such years could have severe consequences, especially since other wild crops might likewise fail. For the most part, however, mesquite pods were predictably available for harvest at the height of the early summer dry season, making this a time of plenty, and they continued to be available through the summer and fall but generally in reduced quantities. Lumholtz (1912:331) reports that Hia C'ed O'odham "used to come as far as Quitovaquito and Santo Domingo to gather mezquite beans (called by the Mexicans *pechita*)."

The pulp (mesocarp) of mesquite pods is rich in calories and carbohydrates. The pod husk (exocarp) is not digestible, but ground up it adds dietary fiber to the flour. The actual seeds are each encased in a tough, leathery-woody pit (endocarp). The seeds were sometimes laboriously separated from the surrounding endocarp by the Seris and likely by the Hia C'ed O'odham. Gyratory crushers found in the Pinacate region were probably used to process mesquite pods and separate the seeds from the leathery pit (Felger 1977, 2000; Hayden 1969). Most reports of people in the Colorado delta and elsewhere eating the seeds should be interpreted with caution. The term *bean* for either the seed or the whole pod is often loosely and uncritically used. In modern times the Cocopahs and others used mesquite pods as fodder or forage for cattle, horses, and pigs.

A whitish or amber-colored gum, oozing from wounds on the branches or trunk, was extensively employed as medicine, especially for eye ailments, and was eaten as candy, chewed as gum, or mixed with saguaro fruit and eaten like jam. The white gum also was used as a mucilage or gargle to soothe a sore throat (Curtin 1949). The black sap or pitch collected from the bark was used as a general-purpose black dye as well as for many medicinal purposes including eye ailments. It was used for decorating pottery but was most commonly boiled to make black hair dye; for example, Cocopahs and Gila River Pimas mixed this black dye with river mud and left it overnight on the hair to keep it black and kill lice (Gifford 1933; Rea 1997).

Bark from the roots was used by Pimas to treat wounds, and they ate the sap to treat respiratory conditions (Curtin 1947; Kearney & Peebles 1960). The O'odham drank a decoction of the powdered white inner bark as an intestinal antispasmodic. The crushed green leaves were mixed into mother's milk and the mixture strained into a baby's inflamed eye. For treating older people, the crushed leaves were mixed with water. The seeds were eaten as a stomachic, and a decoction of the leaves was drunk for bladder trouble. The Gila River Pimas boiled the root and used the liquid to dress

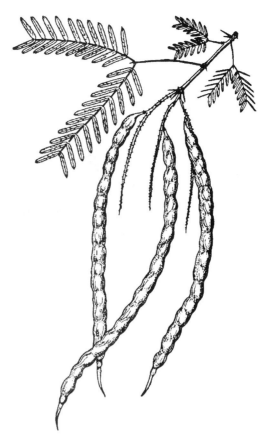

wounds; or they pounded the root, dried it, and then ground it into a fine powder (Rea 1997; Russell 1908). Tea made from the root was also used to treat menstrual problems (Curtin 1949).

Mesquite digging sticks were used for planting, and a similar pole flattened at one end was used for weeding (Kelly 1977). The postcontact plow was made from a single piece of mesquite wood by the O'odham and others. The roots were widely fashioned into multipurpose cordage (Felger 1977). The kickball game was played with a ball made of mesquite wood or a pebble embedded in mesquite gum. Mesquite-wood fishhooks are reported for the Río Colorado (Bourke 1889; Heintzelman 1857). The wood was also used for weapons, including arrow points consisting of sharpened foreshafts (MacDougal 1906), clubs, and maces (Heintzelman 1857). Alarcón (Flint & Flint 2005:190) reported that among the people along the lower Río Colorado "their weapons were bows and arrows made of hard wood and two or three sorts of clubs made from fire-seasoned wood." The hardwood arrows could have been made from various species of trees or shrubs, the bows might have been from screwbean (see next entry), and the clubs most likely were mesquite.

Mesquite continues to be the preferred regional cooking fuel, not only because it is so readily available but because of superior burning qualities and the flavor

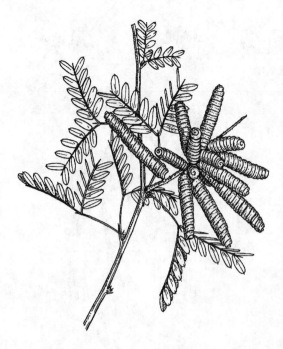

Figure 15.9. Prosopis pubescens. *(Drawing by Lucretia Brezeale Hamilton)*

it imparts to food. House posts most often were made of mesquite trunks, and the forked trunks or main branches were especially popular in local architecture. The Cocopahs fired pottery with mesquite wood, and pottery designs were made by using a chewed end of a mesquite twig to apply black mesquite pitch. Cocopah funeral pyres, fueled with mesquite wood, included two green poles for the sides of the pyre (Gifford 1933). Large basketry granaries, commonplace features on top of traditional houses in the region, were used to store mesquite pods; these granaries were often made with arrowweed *(Pluchea sericea)*, willow *(Salix gooddingii)*, or mesquite stems. Chittenden (1901) reports baskets made by Cocopah women from mesquite-root fiber, but I am skeptical that roots were used. Mesquites thrive under human-disturbed conditions and were common landscape features around regional homes and settlements—many a home was shaded and sheltered by large mesquite trees. Nowadays various South American mesquites, often of hybrid origin, are the most commonly planted urban trees across the Sonoran Desert. PI, AG, CP, GR, OP, SD.

Prosopis pubescens. SCREWBEAN; TORNILLO. Screwbean trees are widespread in the Colorado delta and grow near a few alkaline waterholes elsewhere (Figure 15.9). The pods were harvested in early summer as a significant crop. Screwbean pods were parched or often were buried in a pit to "ripen" or partially ferment, and then were ground into flour. The pods were also sometimes fermented as a beverage (Bell & Castetter 1937; Castetter & Bell 1951). In 1699 people near present-day Yuma gave Manje "some bread" made from screwbean flour (Manje 1954:114), although Kelly (1977:34) says

that "screwbean meal was never made into cakes." Like mesquite pods, whole screwbean pods often were stored for extended periods in large, rooftop basketry granaries. Gila River Pimas used the root bark as remedies for wounds and for menstrual problems (Curtin 1949; Russell 1908).

The hard wood was used in similar ways to that of mesquite, including as weapons, such as war clubs and lances (Gifford 1933:274). On January 1, 1828, James Pattie "examined twenty three bows" of the "Pipi" (River Pai Pai) warriors he and his companions had just killed in a skirmish on the Baja California side of the Colorado delta. He said the bows were "six feet in length, and made of a very tough and elastic kind of wood, which the Spaniards call *Tarnio*" [= tornillo] (Pattie 1988:111). Hardwood bows seen by Alarcón in 1540 might have been made from screwbean or mesquite. AG, OP.

Psorothamnus emoryi. EMORY'S SMOKEBUSH. A fugitive yellow dye was made from the herbage by Seris and Cahuillas (Bean & Saubel 1972; Felger & Moser 1985). PI, AG, CP, GR.

Senna covesii. HOJASEN. The Seris made a tea from the roots to "clean out the stomach," increase appetite, treat measles and kidney disorders, and aid conception. They used tea made from the roots and stems as a liver medicine and to treat chicken pox (Felger & Moser 1985:323). PI, CP, GR, OP, SD.

Sesbania herbacea. COLORADO RIVER HEMP. This robust hot-weather annual often reached more than 2 m tall in the Colorado delta and served as an important fiber plant (Figure 15.10). It was used to make fishing nets (Chittenden 1901) and lines and bow strings (MacDougal 1906). The Yaquis in Sonora ground the entire plant to make soap or detergent to clean the dirt floors of their houses, and the large stems were used to cover the earthen layer of the roofs of their houses. The seeds were ground and used as butter or lard (Felger & F. Molina, field notes). Colorado River hemp was the basis for a large-scale agriculture-based real estate promotion in the Colorado delta during the late nineteenth century (see Colonia Lerdo in Chapter 39, this volume; Bowen 2000; Felger 2000). AG.

*Vigna unguiculata. COWPEA, BLACK-EYED PEA. This early Hispanic introduction became a major agricultural crop for the Cocopahs and others (Castetter & Bell 1951). Several varieties were grown. After threshing and winnowing, the seeds were stored in pottery vessels or baskets inside the house or on the roof. Cowpea fiber string or twine served many purposes, especially for fishnets (two months of work went into making a large net) as well as for carrying nets and snares to capture quail (Gifford 1933).

FAGACEAE – BEECH FAMILY

Quercus spp. OAKS. Acorns were a seasonally significant food resource. The Cocopahs made summertime trips to the Sierra Juárez in Baja California to gather acorns or sometimes traded for them with the Pai Pais and the Digueños (Castetter & Bell 1951; Gifford 1933). Acorns were often ground into meal and consumed as cakes or *atole* (Hodgson 2001). The small groves of *Q. turbinella* in Alamo Canyon and shrubs at higher elevations in the Ajo Mountains were a potential source of small acorns. OP, GR, SD.

Three oak trees occur in the Sierra Juárez: *Q. peninsularis* (the majority), *Q. agrifolia,* and some *Q. chrysolepis. Q. peninsularis* has smaller acorns than *Q. agrifolia* or *Q. chrysolepis. Q. cornelius-mulleri, Q. palmeri,* and *Q. turbinella* are shrubs and have small acorns (Hodgson 2001; Minnich 1987; Tom Oberbauer, personal communication 2004).

FOUQUIERIACEAE – OCOTILLO FAMILY

Fouquieria splendens. OCOTILLO. Flowering is in spring. Nectar was sucked from the flower base as a snack food (Barrows 1900; Felger et al. 1992), and the flowers were steeped in water for a beverage (Bean & Saubel 1972). Nectar pressed from the flowers hardens when dry and was chewed as a delicacy (Castetter & Bell 1935). The Cahuillas parched and ground the seeds to make *atole* or cakes (Bean & Saubel 1972; Standley 1923). The wand-like stems were extensively used for house construction and fences (Bean & Saubel 1972; Castetter & Bell 1935; Betty Melvin in Zepeda 1985:34). Living fences made from the stems continue to be popular in the region. PI, CP, GR, OP, SD.

FRANKENIACEAE – FRANKENIA FAMILY

Frankenia palmeri. The Seris made a tea from the root to treat colds and sometimes used these dwarf shrubs as cooking fuel (Felger & Moser 1985). AG.

GERANIACEAE – GERANIUM FAMILY

*****Erodium cicutarium** and **E. texanum.** FILAREE. The young plants were eaten as greens, fresh or cooked, by the Cahuillas and others (Bean & Saubel 1972; Hodgson 2001). PI, CP, GR, OP, SD.

HYDROPHYLLACEAE – WATERLEAF FAMILY

Phacelia spp. WILD HELIOTROPE. Young, tender plants of these spring annuals were cooked as greens by the Gila River Pimas but were not highly esteemed (Rea 1997). Certain species, especially older plants, can be stinky and highly irritating to the skin. PI, CP, GR, OP, SD.

JUNCACEAE – RUSH FAMILY

Juncus spp., probably **J. acutus** and **J. cooperi.** The slender stems were used for granary baskets (Castetter & Bell

Figure 15.10. Sesbania herbacea. *(Drawing by Lucretia Brezeale Hamilton)*

1951). Lumholtz (1912:331) reports that Hia C'ed O'odham made baskets from bulrushes, perhaps *Juncus* and/or *Scirpus.* PI, AG, OP.

KRAMERIACEAE – RATANY FAMILY

Krameria grayi. WHITE RATANY; CÓSAHUI. The thick roots of this shrub have had widespread use in the Sonoran Desert as a source of dyes and medicines (e.g., Castetter & Underhill 1935; Curtin 1949; Felger & Moser 1985; Felger et al. 1992; Rea 1997) (Figure 15.11). The roots were an important source of reddish to pinkish dye, especially for basketry and fabrics; they were also prepared for cosmetics and as a tanning agent for deer hides. Hia C'ed O'odham women's buckskin dresses were sometimes "made red with a dye made from a small bush which the Mexicans call *Cosawi*" (Childs 1954: 36). Hia C'ed O'odham women "use 'edho (a red dry plant)...[to] paint their cheeks and lips....Women who paint with these plants are women who dance" (Betty Melvion in Bell et al. 1980:101). This plant continues to be used medicinally to treat diabetes among the Gila River Pimas and has been used in numerous remedies, such as for diarrhea, upset stomach, stomach sores (ulcers), skin sores, kidney problems, sore throats or bad colds, arthritic pain, tuberculosis, and to facilitate healing, prevent infection, and purify the blood (Rea 1997). PI, CP, GR, OP, SD.

LAMIACEAE (LABIATAE) – MINT FAMILY

Hyptis albida [*H. emoryi*]. DESERT LAVENDER. It was an important medicinal plant in the Sonoran Desert, used in combination or alone to treat asthma, colds,

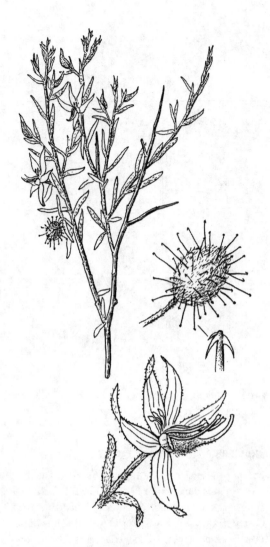

Figure 15.11. Krameria grayi. *(Drawing by Bobbi Angell, ©James Henrickson 1999)*

fever, tooth problems, and hemorrhaging (Bean & Saubel 1972; Felger & Moser 1985). Desert lavender was appreciated for its fragrance (Felger & Moser 1985; Lumholtz 1912:205). The Gila River Pimas smoked the leaves as tobacco (Rea 1997). The seeds have been reported as edible (e.g., Kirk 1970; Uphof 1968), but I believe this is an error based on Lumholtz's (1912:204) misuse of "*hyptis*" for *Salvia columbariae*. PI, CP, GR, OP, SD.

Salvia columbariae. DESERT CHIA. The seeds were "much relished" by the Hia C'ed O'odham (Lumholtz 1912:204) and by many others as a significant food resource in many regions of the Sonoran Desert (Hodgson 2001). Placed in water, the seeds become gelatinous and were consumed as a beverage or food. Parched and ground into flour, they were prepared in various ways and often stored. The seeds were also widely used medicinally, especially to treat eye irritants and ailments (Bean & Saubel 1972; Felger et al. 1992). PI, CP, GR, OP, SD.

LENNOACEAE – LENNOA FAMILY

Pholisma sonorae [*Ammobroma sonorae*]. SANDFOOD. This famous food of the Gran Desierto dunes also

occurs on sand flats and hills (Bell et al. 1980; Castetter & Bell 1941, 1951; Childs 1954; Felger 2000; Havard 1895; Lumholtz 1912; Palmer 1871). Hia C'ed O'odham families often camped in the dunes in spring to gather sandfood. It was generally harvested when the button-like inflorescences appeared at the sand surface in spring, but Lumholtz (1912:331) says the Hia C'ed O'odham located plants "all the year round." Nabhan et al. (1989: 522) clarify this statement: "To find it early in the season one must look for the blackened, withered flower heads from the past year, and dig down in the sand below them to encounter pre-emerged, succulent stalks suitable for eating." Furthermore, except in spring, the plants are generally small and probably not worth harvesting (Felger 2000; also see Yatskievych 1985). The sweet and juicy stems provided food as well as "liquid" for thirsty travelers. Yatskievych (1985) reports that *P. sonorae* accumulates greater amounts of sugars than other species in the family. Sandfood was eaten boiled or after being baked in hot ashes or coals and the thin "bark" peeled away, or it was dried and stored and eaten after boiling. It is delicious when properly prepared, and Cocopahs and Quechans (Yumas) "eagerly sought the sandroot" (Havard 1895:123). Lumholtz (1912) called it "The Great Camote" and even proposed growing it as an agricultural crop, but he did not know the biology of this strange parasitic plant (see Chapter 17, this volume). Hodgson (2001:205) alludes to sandfood being confused with broomrape *(Orobanche cooperi)* as a Cocopah food plant, but this seems unlikely since broomrape is bitter and not especially esteemed. PI, AG, GR.

LILIACEAE (sensu lato) – LILY FAMILY

Allium macropetalum. DESERT ONION. There are reports of this small wild onion being harvested on Table Top Mountain (Rea 1997) and in Organ Pipe Monument (Bell et al. 1980). It also occurs in substantial quantities elsewhere in the region such as granitic hills on the east side of the Cabeza Prieta Refuge. Native wild onions were eaten fresh or cooked or were used as seasoning (Felger & Moser 1985; Hodgson 2001). Some references to edible "wild onions" or "wild garlic" are likely to be *Allium* or in some cases perhaps *Dichelostemma*. In discussion of the name for the town of Ajo, Zepeda (1985:23–24) relates that "*Ajo* (a:sos) 'garlic' was of course named by the Spanish people. Mr. [Miguel] Velasco spoke of a mountain that was very steep and rocky. On this mountain many wild garlic plants grew, and so they called the place *Ajo,* 'garlic'." This *ajo* is likely to be *A. macropetalum,* a small onion that has a garlic-like flavor, rather than *Hesperocallis,* which is slimy and would likely not be common on steep mountain slopes. CP, GR, OP, SD.

Calochortus kennedyi. DESERT MARIPOSA LILY. The corms ("bulbs") were cooked or sometimes eaten fresh but are probably too scarce in the Sonoran Desert to have been a significant source of food (Hodgson 2001). GR, OP, SD.

Dichelostemma capitatum. BLUEDICKS. The flowers and small corms are edible fresh or cooked. Castetter and Underhill (1935:18) say the bulbs are unpleasant tasting but were "eaten largely because they appear in early spring, before other crops are ready." PI, GR, OP, SD.

Hesperocallis undulata. AJO LILY. The relatively large corms ("bulbs") were baked or boiled and also eaten fresh, probably in spring (Castetter & Bell 1951; Hodgson 2001). I found them to be slimy when fresh (also see Rea 1997). PI, AG, CP, GR, OP, SD.

Triteleiopsis palmeri. BLUE SAND LILY. The small cormlets (bulblets) were eaten fresh or cooked by the Seris, generally by children playing on dunes and otherwise rather like snack food (Felger & Moser 1985). They are tasty and abundant on Dry Borders dunes and sand flats. PI, AG, CP, GR.

LOASACEAE – STICK-LEAF FAMILY

Mentzelia spp., including **M. involucrata** and **M. multiflora.** BLAZINGSTAR. The seeds were parched and ground and the flour consumed as *atole*. The seeds are available mostly mid to late spring. There is no direct evidence of use in the Dry Borders area, but the seeds were widely used elsewhere, including southern California (Bean & Saubel 1972), and have been recovered from archaeological caches (Hodgson 2001). PI, AG, CP, GR, OP, SD.

MALVACEAE – MALLOW FAMILY

Abutilon palmeri. The Seris used the roots in an infusion to treat sore throat (Felger & Moser 1985). PI, CP, GR, OP.

Eremalche exilis. The plants were cooked as greens with wheat flour by the Gila River Pimas as emergency food (Rea 1997; see *Malva parvifolia*). This species is generally scarce in the Dry Borders. PI, CP, OP.

Gossypium hirsutum [*G. hopi*] COTTON. Widely cultivated in southwestern North America, along the lower Río Colorado cotton was cultivated and/or traded from upriver agriculturalists. In September 1540 Alarcón found that "these people had cotton, but they did not take much interest in working it, because there was no person among them who knew how to weave in order to make clothing" (Flint & Flint 2005:198). Kino and Manje saw productive cotton cultivation in southern Arizona in the late 1600s and early 1700s (Burrus 1971). Hardy (1829:346) encountered cotton at the Colorado delta in July 1826: "They shortly returned, bringing with them . . . raw cotton . . . which I purchased." Although some south-

ern Arizona people wove fine cotton cloth and blankets, there are no such records from the Dry Borders region (see Rea 1997).

*****Malva parviflora.** CHEESEWEED. This weedy plant is cooked as greens in many parts of the world, and the fruits are also edible (Bean & Saubel 1972; Kirk 1970; Yanovsky 1936). It is uncommon in the Dry Borders except in disturbed habitats. Russell's (1908) report of this species as a Pima emergency food was based on misidentification of *Eremalche exilis* (Rea 1997). PI, GR, OP, SD.

Sphaeralcea ambigua, S. coulteri, and **S. emoryi.** GLOBE MALLOW; MAL DE OJO. These plants have been widely used medicinally, especially the roots for eye ailments, although the herbage is well known to cause eye irritations, as indicated by the common name in Mexico (Felger & Moser 1985; Kearney & Peebles 1960; Rea 1997). PI, AG, CP, GR, OP, SD.

MARTYNIACEAE – DEVIL'S CLAW FAMILY

Proboscidea altheifolia. DEVIL'S CLAW. The large tuberous roots were peeled and the outer portion (cortex) eaten fresh by the Seris (Felger & Moser 1985). The seeds are edible, and the capsules were used in basketry "when the regular kind" (*P. parviflora;* see next entry) was not available (Felger et al. 1992). PI, CP, GR, OP, SD.

Proboscidea parviflora. DEVIL'S CLAW. The seeds were casually eaten after the tough "husk" was peeled and discarded, and the young fruits were sometimes cooked and eaten (Figure 15.12). A black strip in each long claw of the capsule is used in basketry. Wild plants have black seeds and shorter claws whereas plants of the domesticated cultivar, grown in regional gardens and fields, have white seeds and have been selected for extra-long claws (Hodgson 2001; Nabhan et al. 1981; Nabhan & Rea 1987; Rea 1997). PI, GR, OP, SD.

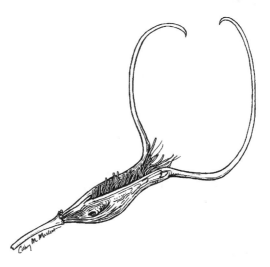

Figure 15.12. Proboscidea parviflora. *(Drawing by Cathy Moser Marlett)*

NOLINACEAE – BEARGRASS FAMILY

Nolina bigelovii. DESERT TREE-BEARGRASS. The young flower stalks were pit-baked by the Cahuillas (Bean & Saubel 1972), and the seeds undoubtedly are edible. These large plants are common in the western part of the Dry Borders. The leaves, often about 1 m long, are flat, strong, and pliable and would be a handy source of tough fiber, but evidence for such use is lacking. PI, CP, GR.

Nolina microcarpa. BEARGRASS. Elsewhere in Arizona the young flower stalks were baked in coals and the flowers and seeds were ground and cooked (Castetter 1935; Hodgson 2001; Yanovsky 1936). The leaves have been used for basketry by the Pimas and Tohono O'odham (Castetter & Bell 1941). It is common at higher elevations in the Ajo Mountains. OP, GR.

NYCTAGINACEAE – FOUR-O'CLOCK FAMILY

Abronia maritima. COASTAL SAND VERBENA. Tea made from the roots was used by Seri women to aid in expulsion of a torn placenta (Felger & Moser 1985). AG.

Allionia incarnata. TRAILING FOUR-O'CLOCK. Seris drank tea made from this plant to treat diarrhea (Felger & Moser 1985). PI, AG, CP, GR, OP, SD.

Boerhavia spp., including **B. erecta** and **B. intermedia.** SPIDERLING. Young plants of native species were used as greens by the Seris (Felger & Moser 1985). The River Pimas identified them as "*makkom je'el* 'mother of the *makkom*', the edible caterpillar" (the sphinx moth, *Hyles lineata*), because they are one of its favorite foods (Rea 1997:215). PI, CP, GR, OP, SD.

ONAGRACEAE – EVENING PRIMROSE FAMILY

Camissonia claviformis. BROWNEYES. Bean and Saubel (1972) report that the plants were eaten as greens; they are often abundant in winter and spring. PI, AG, CP, GR, OP, SD.

Oenothera deltoides. DUNE PRIMROSE. Lumholtz (1912:331) reports that it was cooked as greens (he called it *O. trichocalyx*). It is often abundant on dunes and sand flats during cooler seasons. PI, AG, CP, GR.

OROBANCHACEAE – BROOMRAPE FAMILY

Orobanche cooperi. DESERT BROOMRAPE. The young shoots, available in spring, were apparently widely used, often roasted in coals. The label on a specimen at the Gray Herbarium (Harvard University), collected by Carl Lumholtz in the Pinacate region, reads: "slightly bitter, Papago Indians toast and eat the plant at this stage." It includes the notation "called 'Camote' by Spaniards," indicating that non-Indians also knew of its being edible (see Chapter 17, this volume). The Cahuillas likewise ate them "before the plants blossom . . . roasted in the coals" (Barrows 1900:66) and "peeled prior to eating" (Bean & Saubel 1972). Some friends and I roasted

succulent but mature plants and found them very bitter; too bad we did not know to look for younger ones or to peel them (see *Pholisma sonorae*, sandfood). Caution: some people have adverse reactions to eating these plants (Amadeo Rea, personal communication 2003). PI, CP, GR, OP, SD.

PAPAVERACEAE – POPPY FAMILY

Argemone gracilenta. PRICKLY POPPY. Species in this genus are poisonous and have also been used medicinally. There is no specific information for uses in the Dry Borders. PI, CP, GR, OP, SD.

PHYTOLACCACEAE – POKEWEED FAMILY

Rivina humilis. PIGEON BERRY. The fresh, juicy fruits are sweet (Pennington 1963), but the plants are scarce in the Dry Borders. OP.

PLANTAGINACEAE – PLANTAIN FAMILY

Plantago ovata. WOOLLY PLANTAIN, INDIAN WHEAT. The small seeds were eaten by all Dry Borders groups (Hodgson 2001). They were boiled, parched and ground into flour, or merely soaked in water and consumed as a beverage or eaten as a gelatin-like mass. In favorable years it is abundant in spring and could be a significant food source. The seeds were widely used medicinally. Selections of more robust plants produce the psyllium seed grown commercially. *P. ovata* is native to both the Old World and New World. PI, AG, CP, GR, OP, SD.

Plantago patagonica. PASTORA. The seeds are similar to those of *P. ovata* and have been used in similar ways (Hodgson 2001), but *P. patagonica* is not as widespread or common in the Dry Borders as *P. ovata*. CP, GR, OP, SD.

POACEAE (GRAMINEAE) – GRASS FAMILY

The grains (technically, the caryopsis or fruit with its enclosed seed) of various grasses are edible and were often harvested if the grain was large enough and abundant enough to make the effort worthwhile. Grains were commonly parched and ground, winnowed to separate chaff from flour, and generally consumed as *atole*. Some of the better-known utilitarian grasses are listed below.

Grasses played an important role in regional agriculture and food resources. From pre-Spanish times until the early twentieth century, people along the lower Río Colorado made extensive use of nipa (*Distichlis palmeri*) and cultivated other grasses, including crowfoot grass (*Dactyloctenium aegyptium*), barnyard grass (*Echinochloa muricata*), panicgrass (*Panicum hirticaule*), and corn (*Zea mays*). Jesuit missionaries introduced cattle, which thrived on grasses and other forage, and the cattle contributed to the demise of local stands of grasses and wetland habitats. In historic times wheat, barley, oats, and maize have been grown under irrigation in the Río Sonoyta and Río Colorado valleys. Maize and other crops have been grown at several small dryland and floodwater fields.

Aristida californica. CALIFORNIA THREE-AWN. The Seris fashioned hairbrushes from the wiry roots (Felger & Moser 1985). PI, AG, CP, GR, OP.

Bouteloua aristidoides, NEEDLE GRAMA, and **B. barbata,** SIX-WEEKS GRAMA. The Seris harvested the grain although it is quite small; these grasses can be abundant following summer rains (Felger & Moser 1985). PI, CP, GR, OP, SD.

*****Dactyloctenium aegyptium.** CROWFOOT GRASS. Castetter and Bell (1951:171–72) report that the grain was harvested in summer from seeds planted in receding Río Colorado floodwaters (also see Kelly 1977). Their reports are based in part on a seed collection by W. J. McGee in 1900 when he was among the Cocopahs near the river's mouth (see Chapter 17, this volume). Although native to the Old World, it has long been in western North America, generally in weedy habitats. AG, OP.

Distichlis palmeri. NIPA. The name *nipa*, adapted from the Cocopah term for this species (Castetter & Bell 1951; Crawford 1989), honors Cocopah knowledge and usage (Figure 15.13). This unique saltgrass thrives on pure seawater, and the grain was harvested by the Cocopahs as one of their staples. It is endemic to the northern Gulf of California and extends southward along the Gulf Coast of Baja California and Sonora but is nowhere as extensive as in the tidal reaches of the Colorado delta, where it is daily washed with seawater. The greatest stands are on delta mud flats, especially Islas Gore and Montague and the opposite shores, and in the large tidal wetlands at the western side of Bahía Adair. In these places nipa forms thick mats of nearly 100 percent plant cover. Nearly all stems become reproductive in late spring. Female (grain-producing) and male flowers are borne on separate plants.

Nipa was harvested in substantial quantities prior to the era of large upriver dams; the last harvest was in the 1950s (Juan García Aldama, personal communication 1977, at El Mayor). The harvest extended for about five weeks, from late April to the end of May or early June. Nipa was the first major harvest of the year, occurring when there were no other major harvests and well before mesquite pods ripened. It was a much-appreciated food, and the harvest brought family groups together for festivities and courting (Kelly 1977).

During the first part of the nipa season the stems would be harvested while the grain was still green. Harvesting was often carried out with the aid of rafts (see *Phragmites* and *Typha*), or the people waded into the soft mud at low tide, often sinking nearly to their knees (Vasey 1889). The somewhat brittle stems were severed

Figure 15.13. Distichlis palmeri. *(Drawing by Drylands Institute)*

with wooden or metal knives. The grain-bearing stems were thrown into baskets, then dried in large masses between fires, and finally threshed. Harvesting was done by women, and the burning and threshing by men. Also, when harvested early in the season (the grain would still be "green"), the grain-bearing stems were piled in large heaps on water-dampened hardpan ground, set afire, and stirred and raked frequently so that the grain was parched but not burned; the grain was then swept up (Castetter & Bell 1951:192–194). The grain was also threshed by foot. The sharp-tipped leaves made much of the harvest process painful. This early harvest stage lasted about eight to ten days, after which there was about a two-week period while the grain matured on the plants. This was a time for much socializing, dancing, games, relaxing, and singing, and hunting expeditions for the men.

Later, in May, grain-containing spikelets washed ashore and accumulated in tidal windrows, sometimes "as much as a foot or more high" (Kelly 1977:35), where they were easily gathered. (In the early 1990s I found such tidal windrows near the mouth of the Santa Clara Slough to be about 5 cm high.) This "water-washed" grain was less desirable than the first or early nipa harvest but was appreciated since it provided much larger, and presumably more easily harvested, stores to be carried home. Whenever possible the grain was taken home on rafts.

Nipa grain was ground into coarse flour and, like most seed crops, usually consumed as *atole*. It was also mixed with other plant foods such as cattail pollen or with fish or meat as stew. Nipa flour also was made into cakes and cooked over hot coals (Castetter & Bell 1951; Kelly 1977; Vasey 1889). Hardy (1829:347) reported "wild wheat, the taste of which is very sweet." The nutritional content compares favorably with that of wheat (Yensen & Weber 1986, 1987).

This grass has the potential to become an important world grain crop and in my opinion represents one the world's potentially most valuable resources (Felger 1979, 2000; see also Williams, this volume). Under the auspices of a Rockefeller Foundation Grant to the Environmental Research Laboratory of the University of Arizona in the 1980s, I had the opportunity to search the world for halophytes of potential agronomic value for food production, often collaborating with James Aronson; my conclusion then and now is that nipa is the single most promising species. Nick Yensen and associates (Yensen 2001) have conducted years of research on developing nipa and have even patented certain strains they deem economically superior. Wild nipa, however, cannot be patented, and the world must not be denied access to this valuable future food resource.

Although the plants thrive and produce grain with pure seawater, the seeds germinate best with fresh or only moderately brackish water (Glenn 1987; Glenn in Felger 2000). Present-day populations seem to be maintaining themselves by vegetative propagation. Although delta populations of *D. palmeri* probably diminished during the twentieth century, the population is still extensive and substantial quantities of spikelets still accumulate in tidal windrows in early summer. AG.

*Echinochloa.** Taxonomy of New and Old World members of this genus remains somewhat confused. Castetter and Bell (1951) report *E. colonum* and *E. crusgalli*, species native to the Old World, used by the Cocopahs: the grain was harvested in early summer from wild plants and/or seeds planted in receding Río Colorado floodwaters. Some New World native *Echinochloa* are often confused with the Old World *E. crusgalli* (for example, the New World *E. muricata* is only subtly distinguishable). Apparently the Cocopahs were harvesting both native and non-native *Echinochloa* grasses, although *E. colonum* and *E. crusgalli* are documented for the lower Río Colorado region since the nineteenth century. Even more complication arises because Castetter and Bell (1951:190) report "*E. crus-galli* var. *mitis* ... as a wild grass seed utilized formerly by the Cocopa. This, too, is a native variety." See Gould et al. 1972 and Michael 2003.

*Echinochloa colonum.** JUNGLEGRASS, JUNGLERICE. "The wild seed was gathered and eaten by the Cocopa" (Castetter & Bell 1951:191). PI, AG, CP, OP, SD.

Echinochloa muricata. Gifford (1933:267) says that Cocopahs gathered the "seeds ... on [a] large island near [the] mouth of [the Río] Hardy." Gifford called it *E. crusgalli*, but most likely it is *E. muricata*, as documented by Edward Palmer's 1889 collection at "Horseshoe Bend of Colorado River," which is the type locality for nipa, *Distichlis palmeri*. AG.

Eragrostis pectinacea. CAROLINA LOVEGRASS. Castetter and Bell (1951:191) report grain harvested from "*E. mexicana* ... Native on the lower Colorado." This species does not occur at low elevations in the Sonoran Desert; it was probably *E. pectinacea*, a hot-season annual likely to be found in the region. AG.

Eriochloa aristata. BEARDED CUPGRASS. Castetter and Bell (1951) report that the grain was harvested at the Colorado delta. It is sometimes locally abundant with summer rains elsewhere in the Dry Borders. AG, PI, CP, OP.

Muhlenbergia microsperma. LITTLESEED MUHLY. Seris harvested the grain, which is indeed small, but the plants can be abundant, especially in spring (Felger & Moser 1985). PI, CP, GR, OP, SD.

Panicum hirticaule var. **hirticaule** [*P. hirticaule* var. *miliaceum, P. capillare* var. *hirticaule, P. sonorum*]. MEXICAN PANICGRASS. The grain was harvested in summer from seeds planted in receding Río Colorado floodwaters and also from wild plants. It was a significant food resource. Traveling along the Río Colorado in the summer of 1540, Alarcón reported, "In addition to corn, they had some squash and another seed similar to millet" (Flint & Flint 2005:196). Castetter and Bell (1951) describe this grass (they call it *P. sonorum*) as an important grain crop cultivated (they say "semicultivated") by the Cocopah and other Yuman people along the lower Río Colorado. Gifford (1933:267) reports that it grew wild "among Yuma" (Quechans), that the Cocopahs planted it by blowing the seeds from their mouths while walking "over soft mud," and that it was planted by men "away from wives 4 nights" for "continence to make plants grow without weeds and molestation by birds." (Also see *Taxidea taxus,* badger, for planting ritual.) It has not been cultivated in the delta since the early twentieth century, following the demise of the native agricultural systems that depended on the living river.

The type specimen of *P. capillare* var. *miliaceum* (at the U.S. National Herbarium), collected by Edward Palmer in 1889 near Lerdo, has an annotation, "seeds used for food by the Indians, Sonora." These Colorado delta specimens are robust plants and were recognized as a distinct species called *P. sonorum.* The concept of *P. sonorum* was then extended to other robust specimens from elsewhere in Latin America. All these plants seem to be merely robust specimens of *P. hirticaule* var. *hirticaule,* which is widespread in the Americas (Felger 2000; Zuloaga & Morrone 1996).

Nabhan and de Wet (1984) and Nabhan (1985) describe an endangered, cultivated panicgrass that they and others (Gentry 1942, 1963) have called *P. sonorum.* Their work is based on an unnamed variety or landrace of *P. hirticaule* still grown by a few Guarijíos in remote mountain areas in southeastern Sonora (Felger 2000; Gentry 1963; Yetman & Felger 2002). The plants once grown at the Colorado delta are long gone. PI, AG, CP, GR, OP, SD.

Phragmites australis. COMMON REED, REEDGRASS. Young shoots are edible and may have been harvested by the Cocopahs (see Kelly 1977:39). The sweet "honey-dew" or "manna" on the leaves, an exudate from aphids, was a potential food source along the lower Río Colorado (Drucker 1937; Heizer 1945; Jones 1945; Zigmond 1981). The stems were used for house construction, mats, arrow shafts, containers, tobacco pipes, musical instruments including flutes and whistles, and rafts on the Río Colorado (Castetter & Bell 1951; Densmore 1922; Gifford 1933; Williams 1987). The very lightweight arrows were particularly desirable for hunting birds (Castetter & Underhill 1935). Hia C'ed O'odham "made flutes from the cane that grew in those times around almost any permanent water—spring or river" and drums that "were all round, and were made with circles of cane with some vertical stays in them" (Childs 1954:37; see *Antilocapra,* pronghorn). The stems, or canes, are mature by early summer and would be suitable for harvesting sometime thereafter.

In late August 1540, Alarcón saw people at the Colorado delta wearing armbands and "some cane tubes" and also reported that "they carry their tubes to incense themselves" (Flint & Flint 2005:191, 196). Fishing nets were "buoyed on the surface with wild cane" (Chittenden 1901:201).

People with access to the abundant reedgrass at the delta made *balsa* boats like those of the Seris and more than one kind of raft (see *Typha*). The Seris bound the bundles of reedgrass stems with mesquite-root cordage (Felger & Moser 1985), and the delta people may have done the same. Hardy (1829:381) "observed several reed canoes, similar in construction to those of the island of Tiburow [Tiburon]." The term *reed* and comparison with Seri *balsas* indicates use of *Phragmites.* George Derby recorded Cocopah "reed rafts or balsas" in 1851 (Williams 1975:85). PI, AG, OP.

Setaria macrostachya [*S. leucopila*]. PLAINS BRISTLE-GRASS. The grain is often available in substantial quantities in warmer seasons, generally in Arizona Upland portions of the Dry Borders. It was harvested by the Seris and presumably by others (Felger & Moser 1985). CP, GR, OP, SD.

Sporobolus airoides. ALKALI SACATON. Substantial grain is available in summer and fall. This large grass is locally abundant in low-lying sandy and saline soils, such as at the Colorado delta and near the coast, along the Río Sonoyta, and at Quitobaquito. Castetter and Underhill (1935:24) report that the plants were burned and people would "then sweep the seeds off the ground." Reports of the use of sacaton, tall grasses, and *S. wrightii* in the Dry Borders region probably refer to *S. airoides.* "Trippel, writing in 1889 of the Yuma, reported that the seed of sacaton grass, found along the river bottoms, was baked into a dough, then dried in the sun" (Castetter & Bell 1951:200). PI, AG, CP (scarce), OP.

*****Triticum aestivum.** WHEAT. Before the introduction of wheat there were no significant winter-spring cultivated crops across the Sonoran Desert region. Alarcón brought "wheat and other seeds" to the Colorado delta in 1540 (Flint & Flint 2005:202). There is no indication, however, that this introduction succeeded (see Castetter & Bell 1951:123). Kino successfully introduced wheat into the region in the late seventeenth century (Burrus 1971). It soon became a major crop of people living along the Colorado and Gila rivers (Castetter & Bell 1951; Kelly 1977; Rea 1997). Wheat was also grown at Sonoyta and at Suvuk (Romero floodwater field) (Bell et al. 1980; Childs 1954; Felger 2000; Lumholtz 1912; Nabhan 1985; Julian Hayden, personal communication 1992; also see Chapter 39, this volume).

Zea mays. MAIZE, CORN. Maize, teparies, and squash were the most important indigenous agricultural crops, and there was a rich diversity of kinds, colors, and local landraces of corn (Castetter & Bell 1951; Gifford 1933; Kelly 1977; Kniffen 1931; Lumholtz 1912; Nabhan 1985;

Rea 1997). Cocopahs grew large quantities of maize along the lower Río Colorado (Burrus 1971; Castetter & Bell 1951; Lumholtz 1912). Men, women, and children planted, weeded, and tended the crop, guarding the sprouting plants and corn ears from birds and rabbits. Corn was cooked fresh or was dried for future use and stored in rooftop granaries or in tree branches and platforms. Alarcón provides substantial reference to corn on the lower Río Colorado in 1540, mentioning people inland "on a mountain… where little corn was harvested" who came to the river to get "[corn] through barter with deerskins" (Flint & Flint 2005:195). The Hia C'ed O'odham and others who were unable to grow crops bartered with the Cocopahs for corn (Gifford 1933:262).

Maize was cultivated with summer-fall rains by Hia C'ed O'odham people along the Río Sonoyta, at Quitobaquito, Suvuk, and a few special places in the Pinacate region (Burrus 1971; Castetter & Bell 1942; Felger et al. 1992; Lumholtz 1912). Best known is the Romero floodwater field at Suvuk on the northeast side of the lava fields (Lumholtz 1912; Nabhan 1985). In the 1980s this field was still being planted during years of sufficient rainfall, and in the 1960s there was a small cornfield in deep, sandy soil a few kilometers east and slightly north of MacDougal Pass (Felger 2000). These fields are at the arid limits of agriculture; perhaps only in the monsoon-fed, sandy fields west of Jaisalmer in Rajasthan, India, has dryland agriculture been practiced in such an arid environment.

POLYGONACEAE – BUCKWHEAT FAMILY

Eriogonum spp. Stems and "seeds" (achenes) of various species were eaten by the Cahuillas and others (Bean & Saubel 1972). PI, CP, GR, OP, SD.

Eriogonum inflatum. DESERT TRUMPET, BLADDER STEM. The stems were harvested in spring before flowering and eaten fresh or cooked by the Cahuillas and others (Bean & Saubel 1972; Hodgson 2001). PI, CP, GR, OP, SD.

Rumex spp. DOCK; CAÑAIGRE. The leaves and "stalks" of native and non-native species of dock were sometimes important food plants. They were cooked and eaten as greens, but because of citric, malic, and oxalic acids they were cooked in a change of water. The "seeds" (achenes) were also eaten (Hodgson 2001). Dock was an important food and medicinal plant along the lower Río Colorado (Castetter & Bell 1951; Kelly 1977) and for the Gila River Pimas (Hrdlièka 1908) and Tohono O'odham (Castetter & Bell 1942).

The tuberous roots were one of the more important sources of medicine in the region, and the plants were sometimes transplanted to home gardens (Rea 1997). The Tohono O'odham made yellow dyes for cotton fabrics from *R. crispus* and *R. hymenosepalus* roots

(Castetter & Bell 1942). Most of the earlier reports are not documented with specimens, and species identifications might be questioned. *R. inconspicuus* is known from AG but does not produce tuberous roots; *R. hymenosepalus* is uncommon in OP. At least one tuberous-rooted species was once common along the lower Río Colorado.

PORTULACACEAE – PORTULACA FAMILY

Calandrinia ciliata. RED MAIDS. Elsewhere the plants were eaten as greens in spring (Hodgson 2001). GR, OP, SD.

Claytonia perfoliata [*Montia perfoliata*]. MINER'S LETTUCE. Elsewhere these plants are well-known springtime greens and are eaten fresh or cooked (Kirk 1970). It is seldom abundant in the region, although I have enjoyed it on sandwiches while hiking in Ajo Mountain canyons. GR, OP.

*****Portulaca oleracea.** PURSLANE. This worldwide plant is cooked and eaten as greens (Hodgson 2001; Uphof 1998), and I have enjoyed the similar-appearing native *P. retusa* and *P. umbraticola* as greens. "You would gather it and wash it and boil it until it was tender, the same way as the other grass plants. You refry it with butter and onions and it would be very good" (Betty Melvin in Zepeda 1985:62). PI, CP, OP, SD.

RESEDACEAE – MIGNONETTE FAMILY

Oligomeris linifolia. DESERT CAMBESS. The seeds were eaten by the Seris (Felger & Moser 1985; also see Hodgson 2001) as well as by people living along the shores of ancient Lake Cahuilla (in a reduced phase now the Salton Sea), as shown by Wilke's (1978) analysis of coprolites from prehistoric lakeshore campsites (also see Ebeling 1986). It also may have been a common food resource on the Baja California peninsula (Hodgson 2001). Although the seeds are minute, they are often available in substantial quantity. The Lake Cahuilla record refutes the claim that this species is not native to the New World. AG, CP, GR, OP, SD.

RHAMNACEAE – BUCKTHORN FAMILY

Condalia warnockii. The thin, fleshy part of the small fruits was eaten fresh, probably serving as a minor resource (Castetter & Bell 1935, interpreted in Hodgson 2001). GR, SD.

Ziziphus obtusifolia. WHITE CRUCILLO. The fleshy parts of the fruits were eaten fresh or cooked (Nabhan et al. 1982; Rea 1997), and the Seris obtained sizable quantities of the fruit from packrat nests (Felger & Moser 1985). Among the O'odham the fleshy fruits were boiled to a syrup like that of cactus fruits and the juice was sometimes fermented (Castetter & Underhill 1935). It was probably a minor resource. PI, CP, GR, OP, SD.

SALICACEAE – WILLOW FAMILY

Cottonwood and willow trees were abundant along the lower Río Colorado and locally along the Río Sonoyta near Sonoyta.

Populus fremontii. FRÉMONT COTTONWOOD. This tree was abundant along the Colorado and Gila rivers and locally along the Río Sonoyta near Sonoyta. The trunk was extensively used for heavy construction, such as for house posts, and for fuel. Among the Cocopahs, Tohono O'odham, and Gila River Pimas the usual household utensils included a large mortar fashioned from a cottonwood log and primarily used to grind and pound mesquite pods (Bell & Castetter 1937; Gifford 1933:270; Rea 1997). The Cocopahs crossed the river paddling or swimming alongside cottonwood and willow logs, and rafts "for voyages to [the] mouth of [of the Río] Colorado" were made with "willow and cottonwood roots" (Gifford 1933:272).

Chittenden (1901) reports women wearing cottonwood- or willow-bark skirts, although most reports mention only willow bark. The Gila River Pimas ate the young, developing inner part of the female (pistillate) flowers; it was like chewing gum and served as emergency food (Rea 1997) as well as a widely used snack food (Amadeo Rea, personal communication 2004; also see Drucker 1941; Russel 1908). These flowers served the Pimas for "the worst time of the year… in spring when their stored stuff was gone" (Ruth Giff in Rea 1997:178). The male (staminate) flowers sometimes were also eaten (Rea 1997). Kirk (1970) reports that the inner bark can be eaten as emergency food. AG, *OP (rare).

Salix gooddingii. GOODDING WILLOW. Willow trees were abundant at the Colorado delta and locally along the Río Sonoyta near Sonoyta. Cocopahs made extensive use of these trees. The bark from young plants ("seedlings") was eaten fresh or cooked, probably as a minor or emergency food; the bark and leaves were made into tea; and a beverage was made with the flowers. Honeydew was gathered from branches (probably young leafy branches) in late spring along the "overflow of the river" (Jones 1945).

Willow poles served for house construction of the several kinds of Cocopah houses and shelters (Gifford 1933; MacDougal 1906). "In front of the house, but unconnected," was an arbor or ramada "where cooking was done with roofing of willow and arrowweed" (Gifford 1933:271; also see Chittenden 1901:203). The house "doorway had [a] hanging willow mat" (Gifford 1933: 271), and a domed hut was built "of willow branches, closely woven, erected in summer for mosquito protection" (Gifford 1933:271). The description of the interior of a Kamia house seems typical of those of the people living along the lower Colorado River: "each bed was simply a willow-bark blanket spread on the floor. The bed-covering, when such was necessary, was either a willow-bark blanket or a rabbit-skin blanket" Gifford (1931:20). Among the Cocopahs these blankets were made by men; for willow blankets the warp and weft was made of willow-bark string, and these blankets were "usually larger than 5 × 8 ft. [and] softened with use" (Gifford 1933:276). The inner bark, best harvested in summer, was the principal material for Cocopah garments, including skirts and dresses for women, breechcloths for men, and robes for women and men (Chittenden 1901; Drucker 1941:112; Gifford 1933:275). Women used "thick rings of willow bark… for balancing pots and cradles," and cordage was made from the bark (Gifford 1933:270, 275). Various utensils were fashioned from willow wood, including paddles for pottery making. Pottery might be fired with willow wood, although mesquite was preferred. Smaller vessels were fired with willow and cottonwood bark, and a small "bundle of willow-bark fibers" served as a brush to decorate pottery (Gifford 1933:272). Willow strips were extensively used for binding and fastening.

Cocopah "bows were made from willow, and being less elastic and more liable to break when dry, old ones were seldom seen. Those used for hunting deer were from six to eight feet in length" (Chittenden 1901:203–204). Small hunting bows for birds and smaller game were also made from willow (MacDougal 1906). Cocopahs would cover a "small pond with willow leaves, which discolored water, causing fish to rise in 2 or 3 days." They also made a "fence of willow twigs and arrowweed stems pushed along by 20 to 30 wading men in lagoons to impound fish" (Gifford 1933:268). Rafts on the lower Río Colorado were made of a willow log frame, attached with willow bark strips (Kelly 1977). For the Hia C'ed O'odham, Lumholtz (1912:331–332) reports, "To make bows, these Indians travelled as far as the Colorado River to get willow as material." The Hia C'ed O'odham made fish spears, used at the gulf, from "a small willow branch" (Childs 1954:32; see *Dasyatis* spp. and *Totoaba macdonaldi*). AG, OP.

SAPINDACEAE – SOAPBERRY FAMILY

Sapindus drummondii. SOAPBERRY; JABONCILLO, AMOLILLO. As indicated by the common names, the fruits were widely used for soap (Uphof 1968), although such use is not documented for the Dry Borders. The Tohono O'odham made arrow foreshafts from the straight stems, although creosotebush (*Larrea*) was preferred (see *Baccharis sarothroides;* Castetter & Underhill 1935). OP.

SAURURACEAE – LIZARD-TAIL FAMILY

Anemopsis californica. HIERBA DEL MANSO; VA:VIS (Hia C'ed O'odham). This is one of the most esteemed medicinal plants in western North America (Felger 2000; Felger & Moser 1985; Felger et al. 1992; Moerman 1998; Betty Melvin in Zepeda 1985:42). It has long been cultivated in Sonora and is grown in cool, shaded gardens in Sonoyta as well as kitchen gardens in *ejidos* and farms in the Río Colorado valley. The term *manso* may be translated as "gentle," "lamblike," or "tame."

Lumholtz (1912:264–265) gives an account of his experience with *Anemopsis* at La Salina in February 1910: "A plant … called by the Mexicans *herba del manso* was a singular growth in these pozos. Its large root, which has a strong medicinal scent, like that which characterizes an apothecary shop, is perhaps the most popular of the many favorite remedies of northern Mexico. It is used internally to cure colds, coughs, or indigestion, as well as externally for wounds or swellings, and is employed in a similar way by the Indians. Of the latter, those who lived in the dune country are said to have been in the habit of chewing bits of this root, as elsewhere tobacco is chewed. These plants grew here in great numbers and to enormous proportions; some of their roots were as much as three feet long and very heavy. The root finds a ready sale everywhere and my Mexicans were not long in gathering as many of the plants as they could carry on their animals. One of the men, whose horse was well-nigh exhausted, walked himself in order to put a load of fifty pounds on his horse." Childs recounts that the Hia C'ed O'odham went to La Salina (Salina Grande) for "yerba mansa" (Van Valkenburgh 1945).

Some Hia C'ed O'odham uses recorded by Gary Nabhan are as a remedy for "cold, flu, and impetigo" (Juan Joe Cipriano) and for cough (Betty Melvin in Zepeda 1985:42). It "makes you hot inside and that's what takes care of the sickness" (Delores Lewis in Felger et al. 1992:32). Betty Melvion recalled that the "Indian medication" for smallpox is "wiwi'is," which "they boil and drink" (Bell et al. 1980:101).

Mearns (1892–93) reported that "the Mexicans at the village of Sonoyta … call it '*Yerba del Manzo*,' and assert that it imparts properties to the water which render it deleterious to the teeth. It grows on marshy ground, and emits a strong odor when trodden upon. Mexicans use it medicinally. Found on the boundary line from Lake Palomas (Mimbres Valley) westward to Quitovaquito, in all marshy grounds." The plants also have been used as a source of tannin. Gifford (1931:24) reports that Kamias ate the seeds, which they pulverized in a cottonwood mortar, and the "meal was then cooked as mush in a pot or baked as bread in hot ashes." PI, AG, OP.

SCROPHULARIACEAE – SNAPDRAGON FAMILY

Mimulus guttatus. MONKEY FLOWER. Fresh leaves can be eaten like lettuce (Chestnut 1902; Yanovsky 1936), and young, tender leaves may have a mushroom-like flavor. GR, OP, SD.

SIMMONDSIACEAE – JOJOBA FAMILY

Simmondsia chinensis. JOJOBA. The seeds have been used for food (Castetter & Underhill 1935; Meigs 1939) but are nutritionally marginal or not digestible. The Seris regarded them as an emergency food (Felger & Moser 1985). The Cahuillas made a coffee substitute from the ground seeds (Bean & Saubel 1972). Sonoran Desert people valued the seed oil (actually a liquid wax) for shampoo and hair care (Felger and Moser 1985). There is a long history of medicinal use of the seeds to treat many ailments, including colds, eye problems, and sores, and for women at childbirth (del Barco 1980; Castetter & Underhill 1935; Felger and Moser 1985). The Cocopahs obtained jojoba on their annual summertime treks to Baja California mountains (Castetter & Bell 1951). Kino reports that jojoba was esteemed for its medicinal properties, and in the late seventeenth century it was in demand in Mexico City and even in Spain (Burrus 1954, 1971; also see Kay 1996 and Treutlein 1945). GR, OP, SD.

SOLANACEAE – NIGHTSHADE FAMILY

Capsicum annuum var. **glabriusculum.** CHILTEPIN. These fiery little chilies are widely appreciated as a condiment (Hodgson 2001; Nabhan 1978). Chiltepin occurs in the Ajo Mountains but is more common eastward in the Tohono O'odham region and to the southeast in Sonora. OP.

Datura discolor. POISONOUS NIGHTSHADE. The various daturas and their close relatives in the Americas are widely known for powerful and often dangerously or even deadly hallucinogenic and narcotic properties. *Datura* was ritually used by Cocopah shamans and young men seeking visions. "Persons other than administering shamans drank [*Datura*] only once in [a] lifetime" (Gifford 1933:305). Medicinal application was widespread, including among the Seris and the Hia C'ed O'odham (Felger & Moser 1985; Felger et al. 1992). PI, CP, GR, OP, SD.

Lycium andersonii. DESERT WOLFBERRY. The small fruits were eaten (Chico Suni in Felger et al. 1992). PI, CP, GR, OP, SD.

Lycium berlandieri. SALICIESO. The fruits were probably eaten (Hodgson 2001), and I found them to taste like other lycium fruits. CP, GR, OP, SD.

Lycium brevipes. SALICIESO. The sweet fruits ("*tomatillas*") are eaten fresh (Homero León, Estación López Collada, personal communication 2003). The Seris ate the fruits fresh or cooked (Felger & Moser 1985). PI, AG, OP.

Lycium exsertum. The fruits are edible (Castetter & Bell 1951) and probably were used like those of *L. fremontii*. GR, OP, SD.

Lycium fremontii. FRÉMONT WOLFBERRY. The fruits were eaten fresh but especially cooked. They were also dried like raisins and probably at times served as an important resource in spring (Felger et al. 1992). Most people added sugar to cooked lycium fruits. This species generally yields larger fruits and probably larger yields than most other regional lycium species (Felger & Moser 1985). The Tohono O'odham made hunting bows from the wood (Castetter & Underhill 1935). CP, GR, OP, SD.

Nicotiana. TOBACCO. Traditionally, tobacco smoking was largely ceremonial, often restricted to use by shamans (Castetter & Bell 1951; Rea 1997), "except that the Cocopas and Maricopa [men] seem to have smoked for pleasure to some extent" and "women rarely smoked" (Castetter & Bell 1951:121). The Cahuillas' use of both wild and cultivated tobacco, however, extended to men and women, especially older people, who "smoked it almost daily when the plant was available. Tobacco was considered a relaxing euphoriant as well as a medicinal and ritualistic plant" (Bean & Saubel 1971:93). Tobacco was smoked in cane pipes (see *Phragmites*) or less often in clay pipes in historic times (Castetter & Bell 1951; Spier 1933). Alarcón in 1540 and Hardy in 1826 found tobacco used at the Colorado delta, but it is not possible to know if this was wild or cultivated. Childs (1954:29) wrote that the Hia C'ed O'odham "smoked it from time immemorial. That is why they killed so many immigrants coming and going to California in 1848 and 1849—they wanted to get what tobacco they carried along with them." These events occurred before Tom Childs was born, and perhaps the reasons for these attacks were more complex.

Nicotiana clevelandii. DESERT TOBACCO; TABAQUILLO DE COYOTE. The leaves were smoked but considered inferior to cultivated tobacco, as indicated by its "coyote" name (Bean & Saubel 1972; Felger & Moser 1985). PI, AG, CP, GR, OP.

Nicotiana obtusifolia [*N. trigonophylla*]. DESERT TOBACCO, COYOTE TOBACCO; TABACO DE COYOTE. The leaves were smoked by people across the Sonoran Desert, although it was universally considered inferior to cultivated tobacco, as indicated by its "coyote" name (Bean & Saubel 1972; Castetter & Bell 1951; Castetter & Underhill 1935; Felger & Moser 1985; Betty Melvin in Zepeda 1985:55; Rea 1997) (Figure 15.14). Use of wild tobacco by the Quechans (Yumas) was documented by Palmer in 1885 (Castetter & Bell 1951:120). Cocopahs and Yumans obtained tobacco from mountains in Baja California or California, either by trade or from their travels (Castetter & Bell 1951). PI, CP, GR, OP, SD.

Figure 15.14. Nicotiana obtusifolia. *(Drawing by Bobbi Angell, ©James Henrickson 1999)*

*****Nicotiana rustica** and **N. tabacum.** TOBACCO. Once widely grown in the Sonoran Desert region, domesticated, cultivated tobacco requires high soil moisture and warm or hot weather and is frost-sensitive. Nonagricultural people obtained it by trade. *N. rustica* was grown regionally since prehistoric times, and *N. tabacum* is perhaps more recently cultivated. Among at least the Gila River Pimas, Mohaves, and Quechans, tobacco was not grown publicly but planted in "semi-secret" or "private" places, often protected from herbivores with spiny branches (Castetter & Bell 1951; Rea 1997). Lack of reports in the literature should not be considered conclusive, as its cultivation and use might not have been readily apparent (Rea 1997).

Physalis spp. GROUND CHERRY. The fruits of the several wild species in the region are edible fresh and resemble the domesticated tomatillo in taste but are much smaller in size. They were probably minor resources.

Physalis acutifolia. Gila River Pima children ate the fruits fresh (Rea 1997). PI, CP, OP.

Physalis crassifolia. DESERT GROUND CHERRY. The fresh, ripe fruits are pleasantly tart and were eaten by various Sonoran Desert people (Felger & Moser 1985; Rea 1997). PI, CP, GR, OP, SD.

Physalis lobata. PURPLE GROUND CHERRY. The fruits were possibly eaten and may be the *kukik* fruit eaten by the Mohaves (Castetter & Bell 1951:207; also see Hodgson 2001, who questionably identified it as *Chamaesaracha*). PI, CP, GR, SD.

Physalis pubescens. HAIRY GROUND CHERRY. "Yuma children" ate the fresh fruits from agricultural fields (Castetter & Bell 1951). AG.

***Solanum americanum** [*S. nodiflorum*]. BLACK NIGHTSHADE; CHICHIQUELITE. The leaves were eaten as quelites (greens), and the small fruits, blackish when ripe, were eaten fresh or cooked (Hodgson 2001; Palmer 1887; Watson 1889). I found this plant to be extensively used in Arizona and Sonora by Yaqui and Mexican people. Gila River Pimas used the ripe fruits as a purple dye (Rea 1997). It grows during the warmer seasons and occurs locally at Quitobaquito, where it was probably purposely or accidentally introduced rather than being native. This nightshade, probably native to South America, is found nearly worldwide. Much confusion surrounds the taxonomy of the various species making up the complex of black nightshade in different parts of the world, and it may be difficult to relate proper identification of most ethnographic accounts without adequate specimens. The plants of these species can be toxic (Kinsbury 1964), although cooking the leaves and shoots can remove the toxin, and toxicity of the berries is greatly reduced when they are ripe (e.g., Culpeper 1652; Edmonds & Chweya 1997; Kingsbury 1964). Similar-appearing herbaceous nightshades (e.g., *S. douglasii*) can be highly toxic even when cooked. OP.

TYPHACEAE – CATTAIL FAMILY

Typha domingensis. SOUTHERN CATTAIL; TULE. Cattails are abundant in the Colorado delta wetlands and were locally common along the Río Sonoyta but scarce elsewhere in the Dry Borders. It was a major resource for the Colorado delta people. Many parts and growth stages were eaten either fresh or cooked, including young submerged plants, young shoots, young stem bases, rhizomes, tender developing inflorescences, pollen and flowers, and seeds (achenes) (Bean & Saubel 1972; Gifford 1933; Hodgson 2001; Kelly 1977; Nabhan et al. 1982; Palmer 1878; Rea 1997; Williams 1987). The pollen (called "flower heads" or "pollen heads," which may be flowers as well as the pollen) was eaten in substantial quantities; its collection and preparation was hard work, but it was highly prized for adding a sweet flavor to many dishes (e.g., Curtin 1949; Kelly 1977:39; also see *Leuresthes sardina*, Gulf grunion). Gifford (1933:268) also reports that the fresh "pith of [the] stems" was eaten. Cattail food products were often stored

(Gifford 1933; Hodgson 2001). Kelly (1977:39) mentions that the pollen "was considered a particularly potent medicine and was used in a curing ceremony sponsored by a Yavapai religious leader who made frequent visits to the Cocopa community [in Arizona]."

The leaves were used "to pack interstices of huts, especially...sweat-houses" (MacDougal 1906:13), and cattails were used as roofing for traditional Cocopah houses and cooking ramadas (see *Salix gooddingii*). Cattail fields were extensively burned for hunting purposes: "great smoke [was]...seen almost constantly in the delta" (MacDougal 1906:13). Chittenden (1901:204) reports "a dense growth of tule, which the Indians had set on fire for the purpose of driving out game" (also see Hardy 1829:375; Lumholtz 1912:248–249). Anita Williams (1987) shows a detailed drawing of a Cocopah river raft incorporating bundles of tule, and Gifford (1933:272) describes a "crude balsa, of bundles of tules lashed together; square ended 10 ft long, 2 [ft] wide, [and] paddled and poled, [while] standing." The Hia C'ed O'odham "would use cattail for making baskets" (Betty Melvin in Zepeda 1985:66). PI, AG, CP, GR, OP.

ULMACEAE – ELM FAMILY

Celtis pallida. DESERT HACKBERRY. The small, orange, fleshy fruits were eaten fresh, probably as a minor resource or snack food on the trail. Castetter and Bell (1951:207) and Hodgson (2001) interpret Rogers's report (in Castetter & Bell) of "orange-colored" edible fruits as *C. reticulata* (canyon hackberry), but orange fruits would be from *C. pallida* and not *C. reticulata*, which has hard, reddish-brown fruits. CP, GR, OP, SD.

VISCACEAE – MISTLETOE FAMILY

Phoradendron californicum. DESERT MISTLETOE. The fleshy fruits were eaten fresh or more often cooked; it is often plentiful and easily harvested (Castetter & Bell 1951; Castetter & Underhill 1935; Rea 1997). The Seris selectively harvested the fruits from mistletoe growing on desert legume trees (Felger & Moser 1985). PI, CP, GR, OP, SD.

Phoradendron serotinium [*P. flavescens, P. macrophyllum, P. orbiculatum*]. CHRISTMAS MISTLETOE. Cocopahs used this mistletoe "dried, pulverized in [a] wooden mortar, boiled with clay, [and] plastered on [the] hair to kill lice and dye [it] black" (Gifford 1933:279). This broad-leaved mistletoe grew on cottonwood and willow trees in the forests along the Colorado River, and it is still found in some areas in the vicinity of Yuma. I know of no specimens of this mistletoe from the Mexican portion of the river.

ZYGOPHYLLACEAE – CALTROP FAMILY

Larrea divaricata [*Covillea glutinosa*]. CREOSOTE-BUSH. The wood is very hard, and its uses include arrow foreshafts and arrows for small game hunting (both with a fire-hardened tip), basketry awls, crosspieces of saguaro fruit-gathering poles, drills for the firedrill (see *Carnegiea, Pluchea*), rope twisters (for horsehair and/ or mesquite-root twine), and tool handles. The leafy branches were used for roofing and to cover traditional O'odham "grass houses" (Miguel Velasco in Zepeda 1985: 23). A dark reddish lac, sometimes found on the stems, is plastic when heated and served as an all-purpose sealant for uses such as sealing pottery vessels for food storage and hafting arrows, and it also was used for medicinal purposes. Creosotebush is the most important and universal medicinal plant in the region, and its highly aromatic herbage continues to be extensively employed (Homero León, Estación López Collada, personal communication 2003). It was used to treat many conditions, including congestion, childbirth, sore eyes, snake and spider bites, and scorpion stings (Betty Melvion in Bell et al. 1980; Bean & Saubel 1972; Castetter & Underhill 1935; Felger & Moser 1985; Kearney & Peebles 1960; Moerman 1998; Nabhan 1982; Rea 1997). PI, AG, CP, GR, OP, SD.

Animals
INSECTS

*Apis mellifera. HONEY BEE. Native to Europe, honey bees apparently became established in southern Arizona in the late nineteenth century (Brand 1988; also see Felger & Moser 1985), at which time Native Americans began harvesting honey from feral hives (see Betty Melvin in Zepeda 1985:48, 58–59). PI, AG, CP, GR, OP, SD.

Bombus sonorus. SONORAN DESERT BUMBLEBEE. This large, black and yellow, fuzzy bee is probably the species mentioned by Castetter and Bell (1951:212, 217): the "Lower Colorado . . . people ate without preparation honey found just below the surface of the ground in light amber-colored casings about the size of a marble." These would be the honey storage pots of recycled cocoons, typically dark brown. A large honey-pot nest might contain only 25–50 ml of honey. Robbing a nest would bring a risk of receiving painful stings (Stephen Buchmann, personal communication 2003). AG.

Diceroprocta apache. APACHE CICADA. Gila River Pimas ate cicadas "roasted or fried. . . . This is a summer food, collected after the emergence of the adults. At this season one's ears fairly ring with the droning song of the cicadas" (Rea 1974). "The cicada was also a very common food . . . some Pima Indians children . . . had a whole string of them on a stick. They roasted them over the coals and ate them one by one. That was one of the ways that people used to eat these animals back then . . . they buzzzzz . . . they put salt on it" (Betty Melvin in Zepeda 1985:70,75). This is the common cicada of the Sonoran Desert lowlands.

Eupackardia calleta. CALLETA SILKMOTH. The *hierba de la flecha* shrub was known by western O'odham people to be the host plant for this large native moth. The cocoons were used in making pascola-style leg rattles (Childs 1954; Chico Suni in Felger et al. 1992; see *Sebastiania*). CP, GR?, OP.

Hyles lineata. WHITE-LINED SPHINX MOTH. Caterpillars of this moth commonly appear with the wildflower displays of spring and summer. At such times hordes of these large caterpillars march across the desert in search of food plants or a place in the soil to pupate. They were gathered in baskets, and women often sat around an open hearth twisting off the heads and pulling out the guts to discard, and then braiding the bodies into chains. The caterpillars were pit-roasted, parched in a basket with hot coals, boiled, or dried in the sun and stored for future use. They were much relished (Castetter & Underhill 1935; Childs 1954; Felger & Moser 1985; Rea 1997; Betty Melvin in Zepeda 1985:70, 75). AG, PI, CP, GR, OP, SD.

Grasshoppers. Many people ate certain grasshoppers, which are still considered a delicacy in parts of Mexico, especially Oaxaca. I found that they taste like shrimp. Use of grasshoppers as food among Sonoran Desert people ceased long ago, but there are many brief references to it (Felger & Moser 1985; Manje 1954:111; also see Castetter & Bell 1942:70). Manje mentioned grasshoppers in western Piman (Hia C'ed) diet several times: in 1694, for example, he encountered people near the Sonora coast who "live on roots, locust, and shellfish" (Burrus 1971:175, also 186).

Mosquitoes. The Cocopahs had various means to deal with mosquitoes along the Río Colorado, including a smoldering "smudge of arrowweed" (see *Pluchea sericea*) while tending cornfields, summertime huts with closely woven willow branches (see *Salix gooddingii*), and "smudges of green arrowweed around [the] house [and a] dish of coals and horse manure within" the house (Gifford 1933:263, 271).

Myrmecocystus sp. HONEY ANT. The repletes ("honey pots"), a worker storage caste, were possibly eaten by Cocopahs (Castetter & Bell 1951:212, 217). Repletes are harvested for their honey by many people around the world. AG.

Xylocopa sp. CARPENTER BEE. These large, black bees make nests in large agave and yucca flowering stalks. The nests were harvested for honey by various people, such as the Gila River Pimas (Rea 1977) and Maricopas (Spier 1933).

MOLLUSCS

Extensive shell middens along the Alto Golfo coast demonstrate a deep history of use, and the historic record further documents the importance of molluscs in the local cuisine and culture. Selected mollusc species were collected for food, and the shells of others were transported and traded inland in huge quantities to be made into jewelry; a few species served both purposes (Bowen 1986; Brusca 2004, and this volume; Foster 1975; Foster & Mitchell 2000; Gifford 1946; May 1973; Mitchell & Foster 2000; Vargas 2004). Shells, of course, preserve better than most other kinds of biological resources. Many of the molluscs listed here are nowadays economically harvested in the northern Gulf of California, often in a nonsustainable manner (for example, see discussion below for black murex, *Hexaplex nigritus*).

People in the northern Gulf of California have eaten shellfish for a very long time. Shell mounds at Bahía de los Angeles in Baja California contain shells 6,000 years old (Ritter 1985, 1998). Some midden shells at Estero Morua are about 2,000 years old (dated by radiocarbon analysis; Brusca 2004), but other Alto Golfo middens are younger and some may be recent. Mixed in among discarded shells are artifacts such as potsherds, obsidian and other stone flakes, metates and manos, shell tools, and occasional arrowheads, beads, and shell pendants (Figure 15.15). Hohokam, Patayan, and Trincheras artifacts, especially ceramics, indicate intensive shell gathering for about 1,000 years beginning as early as A.D. 300 or 400. The most intensive use was by Hohokam and Trincheras people, probably between A.D. 800 and 1450. "Although midden deposits are abundant, there is little to suggest any sustained occupation of the area. It is more likely these middens are the result of repeated visits by people who ate local shellfish while collecting other shell for trade and craft production" (Mitchell & Foster 2000:38). If so, this pattern changed after 1450, because historic people visited the shore primarily for subsistence reasons rather than merely to obtain shells for trade. They undoubtedly ate shellfish along with other kinds of food such as fish and plant foods (e.g., Castetter & Bell 1951; Childs 1954; Lumholtz 1912).

The most common northern gulf shells used by the Hohokam and Trincheras people for making ornaments were *Glycymeris*, *Laevicardium*, and *Conus* (Figure 15.16), and *Agropecten*, *Olivella*, *Pecten (sensu lato)*, and *Turritella* were also extensively used (e.g., Nelson 1991; Vargas 2004). Several bivalves are among the most abundant and widespread edible molluscs in coastal middens: *Arca pacifica*, *Chione californiensis*, *Dosinia ponderosa*, and *Myrakeena angelica (Ostrea angelica)*. *Glycymeris* and *Laevicardium* were important for both food and ornament. Species composition varies greatly among middens, reflecting proximity to an existing or extinct *estero* or the open shore. There is usually a preponderance of one or a few kinds of shells at any one place (Mitchell & Foster 2000).

Shells smaller than about 2.5 cm long are scarce in the middens, indicating that people generally didn't bother gathering items with little food value (e.g., Bowen 1986; Foster 1975). Many of the shells were "burned, although not extensively so" (Mitchell & Foster 2000:36), and in some areas the shells show little or no burning (e.g., Bowen 1986). Although many molluscs are quite tasty raw, getting at the meat usually requires heating, especially in the case of clams. A likely common means of preparation would be building a small, quickly burning fire on top of a pile of shells, although other methods of preparation were probably also used (Foster & Mitchell 2000; Mitchell & Foster 2000). One can imagine coastal grasses, croton (see *Croton wigginsii*), and the dwarf shrub *Frankenia palmeri* providing ready sources of fuel (see Felger & Moser 1985). You don't have to heat clams for very long to make them open, and they do not need to be in direct contact with fire. The Seris prepared shellfish by steaming, placing them on or around hot coals, or boiling, and they ate some kinds raw (Felger & Moser 1985:36–37; see *Dosinia*, below). They placed the large, thick-shelled *Dosinia* clams directly on hot coals to make them open (Cathy Moser Marlett, personal communication 2003). In the Alto Golfo middens the heavy, thick shells of large gastropods were broken, obviously to get at the meat inside (Bowen 1986; Gifford 1946; Mitchell & Foster 2000); these include black murex (*Hexaplex nigritus*), pink-mouth murex (*Phyllonotus erythrostomus*), Cortez melongena (*Melongena patula*), and smooth conch (*Strombus gracilior*). Tom Childs (1954:32–33) reported that the Hia C'ed O'odham "ate their Missmire Clams raw, and opened them with their teeth." I doubt that people opened clams with their teeth. Live clams are extremely difficult to open unless the strong adductor muscle is severed, and the more effective method is to heat them, as shown by evidence from middens and ethnographic accounts.

Walking along old footpaths in inland places such as the Pinacate lava fields, and especially in the interior of Isla Tiburón, I would sometimes see clamshells, mostly *Chione*. Maybe these shells were from someone's lunch. On March 12, 1701, Manje reported that people at Quitovac (Bacopa or Quitobac) "lived on shellfish, pitahayas, and other wild fruits" (Burrus 1971:265). Quitovac is about 50 km inland. During the cooler seasons clams can be kept alive and fresh for a number of days out of water. Cooked and dried shellfish meat will keep for several days and, without the shells, will be much lighter than when fresh (Henshilwood et al. 1994; Mitchell & Foster 2000).

Shellfish were collected at low tide and on a seasonal basis (e.g., Castetter & Bell 1951; Mitchell & Foster 2000). In March or April the Kiliwas harvested "clams and mussels" at San Felipe (Meigs 1939:27). The "Cocopa made an annual sojourn to the head of the gulf

Figure 15.15. Midden northeast of La Salina, Bahía Adair. Shells in-clude Arca pacifica *and* Sarcostrea palmula (Ostrea palmula). *Just below the 15-cm rule is an arrowhead. (Photo by Richard S. Felger)*

for the purpose of gathering the abundant clams" (Castetter & Bell 1951:223). Gifford (1933:261) mentions a site on the Sonora coast that was visited by Cocopas and Papagos for shellfish and fish. Childs (1954:32–33) reported that for the Hia C'ed O'odham "the shell fish the Indians ate were mostly clams. They live in the sand and are very easily obtained. The oysters live on coral reefs [rocky reefs]." Hohokam shell-gathering forays were probably from late fall through early spring, a time of cooler weather (Mitchell & Foster 2000). These trips were probably undertaken for multiple purposes. I would add that a trip to the seashore, including the well-known salt-gathering pilgrimages (see Chapter 39, this volume), might also have been recreational, and an abundant supply of shellfish would ensure plenty to eat.

Shells were universally used for jewelry (Jernigan 1978). In 1540 Alarcón reported that the people at the Colorado delta "have their noses pierced at the base from where they attach some pendants. Others wear shells and have their ears pierced with many holes, in which they fix beads and shells" (Flint & Flint 2005: 190–191). At a village on the lower Gila River in 1699 Manje saw beads "from a red shell they obtain from the sea" (Burrus 1971:233). Perhaps the beads were made from spiny oyster *(Spondylus)* or rock oyster *(Chama)*. Cocopahs wore necklaces and other ornaments, includ-ing earrings and nose pendants of shells, sometimes with cutout designs, as well as shell-bead necklaces (Chit-tenden 1901; Gifford 1933; Williams 1983). Fine neck-laces made of shell disk beads were prized by Coco-pahs, and few people had them; these necklaces came

"from Walapai country," and one necklace would buy a horse (Gifford 1933:277). For Cocopahs and Hia C'ed O'odham, Gifford (1933:277) reports that "clam shells [were] obtained on [the] Sonora coast, south of Port Isabel, one day's journey from Cocopa country." Lum-holtz (1912:332) records that the Hia C'ed O'odham made an annual journey "to Yuma to barter with Indi-ans there, and maize, tépari beans, and squash were exchanged for baskets and sea shells." Gifford (1933:262) notes that "a small band of Papago" exchanged shells from the gulf with Cocopahs at Somerton for food, probably in the latter part of the nineteenth century.

Cocopahs fashioned clamshells into knives, and the women used a sharp clam or oyster shell to shape pottery vessels (Gifford 1933:372; Williams 1983). Shells such as *Laevicardium elatum* were used as utensils, and shell tools are common in the archaeological record of the region (e.g., Rosenthal 1977; also see *Dosinia).* Among the Seris "clamshells were indispensable as tools, uten-sils, and containers," medium-sized clams were used as spoons, and "a large clamshell filled with water served as a mirror when placed in the shade" (Felger & Moser 1985:37–38).

Shells were widely transported and traded across North America, especially in the southwestern United States and northwestern Mexico (e.g., Bradley 1995; Ezell 1937; Nelson 1991; Villalpando 1997). The shells of about three dozen species were used by the Hohokam and Trincheras people. Although most were gathered from the Gulf of California, abalones *(Haliotis)* were acquired by trade from the Pacific coast. A well-used

Figure 15.16. Laevicardium elatum *and* Arca pacifica *in midden northeast of La Salina. (Photo by Richard S. Felger)*

Hohokam trail for transporting shells from the coast to the Gila Bend region and major population centers such as Snaketown passed by the east side of the Pinacates (Gifford 1946; Hayden 1972). Some petroglyph figures at two waterholes on shell transport routes include representations of heart shells *(Carditamera affinis)* or pecten shells. Also along this route is Lost City, an extensive prehistoric campsite in the Growler Valley which was a stopover on salt- and shell-gathering trips to and from the gulf (see Chapter 39, this volume). The site was used principally for shell manufacturing and was occupied only seasonally but over a long period of prehistoric time (Fontana 1965). Thousands of shell ornaments recovered at Hohokam sites, such as in the Gila Bend region (Fontana 1965), Snaketown (Haury 1975, 1976), and Pueblo Grande near Phoenix (Andrews & Bostwick 1997), indicate wholesale gathering and transport (Marmaduke & Martynec 1993).

Some of the more common molluscs found in archaeological sites along the coast from Estero Morua westward to Salina Grande as well as at inland sites are listed below (information largely from Bowen 1986; Tom Bowen, personal communication 2004; Richard Brusca, personal communication 2003; Foster 1975; Michael D. Foster, personal communication 2004; Gifford 1946; May 1973; Mitchell & Foster 2000; Richard S. White, personal communication 2004; and my observations).

Bivalves:

Anadara multicostata
Arca pacifica
Argopecten circularis
Barbatia sp.

Carditamera affinis [*Cardita affinis*]
Chama frondosa
Chama buddiana [*C. mexicana*]
Chione californiensis
Chione cortezi
Chione fluctifraga
Chionopsis gnidia [*Chione gnidia*]
Dosinia ponderosa
Glycymeris gigantea
Glycymeris maculata
Laevicardium elatum
Leptopecten sp.
Modiolus capax
Myrakeena angelica [*Ostrea angelica*]
Nodipecten subnodosus [*Lyropecten subnodosus*]
Oppenhelmopecten vogdesi [*Pecten vogdesi*]
Ostreola conchaphila
Pseudochama sp.
Pteria sterna
Saccostrea palmula [*Ostrea palmula*]
Spondylus calcifer
Trachycardium panamense

Gastropods:

Cerithidea californica mazatlanica
Cerithium stercusmuscarum
Conus princeps
Crepidula sp.
Crucibulum spinosum
Ficus ventricosa
Hexaplex nigritus
Malea ringens
Melongena patula
Oliva including *O. undatella*
Olivella including *O. dama*
Phyllonotus erythrostomus [*Hexaplex
    erythrostomus*]
Polinices reluzianus
Strombus gracilior
Turbo fluctuosus
Turritella spp.

A few culturally significant molluscs are briefly discussed below.

Bivalves:

Arca pacifica. PACIFIC ARC SHELL; ARCA. This medium-sized, edible clam is common in coastal middens, where an occasional shell had a drill hole, indicating use as a pendant ornament (Gifford 1946). The shells are common in Hohokam and Trincheras archaeological sites.

Carditamera affinis. HEART SHELL; ALMEJA DE CORAZÓN. This medium-sized, edible clam is abundant in middens and was sometimes fashioned into a pendant (Gifford 1946). It is also common at inland archaeological sites.

Chione spp. VENUS CLAMS; ALMEJA CHINA, ALMEJA CHIRLA, ALMEJA ROÑOSA. Chione shells are abundant at nearly all coastal middens, sometimes in spectacular concentrations (Bowen 1986; Mitchell & Foster 2000). *C. californiensis* outnumbered all others at Estero Morua middens (Foster 1975) (Figure 15.17), and *C. cortezi* and *C. fluctifraga* are also common in regional middens. These clams are abundant and easily collected.

Dosinia ponderosa. DISK SHELL; ALMEJA BLANCA GIGANTE, ALMEJA REINA. This edible clam is often abundant in middens (Figure 15.18). The thick valve margins are generally broken, and many were made into tools (Bowen 1986; Mitchell & Foster 2000; Rosenthal 1977). The Seris have long eaten this clam. They placed the large, thick-shelled *Dosinia* clams directly on hot coals, "side by side in a row (on end, in other words), the hinge side down so the clams would open at the top and not down into the sand" (Cathy Moser Marlett, personal communication 2005).

Glycymeris gigantea and **G. maculata.** BITTERSWEET SHELLS. These heavy, thick-shelled clams are not especially common in coastal middens but were sometimes used for food (Figure 15.19). On several occasions, especially in middens around Estero Morua, Michael Foster and Douglas Mitchell found clusters of glycymeris shells, most of which exhibited some evidence of burning, indicating that the people cooked a group of glycymeris together. The shells are not often found mixed with other species (Michael S. Foster, personal communication 2004). It was an enormously popular trade item in the prehistoric Southwest, and huge quantities of these shells were crafted into jewelry, especially bracelets, by the Hohokam and Trincheras people (e.g., Bradley 1995; Fontana 1965; Haury 1975, 1976; Woodward 1936). The shells were often incised or etched using vinegar from saguaro wine (see *Carnegiea gigantea*).

Laevicardium elatum. GIANT EGG COCKLE; ALMEJA AMARILLA. The shells of these large, edible clams were often used as eating utensils and for ornaments (e.g., Mitchell & Foster 2000; Rosenthal 1977). Tom Bowen and I saw a cache of three nested *Laevicardium* shells at La Salina (Bowen 1986). These and many others in the coastal middens were found entire and not worked (Figure 15.16). Among the Hohokam they were a favored source for cut-shell ornaments (Michael S. Foster, personal communication 2004). Among the Seris the shells served as "all-purpose bowls, dippers for food, containers for pigments and paints... and were used to scoop out dirt to dig or enlarge a well" (Felger & Moser 1985:37).

Myrakeena angelica. This oyster is one of the most common shells in the coastal middens.

Figure 15.17. Chione californiensis. *(Drawing by Cathy Moser Marlett)*

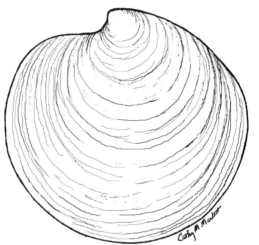

Figure 15.18. Dosinia ponderosa. *(Drawing by Cathy Moser Marlett)*

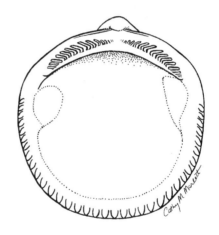

Figure 15.19. Glycymeris gigantea. *(Drawing by Cathy Moser Marlett)*

Spondylus calcifer. SPINY OYSTER; ALMEJA BURRA, CALLO DE ESCARLOPA. This large bivalve occurs in coastal middens (Bowen 1986) but is not common. The colorful shells were crafted into jewelry and ornaments, including the famous Hohokam inlay work.

Gastropods:

Conus princeps. PRINCELY CONE; CONO. This is one of the larger Alto Golfo cone shells. It is rather scarce in Alto Golfo middens (Michael Foster, personal communication 2004) but was collected for ornament, especially pendants, and is found in Hohokam and Trincheras archaeological sites (e.g., Nelson 1991; Vargas 2004).

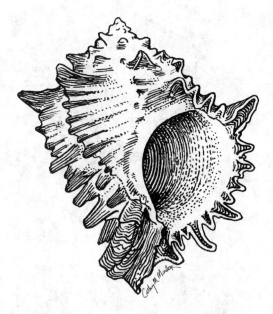

Figure 15.20. Hexaplex nigritus. *(Drawing by Cathy Moser Marlett)*

*Haliotis spp. ABALONE; ABULÓN. The several North American species of this genus occur only along the Pacific coast from Baja California Sur to Oregon. Abalones were prized especially for jewelry and other artwork, and there was an extensive prehistoric trade in these shells between the Pacific coast and the greater Southwest as well as other inland regions across North America (Ives 1961; Haury 1965). Kino first observed abalones in their native habitat on the Pacific shore of Baja California about December 30, 1684 (Ives 1961). He later saw these famous "blue shells" at a village near the Gila-Colorado River junction on February 21, 1699 (Burrus 1971:112). He asked the Indians about them and was told that the shells do not occur in the Gulf of California. At many other villages the Indians told him that the blue shells came from the sea far to the west, in "other lands more remote" (Burrus 1971:116). Kino used this biogeographic information to deduce that California was indeed not an island, and this in turn spurred his determination to explore the Dry Borders region to find a land route from mainland Mexico to the missions of Baja California.

Figure 15.21. Olivella dama. *(Drawing by Cathy Moser Marlett)*

Hexaplex nigritus. LARGE BLACK MUREX; MÚRICE NEGRO, CARACOL CHINO NEGRO. These large, heavy-shelled gastropods are often abundant in coastal middens (Figure 15.20). At some places near Bahía de la Cholla you could stand in one place and see thousands if not tens of thousands of these shells (Foster & Mitchell 2000; Richard S. White, personal communication 2004). The shells are usually broken to allow access to the meat inside (Bowen 1986; Gifford 1946; Mitchell & Foster 2000). There is often a single hole about midway on the main body whorl, broken from the outside, although many have the whole side or both sides broken open to expose the body whorls. Mitchell and Foster (2000:34) found "untold thousands of perforated specimens" along the eastern edge of Bahía Adair, indicating that "it must have been a favored food." The Seris cooked this murex by burning sticks on top of it (Felger & Moser 1985:36–37). The shells were fashioned into trumpets by the Hohokam and also used as ceremonial objects but are not common in Hohokam sites (Michael S. Foster, personal communication 2004). Large-scale commercial harvest of this murex began in 1992, primarily for the Asian market for the meat and the operculum. In 1992 alone, more than 600 metric tons were landed in the Puerto Peñasco area (Cudney-Bueno 2000). By 2005 its importance for the Asian market had declined, but it continued to be harvested for national consumption and "is one of the main catches of the diving fishery in the upper Gulf of California" (Cudney-Bueno 2001:14). Since 2001, season and area closures have been established to protect the breeding aggregations of this species (Cudney-Bueno 2004).

Melongena patula. CORTEZ MELONGENA; CARACOL BURRO. This large, thick-shelled species is common in middens. The shells are often not broken, although some have a pattern of breakage like that seen in the black murex (Mitchell & Foster 2000; Richard S. White, personal communication 2003).

Olivella dama. PIGMY OLIVE; OLIVA CHICA. These small, glossy shells were among the most common necklace beads and were traded far and wide (Figure 15.21). They are not common in coastal middens, probably because they are too small to be worth eating and were removed to be used for necklaces.

Phyllonotus erythrostomus. PINK-MOUTH MUREX; MÚRICE DE BOCA ROSA, CARACOL CHINO ROSA. This species is common in some middens, and the shells frequently show the same pattern of breakage as the black murex (Richard S. White, personal communication 2003).

Polinices recluzianus. GIANT MOON SNAIL; CARACOL DE LUNA. This species is common in middens, and the shells frequently show the same pattern of breakage as the black murex (Richard S. White, personal communication 2003).

Strombus gracilior. SMOOTH CONCH; CARACOL DE UÑA. Shells in middens often have a large part of the outer lip broken away, apparently to obtain the meat (Mitchell & Foster 2000).

Turbo fluctuosus. TURBAN SHELL; CARACOL TURBANTE. This is one of the more common shells in coastal middens, although the "cat's eye" operculas are often more common than the shell (Richard S. White, personal communication 2003).

Turritella gonostoma and **T. leucostoma.** TOWER SHELL; CARACOL TORNILLO. These attractive shells are often found in middens but are seldom common. *Turritella* is not a food resource, and the shells are neither broken nor show signs of being used. They are abundant along the shore and perhaps were picked up just as people do today simply because they are pretty. The Seris used tower shells "in a game in which the shell was flipped into the open end of a piece of reedgrass" (Felger & Moser 1985:38). The shells are common in Hohokam archaeological sites and were used as ornaments (Nelson 1991).

CRUSTACEANS

Callinectes bellicosus. BLUE CRAB; JAIBA AZUL. This was a common food item for Gulf of California people (Felger & Moser 1985) (Figure 15.22). In 1854 A. B. Gray found "a band of Indians (Papagos)...living on fish and crabs in the salt creeks and lagoons" at Bahía Adair (Bailey 1963:58). Gifford (1933:269) says that the Cocopahs did not eat "lobsters and crabs." The Seris used a slender, lightweight pole with a nail as a point to harpoon *Callinectes* in shallow water. "These crabs, esteemed for their sweet-tasting meat, were eaten in substantial quantities. The claws and carapaces were numerous in camp and house refuse" (Felger & Moser 1985:38). Remains of this crab have been found in coastal middens from Estero Morua westward (Bowen 1986; Brusca 2004), often as burned claws in shell mounds containing Hohokam artifacts (Mitchell & Foster 2000; Michael Foster, personal communication 2004). Because only the claws were recovered from Estero Morua middens, Brusca (2004:16) suggests that the people were "ecologically aware, and instead of killing the entire crab they simply broke off the chelipeds, which would grow back at the next molt." I disagree, and base my opinion on ethnographic accounts, on knowing how good these creatures taste, and on the high probability that after more than 1,000 years the rather thin carapaces and walking legs are not as likely to persist as the chelipeds.

Farfantepenaeus californiensis [*Penaeus californiensis*], BROWN SHRIMP; CAMERÓN CAFÉ; and **Litopenaeus**

Figure 15.22. Callinectes bellicosus. *(Drawing by Cathy Moser Marlett)*

stylirostris [*P. stylirostris*], BLUE SHRIMP; CAMERÓN AZUL. These are the common, commercial shrimp species of the Gulf of California. Both can be found in estuaries and shallow lagoons and undoubtedly would have been common in the nineteenth century. At Bahía Adair in 1854 Peter Brady noted that "our guide took us to the camp of fish eating Indians belonging to the Papago tribe and who were called Areneflos [Areneños] or sandy Indians...their commissary stores...consisted principally of dried fish and shrimp put up in little cakes, and wild grass seed" (Bailey 1963:219). This is the only report of Hia C'ed O'odham using shrimp.

FISH

For the river people and those with access to the coast, there was an abundance of fishes. There was, however, considerable seasonal variation in availability. In 1856 Lt. Michler reported that "a sub-tribe of the Papagos, called Areneños, live on the salt lakes near the head of the Gulf of California, and principally subsist on fish" (Michler 1987:123). Lumholtz (1912:330) notes, "At certain seasons they went to the coast for fishing, catching as many fish as they wished." Early travelers, including Anza, Garcés, Hardy, Kino, Manje, and Sedelmayr, observed large quantities of fish at Cocopah camps (Castetter & Bell 1951; Kelly 1977; Williams 1974). All the native freshwater food fishes of the lower Río Colorado have been extirpated from Mexico, and most are endangered on the U.S. side (Mueller & Marsh 2002). The few traditional food fishes reported in the literature are listed here, but there undoubtedly were others.

In 1540 Alarcón recorded, "They have...pots in which they cook the squash and very excellent fish they obtain from the river" (Flint & Flint 2005:196). Kelly (1977:44) reports: "Among the Hwanyak Cocopa, parties of men frequently went to the Gulf to fish. They watched the sea birds to discover where a school of fish was located. When the fish came near the shore, the men ran out into the water and drove the fish further in by beating the water with sticks. When the fish entered shallow water, they were picked up and thrown ashore. These ocean fish were dried before being carried home." In March or April the Kiliwas made an annual excursion to the coast at San Felipe, where they "caught fish and dried them in the sun to take back to their permanent rancherías" (Meigs 1939:27). Freshwater fishes were often taken with bow and arrow (Gifford 1933). Joe Giff, a Gila River Pima, told Rea (1974) that fishing arrows were made "opposite from game arrows, with the heavy part in front instead, so they would go in the water. But they have to be used in shallow water." Rea (1974) further reports: "There were no feathers on fishing arrows.... Pimas have no knowledge of poisoning fish.... Basketry fish traps made from willow were used."

Atractoscion nobilis. WHITE SEABASS (see *Totoaba macdonaldi*).

Balistes polylepis. FINESCALE TRIGGERFISH; COCHI. Remains of this medium-sized marine fish were found at archaeological sites near Puerto Peñasco (Follett 1957, listed as *Verrunculus polylepis*). It is a modern-day preferred food fish, especially for ceviche. AG.

Calamus brachysomus. PACIFIC PORGY; PLUMA MAROTILLA. Material from an archaeological site near Puerto Peñasco is probably this marine species (Follett 1957, listed as *C. taurinus*; see Thomson et al. 2000). AG.

Cynoscion othonopterus. GULF CORVINA (see *Totoaba macdonaldi*).

Cynoscion xanthulus. ORANGEMOUTH CORVINA; CORVINA BOQUINARANJA. Remains of this meter-long marine food fish were found at an archaeological site near Puerto Peñasco (Follett 1957). AG.

*Cyprinus carpio. COMMON CARP (EUROPEAN CARP); CARPA COMÚN. *Siix anyur*, the Cocopah name for this fish, translates as "new fish" (Gifford 1933). This freshwater species was introduced into the lower Colorado River during the nineteenth century (Mueller & Marsh 2002). It was "taken with bow" and arrow (Gifford 1933: 268). AG.

Dasyatis spp. WHIPTAIL STINGRAYS; RAYAS LÁTIGO. Childs (1954:32) describes a unique Hia C'ed O'odham harpoon: "Some of the spears were formed with the barb of the stingaree which is taken from his tail.... They would attach it to a small willow branch and carried it in their hand. When they ran up on the big fish they would jab it in the fish and the barbs on the stinger would keep it from pulling out." *Dasyatis* is the one local genus that has a large spine (Don Thomson, personal communication 2003). The "big fish" was probably totoaba or a similar large fish (see *Totoaba macdonaldi*). AG.

Gila elegans. BONYTAIL; CARPA ELEGANTE. This freshwater fish was taken with dip nets in the lower Río Colorado by the Cocopahs, Mohaves, and Quechans (Castetter & Bell 1951). AG.

Gillichthys mirabilis. LONGJAW MUDSUCKER; CHUPALODO GRANDE. For the Cocopahs, Kelly (1977:44) reports, "In the estuary [Río Colorado delta], a certain species of fish *(šlnyah)* could be captured by digging

them out of soft mud. These fish were quite small and resembled catfish. They were located by looking for an opening in the mud." Castetter and Bell (1951:220) mention a fish used by Cocopahs called "sinyah. When the tide went out these ... were left stranded at low tide and burrowed into the mud, tails sticking up. These resembled catfish although quite small." Although neither Kelly nor Castetter and Bell identified this fish, Lloyd Findley and Don Thomson (personal communication 2003) said it is probably this large goby, which can be caught by digging it out of the mud; it is incredibly hardy and can tolerate relatively high salinity and temperatures. AG.

Girella simplicidens. GULF OPALEYE; CHOPA OJO AZUL. Remains of this common, small marine fish were found at an archaeological site near Puerto Peñasco (Follett 1957). AG.

Leuresthes sardina. GULF GRUNION; PEJERREY SARDINA. Gifford (1933:268) reports, "On [the] Sonora coast ca. 30 miles S. of Shipyard—full day's walk—Cocopa took 'sardines' *(kwiksi)*. As waves swept in, [the] fish were beaten rapidly against [the] sand with [a] 4-ft. stick, then scraped up [the] beach with [a] stick... parched on coals; or beheaded, pulverized in [a] wooden mortar, [and] boiled with pulverized tule [cattail, *Typha domingensis*] root for thickening." Crawford (1989) corrects the orthography to *kuksí*.

In March or April the Kiliwas harvested grunion at San Felipe: "the fish (tesmér, 'sardines') came up on the beach, where they were killed with clubs" (Meigs 1939:27). These are, of course, grunion and not true sardines. Among the Seris "they were cooked in large numbers against coals, dried, and stored in sealed pottery vessels in caves" (Felger & Moser 1985:41).

Gulf grunion actively spawn in the wave wash on beaches at precise tidal phases from January to May (see Hastings & Findley, this volume). In southern California we caught grunion (the closely related *L. affinis*) at night in phosphorescent froth at water's edge, carried them home in our buckets, and the next morning had them fried in butter for the best breakfast ever. AG.

Mugil cephalus. STRIPED MULLET; LISA RAYADA; CAMÁNY. This has been an important fish for the Cocopas and was taken in "the river and land-locked bodies of river water. It lived in the lakes during the winter and thus was available when fish were difficult to get in the river" (Castetter & Bell 1951:219). It was "taken in [the] river with dip net or bow, [and] in lagoons with bow or gill net" (Gifford 1933:268; also see Chittenden 1901). This euryhaline fish occurs mainly in the sea or estuaries but can penetrate far up rivers. Striped mullet remains were found at archaeological sites near Puerto Peñasco (Follett 1957). AG.

Mustelus lunulatus. SICKLEFIN SMOOTHHOUND; CAZÓN SEGADOR. Remains presumably of this small, edible shark were found at an archaeological site near Puerto Peñasco (Follett 1957, listed as *tiburón mamón*). AG.

Mycteroperca jordani. GULF GROUPER; BAYA. Remains of this large, marine food fish were found at an archaeological site near Puerto Peñasco (Follett 1957). AG.

Ptychocheilus lucius. COLORADO PIKEMINNOW; CARPA GIGANTE DEL COLORADO; MWI•LK [*muwilk*, Cocopah]. Formerly also called Colorado squawfish, white salmon of the Colorado, bull salmon. This freshwater fish is actually a giant minnow that often weighed 20–80 pounds. It was said to be the Cocopahs' most important food fish and was taken all year on the lower Río Colorado. Gifford (1933) reports that it was caught with dip nets. In his journal of February 1699 Manje wrote that the lower Gila River "abounds in large fish which resemble trout or salmon, and are the ordinary food of these tribes" (Burrus 1971:236). AG.

Rhizoprionodon longurio. PACIFIC SHARPNOSE SHARK; CAZÓN BIRONCHE. Material "from a fish approximately 16 inches long" was found at an archaeological site near Puerto Peñasco (Follett 1957, listed as *Scoliodon longurio*). This small requiem shark is now often used as a food fish. AG.

Totoaba macdonaldi [*Cynoscion macdonaldi*], TOTOABA; **Atractoscion nobilis,** WHITE SEABASS, CORVINA CABICUCHO; and **Cynoscion othonopterus,** GULF CORVINA, CORVINA GOLFINA. Some of the information below may apply to any of these three large fishes, which could have been found in shallow water, especially in the nineteenth century. The dark coloring reported by Castetter and Bell describes totoaba rather than corvina, but the white ventral coloring seems to describe a corvina (Lloyd Findley, Carlos Navarro, and Don Thomson, personal communication 2003). The "250 pound" fish described by Childs would have been the totoaba, which was a larger and heavier fish than the others. These brief descriptions, however, are too vague to be truly diagnostic.

Cocopahs took "a small-scaled bass (*amuyn* or *a moanyi*)... on the coast of Sonora. This was a large fish, about four feet long.... It was speared with a pointed pole of screwbean by men standing in the water. The color was dark on top, nearly white underneath; the white flesh was cooked with nypa [*Distichlis palmeri*] mush" (Castetter & Bell 1951:220; also see Gifford 1933.)

Tom Childs (1954:32) describes his experiences as a young man with his Hia C'ed O'odham friends on the Sonoran coast in the late nineteenth century: "They showed me how to catch those fish... called Sea Bass, and some of them will lick 250 pounds, and are nearly all meat—hardly any bones in them. They wait until just before the moon changes from full. When it changes to new... on the high tides they go down and wait for the tide to come in, and when it comes in, it comes with a rush, and the large fish come in with it. They come in to get the smaller fish.... The tide breaks and rushes back, and those large fish are left stranded on dry ground, so they rush in with a spear and spear them, and string them on a rope until they get a big load. There's where I learned that fish had teeth. I got my foot caught in one's mouth. We all got a big load of fish, and strung them on ropes, and pulled them in as the tide kept rising." Childs also reports using a harpoon with a stingray point (see *Dasyatis*).

Totoaba remains from archaeological sites near Puerto Peñasco indicate that it was a common food fish (Follett 1957). It seems that totoabas were rather easily obtained. Follett (1957:281) says, "It was reported by Gilbert (1890, p. 65) as being very abundant... and as feeding [and likely spawning] in shallow water, where it was easily approached and speared. Nakashima (1916, p. 85, 86) stated that this species often comes into very shallow water; that it is not very shy; and that when one is hooked or speared, the others crowd around as if in curiosity." AG.

Xyrauchen texanus. RAZORBACK SUCKER; MATALOTE JOROBADO. This large freshwater fish was a food resource for the Cocopahs. Gifford (1933:268) reports "humpbacks... taken with gill net in lagoons, with dip net and bow elsewhere." AG.

Unidentified Fishes.

Castetter and Bell (1951:220) list several unidentified gulf fishes taken at the Colorado delta by Cocopahs: "*kweyah*... whitish in color, rather smooth with inconspicuous scales, about two and one-half feet long"; "*chimo hul*, six inches long, scaly"; "*solalao*, a flat, white, slender fish about fourteen inches long"; and "*karrh ush*, about fourteen inches long."

REPTILES

Crocodylus acutus. AMERICAN CROCODILE; COCODRILO, LAGARTO. These tropical animals extend northward to river deltas in Sinaloa and formerly occurred in southern Sonora, perhaps in the Río Mayo and Yaqui deltas, and occasional strays are known as far north as the vicinity of Guaymas (Navarro 2003a, 2003b). During his expedition to the lower Colorado River in 1540, Alarcón reported, "I asked him whether he had information about a river called Totonteac. He replied to me, 'No,' but that he knew well there was another great river where such large *lagartos* were found that they made round shields out of their skins" (Flint & Flint 2005:198). Baegert (1952) makes a fanciful claim of crocodiles (inaccurately translated as "alligators") at the delta of the Río Colorado in 1751. Baegert never visited the Colorado, and his report is not credible.

Crotalus spp. RATTLESNAKE; CASCABEL. Among the Hia C'ed O'odham, William Merrill said, "Indians don't eat rattlesnakes" (Zepeda 1985:90). Snakes as food were generally taboo among Sonoran Desert people (Rea 1981).

Dipsosaurus dorsalis. DESERT IGUANA. These relatively large lizards are reported as food animals for the Hia C'ed O'odham (Rea 1981). Speaking of the Hia C'ed O'odham, C. Moore, interviewed in 1953 by Thomas (1991:380), said, "They used to eat a big white lizard that lives in the sand." This is probably the desert iguana. PI, AG, CP, GR, OP, SD.

Heloderma suspectum. GILA MONSTER. Zepeda (1985: 15, 70) says that the Hia C'ed O'odham ate the Gila monster, but it is scarce or even absent over much of the Hia C'ed territory. But William Merrill's statement, "They eat the tail. They don't eat the rest of it.... They got a big fat tail" (Zepeda 1985:90), would fit a Gila monster. PI, CP, GR, OP, SD.

Sauromalus obesus. CHUCKWALLA. This large lizard was a common food animal among the Hia C'ed O'odham and people of the lower Río Colorado region (Castetter & Bell 1951; Felger & Moser 1985; Amadeo Rea, personal communication 2003). PI, CP, GR, OP, SD.

Uma notata. COLORADO DESERT FRINGE-TOED LIZARD. This lizard may have been a food animal among the Hia C'ed O'odham. After discussing the sandfood plants (*Pholisma sonorae*), Ramon Anita (in Thomas 1991:374) said, "They would also follow lizard tracks in the sand until the track ended. This is where the lizard buries itself. They would stick a sharp stick down in the sand and pull him out. It has white meat something like an iguana." This may have been the fringe-toed lizard or perhaps the desert iguana. PI, AG, CP, GR.

Turtles. Castetter and Bell (1951:213) mention that the "Mohave and Yuma never ate turtles of any variety," indicating a taboo that also seems to have extended to the Cocopahs (Rea 1981). Yet one page earlier Castetter and Bell refer to Trippel's (1889) report of Yumas eating "land tortoises."

Chelonia mydas, GREEN TURTLE, and **Lepidochelys olivacea,** OLIVE RIDLEY. These two sea turtles were probably once fairly common in the Alto Golfo (Seminoff & Nichols, this volume), but their role in local cultures for the most part remains a mystery. I know of only two brief reports mentioning Hia C'ed O'odham use of sea turtles. Peter Brady and A. B. Gray visited the head of the gulf in 1854 with an O'odham guide, who led them to a waterhole in the Pinacates. Brady wrote, "There were signs of old huts, fish bones, turtle and marine shells, which showed us that we were not very far from the gulf" (Bailey 1963:218–219). In a 1953 interview of his experiences around 1900 with the "Sand Papago," Ramon Anita said, "When the tide came in, they would catch fish and big turtles (cahuamas)" (Thomas 1991:374).

At the Colorado delta in summer 1826 Hardy (1829: 336) observed a "hut...saving only the absence of turtle shells, resembled that of the island of Tiburow [Isla Tiburón]." Seri brush houses invariably had green turtle carapaces stacked against the walls (Felger & Moser 1985). AG.

Gopherus agassizii. DESERT TORTOISE. Desert people relished tortoises for food, usually roasting them in coals. Tortoises were also featured in oral history and song and were used medicinally, and the shells were fashioned into musical instruments (Castetter & Underhill 1935; Felger et al. 1983; Nabhan 2002). Vinito Garcia, a Hia C'ed O'odham man, said, "What will happen if the Anglos discontinued their money system? What will happen to our children? They will not want to eat the mountain turtle, because they have never eaten any. Maybe they will eat it if they get hungry enough" (Bell et al. 1980:73). PI, CP, GR, OP, SD.

Kinosternon sonoriense. SONORAN MUD TURTLE. This small turtle was a food item for the Hia C'ed and Tohono O'odham (Rea 1981) and Gila River Pimas (Rea 1974). It is found at Quitobaquito and is known from the Río Sonoyta and formerly the Río Colorado (Rosen, this volume) and the Gila River (Rea 1974). "The mud turtle and the tortoise were relished by the Pima, who ate legs, head and parts inside the shell. 'They were always fat.' I know of no one today who eats them" (Rea 1974). Nabhan (2002:359), however, reports that Hia C'ed O'odham people he interviewed said the mud turtle "was the 'wrong kind for eating'" when compared with the desert tortoise. Mud turtles smell bad, and a related species with a similar, although somewhat more pungent musk, is called the stinkpot. It is not surprising that people at the end of the twentieth century found mud turtles distasteful, but there is no reason to doubt the validity of the differences in these reports. AG (extirpated?), OP.

BIRDS

The regional cultural significance of bird life is amply demonstrated by the work of Amadeo Rea (1983, in press). Published information on cultural connections of birds among the Hia C'ed O'odham and Cocopah, however, is generally scant and often imprecise. A diversity of birds provided significant food resources, although they were generally less important than other kinds of animals and for the Cocopahs less important than fish. Birds' eggs, especially duck and quail eggs, were eaten boiled and were often important food resources, especially among the Cocopahs, who sometimes traded bird eggs with their neighbors (Gifford 1933; Kelly 1977). Hia C'ed O'odham ate eggs of at least some birds, including quail (see Gambel's quail, *Callipepla gambelii*). There were, however, certain taboos on eating eggs among some people, such as the Tohono O'odham (Rea 1981). Feathers were universally used for decoration and ceremony. In 1540 Alarcón observed, "Everyone, both large and small, wears a cord made of various colors at the level of the navel. In the middle of it is attached a round cluster of feathers, which hangs behind them like a tail. The women . . . wear a covering of painted and glued feathers in back and front" (Flint & Flint 2005:191). Gifford (1933:279) reports that among the Cocopahs feathers of hawks and eagles were "not worn by ordinary" men, and if they did so, it "caused severe headache. Certain shamans and twins wore these. . . . Most distinguished warriors wore crow [probably raven], owl, [and] white heron feathers in [their] hair."

Anatidae. DUCKS AND GEESE. Diverse species were hunted for food, especially in the Colorado delta, where waterfowl served as significant food resources. Cocopahs hunted ducks with wooden-pointed arrows and also gathered their eggs (Gifford 1933). Hia C'ed O'odham hunted ducks "when the people stayed near the water and there would be ducks" (Betty Melvin in Zepeda 1985:53).

Ducks appear to be under-differentiated (different kinds often not distinguished by name) in North American native folk taxonomies that have been carefully studied (Hunn 1999; Amadeo Rea, personal communication 2003). Many ethnographers likewise did not make many distinctions. Gila River Pimas agree that Anatidae were probably not part of the aboriginal diet—they hunted ducks after obtaining shotguns (Rea 1983, in press). AG, and locally in CP, GR, OP.

Aquila chrysaetos. GOLDEN EAGLE. Eagles had special religious significance. Among some O'odham groups eagle feathers were worn by men as a headdress and eagle down was tied in the hair (Castetter & Underhill 1935:50). "A Papago man who had come into contact with the supernatural by killing an enemy or an eagle, or by joining the salt pilgrimage, needed to be purified by a period of segregation and fasting" (Castetter & Bell 1942:221). These are independent, parallel opportunities to get power (Underhill 1946). Eagle down was affixed to prayer sticks (see *Acacia greggii;* Castetter & Underhill 1935). For the Hia C'ed O'odham, the golden eagle was "believed to be a person, has power, and so is not eaten" (Betty Melvin in Zepeda 1985:30). Cocopahs and

O'odham sometimes kept eagles in captivity to obtain feathers (Castetter & Bell 1951:70; Drucker 1941). Among the Cocopahs the feathers were used for war arrows and were worn by a shaman (Kelly 1977). In addition to egret feathers, youths seeking a wife wore eagle feathers in their hair and on necklaces and belts (Kelly 1977). Gifford (1933:279) reports that among the Cocopahs "eagle feathers [were] obtained from Diegueño; shamans who dreamed of eagles kept [the] feathers. Others would sicken" if they kept these feathers. AG, CP, GR, OP, SD.

*****Ara macao.** SCARLET MACAW. Parrot feathers were highly prized, and the scarlet macaw, "a southern Mexican species, was definitely a trade item in the aboriginal Southwest." It was captive-raised by settled people in southern Arizona as late as the mid-seventeenth century (Rea 1983:162–163). The scarlet macaw is well known from the regional archaeological record, including the Hohokam site of Snaketown (Rea 1983). In 1540 Alarcón was given parrot feathers by Río Colorado people (Flint & Flint 2005), who probably got them by trade.

Ardea alba [*Casmerodius egretta*], GREAT EGRET [AMERICAN EGRET], and **Egretta thula** [*E. candidissima*], SNOWY EGRET. Cocopah youths looking for a wife wore egret feathers in their hair and on a necklace. The feathers were also tied on a boy's cradle (Kelly 1977:54). In April 1926 Raymond Gilmore met a Cocopah hunter "killing egrets for their plumes which were expensive and highly desired items in the millinery business" (Williams 1974:137). AG, and locally in CP, GR, OP, SD.

Ardea herodias. GREAT BLUE HERON. One of the largest birds in the region, it was eaten by people at Quitovac (Nabhan et al. 1982) and probably elsewhere. The Seris regarded it as one of the best-tasting birds (Felger & Moser 1985). AG, CP, GR, OP, SD.

Bubo virginianus. GREAT HORNED OWL. The following information undoubtedly refers to the great horned owl (Amadeo Rea, personal communication 2003). Calling of this owl is generally taken as a bad omen (see Rea 1983). For example, among the Cocopahs, an "owl hooting at night near [a] house [was a] death portent for [the] inmates" (Gifford 1933:305). The Hia C'ed O'odham had similar concepts: "During the death ceremony an owl feather is used to wave at the villagers and the deceased for purification. Owl feathers represent healing for the sick or purification during death ceremonies, keeping the evil spirits from entering the dead body. The owl is recognized as a bearer of a bad omen. When he appears in a village hooting loudly, it is a sign that he brings bad news of a death or illness" (Fillman Bell in Bell et al. 1980:103–104). AG, PI, CP, GR, OP, SD.

Callipepla gambelii [*Lophortyx gambelii*]. GAMBEL'S QUAIL. This was one of the most important food birds in the region. The O'odham often trapped them in saguaro-rib cages (Castetter & Underhill 1935). Betty Melvion recalled that the Hia C'ed O'odham trapped birds and ate "the eggs of these birds—even quail eggs" (Bell et al. 1980:101). Cocopahs captured quail "by hand when drenched with rain, or [they were] taken in [a] snare with [a] cowpea-fiber noose." They also collected the eggs (Gifford 1933:269). AG, PI, CP, GR, OP, SD.

*****Chickens.** Alarcón brought "hens and roosters from Castile" to the lower Río Colorado in 1540 (Flint & Flint 2005:202), but there is no evidence that this introduction was successful.

Fulica americana. AMERICAN COOT. It was hunted for food at Quitovac (Nabhan et al. 1982) and probably at wetlands elsewhere in the region. Río Sonoyta, AG, CP, GR, OP.

Hawks. Feathers of various species were prized for arrows (Childs 1954; Gifford 1933:274). Along with eagles, Cocopahs sometimes kept hawks in captivity to obtain feathers (Drucker 1941).

Zenaida macroura. MOURNING DOVE. This dove was widely used for food, often shot with arrows when roosting at night or trapped (Nabhan et al. 1982). Williams (1983) reports doves kept as pets, but the species is not identified. PI, AG, CP, GR, OP, SD.

Zenaida asiatica. WHITE-WING DOVE. Eating this dove was forbidden to all Pimas, although during the twentieth century the taboo was relaxed among some O'odham. The taboo involved this dove's association with saguaro fruit, and perhaps when saguaro wine ceremonies ceased, some people dropped the taboo (Amadeo Rea, personal communication 2003). Kelly (1977:45) reports that "the only game animal not eaten [by Cocopahs] was the dove," and although he does not identify the species, it was probably the white-wing dove. PI, AG, CP, GR, OP, SD.

MAMMALS

Information on the larger, more conspicuous, and culturally important mammals is relatively extensive, but reports for the smaller ones can be casual and nonspecific or even misleading. For example, Castetter and Bell (1951:212) report that lower Colorado tribes used "prairie dogs" and "various rats" in spite of the fact that prairie dogs (*Cynomys*) do not occur in the Sonoran Desert.

Domestic mammals

By the time Alarcón made his second ascent of the Colorado and lower Gila rivers, in September 1540, local Indians already knew about the "new" domestic animals brought to the Pueblo Indian region in present-

day New Mexico by the Coronado expedition a few months earlier. Alarcón reported, "[The locals said] that many of them had cattle like those of Cibola [meaning bison] and other small black animals with wool and horns.... And [they said] that there were some of them who rode horseback who raced a great deal" (Flint & Flint 2005:201). Kino brought cattle, goats, horses, and sheep to the Dry Borders region at the end of the seventeenth century (Bolton 1919; Burrus 1971).

Camels. Feral camels from 1860s U.S. Army and mining operations multiplied, and their descendants roamed southwestern Arizona until the early twentieth century (Boyd 1995; also see *Camel Skeleton* and *Camelback Mountain* in Chapter 39, this volume). "The Sand Papago...saw the camels were grass-eating animals like the cow or the horse, had split hooves the way cows do, and assumed that they were good for eating. So they ate the camels" (Betty Melvin, also William Merrill, in Zepeda 1985:53, 88).

Cattle. The cattle and horses introduced by Kino thrived at places like Sonoyta where there was sufficient water (Burrus 1971) and undoubtedly led to degradation of the native riparian ecosystem. During the mid-nineteenth century the Cocopahs engaged in cattle raiding (see discussion for horses) but apparently were not keeping cattle as late as 1901 (Chittenden 1901). Within the first few decades of the twentieth century, however, the Cocopahs, like their Mexican neighbors, were raising cattle (Anita Williams, personal communication 2003). Castetter and Underhill (1935:73) report that among the O'odham "ownerless cows and horses" were "hunted...like deer."

Dogs. People of the Dry Borders kept dogs, although they were apparently not used for hunting nor were they eaten. There is, however, the questionable report by James Ohio Pattie on January 27, 1828, that his Cocopah hosts "prepared a feast for us by killing a number of fattened dogs...and...the flesh of young and fat dogs was served up" (Pattie 1988:109). Pattie and his companions were unable to communicate by language with the Cocopahs, and there is no indication that he saw dogs being prepared. Richard Batman (Pattie 1988:127), editor of the *Personal Narrative*, asserts that "they did not eat dog meat. They did, however, eat jackrabbits and he may have confused one with the other." I am sure Pattie knew about jackrabbit meat, but whatever was served, it seems unlikely that it was dog.

Across the region dogs were taboo for food (Rea 1981; Betty Melvin in Zepeda 1985:69), and Kroeber (1941) found that dogs were generally not eaten west of the Rocky Mountains. Castetter and Bell (1951:93), however, were told by their Mohave and Quechan (Yuma) consultants that "dogs were kept and eaten by their people." Dogs are well represented in the regional archaeological record. The Spaniards brought their dogs to the Southwest, beginning with the war dogs (mastiffs) of the Coronado entrada of 1540 (Bolton 1949).

Horses. People could keep horses only where there was sufficient forage and especially water, which for the Dry Borders region in early postcontact times pretty much meant along the Colorado, Gila, and the Sonoyta rivers. Smaller numbers could be kept at a few ranches, but that was mostly later in the nineteenth century (Rea 1998). During the nineteenth and early twentieth centuries, horse, burro, and mule meat was eaten by Native Americans and Anglos (Betty Melvin in Zepeda 1985: 70, 75).

Spanish explorers, beginning with Melchior Díaz in 1540, rode into the region on horseback, and Kino introduced horses between 1687 and around 1700 (Burrus 1971). Anza and Garcés found horses and cattle among the Yumans in 1774 (Bolton 1930; also see Castetter & Bell 1951:91).

By the mid-nineteenth century some Hia C'ed O'odham living near Mexican or Anglo settlements had acquired horses (Childs 1954). A small band of "Papago" who lived near Somerton (probably sometime in the nineteenth century) had horses (Gifford 1933).

Hardy (1829:334) observed tame horses at the Colorado delta in 1826. In the 1850s Cocopahs raided herds of horses and cattle being driven across the river near Yuma and drove them "to the lower delta" for fattening and eating (Castetter & Bell 1951:92). This was quite a feat since the raids were carried out in the territory of their perennial enemies, the Quechans (Yumas). In general, the people of the lower Colorado had few horses in the mid-1800s because they had little means to purchase them, they enjoyed horseflesh, and they "slaughtered horses at funerals and in the annual Mourning Ceremony" (Kroeber & Fontana 1986:64). During Cocopah funerals there were "horse races . . . and usually one or more horses were killed for food, providing a relatively rare treat," and at the death of "important men, a horse was killed and buried" (Kelly 1949:163, 157). During the nineteenth and early twentieth centuries the Hia C'ed O'odham had a similar practice. "If the deceased is a man and owns a horse, the horse is also killed so the deceased can ride his horse into the new land" (Fillman Bell in Bell et al. 1980:103). Another record of this practice is from Childs (1954:31), who reports, "When I was a young boy at times I saw them kill his best horse to carry him on to perdition."

After combat with the Quechans (until the mid-nineteenth century) it was "customary [for Cocopahs] to exchange captive boys and girls with Mexicans for horses" (Gifford 1933:269). Chittenden (1901:203) saw "only a few horses" among the Cocopahs. Gifford (1933: 271) mentions Cocopahs hunting deer on horseback

and using a "dish of coals and horse manure" inside the house to ward off mosquitoes. Cocopahs used horsehide as a replacement for deer rawhide for war shields and daily-use sandals (Gifford 1933).

Pigs. During historical times feral pigs became established in densely vegetated areas of the Colorado delta. Boars were hunted by Cocopah men before the mid-twentieth century (Williams 1983).

Wild mammals

Antilocapra americana sonoriensis. SONORAN PRONGHORN; BERRENDO. Now verging on extinction, the Sonoran pronghorn was once common across much of the open lowland plains of the Sonoran Desert. Lumholtz (1912:330) reports that the Hia C'ed O'odham "were even able to approach mule deer and antelope near enough to kill them" with bow and arrow, and Childs (1954:33) tells that "there are lots of tricks in hunting them." Gila River Pimas hunted pronghorn "in the plains . . . all the way to Table Top Mountain" (Rea 1998: 251). Gifford (1933:269) says they were rare in the Cocopah region. Castetter and Bell (1951:215) claim that the Cocopahs "never" hunted these swift animals, although it was a food animal among some Yuman people (Forde 1931; Rea 1981). Seri hunters stalked them "during the mating season, when they could be approached and dispatched by bow and arrow" (Felger & Moser 1985:52).

In 1701 Manje recorded women in the Pinacate area wearing "antelope skin" skirts (Burrus 1971:264, 267; also see Lumholtz 1912:331). Similarly, Childs (1954: 36) reported that "women's buckskin gowns or dresses were tanned, mostly from antelope skins as they were easiest to tan soft." Hia C'ed O'odham drums, both small and large, "were made from antelope hides" (Childs 1954:37). AG, PI, CP, GR, OP.

Bassariscus astutus. RINGTAIL; CACOMISTLE. Nabhan et al. (1982) list the ringtail as a food animal at Quitovac. PI, AG, CP, GR, OP, SD.

Canis latrans. COYOTE. There was a nearly universal taboo against eating coyotes (Rea 1982; Betty Melvin in Zepeda 1985:67). Coyote, the trickster and fool, unable to make up his mind, braggart, mischief maker, deceiver, lecher, or even nice guy features widely in oral traditions of Native Americans (e.g., Felger & Moser 1985; Nabhan 1982; Rea 1998). Things of inferior quality or humor or falsehood were often named as coyote's belongings, such as wild tobaccos (*Nicotiana clevelandii* and *N. trigonophylla*) since they were regarded as inferior to "real" tobacco; also see *Cucurbita digitata, Lyrocarpa coulteri, Pectis papposa, Proboscidea altheaefolia, Salix exigua,* and *Thymophylla concinna* (Chapter 17, this volume). Coyote is a messenger in the Cocopah creation epic, and a coyote calling close to a house at night or in the early morning was "a sign something bad had happened, perhaps [the] death of [a] friend" (Gifford 1933:305). Coyotes were used for medicinal purposes and in shamanism (Felger & Moser 1985; Nabhan et al. 1982; Rea 1998). Cocopahs fashioned arrow quivers from the whole pelt obtained in wintertime, presumably because the fur would be in prime condition, and a lance was sometimes "wrapped with coyote skin" (Gifford 1933: 275). The O'odham also used the pelts for quivers (Castetter & Underhill 1935). PI, AG, CP, GR, OP, SD.

Castor canadensis. BEAVER; CASTOR. These animals, once abundant in the lower Río Colorado (Navarro, this volume; Nelson 1921; Pattie 1988), were eaten by Cocopahs and other river people (Drucker 1941, Pattie 1988). The Maricopas relished the fat tails (Castetter & Bell 1951). Russell (1908) reports that it was a highly esteemed food animal of the Gila River Pimas, but Rea (1998:169) shows that "the role of beaver in Pima dietary is somewhat equivocal." AG.

Dipodomys spp. KANGAROO RAT; RATA CANGURO. As emergency food these small animals were eaten "as a last resource" among the O'odham (Castetter & Underhill 1935:42). AG, PI, CP, GR, OP, SD.

Lepus alleni. ANTELOPE JACKRABBIT; LIEBRE TORDA. This jackrabbit occurs in the eastern part of the Dry Borders region and does not extend into the drier desert areas (Henry, this volume). It was hunted by the Gila River Pimas (Rea 1998) and most likely also at the eastern margins of the Dry Borders.

Lepus californicus. BLACK-TAILED JACKRABBIT; LIEBRE COLA NEGRA. Jackrabbits were significant meat animals and are documented in most of the regional ethnographic works (Burrus 1971; Lumholtz 1912; Rea 1981) (Figure 15.23). For example, Castetter and Underhill (1935:42) report: "The Papago considered cottontail meat sweet and jackrabbit poor. However, jackrabbit was the one meat available at all seasons, though in spring the animals were so thin as to be almost useless." Lumholtz (1912:334), however, provides a different opinion: "The meat of the jack-rabbit is much coveted by the Papagos, who often run these animals down on horseback." Many ethnographic reports do not differentiate between cottontail rabbits and jackrabbits (let alone which of the two jackrabbit species; for example, Betty Melvin in Zepeda 1985:68, 72). Rabbit pelts were prized for blankets (Gifford 1931:276). (Also see *Sylvilagus,* cottontail rabbit.)

The black-tailed jackrabbit is common throughout the desert and was a major food resource for the Hia C'ed O'odham (Nabhan et al. 1982). Kelly (1977) reports that it was the most important game animal of the Cocopahs, who conducted communal rabbit drives, the best time being in fall. PI, AG, CP, GR, OP, SD.

Lynx rufus. BOBCAT; GATO MONTÉS. It is reported as a food animal at Quitovac (Nabhan et al. 1982; Rea 1981) but generally is regarded as taboo for food by Yuman speakers (Castetter & Bell 1951:212; Rea 1981). For the Hia C'ed O'odham, Betty Melvin said, "No one ate the bobcat" (in Zepeda 1985:69). The pelts were widely prized and used for such items as arrow quivers (Castetter & Underhill 1935). PI, AG, CP, GR, OP, SD.

Neotoma albigula, WHITE-THROATED WOODRAT (PACKRAT), and **N. lepida,** DESERT WOODRAT (PACKRAT); COSÓN. These ubiquitous little animals provided significant food resources all across the Dry Borders and elsewhere in the Sonoran Desert region. Their remains are abundant at archaeological sites (see Van Devender, this volume). Cocopahs hunted packrats with bow and arrow or set fire to nests and clubbed them. They also collected their cached seeds and fruits: "When we were awfully hungry we would eat the rat's stores. We got the mesquite beans he had stored and also the rat" (Kelly 1977:45). By collecting stored caches of mesquite (*Prosopis* spp.), palo verde (*Parkinsonia* spp.), desert wolfberry (*Lycium fremontii*), ironwood (*Olneya*), and white crucillo (*Ziziphus*) seeds and fruits, the Seris were able to extend the time of harvest of these crops "for several months or more. The nests were most often robbed in fall" (Felger & Moser 1985:89). Lumholtz (1912) reports that the Hia C'ed O'odham "caught muskrats by burning the accumulations of cactus spines with which those animals keep enemies away from their burrow." These animals, of course, were packrats and not muskrats, and other authors too have confused muskrats *(Ondatra)* with packrats (e.g., Castetter & Bell 1951:70). Packrats were often roasted in coals with the skin on to protect the meat or "skinned and roasted under coals" (Felger and Moser 1985:53). PI, AG, CP, GR, OP, SD.

Odocoileus hemionus. MULE DEER; BURA, VENADO BURA. Across the Dry Borders region mule deer are generally in Arizona Upland and much less common or even absent from drier, lower-elevation regions. Together with the desert bighorn, this was the largest animal hunted across most of the region and featured prominently in local cultures, including creation stories and other oral traditions and rituals (Gifford 1933; Lumholtz 1912:330; Rea 1998; Betty Melvin in Zepeda 1985: 69). Deer were hunted with bow and arrow by a variety of methods, often by men wearing deer-head disguises. The hunting season usually began in fall (Castetter & Underhill 1935:10). Deer were often ambushed at waterholes or tracked, sometimes for as long as two days (Castetter & Bell 1951). The meat was eaten freshly cooked, or strips were sun-dried for later use. Deer fat, as well as that of other animals, sometimes was used in cooking (see *Opuntia chlorotica* and *Parkinsonia microphylla*, and Rea 1998:87).

Cocopah men hunted deer in Baja California mountains (Chittenden 1901; Castetter & Bell 1951). Arthur North, visiting the Colorado delta in August 1908, reported that "some few 'mule' deer and wild hogs live in the cane-breaks" (in Williams 1975:123). Gifford (1933) mentions Cocopahs hunting deer on horseback along the west bank of the Río Colorado.

Among the Cocopahs, Hia C'ed O'odham, and other groups, uses included buckskin for clothing; tendons for fletching, bowstrings, and fastening objects including arrow foreshafts; rawhide for sandals and war shields; brains for tanning hides (see *Bursera microphylla*); and deerskin pouches (Castetter & Underhill 1935; Castetter & Bell 1951; Childs 1954; Gifford 1933; Lumholtz 1912). Deer fat was used to mix paints and grease the body. In 1540 Alarcón recorded, "On their heads they wore a piece of buckskin...like a helmet," and "Some brought me well-dressed hides." He mentions people who "came down to the plain to get [corn] through barter with deerskins. These they wore, along with long garments...sewed with needles made from deer bone" (Flint & Flint 2005:190, 195). Deer featured prominently in the Viigida (Vikita) ceremony of the Tohono and Hia C'ed O'odham (Hayden 1987), and Cocopahs and others danced with deer-hoof rattles (Forde 1931; Kelly 1977). PI, AG (extirpated?), CP, GR, OP, SD.

Odocoileus virginianus. WHITE-TAILED DEER; VENADO COLA BLANCA. The uses and methods of hunting were similar to those of the much more common mule deer. White-tailed deer range into the eastern part of the Dry Borders and generally do not extend into the more arid desert regions. PI, CP, GR, OP, SD.

Ondatra zibethicus. MUSKRAT; RATA ALMIZCLERA. Castetter and Bell (1951:212) mention it as a "secondary" food animal for the Cocopahs, and it may have been eaten by the Gila River Pimas (Rea 1998). Muskrats were apparently not common in the Colorado delta region until the advent of modern agriculture in the twentieth century (Mellink 1995). Some authors confused muskrats with packrats (see *Neotoma*). AG.

Ovis canadensis mexicana. DESERT BIGHORN; BORREGO CIMARRÓN. This was the principal Dry Borders big game animal (Lumholtz 1912; Sheldon 1979; Betty Melvin and Miguel Velasco in Zepeda 1985:24, 68) (Figure 15.24). Men hunted them in the mountains, often ambushing them at waterholes, or waited for them along bighorn trails. Cocopahs journeyed to the Sierra de los Cucapá to hunt bighorn (Castetter & Bell 1951), and the Hia C'ed O'odham "killed mountain-sheep, which were not a difficult quarry, with bows and arrows" (Lumholtz 1912:330). Like most other meat, it was often

dried for later use (Lumholtz 1912:334). The Hia C'ed O'odham made clothing from the hides (Lumholtz 1912:331). The Kiliwas made barbless fishhooks from "the horn of mountain sheep softened in boiling water so that it could be bent into the desired shape" (Meigs 1939:28). There are accounts of several enormous shrine-like piles of horns scattered across western Pimería Alta (Fontana 1974; Hayden 1985). On November 19, 1697, west of Casas Grandes, Manje and Kino came to "Tusonimo, so named from the high pile of wild-sheep horns, which looked like a hill.... The heap towered so high above the dwellings that there must have been more than a hundred thousand antlers [*sic*] piled together" (Burrus 1971:209; also see Manje 1954:87). PI, CP, GR, OP, SD.

Perognathus spp., POCKET MOUSE, and **Peromyscus,** DEER MOUSE; RATÓN. Castetter and Underhill (1935:42) report that the Merriam pocket mouse *(Perognathus spinatus)* was an emergency food among the "Papagos." Rea (1981:72) indicates that one or both genera were Hia C'ed O'odham food animals (information recorded at Quitovac), probably emergency food; Rea (personal communication 2004) notes that *Peromyscus* would be a more likely food source than *Perognathus*. Betty Melvin, however, said that "mice are poisonous" (in Zepeda 1985:71). PI, AG, CP, GR, OP, SD.

Procyon lotor. RACCOON; MAPACHE. A single reference reports that raccoons were eaten by Cocopahs (Drucker 1941). It was also a food animal of the Gila River Pimas (Rea 1998). Betty Melvin said it was not eaten by the Hia C'ed O'odham (in Zepeda 1985:72). PI, AG, OP.

Puma concolor. PUMA, MOUNTAIN LION; LEÓN. Several authors mention mountain lions as a food animal for the Hia C'ed O'odham (Rea 1981), but finding or killing one must have been uncommon. Amadeo Rea (personal communication 2004) comments, "I think all the cats were eaten by all the O'odham when they got them." In contrast, Betty Melvin said, "We wouldn't eat something that would eat you. I've never heard of

Figure 15.24. Ovis canadensis mexicana. *(Drawing by Cathy Moser Marlett)*

anybody eating the mountain lion" (in Zepeda 1985:71). Castetter and Bell (1951:212) say that "none of the River Yuman tribes ate mountain lions." The pelts were prized by the Gila River Pimas (Rea 1998) and were made into arrow quivers by the Tohono O'odham (Castetter & Underhill 1935:72). PI, CP, GR, OP, SD.

Sigmodon arizonae. ARIZONA COTTON RAT; RATA JABALINA. These small animals were numerous in the agricultural fields of the Gila River Pimas and were a common and much-enjoyed food item, "like...pork chops" (Rea 1998:176). They were also eaten by lower Colorado River people (Rea 1981). AG.

Spermophilus tereticaudus [*Citellus tereticaudus*]. ROUND-TAILED GROUND SQUIRREL; JUANCITO. This common, small squirrel was hunted by at least some O'odham (Castetter & Underhill 1935). PI, AG, CP, GR, OP, SD.

Spermophilus variegatus. ROCK SQUIRREL; ARDIL-LÓN. This large squirrel was hunted for food at Quito-vac (Nabhan et al. 1982). It was used for food by Gila River Pimas but "surrounded by sanction," or taboos (Rea 1998:151). PI, CP, GR, OP, SD.

Sylvilagus audubonii [*Lepus arizonicus*]. COTTONTAIL RABBIT; CONEJO. Cottontails were widely hunted, often with bow and arrow and on communal drives (Rea 1998). Cocopahs used feathered arrows to hunt them (Gifford 1933). (See *Lepus.*) PI, AG, CP, GR, OP, SD.

Taxidea taxus. BADGER; TEJÓN. The badger was a food animal of the Hia C'ed O'odham (Nabhan et al. 1982). "They like badger meat too. The woman hunt for meat too. They chase the badger no matter where the badger runs to hide. Even in a hole, the woman digs after the badger and beats him on the head till he dies. My mother told me this" (Betty Melvion in Bell et al. 1980:100; also Betty Melvin in Zepeda 1985:47, 75). They also used badger hair "to plait ribbons for the hair and make twine to be used for the breech cloth" (Lumholtz 1912:331). Castetter and Bell (1951:212) mention it as a "secondary" food animal for lower Colorado River tribes. Cocopah men employed the claws in a magical ritual to ensure a good crop of panicgrass (see *Panicum hirticaule*; Gifford 1933; Kelly 1977). PI, CP, GR, OP.

Tayassu tajacu [*Dicotyles tajacu, Pecari tajacu*]. COLLARED PECCARY, JAVELINA; JABALÍ. There are few records of it as a food animal in the Dry Borders area. Nabhan et al. (1982) list it as a food animal at Quitovac, and Betty Melvin reports that the Hia C'ed O'odham "used to hunt them.... They would roast it in a pit or...make something that is like a tamale or just fry the meat.... It was a very good food source back then" (in Zepeda 1985:70). Gila River Pimas hunted it on Table Top Mountain (Rea 1998:235). It is scarce in the western part of the region and probably was not in most of the Dry Borders area until the twentieth century (Henry, this volume). PI, CP, GR, OP, SD.

Thomomys bottae. VALLEY POCKET GOPHER; TUZA. Castetter and Bell (1951:217) say that "gophers...were hunted" by Cocopahs. Among the O'odham there are taboos against eating gophers (Rea 1981, 1998). AG, PI, CP, GR, OP, SD.

Urocyon cinereoargenteus. GRAY FOX; ZORRA. This animal is mentioned as a "secondary" food animal by Castetter and Bell (1951). AG, PI, CP, GR, OP, SD.

Vulpes velox. KIT FOX; ZORRA. This small fox is listed as a food animal at Quitovac by Nabhan et al. (1982). AG, PI, CP, GR, OP, SD.

Whales. Deer and pronghorn "hides were first grained with the ribs from a large whale, the bones of which lie stranded along the entire length of the Gulf" (Childs 1954:36). AG.

Zalophus californianus. CALIFORNIA SEA LION; LOBO MARINO. The Hia C'ed O'odham "killed sea lions on the rocks by hitting them on the nose, and from their skins sandals and straps were cut" (Lumholtz 1912:331). Punta Pelicano at Bahía de la Cholla, which Lumholtz called "Sea Lion Bluff...was where the sand Papagoes [sic] used to kill sea lions (in Spanish *lobos*)" (Lumholtz 1912:277 and map 2). Sea lions in the northern Gulf of California aggregate on rocky shores in breeding colonies, which no longer occur on the mainland coast. The nearest known colonies are on Rocas Consag and Isla San Jorge (see Navarro, this volume). Seris also killed sea lions by throwing rocks at their heads and made sandals from the hides (Bowen 2000; Felger and Moser 1985). AG.

Part Three

THE DESERT

Sixteen

A Botanist's View of the Center of the Universe

Richard S. Felger

View from the Top

On a warm spring day the desert breeze is alive with buzzing insects and the smell of yellow palo verde flowers. It is a long day's hike from our camp near Tinaja del Tule to Pinacate Peak, long because of the distance and so many things to see and record. From the cinder-cone summit I look out across lava fields, great craters, dunes, distant saw-tooth desert mountains, the sea, and the Sierra San Pedro Mártir more than a hundred miles across the vanquished delta. I imagine a delta still teeming with life as I look across a quiet, primordial empire.

Less than three months later, during late May, I return to find most of the waterholes dry, even Tinaja del Tule. There are animal bones where the last water disappeared. The heat—the searing heat—-the dust and the dryness penetrate everything. The wildflowers are gone. Even creosote-bush leaves are shriveled, brown, and brittle.

The Craters

It was my first trip to El Pinacate. I parked the Jeep, walked up a nondescript hillside, and was suddenly standing at the rim of a great crater. Before me was a mile-wide gaping hole in the earth like nothing I had ever seen—surprising and mysterious because there was no warning. Until you learn to pick out the nearly featureless outer rim, there is nothing special to warn you of the presence of one of these great craters, which seem to exhale an eerie silence. The descent into Mac-Dougal Crater is fairly easy. I scrambled down the steep crumbly tuff breccia, carefully climbing down a partial break in the cliffs that ring the crater and down the rocky talus slope to the flat crater floor. The air was still, there was no wind, there was no view except crater walls and sky. When Captain Juan Mateo Manje discovered a great Pinacate crater on March 20, 1701, he described it as "a big hole of such profundity that it caused terror and fear" (Burrus 1971:476).

Ten major craters are scattered across the northern and western flanks of the lava shield. The six largest craters are Elegante, Sykes, Mac-Dougal, Cerro Colorado, Molina, and Moon. Although their origins probably varied, most are maar (collapse) craters (Hartmann 1989; Kresan, this volume; Lynch 1981). According to current theory, these craters were formed when molten lava encountered groundwater, causing it to boil immediately and generate a great steam explosion. The explosion was followed by deposition of a tuff ring and subsequent collapse into the chamber from which the explosion occurred.

The western craters, such as MacDougal, Molina, and especially Moon, are partially filled with sand blowing in from the dunes of the Gran Desierto. Indeed, there may be undiscovered craters buried in the dunes. Cerro Colorado, the most distinctive of the larger craters, lies slightly apart from the main volcanic shield. The two deepest craters, Elegante and Sykes, farthest from moving dunes, are the least sand-filled. Perhaps as late as thirteen thousand years ago there was a freshwater lake in Elegante Crater, as evidenced by remains of lake sediments and freshwater snail shells. Large cracks or fissures in the playa at the bottom of the crater, some more than thirty centimeters across, are probably due to continuing subsidence. Jahns (1959:27) describes the several larger craters:

> The principal calderas [craters] are steep-walled depressions with circular to broadly oval outlines, and from the air they appear as huge pock-marks on the rough face of the volcanic field. Each has a remarkably even rim from which the ground surface slopes moderately to gently outward, giving the impression of a low, flat-topped hill with wide and symmetrical shoulders when viewed from

adjacent points on the ground. The depressions range…in ratio of diameter to depth from 6:1 to nearly 25:1. Each marks the site of a volcanic cone that was considerably larger than any of the associated earlier cinder cones. Each has an almost flat floor, from the margins of which an essentially continuous apron of talus rises to the base of a cliffed wall; a moderate to steep slope extends upward from the top of this wall to the rim of the caldera.

The vegetation and floras of the various craters are relatively rich and remarkably similar, especially among craters of comparable size and depth. The majority of species present in the entire Pinacate region can be found in just the several larger craters. During a one-day survey I located nearly one hundred plant species in Sykes Crater, which turned out to represent about 90 percent of the total flora of that crater (Felger 2000). This rich assemblage of species undoubtedly is related to the relatively high habitat diversity. The usual lack of wind would reduce transpiration, but this factor might be offset by the generally higher temperatures inside the craters. On a summer afternoon the dark lava on west-facing crater walls can be too hot to touch—yet little herbs such as desert spurge (*Euphorbia polycarpa*) grow out of crevices in these very same rocks.

Small playas, most about two hundred to three hundred meters across in the larger craters, have formed in the lowest point of each crater. The playa flora and vegetation are remarkably predictable from crater to crater and are also similar to those of playas elsewhere in the Pinacate region. Crater playas may develop 100 percent vegetation coverage, mostly ephemerals (short-lived annuals) during wet periods, and remain green weeks after the surrounding vegetation becomes desiccated. There are even vegetational zones in concentric bands within and around the playas, corresponding to soil moisture. Mesquite (*Prosopis glandulosa*) is the most conspicuous and predictable larger perennial. Other common perennials include slimleaf ragweed (*Ambrosia confertiflora*), prickly poppy (*Argemone gracilenta*), rattlesnake weed (*Euphorbia albomarginata*), blue palo verde (*Parkinsonia florida*), and devil's claw (*Proboscidea altheifolia*).

In years of good winter-spring rains the crater playas are carpeted orange with annual globe mallow (*Sphaeralcea coulteri*), often reaching one meter or more in height. Other spring annuals are

likewise abundant. And summer rains often bring head-height, 100 percent cover of another set of ephemerals dominated by amaranth (*Amaranthus palmeri*) and lizard-tail (*Gaura parviflora*), plus the perennial slimleaf ragweed (*Ambrosia confertiflora*). Walking through this amaranth jungle in the hot, still air of a sweaty summer day produces clouds of pollen. Other common summer ephemerals of the crater playas include spiderlings (*Boerhavia* spp.), six-weeks needle grama (*Bouteloua aristidoides*), six-weeks grama (*B. barbata*), dodders (*Cuscuta* spp.), silky dalea (*Dalea mollis*), California caltrop (*Kallstroemia californica*), orange caltrop (*K. grandifolia*), red sprangletop (*Leptochloa panicea*), and desert chinchweed (*Pectis papposa*).

Bighorn sheep, coyotes, and other larger mammals including humans come and go at will from the craters, but desert tortoises living in the bottom of MacDougal Crater are isolated. Indeed, how these tortoises came to occur inside MacDougal Crater is difficult to conjure. Were they put there by earlier people? Because livestock and vehicles do not reach the deeper craters, the natural vegetation is protected. Thus these craters provide important natural laboratories. Long-term vegetation studies in MacDougal Crater by Ray Turner (1990; this volume) demonstrate the dynamic nature of desert vegetation. Stands of mesquites and creosotebushes have grown and perished in cycles responding to climatic change and weather events. Although the crater floors are "pristine" and relatively free of nonnative weedy plants, I was surprised and indignant to find the weedy shrub tamarisk (*Tamarix ramosissima*) established in the bottom of Elegante Crater.

During summer-fall thunderstorms the nearly vertical drainage channels on the crater walls can briefly turn into waterfalls. In an early September storm at MacDougal Crater I witnessed torrential waterfalls spilling into flash floods that ripped across the crater floor. The water flow lasted about ten minutes, and the storm clouds quickly passed. Descending into the hot, steamy crater, I found fresh-cut channels near the crater walls where as much as one meter of sandy soil had washed away.

Desert Legume Trinity

It is mid-September, the tail end of the summer monsoon. We leave Organ Pipe Cactus National Monument and head west into Cabeza Prieta National Wildlife Refuge. Peter Gierlach (a.k.a.

Petey Mesquitey of local radio fame) is helping me with a summer botanical inventory along the southern part of the refuge. Not quite midday and the temperature is 100°F and climbing. We are entering a vast desert realm. We have not seen anyone since leaving the highway at Ajo, two hours and thirty miles to the north, when we meet Lyle Williams, who works for the refuge. We are heading for the San Cristobal Wash. Lyle semi-jokingly calls it "The Jungle" and says it is just a few miles down the road. It seems strange to hear talk of a nearby jungle when we are in the middle of the Sonoran Desert, in fact one of the drier parts of the desert—a sparsely vegetated desert where the landscape is mostly sand, creosotebush, and bursage, with scattered cacti and summer annuals.

You can actually run through this desert vegetation, easily dodging the few widely spaced chollas and other cacti. The low desert shrubs probably cover less than 10 percent of the ground, and the creosotebushes seemingly cast no shadow. Across the desert plain we see a few big, obvious desert legumes, and there are occasional low, scruffy mesquite bushes.

So the mention of a jungle just up the road makes us eager to go have a look. I have been to the San Cristobal Wash before and know that it supports dense vegetation, but I have not seen it in full green glory of summer rain. This wash is like most other large drainageways coursing through Sonoran Desert valley bottoms, except that human-caused impacts here are virtually nil: for many years no woodcutting, no cattle grazing, no off-road vehicles, no diversions of the streamways, no upstream development, and few non-native species of plants. For a botanist at the end of the twentieth century, such a place is a treasure house.

We drive on a bit farther, and entering the great, braided wash system, I find a number of new plant records for the flora of the refuge. After the creosotebush-bursage flats, San Cristobal Wash indeed looks like a jungle—a legume-dominated jungle. You can't run through it. You might pick your way through it, crawling and climbing over shrubs and fallen mesquite limbs, parting vines, and dodging or brushing away spiderwebs while trying not to tear your clothes and flesh on spines. The canopy is only five to seven or eight meters tall, closed in places and open elsewhere, open to the understory shrubs. Because it is the end of the monsoon season in a rather favorable year, the

ground is covered with more than a dozen species of summer annuals (ephemerals) and herbaceous perennials. I can't see the ground; it is covered with green. Amaranths (mostly *Amaranthus palmeri*) and ragweed (*Ambrosia confertiflora*) are in full flower and chest-to-nose-high in "open" areas. Just as in the crater bottom playas, parting and brushing them aside shakes loose yellow clouds of allergenic, nose-running pollen mixing with sweat in the hot, humid still air. Vines festoon the trees, interlacing leafy green mesquites, palo verdes, and scattered ironwoods.

Insects buzz, bite, crawl, and fly. Ants are everywhere, and termites too, invisible except for their dry mud-saliva tunnels covering dead stalks, sticks, and bark. Long-tailed bush lizards make themselves nearly invisible a little higher up on the mesquite bark. Packrats incorporate thorny twigs into their large stick and rubble houses instead of cholla pieces because there are few cacti in the middle of the wash jungle. Since it is midday, the birds aren't very noisy. But early morning and dusk would be different. It seems like quail are everywhere. Red-tailed hawks, turkey vultures, ravens, and barn owls roost in the higher branches of the legume trees. At dusk at Monreal Wash, another large wash on the refuge, I recall a clumsy bunch of turkey vultures jockeying for position on barren snags of blue palo verdes. Unable to close their feet and grasp, they pushed and shoved to balance themselves.

The vine, or liana, growth-form is usually scarce in dry, desert habitats; the number of vining species is low, and their biomass scant. This seems reasonable since deserts have relatively few trees for vines to grow on, and the liana growth-form is usually seen as an adaptation for plants to reach light and potential pollinators in treetops. In the San Cristobal Wash vines are notably conspicuous because of the contrast with the open desert. There are four common vines here, only one of which is a legume. The festooning vines twine and drape over dead mesquite, ironwood, and palo verde branches, lending a decidedly jungle-like appearance to the place. Perennial vines are represented by a milkweed (*Funastrum cynanchoides*) and a desert clematis (*Clematis drummondii*).

In the cooler seasons a cucurbit, desert starvine (*Brandegea bigelovii*), shrouds the desert legume trees, all but smothering them in green curtains. These annual vines are just beginning to reappear. Morning-glory vines *(Ipomoea hederacea)* make the summer scene, spotting the jungle with bright blue flowers shortly after sunrise and fading by midmorning heat. In the still-comfortable hour or so after dawn, large sphinx moths perform on-the-wing pollination services, sucking high-calorie sugary nectar from morning-glory flowers hanging from tree twigs. The one legume vine species, a desert bean *(Phaseolus filiformis)*, spots the lower branches and twigs with pink flowers. It grows largest and most luxuriantly in the washes. It is the only bean species in the middle of the desert and unusual because it grows with winter-spring rains and another generation germinates and matures with summer monsoons. Members of the bean genus *(Phaseolus)* are usually strictly summer or warm-season growers; bean crops die with even the slightest frost. In earlier times the O'odham harvested the seeds of this desert bean for food (Felger et al. 1992).

I stop for a moment and daydream about the small, scattered floodwater-irrigated fields of the O'odham who lived here. We are not far from where Francisco "Chico" Shunie cultivated his fields (see Chico Shunie Temporal and Chico Shunie Well, Chapter 39, this volume). The clearings were planted with the trinity of corn, beans (teparies), and squash. The soil would be rich from all the rotting humus and the nitrogen fixed by legume species, and most years there would be enough water for the crops. And long before their field crops ripened, there would be plenty of pods and seeds to harvest and prepare from the wild legume trio of mesquite, palo verde, and ironwood that makes up the canopy.

Across the Sonoran Desert the ribbons of xeroriparian gallery forest are largely made up of this legume trinity. Because San Cristobal Wash is so large and the elevational gradient so gradual, it is a broad braided wash of many meandering and anastomosing channels. Each channel resembles the often simple desert wash or arroyo. The big legume trinity and sometimes a few other woody desert legumes dominate the wash landscape and provide food and shelter for other plants, animals, and in earlier times Native Americans. Here we find shade, a really rare item in the Cabeza Prieta Refuge in summertime. But we are not alone in seeking the shade and extra moisture that supports so much green vegetation. Insects are abundant and of course annoying, spiders cast nets across

openings in the mesquites, and we can imagine numerous hiding and burrowing creatures. And the ground actually has an accumulation of leaf litter, a humus layer, although it is quickly digested by termites, fungi, and microbes. Walk across the open desert and you won't find leaf litter.

Other desert legume trees and shrubs make their appearances in some of the other xeroriparian scenes: the essentially leafless smoke tree *(Psorothamnus spinosus)* in the drier parts of the desert and acacias (white-thorn, *Acacia constricta;* and catclaw, *A. greggii)* in areas of slightly more rainfall. But across most of the desert it is the trinity of mesquite, ironwood, and palo verde that fuels and feeds the desert drainageways. While not always restricted to the dry desert streamways, they are seldom as dense and large on the open desert as along washes.

On the east side of the refuge the mesquites are readily identified as the velvet mesquite *(Prosopis velutina)*. This is the common mesquite species of the Arizona Upland around Tucson and elsewhere across Pima County. The key identifying characters are leaves bearing two pairs of pinnae and densely hairy twigs and leaves (Figure 16.1). San Cristobal Wash is in western Pima County. Continuing westward along the rough dirt road, in an hour or so we pass O'Neill's Grave and enter Yuma County on the once-infamous Camino del Diablo. David O'Neill's fellow prospectors buried him with his tobacco at his feet and went on prospecting. On their way back, having run out of their own tobacco, they dug up his (see Chapter 39, this volume). We continue westward and soon cross the Pinta Sands and the northern outlier of the Pinacate Lava Flow.

In washes in and around the Pinacate Lava and Pinta Sands, a number of "western" desert or Lower Colorado Valley species have replaced the "eastern" or Arizona Upland species (Felger 2000; also see Rosen, this volume; Shreve 1964). The washes are still much more densely vegetated than the open, creosotebush desert flats, and the trinity of large legumes is still with us. But there are some subtle as well as not-so-subtle changes. Some of the vines, notably the morning glory and desert clematis, are not present. Peter Gierlach remarks that the mesquites here have more beautiful leaves than the ones we saw earlier in the day.

Indeed, the leaves of these mesquites have larger leaflets and seemingly greener leaves with

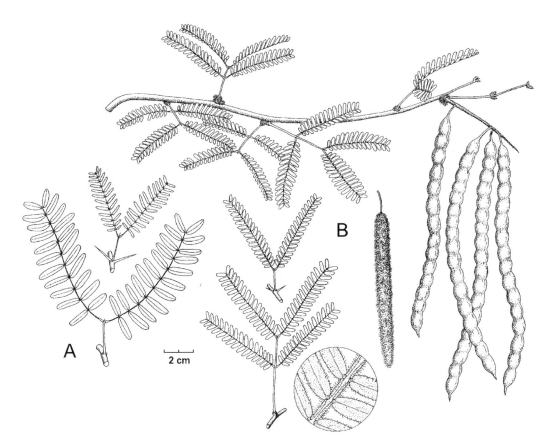

Figure 16.1. Mesquite species in the Dry Borders region. (A) Western honey mesquite, Prosopis glandulosa var. torreyana: *a drought-stunted leaf and a "normal" one. Note that each leaf has only one pair of pinnae.* (B) Velvet mesquite, P. velutina: *branch with several pods; inflorescence with the small, crowded flowers; and two leaves, one drought-stunted and one "normal";* inset *shows leaf hairs. Note that the smaller, "drought" leaf has one pair of pinnae and the "normal" leaf has two pairs. (Drawing by Matthew B. Johnson)*

only one pair of pinnae like those of the western honey mesquite *(Prosopis glandulosa* var. *torreyana).* But the leaves and twigs have the small hairs characteristic of the velvet mesquite *(P. velutina).* Farther west, in the vicinity of the Colorado River and southward along the Sonora coast, the leaves are both hairless (glabrous) and once-pinnate—the two major key characters of the honey mesquite.

Thus the Pinta Sands mesquites share features of the two supposedly different species. There are several possibilities: (1) The mesquites are confused, uncooperative, and don't know that they have been classified; (2) the taxonomy is confused and does not accurately reflect the situation; or (3) it is difficult or indeed impossible to make a "perfect" linear classification system for an evolutionary continuum. Any botanist engaged in taxonomy has struggled with problems of this kind: the mesquites in the western part of the refuge are indeed intermediate in character. In fact, the area of transition, or the intermediate population, is quite large.

Perhaps we should scrap our seemingly artificial taxonomy. Yet we need names in order to communicate about the different kinds of life. As

biologists, we strive to make the classification reflect evolutionary patterns as closely as possible. But a continuum sometimes does not slice up into discrete units—there are fuzzy boundaries.

When I was in high school I thought there was a definite way biologists classified or defined a species. I was sure there was some very scientific knowledge that I would learn—precise and, to me at the time, mysterious—that would enable me to know how to define a species. The old textbook definition about species not interbreeding hardly works in the case of so many plant species. And then we snickered when told that a "good" species is what a good taxonomist recognizes as such. Yet this later definition may be closer to the mark than it seems. Although a "good" taxonomist often arrives at conclusions by using many different kinds of data, having a vast knowledge of the group of organisms in question and often having a lifetime of experience and credentials, the final choice can be subjective.

As a student, I soon came to realize that biologists do not always agree upon classifying the same group of plants or animals. Using Kearney & Peebles's (1960) *Arizona Flora,* I learned that our mesquites were *Prosopis juliflora* and that there were different varieties or subspecies. But Marshall Johnston (1962), of the University of Texas, published a study of the North American mesquites in which the Arizona mesquites are quite differently classified—as *P. velutina* and *P. glandulosa* var. *torreyana*—and this system was followed by the great botanists Arturo Burkart (1976) of Argentina and Jerzy Rzedowski of Mexico and his wife, Graciela Calderón (Rzedowski & Calderón 1988). But Johnston's system was not universally accepted. Lyman Benson, in his revision of *Trees and Shrubs of the Southwest* (Benson & Darrow 1981), continued to treat the Arizona mesquites as varieties of *P. juliflora*. And the story will not end here; new information will undoubtedly call for new alignments and classifications. There is no absolutely right or wrong choice. But the overwhelming evidence now indicates that *P. juliflora* is a tropical species that does not reach the United States or even the Sonoran Desert.

Every few years new techniques come along, new fads in science, and the priests of academia claim that newfound, grant-generating, cutting-edge techniques will solve old mysteries. Indeed, some are solved, or more likely the old mysteries are discarded, and new questions are raised. Long ago we learned that chromosomes would give the "true" answers. Then came biochemistry, with scores of graduate students studying spots on thin, gel-coated glass plates; immunological tests; more and more picking apart and analyzing chemical constituents; and studies of surfaces at incredible magnifications using scanning electron microscopes. With the advent of user-friendly computers, numerical taxonomy and cladistics came into fashion. And at the end of the twentieth century gene jockeys began in-depth work with DNA and RNA, the molecules of the genetic material itself, to produce powerful studies of evolutionary relationships. Over the decades fierce arguments developed about who had the best answer: laboratory people scoffed at the old-fashioned field biologists, who were derided as looking only at natural history. Of course, the best taxonomists are supposed to use all pertinent lines of information in arriving at their conclusions.

The interested public accuses Ivory Tower botanists of changing names as if it were just a whim. When zoologists make taxonomic name changes, or "new combinations," it is not customary to have the combining author's name appear with the new scientific name. But botanists tenaciously include the combining author (look at the checklist in Chapter 17 of this volume). Accordingly, the two mesquites in southern Arizona are *Prosopis glandulosa* Torrey var. *torreyana* (L. Benson) M.C. Johnston [= *P. juliflora* (Swartz) DC. var. *torreyana* L. Benson] and *Prosopis velutina* Wooton [= *P. juliflora* of earlier western American authors, NOT *P. juliflora* (Swartz) DC., a species in southern Mexico to northern South America. *P. juliflora* (Swartz) DC. var. *velutina* (Wooton) Sargent]. Some say that if botanical nomenclature were like zoological nomenclature there would be fewer new combinations (name changes) because there would not be so much glory in it.

What about the other major desert legumes in the San Cristobal Wash, and along the Camino del Diablo and the Sonoran Desert in general? The mesquites belong to a diverse, unwieldy genus of nearly fifty species, but ironwood *(Olneya tesota)* would seem to hold few taxonomic mysteries, since it is the only species in its genus and there are no real close relatives. There is little doubt that the mesquites evolved and spread from drylands in South America. But where did the Sonoran Desert ironwood come from? It is restricted to the Sonoran Desert and immediately adjacent hot, dry places such as the thornscrub of southwestern Sonora.

Matt Lavin's work (Lavin 1988; also see Lavin & Sousa 1995) places our desert ironwood in a group of legume genera that includes sámota *(Coursetia glandulosa),* which are of South American origin. (There are other, quite unrelated, trees called ironwood because they have extremely hard wood, so heavy that it won't float in water.) There is not sufficient variation within *Olneya tesota* to warrant naming subspecies or varieties, although a few years ago Dennis Cornejo, then at the University of Texas, found that ironwood seeds are larger in the north (Arizona) than in the south (southern Sonora). *Olneya* is a very long-lived tree, in fact one of the longest-lived trees in the Sonoran Desert. Its spiny twigs afford protection not only for its leaves, flowers, and fruits but for many other organisms. Ironwood is a prominent "nurse plant" for numerous other plant species, and its overharvest and destruction, largely for clearing for buffelgrass pasture, charcoal production, and wood for Seri or Seri-style sculptures, are leading to a serious decline in recruitment of many long-lived perennials, including various cacti (Búrquez et al. 2002; Búrquez & Martínez, this volume).

Blue palo verde *(Parkinsonia florida, = Cercidium floridum)* is the third member of the desert legume tree trinity. The brilliant yellow flowers in spring make it especially conspicuous, and in the summer growing season we have to look twice to see the trunks among the jungle tangle in San Cristobal Wash. Being a member of the Caesalpinioid subfamily of legumes, it apparently does not fix nitrogen, as do the other two members of the trinity. Like the other two, but especially mesquite, it can grow rapidly if there is sufficient soil moisture during hot weather. It undoubtedly is a much shorter-lived tree than mesquite and certainly does not live as long as ironwood. From one end of the Camino del Diablo to the other there is no discernible difference among the blue palo verdes, and even across most of the Sonoran Desert and into northwestern Sinaloa they are all classified as a single subspecies. However, a second subspecies, *Cercidium floridum* subsp. *peninsulare,* is recognized from the state of Baja California Sur and also occurs on the south side of Isla Tiburón. But the plot thickens because this name (the Baja California Sur subspecies) has not formally been transferred to *Parkinsonia florida* and there is some doubt whether it should be recognized as a subspecies or treated as a distinct species.

And while we are at it, it is worth mentioning that the debate about the ten species of palo verde belonging to a single genus *(Parkinsonia)* or two genera *(Cercidium* and *Parkinsonia)* has been going on for more than a hundred years and the botanical bickering will probably not end any time soon. *Parkinsonia* in the narrow sense *(sensu stricto)* includes three species in Africa plus *P. aculeata,* widespread in both hemispheres. *Cercidium* ranges from the southwestern United States to Argentina. A magnificent selection of a hybrid found in the Tucson region, called *Cercidium* cultivar "Desert Museum," involves hybridization of *P. aculeata, P. florida,* and *P. microphylla* (Dimmitt 1987), and in my opinion hybridization studies support the concept of a single genus (see Felger 2000; Hawkins et al. 1999).

Today the desert legumes flourish in the absence of the people who used to live among them and depend on them for food, fuel, shelter, fiber, dyes, and medicine (e.g., Felger 1977; Felger & Moser 1985; Hodgson 2001; Rea 1997; Chapter 15, this volume). Today, with great increases in human population and overuse of groundwater, fewer and fewer intact stands of the desert legume trinity remain. When Gary Nabhan began alerting us to the problem of the destruction of desert ironwood in the mid-1990s, it seemed that such a common desert plant certainly did not fit the category of an endangered or threatened species (Nabhan & Carr 1994). In some circles mesquites are regarded as more of a pest than a valuable resource, albeit one that will become a major world food crop in the not-too-distant future (Felger 1990). The "fully protected" places such as the Cabeza Prieta Refuge are few, and perhaps safer only from the woodsman's ax than from the governmental budgetary ax. Today management and protection require money and effort, and protected places are becoming unconnected islands, their biotic corridors severed. What will the San Cristobal Wash look like if our population doubles again?

Acknowledgments

"View from the Top" and "The Craters" first appeared in *Journal of the Southwest* (1997) and are reprinted here, in revised form, by permission. "Desert Legume Trinity" first appeared in *Aridus* (Felger 1992) and is reprinted here, in revised form, by permission.

Seventeen

Botanical Diversity of Southwestern Arizona and Northwestern Sonora

Richard Stephen Felger, Susan Rutman, Michael F. Wilson, and Kathryn Mauz

Walk, drive, fly, or crawl across the Dry Borders and the one plant you see most is creosotebush *(Larrea divaricata)*. This hardy shrub defines not only the Sonoran Desert but most of the deserts of North and South America (Mabry et al. 1977; Shreve 1951). Look again and you see veins of denser green along the dry watercourses anastomosing down the bajadas and valley plains and collecting bigger and greener at the drainage bottoms. Most of this green is from double ribbons of gallery trees, most often the legume trinity of mesquites, palo verdes, and ironwood *(Prosopis glandulosa, P. velutina; Parkinsonia microphylla, P. florida;* and *Olneya tesota)*. The distributions of many of the shrubs, trees, and other perennials are limited to the drainageways in the familiar desert xeroriparian pattern. Lowland plains with predominantly sandy soil cover large areas of the region. Over vast areas the most conspicuous larger perennials are creosotebush and bursage *(Ambrosia deltoidea* and/or *A. dumosa)*. The tops of the highest mountains reveal an almost chaparral, grassy, and decidedly nondesertlike vegetation. The two words *mixed desertscrub* cover a potpourri of combinations of the hundreds of species in complex upland habitats. Despite the aridity of the region, the flora and vegetation are diverse (Bowers 1980; Felger 2000; Felger et al. 1992, 2003; Malusa 2003a, 2003b; Warren et al. 1981).

Apart from the seeming monotony of vast plains and distant, barren-looking mountains, a number of unique habitat types contribute greatly to the floristic diversity of the region. A thin vegetation cover of plants adapted to shifting sands speckles the regional dunes. A special vegetation and flora is seen on the several large and many small playas following the rare times of sufficient rains. Coastal wetlands are clogged with essentially evergreen halophytes. Oases and other small wetlands have their own and often highly diverse floras, some of them related to the vanquished riverine floras. The once-mighty Río Colorado had huge wetlands with ever-shifting forests.

These scenes can be generalized to make nice neat stories, but the deviations and complexities of the changing plant life across the gradients and mosaics of the Dry Borders will boggle the mind of anyone wanting a simple classification. Nevertheless, we feel a need to classify or make hierarchies of nature, for this is the means of communicating what we see. One such hierarchy is an annotated taxonomic and distributional listing, the poetry of botany, like the floristic listing (species accounts) in this chapter.

Climate

Rainfall in the Dry Borders region is largely biseasonal. Winter-spring storms originating in the Pacific Ocean can deliver widespread precipitation. Sporadic El Niño events bring exceptional amounts of winter-spring rainfall, which can promote spectacular displays of spring wildflowers. Summer monsoon rains are a northern extension of a tropical phenomenon, yet the moisture that feeds these storms is drawn locally from the warm Gulf of California and neighboring Pacific Ocean. Often highly localized and violent, summer thunderstorms can bring heavy rainfall of brief duration but are sporadic and undependable (Ezcurra & Rodríguez 1986; Shreve 1951). In addition, occasional hurricane-fringe storms in late summer and fall may bring deluges that result in the spectacular development of plant life. Within the region the gradient of total annual rainfall declines from east to west and from higher to lower elevations (Comrie & Broyles 2002). Annual average rainfall is less than 50 mm at the lower (western) elevations and at least 300 mm at the highest (eastern) elevations.

Highest temperatures in the Sonoran Desert rival records set elsewhere in North America, and frequent winds intensify the aridity. Maximum daily temperatures commonly exceed 38–45°C (100–113°F) from late April to early October. The highest temperature recorded for the Sonoran Desert was 56.7°C (134°F), taken in the Sierra Blanca in late June 1971 (May 1973). Winter daytime temperatures often range between 15.5 and 24°C (60–75°F), but temperatures commonly dip several degrees below freezing on a few nights during each of the colder months. Charles Conner's (personal communication 2004) weather records for 2003 in Organ Pipe Cactus National Monument illustrate the range of variation and extremes that can influence the distribution of plant life:

> The coldest day of the year was December 28, with several low valley sites getting down to 19°F and the coldest being Salsola Site, 2 miles east of Blankenship, that got down to 11°F. Alamo Canyon, above the wash bottom, bottomed out at exactly 32°F, and Bull Pasture also never got below freezing! The low there was 33°F, and is actually typical of that site. The hottest two days of the year were July 13 and August 10. The winner was Aguajita Wash, just on the other side of the hills and east of Quitobaquito, at 122°F on August 10. Next was Salsola Site, which topped out at 116°F the same day. On July 13 two other hot sites were Growler Valley, 4 miles west of Bates Well, and Valley Floor, 1 mile west of Armenta Ranch. At both of those sites the temperature reached 115°F. As for rain . . . the wettest sites were Arch Canyon with 16.34 inches and Alamo Canyon with 15.85 inches. The driest was Growler Valley with 8.82 inches. The average for the park was 11.4 inches. The maximum 1 hour rain was at Senita Basin: 1.55 inch on September 5. The maximum 1 day rain was 3.50 inches at Alamo Canyon on September 24. The previous day it rained 2.08 inches there, and this was from Tropical Depression Marty, which was easily the most significant rain event of the year. At many sites it rained continuously for 30 hours! As a side note, during those same two days of Marty, it rained almost 6 inches at Red Cone in the Pinacate, a site that averages little more than 3 inches per year. The maximum wind gust was 75 mph on September 1 at the Growler Valley Site (monsoon related). Most other stations reported yearly maximums in the range of 40–50 mph.

Summers are long and very hot, although temperatures are generally slightly lower near the coast and at peak elevations. Within the regional precipitation gradient, plant distributions at landscape scales are further delimited here by heat, drought, and freezing. The combination of very hot weather and drought in late spring and early summer severely limits the survival and distribution of Sonoran Desert plants. Many species in the region are frost-sensitive. However, certain habitats or microhabitats can be nearly or entirely frost-free, permitting a number of species with subtropical affinities to survive in the region. The frost-sensitive plants found on some rocky slopes, such as *Bursera microphylla*, *Jatropha cinerea*, *J. cuneata*, and *Stenocereus thurberi*, attest to minimal freezing weather (Felger 2000; Turner et al. 1995). Niches around rocks can be virtually frost-free because of stored daytime heat.

Vegetation and Flora

The lower-elevation portions of the Dry Borders region are within Shreve's (1951) Lower Colorado Valley subdivision of the Sonoran Desert—the most arid portion of this desert. This includes the two Mexican biosphere reserves, most of the Cabeza Prieta Refuge, the lower elevations and western four-fifths of the Goldwater Range, the western margin of Organ Pipe National Monument, and the lower elevations of the Sonoran Desert National Monument. The higher-elevation portions of the Dry Borders region are within Shreve's Arizona Upland subdivision of the Sonoran Desert, including most of Organ Pipe National Monument, the eastern one-fifth of the Goldwater Range, and most of the Sonoran Desert National Monument (also see Brown 1982). The entire region falls within the Sonoran Warm Desert Scrub vegetation type identified by Barbour and Christensen (1993) and the Sonoran Biotic Province in use by biogeographers and zoologists (Ramamoorthy et al. 1993).

There are several biological "sky islands" in the region: for example, the Ajo Mountains, Sand Tank Mountains, Table Top Mountains, and Sierra Pinacate. A significant number of species occurring at higher elevations in the mountains do not occur in the surrounding desert lowlands, and a few of the sky island plants are endemic to the region. The Ajo and Sand Tank mountains share a majority of their sky island species, but the high-elevation flora of Sierra Pinacate is unique.

Key references for the regional vegetation

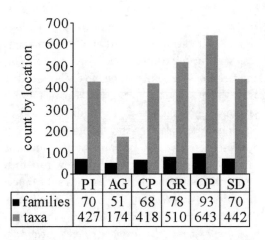

Figure 17.1. *Species richness for plants of the six Dry Borders reserves. PI = Reserva de la Biosfera El Pinacate y Gran Desierto de Altar in Sonora, AG = Reserva de la Biosfera Alto Golfo de California y Delta del Río Colorado, CP = Cabeza Prieta National Wildlife Refuge, GR = Barry M. Goldwater Air Force Range, OP = Organ Pipe Cactus National Monument, SD = Sonoran Desert National Monument.*

	PI	AG	CP	GR	OP	SD
■ families	70	51	68	78	93	70
▪ taxa	427	174	418	510	643	442

and flora include Benson and Darrow 1981, Brown 1982, Felger 2000, Felger et al. 2001, Hickman 1993, Kearney and Peebles 1960, Shreve 1951, Turner et al. 1995, Wiggins 1964 and 1980, and the Vascular Plants of Arizona project in the *Journal of the Arizona-Nevada Academy of Sciences* 1992 to 2005 and *Canotia* beginning 2005.

As might be expected in an arid region, the number of species comprising the flora is relatively small in relation to area size and ecological complexity (Felger 2000; McLaughlin & Bowers 1999). The total Dry Borders area of approximately 26,305 km² (2.63 million ha, or 6.5 million acres) supports a flora of at least 854 vascular plant species, subspecies, varieties, and hybrids in 447 genera and 106 families (Figure 17.1). This is roughly one-third of the total flora of the entire Sonoran Desert region—spanning 310,000 km² across five states in Mexico and the United States (Shreve 1951; Wiggins 1964). The floristic listings here are estimated to be 90 percent complete for the Alto Golfo Reserve, Goldwater Range, and Sonoran Desert Monument and more than 95 percent complete for Organ Pipe Monument and the Pinacate Reserve.

The five largest plant families in terms of number of species are the composites (Asteraceae), grasses (Poaceae), legumes (Fabaceae), cacti (Cactaceae), and euphorbs (Euphorbiaceae) (Table 17.1). The largest genera are *Euphorbia* with 21 species; *Cylindropuntia* with 14 taxa; *Astragalus* with 11 taxa; *Eriogonum* and *Phacelia*, each with 10 species; and *Atriplex, Camissonia,* and *Mentzelia,* each with 9 taxa. The next largest genera are *Lycium* and *Muhlenbergia* (each with 8 species), and *Amaranthus* and *Ambrosia* (each with 7 species).

Although the areas covered include a substantial portion of the Sonoran Desert, endemism

as a proportion of the total flora is not especially high (see Felger 2000). Species endemic or essentially endemic to the region include:

Berberis harrisoniana (Berberidaceae)
Croton wigginsii (Euphorbiaceae)
Dimorphocarpa pinnatifida (Brassicaceae)
Euphorbia platysperma (Euphorbiaceae)
Heterotheca sessiliflora var. *thiniicola* (Asteraceae)
Perityle ajoensis (Asteraceae)
Senecio pinacatensis (Asteraceae)
Stephanomeria schottii (Asteraceae)
Suaeda puertopenascoa (Chenopodiaceae)

Approximately 11 percent of the total flora, represented by 91 species, consists of non-native plants (Figure 17.2). Most of the non-natives, however, are agricultural or urban weeds, or plants in disturbed habitats (Felger 1990, 2000). Furthermore, some of the non-natives in the species accounts are "strays" such as shepherd's purse *(Capsella bursa-pastoris),* safflower *(Carthamus tinctorius),* and wheat *(Triticum aestivum)* and are not established as reproducing populations. Others are persisting from cultivation, such as the figs *(Ficus carica)* and pomegranates *(Punica granatum)* at Quitobaquito (Felger et al. 1992). Non-natives make up only 6 percent of the flora of the Goldwater Range, probably reflecting both its remoteness and its relatively pristine condition. In contrast, non-natives make up 14.6 percent of the Alto Golfo Reserve. This high percentage is attributable largely to its proximity to, and inclusion of, agricultural areas and disturbed habitats in the lower Río Colorado valley.

Only 30 non-native species, or 3.5 percent of the total flora, are present as well-established, reproducing populations in the desert wildlands of the region—the undisturbed (natural) habitats (Table 17.2). Half these species are grasses. Furthermore, only a few, all of Old World origin, are considered invasive species that pose serious threats to the native ecosystems (Felger 1990, 2000; Wilson et al. 2002). Among the most insidious are red brome *(Bromus rubens),* buffelgrass *(Pennisetum ciliare),* Arabian and Mediterranean grass *(Schismus* spp.), Sahara mustard *(Brassica tournefortii),* and tamarisk *(Tamarix ramosissima* or related taxa). Others of concern include *Cynodon dactylon, Eragrostis lehmanniana, Hordeum murinum, Mesembryanthemum crystallinum,* and *Pennisetum setaceum.*

TABLE 17.1. *Distribution of species in the Dry Borders flora across plant families.*

ASTERACEAE	125
POACEAE	98
FABACEAE	57
CACTACEAE	40
EUPHORBIACEAE	37
BRASSICACEAE	30
MALVACEAE	26
BORAGINACEAE	24
CHENOPODIACEAE	24
SOLANACEAE	22
POLYGONACEAE	18
SCROPHULARIACEAE	17
NYCTAGINACEAE	16
HYDROPHYLLACEAE	16
POLEMONIACEAE	14
PTERIDACEAE	14
ONAGRACEAE	14
LOASACEAE	12
PORTULACACEAE	12
AMARANTHACEAE	10
CONVOLVULACEAE	10
LAMIACEAE	10
ASCLEPIADACEAE	9
ZYGOPHYLLACEAE	9
CYPERACEAE	8
VERBENACEAE	8
ACANTHACEAE	7
APIACEAE	7
CARYOPHYLLACEAE	7
CUCURBITACEAE	7
AGAVACEAE	6
CAPPARACEAE	6
"LILIACEAE"	6
RHAMNACEAE	6
PAPAVERACEAE	5
RANUNCULACEAE	5

Number of families (N) with fewer than 5 species (sp) each:

sp	N
4	2
3	7
2	19
1	40

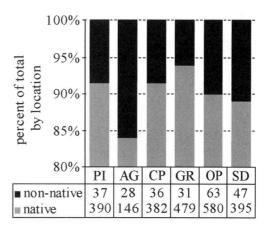

	PI	AG	CP	GR	OP	SD
■ non-native	37	28	36	31	63	47
▪ native	390	146	382	479	580	395

Figure 17.2. Distribution of non-native plants in the Dry Borders (values in the table are counts of species represented as percentages in the graph).

Desert annuals, or ephemerals (short-lived annuals, completing their life cycle in a single season), make up about half the total flora of the Dry Borders region (Felger 2000; Felger et al. 2003), as in the Sonoran Desert generally (Venable & Pake 1999). In some extreme habitats such as the Mohawk Dunes, annuals make up as much as 81 percent of the total flora (Felger et al. 2003). The majority are cool-season (winter-spring) annuals. As pointed out by Exequiel Ezcurra (this volume), desert seeds, especially those of the annuals, are the basis of the desert's food chain. On the rare occasions of abundant rainfall, the desert annuals may form meadowlike expanses of nearly 100 percent plant cover—and we revel in the spectacular displays of wildflowers (Goodpaster & Bowers 2004).

The Six Reserves

Reserva de la Biosfera Alto Golfo de California y Delta del Río Colorado

The documented flora of the Alto Golfo Reserve includes at least 174 species, varieties, and subspecies. Although the original delta flora may have included 200–400 species historically (Ezcurra et al. 1988), only a small fraction of this flora was recorded before large-scale changes to upstream hydrology during the twentieth century decimated the delta ecosystem. The contrasts in habitats and their plant life are profound. Places with plentiful water, such as the tidal marshes and the riverine vegetation (or its recent replacement, irrigated agriculture), can be green and lush and may have nearly 100 percent plant cover. Immediately adjacent to the delta wetlands are the extreme desert drylands—arid mesas, badlands, and dunes—

TABLE 17.2. *Common or well-established non-native plants in natural vegetation (wildlands) in the Dry Borders region.*

FAMILY	SPECIES	PI	AG	CP	GR	OP	SD
AIZOACEAE	Mesembryanthemum crystallinum		AG			OP	
ASTERACEAE	Sonchus asper	PI	AG	CP	GR	OP	SD
	Sonchus oleraceus	PI			GR	OP	SD
BRASSICACEAE	Brassica tournefortii	PI	AG	CP	GR	OP	SD
	Sisymbrium irio	PI	AG	CP	GR	OP	SD
CHENOPODIACEAE	Bassia hyssopifolia		AG				
	Chenopodium murale	PI	AG	CP	GR	OP	SD
EUPHORBIACEAE	Euphorbia prostrata	PI				OP	SD
FABACEAE	Melilotus indica				GR	OP	SD
GERANIACEAE	Erodium cicutarium	PI		CP	GR	OP	SD
NYCTAGINACEAE	Boerhavia coccinea			CP	GR	OP	SD
POACEAE	Bromus rubens	PI		CP	GR	OP	SD
	Chloris virgata	PI		CP		OP	SD
	Cynodon dactylon	PI	AG	CP	GR	OP	SD
	Echinochloa colonum	PI	AG	CP		OP	SD
	Echinochloa crusgalli		AG	CP			
	Eragrostis cilianensis	PI		CP		OP	SD
	Eragrostis lehmanniana	PI		CP	GR	OP	SD
	Hordeum murinum	PI		CP	GR	OP	SD
	Pennisetum ciliare	PI		CP	GR	OP	SD
	Pennisetum setaceum			CP	GR	OP	
	Phalaris minor	PI		CP	GR	OP	SD
	Polypogon monspeliensis		AG	CP	GR	OP	SD
	Schismus arabicus	PI	AG	CP	GR	OP	SD
	Schismus barbatus				GR	OP	
	Sorghum halepense	PI	AG	CP		OP	SD
PORTULACACEAE	Portulaca oleracea	PI		CP		OP	SD
SOLANACEAE	Petunia parviflora					OP	
	Solanum americanum					OP	
TAMARICACEAE	Tamarix ramosissima	PI	AG	CP	GR	OP	SD
TOTAL	30	20	13	22	19	28	23

Note: Table indicates presence only; relative abundance varies among areas and habitat types. PI = Reserva de la Biosfera El Pinacate y Gran Desierto de Altar; AG = Reserva de la Biosfera Alto Golfo de California y Delta del Río Colorado; CP = Cabeza Prieta National Wildlife Refuge; GR = Barry M. Goldwater Range; OP = Organ Pipe Cactus National Monument; SD = Sonoran Desert National Monument.

which have sparse perennial vegetation and far less than 5 percent cover of perennial plants. Rainfall is scant, but maritime dew during the cooler months is often heavy. During winter and spring the coastal plants are more often than not wet at dawn from condensation. The more stable soils near the coast can have notable development of biological soil crusts (see Belnap, this volume), presumably because of the dew.

The diversity of plant species and growth forms in the dry uplands of the Mesa de Sonora, in the southwestern part of the region, is the lowest in any part of the Dry Borders. The relatively low species richness is attributed to aridity as well as to low topographic variability within the reserve—there are no mountains. During dry times (the usual situation), the landscape is dominated by a few species of scruffy shrubs, mostly *Ambrosia dumosa* and *Frankenia palmeri*. There are no trees. There are no ferns and fern relatives. The Alto Golfo is too dry even for cacti, except for a few small populations of teddybear cholla *(Cylindropuntia bigelovii)*, jumping cholla *(C. fulgida)*, and rare individuals of silver cholla *(C. echinocarpa)*. Coastal dunes supporting a unique dune flora extend inland into the sand sea of the Gran Desierto.

Apart from the Río Colorado delta, freshwater and trees are indeed scarce (see El Torneal in the gazetteer, Chapter 39, this volume). Upwellings of freshwater near the coast form widely scattered pools, or *pozos*, in otherwise barren salt flats (Ezcurra et al. 1988; Felger 2000). The plants at these small wetlands, especially at La Salina, represent remnant populations of the original delta flora. Immense gallery forests of cottonwood *(Populus fremontii)* and willow *(Salix gooddingii)* stretched along the Río Colorado and its tributaries, from the myriad channels of the delta to elevations far above the desert. With all that water and heat, the growth of these trees must have been incredibly fast and their biomass enormous, contributing substantially to the teeming life of the delta and the Gulf of California. These riparian forests survived until upriver diversions and dams killed the river and its annual flood regime. Some cottonwoods and willows are recolonizing (Glenn and Nagler, this volume), but most of the associated plants and animals are gone or barely hanging on.

Bordering the cottonwood-willow forests on slightly higher ground were forests of honey mesquite *(Prosopis glandulosa)*, and peripheral to these were expansive thickets of arrowweed *(Pluchea sericea)* and associated plants. The cottonwood forests apparently extended seaward to about the vicinity of the Lerdo settlement, or the inland margin of the present-day Ciénega de Santa Clara. At the end of the twentieth century the ciénega became the largest and richest wetland in the region (Felger 2000; Glenn et al. 1996). This brackish-water marsh of 12,500 to 20,000 ha of wetland supports fish such as mullet and the endangered desert pupfish *(Cyprinodon macularius;* Zengel &

Glenn 1996) and a diverse avifauna (Hinojosa-Huerta et al., this volume). Much of the ciénega is thickly vegetated with cattail *(Typha domingensis),* common reed *(Phragmites australis),* and bulrush *(Scirpus americanus).* Large quantities of submerged aquatic plants, largely holly-leaved water nymph *(Najas marina),* pondweed *(Stuckenia pectinata),* and some widgeon grass *(Ruppia maritima),* provide food for waterfowl. The backwaters and permanently wet soils support dense growth of halophytic and semi-halophytic wetland plants (Felger 2000). Due to upriver diversions and dams, by 1974 the marsh had shrunk to about 210 ha (see Glenn et al. 1992). Since 1977 the ciénega has been fed by the Wellton-Mohawk drainage canal, which carries semi-saline irrigation water drained from fields in the lower Gila River valley in Arizona. The ciénega is threatened by the Yuma Desalting Plant, built to desalinate Colorado River water being delivered to Mexico.

Tidal flats and lagoons in protected embayments and desert estuaries, or *esteros*, still support halophytic plant communities of relatively low species richness and highly consistent composition. Halophytes characteristically form 100 percent plant cover in the saline mud inundated by tidal seawater. Vast but possibly diminishing stands of nipa *(Distichlis palmeri)* and other halophytes cover much of Islas Montague and Gore and other tidal wetlands.

Reserva de la Biosfera El Pinacate y Gran Desierto de Altar

The Pinacate Reserve, including the two core areas and the buffer zones, supports a flora of 427 species, varieties, and subspecies of vascular plants. Major works on the vegetation and flora include Búrquez and Castillo 1994, Ezcurra et al. 1987, Felger 1980, and Felger 2000. Several distinctive habitat areas stand out: the Pinacate volcanic field with its peripheral lava flows, the great maar craters, sky island Pinacate Peak, playas, granitic ranges including the Sierra del Rosario, dunes, desert plains, and large xeroriparian drainageways.

The Pinacate volcanic field, from lowest to highest elevation, supports at least 309 plant species, of which the majority occur mostly below 600 m elevation. Some extreme habitats are notable for being virtually devoid of perennials or having very low perennial diversity and density. On some cinder cones only one or two truly perennial species are present, usually *Ambrosia dumosa* and *Larrea divaricata,* or only *A. dumosa.* Ash flats can also be inhospitable habitats for perennials. These flats are riddled with rodent burrows, whose occupants may prevent the establishment of perennials. For example, the large apron of ash flat surrounding Cerro Colorado is virtually devoid of perennials except for the deep-rooted and apparently unpalatable *Euphorbia polycarpa* and *Tiquilia palmeri.*

Plant life in the Pinacate craters is relatively rich, and the various craters have remarkably similar patterns of species distributions, especially among craters of comparable size and depth. About half the species present in the entire Pinacate region can be found inside just the several larger craters. This rich botanical assemblage seems related to the relatively high habitat diversity. The relative lack of wind would potentially reduce transpiration, but this factor could be offset by the generally higher temperatures inside the craters.

The mountaintop of Sierra Pinacate is a sky island supporting Ice Age relict plants, and some of these species occur nowhere else in mainland Mexico (Felger 2000; Van Devender et al. 1990). *Senecio pinacatensis,* known only from the higher elevations, is the only species endemic to the Pinacate volcanic field.

Characteristic plants of the granitic ranges include a number of species that are not found on the Pinacate lava, such as *Agave deserti, Dudleya arizonica, Hesperoyucca whipplei, Nolina bigelovii,* and *Rhus kearneyi.* The *Hesperoyucca* has one of the narrowest ranges of any plant in the region, occurring only on the north side of Sierra del Viejo (see Felger, this volume, Chapter 15). The isolated Sierra del Rosario is even more arid than other granitic ranges in the region. A notable indicator of its extreme aridity is the absence of teddybear cholla *(Cylindropuntia bigelovii),* present on almost all other mountains in the Dry Borders region.

Before rampant woodcutting during the 1980s, the perennial vegetation along a major wash near the base of the Sierra del Rosario covered 84 percent of the ground surface. Perennial vegetation on nearby desert pavement and sandy-gravel flats supported far less than 10 percent perennial plant cover. In 1980 no non-native plants were found in the Sierra del Rosario, although several non-natives occurred in the nearby dunes (Felger 1980). Sahara

mustard *(Brassica tournefortii),* however, soon arrived on the scene (Felger 2000).

The enormous Gran Desierto dune system has a flora of only 85 species. The relatively low species richness can be attributed to the low habitat diversity, aridity, and harsh conditions brought about by moving sand. During seasons of favorable rains the dunes support spectacular displays of wildflowers.

Fifteen taxa (17.6 percent) of the dune flora are regional dune endemics at the species or infraspecific level or show unique, apparently ecotypic variation. Examples of this pattern are *Astragalus magdalenae* var. *peirsonii, Croton wigginsii, Dimorphocarpa pinnatifida, Eriogonum deserticola, Euphorbia platysperma, Heterotheca sessiliflora* var. *thiniicola, Pholisma sonorae, Stephanomeria schottii,* and *Larrea divaricata* var. *arenaria. Heterotheca sessiliflora* var. *thiniicola* is known from only a small area of dunes northeast of Puerto Peñasco. Only three non-native species, all ephemerals, occur among the dune flora: *Brassica tournefortii, Schismus arabicus,* and *Sonchus asper.*

Cabeza Prieta National Wildlife Refuge

The Cabeza Prieta flora includes 418 species and varieties or subspecies. Reports on the plants include the pioneer work of Simmons (1966). The vegetation has been surveyed by Malusa (2003b), and a comprehensive flora is being prepared by Felger, Rutman, Wilson, and Tom Van Devender.

Although the refuge lacks the sky island and chaparral-like vegetation seen in the Organ Pipe and Sonoran Desert monuments, the tops of the larger mountains support plant species not seen at lower elevations. A spectacular shrubby desert mint *(Salvia vaseyi),* discovered on the Sierra Pinta in 2003, is not known elsewhere in Arizona. This mint and a number of other plants in the granitic mountains in the western part of the refuge have their major populations and closest relatives in Baja California and California. Other western elements creeping into the refuge include the beavertail prickly pear *(Opuntia basilaris),* here every bit as stunted as it is in the nearby Sierra del Viejo in the Pinacate Reserve and near Tinajas Altas in the Goldwater Range (Felger 2000).

Dunes of the Pinta Sands along the southern margin of the refuge support a flora similar to that of the nearby Gran Desierto dunes in the Pinacate

Reserve. Certain widespread Gran Desierto species in Sonora, such as giant sandbur (*Cenchrus palmeri*), long-leaved joint-fir (*Ephedra trifurca*), and the dune creosotebush (*Larrea divaricata* var. *arenaria*), however, have not been found in the refuge. The northern extension of the Pinacate Lava has a flora essentially indistinguishable from that of the larger, low-elevation volcanic areas south of the international border.

On rare occasions, following heavy rains, the usually dry and barren Las Playas supports a carpet of herbaceous plants including *Euphorbia spathulata* and *Sibara virginica,* which are not known anywhere else in the Sonoran Desert. The flora of Las Playas includes more than 40 species. *Sibara angelorum* is known for the Dry Borders region (and indeed, north of Mexico) only by the single Cabeza Prieta specimen cited in the species accounts. Another small desert annual, *Drymaria viscosa,* is also known for the United States only from the refuge.

Barry M. Goldwater Air Force Range

The present listing documents 510 species, varieties, or subspecies and one hybrid for the 749,823-ha (1,733,921-acre) portion of the Goldwater Range outside the Cabeza Prieta Refuge. The floristic inventory reported here is reasonably complete for large areas of the range, although some of the higher elevations and many remote areas remain poorly known botanically.

There is considerable change in vegetation and floristic makeup across the broad span of the range. At its western margin the climate is arid in the extreme. In contrast, the eastern part of the range, at higher elevation and with greater rainfall, supports a number of species not found elsewhere in the range, such as isolated populations of Kofa Mountain barberry (*Berberis harrisoniana*), crucifixion thorn (*Canotia holacantha*), beargrass (*Nolina microcarpa*), and Sonoran Desert rosewood (*Vauquelinia californica* subsp. *sonorensis*).

Sandy soils and dunes in the arid, southwestern part of the range are home to sand-adapted plants of special conservation interest, including sand croton (*Croton wigginsii*), dune spurge (*Euphorbia platysperma*), sandfood (*Pholisma sonorae*), and giant dune-buckwheat (*Eriogonum deserticola*). These plants are far more widespread in the adjacent Gran Desierto of northwestern

Sonora. Other "western" or "Californian" desert plants occurring in the western margin of the range and known nowhere else in the Dry Borders region include desert holly (*Atriplex hymenelytra*) and Schott's dalea (*Psorothamnus schottii*). The Mohawk Dunes support an isolated dune flora of 78 species that is similar in composition as well as species richness to that of the vastly larger Gran Desierto dune field. (The Mohawk Dunes occupy an area that is less than 2 percent that of the Gran Desierto dune field.) This unique dune system, largely unaffected by human activities, has been recommended as a site for baseline studies of plant migrations and population dynamics, including potential effects of global climatic change (Felger et al. 2003). The Tinajas Altas Mountains, which include the famous Tinajas Altas waterholes, are a special place with some plants, such as *Mirabilis tenuiloba*, not known elsewhere in Arizona. Although the immediate area of the Tinajas Altas has been heavily impacted by successive waves of people (see gazetteer, Chapter 39, this volume), the vegetation remains remarkably original, and nearly all the rest of the Tinajas Altas Mountains is virtually pristine. A specimen of *Jacquemontia pringlei,* collected at the "south end of the Gila Mountains" (probably the Tinajas Altas Mountains) in 1938, has otherwise not been found west of the Ajo Mountains.

Organ Pipe Cactus National Monument

The flora of Organ Pipe Cactus National Monument includes at least 643 plant species, varieties or subspecies, and hybrids. The majority of the monument falls within Shreve's (1951) Arizona Upland subdivision of the Sonoran Desert and includes sky island and oasis habitats that contribute to its relatively high floristic diversity. Reports on the flora include Bowers 1980, Felger 1990, and Felger et al. 1992, and vegetation maps have been prepared by Malusa (2003a) and Warren et al. (1981). A comprehensive flora is being prepared by Felger, Rutman, Wilson, and Van Devender.

Of special interest is the well-known oasis of Quitobaquito, with a flora of 261 species in 191 genera and 60 families. In addition, a number of plants were formerly cultivated here. The Quitobaquito region supports approximately 45 percent of the total flora, although the area constitutes only about 3.5 percent of the total area, of

Organ Pipe Monument (Felger et al. 1992). Because it provides dependable water, Quitobaquito has been a crossroads of human activity since early prehistoric times. These same factors have made it a center of biological dynamism and accumulated diversity.

The Ajo Mountain system supports at least 141 species—such as juniper *(Juniperus coahuilensis)*, scrub oak *(Quercus turbinella)*, and Sonoran Desert rosewood—that do not occur farther west in the Dry Borders region. *Perityle ajoensis* is endemic to the Ajo Mountains. The large, west-facing canyons, such as Alamo and Arch canyons and the mid-elevation Bull Pasture, are exceptionally rich botanical enclaves of many nondesert species. For example, scrub oak in Alamo Canyon, usually a mere shrub as the common name indicates, develops groves of well-formed trees often 8 m tall. Sonoran Desert rosewood, generally a shrub or small tree, likewise develops to unusual size—in fact, the largest known individual of the species, 14.3 m in height, occurs in Alamo Canyon (Felger et al. 2001; National Register of Big Trees 1996).

A number of plants that are common in nearby Sonora (e.g., *Atamisquea emarginata, Jatropha cinerea, Matelea cordifolia,* and *Solanum hindsianum*) are not known elsewhere in the United States. Others, such as *Eucnide rupestris, Pachycereus schottii,* and *Peniocereus striatus,* are also rare or of extremely limited distribution in the United States but are widespread in nearby Sonora. Organ pipe cactus *(Stenocereus thurberi)*—the namesake of the monument—is more widespread and common here than anywhere else in the Dry Borders region.

Non-native plants account for about 10 percent of the flora. Arizona Highway 85, which bisects the monument, and the urbanized and disturbed habitats opposite the monument in Sonora serve as major invasion corridors for non-native plants (Felger 1990).

Sonoran Desert National Monument

The known flora of the Sonoran Desert National Monument includes 442 species, varieties or subspecies, and hybrids. This is the first comprehensive, specimen-based listing for the monument. Floristic studies have been conducted by Mauz and Felger, and the vegetation has been surveyed by Morrison et al. (2003) and in the Table Top Mountains by Pendall (1994).

The lowest-elevation valleys can be included in Shreve's Lower Colorado Valley subdivision, but the majority of the monument—the mid-elevations—is the classic Arizona Upland landscape of magazines and calendars. Magnificent saguaro forests are found on many of the upper bajadas and lower-elevation mountain areas. Valley floors are expansive and dissected by watercourses bordered by desert legume trees—ironwood, mesquite, and blue palo verde—and sometimes others including catclaw acacia *(Acacia greggii)* and desert willow *(Chilopsis linearis).* The surrounding flats are dominated by creosotebush and include two (unrelated) shrubs known as crucifixion thorn *(Castela emoryi* and *Koeberlinia spinosa).* Aside from well-developed xeroriparian forests along major valley-floor washes, scattered water-retention features support dense stands of mesquite *(Prosopis velutina* and, in the northern portion, *P. glandulosa).* The standing water and deep shade at these sites enable some plants to establish and persist that otherwise would not in the more ephemeral flows of the desert washes and pools. The valley floors explode with life in wet winters and when the summer monsoon rains arrive. A vast drainage system spreads across the southern reaches of the Vekol Valley, puddling up the valley with deep, poorly draining clay soils. There is a dense but drastically overgrazed tobosa *(Hilaria mutica)* grassland that has been recognized for special conservation status for its regional uniqueness, vulnerability, and importance as wildlife habitat. The grassland may have been larger historically, but it now occupies only 300 acres within the area of the monument (BLM 1988) and extends into adjacent Tohono O'odham lands.

The highest elevations harbor relict populations such as crucifixion thorn *(Canotia),* desert olive *(Forestiera phillyreoides),* juniper, bush penstemon *(Keckiella antirrhinoides),* and scrub oak. Table Top Mountain is best known for its isolated tobosa grassland on the 107-acre mesa top. The unusual combination of plant species at the higher elevations is rarely found in this ecoregion. The lower elevations of Javelina Mountain harbor some of the northernmost individuals of organ pipe cactus *(Stenocereus thurberi).* Given the area yet to be explored, its topographic diversity, and its position on the boundary between two distinct floristic regions of North America, we estimate that new records are still to be found, particularly at the higher elevations.

Acknowledgments

Richard Felger and Michael Wilson thank the Wallace Research Foundation for financial support to Drylands Institute. Over the years many friends and colleagues have provided generous assistance and support with fieldwork, herbarium studies, sharing of data and herbarium specimens, review of taxonomic decisions, and many other aspects of our botanical studies. In this regard we especially thank Marc Baker, Jim Barnett, Bill Broyles, Alberto Búrquez, Travis Columbus, Charles Conner, Mark Dimmitt, Shannon Doan, Erik Enderson, Luke Evans, Exequiel Ezcurra, Carianne Funicelli, Ed Gilbert, Gil Gillenwater, James Henrickson, Wendy Hodgson, Peter A. Holm, Phil Jenkins, Gene Joseph, Linda Leigh, Angelina Martínez Yrízar, Jim Malusa, Gary Maskarinec, Curtis McCasland, Lucinda McDade, Joseph McShane, Peter H. Morrison, Gary Paul Nabhan, Guy Nesom, Bruce Parfitt, Ami Pate, Don Pinkava, Amadeo M. Rea, Charlotte Reeder, John Reeder, Ana Lilia Reina, Andrew Salywon, Linwood Smith, Hans M. Smith IV, Richard Spellenberg, Victor Steinmann, Laura Thompson-Olais, Tim Tibbitts, Dale Turner, Tom Van Devender, Elizabeth "Betsy" Wirt, and George Yatskievych. RSF thanks the curators and staff of herbaria that provided generous assistance, including information and loans of specimens, and especially Phil Jenkins at the University of Arizona (ARIZ), Tucson; Shannon Doan and Don Pinkava at Arizona State University (ASU), Tempe; Lisa Blay at the Center for Environmental Management of Military Lands (CEMML) at Colorado State University, Fort Collins; Wendy Hodgson at the Desert Botanical Garden (DES), Phoenix; Judy Gibson at the San Diego Natural History Museum (SD), San Diego; and the staff of Rancho Santa Ana Botanic Garden (RSA), Claremont, California.

Species Accounts

The plants in this checklist are grouped as ferns and fern relatives, gymnosperms (cone-bearing plants), and angiosperms (flowering plants). Within these categories the plants are listed alphabetically by family, genus, and species. The accepted scientific names, including the variety (var.) or subspecies (subsp.), are in **bold.** The authors of scientific names are not in bold. Selected synonyms of scientific names are in *italics* within brackets [—]. Common names are in SMALL CAPITALS and follow the scientific names, and when known are given in English, Spanish, and O'odham, respectively. A representative herbarium specimen or record is cited for each of the six major conservation areas in which the species occurs. An index of genera and common names of families follows the species accounts.

The Hia C'ed O'odham names are based largely on Gary Nabhan's work in Felger 2000, Felger et al. 1992 and 1997, Nabhan 1983, and Nabhan et al. 1987. The O'odham orthography generally follows that of Alvarez & Hale 1970, with the exception that *v* generally is substituted for *w*. The Hia C'ed dialect, however, is little known. It falls within the /v/ dialect group. (In the /w/ dialects, *w* corresponds to *v* in the /v/ dialects; for example, /waik/ and /vaik/ both mean "three" but are different dialect forms.) Mathiot (1972) and Saxton et al. (1982) cover this variety theoretically, but there has been almost no direct work with it. David Shaul kindly regularized the Hia C'ed spellings given here according to standard sources and word meanings.

This listing is an expansion and refinement of earlier floristic works for the region (Felger 2000; Felger et al. 1997; Felger et al. 2003). Taxonomic choices (which scientific name[s] to accept) reflect the interpretation of one of the authors (RSF) of the available literature as of early 2005. A slightly conservative interpretation is taken for the ever-changing taxonomic revisions—like many art forms, especially those whose creators do not think of themselves as artists, these hierarchies of nature are dynamic. Largely for the sake of convenience, plant families generally follow Cronquist 1981 and the *Flora of North America* format. Also, for the sake of convenience, some admittedly artificial families are used, such as the Liliaceae.

All specimens cited are at the University of Arizona Herbarium (ARIZ), unless otherwise indicated by the abbreviations for herbaria at Cabeza Prieta National Wildlife Refuge (CAB), Organ Pipe Cactus National Monument (ORPI), Center for Environmental Management of Military Lands, Colorado State University (CMML), and the standardized herbarium acronyms given in Holmgren et al. 1990. This is mostly a specimen-based flora, and all specimens cited have been seen by RSF unless otherwise noted. Some records are verified by observation, photo documentation, or published report. The name of the collector and the collection number are given. In cases where more than one collector is listed on a label, generally only the first collector's name is given. If no collection number is provided on the herbarium label, then the specimen is identified by the date of collection; for example, *Ezcurra 30 Oct 1982*. When the date of collection is significant, such as collections of historic interest or type collections, both the collection number and date are given. In a few cases the herbarium accession number follows the herbarium abbreviation in order to avoid confusion in the case of multiple specimens of type collections. Spellings of locations and the like generally follow the original herbarium label; spellings of place-names generally follow the gazetteer in Chapter 39 of this volume. The present flora includes numerous new records for the various reserves as well as for the region.

Area designations are as follows: **PI** = Reserva de la Biosfera El Pinacate y Gran Desierto de Altar, **AG** = Reserva de la Biosfera Alto Golfo de California y Delta del Río Colorado, **CP** = Cabeza Prieta National Wildlife Refuge, **GR** = Barry M. Goldwater Air Force Range, **OP** = Organ Pipe Cactus National Monument, **SD** = Sonoran Desert National Monument. Non-native plants are indicated with an asterisk (*). Hwy = Highway. Rd = road. Rte = route. *N Maricopa Mts* refers to mountains in the North Maricopa Wilderness, and *S Maricopa Mts* refers to mountains in the South Maricopa Wilderness. *Mainland Mexico* refers to Mexico except the Baja California peninsula and associated islands.

FERNS AND FERN RELATIVES

MARSILEACEAE – WATER-CLOVER FAMILY

Marsilea vestita Hook. & Grev. HAIRY WATER-CLOVER. Annuals or perennial herbs, the leaves like a 4-leaf clover.

PI: Playa S of Tinaja de los Pápagos, *Felger 86-495.* **CP:** Las Playas, *Harlan 408.*

PTERIDACEAE – BRAKE FAMILY

Argyrochosma limitanea (Maxon) Windham subsp. **limitanea** [*Notholaena limitanea* Maxon var. *limitanea*] BORDER CLOAK FERN. Small ferns with short rhizomes.

OP: Pitahaya Canyon, *Nichol 23 Feb 1939.* **SD:** Sand Tank Mts, N end Arrowhead Mt, *Rutman 2003-1129-21.*

Astrolepis cochisensis (Goodd.) D.M. Benham & Windham subsp. **cochisensis** [*Notholaena cochisensis* Goodd.] SCALY STAR FERN. Small, sword-leaved ferns.

PI: NE base Pinacate Peak, *Felger 92-89.* **CP:** Childs Mt, *Felger 93-29.* **GR:** Tinajas Altas, above 1500 ft, *Van Devender 10 Mar 1980.* **OP:** Quitobaquito, *Darrow 2418.* **SD:** Javelina Mt, *Felger 00-69.*

Astrolepis sinuata (Lag. ex Sw.) D.M. Benham & Windham subsp. **sinuata** [*Notholaena sinuata* (Lag. ex Sw.) Kaulf.] WAVY STAR FERN. Robust, sword-leaved ferns.

PI: NE base of Pinacate Peak, *Felger 92-90.* **GR:** Tom Thumb, *Felger 02-91.* **OP:** Arch Canyon, *Felger 90-568.* **SD:** Javelina Mt, *Felger 00-68.*

Bommeria hispida (Mett. ex Kuhn) Underw. COPPER FERN. Small ferns with long rhizomes and hairy, leaves pentagonal in outline.

OP: Santa Rosa Peak, *Steenbergh 1 Mar 1962* (ORPI).

Cheilanthes lindheimeri Hook. FAIRY SWORDS. Small, sword-leaved, rhizomatous ferns with gray foliage.

GR: Tom Thumb, *Felger 02-103.* **OP:** Arch Canyon, *Felger 90-559.* **SD:** S Maricopa Mts, *Felger 03-446.*

Cheilanthes parryi (D.C. Eaton) Domin [*Notholaena parryi* D.C. Eaton] PARRY'S LIP FERN. Small desert ferns with short rhizomes and small, gray hairy leaves.

PI: Sierra del Rosario, *Búrquez 14 Mar 1991.* **CP:** Tule Mts, *Felger 92-47.* **GR:** Borrego Canyon, *Felger 92-618.* **OP:** Kino Peak, *Wirt 5 Dec 1990.* **SD:** N Maricopa Mts, *Felger 01-176.*

Cheilanthes villosa Davenp. ex Maxon. VILLOUS LIP FERN. Small tufted ferns.

GR: Sand Tank Mts, *Darrow 13 May 2003.* **OP:** Trail above Bull Pasture, 4025 ft, *Felger 05-267.* **SD:** Table Top Mts, *Felger 01-276.*

Cheilanthes wrightii Hook. WRIGHT'S LIP FERN. Small ferns with long rhizomes.

GR: 4 km N of Coffeepot Mt, *Baker 12235* (ASU). **OP:** Arch Canyon, *Felger 90-567.* **SD:** S Maricopa Mts, *Felger 03-448.*

Cheilanthes yavapensis T. Reeves ex Windham. YAVAPAI LIP FERN. Small ferns with long rhizomes and elongated leaves.

GR: Sand Tank Mts, *Felger 01-388.* **OP:** Above Pitahaya Canyon, *Phillips 76-6.* **SD:** Table Top Mts, *Smith 21 Apr 2003.*

Notholaena californica D.C. Eaton subsp. **californica** [*Cheilanthes deserti* Mickel] INDIAN FERN, CALIFORNIA CLOAK FERN. Small tufted desert ferns with beadlike leaf divisions.

PI: Tinajas de Emilia, *Felger 87-38.* **CP:** Tule Mts, *Felger 92-46.* **GR:** Tinajas Altas, *Reeves 5353* (ASU). **OP:** Quitobaquito, *Felger 88-135* (ORPI).

Notholaena standleyi Maxon [*Cheilanthes standleyi* (Maxon) Mickel] STAR CLOAK FERN. Small tufted desert ferns with leaves pentagonal in outline.

PI: Sierra de los Tanques, *Felger 89-17.* **CP:** Agua Dulce Tank, *Felger 92-575.* **GR:** Tom Thumb, *Felger 02-88.* **OP:** Quitobaquito, *Darrow 2421.* **SD:** Table Top Mts, *Reeves 6405* (ASU).

Pellaea mucronata (D.C. Eaton) D.C. Eaton. BIRD'S-FOOT CLIFFBRAKE. Tufted rock ferns with short rhizomes and firm leaflets.

PI: N side of Pinacate Peak, *Felger 87-51.*

Pellaea truncata Goodd. CLIFFBRAKE. Tufted rock ferns with short rhizomes and firm leaflets.

GR: Sand Tank Mts, *Felger 95-381.* **OP:** Pitahaya Canyon, *Nichol 23 Feb 1939.* **SD:** Table Top Mts, *Felger 01-275.*

Pentagramma triangularis (Kaulf.) Yatsk. et al. var. **maxonii** (Weath.) Yatsk. et al. [*Pityrogramma triangularis* (Kaulf.) Maxon var. *maxonii* Weath.] SILVERBACK FERN. Small tufted ferns.

GR: Sand Tank Mts above Bender Spring, *Holm 15 Mar 2003.* **OP:** Alamo Canyon, *Darrow 3849.*

SELAGINELLACEAE – SPIKE-MOSS FAMILY

Selaginella arizonica Maxon. ARIZONA SPIKE-MOSS; FLOR DE PIEDRA. Matlike plants with scale-like leaves.

CP: Below Agua Dulce Pass, *Felger 92-578.* **GR:** Thanksgiving Day Tank, *Felger 02-116.* **OP:** Bull Pasture trail, *Bezy 25 Oct 1964.* **SD:** W side Javelina Mt, *Rutman 2003-123.*

Selaginella eremophila Maxon. DESERT SPIKE-MOSS; FLOR DE PIEDRA. Matlike plants with scale-like leaves.

PI: Sierra de los Tanques, *Felger 89-28.* **CP:** Eagle Tank, *Felger 92-585.* **GR:** Tinajas Altas Mts, *Felger 90-1.* **OP:** Quitobaquito, *Felger 88 113.*

GYMNOSPERMS – CONE-BEARING PLANTS
CUPRESSACEAE – CYPRESS FAMILY

Juniperus coahuilensis (Martínez) R.P. Adams [*J. erythrocarpa* Cory var. *coahuilensis* Martínez; *J. monosperma* (Engelm.) Sarg. of authors] ROSEBERRY JUNIPER; HUATA, TÁSCATE. Shrubs or small trees with scale leaves.

GR: 1 mi SW of Squaw Tit Peak, 2 Jan 1995, *Jim Malusa,* observation. **OP:** Arch Canyon, *Felger 90-508.* **SD:** Table Top Mts, N side, 21 Apr 2003, *Peter Morrison,* photos.

EPHEDRACEAE – EPHEDRA FAMILY

Ephedra aspera Engelm. ex S. Watson. BOUNDARY EPHEDRA, MORMON TEA; TEPOPOTE. Woody shrubs, often appearing leafless, with scale leaves in 2's.

PI: Sierra Pinacate, *Felger 18659.* **CP:** Childs Mt, *Felger 93-46.* **GR:** Hat Mt, *Felger 03-200.* **OP:** Near Quitobaquito, *Ranzoni 13 Jul 1962* (ORPI). **SD:** S Maricopa Mts, *Felger 01-160.*

Ephedra trifurca Torr. ex S. Watson. LONGLEAF JOINT FIR, MORMON TEA; CANUTILLO, TEPOPOTE. Robust shrubs with scale leaves in 3's.

PI: S of Moon Crater, *Felger 19009.* **AG:** E of López Collada, *Felger 03-590.* **GR:** Mohawk Dunes, *Van Devender 8 Mar 1980.*

ANGIOSPERMS – FLOWERING PLANTS
ACANTHACEAE – ACANTHUS FAMILY

Anisacanthus thurberi (Torr.) A. Gray. DESERT HONEYSUCKLE. Shrubs; flowers orange.

GR: Bender Saddle, *Felger 95-394.* **OP:** Alamo Canyon, *Nichol 4 May 1939.* **SD:** Vekol Valley, *Felger 02-320.*

Carlowrightia arizonica A. Gray. LEMILLA. Herbaceous perennials; flowers white and yellow.

PI: Tinaja de los Pápagos, *Felger 86-485A.* **CP:** Cabeza Prieta Tanks, *Lehto L23542* (ASU). **GR:** Sand Tank Mts, *Felger 95-385.* **OP:** Alamo Canyon, *Nichol 4 May 1939.* **SD:** Vekol Valley, *Felger 01-424.*

Dicliptera resupinata (Vahl) Juss. ALFALFILLA. Herbaceous perennials or annuals; flowers pale lavender with white on lip.

GR: Bender Saddle, *Felger 95-405.* **OP:** Canyon Diablo, *Supernaugh 453.*

Justicia californica (Benth.) D.N. Gibson [*Beloperone californica* Benth.] DESERT HUMMINGBIRD-BUSH; CHUPARROSA, MILTLE CIMARRÓN; WIPISIMAL. Shrubs; flowers red-orange.

PI: Tinaja de Tule, *Felger 19228F.* **CP:** Tule Tank, *Goodding 2074.* **GR:** Tinajas Altas, *Shreve 5940.* **OP:** Arch Canyon, *Lockwood 153.* **SD:** Table Top Mts, *Bolton 94-080.*

Justicia candicans (Nees) L.D. Benson [*Jacobinia ovata* A. Gray]. Shrubs; flowers red-orange.

OP: Alamo Canyon, *Nichol 24 Mar 1941.*

Justicia longii Hilsenb. [*Siphonoglossa longiflora* (Torr.) A. Gray]. Small herbaceous perennials; flowers white.

GR: Tom Thumb, *Felger 02-93.* **OP:** Dripping Springs, *Parker 9753.* **SD:** Javelina Mt, *Holm 2001-09-16-8.*

Ruellia nudiflora (Engelm. & A. Gray) Urb. Herbaceous perennials; flowers lavender.

OP: Canyon Diablo, *Supernaugh 431* (ORPI). **SD:** Vekol Valley, *Mauz 20-014.*

AGAVACEAE – CENTURY PLANT FAMILY

Agave ×ajoensis W.C. Hodgs. AJO MOUNTAIN AGAVE. Rare sterile, putative hybrid of *A. deserti* × *A. schottii.* Flowers yellow.

OP: Ajo Mts, *Hodgson 4478* (Holotype, DES).

Agave deserti Engelm. var. **simplex** (Gentry) W.C. Hodgs. & Reveal. DESERT AGAVE; LECHUGUILLA, MEZCAL; 'A'UD. Perennial rosette succulents; flowers yellow.

PI: Sierra Blanca, *Felger 87-17.* **CP:** Tule Mts, Mexican boundary, *Mearns 305* (US, cited by Gentry 1982: 412). **GR:** "Tinaja Altas," *Goldman 2310* (US, not seen, cited by Gentry 1982:412). **OP:** 18 Mile Drive, *West 27 May 1962.* **SD:** Table Top Mts, 24 May 1999, *Mauz,* photo.

Agave schottii Engelm. var. **schottii.** SHIN DAGGER; AMOLILLO; 'UTKO JE:J. Perennial rosette succulents; flowers yellow.

OP: Bull Pasture, *Baker 7758* (ASU).

Hesperoyucca whipplei (Torr.) Baker [*Yucca whipplei* Torr.] SPANISH BAYONET. Perennial rosette succulents; flowers white, massive flower stalk. A small population in Pinacate region is the only occurrence in mainland Mexico.

PI: Sierra del Viejo, *Felger 88-100.*

Yucca baccata Torr. [*Y. arizonica* McKelvey, misapplied] BANANA YUCCA; DÁTIL; HOWIJ. Shrub-size yucca with thick leaves; flowers large and white; fruits fleshy. Mountaintops.

GR: Above Bender Spring, *Holm 11 Apr 2003.* **OP:** Arch Canyon, *Bowers 1297* (ORPI). **SD:** Javelina Mt, 1 Dec 2000, *Felger,* photo.

Yucca elata Engelm. SOAPTREE YUCCA; DÁTIL. Shrub-size yucca with slender leaves; flowers white, on tall stalks. Valley floors; uncommon in the flora area.

SD: Sand Tank Mts, rd to Johnson Well, *Felger 95-333.*

AIZOACEAE – ICEPLANT FAMILY

*****Mesembryanthemum crystallinum** L. CRYSTAL ICE-PLANT; HIELITOS. Cool-season, succulent annuals; flowers white and pink.

AG: Near El Golfo (Felger 2000). Station Beach, Puerto Peñasco, 19 May 1973, *Felger 20865.* **OP:** La Abra Plain, *Rutman 11 May 1995.*

*****Mesembryanthemum nodiflorum** L. SLENDERLEAF ICEPLANT. Cool-season succulent annuals; flowers white. Localized, recent invader in northwestern Sonora and spreading; in southern Arizona at least since 1980s.

CP: Near Corner Well, 11 May 1995, *Rutman,* observation. **OP:** La Abra Plain, *Rutman 11 May 1995.*

Sesuvium verrucosum Raf. WESTERN SEA-PURSLANE. Succulent annuals, mostly with hot weather; flowers pink.

AG: Lerdo, *Price 3 Dec 1898* (DS).

Trianthema portulacastrum L. HORSE PURSLANE; VER-DOLAGA DE COCHI; KAṢVAÑ. Summer annuals; flowers pink-lavender. Possibly not native in New World.

PI: Los Vidrios, 5 Oct 1985, *Felger,* observation. **AG:** Gustavo Sotelo, *Felger 03-531.* **CP:** Adobe Well (cited by Simmons 1966). **GR:** San Cristobal Valley, *Wilson 7 Oct 2002.* **OP:** Quitobaquito, *Felger 88-431.* **SD:** Free-man Rd and Interstate 8, *Felger 01-478.*

ALISMATACEAE – WATER-PLANTAIN FAMILY

Sagittaria longiloba Engelm. ex J.G. Smith. ARROW-HEAD. Perennial aquatic herb; flowers white. Once common, apparently extirpated from the flora area since the demise of Colorado River wetlands.

AG: Near Lerdo, 1889, *Palmer* (US).

AMARANTHACEAE – AMARANTH FAMILY

*****Amaranthus albus** L. TUMBLEWEED PIGWEED. Hot-weather annuals; flowers inconspicuous.

AG: Ciénega de Santa Clara, *Felger 92-527.* **SD:** N of Antelope Peak, *Mauz 21-024.*

Amaranthus crassipes Schltdl. var. **crassipes.** Hot-weather annuals; flowers inconspicuous.

PI: Rancho Los Vidrios, playa, *Equihua 26 Aug 1982.* **CP:** Jose Juan Tank, *Felger 92-713.* **GR:** Coyote Water, *Felger 04-24.* **OP:** Old field, Armenta Well Ranch, *Bowers 1531* (ORPI). **SD:** Vekol Valley, *Smith 18 Apr 2003.*

Amaranthus fimbriatus (Torr.) Benth. ex S. Watson. FRINGED PIGWEED; BLEDO, QUELITILLO; CUHUKKIA I: VAKĬ. Hot-weather annuals; flowers inconspicuous.

PI: MacDougal Crater, *Felger 10440.* **AG:** Gustavo Sotelo, *Felger 03-550.* **CP:** Daniels Arroyo, *Felger 92-663.* **GR:** Sand Tank Mts, *Felger 95-353.* **OP:** Quitobaquito, *Felger 88-416.* **SD:** Vekol Valley, *Mauz 99-075.*

*****Amaranthus obcordatus** (A. Gray) Standl. Hot-weather annuals; flowers inconspicuous. Roadside.

SD: Hwy 238, 2.7 mi W of Mobile, *Felger 02-348.*

Amaranthus palmeri S. Watson. CARELESS WEED, PIG-WEED; BLEDO, QUELITE DE LAS AGUAS; CUHUGIA. Hot-weather annuals; flowers inconspicuous.

PI: Sykes Crater, *Felger 18919.* **AG:** Colorado delta (Castetter & Bell 1951). **CP:** Daniels Arroyo, *Felger 92-665.* **GR:** Bender Spring, *Felger 95-425.* **OP:** Quitobaquito, *Felger 88-441.* **SD:** Vekol Valley, *Mauz 99-082.*

Amaranthus ×**tucsonensis** Henrickson. TUCSON AMA-RANTH. Hot-weather annuals; flowers inconspicuous. An enigmatic amaranth, widely scattered in southwestern U.S. and Mexico, locally in Organ Pipe.

OP: Alamo Canyon, 13 Dec 1939, *Harbison 26249.*

Amaranthus watsonii Standl. CARELESS WEED; BLEDO, QUELITE DE LAS AGUAS. Warm-weather annuals; flowers inconspicuous.

AG: Lerdo, 1889, *Palmer 953 & 958* (US).

Gomphrena sonorae Torr. SONORAN GLOBE-AMARANTH. Herbaceous perennials; flowers inconspicuous.

OP: Bull Pasture, *Henry probably in 1977* (ORPI).

Tidestromia lanuginosa (Nutt.) Standl. subsp. **eliasso-niana** Sánchez-del Pino & Flores Olvera. HONEYSWEET; HIERBA CENIZA, HIERBA LANUDA. Hot-weather annu-als; flowers minute, yellow.

PI: Sykes Crater, *Felger 18974.* **AG:** Gustavo Sotelo, *Felger 03-530.* **CP:** Daniels Arroyo, *Felger 92-666.* **GR:** 8 mi S of N boundary on Hwy 85, *Felger 03-463.* **OP:** Quito-baquito, *Felger 88-408.* **SD:** Johnson Well, *Funicelli 31.*

Tidestromia suffruticosa (Torr.) Standl. var. **oblongifolia** (S. Watson) Sánchez-del Pino & Flores Olvera [*T. ob-longifolia* (S. Watson) Standl.]. Herbaceous perennials; flowers yellow, minute. One locality for mainland Mexico.

PI: Cerro Pinto, S-facing slopes, *Felger 75-41.*

ANACARDIACEAE – SUMAC FAMILY

Rhus aromatica Aiton var. **trilobata** (Nutt.) A. Gray ex S. Watson [*R. trilobata* Nutt.] SKUNKBUSH. Woody shrubs; flowers white.

> **PI:** N side Pinacate Peak, *Felger 87-439*. **GR:** Above Bender Spring, *Holm 11 Apr 2003*. **OP:** Alamo Canyon, *Harbison 25670*.

Rhus kearneyi F.A. Barkley subsp. **kearneyi.** DESERT SUMAC. Large, woody shrubs; flowers white and pink.

> **PI:** Sierra Nina, *Felger 89-47*. **CP:** Cabeza Prieta Mts, *Simmons 27 Sep 1964*. **GR:** Tinajas Altas Mts, 29 Mar 1930, *Harrison & Kearney 6573* (Isotype).

APIACEAE (UMBELLIFERAE) – CARROT FAMILY

Bowlesia incana Ruiz & Pav. HAIRY BOWLESIA. Cool-season annuals; flowers inconspicuous.

> **PI:** Represo Cipriano, *Felger 89-41*. **CP:** Charlie Bell Rd, *Felger 93-50*. **GR:** SE of Gila Bend Auxiliary Field, *Felger 03-72*. **OP:** Quitobaquito, *Felger 86-101*. **SD:** N Maricopa Mts, *Felger 01-174*.

Daucus pusillus Michx. WILD CARROT; ZANAHORIA SILVESTRE. Cool-season annuals; flowers white, minute.

> **PI:** SE of Carnegie Peak, *Felger 19921*. **CP:** Charlie Bell Pass, *Whipple 3922* (CAB). **GR:** Hwy 85 near Maricopa/Pima County line, *Felger 03-9*. **OP:** Quitobaquito, *Felger 88-137*. **SD:** S Maricopa Mts, *Chamberland 1861*.

Eryngium nasturtiifolium Juss. ex F. Delaroche. Cool-season annuals; flowers white, minute. Only one locality in Arizona.

> **PI:** Ciénega 25 mi W of Sonoyta, *Shreve 7604*. **CP:** Las Playas, *Felger 01-567*.

Hydrocotyle verticillata Thunb. var. **verticillata.** WATER PENNYWORT. Herbaceous perennials, emergent aquatic; flowers inconspicuous.

> **AG:** N of El Doctor, *Felger 93-251*.

Lomatium nevadense (S. Watson) J.M. Coult. & Rose var. **pseudorientale** (M.E. Jones) Heller. NEVADA WILD PARSLEY. Small perennial herbs; flowers dull purplish-white. Mountaintops.

> **GR:** Sand Tank Mts, *Holm 4 Feb 2003-15*. **OP:** Ajo Mts, near crestline, *Rutman 2003-333* (ORPI).

Spermolepis echinata (Nutt.) A. Heller. SCALE-SEED. Cool-season annuals; flowers white, minute.

> **CP:** Charlie Bell Rd, *Felger 93-360* (CAB). **OP:** Between Boulder & Arch canyons, *Bowers 1288a* (ORPI). **SD:** NW of Bender Spring, *Felger 01-362*.

Yabea microcarpa (Hook. & Arn.) Koso-Pol. [*Caucalis microcarpa* Hook. & Arn.] FALSE CARROT. Cool-season annuals; flowers inconspicuous.

> **GR:** Above Bender Spring, *Holm 11 Apr 2003*. **OP:** Estes Canyon, *Wirt 1 Apr 1990*. **SD:** NW of Bender Spring, *Felger 01-363*.

APOCYNACEAE – DOGBANE FAMILY

Apocynum cannabinum L. [*A. sibiricum* Jacq.] INDIAN HEMP. Tall herbaceous perennials; flowers white.

> **AG:** La Salina, *Felger 93-15*.

Haplophyton cimicidum A. DC. [*H. cimicidum* var. *crooksii* L.D. Benson. *H. crooksii* (L.D. Benson) L.D. Benson] COCKROACH PLANT; HIERBA DE LA CUCARACHA. Subshrubs with slender stems; flowers bright yellow.

> **GR:** Bender Spring, *Felger 95-434*. **OP:** Estes Wash in side canyon, *Supernaugh 432*. **SD:** Table Top Mts, *Mauz 99-108*.

*ARECACEAE (PALMAE) – PALM FAMILY

***Phoenix dactylifera** L. DATE PALM. Native to North Africa and widely cultivated in the Sonoran Desert.

> ***AG:** La Salina, one tree ca. 6 m tall, planted and persisting, 28 May 2005, *Felger*, observation.

***Washingtonia filifera** (Lindl. ex André) H. Wendl. DESERT FAN PALM. Large, commonly cultivated palms, native in Arizona, Baja California, and California. Planted at La Salina probably in the late 1980s; three about 5 m tall and potentially reproducing, and several smaller ones.

> ***AG:** La Salina, *Felger 05-315*.

ARISTOLOCHIACEAE – BIRTHWORT FAMILY

Aristolochia watsonii Wooton & Standl. INDIAN-ROOT; HIERBA DEL INDIO; ZAPATITO. Herbaceous perennials from thick root; flowers maroon and yellow.

> **CP:** Jose Juan Tank, *Felger 92-709*. **GR:** Hat Mt, *Rutman 23 Nov 2001*. **OP:** Aguajita, *Felger 86-275*. **SD:** Vekol Valley, *Mauz 99-074*.

ASCLEPIADACEAE – MILKWEED FAMILY

Asclepias albicans S. Watson. WHITE-STEM MILKWEED; JUMETE, CANDELILLA. Tall, reed-stemmed perennials, stems semi-succulent; flowers white and pink.

> **PI:** Moon Crater, *Felger 10587*. **CP:** Childs Mt, *Felger 93-300*. **GR:** Tinajas Altas Mts, *Shreve 5941*.

Asclepias erosa Torr. GIANT SAND MILKWEED; HIERBA DEL CUERVO. Robust annuals; flowers greenish white.

> **PI:** E of San Luis, *Felger 90-174*. **CP:** Tule Well, *Felger 92-622*. **GR:** Lechuguilla Desert, *Simmons 21 May 1965*.

Asclepias linaria Cav. NARROWLEAF MILKWEED. Small shrubs; flowers white.

> **OP:** Pitahaya Canyon, *Nichol 23 Feb 1939*.

Asclepias nyctaginifolia A. Gray. MOJAVE MILKWEED. Herbaceous perennials; flowers yellow-white.

> **OP:** Armenta Well, *Wirt 10 Aug 1990*. **SD:** S Maricopa Mts, *Felger 01-210*.

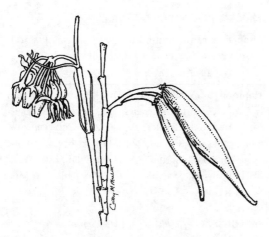

Figure 17.3. Asclepias subulata. *(Drawing by Cathy Moser Marlett)*

Asclepias subulata Decne. RUSH MILKWEED, REEDSTEM MILKWEED; JUMETE, CANDELILLA. Robust reed-stemmed perennials, stems semi-succulent; flowers yellow-white.

PI: Crater de la Luna, *Felger 18639.* **AG:** S of El Doctor, *Ortiz 4 May 1993.* **CP:** Las Playas, *Harlan 447.* **GR:** 8.7 km NNW of Devil Hills, Mohawk Valley, *Arnett 1264* (ASU). **OP:** N of Quitobaquito, *Bowers 1538* (ORPI).

Funastrum cynanchoides (Decne.) Schltr. var. **hartwegii** (Vail) Krings [*F. heterophyllum* (Engelm.) Standl.; *Sarcostemma cynanchoides* Decne. subsp. *hartwegii* (Vail) R.W. Holm] NARROWLEAF CLIMBING MILKWEED; GÜIROTE; VI'IBGAM. Perennial vines; flowers maroon and white.

PI: Hornaday Mts, *Burgess 6861.* **CP:** Papago Well, *Harlan 45* (CAB). **GR:** Butler Mts, *Van Devender 27 Mar 1983.* **OP:** Quitobaquito, *Felger 88-453.* **SD:** Johnson Well, *Funicelli 39.*

Matelea cordifolia Woodson. TALAYOTE. Perennial vines; flowers cream yellow. In U.S. known only in Ajo Mountains.

OP: Canyon Diablo, *Supernaugh 440* (ORPI).

Matelea parvifolia (Torr.) Woodson. Perennial vines; flowers small, brownish or greenish purple.

CP: NE of Little Tule Well, *Felger 94-29.* **GR:** N of Paradise Well, *Smith 12 May 2003.* **OP:** Bull Pasture, *Bowers 1272* (ORPI). **SD:** Table Top Mts, *Bolton 94-092.*

Metastelma arizonicum A. Gray subsp. **arizonicum** [*Cynanchum arizonicum* (A. Gray) Shinners]. Perennial vines; leaves slender and becoming revolute in drought; flowers white, minute.

GR: Tom Thumb, *Felger 02-89.* **OP:** Bull Pasture Trail, *Bowers 947.* **SD:** Javelina Mt, *Felger 00-60.*

ASTERACEAE (COMPOSITAE) – DAISY OR COMPOSITE FAMILY

Acamptopappus sphaerocephalus (Harv. & A. Gray) A. Gray var. **sphaerocephalus.** GOLDENHEAD. Small shrubs; flowers yellow.

OP: Walls Well, *Nichol 28 Apr 1939.*

Acourtia nana (A. Gray) Reveal & R.M. King [*Perezia nana* A. Gray] DESERT HOLLY. Small herbaceous perennials, leaves hollylike; flower heads purplish.

GR: 1.5 mi ENE of Coffeepot Mt, *Butterwick 7416* (ASU). **OP:** Headquarters, *Supernaugh 1 May 1948* (ORPI). **SD:** Vekol Valley, *Mauz 99-133.*

Acourtia wrightii (A. Gray) Reveal & R.M. King [*Perezia wrightii* A. Gray] BROWNFOOT. Tall, herbaceous perennials; flowers lavender.

CP: W of Little Tule Well, *Felger 92-652.* **GR:** Above Bender Spring, *Holm 11 Apr 2003.* **OP:** Bull Pasture, *Bowers 1702.* **SD:** Table Top Mts, *Mauz 21-017.*

Adenophyllum porophylloides (A. Gray) Strother [*Dyssodia porophylloides* A. Gray] DOGWEED. Herbaceous perennials; disk flowers yellow, rays orange-yellow.

CP: Agua Dulce Pass, *Felger 92-735.* **GR:** Hat Mt, *Felger 03-213.* **OP:** Quitobaquito, *Felger 88-447.* **SD:** S Maricopa Mts, *Felger 03-452.*

Ageratina paupercula (A. Gray) R.M. King & H. Rob. [*Eupatorium pauperculum* A. Gray] SANTA RITA SNAKE-ROOT. Herbaceous perennials to ca. 40 cm tall. Flowers heads small, numerous in dense clusters, dull white.

OP: Main canyon N of Alamo Canyon, under oaks, *Gould 4686.*

Ambrosia acanthicarpa Hook. ANNUAL BURSAGE; ESTAFIATE. Annuals, apparently nonseasonal; flowers inconspicuous.

PI: 24 mi SW of Sonoyta on Mex Hwy 8, *Felger 13212.*

Ambrosia ambrosioides (Cav.) W.W. Payne [*Franseria ambrosioides* Cav.] CANYON RAGWEED; CHICURA; ÑUÑUVĬ JEJ. Shrubs; flowers green or yellow.

PI: E of MacDougal Crater, *Felger 10458.* **CP:** Cabeza Prieta Mts, *Van Devender 9 Mar 1980.* **GR:** Tinajas Altas, *Van Devender 9-10 Mar 1980.* **OP:** Quitobaquito, *Mearns 2736* (US). **SD:** Table Top Mts, *Bolton 94-067.*

Ambrosia confertiflora DC. SLIMLEAF RAGWEED; ESTAFIATE; MO'OSTADK. Perennial herbs; flowers green or yellow.

PI: Molina Crater, *Felger 10643.* **CP:** Little Tule Well, *Felger 92-538.* **GR:** Bender Spring Rd, *Felger 95-422.* **OP:** Quitobaquito, *Felger 88-271.* **SD:** Table Top Mts, *Mauz 99-121.*

Ambrosia cordifolia (A. Gray) W.W. Payne [*Franseria cordifolia* A. Gray] SONORAN BURSAGE; CHICURILLA. Small shrubs; flowers green or yellow.

OP: Alamo Canyon, *Tinkham 19 Apr 1942.*

Ambrosia deltoidea (Torr.) W.W. Payne [*Franseria deltoidea* Torr.] TRIANGLELEAF BURSAGE; CHAMIZO FORRAJERO; TAḌSAḌ, va:gita. Small shrubs; flowers green or yellow.

PI: Tinaja Tule, *Felger 18901.* **CP:** Chico Shuni Hills, *Rutman 2003-26.* **GR:** Tinajas Altas, *Van Devender*

26 Mar 1983. **OP:** Quitobaquito, *Nichol 3 Mar 1939* (ORPI). **SD:** Table Top Mts, *Bolton 94-035.*

Ambrosia dumosa (A. Gray) W.W. Payne [*Franseria dumosa* A. Gray] WHITE BURSAGE; CHAMIZO; TAḌSAḌ. Small shrubs; flowers green or yellow.

PI: MacDougal Crater, *Felger 9941.* **AG:** El Golfo, *Burgess 701.* **CP:** Papago Well, *Felger 93-137.* **GR:** Mohawk Dunes, *Reina 96-215.* **OP:** Quitobaquito, *Nichol 3 Mar 1939* (ORPI). **SD:** Table Top Mts, *Bolton 94-037.*

Ambrosia ilicifolia (A. Gray) W.W. Payne [*Franseria ilicifolia* A. Gray] HOLLYLEAF BURSAGE. Shrubs or subshrubs; flowers green or yellow.

PI: Sierra del Rosario, *Felger 20372.* **CP:** Tule Tank, *Goodding 30 Nov 1938.* **GR:** Tinajas Altas, *Vorhies 16 Apr 1924.*

Artemisia dracunculoides Pursh. TARRAGON; ESTRAGÓN. Herbaceous perennials; flowers inconspicuous, minute.

OP: Alamo Canyon, *Goodding 484-45.*

Artemisia ludoviciana Nutt. subsp. **albula** (Wooton) D.D. Keck. WESTERN MUGWEED, WHITE SAGE; ESTAFIATE. Herbaceous perennials; flowers inconspicuous.

PI: Pinacate Peak, *Felger 86-444.* **GR:** Tom Thumb, *Felger 02-95.* **OP:** Alamo Canyon, *Harbison 26269.* **SD:** Table Top Mts, *Felger 01-278.*

Baccharis brachyphylla A. Gray. Low, spreading shrubs; flowers inconspicuous, dull white.

CP: E of Little Tule Well, *Felger 92-533.* **GR:** Tinajas Altas, 5 Dec 1935, *Goodding 1186.* **OP:** Cherioni Wash, *Warren 10 Nov 1983.* **SD:** SW of Big Horn Station, *Felger 95-327.*

Baccharis salicifolia (Ruiz & Pav.) Pers. [*B. glutinosa* Pers.] SEEP WILLOW; BATAMOTE; ṢUṢK KUAGĬ, ṢUṢK KUAGSIG. Leafy shrubs; flowers white.

PI: Pinacate Junction, playa, *Felger 19606.* **CP:** Agua Dulce Spring, *Felger 92-576.* **OP:** Quitobaquito, *Nichol 28 Apr 1939.* **SD:** Vekol Valley, *Felger 01-402.*

Baccharis salicina Torr. & A. Gray [*B. emoryi* A Gray]. Broomlike shrubs; flowers white.

AG: Río Colorado near El Doctor, *Felger 92-1000.*

Baccharis sarothroides A. Gray. DESERT BROOM; ESCOBA AMARGA, ROMERILLO; ṢUṢK KUAGĬ, ṢUṢK KUAGSIG. Broomlike shrubs; flowers white.

PI: 33 mi S[W] of Sonoyta, *Keck 4193* (DS). **CP:** Growler Wash at OP boundary, *Felger 93-78.* **GR:** Ryans Wash, *Felger 02-106.* **OP:** Quitobaquito, *Mearns 2775* (US). **SD:** Vekol Valley, *Felger 02-308.*

Baileya multiradiata Harv. & A. Gray. DESERT MARIGOLD; GI:KO. Nonseasonal annuals or short-lived perennials; flowers yellow.

CP: Daniels Arroyo at Charlie Bell Rd, *Felger 93-74.* **GR:** Crater Range, *Morrison 1055* (ASU). **OP:**

Alamo Canyon, *Tinkham 19 Apr 1942.* **SD:** Vekol Valley, *Felger 01-467.*

Baileya pauciradiata Harv. & A. Gray ex A. Gray. FEW-FLOWERED DESERT MARIGOLD. Spring annuals; flowers yellow.

PI: S of Moon Crater, *Felger 19035A.* **AG:** El Golfo, *Felger 75-81.* **GR:** Mohawk Dunes, *Reichenbacher 601.*

Baileya pleniradiata Harv. & A. Gray ex A. Gray. WOOLLY DESERT MARIGOLD. Annuals, mostly spring; flowers yellow.

PI: MacDougal Crater, *Felger 9901.* **AG:** Gustavo Sotelo, *Ezcurra 14 Apr 1981* (MEXU). **CP:** Las Playas, *Benson 10782.* **GR:** Butler Mts, *Van Devender 27 Mar 1983.* **OP:** Cuerda de Leña Wash, *Bowers 1159* (ORPI).

Bebbia juncea (Benth.) Greene var. **aspera** Greene. SWEETBUSH, CHUCKWALLA DELIGHT; HAUK ʼUʼUS. Small shrubs; flowers yellow.

PI: Tinajas de Emilia, *Felger 19718.* **CP:** Christmas Pass, *Harlan 273* (CAB). **GR:** Tinajas Altas, *Van Devender 5 Mar 1983.* **OP:** Aguajita, *Felger 88-272.* **SD:** Vekol Valley, *Felger 02-307.*

Brickellia atractyloides A. Gray var. **atractyloides.** SPINY-LEAF BRICKELL-BUSH. Small shrubs; flowers pale yellow and purplish.

PI: Sierra del Viejo, *Felger 16879.* **CP:** Eagle Tank, *Felger 92-583.* **GR:** Tinajas Altas, *Kearney 10906.* **SD:** Table Top Mts, *Felger 02-50.*

Brickellia californica (Torr. & A. Gray) A. Gray. CALIFORNIA BRICKELL-BUSH; PACHABA. Small shrubs; flowers whitish, inconspicuous.

GR: Near top of Squaw Tit, *Rorabaugh 27 Nov 1999.* **OP:** Bull Pasture Trail, *Bowers 929* (ORPI).

Brickellia coulteri A. Gray var. **coulteri.** TRIANGLELEAF BRICKELL-BUSH. Small shrubs; flowers yellow and purple.

PI: E of Tinaja Tule, *Felger 19286.* **CP:** Childs Mt, *Felger 93-271.* **GR:** Sauceda Mts, *Felger 03-45.* **OP:** N of Alamo Canyon, *Gould 4689.* **SD:** Table Top Mts, *Bolton 94-045.*

Brickellia frutescens A. Gray. SHRUBBY BRICKELL-BUSH. Semi-shrubby perennials; flowers inconspicuous.

OP: Between Boulder & Arch canyons, *Bowers 1289.*

Calycoseris parryi A. Gray. YELLOW TACKSTEM. Cool-weather annuals; flowers pale yellow.

PI: Pinacate Peak, *Felger 92-446.*

Calycoseris wrightii A. Gray. WHITE TACKSTEM. Cool-weather annuals; flowers white.

PI: E of La Joyita, Mex Hwy 2, *Prigge 7248* (RSA). **CP:** Charlie Bell Rd at Daniels Arroyo, *Felger 93-341.* **GR:** Spook Canyon, *Douglas 891* (ASU). **OP:** Dripping Springs, *Parker 7926.* **SD:** S Maricopa Mts, *Felger 01-211.*

*Carthamus tinctorius L. SAFFLOWER; CÁRTAMO. Spring annuals; flowers bright orange-yellow.

> **PI:** Mex Hwy 2 at rd to Rancho Guadalupe Victoria, *Felger 20405.* **OP:** Quitobaquito, *Bowers 1717* (ORPI).

*Centaurea melitensis L. MALTA STAR-THISTLE. Annuals; flowers yellow, late spring and early summer; locally at some waterholes and roadsides.

> **CP:** Jose Juan Represo, *Felger 92-554.* **OP:** Quitobaquito, *Felger 89-251.* **SD:** Freeman Rd and Interstate 8, *Felger 01-473.*

Chaenactis carphoclinia A. Gray var. **carphoclinia.** PEBBLE PINCUSHION. Cool-season annuals; flowers white to pink.

> **PI:** Elegante Crater, *Felger 19946.* **CP:** Charlie Bell Pass, *Whipple 3942.* **GR:** Tinajas Altas, *Van Devender 26 Mar 1983.* **OP:** N of junction of Bates Well Rd and Puerto Blanco Drive, *Bowers 1118* (ORPI). **SD:** Table Top Mts, trailhead, *Felger 01-327.*

Chaenactis stevioides Hook. & Arn. DESERT PINCUSHION. Cool-season annuals; flowers white to pink.

> **PI:** MacDougal Crater, *Felger 9750.* **CP:** Growler Wash, *Felger 93-369.* **GR:** Mohawk Dunes, *Turner 95-5.* **OP:** Alamo Canyon, *Nichol 14 Mar 1939.* **SD:** Table Top Mts, trailhead, *Felger 01-328.*

Chloracantha spinosa (Benth.) G.L. Nesom var. **spinosa** [*Aster spinosus* Benth. var. *spinosus*] SPINY ASTER. Spiny shrubs, broomlike and nearly leafless; rays white, disk yellow.

> **AG:** Ejido Johnson, 27 May 2005, *Felger,* observation.

Cirsium neomexicanum A. Gray. NEW MEXICO THISTLE; CARDO; GEWEL. Large annuals or biennial herbs; flowers pale lavender.

> **GR:** Sand Tank Mts, *Felger 95-356.* **OP:** N of Alamo Canyon, *Darrow 31 Mar 1948.* **SD:** NW of Bender Spring, *Felger 01-385.*

*Conyza canadensis (L.) Cronquist. var. **glabrata** (A. Gray) Cronquist. HORSEWEED; COLA DEL CABALLO, HIERBA DEL CABALLO. Summer-fall annuals; flowers white, inconspicuous. Uncommon, disturbed habitats.

> **PI:** S of Pinacate Junction, roadside, *Felger 86-383.* **CP:** Jose Juan Represo, *Felger 92-568.* **GR:** Gila Bend Auxiliary Air Force Base, lawn weed, *Felger 03-163.* **OP:** E of Lukeville, *Felger 87-322* (ORPI). **SD:** Smith Rd, *Smith 2 May 2003.*

*Conyza coulteri, see **Laennecia coulteri.**

*Cotula australis (Sieber) Hook.f. Winter-spring annuals; flowers yellow, inconspicuous.

> **GR:** Gila Bend Auxiliary Base, lawn weed, *Felger 03-166.*

Dicoria canescens A. Gray subsp. **canescens** [*D. calliptera* Rose & Standl.] BUGSEED. Nonseasonal annuals; flowers inconspicuous. On dunes.

> **PI:** S of Moon Crater, *Felger 19107B.* **AG:** Sand hills near Adair Bay, 20 Nov 1907, *Sykes 63* (Holotype of *D. calliptera,* US). **GR:** Mohawk Dunes, *Reichenbacher 7 Mar 1980.*

*Dimorphotheca sinuata DC. AFRICAN DAISY. Spring annuals; flowers bright orange and showy. Rare, probably not established.

> **GR:** Ca. 4 mi S of Interstate 8 on State Rte 85, *Rutman 20050306-26.* **SD:** Sand Tank Mts, *Turner 15 Feb 2003.*

Dyssodia concinna, see **Thymophylla concinna.**

Dyssodia porophylloides, see **Adenophyllum porophylloides.**

Dyssodia pentachaeta, see **Thymophylla pentachaeta.**

*Eclipta prostrata (L.) L. [*E. alba* (L.) Hassk.] FALSE DAISY; CHILE DE AGUA, HIERBA DEL TAJO. Warm-weather annuals; flowers white and yellow.

> **AG:** Ejido Johnson, 27 May 2005, *Felger,* observation. **OP:** Quitobaquito, *Niles 724.*

Encelia farinosa A. Gray var. **farinosa** [var. *phenicodonta* (S.F. Blake) I.M. Johnst.] BRITTLEBUSH; INCIENSO, HIERBA DEL BAZO, RAMA BLANCA; TOHAVES. Small shrubs; rays yellow, disk yellow (forma *farinosa*) or purple-brown (forma *phenicodonta*); flowering mostly spring, also with summer-fall rains.

> **PI:** Tinaja Tule, *Felger 18785B.* **AG:** 8 m E of López Collada along RR, *Felger 03-610.* **CP:** N side of Tule Mts, *Felger 92-54a & b.* **GR:** Camino del Diablo, E of Raven Butte, *Felger 01-586.* **OP:** Alamo Canyon, *Nichol 4 May 1939.* **SD:** Table Top Mts, *Bolton 94-048.*

Encelia farinosa × E. frutescens var. **frutescens** [putative hybrid]. Shrubs, rays and disk yellow; occasional.

> **GR:** Camino del Diablo, E of Raven Butte, *Felger 01-586.* **OP:** 2 mi WSW of Bates Well, *Bowers 1131.*

Encelia frutescens A. Gray var. **frutescens.** BUTTON ENCELIA. Small shrubs; flowers yellow.

> **PI:** Rd to Rancho Guadalupe Victoria, *Felger 86-475.* **AG:** NNE of El Golfo, *Felger 92-213.* **CP:** Monreal Well, *Edwards 20 May 1978* (ASU). **GR:** Crater Mts, *Pinkava 10026* (ASU). **OP:** Quitobaquito, *Clark 11477* (ORPI).

Ericameria cuneata (A. Gray) McClatchie var. **spathulata** (A. Gray) H.M. Hall. [*Haplopappus cuneata* A. Gray var. *spathulata* (A. Gray) S.F. Blake] DESERT ROCK-GOLDENBUSH. Perennial herbs; flowers yellow. Crevices in rock walls.

> **GR:** SW of Squaw Tit, T9S, R1W, S11, 2900 ft, *Rutman 16 Mar 2002.* **OP:** Estes Canyon, *Henry 6 Nov 1977* (ORPI).

Ericameria laricifolia (A. Gray) Shinners [*Haplopappus laricifolius* A. Gray] TURPENTINE BUSH. Shrubs; flowers bright yellow.

GR: Tom Thumb, *Felger 02-90.* **OP:** Pitahaya Canyon, *Nichol 23 Feb 1939* (ORPI). **SD:** NW of Bender Spring, *Felger 01-353.*

Erigeron lobatus A. Nelson. DESERT FLEABANE. Cool-season annuals; rays pale violet, disk yellow.

PI: Tinajas de Emilia, *Felger 87-33.* **CP:** Jose Juan Represo, *Felger 92-560.* **GR:** Coyote Water [Well], *Felger 98-118.* **OP:** Quitobaquito, *Felger 86-182.* **SD:** Vekol Valley, *Felger 01-237.*

Erigeron oxyphyllus Greene. Herbaceous perennials; rays white to pale blue, disk yellow. Not known elsewhere in Mexico.

PI: Sierra del Viejo, *Felger 85-733.*

Eriophyllum lanosum (A. Gray) A. Gray. WOOLLY DAISY. Cool-season annuals; rays white, disk yellow.

CP: Charlie Bell Rd, *Felger 93-312.* **GR:** W of Thanksgiving Day Tank, *Rutman 2003-83.* **OP:** Arch Canyon, *Phillips 83-68* (ORPI). **SD:** Table Top Mts, *Bolton 94-001.*

Eupatorium, see **Ageratina** and **Koanophyllon.**

Evax multicaulis DC. var. **multicaulis.** Cool-season annuals, plants small and white-woolly. Flowers minute, inconspicuous; achenes without pappus. Depressions and other places where water temporarily accumulates.

CP: San Cristobal Wash, *Harlan 167.* **OP:** E of Dos Lomitas, *Rutman 2003-438.* **SD:** Vekol Valley, *Felger 01-236.*

Filago arizonica A. Gray [*Logfia arizonica* (A. Gray) Holub] ARIZONA FLUFFWEED. Cool-season annuals; flowers minute, inconspicuous.

PI: Hornaday Mts, *Burgess 6866-A.* **CP:** Jose Juan Tank, *Felger 92-561.* **GR:** Camino del Diablo at Coyote Wash, *Felger 02-9.* **OP:** Aguajita, *Felger 88-274.* **SD:** N Maricopa Mts, *Felger 01-182.*

Filago californica Nutt. [*Logfia californica* (Nutt.) Holub] CALIFORNIA FLUFFWEED. Cool-season annuals; flowers minute, inconspicuous.

PI: W of Tinajas de Emilia, *Felger 19803.* **CP:** Near Agua Dulce Pass, *Felger 92-573.* **GR:** Tinajas Altas, *Van Devender 86-14.* **OP:** Quitobaquito, *Felger 88-128.* **SD:** S Maricopa Mts, *Chamberland 1854.*

Filago depressa A. Gray [*Logfia depressa* (A. Gray) Holub]. Cool-season annuals; flowers minute, inconspicuous.

CP: Pinta Sands at E side of Pinacate Lava, *Felger 93-400.* **OP:** Puerto Blanco Drive, *Bowers 1219* (ORPI). **SD:** N Maricopa Mts, *Felger 01-184.*

Gaillardia arizonica A. Gray [*G. arizonica* var. *pringlei* (Rydb.) S.F. Blake] ARIZONA BLANKET-FLOWER. Spring annuals; flowers showy, yellow. Widely scattered.

PI: 8.5 km NNE of Elegante Crater, *Felger 88-259.* **CP:** Charlie Bell Rd at Daniels Arroyo, *Felger 93-345.*

GR: Crater Range, *Felger 03-386.* **OP:** Dripping Springs, *Parker 7924.* **SD:** 30 mi E of Gila Bend, *Parker 7416.*

Gamochaeta stagnalis (I.M. Johnst.) Anderb. [*Gnaphalium stagnale* I. M. Johnst.] DESERT CUDWEED. Small spring annuals, the flowers inconspicuous. Known in the flora area from only one locality.

OP: Bull Pasture, *Rutman 20050318-9.*

Geraea canescens Torr. & A. Gray. DESERT SUNFLOWER, DESERT GOLD. Coarse spring annuals; flowers bright yellow, sunflower-like.

PI: Sykes Crater, *Felger 18954.* **AG:** NNW of El Golfo, *Felger 92-219.* **CP:** Pinta Sands, *Felger 93-425.* **GR:** Mohawk Dunes, *Turner 95-27.* **OP:** E of Aguajita Wash, *Baker 7773* (ORPI). **SD:** Table Top Mts, *Bolton 94-085.*

Gnaphalium palustre Nutt. [*Filaginella palustris* (Nutt.) Holub] LOWLAND CUDWEED. Cool-season annuals; flowers inconspicuous.

PI: Tinaja de los Chivos, *Felger 18787.*

*****Grindelia squarrosa** (Pursh) Dunal. GUM-PLANT, RESIN-WEED. Coarse winter-spring annuals. Flowers yellow. About one dozen dead plants from previous season in rain-filled cattle pond, probably not native in the region; this is the only Sonoran Desert record for this genus.

SD: Vekol Valley, 11 Jul 2001, *Felger 01-400.*

Gutierrezia arizonica (A. Gray) M.A. Lane [*Greenella arizonica* A. Gray; *Xanthocephalum arizonicum* (A. Gray) Shinners]. Spring annuals; rays white, disk yellow.

CP: Growler Wash, *Felger 93-367.* **OP:** Bates Well, *Nichol 26 Apr 1939.* **SD:** Vekol Valley, *Felger 01-233.*

Gutierrezia microcephala (DC.) A. Gray. STICKY SNAKEWEED. Perennial subshrubs; flowers yellow.

SD: Johnson Well, *Felger 95-335.*

Gutierrezia sarothrae (Pursh) Britton & Rusby. BROOM SNAKEWEED; HIERBA DE LA VÍBORA; SIW TADṢAGĬ. Perennial subshrubs; flowers yellow.

PI: N side of Pinacate Peak, *86-451A.* **CP:** Eagle Tank, *Felger 92-584.* **GR:** Thanksgiving Day Tank, *Rutman 24 Dec 2001.* **OP:** Alamo Canyon, *Baker 7567* (ORPI). **SD:** Table Top Mts, *Felger 01-301.*

Gymnosperma glutinosum (Spreng.) Less. GUMHEAD. Small shrubs or subshrub perennials; flowers yellow.

PI: Sierra Nina, *Felger 89-50.* **CP:** Eagle Tank, *Felger 92-90.* **GR:** Tinajas Altas, *McLaughlin 1969.* **OP:** Pitahaya Canyon, *Nichol 23 Feb 1939.* **SD:** Table Top Mts, *Felger 01-287.*

*****Helianthus annuus** L. subsp. **lenticularis** (Douglas) Cockerell. COMMON SUNFLOWER; GIRASOL, MIRASOL. Nonseasonal annuals; flowers yellow. Uncommon weed, disturbed habitats.

PI: Suvuk, Romero floodwater field, *Nabhan 374.*

Helianthus niveus (Benth.) Brandegee subsp. **tephrodes** (A. Gray) Heiser [*Viguiera sonorae* Rose & Standl.] DUNE SUNFLOWER; MIRASOL DE LAS DUNAS; HI:WAI. Nonseasonal annuals or short-lived perennials; flowers yellow, sunflower-like.

PI: Papago Tanks, 20 Nov 1908 [=1907], *MacDougal 57* (Holotype of *Viguiera sonorae*, US). AG: NNE of El Golfo, 5 Mar 1992, *Felger,* observation. CP: Pinta Sands, *Felger 92-775*. GR: Gila Mts, *Crooks 9200*.

Heterotheca sessiliflora (Nutt.) Shinners var. **thiniicola** (Rzed. & Ezcurra) G.L. Nesom [*Haplopappus thiniicola* Rzed. & Ezcurra; *Heterotheca thiniicola* (Rzed. & Ezcurra) B.L. Turner] GRAN DESIERTO CAMPHORWEED. Cool-season annuals to woody shrubs; flowers yellow. Known only from two nearby dune localities.

PI: 8 km NE de Gustavo Sotelo, 17 Dec 1984, *Ezcurra 84001* (Holotype, ENCB).

Hymenoclea monogyra Torr. & A. Gray ex A. Gray [*Ambrosia monogyra* (Torr. & A. Gray ex A. Gray) Strother & B.G. Baldwin] SLENDER BURROBUSH; JÉCOTA; 'I:VADHOD̦. Upright, broomlike shrubs; flowers straw-colored, fall; in some larger washes.

CP: Growler Wash at OP boundary, *Felger 92-553*. GR: Tenmile Wash, WNW of Deadman Gap, *Morrison 484* (ASU). OP: Aguajita, *Felger 87-261*.

Hymenoclea salsola Torr. & A. Gray ex A. Gray var. **pentalepis** (Rydb.) L.D. Benson [*Ambrosia salsola* (Torr. & A. Gray) Strother & B.G. Baldwin var. *pentalepis* (Rydb.) Strother & B.G. Baldwin] WHITE BURROBUSH; 'I:VADHOD̦. Globose shrubs; flowers straw-colored, spring. Widespread, common.

PI: S of Moon Crater, *Felger 19088*. CP: Bates Wash, Papago Well Rd, *Simmons 7 Mar 1963* (CAB). GR: Crater Range, *Van Devender 18 Mar 1973*. OP: Quitobaquito, *Mearns 2768* (US). SD: Vekol Valley, *Bolton 94-020*.

Hymenothrix wislizeni A. Gray. Annuals or perennial herbs; flowers yellow.

CP: Little Tule Well, *Felger 92-536*. GR: 5 km NW of Coffeepot Mt, *Morrison 1093* (ASU). OP: Aguajita Spring, *Felger 87-266* (ORPI).

Hymenoxys odorata DC. BITTERWEED. Spring annuals; flower yellow.

PI: Ciénega 25 mi W of Sonoyta, *Shreve 7601*. CP: Las Playas, *Felger 93-382*. GR: 10 mi S of Wellton, *Shreve 6235*.

Isocoma acradenia (Greene) Greene [*Haplopappus acradenius* (Greene) S.F. Blake] ALKALI GOLDENBUSH. Small shrubs; flowers yellow. Two varieties.

Isocoma acradenia var. **acradenia** [*Haplopappus acradenius* (Greene) S.F. Blake]

GR: Playa E of Mohawk Dunes, *Reina 96-214*. OP: Quitobaquito, *Bowers 903* (ORPI).

Isocoma acradenia var. **eremophila** (Greene) G.L. Nesom [*Haplopappus acradenius* subsp. *eremophilus* (Greene) H.M. Hall]

AG: Beach cliffs E of El Golfo, *Felger 86-559*. GR: Tenmile Wash, 14 km SW of Sentinel, *Walter 574* (ASU). SD: Vekol Valley, *Felger 01-223*.

Koanophyllon palmeri (A. Gray) R.M. King & H. Rob. var. **palmeri** [*Eupatorium palmeri* A. Gray. *E. solidaginifolium* A. Gray as it occurs west of Texas and north-central Mexico] UMBRELLA THOROUGHWORT. Low, spreading subshrubs or bushy perennials. Flower heads small, whitish, and inconspicuous.

OP: Alamo Canyon, *Nichol 4 May 1939* (ORPI).

*****Lactuca serriola** L. PRICKLY LETTUCE, COMPASS PLANT. Warm-weather annuals; flowers pale yellow.

AG: Ciénega de Santa Clara, *Felger 92-519*. CP: San Cristobal Wash at Camino del Diablo, *Felger 93-375*. OP: Puerto Blanco Drive, *Bowers 1756* (ORPI). SD: N of Antelope Peak, *Mauz 21-026*.

*****Laennecia coulteri** (A. Gray) G.L. Nesom [*Conyza coulteri* A. Gray]. Warm-weather annuals; flowers inconspicuous.

PI: Playa Díaz, *Felger 86-368*. CP: N of Christmas Pass, *Harlan 269* (CAB). GR: Coyote Wash at Camino del Diablo, *Felger 02-14*. OP: Quitobaquito, *Felger 87-291*. SD: Vekol Valley, *Felger 01-430*.

Machaeranthera asteroides (Torr.) Greene var. **glandulosa** B.L. Turner [*Dicentra asteroides* Torr. var. *glandulosa* (B.L. Turner) D.R. Morgan & R.L. Hartman]. Annuals or short-lived perennial herbs to 80 cm tall; rays violet, disk yellow.

OP: Puerto Blanco Drive, *Bowers 1756* (ORPI).

Machaeranthera carnosa (A. Gray) G.L. Nesom var. **carnosa** [*Aster carnosus* (A. Gray) A. Gray ex Hemsl.; *Arida carnosa* (A. Gray) D.R. Morgan & R.L. Hartman] ALKALI ASTER. Semi-herbaceous perennials; flowers yellow. Localized and widely scattered.

PI: Río Sonoyta, S of Cerro El Huérfano, *Felger 92-971*. AG: La Soda, *Felger 86-521*. OP: Quitobaquito, *Felger 86-219*.

Machaeranthera coulteri (A. Gray) B.L. Turner & D.B. Horne var. **arida** (B.L. Turner & D.B. Horne) B.L. Turner [*M. arida* B.L. Turner & D.B. Horne; *M. arizonica* R.C. Jackson & R.R. Johnson; *Arida arizonica* (R.C. Jackson & R.R. Johnson) D.R. Morgan & R.L. Hartman]. Nonseasonal annuals to short-lived herbaceous perennials; rays violet, disk yellow.

PI: 21 mi SW of Sonoyta on Mex Hwy 8, *Bowers 2590*. AG: 10 km W of Gustavo Sotelo, *Felger 84-3*. CP: Tule Well, *Felger 93-435*. GR: Black Gap, *Cooper 553*. OP: Quitobaquito, 31 Mar 1962, *Jackson 3043-2* (Isotype of *M. arizonica*).

Machaeranthera gracilis (Nutt.) Shinners [*Haplopappus gracilis* (Nutt.) A. Gray]. Annuals; flowers yellow.

OP: Trail to Bull Pasture, *Bowers 1698.*

Machaeranthera pinnatifida (Hook.) Shinners var. **gooddingii** (A. Nelson) B.L. Turner & D.B. Horne [*Haplopappus spinulosus* (Pursh) DC. subsp. *gooddingii* (A. Nelson) H.M. Hall; *Sideranthus viridis* Rose & Standl.; *Xanthisma spinulosus* (Pursh) D.R. Morgan & R.L. Hartman var. *gooddingii* (A. Nelson) D.R. Morgan & R.L. Hartman] SPINY GOLDENWEED. Herbaceous perennials, also flowering in first season; flowers yellow.

PI: Pinacate Mts, *MacDougal 21 Nov 1907* (Holotype of *Sideranthus viridis,* US). CP: Charlie Bell Pass, *Whipple 3932.* GR: Borrego Canyon, *Felger 92-617.* OP: Trail to Bull Pasture, *Bowers 1697.* SD: Table Top Mts, *Felger 02-53.*

Machaeranthera tagetina Greene [*Aster tagetinus* (Greene) S.F. Blake]. Annuals, spring-summer; rays violet, disk yellow.

GR: Paradise Well, *Smith 14 May 2003.* OP: Cherioni Well, *McDougall 65* (ORPI).

Malacothrix coulteri A. Gray. SNAKE'S HEAD. Cool-season annuals; leaves and stems semi-succulent, blue-green. Flower heads globose, bracts (phyllaries) silvery with purplish midstripes; flowers pale yellow with pink bases.

SD: Vekol Valley, *Felger 01-229.*

Malacothrix fendleri A. Gray. Spring annuals; flowers yellow.

CP: San Cristobal Wash, Camino del Diablo, *Harlan 153* (CAB). GR: Sand Tank Mts, *Shreve 10157.* OP: Hwy 85 near N boundary, *Bowers 1611* (ORPI). SD: Table Top Mts, summit, *Felger 01-289.*

Malacothrix glabrata (A. Gray ex D.C. Eaton) A. Gray [*M. californica* DC. var. *glabrata* A. Gray ex D.C. Eaton] SMOOTH DESERT-DANDELION. Spring annuals; flowers white and yellow.

PI: MacDougal Crater, *Turner 86-20.* CP: Pinta Sands, *Felger 93-401.* GR: Mohawk Dunes, *Reichenbacher 603.* OP: Aguajita, *Felger 92-115.* SD: S Maricopa Mts, *Felger 01-151.*

Malacothrix sonorae W.S. Davis & P.H. Raven. SONORAN DESERT-DANDELION. Spring annuals; flowers yellow.

PI: Sierra Pinacate, 950 m, *Felger 92-496.* CP: Salazaria Wash, *Harlan 220.* GR: 1.5 km SE of Squaw Tit Peak, *Felger 01-336.* OP: Arch Canyon, *Niles 554.* SD: S Maricopa Mts, *Chamberland 1853.*

***Matricaria discoidea** DC. [*Chamomilla suaveolens* (Pursh) Rydb.] PINEAPPLE WEED, FALSE CHAMOMILE; MANZANILLA. Spring annuals; flowers yellow. Rare in the flora area.

CP: San Cristobal Wash, *Harlan 27* (CAB). SD: Flats E of N Maricopa Mts, *Felger 01-202.*

Monoptilon bellioides (A. Gray) H.M. Hall. MOJAVE DESERTSTAR. Spring annuals; rays white to lavender, disk yellow.

PI: Sykes Crater, *Felger 18955.* CP: Pinta Sands, *Felger 93-430.* GR: Crater Range, *Van Devender 18 Mar 1973.* OP: W base of Ajo Mts, *Benson 10625.* SD: Table Top Mts, *Bolton 94-036.*

Palafoxia arida B.L. Turner & M.I. Morris. Nonseasonal annuals; flowers white to pale pink. Two varieties.

Palafoxia arida var. **arida.** SPANISH NEEDLES.

PI: Sykes Crater, *Felger 18970.* AG: W of El Golfo, *Felger 93-06.* CP: Pinta Sands, *Felger 92-781.* GR: Mohawk Dunes, *Turner 95-4.* OP: Aguajita, *Felger 88-406.*

Palafoxia arida var. **gigantea** (M.E. Jones) B.L. Turner & M.I. Morris. GIANT PALAFOXIA. Robust annuals, mostly in spring. Dunes.

PI: N of Sierra del Rosario, *Felger 20347.*

Parthenice mollis A. Gray. Robust hot-weather annuals; flowers inconspicuous, gray-green.

OP: Estes Canyon, *Bowers 961* (ORPI).

Pectis cylindrica (Fern.) Rydb. Hot-weather annuals; flowers minute, yellow.

PI: Playa Díaz, *Felger 86-367.* CP: Las Playas, *Felger 01-566.* SD: Vekol Valley, *Felger 01-445.*

Pectis linifolia L. var. **linifolia.** Hot-weather annuals; flowers minute, yellow tinged with purple.

OP: East Loop, 3 mi from Rte (Hwy) 85, *Pinkava 9970* (ORPI). SD: Johnson Well, *Funicelli 15.*

Pectis papposa Harv. & A. Gray var. **papposa.** DESERT CHINCHWEED; MANZANILLA DEL COYOTE; BAN MANSANI: YA. Hot-weather annuals; flowers yellow.

PI: Cerro Colorado, *Felger 10803.* AG: Gustavo Sotelo, *Felger 03-557.* NE corner of Reserva AG, *Felger 03-501.* CP: Pinacate Lava, *Felger 92-768.* GR: 2.4 mi WSW of Coyote Peak, *Morrison 426* (ASU). OP: Quitobaquito, *Felger 87-304.* SD: Johnson Well, *Funicelli 29.*

Perityle ajoensis T.K. Todsen. AJO ROCK-DAISY. Herbaceous perennials; flowers yellow. Known only from Ajo Mountains, rock crevices.

OP: Bull Pasture Trail, N face cliff, 22 Oct 1972, *Todsen 2292* (Isotype).

Perityle emoryi Torr. DESERT ROCK-DAISY. Cool-season annuals; rays white, disk yellow.

PI: Elegante Crater, *Felger 19682.* AG: Gustavo Sotelo, *Felger 03-556.* CP: Charlie Bell Pass, *Whipple 3912.* GR: Crater Range, *Van Devender 18 Mar 1973.* OP: Aguajita, *Beale 8 Apr 1988* (ORPI). SD: North of Antelope Peak, *Mauz 21-030.*

Peucephyllum schottii A. Gray. DESERT-FIR, PYGMY-CEDAR; ROMERO DEL DESIERTO. Woody shrubs resembling a dwarf conifer; flowers yellow.

PI: Sierra Extraña, *Felger 19042*. CP: Cabeza Prieta Mts, *Hodgson 2752* (DES). GR: Tinajas Altas, *Van Devender 5 Mar 1983*.

Pleurocoronis laphamioides (Rose) R.M. King & H. Rob. [*Hofmeisteria laphamioides* Rose] ARROW-LEAF. Subshrub perennials; flowers pale yellow.

GR: Thanksgiving Day Tank, *Felger 02-136*. OP: Alamo Canyon, *Baker 7562* (ORPI).

Pleurocoronis pluriseta (A. Gray) R.M. King & H. Rob. [*Hofmeisteria pluriseta* A. Gray] ARROW-LEAF. Subshrub perennials; flowers pale yellow.

PI: Cerro Colorado, *Felger 10779*. CP: Tule Tank, *Darrow & Benson 10804*. GR: Tinajas Altas, *Goodding 2103*.

Pluchea odorata (L.) Cass. var. **odorata** [*P. purpurascens* (Sw.) DC.; *P. camphorata* of various authors, not *P. camphorata* (L.) DC.] MARSH FLEABANE, ALKALI CAMPHORWEED; JARA. Warm-weather annuals or perennial herbs; flowers rose-lavender. Wetlands.

AG: S of El Doctor, *Felger 85-1048*. OP: Quitobaquito, *Anderson 4*.

Pluchea sericea Nutt. [*Tessaria sericea* (Nutt.) Shinners] ARROWWEED; CACHANILLA; KOMAGĬ 'U'US, 'U'US KOKOMAḌK. Woody shrubs; flowers pink.

PI: Pinacate Junction, *Felger 19607*. AG: La Salina, *Felger 86-553*. OP: Quitobaquito, *Nichol 28 Apr 1939*. SD: Cattle tank N of Hwy 238, young plants, rare, *Felger 02-365*.

Porophyllum gracile Benth. ODORA, HIERBA DEL VENADO. Aromatic, herbaceous perennials; flowers purplish or whitish.

PI: S of Pinacate Peak, *Felger 19304*. CP: Chico Shuni Well, *Rutman 2003-19*. GR: Tinajas Altas Mts, *Van Devender 5 Mar 1983*. OP: Quitobaquito, *Felger 88-118* (ORPI). SD: Table Top Mts, *Bolton 94-041*.

Prenanthella exigua (A. Gray) Rydb. Cool-season annuals; flowers minute, white with violet tips.

PI: Sierra Extraña, *Felger 19058*. CP: Agua Dulce Mts, *Darrow & Benson 10753*. GR: Tinajas Altas, *Felger 98-132*. OP: NE of Quitobaquito, *Gould 2990*.

Psathyrotes ramosissima (Torr.) A. Gray. DESERT VELVET. Cool-season annuals; flowers yellow.

PI: S of Pinacate Junction, *Felger 20617*. AG: Mesa de Andrade, *Felger 93-255*. CP: NW of Tule Well, *Yeatts 3246* (CAB). GR: Camino del Diablo, E edge Davis Plains, *Halse 31 Mar 1973*.

Pseudognaphalium canescens (DC.) W.A. Weber [*Gnaphalium canescens* DC.; *G. wrightii* A. Gray] WRIGHT'S CUDWEED. Herbaceous perennials; flowers inconspicuous.

OP: Bull Pasture Trail, *Bowers 1927*.

Psilostrophe cooperi (A. Gray) Greene. PAPER DAISY, PAPER FLOWER. Herbaceous perennials; flowers yellow.

PI: N of Pinacate Peak, *Felger 86-431*. CP: Childs Mt, *Felger 93-302*. GR: 5 mi W of Sand Tanks, *Stitt 5 May 1935* (ASU). OP: S of Growler Well, *Nichol 17 Apr 1939* (ORPI). SD: Big Horn, *Peebles 9981*.

Rafinesquia californica Nutt. CALIFORNIA CHICORY. Cool-season annuals; flower heads white with pale yellow center.

PI: Pinacate Peak, *Felger 19392*. CP: Childs Mt, *Felger 93-299*. GR: SE of Squaw Tit Peak, *Felger 01-337*. OP: Estes Canyon, *Bowers 1203* (ORPI).

Rafinesquia neomexicana A. Gray. DESERT CHICORY. Cool-season annuals; flowers white tinged with pale rose-purple and yellow.

PI: NE of Elegante Crater, *Felger 92-156*. CP: Papago Well, *Felger 93-139*. GR: Tinajas Altas Pass, *McLaughlin 1974*. OP: Alamo Canyon, *Nichol 14 Mar 1939*. SD: S Maricopa Mts, *Felger 01-162*.

Senecio flaccidus Less. var. **monoensis** (Greene) B.L. Turner & T.M. Barkley [*S. monoensis* Greene] SAND-WASH GROUNDSEL; HIERBA CENIZA. Cool-season annuals; flowers yellow.

GR: Tenmile Wash, 0.5 km WSW of Burro Gap, *Walter 209* (CMML). OP: Growler Canyon, *Bowers 1600* (ORPI).

Senecio lemmonii A. Gray. LEMMON GROUNDSEL. Annuals, mostly spring, to weakly perennial; flowers yellow.

CP: Sierra Agua Dulce, *Simmons 24 Jan 1965*. GR: Hat Mt, *Felger 03-198*. OP: Canyon Diablo, *Kearney 10849*. SD: Sand Tank Well, 9 Oct 1995, *Felger, observation*.

Senecio mohavensis A. Gray. MOJAVE GROUNDSEL. Cool-season annuals; flowers yellow.

PI: MacDougal Crater, *Fishbein 913*. CP: Agua Dulce Spring, *Felger 93-91*. GR: Tinajas Altas, *Van Devender 26 Mar 1983*. OP: Quitobaquito, *Gould 2995*.

Senecio pinacatensis Felger. PINACATE GROUNDSEL. Annuals or short-lived subshrub perennials; flowers yellow. Known only from higher elevations on Sierra Pinacate.

PI: N of Pinacate Peak, 935 m, 13 Oct 1986, *Felger 86-426* (Holotype).

Senecio quercetorum Greene [*Packera quercetorum* (Greene) C. Jeffrey]. Herbaceous perennials; flowers yellow.

GR: Above Bender Spring, *Holm 11 Apr 2003*. OP: Boulder Canyon, *Bowers 1284*.

*****Sonchus asper** (L.) Hill subsp. **asper.** SPINY SOW-THISTLE; CHINITA; HO'IDKAM 'I:VAKĬ. Winter-spring annuals; flowers pale yellow.

PI: Tinaja Huarache, *Felger 19556*. CP: Jose Juan Tank, *Felger 93-98*. GR: Coyote Wash at Camino del

Diablo, *Felger 01-10.* **OP:** Quitobaquito, *Felger 87-301.*
SD: N of Antelope Peak, 3 Apr 2001, *Felger,* observation.

*****Sonchus oleraceus** L. COMMON SOWTHISTLE; CHINITA;
HAUVĬ HEHEWO. Winter-spring annuals; flowers pale
yellow.

PI: Tinaja Tule, *Felger 19202.* **AG:** 5 km W of Tornillal, *Felger 05-308A.* **GR:** SW of Midway Peak, *Walter
1365* (ASU). **OP:** Quitobaquito, *Felger 7654.* **SD:** S Maricopa Mts, *Chamberland 1863.*

Stephanomeria exigua Nutt. subsp. **exigua.** WIRE-
LETTUCE. Cool-season annuals; flowers pink.

GR: Crater Range, *Felger 03-389.* **OP:** S of Growler
Well, *Nichol 17 Apr 1939.*

Stephanomeria pauciflora (Torr.) A. Nelson var.
pauciflora. DESERT STRAW. Bushy perennials; flowers
pale pink.

PI: Base of Carnegie Peak, *Felger 19913.* **CP:** Tule
Wells, *Goodding 4 Dec 1935.* **GR:** Tinajas Altas Mts, *Van
Devender 84-144.* **OP:** Aguajita Spring, *Felger 86-293.*
SD: Table Top Mts, *Felger 02-51.*

Stephanomeria schottii (A. Gray) A. Gray. SCHOTT's
WIRE-LETTUCE. Cool-season annuals; flowers white
tinged with violet. Dunes and sand flats, known only
from the flora area in northwestern Sonora and southwestern Arizona.

PI: Moon Crater, *Felger 19274.* **AG:** Gustavo Sotelo,
Ezcurra 14 Apr 1981 (MEXU). **CP:** Pinta Sands, *Lehto
L22764.* **GR:** Mohawk Dunes, *Turner 95-14.*

Stylocline micropoides A. Gray. DESERT NESTSTRAW.
Small spring annuals; flowers minute, inconspicuous.

PI: S of Pinacate Peak, *Felger 19926.* **CP:** Pinta
Sands, *Felger 93-399.* **GR:** Tinajas Altas, *Van Devender 5
Mar 1983.* **OP:** Quitobaquito, *Felger 88-115.* **SD:** S Mari-
copa Mts, *Chamberland 1844.*

Thymophylla concinna (A. Gray) Strother [*Dyssodia
concinna* (A. Gray) B.L. Robinson] DOGWEED; MAN-
ZANILLA DEL COYOTE; BAN MANSANI:YA. Cool-season
annuals, pungently aromatic; rays white, disk yellow.

CP: S edge Agua Dulce Mts, *Niles 341.* **OP:** Quitobaquito, *Felger 88-119.*

Thymophylla pentachaeta (DC.) Small var. **belenidium** (DC.) Strother [*Dyssodia pentachaeta* (DC.) B.L.
Rob. var. *belenidium* (DC.) Strother]. Short-lived herbaceous perennials; flowers bright yellow.

CP: Childs Mt, *Felger 92-636A.* **OP:** North Puerto
Blanco Drive, *Beale 10 Mar 1987* (ORPI). **SD:** Table Top
Mts, *Felger 01-290.*

Townsendia annua Beaman. Small, low-growing annuals; rays white to pink or pale lavender, disk yellow.
Plants resemble *Monoptilon.* Highly localized in the
flora area.

OP: Near Cherioni Well, 9 Apr 1941, *McDougall 64.*

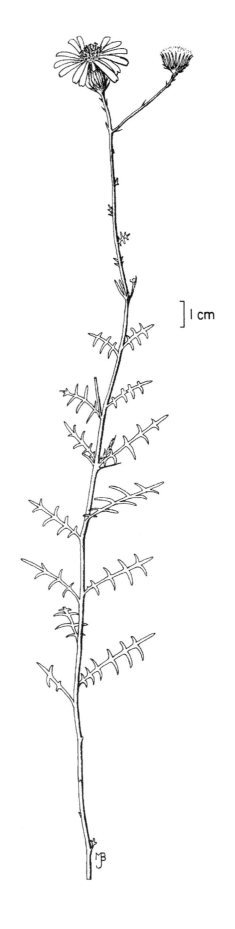

Figure 17.4. Senecio
pinacatensis. *(Drawing
by Matthew B. Johnson)*

] 1 cm

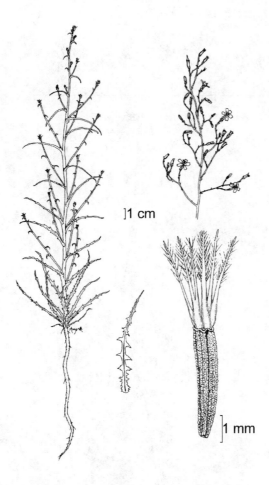

Figure 17.5. Stephano-meria schottii. *(Drawing by Amy Eisenberg)*

]1 cm

]1 mm

Trichoptilium incisum (A. Gray) A. Gray. YELLOW HEAD. Nonseasonal annuals; flowers yellow.

PI: Moon Crater, *Fishbein 911.* **CP:** Cabeza Prieta Tanks, *Simmons 3 May 1964* (CAB). **GR:** Tinajas Altas, *Van Devender 10 Mar 1980.* **OP:** N of Bonita Well, *McDougall 58* (ORPI).

Trixis californica Kellogg var. **californica.** CALIFORNIA THREEFOLD. Small shrubs or subshrubs; flowers yellow.

PI: Tinaja de los Chivos, *Felger 18814.* **CP:** E of Tule Well, *Reichenbacher 470.* **GR:** Tinajas Altas, *Vorhies 16 Apr 1924.* **OP:** Arch Canyon, *Lockwood 162.* **SD:** Johnson Well, *Funicelli 26.*

Uropappus lindleyi (DC.) A. Gray [*Microseris lindleyi* (DC.) A. Gray; *M. linearifolia* (DC.) Sch.-Bip.] SILVER PUFFS. Winter-spring annuals; flowers yellow.

PI: Sierra Pinacate, *Felger 92-469.* **CP:** Charlie Bell Rd, *Felger 93-352.* **GR:** Above Bender Spring, *Holm 11 Apr 2003.* **OP:** Arch Canyon, *Niles 544.* **SD:** Vekol Valley, *Felger 01-228.*

*****Verbesina encelioides** (Cav.) Benth. & Hook. ex A. Gray. GOLDEN CROWNBEARD. Nonseasonal annuals, stinky; flowers yellow. Disturbed habitats.

AG: El Golfo, empty lot, 27 May 2005, *Felger,* observation. **OP:** Quitobaquito, *Harbison 30 Nov 1939* (SD).

Viguiera parishii Greene [*V. deltoidea* A. Gray var. *parishii* (Greene) Vasey & Rose] PARISH GOLDENEYE; ARIOSA. Small shrubs; flowers yellow.

PI: Tinajas de Emilia, *Felger 19720.* **CP:** Childs Mt, *Felger 93-295.* **GR:** NE of Hat Mt, *Rutman 25 Nov 2001.* **OP:** Arch Canyon, *Niles 546.* **SD:** N Maricopa Mts, *Felger 03-121.*

*****Xanthium strumarium** L. COCKLEBUR; HUACHAPORI; VAIWA. Robust, nonseasonal annuals mostly in hot weather. Female flowers enclosed in a bur. Disturbed habitats.

PI: Rancho los Vidrios, *Ezcurra 26 Sep 1982.* **SD:** Vekol Valley, *Felger 01-401.*

Zinnia acerosa (DC.) A. Gray. DESERT ZINNIA; ZINIA DEL DESIERTO. Dwarf, shrublike perennials; flowers white.

GR: Tom Thumb, *Felger 02-77.* **OP:** Walls Well, *Nichol 28 Apr 1939.* **SD:** Vekol Valley, *Felger 02-337.*

BATACEAE – SALTWORT FAMILY

Batis maritima L. SALTWORT. Succulent perennial herbs or subshrubs; flowers green, inconspicuous. Tidal marshes.

AG: Bahía Adair, *López-Portillo 9 Jul 1984.*

BERBERIDACEAE – BARBERRY FAMILY

Berberis haematocarpa Wooton. RED BARBERRY. Shrubs; flowers yellow.

PI: Pinacate Peak, *Felger 86-451.* **OP:** Pitahaya Canyon, *Nichol 23 Feb 1939.*

Berberis harrisoniana Kearney & Peebles. KOFA MOUNTAIN BARBERRY. Shrubs; flowers yellow. Known only from southwestern Arizona in the Ajo, Sand Tank, and Kofa mountains, and southeastern California in the Whipple Mountains.

GR: 1 mi SW of Squaw Tit Peak, *Malusa 2 Jan 1995.* **OP:** Pitahaya Canyon, *Nichol 23 Feb 1939.*

BIGNONIACEAE – BIGNONIA FAMILY

Chilopsis linearis (Cav.) Sweet subsp. **arcuata** (Fosberg) Henrickson. DESERT WILLOW; MIMBRE. Large shrubs or trees to 8 (10) m; flowers pink to purple and white.

CP: Daniels Arroyo at Charlie Bell Rd, *Felger 92-547.* **GR:** Tenmile Wash, N of Ajo Airport, *Rutman 2003-477.* **OP:** Bates Mts, *Nichol 17 Apr 1939* (ORPI). **SD:** Vekol Valley, *Mauz 21-021.*

BORAGINACEAE – BORAGE FAMILY

Amsinckia intermedia Fisch. & C.A. Mey. var. **echinata** (A. Gray) Wiggins. DEVIL'S LETTUCE, FIDDLENECK; CEDKAM. Cool-season annuals; flowers yellow-orange. Calyx lobes 5, about equal in size; nutlets ragged-edged.

PI: Cerro Colorado, *Felger 93-237.* **CP:** Charlie Bell Rd near E boundary, *Felger 93-58.* **GR:** Tinajas Altas

Mts, *Van Devender 5 Mar 1983.* **OP:** Aguajita, *Felger 88-305.* **SD:** Table Top Mts, *Felger 01-323.*

Amsinckia tessellata A. Gray. CHECKER FIDDLENECK; CEDKAM. Cool-season annuals; flowers yellow-orange. Calyx lobes 3 or 5, unequal in size; nutlets smooth-edged and bumpy-surfaced.

PI: Vicinity of Carnegie Peak, *Felger 19816.* **CP:** Jose Juan Tank, *Felger 93-104.* **GR:** Camino del Diablo near W boundary, *Felger 93-197.* **OP:** Aguajita, *Beale 8 Apr 1988* (ORPI). **SD:** Table Top Mts, *Bolton 94-012.*

Cryptantha angustifolia (Torr.) Greene. NARROWLEAF CRYPTANTHA, DESERT CRYPTANTHA. Cool-season annuals; flowers white.

PI: Sykes Crater, *Felger 18938.* **AG:** Near Gustavo Sotelo, *Ezcurra 14 Apr 1981* (MEXU). **CP:** Pinacate Lava Fields, *Shreve 6219.* **GR:** Mohawk Dunes, *Turner 95-12.* **OP:** Senita Basin, *Bowers 1093.* **SD:** S Maricopa Mts, *Felger 01-144.*

Cryptantha barbigera (A. Gray) Greene. BEARDED CRYPTANTHA. Cool-season annuals; flowers white.

PI: Elegante Crater, *Felger 19686.* **CP:** Tule Mts, *Kearney 10880.* **GR:** Tinajas Altas, *Felger 98 137.* **OP:** Agua jita, *Felger 88-268.* **SD:** S Maricopa Mts, *Felger 01-143.*

Cryptantha costata Brandegee. RIBBED CRYPTANTHA. Cool-season annuals; flowers white. Dunes; rare in Arizona.

PI: N of Sierra del Rosario, *Felger 89-66.* **AG:** E of El Golfo, *Felger 75-89.* **GR:** Yuma Dunes, 0.4 km N of Mexico border, *Morrison 67* (ASU).

Cryptantha ganderi I.M. Johnst. DUNE CRYPTANTHA. Cool-season annuals; flowers white. Sand flats and dunes, common at interfaces; in Arizona known from only two localities, widespread in Gran Desierto.

PI: Base of Hornaday Mts, *Burgess 6795.* **CP:** Pinta Sands, *Felger 93-388.* **GR:** Mohawk Dunes, *Felger 98-64.*

Cryptantha holoptera (A. Gray) J.F. Macbr. WINGED CRYPTANTHA. Cool-season annuals to short-lived perennial herbs or subshrubs; flowers white.

PI: Sykes Crater, *Felger 18961.* **CP:** Tule Mts, *Benson 10791.* **GR:** SE slopes of Wellton Hills, *Van Devender 14 Jan 1973.*

Cryptantha maritima (Greene) Greene [var. *maritima* and var. *pilosa* I.M. Johnst.] WHITE-HAIRED CRYPTANTHA. Cool-season annuals; flowers white.

PI: Tinajas de Emilia, *Felger 19742.* **CP:** Agua Dulce Mts, *Benson 10758.* **GR:** Tinajas Altas, *Kearney 10905.* **OP:** Aguajita, *Felger 88-269.* **SD:** N Maricopa Mts, *Felger 01-170.*

Cryptantha micrantha (Torr.) I.M. Johnst. subsp. **micrantha.** DWARF CRYPTANTHA. Cool-season annuals; flowers white.

PI: Rd to Rancho Guadalupe Victoria (Grijalva), *Felger 18716-A.* **AG:** NNE of El Golfo, *Felger 92-163A.*

CP: Pinacate Lava Fields, *Shreve 6217.* **GR:** NW Yuma Dunes, 7.4 km N of Mexico border, *Douglas 873* (ASU). **SD:** S Maricopa Mts, 24 Mar 2001, *Chamberland*,photo.

Cryptantha pterocarya (Torr.) Greene var. **cycloptera** (Greene) J.F. Macbr. WING-NUT CRYPTANTHA. Cool-season annuals; flowers white.

PI: Sykes Crater, *Felger 18940.* **CP:** Bassarisc Tank, *Felger 93-123.* **GR:** Tinajas Altas, *Van Devender 5 Mar 1983.* **OP:** Quitobaquito, *Felger 88-122.* **SD:** S Maricopa Mts, *Felger 01-145.*

Cryptantha racemosa (S. Watson ex A. Gray) Greene. Cool-season annuals to short-lived perennial herbs or subshrubs; flowers white.

PI: Hornaday Mts, *Burgess 6519.* **CP:** W of Tule Tank, *Harlan 290.* **GR:** Tinajas Altas, *Van Devender 10 Mar 1980.*

Harpagonella palmeri A. Gray. GRAPPLING-HOOK BORAGE. Cool-season annuals; flowers inconspicuous.

OP: Bull Pasture, *Felger 05-218.*

Heliotropium convolvulaceum (Nutt.) A. Gray [*H. convolvulaceum* var. *californica* (Greene) I.M. Johnst.; *Euploca aurea* Rose & Standl.] MORNING-GLORY HELIOTROPE. Nonseasonal annuals, mostly in warm weather; flowers white.

AG: Sand hills near Adair Bay, 20 Nov 1907, *Sykes 61* (Holotype of *E. aurea*, US). **GR:** Mohawk Dunes, *Van Devender 92-644.*

Heliotropium curassavicum L. [*H. c.* var. *oculatum* (A. Heller) I.M. Johnst. ex Tidestr.] ALKALI HELIOTROPE; HIERBA DEL SAPO; BABAD 'I:VAKĬ, KAKAICU 'I:VAKĬ. Semi-succulent perennial herbs or annuals; flowers white with yellow center fading purplish.

PI: Playa los Vidrios, *Ezcurra 19 Apr 1981* (MEXU). **AG:** La Soda, *Felger 86-523.* **CP:** Agua Dulce Spring, *Felger 92-577.* **GR:** Playa, Mohawk Dunes, *Turner 94-1.* **OP:** Quitobaquito, *Felger 87-298.*

Lappula occidentalis (S. Watson) Greene [*Echinospermum redowskii* (Hornem.) Greene var. *occidentale* S. Watson; *Lappula redowskii* (Hornem.) Greene, misapplied] STICKSEED. Cool-season annuals; flowers pale blue or white.

CP: Charlie Bell Rd, *Felger 93-57.* **GR:** Tenmile Wash at Hwy 85, *Felger 03-31.* **OP:** Quitobaquito, *Felger 86-178.* **SD:** Vekol Valley, *Harrison 8451.*

Lappula texana (Scheele) Britton. Cool-season annuals; flowers white.

SD: Table Top Mts, 3755 ft, *Felger 01-273.*

Pectocarya heterocarpa (I.M. Johnst.) I.M. Johnst. MIXED-NUT COMB-BUR. Cool-season annuals; flowers minute, white.

PI: Tinaja Huarache, *Felger 19125.* **CP:** Charlie Bell Pass, *Whipple 3953.* **GR:** Tinajas Altas, *Van Devender 5*

Mar 1983. **OP:** Quitobaquito, *Felger 86-183.* **SD:** S Maricopa Mts, *Felger 01-149.*

Pectocarya platycarpa (Munz & I.M. Johnst.) Munz & I.M. Johnst. BROAD-WING COMB-BUR. Cool-season annuals; flowers minute, white.

PI: Sykes Crater, *Felger 18948.* **CP:** Heart Tank, *Felger 93-167.* **GR:** Tinajas Altas, *Van Devender 5 Mar 1983.* **OP:** Quitobaquito, *Felger 88-127.* **SD:** Table Top Mts, *Bolton 94-002.*

Pectocarya recurvata I.M. Johnst. ARCHED COMB-BUR. Cool-season annuals; flowers minute, white.

PI: Pinacate Peak, *Felger 19467.* **CP:** Childs Mt, *Felger 93-32A.* **GR:** Sauceda Mts, *Johnson 27 Mar 1960.* **OP:** Quitobaquito, *Felger 88-126.* **SD:** Table Top Mts, *Bolton 94-061.*

Plagiobothrys arizonicus (A. Gray) A. Gray. ARIZONA POPCORN-FLOWER. Cool-season annuals; flowers white.

GR: Hat Mt, *Felger 03-228.* **OP:** Armenta Rd, 2 mi W of Hwy 85, *Rutman 18 Mar 1998* (ORPI). **SD:** S Maricopa Mts, *Felger 01-146.*

Plagiobothrys jonesii A. Gray. Cool-season annuals; flowers white.

GR: Hat Mt, *Felger 03-229.* **OP:** Twin Peaks, *Van Devender 19 Feb 1984.* **SD:** S Maricopa Mts, *Felger 01-142.*

Tiquilia canescens (A. DC.) A.T. Richardson [*Coldenia canescens* A. DC.] WOOLLY CRINKLEMAT. Dwarf, subshrub perennials; flowers lavender.

CP: Childs Mt, *Felger 92-643A.* **GR:** Squaw Tit Mt, *Felger 95-449.* **OP:** NW of Visitor Center, *Bowers 1716* (ORPI). **SD:** Table Top Mts, near summit, *Felger 02-62.*

Tiquilia palmeri (A. Gray) A.T. Richardson [*Coldenia palmeri* A. Gray] PALMER'S CRINKLEMAT. Perennial herbs; flowers lavender.

PI: Moon Crater, *Felger 19029.* **AG:** N of El Golfo, *Felger 75-75.* **CP:** Pinta Sands, *Felger 93-410.* **GR:** Yuma Desert, 15 km N of Mexico border, *Douglas 885* (ASU).

Tiquilia plicata (Torr.) A.T. Richardson [*Coldenia plicata* Torr.] FANLEAF CRINKLEMAT. Perennial herbs; flowers lavender.

PI: Moon Crater, *Felger 19022.* **AG:** El Golfo, *Felger 75-85.* **GR:** Mohawk Dunes, *Felger 93-136.*

BRASSICACEAE (CRUCIFERAE) – MUSTARD FAMILY

Boechera perennans (S. Watson) W.A. Weber [*Arabis perennans* S. Watson] ROCK CRESS. Perennials herbs; flowers pink-purple.

GR: Hat Mt, *Walter 844* (ASU). **OP:** Alamo Canyon, *Bowers 1242* (ORPI).

*****Brassica nigra** (L.) W.D.J. Koch. BLACK MUSTARD; MOSTAZA NEGRA. Cool-season annuals; flowers yellow. Agricultural weed and one record from Organ Pipe.

OP: Alamo Wash-Sonoyta Rd, 22 Apr 1941, *Supernaugh 6* (ORPI).

*****Brassica tournefortii** Gouan. SAHARA MUSTARD, WILD TURNIP; MOSTAZA; MOSTA:S. Cool-season annuals; flowers pale yellow.

PI: Moon Crater, *Felger 18826.* **AG:** E of López Collada, *Felger 84-17.* **CP:** Pinta Sands, *Felger 93-418.* **GR:** Mohawk Dunes, *Turner 95-10.* **OP:** Quitobaquito, *Bowers 1030.* **SD:** Rainbow Valley, *Felger 03-95.*

*****Capsella bursa-pastoris** (L.) Medik. SHEPHERD'S PURSE; HIERBA DEL PASTOR. Cool-season annuals; flowers minute, white. Rare and not established in the flora area.

CP: Bajada S of Tordillo Butte, from discarded hay, did not reproduce, *Felger 92-201.* **GR:** Baker Tanks, "only plant [of this species] seen in area," *Walter 764* (CMML).

Caulanthus lasiophyllus (Hook. & Arn.) Payson [*Thelypodium lasiophyllus* (Hook. & Arn.) Greene]. Cool-season annuals; flowers minute, white.

PI: Chivos Tank, *Felger 18806.* **CP:** Papago Well, *Felger 93-132.* **GR:** Tinajas Altas, *Van Devender 5 Mar 1983.* **OP:** Quitobaquito, *Felger 7673.* **SD:** N Maricopa Mts, *Felger 01-175.*

*****Chorispora tenella** (Pall.) DC. Winter-spring annuals; small pink flowers. Cattle tanks and borrow pits.

SD: North of Antelope Peak, *Felger 01-255.*

Descurainia pinnata (Walter) Britton. TANSY MUSTARD; PAMITA; ṢU'UVAḌ. Cool-season annuals; flowers minute, pale yellow.

PI: S of Pinacate Peak, *Felger 19935B.* **CP:** Childs Mt, *Felger 93-277.* **GR:** Tinajas Altas, *Van Devender 5 Mar 1983.* **OP:** Alamo Canyon, *Nichol 14 Mar 1939.* **SD:** Table Top Mts, *Felger 01-284.*

Dimorphocarpa pinnatifida Rollins [*Dithyrea wislizeni* Engelm., in part] DUNE SPECTACLE-POD. Cool-season annuals; flowers white. Not known elsewhere in Mexico, otherwise in southwestern Arizona.

PI: MacDougal Crater, *Felger 9923.* **AG:** E of Estación López Collada, *Felger 84-13.* **CP:** Pinta Sands, *Felger 92-27.* **GR:** Mohawk Dunes, *Turner 95-7.*

Dithyrea californica Harv. CALIFORNIA SPECTACLE-POD. Cool-season annuals; flowers white.

PI: MacDougal Crater, *Felger 9923.* **AG:** N of El Golfo, *Felger 75-74.* **CP:** Pinta Sands, *Felger 92-27.* **GR:** Mohawk Dunes, *Felger 98-5.*

Draba cuneifolia Nutt. ex Torr. & A. Gray [*D. cuneifolia* var. *integrifolia* S. Watson; var. *sonorae* (Greene) Parish] WEDGELEAF DRABA. Cool-season annuals; flowers minute, white.

PI: S of Pinacate Peak, *Felger 19346.* **CP:** Adobe Windmill, *Felger 93-62.* **GR:** Tinajas Altas, *Van Devender 10 Mar 1980.* **OP:** Quitobaquito, *Nichol 10 Mar 1939.* **SD:** Table Top Mts, *Felger 01-280.*

*****Eruca vesicaria** (L.) Cav. subsp. **sativa** (Mill.) Thell. [*E. sativa* Miller] GARDEN ROCKET, SALAD ROCKET,

ARUGULA. Cool-season annuals; flowers pale yellow to whitish. Often abundant west of Gila Bend during El Niño years.

OP: Bates Well Rd, 1 mi S of N boundary of monument, rare, roadside, *Conner 16 Feb 2005*. **SD:** Interstate 8, 4 mi E of Big Horn Station, roadside, 18 Feb 2005, *Felger*, observation.

Erysimum capitatum (Douglas ex Hook.) Greene [*E. capitatum* var. *purshii* (Durand) Rollins] WESTERN WALLFLOWER. Winter-spring annuals, perhaps short-lived perennials. Flowers yellow-orange.

OP: Alamo Canyon, *Tinkham 15 Apr 1942*.

Lepidium densiflorum Schrader. Cool-season annuals; flowers minute, white.

PI: Pinacate Peak, *Felger 19437*. **GR:** Thanksgiving Tank, *Felger 02-127*. **OP:** Arch Canyon, *Bowers 1063*.

Lepidium lasiocarpum Nutt. SAND PEPPERGRASS; LENTESILLA; KA:KOWANI. Cool-season annuals; flowers minute, white.

PI: Sykes Crater, *Felger 18916*. **CP:** Pinta Sands, *Felger 93-426*. **GR:** Tinajas Altas, *Van Devender 5 Mar 1983*. **OP:** Growler Valley, *Shreve 6203*. **SD:** N of Antelope Peak, *Bolton 94-013*.

Lepidium thurberi Wooton. ARIZONA PEPPERGRASS. Annuals (short-lived perennial herbs elsewhere); flowers white.

OP: Cuerda de Leña Wash, *Bowers 1158*.

Lesquerella, see **Physaria**.

Lyrocarpa coulteri Hook. & Harv. ex Harv. var. **coulteri**. LYRE-POD; BAN CENṢAÑIG. Perennial herbs; flowers yellow-green to yellow-brown.

PI: Sierra Extraña, *Felger 19082*. **CP:** E of Papago Well, *McLaughlin 1034*. **GR:** Tinajas Altas Mts, *Kearney 6563*. **OP:** Quitobaquito, *Felger 86-284*. **SD:** N Maricopa Mts, *Mauz 21-031*.

*****Nasturtium officinale** R. Br. [*Rorippa nasturtium-aquaticum* (L.) Hayek] WATERCRESS; BERRO. Perennial herbs; flowers white. Extirpated from the flora area.

OP: Williams Spring (Felger et al. 1992).

Physaria gordonii (A. Gray) O'Kane & Al-Shehbaz [*Lesquerella gordonii* (A. Gray) S. Watson var. *gordonii*] BLADDERPOD. Cool-season annuals; flowers bright yellow.

SD: Table Top Mts, *Felger 01-309*.

Physaria purpurea (A. Gray) O'Kane & Al-Shehbaz [*Lesquerella purpurea* (A. Gray) A. Nelson] WHITE BLADDERPOD. Cool-season annuals or short-lived perennials; flowers white.

SD: S Maricopa Mts, *Felger 01-154*.

Physaria tenella (A. Nelson) O'Kane & Al-Shehbaz [*Lesquerella tenella* A. Nelson] DESERT BLADDERPOD. Cool-season annuals; flowers yellow.

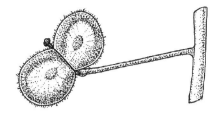
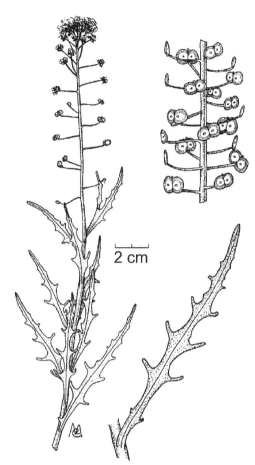

Figure 17.6. Dimorpho-carpa pinnatifida. *(Drawing by Amy Eisenberg)*

2 cm

PI: S of Pinacate Junction, *Felger 20580*. **CP:** Tule Mountains, *Felger 92-60*. **GR:** Tinajas Altas, *Van Devender 5 Mar 1983*. **OP:** N of Sonoyta, *McDougall 15*. **SD:** N Maricopa Mts, *Felger 01-187*.

Sibara angelorum (S. Watson) Greene. Cool-season annuals; flower small and pale lavender. Only record for this species in U.S.

CP: Cabeza Prieta Tanks, canyon, *Lehto L23523* (ASU).

Sibara virginica (L.) Rollins. Cool-season annuals; flowers minute, whitish. Only known locality for this species in the Sonoran Desert.

CP: Las Playas, *Harlan 495*.

*****Sinapis arvensis** L. CHARLOCK. Cool-season annuals; flowers bright yellow. Scarce in the flora area; roadsides.

PI: Mex Hwy 2, W of Sonoyta, *Felger 92-144*.

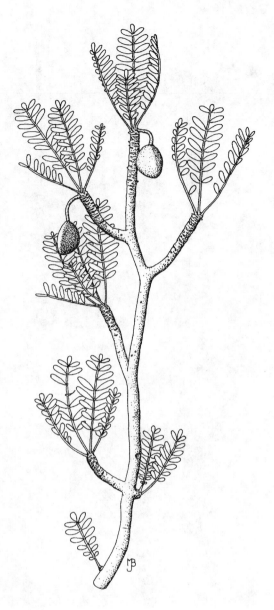

Figure 17.7. Bursera
microphylla. *(Drawing by
Matthew B. Johnson)*

*Sisymbrium irio** L. LONDON ROCKET; PAMITÓN; BAN
CENSAÑIG. Cool-season annuals; flowers yellow.

PI: Pinacate Junction, *Felger 19612.* AG: Ciénega de
Santa Clara, *Ortiz 21 Mar 1993.* CP: Tule Tank, *Felger
92-64.* GR: Tenmile Wash at Hwy 85, *Felger 03-36.* OP:
Canyon Diablo, *Kearney 10830.* SD: Table Top Mts, *Bolton
94-065.*

*Sisymbrium orientale** L. Cool-season annuals; flowers
yellow.

OP: State Rte 85, ca. 6.5 mi N of park headquarters, dozens of plants in imported soil at construction
site, *Rutman 20050315-1.*

Streptanthella longirostris (S. Watson) Rydb. LONG-
BEAK TWIST-FLOWER. Cool-season annuals; flowers
minute, whitish.

PI: MacDougal Crater, *Felger 9700.* CP: Dos Playas,
Felger 93-143. GR: Mohawk Dunes, *Felger 98-7.* OP: Bull
Pasture, *Baker 7701* (ORPI).

Streptanthus carinatus A. Gray subsp. **arizonicus** (S.
Watson) Kruckeb. et al. [*S. arizonicus* S. Watson var.
luteus Kearney & Peebles] ARIZONA JEWELFLOWER. Cool-
season annuals; flowers yellow or white.

GR: Hat Mt, *Felger 03-195.* OP: Arch Canyon, *Niles
548.* SD: Table Top Mts, *Felger 01-295.*

Thelypodiopsis linearifolia (A. Gray) Al-Shehbaz
[*Schoenocrambe linearifolia* (A. Gray) Rollins; *Sisymbrium linearifolium* (A. Gray) Payson] PURPLE ROCK
MUSTARD. Tall, robust perennial herbs; flowers purple,
fading white.

OP: Alamo Canyon *Darrow 3865.*

Thelypodium wrightii A. Gray subsp. **wrightii** [*Stanleya
wrightii* (A. Gray) Rydb.]. Robust cool-season annuals
(perhaps biennials) to 2 m tall; flowers purple and white.

OP: Alamo Canyon, *Goodding 290-41.*

Thysanocarpus curvipes Hook. LACEPOD. Cool-season
annuals; flowers minute, white.

CP: Below Agua Dulce Pass, *Felger 93-93.* GR: Hat
Mt, *Felger 02-203.* OP: Alamo Canyon, *Nichol 14 Mar
1939* (ORPI). SD: Table Top Mts, *Mauz 21-007.*

BURSERACEAE – FRANKINCENSE FAMILY

Bursera microphylla A. Gray. ELEPHANT TREE; TOROTE;
'USABKAM. Treelike shrubs with thick, semi-succulent
limbs, highly aromatic foliage and sap; flowers minute,
white.

PI: MacDougal Crater, *Felger 9755.* CP: Agua
Dulce Mts, *Simmons 9 Oct 1962* (CAB). GR: Tinajas
Altas Mts, *Van Devender 86-12.* OP: Senita Basin, *Baker
7627* (ORPI). SD: Javelina Mt, 3 Dec 2000, *Felger,* photo.

CACTACEAE – CACTUS FAMILY

Carnegiea gigantea (Engelm.) Britton & Rose. SAGUARO;
SAHUARO; HA:ṢAÑ, BAHIDAJ (fruit). Giant columnar
cactus. Flowers white; fruits with small, black seeds in
sweet, edible, red, juicy pulp.

Widespread in **PI, CP, GR, OP, SD.** Not in **AG.**

Cylindropuntia acanthocarpa (Engelm. & J.M. Bigelow)
F.M. Knuth [*Opuntia acanthocarpa* Engelm. & J.M.
Bigelow] BUCKHORN CHOLLA; CHOYA; CIOLIM. Shrub-
size chollas; flowers yellow (gold), orange, reddish, or
purplish on different plants, filaments usually red-
purple. Fruits dry soon after maturity. Two varieties.

Cylindropuntia acanthocarpa var. **coloradensis** (L.D.
Benson) Pinkava. Spines and spine sheaths yellow,
sheaths more inflated; plants more robust and upright
than var. *major.* Replaces var. *major* westward; Lower
Colorado Valley of most of Cabeza Prieta and Tinajas
Altas Mountains.

PI: Cerro Pinto, *Felger 75-91.* **CP:** Buckhorn Tank, 14 Jun 1992, *Felger,* observation. **GR:** Tinajas Altas, 19 Mar 1998, *Felger,* observation.

Cylindropuntia acanthocarpa var. **major** (Engelm. & J.M. Bigelow) Pinkava. Spines yellowish to dark, spine sheaths dark and tightly fitting (not baggy). Differs from var. *coloradensis* by generally being less robust, branches more spreading, joints shorter and more densely spiny. Primarily Arizona Upland of most of Organ Pipe and eastern Cabeza Prieta.

PI: 23 mi W of Sonoyta, *Felger 16854.* **CP:** Agua Dulce Pass, 13 Jun 1992, *Felger,* observation. **OP:** Headquarters, 26 May 1962, *Steenbergh 5-2662-1* (Neotype, POM). **SD:** Bajada W side Table Top Mts, *Felger 02-163.*

Cylindropuntia acanthocarpa × C. leptocaulis [putative hybrid]. Shrub-size chollas, stems green, fruits fleshy; rather rare.

SD: Bajada W side Table Top Mts, *Felger 02-162.*

Cylindropuntia acanthocarpa × C. spinosior. One record known from the flora area.

OP: S of Dos Lomitas, 1.8 m tall, flowers red-purple, *Baker 8366* (SD).

Cylindropuntia arbuscula (Engelm.) F.M. Knuth [*Opuntia arbuscula* Engelm.] PENCIL CHOLLA; SIVIRI; VIPINOI. Shrub-size chollas, rarely 3-3.5 m tall with well-formed trunk; flowers yellow-green; fruits green, fleshy.

PI: S of Pinacate Junction, *Felger 88-261.* **GR:** Tom Thumb Quadrangle, N36 01 400 E3 48 000, 2180 ft, rhyolitic hill, 2 Aug 1996, *Baker 12232* (SD). **OP:** Aguajita, *Felger 88-321.* **SD:** Upper bajada W side Table Top Mts, *Felger 02-169.*

Cylindropuntia arbuscula × C. leptocaulis [putative hybrid]. Shrub-size chollas, stems green, fruits fleshy; rather rare.

SD: Upper bajada, W side Table Top Mts, *Felger 02-168.*

Cylindropuntia bigelovii (Engelm.) F.M. Knuth var. **bigelovii** [*Opuntia bigelovii* Engelm.] TEDDYBEAR CHOLLA; CHOYA GÜERA; HAḌSADKAM (also called HANAMĬ, the general term for cholla). Shrub-size chollas; flowers pale yellow-green; fruits generally dry soon after maturity.

PI: Cactus flat, 32 mi W of Sonoyta, *Lehto 15507* (ASU). **AG:** 2 km W of El Golfo, 6 Jan 1993, *Felger,* observation. **CP:** Agua Dulce Mts, *Benson 10766.* **GR:** Tinajas Altas, *Harbison 6 Mar 1937* (SD). **OP:** Puerto Blanco Mts, *Baker 7588* (ORPI). **SD:** Table Top Mts, 4 Apr 2001, *Felger,* observation.

Cylindropuntia echinocarpa (Engelm. & J.M. Bigelow) F.M. Knuth [*Opuntia echinocarpa* Engelm. & J.M. Bigelow; *O. wigginsii* L.D. Benson] SILVER CHOLLA.

Small chollas, sometimes to 1+ m tall; flowers silvery white, filaments green; fruits dry soon after maturity.

PI: Sierra Blanca, 31 Mar 1988, *Felger,* observation. **AG:** 5 mi W of Gustavo Sotelo, *Felger 20205.* **CP:** E of Tule Well on El Camino del Diablo, *Felger 92-623.* **GR:** Mohawk Dunes, 24 Sep 1996, *Felger,* observation.

Cylindropuntia fulgida (Engelm.) F.M. Knuth [*Opuntia fulgida* Engelm.] JUMPING CHOLLA, CHAIN-FRUIT CHOLLA; CHOYA; HANAMĬ. Shrub- to small tree-size chollas; flowers pink; fruits green, fleshy, in persistent chains. Two varieties.

Cylindropuntia fulgida var. **fulgida** [*O. fulgida* var. *fulgida*]. Common and widespread; very spiny with large, papery-sheathed spines.

PI: Cactus flat, 32 mi W of Sonoyta, *Lehto 15508* (ASU). **AG:** Punta Borrascosa, ca. 1 mi E of lighthouse, 27 May 2005, *Felger,* observation. **CP:** 7 mi E of Papago Well, 14 Mar 1937, *Harbison 17059* (SD). **GR:** Black Gap, 10 Jan 2002, *Felger,* observation. **OP:** Aguajita, *Felger 87-264.* **SD:** 44 mi W of Casa Grande, *Tschirley T-75.*

Cylindropuntia fulgida var. **mamillata** (Schott ex Engelm.) Backeb. [*O. fulgida* var. *mamillata* (Schott ex Engelm.) J.M. Coult.] Spines slender, the sheaths inconspicuous. Rare in flora area.

OP: Near Kuakatch, ca. 2 m tall, 10 Apr 2000, *Rutman,* photo.

Cylindropuntia leptocaulis (DC.) F.M. Knuth [*Opuntia leptocaulis* DC.] DESERT CHRISTMAS CHOLLA; TASAJILLO; ʼAJĬ VIPINOI, CEʼECEM VIPINOI. Small shrub-size chollas; flowers cream-white; fruits small, red, fleshy, midwinter and spring.

PI: Cactus flat, 32 mi W of Sonoyta, *Lehto 15506* (ASU). **CP:** Tule Wells, *Harbison 12 Mar 1937* (SD). **GR:** 2.7 km W of Hat Mt, *Walter 819* (ASU). **OP:** Quitobaquito, *Felger 88-470.* **SD:** Bajada W side Table Top Mts, *Felger 02-165.*

Cylindropuntia ramosissima (Engelm.) F.M. Knuth [*Opuntia ramosissima* Engelm.] DIAMOND CHOLLA. Subshrub to shrub chollas; flowers yellow-brown; fruits very spiny, generally dry soon after maturity.

PI: Cactus flat, 32 mi W of Sonoyta, *Lehto 15505* (ASU). **CP:** Lower Well, *Simmons 17 May 1963* (CAB). **GR:** Camino del Diablo, SE of Raven Butte, *Felger 04-09.* **OP:** W of Bates Mts, *Baker 7776* (ORPI).

Cylindropuntia spinosior (Engelm.) F.M. Knuth [*Opuntia spinosior* (Engelm.) Toumey] CANE CHOLLA. Shrub-size chollas; flowers purple; fruits fleshy, yellow, knobby. Not common in the flora area.

CP: E of Adobe Well, *Felger 92-546.* **OP:** Bates Well Rd, *Felger 90-579.* **SD:** Vekol Valley grassland, *Felger 02-157.*

Cylindropuntia versicolor (Engelm. ex J.M. Coult.) F.M. Knuth [*Opuntia versicolor* Engelm. ex J.M. Coult.]

STAGHORN CHOLLA; SIVIRI. Shrub-size cholla; flowers yellow (in flora area); fruits green and fleshy. Scarcely entering the eastern margin of Dry Borders area.

OP: W of Diablo Mts, *Baker 7752* (ASU).

Echinocactus polycephalus Engelm. & J.M. Bigelow var. **polycephalus**. MANY-HEADED BARREL CACTUS. Multiple-headed, mound-forming barrel cactus; flowers yellow.

PI: SW of Los Vidrios, *Pinkava 15510* (ASU). CP: NE of Tule Well on Christmas Pass Rd, *Felger 92-596*. GR: Mohawk Valley, Christmas Pass Rd, *Turner 95-35*.

Echinocereus coccineus Engelm. [*E. triglochidiatus* Engelm. var. *melanacanthus* (Engelm.) L.D. Benson; *E. santaritensis* W. Blum & Rutow] CLARETCUP CACTUS. Multiple-stem cactus; flowers red, bisexual. Higher elevations in the Ajo Mountains.

OP: Near Mt Ajo, *Baker 14050* (ASU).

Echinocereus engelmannii (Parry ex Engelm.) Lem. STRAWBERRY HEDGEHOG CACTUS; PITAYITA; 'ISVIGĬ. Multiple-stem cactus; flowers deep magenta, large and showy. Two varieties in the flora area.

Echinocereus engelmannii var. **acicularis** L.D. Benson. Plants have fewer major spines than var. *chrysocentrus*.

GR: SSW of Tom Thumb, 2 Feb 2002, *Felger,* observation. OP: Puerto Blanco Drive, *Bowers 1256*. SD: N Maricopa Mts, 3 Apr 2001, *Felger,* photo.

Echinocereus engelmannii var. **chrysocentrus** (Engelm. & J.M. Bigelow) Rümpler. Plants have more major spines than var. *acicularis*.

PI: NE of Elegante Crater, 1 Apr 1988, *Felger,* observation. CP: Agua Dulce Pass, 12 Jun 1992, *Felger,* observation. GR: Tinajas Altas, *Blackwell 709*.

Echinocereus nicholii (L.D. Benson) B.D. Parfitt. GOLDEN HEDGEHOG CACTUS. Multiple-stem cactus; spines yellowish; flower pink.

CP: Childs Mt, *Felger 93-280*. OP: Quitobaquito, *Felger 90-39*.

Echinomastus erectocentrus (J.M. Coult.) Britton & Rose var. **acunensis** (W.T. Marshall) Bravo [*Neolloydia erectocentra* var. *acunensis* (W.T. Marshall) L.D. Benson] ACUÑA CACTUS. Dwarf barrel cactus; flowers rose-pink. Rare. Candidate for federal designation as threatened or endangered.

GR: Vicinity of Coffeepot Mt, *Anderson 93-27*. OP: Acuña Valley, *Supernaugh 2 Jan 1951* (Lectotype, DES). SD: Butte S of Javelina Mt, *Holm 2000-0914-3*.

Ferocactus cylindraceus (Engelm.) Orcutt [*F. acanthodes* (Lem.) Britton & Rose. *F. acanthodes* var. *eastwoodiae* L.D. Benson] DESERT BARREL CACTUS; BIZNAGA; JIAVUL. Unbranched barrel cactus to 1.6 m tall; flowers yellow, orange, or red.

PI: W of Sonoyta on Mex Hwy 2, *Lehto 15487* (ASU). CP: Tule Tank, *Benson 10809*. GR: 2.4 km SE of

Hat Mt, *Arnett 1243* (ASU). OP: Quitobaquito, *Felger 88-456*. SD: Maricopa Mts, *Barr 62-405*.

Ferocactus emoryi (Engelm.) Orcutt [*F. covillei* Britton & Rose] EMORY'S BARREL CACTUS; BIZNAGA; JIAVUL. Unbranched large barrel cactus; flowers red to red-orange.

PI: Presa Cipriano, 11 Feb 1989, *Felger,* observation. CP: Bajada near wash, 19 Mar 1975, *Lehto L18392* (ASU). GR: Tom Thumb, 2 Feb 2002, *Felger,* observation. OP: Quitobaquito, *Nichol 28 Apr 1939* (ORPI). SD: SW of Sand Tank Wash, 32°45′32″N, 112°29′42″W, *Baker 12245* (ASU).

Ferocactus wislizeni (Engelm.) Britton & Rose. COMPASS BARREL, FISHHOOK BARREL CACTUS; BIZNAGA; JIAVUL. Unbranched large barrel cactus; flowers red to red-orange.

PI: "Cactus flat" E of Pinacate Junction, 24 Feb 1990, *Felger,* observation. CP: 7 mi E of Papago Well, *Harbison 20 Mar 1937* (SD). GR: Mohawk Mts, *Salywon 563* (ASU). OP: Quitobaquito, *Felger 88-306*. SD: Table Top Mts, *Loomis & Peebles SF 231*.

Grusonia kunzei (Rose) Pinkava [*Opuntia kunzei* Rose. *O. stanlyi* var. *kunzei* (Rose) L.D. Benson; *Corynopuntia kunzei* (Rose) M.P. Griffiths] DESERT CLUB CHOLLA. Large club chollas; flowers cream.

PI: Cactus flat, 32 mi W of Sonoyta, *Lehto 15504* (ASU). CP: 26 mi S of Copper Mine [Ajo], 1913, *R.E. Kunze* (Holotype, US). GR: Tinajas Altas,9 Mar 1937, *Harbison 17000* (SD). OP: Quitobaquito, *Mearns 2735* (DS).

Grusonia parishii (Orcutt) Pinkava [*Opuntia parishii* Orcutt; *O. stanlyi* var. *parishii* (Orcutt) L.D. Benson; *Corynopuntia parishii* (Orcutt) F.M. Knuth] PARISH CLUB CHOLLA. Low-growing club chollas; flowers cream.

OP: Near N boundary of OP, near Hwy 85, *Felger 88-110*. SD: Bajada W side Table Top Mts, *Puente 2168* (ASU).

Lophocereus, see **Pachycereus.**

Mammillaria grahamii Engelm. [*M. microcarpa* Engelm.] ARIZONA FISHHOOK CACTUS; CABEZA DE VIEJO; BAN 'ISVIG, BAN CEKIDA. Small globose to cylindrical cactus; flowers pink.

PI: 32 mi W of Sonoyta, *Pinkava 15502* (ASU). CP: N side Sheep Peak, 31 Jan 1992, *Felger,* observation (seeds examined). GR: Tinajas Altas, *Reeves 5391* (ASU). OP: Quitobaquito, *Felger 86-173*. SD: Bajada W side Table Top Mts, 26 Mar 2001, *Felger,* photo (seeds examined).

Mammillaria tetrancistra Engelm. CORKSEED FISHHOOK CACTUS. Small globose to cylindrical cactus; flowers pink.

PI: Sierra del Rosario, *Felger 20395*. CP: 4 mi E of Tule Well, *Fugate 688*. GR: Granite hills, SW side Tinajas Altas Mts, *Felger 02-6*. OP: E of Lukeville, *Steenbergh*

1-662-1 (ORPI). **SD:** N Maricopa Mts, 19 Aug 2001, *Chamberland,* photo (seeds examined).

Mammillaria thornberi Orcutt. SLENDER FISHHOOK CACTUS; CABEZA DE VIEJO; BAN MAUPPA. Small globose to cylindrical cactus; flowers pink.

OP: Quitobaquito, *Felger 86-174.* **SD:** Bajada on W side Table Top Mts, *Felger 01-252.*

Mammillaria viridiflora (Britton & Rose) Boed. Small depressed-globose cactus. Flowers probably greenish, yellowish, or pink with lighter margins. Known from only one locality in the flora area.

SD: Sand Tank Mts, partially barren rock headland above 730 m, *Felger 01-372* (growing with the more common *M. grahamii*).

Opuntia basilaris Engelm. & J.M. Bigelow var. **basilaris.** BEAVERTAIL CACTUS. Small prickly pear; flowers rose-pink; relatively dwarfed, with an enlarged caudex and drought-deciduous pads (cladodes).

PI: Cerro Pinto, 11 Feb 1989, *Felger,* observation. **CP:** Bajada of Tordillo Butte, *Felger 92-621.* **GR:** Borrego Canyon, 3 Feb 1990, *Felger,* observation.

Opuntia chlorotica Engelm. & J.M. Bigelow. PANCAKE PRICKLY PEAR; NOPAL RASTRERO. Shrub-size prickly pear; flowers yellow; higher elevations.

PI: "Near summit of Pinacate Mountains" (Rose & Standley 1912:16). **CP:** 7 mi E of Papago Well, *Harbison 16 Mar 1937* (SD). **GR:** Tom Thumb, 2 Feb 2002, *Felger,* observation. **OP:** Ajo Mts, *Nichol 28 Mar 1939* (ORPI). **SD:** Table Top Mts, 17 Mar 1999, *Mauz,* photo.

Opuntia engelmannii Salm-Dyck ex Engelm. DESERT PRICKLY PEAR; NOPAL; NAV, 'I:BHAI (FRUIT). Shrub-size prickly pear; flowers uniformly yellow, fading to pale orange. Two varieties in the flora area.

Opuntia engelmannii var. **engelmannii.** DESERT PRICKLY PEAR. Common and widespread in Arizona Upland region.

CP: Agua Dulce Pass, 13 Jun 1992, *Felger,* observation. **GR:** 1.8 km SSW of Tom Thumb, 2 Feb 2002, *Felger,* observation. **OP:** Quitobaquito, *Felger 90-430.* **SD:** E of Johnson Well, *Felger 01-381.*

Opuntia engelmannii var. **flavispina** (L.D. Benson) B.D. Parfitt & Pinkava. YELLOW-SPINE DESERT PRICKLY PEAR; NOPAL; NAV. Distinguished from previous variety by fewer and yellow spines, often larger fruits, robust habit, branches held well above ground. Scarce; former settlements (Felger et al. 1992; see Chapter 15, this volume).

CP: Agua Dulce Pass, *Felger 92-737.* **OP:** Alamo Canyon, 2300 ft, *Nichol 27 Apr 1939* (Isotype).

*****Opuntia engelmannii** var. **linguiformis** (Griffiths) B.D. Parfitt & Pinkava [*O. linguiformis* Griffiths] COWTONGUE PRICKLY PEAR. Large, sprawling plants with elongated pads. Escaping from cultivation and growing from dumped trash.

OP: Hills between Lukeville and Dowling Ranch, 3 Nov 2003, *Rutman,* observation.

Opuntia phaeacantha Engelm. BROWN-SPINE PRICKLY PEAR; NOPAL. Subshrub prickly pear; flowers yellow with reddish center.

GR: 1.8 km SSW of Tom Thumb, *Felger 02-76.* **OP:** N of Alamo Canyon campground, *Rutman 26 Apr 2002.* **SD:** E of Johnson Well, *Felger 01-380.*

Pachycereus schottii (Engelm.) D.R. Hunt [*Lophocereus schottii* (Engelm.) Britton & Rose var. *schottii*] SENITA; SINITA; CE:MĬ. Multiple-stem columnar cactus; flowers pinkish white. In U.S. only near the Mexico border in Organ Pipe and Cabeza Prieta.

PI: Campo Rojo, *Sanders 5706* (UCR). **CP:** 7 mi E of Papago Well, *Harbison 14 Mar 1937* (SD). **OP:** 1 mi E of Quitobaquito, *Blakley 323* (DES).

Peniocereus greggii (Engelm.) Britton & Rose var. **transmontanus** (Engelm.) Backeb. DESERT NIGHT-BLOOMING CEREUS; REINA DE LA NOCHE, SARRAMATRACA; HO'OK WA:'O. Slender-stem cactus from a large, tuberous root; flowers white. Scarce and widely scattered.

PI: Cactus flat, 32 mi W of Sonoyta, *Lehto 15503* (ASU). **CP:** Near Tule Tank, *Rebman 2890* (ASU). **GR:** Tinajas Altas, *Mearns 2811* (US). **OP:** Aguajita, *Felger 90-574.* **SD:** Big Horn Reservoir rd, *Felger 03-438.*

Peniocereus striatus (Brandegee) Buxb. [*Neoevansia striata* (Brandegee) Sánchez-Mej.; *Wilcoxia diguetii* (F.A.C. Weber) Diguet & Guillaumin] SACAMATRACA, SARRAMATRACA; 'I:KULĬ. Slender-stem cactus, multiple tuberous roots; flowers white. In U.S. only near the Mexico border in Organ Pipe and in the Tohono O'odham lands. Widespread and more common southward in Mexico.

OP: NE of Sonoyta, *Nichol 20 Apr 1939.*

Stenocereus thurberi (Engelm.) Buxb. [*Lemaireocereus thurberi* (Engelm.) Britton & Rose] ORGAN PIPE; PITAHAYA, PITAYA, PITAHAYA DULCE; CUCUVIS. Multiple-stem columnar cactus; flowers white to pink.

PI: Cerros Batamote, 28 Apr 1991, *Felger,* observation. **CP:** Agua Dulce Pass, 13 Jun 1992, *Felger,* observation. **GR:** 5 km N of Coffeepot Mtn and 2 km N of county line, *Baker 12237* (ASU). **OP:** Quitobaquito, *Hodgson 14* (ASU). **SD:** Javelina Mt, *Tibbitts 23 Apr 1994* (ASU).

CAMPANULACEAE – BELLFLOWER FAMILY

Nemacladus glanduliferus Jeps. var. **orientalis** McVaugh. REDTIP THREADSTEM, THREAD PLANT. Diminutive, cool-season annuals; flowers white with red-tipped petals.

PI: Moon Crater, *Felger 19280.* **CP:** Sierra Pinta, *Monson 20 Mar 1958.* **GR:** Crater Range, *Felger 03-388.* **OP:** Bull Pasture Trail, *Bowers 1202.* **SD:** Table Top Mts, *Bolton 94-083.*

Triodanis biflora (Ruiz & Pav.) Greene. SMALL VENUS' LOOKING-GLASS. Diminutive, cool-season annuals. Flowers blue.

OP: Bull Pasture, *Bowers 1278* (ORPI).

CAPPARACEAE – CAPER FAMILY

Atamisquea emarginata Miers ex Hook. & Arn. [*Capparis atamisquea* Kuntze] DESERT TREE-CAPER; PALO HEDIONDO. Shrubs; flowers cream-white.

OP: Aguajita Spring, *Bowers 1335*.

***Cleome viscosa** L. STICKY BEE-PLANT. Hot-weather annuals; flowers yellow. Uncommon, roadsides. In U.S. only near Aguajita and Quitobaquito; common in Sonora.

PI: 19 mi W of Sonoyta on Mex Hwy 2, *Felger 86-338*. **AG:** W of Gustavo Sotelo, *Felger 03-607*.

Isomeris arborea Nutt. var. **angustata** Parish [*Cleome isomeris* Greene] BLADDERPOD BUSH; EJOTILLO. Shrubs; flowers yellow. Known from mainland Mexico only at higher elevations in Sierra Pinacate.

PI: Carnegie Peak, *Felger 86-460*.

Polanisia dodecandra (L.) DC. [*P. trachysperma* Torr. & A. Gray] WESTERN CLAMMYWEED. Hot-weather annuals; flowers lavender.

OP: Hwy 85 and Alamo Canyon Bridge, *Rutman 23 Nov 1994*.

Wislizenia refracta Engelm. JACKASS CLOVER. Herbs to shrubs, foul-smelling; flowers bright yellow. Two subspecies.

Wislizenia refracta subsp. **refracta.** Annual to perennial herbs, leaves with three leaflets.

PI: Elegante Crater, *Soule 31 Jan 1983*. **CP:** Corner Well (cited by Simmons 1966). **OP:** Quitobaquito, *Benson 9935*.

Wislizenia refracta subsp. **palmeri** (A. Gray) S. Keller. Annuals to mostly perennial shrubs, leaves mostly with one leaflet.

AG: Lower Colorado [River; probably near Puerto Isabel], *Palmer in 1889* (Isotypes, US).

CAPRIFOLIACEAE – HONEYSUCKLE FAMILY

***Sambucus nigra** L. subsp. **cerulea** (Raf.) Bolli [*S. cerulea* Raf.; *S. mexicana* Presl ex DC.; *S. neomexicana* Wooton] BLUE ELDERBERRY; TÁPIRO. Small trees; flowers white. One record in the flora area, at former ranch and probably planted.

OP: Alamo Canyon, *Tinkham Apr 1942*.

CARYOPHYLLACEAE – PINK FAMILY

Achyronychia cooperi Torr. & A. Gray. SANDMAT, FROSTMAT. Cool-season annuals; flowers white.

PI: MacDougal Crater, *Burgess 6327*. **AG:** N of El Golfo, *Felger 75-76*. **CP:** Pinta Sands, *Bowers 1578*. **GR:**
Tinajas Altas, *Reichenbacher 605*. **OP:** Growler Mts, foothills, *Parker 7984*.

Cerastium texanum Britton. MOUSE-EAR CHICKWEED. Small, nonseasonal annuals; flowers white.

OP: Bull Pasture Trail, *Bowers 1231* (ORPI).

Drymaria viscosa S. Watson. Small, cool-season annuals; flowers white.

PI: Moon Crater, *Felger 19034*. **AG:** E of Estación López Collada, *Felger 84-15*. **CP:** Pinacate lava flow, *Hodgson 2080* (DES).

***Herniaria hirsuta** L. var. **cinerea** (DC.) Loret & Barrandon. BURST-WORT. Cool-season annuals; small and prostrate; flowers minute, inconspicuous. Disturbed habitats.

OP: Park headquarters, *Felger 03-245*. **SD:** E of N Maricopa Mts, near cattle tank, *Felger 01-201*.

Loeflingia squarrosa Nutt. [*L. squarrosa* subsp. *cactorum* Barneby & Twisselm.] Diminutive, cool-season annuals; flowers inconspicuous.

CP: N end Agua Dulce Mts, *McLaughlin 1951*. **GR:** Tinajas Altas, *Felger 92-608*. **OP:** SW base Santa Rosa Mts, *Felger 03-355*. **SD:** S Maricopa Mts, *Felger 01-495*.

Silene antirrhina L. SLEEPY CATCHFLY. Cool-season annuals; flowers dark red-purple.

CP: Charlie Bell Rd, *Felger 93-330*. **GR:** Thanksgiving Day Tank, *Felger 02-137*. **OP:** Arch Canyon, *Bowers 1193* (ORPI). **SD:** S Maricopa Mts, *Felger 01-206*.

Spergularia salina J. Presl & C. Presl [*S. marina* (L.) Griseb.] SALT-MARSH SAND-SPURRY. Cool-season annuals; flowers pink.

PI: Río Sonoyta W of Sonoyta, *Felger 86-164*. **AG:** Ciénega de Santa Clara, *Felger 90-206*.

CELASTRACEAE – STAFF-TREE FAMILY

Canotia holacantha Torr. CANOTIA, CRUCIFIXION THORN. Small, leafless trees; flowers white; capsules persistent and woody. Higher elevations.

GR: Bender Saddle, N-facing slope, *Felger 95-388*. **SD:** Table Top Mts, *Butterwick 7434* (ASU).

CHENOPODIACEAE – GOOSEFOOT FAMILY

Allenrolfea occidentalis (S. Watson) Kuntze. IODINE BUSH; CHAMIZO DE AGUA. Succulent shrubs, appearing leafless, branching alternate; flowers inconspicuous.

AG: N of El Golfo, banks of Río Colorado, *Felger 75-61*.

Atriplex barclayana (Benth.) D. Dietr. COAST SALTBUSH; SALADILLO. Perennial herbs or subshrubs; flowers inconspicuous.

AG: La Salina, *Felger 86-557*.

Atriplex canescens (Pursh) Nutt. FOUR-WING SALTBUSH; CHAMIZO CENIZO; 'ONK 'I:VAKĬ. Shrubs; flowers inconspicuous.

PI: S of Moon Crater, *Felger 19102*. **AG:** E of López Collada, *Felger 03-583*. **CP:** Packrat Hill, *Felger 93-61*. **GR:** Sand Tank Mts, *Felger 95-355*. **OP:** Alamo Canyon, *Nichol 4 May 1939* (ORPI). **SD:** Table Top Mts, *Felger 01-306*.

Atriplex elegans (Moq.) D. Dietr. [*A. elegans* subsp. *fasciculata* (S. Watson) H.M. Hall & Clem.] WHEELSCALE; CHAMIZO CENIZO; 'ONK 'I:VAKĬ. Warm-weather annuals; flowers inconspicuous.

PI: Playa Díaz, *Felger 88-398A*. **CP:** Tule Well, *Harlan 253* (CAB). **GR:** Entrance, Gila Bend Air Force Auxiliary Field, *Felger 95-331*. **OP:** Quitobaquito, *Felger 86-271*. **SD:** Antelope Peak, *Felger 01-470*.

Atriplex hymenelytra (Torr.) S. Watson. DESERT HOLLY. Subshrubs; leaves hollylike, thickish and whitish; flowers inconspicuous.

GR: Spook Canyon, *Douglas 890* (ASU).

Atriplex lentiformis (Torr.) S. Watson. QUAIL BUSH, LENS SCALE; CHAMIZO GRANDE. Shrubs; flowers inconspicuous.

PI: E side Pinacate region, *Felger 87-30*. **AG:** W of Mesa de Andrade, 23 Mar 1993, *Felger, observation*. **OP:** Quitobaquito, *Nichol 28 Apr 1939* (ORPI).

Atriplex linearis S. Watson [*A. canescens* subsp. *linearis* (S. Watson) H.M. Hall & Clem.] NARROWLEAF SALTBUSH. Small shrubs; flowers inconspicuous.

PI: Moon Crater, *Felger 10589*. **AG:** Ciénega de Santa Clara, *Felger 92-988*. **CP:** Las Playas, 31 Jan 1992, *Felger, observation*. **OP:** Quitobaquito, *Felger 88-450*.

Atriplex pacifica A. Nelson. PACIFIC ORACH. Cool-season to early summer annuals; flowers inconspicuous.

PI: Moon Crater, *Felger 19229*. **CP:** Camino del Diablo, E of Papago Well, *Hodgson 2050*. **OP:** Puerto Blanco Drive, *Bowers 1225*.

Atriplex polycarpa (Torr.) S. Watson. DESERT SALTBUSH; CHAMIZO CENIZO; 'ONK 'I:VAKĬ. Shrubs; flowers inconspicuous.

PI: Moon Crater, *Felger 10586*. **AG:** Gustavo Sotelo, *Felger 03-539*. **CP:** Charlie Bell Well, *Harlan 311* (CAB). **GR:** Camino del Diablo, E of Raven Butte, *Felger 02-04*. **OP:** Quitobaquito, *Felger 5725*.

*****Atriplex rosea** L. Robust annuals or perennial herbs or subshrubs; flowers inconspicuous.

SD: Cattle tank, N of Hwy 238, *Felger 02-364*.

*****Bassia hyssopifolia** (Pall.) Kuntz. SMOTHER-WEED. Warm-weather annuals; flowers inconspicuous.

AG: Ciénega de Santa Clara, *Felger 92-518*.

*****Chenopodium murale** L. NETLEAF GOOSEFOOT; CHUAL, CUHAL; 'ONK 'I:VAKĬ, KAUPDAM. Cool-season annuals, sometimes surviving through summer; flowers inconspicuous.

PI: Tinaja de los Pápagos, *Turner 59-21*. **AG:** Gustavo Sotelo, *Felger 03-523*. **CP:** Tule Tank, *Felger 92-65*.

GR: Tinajas Altas, parking lot, *Felger 98-149*. **OP:** Quitobaquito, *Felger 86-269*. **SD:** Big Horn Station, *Felger 03-82*.

Chenopodium pratericola Rydb. NARROWLEAF GOOSEFOOT. Cool-season annuals; herbage grayish, leaves slender, much longer than wide; flowers minute, inconspicuous. Disturbed habitats.

GR: Tenmile Wash, 1.5 mi E of Hwy 85, gravel, borrow pit, *Rutman 20 Apr 2003*. **SD:** Cattle charco, N of Antelope Peak, *Felger 01-258*.

Chenopodium watsonii A. Nelson. Nonseasonal or spring annuals; flowers inconspicuous; plants stink like dead fish.

GR: Tom Thumb, *Felger 02-83*. **OP:** Alamo Canyon, *Van Devender 31 Aug 1978* (ORPI). **SD:** Table Top Mts, *Felger 02-46*.

Monolepis nuttalliana (Schult.) Greene. POVERTY WEED; 'OPOÑ. Cool-season succulent annuals; flowers inconspicuous.

CP: Redtail Tank, *Felger 93-77*. **GR:** S Tactical Range, E of H.E. Hill, *Felger 03-13*. **OP:** Old ranch, Kuakatch Wash, *Bowers 1160* (ORPI). **SD:** Vekol Valley, *Felger 01-222*.

Nitrophila occidentalis (Moq.) S. Watson. ALKALI WEED. Perennial herbs; stems and leaves succulent; flowers pink.

PI: Río Sonoyta S of Cerro El Huérfano, *Felger 92-980*. **AG:** La Salina, *Felger 86-539*. **OP:** Quitobaquito, *Nichol 28 Apr 1939*.

Salicornia bigelovii Torr. PICKLEWEED. Annuals; member of this genus have opposite-branching, succulent stems, and appear leafless. Tidal marshes.

AG: Bahía Adair, *López-Portillo 9 Jul 1984*.

Salicornia subterminalis Parish [*Arthrocnemum subterminale* (Parish) Standl.]. Shrubs. Margins of tidal marshes and coastal wetlands.

AG: NE of La Salina, *Felger 86-533*.

Salicornia virginica L. [*S. ambigua* Michx. (may be correct name); *S. pacifica* Standl.; *Sarcocornia pacifica* (Standl.) A.J. Scott]. Herbaceous perennials. Tidal marshes.

AG: NE of La Salina, *Felger 86-532*.

*****Salsola tragus** L. [*S. australis* R. Br.; *S. iberica* Senn. & Pau; *S. kali* of authors, not *S. kali* L.] RUSSIAN THISTLE, TUMBLEWEED; CHAMIZO VOLADOR; HEJEL 'E'EṢADAM, VO: PO'ODAM ṢA'I. Warm-season annuals; flowers inconspicuous. Infrequent roadside weed in the flora area.

CP: Childs Mt, *Simmons 30 Oct 1963* (CAB). **GR:** Gila Bend Air Force Auxiliary Field, *Felger 03-77*. **OP:** Quitobaquito, *Felger 88-407*. **SD:** Freeman Rd and Interstate 8, *Felger 01-477*.

Sarcobatus vermiculatus (Hook.) Torr. GREASEWOOD. Shrubs; flowers greenish. Some authors (e.g., Lumholtz

Figure 17.8. Suaeda puertopenascoa. *(Drawing by Kristina Schierenbeck, in Watson & Ferren 1991)*

1912) have applied the common name *greasewood* to creosotebush (*Larrea divaricata*).

AG: W of Gustavo Sotelo, *Felger 84-10*.

Suaeda esteroa Ferren & Whitmore. Annuals or short-lived herbaceous perennials; stems and leaves succulent; flowers inconspicuous. Tidal marshes.

AG: Estero Cerro Prieto, *Felger 86-515*.

Suaeda nigra (Raf.) J.F. Macbr. [*S. moquinii* (Torr.) Greene. *S. torreyana* S. Watson] SEEPWEED; S-CUK ONK. Shrubs; stems and leaves succulent; flowers inconspicuous.

AG: Coast S of Gustavo Sotelo, *Felger 03-615*. **CP:** Tule Well, *Felger 01-544*. **OP:** Quitobaquito, *Darrow 2926*.

Suaeda puertopenascoa M.C. Watson & Ferren. ALTO GOLFO SEEPWEED. Perennial subshrubs; stems and leaves succulent; flowers inconspicuous. Known only from tidal marshes ca. 25 km SE to ca. 40 km NW of Puerto Peñasco.

AG: Estero las Lisas, *Watson 891010-1*.

COMMELINACEAE – SPIDERWORT FAMILY

Commelina erecta L. DAY FLOWER; HIERBA DEL POLLO. Herbaceous perennials; flowers blue.

OP: Bull Pasture trail, *Wilson 191*.

CONVOLVULACEAE – MORNING GLORY FAMILY

Cressa truxillensis Kunth. ALKALI WEED. Perennial herbs; flowers white.

AG: Colorado River, Sonora, opposite mouth of Hardy River, *Mearns 2842* (DS).

Cuscuta californica Hook. & Arn. CALIFORNIA DODDER; FIDEO. Warm-season annual parasitic vines; flowers white.

OP: Bull Pasture, *Bowers 1712*.

Cuscuta salina Engelm. var. **salina.** DODDER; FIDEO; VEPEGĬ VAṢAI. Warm-season annual parasitic vines; flowers white.

OP: Quitobaquito, *Felger 89-241*.

Cuscuta tuberculata Kunth. DODDER; FIDEO; VEPEGĬ VAṢAI. Warm-season annual parasitic vines; flowers white.

PI: Sykes Crater, *Felger 19998*. **GR:** Sauceda Mts, *Arnett 1242* (ASU). **OP:** N of Lukeville, *Felger 10532*.

Cuscuta umbellata Kunth [*C. umbellata* var. *reflexa* Yuncker] DESERT DODDER; FIDEO; VEPEGĬ VAṢAI. Warm-season annual parasitic vines; flowers white.

PI: Sykes Crater, *Felger 20035*. **CP:** Rd to Jose Juan Tank, *Felger 92-740*. **OP:** Armenta Well, *Warren 16 Nov 1974* (ORPI). **SD:** Vekol Valley, *Mauz 99-081*.

Evolvulus alsinoides L. var. **angustifolia** Torr. [*E. alsinoides* var. *acapulcensis* (Willd.) van Oost.] ARIZONA BLUE-EYES; OREJA DE RATÓN. Perennial herbs; flowers blue.

PI: NE of Tezontle Cinder Mine, 14 Sep 1986, *Felger*, observation. **GR:** Sand Tank Mts, *Felger 95-374*. **OP:** Alamo Canyon, *Nichol 26 Mar 1938*. **SD:** Table Top Mts, *Mauz 99-106*.

Ipomoea costellata Torr. Summer annual vines; flowers pink to purple.

OP: Bull Pasture, *Wirt 12 Aug 1990* (ORPI).

Ipomoea cristulata Hallier f. SCARLET CREEPER. Summer annual vines; flowers red.

OP: Arch Canyon, *Wirt 19 Oct 1990* (ORPI).

Ipomoea hederacea Jacq. MORNING GLORY; TROMPILLO; BI:BHIAG. Summer annual vines; flowers blue.

PI: 6 km W of Los Vidrios, *Felger 92-965*. **CP:** San Cristobal Wash, *Felger 92-746*. **OP:** Bull Pasture trail, *Wilson 189*. **SD:** Vekol Valley, *Felger 01-246*.

Jacquemontia pringlei A. Gray. Scandent shrubs or perennial vines; flowers pale lavender.

GR: "South end of Gila Mountains," *Nichol 25 April 1938*. **OP:** Alamo Canyon, *Van Devender 31 Aug 1978* (ORPI).

CRASSULACEAE – STONECROP FAMILY

Crassula connata (Ruiz & Pav.) Berger [*Tillaea erecta* Hook. & Arn.] PYGMY STONECROP. Diminutive, cool-season annual succulents; flowers white.

PI: Elegante Crater, *Felger 19672.* **AG:** 10 km W of Gustavo Sotelo, *Felger 84-2.* **CP:** Below Heart Tank, *Felger 93-162.* **GR:** Camino del Diablo SSE of Raven Butte, *Felger 05-26.* **OP:** Santa Rosa Mts, *Felger 03-356.* **SD:** Table Top Mts, *Felger 01-321.*

Dudleya arizonica Rose. ARIZONA LIVEFOREVER. Perennial rosette herbs, leaves succulent; flowers yellow and orange-red.

PI: Sierra Blanca, *Felger 87-27.* **CP:** Cabeza Prieta Peak, *Simmons 27 Oct 1962.* **GR:** Tinajas Altas, *Vorhies 16 Apr 1924.* **OP:** Canyon Diablo, *Steenbergh 25 Apr 1962* (ORPI).

Graptopetalum rusbyi (Greene) Rose. Small, perennial rosette herbs, leaves succulent; flowers cream-yellow and red-brown.

OP: N of Alamo Canyon, *Darrow 3863.*

CROSSOSOMATACEAE – CROSSOSOMA FAMILY

Crossosoma bigelovii S. Watson. RAGGED ROCK-FLOWER. Shrubs; flowers white.

PI: Sierra del Viejo, *Felger 85-722.* **CP:** Agua Dulce Tank, *Felger 93-86.* **GR:** Borrego Canyon, *Felger 93-194.* **OP:** N end Ajo Mts, *Rutman 15 Apr 1995* (ORPI). **SD:** N Maricopa Mts, *Felger 03-112.*

CUCURBITACEAE – GOURD FAMILY

Apodanthera undulata A. Gray. Perennials, sprawling seasonal vines, herbage stinky; flowers yellow.

SD: Vekol Valley, *Felger 01-407.*

Brandegea bigelovii (S. Watson) Cogn. DESERT STARVINE. Cool-season annual vines; flowers white.

PI: Cerro Colorado, *Webster 22316.* **CP:** Monreal Well, *Felger 92-591.* **GR:** Tinajas Altas, *Goodding 2092.* **OP:** S of Bates Well, *Benson 9932.* **SD:** N Maricopa Mts, *Felger 01-171.*

Cucurbita digitata A. Gray. COYOTE GOURD; CALABACILLA, CHICHICAYOTE; 'ADAVĬ, 'AḌ. Perennial vines from large, tuberous root; flowers yellow.

PI: NE of Pinacate Peak, *Felger 86-419.* **CP:** Daniels Arroyo, *Felger 92-671.* **GR:** Ryans Wash, *Felger 02-105.* **OP:** Armenta Well, *Warren 16 Nov 1974.* **SD:** Big Horn Service Station, *Peebles 9979.*

Cucurbita palmata S. Watson. Like *C. digitata* but leaf segments or lobes much broader and relatively shorter.

GR: Camino del Diablo, E of Raven Butte, *Felger 01-584.*

Echinopepon wrightii (A. Gray) S. Watson. WILD BALSAM APPLE. Warm-weather annual vines; flowers small, white.

OP: Arch Canyon, *Felger 90-563.*

Marah gilensis Greene. BIG ROOT. Robust perennial vines from large tuberous root; flowers white.

OP: Arch Canyon, *Niles 555.*

Figure 17.9. Dudleya arizonica. *(Drawing by Matthew B. Johnson)*

Tumamoca macdougalii Rose. TUMAMOC GLOBEBERRY. Delicate, summer rainy-season vines from tuberous root; flowers yellow.

OP: E of Dos Lomitas, *Baker 7638* (ORPI). **SD:** Vekol Valley, S of Interstate 8 (Reichenbacher 1990).

CYPERACEAE – SEDGE FAMILY

Cyperus esculentus L. var. **leptostachyus** Boeck. YELLOW NUTGRASS; COQUILLO AMARILLO, CEBOLLÍN; VAṢAI ṢU:VĬ. Hot-weather annuals; many rhizomes ending in a small, rounded tuberous root.

PI: Tinaja de los Pápagos, *Felger 86-480.* **AG:** Lower Río Colorado (Kelly 1977). **CP:** Las Playas, *Monson 8.* **SD:** Vekol Valley, *Felger 01-457.*

Cyperus laevigatus L. FLAT SEDGE; COQUITO. Perennial herbs.

AG: La Salina, *Felger 86-549.* **OP:** Quitobaquito, *Gould 2983.*

Cyperus mutisii (Kunth) Griseb. Perennial herbs.

OP: Ajo Mts, near summit, *Clark 10918* (ORPI).

Cyperus squarrosus L. [*C. aristatus* Rottb.] DWARF SEDGE. Nonseasonal annuals; flowers inconspicuous.

PI: Tinaja de los Pápagos, *Felger 86-479*. CP: Las Playas, *Monson 9*. GR: Coyote Water, *Felger 04-41*. OP: N border of Organ Pipe, *Clark 10990* (ORPI).

Eleocharis geniculata (L.) Roem. & Schult. [*E. caribaea* (Rottb.) S.F. Blake] SPIKERUSH; TULILLO. Nonseasonal annuals; flowers inconspicuous.

AG: La Salina, *Felger 93-14*. OP: Quitobaquito, *Darrow 2403*.

Eleocharis rostellata (Torr.) Torr. TRAVELING SPIKERUSH. Herbaceous perennials, rootstocks tough; dense, grass-like, mounded colonies.

AG: N of El Doctor, *Felger 92-250C*. OP: Quitobaquito, *Felger 20591*.

Scirpus americanus Pers. [*S. olneyi* A. Gray of western authors] THREE-SQUARE BULRUSH; TULE; VA:K. Herbaceous perennials; stems triangular to 2+ m tall.

PI: S of Cerro El Huérfano, *Felger 92-973*. AG: La Soda, *Felger 86-520*. OP: Quitobaquito, *Peebles 14564*.

Scirpus maritimus L. SALT MARSH BULRUSH. Herbaceous perennials, roots tuberous, stems triangular.

AG: La Salina, *Felger 93-12*.

EUPHORBIACEAE – SPURGE FAMILY

Acalypha californica Benth. [*A. pringlei* S. Watson] COPPERLEAF; HIERBA DEL CÁNCER. Small shrubs; flowers small, red or yellow.

CP: Little Tule Well, *Felger 92-534*. GR: Tinajas Altas, *Goodding 5 Dec 1935*. OP: Aguajita, *Felger 88-275*.

Bernardia incana C.V. Morton. Shrubs; flowers inconspicuous.

GR: NW of Hat Mt, *Rutman 24 Dec 2001*. SD: Table Top Mts, *Felger 01-277*.

Croton sonorae Torr. SONORA CROTON. Small shrubs; flowers green or white.

CP: Agua Dulce Tank, *Felger 92-566*. GR: 4 mi W of Tom Thumb, *Rutman 6 Jan 2002*. OP: Bull Pasture trail, *Bowers 944*. SD: Table Top Mts, *Kearney 7298*.

Croton wigginsii L.C. Wheeler [*C. arenicola* Rose & Standl., 1912. Not *C. arenicola* Small, 1905] DUNE CROTON. Shrubs; flowers green or white. Dunes and sand flats of Gran Desierto, adjacent Yuma County, and Algodones Dunes in California.

PI: N of Sierra del Rosario, *Felger 75-30*. AG: Sand hills, Adair Bay, 20 Nov 1908, *Sykes 62* (Holotype, US). CP: Pinta Sands, *Felger 93-386*. GR: N of Border Monument 198, *Felger 16702*.

Ditaxis adenophora (A. Gray) Pax & K. Hoffm. [*Argythamnia adenophora* A. Gray]. Herbaceous to subshrub perennials; flowers inconspicuous. In flora region, few local populations in basalt hills and mountains.

GR: W end of Crater Range, near East Pass, *McLaughlin 10077*. OP: Ajo Loop Rd, *Van Devender 85-*

107. SD: N end Sand Tank Mts, N of Interstate 8, T6S, R3W, rare, *Butterwick 7513* (ASU).

Ditaxis brandegeei (Millsp.) Rose & Standl. var. **intonsa** I.M. Johnst. [*Argythamnia brandegeei* Millsp. var. *intonsa* (I.M. Johnst.) J.W. Ingram] SONORAN SILVERBUSH. Tall, slender, shrubby perennials, stems few, foliage sparse; flowers inconspicuous.

PI: Sykes Crater, *Felger 18999*. CP: Tule Tanks, *Goodding 4358*. GR: Spook Canyon, *Arnett 1266* (ASU).

Ditaxis lanceolata (Benth.) Pax & K. Hoffm. [*Argythamnia lanceolata* (Benth.) Müll. Arg.] NARROWLEAF SILVERBUSH. Perennial herbs to subshrubs; flowers greenish.

PI: Sykes Crater, *Felger 18930*. CP: Near Cabeza Prieta Tanks, *Simmons 25 Oct 1962* (CAB). GR: Tom Thumb, *Felger 02-84*. OP: Quitobaquito, *Felger 86-291*. SD: Table Top Mts, *Bolton 94-046*.

Ditaxis neomexicana (Müll. Arg.) A. Heller [*Argythamnia neomexicana* Müll. Arg.]. Nonseasonal annuals; flowers green and white, inconspicuous.

PI: Cerro Colorado, *Felger 10793*. CP: Tule Mts, *Felger 92-61*. GR: Camino del Diablo, E of Raven Butte, *Felger 01-589*. OP: Quitobaquito, *Felger 86-291*. SD: Table Top Mts, *Felger 01-463*.

Ditaxis serrata (Torr.) A. Heller var. **serrata** [*Argythamnia serrata* (Torr.) Müll. Arg.]. Nonseasonal annuals; flowers green and white, inconspicuous.

PI: Moon Crater, *Felger 18642*. AG: N of El Golfo, *Felger 85-1062*. CP: Pinta Sands, *Felger 92-783*. GR: Mohawk Dunes, *Felger 96-135*.

Euphorbia abramsiana L.C. Wheeler [*Chamaesyce abramsiana* (L.C. Wheeler) Koutnik] GOLONDRINA. Hot-weather annuals; flowers inconspicuous.

PI: Playa Díaz, *Felger 86-364*. CP: Daniels Arroyo at Charlie Bell Rd, *Felger 92-658* (CAB). GR: Gila Bend Air Force Auxiliary Field, *Felger 95-325*. OP: Aguajita, *Felger 86-277*. SD: Vekol Valley, *Felger 01-410A*.

Euphorbia albomarginata Torr. & A. Gray [*Chamaesyce albomarginata* (Torr. & A. Gray) Small] RATTLESNAKE WEED; GOLONDRINA. Perennial herbs; "flowers" white.

PI: Sykes Crater, playa, *Felger 20020*. CP: Jose Juan Tank, *Felger 92-562*. GR: SE Crater Range, *Arnett 1250* (ASU). OP: Bates Well, *Nichol 26 Apr 1939*. SD: Vekol Valley, *Felger 01-411*.

Euphorbia arizonica Engelm. [*Chamaesyce arizonica* (Engelm.) Arthur] GOLONDRINA. Perennial herbs; "flowers" pink.

PI: Sierra Pinacate, 875 m, *Felger 19305*. GR: 3 mi S of Black Gap, *Felger 02-1*. OP: Estes Canyon, *Bowers 1238* (ORPI). SD: Table Top Mts, *Mauz 99-110*.

Euphorbia capitellata Engelm. [*Chamaesyce capitellata* (Engelm.) Millsp.] GOLONDRINA. Perennial herbs; "flowers" white.

GR: 3.5 km NE of Coffeepot Mt, *Douglas 1010* (ASU). **OP:** Estes Canyon, *Beale 15 Feb 1987* (ORPI). **SD:** Table Top Mts, 868 m, *Felger 02-45*.

Euphorbia eriantha Benth. BEETLE SPURGE. Nonseasonal annuals or short-lived perennials; flowers inconspicuous.

PI: Sierra Pinacate, ca. 875 m, *Felger 19353*. **CP:** Pinta Sands, *Felger 93-424*. **GR:** Camino del Diablo, E of Raven Butte, *Felger 02-5*. **OP:** Quitobaquito, *Felger 88-430*. **SD:** Table Top Mts, *Felger 01-465*.

Euphorbia florida Engelm. [*Chamaesyce florida* (Engelm.) Millsp.]. Summer annuals; "flowers" white.

CP: Daniels Arroyo at Charlie Bell Rd, *Felger 92-660* (CAB). **GR:** Sand Tank Mts, *Felger 95-362*. **OP:** Twin Peaks, *Baker 7884* (ORPI). **SD:** Table Top Mts, *Mauz 99-098*.

Euphorbia heterophylla L. WILD POINSETTIA. Warm-weather annuals; "flowers" green.

OP: Senita Basin, *Rutman 95-53* (ORPI). **SD:** Vekol Valley, *Felger 01-420*.

Euphorbia hyssopifolia L. [*Chamaesyce hyssopifolia* (L.) Small] HYSSOP SPURGE. Robust, warm-season annuals; flowers inconspicuous.

CP: Daniels Arroyo, *Harlan 309*. **GR:** Bender Spring, *Felger 95-438*. **OP:** Alamo Canyon, *Wirt 27 Jul 1990*. **SD:** Vekol Valley, *Mauz 99-078*.

Euphorbia melanadenia Torr. [*Chamaesyce melanadenia* (Torr.) Millsp.] GOLONDRINA. Herbaceous perennials; "flowers" pink.

GR: Sand Tank Mts, *Felger 95-348*. **OP:** Canyon Diablo, *Peebles 10836*. **SD:** Table Top Mts, *Felger 01-265C*.

Euphorbia micromera Boiss. ex Engelm. [*Chamaesyce micromera* (Boiss. ex Engelm.) Wooton & Standl.] GOLONDRINA. Nonseasonal annuals or herbaceous perennials; flowers minute.

PI: MacDougal Crater, *Felger 10477*. **CP:** Packrat Hill, *Harlan 300*. **GR:** 20 mi S of Gila Bend, *Harrison 7990*. **OP:** Aguajita, *Felger 86-294*. **SD:** Maricopa Rd (Hwy 238), 4.6 mi W of 91st Ave, *Felger 01-507*.

Euphorbia pediculifera Engelm. var. **pediculifera** [*Chamaesyce pediculifera* (Engelm.) Rose & Standl.] LOUSE SPURGE; GOLONDRINA. Nonseasonal annuals to herbaceous perennials; "flowers" white and maroon.

PI: Sykes Crater, *Felger 19999*. **CP:** Agua Dulce Spring, *Felger 92-733*. **GR:** 3 mi S of Black Gap, *Felger 02-2*. **OP:** Quitobaquito, *Mearns 2746* (US). **SD:** Antelope Peak, *Darrow 23 Dec 1940*.

Euphorbia petrina S. Watson [*Chamaesyce petrina* (S. Watson) Millsp.] GOLONDRINA. Nonseasonal annuals; flowers inconspicuous.

AG: 2 km W of El Golfo, *Felger 93-05*.

Euphorbia platysperma Engelm. ex S. Watson [*Chamaesyce platysperma* (Engelm. ex S. Watson) Shinners]

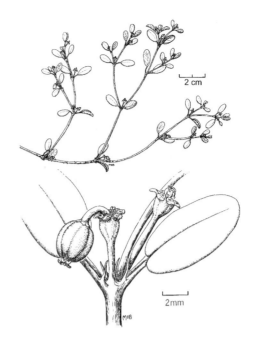

Figure 17.10. Euphorbia platysperma. (*Drawing by Marlo D. Buchmann*)

DUNE SPURGE. Nonseasonal annuals to herbaceous perennials; "flowers" yellowish, inconspicuous. Endemic to the Gran Desierto dunes plus a few waifs recorded from northeastern Baja California and southeastern California dunes (Felger 2000), and Arizona on dunes west of Tinajas Altas Mountains near Mexico border.

PI: S of Moon Crater, *Felger 19011*. **AG:** 2 km W of El Golfo, *Felger 93-08*. **GR:** NW corner of Yuma Dunes, 7.4 km N of Mexico border, *Douglas 876* (ASU).

Euphorbia polycarpa Benth. [*Chamaesyce polycarpa* (Benth.) Parish; *E. polycarpa* var. *hirtella* (Boiss.) Parish] DESERT SPURGE; GOLONDRINA; VI'IBAM. Nonseasonal annuals to herbaceous perennials; "flowers" white and maroon. The most widespread and common spurge in the region.

PI: MacDougal Crater, *Felger 10470*. **AG:** Near NE corner of Reserva, *Felger 03-498*. **CP:** Tule Mts, *Felger 92-59*. **GR:** Gila Bend Air Force Auxiliary Field, *Felger 95-332*. **OP:** Quitobaquito, *Felger 88-459*. **SD:** Johnson Well, *Funicelli 36*.

*****Euphorbia prostrata** Aiton [*Chamaesyce prostrata* (Aiton) Small]. Warm-weather annuals; flowers inconspicuous.

PI: Pinacate Junction, *Felger 86-343B*. **OP:** Armenta Ranch, *Wirt 20 Jul 1990* (ORPI). **SD:** Table Top Mts, *Mauz 99-130*.

Euphorbia revoluta Engelm. [*Chamaesyce revoluta* (Engelm.) Small]. Delicate summer annuals; flowers minute. A single population known from the flora area.

SD: S Maricopa Mts, *Felger 03-444*.

Euphorbia robusta (Engelm.) Small. Herbaceous perennials; "flowers" green. A single record known from the flora area.

OP: Alamo Canyon, *Tinkham 15 Apr 1942*.

*Euphorbia serpens Kunth [*Chamaesyce serpens* (Kunth) Small]. Annuals; flowers inconspicuous. Worldwide weed, one record within the flora area.

AG: Lerdo, 1889, *Palmer 954* (F).

Euphorbia setiloba Engelm. ex Torr. [*Chamaesyce setiloba* (Engelm. ex Torr.) Millsp. ex Parish] FRINGED SPURGE; GOLONDRINA. Nonseasonal annuals; "flowers" white or pink.

PI: Sykes Crater, *Felger 18928*. CP: Little Tule Well, *Felger 92-535*. GR: Sand Tank Mts, *Felger 95-365*. OP: Quitobaquito, *Felger 86-276*. SD: Table Top Mts, *Mauz 20-010*.

Euphorbia spathulata Lam. Cool-season annuals; flowers inconspicuous. Abundant in favorable seasons at Las Playas, no other records for the Sonoran Desert.

CP: Las Playas, *Felger 01-569*.

Euphorbia trachysperma Engelm. [*Chamaesyce trachysperma* (Engelm.) Millsp.]. Hot-weather annuals; "flowers" white. Fine-textured soils of playas and where water temporarily accumulates.

PI: S of Tinaja de los Pápagos, *Felger 86-491*. CP: Las Playas, *Felger 01-568*. SD: Vekol Valley, *Felger 01-439*.

Jatropha cardiophylla (Torr.) Müll. Arg. LIMBERBUSH; SANGRENGADO. Small shrubs; flowers white.

GR: 3.3 km NE of Coffeepot Mt, *Arnett 1208* (ASU). OP: Visitor Center, *Van Devender 30 Aug 1978*. SD: Table Top Mts, *Mauz 99-086*.

Jatropha cinerea (Ortega) Müll. Arg. ASHY LIMBERBUSH; SANGRENGADO; KOMAGĬ VA:S. Shrubs; flowers pink.

PI: NE of Pinacate Peak, 925 m, *Felger 86-422*. OP: Quitobaquito, *Nichol 28 Apr 1939*.

Jatropha cuneata Wiggins & Rollins. LIMBERBUSH; SANGRENGADO, MATACORA; VA:S. Shrubs; flowers white. Stems semi-succulent, flexible, staining clothes.

PI: S of Pinacate Peak, 875 m, *Felger 19352*. CP: 7 mi E of Papago Well, *Peebles & Kearney 10862*. GR: Tinajas Altas, *Kearney 6567*. OP: Quitobaquito, *Felger 86-217*.

Sebastiania bilocularis S. Watson [*Sapium biloculare* (S. Watson) Pax] HIERBA DE LA FLECHA; 'INA HITÁ. Shrubs; flowers green or yellow. Milky sap poisonous, used for arrow poison.

PI: 35 mi W of Sonoyta, *Webster 19700*. CP: Little Tule Well, *Felger 94-31*. GR: Thanksgiving Day Tank, *Felger 02-109*. OP: Pitahaya Canyon, *Nichol 23 Feb 1939*. SD: Hills W of Maricopa Mts, Gila Bend-Mobile Rd, *Christy 1241* (ASU).

Stillingia linearifolia S. Watson. Perennial herbs to subshrubs; flowers green or yellow, inconspicuous.

PI: Sierra del Rosario, *Felger 20698*. AG: NW of La Salina, *Felger 93-11*. CP: East Pinta Sands, *Felger 92-751*. OP: Acuña Basin, *Baker 8787A* (ORPI).

Stillingia spinulosa Torr. Winter-spring annuals; flowers green or yellow, minute.

PI: NE of Sierra del Rosario, *Felger 20357*. AG: N of El Golfo, *Felger 75-73*. GR: Yuma Desert, 15 km N of Mexico border, *Douglas 872* (ASU).

Tragia nepetifolia Cav. var. dissecta Müll. Arg. NOSE-BURN; ORTIGA. Perennial vines with stinging hairs; flowers inconspicuous.

GR: Tom Thumb, *Felger 02-88A* (ASU). OP: Alamo Canyon, *Baker 7554*. SD: Table Top Mts, *Mauz 99-101*.

FABACEAE (LEGUMINOSAE) – LEGUME FAMILY

Acacia angustissima (Mill.) Kuntze. WHITE-BALL ACACIA. Shrubs and subshrubs; flowers white.

GR: Tom Thumb, *Felger 02-92*. OP: Bull Pasture, *Bowers 1793*.

Acacia constricta Benth. WHITE-THORN ACACIA; MEZQUITILLO; GIDAG. Shrubs; flowers bright yellow.

CP: Charlie Bell Rd 1 km W of boundary, *Felger 94-23*. GR: Tom Thumb, *Felger 02-79*. OP: NE of Visitor Center, *Bowers 928*. SD: Vekol Valley, *Felger 02-302*.

Acacia greggii A. Gray [*A. greggii* var. *arizonica* Isely] CATCLAW ACACIA; UÑA DE GATO, GATUÑO; 'U:PAD. Shrubs or small trees; flowers pale yellow.

PI: Tinajas de Emilia, *Felger 19729*. CP: Little Tule Well, *Felger 92-537* (CAB). GR: Rd to Hat Mt, *Felger 03-245*. OP: Alamo Canyon, *Cooper 564*. SD: Vekol Valley, *Felger 02-303*.

*Alhagi maurorum Med. [*A. camelorum* Fischer] CAMEL THORN. Spinescent, weedy subshrubs, here probably annuals. Flowers reddish purple. Occasionally spreading into northern part of Goldwater Range from nearby farmland.

GR: 10.3 mi S of N boundary on Tacna Rd, rare, 4 Feb 1990, *Felger*, observation.

Astragalus aridus A. Gray. PARCHED MILKVETCH. Cool-season annuals; pubescence silvery-satiny, flowers small, whitish tinged with lavender-pink, drying straw-colored. Primarily a Salton Trough species, known from Arizona only by several specimens in southwestern Yuma County.

GR: SE corner Yuma Dunes, 1.6 km N of Mexico border, 15 Apr 1993, *Walter 115B* (ARIZ).

Astragalus arizonicus A. Gray. ARIZONA MILKVETCH. Herbaceous perennials, herbage silvery; flowers pale lavender-blue.

GR: Near Burro Spring, *Smith 8 May 2003* (specimen not curated). SD: Bender Spring Canyon, 3300 ft, *Felger 01-382*.

Astragalus didymocarpus Hook. & Arn. var. dispermus (A. Gray) M.E. Jones. Cool-season annuals; flowers pale violet-pink.

OP: N end Ajo Range, *Holmgren 6735*. SD: Vekol Valley, *Felger 01-231*.

Astragalus insularis Kellogg var. **harwoodii** Munz & McBurney ex Munz. SAND LOCOWEED; KOPONDAKUḌ. Cool-season annuals; flowers indigo purple.

PI: Hornaday Mts, *Burgess 6825*. CP: Pinta Sands, *Yatskievych 79-243*. GR: Mohawk Dunes, *Turner 95-24*.

Astragalus lentiginosus Douglas ex Hook. FRECKLED MILKVETCH. Cool-season annuals. Three varieties in the flora area; two in Organ Pipe, each documented by only a single specimen.

Astragalus lentiginosus var. **australis** Barneby. Flowers pale pink-purple.

OP: Wash, 1798 ft, *Walden 19 Apr 1964* (ASU).

Astragalus lentiginosus var. **borreganus** M.E. Jones. Cool-season annuals; flowers purple. Dunes.

AG: NNE of El Golfo, *Felger 92-181*. GR: E of Yuma, T11S, R22W, *Phillips 16 Apr 2001*.

Astragalus lentiginosus var. **yuccanus** M.E. Jones. Cool-season annuals; flowers pale yellow.

OP: Alamo Canyon, *Tinkham 18 Apr 1942*.

Astragalus magdalenae Greene. Cool-season annuals; flowers magenta to lilac. Two varieties in the flora area.

Astragalus magdalenae var. **magdalenae** [*A. magdalenae* var. *niveus* (Rydb.) Barneby] SATINY MILKVETCH.

AG: El Golfo, *Conner 14 Mar 1990*.

Astragalus magdalenae var. **peirsonii** (Munz & McBurney) Barneby. DUNE MILKVETCH. Dune endemic. Seeds apparently largest of any of the more than 375 American species (Barneby 1964).

PI: S of Moon Crater, *Felger 19010*. AG: 5.8 mi by rd S of Estación López Collada, *Felger 05-318*.

Astragalus nuttallianus DC. var. **imperfectus** (Rydb.) Barneby. SMALL-FLOWERED MILKVETCH. Cool-season annuals; flowers blue and white.

PI: Campo Rojo, *Felger 92-481B*. CP: Childs Mt, *Felger 93-270*. GR: Mohawk Dunes, *Felger 98-74*. OP: Grass Canyon, *Bowers 1085*. SD: Table Top Mts, *Bolton 94-007*.

Astragalus sabulonum A. Gray. GRAVEL MILKVETCH. Cool-season annuals; flowers lavender-purple.

AG: NNE of El Golfo, *Felger 92-185*.

Calliandra eriophylla Benth. FAIRY DUSTER; HUAJILLO, MEZQUITILLO. Small shrubs; flowers pink.

PI: Cerro basáltico, 32°09′N, 113°52′W, *Ezcurra 29 Apr 1981* (MEXU). CP: Charlie Bell Rd at E boundary, *Felger 93-48*. GR: Tom Thumb, 2 Feb 2002, *Felger, observation*. OP: Ajo Mt Drive, *McCarten 2058*. SD: Table Top Mts, *Bolton 94-043*.

Cercidium, see **Parkinsonia.**

Coursetia glandulosa A. Gray [*C. microphylla* A. Gray] SÁMOTA. Shrubs; flowers yellow and pink.

GR: N of Paradise Well, *Darrow 13 May 2003*. OP: Alamo Canyon, *Nichol 4 May 1939*. SD: Bender Spring Canyon, 17 Apr 2001, *Felger, observation*.

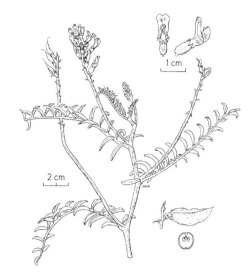

Figure 17.11. Astragalus magdalenae *var.* magdalenae. *(Drawing by Nancy N. Nicholson)*

Dalea mollis Benth. SILKY DALEA. Nonseasonal annuals; flowers violet. Widespread.

PI: Vicinity Elegante Crater, *Sherbrooke 10 Apr 1983*. AG: Vicinity Santa Clara Slough, *Ortiz 5 May 1993*. CP: Pinta Sands, *Felger 92-779*. GR: Mohawk Dunes, *Reichenbacher 437*. OP: Quitobaquito, *Warren 10 Nov 1983*. SD: Table Top Mts, *Bolton 94-059*.

Dalea mollissima (Rydb.) Munz. Nonseasonal annuals; flowers violet. Sand soils.

GR: Camino del Diablo, 6 mi SW of Wellton Mohawk Canal, *Van Devender 10 Mar 1980*. SD: 9 mi E of Gila Bend, *Shreve 10153*.

Dalea pogonathera A. Gray var. **pogonathera.** Herbaceous perennials, low and bushy, from a thick, knotty rootstock; flowers violet, at least in spring. One record in the flora area.

OP: Near Dripping Springs, gravelly wash on desert plain, 16 Apr 1952, *Parker 7922*.

Dalea pringlei A. Gray var. **pringlei.** Herbaceous perennials, stems erect, foliage sparse; flowers purple with yellow anthers.

OP: Alamo Canyon, *Nichol 16 May 1937*.

Desmodium procumbens (Mill.) Hitchc. TICK CLOVER. Summer annuals; flowers yellow to green.

GR: Sand Tank Mts, *Felger 95-376*. OP: Bull Pasture Trail, *Bowers 1549* (ORPI).

Galactia wrightii A. Gray. Perennial vines; flowers pale purple and yellow-green.

GR: Sand Tank Mts, *Felger 95-345*. OP: Bull Pasture Trail, *Bowers 1543*.

Hoffmannseggia glauca (Ortega) Eifert [*Caesalpinia glauca* (Ortega) Kuntze] HOG POTATO; CAMOTE DE RATÓN; 'I:KOVĬ. Perennial herbs from tuberous roots; flowers yellow. Playas.

PI: Sierra Blanca, *Equihua 24 Aug 1982*. AG: NE of Sánchez Islas, *Felger 92-214*. CP: Las Playas, *Reeves 6808* (ASU). GR: Playa E side Mohawk Dunes, *Turner 95-23*.

Hoffmannseggia microphylla Torr. [*Caesalpinia virgata* Fisher]. Shrubs, stems wandlike; flowers yellow.

PI: Sierra del Rosario, *Felger 75-20*. GR: E Gila Mts, 1.6 km E of Dripping Springs, *Walter 784* (ASU).

Lotus humistratus Greene [*Hosackia brachycarpa* Benth.] HILL LOCUST. Cool-season annuals; flowers yellow.

GR: Crater Range, *Van Devender 18 Mar 1973*. OP: Dripping Springs, *Clark 11459* (ORPI). SD: NW of Bender Spring, *Felger 01-376*.

Lotus rigidus (Benth.) Greene. DESERT ROCK-PEA. Perennial subshrubs; flowers yellow.

PI: Cerro Pinto, *Felger 89-55*. CP: Tule Tanks, *Shreve 6228*. GR: Tinajas Altas, 5 Mar 1927, *Harrison 3610*. OP: Arch Canyon, *Felger 90-547*. SD: NW of Bender Spring, *Felger 01-367*.

Lotus salsuginosus Greene var. **brevixillus** Ottley. Cool-season annuals; flowers yellow.

PI: Tinajas de Emilia, *Felger 19752*. CP: Bassarisc Tank, *Felger 93-122A*. GR: Sauceda Mts, *Arnett 1381* (ASU). OP: Tres Alamos Canyon, *Nichol 24 Feb 1939*. SD: Between Indian Butte and Table Top Mts, *Butterwick 7247* (ASU).

Lotus strigosus (Nutt.) Greene var. **tomentellus** (Greene) Isely. HAIRY LOTUS. Cool-season annuals; flowers yellow.

PI: MacDougal Crater, *Turner 86-1*. CP: Bassarisc Tank, *Felger 93-124*. GR: Tinajas Altas, *Van Devender 9 Mar 1980*. OP: Aguajita, *Beale 8 Apr 1988* (ORPI). SD: Table Top Mts, *Bolton 94-006*.

Lupinus arizonicus S. Watson [*L. arizonicus* subsp. *sonorensis* J.A. Christian & D.B. Dunn] ARIZONA LUPINE; LUPINO; TAṢ HA:HAG. Cool-season annuals; flowers lavender-pink, rarely white.

PI: Elegante Crater, *Felger 9699*. AG: NW of Gustavo Sotelo, *Ezcurra 4 Apr 1981* (MEXU). CP: Bassarisc Tank, *Felger 93-119*. GR: Tinajas Altas, *Van Devender 25 Mar 1983*. OP: Alamo Canyon, *Nichol 14 Mar 1939*. SD: N Maricopa Mts, *Felger 01-190*.

Lupinus concinnus J. Agardh. ELEGANT LUPINE. Cool-season annuals; flowers blue.

CP: Charlie Bell Rd at Daniels Arroyo, *Felger 93-349*. OP: Growler Canyon, Bates Mts, *Bowers 1601* (ORPI). SD: S Maricopa Mts, 24 Mar 2001, *Felger*, observation.

Lupinus sparsiflorus Benth. MOJAVE LUPINE; CHICHARITO. Cool-season annuals; flowers blue.

CP: Bassarisc Tank, *Felger 93-120*. GR: Rd to Hat Mt, *Felger 03-191*. OP: Alamo Canyon, *McDougall 20*. SD: N Maricopa Mts, *Felger 01-192*.

Macroptilium atropurpureum (DC.) Urban. Perennial vines; flowers dark red-brown.

GR: Tom Thumb, *Felger 02-98*.

Marina parryi (Torr. & A. Gray ex A. Gray) Barneby [*Dalea parryi* Torr. & A. Gray ex A. Gray]. Nonseasonal annuals or short-lived herbaceous perennials; flowers dark blue.

PI: Carnegie Peak, *Felger 19804*. CP: Little Tule Well, *Felger 92-651A* (CAB). GR: Thanksgiving Day Tank, *Felger 02-135*. OP: Quitobaquito, *Felger 86-286*. SD: Table Top Mts, *Bolton 94-082*.

***Medicago polymorpha** L. [*M. hispida* Gaertn.] BUR CLOVER. Annuals, mostly in spring; flowers yellow. Garden weed, not in natural areas in the flora area.

OP: Research Center, *Felger 88-142B* (ORPI).

***Melilotus indica** (L.) All. SOUR-CLOVER; TRÉBOL AGRIO. Nonseasonal annuals; flowers yellow.

GR: Gila Bend Air Force Auxiliary Field, *Felger 03-165*. OP: Quitobaquito, *Bowers 1607* (ORPI). SD: NW of Bender Spring, *Felger 01-347*.

Mimosa distachya Cav. var. **laxiflora** (Benth.) Barneby [*M. laxiflora* Benth.] GARABATILLO. Shrubs; flowers pink-lavender.

OP: Estes Canyon, *Bowers 1517*.

Nissolia schottii (Torr.) A. Gray. Perennial vines; flowers yellow.

GR: Tom Thumb, *Felger 02-99*. OP: Bull Pasture Trail, *Bowers 939*. SD: Between Johnson Well and Bender Spring, *Holm 2001-09-16-26*.

Olneya tesota A. Gray. IRONWOOD; PALO FIERRO; HO'IDKAM. Trees; flowers pink-lavender. Common and widespread, especially washes.

PI: Sierra del Rosario, *Felger 20369*. CP: N of Sheep Peak, 31 Jan 1992, *Felger*, observation. GR: Borrego Canyon, 16 Jun 1992, *Felger*, observation. OP: S Puerto Blanco Drive, *Felger 90-403*. SD: Vekol Valley, *Felger 02-301*.

***Parkinsonia aculeata** L. MEXICAN PALO VERDE; BAGOTE, RETAMA, GUACAPORA, HUACAPORI. Trees; flowers yellow. Disturbed habitats, rare and not well established in the flora area.

PI: Rancho los Vidrios, *Ezcurra 20 Sep 1980* (MEXU). AG: Gustavo Sotelo, 1 juvenile plant, *Felger 03-553*. OP: Hwy 85 ca. 1.5 mi S of visitor center, two plants, 4 Nov 2003, *Rutman*, observation.

Parkinsonia florida (A. Gray ex A. Gray) S. Watson [*Cercidium floridum* A. Gray ex A. Gray subsp. *floridum*] BLUE PALO VERDE; PALO VERDE; KO'OKOMAḌK, KALISP. Trees or large shrubs; flowers yellow. Common and widespread mostly along washes.

PI: E of MacDougal Crater, *Felger 10437*. CP: Pinta Sands, *Felger 93-415*. GR: Crater Range, *Morrison 1061* (ASU). OP: Puerto Blanco Drive, *Felger 89-228*. SD: Vekol Valley, *Felger 02-304*.

Parkinsonia microphylla Torr. [*Cercidium microphyllum* (Torr.) Rose & I.M. Johnst.] FOOTHILL PALO VERDE; PALO VERDE; KEK CEHEDAGĬ. Small trees; flowers pale yellow and white. Common and widespread, often on slopes and bajadas.

PI: Campo Rojo (Red Cone Camp), *Sanders 5643* (UCR). **CP:** Charlie Bell Rd, 12 June 1990, *Felger,* observation. **GR:** Tinajas Altas, 18 March 1998, *Felger,* observation. **OP:** Alamo Canyon, *Cooper 561.* **SD:** Big Horn Reservoir, *Felger 02-388.*

*Pediomelum rhombifolium (Torr. & A. Gray) Rydb. [*Psoralea rhombifolia* Torr. & A. Gray]. Herbaceous perennials; flowers orange. Scarce in the flora area.

PI: Romero field, Suvuk, *Nabhan 25 Sep 1982* (DES).

Phaseolus acutifolius A. Gray. WILD TEPARY; TÉPARI; BAVĬ. Warm-weather annual vines; flowers pink.

OP: Arch Canyon, *Wirt 13 Oct 1990* (ORPI).

Phaseolus filiformis Benth. [*P. wrightii* A. Gray] DESERT BEAN; BAN BAVĬ, CEPULIŇ BAVĬ. Nonseasonal annual vines; flowers pink.

PI: Elegante Crater, *Felger 19679.* **CP:** Pinta Sands, *Felger 92-780.* **GR:** Bender Spring rd, *Felger 95-440.* **OP:** Alamo Canyon, *Parker 7747.* **SD:** Table Top Mts, *Mauz 99-109.*

Prosopis glandulosa Torr. var. **torreyana** (L.D. Benson) M.C. Johnst. [*P. juliflora* (Sw.) DC. var. *torreyana* L.D. Benson] WESTERN HONEY MESQUITE; MEZQUITE; KUI. Large shrubs to trees; flowers yellow. Common and widespread in the western part of the flora area; often along washes.

PI: MacDougal Crater, *Felger 9946.* **AG:** 7 mi W of Gustavo Sotelo, *Felger 03-612.* **CP:** Salazaria Wash, *Harlan 213* (CAB). **GR:** Borrego Canyon, *Felger 92-615.* **OP:** Aguajita, *Bowers 1337.* **SD:** N Maricopa Mts, *Mauz 23-025.*

Prosopis pubescens Benth. SCREWBEAN; TORNILLO; KUJEL. Large shrubs or small trees; flowers yellow, pods tightly coiled.

AG: La Salina ("Pozo Borrascosa"), *Felger 86-535.* **OP:** Quitobaquito, *Nichol 28 Apr 1939* (ORPI).

Prosopis velutina Wooton [*P. juliflora* var. *velutina* (Wooton) Sargent] VELVET MESQUITE; MEZQUITE; KUI. Large shrubs or trees; flowers yellow. Common and widespread except western part of the flora area; best developed along washes.

CP: Bates Well to Papago Well, 31 Jan 1992, *Felger,* observation. **GR:** Mohawk Dunes, *Reina 96-207.* **OP:** Quitobaquito, *Felger 86-179.* **SD:** Vekol Valley, *Felger 02-314.*

Psorothamnus emoryi (A. Gray) Barneby var. **emoryi** [*Dalea emoryi* A. Gray] EMORY'S INDIGO-BUSH, EMORY'S SMOKEBUSH; OJO DE VENADO. Shrubs, essentially leafless; flowers purple and white.

PI: N of Sierra del Rosario, *Felger 75-37.* **AG:** López Collada, *Felger 03-594.* **CP:** East Pinta Sands, *Felger 92-757.* **GR:** Mohawk Dunes, *Felger 96-141.*

Psorothamnus schottii (Torr.) Barneby [*Dalea schottii* Torr.] SCHOTT'S SMOKEBUSH. Shrubs, foliage sparse,

leaves simple (one leaflet), linear; flowers bright blue. One record known from the flora area.

GR: Spook Canyon, *Douglas 927* (ASU).

Psorothamnus spinosus (A. Gray) Barneby [*Dalea spinosa* A. Gray] SMOKE TREE; PALO CENIZO. Large shrubs or small trees; flowers dark blue. Mostly in large washes and on roadsides.

PI: Moon Crater, 21 Feb 1988, *Felger,* observation. **CP:** W of Senita Tank, *Felger 92-595.* **GR:** Sauceda Wash, E Tactical Range, *Felger 03-65.* **OP:** Aguajita, *Darrow 2398.*

Rhynchosia senna Gillies ex Hook. & Arn. var. **texana** (Torr. & A. Gray) M.C. Johnst. [*R. texana* Torr. & A. Gray] ROSARY BEAN. Perennial herbaceous vines; flowers yellow.

GR: Above Bender Spring, 3300 ft, *Holm 2001-0917-3.* **OP:** Alamo Canyon, *Baker 7552* (ORPI).

Senna covesii (A. Gray) Irwin & Barneby [*Cassia covesii* A. Gray] DESERT SENNA; HOJASÉN, DAISILLO; KO'OVĬ TA: TAMĬ. Herbaceous perennials; flowers yellow.

PI: SW of Tinaja de los Pápagos, *Felger 20161.* **CP:** NE of Little Tule Well, *Felger 94-28.* **GR:** Sauceda Mts, *Felger 02-145.* **OP:** Alamo Canyon, *Nichol 4 May 1939.* **SD:** Table Top Mts, *Mauz 99-097.*

Sesbania herbacea (Mill.) McVaugh. COLORADO RIVER HEMP, COFFEE WEED; BEQUILLA, BAIQUILLO, CÁÑAMO SILVESTRE. Robust, hot-weather annuals; flowers pale yellow. Basis for nineteenth-century development promotion (see Colonia Lerdo, Chapter 39, this volume; Chapter 15, this volume; also Felger 2000).

AG: Colorado River, Sonora below mouth of Hardy River, 27 Mar 1894, *Mearns 2837* (DS).

Tephrosia vicioides Schlecht. [*T. tenella* A. Gray]. Annuals or herbaceous perennials; flowers lavender-pink.

OP: Alamo Canyon, cracks in bedrock, *Rutman 5 Sep 1999* (ORPI).

Trifolium wormskioldii Lehm. var. **arizonicum** (Greene) Barneby [*T. lacerum* Greene] COW CLOVER. Cool-season annuals. Flowers small, lavender and white.

OP: Bull Pasture, *Bowers 1205* (ORPI). **SD:** NW of Bender Spring, 3490 ft, *Felger 01-374.*

Vicia ludoviciana Nutt. var. **ludoviciana** [*V. exigua* Nutt.] DEER-PEA VETCH. Delicate cool-season annual vines, with tendrils and very slender stems; flowers lavender.

GR: Tom Thumb, *Felger 02-94.* **OP:** Bull Pasture Trail, *Bowers 1233.*

FAGACEAE – BEECH FAMILY

Quercus turbinella Greene [*Q. ajoensis* C.H. Muller; *Q. turbinella* Greene subsp. *ajoensis* (C.H. Muller) Felger & C.H. Lowe] SCRUB OAK; ENCINILLO. Trees in Alamo Canyon, shrubs elsewhere; flowers inconspicuous.

GR: Above Bender Spring, N-facing slope, 3280 ft, *Holm 2001-09-17-1.* **OP:** Alamo Canyon, 15 Aug 1952,

Muller 9519 (Isotype of *Q. ajoensis*). **SD:** Javelina Mt, near summit, *Felger & Broyles 00-70*.

FOUQUIERIACEAE – OCOTILLO FAMILY

Fouquieria splendens Engelm. subsp. **splendens.** OCOTILLO; MELHOG. Shrubs; flowers red-orange.

PI: MacDougal Crater, *Felger 10764*. **AG:** 2 mi S of Gustavo Sotelo, *Felger 03-613*. **CP:** Pinta Sands, 1 Feb 1992, *Felger*, observation. **GR:** Camino del Diablo, SE of Raven Butte, *Felger 04-15*. **OP:** Quitobaquito, *Felger 88-132*. **SD:** White Hills, *Doan 1438* (ASU).

FRANKENIACEAE – FRANKENIA FAMILY

Frankenia palmeri S. Watson. SALADITO. Dwarf shrubs along coast; flowers white.

AG: S of López Collada, *Felger 86-600*.

Frankenia salina (Molina) I.M. Johnst. [*F. grandifolia* Cham. & Schltdl.]. Herbaceous perennials with thickened roots; flowers white. Tidal marshes.

AG: SW of Gustavo Sotelo, *López-Portillo 9 Jul 1984* (MEXU).

GENTIANACEAE – GENTIAN FAMILY

Centaurium calycosum (Buckley) Fern. CENTAURY. Annuals; flowers pink. In the flora area only at Quitobaquito.

OP: Quitobaquito, *Felger 86-212*.

Eustoma exaltatum (L.) G. Don forma **albiflorum** Benke. CATCHFLY GENTIAN; HAWAŇ TA:TAḌ. Herbaceous perennials; flowers cream-white. In the flora area only at Quitobaquito.

OP: Quitobaquito, *Baker 7623* (ASU).

GERANIACEAE – GERANIUM FAMILY

*****Erodium cicutarium** (L.) L'Hér. ex Aiton. FILAREE, STORKSBILL, HERONSBILL; ALFILERILLO; HOHO'IBAD. Cool-season annuals; flowers pink-lavender.

PI: Pinacate Peak, *Felger 19441*. **CP:** San Cristobal Wash, *Harlan 19* (CAB). **GR:** Crater Range, *Van Devender 18 Mar 1973*. **OP:** Quitobaquito, *Felger 88-279*. **SD:** Table Top Mts, *Bolton 94-032*.

Erodium texanum A. Gray. FALSE FILAREE, DESERT STORKSBILL. Cool-season annuals; flowers pink-lavender.

PI: Moon Crater, *Felger 19237*. **CP:** Pinta Sands, *Felger 93-398*. **GR:** NE of Mohawk Dunes, *Felger 98-18*. **OP:** Dripping Springs, *Phillips 86-8* (ORPI). **SD:** 20 mi W of Casa Grande, *Peebles 9103*.

Geranium carolinianum L. CRANESBILL. Annuals; flowers pale pink.

OP: Estes Canyon, *Bowers 1711*.

GROSSULARIACEAE – GOOSEBERRY FAMILY

Ribes quercetorum Greene. OAK-BELT GOOSEBERRY. Shrubs; flowers yellow.

OP: Ajo Mts, canyon S of arch, *Fay 739*.

HALORAGACEAE – WATER-MILFOIL FAMILY

*****Myriophyllum spicatum** L. WATER-MILFOIL. Submerged perennial herbs, leaves feathery; flowers small, inconspicuous. Native to Eurasia. Established in Colorado River in Arizona.

AG: Irrigation canal, SE of Indiviso (Oveido Mota), Baja California, *Felger 02-300*.

HYDROPHYLLACEAE – WATERLEAF FAMILY

Eucrypta chrysanthemifolia (Benth.) Greene var. **bipinnatifida** (Torr.) Constance. Cool-season annuals; flowers small, pale lavender.

PI: Carnegie Peak, *Felger 19891*. **CP:** Heart Tank, *Felger 93-158*. **GR:** Hat Mt, *Felger 03-214*. **OP:** Quitobaquito, *Felger 88-134*. **SD:** N Maricopa Mts, *Felger 01-180*.

Eucrypta micrantha (Torr.) A. Heller. PELUDA. Cool-season annuals; flowers small, white to pale violet or lavender.

PI: Sykes Crater, *Felger 18945*. **CP:** Charlie Bell Pass, *Whipple 3921*. **GR:** Tinajas Altas, *Van Devender 5 Mar 1983*. **OP:** Valley back of Montezuma Head, *McDougall 43*. **SD:** N Maricopa Mts, *Felger 01-179*.

Nama demissum A. Gray. PURPLEMAT. Cool-season annuals; flowers bright lavender-pink.

PI: Sykes Crater, *Felger 18995*. **CP:** N of Tule Well, *Felger 93-442*. **GR:** SE of Borrego Canyon, *Felger 98-112*. **SD:** S Maricopa Mts, *Chamberland 1852*.

Nama hispidum A. Gray. BRISTLY NAMA. Cool-season annuals; flowers pale lavender.

PI: MacDougal Crater, *Felger 9724*. **AG:** Gustavo Sotelo, *Felger 03-552*. **CP:** Pinta Sands, *Felger 93-431*. **GR:** Mohawk Dunes, *Felger 98-71*. **OP:** Quitobaquito, *Felger 7682*. **SD:** S Maricopa Mts, *Chamberland 1851*.

Nama stenocarpum A. Gray. Cool-season annuals; flowers rather inconspicuous, pale bluish-white or lavender. Rare in flora area.

PI: Tinaja Tule, *Felger 19194*.

Phacelia affinis A. Gray. Cool-season annuals; flowers white.

PI: Elegante Crater, *Felger 19673*. **OP:** Estes Canyon, *Bowers 1069* (ORPI). **SD:** S Maricopa Mts, *Felger 01-148*.

Phacelia ambigua M.E. Jones [*P. crenulata* Torr. ex S. Watson; *P. crenulata* var. *ambigua* (M.E. Jones) J.F. Macbr.] DESERT HELIOTROPE. Cool-season annuals; herbage smelly, irritating; flowers pale lavender.

PI: MacDougal Crater, *Felger 9697*. **CP:** Charlie Bell Rd at E boundary, *Felger 93-318*. **GR:** Mohawk Dunes, *Felger 98-89*. **OP:** Quitobaquito, *Felger 86-102*. **SD:** N Maricopa Mts, *Felger 01-198*.

Phacelia bombycina Wooton & Standley. MANGAS SPRING PHACELIA. Cool-season annuals; flowers lavender. Known from the flora area by a single record.

SD: White Hills, *Doan 1444* (ASU).

Phacelia coerulea Greene. Cool-season annuals; flowers pale lavender.

CP: Cabeza Prieta Tanks, *Lehto L23535* (ASU). GR: Sauceda Mts, *Weaver & Lehto 2 Apr 1970* (ASU). OP: Canyon Diablo, *Kearney & Peebles 10824*. SD: Table Top Mts, *Felger 01-267A*.

Phacelia cryptantha Greene. Cool-season annuals; flowers pale lavender.

PI: Pinacate Peak, *Felger 19431*.

Phacelia distans Benth. CATERPILLAR PHACELIA, FERN-LEAF PHACELIA. Cool-season annuals; flowers pale violet to blue.

CP: Papago Well, *Felger 93-128*. GR: Hat Mt, *Felger 03-220*. OP: Quitobaquito, *Felger 86-102*. SD: Table Top Mts, *Bolton 94-022*.

Phacelia neglecta M.E. Jones. Cool-season annuals, stems and leaves short, semi-succulent; flowers white.

PI: Tinaja de los Chivos, *Felger 18801*. CP: Packrat Hill, *Felger 93-59*. GR: W side N Mohawk Mts, 0.3 km E of GR border, *Arnett 1311* (ASU). OP: Bates Well, *Bowers 1128* (ORPI).

Phacelia pedicellata A. Gray. Cool-season annuals, herbage smelly, irritating; flowers pale lavender-blue.

PI: Sykes Crater, *Felger 18963*. CP: T13S, R13W, *Irwin 93* (ASU). GR: Tinajas Altas, *Felger 98-145*. OP: Arch Canyon, *Niles 552* (ORPI).

Phacelia ramosissima Douglas ex Lehm. Robust perennial herbs; flowers white to blue.

OP: Trail above Bull Pasture, 4025 ft, *Felger 05-265*.

Phacelia rotundifolia Torr. Cool-season annuals; flowers white. One record at the boundary of the flora area, and one of the southernmost records for this species.

OP: 100 m N of OP and 0.5 km E of CP, rock crevice, *Christy 1263* (ASU).

Pholistoma auritum (Lindl.) Lilja var. **arizonicum** (M.E. Jones) Constance. Cool-season annuals; flowers pale lavender.

PI: Pinacate Peak, *Felger 19439*. CP: Agua Dulce Mts, *Felger 93-94*. GR: Tom Thumb, *Felger 02-85*. OP: Bull Pasture Trail, *Beale 18 Mar 1988* (ORPI). SD: S Maricopa Mts, *Felger 01-215*.

JUNCACEAE – RUSH FAMILY

Juncus acutus L. subsp. **leopoldii** (Parl.) Snogerup. SPINY RUSH. Large perennials resembling a giant pincushion.

AG: La Salina, *Felger 93-17*.

Juncus arcticus Willd. var. **mexicanus** (Willd. ex Roem. & Scult.) Balslev [*J. balticus* Willd. var. *mexicanus* (Willd. ex Roem. & Scult.) Kuntze] WIRE RUSH. Perennials with blackish creeping rhizomes.

PI: Río Sonoyta S of Cerro El Huérfano, *Felger 92-979*. OP: Quitobaquito, *Felger 86-211*.

Juncus bufonius L. TOAD RUSH. Annuals; locally extirpated.

OP: Quitobaquito, edge of pond, 25 Mar 1944, *Clark 11501* (ORPI).

Juncus cooperi Engelm. SPINY RUSH. Large perennials resembling a giant pincushion.

AG: Ciénega de Santa Clara, *Felger 92-986*. OP: Quitobaquito, *Bowers 1309* (ORPI).

KOEBERLINIACEAE – KOEBERLINIA FAMILY

Koeberlinia spinosa Zucc. ALLTHORN; CORONA DE CRISTO. Spinescent shrubs, essentially leafless; flowers cream-yellow.

PI: Playa Díaz, rare, *Felger 88-398*. GR: Ca. 1 mi S of Pistol Pass, 18 Dec 2002, *Rutman*, photo. SD: Vekol Valley, *Felger 02-338*.

KRAMERIACEAE – RATANY FAMILY

Krameria erecta Willd. ex Schult. [*K. parvifolia* Benth.] RANGE RATANY; CÓSAHUI. Shrubs; flowers pink.

PI: Tinaja Huarache, *Felger 19560*. CP: Pinacate Lava, *Felger 92-766*. GR: N of Mohawk Dunes, *Felger 96-148*. OP: Quitobaquito, *Felger 88-468*. SD: Table Top Mts, *Bolton 94-063*.

Krameria grayi Rose & Painter. WHITE RATANY; CÓSAHUI; EDHO, HE:Ḍ. Shrubs; flowers purple.

PI: MacDougal Crater, *Felger 9741*. CP: Christmas Pass, *Harlan 271* (CAB). GR: N of Mohawk Dunes, *Felger 96-147*. OP: South Puerto Blanco Drive, *Felger 90-4067*. SD: Table Top Mts, *Bolton 94-038*.

LAMIACEAE (LABIATAE) – MINT FAMILY

Hedeoma nanum (Torr.) Briq. var. **macrocalyx** W.S. Stewart. FALSE PENNYROYAL; ORÉGANO. Perennial herbs; flowers lavender.

CP: Childs Mt, *Felger 94-11*. GR: Tom Thumb, *Felger 02-97*. OP: Alamo Canyon, *Parker 8000*. SD: Table Top Mts, *Bolton 94-121*.

Hyptis albida Kunth [*H. emoryi* Torr.] DESERT LAVENDER; SALVIA. Shrubs; flowers lavender.

PI: MacDougal Crater, *Felger 9728*. CP: Eagle Tank, *Felger 92-589*. GR: N of Tinajas Altas, *Kurtz 1161*. OP: Quitobaquito, *Felger 90-483*. SD: Table Top Mts, *Bolton 94-075*.

Monardella arizonica Epling. Herbaceous perennials; flowers white spotted with purple.

OP: Arch Canyon, *Baker 7640* (ORPI).

Salazaria mexicana Torr. [*Scutellaria mexicana* (Torr.) A.J. Paton] BLADDER SAGE. Shrubs; flowers white and blue; unique fruiting calyx inflated like a paper bag.

PI: Carnegie Peak, *Felger 19936*. CP: N side Tule Mts, *Felger 92-51*. GR: Tinajas Altas, *Gentry 3524*. OP: Saddle N of Kino Peak, *Wilson 26 Apr 1993* (ORPI).

Salvia columbariae Benth. DESERT CHIA; CHÍA; DA:PK. Cool-season annuals; flowers blue.

PI: Vicinity Pinacate Peak, *Felger 19465.* **CP:** Pinacate Lava flow (cited by Simmons 1966). **GR:** Midway Wash, E of Hwy 85, *Rutman 2003-6.* **OP:** Quitobaquito, *Felger 88-281.* **SD:** Table Top Mts, *Bolton 94-024.*

Salvia mohavensis Greene. MOJAVE SAGE. Small shrubs; flowers pale to dark violet-blue.

PI: Pinacate Peak, *Felger 86-455.* **GR:** Mohawk Mts, *Holm 2003-0210-8.* **SD:** S Maricopa Mts, *Felger 01-218.*

Salvia pinguifolia (Fern.) Wooton & Standl. ROCK SAGE. Small shrubs; flowers lavender.

GR: Squaw Tit Mt, *Felger 95-455.* **OP:** Alamo Canyon, *Goodding 299-41.* **SD:** Sand Tank Mts, *Felger 95-455.*

Salvia vaseyi (Porter) Parish. Extremely aromatic shrubs; flowers white. Otherwise known only from the west side of Sonoran Desert in California and Baja California.

CP: Top of Sierra Pinta, S of Sunday Pass, *Cain & Jansen 11 Feb 2003.*

Teucrium cubense Jacq. subsp. **depressum** (Small) E.M. McClint. & Epling. Nonseasonal annuals; flowers pale blue to nearly white. Wet soil.

PI: Ciénega 25 mi W of Sonoyta [Pinacate Junction], *Shreve 7603.* **CP:** Jose Juan Tank, *Felger 93-99.* **GR:** Paradise Well, *Smith 13 May 2003.* **OP:** Dos Lomitas, *Wirt 12 Apr 1989.* **SD:** N of Antelope Peak, *Mauz 21-029.*

Teucrium glandulosum Kellogg. Perennial herbs; flowers showy, white with a pale lavender nectar guide.

PI: Pinacate Peak, *Felger 86-441.* **CP:** Eagle Tank, *Felger 92-586.* **GR:** Coyote Wash at Camino del Diablo, *Felger 02-14.* **OP:** Canyon SW of Kino Peak, *Rutman 31 Mar 2005.* **SD:** Javelina Mt, above 3600 ft, *Felger 00-70.*

LEMNACEAE – DUCKWEED FAMILY

Lemna sp. DUCKWEED; LAMITA. Minute floating aquatics.

GR: Thanksgiving Day Tank, *Rutman 24 Dec 2002.*

LENNOACEAE – LENNOA FAMILY

Pholisma sonorae (Torr.) Yatsk. [*Ammobroma sonorae* Torr. ex A. Gray] SANDFOOD; CAMOTE DE LOS MÉDANOS; HIA TAḌK. Parasitic perennial herbs; flowers lavender. Endemic to dunes and sand flats in drier areas of Lower Colorado Valley.

PI: "The Great Camote, sand dunes of Sierra del Rosario," Mar 1910, *Lumholtz 4* (G). **AG:** Hills around Adair Bay, *A. B. Gray 17-19 May 1854* (NY, not seen; photos, ARIZ). Lerdo, 1899, *Palmer 7616* (SD). **GR:** NNE of Border Monument 198, *Reichenbacher 644.*

LILIACEAE (sensu lato) – LILY FAMILY

Allium macropetalum Rydb. DESERT ONION; CEBOLLÍN; HUHUDAJ SIWOL. Perennials, small onion bulbs; flowers white and red-purple. Growing and flowering in spring.

CP: S of Charlie Bell Pass, *Felger 93-336.* **GR:** 3.5 km NE of Coffeepot Mt, *Morrison 991* (ASU). **OP:** W of Dripping Springs, *Steenbergh 15 Mar 1962* (ORPI). **SD:** Table Top Mts, *Felger 01-272.*

Calochortus kennedyi Porter. DESERT MARIPOSA LILY; COBENA AMARILLA; HA:DKOS. Perennials from a bulb; flowers orange-red, large and showy. Growing and flowering in spring.

GR: Squaw Tit Mt, *Felger 96-444.* **OP:** Bull Pasture, *Bowers 1200* (ORPI). **SD:** Table Top Mts, *Felger 01-300.*

Dichelostemma capitatum (Benth.) Wood subsp. **pauciflorum** (Torr.) Keator [*D. pulchellum* (Salisbury) A. Heller var. *pauciflorum* (Torr.) Hoover; *Brodiaea capitata* Benth. var. *pauciflora* Torr.] BLUE DICKS, WILD-HYACINTH; COBENA, COBERIA; HA:D. Perennials from a bulb; flowers violet-blue. Growing and flowering winter and spring.

PI: Sierra Pinacate, higher elevation, *Felger 92-464.* **CP:** 1 mi NE of Agua Dulce Pass (cited by Simmons 1966). **GR:** Squaw Tit Mt, *Felger 95-463.* **OP:** Alamo Canyon, *Nichol 14 Mar 1939.* **SD:** Table Top Mts, *Felger 01-299.*

Hesperocallis undulata A. Gray. AJO LILY, DESERT LILY; AJO SILVESTRE; A:SOS. Perennials from a relatively large bulb; flowers white. Growing and flowering winter and spring.

PI: N of Moon Crater, *Felger 88-78.* **AG:** N of El Doctor, *Bezy 359A.* **CP:** N of Tule Well, *Yeatts 3241* (CAB). **GR:** Crater Range, *Walter 1407* (ASU). **OP:** Growler Mts, *Crooks 31 Mar 1937.* **SD:** S Maricopa Mts, 24 Mar 2001, *Felger,* photo.

Triteleiopsis palmeri (S. Watson) Hoover. BLUE SAND LILY. Perennials, numerous small bulbs; flowers blue. Growing and flowering winter and spring. Dunes and sand flats.

PI: Sierra del Rosario, *Felger 20797.* **AG:** NNW of El Golfo, *Felger 92-218.* **CP:** Pinta Sands, *Felger 93-384.* **GR:** Butler Mts, *Van Devender 27 Mar 1983.*

Zephyranthes longifolia Hemsl. YELLOW ZEPHYR LILY. Summer growing and flowering from a single bulb; flowers yellow.

PI: N of Pinacate Peak, *Felger 86-429.* **OP:** Bull Pasture, *Bowers 1802.*

LINACEAE – FLAX FAMILY

Linum perenne L. subsp. **lewisii** (Pursh) Hulten [*L. lewisii* Pursh] BLUE FLAX. Cool-season annuals (elsewhere often perennials); flowers blue.

OP: Bates Well, *McDougall 67* (ORPI). **SD:** S Maricopa Mts, *Chamberland 1864.*

LOASACEAE – STICK-LEAF FAMILY

Eucnide rupestris (Baill.) H.J. Thomps. & W.R. Ernst [*Sympetaleia rupestris* (Baill.) S. Watson] VELCRO PLANT.

Nonseasonal annuals; flowers yellow and green. Rare in U.S., known only from vicinity of Cabeza Prieta Tanks, two records from Organ Pipe, and SE California; common in nearby Mexico.

PI: Elegante Crater, *Felger 19692*. **CP:** Cabeza Prieta Tanks, *Monson 1*. **OP:** Kino Peak, *Wirt 5 Dec 1990*.

Mentzelia adhaerens Benth. PEGAPEGA. Nonseasonal annuals; flowers orange to yellow-orange.

PI: Tinaja Tule, *Felger 19214*.

Mentzelia affinis Greene. TRIANGLE-SEED BLAZINGSTAR; PEGAPEGA. Cool-season annuals; flowers yellow.

PI: Arroyo Tule, *Felger 19540*. **CP:** Camino del Diablo 1.7 mi E of W border, *Felger 92-620*. **GR:** Paradise Well, *Smith 13 May 2003*. **OP:** Aguajita, *Felger 88-287*. **SD:** N Maricopa Mts, *Felger 01-194*.

Mentzelia albicaulis Douglas ex Hook. [species complex including *M. desertorum* (Davidson) H.J. Thomps. & J. Roberts] WHITE-STEM BLAZINGSTAR; PEGAPEGA. Cool-season annuals; flowers bright yellow.

CP: Pinacate lava flow, *McLaughlin 2986*. **GR:** Mohawk Dunes, *Felger 98-82*. **OP:** Alamo Wash, *Beale 22 Feb 1986* (ORPI). **SD:** S Maricopa Mts, *Chamberland 1858*.

Mentzelia isolata Gentry. Hot-season annuals; flowers yellow-orange.

OP: Dripping Springs, *Supernaugh-Leding 27 Oct 1951* (ORPI).

Mentzelia involucrata S. Watson [*M. involucrata* var. *megacantha* I.M. Johnst.] SILVER STICKLEAF, SILVER BLAZINGSTAR; PEGAPEGA. Cool-season annuals; flowers silvery white.

PI: Pinacate Peak, *Felger 19384*. **CP:** Sheep Tanks, *Kearney 11012*. **GR:** Baker Tanks, *Walter 742* (ASU). **OP:** Quitobaquito, *Clark 25 Mar 1944*. **SD:** Sand Tank Well, *Rutman 2003-158*.

Mentzelia jonesii (Urb. & Gilg) H.J. Thomps. & J. Roberts. Cool-season annuals; flowers yellow.

SD: Table Top Mts, *Bolton 94-097*.

Mentzelia multiflora (Nutt.) A. Gray [*M. multiflora* subsp. *longiloba* (J. Darl.) Felger; *M. pumila* (Nutt.) Torr. & A. Gray, in part] BLAZINGSTAR; PEGAPEGA. Cool-season annuals to short-lived herbaceous perennials; flowers yellow.

PI: Campo Rojo, *Felger 87-56*. **AG:** E of López Collada, *Felger 03-567*. 3.5 km NW of La Salina, 6 Jan 1993, *Felger*, observation. **CP:** Pinta Sands, *Felger 93-428A*. **GR:** Mohawk Dunes, *Turner 92-5*. **OP:** Rancho Bonito, La Abra Valley, *Harbison 26217*.

Mentzelia puberula J. Darl. Facultative annuals to short-lived perennials, base often woody; flowers yellow.

PI: Cerro Pinto, *Felger 89-57*. **CP:** Sierra Pinta, summit, *Cain 15 Nov 2003*. **GR:** Tinajas Altas, *Reichenbacher 480*. **SD:** Table Top Mts, *Felger 02-48*.

Figure 17.12. Pholisma sonorae *visited by a bee fly (Bombyliidae). (Drawing by Cathy Moser Marlett, based on a video by Eduardo Gómez-Limón)*

Mentzelia veatchiana Kellogg. Cool-season annuals; flowers yellow-orange with red-orange center.

PI: Pinacate Peak, *Felger 19389*.

Petalonyx linearis Greene. NARROWLEAF SANDPAPER PLANT. Small shrubs; flowers white.

PI: Sykes Crater, *Felger 18992*. **GR:** Tinajas Altas, *Reichenbacher 479*. **OP:** NW of Dripping Springs, *Baker 7589* (ORPI).

Petalonyx thurberi A. Gray. SANDPAPER PLANT; HADSADKAM. Shrubs; flowers white.

PI: High dunes, 5 mi SSE of Moon Crater, *Felger 20199*. **AG:** Dunes, NNE of El Golfo, 5 Mar 1992, *Felger*, observation. **CP:** Daniels Arroyo at Charlie Bell Rd, *Felger 92-548*. **GR:** 10.3 mi S of Gila Bend, *Van Devender 26 Sep 1974*. **OP:** Aguajita Wash, *Felger 86-288*. **SD:** North of Antelope Peak, *Mauz 21-020*.

LYTHRACEAE – LOOSESTRIFE FAMILY

Lythrum californicum Torr. & A. Gray. CALIFORNIA LOOSESTRIFE. Perennial herbs or shrubs; flowers purple.

AG: La Salina, *Felger 93-17*.

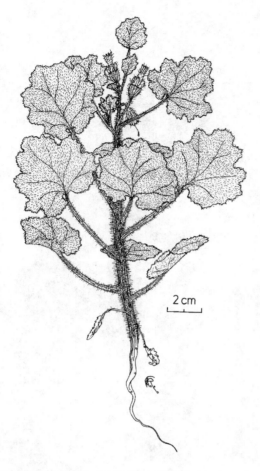

Figure 17.13. Eucnide rupestris. *(Drawing by Frances Runyan)*

2 cm

MALPIGHIACEAE – MALPIGHIA FAMILY

Janusia gracilis A. Gray. FERMINA. Perennial vines; flowers yellow.

    PI: W of Tinajas de Emilia, *Felger 19791*. **CP:** Childs Mt, *Felger 92-643C* (CAB). **GR:** Thanksgiving Day Tank, *Felger 02-138*. **OP:** Quitobaquito, *Felger 88-125*. **SD:** Table Top Mts, *Bolton 94-050*.

MALVACEAE – MALLOW FAMILY

Abutilon abutiloides (Jacq.) Britton & Wilson. PINTAPÁN. Shrubs; flowers yellow to orange.

    OP: Ajo Mts, *Bowers 990* (ORPI).

Abutilon californicum Benth. Shrubs; flowers yellow to orange.

    PI: Tinaja de los Chivos, *Felger 18622*.

Abutilon incanum (Link) Sweet. Small shrubs; flowers pale orange with maroon center.

    PI: Sierra de los Tanques, *Felger 89-16*. **CP:** Agua Dulce Mts, *Felger 92-728* (CAB). **GR:** Thanksgiving Day Tank, *Felger 02-115*. **OP:** Alamo Canyon, *Bowers 983*. **SD:** Table Top Mts, *Harrison 7294*.

Abutilon malacum S. Watson. Perennial subshrubs; flowers pale yellow-orange.

    CP: Agua Dulce Tank, *Felger 92-565*. **GR:** Sauceda Mts, *Felger 03-39*. **OP:** 40 Mile Drive, *Ranzoni 192* (ORPI). **SD:** Vekol Valley, *Felger 01-403*.

Abutilon palmeri A. Gray [*A. macdougalii* Rose & Standl.]. Sparsely branched shrubs or subshrubs, leaves velvety, rather large; flowers yellow-orange.

    PI: Pinacate Mts, 22 Nov 1907, *MacDougal 47* (Holotype of *A. macdougalii*, US). **CP:** Cabeza Prieta Tanks, *Lehto L23521*. **GR:** Thanksgiving Day Tank, *Felger 02-113*. **OP:** Dripping Springs, *Wirt 4 Mar 1989* (ORPI).

Anoda abutiloides A. Gray. Perennial subshrubs; flowers pale yellow, drying rose.

    OP: Arch Canyon, *Rutman 8 Nov 1995* (ORPI).

Anoda pentaschista A. Gray. Sparsely branched summer-fall annuals. Flowers small, pale yellow-orange. One record in the flora area.

    OP: Bull Pasture, *Wirt 12 Aug 1990*.

Eremalche exilis (A. Gray) Greene. Cool-season annuals; flowers white to pale lavender.

    PI: MacDougal Pass, *Felger 92-314*. **CP:** Pinta Sands, *Mason 3370*. **OP:** Alamo Canyon, *Nichol 26 Mar 1939* (ORPI).

Eremalche rotundifolia (A. Gray) Greene. DESERT FIVE-SPOT. Cool-season annuals; flowers pale pink-lavender with dark spots in center.

    PI: Moon Crater, *Felger 19232*. **GR:** Camino del Diablo, W side Gila Mts, *Eiber 44*.

Herissantia crispa (L.) Brizicky. BLADDER MALLOW. Perennial herbs; flowers pale yellow; fruits like a miniature paper lantern, falling apart at maturity.

    PI: N of Moon Crater, *Felger 10573*. **CP:** Pinacate Lava, *Felger 92-770*. **GR:** Thanksgiving Day Tank, *Felger 02-122*. **OP:** Dripping Springs, *Parker 7949*. **SD:** S Maricopa Mts, 21 Feb 2001, *Felger*, observation.

Hibiscus biseptus S. Watson. Perennial herbs or subshrubs; flowers yellow. One specimen known from the flora area, perhaps widespread in Ajo Mountain canyons.

    OP: N fork Alamo Canyon, *Baker 7557* (ASU, mixed with *H. coulteri*).

Hibiscus coulteri Harvey. DESERT ROSE-MALLOW. Perennial herbs or subshrubs; flowers yellow.

    CP: Childs Mt, *Felger 93-286*. **GR:** Sand Tank Mts, *Felger 95-357*. **OP:** Dripping Springs, *Parker 7947*. **SD:** Between Indian Butte and Table Top Mts, *Butterwick 7263* (ASU).

Hibiscus denudatus Benth. var. **denudatus.** ROCK HIBISCUS. Perennial subshrubs; flowers white to pinkish with maroon spots in the center.

    PI: MacDougal Crater, *Felger 9735*. **CP:** Hills E of Papago Well, *Shreve 5924*. **GR:** Cipriano Pass, *Reeves R5431* (ASU). **OP:** Aguajita, *Beale 23 Feb 1986* (ORPI). **SD:** Table Top Mts, *Felger 01-265*.

Horsfordia alata (S. Watson) A. Gray. PINK VELVET-MALLOW. Tall, slender shrubs; flowers pale lavender-white to pink.

PI: N of Moon Crater, *Felger 10572*. **CP:** Tule Tank, *Lehto 23550*. **GR:** Tinajas Altas, *Van Devender 25 Mar 1983*. **OP:** W of Quitobaquito, *Bowers 1526* (ORPI).

Horsfordia newberryi (S. Watson) A. Gray. ORANGE VELVET-MALLOW. Slender shrubs; flowers yellow orange.

PI: Sierra Blanca, *Felger 20225*. **CP:** Tule Tank, *Lehto 23549*. **GR:** Thanksgiving Day Tank, *Rutman 24 Dec 2001*. **OP:** Quitobaquito, *Darrow 2411*. **SD:** S Maricopa Mts, *Felger 03-442*.

*****Malva parviflora** L. CHEESEWEED; MALVA, QUESITOS; TAṢH MA:HAG, HA:HAG CU'IGKAM. Cool-season annuals; flowers white. Disturbed habitats.

PI: Pinacate Junction, *Felger 88-61B*. **AG:** Gustavo Sotelo, *Felger 03-560*. **GR:** Tenmile Wash at Hwy 85, *Felger 03-28*. **OP:** Alamo Canyon, old corral, *Bowers 1563* (ORPI). **SD:** Big Horn, *Felger 03-81*.

Malvastrum bicuspidatum (S. Watson) Rose subsp. **bicuspidatum.** Shrubs; flowers pale yellow-orange.

GR: Sand Tank Mts, *Felger 95-350*. **OP:** Arch Canyon, *Felger 90-553*. **SD:** NW of Bender Spring, *Felger 373*.

Malvella leprosa (Ortega) Krapov. [*Sida leprosa* var. *hederacea* (Douglas) K. Schum.] ALKALI MALLOW. Perennial herbs; deep-seated roots; flowers white. Playas.

PI: Playa Díaz, *Felger 86-366*. **AG:** Ejido Johnson, 27 May 2005, *Felger*, observation. **CP:** Las Playas, *Reeves 6811*.

Malvella sagittifolia (A. Gray) Fryxell [*Sida lepidota* A. Gray var. *sagittifolia* A. Gray] ARROWLEAF ALKALI MALLOW. Perennial herbs; deep-seated roots; flowers white to pink. Playas.

PI: S of Tinajas de los Pápagos, *Felger 18735*. **CP:** Pinta Playa, *Simmons 4 Oct 1964*. **GR:** Playa E side Mohawk Dunes, *Turner 95-18*. **SD:** Vekol bosque, *Mauz 20-004*.

Rhynchosida physocalyx (A. Gray) Fryxell. Perennial herbs; flowers yellow.

OP: Cherioni Wash, *Warren 10 Nov 1983*. **SD:** Vekol Valley, *Felger 01-425*.

Sida abutifolia Mill. [*S. filicaulis* Torr. & A. Gray; *S. procumbens* Sw.]. Perennial herbs; flowers white to pale yellow.

OP: Between Boulder and Arch canyons, *Bowers 1287* (ORPI). **SD:** Table Top Mts, *Felger 01-302*.

Sphaeralcea ambigua A. Gray. DESERT GLOBE MALLOW. Shrub or subshrub perennials. Two subspecies in the flora area.

Sphaeralcea ambigua subsp. **ambigua.** Flowers orange.

PI: Sykes Crater, *Felger 18966*. **CP:** Tule Tank, *Shreve 6223*. **GR:** Tinajas Altas, *Reichenbacher 481*. **OP:** Puerto Blanco Drive, *Felger 89-229A*. **SD:** Table Top Mts, *Bolton 94-069*.

Sphaeralcea ambigua subsp. **rosacea** (Munz & I.M. Johnst.) Kearney. Flowers pinkish-lavender to lavender.

PI: S of Carnegie Peak, *Felger 19879*. **SD:** Margies Cove, *Smith 3 May 2003*.

Sphaeralcea coulteri (S. Watson) A. Gray var. **coulteri** [*S. orcuttii* Rose] COULTER'S GLOBE MALLOW; MAL DE OJO; HAḌAM TATK, ÑIATUM. Cool-season or sometimes summer annuals, sometimes persisting as bushy annuals; flowers orange. Large, robust dune and sand-flat plants have been called *S. orcuttii.*

PI: MacDougal Crater, *Felger 9907*. **AG:** Gustavo Sotelo, *Felger 03-562*. **CP:** Near Tule Tank, *Kearney 10900*. **GR:** Mohawk Dunes, *Felger 98-75*. **OP:** Quitobaquito, *Felger 7650*. **SD:** Table Top Mts, *Bolton 94-008*.

Sphaeralcea emoryi Torr. MAL DE OJO. Annuals to short-lived perennial herbs or subshrubs; flowers orange to red-orange.

PI: Pinacate Junction, *Felger 19596*. **CP:** San Cristobal Wash, *Felger 92-689*. **GR:** Playa E side Mohawk Dunes, *Turner 95-17*. **OP:** Quitobaquito, *Felger 86-176*. **SD:** Vekol Valley, *Felger 01-228*.

Sphaeralcea laxa Wooton & Standl. CALICHE GLOBE MALLOW. Perennials; flowers orange.

GR: Paradise Well, *Smith 13 May 2003*. **OP:** Alamo Canyon, *Bowers 1252* (ORPI).

MARTYNIACEAE – DEVIL'S CLAW FAMILY

Proboscidea altheifolia (Benth.) Decne. DEVIL'S CLAW; CUERNITOS, UÑA DE GATO; BAN 'IHUGGA. Perennial herbs from a tuberous root; flowers yellow.

PI: MacDougal Crater, *Felger 10498*. **CP:** Tule Tank, 2 Feb 1992, *Felger 92-66*. **GR:** Mohawk Dunes, *Felger 96-146*. **OP:** Quitobaquito, *Bowers 1387*. **SD:** Table Top Mts, bajada, *Mauz 99-085*.

Proboscidea parviflora (Wooton) Wooton & Standl. subsp. **parviflora.** DEVIL'S CLAW; CUERNITOS, UÑA DE GATO; 'IHUG. Hot-weather annuals; flowers lavender with purple, white, and yellow.

PI: Suvuk, N of Campo de Romero, *Equihua 22 Sep 1982* (MEXU). **GR:** 3 mi S of Black Gap, 26 Nov 2001, *Felger*, observation. **OP:** Armenta Well, *Warren 16 Nov 1974*. **SD:** Vekol Valley, *Mauz 99-111*.

MOLLUGINACEAE – CARPETWEED FAMILY

*****Glinus lotoides** L. Nonseasonal annuals; flowers inconspicuous. Locally in cattle tanks.

CP: Redtail Tank, *Felger 92-552*. **SD:** Vekol Valley Ranch, *Hahn 15 Apr 2003*.

Mollugo cerviana (L.) Sér. THREADSTEM CARPETWEED, INDIAN CHICKWEED. Hot-weather annuals; flowers white, minute. Sometimes considered non-native in the New World.

PI: MacDougal Crater, *Felger 10476*. **AG:** Near NE corner of the Reserva, *Felger 03-494*. **CP:** Jose Juan Tank,

Felger 92-715. **GR:** Mohawk Dunes, *Felger 97-62*. **OP:** Aguajita, *Felger 88-419*. **SD:** Vekol Valley, *Mauz 99-076*.

MORACEAE – MULBERRY FAMILY

*****Ficus carica** L. FIG; HIGUERA; SU:NA. Shrubs or small trees; flowers inconspicuous.

OP: Quitobaquito, persisting from cultivation, *Felger 88-452*.

Morus microphylla Buckley. LITTLELEAF MULBERRY; MORA CIMARRONA; GOHI. Shrubs; flowers inconspicuous.

OP: Alamo Canyon, *Clark 10916* (ORPI).

NAJADACEAE – WATER-NYMPH FAMILY

Najas marina L. HOLLYLEAF WATER-NYMPH, SPINY NAIAD; SARGAZO. Submerged herbs with prickly stems and leaves; flowers inconspicuous. Abundant in Ciénega de Santa Clara and common in the pond at Quitobaquito.

AG: Ciénega de Santa Clara, *Felger 93-214*. **OP:** Quitobaquito, *Pinkava 2363* (ASU).

NOLINACEAE – BEARGRASS FAMILY

Nolina bigelovii (Torr.) S. Watson. DESERT TREE-BEARGRASS. Yucca-like plants to 3 m tall (rarely to 4+ m tall) with woody trunk; flowers cream color.

PI: Sierra del Rosario, *Felger 20396*. **CP:** Buckhorn Tank, *Felger 92-601*. **GR:** Tinajas Altas, *Shreve 6233*.

Nolina microcarpa S. Watson. BEARGRASS; SACAHUISTE; MOHO. Large perennials with underground caudex; flowers white.

GR: 1 mi SW of Squaw Tit Peak, 3340 ft, *Holm 2001-0917-10*. **OP:** Boulder Canyon, *Bowers 1296* (ORPI).

NYCTAGINACEAE – FOUR-O'CLOCK FAMILY

Abronia maritima Nutt. ex S. Watson subsp. **maritima.** COASTAL SAND VERBENA. Succulent perennial herbs; flowers bright purple-magenta. Beaches.

AG: Beach 5 km NW of El Tornillal, *Felger 92-193*.

Abronia villosa S. Watson var. **villosa.** SAND VERBENA; VERBENA DE LA ARENA. Cool-season annuals; flowers magenta.

PI: MacDougal Crater, *Felger 9906*. **AG:** E of López Collada, *Felger 03-564*. NE corner of Reserva AG, *Felger 03-491*. **CP:** E of Pinacate Lava Flow, *Niles 348*. **GR:** Mohawk Dunes, *Turner 95-15*.

Acleisanthes longiflora A. Gray. ANGELS' TRUMPETS. Perennial herbs from thickened roots; flowers white with a long tube, nocturnal and pollinated by hawk moths during hot weather with sufficient soil moisture; also selfing, short and non-opening (cleistogamous) flowers during drought and cooler weather.

CP: W of Agua Dulce Pass, *Felger 92-564*. **GR:** Blue Plateau, *Smith 6 May 2003*. **SD:** Table Top Mts, *Mauz 99-059*.

Allionia incarnata L. [*A. incarnata* var. *nuda* (Standl.) Munz, *A. incarnata.* var. *villosa* (Standl.) B.L. Turner] TRAILING WINDMILLS, TRAILING FOUR-O'CLOCK. Short-lived perennials or annuals; flowers bright pink-purple.

PI: Sykes Crater, *Felger 18974A*. **AG:** Gustavo Sotelo, *Felger 03-525*. **CP:** Bates Well Rd at OP boundary, *Felger 92-678*. **GR:** Tenmile Wash, N of Ajo Airport, *Rutman 2003-473*. **OP:** Quitobaquito, *Felger 88-403*. **SD:** Vekol Valley, *Felger 02-313*.

*****Boerhavia coccinea** Mill. SCARLET SPIDERLING. Short-lived perennial herbs; flowers red-purple.

CP: Childs Mt, *Felger 92-637* (CAB). **GR:** Tinajas Altas, *Felger 92-609*. **OP:** W of Bates Mts, *Bowers 1165* (ORPI). **SD:** Papago Indian Chief Mine, *Felger 95-329*.

Boerhavia erecta L. SPIDERLING; MAKKUMĬ HA-JEVEḌ. Hot-weather annuals; flowers pink. Two varieties, often treated as distinct species.

Boerhavia erecta var. **erecta**

PI: MacDougal Crater, *Felger 10452*. **CP:** San Cristobal Wash, *Felger 92-692*. **GR:** Coyote Water, *Felger 04-28*. **OP:** Aguajita, *Felger 88-424*. **SD:** Table Top Mts, *Mauz 99-079*.

Boerhavia erecta var. **intermedia** (M.E. Jones) Kearney & Peebles [*B. intermedia* M.E. Jones; *B. triqueta* S. Watson].

PI: Cerro Colorado, *Felger 10787*. **CP:** Las Playas, *Felger 01-572*. **GR:** Mohawk Dunes, *Felger 97-75*. **OP:** Aguajita, *Felger 88-413*. **SD:** Vekol Valley, *Felger 02-322*.

Boerhavia megaptera Standl. Hot-weather annuals; flowers pink.

OP: Bull Pasture Trail, *Bowers 954*.

Boerhavia pterocarpa S. Watson. Hot-weather annuals; flowers pink. One record from the flora area.

OP: Armenta Well Ranch, *Bowers 1533* (ORPI).

Boerhavia spicata Choisy [*B. coulteri* (Hook. f.) S. Watson; *B. coulteri* var. *palmeri* (S. Watson) Spellenb.; *B. spicata* var. *palmeri* S. Watson; *B. watsonii* Standl.] SPIDERLING. Hot-weather annuals; flowers white to pink. Often ravaged by caterpillars of white-lined sphinx moth (*Hyles lineata*).

PI: MacDougal Crater, *Felger 10478*. **CP:** Daniels Arroyo at Charlie Bell Rd, *Felger 92-656*. **GR:** Mohawk Dunes, *Felger 96-166*. **OP:** Aguajita Wash, *Felger 88-415*. **SD:** Vekol Valley, *Felger 01-417*.

Boerhavia wrightii A. Gray. DESERT SPIDERLING. Hot-weather annuals; flowers pink.

PI: MacDougal Crater, *Felger 10761*. **CP:** Daniels Arroyo at Charlie Bell Rd, *Felger 92-655*. **GR:** Camino del Diablo, E of Raven Butte, *Felger 01-588*. **OP:** Aguajita, *Felger 88-412*. **SD:** Table Top Mts, *Mauz 99-116*.

Commicarpus scandens (L.) Standl. Bushy perennials. Flowers pale yellow-green.

GR: Sauceda Mts, *Holm 2001-0906-19.* **OP:** Estes Canyon, *Supernaugh 446.* **SD:** Vekol Valley, *Mauz 99-077.*

Mirabilis albida (Walter) Heimerl, sensu lato [*M. comata* (Small) Standl., sensu stricto; *M. oblongifolia* (A. Gray) Heimerl, sensu Reed] WHITE FOUR-O'CLOCK. Perennial herbs; flowers purple-red or rose. One record from the flora area; nearest known population in the Sierra Estrella.

GR: Squaw Tit Mt, summit, *Smith 16 May 2003.*

Mirabilis laevis (Benth.) Curran var. **villosa** (Kellogg) Spellenb. [*M. bigelovii* A. Gray] DESERT FOUR-O'CLOCK. Perennial herbs; flowers white.

PI: Pinacate Peak, *Felger 19410.* **CP:** Eagle Tank, *Simmons 24 Feb 1964* (CAB). **GR:** Borrego Canyon, *Felger 92-614.* **OP:** Quitobaquito, *Felger 86-180.* **SD:** Sand Tank Mts, Big Horn Rd, *Funicelli 59.*

Mirabilis multiflora (Torr.) A. Gray. COLORADO FOUR-O'CLOCK. Perennial herbs; flowers pink.

OP: Boulder Canyon, *Bowers 1279.*

Mirabilis tenuiloba S. Watson. LONG-LOBED FOUR-O'CLOCK. Perennial herbs; flowers white. Baja California and southeastern California, otherwise known only from one locality in Arizona and one in Sonora.

PI: Sierra del Rosario, *Felger 20652.* **GR:** Borrego Canyon, *Felger 92-614.*

OLEACEAE – OLIVE FAMILY

Forestiera phillyreoides (Benth.) Torr. [*F. shrevei* Standl.] DESERT OLIVE. Hardwood shrubs. Flowers inconspicuous.

GR: Sand Tank Mts, Bender Saddle, *Felger 95-392.* **OP:** Above Alamo Ranch, Ajo Mountains, 19 Apr 1933, *Shreve 6201* (Isotype of *F. shrevei*). **SD:** N Maricopa Mts, *Mauz 24-003.*

Fraxinus velutina Torr. ARIZONA ASH; FRESNO. Trees; flowers yellow or green. Known from the flora area by one specimen; perhaps extirpated or planted at former ranch.

OP: Alamo Canyon, 3000 ft, 14 Mar 1940, *Benson 10686.*

Menodora scabra A. Gray. TWINBERRY. Small shrubs or subshrubs; flowers yellow.

PI: Sierra del Viejo (Hwy 2), *Felger 85-730.* **CP:** Tuseral Tank, *Felger 92-598.* **GR:** Sauceda Mts, *Holm 2001-0906-12.* **OP:** Senita Pass, *McDougall 85.* **SD:** NE slope Javelina Mt, *Walter 1259* (ASU).

ONAGRACEAE – EVENING PRIMROSE FAMILY

Camissonia arenaria (A. Nelson) P.H. Raven. Cool-season annuals to short-lived perennial herbs; flowers yellow, fading pink.

PI: Sierra del Rosario, *Felger 20663.* **CP:** Tule Tank, *Hinckley 26 Mar 1932.* **GR:** Tinajas Altas, *Harrison 3608.*

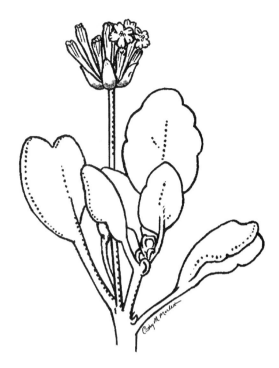

Figure 17.14. Abronia maritima. *(Drawing by Cathy Moser Marlett)*

Camissonia boothii (Douglas) P.H. Raven subsp. **condensata** (Munz) P.H. Raven. WOODY BOTTLE-WASHER. Cool-season annuals; flowers white.

PI: S of Papago Tanks, *Felger 18911.* **CP:** Las Playas, *Niles 356.* **GR:** Mohawk Dunes, *Felger 98-92.* **OP:** N of Pozo Nuevo, *Bowers 1097.* **SD:** Vekol Valley, *Felger 01-253.*

Camissonia brevipes (A. Gray) P.H. Raven subsp. **arizonica** (P.H. Raven) P.H. Raven. Cool-season annuals; flowers yellow.

GR: Baker Tanks, *Halse 4 Mar 1973.*

Camissonia californica (Nutt. ex Torr. & A. Gray) P.H. Raven. Cool-season annuals; flowers yellow.

PI: Sykes Crater, *Felger 18939.* **CP:** Charlie Bell Pass, *Whipple 3914.* **GR:** Tinajas Altas, *Van Devender 5 Mar 1983.* **OP:** Quitobaquito, *Felger 88-312.* **SD:** Table Top Mts, *Mauz 21-011.*

Camissonia cardiophylla (Torr.) P.H. Raven subsp. **cardiophylla.** Cool-season annuals to short-lived perennial herbs; flowers yellow, drying pink.

PI: Elegante Crater, *Felger 19680.* **GR:** Mohawk Mts, *Salywon 542* (ASU).

Camissonia chamaenerioides (A. Gray) P.H. Raven. WILLOW-HERB PRIMROSE. Cool-season annuals; flowers pink.

PI: Sykes Crater, *Felger 18982.* **CP:** Bassarisc Tank, *Felger 93-121.* **GR:** Tinajas Altas, *Van Devender 5 Mar 1983.* **OP:** Quitobaquito, *Darrow 2412.* **SD:** Table Top Mts, *Felger 01-315.*

Camissonia claviformis (Torr. & Frém.) P.H. Raven. BROWNEYES. Cool-season annuals. Widespread and common. Three of the 12 subspecies occur in the flora area.

Camissonia claviformis subsp. **peeblesii** (P.H. Raven) P.H. Raven. Flowers white, some with pink tinges, throat red-brown.

PI: SW of Sierra Extraña, *Felger 88-70.* **CP:** Papago Well, *Felger 93-380.* **GR:** Mohawk Dunes, *Felger 98-14.* **OP:** Alamo Canyon, *Nichol 26 Mar 1939.* **SD:** S Maricopa Mts, *Felger 01-141.*

Camissonia claviformis subsp. **rubescens** (P.H. Raven) P.H. Raven. Flowers yellow, fading orange-red, throat maroon.

PI: Sykes Crater, *Felger 18959.* **CP:** Pinacate Lava Fields, *Shreve 6211.* **GR:** W side N Mohawk Mts, *Arnett 1319* (ASU). **OP:** Junction Bates Well Rd and rd to Cabeza Prieta, *Bowers 1138.*

Camissonia claviformis subsp. **yumae** (P.H. Raven) P.H. Raven. Flowers pale yellow, sometimes fading reddish.

PI: Sierra Extraña, *Felger 88-71A.* **AG:** N of El Golfo, *Felger 75-77.* **GR:** Butler Mts, *Van Devender 27 Mar 1983.*

Epilobium canum (Greene) P.H. Raven subsp. **latifolium** (Hook.) P.H. Raven [*Zauschneria californica* Presl subsp. *latifolia* (Hook.) D.D. Keck] HUMMING-BIRD TRUMPET. Perennial subshrubs; flowers red.

OP: South Alamo Canyon, *Wilson 199.*

Gaura parviflora Hook. LIZARD TAIL, VELVET-LEAF GAURA. Tall, slender, nonseasonal annuals; flowers pink.

PI: Sykes Crater, *Felger 18917.* **CP:** Jose Juan Tank, *Felger 93-105.* **OP:** Quitobaquito, *Felger 86-174A.*

Oenothera arizonica (Munz) W.L. Wagner [*O. deltoides* Torr. & Frém. var. *arizonica* Munz; *O. californica* S. Watson subsp. *arizonica* (Munz) W. Klein; *O. avita* (W. Klein) W. Klein subsp. *arizonica* (Munz) W. Klein] ARIZONA EVENING PRIMROSE. Cool-season annuals; flowers white.

CP: N of Las Playas, *Darrow 15 Apr 1941.* **OP:** Wash near Sonoita [sic] Rd, *McDougall 10 Apr 1941.*

Oenothera deltoides Torr. & Frém. subsp. **deltoides.** DUNE EVENING PRIMROSE, WHITE DESERT PRIMROSE, DEVIL'S LANTERN. Cool-season annuals; flowers white. Abundant on dunes and sand flats.

PI: Moon Crater, *Felger 18828.* **AG:** El Golfo, *Bezy 364.* **CP:** Pinta Sands, *Felger 92-37.* **GR:** Tinajas Altas, *Reichenbacher 609.*

Oenothera primiveris A. Gray subsp. **primiveris.** YELLOW EVENING PRIMROSE. Cool-season annuals; flowers yellow.

PI: MacDougal Crater, *Felger 9716.* **CP:** Pinta Sands, *Felger 92-35.* **GR:** Mohawk Dunes, *Felger 98-84.* **OP:** Tres Alamos Canyon, *Nichol 24 Feb 1939.* **SD:** Table Top Mts, 17 Feb 2001, *Mauz,* photo.

OROBANCHACEAE – BROOMRAPE FAMILY

Orobanche cooperi (A. Gray) A. Heller. DESERT BROOM-RAPE; FLOR DE TIERRA; MO'OTAṢK. Winter-spring annuals ("North American *Orobanche* are annuals," George Yatskievych, personal communication 2002); parasitic on *Ambrosia* spp.; flowers purple and white.

PI: Sierra Blanca near Pinacate, "called 'camote' by Spaniard," Feb 1910, *Lumholtz 5* (GH, photocopy). **AG:** Lerdo, 1889, *Palmer 937* (GH, photocopy). **CP:** Heart Tank, *Simmons 27 Mar 1955* (CAB). **GR:** W slope Tinajas Altas Mts, *Van Devender 6 Mar 1983.* **OP:** Aguajita, *Felger 88-300.* **SD:** Bender Spring Rd, *Felger 95-421.*

Orobanche fasciculata Nutt. YELLOW BROOMRAPE. Annuals, spring, several slender stems, each bearing one to several rather large, bright yellow flowers. In the flora area known by several records from near the mouth of Alamo Canyon.

OP: S fork Alamo Canyon, *Rutman 2003-497* (ORPI).

OXALIDACEAE – OXALIS FAMILY

Oxalis albicans Kunth. WOOD SORREL. Perennial herbs; flowers yellow.

OP: Bull Pasture Trail, *Wilson 190.*

PAPAVERACEAE – POPPY FAMILY

Argemone gracilenta Greene. PRICKLY POPPY, COW-BOY'S FRIED EGGS; CARDO. Large perennial herbs; petals white, stamens yellow.

PI: Papago Tanks, *Burgess 6288.* **CP:** Daniels Arroyo at Charlie Bell Rd, *Felger 93-365.* **GR:** Mohawk Dunes, *Felger 98-77.* **OP:** Walls Well, *Nichol 28 Apr 1939.* **SD:** Roadside, E of Gila Bend, 19 Mar 2001, *Chamberland,* photo.

*****Argemone ochroleuca** Sweet subsp. **ochroleuca.** MEXI-CAN PRICKLY POPPY; CARDO. Facultative annuals or perennials; petals and stamens yellow. Scarce, not established in the flora area; weedy elsewhere.

OP: Growler Wash downstream from Bates Well, *Johnson 25 Apr 1992* (ASU).

Eschscholzia californica Chamisso subsp. **mexicana** (Greene) C. Clark. MEXICAN GOLD POPPY; AMAPOLITA DEL CAMPO; HO:HI 'E'ES. Cool-season annuals; flowers showy, gold-yellow.

GR: Rd to Hat Mt, *Felger 03-227.* **OP:** E of Lukeville, *Felger 88-07.* **SD:** Table Top Mts, *Bolton 94-033.*

Eschscholzia glyptosperma Greene. DESERT GOLD POPPY. Cool-season annuals; flowers gold-yellow. Similar to *E. californica,* distinguished in part by different pattern on seed surface.

GR: 5 mi W of Mohawk Pass, *Salywon 560* (ASU).

Eschscholzia minutiflora S. Watson. LITTLE GOLD POPPY. Cool-season annuals; flowers small, yellow-orange.

PI: Pinacate Peak, *Felger 19400.* **CP:** Heart Tank, *Simmons 6 Mar 1964* (CAB). **GR:** Mohawk Dunes, *Turner 95-33.* **OP:** Aguajita Wash, *Felger 88-290.*

PEDALIACEAE – SESAME FAMILY

*Sesamum orientale L. [*S. indicum* L.] SESAME; AJONJOLÍ. Hot-season annuals; flowers white. Occasionally along roadsides, growing from seeds from passing trucks; not reproducing.

PI: W of Sonoyta, *Felger 85-958.*

PHYTOLACCACEAE – POKEWEED FAMILY

Rivina humilis L. PIGEON BERRY. Perennial subshrubs; flowers red-purple.

OP: Alamo Canyon, *Goodding 294-41.*

Stegnosperma halimifolium Benth. [*S. watsonii* D.J. Rogers] CHAPACOLOR. Shrubs; flowers white.

PI: Tinaja Huarache, *Felger 19128.*

PLANTAGINACEAE – PLANTAIN FAMILY

Plantago ovata Forssk. [*P. insularis* Eastw. var. *fastigiata* (Morris) Jeps.] WOOLLY PLANTAIN, INDIAN WHEAT; PASTORA; MUMṢA. Cool-season annuals; flowers straw-colored.

PI: Moon Crater, *Felger 19276.* **AG:** N of El Golfo, *Felger 75-66.* **CP:** Pinta Sands, *Felger 92-25.* **GR:** E of Mohawk Dunes, *Turner 95-19.* **OP:** Tres Alamos Canyon, *Nichol 24 Feb 1939.* **SD:** Table Top Mts, *Bolton 94-003.*

Plantago patagonica Jacq. [*P. purshii* Roem. & Schult.] PASTORA. Cool-season annuals; flowers straw-colored.

CP: Jose Juan Represo, *Felger 92-560.* **GR:** Above Bender Spring, *Holm 11 Apr 2003.* **OP:** Alamo Canyon, *Benson 10683.* **SD:** Table Top Mts, *Felger 01-288.*

Plantago rhodosperma Decne. Cool-season annuals; leaves broad, margins toothed; flowers white with pale red ovary.

SD: Vekol Valley, *Felger 01-226.*

PLUMBAGINACEAE – PLUMBAGO FAMILY

Plumbago zeylanica L. [*P. scandens* L.] DOCTOR BUSH; ESTRENINA. Perennial herbs or subshrubs; flowers white.

OP: Arch Canyon, *Bowers 1299.*

POACEAE (GRAMINEAE) – GRASS FAMILY

Aristida adscensionis L. SIX-WEEKS THREE-AWN; ZACATE TRES BARBAS. Nonseasonal annuals.

PI: MacDougal Crater, *Felger 10463.* **AG:** 8 mi E of López Collada along RR, *Felger 03-618.* Cerro Prieto, *Felger 03-475.* **CP:** Charlie Bell Pass, *Whipple 3954.* **GR:** Crater Range, *Van Devender 18 Mar 1973.* **OP:** Quitobaquito, *Felger 87-299.* **SD:** Table Top Mts, *Bolton 94-084.*

Aristida californica Thurb. CALIFORNIA THREE-AWN; TRES BARBAS DE CALIFORNIA. Nonseasonal tufted perennials, sometimes flowering in first season. Awn column long, articulated (breaking apart at joint), awns long and slender. Two varieties.

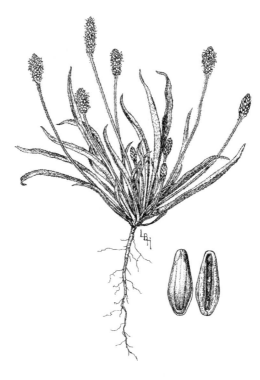

Figure 17.15. Plantago ovata. *(Drawing by Lucretia Brezeale Hamilton)*

Aristida californica var. **californica**

PI: MacDougal Crater, *Felger 10463.* **AG:** W of El Golfo, *Felger 93-05.* **CP:** Pinta Sands, *Felger 92-628.* **GR:** Tinajas Altas, *Reichenbacher 602.*

Aristida californica var. **glabrata** Vasey

OP: Hwy 85, 4 mi S of N boundary, *Felger 87-334.*

Aristida parishii Hitchc. [*A. purpurea* var. *parishii* (Hitchc.) Allred] PARISH THREE-AWN. Tufted perennials.

CP: Papago Well, *Felger 92-10.* **GR:** East Tactical Range, Sauceda Wash drainage, *Felger 03-37.* **OP:** Aguajita, *Felger 92-102.* **SD:** N slope of Javelina Mt, *Morrison 1044* (CMML).

Aristida purpurea Nutt. var. **nealleyi** (Vasey) Allred [*A. glauca* (Nees) Walpers] PURPLE THREE-AWN; TRES BARBAS. Tufted perennials.

PI: S of Pinacate Peak, *Felger 19301.* **CP:** Rd to Christmas Pass, *Felger 92-73.* **GR:** Butler Mts, *Van Devender 27 Mar 1983.* **OP:** Quitobaquito, *Felger 90-49.* **SD:** Table Top Mts, *Mauz 99-120.*

Aristida ternipes Cav. Tufted perennials. Two varieties.

Aristida ternipes var. **gentilis** (Henrard) Allred [*A. hamulosa* Henrard] POVERTY THREE-AWN; ZACATE ARAÑA DE TRES BARBAS. Localized in widely scattered places.

PI: 6 km W of Los Vidrios, *Felger 92-964.* **CP:** Jose Juan Tank, *Felger 92-710.* **GR:** E Tactical Range, valley plain E of Sauceda Mts, *Felger 03-37.* **OP:** Bull Pasture, *Wirt 12 Nov 1989* (ORPI). **SD:** Maricopa Rd (Hwy 238), 7.3 mi W of 91st Ave., *Felger 01-496.*

Aristida ternipes var. **ternipes.** SPIDERGRASS; ZACATE ARAÑA. Widespread, especially mountains and hills.

CP: Agua Dulce Tank, *Felger 92-567*. **GR:** Thanksgiving Day Tank, *Felger 02-111*. **OP:** Alamo Canyon, *Gould & Darrow 4691*. **SD:** Table Top Mts, *Felger 01-464*.

*****Avena fatua** L. WILD OAT; AVENA LOCA; 'AKṢĬ MUḌADT-KAM, KO:KṢAM. Cool-season annuals. Mostly roadsides.

GR: Crater Range, *Morrison 1056* (ASU). **OP:** Bull Pasture, *Bowers 1275*. **SD:** Vekol Rd and Interstate 8, *Felger 01-254*.

Bothriochloa barbinodis (Lag.) Herter [*Andropogon barbinodis* Lag.] CANE BLUESTEM; ZACATE POPOTILLO. Perennials with cottony inflorescences.

PI: Pinacate Peak, *Felger 92-86*. **CP:** Cabeza Prieta Tanks, *Felger 92-605*. **GR:** Sand Tank Mts, *Felger 95-387*. **OP:** Arch Canyon, *Felger 90-522*. **SD:** N of Butterfield Pass, 1993, *Wirt*, observation.

Bouteloua aristidoides (Kunth) Griseb. SIX-WEEKS NEEDLE GRAMA; ACEITILLA, NAVAJITA AGUJA. Summer annuals.

PI: Molina Crater, *Felger 10651*. **AG:** Gustavo Sotelo, *Felger 03-546*. **CP:** Childs Mt, *Felger 92-643*. **GR:** Sand Tank Mts, *Felger 95-422*. **OP:** Quitobaquito, *Felger 86-280*. **SD:** Vekol Valley, *Felger 01-436*.

Bouteloua barbata Lag. Two varieties.

Bouteloua barbata var. **barbata**. SIX-WEEKS GRAMA; NAVAJITA, ZACATE LIEBRERO; S-CUK MUḌADT-KAM. Summer annuals.

PI: Molina Crater, *Felger 10650*. **AG:** Gustavo Sotelo, *Felger 03-545*. **CP:** Jose Juan Represo, *Felger 92-561*. **GR:** Fortuna Mine, *Goodding & Hardies 719*. **OP:** Aguajita, *Felger 86-279*. **SD:** Johnson Well, *Funicelli 32*.

Bouteloua barbata var. **rothrockii** (Vasey) Gould [*B. rothrockii* Vasey] ROTHROCK GRAMA; ZACATE LIEBRERO. Tufted perennials, higher elevations in mountains.

GR: Sand Tank Mts, *Felger 95-364*. **OP:** Bull Pasture, *Bowers 1708*. **SD:** Table Top Mts, *Mauz 17 Mar 1999* (specimen not curated).

Bouteloua curtipendula (Michx.) Torr. SIDEOATS GRAMA; BANDERILLA; DA:PK VAṢAI. Tufted perennials, in mountains.

GR: Sand Tank Mts, *Felger 95-384*. **OP:** Alamo Canyon, *Nichol 4 May 1939*. **SD:** Table Top Mts, 4 Apr 2001, *Felger*, observation.

Bouteloua repens (Kunth) Scribn. [*B. filiformis* (E. Fournier) Griffiths] SLENDER GRAMA; NAVAJITA DELGADA. Tufted perennials.

GR: Thanksgiving Day Tank, *Felger 02-112*. **OP:** Alamo Canyon, *Bowers 980*. **SD:** N slope Javelina Mts, *Morrison 233* (CMML).

Bouteloua trifida Thurb. RED GRAMA; NAVAJITA CHINA. Small tufted perennials.

PI: Arroyo below Tinaja Tule, *Felger 19190*. **CP:** Eagle Tank, *Felger 92-587*. **GR:** Gila Mts, ENE of Drip-

ping Springs, *Walter 1069* (ASU). **OP:** Gunsight Hills, *Rutman 4 Apr 1988* (ORPI). **SD:** Johnson Well, *Funicelli 9*.

Brachiaria arizonica (Scribn. & Merr.) S.T. Blake [*Panicum arizonicum* Scribn. & Merr.; *Urochloa arizonica* (Scribn. & Merr.) Morrone & Zuloaga] ARIZONA SIGNALGRASS; PIOJILLO DE ARIZONA. Hot-weather annuals.

CP: Pinta Sands, *Felger 92-759*. **GR:** NE Sauceda Mts, *Arnett 1219* (ASU). **OP:** Armenta Well, *Bowers 1532*. **SD:** Johnson Well, *Funicelli 28*.

Bromus berterianus Colla [*B. trinii* Desv.] CHILEAN CHESS. Cool-season annuals. Known from mainland Mexico and the flora area only from Pinacate Peak.

PI: Pinacate Peak, *Felger 19449*.

Bromus carinatus Hook. & Arn. [*B. carinatus* var. *arizonicus* Shear; *B. arizonicus* (Shear) Stebb.] CALIFORNIA BROME. Cool-season annuals.

CP: San Cristobal Wash, *Felger 92-2*. **GR:** SE Crater Range, *Walter 1047* (ASU). **OP:** Quitobaquito, *Felger 7676*. **SD:** Table Top Mts, *Felger 01-307*.

*****Bromus catharticus** Vahl var. **catharticus** [*B. unioloides* Kunth; *B. willdenowii* Kunth] RESCUE BROME; BROMO CEBADILLA. Cool-season annuals.

PI: Playa los Vidrios, *Ezcurra 7 Oct 1981*. **SD:** NW of Bender Spring, *Felger 01-361*.

*****Bromus rubens** L. [*B. madritensis* L. subsp. *rubens* (L.) Husn.] FOXTAIL BROME, RED BROME; BROMO ROJO. Cool-season annuals.

PI: Pinacate Peak, *Felger 87-53*. **CP:** Daniels Arroyo, *Felger 92-543*. **GR:** 4 km WSW of Hat Mt, *Morrison 145* (ASU). **OP:** Alamo Canyon, *Tinkham 18 Apr 1942*. **SD:** Antelope Peak, *Bolton 94-039*.

*****Bromus tectorum** L. DOWNY CHESS. Cool-season annuals. Not established in the flora area.

OP: Quitobaquito, *Felger 86-133*.

Cenchrus ciliaris, see **Pennisetum ciliare.**

*****Cenchrus echinatus** L. SOUTHERN SANDBUR; GUACHAPORI. Warm-weather annuals. Weed, primarily on Mexico side of border.

OP: E of Lukeville, *Felger 87-319*.

Cenchrus palmeri Vasey. GIANT SANDBUR; HUIZAPORI, GUACHAPORI. Nonseasonal annuals.

PI: MacDougal Crater, *Felger 10441*. **AG:** Gustavo Sotelo, *Felger 03-521*.

*****Cenchrus spinifex** Cav. [*C. incertus* M.A. Curtis; *C. pauciflorus* Benth.] FIELD SANDBUR; HUIZAPORI, GUACHAPORI. Warm-weather annuals or perennials. In the flora area known from two nearby local areas.

PI: Rd to Rancho Guadalupe Victoria, *Felger 92-963*. **CP:** 8 mi W of O'Neill's grave, *Reeder 6836*.

Chloris crinita Lag. [*Trichloris crinita* (Lag.) Parodi] FEATHER FINGERGRASS. Large, tufted perennials.

OP: W of Lukeville, *Felger 87-280*.

*Chloris virgata Sw. FEATHER FINGERGRASS; COLA DE ZORRA, ZACATE LAGUNERO. Warm-weather annuals.

PI: S of Tinaja de los Pápagos, *Felger 86-488*. CP: Redtail Tank, *Felger 92-550*. OP: Quitobaquito, *Felger 90-487*. SD: Vekol Valley, *Felger 01-419*.

Cottea pappophoroides Kunth. COTTEA; ZACATE PAPO. Tufted perennials or perhaps annuals from cleistogenes at base of plant, winter or dry-season dormant; roots tough and wiry.

CP: Papago Well, *Felger 02-38*. GR: Crater Mts, *Pinkava 10028* (ASU). OP: Armenta Ranch Rd, *Felger 02-73*.

*Cynodon dactylon (L.) Pers. var. dactylon. BERMUDA GRASS; ZACATE BERMUDA, ZACATE INGLÉS; KI:WECO VAṢAI, 'A'AI HIHIMDAM VAṢAI. Creeping perennials.

PI: Tinaja Chivos, *Felger 18786*. AG: Gustavo Sotelo, *Felger 03-522*. CP: Eagle Tank, 13 Jun 1992, *Felger*, observation. GR: Gila Bend Air Force Auxiliary Field, *Felger 03-72*. OP: Quitobaquito, *Felger 7665*. SD: Vekol Valley, *Mauz 99-124*.

*Dactyloctenium aegyptium (L.) Willd. CROWFOOT GRASS; ZACATE DE CUERVO; KACHA (COCOPAH). Hot-weather annuals. Although native to the Old World, it has long been in western North America, generally in weedy places.

AG: Río Colorado delta (U.S. National Museum, catalogue no. 209,823, "grass seed. Lower California, W. J. McGee, collector, acc. 9 April 1901, 81-34-5."). In late 1900 McGee was among the Cocopahs on the west side of the river near the river's mouth (Fontana & Fontana 2000; Kelly 1977; Williams 1975). OP: Quitobaquito, *Felger 87-289*.

Dasyochloa pulchella (Kunth) Willd. ex Steud [*Erioneuron pulchellum* (Kunth) Tateoka; *Tridens pulchellum* (Kunth) Hitchc.] FLUFF-GRASS; ZACATE BORREGUERO. Dwarf tufted perennials.

PI: Hourglass Canyon, *Felger 19174*. CP: Charlie Bell Pass, *Whipple 3937* (CAB). GR: Thanksgiving Day Tank, *Felger 02-131*. OP: Quitobaquito, *Felger 87-290*. SD: Table Top Mts, *Bolton 94-062*.

Digitaria californica (Benth.) Henrard var. californica [*Trichachne californica* (Benth.) Chase] COTTONTOP; ZACATE PUNTA BLANCA. Tufted perennials; winter or dry-season dormant.

PI: Pinacate Peak, *Felger 87-47*. CP: E of Papago Well, *Goodding 924-G*. GR: Sand Tank Mts, *Felger 95-359*. OP: Alamo Canyon, *Nichol 4 May 1939*. SD: Table Top Mts, near summit, *Mauz 99-113*.

Distichlis palmeri (Vasey) Fassett. NIPA; ZACATE SALADO, ZACATE ESPINOSO; ÑIPÁ (COCOPAH). Perennials with creeping rhizomes and firm, sharp-tipped leaves. Male and female flowers on different plants. Endemic to northern Gulf of California, especially Alto Golfo (see Chapter 15, this volume).

AG: Head of Gulf of California, Horseshoe Bend of the Colorado River, about 35 mi S of Lerdo, "seeds shelled out from the chaff, and used as food by the Cocopa Indians," *Palmer Apr 1889* (Lectotype, US 81764 [see Felger 2000]); *Palmer Apr 28-30, 1889* (UC).

Distichlis spicata (L.) Greene. SALTGRASS; ZACATE SALADO; 'ONK VAṢAI. Perennials with creeping rhizomes.

PI: Río Sonoyta, E of Cerro Colorado, *Ezcurra 19 Apr 1981* (MEXU). AG: S of El Doctor, *Felger 85-1054*. OP: Quitobaquito, *Felger 86-274*.

*Echinochloa colonum (L.) Link. JUNGLEGRASS, JUNGLERICE, LEOPARD GRASS; ZACATE RAYADO, ZACATE PINTO, ZACATE TIGRE; SO-O'OI VAṢAI. Hot-weather annuals.

PI: Río Sonoyta 21 km W of Sonoyta, *Felger 85-973*. AG: Río Colorado delta (Castetter & Bell 1951). CP: Redtail Tank, *Felger 92-549*. OP: Williams Spring, *Van Devender 31 Aug 1978*. SD: Vekol Valley, *Felger 01-461*.

*Echinochloa crusgalli (L.) P. Beauv. var. crusgalli. BARNYARD GRASS; ZACATE DE AGUA, ZACATE DE CORRAL. Hot-weather annuals.

AG: M.O.D.E. Canal, Site of Rillito Salado, *Felger 95-513*. CP: Jose Juan Represo, *Felger 92-718*.

Elymus elymoides (Raf.) Swezey [*Sitanion hystrix* (Nutt.) J.G. Smith] BOTTLEBRUSH SQUIRRELTAIL. Tufted perennials.

GR: Bender Saddle, *Felger 95-389*. OP: Arch Canyon, *Bowers 1302*. SD: NW of Bender Spring, *Felger 01-383*.

Enneapogon desvauxii P. Beauv. SPIKE PAPPUSGRASS; ZACATE LOBERO. Dwarf tufted perennials.

PI: Sierra Extraña, *Felger 19071*. CP: Childs Mt, *Felger 92-643B*. GR: Sand Tank Mts, *Felger 95-358*. OP: Arch Canyon, *Felger 90-524*. SD: Table Top Mts, near summit, *Felger 02-55*.

*Eragrostis barrelieri Dav. MEDITERRANEAN LOVEGRASS. Warm-weather annuals.

OP: Lukeville, *Felger 87-276* (ORPI). SD: Cattle tank, N of Maricopa Rd, *Felger 02-363*.

*Eragrostis cilianensis (All.) Vignolo ex Janch. STINKING LOVEGRASS; ZACATE APESTOSO. Hot-weather annuals.

PI: Tinaja de los Pápagos, *Felger 86-485*. CP: Jose Juan Represo, *Felger 92-567*. GR: Coyote Water, *Felger 04-21*. OP: W of Lukeville, *Felger 87-282*. SD: Vekol Valley, *Mauz 99-128*.

*Eragrostis lehmanniana Nees. LEHMANN LOVEGRASS; ZACATE AFRICANO. Tufted, stoloniferous perennials.

PI: Campo Rojo, *Felger 92-476A* (not established). CP: Childs Mt, *Felger 92-647*. GR: Crater Range, *Morrison 1045* (ASU). OP: Hwy 85, 1 mi S of Visitor Center, *Rutman 9 May 1996* (ORPI). SD: Interstate 8 at rd to Big Horn Reservoir, *Felger 02-381*.

Eragrostis lugens Nees [*E. intermedia* Hitchc.] MOURNING LOVEGRASS. Tufted perennials. Ajo Mountains.

OP: Arch Canyon, *Felger 90-532*.

Eragrostis pectinacea (Michx.) Nees var. **pectinacea** [*E. diffusa* Buckley; *E. tephrosanthos* Schult.; *E. arida* Hitchc.; *E. pectinacea* var. *miserrima* (E. Fourn.) J. Reeder] CAROLINA LOVEGRASS. Hot-weather annuals.

PI: Campo Rojo, *Felger 92-476B.* AG: Reported as *E. mexicana* by Castetter & Bell (1951:191). CP: Las Playas, *Felger 01-560.* GR: Thanksgiving Day Tank, *Felger 02-118.* SD: Johnson Well, *Funicelli 35.*

*Eriochloa acuminata (J. Presl) Kunth var. **acuminata** [*E. gracilis* (E. Fourn.) Hitchc.; *E. lemmonii* Vasey & Scribn. var. *gracilis* (E. Fourn.) Gould] SOUTHWESTERN CUPGRASS; ZACATE TAZA. Hot-weather annuals. Apparently not native in the flora area.

OP: W of Lukeville, *Felger 87-281.*

Eriochloa aristata Vasey var. **aristata.** BEARDED CUPGRASS; ZACATE TAZA. Hot-weather annuals. Often common after rains.

PI: NW of Tezontle Cinder Mine, *Felger 86-376.* CP: Jose Juan Tank, *Felger 92-719.* OP: Growler Canyon, *Wirt 13 Oct 1988.* SD: Vekol Valley, *Felger 01-409.*

Festuca microstachys Nutt. [*Vulpia microstachys* (Nutt.) Benth. including var. *ciliata* (Beal) Lonard & Gould] SMALL FESCUE. Cool-season annuals.

GR: W Sauceda Mts, *Rutman 2003-97.* OP: Alamo Canyon, *Felger 03-426.*

Festuca octoflora Walter [*Vulpia octoflora* (Walter) Rydb.; *V. octoflora* var. *hirtella* Piper] SIX-WEEKS FESCUE, EIGHT-FLOWERED FESCUE. Cool-season annuals.

PI: Elegante Crater, *Felger 19683.* CP: Bassarisc Tank, *Felger 93-125.* GR: Rd to Hat Mt, *Felger 03-189.* OP: Quitobaquito, *Felger 88-116.* SD: Table Top Mts, *Bolton 94-040.*

Heteropogon contortus (P. Beauv. ex L.) Roem. & Schult. TANGLEHEAD; ZACATE COLORADO. Robust tufted perennials.

PI: Tinajas de los Pápagos, *MacDougal 52* (US). CP: Little Tule Well, *Felger 92-651.* GR: Thanksgiving Day Tank, *Felger 02-117.* OP: Quitobaquito, *Mearns 2752* (US). SD: S Maricopa Mts, *Doan 1621* (ASU).

Hilaria belangeri (Steud.) Nash. CURLY MESQUITE; ZACATE CHINO. Stoloniferous perennials, leaves often curling and relatively short.

GR: Squaw Tit Mt, *Felger 95-451.* OP: Bull Pasture, *Wirt 28 Jul 1990* (ORPI). SD: Table Top Mts, near summit, *Felger 02-57.*

Hilaria mutica (Buckley) Benth. [*Pleuraphis mutica* Buckley] TOBOSA. Coarse perennials. Tobosa in Vekol Valley grassland ACEC seems to be the most extensive stand of this species within a national monument; also abundant on summit mesas of Table Top Mts.

GR: 3 km SE of Squaw Tit Peak, *Felger 01-330.* SD: Vekol Valley, *Mauz 21-022.*

Hilaria rigida (Thurb.) Benth. ex Scribn. [*Pleuraphis rigida* Thurb.] BIG GALLETA; TOBOSA. Large, tufted or bushy perennials. Characteristic of Lower Colorado Valley, especially sandy habitats including lower dunes, and infrequent on rocky slopes; scarce in SD.

PI: Sykes Crater, *Felger 20030.* AG: Near Santa Clara Slough, *Ortiz 5 May 1993.* CP: Charlie Bell Pass, *Whipple 3931* (CAB). GR: Crater Range, *Van Devender 18 Mar 1973.* OP: Quitobaquito, *Felger 88-466.* SD: S Maricopa Mts, *Felger 03-450.*

*Hordeum murinum L. subsp. **glaucum** (Steud.) Tzvelev [*H. stebbinsii* Cov.; *H. leporinum* Link subsp. *glaucum* (Steud.) Booth & Richards] WILD BARLEY; CEBADILLA SILVESTRE. Cool-season annuals.

PI: Campo Rojo, not established, *Felger 92-478.* CP: Daniels Arroyo, *Felger 93-72.* GR: Gila Bend Air Force Auxiliary Field, *Felger 03-168.* OP: Quitobaquito, *Nichol 28 Apr 1939.* SD: Table Top Mts, *Bolton 94-073.*

Hordeum pusillum Nutt. LITTLE BARLEY. Small, cool-season annuals.

GR: Sand Tank Mts, *Felger 01-348.* SD: Table Top Mts, *Felger 01-308.*

Leptochloa dubia (Kunth) Nees [*Diplachne dubia* (Kunth) Scribn.] GREEN SPRANGLETOP. Tufted perennials.

PI: W of Los Vidrios, small playa, *Felger 92-966.* GR: Squaw Tit Mt, *Felger 95-446.* OP: Canyon N of Alamo Canyon, *Gould 4690.* SD: NW of Bender Spring, 3475 ft, *Felger 01-384.*

Leptochloa fusca (L.) Kunth subsp. **uninervia** (J. Presl) N. Snow [*L. uninervia* (J. Presl) Hitchcock & Chase; *Diplachne uninervia* (J. Presl) Parodi] MEXICAN SPRANGLETOP. Coarse, warm-weather annuals (often appearing perennial).

PI: Río Sonoyta, SW of Quitobaquito, *Felger 85-972.* AG: Ciénega de Santa Clara, *Felger 92-524.* GR: Near Bender Spring, *Felger 95-426.* OP: Rincon Spring, *McDougall 89.*

Leptochloa panicea (Retz.) Ohwi subsp. **brachiata** (Steud.) N. Snow [*L. filiformis* (Pers.) P. Beauv. Previously also known as *L. mucronata* (Michx.) Kunth or *L. panicea* subsp. *mucronata* (Michx.) Nowack (in part): subsp. *mucronata* now restricted to SE and central U.S.] RED SPRANGLETOP; DESPARRAMO ROJO. Hot-weather annuals; often delicate and filmy.

PI: MacDougal Crater, *Felger 10638.* CP: Jose Juan Represo, *Felger 92-564.* GR: Base of Tom Thumb, 2 Feb 2002, *Felger,* observation. OP: Aguajita, *Felger 88-402.* SD: SW of Big Horn Station, *Felger 95-328.*

Leptochloa viscida (Scribn.) Beal. STICKY SPRANGLETOP. Hot-weather annuals; spikelets with short awns. Often in playas.

PI: Tinaja de los Pápagos, *Ezcurra 5 Nov 1982.* CP: Las Playas, *Monson 7.* GR: 25 mi N of Ajo, T8S, R6W, *Perrill 5869.* SD: Vekol Valley, *Mauz 99-125.*

Lycurus setosus (Nutt.) C. Reeder. WOLFTAIL, TEXAS TIMOTHY. Tufted perennials; leaves end in a slender bristle.

> **OP:** Bull Pasture, *Wirt 29 Oct 1989* (ORPI).

Melica frutescens Scribn. BUSHY MELIC. Coarse, tufted perennials, panicles slender, spikelets large and silvery-papery. Otherwise known in Arizona only from the Estrella and Superstition Mountains.

> **OP:** Alamo Canyon, *Goodding 302-41.*

Monanthochloë littoralis Engelm. SHORE GRASS; ZACATE PLAYERO. Perennials, creeping rhizomes and short leaves (smallest leaves of any grass in region). Tidal marshes.

> **AG:** 5.8 mi by rd S of López Collada, *Felger 86-601.*

Muhlenbergia appressa C. Goodd. Small, delicate cool-seasonal annuals (perhaps nonseasonal). Locally in Ajo Mountains. Resembling *M. microsperma* but panicles contracted (branches close together) and spikelets with larger glumes and lemma.

> **OP:** Alamo Canyon, *Goodding 472-45.*

Muhlenbergia dumosa Scribn. ex Vasey BAMBOO MUHLY; OTATILLO. Robust, bamboo-like tufted to rhizome-forming perennials.

> **GR:** Tom Thumb, *Felger 02-102.* **OP:** Arch Canyon, *Felger 90-557.*

Muhlenbergia emersleyi Vasey. BULL GRASS; ZACATE DE TORO. Robust tufted perennials; inflorescences large and plumose.

> **OP:** Arch Canyon, *Felger 90-535.*

Muhlenbergia fragilis Swallen. Small, summer-fall annuals; inflorescences with numerous slender, spreading branches.

> **OP:** Ajo Mt crestline, *Rutman 8 Oct 1999* (ORPI).

Muhlenbergia microsperma (DC.) Trin. LITTLESEED MUHLY; LIENDRILLA. Nonseasonal annuals. Widespread and common, panicles feathery, spikelets awned; cleistogenes at base of plant.

> **PI:** Elegante Crater, *Felger 19694.* **CP:** Jose Juan Represo, *Felger 92-569.* **GR:** Thanksgiving Day Tank, *Felger 02-132.* **OP:** Aguajito, *Felger 86-281.* **SD:** NW of Bender Spring, *Felger 01-368.*

Muhlenbergia porteri Scribn. ex Beal. BUSH MUHLY; ZACATE APAREJO; KU:KPAḎAG. Bushy perennials, branches spreading and wiry.

> **PI:** Pinacate Peak, *Felger 18663.* **CP:** Childs Mt, *Felger 93-45.* **GR:** 3 km SE of Copper Mt, *Walter 340* (ASU). **OP:** Puerto Blanco Drive, *Felger 86-227.* **SD:** Vekol Valley, *Felger 01-423.*

Muhlenbergia rigens (Benth.) Hitchc. DEER GRASS; ZACATE DEL VENADO. Large tufted perennials. Panicles long and slender.

> **OP:** Alamo Canyon, *Goodding 479-45.*

Muhlenbergia tenuifolia (Kunth) Trin. Tufted perennials. One specimen known from the flora area.

> **OP:** Arch Canyon, 800 m, *Reeder & Reeder 8910.*

Panicum alatum Zuloaga & Morrone. Hot-weather annuals; plants resemble *P. hirticaule,* but upper (fertile) floret has a short stalk and two fleshy expansions (like little ears) at its base. Two varieties in the flora area; playas.

Panicum alatum var. **alatum**

> **PI:** Cerro Colorado, *Felger 10781.* **CP:** Pinta Playa, *Edwards 9 Oct 1977.*

Panicum alatum var. **minus** (Andersson) Zuloaga & Morrone

> **PI:** Pinacate Junction, *Felger 86-339.*

***Panicum antidotale** Retz. GIANT PANICGRASS, BLUE PANICGRASS; PANIZO AZUL. Robust, tall perennials with short rhizomes.

> **OP:** E of Lukeville, *Felger 87-329.* **SD:** Freeman Rd and Interstate 8, *Felger 01-481.*

Panicum hallii Vasey var. **hallii** [*P. lepidulum* Hitchc. & Chase]. Tufted perennials.

> **OP:** Ajo Mts, *Goodding 31 Oct 1938.* **SD:** Table Top Mts, near summit, *Felger 02-58.*

Panicum hirticaule J. Presl var. **hirticaule** [*P. capillare* L. var. *hirticaule* (J. Presl) Gould; *P. hirticaule* var. *miliaceum* (Vasey) Beetle; *P. hirticaule* subsp. *sonorum* (Vasey) Freckmann & Lelong; *P. sonorum* Beal] MEXICAN PANICGRASS; ŠIMČHÁ (COCOPAH). Hot-weather annuals; widespread and common.

> **PI:** NW of Tezontle Cinder Mine, *Felger 86-378.* **AG:** Near Lerdo, 1889, *Palmer 947* (US). **CP:** Daniels Arroyo, *Felger 92-657.* **GR:** 3 mi S of Black Gap, *Felger 01-520.* **OP:** Aguajita, *Felger 88-428.* **SD:** Vekol Valley, *Mauz 99-123.*

Panicum obtusum Kunth. VINE MESQUITE; ZACATE DE GUÍA. Stoloniferous perennials.

> **OP:** Bull Pasture, *Bowers 1796.* **SD:** Vekol Valley, arroyo bank, *Felger 01-458.*

Pappophorum vaginatum Buckley. PAPPUS GRASS. Tufted perennials.

> **OP:** Ajo Mts (probably in OP), *Albee Apr 1937.* **SD:** Vekol Valley, *Felger 01-429.*

***Pennisetum ciliare** (L.) Link [*Cenchrus ciliaris* L.] BUFFELGRASS; ZACATE BUFFEL. Tufted perennials. Highways and variously spreading into natural habitats.

> **PI:** Pinacate Junction, *Felger 86-374.* **CP:** S of Jose Juan Tank, *Felger 92-727.* **GR:** Hwy 85 near Pima County line, *Felger 03-6.* **OP:** Quitobaquito, *Felger 86-326.* **SD:** Freeman Rd at Interstate 8, *Felger 01-486.*

***Pennisetum setaceum** (Forssk.) Chiov. [*P. ruppelii* Steud.] FOUNTAIN GRASS. Robust tufted perennials. Occasional at roadsides; once common along Childs

Mountain Rd (nearly eradicated by CP staff); also spreading into some natural areas.

CP: Childs Mt, *Felger 92-646.* **GR:** Ca. 2 mi SSE of Tom Thumb Butte, ca. 2600 ft, reproducing population of ca. 100 plants, *Rutman 1 Jan 2005.* **OP:** Hwy 85, *Felger 87-333.*

*__Phalaris caroliniana__ Walter. CAROLINA CANARY GRASS; ALPISTILLO. Cool-season annuals. Two collections, from playas.

PI: Playa los Vidrios, *Ezcurra 7 Oct 1981* (MEXU). **CP:** Las Playas, not common, 1 Mar 1998, *Harlan 494.*

*__Phalaris minor__ Retz. LITTLE-SEED CANARY GRASS; ALPISTILLO; BA:BKAM. Cool-season annuals.

PI: Pinacate Junction, *Felger 93-215.* **CP:** Redtail Tank, *Felger 92-551.* **GR:** Crater Range, roadside, *Morrison 1063* (ASU). **OP:** Gachado Line Camp, *Felger 87-328.* **SD:** Table Top Mts, summit, *Felger 01-294.*

Phragmites australis (Cav.) Trin. ex Steud. [*P. communis* Trin.] COMMON REED, REEDGRASS; CARRIZO; VA:PK. Bamboo-like perennials.

PI: Río Sonoyta, S of Cerro El Huérfano, *Felger 92-973.* **AG:** La Salina, *Felger 86-544.* **OP:** Burro Spring, *Bowers 1316* (ORPI).

Pleuraphis, see **Hilaria.**

*__Poa annua__ L. ANNUAL BLUEGRASS, WINTERGRASS; PASTITO DE INVIERNO. Cool-season annuals. Not established in natural areas.

GR: Gila Bend Air Force Auxiliary Field, *Felger 03-164.* **OP:** Quitobaquito, *Darrow 2405.* **SD:** Vekol Valley, margin of cattle pond, *Felger 01-238.*

Poa bigelovii Vasey & Scribn. BIGELOW BLUEGRASS; ZACATE AZUL. Cool-season annuals.

CP: Charlie Bell Rd, *Felger 93-54.* **GR:** Hat Mt, *Felger 03-202.* **OP:** E of Lukeville, *Felger 88-04.* **SD:** N Maricopa Mts, *Felger 01-197.*

*__Polypogon monspeliensis__ (L.) Desf. RABBITFOOT GRASS; COLA DE ZORRA. Cool-season annuals.

AG: Ciénega de Santa Clara, *Felger 90-196.* **CP:** Agua Dulce seep, Agua Dulce Mts, *Henry 8 May 1966* (CAB). **GR:** Baker Tanks, *Walter 744* (CMML). **OP:** Burro Spring, *Felger 86-215B.* **SD:** Near Bender Spring, *Felger 95-422.*

*__Polypogon viridis__ (Gouan) Breistr. [*Agrostis semiverticillata* (Forssk.) C. Chrs.] WATER BENTGRASS. Perennials with creeping rootstocks. Known from one locality in the flora area.

OP: Quitobaquito, *Darrow 2409.*

*__Schismus arabicus__ Nees. ARABIAN GRASS. Small, cool-season annuals.

PI: MacDougal Crater, *Turner 86-18.* **AG:** NNE of El Golfo, *Felger 92-179.* **CP:** E Pinta Sands, *Felger 93-411.* **GR:** SE of Gila Bend Auxiliary Field, *Felger 03-69.* **OP:**

N of Pozo Nuevo, *Bowers 1109.* **SD:** N Maricopa Mts, *Felger 01-196.*

*__Schismus barbatus__ (L.) Thell. MEDITERRANEAN GRASS. Small, cool-season annuals. Distinguished from previous species by technical features of the spikelets.

GR: Tenmile Wash, *Walter 730* (ASU). **OP:** Bates Well, disturbed habitat, *Felger 03-297.*

Setaria grisebachii E. Fourn. SUMMER BRISTLEGRASS; COLA DE ZORRA. Summer annuals. Ajo Mountains.

OP: Arch Canyon, *Felger 90-551.*

Setaria liebmannii E. Fourn. SUMMER BRISTLEGRASS; COLA DE ZORRA. Summer annuals. Ajo Mountains.

OP: Alamo Canyon, *Goodding 25 Sep 1943.*

Setaria macrostachya Kunth [*S. leucopila* (Scribn. & Merr.) K. Schum.] PLAINS BRISTLEGRASS; ZACATE TEMPRANERO. Tufted perennials; warm weather.

CP: Agua Dulce Tank, *Felger 92-570.* **GR:** 6 km NW of Coffeepot Mt, *Morrison 1103* (ASU). **OP:** Boulder Canyon, *Bowers 1294.* **SD:** Table Top Mts, *Mauz 20-013.*

*__Sorghum halepense__ (L.) Pers. JOHNSON GRASS; ZACATE JOHNSON. Robust, warm-weather annuals.

PI: Pinacate Junction, *Felger 85-996.* **AG:** 8 m E of López Collada along RR, *Felger 03-619.* **CP:** Childs Mt, *Simmons 30 Oct 1962* (CAB). **OP:** E of Lukeville, *Felger 87-325* (ORPI). **SD:** Freeman Rd and Interstate 8, *Felger 01-483.*

Sphenopholis interrupta (Buckley) Scribn. subsp. **interrupta** [*Trisetum interruptum* Buckley] Small, delicate cool-season annuals. Known from the flora area by two collections in close proximity. Generally above the desert; nearest known populations are on Ragged Top and Tucson Mountains in Pima County.

GR: Rocky hill W of Dragon's Tooth, 2060 ft, *Morrison 8 May 2003.*

Sporobolus airoides (Torr.) Torr. subsp. **airoides.** ALKALI SACATON; ZACATÓN ALCALINO. Large, tufted perennials.

PI: Río Sonoyta S of Cerro El Huérfano, *Felger 92-983.* **AG:** La Salina, *Felger 86-528.* **CP:** Cabeza Prieta Tanks, *Felger 92-604.* **GR:** Baker Tanks, *Schulz 463* (CMML). **OP:** Quitobaquito, *Felger 87-288.*

Sporobolus cryptandrus (Torr.) A. Gray. SAND DROPSEED; ZACATE ARENERO. Tufted perennials.

PI: Pinacate Peak, *Felger 19300.* **AG:** Gustavo Sotelo, *Felger 03-537.* **CP:** Childs Mt, *Felger 92-643D.* **GR:** Tinajas Altas, *Goodding 599.* **OP:** Quitobaquito, *Felger 90-474.* **SD:** Table Top Mts, 4 Apr 2001, *Felger,* observation.

Sporobolus flexuosus (Thurb. ex Vasey) Rydb. MESA DROPSEED. Tufted perennials.

PI: 19 mi SW of Sonoyta, *Felger 86-507.* **OP:** Sonoyta Valley, *Rutman 29 Aug 2001* (ORPI).

Sporobolus pyramidatus (Lam.) Hitchc. [*S. patens* Swallen; *S. pulvinatus* Swallen] WHORLED DROPSEED. Hot-weather annuals.

OP: Aguajita, *Felger 88-420*.

Stipa speciosa Trin. & Rupr. var. **speciosa** [*Achnatherum speciosum* (Trin. & Rupr.) Barkw.; *Jarava speciosa* (Trin. & Rupr.) Peñailillo] DESERT NEEDLEGRASS. Tufted perennials.

PI: Pinacate Peak, *Felger 86-446*. **GR:** Borrego Canyon, *Felger 92-616*. **OP:** Arch Canyon, *Felger 90-529*.

Tridens eragrostoides (Vasey & Scribn.) Nash. LOVEGRASS TRIDENS. Tufted perennials. Ajo Mountains.

OP: Arch Canyon, *Felger 90-539*.

Tridens muticus (Torr.) Nash var. **muticus**. SLIM TRIDENS. Tufted perennials.

PI: Tinaja de los Pápagos, *Ezcurra 5 Nov 1982*. **CP:** Charlie Bell Pass, *Whipple 3955*. **GR:** Thanksgiving Day Tank, *Felger 02-133*. **OP:** Alamo Canyon, *Bowers 1559*. **SD:** Table Top Mts, *Mauz 99-091*.

*****Triticum aestivum** L. WHEAT; TRIGO; PILKAÑ. Cool-season annuals. Occasionally growing from grain falling from trucks or roadside seeding; not reproducing.

PI: Mex Hwy 2 at rd to Rancho Guadalupe Victoria, *Felger 20405*. **OP:** Hwy 85, roadside seeding, *Felger 05-159*. **SD:** Along Interstate 8, *Francis 30 Apr 2003*.

Vulpia, see **Festuca**.

POLEMONIACEAE – PHLOX FAMILY

Aliciella latifolia (S. Watson) J.M. Porter subsp. **latifolia** [*Gilia latifolia* S. Watson] BROADLEAF GILIA. Cool-season annuals; flowers pink.

PI: Sykes Crater, *Felger 18966*. **CP:** N of Tule Well, *Felger 93-441*. **GR:** N of Tinajas Altas Pass, *Halse 31 Mar 1973*.

Eriastrum diffusum (A. Gray) H. Mason. Cool-season annuals; flowers blue.

PI: Pinacate Peak, *Felger 19472*. **CP:** Papago Well, *Kearney 10870*. **GR:** Mohawk Dunes, *Felger 98-55*. **OP:** Aguajita, *Felger 88-293*. **SD:** N Maricopa Mts, *Felger 01-177*.

Eriastrum eremicum (Jeps.) H. Mason. Cool-season annuals; flowers blue.

GR: Mohawk Dunes, *Turner 95-32*. **OP:** Alamo Canyon, *Tinkham Apr 1942*.

Gilia flavocincta A. Nelson subsp. **australis** (A.D. & V.E. Grant) A.G. Day & V.E. Grant. Annuals; flowers bluish pink.

GR: 12 mi N of Ajo, *Elias 9303*. **OP:** Sonoyta Rd, *McDougall 80*. **SD:** S Maricopa Mts, *Felger 01-156*.

Gilia minor A.D. Grant & V.E. Grant. Cool-season annuals; flowers white to pale pink.

PI: Sierra Pinacate, *Felger 19814*.

Gilia stellata A. Heller. STAR GILIA. Cool-season annuals; flowers white tinged with violet.

PI: Tinajas de Emilia, *Felger 19712*. **CP:** Charlie Bell Pass, *Whipple 3915*. **GR:** Tinajas Altas Pass, *McLaughlin 1972*. **OP:** Canyon Diablo, *Kearney & Peebles 10811*. **SD:** N Maricopa Mts, *Felger 01-185*.

Ipomopsis multiflora (Nutt.) V.E. Grant [*Gilia multiflora* Nutt.]. Perennial herbs; flowers violet-blue. Ajo Mountains.

OP: Boulder Canyon, *Baker 7645* (ORPI).

Langloisia setosissima (Torr. & A. Gray) Greene subsp. **setosissima**. Cool-season annuals; flowers lavender-pink.

PI: Elegante Crater, *Felger 19949*. **CP:** Charlie Bell Pass, *Whipple 3941*. **GR:** Baker Tanks, *Halse 4 Mar 1973*. **OP:** Near Bates Well Rd and Puerto Blanco Drive, *Bowers 1119*. **SD:** Margies Cove, *Smith 4 May 2003*.

Linanthus aureus (Nutt.) Greene. DESERT GOLD. Cool-season annuals; flowers yellow. Two records from NE part of OP in 1941.

OP: Rd to Wall's Well, *McDougall 39*.

Linanthus bigelovii (A. Gray) Greene [*L. jonesii* (A. Gray) Greene]. Cool-season annuals; flowers white, relatively small, nocturnal and highly fragrant.

PI: Sykes Crater, *Felger 18994*. **CP:** Pinta Sands, *Felger 92-39*. **GR:** Mohawk Dunes, *Reichenbacher 273*. **OP:** Bull Pasture Trail, *Bowers 1128*. **SD:** N Maricopa Mts, *Felger 01-188*.

Linanthus demissus (A. Gray) Greene. Cool-season annuals; flowers white.

OP: Bull Pasture Trail, *Bowers 932*. **SD:** S Maricopa Mts, *Felger 01-213*.

Linanthus dichotomus Benth. EVENING SNOW. Cool-season annuals; flowers white and relatively large, nocturnal and fragrant.

SD: N Maricopa Mts, *Felger 01-189*.

Loeseliastrum schottii (Torr.) Timbrook [*Langloisia schottii* (Torr.) Greene]. Cool-season annuals; flowers white to pink.

PI: N of Sierra del Rosario, *Felger 20769*. **AG:** 10 mi N of El Golfo, *Felger 76-65*. **GR:** Mohawk Dunes, *Turner 95-34*.

Phlox tenuifolia E. Nelson. Herbaceous perennials; flowers white. Ajo Mountains.

OP: Arch Canyon, *Niles 550*.

POLYGALACEAE – MILKWORT FAMILY

Polygala macradenia A. Gray. MILKWORT. Small perennial herbs, woody at base; flowers purple.

GR: Tom Thumb, *Felger 02-86*. **OP:** N of Alamo Canyon, *Darrow 3857*. **SD:** Table Top Mts, *Felger 02-56*.

Figure 17.16. Eriogonum deserticola. *(Drawing by Amy Eisenberg)*

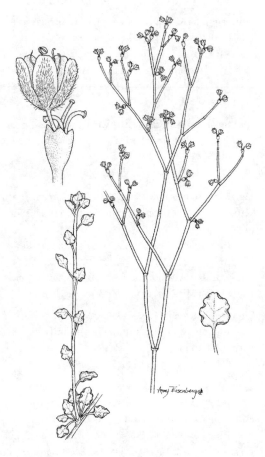

POLYGONACEAE – BUCKWHEAT FAMILY

Chorizanthe brevicornu Torr. subsp. **brevicornu.** BRITTLE SPINEFLOWER, SHORT-HORN SPINEFLOWER. Cool-season annuals; flowers white, minute.

PI: Elegante Crater, *Felger 19671.* **CP:** Pinta Sands, *Felger 93-395.* **GR:** Mohawk Dunes, *Felger 98-81.* **OP:** Alamo Canyon, *Benson 10675.* **SD:** Table Top Mts, *Bolton 94-023.*

Chorizanthe corrugata (Torr.) Torr. & A. Gray. WRINKLED SPINEFLOWER; TAPACOLA. Cool-season annuals; flowers white, minute.

PI: MacDougal Crater, *Turner 86-28.* **CP:** Pinta Sands, *Felger 93-394.* **GR:** 6.8 km NW of Monreal Peak, *Morrison 306* (ASU). **OP:** 1.4 mi WSW of Bates Well, *Rutman 6 Apr 1998* (ORPI).

Chorizanthe rigida (Torr.) Torr. & A. Gray. DEVIL'S SPINEFLOWER. Cool-season annuals; flowers white, minute.

PI: Sykes Crater, *Felger 18958.* **CP:** Pinta Sands, *Felger 93-396.* **GR:** Mohawk Dunes, *Reichenbacher 271.* **OP:** Dripping Springs, *Parker 7923.* **SD:** Table Top Mts, *Bolton 94-057.*

Eriogonum abertianum Torr. ABERT'S WILD BUCKWHEAT. Annuals or short-lived perennial herbs; flowers pink.

GR: Tom Thumb, *Felger 02-87.* **OP:** Canyon Diablo, *Bowers 1059.* **SD:** Table Top Mts, *Felger 01-283.*

Eriogonum deflexum Torr. var. **deflexum** [*E. deflexum* var. *turbinatum* (Small) Reveal] SKELETON WEED. Cool-season annuals and often persisting in summer and flowering summer and fall; flowers white to pink.

PI: Pinacate Peak, *Felger 19444.* **CP:** Childs Mt, *Felger 92-642.* **GR:** Ryan's Canyon, *Holm 2001-0906-1.* **OP:** Quitobaquito, *Felger 86-267.* **SD:** Table Top Mts, *Bolton 94-034.*

Eriogonum deserticola S. Watson. GIANT DUNE BUCKWHEAT. Spindly shrubs; flowers yellow. Dune endemic; highly localized in Arizona.

PI: S of Moon Crater, *Felger 19016.* **AG:** SE of López Collada, *Felger 86-527.* **GR:** Near Border Monument 198, *Reichenbacher 590.*

Eriogonum fasciculatum Benth. var. **polifolium** (Benth.) Torr. & A. Gray. FLAT-TOP BUCKWHEAT. Small shrubs; flowers white to pink.

PI: Sierra del Rosario, *Felger 20383.* **CP:** N side Tule Mts, *Felger 92-52.* **GR:** N of Hat Mt, *Rutman 24 Nov 2001.* **OP:** Alamo Canyon, *Parker 8009.* **SD:** Table Top Mts, *Bolton 94-052.*

Eriogonum inflatum Torr. & Frém. DESERT TRUMPET, BLADDER STEM. Perennial herbs; stems often inflated; flowers yellow.

PI: Elegante Crater, *Felger 19693.* **CP:** Pinacate Lava, *Simmons 17 Oct 1962* (CAB). **GR:** S of Wellton, *Van Devender 14 Jan 1973.* **OP:** Quitobaquito, *Felger 88-291.* **SD:** NW side Javelina Mt, *Rutman 2003-155.*

Eriogonum maculatum A. Heller. SPOTTED WILD BUCKWHEAT. Cool-season perennials; flowers red. In the flora area known only from Table Top Mountains.

SD: Table Top Mts, *Felger 01-266A.*

Eriogonum thomasii Torr. Small, cool-season annuals; flowers yellow and pink.

PI: Elegante Crater, *Felger 19684.* **AG:** 1 km W of Lerdo, 27 May 2005, *Felger,* observation. **CP:** Copper Wash, *Felger 93-333.* **GR:** W Sauceda Mts, *Rutman 2003-92.* **OP:** Growler Mts, *Parker 7968.* **SD:** N Maricopa Mts, *Felger 01-178.*

Eriogonum thurberi Torr. Small, cool-season annuals; flowers white to pink.

PI: 18 mi S[W] of Sonoyta on rd to Puerto Peñasco, *Shreve 7580.* **CP:** N of Tule Well, *Felger 93-438.* **GR:** Davis Plain adjacent to Gila Mts, *Felger 05-84.*

Eriogonum trichopes Torr. var. **trichopes.** LITTLE DESERT TRUMPET. Cool-season annuals, occasionally surviving through summer; flowers yellow.

PI: MacDougal Crater, *Turner 86-17.* **CP:** Pinta Sands, *Felger 92-776.* **GR:** Tinajas Altas, *Reichenbacher 608.* **OP:** Puerto Blanco Drive, *Bowers 1253.* **SD:** Table Top Mts, *Bolton 94-009.*

Eriogonum wrightii Torr. ex Benth. var. **nodosum** (Small) Reveal [*E. wrightii* var. *pringlei* (J.M. Coult. & Fisher) Reveal] BASTARD SAGE. Small shrubs; flowers white to pink.

PI: Campo Rojo, *Ezcurra 16 Apr 1981* (MEXU). CP: Agua Dulce Tank, *Felger 92-568*. GR: Tinajas Altas, *Reichenbacher 594*. OP: Bull Pasture Trail, *Bowers 931*. SD: S Maricopa Mts, *Felger 01-216*.

Nemacaulis denudata Nutt. var. **gracilis** Goodman & L.D. Benson. WOOLLY HEADS. Cool-season annuals; flowers yellow. Dunes.

PI: Moon Crater, *Felger 19244*. AG: NNE of El Golfo, 5 Mar 1992, *Felger,* observation. CP: Pinta Sands, *Felger 93-392*. GR: Mohawk Dunes, *Felger 98-73*.

*****Polygonum argyrocoleon** Steud. ex Kunze. SILVER-SHEATH KNOTWEED. Nonseasonal annuals; flowers white.

PI: Pinacate Junction, *Felger 19605*. AG: Ciénega de Santa Clara, *Ortiz 9 Apr 1993*. CP: Jose Juan Tank, *Felger 92-562* (CAB). OP: Hwy 85, roadside seeding, N of park headquarters, *Felger 05-161*.

Pterostegia drymarioides Fisch. & C.A. Mey. WOOD-LAND THREADSTEM. Cool-season annuals; slender, sprawling stems; fan-shaped leaves like a miniature ginkgo leaf; flowers inconspicuous.

OP: Alamo Canyon, *Darrow 3861*.

Rumex hymenosepalus Torr. ARIZONA DOCK; CAÑAIGRE; WAKONDAM. Robust, herbaceous perennials from tuber-ous roots. Flowers greenish.

AG: Harvested by Cocopahs in Colorado delta, plants reported as the Eurasian *R. crispus* by Castetter & Bell (1951) may have been this species. OP: Sonoyta rd 1 m S of N entrance, *McDougall 82*.

Rumex inconspicuus Rech. f. DOCK; CAÑAIGRE, HIERBA COLORADA. Cool-season annuals; flowers greenish.

PI: Pinacate Junction, *Felger 93-218*. AG: Ciénega de Santa Clara, *Felger 92-522*.

PORTULACACEAE – PORTULACA FAMILY

Calandrinia ciliata (Ruiz & Pav.) DC. RED MAIDS. Cool-season, succulent annuals; flowers rose-red.

GR: N of Hat Mt, *Felger 03-223*. OP: Bull Pasture Trail, *Bowers 1208* (ORPI). SD: Freeman Rd and Inter-state 8, *Felger 01-479*.

Cistanthe ambigua (S. Watson) Carolin ex Hershkovitz [*Calandrinia ambigua* (S. Watson) Howell]. Cool-season, succulent annuals; flowers white. In mainland Mexico known only from Sierra del Rosario.

PI: Sierra del Rosario, *Felger 92-383*.

Cistanthe monandra (Nutt.) Hershkovitz [*Calyptridium monandrum* Nutt.]. Cool-season, succulent annuals; flowers minute, white and yellow.

PI: W of MacDougal Crater, *Felger 92-339*. OP: Alamo Canyon, *Benson 14 Mar 1941*. SD: S Maricopa Mts, *Felger 01-221*.

Cistanthe parryi (A. Gray) Hershkovitz [*C. parryi* var. *arizonica* (J.T. Howell) Kart. & S.K. Gandhi; *Calyptridium parryi* A. Gray var. *arizonicum* J.T. Howell]. Cool-season, succulent annuals; flowers pink.

PI: Campo Rojo, *Felger 92-478*.

Claytonia perfoliata Donn ex Willd. subsp. **mexicana** (Rydb.) John M. Miller & K.L. Chambers [*Montia perfoliata* (Donn ex Willd.) Howell] MINER'S LETTUCE. Cool-season, succulent annuals; flowers white.

GR: Sauceda Mts, 1 mi S of GR border, *Holm 13 Apr 2003*. OP: Alamo Canyon, *Nichol 14 Mar 1939*.

Portulaca halimoides L. [*P. parvula* A. Gray] DWARF PURSLANE. Hot-season, succulent annuals; flowers yellow.

PI: Tinaja de los Chivos, *Felger 18616*. CP: Daniels Arroyo, 1310 ft, *Harlan 305*. GR: Coyote Water, *Felger 04-61*. OP: Aguajita, *Felger 88-433*.

*****Portulaca oleracea** L. PURSLANE; VERDOLAGA; KU'UK-PALK. Hot-season, succulent annuals; flowers yellow.

PI: Pinacate Junction, *Felger 85-993*. CP: Las Playas, *Felger 01-554*. OP: E of Lukeville, *Felger 87-318*. SD: Vekol Valley, *Felger 01-447*.

Portulaca retusa Engelm. PURSLANE; VERDOLAGA. Hot-season, succulent annuals; flowers yellow. (It is sepa-rated from *P. oleracea* on excellent seed characters; J. Henrickson, personal communication 2002).

PI: Rancho Los Vidrios, *Equihua 26 Sep 1982*.

Portulaca suffrutescens Engelm. Hot-season, succu-lent annuals; tuberous roots; flowers orange.

OP: Bull Pasture, *Bowers 1799* (ORPI). SD: Bender Spring, *Felger 95-414*.

Portulaca umbraticola Kunth subsp. **lanceolata** J.F. Matthews & Ketron. Hot-season, succulent annuals; flowers yellow. Ajo Mountains.

OP: Bull Pasture, *Wirt 23 Aug 1990* (ORPI).

Talinum aurantiacum Engelm. [*T. angustissimum* (Engelm.) Wooton & Standl.; *Phemeranthus aurantiacus* (Engelm.) Kiger]. Perennial herbs; flowers yellow.

OP: Bull Pasture, *Bowers 1798* (ORPI). SD: Table Top Mts, *Mauz 99-099*.

Talinum paniculatum (Jacq.) Gaertn. RAMA DEL SAPO. Perennial herbs; flowers red-pink. Ajo Mountains.

OP: Bull Pasture, *Wirt 8 Aug 1990* (ORPI).

POTAMOGETONACEAE – PONDWEED FAMILY

Stuckenia pectinata (L.) Börner [*Potamogeton pectina-tus* L.] SAGO PONDWEED. Submerged perennial herbs; flowers inconspicuous.

AG: Ciénega de Santa Clara, *Felger 05-304*. OP: Quitobaquito, *Felger 86-270* (ORPI).

PRIMULACEAE – PRIMROSE FAMILY

*****Anagallis arvensis** L. SCARLET PIMPERNEL. Cool-season annuals; flowers orange. Not in natural areas.

OP: Weed at Resource Center, *Beale 2 Apr 1988* (ORPI).

Androsace occidentalis Pursh. ROCK JASMINE. Cool-season annuals; flowers white.

GR: SW of Tom Thumb, *Arnett 1377* (ASU). **OP:** Alamo Canyon, *Clark 11566* (ORPI). **SD:** Between Indian Butte and Table Top Mts, *Butterwick 7262* (ASU).

PUNICACEAE – POMEGRANATE FAMILY

*****Punica granatum** L. POMEGRANATE; GRANADA; GALNA: YU. Large shrubs; flowers red.

OP: Quitobaquito, persisting from cultivation, *Felger 86-205.*

RAFFLESIACEAE – RAFFLESIA FAMILY

Pilostyles thurberi A. Gray. Minute parasitic plants on *Psorothamnus emoryi*; flowers red-brown; spring.

PI: Interdune corridor, 5 mi SSE of Moon Crater, *Felger 20188.* **AG:** Punta Borrascosa, *Felger 84-38.*

RANUNCULACEAE – RANUNCULUS FAMILY

Anemone tuberosa Rydb. DESERT WINDFLOWER. Herbaceous root perennials, winter-spring; flowers pink.

GR: SW of Tom Thumb, *Arnett 1375* (ASU). **OP:** Alamo Canyon, *McDougall 16 Apr 1941.* **SD:** Table Top Mts, *Felger 17 Jan 02* (specimen not curated).

Clematis drummondii Torr. & A. Gray. TEXAS VIRGIN-BOWER; BARBA DE CHIVATO. Robust, perennial vines; flowers cream-white, fruits in feathery clusters.

CP: Rd to Lower Well, *Felger 93-71.* **GR:** Sand Tank Mts, *Felger 95-378.* **OP:** E of Lukeville, *Felger 87-326.* **SD:** Vekol Valley, *Felger 01-239.*

Delphinium scaposum Greene. BARESTEM LARKSPUR; ESPUELITA CIMARRONA. Herbaceous root perennials, winter-spring; flowers dark blue and showy.

CP: N end of Growler Mts, *Felger 93-336.* **GR:** Hat Mt, *Felger 03-212.* **OP:** Dripping Springs, *Parker 7960.* **SD:** Table Top Mts, *Bolton 94-095.*

Myosurus cupulatus S. Watson. MOUSE-TAIL. Diminutive cool-season annuals; flowers green.

GR: Above Bender Spring, *Holm 11 Apr 2003.* **OP:** Bull Pasture Trail, *Bowers 1758* (ORPI). **SD:** NW of Bender Spring, *Felger 01-359.*

Myosurus minimus L. DWARF MOUSE-TAIL. Diminutive cool-season annuals; flowers green. One record from the flora area, locally extirpated.

OP: Quitobaquito, with *Poa annua* in marshy area bordering alkaline pool, 18 Mar 1945, *Gould 2986.*

RESEDACEAE – MIGNONETTE FAMILY

Oligomeris linifolia (Vahl) J.F. Macbr. DESERT CAMBESS, SLENDERLEAF CAMBESS. Nonseasonal annuals; flowers minute, green and white.

PI: Moon Crater, *Felger 19236.* **AG:** Ciénega de Santa Clara, *Ortiz 21 Mar 1993.* **CP:** Las Playas, *Benson*

10776. **GR:** Baker Tanks, *Halse 4 Mar 1973.* **OP:** Quitobaquito, *Felger 86-185.* **SD:** Table Top Mts, *Felger 01-325.*

RHAMNACEAE – BUCKTHORN FAMILY

Colubrina californica I.M. Johnst. CALIFORNIA SNAKE-BUSH. Slender-stemmed, large woody shrubs; flowers small, yellow-green.

GR: S of Thanksgiving Day Tank, *Felger 02-141.* **OP:** Ajo Mts (reported by Benson & Darrow 1945). **SD:** Sand Tank Mts, 1.5 mi S of Interstate 8, *Butterwick 7511* (ASU).

Condalia globosa I.M. Johnst. var. **pubescens** I.M. Johnst. CRUCILLO; KAWK KUAVULĬ. Large, thorny hardwood shrubs and small trees; flowers small, yellow-green. Pedicels 4-7 mm long.

PI: NE of Elegante Crater, *Felger 10062.* **CP:** Wash at Packrat Hill, *Felger 93-60.* **GR:** Thanksgiving Day Tank, *Felger 02-130.* **OP:** Aguajita, *Bowers 1046* (ORPI). **SD:** Sand Tank Wash, NNE of Round Butte, *Rutman 2003-135.*

Condalia warnockii M.C. Johnst. var. **kearneyana** M.C. Johnst. Large thorny shrubs similar to *C. globosa* but replacing it to east and at slightly higher elevations, with distinctive leaves, flowers, and fruits; flowers small, yellow-green. Pedicels 0.5-3 mm long.

GR: Tom Thumb, *Felger 02-80.* **SD:** Table Top Mts, near summit, *Felger 02-60.*

Rhamnus betulifolia Greene. BIRCHLEAF BUCKTHORN. Large shrubs; flowers green.

OP: Arch Canyon, *Felger 90-542.*

Rhamnus ilicifolia Kellogg [*R. crocea* Nutt. subsp. *ilicifolia* (Kellogg) C.B. Wolf] HOLLYLEAF BUCKTHORN. Shrubs; flowers yellow.

OP: Bull Pasture Trail, *Bowers 1210.*

Ziziphus obtusifolia (Hook. ex Torr. & A. Gray) A. Gray var. **canescens** (A. Gray) M.C. Johnst. [*Condalia lycioides* (A. Gray) Weberb. var. *canescens* (A. Gray) Trel.] WHITE CRUCILLO, GRAYTHORN; ABROJO; 'U:SPAD, 'US JEVEDPAD. Spinescent shrubs; flowers small, yellow-green.

PI: W of Los Vidrios, *Felger 86-384.* **CP:** Tule Well, *Harlan 283* (CAB). **GR:** 3.3 km NE of Coffeepot Mt, *Walter 1007* (ASU). Tinajas Altas, 19 Mar 1998, *Felger,* observation. **OP:** Quitobaquito, *Felger 86-186A.* **SD:** Javelina Mt, *Holm 2001-0916-21.*

ROSACEAE – ROSE FAMILY

Vauquelinia californica (Torr.) Sarg. subsp. **sonorensis** W.J. Hess & Henrickson. SONORAN DESERT ROSEWOOD. Large shrubs to small trees; flowers white.

GR: Sand Tank Mts, S of Squaw Tit Peak, *Felger 95-337.* **OP:** Arch Canyon, 850 m, 2 Jun 1978, *Hess & Wilhelm 4259* (Holotype, MOR, not seen). Arch Canyon, *Felger 90-543.*

RUBIACEAE – MADDER FAMILY

Galium aparine L. DESERT BEDSTRAW. Annuals; flowers small, white.

> **GR:** 1.5 km SE of Squaw Tit Peak, *Felger 01-338*. **OP:** Canyon Diablo, *Kearney 10845*. **SD:** NW of Bender Spring, *Felger 01-365*.

Galium microphyllum A. Gray. Perennial herbs; flowers minute, greenish white. Ajo Mountains.

> **OP:** Alamo Canyon, *Van Devender 31 Aug 1978* (ORPI).

Galium stellatum Kellogg var. **eremicum** Hilend & J.T. Howell. STARRY BEDSTRAW. Subshrub perennials; flowers minute, yellow green. Rocky slopes.

> **PI:** Elegante Crater, *Felger 19697*. **CP:** Tule Tank, *Darrow & Benson 10803*. **GR:** Tinajas Altas, *Kearney 6574*. **OP:** Alamo Canyon, *Bowers 1251*. **SD:** N Maricopa Mts, *Felger 03-109*.

RUPPIACEAE – DITCH-GRASS FAMILY

Ruppia maritima L. DITCH-GRASS. Submerged annuals or perennial herbs; flowers inconspicuous.

> **AG:** Lerdo, lagoon of brackish water, Apr 1889, *Palmer 935* (US). **OP:** Quitobaquito, *Felger 86-222*.

RUTACEAE – RUE OR CITRUS FAMILY

Ptelea trifoliata L. [*P. trifoliata* subsp. *angustifolia* (Benth.) V.L. Bailey] HOPTREE. Shrubs; flowers small, greenish white.

> **OP:** Alamo Canyon, *Darrow 3848*.

Thamnosma montana Torr. & Frém. TURPENTINE BROOM. Small aromatic shrubs, nearly leafless; flowers indigo blue.

> **PI:** Sierra Nina, *Felger 89-48*. **CP:** 3 mi W of Tule Well on Camino del Diablo, *Engard 914* (DES). **GR:** Tinajas Altas Mts, *Van Devender 6 Mar 1983*.

SALICACEAE – WILLOW FAMILY

Populus fremontii S. Watson subsp. **fremontii**. FRÉMONT COTTONWOOD; ÁLAMO; 'AUPPA. Large trees; flowers yellow-green. Former forest tree in Colorado delta, sparse along Río Sonoyta near Sonoyta. The several trees at Quitobaquito may have been planted. A tree planted at Lower Well (CP; cited by Simmons 1966) is no longer present.

> **AG:** Colonia Lerdo, *MacDougal Feb 1904* (US). **GR:** Playa on E side of Mohawk Dunes, saplings from 1992 to 1993, perished by 1995, *Felger 96-153*. **OP:** Quitobaquito, 5 Mar 1940, *Peebles 14563*.

Salix exigua Nutt. subsp. **exigua**. SANDBAR WILLOW, COYOTE WILLOW; SAUCE DEL COYOTE. Shrubs; flowers yellow.

> **AG:** La Salina, *Felger 93-13*.

Salix gooddingii C.R. Ball [*S. nigra* Marsh var. *vallicola* Dudley] GOODDING WILLOW; SAUCE, SÁUZ; CE'UL.

Large shrubs to large trees; flowers yellow. Former forest tree in Colorado delta, sparse along Río Sonoyta near Sonoyta.

> **AG:** Colonia Díaz, 29 Mar 1894, *Mearns 2840* (UC). **OP:** Quitobaquito, *Peebles 14562*.

SAPINDACEAE – SOAPBERRY FAMILY

Dodonaea viscosa Jacq. HOP BUSH; TARACHICO, SAUCILLO. Shrubs; flowers yellow-green, inconspicuous.

> **GR:** Tom Thumb, *Felger 02-101*. **OP:** Alamo Canyon, *Harbison 26240*.

Sapindus drummondii Hook. & Arn. [*S. saponaria* L. var. *drummondii* (Hook. & Arn.) L.D. Benson] SOAPBERRY; JABONCILLO, AMOLILLO. Slender shrubs or small trees; flowers small, white. In the flora area known only in Alamo Canyon and along Cherioni Wash in OP.

> **OP:** Alamo Canyon, *Bowers 1340*.

SAURURACEAE – LIZARD-TAIL FAMILY

Anemopsis californica (Nutt.) Hook. & Arn. HIERBA DEL MANSO; VA:VIS. Perennial herbs; flower heads white. Wetland habitats; major medicinal plant.

> **PI:** Río Sonoyta S of Cerro El Huérfano, *Felger 92-978*. **AG:** La Salina, *Felger 86-540*. **OP:** Quitobaquito, *Mearns 2786* (US).

SCROPHULARIACEAE – SNAPDRAGON FAMILY

Antirrhinum cyathiferum Benth. [*Pseudorontium cyathiferum* (Benth.) Rothm.] DESERT SNAPDRAGON. Nonseasonal annuals; flowers purple.

> **PI:** MacDougal Crater, *Felger 10730*. **CP:** Near Tule Well, *Yeatts 3236* (CAB). **GR:** Hat Mt, *Arnett 1391* (CMML). **OP:** Quitobaquito, *Harbison 27 Nov 1939* (SD).

Antirrhinum filipes A. Gray [*Neogaerrhinum filipes* (A. Gray) Rothm.] CLIMBING SNAPDRAGON. Cool-season annuals; flowers bright yellow.

> **PI:** S of Pinacate Peak, *Felger 19369*. **CP:** Chico Shuni Wash, *Rutman 2003-27*. **GR:** 1 mi W of Thanksgiving Day Tank, *Rutman 2003-84*. **OP:** Quitobaquito, *Felger 88-124*. **SD:** Margies Cove, *Smith 3 May 2003* (specimen not curated).

Antirrhinum nuttallianum Benth. subsp. **subsessile** (A. Gray) D.M. Thomps. Cool-season annuals; flowers lavender to violet, or not-opening and selfing.

> **OP:** Boulder Canyon, *Thomson 264*.

Antirrhinum watsonii Vasey & Rose [*A. kingii* S. Watson var. *watsonii* (Vasey & Rose) Munz]. Cool-season annuals; flowers lavender-purple with white center. Gulf of California region; in U.S. known only from south end of Ajo Mountains.

> **OP:** W of Sweetwater Pass, *Baker 7707* (ORPI).

Castilleja exserta (A. Heller) Chuang & Heckard subsp. **exserta** [*Orthocarpus purpurascens* Benth.] OWL'S

CLOVER; CU:VĬ TAḌPO. Spring annuals; flowers and bracts pink-purple and yellow.

CP: Jose Juan Charco, *Cutler 17 Mar 1995* (CAB). **GR:** Rd to Hat Mt, *Felger 03-183*. **OP:** W base of Ajo Mts, *Benson 10656*. **SD:** Just E of Maricopa Mts, Rte [Hwy] 238, *Doan 1421* (ASU).

Castilleja lanata A. Gray subsp. **lanata.** INDIAN PAINT-BRUSH. Herbaceous perennials; bracts red, flowers yellow and red, spring. Mountain slopes and canyons.

GR: Tom Thumb, *Felger 02-100*. **OP:** Boulder Canyon, *Bowers 1283*. **SD:** NW of Bender Spring, *Felger 02-100*.

Keckiella antirrhinoides (Benth.) Straw subsp. **microphylla** (A. Gray) Straw [*Penstemon antirrhinoides* Benth. subsp. *microphyllus* (A. Gray) D.D. Keck] BUSH PEN-STEMON. Shrubs; flowers yellow, spring. North-facing mountaintop slopes and canyons. In mainland Mexico known only from Pinacate Peak.

PI: NE slope of Pinacate Peak, *Felger 92-500*. **OP:** Boulder Canyon, *Bowers 1281* (ORPI). **SD:** Table Top Mts, *Felger 01-279*.

Linaria canadensis (L.) Dum.-Cours. var. **texana** (Scheele) Pennell [*L. texana* Scheele. *Nuttallanthus texanus* (Scheele) D.A. Sutton] TEXAS TOADFLAX. Cool-season annuals; flowers blue.

GR: Hat Mountain Rd 2.5 mi E of Ariz Hwy 85, *Felger 03-187*. **OP:** Montezuma's Head, *Van Devender 10 Mar 1978*. **SD:** Vekol Valley, *Christy 898a* (ASU).

Maurandya antirrhiniflora Humb. & Bonpl. ex Willd. subsp. **antirrhiniflora.** SNAPDRAGON VINE. Annual vines; flowers blue.

CP: Daniels Arroyo N of Lower Well, *Felger 92-544*. **GR:** Ryans Wash, *Felger 02-104*. **OP:** Bull Pasture Trail, *Bowers 933*. **SD:** NW of Bender Spring, *Felger 95-428*.

Mimulus guttatus DC. MONKEY FLOWER. Spring annuals; flowers yellow.

GR: Above Bender Spring, *Holm 11 Apr 2003*. **OP:** Estes Canyon, *Bowers 1206*. **SD:** NW of Bender Spring, 11 Oct 1995, *Felger*, observation.

Mimulus rubellus A. Gray. Small, cool-season annuals; flowers yellow or pink.

PI: NE of Elegante Crater, *Felger 92-147*. **OP:** Alamo Canyon, *Shreve 6202*. **SD:** S Maricopa Mts, 21 Feb 2001, *Felger*, observation.

Mohavea confertiflora (Benth.) A. Heller. GHOST FLOWER. Cool-season annuals; flowers pale yellow.

PI: Chivos Butte, *Felger 19620*. **GR:** Ripoff Canyon, *Felger 05-113*.

Penstemon parryi A. Gray. DESERT PENSTEMON; JAR-RITOS, VARITA DE SAN JOSÉ; HEVEL 'E'ES. Cool-season annuals or short-lived perennial herbs, spring; flowers rose-pink.

CP: Childs Mt, Mar 2004, *Curtis McCasland*, observation. **GR:** Sauceda Mts, *Johnson 27 Mar 1960*. **OP:**

Quitobaquito, *Felger 88-296*. **SD:** Vekol Valley, *Peebles 9116*.

Penstemon pseudospectabilis M.E. Jones var. **pseudospectabilis.** MOJAVE BEARDTONGUE. Cool-season annuals or short-lived perennial herbs; flowers rose-purple, spring.

PI: Base of Carnegie Peak, *Felger 86-459*. **CP:** Heart Tank, *Felger 93-160*. **GR:** Above Bender Spring, *Holm 11 Apr 2003*. **OP:** Arch Canyon, *Lockwood 161*. **SD:** Table Top Mts, near summit, *Schrock 21 Apr 2003*.

Penstemon subulatus M.E. Jones. ARIZONA SCARLET-BUGLER. Herbaceous perennials, also flowering in first season, spring. Flowers bright red.

SD: NW of Bender Spring, *Felger 01-375*.

Stemodia durantifolia (L.) Sw. Herbaceous perennials; flowers blue.

OP: Alamo Canyon, *Van Devender 87-5* (ORPI).

Veronica peregrina L. subsp. **xalapensis** (Kunth) Pennell. PURSLANE SPEEDWELL, NECKLACE-WEED. Cool-season annuals; flowers white.

PI: Tinajas de Emilia, *Felger 87-39*. **CP:** Jose Juan Represo, *Felger 92-563*. **GR:** Above Bender Spring, *Holm 11 Apr 2003*. **OP:** Quitobaquito, *Gould 2987*. **SD:** Vekol Valley, *Felger 01-240*.

SIMAROUBACEAE – QUASSIA FAMILY

Castela emoryi (A. Gray) Moran & Felger [*Holacantha emoryi* A. Gray] CRUCIFIXION THORN; CORONA DE CRISTO. Thorny large shrubs or small trees, essentially leafless; flowers whitish, summer.

CP: Adobe Windmill, *Felger 92-545*. **GR:** E of Mohawk Dunes, *Reina 96-216*. **OP:** Bates Well, *Harbison 20 Nov 1939* (SD). **SD:** Vekol Valley, *Felger 02-339*.

SIMMONDSIACEAE – JOJOBA FAMILY

Simmondsia chinensis (Link) C.K. Schneid. JOJOBA; HOHOVAI. Shrubs; flowers green or yellow.

GR: Tom Thumb, *Felger 02-81*. **OP:** Alamo Canyon, *Nichol 4 May 1939* (ORPI). **SD:** 1 km E of Javelina Mt, 2 Dec 2000, *Felger*, observation.

SOLANACEAE – NIGHTSHADE FAMILY

Capsicum annuum L. var. **glabriusculum** (Dunal) Heiser & Pickersgill [*C. indicum* L. forma *aviculare* Dierb.; *C. annuum* var. *aviculare* D'Arcy & Eshb.] CHILTEPIN; CHILTEPÍN; A'AL KO'OKOL. Small shrubs or subshrubs; flowers white.

OP: Alamo Canyon, *Goodding 310-41* (ASU).

Chamaesaracha coronopus (Dunal) A. Gray. FALSE NIGHTSHADE. Perennial herbs; flowers pale yellow.

CP: Pinacate Flats, *Hardy* [*Hardies*] *& Goodding 3 Dec 1935*. **GR:** Coyote Wash, *Felger 04-63*.

Datura discolor Bernh. POISONOUS NIGHTSHADE, DESERT THORN-APPLE; TOLOACHE; KOTADOPI. Nonseasonal annuals; flowers white, nocturnal; the largest flowers in the flora area.

PI: Sykes Crater, *Felger 20026*. **CP:** Pinta Sands, *Felger 92-778*. **GR:** 3 mi S of Black Gap, *Felger 01-523*. **OP:** Aguajita, *Felger 86-282*. **SD:** North of Antelope Peak, *Mauz 21-025*.

Lycium andersonii A. Gray var. **andersonii.** DESERT WOLFBERRY; SALICIESO; S-TOHA KUAVULĬ. Shrubs; flowers white and lavender.

PI: Tinaja de los Chivos, *Felger 18627*. **CP:** Pinacate Plateau, *Goodding 253G*. **GR:** Sauceda Mts, *Felger 02-144*. **OP:** Quitobaquito, *Felger 90-47*. **SD:** Vekol Valley, *Peebles 7500*.

Lycium berlandieri Dunal var. **longistylum** C.L. Hitchc. BACHATA, SALICIESO. Shrubs; flowers cream-white.

CP: Christmas Pass, *Van Devender 9 Mar 1980*. **GR:** NE Sauceda Mts, *Arnett 1228* (CMML). **OP:** SW of Visitor Center, *Bowers 1522*. **SD:** Table Top Mts, *Kearney 7295*.

Lycium brevipes Benth. var. **brevipes.** SALICIESO. Shrubs; flowers lavender.

PI: Río Sonoyta S of El Papalote, *Felger 86-197*. **AG:** 5 km S of El Doctor, *Felger 85-1056*. **OP:** Senita Basin, *Wirt 31 Mar 1989* (ORPI).

Lycium californicum Nutt. ex A. Gray var. **californicum** [*L. californicum* var. *arizonicum* A. Gray]. Small shrubs; flowers white.

PI: La Abra Valley near Santo Domingo, *McDougall 87*. **CP:** Wash at Camino del Diablo ca. 1.5 mi W of Tule Tank, *Rutman 20050115-8*. **OP:** E of Aguajita, *Felger 90-42*.

Lycium exsertum A. Gray. Shrubs; flowers white.

GR: Sauceda Mts, *Felger 03-47*. **OP:** Alamo Canyon, *Bowers 1564*. **SD:** N Maricopa Mts, *Felger 01-193*.

Lycium fremontii A. Gray var. **fremontii.** FRÉMONT WOLFBERRY; SALICIESO; KUAVULĬ. Shrubs; flowers lavender.

CP: Tule Tank, *Felger 92-63*. **GR:** Tinajas Altas, *McLaughlin 1967*. **OP:** Near Dos Lomitas, *Bowers 1011*.

Lycium macrodon A. Gray var. **macrodon.** S-CUK KUAVULĬ. Shrubs; flowers white and green.

PI: MacDougal Pass, *Turner 59-2*. **CP:** Monreal Well, *Simmons 20 Oct 1962* (CAB). **GR:** Tinajas Altas, *Felger 93-203*. **OP:** Growler Canyon, *Bowers 1604*. **SD:** S Maricopa Mts, *Felger 02-398*.

Lycium parishii A. Gray var. **parishii.** PARISH WOLFBERRY; SALICIESO. Shrubs; flowers lavender.

PI: Sierra de los Tanques, *Felger 89-24*. **CP:** O'Neill Hills, *Darrow 14 Apr 1941*. **GR:** Tinajas Altas, *Bowers 1584*. **OP:** Growler Valley, *Shreve 6208*. **SD:** Vekol Valley, *Peebles 7498*.

Nicotiana clevelandii A. Gray. DESERT TOBACCO; TABAQUILLO DE COYOTE; BAN VIVGA. Cool-season annuals; flowers white.

PI: MacDougal Crater, *Turner 86-4*. **CP:** Papago Well, *Felger 93-136*. **GR:** Tinajas Altas, *Kearney 10913*. **OP:** Quitobaquito, *Bowers 1044* (ORPI).

Nicotiana obtusifolia Mart. & Gal. [*N. trigonophylla* Dunal] COYOTE TOBACCO, DESERT TOBACCO; TABACO DE COYOTE; O'ODHAM HA-VIVGA. Perennial herbs, also flowering in first season; flowers cream-white.

PI: Sierra Extraña, *Felger 19046*. **CP:** Salazaria Wash, *Harlan 202*. **GR:** Crater Range, *Van Devender 18 Mar 1973*. **OP:** Quitobaquito, *Mearns 2744* (DS). **SD:** Table Top Mts, *Mauz 99-117*.

*****Petunia parviflora** Juss. [*Calibrachoa parviflora* (Juss.) D'Arcy]. Warm-season annuals; flowers yellow and purple. One locality in the flora area. Apparently not native in North America.

OP: Quitobaquito, *Felger 88-317*.

Physalis acutifolia (Miers) Sandwith [*P. wrightii* A. Gray; *P. acutifolia* may be a synonym of *P. lanceifolia* Nees]. Hot-weather annual; flowers white with a yellow center. Agricultural weed sometimes spreading into natural areas.

PI: Rancho Los Vidrios, *Equihua 26 Sep 1982*. **CP:** Las Playas (cited by Simmons 1966), no specimen located; it occurs in nearby Sonora (Felger 2000). **OP:** Dos Lomitas, *Warren & S. Anderson 17 Nov 1979*.

Physalis crassifolia Benth. var. **versicolor** (Rydb.) Waterf. [*P. versicolor* Rydb.] DESERT GROUND CHERRY; TOMATILLO DEL DESIERTO. Perennial herbs; flowers pale yellow.

PI: MacDougal Crater, *Felger 9731*. **CP:** Tule Tank, *Shreve 5930*. **GR:** Tinajas Altas, *Goodding 4902*. **OP:** Alamo Canyon, *Parker 7731*. **SD:** Smith Rd 5 mi S of N boundary, *Smith 2 May 2003*.

Physalis lobata Torr. [*Quincula lobata* (Torr.) Raf.] HAIRY GROUND CHERRY. Perennial herbs; flowers purple with a white eye.

PI: S of Pinacate Junction, *Felger 86-360*. **CP:** Las Playas, *Felger 92-14*. **GR:** Playa E of Mohawk Dunes, *Turner 95-29*. **SD:** Vekol Valley, *Mauz 99-084*.

Physalis pubescens L. HAIRY GROUND CHERRY. Hot-weather annuals; flowers pale yellow. Agricultural weed.

AG: "Delta of the Colorado River" (Wiggins 1964: 1312).

*****Solanum americanum** Mill. [*S. nodiflorum* Jacq.] BLACK NIGHTSHADE; CHICHIQUELITE; CU:WĬ WU:PUI. Warm-weather annuals or perennial herbs; flowers white. One locality in the flora area (see Chapter 15, this volume).

OP: Quitobaquito, *Bowers 1329*.

Solanum douglasii Dunal. NIGHTSHADE. Perennial herbs; flowers white.

OP: Alamo Canyon, *Nichol 4 May 1939*.

Figure 17.17. Solanum hindsianum. *(Drawing by Matthew B. Johnson)*

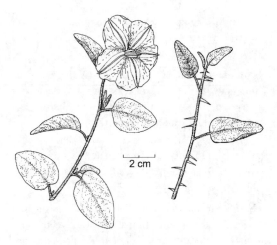

2 cm

***Solanum elaeagnifolium** Cav. WHITE HORSE-NETTLE, BULL NETTLE; MALA MUJER, SACA MANTECA. Spiny, perennial herbs; flowers lavender.

SD: Vekol Valley, *Felger 01-460.*

Solanum hindsianum Benth. MALA MUJER, TOMATILLO ESPINOSO. Shrubs; flowers lavender, rarely white. Widespread in western Sonora and Baja California peninsula; in U.S. known only from Puerto Blanco Mountains in OP.

PI: Pinacate Mts, *MacDougal 19 Nov 1907* (US). OP: S of Pinkley Peak, *Lechner 28 Jan 1986.*

Solanum xanti A. Gray. PURPLE NIGHTSHADE. Herbaceous perennials; flowers purple.

OP: Alamo Canyon, *Tinkham Apr 1942.*

STERCULIACEAE – CACAO FAMILY

Ayenia compacta Rose. Herbaceous perennials; flowers maroon, minute.

PI: 67 mi W of Sonoyta, *Prigge 7262* (UCLA).

Ayenia filiformis S. Watson [*A. pusilla* of authors, not L.]. Herbaceous perennials to slender subshrubs; flowers maroon, minute.

CP: Agua Dulce Pass, *Felger 92-736.* GR: NE of Hat Mt, *Rutman 25 Nov 2001.* OP: Diablo Canyon, *Baker 7607* (ORPI). SD: S Maricopa Mts, *Felger 02-405.*

Ayenia microphylla A. Gray. Small shrubs with slender, rigid stems; flowers maroon, minute.

GR: Squaw Tit Mts, *Felger 95-443.* OP: Canyon Diablo, *Supernaugh 441* (ORPI). SD: Table Top Mts, *Mauz 99-089.*

TAMARICACEAE – TAMARISK FAMILY

*****Tamarix aphylla** (L.) Karsten. ATHEL TREE, SALT CEDAR; PINO. Large trees; flowers white. Persisting from plantings, not known to reproduce in the flora area.

AG: W of Gustavo Sotelo along RR, *Felger 84-8.* CP: Tule Well, one tree, *Felger 02-15.* OP: Bates Well, one tree, *Rutman 20 Apr 2001* (ORPI).

*****Tamarix ramosissima** Ledeb. (or related taxa). SALT CEDAR, TAMARISK; SALADO, PINO SALADO; 'ONK 'U'US, VEPEGĬ 'U'US. Large shrubs; flowers pink or white. Abundant in Colorado delta and along Río Sonoyta, localized to rare elsewhere in the flora area.

PI: Elegante Crater, crater floor, Mar 1985, *Chris Eastoe,* photo. AG: S of El Doctor, *Felger 85-1057.* CP: Eagle Tank, *Simmons 28 Oct 1962* (CAB). GR: Baker Tanks, *Walter 746* (ASU). OP: Quitobaquito, *Bowers 1391.* SD: Gap Tank, *Hahn 13 Apr 2003.*

TYPHACEAE – CATTAIL FAMILY

Typha domingensis Pers. SOUTHERN CATTAIL; TULE; 'UDUVHAG. Robust, emergent perennials; flowers yellow-brown.

PI: Tinaja del Bote (Hayden 1997; Chapter 38, this volume). AG: Ciénega de Santa Clara, *Felger 92-526.* CP: Granite Pass Tank, 12 Jun 1992, *Felger,* observation. GR: Baker Tanks, *Schulz 470* (ASU). OP: Aguajita, *Felger 89-235.*

ULMACEAE – ELM FAMILY

Celtis pallida Torr. subsp. **pallida** [*C. tala* Gillies var. *pallida* (Torr.) Planch.] DESERT HACKBERRY; GARAMBULLO; KUAVULĬ. Shrubs; flowers green, inconspicuous.

CP: Cameron Tank, *Simmons 22 Sep 1963* (CAB). GR: Bender Saddle, *Felger 95-399.* OP: South Puerto Blanco Drive, *Felger 87-285.* SD: Table Top Mts, *Felger 01-466.*

Celtis reticulata Torr. CANYON HACKBERRY; CÚMARO. Trees; flowers inconspicuous, green. Ajo Mountains.

OP: Alamo Canyon, *Clark 10911* (ORPI).

URTICACEAE – NETTLE FAMILY

Parietaria floridana Nutt. [*P. hespera* Hinton] DESERT PELLITORY. Cool-season annuals; flowers inconspicuous, green.

PI: Sykes Crater, *Felger 19507.* CP: Heart Tank, *Felger 93-151.* GR: Thanksgiving Day Tank, *Felger 02-134.* OP: Quitobaquito, *Felger 86-106.* SD: N Maricopa Mts, *Felger 03-156.*

VERBENACEAE – VERBENA FAMILY

Aloysia wrightii (A. Gray) A. Heller ex Abrams. OREGANILLO. Shrubs; flowers minute, white.

CP: Childs Mt, *Felger 93-39.* GR: Hat Mt, *Felger 03-208.* OP: Arch Canyon, *Wirt 30 Sep 1989* (ORPI). SD: S Maricopa Mts, *Felger 03-443.*

Glandularia bipinnatifida (Nutt.) Nutt. var. **ciliata** (Benth.) B.L. Turner [*Verbena ciliata* Benth.]. Annuals or short-lived perennials. Flowers lavender-purple.

OP: Bates Well, 18 Mar 1944, *Clark 11427* (ORPI).

Glandularia gooddingii (Briq.) Solbrig [*Verbena gooddingii* Briq.] DESERT VERBENA. Short-lived perennial herbs or nonseasonal annuals; flowers lavender-pink.

PI: Pinacate Peak, *Joseph 20 Mar 1983.* **CP:** S of Chico Suni (Shuni) temporal, *Felger 93-65.* **OP:** Diablo Canyon, *Kearney 10842.*

*Lantana camara L. CONFITURILLA NEGRA. Shrubs; flowers pink and yellow. Rarely escaping from cultivation.

OP: Headquarters, *Rutman 24 Mar 2003.*

Tetraclea coulteri A. Gray. Herbaceous perennials; flowers white. Widely scattered, localized populations.

CP: Camino del Diablo 2.4 mi SW of E boundary, *Felger 92-741.* **GR:** Childs Valley, main tower in Manned Range, *Felger 03-22.* **OP:** Plain S of Acuña Wash, W of Pozo Nuevo Rd, *Rutman 24 Nov 1997* (ORPI). **SD:** Vekol Valley, *Mauz 99-132.*

Verbena bracteata Lag. & Rodr. Cool-season annuals; flowers pink.

PI: Tanque Romero (Víboras), *Webster 24263.* **CP:** Jose Juan Represo, *Felger 92-555.* **SD:** N of Antelope Peak, *Felger 01-259.*

Verbena neomexicana (A. Gray) Small. HILLSIDE VERVAIN. Perennial herbs; flowers blue purple.

GR: Near Bender Spring, *Felger 95-437.* **OP:** Alamo Canyon, *Nichol 4 May 1939.* **SD:** Table Top Mts, *Felger 01-304.*

Verbena officinalis L. subsp. **halei** (Small) S. Barber. Nonseasonal annuals to short-lived perennial herbs; flowers blue.

PI: Tinajas de los Pápagos, *Turner 59-22.* **CP:** Jose Juan Represo, *Felger 92-556.* **OP:** Quitobaquito, *Felger 88-454.*

VIOLACEAE – VIOLET FAMILY

Hybanthus verticillatus (Ortega) Baill. var. **verticillatus.** Herbaceous perennials. Flowers small, white or yellowish and purple. One record in the flora area but likely on other mountains.

GR: 1 mi S of Squaw Tit, N-facing slope with *Canotia, Smith 15 May 2003.*

VISCACEAE – MISTLETOE FAMILY

Phoradendron californicum Nutt. DESERT MISTLETOE; TOJI; HA:KVAD. Epiphytic parasites, perennial; leaves reduced to scales; flowers yellow-green. Berries are major food resources for phainopepla and other birds.

PI: MacDougal Crater, *Felger 9764.* **CP:** Papago Well, *Felger 92-9.* **GR:** Crater Range, *Van Devender 18 Mar 1973.* **OP:** Quitobaquito, *Mearns 220* (US). **SD:** Bajada W of Table Top Mts, *Felger 02-166.*

ZANNICHELLIACEAE – HORNED PONDWEED FAMILY

Zannichellia palustris L. HORNED PONDWEED. Submerged perennial herbs; flowers inconspicuous.

AG: N of El Doctor, *Felger 93-248.* **CP:** Little Tule "Guzzler," Charlie Bell Area, *Harlan 471.* **OP:** Quitobaquito, *Benson 9939.*

ZYGOPHYLLACEAE – CALTROP FAMILY

Fagonia californica Benth. CALIFORNIA OTAT. Perennial herbs; flowers lavender. Two subspecies in the flora area.

Fagonia californica subsp. **californica** [*F. laevis* Standl. *F. californica* subsp. *laevis* (Standl.) Wiggins]

PI: Sierra Extraña, *Felger 19072.* **CP:** N side Tule Mts, *Felger 92-53.* **GR:** Borrego Canyon, *Felger 93-195.* **SD:** N Maricopa Mts, *Felger 01-181.*

Fagonia californica subsp. **longipes** (Standl.) Felger & C.H. Lowe [*F. longipes* Standl.]

CP: Agua Dulce Pass, *Felger 92-572.* **OP:** Quitobaquito, *Felger 88-131.* **SD:** Big Horn–Papago Chief Mine Rd, *Felger 95-326.*

Fagonia densa I.M. Johnst. Dwarf shrubs; flowers lavender; locally common. Known from mainland Mexico at only one locality.

PI: Sierra del Rosario, *Felger 89-63.*

Fagonia pachyacantha Rydb. THICKLEAF OTAT. Perennial herbs; flowers lavender.

PI: Tinaja Tule, *Felger 18908.* **CP:** Drift Hills, *Felger 93-169.* **GR:** Tinajas Altas Mts, *Lindquist 25 Mar 1983.*

Kallstroemia californica (S. Watson) Vail. CALIFORNIA CALTROP; BAIBURÍN, MAL DE OJO. Hot-weather annuals; flowers yellow.

PI: MacDougal Crater, *Felger 10745.* **AG:** Near NE corner of Reserva, *Felger 03-496.* **CP:** Pinta Sands, *Felger 92-774.* **GR:** Mohawk Dunes, *Felger 96-129.* **OP:** Quitobaquito, *Felger 88-411.* **SD:** Maricopa Rd, *Felger 02-341.*

Kallstroemia grandiflora Torr. ORANGE CALTROP, SUMMER POPPY; BAIBURÍN, MAL DE OJO. Hot-weather annuals; flowers orange.

PI: MacDougal Crater, *Felger 10484.* **CP:** San Cristobal Wash, *Felger 92-686.* **GR:** 3 mi S of Black Gap, *Felger 01-524.* **OP:** Armenta Well, *Bowers 1528.* **SD:** Maricopa Rd, *Felger 02-342.*

Larrea divaricata Cav. subsp. **tridentata** (Sessé & Moç. ex DC.) Felger & C.H. Lowe [*L. tridentata* (Sessé & Moç. ex DC.) Cov.] CREOSOTEBUSH; HEDIONDILLA, GOBERNADORA; SEGAI, SEGOI. Shrubs; flowers yellow. Two varieties.

Larrea divaricata subsp. **tridentata** var. **tridentata.** Widespread across the flora area.

PI: Pinacate Peak, *Felger 19387.* **AG:** El Golfo, *Bezy 371.* **CP:** Cabeza Prieta Peak, *Yeatts 3657.* **GR:** 8 mi S of N boundary on Hwy 85, *Felger 03-462.* **OP:** Quitobaquito, *Felger 88-467.* **SD:** S Maricopa Mts, *Felger 02-402.*

Larrea divaricata subsp. **tridentata** var. **arenaria** (L.D. Benson) Felger [*L. tridentata* var. *arenaria* L.D. Benson] DUNE CREOSOTEBUSH. Slender shrubs 5-6 m tall.

PI: Dunes W Sierra del Rosario (Felger 2000).

Tribulus terrestris L. PUNCTURE VINE, GOATHEAD; TORITO, TOBOSO. Hot-weather annuals; flowers yellow. Locally in disturbed habitats; rare in natural habitats.

PI: W of Pinacate Junction on Mex Hwy 2, *Felger 86-334.* AG: Gustavo Sotelo, *Felger 03-520.* CP: Tule Desert, 3 Oct 1963, *Simmons 7.* GR: Range 2 Main Tower, *Holm 12 Nov 2002-13.*

EXCLUDED, QUESTIONABLE, AND MARGINAL PLANT RECORDS:

FABACEAE

Acacia farnesiana (L.) Willd. [*A. minuta* (M.E. Jones) R.M. Beauch. subsp. *densiflora* (Alexander ex Small) Beauch.; *A. smallii* Isely] SWEET ACACIA; HUIZACHE, VINORAMA. Shrubs; flowers yellow, very fragrant.

A single record from the flora area just south of Goldwater Range: Sauceda Mts, arroyo just N of charco, *Holm 2000-0928-1.* Perhaps associated with cattle grazing.

ROSACEAE

Coleogyne ramosissima Torr. BLACK BRUSH. Small shrubs.

Brown (1978) reports finding three plants on Javelina Mountain (SD), a spectacular southern outpost for this Mojavean species; no specimen has been located, and the report is doubtful.

VISCACEAE

Phoradendron serotinum (Raf.) M.C. Johnst. subsp. **macrophyllum** (Engelm. ex Rothr.) Kuijt [*P. macrophyllum* (Engelm. ex Rothr.) Cockerell; *P. flavescens* Nutt.; *P. orbiculatum* Engelm.] BIGLEAF MISTLETOE. Epiphytic parasites on cottonwood and willow trees.

Probably once present near the Colorado delta (see Chapter 15, this volume). Presently found near Yuma, AZ: Laguna Dam, on *Salix gooddingii,* locally common, 14 Mar 2004, *Elam AZ050-150.*

Generic and Family Index (with selected synonyms)

BELLFLOWER FAMILY – **CAMPANULACEAE**
Berberis – **BERBERIDACEAE**
Bernardia – **EUPHORBIACEAE**
BIGNONIA FAMILY – **BIGNONIACEAE**
BIRTHWORT FAMILY – **ARISTOLOCHIACEAE**
Boechera – **BRASSICACEAE**
Boerhavia – **NYCTAGINACEAE**
BORAGE FAMILY – **BORAGINACEAE**
Bothriochloa – **POACEAE**
Bouteloua – **POACEAE**
Bowlesia – **APIACEAE**
Brachiaria – **POACEAE**
Brandegea – **CUCURBITACEAE**
Brassica – **BRASSICACEAE**
Brickellia – **ASTERACEAE**
Bromus – **POACEAE**
BROOMRAPE FAMILY – **OROBANCHACEAE**
BUCKTHORN FAMILY – **RHAMNACEAE**
BUCKWHEAT FAMILY – **POLYGONACEAE**
Bursera – **BURSERACEAE**
CACAO FAMILY – **STERCULIACEAE**
CACTUS FAMILY – **CACTACEAE**
Calandrinia – **PORTULACACEAE**
Calliandra – **FABACEAE**
Calochortus – **LILIACEAE**
CALTROP FAMILY – **ZYGOPHYLLACEAE**
Calycoseris – **ASTERACEAE**
Camissonia – **ONAGRACEAE**
Canotia – **CELASTRACEAE**
CAPER FAMILY – **CAPPARACEAE**
Capsella – **BRASSICACEAE**
Capsicum – **SOLANACEAE**
Carlowrightia – **ACANTHACEAE**
Carnegiea – **CACTACEAE**
CARPETWEED FAMILY – **MOLLUGINACEAE**
CARROT FAMILY – **APIACEAE**
Carthamus – **ASTERACEAE**
Castela – **SIMAROUBACEAE**
Castilleja – **SCROPHULARIACEAE**
CATTAIL FAMILY – **TYPHACEAE**
Celtis – **ULMACEAE**
Cenchrus – **POACEAE**
Centaurea – **ASTERACEAE**
Centaurium – **GENTIANACEAE**
CENTURY PLANT FAMILY – **AGAVACEAE**
Cerastium – **CARYOPHYLLACEAE**
Cercidium, see **Parkinsonia**
Chaenactis – **ASTERACEAE**
Chamaesaracha – **SOLANACEAE**
Chenopodium – **CHENOPODIACEAE**
Chilopsis – **BIGNONIACEAE**
Chloracantha – **ASTERACEAE**
Chloris – **POACEAE**
Chorispora – **BRASSICACEAE**
Chorizanthe – **POLYGONACEAE**

Cirsium – **ASTERACEAE**
Cistanthe – **PORTULACACEAE**
Claytonia – **PORTULACACEAE**
Clematis – **RANUNCULACEAE**
Cleome – **CAPPARACEAE**
Colubrina – **RHAMNACEAE**
Commelina – **COMMELINACEAE**
Commicarpus – **NYCTAGINACEAE**
Condalia – **RHAMNACEAE**
Conyza – **ASTERACEAE**
Cottea – **POACEAE**
Cotula – **ASTERACEAE**
Coursetia – **FABACEAE**
Crassula – **CRASSULACEAE**
Cressa – **CONVOLVULACEAE**
Crossosoma – **CROSSOSOMATACEAE**
CROSSOSOMA FAMILY – **CROSSOSOMATACEAE**
Croton – **EUPHORBIACEAE**
Cryptantha – **BORAGINACEAE**
Cucurbita – **CUCURBITACEAE**
Cuscuta – **CONVOLVULACEAE**
Cylindropuntia – **CACTACEAE**
Cynodon – **POACEAE**
Cyperus – **CYPERACEAE**
Dactyloctenium – **POACEAE**
DAISY OR COMPOSITE FAMILY – **ASTERACEAE**
Dalea – **FABACEAE**
Dasyochloa – **POACEAE**
Desmodium – **FABACEAE**
Datura – **SOLANACEAE**
Daucus – **APIACEAE**
Delphinium – **RANUNCULACEAE**
Descurainia – **BRASSICACEAE**
DEVIL'S CLAW FAMILY – **MARTYNIACEAE**
Dichelostemma – **LILIACEAE**
Dicliptera – **ACANTHACEAE**
Dicoria – **ASTERACEAE**
Dimorphocarpa – **BRASSICACEAE**
Dimorphotheca – **ASTERACEAE**
Distichlis – **POACEAE**
Ditaxis – **EUPHORBIACEAE**
DITCH-GRASS FAMILY – **RUPPIACEAE**
Dithyrea – **BRASSICACEAE**
Dodonaea – **SAPINDACEAE**
DOGBANE FAMILY – **APOCYNACEAE**
Draba – **BRASSICACEAE**
Drymaria – **CARYOPHYLLACEAE**
DUCKWEED FAMILY – **LEMNACEAE**
Dudleya – **CRASSULACEAE**
Dyssodia – **ASTERACEAE**
Echinocactus – **CACTACEAE**
Echinochloa – **POACEAE**
Echinomastus – **CACTACEAE**
Echinopepon – **CUCURBITACEAE**
Eclipta – **ASTERACEAE**

Eleocharis – **CYPERACEAE**
ELM FAMILY – **ULMACEAE**
Elymus – **POACEAE**
Encelia – **ASTERACEAE**
Enneapogon – **POACEAE**
Epilobium – **ONAGRACEAE**
Eragrostis – **POACEAE**
Eremalche – **MALVACEAE**
Eriastrum – **POLEMONIACEAE**
Ericameria – **ASTERACEAE**
Erigeron – **ASTERACEAE**
Eriochloa – **POACEAE**
Eriogonum – **POLYGONACEAE**
Erioneuron – see **DASYOCHLOA**
Eriophyllum – **ASTERACEAE**
Erodium – **GERANIACEAE**
Eruca – **BRASSICACEAE**
Eryngium – **APIACEAE**
Erysimum – **BRASSICACEAE**
Eschscholzia – **PAPAVERACEAE**
Eucnide – **LOASACEAE**
Eucrypta – **HYDROPHYLLACEAE**
Eupatorium – see **AGERATINA, KOANOPHYLLON**
Euphorbia – **EUPHORBIACEAE**
Eustoma – **GENTIANACEAE**
Evax – **ASTERACEAE**
EVENING PRIMROSE FAMILY – **ONAGRACEAE**
Evolvulus – **CONVOLVULACEAE**
Fagonia – **ZYGOPHYLLACEAE**
Ferocactus – **CACTACEAE**
Festuca – **POACEAE**
Ficus – **MORACEAE**
Filago – **ASTERACEAE**
FLAX FAMILY – **LINACEAE**
FLOWERING PLANTS – **ANGIOSPERMS**
Forestiera – **OLEACEAE**
Fouquieria – **FOUQUIERIACEAE**
FOUR-O'CLOCK FAMILY – **NYCTAGINACEAE**
Frankenia – **FRANKENIACEAE**
FRANKENIA FAMILY – **FRANKENIACEAE**
FRANKINCENSE FAMILY – **BURSERACEAE**
Fraxinus – **OLEACEAE**
Funastrum – **ASCLEPIADACEAE**
Gaillardia – **ASTERACEAE**
Galactia – **FABACEAE**
Galium – **RUBIACEAE**
Gamochaeta – **ASTERACEAE**
Gaura – **ONAGRACEAE**
GENTIAN FAMILY – **GENTIANACEAE**
Geraea – **ASTERACEAE**
Geranium – **GERANIACEAE**
GERANIUM FAMILY – **GERANIACEAE**
Gilia – **POLEMONIACEAE**
Glandularia – **VERBENACEAE**
Glinus – **MOLLUGINACEAE**

Gnaphalium – **ASTERACEAE**
Gomphrena – **AMARANTHACEAE**
GOOSEBERRY FAMILY – **GROSSULARIACEAE**
GOOSEFOOT FAMILY – **CHENOPODIACEAE**
GOURD FAMILY – **CUCURBITACEAE**
Graptopetalum – **CRASSULACEAE**
GRASS FAMILY – **POACEAE**
Grindelia – **ASTERACEAE**
Grusonia – **CACTACEAE**
Gutierrezia – **ASTERACEAE**
Gymnosperma – **ASTERACEAE**
Haplophyton – **APOCYNACEAE**
Harpagonella – **BORAGINACEAE**
Hedeoma – **LAMIACEAE**
Helianthus – **ASTERACEAE**
Heliotropium – **BORAGINACEAE**
Herissantia – **MALVACEAE**
Herniaria – **CARYOPHYLLACEAE**
Hesperocallis – **LILIACEAE**
Hesperoyucca – **AGAVACEAE**
Heteropogon – **POACEAE**
Heterotheca – **ASTERACEAE**
Hibiscus – **MALVACEAE**
Hilaria – **POACEAE**
Hoffmannseggia – **FABACEAE**
HONEYSUCKLE FAMILY – **CAPRIFOLIACEAE**
Hordeum – **POACEAE**
HORNED PONDWEED FAMILY – **ZANNICHELLIACEAE**
Horsfordia – **MALVACEAE**
Hybanthus – **VIOLACEAE**
Hydrocotyle – **APIACEAE**
Hymenoclea – **ASTERACEAE**
Hymenothrix – **ASTERACEAE**
Hymenoxys – **ASTERACEAE**
Hyptis – **LAMIACEAE**
ICEPLANT FAMILY – **AIZOACEAE**
Ipomoea – **CONVOLVULACEAE**
Ipomopsis – **POLEMONIACEAE**
Isocoma – **ASTERACEAE**
Isomeris – **CAPPARACEAE**
Jacquemontia – **CONVOLVULACEAE**
Janusia – **MALPIGHIACEAE**
Jatropha – **EUPHORBIACEAE**
JOJOBA FAMILY – **SIMMONDSIACEAE**
Juncus – **JUNCACEAE**
Justicia – **ACANTHACEAE**
Kallstroemia – **ZYGOPHYLLACEAE**
Keckiella – **SCROPHULARIACEAE**
Koanophyllon – **ASTERACEAE**
Koeberlinia – **KOEBERLINIACEAE**
KOEBERLINIA FAMILY – **KOEBERLINIACEAE**
Krameria – **KRAMERIACEAE**
Lactuca – **ASTERACEAE**
Laennecia – **ASTERACEAE**
Langloisia – **POLEMONIACEAE**

Lantana – **VERBENACEAE**
Lappula – **BORAGINACEAE**
Larrea – **ZYGOPHYLLACEAE**
LEGUME FAMILY – **FABACEAE**
Lemna – **LEMNACEAE**
LENNOA FAMILY – **LENNOACEAE**
Lepidium – **BRASSICACEAE**
Leptochloa – **POACEAE**
Lesquerella, see **Physaria**
LILY FAMILY – **LILIACEAE**
Linanthus – **POLEMONIACEAE**
Linaria – **SCROPHULARIACEAE**
Linum – **LINACEAE**
LIZARD-TAIL FAMILY – **SAURURACEAE**
Loeflingia – **CARYOPHYLLACEAE**
Loeseliastrum – **POLEMONIACEAE**
Lomatium – **APIACEAE**
LOOSESTRIFE FAMILY – **LYTHRACEAE**
Lophocereus, see **Pachycereus**
Lotus – **FABACEAE**
Lupinus – **FABACEAE**
Lycium – **SOLANACEAE**
Lycurus – **POACEAE**
Lyrocarpa – **BRASSICACEAE**
Lythrum – **LYTHRACEAE**
Machaeranthera – **ASTERACEAE**
Macroptilium – **FABACEAE**
MADDER FAMILY – **RUBIACEAE**
Malacothrix – **ASTERACEAE**
MALLOW FAMILY – **MALVACEAE**
MALPIGHIA FAMILY – **MALPIGHIACEAE**
Malva – **MALVACEAE**
Malvastrum – **MALVACEAE**
Malvella – **MALVACEAE**
Mammillaria – **CACTACEAE**
Marah – **CUCURBITACEAE**
Marina – **FABACEAE**
Matelea – **ASCLEPIADACEAE**
Matricaria – **ASTERACEAE**
Maurandya – **SCROPHULARIACEAE**
Medicago – **FABACEAE**
Melica – **POACEAE**
Melilotus – **FABACEAE**
Menodora – **OLEACEAE**
Mentzelia – **LOASACEAE**
Mesembryanthemum – **AIZOACEAE**
Metastelma – **ASCLEPIADACEAE**
MIGNONETTE FAMILY – **RESEDACEAE**
MILKWEED FAMILY – **ASCLEPIADACEAE**
MILKWORT FAMILY – **POLYGALACEAE**
Mimulus – **SCROPHULARIACEAE**
MINT FAMILY – **LAMIACEAE**
Mirabilis – **NYCTAGINACEAE**
MISTLETOE FAMILY – **VISCACEAE**
Mohavea – **SCROPHULARIACEAE**

Mollugo – **MOLLUGINACEAE**
Monanthochloë – **POACEAE**
Monardella – **LAMIACEAE**
Monolepis – **CHENOPODIACEAE**
Monoptilon – **ASTERACEAE**
MORNING GLORY FAMILY – **CONVOLVULACEAE**
Morus – **MORACEAE**
Muhlenbergia – **POACEAE**
MULBERRY FAMILY – **MORACEAE**
MUSTARD FAMILY – **BRASSICACEAE**
Myosurus – **RANUNCULACEAE**
Myriophyllum – **HALORAGACEAE**
Najas – **NAJADACEAE**
Nama – **HYDROPHYLLACEAE**
Nasturtium – **BRASSICACEAE**
Nemacaulis – **POLYGONACEAE**
Nemacladus – **CAMPANULACEAE**
NETTLE FAMILY – **URTICACEAE**
Nicotiana – **SOLANACEAE**
NIGHTSHADE FAMILY – **SOLANACEAE**
Nissolia – **FABACEAE**
Nitrophila – **CHENOPODIACEAE**
Nolina – **NOLINACEAE**
OCOTILLO FAMILY – **FOUQUIERIACEAE**
Oenothera – **ONAGRACEAE**
Oligomeris – **RESEDACEAE**
OLIVE FAMILY – **OLEACEAE**
Olneya – **FABACEAE**
Opuntia – **CACTACEAE**
Orobanche – **OROBANCHACEAE**
Oxalis – **OXALIDACEAE**
OXALIS FAMILY – **OXALIDACEAE**
Pachycereus – **CACTACEAE**
Palafoxia – **ASTERACEAE**
PALM FAMILY – **ARECACEAE**
Panicum – **POACEAE**
Pappophorum – **POACEAE**
Parietaria – **URTICACEAE**
Parkinsonia – **FABACEAE**
Parthenice – **ASTERACEAE**
Pectis – **ASTERACEAE**
Pectocarya – **BORAGINACEAE**
Pediomelum – **FABACEAE**
Peniocereus – **CACTACEAE**
Pennisetum – **POACEAE**
Penstemon – **SCROPHULARIACEAE**
Perityle – **ASTERACEAE**
Petalonyx – **LOASACEAE**
Petunia – **SOLANACEAE**
Peucephyllum – **ASTERACEAE**
Phacelia – **HYDROPHYLLACEAE**
Phalaris – **POACEAE**
Phaseolus – **FABACEAE**
Phlox – **POLEMONIACEAE**
PHLOX FAMILY – **POLEMONIACEAE**

Phoenix – **ARECACEAE**

Pholisma – **LENNOACEAE**

Pholistoma – **HYDROPHYLLACEAE**

Phoradendron – **VISCACEAE**

Phragmites – **POACEAE**

Physalis – **SOLANACEAE**

Physaria – **BRASSICACEAE**

Pilostyles – **RAFFLESIACEAE**

PINK FAMILY – **CARYOPHYLLACEAE**

Plagiobothrys – **BORAGINACEAE**

Plantago – **PLANTAGINACEAE**

PLANTAIN FAMILY – **PLANTAGINACEAE**

Pleurocoronis – **ASTERACEAE**

Pluchea – **ASTERACEAE**

Plumbago – **PLUMBAGINACEAE**

PLUMBAGO FAMILY – **PLUMBAGINACEAE**

Poa – **POACEAE**

POKEWEED FAMILY – **PHYTOLACCACEAE**

Polanisia – **CAPPARACEAE**

Polygala – **POLYGALACEAE**

Polygonum – **POLYGONACEAE**

Polypogon – **POACEAE**

POMEGRANATE FAMILY – **PUNICACEAE**

PONDWEED FAMILY – **POTAMOGETONACEAE**

POPPY FAMILY – **PAPAVERACEAE**

Populus – **SALICACEAE**

Porophyllum – **ASTERACEAE**

Portulaca – **PORTULACACEAE**

PORTULACA FAMILY – **PORTULACACEAE**

Prenanthella – **ASTERACEAE**

PRIMROSE FAMILY – **PRIMULACEAE**

Proboscidea – **MARTYNIACEAE**

Prosopis – **FABACEAE**

Psathyrotes – **ASTERACEAE**

Pseudognaphalium – **ASTERACEAE**

Psilostrophe – **ASTERACEAE**

Psorothamnus – **FABACEAE**

Ptelea – **RUTACEAE**

Pterostegia – **POLYGONACEAE**

Punica – **PUNICACEAE**

QUASSIA FAMILY – **SIMAROUBACEAE**

Quercus – **FAGACEAE**

RAFFLESIA FAMILY – **RAFFLESIACEAE**

Rafinesquia – **ASTERACEAE**

RANUNCULUS FAMILY – **RANUNCULACEAE**

RATANY FAMILY – **KRAMERIACEAE**

Rhamnus – **RHAMNACEAE**

Rhus – **ANACARDIACEAE**

Rhynchosia – **FABACEAE**

Rhynchosida – **MALVACEAE**

Ribes – **GROSSULARIACEAE**

Rivina – **PHYTOLACCACEAE**

ROSE FAMILY – **ROSACEAE**

RUE OR CITRUS FAMILY – **RUTACEAE**

Ruellia – **ACANTHACEAE**

Rumex – **POLYGONACEAE**

Ruppia – **RUPPIACEAE**

RUSH FAMILY – **JUNCACEAE**

Sagittaria – **ALISMATACEAE**

Salazaria – **LAMIACEAE**

Salicornia – **CHENOPODIACEAE**

Salix – **SALICACEAE**

Salsola – **CHENOPODIACEAE**

SALTWORT FAMILY – **BATACEAE**

Salvia – **LAMIACEAE**

Sambucus – **CAPRIFOLIACEAE**

Sapindus – **SAPINDACEAE**

Sarcobatus – **CHENOPODIACEAE**

Schismus – **POACEAE**

Scirpus – **CYPERACEAE**

Sebastiania – **EUPHORBIACEAE**

SEDGE FAMILY – **CYPERACEAE**

Senecio – **ASTERACEAE**

Senna – **FABACEAE**

SESAME FAMILY – **PEDALIACEAE**

Sesamum – **PEDALIACEAE**

Sesbania – **FABACEAE**

Sesuvium – **AIZOACEAE**

Setaria – **POACEAE**

Sibara – **BRASSICACEAE**

Sida – **MALVACEAE**

Silene – **CARYOPHYLLACEAE**

Simmondsia – **SIMMONDSIACEAE**

Sinapis – **BRASSICACEAE**

Sisymbrium – **BRASSICACEAE**

SNAPDRAGON FAMILY – **SCROPHULARIACEAE**

SOAPBERRY FAMILY – **SAPINDACEAE**

Solanum – **SOLANACEAE**

Sonchus – **ASTERACEAE**

Sorghum – **POACEAE**

Spergularia – **CARYOPHYLLACEAE**

Spermolepis – **APIACEAE**

Sphaeralcea – **MALVACEAE**

Sphenopholis – **POACEAE**

SPIDERWORT FAMILY – **COMMELINACEAE**

Sporobolus – **POACEAE**

SPURGE FAMILY – **EUPHORBIACEAE**

STAFF-TREE FAMILY – **CELASTRACEAE**

Stegnosperma – **PHYTOLACCACEAE**

Stemodia – **SCROPHULARIACEAE**

Stenocereus – **CACTACEAE**

Stephanomeria – **ASTERACEAE**

STICK-LEAF FAMILY – **LOASACEAE**

Stillingia – **EUPHORBIACEAE**

Stipa – **POACEAE**

STONECROP FAMILY – **CRASSULACEAE**

Streptanthella – **BRASSICACEAE**

Streptanthus – **BRASSICACEAE**

Stuckenia – **POTAMOGETONACEAE**

Stylocline – **ASTERACEAE**

Suaeda – **CHENOPODIACEAE**
SUMAC FAMILY – **ANACARDIACEAE**
Talinum – **PORTULACACEAE**
TAMARISK FAMILY – **TAMARICACEAE**
Tamarix – **TAMARICACEAE**
Tephrosia – **FABACEAE**
Tetraclea – **VERBENACEAE**
Teucrium – **LAMIACEAE**
Thamnosma – **RUTACEAE**
Thelypodiopsis – **BRASSICACEAE**
Thelypodium – **BRASSICACEAE**
Thymophylla – **ASTERACEAE**
Thysanocarpus – **BRASSICACEAE**
Tidestromia – **AMARANTHACEAE**
Tiquilia – **BORAGINACEAE**
Townsendia – **ASTERACEAE**
Tragia – **EUPHORBIACEAE**
Trianthema – **AIZOACEAE**
Tribulus – **ZYGOPHYLLACEAE**
Trichoptilium – **ASTERACEAE**
Tridens – **POACEAE**
Trifolium – **FABACEAE**
Triodanis – **CAMPANULACEAE**
Triteleiopsis – **LILIACEAE**
Triticum – **POACEAE**
Trixis – **ASTERACEAE**

Tumamoca – **CUCURBITACEAE**
Typha – **TYPHACEAE**
Uropappus – **ASTERACEAE**
Vauquelinia – **ROSACEAE**
Verbena – **VERBENACEAE**
VERBENA FAMILY – **VERBENACEAE**
Verbesina – **ASTERACEAE**
Veronica – **SCROPHULARIACEAE**
Vicia – **FABACEAE**
Viguiera – **ASTERACEAE**
VIOLET FAMILY – **VIOLACEAE**
Vulpia, see **Festuca**
Washingtonia – **ARECACEAE**
WATERLEAF FAMILY – **HYDROPHYLLACEAE**
WATER-MILFOIL FAMILY – **HALORAGACEAE**
WATER-NYMPH FAMILY – **NAJADACEAE**
WATER-PLANTAIN FAMILY – **ALISMATACEAE**
WILLOW FAMILY – **SALICACEAE**
Wislizenia – **CAPPARACEAE**
Xanthium – **ASTERACEAE**
Yabea – **APIACEAE**
Yucca – **AGAVACEAE**
Zannichellia – **ZANNICHELLIACEAE**
Zephyranthes – **LILIACEAE**
Zinnia – **ASTERACEAE**
Ziziphus – **RHAMNACEAE**

Addundum: The following records and information are added in proofs. This results in two additional families for the flora, three additional genera, and one more species for AG, three more for GR, and one more for OP.

CYPERACEAE

Scirpus. Species in the flora area seem best treated as:

Bolboschoenus maritimus (L.) Palla [*Scirpus maritimus* L.]

Schoenoplectus americanus (Pers.) Volkart ex Schinz & Keller [*Scirpus americanus* Pers.]

FUMARIACEAE – FUMATORIA FAMILY

Corydalis aurea Willd. var. **occidentalis** (Engelm. ex A. Gray) Rydb. Cool season annuals; flowers yellow.
    GR: N side of Crater Range, *McLaughlin 10300.*

IRIDACEAE – IRIS FAMILY

Sisyrinchium demissum Greene. Blue-eyed grass. Small, perennial herbs; leaves grass-like; flowers blue with a yellow center. One colony discovered 1999.
    OP: Quitobaquito, *Rutman 23 Apr 1999* (ORPI).

MALVACEAE

Eremalche exilis
    GR: S side of Crater Range, *McLaughlin 10356.*

Sida abutifolia
    GR: Sauceda Mts, 1.4 km NW of Pistol Pass, *Holm 2001-0905-16.*

POACEAE

Echinochloa muricata (P. Beauv.) Fern. var. **microstachya** Wiegand. Hot-weather annuals. It is significant that this native species was in the delta region in the nineteenth century (see Felger, this volume, chapter 15).
    AG: Horseshoe Bend of Colorado River, 1889, *Palmer 949.*

Eighteen

Mammals of the Sonoran Desert Borderland Reserves

Robert S. Henry

All of the Sonoran Desert is dry by definition. Most all of it is hot in the summer.
But there's a great variety of landscapes
and plant communities in this expansive desert,
ranging from relatively lush cactus forests near
Tucson, deep canyons, mountaintops, riparian ribbons along the few rivers, to the other extreme of
seemingly endless creosotebush flats, the dunefields
of the Gran Desierto, and the salt- and mudflats
of the Colorado delta. It's this driest, hottest end
of the Sonoran Desert spectrum in the southwestern corner of Arizona and the northwestern
corner of Sonora that we are concerned with here.
This is the low desert, the region that is often
described with words like *bleak, barren, hellish.*
And yet this area can be beautiful, too: crystalline
air and deep blue skies; red, black, or white mountains; and hillsides covered with wildflowers.
There's a string of protected lands that runs from
the Sonoran Desert National Monument near
Phoenix all the way southwest to the two Mexican
biosphere reserves that hug the upper end of the
Gulf of California. Despite the extreme aridity of
this region, mammals from tiny rodents to bighorn
sheep and pronghorns have found ways to cope
with a scarcity of food and moisture. These reserves
are home to some sixty species of terrestrial mammals, and maybe more that haven't been recorded
yet, for few scientists have cared to work here.

The earliest collections of mammals from
these borderlands were made in the middle to late
1800s, not by biologists per se but by soldiers and
surveyors. In 1894, barely a century ago, the U.S.-
Mexican boundary west of Sonoyta, Sonora, occupied a mostly blank space on the maps. Through
the heart of this country traveled Edgar Mearns
(1907), collecting plants and mammals at every
stop along the way. His primary responsibility
was to serve as chief medical officer for a U.S. Army
detachment that was accompanying the survey of
the international boundary. But his real interest
lay in the natural sciences, and the result was the
most complete description yet of the mammals
that occurred from El Paso, Texas, to the Pacific
coast at San Diego. Mearns was fortunate that the
workers and troops of the survey stayed healthy,
for he was left free to wander widely. During such
forays he made significant collections from the
area of Yuma and the delta of the Colorado River.

In the early 1800s fur trappers and explorers
such as James Ohio Pattie (1988) worked along the
Gila and Colorado rivers and sometimes kept journals of their observations. In the 1850s and 1860s
the first U.S.-Mexico boundary survey brought
military officer–naturalists into the heart of the
desert for the first time, and others collected near
scattered military outposts like those at Forts
Yuma, Whipple, and Grant. After the turn of the
century a new kind of scientist arrived, the hunter-
naturalist, who came into the country in search of
adventure, knowledge, and big game. William Hornaday (1908) wrote a classic account of his trek
into the Organ Pipe, Cabeza Prieta, and Pinacate
country in search of bighorn sheep for the Carnegie
Museum. He was followed by Charles Sheldon,
who explored much of the border country, including the incredibly remote Sierra del Rosario in the
heart of the Gran Desierto, also in search of bighorns (Sheldon 1979). Finally, modern mammalogists E. A. Goldman, Laurence Huey, Donald
Hoffmeister, and E. Lendell Cockrum have more
recently added to our knowledge of the mammals
of the low desert.

The Hoofed Megafauna (Order Artiodactyla)

The rotor of the Bell Jet Ranger helicopter had just
started to wind down after landing at our camp-

site next to a big wash. We were based just south of the old crumbling gas station at Big Horn (see Chapter 7, this volume). My Game and Fish colleagues and I unbuckled our seat belts and hopped out of the doorless ship. We had just completed an aerial survey of the Sand Tank Mountains, and we had seen fewer bighorn sheep (*Ovis canadensis*) than on the last survey three years ago, fewer than we'd ever counted. But our talk, as soon as we got far enough away from the noise of the machine to hear each other, was not about the sheep but about something else we'd seen—a mountain lion. We'd just come around the base of an isolated hill north of Dragon's Tooth when Bob Achee and I, on the same side of the helicopter, looked down into the eyes of the big cat about fifty feet below us. The cat was likewise looking up at us. All three of us were frozen motionless and speechless for a moment. One of us got his voice and called out "lion!" into the microphone, and the pilot was able to turn us back quickly enough to watch the magnificent big cat as he bounded away into a little cave, then came back out and headed for better cover. Was this big predator the reason for our declining bighorn sheep population? Though lions can and do kill plenty of sheep, the two species have successfully coexisted for many centuries. There must be other factors at work here.

At the beginning of the twenty-first century, approximately 1,000 bighorn sheep are living in the six low desert reserves. About 900 live on the U.S. side, and an unknown number live in the mountains just below the border in the Pinacate of Mexico—probably at least 100. By area, the estimates run (1) about 90 in the Sonoran Desert National Monument, (2) 340 in the Goldwater Range, (3) about 100 in Organ Pipe Cactus National Monument (1994 estimate), and (4) 380 in the Cabeza Prieta National Wildlife Refuge (AGFD data). Though this sounds like a lot of sheep, their populations are not really secure. Bighorn populations, especially on the eastern and northern edges of their range, have a tendency to enter into precipitous declines from which they sometimes don't recover. Sheep in the Sauceda, Sand Tank, Table Top, and Maricopa mountains are currently in decline. Though drought and predators may be factors, the main culprit in these declines seems often to be disease. At first look, the area protected within the boundaries of the national monuments,

biosphere reserves, refuge, and military reservation appears to be huge. But for large, mobile mammals like sheep, deer, and pronghorn, the area is not large enough. Roads, railways, canals, agriculture, and towns have dissected their traditional ranges. These animals can no longer travel freely to areas that have greened up after rains, or to get to the few historically permanent water sources like the Gila and Sonoyta rivers, or to exchange genetic information across the landscape. Additionally, and perhaps more devastating, is the suite of diseases that were introduced with domestic livestock and that still persist within the native wildlife populations. The environment will never again be "natural" or "pristine" for these large ungulates.

Besides bighorn sheep, four other artiodactyls occur within the borderland deserts: mule deer, white-tailed deer, pronghorn, and javelina. The two species of deer occupy very different habitats and probably compete little in this environment. Desert mule deer, *Odocoileus hemionus crooki*, live in the lowlands, the valleys between and around the mountains, while the white-tailed deer, *Odocoileus virginianus couesi*, occupy only the easternmost mountain ranges.

Mule deer are much the larger of the two and are common in the eastern part of this region, but their abundance gradually decreases to the west. Presently, a few deer can be found around the Mohawk and Sierra Pinta mountains, but no farther west. The habitat becomes too dry: deer need high-quality forage and free water. The mule deer of southwestern Arizona and northwestern Mexico have often been thought to be unique. They've been called "bura" or "burro" deer and were originally described as a separate subspecies, *O. h. eremicus,* and some researchers have even maintained that *bura* deer coexist with the more typical mule deer. More recent thinking is that only one mule deer exists here and is not sufficiently different to warrant subspecific status (Hoffmeister 1986).

The dainty little Coues white-tailed deer is at the western edge of its range in the Ajo, Sauceda, and Sand Tank mountains. Once in a while whitetails will be reported farther west, in the Puerto Blanco, Growler, or even Agua Dulce mountains, but these are probably dispersing individuals, and in recent times populations have not persisted in these areas. It's a miracle that these little deer can persist at all in these isolated desert ranges, for this is really a deer of the oak woodland and above, habitats that are found in the sky islands of southeastern Arizona and south through the Sierra Madre of Mexico. Yet here they are, sharing the desert mountains with bighorn sheep, surviving in small populations with as few as ten to twenty animals (Henry & Sowls 1980), living on mountain islands surrounded by a sea of low "mule deer" desert. The local history of this species is probably one of repeated local extinctions and recolonizations of these isolated populations (Brown and Henry 1981). I once interviewed Bob Montgomery, a lifelong resident of the Organ Pipe country and then living in Sonoyta, to learn more about the historical range of the whitetails. He described an even smaller deer that lived in the area, "not much larger than the antelope jackrabbit," known as "*chifladeros*," or whistlers. I suspect that the diminutive Coues whitetail appeared smaller than life at times.

One of the rarest of North American mammals is the Sonoran pronghorn, *Antilocapra americana sonoriensis,* a subspecies of the more widespread American pronghorn. Commonly called antelope, this subspecies in the United States is currently found only in Organ Pipe, Cabeza Prieta, and the Goldwater Range. In Mexico these pronghorn are found in the Pinacate and Gran Desierto biosphere reserve and in the *ejido* lands north and east of Puerto Peñasco. Their current population is less than 100 in the United States and around 650 in Mexico (Bright & Hervert 2005, 2006). Few of these details about their range and numbers were known in 1992 when a group of biologists from the United States and Mexico gathered in Ajo to conduct the first systematic survey of suspected Sonoran pronghorn habitat. This and subsequent surveys finally gave us a true picture of just how limited this species' range and numbers were. Every Sunday morning for seven years an Arizona Game and Fish Department airplane took off at daybreak from the Yuma airport, and a biologist on board (about four of us rotated the task) located each of 6 to 15 radio-collared pronghorn scattered between Yuma and Ajo. We took a GPS fix of their location and, using image-stabilized binoculars from 1,000 feet above, visually noted their group composition, behavior, and habitat. They got so used to that Cessna circling above them on Sunday mornings that they would rarely bother to look up and often lay down to nap while we were watching them.

Sonoran pronghorn are truly living on the edge. Normally inhabitants of the grassland, here they live entirely in some of the driest desert in North America. Like the bighorn, these are animals that are used to traveling huge distances to satisfy their needs. They can no longer reach the rivers if they need to or move to the areas that received the most rainfall: highways, canals, and fences block their way. Though occupying contiguous habitat, the U.S. and Mexican populations have almost no interchange. Their way is blocked by Highway 2, which runs between Sonoyta and San Luis Río Colorado (and which Mexico wants to widen), and a barbed-wire fence along the border. Here's a management dilemma: if we could, should we remove the border fence to allow pronghorns to cross freely but then subject them to the dangers of crossing Highway 2? They might not cross it anyway; these animals are not used to paved roads.

The other hoofed beast of the desert is the collared peccary *(Pecari tajacu),* known locally as the javelina or *jabalí.* Like the deer, they are most common to the east and become scarcer in the western, drier areas, though unlike the mule deer, a few can be found as far west as the Cabeza Prieta and Tinajas Altas mountains. The javelina is thought to be a relative newcomer to the U.S. Southwest, dispersing northward during the last century from the more tropical lands to the south in Mexico (Sowls 1997). These are typically animals of thornscrub and woodland. In our desert they are restricted primarily to the major washes and mountain canyons.

The Predators (Order Carnivora)

The order of carnivores includes a wide variety of mammal types, mostly medium to large in size. In our area of interest it includes four families: (1) the canids, or doglike mammals, with three species in the area: coyote, kit fox, and gray fox; (2) the felids, or cats, with two species: the mountain lion and bobcat, and old records of a third, the jaguar; (3) the procyonids, or raccoonlike mammals, which here include the raccoon and the ringtail, or *cacomixtle;* and (4) the mustelids, which include the badger and skunks.

The mountain lion, or cougar, or puma *(Puma*

concolor), is an animal that is always surrounded by controversy, as are the carnivores as a group. Hated by many as a killer of livestock and game, mountain lions are revered by others as a symbol of wildness and beauty. In southwestern Arizona the controversy reaches into the taxonomic realm, as the lions that were found along the lower Colorado River were first described by Merriam in 1903 as representing a separate subspecies, *P. c. browni,* also called the Yuma puma. Because of habitat changes along the lower river, few lions can now be found there, and that led the federal and state governments and other agencies to consider the subspecies imperiled and deserving of protection. However, the original description of the subspecies was based on only a single, young animal, and few specimens were ever collected, so many have questioned whether the Yuma puma is deserving of distinction. More recent DNA and morphometric analysis does not support subspecific status (Arizona Game and Fish Department, unpublished data). Nevertheless, the mountain lion, like most of the large mammals, is much more common in the easterly parts of our study area and is known only as an occasional wanderer to the western Cabeza Prieta and Pinacate areas. Lion populations go as deer populations go, so the areas that have few deer have few lions. Though mountain lions will prey on bighorn sheep, as they often do in the Sand Tank and Sauceda mountains, and anything else they can catch, it is doubtful that they can do so for long without an adjoining deer herd.

The other big cat, the jaguar *(Panthera onca),* could appear on our list of mammals of the desert borderlands based on some old records and the admittedly remote prospect of future visits. There's a record from the Ajo Mountains in Organ Pipe Cactus National Monument from about 1918 (cited in Hoffmeister 1986), as well as Aldo Leopold's observations from the "green lagoons" of the Colorado River delta in 1922 (Leopold 1966). A few years ago most of us thought the jaguar was probably gone from Arizona for good, but a couple of these magnificent cats have recently been photographed in the southeastern part of the state (AGFD 2002), and that raises the expectation that they can still appear almost anywhere. Of the smaller cats, only the bobcat is common across the entire borderland region. The ocelot *(Leopardus pardalis)* and jaguarundi *(Herpailurus yaguarondi),*

though occasionally reported, have never had a verified record in southwestern Arizona (Brown & López González 2000) and probably don't find our arid habitat much to their liking.

The three species of canids—the coyote *(Canis latrans),* gray fox *(Urocyon cinereoargenteus),* and kit fox *(Vulpes velox)*—can be found across the entire region. Coyotes are just about everywhere, though during the summer they can't get too far from a source of water (Golightly 1981). The two foxes are more specialized and use different habitats: the kit prefers the more openly vegetated valleys while the slightly larger gray prefers rougher country in and around the mountains. I helped a graduate student live-trap kit foxes for a research project (Zoellick et al. 1989): they are surprisingly small underneath that great coat of fur, only about the size of a small housecat.

Of the three possible species of procyonids, only the ringtail *(Bassariscus astutus)* is widespread across our area. The ringtail is highly nocturnal and rarely seen but probably occurs in all the desert mountain ranges. Specimens collected near the Colorado River, in the Gila and Tinajas Altas mountains, have been described as a separate subspecies, *B. a. yumanensis,* but how far east this form gets has not been ascertained. The raccoon *(Procyon lotor)* is restricted to areas near water, is common only along the Colorado River, and probably actually enters one of our borderland reserves only in the delta area. The coatimundi *(Nasua narica),* coming from the other direction, may just barely enter our area, and only occasionally as a wanderer, in the Organ Pipe country.

The family Mustelidae—the skunks, weasels, and relatives—is represented by two species that live throughout the region; a third that, like the raccoon, occurs on the periphery; and a fourth that has been extirpated. The badger *(Taxidea taxus)* and spotted skunk *(Spilogale putorius)* can be found in all the desert zones, the badger in particular being quite common though rarely seen. Once one learns to recognize the telltale diggings that badgers create as they try to dig rodents out of their burrows, one can appreciate how widespread they really are. The spotted skunk is also not often seen but can occur almost anywhere in the desert. Not so the striped skunk *(Mephitis mephitis):* it's found only along the rivers and irrigated areas. A species that once occurred along the lower Colorado, but is now gone, is the river otter *(Lontra canadensis)*. These animals could possibly be reestablished if permanent flows are ever returned to the lower river.

The Rabbits and Hares (Order Lagomorpha)

Three species of these ubiquitous and well-known animals occur in the desert borderlands. The desert cottontail *(Sylvilagus audubonii)* can be found anywhere there is thick cover, especially near the rivers but also in desert canyons and densely vegetated washes. The black-tailed jackrabbit *(Lepus californicus)* likewise can be found throughout the desert out on the open flats. Another species of jackrabbit, Allen's *(Lepus alleni)*, is more characteristic of the desert grasslands east of our region but reaches the dry desert in the Organ Pipe, Cabeza Prieta, and eastern Pinacate areas.

Bats (Order Chiroptera)

The distinctive aroma of a major bat roost drifted out to meet us as we approached the black hole in the lava. We had hiked across a mile and a half of one of the jumbled, jagged lava flows that emanate from the flanks of the Pinacate volcano to check out a promising cave. It was Thanksgiving 1989, and I was here with my wife, Susanna, and our old caving friends from Tucson: Bill Peachey, Tom and Cyndi Bethard, and their two children, Steve and Laura. Bill, an indefatigable desert explorer and perennial student of all things natural, had found this lava tube on a previous trip but had not gone beyond the entrance. It had promise, though, so we were back to check it out. Before the day was out, we explored more than 2,000 feet of cave and found several areas where large numbers of bats apparently roosted. None were there at that time of year, but what excited us was that a number of little bat skulls on the floor of the cave had the elongated snout that is characteristic of the lesser long-nosed bat *(Leptonycteris curasoae)*. This species is listed as endangered, and only a few roost sites are known in the region. Their long snout allows them to probe into the flowers of cacti and agaves to get at the nectar and pollen and at the same time serve as the primary pollinator of some of these plants. They also consume the cacti fruit later in the season, which colors their droppings bright red.

We returned the next May with University of Arizona mammalogist Yar Petryszyn and bat expert Dave Dalton, and this time the roost areas were carpeted with long-nosed bat females and their young. By counting the bats in a square foot of ceiling and multiplying by the number of square feet of ceiling space occupied by the hordes, Yar estimated that there were more than 20,000 bats. This was truly exciting, for it meant that this was one of the largest roosts known, and this one a natural cave rather than a mine tunnel. Later in the season, when the number of females was bolstered by juveniles and males, the number of bats exiting the cave in the evening surpassed 100,000. We experienced this one July night when we camped by the entrance and counted them as they left for their nightly foraging run. As darkness settled, we first could hear the rustle of thousands of flapping wings from inside the entrance as the bats swirled back and forth, right up to the entrance, then back inside, testing the light level, waiting for just the right time to leave. When that time arrived, they streamed from the entrance, thousands of them, their wings making a whistling sound as they picked up speed and dispersed into the dark desert night. We woke ourselves up at four in the morning to watch the return flight. We could just make out their shadows against the starry sky as they dove down toward the entrance with a roaring sound and disappeared inside. Left behind as evidence of their passing, all over the rocks and our sleeping bags, were myriad little red-colored splotches.

Many other bat species occur in the borderlands: at least 15 to 20 different species have been recorded in the six reserves, most of them insectivores, and all of them play a crucial role in the proper functioning of the desert ecosystem.

The Rodents and Shrews (Orders Rodentia and Insectivora)

This is the largest group of mammals in the borderlands, with at least 25 species of rodents recorded in the six reserves. As with the bats, other species will likely be added to the known fauna as more investigations are conducted. In a way, desert rodents function like the engine that drives the desert ecosystem. Rainfall and the plants that it causes to grow are the fuel for that engine. Rodent populations, in particular the heteromyids of the plains (the pocket mice and kangaroo rats) and the murids of the mountains and washes (represented by the cactus mouse and woodrats), rise and fall in tune with rainfall. In turn, many carnivore populations—mammal, bird, and reptile—rise and fall with the rodents, though lagging behind a bit. And the rodents have an impact on the plants themselves, redistributing seeds and consuming huge amounts of vegetation. Petryszyn & Russ (1996) estimate that 3 million rodents, with a biomass of 100,000 kilograms, live in Organ Pipe Cactus National Monument.

One little rodent, called the mesquite or Merriam's mouse *(Peromyscus merriami),* was first discovered in 1894 by Edgar Mearns in the Sonoyta River valley along the southern edge of Organ Pipe (Mearns 1907). It's very similar to the common cactus mouse *(P. eremicus),* but it lives only in dense mesquite thickets that grow in river and stream bottoms. These riparian habitats have nearly disappeared from southern Arizona and Sonora, and so has the mesquite mouse. After Mearns's discovery, the mouse was not seen again in Organ Pipe until 1988 (Petryszyn & Russ 1996). Several more have been trapped since. It would be nice to think that the protection afforded the lands in the monument has helped to restore some of this rodent's habitat and that this is just an example of what can happen in all six of the borderland reserves.

Checklist of Mammals of the Sonoran Desert Borderland Reserves

Following is a list of mammals that have been documented in at least one of the six borderland reserves in southwest Arizona, northwest Sonora, and extreme northeast Baja California. Records have been accumulated from numerous sources: Cockrum 1960, 1981; Cockrum & Petryszyn 1986, 1992; Dalton & Dalton 1994; Grinnell 1914; Hoffmeister 1986; Huey 1942; Instituto Nacional de Ecología n.d.; Mellink et al. 1999; Roman & Campoy 1998; USDI 1997, 1998; and personal knowledge. The order and nomenclature follow Wilson and Reeder 1993, as displayed on the Mammal Species of the World website of the Smithsonian National Museum of Natural History (http://nmnhgoph.si.edu/msw/).

Abbreviations: OP = Organ Pipe Cactus National Monument; SD = Sonoran Desert National Monument; CP = Cabeza Prieta National Wildlife Refuge; GR = Barry M. Goldwater Range (U.S. Department of De-

fense); PI = Reserva de la Biosfera El Pinacate y Gran Desierto de Altar; AG = Reserva de la Biosfera Alto Golfo de California y Delta del Río Colorado.

Order Insectivora – Insectivores
Soricidae – Shrews
   Notiosorex crawfordi crawfordi. Desert shrew. Throughout but rarely seen (OP, PI, AG).
Order Chiroptera – Bats
Phyllostomidae – Leaf-nosed Bats
   Macrotus californicus. California leaf-nosed bat. Throughout (OP, CP, GR, PI, AG).
   Leptonycteris curasoae yerbabuenae. Lesser long-nosed bat. Eastern half of area where agaves and columnar cacti are abundant (OP, CP, PI).
Vespertilionidae – Plain-nosed Bats
   Antrozous pallidus pallidus. Pallid bat. Throughout (OP, CP, GR, PI, AG).
   Eptesicus fuscus pallidus. Big brown bat. Throughout (OP, CP, GR, PI, AG).
   Lasionycteris noctivagans. Silver-haired bat. Mostly in high mountains; rare in our area; recent record in CP (CP).
   Lasiurus cinereus cinereus. Hoary bat. Uncommon, prefers areas with large trees, record from Yuma (OP, CP).
   [*Lasiurus ega xanthinus.* Southern yellow bat. Prefers trees, especially fan palms, record from Yuma, possible in AG.]
   Myotis californicus stephensi. California myotis. Throughout (OP, CP, GR, PI, AG).
   Myotis velifer velifer. Cave myotis. Mostly eastern parts, never far from water (OP, SD).
   [*Myotis vivesi.* Fish-eating bat. Gulf of California, possible in AG.]
   Myotis yumanensis yumanensis. Yuma myotis. Forages over water, most records near rivers (AG).
   Pipistrellus hesperus hesperus. Western pipistrelle. Throughout (OP, CP, GR, PI, AG).
   Plecotus townsendii pallescens (= *Corynorhinus townsendii*). Townsend's big-eared bat. Prefers forests, uncommon in desert (OP, CP).
Molossidae – Free-tailed Bats
   Eumops perotis californicus. Western mastiff bat. Uncommon, prefers cliff areas near water (OP, GR).
   Eumops underwoodi sonoriensis. Underwood's mastiff bat. Very rare, only in OP area (OP).
   Nyctinomops femorosaccus. Pocketed free-tailed bat. Possible throughout but uncommon (OP, CP).
   Nyctinomops macrotis. Big free-tailed bat. Uncommon throughout (CP).
   Tadarida brasiliensis mexicana. Brazilian free-tailed bat. Uncommon throughout (CP, GR, PI, AG).

Order Carnivora – Carnivores

Canidae – Dogs and Allies

Canis latrans mearnsi. Coyote. Throughout (OP, CP, SD, GR, PI, AG).

Urocyon cinereoargenteus scottii. Gray fox. Throughout, especially in rocky or brushy areas (OP, CP, SD, GR, PI, AG).

Vulpes velox macrotis (= *V. macrotis*). Kit fox. Throughout, in open habitats (OP, CP, SD, GR, PI, AG).

Felidae – Cats

Lynx rufus baileyi. Bobcat. Throughout (OP, CP, SD, GR, PI, AG).

Puma concolor azteca, P. c. browni. Mountain lion. Throughout but more common in eastern parts (OP, CP, SD, GR, PI).

Mustelidae – Skunks and Allies

Conepatus mesoleucus venaticus. Western hog-nosed skunk. Mostly east of our area, recorded in OP.

Mephitis macroura milleri. Hooded skunk. Mostly east of our area, recorded in OP.

Mephitis mephitis estor. Striped skunk. Near water along Colorado and Sonoyta rivers (OP, PI).

Spilogale putorius leucoparia. Spotted skunk. Uncommon throughout (OP, GR, PI, AG).

Taxidea taxus berlandieri. American badger. Throughout (OP, CP, GR, PI).

Procyonidae – Raccoons and Allies

Bassariscus astutus arizonensis, B. a. yumanensis. Ringtail. Throughout, in mountains (OP, CP, SD, GR, PI, AG).

Procyon lotor pallidus. Raccoon. Restricted to areas near permanent water (OP, PI, AG).

Order Artiodactyla – Even-toed Hoofed Mammals

Tayassuidae – Peccaries

Pecari tajacu sonoriensis. Collared peccary, javelina. Eastern areas, in canyons and washes (OP, CP, SD, GR, PI).

Cervidae – Deer

Odocoileus hemionus eremicus. Desert mule deer. Eastern half of area, not in steep mountains (OP, CP, SD, GR, PI).

Odocoileus virginianus couesi. White-tailed deer. Eastern areas, in mountains and foothills (OP, CP, SD, GR, PI).

Antilocapridae – Pronghorns

Antilocapra americana sonoriensis. Pronghorn. Throughout much of area but currently not east of Highway 85 or in extreme west (OP, CP, GR, PI).

Bovidae – Sheep, Cattle, and Allies

Ovis canadensis mexicana (= *O. c. nelsoni*). Desert bighorn sheep. Throughout, in mountains (OP, CP, SD, GR, PI).

Order Rodentia – Rodents

Sciuridae – Squirrels

Ammospermophilus harrisii. Harris' antelope squirrel. Throughout, in rocky or gravelly habitats (OP, CP, SD, GR, PI, AG).

Spermophilus tereticaudus tereticaudus, S. t. neglectus. Round-tailed ground squirrel. Throughout, in valleys; subsp. *tereticaudus* only in Colorado and lower Gila river valleys (OP, CP, SD, GR, PI, AG).

Spermophilus variegatus grammurus. Rock squirrel. Eastern half, in rocky habitats (OP, CP, SD, GR, PI).

Castoridae – Beavers

Castor canadensis frondator. Beaver. Along Colorado and Gila rivers, possibly in AG.

Geomyidae – Pocket Gophers

Thomomys bottae albatus, cervinus, pusillus. Botta's pocket gopher. Throughout, in fine-grained soils; many variants (OP, CP, SD, GR, PI, AG).

Heteromyidae – Kangaroo Rats and Pocket Mice

Dipodomys deserti deserti, D. d. arizonae. Desert kangaroo rat. Throughout, in fine-grained valley soils (OP, CP, SD, GR, PI, AG).

Dipodomys merriami merriami. Merriam's kangaroo rat. Throughout, in fine-grained soils (OP, CP, SD, GR, PI, AG).

Dipodomys spectabilis perblandus. Banner-tailed kangaroo rat. Barely enters our area from the east in OP (OP).

Chaetodipus baileyi baileyi. Bailey's pocket mouse. Nearly throughout but maybe not west of Gila Mountains (OP, CP, SD, GR, PI).

Chaetodipus intermedius phasma. Rock pocket mouse. Throughout, in rocky or gravelly habitats (OP, CP, SD, GR, PI, AG).

Chaetodipus penicillatus pricei, C. p. penicillatus. Desert pocket mouse. Throughout, on valley floors (OP, CP, SD, GR, PI, AG).

Perognathus amplus amplus, P. a. taylori. Arizona pocket mouse. Nearly throughout, except along Colorado River, on valley floors (OP, CP, SD, GR, PI, AG).

Perognathus longimembris bombycinus. Little pocket mouse. Colorado River valley, in sandy soils, doubtful in OP or PI (AG).

Muridae – Mice and Rats

Ondatra zibethicus pallidus. Muskrat. Along Colorado River (AG).

Mus musculus. House mouse. Restricted to towns and agricultural areas (AG).

Neotoma albigula mearnsi, N. a. venusta. White-throated woodrat, "packrat." Throughout; subsp. *venusta* in Colorado River valley (OP, CP, SD, GR, PI, AG).

Neotoma lepida auripila. Desert woodrat, "packrat." Throughout, except extreme east; prefers rocky habitats (OP, CP, GR, PI, AG).

Onychomys torridus torridus. Southern grasshopper mouse. Throughout (OP, CP, SD, GR, PI, AG).

Peromyscus crinitus disparilis. Canyon mouse. Western half of area, in rocky habitats (CP, GR, PI).

Peromyscus eremicus eremicus. Cactus mouse. Throughout (OP, CP, SD, GR, PI, AG).

Peromyscus maniculatus sonoriensis. Deer mouse. Mostly along waterways, not in desertscrub (SD, PI, AG).

Peromyscus merriami merriami. Mesquite mouse. Known only from southern boundary of OP and Sonoyta valley, in thick mesquite (OP).

Reithrodontomys megalotis megalotis. Western harvest mouse. Along waterways and around agriculture (PI, AG).

Sigmodon arizonae cienegae. Arizona cotton rat. Mostly near waterways north and east of our area, recent record from OP (OP).

Sigmodon hispidus subsp. *eremicus.* Yuma cotton rat. Colorado River valley, possible in AG.

Order Lagomorpha – Rabbits and Hares

Leporidae – Rabbits and Hares

Lepus alleni alleni. Antelope jackrabbit. Open habitats in southeast part of area (OP, CP, PI).

Lepus californicus eremicus. Black-tailed jackrabbit. Throughout, in open habitats (OP, CP, SD, GR, PI, AG).

Sylvilagus audubonii arizonae. Desert cottontail. Throughout, in brushy habitats (OP, CP, SD, GR, PI, AG).

Nineteen

Birds of Arizona's Southwestern Borderland

David J. Griffin

Because of its southern location, year-round warm climate, biseasonal rainfall, and vegetation links to tropical thornscrub regions to the south, the Sonoran Desert is the most diverse of the North American deserts (Dimmitt 1999; Ohmart & Anderson 1982). The vegetation communities provide a varied assemblage of resources and habitats for a variety of wildlife, particularly for the birds of the region, resulting in a relatively high avian diversity in comparison with other North American deserts (Ohmart & Anderson 1982; Parker 1986). These habitats provide resident and migrant birds with places to forage, nest, and shelter from the physiological stresses of the harsh desert environment. Approximately 305 bird species have been reported from the region, representing 15 orders and 55 families. About 25 percent (72 to 79) are resident breeders, and the remaining 75 percent (226 to 233) are migrants or winter residents. For this chapter, records of birds for the region came from numerous sources, including published and unpublished literature as well as the author's and others' personal observations and experience conducting wildlife surveys.

The diverse habitats are used by many different species, which employ differing behavioral strategies for foraging and nesting in order to partition the resources (Parker 1986; Vander Wall & Mac-Mahon 1984). For instance, while walking along a large desert wash, you might spot two flycatchers up ahead in a mesquite tree. The first bird you note to be a phainopepla *(Phainopepla nitens);* the other, an ash-throated flycatcher *(Myiarchus cinerescens)*. And although these two birds may be observed in the same tree at the same time and may even be feeding on the same insect prey, the ash-throated flycatcher, you'll notice, typically forages from the *lower edges* of the tree outward, while the phainopepla usually sallies outward from *higher perches* and back again to a favorite spot (Parker

1986; author's observation). And while the ash-throated flycatcher uses *cavities* in plants such as mesquite in which to nest, the phainopepla nests *on top* of the horizontal branches of the tree. So although both flycatchers occur in the same areas, and sometimes even in the same tree, they avoid direct competition with each other by choosing different features of the desert vegetation. This subtle difference in habitat selection is repeated over and over again by numerous bird species in the Sonoran Desert, allowing for great overall diversity.

The area covered by the Barry M. Goldwater Range (GR), Cabeza Prieta National Wildlife Refuge (CP), Organ Pipe Cactus National Monument (OP), and Sonoran Desert National Monument (SD) is approximately 13,876 km² (1.39 million ha, or 3.43 million acres). Elevations in the region range from about 60 m (180 ft) in the southwest corner near Yuma to 1,382 m (4,808 ft) at the top of Mount Ajo. Although the region is known worldwide for its spring display of wildflowers, especially at OP, most visitors to the region are unaware of the great avian riches that await them in the same areas. And while the "Sky Islands" in southeastern Arizona have become a bird-watcher's paradise over the years, attracting the attention of amateurs and professionals alike, the birdlife of our region has remained for the most part out of the public spotlight. Nevertheless, the region's birdlife has attracted the attention of a few hardy ornithologists and naturalists, and it is beginning to catch a wider audience of birders.

The landforms and vegetation of this vast area provide diverse habitats for bird species. The Basin and Range topography, with long, steeply sloped, rugged mountain ranges separated by broad valleys, appeals to golden eagles *(Aquila chrysaetos)*, which use the ridges and cliffs as routes of travel and for nest sites, as well as horned larks *(Eremo-*

Figure 19.1. *Desert riparian habitat, Sauceda Mountains (Ryans Canyon). (Photo by David J. Griffin)*

phila alpestris), which use the open valley floors for foraging and nesting. The valleys are dissected by riparian ribbons of xeric trees, which in turn are some of the favored nesting areas for mourning and white-winged doves *(Zenaida macroura, Z. asiatica).*

High summer temperatures, warm winter temperatures, and low rainfall characterize the climate resident and migratory birds must face. Winter temperatures are mild, and daily highs average about 21°C (70°F). There are few days with below-freezing temperatures, although temperatures as low as −4°C (25°F) can occur even into March (author's observation). But the Sonoran Desert is often thought of as a hot place, and rightly so, with typical daily temperatures of 40°C to 46°C (105°F to 115°F) from May through September, and maximum daily temperatures in midsummer that approach 51°C (123°F) (author's observation)! Even with what appear to be drastic temperature changes both within and between seasons, nesting by some permanent residents such as crissal and Le Conte's thrashers *(Toxostoma crissale, T. lecontei)* can begin as early as mid-January as a response to spring green-up and temperatures favorable to nesting, and when conditions are favorable in late spring, these species may breed as late as July (author's observation). Temperatures also vary greatly on a daily basis, and temperature fluctuations can be as great as 19°C to 25°C (35°F to 45°F) between night and day; thus, in dove nests exposed to direct sun, the parent has to cool the eggs by day and warm them by night.

Rainfall amounts are highly variable throughout the region and typically occur in a biseasonal pattern. The summer rain season usually begins in early July and continues through August and September. Summer rains are typically from short, intense thunderstorms and generally produce a great deal of run-off. Rain can also fall as prolonged showers during the winter period, from December to March. Winter rains trigger the growth of annual plants, which produce the seeds, fruits, and nuts that are important to granivorous birds such as Gambel's quail *(Callipepla gambelii).* The quail also eat the fresh growth of leafy plants, ingesting great quantities of vitamin A, which is essential to virility and egg production. Annual numbers of many birds, especially Gambel's quail, correlate closely with winter rainfall and the subsequent annual plant production. Similarly, the production of late summer plants following the warm-season rains ("monsoon") plays a part in determining the number of species and individuals (e.g., winter residents) that will remain over winter in the region.

One of the first efforts at characterizing the birds of the region was done in the early 1890s by Edgar A. Mearns as part of the International Boundary Commission's survey of the U.S.-Mexico boundary (Phillips 1940), although many of his observations were likely within a short distance of the boundary. More focused work specifically directed at the birdlife in the Southwest wasn't begun until just after the early 1900s. For the next twenty to thirty years ornithologists generally overlooked our Sonoran Desert region because much of their attention was directed at higher-elevation mountain ranges nearer Tucson or to the north and west along portions of the Gila and Colorado rivers (see Amadeo M. Rea's classic 1983 book, *Once a River: Bird Life and Habitat Changes on the Middle Gila,* for an excellent description of the historic work of ornithologists, which he compares with his own findings nearly fifty years later).

Throughout much of North America the period from the 1930s through the 1950s marked a transition when many naturalists and ornithologists began to shift their studies from the systematics and biogeography of birds to ecology, behavior, and physiology (Ehrlich et al. 1988), and the southwestern Arizona region was no exception. Early work by Gale Monson (1936), George M. Sutton and Allan R. Phillips (1942), Laurence M. Huey (1936, 1942), and Phillips and Warren M. Pulich (1948) focused on basic inventories of the region and portions of the Tohono O'odham reservation, which included the collection of voucher specimens for museums and documentation of the distribution, abundance, and breeding status for many of the common species. Their work was carried out during field trips to the region that typically lasted from a few days to a couple of months, and in the case of Monson, for a number of years while he was employed by the U.S. Bureau of Sport Fisheries and Wildlife (today's Fish and Wildlife Service) as the manager of the national wildlife refuges in southwestern Arizona, which included Cabeza Prieta.

It wasn't until the early 1950s that biologists attempted to characterize avian habitat selection and ecological associations for a number of resident species in the region. M. Max Hensley (1954, 1959) studied bird communities at Organ Pipe and quantified the ecological relationships and nesting characteristics of many of the area's breeding birds. He was the first ornithologist to report on the nesting by ferruginous pygmy-owls *(Glaucidium brasilianum cactorum)* at OP and on the low incidence of nest parasitism by brown-headed cowbirds *(Molothrus ater)* on desert birds. Hensley also was the first to suggest that the trees that lined desert washes (e.g., xeroriparian areas) were used by a larger percentage of breeding birds (something that wasn't fully investigated until the early 1980s; see below) and that the xeroriparian areas may be used as movement corridors for migratory birds.

In the mid-1960s Alan Gubanich (1966) studied a local bird community in the Growler Valley at a recently established water source on the Cabeza Prieta. He found that many of the species observed using the waterhole were also found in the open creosotebush vegetation away from the water source, suggesting that some species may be able to derive a large portion of their moisture from their diets. In January 1969 Benjamin B. Beck and his colleagues (1973) conducted a brief study of the behavior and activity cycles of Gambel's quail and diurnal raptors at the same waterhole studied by Gubanich. By recording the frequency and timing of visits to water, they found that the timing of the quails' water use was inversely correlated with the presence of raptors, thus reducing the probability of quail encountering avian predators.

Besides the more rigorous studies that were being conducted during the 1950s and 1960s, a number of local volunteers, or "citizen scientists," as they are now called, began to organize and conduct Christmas Bird Counts at CP and OP in association with the National Audubon Society. These annual counts, centered at Lukeville, Alamo Canyon, and places in between, provided many new records for the region and helped define the distributions of some of the more common species. The most long-lived of these counts, the Sierra Pinta–Cabeza Prieta NWR Count, was initiated in 1955 by Monson. And though this count area incorporates some of the most isolated portions of Sonoran Desert in the region, it still manages to attract volunteer interest and has been conducted nearly every year since.

From the late 1950s to the early 1980s ornithologists and ecologists conducted groundbreaking studies of the ecology of avian community structure and resource partitioning in the temperate forests of North America (MacArthur 1958). However, it wasn't until the early 1980s that researchers began to conduct more in-depth studies of the habitat requirements and associations of resident desert birds in southwestern Arizona. Stephen B. Vander Wall and James A. MacMahon (1984) were the first to conduct a study of bird community structure across different elevation gradients at OP. They found that breeding bird species diversity was positively correlated with foliage height diversity and cover diversity, which simply meant that a higher diversity of birds could be found in the more heavily vegetated areas of the upper bajada. Kathleen C. Parker (1986) also studied birds at OP, examining the foraging behavior and habitat partitioning of breeding birds and how they related to the overall structuring of desert-scrub bird communities. She found that the presence of large trees and cacti enhanced species richness in two ways: the habitats with large trees and cacti were generally more productive than surrounding areas, which provided spatial resource partitioning; and they provided most of the nest sites for birds.

In the mid-1990s Patricia L. Cutler (1996) studied wildlife use at two water sources on the CP, Jose Juan Charco and Redtail Charco. Over an eighteen-month period she observed 150 species of birds and found that bird abundance and species diversity were positively associated with the water sources and the lush mesquite-dominated vegetation that was present (Cutler & Morrison 1998). Interestingly, a portion of Cutler's study took place at the same water source where Gubanich's study had been conducted thirty years before. During Gubanich's study the vegetation surrounding Jose Juan Charco was mostly creosotebush, small scattered mesquite shrubs, and a few older mesquite trees. But by the early 1990s the area around the water source had become heavily vegetated with a dense woodland, or bosque, of large mesquite trees. The combination of open water and a mature bosque provided habitat for greater than 40 percent more bird species than Gubanich had recorded: about 150 species compared with 65 reported by Gubanich. Cutler also recorded numerous species occurrences new to the CP and documented nesting by a number of species not previously recorded such as white-tiled kite *(Elanus leucurus)*, Anna's hummingbird *(Calypte anna)*, vermilion flycatcher *(Pyrocephalus rubinus)*, and burrowing owl *(Athene cunicularia)* (Cutler et al. 1996).

Between 1994 and 1998 I had the opportunity to work with other researchers on the GR and was involved with some of the most recent work conducted on birds in the region. There we monitored the population trends and habitat use of Neotropical migrant birds at four locations in the Sauceda and Sand Tank mountains (Bibles & Harris 1999; Hardy et al. 2003; Morrison et al. 1996). Although these mountains are prominent physical landmarks in the region, I was surprised to learn that their avian communities had never been investigated or well described by earlier observers. Consequently, we made many new distribution and breeding records during our monitoring surveys. For instance, we documented breeding by varied buntings *(Passerina versicolor)* in the Sauceda and Sand Tank mountains, which were the first records for Maricopa County (Witzeman et al. 1997) and likely represented the most northwestern point of the species' breeding range in the United States (National Geographic Society 2003; Rappole 2000; Sibley 2000). We also located previously unknown breeding "colonies" of purple martins *(Progne subis)* and observed more widespread breeding by rufous-crowned sparrows *(Aimophila ruficeps)*. We documented the use of large desert mistletoe *(Phoradendron californicum)* clumps as nest substrates by hooded orioles *(Icterus cucullatus)*, a species that was long believed not to nest along the dry desert washes in the region (Troy Corman, Arizona Game and Fish Department, personal communication 1996). We also documented the use of xeroriparian areas by some migratory species that had not been observed previously in the region, such as northern parula *(Parula pitiayumi)* and winter wren *(Troglodytes troglodytes)*.

The results of our study were similar to Kathleen Parker's (1986) findings and reminiscent of M. Max Hensley's suggestion from the 1950s that bird species diversity and numbers were greater in xeroriparian and paloverde–mixed cactus communities, where larger-profile plants and more diverse vegetation occurred, than in areas with less diverse vegetation such as creosotebush flats and open rocky and cliff areas (Hardy et al. 2003).

From 1995 to 1998 Paul Hardy and his colleagues conducted an intensive study of the distribution, abundance, and habitat selection of small owls in the Sauceda and Sand Tank mountains (Hardy 1997; Hardy et al. 1999). They used tape playback calls to survey for western screech-owls *(Otus kennicottii)*, elf owls *(Micrathene whitneyi)*, and cactus ferruginous pygmy-owls along large washes. They didn't locate any pygmy owls but found that elf owls exclusively used cavities in saguaros for nesting whereas western screech-owls used cavities in both saguaros and trees. These two diminutive species further partitioned their resources by choosing specific sizes of cavities: elf owls used smaller-diameter cavities that had been excavated by Gila woodpeckers *(Melanerpes*

uropygialis) whereas western screech-owls used larger cavities that had been excavated by gilded flickers *(Colaptes chrysoides)*. Hardy speculated that elf owls nested only in saguaros because such microclimates were cooler and moister than a more exposed cavity in a woody tree. The larger cavities chosen by western screech-owls may have been needed to house the species' nestlings, which grow larger than those of the tiny elf owls (Hardy & Morrison 2001). Hardy also found that elf owl nest cavities were in locations where there were greater local abundances of mature saguaros with more cavities. He suggested that because of frequent losses of mature saguaros during storms in the nonbreeding season, elf owls would have a better choice of nest sites when they returned to their breeding territory the following spring (Paul referred to these alternate saguaros and nest sites as "back-up cavities" and "back-up saguaros"). Under the same circumstances western screech-owls could choose a cavity in a tree if their nest saguaro had been toppled.

When Hardy looked at the factors that affected the detection of the small owls, he found that elf owls were much more affected by moon cycles and moonlight than western screech-owls (Hardy & Morrison 2000). He noted that there was a seasonal difference in when the owls sang; screech-owls were more easily detected from late February through late March whereas elf owls

were more detectable during April. Paul found that elf owls sang more frequently nearer the full moon than did screech-owls and that their singing behavior was affected by whether or not the moon was visible in the sky. For example, on a full-moon night elf owls were reluctant to sing before the moon had risen or if the moon was behind a cloud but "would bust out singing when the light came out!" (Paul C. Hardy, personal communication 2003).

Hardy and his colleagues were also able to record data on the abundance and habitat associations of common poorwills *(Phalaenoptilus nuttallii)*. Hardy et al. (1998) found these secretive birds to be very abundant when compared with previously reported numbers (0.5 birds/survey station versus 0.15 birds/survey station in Alberta, Canada). The abundance of poorwills in the Sauceda and Sand Tank mountains had a significant positive association with the amount of xeroriparian cover, and the highest numbers were associated with areas that had a great deal of physiographic interspersion (e.g., areas where at least three physiographic types were found within 300 m of a survey station, in other words, where a wash, steep upland, and bajada were all found in close proximity). The overall abundance of poorwills had a positive association with gravel and perennial vegetation cover and a negative association with grass cover. Poorwill abundance was nega-

Figure 19.3. Sand Tank Mountains. (Photo by David J. Griffin)

tively correlated with numbers of great horned owl *(Bubo virginianus),* western screech-owl, and lesser nighthawks *(Chordeiles acutipennis)* and was positively correlated with numbers of elf owls. And as with elf owls, Hardy found that common poorwills "love to sing when the moon is out" (Paul C. Hardy, personal communication 2003).

Between 1995 and 2001 much of the region was thoroughly surveyed as part of the Arizona Breeding Bird Atlas (ABBA) project, which recorded the distribution and relative abundance of the region's breeding species. The ABBA covered many remote areas that had never or only rarely been visited by ornithologists. The project filled many of the knowledge gaps about the distribution and breeding ranges of resident species and provided an extensive list of resident and migratory species (AGFD 2002). Many of the breeding records that were reported could be construed by some in the bird-watching crowd as "uneventful," but there were a few surprises. For example, at OP and GR the ABBA found black-chinned hummingbirds *(Archilochus alexandri)* nesting in xeroriparian areas. This species is generally found in less arid areas near water, such as riparian areas, oak woodlands, and chaparral; and its use of the desert washes was most unexpected. Before this discovery by the ABBA, only one nesting attempt by black-chinned hummingbirds had been recorded in the region (at Jose Juan Charco in 1994; Tricia L.

Griffin, personal communication 1994). The most interesting discovery by the ABBA project was that of multiple nesting records for violet-green swallows *(Tachycineta thalassina),* a species that is typically found in more temperate areas in forests, on cliffs, and in human developments. Violet-green swallows were found nesting in woodpecker cavities in saguaros at OP and GR. Remarkably, over the past sixty years many astute observers had seen this species during migration but no one had included it in the region's resident breeding community. A diminutive race, *T. t. brachyptera,* is known to nest in large cacti along the gulf coast of northwestern Sonora, Mexico, however, and perhaps during wet winters some individuals of this race periodically move into southern Arizona to nest (Troy Corman, Arizona Game and Fish Department, personal communication 2001). Like many discoveries in the natural sciences, this one may have been the result of an observer being in the right place at the right time.

Many desert inhabitants and visitors in the region wonder how the resident wildlife survive in such a harsh environment. "Where do they get water?" "Do they need to drink water?" "What do they eat?" and "How do they avoid the heat?" The answers are variable and multifaceted, but we can begin by looking at how one species overcomes the rigors of the Sonoran Desert. One of the most frequently encountered species in the region is the

Figure 19.4. *Arizona Upland habitat, Sand Tank Mountains. (Photo by David J. Griffin)*

black-throated sparrow *(Amphispiza bilineata)*. This boldly marked bird is a year-round resident and is truly a desert-adapted species that does not require free (drinking) water for its survival, choosing instead to get most or all of its required moisture from the seeds and insects on which it forages (Smyth & Bartholomew 1966). The ability of the black-throated sparrow to efficiently convert food to water allows it to occur in most of the plant communities in the region, no matter how dry or lacking in vegetation they may appear. Van-der Wall and MacMahon (1984) found that along an elevation gradient of a bajada on OP, the number of resident bird species "dropped out" of the community as the vegetation structure and composition became simpler (e.g., from higher elevations to lower), but the black-throated sparrow was one of the few breeding species that occurred along the entire gradient. Cutler (1996) and Cutler and Morrison (1998) found that black-throated sparrows were not associated with free-standing water or lush vegetation, as were most of the species at their study sites on CP, but instead occurred in all plant communities in equal proportions to their availability. Black-throated sparrows not only have physiological adaptations that allow them to exist in one of the harshest environments in North America but also incorporate certain behaviors to withstand and in some cases avoid high temperatures during the hottest times of the day. Like many birds, when ambient temperatures approach about 35°C (95°F), black-throated sparrows will roost or stand in the shade of a shrub, dropping their wings out and away from their body in an effort to dissipate heat; and they'll open their mouths and begin to flutter their tongues, using evaporation across their mouths and throats to cool down. Under extremely hot circumstances this desert denizen has even been known to enter small mammal burrows to avoid the heat (Austin & Smith 1974)! All these remarkable attributes lend support to the anecdotal observations of many desert bird-watchers through the years about the hardiness of the ubiquitous black-throated sparrow and explain why not too long ago this species was appropriately known as "desert sparrow."

Many resident species rely on the "pulse" of productivity that results from the winter and summer rains. This pulse includes plants, insects, and vertebrates, all of which make up the diet of some or all of the birds in the region. For example, in late fall granivorous species such as sparrows and quail can subsist on seeds that may have been produced as a result of the summer rains, and if the rains have failed, the birds will likely still find seeds from the previous winter or summer. Other species, such as the phainopepla, can switch their diets to reflect what resources are available. The phainopepla is mostly thought of as an insectivore, and it breeds in the region during late winter to early spring. During this time phainopeplas feed largely on flying insects, which they also feed to their young. After their breeding season most phainopeplas leave the region to breed in other areas away from the low Sonoran Desert. By the time phainopeplas return in the fall following the summer rains, many of the region's plants have grown and become more lush than in the late spring; many have flowered, set seed, and produced fruits. At this time phainopeplas don't have young to tend to, and they can often be seen eating items other than insects, such as I witnessed in 1995, when they were gorging themselves on the fruit of desert hackberry *(Celtis pallida)*.

Another resident species that makes use of a change in the available resources is the long-eared owl *(Asio otus)*. This species has been known to nest in the region (Groschupf et al. 1988) but typically occurs as a winter resident. On their breeding grounds long-eared owls usually concentrate their diet on a single species of rodent such as voles *(Microtus* spp.). During Cutler's study of wildlife use of water sources at CP, long-eared owls began to appear in late August 1994, following abundant summer rains. Ten to twenty owls remained at one site until June 1995. As the season passed, the results from Cutler's small-mammal trapping showed that many of the pocket mouse species *(Perognathus* sp., *Chaetodipus* spp.) had entered hibernation and were no longer being captured. By midwinter nearly 90 percent of all captures were of Merriam's kangaroo rat *(Dipodomys merriami)*, a species that is larger and more cold-tolerant than the smaller pocket mice. Cutler monitored the roosting activities of the long-eared owls and in midwinter noted that on more than one occasion, on emerging from their daily roost, some of the owls would begin foraging above her recently baited small-mammal traps. She suggested that individual owls may have learned that there was a potential source of food nearby (e.g., small mammals attracted to the bait), and she speculated that the owls may have remained at the roost site longer than they normally would had it not been for the overwhelming presence of a single species of small mammal (Tricia L. Griffin, personal communication 1998, 2001). This hypothesis was strengthened on examination of cast pellets collected at the roost site, which were about 90 percent Merriam's kangaroo rat (author's unpublished data).

Partitioning of resources allows some year-round resident species to coexist. The northern cardinal *(Cardinalis cardinalis)* and pyrrhuloxia *(C. sinuatus)*, for example, occupy essentially the same environment in the same way. At first glance these species appear to be very similar: males of both species are red or reddish; females are gray with slight washes of red; both have large, powerful beaks and crested heads; and both sing a loud, rich song. Although the pyrrhuloxia is typically found in drier areas, in many places both species can be found in dense thickets of legume trees and shrubs and along watercourses (Ehrlich et al. 1988; Russell & Monson 1998; author's observation). The diet of both species consists of seeds, fruits, and insects. On closer examination, we find that northern cardinals tend to be highly sedentary and are rarely observed in areas where they do not breed (Russell & Monson 1998) whereas the pyrrhuloxia is considered an opportunistic species and moves into or out of an area in search of favorable conditions. There are exceptions to these generalizations, such as the northern cardinals that were observed during Christmas Bird Counts in a canyon on the west front of the Sierra Pinta and as far west as Tule Well (author's observation). Pyrrhuloxias are single-brooded, and their nesting season can begin anytime after mid-March (Ehrlich et al. 1988; Rea 1983), while the northern cardinal regularly breeds from March through August–September and can have up to four broods. These species are known to hybridize when found in the same areas (Rea 1983), but generally, when they are found breeding in the same areas, they partition their resources.

On the San Xavier Indian Reservation, Patrick J. Gould (1961) studied the territorial relationships between these two species and found that pyrrhuloxias chose more open nest areas than northern cardinals and used slightly differing methods of nest construction to reduce competition between them. For example, pyrrhuloxias used more open habitats, and their nests were more tightly constructed and placed farther out on tree limbs than were those of cardinals. More interestingly, he discovered that males of both species defended their territories only against conspecifics. For these reasons, both species often remain as year-round residents in the same areas.

Some resident breeding species escape many of the hardships of year-round desert life by being present only for their breeding seasons, during the summer period before and after summer rains. With this strategy purple martins, brown-crested flycatchers *(Myiarchus tyrannulus),* rufous-winged sparrows *(Aimophila carpalis),* and varied buntings avoid having to endure the annual "boom and bust" cycles that can occur in the Sonoran Desert. And by arriving in late spring, these species may not have to compete for breeding territories with local resident species, many of which will have finished their breeding seasons; the latecomers can also take full advantage of the peak in productivity that usually occurs in mid to late summer. Typically, these summer birds don't waste time, and by late August or early September most of them begin migration and leave the area.

Though the greater proportion of the region's avifauna is made up of migratory species, non-migratory year-round resident birds such as the black-throated sparrow; cactus wren *(Campylo-rhynchus brunneicapillus);* curve-billed *(Toxostoma curvirostre),* crissal, and Le Conte's thrashers; red-tailed hawk *(Buteo jamaicensis);* northern cardinal; gilded flicker; Gila woodpecker; ladder-backed woodpecker *(Picoides scalaris);* and canyon towhee *(Pipilo fuscus)* are all able to survive during winter cold spells as well as summer furnacelike heat and dryness. And for everything that migratory birds have in terms of species diversity, attractiveness, colorful appeal, and ability to travel, the year-round resident birds more than compensate for by their ability to survive and even prosper in some of the harshest desert conditions in North America, making them truly special birds.

Now that we've reviewed some of the strategies and mechanisms resident species use to exist in the region, it may seem as though migratory birds have an easier existence in the Sonoran borderlands. After all, migrants are here for only a short period, they can pick up and leave whenever they want to, and they don't have to survive here during the hot summer months. Bear in mind, however, that migration can be one of the most physically challenging times for land birds, especially when they must cross large expanses of unsuitable habitat like open water and harsh arid environments. Many species must be able to stop and rest for a time to refuel and repay oxygen debt to their worn muscles (Moore & Simons 1992). Some birds may become too weak and may not be able to compensate for their losses in fat and muscle during long periods of flight, succumbing to the elements or local predators (Moore et al. 1993). Others, like the group of grosbeaks I describe below—no matter how shabby they may seem—are able to rest, refuel, and again make their way across the desert. The CP, GR, OP, and SD not only contain diverse habitats for resident species but also provide stopover habitat for migratory birds; together they make up a major link used annually by thousands of birds that travel between Central and South America and much of western North America.

In our area of the dry borderlands approximately 75 percent of the avifauna (i.e., about 230 species) are migratory species. Different species have different times or periods of migration through the region, but some migrant birds can generally be found during every month. As Gale Monson (1965:310) stated forty years ago, "One of the unexpected distinctions of bird watching in southwestern Arizona is that of the migrants that literally swarm in the desert trees and shrubbery along the washes and canyons." The peak periods of migration are from mid-April to late May and from mid-August through October. During these times it is a joy to go bird-watching, and it's not unusual to observe 45 to perhaps 65 species of birds on a morning's walk along a well-vegetated wash. Spending a few hours watching birds during migration can be quite rewarding, just for their sheer variety: the buzzing, iridescent hummingbirds; colorful, singing wood warblers and vireos; elusive *Empidonax* flycatchers; sometimes drab sparrows; dabbling ducks and geese; herons and egrets; and shorebirds of all shapes and sizes. Occasionally, an unusual, stray, or late migratory species will be spotted, piquing the interest of any observer, and seasoned observers can begin to mark time by the regular passing of certain species, such as the spring northward and fall southward mass movement of turkey vultures over the Sierra Pinta.

A Personal Reminiscence

You would not believe how hot it is out here. It's a little past midday in late June, and we're lying on cots in a bosque of mesquite trees in the Growler Valley. We finished work before noon and decided to try and get some rest before we start up again at sundown. For her graduate research project, Trish is studying the use of water sources by desert wildlife, and I have been assisting her with fieldwork at this waterhole on CP. And because of the diversity of wildlife at this site, that means being up at all hours of the day and night, day after day. We're tired now because we were up late last night mist-netting bats at the waterhole. Prior to mist-netting, we had been setting and baiting small-mammal traps in and around the bosque. We got to bed far past midnight and woke at 4:00 a.m. to check the small-mammal traps. For the health and well-being of the small mammals, it was imperative to inspect all traps before the heat of the summer sun cooked them up. Running the traps lasted a couple of hours. After trapping, I conducted a bird survey of the area surrounding the waterhole from about 6:00 a.m. to 9:30 a.m. While I was recording birds, Trish was collecting equipment and recoding data; I caught up with her, and we completed our morning's work around 10:30 a.m. We then inspected our remote cameras, recorded pertinent data, and changed camera film and batteries. It was 11:00 a.m., already over 100°F, and we had been up for seven hours after three or four hours of fitful sleep. Much of this routine had been going on for about a week now, and we were getting tired. We were ready for a siesta.

Because the temperature would likely reach 110°F within a couple of hours, we needed a slightly cooler place to rest. We walked the mile back to our camp and grabbed our cots, some water, and snacks and headed back to the bosque and much-needed shade. There the temperature might be only somewhere between 105°F and 108°F, which may not sound like much of a relief, but over the long haul it can make all the difference in maintaining one's peaceful state of mind. We typically would place the cots under the densest shade, usually provided by the largest trees. We located our "favorite" clump of trees, and Trish was so tired that she fell into a deep sleep nearly as soon as she stretched out on the cot. As I began to drift off to sleep, I was harshly awakened by the steady droning of bees flying around me. It was so hot that our sweat began to soak the cots, attracting the bees. Trish was awakened as well but was again able to get back to sleep. I wasn't so lucky.

By now the sun had changed its position in the sky, and I had to reposition the cot in order to take full advantage of the shade. As I relaxed back onto my cot and flip-flopped around trying to avoid the bees and the heat, I heard a shuffling on the ground in the duff behind me. I turned toward the sound and was surprised to see a male black-headed grosbeak (*Pheucticus melanocephalus*) huddled next to the trunk of the tree, no more than six feet away. The bird looked to be in terrible condition but probably was no worse off than I was at that point: its feathers were all matted and out of place (as was my hair), its wings were drooping (as were my arms over the edge of the cot), and most evident was the wide-open mouth and constant fluttering of the bird's throat. This bird was not enjoying itself, and to me it looked about ready to die. As I was thinking about how the bird must be feeling, two other grosbeaks appeared from within the bosque to join the male under the mesquite. Both were females. All the grosbeaks looked to be in the same condition. I was a bit excited by their appearance because it was rather late in the spring migration season and it had been a while since I had encountered many nonresident, northbound birds on my surveys. But alas, black-headed grosbeaks are known to begin moving south through the region beginning in early July, so these may well have been southbound birds! Though why they would be moving south into the heart of the inferno was beyond my comprehension. There we all stayed, as the bees buzzed by, resting in the shade of the mesquite trees.

Eventually, I was able to drift off, and I may have actually got a couple of hours of sleep. When I woke up, it was still amazingly hot and the bees were still buzzing, but the grosbeaks were gone. Trish was waking up, and we were going to have to prepare for the late afternoon and evening's work. I paused to reflect on the three grosbeaks and at first thought to myself that the birds probably marked the end of the spring migration; however, I also knew that they may have represented the beginning of the fall migration, and in a few weeks we would certainly be seeing other migrants working their way south for the winter, marking the beginning of a new season. Were the grosbeaks traveling north or south? It doesn't really matter which, because it was now a time of migration, and to me migration provides one of the greatest joys of bird-watching and study. And for the hardy wildlife watcher, bird migration can be especially enjoyable when you're camped in a mesquite bosque in the Sonoran Desert.

There have been a lot of changes in the southwestern Arizona borderlands since the late 1990s, when I last spent considerable time there. Between February 1994 and August 1995 my wife, Tricia, and I worked on the CP and spent about 300 days camped in the vast Cabeza Prieta Wilderness. During all seasons we conducted wildlife surveys and spent "free" time walking through the desert. During that period we had encounters with three people: a young couple from Oregon and a young Mexican man. The backpackers were spending a week traversing a route from the Bates Mountains to the Agua Dulce Mountains, across Growler Valley to the Growler Mountains, and then back to Bates Well. They spent the late afternoon assisting us and spent the night watching us mist-net bats. The next morning, their water cans filled from our plentiful supply, they resumed their trip, fully prepared for whatever the desert might dish out and anticipating their arrival at a cave visible on the face of the distant mountains. A few weeks later I encountered the young Mexican man while I was conducting work in the middle of the Growler Valley. I had been camped out for a week and was preparing for my last day in the field. Although it was January and conditions were relatively mild, when I found "Andreas," he was beginning to feel the effects of being lost in the desert for four or five days. His partner was a small horse named Pancho and was in very poor condition. I shared water and food with him and his horse, and we even traded candy from our larders. Andreas did not have a map, had never spent time roughing it in the desert, and had been given bad advice from an unscrupulous person back in his town of departure. Ajo was his destination, but he was out of water and had been traveling by night, using the city lights for navigation. Unfortunately, he had confused the light pollution from Yuma with that of Ajo and had been heading northwest for two days. An additional day would likely have killed his horse, and he too would probably have perished. He broke down and cried when I pulled out my maps and showed him where we were and where he would have been headed had I not encountered him.

As I did with the young backpacking couple, Andreas and I spent some quality time together. We discussed our families, life in the desert, mythical creatures, and the current situation in Mexico (this was 1995, and the value of the peso had just crashed). But unlike the case of the backpackers,

Andreas's departure from my camp later that day did not portend a promising adventure. He and I had made a decision that would be most beneficial to him and his family. After midday I never saw him again. I think about him regularly and wonder if his life is any better now than on that fateful January day in 1995.

The reason I bring up this comparison of circumstances is that there have been great changes in the integrity of the desert ecosystem along the borderlands. Over the last few years we have learned of increasing destruction of the fragile ecosystem, of numerous illegal roads and trails, garbage, and dangerous situations that have led to an unknown number of innocent deaths and the malicious death of one of those who had chosen to protect the resources of the area. I have no idea what circumstances will bring about a change so that these beautiful borderlands will not have to endure continued, unmitigated destruction and people don't regularly risk their lives. When I consider the current situation, I am drawn to an almost innocent reminiscence given by Gale Monson in 1965, when he wondered "what this border area will be like in the future" and noted that much of the region was "essentially as it was before the advent of the white man, and it is so wild that it is still possible to camp in the realization that the nearest fellow human is thirty to forty miles away.... Undoubtedly there are going to be changes. But let us hope...for all forthcoming bird watchers and their fellow naturalists...that they will be few and of such nature that the essential feeling of space and time and distance will always be there to savor, with all the interesting plants and insects and mammals—and birds" (Monson 1965:311).

Acknowledgments

I am especially grateful to these observers who provided information through personal communications: Troy Corman (non–game bird coordinator for Arizona Game and Fish Department), Tricia L. Griffin (formerly T. L. Cutler, currently wildlife biologist at White Sands Missile Range, New Mexico), Paul C. Hardy (executive director of the Feather River Land Trust, Quincy, California), Gale W. Monson (U.S. Fish and Wildlife Service/U.S. Bureau of Sport Fisheries and Wildlife [retired] and expert on southwestern birds), and Timothy J. Tibbitts (wildlife biologist at OP).

Checklist of the Birds of Arizona's Southwestern Borderlands

Areas Included

CP = Cabeza Prieta National Wildlife Refuge; data from USFWS 1991; Cutler 1996; Cutler et al. 1996; *Audubon Field Notes/American Birds* 1956–2000 (for the Sierra Pinta–Cabeza Prieta Christmas Bird Count); *American Birds* 1998–2000 (for the Ajo–Cabeza Prieta Christmas Bird Count); Ganley 2001a, 2001b; Arizona Game and Fish Department, unpublished data 2002 (Arizona Breeding Bird Atlas); and the author's field notes, 1994–2002.

GR = Barry M. Goldwater Air Force Range; data from Department of Defense n.d.; Morrison et al. 1996; Witzeman et al. 1997; Bibles and Harris 1999; Hall et al. 2001; Arizona Game and Fish Department, unpublished data 2002 (Arizona Breeding Bird Atlas); Hardy et al. 2003; and the author's field notes, 1993–2002.

OP = Organ Pipe Cactus National Monument; data from Huey 1942; Hensley 1954, 1959; Groschupf et al. 1988; Tim Tibbitts (OP wildlife biologist), personal communication 2001, 2002; Arizona Game and Fish Department, unpublished data 2002 (Arizona Breeding Bird Atlas); and the author's field notes, 1993–96.

SD = Sonoran Desert National Monument; data from Witzeman et al. 1997; Turner et al. 2000; Arizona Game and Fish Department, unpublished data 2002 (Arizona Breeding Bird Atlas); and the author's field notes, 1994–2002.

Status and Abundance

Status and abundance codes were developed and modified from a number of sources (Andrews et al. 1992; Groschupf et al. 1988; Monson & Phillips 1981; Phillips et al. 1964; Rappole 2000; Russell & Monson 1998; Unitt 1984; Witzeman et al. 1997) but most closely follow those of Russell & Monson 1998. As Russell and Monson note, codes indicating relative abundance are useful, but it is important to keep in mind that bird numbers can vary within a species' range. Additionally, some species can be highly localized in distribution and/or restricted to habitats with limited extent, and the number of species can fluctuate with changing seasons, especially in desert communities. The following status and abundance codes are subjective and are intended to be used to represent the results in a single day's effort by a practiced observer familiar with the region, in appropriate habitat. An asterisk (*) beside a species' name indicates that it is known to breed in the region; a question mark (?) indicates the species may nest in the region but nests have not been documented. An exclamation point (!) beside a species' name indicates that it

is an introduced (exotic) species. Nomenclature and organization follow that of the American Ornithologists' Union *Check-list of North American Birds* (7th edition, 1998).

Status Codes

Permanent resident: Birds that are typically present in the region all year, usually breeding.

Summer resident: Birds that are typically present in the region from late March through October, usually breeding.

Summer visitor: Birds that typically breed south of the region and migrate north in late summer or fall, then return south in winter; or birds that remain in the region during summer but do not breed here.

Winter resident: Birds that remain in the region during winter, typically from October through March or later.

Winter visitor: Birds that occur temporarily in the region during winter.

Passage migrant: Birds that typically pass through the region in spring (i.e., late February to mid-June) and/or fall (i.e., late July through October); individuals may remain for one or more days, rarely more than a week.

Abundance Codes

Abundant: Invariably seen, often in conspicuous flocks (e.g., more than 100 birds/day)

Common: Frequently encountered, either as individuals or in pairs or small groups (e.g., 25–100 birds/day)

Fairly common: A few individuals or pairs may be seen (e.g., 10–25 birds/day)

Uncommon: Present in the area (region, habitat) but may not be found in one or two days of observations (e.g., 1–10 birds/day)

Rare: Present in the area but infrequently seen; several days may be required to find it (e.g., 1–5 birds/day and 1–10 birds/season)

Casual: Out of its usual range but could be expected every year or two (e.g., 5 or more records within the region)

Irregular: Within its range but not present every year

Accidental: Far from its usual range and not expected again (e.g., 1–5 records within the region)

Habitats

For each species, habitats (i.e., places and components that make up where the species forages, nests, rests, etc.) are listed in accordance with their relative importance. Major habitats are listed before the slash and minor habitats after the slash; underlined habitats are where breeding most often occurs. Habitats are designated by the following codes:

Dune = Dune

Creosote = Creosotebush scrub (and/or saltbush scrub)

Riparian = Desert riparian/xeroriparian/riparian

Paloverde mixed = Paloverde/mixed cactus

Sand Tanks = Sand Tank Mountains Uplands (Sand Tank and Table Top mountains)

Ajo = Ajo Mountains juniper-oak woodland/mixed mountain scrub

Cliffs = Rocks and cliffs

Developed = Developed areas

Open water = Open water/freshwater marsh (includes Quitobaquito Springs, cattle tanks, *represos* [dirt water-catchments], and sewage ponds)

Checklist of the Birds

Gaviiformes

Gaviidae—Loons

Common loon *(Gavia immer)*. Passage migrant (fall). Accidental. Open water, developed. OP (observed October 23, 1975, near OP in a Lukeville parking lot).

Podicipediformes

Podicipedidae—Grebes

Least grebe *(Tachybaptus dominicus)*. Passage migrant (fall). Accidental. Open water. OP.

Pied-billed grebe *(Podilymbus podiceps)*. Passage migrant (fall)/winter resident. Uncommon to rare. Open water. CP, GR, OP.

Eared grebe *(Podiceps nigricollis)*. Passage migrant (spring/fall)/winter resident. Uncommon. Open water. CP, GR, OP.

Western grebe *(Aechmophorus occidentalis)*. Passage migrant (spring/fall). Accidental. Open water. OP.

Pelicaniformes

Pelicanidae—Pelicans

American white pelican *(Pelecanus erythrorhynchos)*. Passage migrant (fall). Accidental. Open water/creosote. CP, OP.

Brown pelican *(Pelecanus occidentalis)*. Summer visitor/passage migrant (fall). Accidental to casual. Open water/creosote. OP.

Phalacrocoracidae—Cormorants

Double-crested cormorant *(Phalacrocorax auritus)*. Passage migrant/summer visitor. Accidental. Open water. OP.

Fregatidae—Frigatebirds

Magnificent frigatebird *(Fregata magnificens)*. Summer visitor. Accidental to casual. Open water/creosote. CP.

Ciconiiformes

Ardeidae--Herons, Bitterns

Least bittern *(Ixobrychus exilis)*. Passage migrant. Accidental. Open water. OP.

Great blue heron *(Ardea herodias)*. Passage migrant (spring and fall)/summer and winter visitor. Uncommon to rare. Open water/riparian/creosote. CP, GR, OP, SD.

Great egret *(Ardea alba)*. Passage migrant (spring and fall). Uncommon to rare. Open water. CP, OP.

Snowy egret *(Egretta thula)*. Passage migrant (spring and fall). Uncommon to rare. Open water/riparian. CP, GR, OP, SD.

Cattle egret *(Bubulcus ibis)*. Passage migrant (spring and fall)/winter visitor. Casual to accidental. Open water/developed/creosote/riparian. CP, OP.

Green heron *(Butorides virescens)*. Passage migrant (spring and fall). Uncommon. Open water/creosote/riparian. CP, OP.

Black-crowned night-heron *(Nycticorax nycticorax)*. Passage migrant (spring and fall). Irregular. Open water/creosote/riparian. CP, OP.

Threskiornithidae—Ibises, Spoonbills

White-faced ibis *(Plegadis chihi)*. Passage migrant (spring and fall). Irregular. Open water. CP, OP.

Roseate spoonbill *(Ajaia ajaja)*. Passage migrant (spring). Accidental. Open water. OP.

Ciconiidae—Storks

Wood stork *(Mycteria americana)*. Summer visitor. Casual. Open water. CP, OP.

Carthartidae—New World Vultures

Black vulture *(Coragyps atratus)**. Permanent resident. Fairly common. Riparian/paloverde mixed/cliffs/creosote. CP, OP.

Turkey vulture *(Cathartes aura)**. Permanent resident/passage migrant (spring and fall). Common. Riparian/paloverde mixed/cliffs/creosote. CP, GR, OP, SD.

Anseriformes

Anatidae—Ducks, Geese, Swans

Snow goose *(Chen caerulescens)*. Winter visitor. Accidental. Open water/developed. CP.

Canada goose *(Branta canadensis)*. Winter visitor, passage migrant (fall). Casual. Open water/developed. CP, OP.

Wood duck *(Aix sponsa)*. Winter visitor. Accidental. Open water. OP.

Gadwall *(Anas strepera)*. Passage migrant (spring and fall)/winter visitor. Casual. Open water. CP, OP.

American wigeon *(Anas americana)*. Passage migrant (spring and fall)/winter visitor. Rare to uncommon. Open water. CP, GR, OP.

Mallard *(Anas platyrhynchos)*. Passage migrant (spring and fall)/winter visitor. Rare to irregular. Open water/developed. CP, OP.

Blue-winged teal *(Anas discors)*. Passage migrant (spring and fall). Uncommon. Open water. OP.

Cinnamon teal *(Anas cyanoptera)*. Passage migrant (spring and fall). Uncommon. Open water. CP, GR, OP.

Northern shoveler *(Anas clypeata)*. Passage migrant (spring and fall). Rare. Open water. CP, GR, OP.

Northern pintail *(Anas acuta)*. Passage migrant (spring and fall). Rare. Open water. CP, GR, OP.

Green-winged teal *(Anas crecca)*. Passage migrant (spring and fall)/winter visitor. Uncommon. Open water. CP, GR, OP.

Canvasback *(Aythya valisineria)*. Passage migrant (spring and fall)/winter visitor. Accidental. Open water. OP.

Redhead *(Aythya americana)*. Passage migrant (spring and fall)/winter visitor. Uncommon. Open water. CP, OP.

Ring-necked duck *(Aythya collaris)*. Passage migrant (spring and fall)/winter visitor. Uncommon to rare. Open water. OP, SD.

Lesser scaup *(Aythya affinis)*. Passage migrant (spring and fall)/winter visitor. Uncommon to rare. Open water. CP, OP.

Bufflehead *(Bucephala albeola)*. Passage migrant (spring and fall). Rare. Open water. CP, OP.

Common goldeneye *(Bucephala clangula)*. Winter visitor. Rare. Open water. CP, OP.

Hooded merganser *(Lophodytes cucullatus)*. Winter visitor. Rare. Open water. OP.

Common merganser *(Mergus merganser)*. Winter visitor. Accidental. Open water. CP, OP.

Red-breasted merganser *(Mergus serrator)*. Winter visitor. Accidental. Open water. CP, OP.

Ruddy duck *(Oxyura jamaicensis)*. Passage migrant (spring and fall)/winter visitor. Uncommon to fairly common. Open water. CP, GR, OP.

Falconiformes

Accipitridae—Hawks, Kites, Eagles

Osprey *(Pandion haliaetus)*. Passage migrant (spring and fall). Rare. Creosote, open water. CP, GR, OP.

White-tailed kite *(Elanus leucurus)**. Accidental resident/casual. Accidental. Creosote, paloverde mixed. CP (nested spring 1994 in southern Growler Valley).

Northern harrier *(Circus cyaneus)*. Passage migrant (spring and fall)/winter visitor. Uncommon to rare. Creosote, dune. CP, GR, OP, SD.

Sharp-shinned hawk *(Accipiter striatus)*. Passage migrant (spring and fall)/winter visitor. Uncommon to rare. Creosote, riparian, paloverde mixed. CP, GR, OP, SD.

Cooper's hawk *(Accipiter cooperii)**?. Passage migrant (spring and fall)/winter visitor/summer resident. Fairly common to uncommon/potential breeder. Creosote, riparian, paloverde mixed, developed. CP, GR, OP, SD.

Northern goshawk *(Accipiter gentilis)*. Winter visitor. Accidental. Ajo. OP.

Common black-hawk *(Buteogallus anthracinus)*. Passage migrant (spring and fall). Casual. Riparian, open water, paloverde mixed. OP.

Harris's hawk *(Parabuteo unicinctus)**. Permanent resident. Fairly common to uncommon. Paloverde mixed, riparian, Ajo. CP, GR, OP, SD.

Swainson's hawk *(Buteo swainsoni)*. Passage migrant (spring and fall). Rare. Creosote, paloverde mixed, dune, riparian. CP, GR, OP, SD.

White-tailed hawk *(Buteo albicaudatus)*. Accidental winter visitor. Accidental. Creosote, paloverde mixed, riparian. OP.

Zone-tailed hawk *(Buteo albonotatus)**. Passage migrant (spring and fall)/permanent resident. Casual. Creosote, paloverde mixed, riparian, Ajo. OP.

Red-tailed hawk *(Buteo jamaicensis)**. Permanent resident/winter visitor. Common to fairly common. Paloverde mixed, creosote, riparian, cliffs. CP, GR, OP, SD.

Ferruginous hawk *(Buteo regalis)*. Passage migrant (spring and fall)/winter visitor. Rare. Creosote, paloverde mixed, riparian. CP, GR, OP, SD.

Golden eagle *(Aquila chrysaetos)**. Permanent resident/passage migrant (spring and fall). Uncommon to rare. Paloverde mixed, creosote, Ajo, Sand Tanks, cliffs, open water. CP, GR, OP, SD.

Falconidae—Falcons

Crested caracara *(Caracara plancus)**?. Permanent resident/summer resident. Rare/potential breeder. Creosote, paloverde mixed, riparian, developed, open water. CP, OP (suspected breeding in southern portion of OP near Sonoyta, Mexico; Tim Tibbitts, personal communication).

American kestrel *(Falco sparverius)**. Permanent resident/winter visitor. Common. Paloverde mixed, creosote, riparian, cliffs. CP, GR, OP, SD.

Merlin *(Falco columbarius)*. Passage migrant (spring and fall)/winter visitor. Rare. Creosote, paloverde mixed, riparian, Ajo, open water. CP, OP.

Peregrine falcon *(Falco peregrinus)**. Permanent resident/passage migrant (spring and fall). Rare to casual. Ajo, Sand Tanks, open water, paloverde mixed, cliffs. CP, GR, OP (historic and recent nest records from Ajo Mountains).

Prairie falcon *(Falco mexicanus)**. Permanent resident/winter visitor. Uncommon to rare. Creosote, paloverde mixed, open water, cliffs. CP, GR, OP, SD.

Galliformes

Phasianidae—Partridges, Grouse, Turkeys

Gambel's quail *(Callipepla gambelii)**. Permanent resident. Common to abundant. Creosote, riparian, paloverde mixed, Sand Tanks, Ajo, developed. CP, GR, OP, SD.

Gruiformes

Rallidae—Rails, Gallinules, Coots

Black rail *(Laterallus jamaicensis)*. Passage migrant (spring and fall). Accidental. Open water. OP (observed at Quitobaquito Springs).

Virginia rail *(Rallus limicola)*. Passage migrant (spring and fall)/winter visitor. Accidental to casual. Open water. CP, OP.

Sora *(Porzana carolina)*. Passage migrant (spring and fall)/winter visitor. Accidental to casual. Open water. CP, OP.

Common moorhen *(Gallinula chloropus)*. Winter visitor/passage migrant (spring). Accidental to casual. Open water. OP.

American coot *(Fulica americana)**. Permanent resident/passage migrant (fall). Fairly common/casual. Open water, creosote, dune, developed. CP, GR, OP.

Gruidae—Cranes

Sandhill crane *(Grus canadensis)*. Passage migrant (spring and fall). Accidental. Creosote, paloverde mixed, open water. OP.

Charadriiformes

Charadriidae—Lapwings, Plovers

Semipalmated plover *(Charadrius semipalmatus)*. Passage migrant (spring). Accidental. Open water. OP.

Killdeer *(Charadrius vociferus)**. Winter visitor/permanent resident/passage migrant (spring and fall). Uncommon to rare. Open water, developed. CP, GR, OP, SD.

Recurvirostridae—Stilts, Avocets

Black-necked stilt *(Himantopus mexicanus)*. Passage migrant (spring and fall). Rare. Open water. CP, GR, OP, SD.

American avocet *(Recurvirostra americana)*. Passage migrant (spring and fall). Rare. Open water. CP, GR, OP.

Scolopacidae--Sandpipers, Phalaropes

Greater yellowlegs *(Tringa melanoleuca)*. Passage migrant (spring and fall). Rare. Open water. CP, GR, OP.

Lesser yellowlegs *(Tringa flavipes)*. Passage migrant (fall). Casual to rare. Open water. OP.

Solitary sandpiper *(Tringa solitaria)*. Passage migrant (spring and fall). Rare. Open water. CP, GR, OP.

Willet *(Catoptrophorus semipalmatus)*. Passage migrant (spring and fall). Casual. Open water. CP, OP.

Spotted sandpiper *(Actitis macularia)*. Passage migrant (spring and fall)/winter visitor. Uncommon to rare. Open water. CP, GR, OP, SD.

Long-billed curlew *(Numenius americanus)*. Passage migrant (spring and fall). Casual. Open water, creosote. CP, OP.

Western sandpiper *(Calidris mauri)*. Passage migrant (spring and fall). Uncommon. Open water. CP, GR, OP.

Least sandpiper *(Calidris minutilla)*. Passage migrant (spring and fall)/winter visitor. Uncommon. Open water. CP, GR, OP, SD.

Baird's sandpiper *(Calidris bairdii)*. Passage migrant (spring and fall). Rare to casual. Open water. CP, OP.

Stilt sandpiper *(Calidris himantopus)*. Passage migrant (fall). Accidental. Open water. OP.

Long-billed dowitcher *(Limnodromus scolopaceus)*. Passage migrant (spring and fall). Casual. Open water. CP, OP.

Common snipe *(Gallinago gallinago)*. Passage migrant (spring and fall)/winter visitor. Uncommon to rare. Open water. CP, OP.

Wilson's phalarope *(Phalaropus tricolor)*. Passage migrant (spring and fall). Uncommon. Open water. CP, GR, OP.

Red-necked phalarope *(Phalaropus lobatus)*. Passage migrant (fall). Accidental. Open water. OP.

Red phalarope *(Phalaropus fulicaria)*. Passage migrant (fall). Accidental. Open water. OP.

Laridae—Skuas, Gulls, Terns, Skimmers

Bonaparte's gull *(Larus philadelphia)*. Passage migrant (spring). Accidental. Open water. OP.

Heermann's gull *(Larus heermanni)*. Passage migrant (spring and fall). Accidental. Open water. OP.

Ring-billed gull *(Larus delawarensis)*. Passage migrant (spring and fall). Casual. Open water. CP, GR, OP.

California gull *(Larus californicus)*. Passage migrant (spring). Accidental. Open water. OP.

Herring gull *(Larus argentatus)*. Passage migrant (spring). Accidental. Open water. OP.

Common tern *(Sterna hirundo)*. Passage migrant (spring and fall). Casual. Open water, paloverde mixed. OP.

Forster's tern *(Sterna forsteri)*. Passage migrant (spring). Accidental. Open water. OP.

Least tern *(Sterna antillarum)*. Passage migrant (fall). Accidental. Open water. OP.

Black tern *(Chlidonias niger)*. Passage migrant (spring and fall). Casual. Open water. CP, GR, OP.

Columbiformes

Columbidae—Pigeons, Doves

Rock pigeon *(Columba livia)*!*. Permanent resident. Fairly common to common. Developed, paloverde mixed, open water. CP, GR, OP, SD.

Band-tailed pigeon *(Columba fasciata)*. Passage migrant (spring and fall)/winter visitor. Casual/irregular. Ajo, developed, paloverde mixed, riparian. CP, OP, SD.

White-winged dove *(Zenaida asiatica)**. Summer resident/winter resident. Common to abundant/rare. Paloverde mixed, riparian, Ajo. CP, GR, OP, SD.

Mourning dove *(Zenaida macroura)**. Permanent resident/winter visitor. Abundant to common/fairly common to common. Creosote, riparian, paloverde mixed, Sand Tanks, Ajo, developed, open water. CP, GR, OP, SD.

Inca dove *(Columbina inca)**. Permanent resident/winter visitor. Uncommon to fairly common. Developed, Ajo, riparian, paloverde mixed. OP, SD.

Common ground-dove *(Columbina passerina)**. Summer resident/winter visitor. Rare to uncommon. Riparian, Ajo, paloverde mixed. CP, GR, OP.

Cuculiformes

Cuculidae—Cuckoos, Roadrunners, Anis

Greater roadrunner (Geococcyx californianus)*. Permanent resident. Fairly common. Creosote, riparian, paloverde mixed, Sand Tanks, Ajo, developed. CP, GR, OP, SD.

Strigiformes

Tytonidae—Barn owls

Barn owl (Tyto alba)*. Permanent resident. Rare. Riparian, paloverde mixed, Ajo, developed. CP, GR, OP, SD.

Strigidae—Typical owls

Flammulated owl (Otus flammeolus). Passage migrant (spring and fall). Accidental to casual. Riparian. SD.

Western screech-owl (Otus kennicottii)*. Permanent resident. Fairly common to common. Riparian, paloverde mixed, Ajo, Sand Tanks. CP, GR, OP, SD.

Great horned owl (Bubo virginianus)*. Permanent resident. Fairly common to common. Riparian, paloverde mixed, Ajo, Sand Tanks, cliffs, developed. CP, GR, OP, SD.

Cactus ferruginous pygmy-owl (Glaucidium brasilianum cactorum)*. Permanent resident. Rare to irregular. Riparian, paloverde mixed, Ajo. CP, OP (expected at GR, potential at SD).

Elf owl (Micrathene whitneyi)*. Summer resident/winter resident. Common to abundant/rare. Riparian, paloverde mixed, Sand Tanks, Ajo, developed. CP, GR, OP, SD.

Burrowing owl (Athene cunicularia)*. Permanent resident/winter resident. Rare/uncommon to irregular. Creosote, paloverde mixed, developed. CP (nested in Growler Valley in 1995).

Mexican spotted owl (Strix occidentalis lucida)?. Winter visitor. Accidental. Ajo. OP (unconfirmed observation from Ajo Mountains in winter 1999–2000; Tim Tibbitts, personal communication).

Long-eared owl (Asio otus)*. Winter resident/summer resident. Rare to fairly common/accidental and/or irregular. Riparian, paloverde mixed, Sand Tanks, Ajo. CP, GR, OP, SD.

Short-eared owl (Asio flammeus). Winter resident. Rare. Creosote, dune, riparian. CP.

Caprimulgiformes

Caprimulgidae—Nighthawks, Nightjars

Lesser nighthawk (Chordeiles acutipennis)*. Summer resident/passage migrant (spring and fall). Fairly common to common. Creosote, dune, riparian, paloverde mixed, Sand Tanks, open water, developed. CP, GR, OP, SD.

Common poorwill (Phalaenoptilus nuttallii)*. Summer resident/winter resident. Common/casual to rare. Paloverde mixed, creosote, riparian, open water, Sand Tanks, Ajo, developed. CP, GR, OP, SD.

Buff-collared nightjar (Caprimulgus ridgwayi)*?. Summer visitor/summer resident. Accidental to irregular/casual. Paloverde mixed, Ajo. OP (an adult bird was mist-netted near mouth of Alamo Canyon in 1998, a potential breeder there; Tim Tibbitts, personal communication).

Apodiformes

Apodidae—Swifts

Vaux's swift (Chaetura vauxi). Passage migrant (spring and fall). Uncommon. Creosote, riparian, Ajo, paloverde mixed, open water. CP, GR, OP, SD.

White-throated swift (Aeronautes saxatalis)*. Permanent resident/passage migrant (spring and fall). Fairly common to common/uncommon. Cliffs, creosote, paloverde mixed, riparian, open water. CP, GR, OP, SD.

Trochilidae—Hummingbirds

Broad-billed hummingbird (Cynanthus latirostris). Passage migrant (spring and fall). Casual. Riparian, paloverde mixed, open water. OP.

Black-chinned hummingbird (Archilochus alexandri)*. Passage migrant (spring and fall)/accidental summer resident. Fairly common to uncommon/accidental breeder. Riparian, paloverde mixed, open water. CP, GR, OP, SD.

Anna's hummingbird (Calypte anna)*. Winter resident/accidental summer resident. Common to fairly common/accidental breeder. Riparian, paloverde mixed, developed, open water. CP (nested in Growler Valley in 1995), GR, OP, SD.

Costa's hummingbird (Calypte costae)*. Winter resident/permanent resident. Common/uncommon to common. Riparian, paloverde mixed, creosote, Sand Tanks, Ajo. CP, GR, OP, SD.

Calliope hummingbird (Stellula calliope). Passage migrant (spring). Rare to uncommon. Riparian, paloverde mixed. CP, GR, OP, SD.

Broad-tailed hummingbird (Selasphorus platycercus). Passage migrant (spring). Casual to rare. Riparian, Ajo, Sand Tanks, paloverde mixed. GR, OP, SD.

Rufous hummingbird (Selasphorus rufus). Passage migrant (spring and fall). Uncommon. Riparian, Ajo, Sand Tanks, paloverde mixed. CP, GR, OP, SD.

Allen's hummingbird (Selasphorus sasin). Passage migrant (spring and fall). Rare to uncommon. Riparian, open water, paloverde mixed. CP, GR, OP, SD.

Coraciiformes

Alcedinidae—Kingfishers

Belted kingfisher (Ceryle alcyon). Passage migrant (spring and fall)/winter visitor. Casual to rare/casual. Open water, Ajo. CP, GR, OP.

Piciformes

Picidae—Woodpeckers

Lewis's woodpecker *(Melanerpes lewis)*. Winter resident/passage migrant (fall). Irregular to casual. Ajo, creosote, riparian, paloverde mixed. OP.

Acorn woodpecker *(Melanerpes formicivorus)*. Passage migrant (fall)/winter visitor. Accidental to casual. Ajo, riparian, paloverde mixed. OP.

Gila woodpecker *(Melanerpes uropygialis)**. Permanent resident. Common. Ajo, riparian, paloverde mixed, Sand Tanks, developed. CP, GR, OP, SD.

Yellow-bellied sapsucker *(Sphyrapicus varius)*. Passage migrant (spring and fall). Rare to uncommon. Riparian, Ajo, open water. OP.

Red-naped sapsucker *(Sphyrapicus nuchalis)*. Passage migrant (spring). Rare. Riparian, paloverde mixed, developed. CP, SD.

Red-breasted sapsucker *(Sphyrapicus ruber)*. Passage migrant (fall)/winter visitor. Rare. Riparian, open water. OP.

Ladder-backed woodpecker *(Picoides scalaris)**. Permanent resident. Fairly common to common. Ajo, riparian, paloverde mixed, Sand Tanks. CP, GR, OP, SD.

Northern flicker *(Colaptes auratus)*. Winter resident. Fairly common to common. Ajo, paloverde mixed, riparian, Sand Tanks, creosote. CP, GR, OP, SD (all records from the area are of the red-shafted subspecies).

Gilded flicker *(Colaptes chrysoides)**. Permanent resident. Fairly common to common. Paloverde mixed, riparian, Sand Tanks, creosote. CP, GR, OP, SD.

Passeriformes

Tyrannidae—Tyrant flycatchers

Olive-sided flycatcher *(Contopus cooperi)*. Passage migrant (spring and fall). Rare to uncommon. Riparian, Ajo, Sand Tanks, open water. CP, GR, OP, SD.

Western wood-pewee *(Contopus sordidulus)*. Passage migrant (spring and fall). Uncommon. Riparian, Ajo, open water. CP, GR, OP, SD.

Willow flycatcher *(Empidonax traillii)*. Passage migrant (spring and fall). Uncommon to rare. Riparian, open water. CP, GR, OP, SD (the endangered "southwestern" subspecies [*E.t. extimus*] is a presumed rare to irregular summer resident at OP, where breeding was presumed but not confirmed at Quitobaquito Springs in 2000 and 2001; Tim Tibbitts, personal communication).

Least flycatcher *(Empidonax minimus)*. Passage migrant (spring and fall). Accidental. Riparian, paloverde mixed. CP, OP.

Hammond's flycatcher *(Empidonax hammondii)*. Passage migrant (spring and fall). Uncommon. Riparian, Ajo, paloverde mixed. CP, GR, OP, SD.

Gray flycatcher *(Empidonax wrightii)*. Passage migrant (spring and fall)/winter resident. Uncommon to fairly common/uncommon. Ajo, riparian. CP, GR, OP, SD.

Dusky flycatcher *(Empidonax oberholseri)*. Passage migrant (spring and fall)/winter visitor. Rare/accidental. Riparian. CP, GR, SD.

Pacific-slope flycatcher *(Empidonax difficilis)*. Passage migrant (spring and fall)/winter resident. Common/rare to uncommon. Ajo, riparian, paloverde mixed, open water. CP, GR, OP, SD.

Cordilleran flycatcher *(Empidonax occidentalis)*. Passage migrant (spring and fall). Common. Ajo, riparian, paloverde mixed. CP, GR, OP, SD.

Black phoebe *(Sayornis nigricans)**. Summer resident/winter resident/passage migrant (spring and fall). Rare to uncommon/uncommon/fairly common to common. Open water, riparian, developed. CP, GR, OP, SD.

Eastern phoebe *(Sayornis phoebe)*. Passage migrant (spring). Accidental. Open water, riparian. OP.

Say's phoebe *(Sayornis saya)**. Permanent resident/winter resident. Fairly common to common. Creosote, riparian, paloverde mixed, Ajo, cliffs, developed. CP, GR, OP, SD.

Vermilion flycatcher *(Pyrocephalus rubinus)**. Summer resident/winter resident. Uncommon. Open water, riparian, Ajo, developed. CP, GR, OP, SD.

Ash-throated flycatcher *(Myiarchus cinerascens)**. Permanent resident/winter resident. Fairly common to common/uncommon. Riparian, paloverde mixed, Sand Tanks, Ajo, creosote. CP, GR, OP, SD.

Brown-crested flycatcher *(Myiarchus tyrannulus)**. Summer resident/winter visitor. Uncommon to fairly common/casual. Riparian, paloverde mixed, Ajo, Sand Tanks. CP, GR, OP, SD.

Tropical kingbird *(Tyrannus melancholicus)**. Passage migrant (spring)/ accidental breeder. Casual/accidental. Open water, riparian. CP, OP.

Cassin's kingbird *(Tyrannus vociferans)*. Passage migrant (spring and fall). Rare. Riparian, paloverde mixed, open water. OP, SD.

Thick-billed kingbird *(Tyrannus crassirostris)*. Passage migrant (spring). Accidental. Open water, riparian. OP.

Western kingbird *(Tyrannus verticalis)**. Summer resident/passage migrant (spring and fall). Rare to uncommon/fairly common. Riparian, open water, paloverde mixed, developed. CP, GR, OP, SD.

Scissor-tailed flycatcher *(Tyrannus forticatus)*?*. Passage migrant (spring). Casual. Riparian, open water, paloverde mixed. OP (undocumented nesting at Lukeville store in May–June 1966).

Laniidae—Shrikes

Loggerhead shrike *(Lanius ludovicianus)**. Permanent resident/winter resident. Uncommon/fairly common. Creosote, riparian, paloverde mixed, Sand Tanks, Ajo. CP, GR, OP, SD.

Vireonidae—Vireos

Bell's vireo *(Vireo bellii)**. Summer resident/passage migrant (spring and fall). Uncommon to fairly common. Riparian, open water, Ajo. CP, GR, OP, SD.

Gray vireo *(Vireo vicinior)*. Passage migrant (spring and fall)/winter resident. Rare/fairly common. Ajo, riparian, paloverde mixed. CP, GR, OP, SD.

Yellow-throated vireo *(Vireo flavifrons)*. Passage migrant (spring). Casual to accidental. Riparian, paloverde mixed. CP (one observed by Gale Monson in the Sierra Pinta on June 4, 1956).

Plumbeous vireo *(Vireo plumbeus)*. Passage migrant (spring and fall)/winter visitor. Uncommon to fairly common/casual. Riparian, paloverde mixed. CP, GR, OP, SD.

Cassin's vireo *(Vireo cassinii)*. Passage migrant (spring and fall). Uncommon to fairly common. Riparian, paloverde mixed. CP, GR, OP, SD.

Hutton's vireo *(Vireo huttoni)*. Passage migrant (spring and fall)/winter resident. Rare/irregular. Riparian, paloverde mixed. CP, OP.

Warbling vireo *(Vireo gilvus)*. Passage migrant (spring and fall). Fairly common to uncommon. Riparian, open water, paloverde mixed. CP, GR, OP, SD.

Red-eyed vireo *(Vireo olivaceus)*. Passage migrant (fall). Accidental. Riparian, paloverde mixed. OP.

Corvidae—Crows, Jays

Steller's jay *(Cyanocitta stelleri)*. Passage migrant (spring and fall)/winter visitor. Accidental/irregular. Paloverde mixed, riparian. CP, OP.

Western scrub-jay *(Aphelocoma californica)*. Passage migrant (fall)/winter visitor. Casual/irregular. Riparian, paloverde mixed. CP, OP.

Pinyon jay *(Gymnorhinus cyanocephalus)*. Passage migrant (fall). Accidental. Riparian, paloverde mixed. CP.

Clark's nutcracker *(Nucifraga columbiana)*. Passage migrant (spring and fall). Accidental. Riparian, paloverde mixed. CP, OP.

Chihuahuan raven *(Corvus cryptoleucus)*. Winter visitor/possible summer resident. Uncommon. Paloverde mixed, riparian (possible resident breeder in Vekol Valley and eastern OP). OP.

Common raven *(Corvus corax)**. Permanent resident. Fairly common to abundant. Creosote, riparian, paloverde mixed, Sand Tanks, Ajo, cliffs, developed. CP, GR, OP, SD.

Alaudidae—Larks

Horned lark *(Eremophila alpestris)**. Permanent resident/winter resident. Fairly common to abundant. Dune, creosote, developed, open water. CP, GR, OP, SD.

Hirundinidae—Swallows

Purple martin *(Progne subis)**. Summer resident. Fairly common to common. Paloverde mixed, riparian, Sand Tanks, open water. CP, GR, OP, SD.

Tree swallow *(Tachycineta bicolor)*. Passage migrant (spring). Uncommon. Creosote, open water. CP, GR, OP, SD.

Violet-green swallow *(Tachycineta thalassina)**. Passage migrant (spring and fall)/summer resident. Fairly common to common/rare breeder. Riparian, paloverde mixed, creosote, open water. CP, GR, OP, SD (a diminutive race, *T. t. brachyptera*, nests in large cacti along the coast of northwestern Mexico, and periodically, perhaps during wet winters, some individuals of this race move into southern Arizona to nest; Troy Corman, personal communication 2001). This species was documented nesting in saguaros at GR and OP during the Arizona Breeding Bird Atlas project.

Northern rough-winged swallow *(Stelgidopteryx serripennis)**?. Passage migrant (spring and fall)/summer visitor. Fairly common to common/casual. Creosote, riparian, open water, paloverde mixed. CP, GR, OP, SD (this species has nested a short distance south of the OP boundary along the Rio Sonoyta [Russell & Monson 1998] and could potentially nest in steep cut-banks of some of the larger washes in the region).

Bank swallow *(Riparia riparia)*. Passage migrant (spring and fall). Rare. Open water, creosote, riparian. CP, GR, OP.

Cliff swallow *(Petrochelidon pyrrhonota)**?. Passage migrant (spring and fall)/summer visitor. Common/rare. Creosote, riparian, open water. CP, GR, OP, SD (this species has nested a short distance south of the OP boundary along the Rio Sonoyta [Russell and Monson 1998] and could potentially nest on cliffs or human structures in areas near sources of nest material [mud] at some of the larger, permanent water sources in the region).

Barn swallow *(Hirundo rustica)*. Passage migrant (spring and fall). Fairly common to common. Creosote, riparian, open water, paloverde mixed. CP, GR, OP, SD.

Paridae—Chickadees, Titmice

Mountain chickadee *(Poecile gambeli)*. Winter visitor. Accidental/irregular. Riparian, paloverde mixed. SD.

Remizidae—Verdins

Verdin *(Auriparus flaviceps)**. Permanent resident. Common. Creosote, riparian, paloverde mixed, Sand Tanks, Ajo, developed. CP, GR, OP, SD.

Aegithalidae—Bushtits

Bushtit *(Psaltriparus minimus)*. Passage migrant (spring). Accidental/irregular. Riparian, paloverde mixed. OP.

Sittidae—Nuthatches

Red-breasted nuthatch (*Sitta canadensis*). Passage migrant (fall)/winter visitor. Accidental/irregular. Riparian, paloverde mixed, open water. CP, OP.

Certhiidae—Creepers

Brown creeper (*Certhia americana*). Winter visitor. Accidental. Riparian, Ajo. OP.

Troglodytidae—Wrens

Cactus wren (*Campylorhynchus brunneicapillus*)*. Permanent resident. Common. Paloverde mixed, riparian, Sand Tanks, Ajo, creosote, developed. CP, GR, OP, SD.

Rock wren (*Salpinctes obsoletus*)*. Permanent resident. Common. Cliffs, creosote, paloverde mixed, Sand Tanks, Ajo, developed. CP, GR, OP, SD.

Canyon wren (*Catherpes mexicanus*)*. Permanent resident. Fairly common. Cliffs, riparian, paloverde mixed, Sand Tanks, Ajo, developed. CP, GR, OP, SD.

Bewick's wren (*Thryomanes bewickii*). Passage migrant (spring and fall)/winter resident. Rare/uncommon to fairly common. Riparian, Ajo, paloverde mixed, creosote. CP, GR, OP, SD.

House wren (*Troglodytes aedon*). Passage migrant (spring and fall)/winter resident. Rare/uncommon to fairly common. Riparian, Ajo, paloverde mixed, creosote. CP, GR, OP, SD.

Winter wren (*Troglodytes troglodytes*). Passage migrant (fall). Accidental. Riparian. GR (author observed one at Midway Wash in October 1995).

Marsh wren (*Cistothorus palustris*). Passage migrant (spring and fall)/winter resident. Rare/fairly common. Open water, riparian. OP.

Regulidae—Kinglets

Golden-crowned kinglet (*Regulus satrapa*). Winter visitor. Accidental/irregular. Riparian, paloverde mixed. CP, OP.

Ruby-crowned kinglet (*Regulus calendula*). Winter resident/passage migrant (spring and fall). Fairly common to common/common. Riparian, paloverde mixed, Sand Tanks, Ajo. CP, GR, OP, SD.

Sylviidae—Old World warblers, Gnatcatchers

Blue-gray gnatcatcher (*Polioptila caerulea*)*. Summer resident/passage migrant (spring and fall)/winter resident. Rare/uncommon. Creosote, riparian, paloverde mixed, Ajo, Sand Tanks. CP, GR, OP, SD (breeds in Ajo Mountains and is a possible breeder in portions of the Sand Tank Mountains).

Black-tailed gnatcatcher (*Polioptila melanura*)*. Permanent resident. Common. Creosote, riparian, paloverde mixed, Ajo, Sand Tanks. CP, GR, OP, SD.

Turdidae—Thrushes

Eastern bluebird (*Sialia sialis*). Winter visitor. Casual to rare. Creosote, riparian, paloverde mixed. OP.

Western bluebird (*Sialia mexicana*). Winter visitor/passage migrant (spring). Rare to fairly common. Creosote, riparian, paloverde mixed, Ajo, open water. CP, GR, OP, SD.

Mountain bluebird (*Sialia currucoides*). Winter visitor/passage migrant (spring). Rare to uncommon. Creosote, paloverde mixed, riparian. CP, GR, OP, SD.

Townsend's solitaire (*Myadestes townsendi*). Winter visitor/passage migrant (spring and fall). Casual to uncommon. Paloverde mixed, riparian, Ajo, Sand Tanks, creosote. CP, GR, OP, SD.

Swainson's thrush (*Catharus ustulatus*). Passage migrant (spring and fall). Rare to uncommon. Riparian, paloverde mixed, Ajo. CP, GR, OP, SD.

Hermit thrush (*Catharus guttatus*). Passage migrant (spring and fall)/winter visitor/winter resident. Fairly common/uncommon/fairly common. Riparian, Ajo, creosote, paloverde mixed. CP, GR, OP, SD.

American robin (*Turdus migratorius*). Winter visitor/winter resident. Fairly common to common. Riparian, Ajo, paloverde mixed. CP, GR, OP, SD.

Varied thrush (*Ixoreus naevius*). Winter visitor. Casual to irregular. Paloverde mixed, riparian, open water. OP.

Mimidae—Mockingbirds, Thrashers

Gray catbird (*Dumetella carolinensis*). Passage migrant (spring). Accidental. Riparian, paloverde mixed. OP (one caught in mist-net at Bates Well in 1997; Tim Tibbitts, personal communication).

Northern mockingbird (*Mimus polyglottos*)*. Permanent resident/winter resident. Fairly common/common. Riparian, Ajo, Sand Tanks, paloverde mixed, creosote. CP, GR, OP, SD.

Sage thrasher (*Oreoscoptes montanus*). Winter visitor/winter resident. Uncommon/rare. Creosote, riparian, paloverde mixed. CP, GR, OP, SD (author observed an albino bird in the Growler Valley in February 1995).

Brown thrasher (*Toxostoma rufum*). Winter visitor. Accidental. Riparian, open water. OP (one bird reported from Quitobaquito Springs in 1977).

Bendire's thrasher (*Toxostoma bendirei*)*. Summer resident/winter visitor/ permanent resident. Irregular/rare to uncommon. Riparian, Ajo, paloverde mixed, creosote, Sand Tanks. CP, GR, OP, SD.

Curve-billed thrasher (*Toxostoma curvirostre*)*. Permanent resident. Common to abundant. Paloverde mixed, riparian, Ajo, Sand Tanks, developed. CP, GR, OP, SD.

Crissal thrasher (*Toxostoma crissale*)*. Permanent resident. Uncommon. Riparian, Ajo, Sand Tanks. CP, GR, OP, SD.

Le Conte's thrasher (*Toxostoma lecontei*)*. Permanent resident. Uncommon to fairly common. Dune, creosote, riparian. CP, GR, OP, SD.

Sturnidae—Starlings

European starling (Sturnus vulgaris)*!. Permanent resident (at/near human settlements)/winter visitor (in native habitats). Uncommon to common/casual. Developed, paloverde mixed, riparian. CP, GR, OP, SD.

Motacillidae—Wagtails, Pipits

American pipit (Anthus rubescens). Passage migrant (spring and fall)/winter visitor. Rare to uncommon. Open water, developed, riparian. CP, GR, OP.

Sprague's pipit (Anthus spragueii). Passage migrant (spring and fall)/winter visitor. Casual. Open water, developed, riparian. CP, OP.

Bombycillidae—Waxwings

Cedar waxwing (Bombycilla cedrorum). Passage migrant (spring and fall)/winter visitor. Rare to uncommon. Riparian, paloverde mixed, Ajo. CP, OP.

Ptilogonatidae—Silky-flycatchers

Phainopepla (Phainopepla nitens)*. Summer resident/winter resident. Uncommon/common to abundant. Riparian, Ajo, paloverde mixed, Sand Tanks. CP, GR, OP, SD.

Parulidae—Wood-warblers

Golden-winged warbler (Vermivora chrysoptera). Passage migrant (fall). Accidental. Open water, riparian. OP.

Tennessee warbler (Vermivora peregrina). Passage migrant (spring and fall). Accidental. Open water, riparian. OP.

Orange-crowned warbler (Vermivora celata). Passage migrant (spring and fall)/winter visitor. Fairly common. Riparian, paloverde mixed, Ajo, creosote. CP, GR, OP, SD.

Nashville warbler (Vermivora ruficapilla). Passage migrant (spring and fall)/winter visitor. Fairly common/casual. Riparian, paloverde mixed, creosote. CP, GR, OP, SD.

Virginia's warbler (Vermivora virginiae). Passage migrant (spring). Casual to rare. Open water, riparian, Ajo, Sand Tanks. CP, GR, OP, SD.

Lucy's warbler (Vermivora luciae)*. Summer resident. Common. Riparian, paloverde mixed, open water. CP, GR, OP, SD.

Northern parula (Parula americana). Passage migrant (spring). Casual to rare. Riparian, Sand Tanks. GR (Paul Hardy observed a singing male in the Sand Tank Mountains in July 1995).

Yellow warbler (Dendroica petechia). Passage migrant (spring and fall)/summer visitor. Fairly common/accidental. Riparian, open water, paloverde mixed. CP, GR, OP, SD.

Magnolia warbler (Dendroica magnolia). Passage migrant (spring and fall). Accidental to casual. Riparian, Ajo, paloverde mixed. OP.

Black-throated blue warbler (Dendroica caerulescens). Passage migrant (spring and fall). Accidental. Ajo, riparian. OP.

Yellow-rumped warbler (Dendroica coronata). Passage migrant (spring and fall)/winter visitor. Common/fairly common. Riparian, Ajo, paloverde mixed, creosote, open water. CP, GR, OP, SD.

Black-throated gray warbler (Dendroica nigrescens). Passage migrant (spring and fall)/winter visitor. Uncommon to fairly common/rare. Riparian, paloverde mixed, Ajo. CP, GR, OP, SD.

Black-throated green warbler (Dendroica virens). Passage migrant (spring). Accidental. Ajo, riparian. OP.

Townsend's warbler (Dendroica townsendi). Passage migrant (spring and fall). Uncommon to fairly common. Riparian, paloverde, Ajo, Sand Tanks. CP, GR, OP, SD.

Hermit warbler (Dendroica occidentalis). Passage migrant (spring and fall). Uncommon. Riparian, paloverde mixed, Ajo, Sand Tanks. CP, GR, OP, SD.

Blackburnian warbler (Dendroica fusca). Passage migrant (fall). Accidental. Creosote, riparian. CP (undocumented observation by author in Growler Valley in 1994).

Grace's warbler (Dendroica graciae). Passage migrant (spring and fall). Accidental. Open water, riparian, paloverde mixed. OP.

Blackpoll warbler (Dendroica striata). Passage migrant (spring and fall). Accidental. Open water, riparian. CP, OP.

Black-and-white warbler (Mniotilta varia). Passage migrant (spring). Accidental to casual. Open water, riparian. OP.

American redstart (Setophaga ruticilla). Passage migrant (spring and fall). Rare. Ajo, riparian, paloverde mixed. OP.

Ovenbird (Seiurus aurocapillus). Passage migrant (spring). Accidental. Riparian, paloverde mixed. OP (one caught in mist-net at Bates Well in 1997; Tim Tibbitts, personal communication).

Northern waterthrush (Seiurus noveboracensis). Passage migrant (spring and fall). Casual. Riparian, Ajo, open water. OP.

MacGillivray's warbler (Oporornis tolmiei). Passage migrant (spring and fall). Fairly common. Riparian, Ajo, paloverde mixed. CP, GR, OP, SD.

Common yellowthroat (Geothlypis trichas). Passage migrant (spring and fall)/winter visitor. Uncommon. Open water, riparian, paloverde mixed. CP, GR, OP, SD.

Wilson's warbler (Wilsonia pusilla). Passage migrant (spring and fall)/winter visitor. Common to abundant/casual. Riparian, open water, paloverde mixed, creosote. CP, GR, OP, SD.

Painted redstart (Myioborus pictus). Passage migrant

(spring and fall). Casual. Riparian, Ajo, paloverde mixed, open water. OP.

Yellow-breasted chat (Icteria virens)*?. Passage migrant (spring and fall)/accidental summer resident/winter visitor. Uncommon/casual to irregular. Riparian, open water. CP, GR, OP, SD (suspected but not confirmed breeder at Quitobaquito Springs; Tim Tibbitts, personal communication).

Thraupidae—Tanagers

Summer tanager (Piranga rubra). Passage migrant ("late" spring). Casual. Riparian, open water, creosote. CP, OP.

Scarlet tanager (Piranga olivacea). Passage migrant (spring and fall). Accidental. Riparian, open water. OP.

Western tanager (Piranga ludoviciana)*?. Passage migrant (spring and fall)/summer visitor. Common/rare. Riparian, Ajo, Sand Tanks, paloverde mixed. CP, GR, OP, SD (potential breeder in higher elevations of Alamo Canyon, but because of protracted migrations, this species can be present in the region during all months; see also black-headed grosbeak).

Emberizidae—Emberizids

Green-tailed towhee (Pipilo chlorurus). Winter resident/winter visitor/passage migrant (spring and fall). Uncommon to common. Riparian, paloverde mixed, creosote, Ajo, Sand Tanks. CP, GR, OP, SD.

Spotted towhee (Pipilo maculatus). Winter resident/passage migrant (spring and fall). Uncommon to fairly common. Riparian, Ajo, paloverde mixed, Sand Tanks. CP, GR, OP, SD.

Canyon towhee (Pipilo crissalis)*. Permanent resident. Fairly common to common. Riparian, Ajo, Sand Tanks, paloverde mixed. CP, GR, OP, SD.

Abert's towhee (Pipilo aberti)*. Permanent resident. Uncommon to common. Riparian, developed, open water. OP, SD.

Rufous-winged sparrow (Aimophila carpalis)*?. Winter resident/summer visitor. Irregular/rare. Riparian, paloverde mixed, creosote. GR, OP, SD (likely breeder in Sand Tank and Table Top mountains and Vekol Valley).

Cassin's sparrow (Aimophila cassinii). Winter visitor/possible summer resident/passage migrant (fall). Irregular/casual to rare. Creosote, paloverde mixed, riparian (possible breeder in Vekol Valley following ample rain). CP, GR, OP, SD.

Rufous-crowned sparrow (Aimophila ruficeps)*. Permanent resident/winter visitor. Fairly common to common/casual. Ajo, Sand Tanks, paloverde mixed, riparian. CP, GR, OP, SD (breeds in Ajo, Sauceda, Sand Tank, and Table Top mountains, and possibly as far west as the Sierra Pinta and Mohawk mountains, where they have been observed during winter and spring, respectively).

Chipping sparrow (Spizella passerina). Winter resident/passage migrant (spring and fall). Uncommon. Ajo, Sand Tanks, riparian, paloverde mixed. CP, GR, OP, SD.

Clay-colored sparrow (Spizella pallida). Passage migrant (spring)/winter visitor. Accidental. Paloverde mixed, riparian. OP.

Brewer's sparrow (Spizella breweri). Winter resident. Common to abundant. Creosote, dune, riparian. CP, GR, OP, SD.

Black-chinned sparrow (Spizella atrogularis). Winter resident. Uncommon/irregular. Riparian, Ajo, Sand Tanks, paloverde mixed. CP, GR, OP, SD.

Vesper sparrow (Pooecetes gramineus). Winter resident. Uncommon to abundant. Creosote, dune, riparian, paloverde mixed. CP, GR, OP, SD.

Lark sparrow (Chondestes grammacus)*. Winter resident/summer resident. Uncommon/casual. Riparian, creosote, paloverde mixed, Ajo. CP, GR, OP, SD (nested at Quitobaquito Springs in 1939).

Black-throated sparrow (Amphispiza bilineata)*. Permanent resident. Fairly common to abundant. Creosote, dune, riparian, paloverde mixed, Sand Tanks, Ajo. CP, GR, OP, SD.

Sage sparrow (Amphispiza belli). Winter resident. Uncommon to abundant. Creosote, dune, riparian. CP, GR, OP, SD.

Lark bunting (Calamospiza melanocorys). Winter resident/winter visitor. Uncommon to common. Creosote, dune, riparian. CP, GR, OP, SD.

Savannah sparrow (Passerculus sandwichensis). Winter visitor. Uncommon. Riparian, creosote, developed, open water. CP, GR, OP, SD.

Grasshopper sparrow (Ammodramus savannarum). Winter visitor/winter resident. Casual. Creosote, paloverde mixed, riparian. CP, GR, OP.

Fox sparrow (Passerella iliaca). Winter visitor/winter resident. Irregular to uncommon. Riparian, creosote, paloverde mixed, Ajo. CP, GR, OP, SD.

Song sparrow (Melospiza melodia). Winter visitor. Rare to uncommon. Riparian, open water. OP, SD.

Lincoln's sparrow (Melospiza lincolnii). Passage migrant/winter visitor. Uncommon to fairly common. Riparian, open water, Ajo. CP, GR, OP, SD.

Swamp sparrow (Melospiza georgiana). Winter visitor/winter resident. Irregular/rare. Open water, riparian. OP, SD.

White-throated sparrow (Zonotrichia albicollis). Winter resident. Rare. Riparian, Ajo. OP.

White-crowned sparrow (Zonotrichia leucophrys). Winter resident. Fairly common to abundant. Creosote, riparian, paloverde mixed, Sand Tanks, Ajo, developed. CP, GR, OP, SD.

Golden-crowned sparrow (Zonotrichia atricapilla). Passage migrant (spring)/winter visitor. Rare. Riparian, Ajo. OP.

Dark-eyed junco *(Junco hyemalis)*. Winter resident. Fairly common to common. Creosote, riparian, Ajo, Sand Tanks, paloverde mixed. CP, GR, OP, SD (of the four races that occur in our region, "Oregon" is most common, "Gray-headed" and "Pink-sided" are less common, and "Slate-colored" is casual).

Chestnut-collared longspur *(Calcarius ornatus)*. Passage migrant (fall). Casual/irregular. Creosote, riparian. CP, GR.

Cardinalidae—Cardinals

Northern cardinal *(Cardinalis cardinalis)**. Permanent resident/winter visitor. Fairly common to common/casual to rare. Riparian, Ajo, paloverde mixed, Sand Tanks. CP, GR, OP, SD (in the region, northern cardinals breed as far west as Daniel's Arroyo and the southern Growler Wash, near Bates Well).

Pyrrhuloxia *(Cardinalis sinuatus)**. Permanent resident. Fairly common. Riparian, Ajo, paloverde mixed. CP, GR, OP, SD.

Rose-breasted grosbeak *(Pheucticus ludovicianus)*. Passage migrant (spring and fall). Irregular/accidental. Riparian, paloverde mixed. GR, OP, SD.

Black-headed grosbeak *(Pheucticus melanocephalus)**?. Passage migrant (spring and fall)/summer visitor/ winter visitor. Fairly common to common/rare. Riparian, paloverde mixed, Ajo, Sand Tanks. CP, GR, OP, SD (a potential breeder in higher elevations of Alamo Canyon, but because of protracted migrations, this species can be present in the region during all months; see also western tanager).

Blue grosbeak *(Guiraca caerulea)**?. Passage migrant (spring and fall)/summer resident. Rare. Riparian, open water, Ajo. CP, OP (a potential breeder at Quitobaquito Springs).

Lazuli bunting *(Passerina amoena)*. Passage migrant (spring and fall). Uncommon to fairly common. Riparian, creosote, Ajo. CP, GR, OP, SD.

Indigo bunting *(Passerina cyanea)*. Passage migrant (spring and fall). Casual. Riparian, paloverde mixed. CP, OP.

Varied bunting *(Passerina versicolor)**. Summer resident. Rare/irregular. Riparian, Ajo, Sand Tanks, paloverde mixed, creosote. CP, GR, OP, SD.

Painted bunting *(Passerina ciris)*. Summer visitor. Accidental/casual. Riparian, open water. OP.

Dickcissel *(Spiza americana)*. Passage migrant (fall). Accidental. Paloverde mixed, riparian. OP.

Icteridae—Blackbirds

Red-winged blackbird *(Agelaius phoeniceus)*. Passage migrant (spring and fall)/winter visitor/summer visitor. Uncommon/uncommon/rare. Open water, riparian. CP, GR, OP, SD.

Eastern meadowlark *(Sturnella magna)*. Passage migrant (spring)/winter visitor. Casual/rare to irregular. Creosote, dune, paloverde mixed. OP.

Western meadowlark *(Sturnella neglecta)**. Winter resident/summer resident. Uncommon to abundant/ irregular. Creosote, dune, open water, developed. CP, GR, OP, SD (during years with above-average rainfall, will breed in some valleys and basins, such as occurred in 1958 in the Growler Valley and Las Playas on CP and in 1998 on the Ranegras Plain to the north of the region).

Yellow-headed blackbird *(Xanthocephalus xanthocephalus)*. Passage migrant (spring and fall)/winter visitor/summer visitor. Uncommon to fairly common/ rare. Open water, creosote, developed. CP, GR, OP, SD (on January 2, 2001, the author and others in his field party observed a flock of approximately 10,000 birds north of GR at the intersection of Interstate 8 and Paloma Road, near the agricultural town of Theba).

Rusty blackbird *(Euphagus carolinus)*. Passage migrant (fall). Accidental. Riparian, paloverde mixed. CP.

Brewer's blackbird *(Euphagus cyanocephalus)*. Passage migrant (spring and fall)/winter visitor. Uncommon. Open water, riparian, paloverde mixed. CP, GR, OP, SD.

Great-tailed grackle *(Quiscalus mexicanus)**. Permanent resident/summer resident. Uncommon to common. Open water, riparian, developed. CP, GR, OP, SD.

Bronzed cowbird *(Molothrus aeneus)**. Summer resident. Fairly common to common. Riparian, developed. CP, GR, OP.

Brown-headed cowbird *(Molothrus ater)**. Summer resident/winter resident. Common/uncommon. Riparian, paloverde mixed, developed. CP, GR, OP, SD.

Hooded oriole *(Icterus cucullatus)**. Summer resident/ winter visitor. Fairly common/casual. Riparian, Ajo, Sand Tanks, open water. CP, GR, OP, SD.

Bullock's oriole *(Icterus bullockii)**. Passage migrant (spring and fall)/summer resident. Fairly common/ irregular. Riparian, Ajo, developed, open water. CP, GR, OP, SD.

Scott's oriole *(Icterus parisorum)**. Summer resident/ passage migrant (spring and fall). Uncommon to common. Ajo, riparian, Sand Tanks, paloverde mixed. CP, GR, OP, SD.

Fringillidae—Finches

Purple finch *(Carpodacus purpureus)*. Winter visitor. Casual/irregular. Riparian, paloverde mixed, Ajo. OP.

Cassin's finch *(Carpodacus cassinii)*. Winter visitor/passage migrant (fall). Casual/irregular. Riparian, paloverde mixed. CP.

House finch *(Carpodacus mexicanus)**. Permanent resident. Fairly common to abundant. Creosote, riparian, paloverde mixed, Sand Tanks, Ajo, cliffs, developed. CP, GR, OP, SD.

Pine siskin *(Carduelis pinus)*. Passage migrant (spring and fall). Rare. Riparian, paloverde mixed, creosote, Ajo. CP, OP.

Lesser goldfinch *(Carduelis psaltria)**. Winter resident/ summer visitor. Fairly common to common/uncommon. Riparian, paloverde mixed, Ajo. CP, GR, OP, SD.

Lawrence's goldfinch *(Carduelis lawrencei)*. Passage migrant/winter visitor. Rare to uncommon/casual. Riparian, paloverde mixed, creosote, Ajo. CP, GR, OP.

American goldfinch *(Carduelis tristis)*. Passage migrant (spring)/winter visitor. Casual/rare. Creosote, riparian, paloverde mixed, Ajo. CP, GR, OP.

European goldfinch *(Carduelis carduelis)*. Winter visitor (escaped cage bird?). Accidental. Developed, paloverde mixed. None at CP, GR, OP, or SD, but photos and video taken in January 2001 of one bird at a feeder in the backyard of Henry and Dorothy Jorgensen of Ajo.

Evening grosbeak *(Coccothraustes vespertinus)*. Passage migrant (spring). Accidental. Riparian, paloverde mixed. OP.

Passeridae—Old World sparrows

House sparrow *(Passer domesticus)**!. Permanent resident/summer visitor/winter visitor. Fairly common to common/casual. Developed, creosote, riparian, paloverde mixed. CP, GR, OP, SD (this species is a resident of human settlements, and in the past Huey [1942] found house sparrows to be much more common at centers of ranching and mining operations such as Bates Well and Growler Mine, where now, as in other native habitats, they are only casual visitors).

Twenty

Long-Nosed Bats and White-Winged Doves:

Travels and Tribulations of Two Migrant Pollinators

Carlos Martínez del Rio

I grew up in a place where wintering warblers fed on flowers and where they very rarely sang. Yellow-rumped and orange-crowned warblers fed among the red flowers of coral-bean trees. The warblers' heads were covered with pollen—so much pollen that they were often hard to identify. They defended territories with furious energy and loud chips, and they flitted from flower to flower, sipping nectar. They behaved a lot like humming-birds. Later in life, during my first visit to the eastern forest in Maine, I discovered with astonishment that in the summer my old cantankerous friends fed on insects (Morse 1971). Perhaps more surprisingly, I also found that instead of chipping, they sang. I had a Mesoamerican perspective on warblers, but they had dual citizenship!

Because like them I traveled north, I have come to realize that the birds I grew up with play different ecological roles in summer and winter. In the summer they are typical insectivorous warblers whereas in the winter they are frequently nectarivorous. Moreover, they are often the main pollinators of many plants. Recently, I have encountered another migratory species that, like many warblers, plays different roles in its breeding and wintering grounds. The white-winged doves that I study are pollinators while breeding in the Sonoran Desert and become typical doves in the winter in western Mexico.

Migratory pollinators, like billions of other animals in hundreds of species, fly across the earth to populate regions that are inhabitable only seasonally. In the spring they travel to take advantage of the long days and high productivity of high latitudes. In the fall they move to lower latitudes to avoid the cold and unproductive winter. We know a good deal about migration, and there are many excellent reviews that describe its hows and whys. I will not dwell on the best-studied aspects of migration, such as how animals know when and where to migrate. Readers interested in these aspects can consult the wonderful book edited by Kenneth Able (1999) and the comprehensive survey by Peter Berthold (1993). I will concentrate on an important, albeit relatively neglected, consequence of migration: many migrant animals play the role of keeping distant areas biologically connected by acting as pollinators. Events that impact the populations of migrant birds and bats in one place can have biological consequences for the plants that they pollinate thousands of kilometers away. Migratory pollinators are the glue that binds distant wild lands.

In the 1990s Gary Nabhan and Steve Buchmann wrote an influential book that popularized the vulnerability of pollinators (Buchmann & Nabhan 1996). In *The Forgotten Pollinators* Gary and Steve argued that we were heading toward a pollination crisis. They contended that if no action were taken to protect pollinators, the reproduction of both wild and cultivated plants would suffer. Their plea has been heeded: the pollination crisis is acknowledged by scientists (see Kearns et al. 1998 for a technical and literature review), and the word *pollination* is recognized by at least the most enlightened members of government. Gary realized that migrant pollinators face unique threats: these animals can be at risk while breeding in the temperate zone, while in their winter tropical quarters, and while they are in transit. He also recognized that we knew very little about the biology of these important animals. Because effective conservation must be informed by solid science, any conservation recommendations and actions had to be preceded by research. In the spring of 1999 Gary convened a diverse group of researchers and conservationists at the Arizona-Sonora Desert Museum in Tucson. In that meeting we discussed the research needed to face the conservation challenges posed by migrant pollinators.

The biological tales that make up this chapter are outcomes of the Tucson meeting. I use two North American species, long-nosed bats (*Leptonycteris curasoae*) and white-winged doves (*Zenaida asiatica*), to illustrate the travails of migratory animals that are also pollinators. I chose to write about bats and doves not because they are the most important or the best-known migrant pollinators but because they are animals that have shaped my life.

In my feral youth I hunted white-winged doves wintering in western Mexico. They fed on the fruit of guava trees gone wild. I chased them with a slingshot and later with an ancient .410 single-shot shotgun. They were delicious grilled in a stick fire, spiced with ashes and accompanied by hard green guavas and cold water. Later, as a budding naturalist, I spent hours sitting on the branches of a calabash tree (*Crescentia alata*) studying its pollination: I watched stingless bees steal pollen from the huge fleshy flowers and counted the soft hovering visits of bats. One evening a jaguar wandered under my tree. It stopped to watch me before ambling into the forest, its curiosity satisfied. I was paralyzed with joy and fear until the velvet wings of a bat brushed my face. A shiver brought me back to my task. I kept measuring and counting, but at dawn I ran to the field station singing, stinking like a calabash blossom, blessed by bats and by the sacred cat. I write about doves and bats because they are species that I know well and, perhaps more important, because they are species for which I have deep affection. This essay is a biologist's grateful tribute to nectar-feeding bats and doves.

Nectar-Feeding Bats and Their Nectar Corridors

Long-distance migration is very common among birds, but it is much less common among bats. Almost half of all North American north-temperate songbirds migrate to the tropics. In contrast, most species of north-temperate bats migrate only short distances. Rather than migrate, most bats evade the harsh winter by hibernating. In North America only four bat species migrate long distances. Two species, hoary bats (*Lasiurus cinereus*) and Mexican free-tailed bats (*Tadarida brasiliensis*), feed on insects. The remaining two species, lesser long-nosed bats (*L. curasoae*) and Mexican long-tongued bats (*Choeronycteris mexicana*), feed on nectar, pollen, and fruit. Lesser long-nosed bats form maternity roosts in southern Arizona and northern Sonora and spend the fall and winter in south-central Mexico. Not all populations of lesser long-nosed bats are comprised of long-distance migrants; some populations are sedentary. Furthermore, some populations contain both migratory and sedentary individuals. Many populations in central Mexico stay in one place or perform short-distance movements up and down the mountains (Rojas-Martínez et al. 1999). The populations of western Mexico migrate from their fall and winter roosts in south and central Mexico to summer roosts in the Sonoran Desert. Lesser long-nosed bats feed almost exclusively on pollen and nectar, and their morphology and physiology reflect this specialized diet. Nectar-feeding bats have long snouts, a long brush-tipped tongue well suited to sop up nectar, and a small number of tiny teeth. They seem to rely more on vision than echolocation to find flowers, and therefore they have relatively large eyes. Few people consider most bats attractive. I find nectar-feeding bats exceedingly good-looking.

Bats get thoroughly dusted with pollen while they feed on flowers. As they move from flower to flower, they fertilize them. In the spring and early summer migratory lesser long-nosed bats feed on the flowers of desert columnar cacti such as cardon (*Pachycereus pringlei*), saguaro (*Carnegeia gigantea*), and organ pipe (*Stenocereus thurberi*). In the early to late summer they literally feed on the fruits of their labor—they eat the nutritious juicy fruit of the same columnar cacti whose flowers they pollinated. Bats have gentle guts. After assimilating the fruit pulp, they defecate the cactus seeds intact. Migratory bats are not only important pollinators; they are also significant seed dispersers. When the abundance of cactus flowers and fruit winds down in the Sonoran Desert, the bats move south, feeding on the nectar and pollen of several species of paniculate century plants (*Agave spp.*). These plants appear to bloom in a southward progression in the foothills and on the western flank of the Sierra Madre Occidental. Ted Fleming has speculated that lesser long-nosed bats fuel their spring migration with columnar cacti that bloom in a northward progression (see Fleming & Soza 1994; Fleming et al. 1996; Wilkinson & Fleming 1996). In the fall they fuel their migration with agave nectar and pollen. Migrant nectar-feeding bats seem to follow broad paths of blooming plants, which Fleming calls nectar corridors. In the absence of migrant bats, it is likely that many plants along these corridors would suffer from reduced reproduction.

Although lesser long-nosed bats are listed as endangered in the United States, they maintain relatively large populations on both sides of the border. As a species, they are probably relatively secure. However, the migration of lesser long-nosed bats from south-central Mexico to the Sonoran Desert may be a phenomenon at risk, for it hinges on the existence of safe roosts along the migratory route and on habitats with sufficient densities of food plants. Both roosts and plants are far from secure. Lesser long-nosed bats are very picky about the sites that they choose to roost. They prefer large, hot (hotter than about 30°C), and humid caves that are safe from predators and human disturbance. These caves are rare. A few important roosting sites in Mexico and the Sonoran Desert are protected. However, we know little about the location and vulnerability of the roosts used by bats along their migratory route. Migrating nectar-feeding bats travel through prime poppy- and marijuana-growing areas. The presence of territorial *narcotraficantes* makes research difficult, although it may have the ironical positive consequence of keeping people away from caves. In Mexico, bat roosts are often at risk because of misguided vampire bat eradication programs. Ranchers use fire and even dynamite to drive bats away from roosting caves. Bat Conservation International and a Mexican program, Programa Para la Conservación de Murcielagos Migratorios (PCMM), are conducting a large-scale educational program to stress the beneficial aspects of most bats. The work of these fine organizations will do much to protect nectar-feeding bats.

Safe roost sites are essential for the conservation of migratory bats, but they are not sufficient. Migratory bats must find adequate density of food plants along their routes. Threats to columnar cacti and paniculate agaves include the familiar catalog of wildland destruction and fragmentation: conversion into agriculture, recreation, and urban development, all of which are in full swing in western Mexico. The importance of large areas containing food plants is illustrated by Fleming's study of a smallish (7,000 individuals) "transient" roost on the coast of Sonora, where bats spend three to four weeks before moving north (Fleming et al. 1996). At this site the radius of the foraging area used by the bats is probably larger than 30 kilometers. Because lesser long-nosed bats take their time to get from winter to summer roosts, finding and protecting their transient roosts and safeguarding the plants around them are critical for their conservation.

White-Winged Doves, Saguaros, and Men: An Uneasy Partnership

The song of white-winged doves is the lusty sound of summer in the Sonoran Desert. With Egyptian blue eyeliner and iridescent breast feathers, males belt their sonorous "who-cooks-for-you!" from the top of saguaros all through the summer. I love white-wings, and my love for them is shared by many in the desert. Images of doves plunging their heads into saguaro flowers and messily eating the bright red pulp of saguaro fruit adorn postcards, magazine covers, and even children's books. Although doves are dearly loved, in Arizona hordes of hunters kill them by the thousands in the fall. I am fascinated by white-winged doves because their natural history is full of quirks. White-winged doves are a beloved migrant pollinator that is also a game species. Their relationship with the mighty saguaro is tight but also ambiguous (Martínez del Rio et al. 2004; Wolf & Martínez del Rio 2000). They are saguaro mutualistic pollinators, but they are also parasitic seed predators. White-winged doves are wild desert denizens, but they can take advantage of human crops, and therefore the fate of their populations has been shaped by humans. Curiously, and unlike the case for most wild organisms, the interaction of doves with humans has not always been to the doves' disadvantage.

There is little doubt that white-winged doves were the most important pollinators of saguaros in the past. Now they share the pollination of saguaro flowers with introduced feral honeybees and to a much lesser extent with long-nosed and long-tongued bats. Their importance as saguaro pollinators may increase in the future if, as predicted, the population of feral honeybees decreases in the desert as a result of mite infections. The value of doves as saguaro pollinators is difficult to assess. I suspect that it varies from place to place, depending on the local density of feral bee colonies. Although saguaros receive significant pollination services from doves, doves feed on saguaro fruit and destroy an enormous number of saguaro seeds. Unlike nectar-feeding bats, doves have powerful

guts, and no saguaro seeds survive the passage through their gizzards. The balance between the pollination benefits that saguaros receive from doves and the seed damage that doves cause probably varies in space. It certainly has varied in time as a result of the ecological success of a feral invader. The canvas of biological interactions is not painted in black and white.

Although the balance sheet of the saguaro-dove interaction is mixed for saguaros, desert doves are crucially dependent on the mighty cactus. Doves arrive in Arizona in early to mid-April, and they start to breed by early May when the desert is getting really hot and when water is the most scarce. Why do white-winged doves do something as insane as migrating into a sweltering subtropical desert to breed at the hottest and most stressful time of the year? The answer seems to be that the dove's breeding cycle is synchronized with the reproductive cycle of the saguaro. Doves appear in the desert as the saguaros start blooming. The doves feed extensively at the saguaro flowers, and when saguaro fruit is available they eat it almost exclusively. Doves can breed in the desert because saguaros provide them with nectar and fruit pulp, which are both watery and nutritious.

The ecological dependence of white-winged doves on saguaros (and other columnar cacti farther south in the southern portion of the Sono-ran Desert) is recognized in the Spanish (or more properly, Sonoran) name for the white-winged dove, *paloma pitayera* ("dove that eats columnar cactus fruit"). White-winged doves are widespread in North and South America and have twelve morphologically distinct subspecies. To my knowledge, only Sonoran Desert white-winged doves rely on saguaro nectar and fruit. The remaining eleven populations feed on a variety of seeds and agricultural grains. The subspecies of white-winged doves that inhabits Arizona and Sonora has a much longer bill than other subspecies. I suspect that the longer bills of western white-winged doves facilitate probing efficiently into the deep flowers and fruits of saguaros. The Sonoran Desert white-winged doves seem to be saguaro specialists deserving of their Spanish common name.

The fate of white-winged doves is not only linked to that of saguaros; it is also dependent on the vagaries of the relationship of humans with the land. In the last 150 years white-winged dove populations have experienced rollercoaster-like population fluctuations (see Alcock 1993; Brown 1989). These cycles of boom and bust can be explained by changes in how humans have perceived doves (as pests, quarry, and fragile resource) and how they have used the land. The size of white-winged dove populations before large-scale agriculture started in Arizona are unknown. Naturalists from the early and mid-nineteenth century reported white-wings as common, even numerous, but their numbers seem to have been lower than in the late 1800s, when increased cereal production appears to have led to a population surge. Like South American eared doves *(Zenaida auriculata)*, white-wings are facultative colonial nesters. They can nest singly, but if food is concentrated and abundant, and dense vegetation for nesting is available, they can form large, raucous colonies. By the beginning of the twentieth century several vast colonies were well established in the then extensive riparian mesquite bosques along the Santa Cruz and Gila rivers.

Before 1941 white-winged doves were managed as pests. Squabs were plucked from nests, and adults were hunted in a long and loosely enforced season. Colonial nesting white-wings almost suffered the fate of the passenger pigeon. Overhunting and destruction of nesting habitat, aided by the conversion of grain fields to cotton, led to such a dramatic population collapse in the forties that wildlife biologists feared that the population was becoming extinct. The hunting season opening date was moved from August 1 (when doves are still nesting) to September 1. White-winged dove populations rebounded, and in the absence of mesquite bosques that were cleared for firewood, they formed nesting colonies in citrus groves. They increased again. In the 1960s white-winged doves were so abundant that the bag was set at 25 birds per day (the bag is now 6 birds per day). By 1968 the population began to decline again, apparently as a result of the combined effect of nesting habitat loss, a dramatic reduction in cereal production, and overharvest. Citrus farming followed the usual fate of desert agriculture: it became unprofitable as water costs increased. A few small white-winged dove colonies still hang on precariously in salt cedar thickets along the Gila River.

From 1967 to 1980 the number of birds killed annually by hunters dropped precipitously, from 700,000 to fewer than 100,000. Recent data on white-winged dove populations are unavailable, but the numbers killed by hunters in Arizona remain low. The morning feeding flights of white-winged doves that took place in the fifties and early sixties have been described as one of the great natural wonders of Arizona. The historical evidence suggests that they may have been artificial, the result of short-lived increases in cereal production

that coincided with the presence of huge mesquite riparian bosques and citrus groves that allowed colonial nesting. Cereal production is almost extinct in the Sonoran Desert, and the mesquite bosques and citrus plantations are all but gone. So are the magnificent, albeit human-induced, dove flights that filled the desert sky with birds—and the hotels of Gila Bend and Tucson with hunters.

These dramatic fluctuations portray more or less accurately the fluctuations in abundance of white-winged doves that were closely associated with agricultural fields and riparian thickets. It is not certain that desert-dwelling, saguaro-dependent, white-winged doves followed the same trends. The foraging habits, social behavior, and demography of desert-dwelling doves appear to differ from those of birds dependent on agricultural products. The enormous population fluctuations exhibited by white-winged doves can be explained only by a very productive population that depended strongly on clumped abundant resources and had large tracts of dense nesting habitat. These are not characteristics that typify desert-nesting doves. I suspect that the populations of desert-dwelling and saguaro-dependent doves have fluctuated much less than those of birds that nested colonially and relied on cereals. During the breeding season most of the diet of desert-dwelling white-winged doves is saguaro. Although saguaro groves can produce large amounts of fruit, this productivity cannot be compared with the enormous productivity of irrigated cereal fields. Saguaro represents only 2–5 percent of the diet of the last few white-winged dove colonies that still depend on agricultural products in Arizona. Nesting pairs of desert-dwelling doves are scattered rather than clumped in colonies. Birds feeding in agricultural fields are noticeably gregarious whereas desert doves feeding on saguaro feed singly or, more rarely, in pairs. Finally, the number of clutches per season, and hence the productivity, of white-winged doves nesting in the desert is lower (one clutch per season) than that of colonially nesting birds that feed on grain (sometimes two clutches per season). The high productivity of "agricultural" doves may explain the remarkable ability of their populations to rebound after approaching extinction. White-winged doves in the Sonoran Desert may be unique in that, at least during the twentieth century, a colonially nesting population that fed on cultivated grain coexisted with a solitary nesting population that fed primarily on the fruit and nectar of a single plant species.

It is highly likely that desert-dwelling white-winged doves were spared the demographic turmoil of their agricultural relatives. This does not mean that all is fine with them. Because they are scattered and much harder to hunt, wildlife biologists have paid less attention to their long-term population trends. We have just begun to understand their complex interaction with saguaros, and hence with the varied coterie of insects, birds, and mammals that rely on these keystone giants for food, water, and shelter. Hunting in the United States probably has a minimal effect on desert white-wings. By the time the early dove-hunting season starts, most of the desert doves have left for Mexico. Most of the birds banded in Arizona spend the winter in the Pacific coastal plains and foothills from southern Sinaloa to Guerrero and Oaxaca. They appear to winter in deciduous and subdeciduous tropical woodlands, although they probably also use expanding pockets of agriculture and secondary vegetation as well as small areas with thornscrub and, at higher elevations, pine-oak forests. Native forests in western Mexico are rapidly being cleared for agricultural fields and pasture, and white-winged doves are hunted by both subsistence and sport hunters. Is habitat destruction and hunting in Mexico having an impact on saguaro doves? No one knows.

Conclusion: Conservation of Migratory Pollinators Needs Science, International Cooperation, and Pragmatism

It is clear that we will not be able to protect the migration of nectar-feeding bats along the Sierra Madre Occidental until we understand it much better. First, we must identify the transient roosts used by these bats on their spring and fall migration. Second, we must gather the political will and garner the force to protect extensive areas around these roosts. What we know about white-winged doves is even more rudimentary than what we know about bats, and hence protecting them (if needed) and managing their populations wisely requires that we do a significant amount of research. Given the game status of white-wings and their importance as saguaro pollinators, a program of population monitoring in Arizona is needed. However, information on the habitats and resources that the doves use in the winter, as well as

data on the numbers of birds killed by Mexican hunters, is also required to interpret their population trends in the breeding grounds and to provide guidelines for their management in both Mexico and Arizona. The populations of migratory animals like white-wing doves and long-nosed bats depend on conditions at both the breeding and wintering areas. Their conservation and management demand that we abandon isolationist delusions and embrace international cooperation. Like other migratory animals, pollinators remind us of the biological wholeness of this continent.

When it comes to conservation issues, I tend to be a purist. I believe in conserving as much wilderness as possible. The words *wilderness* and *management* used in the same sentence make me uneasy. But thinking about migratory nectar-feeding doves and bats, and of the conservation of processes that take place at the level of our continent, has tempered my purity. In their yearly travels doves and bats use a huge area that is a complex tapestry of wild, semi-wild, and domesticated lands. The populations of both species can be injured by human activities, yet both bats and doves can take advantage of human-produced resources when they are available. I have discussed at length how doves are capable of adjusting their feeding and reproductive behavior in response to human land uses. Given the level of land destruction in western Mexico, I would be very surprised if wintering desert white-wings are restricted to and rely solely on pristine forests. Similarly, long-nosed bats often use abandoned mine shafts and adits to roost and to reproduce. I suspect that banana monocultures are disliked by most conservationists. In western Mexico, however, they can be great places to catch long-nosed bats. Banana plants produce huge amounts of nectar, pollen, and fruit, and bats feed on them. When I have suggested to conservation audiences the possibility that banana plantations in western Mexico might play a positive role for nectar-feeding bats, I have always felt a ripple of distaste in response. I am not advocating bulldozing forests to plant bananas. I am suggesting that it is likely that some long-nosed bat roosts rely on banana plantations. Under some conditions, maintaining a viable roost in a heavily agricultural area might require subsidizing it by favoring banana plantations over other land uses. Conserving migratory pollinators demands pragmatism, leaving preconceptions aside, and letting the organisms tell us what their needs are in the sometimes messed-up environment in which they live and travel. We must face the possibility that the bats and doves that play a central role in the ecological integrity of the most pristine and isolated corners of the Sonoran Desert may rely on semi-wild or even agricultural habitats in the winter.

I have used the word *management* more than once in this chapter when referring to wild white-winged doves. This is because doves are both wild pollinators and a game species. I doubt that I will abandon the "M" word any time soon. White-wings will be hunted on both sides of the border whether I wish it or not. With proper restrictions, hunting may still allow doves to fulfill their role in the interaction with saguaros and other columnar cacti. White-winged doves and bats have taught me a supremely important lesson. Even our most heavily protected areas are leaky. The populations of some of the species that play key roles in them (such as saguaros) are intertwined with those of others whose fates depend on management and conservation outside parks and reserves (such as doves and bats). The doves that pollinate the flowers and crush the seeds of saguaros in Organ Pipe National Monument and Cabeza Prieta National Wildlife Refuge are hunted as soon as they step out of the monument and refuge boundaries. And they all step out every year on their way south.

The challenge of conservation biologists and wildlife managers is to define the level of hunting in Mexico and Arizona that is compatible with a population of doves that can fulfill its role in the ecosystem. We have emphasized for too long the management and conservation of populations at the minimal level that allows persistence. This strategy is inappropriate for animals the play important roles in biological communities. For these species, the goal of conservation biologists should be to ensure the existence of populations that are large enough to fulfill their ecological vocation in natural ecosystems. This is not a trivial enterprise, and we must approach it humbly because we know so damn little that all attempts at managing wild organisms seem like hubris. Wildlife management often appears a contradiction in terms. Yet it is something we have to do.

Unlike some conservationists, I think there is a role for management in conservation biology.

The doves and the bats have convinced me of it. Every time I encounter an invasive exotic in a remote wilderness area, my conviction strengthens. Developing a biocentric wildlife management discipline is not a simple enterprise. Perhaps the central difference between conservation (biocentric) management of wildlife and control (anthropocentric) management for recreation and profit is one of values. Biocentric wildlife managers intervene only when absolutely necessary, and then they do so with the scientific humility of adaptive management. Their goal is to uphold the function of interacting populations in living landscapes.

Human activity is widespread and penetrating. No ecosystem is free from it, making intervention almost inevitable. The biocentric manager will intervene not for us only but for the saguaros, the bats, and the doves.

Acknowledgments

The migrant pollinator initiative was funded the Turner Endangered Species Fund. My thoughts on doves have been shaped by many sweltering days in the desert in the company of Blair Wolf; the ideas expressed here are as much his as they are mine. Gary Nabhan started the migrant pollinator strategy. Those that travel the land owe him much. Steve Buskirk, Chris Lotz, Todd McWhorter, and Blair Wolf reviewed previous versions of this chapter. I am grateful to have such insightful and constructively critical friends. This essay is dedicated to the newly created Sonoran Desert National Monument, a wild place that gives shelter to doves, bats, and saguaros.

This essay first appeared in a slightly different form in *WildEarth* (Summer 2001): 14–21; it is used here by permission.

Poems
Ofelia Zepeda

Bat
Gently
The water is kissed.
By moonlight,
The courting
of Saguaro Flowers

Dove
She is the first one.
She is the first one.
The one who tastes the beautiful fruit.
See here, see here, she breathes clouds of wetness

Twenty-One

Reptiles and Amphibians in Arid Southwestern Arizona and Northwestern Sonora

PHILIP C. ROSEN

I stand in a high desert pass, tired and sweating, my boot soles baking from contact with the ground. It is late morning, and I'm mapping the transitions between two species of whiptail lizards in an isolated part of southwestern Arizona. As if to heighten my sensation of deadly heat, the sound of a distant breeze grows, in a few instants, to an explosive roar—a jet slips through the rocky notch I'm on, angling down to its practice target. Everything jumps—the warbler I'm watching, me, and a side-blotched lizard on a stone nearby—then stillness and heat regain position. I'm at the very edge of real heat and aridity, and as the now-distant jet goes to target, I notice instead a breadth of valley, range, horizon, and butte that extends into the true desert hinterland.

The "dead ranges" of southwestern Arizona, so-called by Howard Gloyd (1937), into which recent work has drawn me, turn out to be anything but dead for true desert reptiles. As I gaze west and south, my mind is drawn to an image of many chuckwallas, perched vigilant despite the inferno, on rocks black or white; to rock-and-boulder fields whose every prominence is occupied by a male side-blotched lizard, except where ruled by a predatory collared lizard. As I consider my own potential mistakes with heat and dryness, I recall stories of "forty sidewinders in a few miles of road," and dozens of little coral-banded shovel-nosed snakes, and rock reefs in the sand crawling with chucks. For these true desert reptiles, the more moderate climate of Tucson is anything but hospitable.

There at Tucson, they find the end of their distributions and are local and uncommon. As I headed west and south from there, I left behind a great aggregation of humanity, which now administers coups de grâce to true desert reptile species populations in the northeastern Sonoran Desert. Like these species, I escape into the heat, into the dryness; and escape from beasts too predatory or competitive, or at least too numerous, for my health and welfare. In this hyper-arid place, a drought is severely stressful, even for reptiles—potentially even lethal (Figure 21.1). In ordinary droughts at Tucson or Organ Pipe, lizards may flourish as their predators recede (Rosen 2000), while here the climate seems too challenging to support that response. But in better times these lands are teeming with a visible abundance of reptiles rarely exceeded elsewhere (Camp 1916). When times are good, whiptails, iguanas, zebra-tails, and fringe-toed lizards can seem literally to scatter underfoot; sidewinder rattlesnakes are so numerous they become a chore; and western shovel-nosed snakes appear and disappear in the sands like dune flowers at dusk.

My business here is pretty mundane. I must "survey" the herpetofauna of this place. It is my task to recommend ways that modern management can "monitor" the system, potentially in a very mundane, even mechanical, way. I have big ideas about deriving an understanding of how this rich ecosystem works, but that is an ambitious proposal. It took four years of waiting, just to get out to work, in August 1987, in the desert at Organ Pipe Cactus National Monument (Rosen & Lowe 1996). By then I was working with Charles Lowe, and when we were told to wait until the following year, we simply went to work. The business of moving organizations to action is slow; more effort goes into that than toward observation in the ecosystem. Lots of time is spent talking and theorizing, while few people actually see what is happening.

It's taken me another decade to get out here into the real desert wilderness: at Organ Pipe I worked in a thornscrub-like "desert." There's a certain difficulty in working on reptiles in this hottest part of the continent. Waiting for winter just won't do, and most of the few existing roads are off limits nowadays. There are big highways, down the Gila River, and just south of the border, and through Organ Pipe to Peñasco, and around Yuma. John Van Denburgh (1922) and Joseph Slevin (1928) braved the heat at Yuma, making early collections, and by now the Yuma region's herpetofauna has been extensively documented, not to mention decimated. There are large collections from all along the pavement, but since Gloyd's sojourn near Tinajas Altas in 1936, not many have ventured into the vast interiors between the Gila River and Gulf of California. Not much organized herpetological survey and collecting has been carried out in the blazing backcountry for several decades.

Even in relatively mild Organ Pipe, early surveys like those of Lawrence Huey (1942) avoided the warmer months. M. Max Hensley (1950) was the first to report many of the amphibian and reptile species there, even though his original work had a springtime slant, largely bypassing the all-important summer monsoon. Hensley reported several species populations thought to be highly isolated from more easterly populations, some of which are still incorrectly viewed as isolated (although the black-necked garter snake does seem to be). One of the herpetofauna's most striking animals—the red-backed whiptail—was not even recognized by scientists until 1951 (Duellman & Lowe 1953).

Philip Smith and Hensley (1958:201), remarking on their "good fortune to discover that a new blacktop highway had just been completed between Sonoyta and San Luis," noted that "excessive temperatures prohibited collecting at any great distance from the paved road." The situation is not that different today, and recent work has just begun to open up our knowledge of reptile distributions across the great desert's interior. Norm Scott collected in Cabeza Prieta NWR intermittently during 1971–87. In 1980 Charles Lowe, Peter Holm, and Cecil Schwalbe (whom they abandoned at Tule Well for several days!) toughed out a two-week August trip along Camino del Diablo. (Much earlier, the Gloyds had turned back from this route, after "learning of the almost impassable condition of the road" [Gloyd 1937:92]).

In Mexico formal zoological survey of the arid border region began later (Burger & Hensley 1949; May 1973, 1976), and a great many key details about

Figure 21.1. Chuckwalla, dehydrated but not enfeebled on April 7, at Growler Pass in Organ Pipe Cactus National Monument, during the marked heat and drought of 1990. The drought did not break until July 6–7. (Photo by P. C. Rosen)

species occurrence and habitat patterns remain to be documented (Gonzáles-Romero & Alvarez-Cárdenas 1989; Gonzáles-Romero et al. 1989; Ortega et al. 1986), with few voucher specimens available for the core of the Pinacate and Gran Desierto. Herpetological survey remains difficult and even hazardous in both countries, particularly on desert mountains and out in the great sand field. One wishing to shirk administrative paperwork does not relish enumerating for risk managers the rigors of backcountry herpetology in the continent's deepest deserts.

Field guides still incorrectly show fragmented distributions of many rock-dwelling reptiles across the Tohono O'odham lands, Organ Pipe and surrounding areas, Sonoran Desert National Monument, and the region of Sonoyta. Meanwhile, other species, such as the tree lizard, are assumed to have continuous distributions through the most arid part of the desert, where they are actually rare or absent. I explore these distributions herein, with an eye toward defining the structure of the herpetofauna in relation to macrohabitat and geography. I do this reluctantly, for despite a couple of years of modest effort on my part, with the help of some of Arizona's outstanding field herpetologists and a nationwide survey of museum records, I am stung by my ignorance of what lives in, and what may really be absent from, the vast hyper-arid area. Though I have worked in the region for more than twenty years, with several visits to most of the major environmental zones, what I write will surely be subject to revision, in some cases immediately, by some who know what I do not.

Although the focus here is on a herpetofauna living in great arid reaches of true desert, I cannot isolate this fauna from its setting near two great desert rivers, the Gila and Colorado. Though they are now degraded, they were key features of the region for many species. Thus I have included areas of the Gila River bottom and Río Colorado adjoining the dry borderlands, both as contrast to the interior and to offer insight into the penetration of less desert-oriented species into the hyper-arid core. Perhaps some of the amphibian and reptile species present in the desert proper would be regionally absent if not for the rivers and their floodplains. For completeness, I have also listed marine reptiles from the adjoining Gulf of California. Although I have not included Baja California Norte or California, no additional species would be added until the west margin of the Lower Colorado Valley is passed near the rocks of the Jacumba Mountains, where the distinctive Baja California herpetofauna appears (Grismer 2002; Stebbins 2003).

A total of 72 species are listed here as occurring or expected in the regional herpetofauna of the dry borderlands. Included are 5 introduced species (4 of them aquatic) and 2 apparently extirpated species (also both aquatic). Table 21.1 summarizes the available data for the various reserves and sub-areas. The list includes frogs and toads (12), salamanders (1), turtles (9), lizards (21), and snakes (29) living in the core of the North American Desert. Excluding species found only in aquatic, riparian, urban, and agricultural environments of the Gila and Colorado rivers, the list consists of 63 species, 57 in the desert and 6 marine, of which 61 are confirmed. Not surprisingly, where "every plant and animal is protected by sting or spine," it is the rattlesnakes, at 6 species total and often 3 species per plot of ground, that are the most diverse in this arid region, and they are all closely tied to the deserts. These deserts, now revered as a last intact wilderness, are the central focus of this chapter.

Structure and Ecogeography of the Herpetofauna

Desert-ness of the Fauna

In a region as arid as the dry borderlands of western Sonora and Arizona, it is worth asking what a "true" desert animal is. Lowe (1968, 1989) and Lowe et al. (1986) distinguished between desert-included and true desert species. True (or "obligate") desert species (practically never occurring outside desert environments) contrast with desert-centered species that also occur significantly in other biomes. Our list of obligate desert vertebrate species is surprisingly short, without even a single amphibian and with but one bird, Le Conte's thrasher (*Toxostoma lecontei*). Even among reptiles, there are only about 9 in the area (4 snakes—sidewinder, Sonoran and western shovel-nosed snakes, and spotted leaf-nosed snake; and 5 lizards—desert iguana, chuckwalla, Colorado Desert fringe-toed lizard, flat-tailed horned lizard, and long-tailed brush lizard). Neither do mammals count high against this rigorous standard: desert kangaroo rat (*Dipodomys deserti*) is the only clear choice, although Arizona pocket mouse (*Perognathus longimembris*) and round-tailed ground squirrel (*Spermophilus tereticaudus*) may also qualify (Hoffmeister 1986). One must know the animals inordinately well to whittle down a regional list to obligate desert species. George Bradley pointed out to me that chuckwallas, outside the dry borderlands, occasionally occupy non-desert environments. We recently photographed a desert iguana at 3,702 ft elevation, in desert grassland near Ban Thak ("Pan Tak") Pass at the base of the Baboquivari Mountains, and found a zebra-tailed lizard that had followed the same dirt road to the even loftier elevation—for the Sonoran Desert region—of 4,301 ft. These examples I attribute to the road, and thus retain the desert iguana as a desert obligate.

If we add desert-centered species, including only species that occur primarily in, and have probably evolved primarily under, xeric (dry and desertlike) conditions, we add three amphibians (Sonoran desert toad, Sonoran green toad, Couch's spadefoot), a turtle (desert tortoise), and about 15 squamate reptiles (speckled and Mojave rattlers, rosy boa, western patch-nosed snake, and banded sand snake; desert horned lizard, desert spiny lizard, zebra-tailed lizard, side-blotched lizard, long-nosed leopard lizard, Sonoran Desert and Basin and Range collared lizards, western banded gecko, desert night lizard, and tiger whiptail). Several others living astride the thornscrub–desert-scrub transition belong here by dint of their prominence in the xeric thornscrub that is the Arizona Upland: Gila monster, red-backed whiptail, regal horned lizard, tiger rattlesnake, Sonoran coral snake, and saddled leaf-nosed snake. Summing all these, the "desert" list is 34 species (3 toads, 1 tortoise, 12 snakes, and 18 lizards). These num-

TABLE 21.1. *Confirmed occurrence of taxa within protected area boundaries and on the major river floodplains.*

TAXON	SonDes NM	Organ Pipe	Cabeza Prieta	Goldwater Range	Pinacate-GranDes	Colorado and Gila R	Alto Golfo (marine)
FROGS AND TOADS							
Bufo alvarius	X	X	X	X	?	X	O
Bufo cognatus	X	X	X	X	?	X	O
Bufo punctatus	X	X	X	X	X	X	O
Bufo retiformis	X	X	?	O	O	O	O
Bufo woodhousii	O	O	O	O	O	X	O
Gastrophryne olivacea	X	?	O	O	?	O	O
Pternohyla fodiens	X	O	O	O	O	O	O
Rana berlandieri	I	O	O	O	O	I	O
Rana catesbeiana	O	O	O	O	O	I	O
Rana yavapaiensis	O	O	O	O	O	E	O
Scaphiopus couchii	X	X	X	X	X	X	O
Spea multiplicata	?	O	O	O	O	X	O
SALAMANDER							
Ambystoma tigrinum	O	O	I	O	O	I	O
LIZARDS							
Callisaurus draconoides	X	X	X	X	X	X	O
Cnemidophorus burti	X	X	X	X	?	O	O
Cnemidophorus tigris	X	X	X	X	X	X	O
Coleonyx variegatus	X	X	X	X	X	X	O
Crotaphytus bicinctores	O	O	O	?	O	X	O
Crotaphytus nebrius	X	X	X	X	X	X	O
Dipsosaurus dorsalis	X	X	X	X	X	O	O
Gambelia wislizenii	X	X	X	X	X	X	O
Heloderma suspectum	?	X	X	X	X	X	O
Hemidactylus turcicus	O	O	O	O	O	I	O
Phrynosoma mcallii	O	O	?	X	X	O	O
Phrynosoma platyrhinos	X	X	X	X	X	X	O
Phrynosoma solare	X	X	X	X	X	O	O
Sauromalus obesus	X	X	X	X	X	O	O
Sceloporus clarkii	X	X	?	?	?	O	O
Sceloporus magister	X	X	X	X	X	X	O
Uma notata	O	O	X	X	X	O	O
Urosaurus graciosus	X	X	X	X	X	X	O
Urosaurus ornatus	X	X	X	X	X	X	O
Uta stansburiana	X	X	X	X	X	X	O
Xantusia vigilis	?	?	X	?	?	O	O
SNAKES							
Arizona elegans	O	X	X	X	X	X	O
Charina trivirgata	X	X	X	X	X	O	O

TAXON	SonDes NM	ORGAN PIPE	CABEZA PRIETA	GOLDWATER RANGE	PINACATE-GRANDES	COLORADO AND GILA R	ALTO GOLFO (MARINE)
Chilomeniscus cinctus	?	x	x	?	o	x	o
Chionactis occipitalis	x	x	x	x	x	x	o
Chionactis palarostris	o	x	?	o	o	o	o
Crotalus atrox	x	x	x	x	x	x	o
Crotalus cerastes	x	x	x	x	x	x	o
Crotalus mitchellii	x	x	x	x	x	o	o
Crotalus molossus	x	x	x	x	?	o	o
Crotalus scutulatus	x	x	x	x	x	x	o
Crotalus tigris	x	x	x	?	x	o	o
Hypsiglena torquata	x	x	x	x	x	x	o
Lampropeltis getula	?	x	x	x	?	x	o
Leptotyphlops humilis	?	x	?	x	x	x	o
Masticophis bilineatus	x	x	x	x	x	o	o
Masticophis flagellum	x	x	x	x	x	x	o
Micruroides euryxanthus	?	x	x	?	?	?	o
Pelamis platurus	o	o	o	o	o	o	x
Phyllorhynchus browni	?	x	?	x	x	o	o
Phyllorhynchus decurtatus	x	x	x	x	x	x	o
Pituophis catenifer	x	x	x	x	x	x	o
Rhinocheilus lecontei	x	x	x	x	x	x	o
Salvadora hexalepis	x	x	x	x	x	x	o
Sonora semiannulata	x	?	?	x	o	x	o
Tantilla hobartsmithi	?	x	?	o	?	x	o
Thamnophis cyrtopsis	o	x	o	o	o	o	o
Thamnophis eques	o	o	o	o	o	E	o
Thamnophis marcianus	o	o	o	o	o	x	o
Trimorphodon biscutatus	x	x	x	x	x	o	o
TURTLES							
Apalone spinifera	o	o	o	o	o	I	o
Caretta caretta	o	o	o	o	o	o	?
Chelonia mydas	o	o	o	o	o	o	x
Dermochelys coriacea	o	o	o	o	o	o	x
Eretmochelys imbricata	o	o	o	o	o	o	x
Gopherus agassizii	x	x	x	x	x	o	o
Kinosternon flavescens	?	o	o	o	o	?E	o
Kinosternon sonoriense	o	x	o	o	x	E?	o
Lepidochelys olivacea	o	o	o	o	o	o	x
TOTAL SPECIES CONFIRMED	41	48	43	42	38	43	5
OCCURRENCE POSSIBLE	10	3	8	6	10	2	1
POSSIBLE MAXIMUM TOTAL	51	51	51	48	48	45	6

X = confirmed native ?E = questionably native, ? = possibly present
E = extirpated native   not currently present   o = not present
E? = presumed extirpated I = introduced non-native

bers reinforce what we know and see: although the regional snake fauna is diverse, a closer look shows that lizards predominate among desert species.

Species in Ecological Regions and Landscapes

In this section I take a more analytical approach. "Desert species" here include all those maintaining successful populations within the confines of the truly arid desert interior. These confines are highlighted by a demonstration of the abrupt herpetofaunal transition from the Arizona Upland (sensu Shreve 1951; Brown 1994) to the real, world-class desert conditions found in the Mojave Desert and the Lower Colorado Valley subdivision of the Sonoran Desert (sometimes equated with the "Colorado Desert"; or alternatively, subsuming California's "Colorado Desert"; see Shreve 1951; also MacDougal 1908 and Stewart 1993). One part of the herpetofauna corresponds geographically with the Arizona Upland whereas a second, distinctive part occupies both the Lower Colorado Valley and Mojave Desert. It is this unique "Colorado-Mojave Desert herpetofauna" (occupying two desert areas that are usually treated separately) that I identify as the true desert herpetofauna of southwestern North America.

A prime consideration in defining this desert herpetofauna is the relationship of species to the mesic riparian corridors adjoining the true desert, especially the floodplains of the Gila Valley and Colorado River, but also at Río Sonoyta. Are some species in the region restricted to these areas? Trivially, yes for the aquatics and riparian obligates. Are yet others present in the desert only because of the influence of these wet and semiarid corridors? A third consideration in defining the true desert herpetofauna is the marked transition, within the arid desert proper, between sand-dwelling species of the Gran Desierto's core and those of the Colorado-Mojave Desert. The sand field has a special herpetofaunal assemblage, though it is one contained within the Colorado-Mojave Desert herpetofauna.

I address these faunal and biogeographic questions using museum records accumulated during a century and a half, along with my own observations, to derive a relatively precise mapping of species boundaries and faunal transitions. Then I use the summed museum records to derive an account of the relative abundances of species in the Lower Colorado Valley and Arizona Upland

subdivisions of the Sonoran Desert, and I contrast these with literature data for the Colorado-Mojave Desert from California and Nevada. Holes remain in these analyses: secretive snakes and lizards (rosy boas, tantillas, ground snakes, blind snakes, and night lizards) are not adequately sampled even in museum records; nonetheless, enough data are available to draw meaningful comparisons.

Based on the herpetofauna, I recognize four major desert ecological formations in the area (more, if you add marine, riverine aquatic, and riparian environments). The four are the xeric thornscrub (Arizona Upland subdivision), the desert environs of the river valley bottoms (Gila, Colorado, and perhaps Sonoyta), the arid desert (Lower Colorado Valley subdivision), and the hyper-arid sand desert (Gran Desierto). However, to see these clearly, one must focus first at a great dividing line within arid lands herpetofaunas, the slope inflection point between rock slope and bajada that divides desert mountain from desert valley (Figures 21.2, 21.3). Although sites where level, shallow lava flows overlie sandy flats have admixtures of rock slope and valley lizard assemblages (Bury 1977; Gonzáles-Romero et al. 1989), overall the landscape structure of herpetofaunal assemblages in the dry borderlands is tightly organized, with many examples of "species for species" matching (Schluter 1990) easily seen in Table 21.2. The table illustrates the structure of the lizard and snake assemblages in the dry borderlands (based primarily on my observations in the Sonoran Desert of southern Arizona), although many important ecological and regional details remain to be learned.

In the Arizona Upland there are 12 pairs (6 lizards and 6 snakes) of ecologically similar species that switch at the transition from rocky slope to valley fill habitat types (Table 21.2); in the arid Lower Colorado Valley, only 6 pairs are known (2 lizards and 4 snakes), although some may be added when snakes are better studied in rocks. Several rock-dwelling species, especially lizards, are present in the Arizona Upland but lack ecological counterparts in the Lower Colorado Valley, including such prominent ones as the red-backed whiptail, Clark's spiny lizard, tree lizard, and Sonoran whipsnake. Nevertheless, total lizard diversity in the arid desert (Lower Colorado Valley and Gran Desierto; 15 species) is remarkably similar to that in the Arizona Upland (16 species); in the arid

Figure 21.2. Contrasting rocky canyon environments, in the Arizona Upland (top, *in Alamo Canyon, Ajo Mountains*) and Lower Colorado Valley (bottom, *in Cabeza Prieta Tanks Canyon, Cabeza Prieta Mountains*). Both are productive canyons relative to their surroundings. Alamo Canyon has tiger rattlesnakes, Sonoran coralsnakes, Sonoran whipsnakes, southwestern black-headed snakes, black-necked garter snakes, red-backed whiptails, tree lizards, and Clark's spiny lizards, all absent from the arid desert. Cabeza Prieta Tanks Canyon and other less productive rock environments in the arid desert support populations of speckled rattlesnakes, rosy boas, side-blotched lizards, chuckwallas, and, at least locally, desert night lizards, all absent from Alamo Canyon or confined to its mouth, as well as a number of species that are, surprisingly, shared with Alamo Canyon, including the black-tailed rattlesnake, western lyre snake, and red-spotted toad. (Photos by P. C. Rosen)

desert arenicolous (sand-dwelling) lizards and the rare and secretive night lizard make up for the fewer rock-dwelling species. Rocky slopes deep in the Lower Colorado Valley apparently support few lizard species, with only the chuckwalla and side-blotched lizard being truly prominent.

Snakes are found to be more diverse in the Arizona Upland (24 species) than in the true desert (18 species), and the speckled rattlesnake and western shovel-nosed snake are the only species that are restricted, here, to the true desert (Table 21.2). Moreover, 4 snake species listed within the Lower Colorado Valley in Arizona are rare there. Snake diversity is markedly lower and more restricted than in the snake-rich Arizona Upland.

Tropical deciduous (dry) forest in Sonora (Schwalbe & Lowe 2000) has about 19 lizard species, just 19 percent more than the Arizona Upland, whereas there are 36 snake species, 50 percent more than the Arizona Upland. This is part of a pattern—relatively unchanging lizard diversity from hyper-arid desert to xeric thornscrub and dry tropical forest—that continues as far south as Costa Rica (Figure 21.4), where tropical dry forest supports something like 16 lizard species, and the phenomenally diverse lowland moist-wet forest formations still average only about 27 lizard species (Savage 2002). (Some caveats should be specified. The desert values in Figure 21.4 are derived from museum records, but I assumed that the rock-dwelling reptiles of the Lower Colorado Valley, plus the gopher snake and Mojave rattlesnake, will be found in the core of Gran Desierto with further work; I eliminated "spillover species" in the

Figure 21.3. Characteristic desert valley environments in the Arizona Upland (above, trap at snake mark-recapture site in Valley of the Ajo) and Lower Colorado Valley (below, looking east up Mohawk Mountain bajada). Although many species occur in both environments, notably abundant at the Arizona Upland site are western diamondbacks, Sonoran coralsnakes, coachwhips, long-nosed snakes, tree lizards, and regal horned lizards, whereas Lower Colorado Valley floors support greater abundances of sidewinders, glossy snakes, long-tailed brush lizards, and desert horned lizards. The Mohawk Mountains upper bajada (across middle of lower picture) supports a western diamondback population in ironwood, palo verde, and saguaro within the arid desert. (Upper photo by S. S. Sartorius; lower photo by P. C. Rosen)

Lower Colorado Valley (saddled leaf-nosed snake and tiger rattlesnake) and Arizona Upland (western shovel-nosed snake and desert horned lizard); and included the ground snake in the Arizona Upland fauna.)

Figure 21.4 shows a surprising trend: reptile diversity increases rather modestly with increasing vegetation structure diversity and density until the rainforest is considered. Most striking of all, lizard diversity is nearly as high in the most barren, arid environments as it is in Arizona Upland and tropical dry forest. Lizards truly thrive in the aridity and heat (see the appendix), whereas snakes become much more diverse (and likely much more abundant) in the dense protective vegetation of the thornscrub and tropical forest. Even more

marked increases along this gradient are seen in amphibians and turtles, as expected for animals tied so directly to water and moisture, although the Central American tropics are not well endowed with turtle species.

Another feature of the true desert herpetofauna is its elevated diversity in the open flats, bajadas, and sands (13 snakes and 11 lizards), compared with arid desert mountains (9 snakes, 8 lizards). The valleys, with monotonous perennial vegetation and few bird species, are herpetofaunally rich. In the rockpiles there seem to be many plants relictual from wetter, cooler times but fewer such reptiles (the black-tailed rattlesnake, lyre snake, Gila monster, desert tortoise, and desert night lizard may be examples). This is a paradox:

TABLE 21.2. *Landscape structure of the Sonoran Desert lizard assemblage in two floristic provinces, in the dry borderlands of southwestern Arizona and northwestern Sonora.*

ECOLOGICAL TYPE	ARIZONA UPLAND		LOWER COLORADO VALLEY	
	VALLEY	MOUNTAIN	VALLEY	MOUNTAIN
LIZARDS				
1. Small arboreal insectivore	***Urosaurus ornatus***	***Urosaurus ornatus***	*Urosaurus graciosus*	
2. Small saxicolous / terrestrial insectivore	***Uta stansburiana***	*U. ornatus* (*Uta stansburiana*)	*Uta stansburiana*	***Uta stansburiana***
3. Large arboreal / saxicolous insectivore	***Sceloporus magister***	*Sceloporus clarkii*	***Sceloporus magister***	(*Sceloporus magister*)
4. Terrestrial runner, insectivore	***Callisaurus draconoides***	(*Holbrookia maculata*)	***Callisaurus draconoides***	—
5. Arenicolous omnivore	—	—	***Uma notata***	—
6. Terrestrial / saxicolous carnivore-insectivore	***Gambelia wislizenii***	***Crotaphytus nebrius***	***Gambelia wislizenii***	***Crotaphytus nebrius***
7. Armored terrestrial ant eater	***Phrynosoma solare***	(*Phrynosoma solare*)	***Phrynosoma platyrhinos***	—
8. Arenicolous armored terrestrial ant-eater	—	—	*Phrynosoma mcallii*	—
9. Large heat-loving herbivore	*Dipsosaurus dorsalis*	(*Sauromalus obesus*)	***Dipsosaurus dorsalis***	***Sauromalus obesus***
10. Active-foraging diurnal insectivore	*Cnemidophorus tigris*	*C. xanthonotus* (*C. tigris*) (*C. sonorae*)	*C. tigris*	(*C. tigris*)
11. Venomous nest predator	*Heloderma suspectum*	***Heloderma suspectum***	—	(*Heloderma suspectum*)
12. Nocturnal terrestrial insectivore	***Coleonyx variegatus***	***Coleonyx variegatus***	***Coleonyx variegatus***	*Coleonyx variegatus*
13. Nocturnal cover-dwelling insectivore	—	—	?.–	(*Xantusia vigilis*)
SNAKES				
1. Small fossorial arthropod eater	*Chilomeniscus cinctus* (*Sonora semiannulata*) (*Chionactis palarostris*)	*Chilomeniscus cinctus* *Tantilla hobartsmithi*	***Chionactis occipitalis*** (*Sonora semiannulata*) (*Chilomeniscus cinctus*)	? (*Sonora semiannulata*) ? (*Chionactis occipitalis*)
2. Small fossorial ant-termite eater	*Leptotyphlops humilis*	?.–	*Leptotyphlops humilis*	?.–
3. Semi-aquatic anuran eater	—	(*Thamnophis cyrtopsis*)	—	—
4. Medium mammal-lizard-eating racer	***Salvadora hexalepis***	***Salvadora hexalepis***	***Salvadora hexalepis***	***Salvadora hexalepis***
5. Large lizard-snake-eating racer	***Masticophis flagellum***	***Masticophis bilineatus***	***Masticophis flagellum***	—
6. Small nocturnal lizard-anuran eater	***Hypsiglena torquata***	*Hypsiglena torquata*	(*Hypsiglena torquata*)	(*Hypsiglena torquata*)
7. Medium lizard-mammal-eating constrictor	*Rhinocheilus lecontei*	*Trimorphodon biscutatus*	(*Rhinocheilus lecontei*)	*Trimorphodon biscutatus*
8. Medium mammal-lizard- eating constrictor	*Arizona elegans*	(*Charina trivirgata*)	*Arizona elegans*	*Charina trivirgata*
9. Small snake eater	*Micruroides euryxanthus*	*Micruroides euryxanthus*	—	—
10. Medium-large snake-mammal eater	*Lampropeltis getula*	*Lampropeltis getula*	?.–	?.–
11. Large mammal-bird egg-eating constrictor	*Pituophis catenifer*	*Pituophis catenifer*	*Pituophis catenifer*	? (*Pituophis catenifer*)
12. Small mammal-lizard-eating pit viper	*Crotalus cerastes*	*Crotalus tigris*	*Crotalus cerastes*	*Crotalus mitchellii*
13. Medium mammal-eating pit viper	*Crotalus scutulatus*	*Crotalus molossus*	*Crotalus scutulatus*	*Crotalus molossus*
14. Large mammal-eating pit viper	*Crotalus atrox*	(*Crotalus atrox*)	(*Crotalus atrox*)	?.–
15. Small lizard-egg eater	*Phyllorhynchus browni* *Phyllorhynchus decurtatus*	—	*Phyllorhynchus decurtatus*	—

Species in bold are abundant, while those in parentheses are uncommon or of regionally and locally variable occurrence.

vegetational flux has been rapid, yet reptile distributions have tended to be stable during the Wisconsin glacial cycle (Betancourt et al. 1990). Why should the animals display distributional stasis, and why should there be relatively fewer relict populations among them? Perhaps their shorter generation time makes them decline faster than plants (especially long-lived perennials), leaving fewer relicts; and perhaps climatic shifts are less likely to produce deterministic species replacements in animal populations, instead producing compensatory behavioral changes. If so, the sharp, apparently climate-related distributional boundary between Arizona Upland and true desert reptile assemblages (see below) would have a long, spatially static history despite climate flux and the resultant reshaping of the vegetation. Montane skinks, whipsnakes, alligator lizards, and other reptiles do penetrate both the Sonoran and Mojave deserts from woodland or grassland redoubts, and at least some of these were indeed more widespread during the Wisconsin glacial period. Perhaps further study will demonstrate that several of the snakes, and perhaps some lizards, are really just as relictual as certain plants, persisting by tapping moister crevices in the most mesic canyons and on high slopes.

How many species of reptiles in the hyperarid interior are spillovers from the Arizona Upland and the floodplains of the Gila and Colorado? Records from museums, my own notes, and Dale Turner et al. (1997) demonstrate that the long-nosed snake, Mojave rattlesnake, western diamondback, common kingsnake, and banded sand snake do occur at least 5 to 20 miles into the aridity and away from the Gila River. They are, however, so infrequently reported that they may depend on recolonization (or even immigration) from the great linear riverine oases. Deep within the arid desert of the Cabeza Prieta and the Goldwater Range there are no records of western diamondbacks, long-nosed snakes or kingsnakes— all conspicuous animals. For the great sand field of the Gran Desierto proper—west of the Pinacate lava—I have no records of any large rattlesnake, or long-nosed snake, or kingsnake, or even a gopher snake (appendix). These species are to be found in similar but less uniformly sandy environments near Puerto Peñasco and the Mohawk Dunes, but within the hyper-arid quarter they may be rare or possibly even absent.

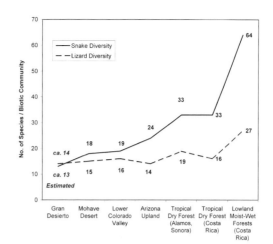

Figure 21.4. Changes in reptile diversity across biotic community type and over latitude, from the most arid part of North America to the lowland rainforests of Costa Rica. The Gran Desierto here includes only the core area—the sand field and rock piles west of the Pinacate lava. The Mojave Desert is as delineated in Brown & Lowe 1980. Species totals for the Lower Colorado Valley and Arizona Upland do not include the transitional region of overlap between these two faunas. For moist-wet forests in Costa Rica, the value is a mean per community type rather than a sum of all species in this broad forest category.

Is There a Unique Mojave Desert Herpetofauna?

The Mojave Desert might be viewed as simply a more elevated portion of the Sonoran Desert, one that is also transitional in some areas to Great Basin Desert. Although ephemeral plants show marked endemism in the Mojave, few other groups of organisms seem to (R. M. Turner 1994). From the driest part of the Lower Colorado Valley to the northeastern margin of the Mojave in southern Nevada (and eastern California; Banta 1962), where the Mojave grades into Great Basin Desert, herpetofaunal consistency is striking (Table 21.3). Most seeming "exceptions" in Table 21.3 are actually only local in nature. For example, the rosy boa is as much Mojavean as Sonoran; the obligate sand-dwelling fringe-toed lizards are distributed across the Gran Desierto, Lower Colorado Valley, and Mojave Desert, and the distribution of the Mojave fringe-toed lizard (*Uma scoparia*) crosses decisively into the Lower Colorado Valley province. Identifiably Sonoran elements in the Lower Colorado Valley include the banded sand snake, black-tailed rattlesnake, and western diamondback, but these only weakly penetrate the dry borderlands, and only the diamondback is in Sonoran Desert west of the Colorado River. Table 21.3 (and see Banta 1962) shows contact of montane and woodland species (those in Category III) with the Mojave Desert fauna (Greene and Luke 1996). Such contact is not seen in the dry borderlands, but analogous penetration of montane species into the Arizona Upland is found at Tucson and in La Paz County, Arizona.

Equally striking is the consistency of relative species abundances (Figures 21.5, 21.6; appendix).

TABLE 21.3. *Comparison of the reptile fauna of southern Nevada (Mojave and Great Basin elements) with that of dry borderlands deserts of southwestern Arizona and northwestern Sonora (Sonoran Desert).*

	LIZARDS		SNAKES	
	SW ARIZONA	S NEVADA	SW ARIZONA	S NEVADA
I. Taxa in common	*Uta stansburiana*	*Uta stansburiana*	*Chionactis occipitalis*	*Chionactis occipitalis*
	Cnemidophorus tigris	*Cnemidophorus tigris*	*Masticophis flagellum*	*Masticophis flagellum*
	Sceloporus magister	*Sceloporus magister*	*Salvadora hexalepis*	*Salvadora hexalepis*
	Sauromalus obesus	*Sauromalus obesus*	*Crotalus mitchellii*	*Crotalus mitchellii*
	Gambelia wislizenii	*Gambelia wislizenii*	*Crotalus cerastes*	*Crotalus cerastes*
	Callisaurus draconoides	*Callisaurus draconoides*	*Pituophis catenifer*	*Pituophis catenifer*
	Dipsosaurus dorsalis	(*Dipsosaurus dorsalis*)	*Arizona elegans*	*Arizona elegans*
	Phrynosoma platyrhinos	*Phrynosoma platyrhinos*	*Phyllorhynchus decurtatus*	*Phyllorhynchus decurtatus*
	Coleonyx variegatus	*Coleonyx variegatus*	(*Rhinocheilus lecontei*)	*Rhinocheilus lecontei*
	(*Xantusia vigilis*)	*Xantusia vigilis*	*Sonora semiannulata*	*Sonora semiannulata*
	Crotaphytus nebrius	*Crotaphytus bicinctores*	*Trimorphodon biscutatus*	(*Trimorphodon biscutatus*)
	Urosaurus graciosus	*Urosaurus graciosus*	*Crotalus scutulatus*	(*Crotalus scutulatus*)
	(*Heloderma suspectum*)	(*Heloderma suspectum*)	(*Hypsiglena torquata*)	(*Hypsiglena torquata*)
			Leptotyphlops humilis	*Leptotyphlops humilis*
			— ?	(*Lampropeltis getula*)
			— ?	(*Tantilla hobartsmithi*)
II. Uniquely Sonoran or uniquely Mojavean	*Uma notata*		(*Chilomeniscus cinctus*)	
	Phrynosoma mcallii		*Charina trivirgata*	
			(*Crotalus atrox*)	
			Crotalus molossus	
III. Great Basin and montane		*Sceloporus occidentalis*		*Masticophis taeniatus*
		Sceloporus graciosus		*Diadophis punctatus*
		Eumeces skiltonianus		

Sources for Nevada: Allred et al. 1963, Stebbins 2003, Tanner 1969, Tanner & Jorgensen 1963.

Note: Species prominent in these desert herpetofaunas are shown in boldface; rare or uncommon species are in parentheses.

The red-spotted toad has been vouchered from deep within the arid deserts of the dry borderlands and Mojave Desert, whereas Couch's spadefoot occurs as a rare species in the most arid parts of only the Sonoran Desert. In both deserts many other amphibians are found in or near the major waterways. The lizard fauna is strikingly similar from the Lower Colorado Valley through the heart of the Mojave Desert: it is ruled by chuckwallas, tiger whiptails, and side-blotched, collared, zebra-tailed, and desert horned lizards, with consistent appearances of western banded geckos, desert iguanas, and leopard, desert spiny, and long-tailed brush lizards. Sidewinders, speckled rattlesnakes, and western shovel-nosed snakes are the fully characteristic snake species of both deserts, and the abundances of other snake species correspond too closely to allow us to confidently identify any substantial differences. In the Mojave Desert, Lower Colorado Valley, and, separately, Gran Desierto, museum data suggest that lizards are relatively more abundant than in the Arizona Upland (appendix). Nearly a century ago Charles Lewis Camp wrote of the "Colorado Desert" (in a broad sense), perhaps justifiably, "Nowhere in the United States are lizards so numerous" (1916:505).

My answer to the question heading this section is "No!" From the herpetofaunal viewpoint, we can speak of a consistent, true desert fauna occupying the whole of the Lower Colorado Valley subdivision of the Sonoran Desert and the Mojave Desert. In this chapter I refer to this true desert assemblage as the Colorado-Mojave Desert herpetofauna. It is a unique herpetofaunal entity, and one with a definite Sonoran, as opposed to more northern, affinity. It has species-level endemism (three species of fringe-toed lizards, the flat-tailed horned lizard); and many species whose distribution and abundance center squarely over its combined extent (long-tailed brush lizard, chuckwalla, and desert iguana; western shovel-nosed snake, spotted leaf-nosed snake, sidewinder, and speckled rattlesnake). Ironically, the Mojave rattlesnake, the biggest rattler in Mojavean valleys, is not consistently or uniquely abundant there but rather in Arizona Upland and Desert Grassland valleys. Nor do subspecies (as tabulated from Stebbins 1966, 1985, 2003) bespeak a well-marked Mojave Desert herpetofauna: there are about four subspecies with boundaries nicely matching the Sonoran-Mojavean transition, although two of them then extend well into the Great Basin; many other subspecific boundaries occur well within either the Mojave or Sonoran Desert, or even correspond with the Colorado-Mojave Desert herpetofauna. More refined analysis at this subspecific level must await future phylogeographic and ecogeographic study.

Compared with the Sonoran Desert, the desert floor in the Mojave Desert is higher and perhaps less deeply heated and dried. The characteristic winter rains of the Mojave Desert infiltrate well into its sandy soils. The Sonoran heat is particularly potent in the Lower Colorado Valley (including especially Gran Desierto, southeastern California's "Colorado Desert," and the arid interior of the lower Gila Valley). Associated with some of these climatic differences are marked intraspecific ecological differences, notably in the desert tortoise and desert night lizard.

The desert tortoise in the Mojave Desert thrives on broad sandy valleys in soil burrows (Germano et al. 1994), whereas it is largely absent from such environments in the Lower Colorado Valley and Arizona Upland (except on the east desert margins, where it is also found on high [ca. 2,800–3,000 ft elevation] sandy-loamy Sonoran Desert Grassland bajadas). In the Mojave Desert (Luckenbach 1982), as in the Sonoran Desert, tortoises are most abundant between 2,000 and 3,000

ft; but in the Mojave, expansive valleys with friable soils are found at these elevations, whereas in the Sonoran Desert rocky environments predominate. However, this difference alone cannot explain the marked scarcity of tortoises on Sonoran bajadas and valley floors: locally in the Mojave Desert, tortoises reach moderate or high densities in low (1,100–1,500 ft elevation; see Luckenbach 1982), hot valleys that are probably fully as arid (Rowlands 1995) as some major, unoccupied valleys in the Sonoran Desert.

Among several hypotheses for why valley soils are largely unoccupied in the Sonoran Desert, the most plausible is McCord's (2002) suggestion that habitat partitioning with the recently (but prehistorically) extirpated Bolson tortoise (*G. flavomarginatus;* an occupant of valley soil burrows) in the Sonoran region may still be reflected in

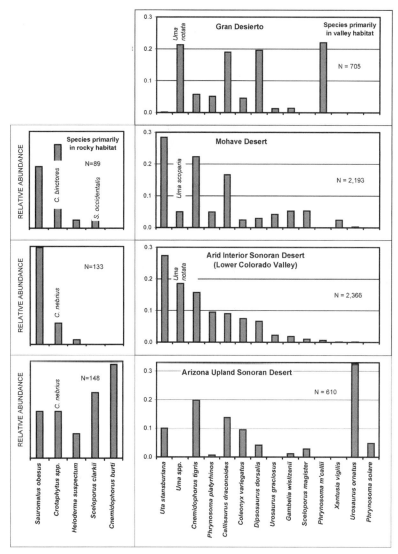

Figure 21.5. Relative abundance of lizards within the dry borderlands (based on museum locality data) and the Mojave Desert (sources as in Figure 21.6). Data from ecotones between Arizona Upland and arid interior desert are omitted. Sample sizes are number of data points for primarily valley (right column) or rock (left column) species. Large value for Uma *in the Lower Colorado Valley museum sample reflects known sampling bias.* Uma *and* Crotaphytus *are represented by sister taxa in the Sonoran and Mojave regions.*

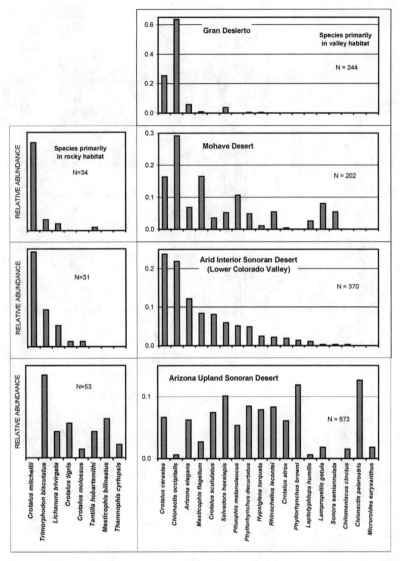

Figure 21.6. *Relative abundance of snakes within the dry borderlands (based on museum locality data) and the Mojave Desert (a composite based on localities and numerical species observations reported in Brown & Nagy 1995, Camp 1916, Linsdale 1940, Morafka 1996, Tanner & Jorgenson 1963). No data were available for rock-dwelling reptiles in Gran Desierto. Major river riparians and associated agricultural and adjoining desert areas are not included.*

genetically fixed habitat selection of the Sonoran tortoise. Ancient (ca. 5 million years) genetic differences between Mojave and Sonoran tortoises (Lamb & McLuckie 2002) are not inconsistent with this idea.

The desert floor in the Mojave is also, famously, home to abundant night lizards (Zweifel & Lowe 1966), most often under yucca (Joshua tree, Mojave yucca) debris, a phenomenon not reported for the Lower Colorado Valley. History seems a probable explanation for this (Robert Bezy, personal communication 2002), with the scanty relictual night lizard populations in the dry borderlands left behind with the disappearance of Joshua trees and waning of other Mojave conditions (see Van Devender, this volume). We don't know the ecological causes, however, which might involve subsurface temperature, predation, or

other biotic interactions. Aridity is as pronounced in parts of the Mojave as in arid parts of the Lower Colorado Valley, and predominates at elevations that, in the Sonoran Desert, support less arid Arizona Upland and Desert Grassland formations. True desert species don't occupy these elevated aspects of the Sonoran Desert, but in the drier Mojave they follow the aridity to equivalent elevations (e.g., shovel-nosed snake, sidewinder, and others).

The warmth, or more properly the infrequency of freezes, and the occurrence of summer rains in the Lower Colorado Valley subdivision have allowed Sonoran Desert plants such as ironwood and saguaro to persist (perhaps as contracting populations), if not really to flourish. At the same time, the attendant aridity has driven Mojavean floristic indicators out or into refugia (see Van Devender 1990 and this volume; Felger 2000). The Colorado-Mojave Desert herpetofauna also displays some evidence of similar Sonoran relictualization, especially in such large and characteristic Arizona Upland species as the Gila monster, desert tortoise, western diamondback, and black-tailed rattlesnake (see species accounts in annotated checklist). Our knowledge of distributions within the arid core remains insufficient, but these examples are likely matched by others involving species such as the common kingsnake and long-nosed snake. Many species have likely been decimated, since 5,000–8,000 years ago, by the postglacial aridity and heat.

Transitions between Colorado-Mojave and Arizona Upland Herpetofaunas

In contrast to herpetofaunal homogeneity within the Colorado-Mojave Desert, the transition to the Arizona Upland herpetofauna is marked and spatially consistent (Table 21.2; Figures 21.7, C21.8). It is clearest in the rocks; in valleys perhaps more varied, although this might reflect ambiguities in the defining boundaries of biotic communities. There is, of course, a transitional area, but the maps (see especially Brown & Lowe 1980) have sharp linear edges. For rocky areas, maps extend the Arizona Upland deep into the arid desert. Conversely, in valleys (much affected by grazing, which, presumably, has permitted creosotebush, bursages [*Ambrosia deltoidea, A. dumosa*], and burrow weed [*Isocoma tenuisecta*] to move up in elevation at the expense of damaged Desert Grassland) the mapped

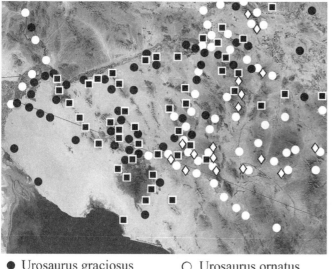

- ● Urosaurus graciosus
- ■ Sauromalus obesus
- ○ Urosaurus ornatus
- ◇ C. burti xanthonotus

- □ Crotalus mitchellii
- ◐ Charina trivirgata
- ■ Crotalus tigris
- ◆ Masticophis bilineatus

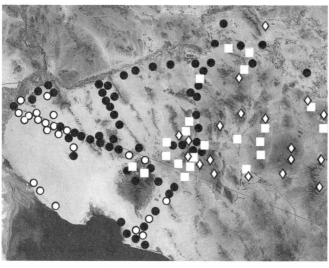
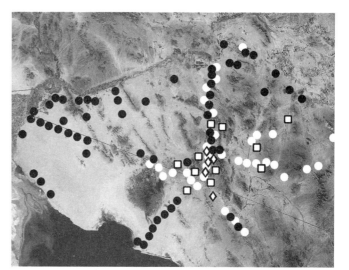

- ● Phrynosoma platyrhinos
- ○ Phrynosoma mcallii
- □ Phrynosoma solare
- ◇ Sceloporus clarkii

- ● Chionactis occipitalis
- ◇ Chionactis palarostris
- ○ Phyllorhynchus browni
- □ Micruroides euryxanthus

lines tend to reflect the extreme extent of Lower Colorado Valley floristic influences. The ambiguity is so great that R. M. Turner and Brown's (1994) climographs and tables include Arizona Upland–like sites (e.g., Santa Rosa, Arizona, and Pitiquito, Sonora) in the Lower Colorado Valley and even show one site (Tajitos, Sonora) in both! Transitional areas at higher elevations of the Lower Colorado Valley are occupied by a few characteristic subspecies such as the Tucson shovel-nosed snake (*Chionactis occipitalis klauberi*), Maricopa leaf-nosed snake (*Phyllorhynchus browni lucidus*), clouded leaf-nosed snake (*P. decurtatus nubilis*), and Sonoran sidewinder (*Crotalus cerastes cercobombus*).

In rocky desert the transition from true desert to thornscrub-like Arizona Upland involves seven or more species-pairs in concert. In valleys the tree lizard and regal horned lizard replace their congeners, and the western shovel-nosed snake drops from the herpetofauna (at about 2,100 ft elevation) on the cusps of this transition. Other species, such as the sidewinder and desert iguana, extend farther up into the mapped Arizona Upland, as does the chuckwalla: these extensions likely occur because such species face no congeners or closely equivalent species constraining them within most favorable habitat. Transitional desert-floor environments have the Colorado-Mojave Desert herpetofauna—with desert iguanas, desert horned

Figure 21.7.
Distributional records for 16 reptile species with range margins in the dry borderlands, based on museum locality records and verified unpublished observations. Each region in which a species occurs is represented, but not all records could be plotted at this scale.

lizards, long-tailed brush lizards, western shovel-nosed snakes, and sidewinders all present. However, they also contain a strong representation of Arizona Upland valley herpetofauna.

The precise nature of the transition from Colorado-Mojave Desert to Arizona Upland herpetofauna is somewhat beyond the geographic scope of this chapter, but some comment is needed. In the core of the Arizona Upland—in the Tohono O'odham Nation and along the Pinal Pioneer Parkway northwest of Oracle—baseline valley elevations rise toward 2,000 ft elevation and more; desert trees prevail, and even today, in ungrazed corners, perennial grasses are abundant. The herpetofauna there is distinctively that of the Arizona Upland: the spotted leaf-nosed snake goes through its subspecific transition; saddled leaf-nosed snakes and banded sand snakes become prominent; the sidewinder becomes uncommon; coral snakes appear; big rattlers (especially the diamondback) assume full dominance in valley snake assemblages; and king snakes and long-nosed snakes also become prominent.

Moving west and down in elevation, thornscrub-oriented snakes such as the diamondback and longnose dwindle rather than disappear, penetrating the Colorado-Mojave assemblage in the broad environs of the lower Gila and Colorado rivers. This pattern does not, however, invalidate the concept of a Colorado-Mojave Desert herpetofauna any more than penetration of grassland, thornscrub, and woodland species in the Santa Cruz River environs at Tucson (Ruthven 1907; Van Denburgh & Slevin 1913) invalidates the concept of an Arizona Upland herpetofauna.

Herpetofauna of the Great River Valleys in the Colorado Desert

The lower Colorado and Gila rivers originally contained a diverse riparian and aquatic amphibian and reptile assemblage, along with their unique native fish fauna. The waterways of the Southwest supported one of the world's outstanding desert river and wetland faunas. Eleven species of native fishes were recorded in the lower Gila and Colorado (Minckley 1973, 1999; Mueller & Marsh 2002), plus two more in Río Sonoyta, along with two garter snakes, one or two mud turtles, a leopard frog, and three toads (Woodhouse, Sonoran Desert, and Great Plains toads), which may have been regionally absent or rare but for the rivers.

This sums to a stream-dependent herpetofauna of up to eight species in the continent's deepest desert. In addition, two lizard species, the tree lizard and Clark's spiny lizard, occupied the region in the riparian corridor (the tree lizard still does), and two to four snakes (the western diamondback, common kingsnake, and perhaps the longnosed snake and ground snake) penetrate the most arid region, primarily along the perennial rivers and streams. The ground snake follows the formerly rich (now heavily damaged and farmed) rivers and valley flats with mesquite and grassland up into Phoenix, Avra Valley, and relict tobosa grasslands in Arizona Upland valleys, yet it is largely absent from most of the Arizona Upland. Thus the rivers may have added fourteen species to the dry borderlands assemblage. Today the most aquatic species are gone, and two non-native ranid frogs and a turtle have been added. Among the riparian-associated species, however, only the ground snake is centered in the lower basins; none are endemic; and all have much larger ranges and population centers elsewhere. Their disappearances in the lower basins are part of wider declines some of them have suffered.

Conclusion

This chapter presents an analysis and summary of the herpetology of the dry borderlands of southwestern Arizona and northwestern Sonora, encompassing the hottest, driest desert region of North America and its transition to the rich Arizona Upland province of the Sonoran Desert. It is based on my data and experience added to a survey of museum voucher localities and literature pertaining to the Sonoran and Mojave deserts in and surrounding this region. The dry borderlands supports a herpetofauna of 70 verified species, including 9 verified only from the big rivers.

The analysis highlights three major desert herpetological formations in the dry borderlands. (1) The Arizona Upland assemblage, thornscrub-associated and mostly to the east and north, is present in important part. It shows a marked transition to the true desert herpetofauna, which is represented by (2) the combined Lower Colorado Valley–Mojave Desert herpetofauna. This true desert herpetofauna, which is characteristic of the dry borderlands, contains (3) a distinctive sand-associated herpetofauna in its hyperthermic and hyper-arid portion, the Gran Desierto.

The Lower Colorado Valley herpetofauna is not markedly distinct from that of the Mojave Desert: the principal true desert species are centered over the combined area of these two recognized desert areas. This finding points toward a concept of the Colorado-Mojave Desert as a valid, arid entity, with a blazing subtropical core that in hot dry times drives its less tolerant species toward the periphery or out to their primary distributional centers. The dry borderlands area is essential to the survival of the biota most central to it—the true desert biota of North America's most arid region.

Acknowledgments

I thank the many museum curators who have generously supplied me with data and given permission to examine key specimens. By acronym (see Leviton et al. 1985), the museums are AMNH, ANSP, ASU, BYU, CAS, CM, FMNH, INHS, KU, LACM, LSU, MSB, MVZ, SDNHM, UAZ, UIMNH, UMMZ, USNM, and UTEP. Dale Turner and David Wake kindly examined and photographed specimens from questioned localities for me. I thank Harry Greene, Bill Broyles, and Richard Felger for reviewing the manuscript, and Richard Felger for clarifying some of the botanical and biogeographic points, for which, of course, I take final responsibility. Charles H. Lowe's knowledge and ideas have contributed strongly to my thinking, directly as well as indirectly through many others listed here, and are noted especially. In addition, I acknowledge Selso Villegas, Curt Mc-Casland, John Morgart, and Don Tiller, Cabeza Prieta National Wildlife Refuge, for support during this project; those who have participated in work at Río Sonoyta, including Israel Barba, Pepé Davila, Glen Knowles, Keno Larios, Juan Miranda, Rafaela Paredes Aguilar, Daren Riedle, and Jim Rorabaugh; colleagues who have given me a view of the Tohono O'odham lands, including Scott Bailey and Jefford Francisco; and the many who have assisted my work at Organ Pipe Cactus National Monument and contributed information over the years, especially Roy Averill-Murray, Randy Babb, James Barnett, Daniel Beck, Peter Bennett, Robert Bezy, George Bradley, Steve Booth, Dennis Caldwell, Charles Conner, Mark Daniels, Roger Eagan, Erik Enderson, Richard Felger, Steve Goldberg, Steve Hale, David Hall, Max Hensley, Peter Holm, Roy Johnson, Thomas R. Jones, Michael Kunzmann, David Lazaroff, Michael Lee, Charles A. (Cal) Lowe, Charles H. Lowe, Margaret Marshall, Brent Martin, Clay May, Robert McCord, Danny Mello, Bill Mikus, Wendell Minckley, Gary Nabhan, David Parizek, Julie Parizek, Ami Pate, William Peachy, Trevor Persons, Yar Petrysyzn, Lin Piest, Karen Reichhardt, Roger Repp, Jim Rorabaugh, Julia Rosen, Shawn Sartorius, Cecil Schwalbe, Harold Smith, Tim Tibbitts, Dale Turner, Tom Van Devender, Mercy Vaughn, Elizabeth Wirt, and John Wright.

CHAPTER 21 APPENDIX. *Numerical summary of museum records used in the analyses, with selected subtotals.*

TAXON	GRAN DESIERTO (CORE)	ARID INTERIOR DESERT	UPLAND-ARID TRANSITION	ARIZONA UPLAND	Σ (NON-RIVER/FLOODPLAIN)	BIG RIVER-ASSOCIATED AREAS	DRY BORDERS TOTAL	MOJAVE DESERT TAXA (INCLUDING COGNATE SPECIES)	MOJAVE DESERT COMPOSITE
AMPHIBIANS									
Ambystoma tigrinum	0	1	5	0	6	1	7		0
Bufo cognatus	0	1	103	69	173	210	383	*Bufo cognatus*	0.089
Bufo alvarius	0	3	50	44	97	83	180		0
Scaphiopus couchii	0	9	79	45	133	34	167		0.089
Bufo woodhousii	0	0	0	0	0	157	157	*Bufo woodhousii*	0.089
Bufo punctatus	0	31	26	52	109	6	115	*Bufo punctatus*	0.607
Rana berlandieri	0	0	2	0	2	49	51		0
Bufo retiformis	0	0	20	8	28	0	28	*Bufo microscaphus*	0.054
Spea multiplicata	0	0	4	5	9	2	11	*Spea* spp.	0.036
Rana yavapaiensis	0	0	0	0	0	11	11	*Rana pipiens* complex	0.089
Rana catesbeiana	0	0	1	0	1	4	5	*Rana catesbeiana*	0.036
Gastrophryne olivacea	0	0	4	1	5	0	5		0
Pternohyla fodiens	0	0	1	0	1	0	1		0
Total amphibian records:	0	45	295	224	564	557	1,121		71
Total amphibian species	0	5	11	7	11	10	13		7
TURTLES (NONMARINE)									
Apalone spinifera	0	0	0	0	0	28	28		0
Kinosternon sonoriense	0	0	1	12	13	11	24		0
Gopherus agassizii	0	1	5	1	7	2	9	*Gopherus agassizii*	1.000
Kinosternon flavescens	0	0	0	1	1	1	2		0
LIZARDS									
I. Primarily Valley Dwellers									
Uta stansburiana	1	648	136	61	846	305	1,151	*Uta stansburiana*	0.284
Cnemidophorus tigris	40	370	172	121	703	398	1,101	*Cnemidophorus tigris*	0.222
Callisaurus draconoides	134	213	112	84	543	317	860	*Callisaurus draconoides*	0.166
Uma notata	150	439	0	0	589	28	617	*Uma notata*	0.050
Dipsosaurus dorsalis	138	157	36	25	356	225	581	*Dipsosaurus dorsalis*	0.030
Coleonyx variegatus	32	177	63	58	330	72	402	*Coleonyx variegatus*	0.024
Urosaurus ornatus	0	2	52	199	253	199	452	*Urosaurus ornatus*	0.003
Urosaurus graciosus	9	52	25	0	86	62	148	*Urosaurus graciosus*	0.042

CHAPTER 21 APPENDIX (CONT'D). *Numerical summary of museum records used in the analyses, with selected subtotals.*

TAXON	GRAN DESIERTO (CORE)	ARID INTERIOR DESERT	UPLAND-ARID TRANSITION	ARIZONA UPLAND	Σ (NON-RIVER/FLOODPLAIN)	BIG RIVER-ASSOCIATED AREAS	DRY BORDERS TOTAL	MOJAVE DESERT TAXA (INCLUDING COGNATE SPECIES)	MOJAVE DESERT COMPOSITE
Sceloporus magister	0	24	50	17	91	100	191	*Sceloporus magister*	0.053
Phrynosoma platyrhinos	36	224	31	4	295	26	321	*Phrynosoma platyrhinos*	0.050
Phrynosoma mcallii	155	15	0	0	170	14	184	0	0
Phrynosoma solare	0	0	22	29	51	0	51	0	0
Gambelia wislizenii	10	43	13	7	73	13	86	*Gambelia wislizenii*	0.053
Xantusia vigilis	0	2	4	0	6	0	6	*Xantusia vigilis*	0.024
Valley subtotal	705	2,366	716	605	4,392	1,759	6,151		**2,193**
Valley species count	10	13	12	10	14	12	14		12
II. Primarily Rock Dwellers									
Sauromalus obesus	?	105	27	25	157	16	173	*Sauromalus obesus*	0.382
Cnemidophorus burti	0	0	15	50	65	0	65		0
Crotaphytus nebrius	?	23	12	25	60	5	65		0
Crotaphytus bicinctores	0	0	0	0	0	10	10	*Crotaphytus bicinctores*	0.519
Sceloporus clarkii	0	0	2	35	37	1	38	*Sceloporus occidentalis*	0.050
Heloderma suspectum	0	5	8	13	26	3	29	*Heloderma suspectum*	0.050
SNAKES (NONMARINE)									
I. Primarily Valley Dwellers									
Crotalus cerastes	62	88	85	45	280	132	412	*Crotalus cerastes*	0.163
Chionactis occipitalis	155	81	56	4	296	50	346	*Chionactis occipitalis*	0.292
Arizona elegans	14	45	33	42	134	60	194	*Arizona elegans*	0.069
Phyllorhynchus decurtatus	1	18	80	57	156	28	184	*Phyllorhynchus decurtatus*	0.049
Crotalus scutulatus	0	30	36	50	116	55	171	*Crotalus scutulatus*	0.036
Pituophis catenifer	0	19	21	36	76	88	164	*Pituophis catenifer*	0.106
Rhinocheilus lecontei	0	8	26	56	90	63	153	*Rhinocheilus lecontei*	0.054
Salvadora hexalepis	9	22	25	68	124	14	138	*Salvadora hexalepis*	0.052
Crotalus atrox	0	7	19	41	67	58	125	*Crotalus atrox*	0.004
Masticophis flagellum	2	31	22	18	73	50	123	*Masticophis flagellum*	0.165
Phyllorhynchus browni	0	5	25	80	110	0	110	0	0
Hypsiglena torquata	1	9	34	53	97	6	103	*Hypsiglena torquata*	0.010
Chionactis palarostris	0	0	3	85	88	0	88	0	0
Lampropeltis getula	0	1	6	12	19	65	84	*Lampropeltis getula*	0.080

CHAPTER 21 APPENDIX (CONT'D). *Numerical summary of museum records used in the analyses, with selected subtotals.*

TAXON	GRAN DESIERTO (CORE)	ARID INTERIOR DESERT	UPLAND-ARID TRANSITION	ARIZONA UPLAND	Σ (NON-RIVER/ FLOODPLAIN)	BIG RIVER-ASSOCIATED AREAS	DRY BORDERS TOTAL	MOJAVE DESERT TAXA (INCLUDING COGNATE SPECIES)	MOJAVE DESERT COMPOSITE
Sonora semiannulata	0	1	1	0	2	31	33	*Sonora semiannulata*	0.054
Chilomeniscus cinctus	0	1	11	10	22	5	27		0
Leptotyphlops humilis	0	4	3	4	11	16	27	*Leptotyphlops humilis*	0.025
Microroides euryxanthus	0	0	4	12	16	0	16		0
Valley subtotal	244	370	490	673	1,777	721	2,498		202
Valley species count	7	16	18	17	18	15	18		14
II. Primarily Rock Dwellers									
Trimorphodon biscutatus	?	7	13	19	39	1	40	*Trimorphodon biscutatus*	0.102
Crotalus mitchellii	?	18	11	0	29	4	33	*Crotalus mitchellii*	0.806
Crotalus tigris	0	1	14	8	23	0	23		0
Masticophis bilineatus	0	0	8	9	17	0	17		0
Charina trivirgata	?	4	6	6	16	0	16	*Charina trivirgata*	0.063
Tantilla hobartsmithi	0	0	1	6	7	5	12	*Tantilla hobartsmithi*	0.029
Crotalus molossus	?	1	5	2	8	1	9		0
III. Aquatic Snakes									
Thamnophis marcianus	0	0	0	0	0	45	45		0
Thamnophis cyrtopsis	0	0	0	3	3	0	3		0
Thamnophis eques	0	0	0	0	0	2	2		0
Total snake records	244	401	548	726	1,919	779	2,698		236
Total snake species	7	21	25	24	26	21	28		18
Total lizard records	705	2,499	780	753	4,737	1,794	6,531		2,282
Total lizard species	10	16	17	15	19	17	20		16
Ratio of snakes : lizards									
Individual records	0.35	0.16	0.70	0.96	0.41	0.43	0.41		0.10
Species	0.7	1.3	1.5	1.6	1.4	1.2	1.4		1.1

Note: The Mojave Desert relative abundance composite is from the literature (sources in Figure 21.6 caption) and includes only species recorded in available studies that list total observations by species. The Gran Desierto (Core) is defined as the great sand field west of the Pinacate lava. Arid Interior Desert thus includes areas transitional between the Gran Desierto (Core) and the herpetofauna outside the sand field. The Σ (sum) of non-river/floodplain records is the sum of the preceding four columns. Number of voucher records for marine reptiles (not shown here) can be found in the annotated checklist.

Annotated Checklist of the Herpetofauna of the Dry Borderlands

This checklist highlights distribution and habitat relationships within the dry borderlands for each species. First, the annotations should help readers identify significant observations, some already in their notes or photographic collections, particularly for undersampled areas. Second, the annotations highlight the transition between the Colorado-Mojave Desert herpetofauna and that of the Arizona Upland (Figures 21.7, C21.8).

Third, the annotations discuss the relationship of the herpetofauna to desert grasslands of Arizona Upland valley floors. This issue arose in the context of defining a characteristic valley floor environment for the Arizona Upland. Shreve's (1951) line between the Arizona Upland and Lower Colorado Valley leaves environments dominated by creosotebush and bursage extending deep into the Arizona Upland map, and even Brown and Lowe (1980) leave one with some difficulty defining a valley floor community for the Arizona Upland. Remaining stands of grass within the heart of the Arizona Upland (see photo in Lowe 1964:44) may be only recently relictual, a consequence of livestock grazing during the past 300 years. Emory's (1856–59) reports suggest widespread, quite severe overgrazing at an early date, in an area as remote as upper Vamori Wash. Today, in rare areas protected from grazing effects, an abundance and diversity of perennial grass and obvious fence-line contrasts (McAuliffe 1997) suggest a formerly wider occurrence of Sonoran Desert grasslands, often at baseline elevations around 2,000 ft, in areas that now may be lumped within Arizona Upland or mapped as Lower Colorado Valley Sonoran Desert. Thus some of the annotations are set within the context of a hypothesis that Arizona Upland valley floors significantly included desert grassland whereas those of the Colorado-Mojave Desert were (and are) short-stature desertscrub.

Also included here are miscellanea that may help orient the reader or that are not necessarily readily available in the literature. Voucher specimens document the species occurrence in the region, except where noted for marine species. Introduced species are marked with an asterisk (*), extirpated species by a cross (+), and the nine dangerously venomous species (8 snakes and 1 lizard) by the pound symbol (#).

CLASS AMPHIBIA – The Amphibians

ORDER ANURA – Frogs and Toads

FAMILY PELOBATIDAE – Spadefoot Toads

Couch's spadefoot – *Scaphiopus couchii*. The only museum records for this desert and desert grassland anuran in the interior deserts west of the Gila Bend–Ajo highway are from near Río Sonoyta and the Pinacates on Mexican Highway 2. However, breeding occurs at Las Playas near Pinta Sands (Laura Thompson-Olais, photo voucher; Curt McCasland, personal communication 2001) and near the Mohawk Dunes (Cecil Schwalbe, personal communication 1980), and likely in other playas within the arid interior. Specimens have been collected in the Gila River environs at Gila Bend, Aztec, Wellton, and Dome, but Vitt and Ohmart (1978) did not find it near the Colorado River. They refer to California specimens from the Lower Colorado Valley near Glamis (east base of Algodones Dunes) and at Chemehuevi Wash west of Lake Havasu. This is the quintessential desert amphibian, with an ability to reach metamorphosis in less than 10 days (Newman 1989), yet it appears to be absent from the Mojave Desert. Its presence with even the scant summer rains of the Lower Colorado Valley underlines the importance of the Sonoran summer rainy season for desert anurans.

Mexican spadefoot – *Spea* (formerly *Scaphiopus*) *multiplicata*. There are several locality records for this species in the dry borderlands, but the only ones likely to be accurate were vouchered by J. Fouquette southwest of Casa Grande, Pinal County. Juvenile *S. couchii* are easily mistaken for this species, and 1971 specimens for this species for Jose Juan Tank, CPNWR (MSB 31269–70), appear to be juvenile *S. couchii*.

FAMILY BUFONIDAE – Toads

Sonoran desert toad – *Bufo alvarius*. This toad occurs in desert canyons, charcos, and stock ponds, as well as along the rivers. I lack records for it in the arid interior west of Jose Juan Tank and Quitobaquito, although it has been collected at localities along the Gila and lower Colorado. It is also called the Colorado River toad.

Great Plains toad – *Bufo cognatus*. There is a single record for this species in the arid interior at 6 mi SW of Gila Bend, and it is also reported at Mohawk Dunes Playa (D. S. Turner et al. 1997). Both are sites where it may occur by virtue of proximity to the Gila River. It is not otherwise recorded (outside the big river environs) desert-ward of the Arizona Upland–Lower Colorado Valley transition.

Red-spotted toad – *Bufo punctatus*. Primarily occurring in rocky canyons and foothill arroyos throughout the Sonoran Desert region, this is the principal amphibian recorded in the arid interior of the Colorado-Mojave Desert. It is associated with tinajas.

Sonoran green toad – *Bufo retiformis*. This toad of the Arizona Upland, in current or former desert grassland, barely enters the Organ Pipe area in stock tanks it may have recently colonized. It is also found in or near the relict tobosa grassland of Vekol Valley (see Enderson & Bezy, this volume) and may be in Río Sonoyta. A presumably isolated population, possibly still extant, was found near San Xavier, near Tucson. Norm Scott collected a specimen at Jose Juan Tank, CPNWR (MSB 31268) in 1971, beyond its expected geographic range. I have seen only *S. couchii* and *B. alvarius* at the site (2000); however, introduced *Ambystoma tigrinum* were collected there in 1969, and this introduction could have inadvertently brought extralimital anurans. Alternatively, during the mid-1950s to early 1970s there were strong summer rains in the Arizona Upland (R. M. Turner et al. 2003:271), often arriving with a regularity like fireworks on the Fourth of July (Charles Lowe, personal communication 1989), possibly allowing this toad to extend its range over Growler Pass from the Valley of the Ajo.

Woodhouse toad – *Bufo woodhousii*. Not found in the desert proper or in the Arizona Upland desert grassland, this toad lives along perennial (and formerly perennial) rivers such as the Santa Cruz, Gila, and Colorado and in associated irrigation agriculture.

FAMILY HYLIDAE – Treefrogs

Burrowing treefrog – *Pternohyla fodiens*. Found in the former and relictual grasslands of the Arizona Upland on the Tohono O'odham Nation and (primarily) in subtropical scrub and woodland farther south, this remarkable frog was recently confirmed in Vekol Valley (Enderson & Bezy, this volume). It is also called the northern casque-headed frog.

FAMILY MICROHYLIDAE – Microhylid Frogs

Great Plains narrow-mouthed toad – *Gastrophryne olivacea*. Much like the burrowing treefrog and Sonoran green toad, this small frog is in current and former desert grasslands in and near the Arizona Upland, including in relict tobosa grassland of Vekol Valley. It is not rare in desert grassland in Altar Valley and encinal in the Pajarito Mountains, and it remains in isolated populations near the Santa Cruz River at Tucson and, presumably, San Xavier. It occurs at Lukeville (Sullivan et al. 1996) and near Sonoyta.

FAMILY RANIDAE – "True" Frogs

+Lowland leopard frog – *Rana yavapaiensis* (extirpated). Here is a prime example of the fate of native aquatic vertebrates in the Sonoran Desert region. This frog once supported lowland desert river populations of the Mexican garter snake, down to Yuma and possibly beyond; now both are extirpated.

*Rio Grande leopard frog – *Rana berlandieri* (introduced). Accidentally introduced into the Gila River and rapidly expanding into the Colorado River and the Phoenix region (Platz et al. 1990), this frog occupies areas formerly occupied by the lowland leopard frog. Why it succeeds where the native had failed is not well understood.

*American bullfrog – *Rana catesbeiana* (introduced). This is a harmful invader that has joined the almost exclusively non-native vertebrate fauna in perennial waters of the lower Gila and Colorado, where it can be moderately abundant (Clarkson & deVos 1986).

ORDER CAUDATA – Salamanders
FAMILY AMBYSTOMATIDAE – Mole Salamanders

*Tiger salamander – *Ambystoma tigrinum* (introduced). Spread as fish bait, this animal inevitably turns up in every region. Although perhaps not established within the dry borderlands, it has been recorded at Yuma, Puerto Peñasco, Jose Juan Tank, and on the Tohono O'odham Nation.

CLASS REPTILIA – The Reptiles
ORDER TESTUDINES – Turtles
FAMILY TESTUDINIDAE – Tortoises

Desert tortoise – *Gopherus agassizii*. Tortoises are abundant in rocky environments of the Arizona Upland but rare in this habitat in the Lower Colorado Valley. Records for the dry borderlands are very sparse, including a single specimen from the floor of MacDougal Crater collected by Wade Sherbrooke, observations of a live and a dead tortoise from there (Richard Felger, personal communication 2003), and dried scat found in the Sierra Pinta and Mohawk mountains (Peter Holm, personal communications 1997, 2001). In the eastern Mojave Desert they occur on rocky bajadas and slopes (Bury et al. 1994), probably because the summer rainfall there, as in the Sonoran Desert, permits them to survive outside the deep soil burrows that are more exclusively used elsewhere in the Mojave (e.g., Germano et al. 1994). Tortoises occur at low population densities even in the best habitat in and near the Lower Colorado Valley in Arizona (Averill-Murray et al. 2002). The dry borderlands, like the "Colorado Desert" in California and most arid parts of the Mojave Desert (Luckenbach 1982), are at best marginal for tortoises. Severe population collapses and mass die-offs have been reported during the past fifteen years at the transition between the Arizona Upland and Lower Colorado Valley, in the Maricopa, Silverbell, and possibly the Sawtooth mountains (Wirt & Holm 1997; Roger Repp, David Lazaroff, personal communication 2003). Heat and drought seem to be responsible for these die-offs, and they are possibly related to climate change.

FAMILY KINOSTERNIDAE – Mud and Musk Turtles

Yellow mud turtle – *Kinosternon flavescens arizonense* (not confirmed). An early record ("pre-1856") of this species, labeled "Camp Yuma," could be inaccurate

(Iverson 1978). A vouchered pair that loved and died for science at Quitobaquito (Smith & Hensley 1957) could reflect a release of animals collected in the former desert grasslands of the Tohono O'odham Nation. Yet it is possible this turtle was formerly more widespread than today in ephemeral waters of the Colorado and Sonoyta floodplains, and it also remains conceivable that the species could still occur there. I presume its original habitat comprised summer flood-filled lakes and scour holes associated with playas and major valley arroyos. East of the dry borderlands, it can still be found in the latter, although today it lives principally in stock ponds.

Sonoran mud turtle – *Kinosternon sonoriense.* A turtle of perennial or nearly perennial waters, this hardy species is at Quitovac, Quitobaquito, and Río Sonoyta, but it formerly inhabited the lower Gila and Colorado rivers. In fact, it was abundant there: six of Van Denburgh's (1922) Arizona localities for this species (23%) are from the dry borderlands region, and Edgar A. Mearns and others collected several specimens from the lower Gila River, from above Gila Bend to well below Wellton, between 1894 and 1934. The most recent plausible report for a native turtle in the lower river basins is a report of this species from 1 mi SW of Laguna Dam by Richard S. Funk (in Vitt & Ohmart 1978), though it is still to be sought, and its conservation would be a priority in the lower basins. A described subspecies, the Sonoyta mud turtle (*K. s. longifemorale),* lives in the Sonoyta basin and is a candidate for Endangered Species Act listing.

FAMILY CHELONIIDAE – Sea Turtles

Green turtle – *Chelonia mydas.* One museum record, from Colorado River below Hardy's River, documents the regional occurrence of this turtle, which remains an important part of the Gulf of California's marine ecosystem despite massive overexploitation (see Seminoff & Nichols this volume).

Loggerhead – *Caretta caretta.* No museum specimens exist for this species in the Alto Golfo region of the Gulf of California, but its presence not far to the south (Seminoff & Nichols, this volume) suggests a strong likelihood that individuals are present in the Alto Golfo on occasion.

Hawksbill turtle – *Eretmochelys imbricata.* Well known in the Gulf of California, and apparently in the Alto Golfo region (Seminoff & Nichols, this volume), but with no museum voucher records.

Olive ridley – *Lepidochelys olivacea.* Eleven museum vouchers include hatchlings that confirm nesting in at least two sites in the vicinity of Puerto Peñasco.

FAMILY DERMOCHELYIDAE – Leatherback Sea Turtle

Leatherback – *Dermochelys coriacea.* Well known in much of the Gulf of California (see Seminoff & Nichols, this volume), with a single voucher photo available for the Alto Golfo region (Richard Felger, personal communication 2004).

FAMILY TRIONYCHIDAE – Soft-shelled Turtles

*****Spiny softshell – *Apalone spinifera* (introduced, formerly in genus *Trionyx*).** Yet another example of an exotic succeeding in modified aquatic habitat where native species have failed, this species is moderately abundant in the lower Gila and Colorado.

ORDER SQUAMATA – Lizards and Snakes

SUBORDER SAURIA – Lizards

FAMILY HELODERMATIDAE – Beaded Lizards

#Gila monster – *Heloderma suspectum.* This large subtropical lizard lives primarily in the Arizona Upland and in the transition between Arizona Upland and Lower Colorado Valley, yet there are verified records from the Pinacate region and Tinajas Altas. I know of no other records for the arid interior and from no farther down the big river valleys than Gila Bend. Vitt and Ohmart (1978) found none near the Colorado River, although Van Denburgh (1922) and Stebbins (1985) refer to two old localities right along the river at Imperial Dam and La Paz (both above the Gila River confluence), and Lowe et al. (1986) imply that the species should be near San Luis in Mexico. These indications of a former river riparian population are not unbelievable; the lizard has also been found to the north, in the mountains of the northern East Mojave (Stebbins 2003).

FAMILY EUBLEPHARIDAE – Eyelidded Geckos

Western banded gecko – *Coleonyx variegatus.* This terrestrial gecko is abundant throughout all the desert formations of the dry borderlands, and especially abundant in museum records for the Lower Colorado Valley. It is widespread and abundant in the Gran Desierto. Individuals seen in parts of the arid interior and the Gran Desierto are pallid and, as older adults, purprescent, although they have not been described as a separate taxon.

FAMILY GEKKONIDAE – Geckos

*****Mediterranean gecko – *Hemidactylus turcicus* (introduced).** This is a plentiful species in cities, where it lives around houses, and is widespread in Yuma (Karen Reichhardt, Lin Piest photo vouchers, 2003). It is not reported to invade non-urban environments in the Sonoran Desert region.

FAMILY XANTUSIIDAE – Night Lizards

Desert night lizard – *Xantusia vigilis.* The quintessential Mojave Desert lizard, this species is known from a locality in Cabeza Prieta National Wildlife Refuge and may occur more widely. It is relictual in the dry borderlands, reflecting recent past environments with ameliorated thermal extremes and more winter rainfall (Van Devender 1990).

FAMILY TEIIDAE – Whiptails and Allies

Tiger whiptail – *Cnemidophorus (Aspidoscelis) tigris.* This is the common, widespread whiptail lizard of the North American desert, and it is plentiful from Sonoran Desert grasslands in valleys, down through the Gran Desierto, and in riparian and xeroriparian environments. Where the following species does not predominate, the tiger whiptail is also found, sometimes in abundance, on desert mountains. It is also called, less colorfully, the western whiptail.

Red-backed whiptail – *Cnemidophorus (Aspidoscelis) burti xanthonotus.* This medium-large, handsome lizard inhabits richly vegetated slopes and canyons throughout most of the Arizona Upland, ascending upward to productive habitat in montane Sonoran Desert grassland. It extends west to the summit of Agua Dulce Peak and is in the Sierra Cipriano southwest of Sonoyta (Ami Pate, personal communication 2002); its occurrence in the Pinacates (Cochran et al. 1990) has not been unequivocally demonstrated. Populations are isolated from one another and appear distinctive. Its young have much more numerous spots than those of the Sonoran spotted whiptail *(C. sonorae)*, with which they have been confused, and a slate-blue tail; these species are syntopic (living in the same place and same environment) in some eastern portions of the Arizona Upland.

FAMILY IGUANIDAE – Iguanas and Related Lizards

SUBFAMILY IGUANINAE - Iguanas

Desert iguana – *Dipsosaurus dorsalis.* The large herbivorous lizard of desert valleys, the iguana is most prominent in the Gran Desierto and Lower Colorado Valley and occurs in creosotebush-dominated flats that finger deeply into the Arizona Upland nearly to Tucson. It is also seen in modest numbers on desert tree-studded bajadas, sometimes including upper bajadas, in many parts of the Arizona Upland.

Common chuckwalla – *Sauromalus obesus* (or, in a still-debated name shuffle, *S. ater*). The large herbivorous lizard of rocky desert mountains, the chuck is most prominent in the Colorado-Mojave Desert; it may occur in mountains within the Gran Desierto, although these have not been well surveyed. The chuckwalla appears to be absent from much of the core of the Arizona Upland, but it extends well into it at Organ Pipe, in and south of Sonoran Desert NM, and in Ironwood Forest NM. Poachers, some of whom may severely damage the environment, are often interested in chuckwallas.

SUBFAMILY CROTAPHYTINAE – Collared and Leopard Lizards

Basin and Range collared lizard – *Crotaphytus bicinctores.* In the dry borderlands this modestly differentiated species is almost precisely separated from the next species by the Gila River. It is known to cross only at Sentinel, although an occurrence at Black Gap (north of Ajo) is suggested, and it is to be sought in Sonoran Desert NM (McGuire 1996).

Sonoran Desert collared lizard – *Crotaphytus nebrius.* This collared lizard can be regularly found on rock-and-boulder slopes in arid desert areas, where the side-blotched lizard, which it eats, is remarkably abundant. I have not found it away from rocky environments.

Long-nosed leopard lizard – *Gambelia wislizenii.* This is the other important lizard-eating lizard, the valley-dwelling crotaphytine. It is quite prominent in the arid deserts and has been identified as a key predator affecting populations of other lizards (F. B. Turner et al. 1982).

SUBFAMILY PHRYNOSOMATINAE – Other Iguanids

Zebra-tailed lizard – *Callisaurus draconoides.* This species is abundant throughout Sonoran Desert valleys, especially in arid regions, and is in lower parts of some canyons. Outside the dry borderlands it may be replaced in Arizona Upland desert canyons and on slopes by the lesser earless lizard *(Holbrookia maculata)* or greater earless lizard *(Cophosaurus texanus)*, but within the area covered here, there is no ecologically equivalent species in the desert mountains.

Flat-tailed horned lizard – *Phrynosoma mcallii.* This species is endemic to the Gran Desierto, where it apparently lives primarily on sandy flats rather than on major dunes. A much-discussed lizard, it has lost large portions of its habitat in the United States to housing developments and agriculture. It is a litigation subject as well as the object of conservation agreements (Foreman 1997) that aim to defang said litigation.

Desert horned lizard – *Phrynosoma platyrhinos.* Although this horned lizard penetrates the Gran Desierto stronghold of the preceding species and the Arizona

Upland redoubt of the succeeding one, its metropolis is in the Colorado-Mojave Desert, where it can be found in truly remarkable numbers, especially around sandy areas.

Regal horned lizard – *Phrynosoma solare.* This is the horned lizard of Arizona Upland and thornscrub formations in the Sonoran Desert region. It extends sparingly into dry forest at the southern end of its range (Schwalbe & Lowe 2000) and similarly into the Lower Colorado Valley at the dry northwestern edge of its existence, reaching its vanishing point, as many Arizona Upland floristic elements do, in the Pinacates and western portion of the Agua Dulce Mountains complex.

Clark spiny lizard – *Sceloporus clarkii.* Here is a reptile from the subtropical thornscrub and lower Madrean woodland that is moderately abundant on rock slopes in much (or all) of the Arizona Upland. Its known, desert-ward outposts are in western Organ Pipe and the Sand Tank Mountains, but it might be in the Agua Dulce Mountains and Pinacates. It also still persists along some major valley riparian corridors in the desert at Tucson, and there is a record at "St. John's Mission" (= Komatke) that demonstrates its persistence at least into recent times (1968) in an analogous setting in Gila Valley. Degradation of the Gila River may have eliminated it there, but it is still to be sought.

Desert spiny lizard – *Sceloporus magister.* This species' ecological relationship to Clark's spiny lizard parallels the macrohabitat partitioning between tiger and red-backed whiptails. Though primarily in arborescent desert, the desert spiny lizard is seen at packrat nests in creosotebush-dominated environments at least as far west as Organ Pipe. In the arid interior of the dry borderlands it is seen in surprising though moderate abundance along major desert washes; and it reaches mountain-base rock environments, but whether it uses rock slopes per se remains to be learned.

Colorado Desert fringe-toed lizard – *Uma notata.* Highly specialized, this species and its closely related congeners *U. scoparia* and *U. inornata* are sand dune endemics in the Gran Desierto and elsewhere in the Colorado-Mojave Desert. Remarkably, a fourth species, *U. exsul*, is in a localized region of the Chihuahuan Desert of north-central Mexico. *U. notata* is found on most sand dunes in the dry borderlands, including Pinta Sands (D. S. Turner & Schwalbe 1998) and dunes on both sides of the Mohawk Mountains (D. S. Turner & Schwalbe 1998; D. S. Turner et al. 1997). The Mohawk Dunes region populations have recently been elevated to the status of cryptic species, *Uma rufopunctata*, the Yuman Desert fringe-toed lizard (see Crother 2003).

Long-tailed brush lizard – *Urosaurus graciosus.* This is the "anole" of the desert, dwelling on branches and stems as well as desert tree trunks in the Colorado-Mojave Desert, including on sand dunes and in the Gran Desierto. Where it contacts the tree lizard in the easterly portions of its distribution, the tree lizard, which is less gracile, occupies larger trees and trunk surfaces (Vitt & Ohmart 1974, 1975; Vitt et al. 1981), as do juvenile desert spiny lizards in the dry borderlands; the brush lizard is often on smaller shrubs. In the dry borderlands I have not observed brush lizards in anything like the high abundances often achieved by the tree lizard. The brush lizard occurs along the Colorado and Gila rivers, but reportedly in relatively low numbers, primarily occupying diverse desert washes (Vitt & Ohmart 1978).

Tree lizard – *Urosaurus ornatus.* This lizard occurs from forest and woodland down to the edge of the Colorado-Mojave Desert in the Agua Dulce Mountains and at Gila Bend, thriving on rocky slopes and boulder-strewn flats and in riparian zones, as well as occupying xeroriparian and other desert tree environments within its range. In the arid parts of the dry borderlands it is replaced by the long-tailed brush lizard in desert valleys and by the side-blotched lizard on rocky slopes, with a transitional area in Valley of the Ajo. There are specimens as far west as Los Vidrios, and it might therefore be confirmed more widely in the Pinacates (see May 1973) and near Sierra Blanca (see Gonzáles-Romero et al. 1989). It occurs along the Colorado River north to Nevada but is restricted to a zone within 100 yd of the river (Vitt & Ohmart 1978). I have no records for the Gila River below Gila Bend, suggesting either that the Gila has been much less suitable than the Colorado (Hendrickson and Minckley 1985; Mueller & Marsh 2002; but see Emory 1848; Mearns 1907; Ohmart 1982) or that massive agricultural damage to the river bottom, along with limited sampling effort, has obscured its presence.

Side-blotched lizard – *Uta stansburiana.* Probably the most abundant herp in the Colorado-Mojave Desert, this species is, remarkably, all but absent (a single museum record) from the core of the Gran Desierto west of the Pinacate lava. The side-blotched lizard is also uncommon at Tucson, increasing with decreasing elevation within the Arizona Upland as primarily a valley-floor species. In the Lower Colorado Valley it also occupies rock slope and boulder field habitat, achieving impressive abundances and replacing the tree lizard in that habitat. This lizard ranges north to central Washington and south through the Sonoran and Chihuahuan deserts in Mexico (Stebbins 2003); here in the southern heat it is a late winter–early spring breeder (Asplund & Lowe 1964) and is found active in numbers year round (Charles Conner, personal communication 2000).

SUBORDER SERPENTES – Snakes

FAMILY LEPTOTYPHLOPIDAE – Slender Blind Snakes

Western blind snake – *Leptotyphlops humilis*. This small, subterranean species is much more abundant than its record indicates and is recorded from throughout the dry borderlands, though not yet definitively in the Gran Desierto core. I have no records demonstrating its occupancy of rocky slopes or canyons.

FAMILY BOIDAE – Boas

Rosy boa – *Charina trivirgata*. Until recently placed in its own genus, *Lichanura,* this rock slope and upper bajada dweller is part of an apparently ancient radiation of small boid snakes (the Erycinae; see Kluge 1993) found in western North America, Asia, and Africa. This one occurs deep within the driest desert, extending east into the margin of the Arizona Upland at Organ Pipe and Sonoran Desert NM. See Figure C21.9, which shows a Mexican rosy boa (*C. t. trivirgata).* Another subspecies, the desert rosy boa (*C. t. gracia)* also occurs in the dry borderlands, but subspecies distributional and genetic relationships are poorly known.

FAMILY COLUBRIDAE – Northern Colubrid Snakes

Glossy snake – *Arizona elegans*. A medium-sized constrictor that eats rodents and lizards, the glossy snake lives on sandy and loamy valley soils. Although its overall geographic distribution shows slightly more grassland association than the ecologically similar long-nosed snake, it is much more prominent than that species, and fully documented by specimens, in the most arid areas, including the Gran Desierto.

Banded sand snake – *Chilomeniscus cinctus*. Living more often in mesquite and acacia duff (dry organic debris and soil) than in pure sand, and not well documented from dunes in our area, this is a small, stout swimmer in loose dry substrata. It is primarily a creature of rich desertscrub and thornscrub, in some areas found high on rock slopes. Museum records confirm it in hyper-arid areas 52 mi ESE of San Luis, near Wellton, and Cholla Bay near Peñasco, and I found it along Mohawk Wash, at a productive valley-floor site deep within the arid interior desert.

Western shovel-nosed snake – *Chionactis occipitalis*. Another sand-swimmer, this is the most abundant snake in the Gran Desierto, and also very abundant in other parts of the Colorado-Mojave Desert, where it lives on dunes and sandy to loamy, friable valley-floor soils. It occurs in creosotebush flats and often in productive areas of open mesquite, with a named pattern class (the Tucson shovel-nosed snake, *C. o. klauberi)* on valley floors transitional to the Arizona Upland. How-

ever, it is largely or entirely absent from the Arizona Upland proper. Funk (1967) described a species of shovel-nosed snake, *C. saxatilis,* from high in the Gila Mountains near Fortuna Mine, but further specimens have yet to come to light, and Mardt et al. (2001) relegated it to the synonymy of the western shovel-nosed snake. See Figure C21.9.

Sonoran shovel-nosed snake – *Chionactis palarostris*. This brilliant little coralsnake mimic has been found principally on middle bajadas. It is known within a narrow band from Guaymas and Hermosillo (on the Plains of Sonora, which Shreve [1951] described as having up to 75% summer grass coverage and which D. E. Brown [1994] used to exemplify desertified Sonoran Savannah Grassland), and in Central Gulf Coast Sonoran desertscrub (with desert trees and organ pipe cactus), to a northern distributional terminus just .5 mi north of Organ Pipe Cactus NM. Its known range is on western, transitional margins of the Arizona Upland and not in the Lower Colorado Valley. Less specialized for sand burrowing than *C. occipitalis,* but slightly more so than the ground snake (*Sonora semiannulata,* another close relative), this snake is parapatric (occurring adjacent to but not overlapping with) to both. Other than on Highway 85 at Organ Pipe, it is rarely observed in the dry borderlands. It appears to be narrowly and patchily distributed in Sonora and might possibly be found east and northeast of Ajo or near the Quijotoa Mountains.

Common kingsnake – *Lampropeltis getula*. Common kingsnakes are often found around water, even in eastern North America, yet in the dry borderlands they occur at least into the fringe of the arid interior at San Cristobal Wash and Río Sonoyta and in the great river valleys. Perhaps they occur deep in the arid interior along the most productive arroyos, but I lack records there.

Sonoran whipsnake – *Masticophis bilineatus*. Well known in Madrean woodland and tropical deciduous forest, this snake was thought to occur as a relictual isolate in the desert at Alamo Canyon at Organ Pipe (see Hensley 1950). It is not: this is a widespread and often abundant species on rock slopes and in canyons of the Arizona Upland, from Tucson and the Agua Caliente Mountains to at least Quitobaquito, and in the Pinacate Mountains (William Peachy, photo voucher; Charles Conner, personal communication 2003). It is fast, and it operates at high temperatures and in steep environments (Parizek et al. 1995) not preferred by most investigators.

Coachwhip – *Masticophis flagellum*. This is the red racer and, at least until one reaches as far desert-ward as western Organ Pipe, sometimes the black racer. It is an active, abundant snake, especially in the Arizona Upland along arroyos, where it is a fearsome predator of lizards and snakes. It is also abundant in valley-floor, dune, and bajada environments in more arid parts of the region, ascending into the mouths of canyons. I have no records of it on rock slopes.

Saddled leaf-nosed snake – *Phyllorhynchus browni.* Here is a species of Arizona Upland, thornscrub, and tropical deciduous forest that extends into the edge of the Gran Desierto near Los Vidrios and co-occurs broadly with the next species in productive desert valleys that rise into Arizona Upland. The two leaf-nosed snakes are highly similar in ecology (Rosen et al. 1995), but this one ascends well into Sonoran Desert grasslands on high bajadas and is prominent in valley bottoms that were presumably once grown to tobosa and grama (see Thornber 1910, esp. 274–280 and 327, lines 10–13; and G. E. Smith 1910, esp. 97–100). It is also much more abundant than its congener on productive, cobbly-gravelly upper bajada desertscrub. It is not reported on the floodplains of the Colorado, Gila, or Santa Cruz rivers in the region under consideration. See Figure C21.10.

Spotted leaf-nosed snake – *Phyllorhynchus decurtatus.* This is the leaf-nosed snake of the Gran Desierto and Colorado-Mojave Desert. At Organ Pipe it ascends only sparingly above middle bajadas, yet there and at other low valley floors within the Arizona Upland it is remarkably abundant.

Gopher snake – *Pituophis catenifer.* Often diurnal as an adult, this large snake may seem more abundant in the Sonoran Desert than it really is: its frequent morning activity makes it highly visible to us. Many people recognize it as distinct from rattlesnakes, and it is able to survive in some urban and agricultural areas in the dry borderlands. It is well represented among snake specimens from the arid interiors of the dry borderlands, although I lack records from the Mohawk Dunes proper (D. S. Turner et al. 1997) or the central core of the Gran Desierto.

Long-nosed snake – *Rhinocheilus lecontei.* Records exist for Papago Tanks and both east and west of Los Vidrios, suggesting that this medium-small lizard and mammal-eater may occur deep in the arid desert interior, but I have no other records confirming this. It is primarily found in a diversity of less arid environments and is one of the most abundant snakes in the Arizona Upland, in valleys and up to the base of rock slopes.

Western patch-nosed snake – *Salvadora hexalepis* (sensu strictu). For a smallish racer-like snake, this species does many things surprisingly well, including feeding on small mammals (as well as lizards), being active on desert summer afternoons, and occurring in numbers through much of the Sonoran and Colorado-Mojave deserts, on rock slopes, bajadas, flats, and dunes, including in the sand-field core of the Gran Desierto.

They are not infrequently seen in the talons of red-tailed hawks and are preyed on by *Masticophis.*

Ground snake – *Sonora semiannulata.* Often viewed as a "trash snake" and used as fodder for captive coral-snakes, this attractive little beast is infrequently seen in arid south-central and southwestern Arizona. It occupies the lower, grassy oak woodland and hilly desert grassland, extending down the Santa Cruz Flats and parts of the Gila River to Yuma itself, with many records from both Yuma and the urbanized Phoenix area. Perhaps a key to understanding its distribution lies in the recent descent of oaks into grassland hills (Hastings & Turner 1965) and the conversion of arid valley grasslands to desertscrub. This species is found on desert floors that we may infer (Brown 1994), or occasionally demonstrate (McAuliffe 1997), to have originally been arid grasslands, prior to the heavy imprint of livestock. I suspect this species does not penetrate the arid interior but has persisted near the periphery of the once-great Gila floodplain, near the sites of Gila Bend, the Gila Mountains, and Kim (near Mohawk and the site of the now defunct Texas Hill bosque [see Brown et al. 1977]), where specimens have been obtained. It is unknown in the region of Organ Pipe but occupies relict and former tobosa grasslands to the northeast, thus segregating ecologically from its former congeners, which now constitute the genus *Chionactis.*

Southwestern black-headed snake – *Tantilla hobartsmithi.* A small species fond of eating centipedes, this snake is more prominent in higher, less xeric regions than in the dry borderlands. Its desert distribution is poorly known outside the Ajo Mountains, but I have museum records from the base of Oatman Mountain adjoining the Gila River floodplain west of Gila Bend; general, and possibly questionable, localities at "Yuma" and "near Sonoita"; and at 3,760 ft in the Sierra Estrella. Perhaps it is more widespread than the meager record indicates, in relatively productive desert mountain environments and on major river floodplains, which it is known to inhabit at Tucson, Phoenix, and Florence.

Lyre snake – *Trimorphodon biscutatus.* This species, which lives from Costa Rica to southern Utah, seemed rare in the desert at Organ Pipe during 1987–92; in succeeding wet years individuals moved away from rock slopes, crossing paved roads where we readily found them in numbers. Numerous museum records from the arid rock slopes make it clear that this primarily dry tropical species is widespread and not rare in its habitat deep within North America's most severe desert.

FAMILY XENODONTIDAE – Neotropical Colubrids

Night snake – *Hypsiglena torquata.* This small, *Uta*-eating, undercover diurnal ambush hunter (Rodríguez-

Robles et al. 1999) is found active and crawling almost exclusively at night, and often very late at night. It occurs from southwestern Mexico to extreme southwestern Canada, and in Arizona even in wooded environments above 6,400 ft (Lowe 1964). It is most abundant in the desert, including Arizona Upland and the most arid interiors of the dry borderlands. I have a museum record for "summit of the Gila Mountains" but no other records for it from rock slopes.

FAMILY NATRICIDAE – Northern Aquatic Snakes

Black-necked garter snake – *Thamnophis cyrtopsis.* In the dry borderlands this species is known only from the Ajo Mountains, where it lives around tinajas with red-spotted and Sonoran Desert toads and, presumably, feeds on lizards when anurans are unavailable. It is apparently isolated from nearest populations in the Baboquivari and South Comobabi mountains and has not been recorded at Río Sonoyta.

+Mexican garter snake – *Thamnophis eques* (extirpated). This was the water snake of lowland desert rivers, once occurring along much of the lower Colorado River (see de Queiroz & Smith 1996) and presumably along the Gila, but it has long since disappeared. There are voucher records from Yuma in 1889 and 1890 and near old Fort Mohave in 1904 and 1911. It suffered under the various assaults of habitat desiccation and modification and the introduction of predatory and competing species (Rosen & Schwalbe 2002). Mearns obtained only *T. marcianus,* five of them, at Yuma in 1894: the decline of *T. eques* could conceivably have been already under way in areas convenient to sample.

Checkered garter snake – *Thamnophis marcianus.* Prior to Mearns in 1894 only one checkered garter snake specimen had come from near Yuma. This species persists better under our assault on the environment than does the Mexican garter snake. Although it still occurs in the Yuma area, as well as in other river-associated agricultural zones from Tucson on downstream, it is apparently not common (Vitt & Ohmart 1978). It is less strictly aquatic than the Mexican garter snake, more apt to exploit summer-breeding toads and frogs in temporary waters, and thus better at avoiding introduced species that predominate in perennial waters.

FAMILY ELAPIDAE – Cobras and Their Relatives

#Sonoran coralsnake – *Micruroides euryxanthus.* This attractive and somewhat dangerous small coralsnake occasionally reaches 30 inches in length and is commonly 20–24 inches long. It occurs in the Arizona Upland, extending west to the Agua Dulce Mountains. It is found in canyons and on productive bajadas and can be surprisingly abundant, considering it is a secretive animal that primarily eats relatively rare prey (other snakes). I have no coralsnake records from the major riverine floodplains that penetrate the Colorado-Mojave Desert.

#Yellow-bellied seasnake – *Pelamis platurus.* I have two museum records of this lone New World seasnake species for the Gulf of California, both from near Puerto Peñasco. The species is well known among the coast-dwelling Seris (Felger & Moser 1985; Nabhan 2003). Though not an aggressive animal, this seasnake has a deadly venom. It is also called pelagic seasnake.

FAMILY VIPERIDAE – Vipers

#Western diamondback rattlesnake – *Crotalus atrox.* Wide-ranging, abundant, and conspicuous, this is the dominant snake predator on rodents in much of the Sonoran Desert (Rosen 2000). It occurs on Arizona Upland bajadas and in canyon mouths, as well as on productive valley floors, including those transitional between the Lower Colorado Valley and Arizona Upland. However, it only barely enters the Mojave Desert and is the only reptile species with a range margin closely approximating the Sonoran-Mojave desert line. The western diamondback is abundant, and often large, along the major riverine corridors but is not well documented within the arid interior of the dry borderlands. Museum records verify it only to the west end of the Agua Dulce Mountains, near Papago Well. Elsewhere outside the Gila River floodplain environs I have records only from the bajada between the Mohawk Dunes and Mohawk Mountains (and see D. S. Turner et al. 1997) and at the south end of the Mohawk Mountains bajada (D. S. Turner, personal communication 2003). It is recorded at Puerto Peñasco and 9 mi northeast in outlying parts of the Gran Desierto, where mesquite-capped dune hummocks (see Lowe 1964:29) may support it, as they do in arid California (Lowe, personal communication 1992, and unpublished field notes 1938). It may also occur in the environs of the Pinacate and Cabeza Prieta mountains, but I lack confirming records or reports. Its use of desert trees and association with productive desert woodlands may explain its limited occurrence in the dry borderlands and its absence from the Mojave Desert.

#Sidewinder – *Crotalus cerastes.* This is the preeminent snake of valleys in the Colorado-Mojave Desert, yielding this distinction in numbers but perhaps not biomass to the western shovel-nosed snake in the Gran Desierto. It is especially abundant around sandy flats and dunes but also may be prominent on loamy, richly grown bajadas in the lower valleys of the Arizona Upland proper. In the Arizona Upland it often avoids desert washes, which are heavily used by most other snake species, including the coachwhip (Rosen 2000), a dangerous predator of small rattlesnakes (see Secor 1994). It is abundant around Yuma and in the arid environs of the Gila River.

#**Speckled rattlesnake – *Crotalus mitchellii*.** This is the preeminent snake of rock slopes in the Colorado-Mojave Desert, probably occurring in abundance in every major mountainous area from the Maricopas and Growlers on down throughout the Lower Colorado Valley. (Sierra del Rosario, in the Gran Desierto, has not been adequately sampled for this or other rock-dwelling reptiles.) Its background-matching proclivities and color polymorphism often make this a strikingly or even shockingly beautiful animal.

#**Black-tailed rattlesnake – *Crotalus molossus*.** Often associated with mesic Madrean and riparian environments, this snake has been found in rocky places throughout the Arizona Upland and, surprisingly, with modest consistency in the arid ranges of the Lower Colorado Valley. I have museum records for the western Agua Dulce Mountains and Gila Mountains; and I nearly stepped on one in Cabeza Prieta Tanks Canyon in the dark, my film yielding up an image of the critical rear half of the snake. It frequently delights mammalogists looking for bats in mine tunnels, but its ecology in the arid desert has not been reported.

#**Mojave rattlesnake – *Crotalus scutulatus*.** Based on its name, one imagines the arid valleys of the Colorado-Mojave Desert to be crawling with this animal. It does occur, but its abundance does not approach the sidewinder's. Although I have no records from the core of the Gran Desierto, it is reasonably abundant on and near the Mohawk Dunes (D. S. Turner et al. 1997). Records from the arid interior are notably few compared with the numbers from valleys throughout the Arizona Upland, the transition to the Colorado-Mojave Desert, and in Sonoran and Chihuahuan desert grasslands. It seems to be more abundant in the environs of the lower Gila River, and less so near Yuma and lower the Colorado River, than the diamondback (see also Vitt & Ohmart 1978).

#**Tiger rattlesnake – *Crotalus tigris*.** This is the preeminent rattlesnake of rock slopes in the Arizona Upland, probably occurring in abundance in every major mountainous area from the Agua Dulces, Maricopas, and Growlers on up into the palo verde–saguaro and desert grasslands just east of Tucson. This is yet another Arizona Upland and thornscrub reptile that is absent from the Colorado-Mojave Desert past an observed terminus in the Agua Dulce Mountains and near Los Vidrios. See Figure C21.10.

Twenty-Two

Amphibians of Vekol Valley

Erik F. Enderson and Robert L. Bezy

I t's the kind of place you can get stuck in for days—vast and remote, harsh and mysterious—a place where even the heartiest can become queasy. And although today a few reminders of civilization can be seen, there still remains a sense of total isolation when you are within its confines. It is Vekol Valley, an untamed, unique, bizarre, and ecologically rich enclave of Sonoran Desert. It is the uniqueness of the Vekol that lured us, specifically, one frog—one toad, to be exact.

We were drawn into the valley by an animal known as *Bufo debilis* (the green toad). This amphibian occurs throughout the Chihuahuan Desert from northern Mexico through Texas and New Mexico to southeastern Arizona. Sometimes considered a Chihuahuan indicator species, in Arizona it thrives in the semiarid grasslands of the state's southeast corner and had not been found west of the upper San Pedro Valley. That changed, however, in 1983 when three BLM biologists reported the surprising occurrence of *B. debilis* in the Vekol together with its nearest relative, *Bufo retiformis* (the Sonoran green toad; Jones et al. 1983).

The Vekol Valley lies well within the Sonoran Desert with luxuriant Arizona Upland Desert on the upper bajadas and stands of creosotebush (*Larrea divaricata*) dominating the lower slopes. The latter are mapped as Lower Colorado Desert, the hottest, driest of the North American deserts, where highs may reach 50°C (120°F) and some years rain does not reach the ground, not exactly where one would expect to find *Bufo debilis*. But the Vekol holds a wild card. In its southern reaches there exists today the remnant of what once may have been an expansive and spectacular tobosa grassland community. It is this same grassland community that supports *Bufo debilis* in the Chihuahuan Desert regions to the east. We wondered if the green toad, like the tobosa grassland and antelope jack rabbits (*Lepus alleni)* we had observed

in the Vekol, may be a relict that has been isolated in the Sonoran Desert since wetter times prevailed perhaps over 10,000 years ago (Van Devender 1990, this volume). The question intrigued us, and in the summer of 2000 the time seemed right to investigate.

What ensued were three summers of axle-grinding, tire-spinning muddy roads and endless nights sloshing through the sloughs of rain-hydrated cow excrement, fending off ravenous mosquitoes, and crawling through some of the densest mesquite bosques in the Southwest. The nights yielded adventure, surprise, and sometimes disappointment.

Doppler-mania

Ominous red-centered masses ringed with yellow and green slowly develop in the late afternoon over Sonora's rugged Sierra Madre Occidental and begin moving north. The monsoon had arrived, and bright Doppler radar images were again lighting up our favorite online weather maps. We watched and waited, sometimes for the entire night. It's like a card game in which you evaluate your chances every fifteen minutes as a new image unfolds on your screen. Some nights the colorful masses appeared to be right on target, sweeping slowly northwest, their size and intensity growing as they approached the Vekol, only to burst and whither away when they hit what we estimated to be the position of Table Top Mountain. Whether any rain may have spilled over into the Vekol was a judgment call. In desperation we sometimes decided to head out on the tiring 99-mile (160-km) excursion just to verify that the cells did not reach the Vekol. On more than one occasion large rain-filled puddles and the smell of wet creosotebush greeted us as we passed north of Table Top on the highway, only to find parchment–like conditions as we dropped into the Vekol.

338

Eventually, our persistence paid off and the torrential summer rains struck the valley, bringing with them an amphibian breeding frenzy, the likes of which we had not previously seen or heard outside the tropics. The normal nocturnal silence was replaced by the calls of thousands, perhaps tens of thousands, of vocalizing frogs. Some nights their numbers were so great, it was difficult to avoid stepping on them. The once-dry pools and ponds were now filled to the rim. Mesquite trees stood like the giant cypress trees in the bayous of the Southeast, with 2 feet (0.6 m) of water extending up the trunks. The ponds were soon to be bursting with tadpoles. A week would pass, and the tadpoles will have metamorphosed into toadlets, so small they fit into the cracks of drying mud, protecting their porous skin from the relentless desert sun. Come nightfall, those same cracks serve as a hub to the new community bustling with nocturnal activity.

It all sounds so pleasant—nature at harmony with itself, sharing its wonders with the eager biologists. But don't be fooled. The thorny Vekol is not a gracious host, and many of our trips were full of all manner of pain and anguish, cruel and unusual punishment.

Follow That Call

During our anuran (frogs and toads) surveys in the valley we use a common technique to locate our subjects. It involves driving short intervals, stopping the vehicle, silencing the engine, and listening for a frog chorus. When the time and conditions are right, anurans can be heard vocalizing from great distances. Using our ears to home in, we would set off on foot to locate the breeding aggregations, which, more often than not, were buried deep within the thorny armor of Vekol's immense mesquite bosque.

We left a glowing flashlight on the roof of the truck as we headed out into the darkness with our headlamps, camera, tape recorder, and high hopes. We crossed the open grassland, following the frog vocalizations arising somewhere deep in the mesquite grove dead ahead. At first the young mesquites were just shrubs, scarcely 9 feet (3 m) tall and widely scattered across the open terrain. As the chorus grew louder, the mesquites became large trees with interlocking branches. After eons of evolution, it is difficult to forsake our noble upright posture and return to our hands and knees—like

Figure 22.1. Wet season. (Photo by Erik F. Enderson)

"animals" or infants. But what alternative is there when the branches become unbending and the thorns have ripped your clothes and gouged your arms and face? It's really a lot easier to make progress below the mesquite branches, crawling along with the harvester ants over the cow pies, at eye level with the occasional Mohave rattlesnake (*Crotalus scutulatus*) out on its nightly search for a packrat.

The bosque crawl was particularly grueling that night. At each pause the chorus seemed just a few meters ahead, like a mountain peak that keeps receding as you climb. We went on, placing faith in our standard creed—"The mesquite is thickest just before you reach the levee"—and eventually we burst free, staggering up the bank on our feet at last. To our utter disappointment, there on the other side was a sea of inflated vocal sacs of the odious *Bufo cognatus* (Great Plains toad) floating in the tank. From the onset of the long trek we had recognized that the chorus was composed largely of these ubiquitous, obnoxious, deafening toads, but we wanted to make sure that their din was not drowning out the calls of any other species.

Having satisfied ourselves that only *Bufo cognatus* and a few *B. alvarius* (Sonoran Desert toad) were present in the tank, we faced the depressing prospect of the return crawl. In a desperate attempt to avoid the mesquite thicket, we explored the full length of levee, but nowhere around the enormous horseshoe-shaped structure did the bosque appear any more penetrable. We returned to our original point on the bank and began the long crawl out.

Soon after, we heard it. At first it sounded like a hiss—maybe that of a gopher snake (*Pituophis*

THE DESERT *AMPHIBIANS OF VEKOL VALLEY* 339

Figure 22.2. Tobosa plain, Vekol Valley. (Photo by Erik F. Enderson)

catenifer) intimidating a potential predator. The sound seemed to come from all directions. Pausing in mid-crawl, we turned off our headlamps and listened intently—nothing but silence. We switched the lights back on, and the hiss resumed. As we crouched, the noise seemed to grow louder, now only a few feet away. We scanned the ground around us and saw nothing that could explain the ominous sound. Finally, we shined the beam up into the trees and saw it—a massive, hissing swarm of honey bees on the mesquite just above our heads. Carefully and silently, we turned off the lights and slowly crawled away. We were unsure whether or not the bees in the Vekol were "Africanized," but the thought of trying to escape a swarm by crashing through the dense thorny mesquite tangle was not reassuring. Had the swarm turned defensive, our chances of escape would have been slim.

The lantern on the hood of the truck was very dim when we finally reached the road after 1 a.m. From then on we tried to avoid crawling through the mesquite. But it was impossible; anurans are integral members of the bosque community in the Vekol.

The Levees

Amazing, complex, industrious, and just plain bizarre. These are the adjectives that come to mind when trying to describe the levees that now constitute the Vekol Wash. The construction of earthen dams to collect and retain water for cattle is a centuries-old practice in the Southwest, but the levees in the Vekol are truly remarkable in size and complexity. It would be interesting to have the opportunity to hear a resident rancher's perspective on the valley and particularly the history of the complex levees, but on none of our trips to the Vekol have we ever encountered another human being. The history behind these industrious constructions remains a story to be told by others.

The wash, as it still appears on maps, transects the valley from south to north and long ago emptied into the Gila River. Today the wash flows only during the most torrential storms, one of which we observed the night of 6 July 2001. This is largely due to the labyrinth of about eight levee-formed tanks that capture most of the rainfall and its runoff. The levees themselves are situated in the wash and are formed by long rows of earth approximately 4–8 feet (1.5–2.5 m) high, and some extend and bend to over 500 feet (150 m) long. Each creates large, long-standing pools, and our observations on 24 June 2001 indicate that at least one of the tanks is likely a semi-permanent water source. However, in June 2002, one of the driest years on record, we found the tank dry. The ecological effects of these levees have not been studied. Our casual observations suggest that they have likely had a major impact on the valley. There are several areas adjacent to the levees (and clearly outside the wash and associated impoundments) that are virtually devoid of vegetation. Although these may be the result of overgrazing of the tobosa grassland, in places it appears as if the topsoil might have been scraped off to form the levees.

The levees, tanks, and associated heavy grazing have very likely been a major factor in converting the grassland to mesquite bosques (see Turner et al. 2003). Because the levees usually prevent Vekol Wash from flowing, the surrounding floodplain has expanded to create a mesquite bosque of extraordinary size and density. What impact this may have had on the anurans is difficult to determine. We conjecture that the presence of permanent to near-permanent tanks has increased the densities of the Great Plains toad *(Bufo cognatus)* and Sonoran Desert toad *(Bufo alvarius)*, species that are known to breed independently of rainfall, particularly in the late spring and early summer. The abundance in the Vekol of *Gastrophryne olivacea* and *Pternohyla fodiens,* two anuran species found in the Sinaloan thornscrub, may also be related to the extensive mesquite bosques resulting from the levees.

TABLE 22.1. *Anuran species in the Vekol Valley.*

Bufo alvarius	Sonoran Desert toad
Bufo cognatus	Great Plains toad
Bufo debilis (?)	Green toad
Bufo punctatus	Red-spotted toad
Bufo retiformis	Sonoran green toad
Gastrophryne olivacea	Great Plains narrowmouth toad
Pternohyla fodiens	Lowland burrowing treefrog
Scaphiopus couchii	Couch's spadefoot

Note: (?) indicates a species reported from previous works but not observed by the authors.

The Anurans

We have documented eight species of frogs and toads in the Vekol Valley (Table 22.1). Although this anuran fauna is not overly rich in terms of species diversity, it includes several amphibians that are biogeographically quite remarkable. Southern Arizona is home to a number species of amphibians and reptiles whose heartland lies in the Neotropics. While some of these species occur in the lowlands of tropical Mexico, at the latitude of Arizona they are largely restricted to high elevations, where relictual populations persist in the Madrean Archipelago due to the presence of monsoonal moisture combined with moderate summer temperatures. Surprisingly, three species of Neotropical frogs that extend into southern Arizona meet the challenges of the arid Sonoran Desert lowlands head-on. These are the lowland burrowing treefrog *(Pternohyla fodiens)*, the Great Plains narrow-mouthed toad *(Gastrophryne olivacea)*, and the Sonoran green toad *(Bufo retiformis)*, all reaching their northern limits in or very near the Vekol Valley (Sullivan et al. 1996). The Vekol thus represents the northern terminus in the American Southwest of the great lowland Neotropical anuran fauna.

The most interesting of these frogs is *Pternohyla fodiens,* which was discovered in the Vekol in August 2000 (Enderson & Bezy 2000). This bizarre amphibian is one of several species of casque-headed frogs of the family Hylidae that are found in the American tropics. The casque head is a heavily boned skull that has protruding lip flanges and that is solidly connected ("co-ossified") with the skin (Duellman & Trueb 1994). This feature facilitates burrowing in the wet soil of temporary ponds. Once buried in the mud at the end of the monsoon, the frog secretes a thick, clear epidermal "cocoon" that retards dehydration (Ruibal & Hillman 1981). This frog is primarily a species of the thornscrub, ranging from Colima, Mexico, to the Vekol Valley. Consistent with its occurrence in the Mexican thornscrub, within Arizona it is virtually restricted to dense mesquite bosques. We heard only two or three calling in 2000, but on the nights of 11 and 17 July 2001 we encountered a very large aggregation. Most of the calling males were stationed on small (about 1 m^2) islands at the base of mesquites, but some individuals were perched on mesquite branches as high as ca. 2 m above the water. Hearing the distinctive ducklike quack issuing from this broad-billed amphibian is truly one of the most thrilling experiences in the Sonoran Desert.

The second Neotropical frog that reaches its northern limit in the Vekol (Jones et al. 1983) is the Great Plains narrow-mouthed toad, *Gastrophryne olivacea* (formerly *Gastrophryne olivacea mazatlanensis,* Sinaloan narrow-mouthed toad). It is an interesting example of an amphibian that combines two biogeographic patterns. As indicated by its former subspecies name, it occurs in thornscrub on the Pacific lowlands of Mexico. In Arizona there are two population clusters. One is in the Madrean Woodland of the Pajarito and Patagonia mountains, a typical thornscrub to Madrean Archipelago pattern. The other northern populations occur in dense mesquite bosques from the Arizona-Sonora border, north through the Tohono O'odham lands to the Vekol (Jones et al. 1983; Sullivan et al. 1996). The population in the Vekol appears to be denser than any other we have observed in the Southwest, and individuals were even encountered on the road surface. The species

Figure 22.3. *Lowland burrowing treefrog* (Pternohyla fodiens). *(Photo by Erik F. Enderson)*

seemed to be more abundant in the summer of 2000 than in 2001 and 2002, literally carpeting the ground in some areas. These frogs are primarily ant predators, and their skin secretions are quite toxic. They emit a high-pitched buzzing advertisement call while immersed in water with only the tips of their pointed snouts protruding from a tangle of mesquite branches and detritus.

The third species is *Bufo retiformis,* the magnificent gold and black jewel of the Vekol. Its heartland lies in the Sonoran Desert of Sonora and northern Sinaloa, extending into Arizona primarily on Tohono O'odham lands north to the vicinity of the eastern flank of the North Maricopa Mountains, Maricopa County (Sullivan et al. 1996). It is less restricted to mesquite bosques than the previous two species, occurring also on rocky

bajadas. This shy toad often calls from beneath a small bush some distance from the edge of the water, and one or two noncalling (satellite) males may be present (Sullivan et al. 1996, 2000; Enderson, personal observation). Although they breed in cattle tank impoundments, we have observed them calling also from newly formed shallow rain ponds on the flats far from the Vekol Wash.

The last species we wish to comment on is *Bufo debilis,* the anuran that originally attracted us to the Vekol. Sullivan et al. (1996) reexamined the one Vekol specimen (USNM 252797) and compared measurements to those presented by Ferguson and Lowe (1969), concluding that it is a *Bufo debilis.* We spent many hours during the monsoons of 2000–2001 searching for additional specimens of the species in the Vekol. We observed, photographed, tape-recorded vocalizations, and obtained tissue samples of numerous (approximately 15) *Bufo retiformis* but found no frogs in the area resembling *Bufo debilis* in color and color pattern or in vocalization (see Sullivan et al. 2000). We also reexamined the one existing specimen of *Bufo debilis* from the Vekol, and our data support the conclusions of Sullivan et al. (1996) that it is indeed a *Bufo debilis.* We also considered the possibility that the specimen might represent a hybrid between *Bufo retiformis* and *Bufo punctatus* similar to those that have been found elsewhere in Arizona (Bowker and Sullivan 1991; Sullivan et al. 1996), but our comparisons and analyses indicate that this is not the case. Although negative evidence is never conclusive, we have found nothing beyond the one preserved specimen to indicate that *Bufo debilis* actually occurs in the Vekol. It appears that the record that first lured us into the Vekol was most likely an error, but this has not diminished our fascination with the thorny Vekol.

Twenty-Three

From the Ground Up:

Biological Soil Crusts in the Sonoran Desert

Jayne Belnap

Ever walk across the desert and hear a little crunch under your feet? Or pick up a small piece of soil and notice fibers in it? If so, you've just discovered biological soil crusts (also called cryptogamic, cryptobiotic, microphytic, or microbiotic crusts). Biological soil crusts are a complex mosaic of living organisms—cyanobacteria (formerly called blue-green algae), green algae, lichens, mosses, liverworts, bacteria, and fungi—that weave throughout the top few millimeters of the soil surface. Most of the organisms in soil crusts are invisible, especially in hot deserts such as the Sonoran. Despite their small size, they perform many essential ecosystem services, including providing the glue that holds the desert soils together. These soil crust communities are common all over Earth, occurring in most habitats where light can reach the soil surface, including shrublands, grasslands, and woodlands.

Biological crusts are very different from physical or chemical crusts. Physical and chemical crusts look like a thin layer of cement. They are nonliving and are formed by raindrop impact onto unprotected soils, compaction, or evaporation of water that leaves salts behind on the soil surface. They have very different characteristics than biological crusts, but the two are often confused.

Biological soil crusts, once called cryptogamic crusts, have lots of names these days. Thirty years ago, scientists classified organisms into only two kingdoms: plants and animals. When it became clear many organisms were neither plants nor animals, five kingdoms were established. Under the old system, most crust species were classified as cryptogams and the soil crusts called cryptogamic crusts. Under the new system, these species were no longer considered plants, making the original name inaccurate. Many alternative names came into use, including microbiotic, cryptobiotic, and others. *Biological soil crust* is often used

because it has no taxonomic implications, it reminds us that these soil crusts are different from physical crusts, and people have complained that the other names are difficult to remember (see Keener letter at end of chapter).

Biological crusts can be highly variable in appearance, depending on what organisms are dominant and whether soils freeze in winter. In hot deserts without freezing soils, crusts are either smooth or only slightly roughened by occasional lichen patches. However, in cool deserts where soils freeze, cyanobacterially dominated crusts can form pinnacles up to 10 cm (4 in) high. Disturbance to these soils flattens most surface roughness.

It may seem that finding soil crusts would be difficult, as most cyanobacteria are too small to be seen with the unaided eye, and in hot deserts there are not many lichens, mosses, or soil bumps to attract your attention. However, you are saved from this dilemma by the amazing ability of cyanobacteria to live almost anywhere in deserts. They cover the soil, are in the water, and can live on plant leaves and stems. They are found on, under, or in most light-colored rocks, whether the rocks are on the ground or forming cliffs. The only places that are likely to lack cyanobacteria are areas of active disturbance (e.g., wash bottoms) or where something prevents light from reaching the soil surface (e.g., a dark rock or thick plant litter). Truly, these tiny living creatures form a living skin over the desert. So all that soil really isn't barren; instead, it is covered with a thin layer of living organisms vitally important to the healthy functioning of this ecosystem. What's the best way to see them? First, look for darker spots of soils and then pick up a piece. Hold it up and look for tiny, threadlike, dangling fibers. If the fibers blow freely in the breeze, you are probably looking at cyanobacteria. If they are stiff and show resistance to blowing, you probably are looking at a plant root.

Figure 23.1. *Soil cyano-bacteria can be either on or beneath the soil surface. (Photo courtesy Jayne Belnap)*

Figure 23.2. *Scanning electron micrograph of cyanobacterial sheath material sticking to sand grains. x90. (Photo courtesy Jayne Belnap)*

Cyanobacteria have long been an essential part of the Earth's ecosystems. They are one of the oldest forms of life known; in fact, they dominated the planet for well over 3 billion years. Fossil marine stromatolites, more than 3.5 billion years old, are extremely thick mats of cyanobacteria. These mats are believed to have converted the Earth's original carbon dioxide–rich atmosphere into the oxygen-rich atmosphere necessary for the evolution of life as we know it today. These organisms were also one of the early colonizers of Earth's land masses. We have found terrestrial cyanobacterial fossils over 1.1 billion years old, whereas plants appeared only 700 million years ago. These early cyanobacteria were likely integral in the formation and stabilization of the Earth's first soils, just as they are today.

What species are found in Sonoran Desert soil crusts? First, this region has an incredibly rich cyanobacterial flora. A tiny piece of soil can con-tain 20 or more of the up to 100 species found in the Sonoran Desert. The most commonly encountered cyanobacteria in Baja California are *Nostoc commune* and *Schizothrix calcicola*, followed by *Microcoleus vaginatus*, *Nostoc piscinale*, and *Plectonema tomasinianum* var. *gracile*. Farther north, in Arizona, commonly occurring species include *Calothrix parietina*, *Microcoleus vaginatus*, *M. paludosus*, *M. sociatus*, *Nostoc commune*, *N. microscopium*, *N. muscorum*, *Schizothrix calcicola*, and *Scytonema hofmannii*. Other common species are *Lyngbya aestuari*, *Plectonema nostocorum*, *Phoridium* sp., *Porphyrosiphon fuscus*, *Oscillatoria* sp., and *Tolypothrix tenuis*. The diverse and fairly even mix of cyanobacterial species found in the Sonoran Desert differs from that of other U.S. desert areas, including the similarly hot Mojave, as the cyanobacterial floras of those deserts are heavily dominated by *Microcoleus vaginatus*.

Green algae are much too small to see without a microscope. In addition, their numbers are very low in the alkaline soils that characterize most deserts. The most common soil green algal species in Baja California are the chlorophytes *Myrmecia astigmatica*, *M. biatorellae*, and *Bracteacoccus minor* and the diatoms *Hantzschia amphioxys*, *Hantzschia amphioxys* f. *capitata*, *Luticola cohnii*, *Luticola mutica*, and *Pinnularia borealis* var. *scalaris*. Chrysophyte cysts are also very common. Farther north, in Arizona, the most common coccoid green algae include *Chlorella vulgaris*, *Navicula* sp., *Nitzschia* sp., *Palmogloea protuberans*, *Pinnularia* sp., *Protococcus grevillei*, *Stichococcus subtilis*, and *Trochiscia hirta*.

The cyanobacteria and green algae found under the diaphanous rocks in the Sonoran Desert include *Anacystis* spp., *Bracteacoccus* spp., *Calothrix parietina*, *Chlorococcum* spp., *Coccochloris* spp., *Nostoc* spp., *Protococcus grevillei*, *Protosiphon cinnamomeus*, *Scytonema hofmannii*, and *Trochiscia hirta*.

Although soil lichens and mosses are less common than cyanobacteria and green algae, they are certainly present. Lichens come in many forms, but in desert soils the forms most often seen are crustose, squamulose, and gelatinous. Crustose and squamulose lichens firmly adhere to the soil surface so that if you try to pull them away, the soil will come too. Crustose species look like little dots scattered on the soil surface. Squamulose species consist of little flat plates. Neither of them changes color or shape when wetted. Most gelatinous species are black, and when wetted, they swell up. When you hold them up to the light, they are a translucent green. The most common lichens in the Sonoran Desert include *Catapyrenium squamulosum* (squamulose) and *Collema coccophorum* and *C. tenax* (both gelatinous). Other, less common lichens include *Heppia lutosa, H. adglutinata, H. despreauxii, Peltula richardsii,* and *P. patellata* (all squamulose). In coastal fog deserts of Baja California, rugose lichen crusts are replaced by extensive carpets of the fruticose lichen *Desmazieria* spp.

Mosses, when dry, either look like a mat of very short grass or have spaces between the spikes of tissue, making them look like spruce trees from 25,000 feet in the air. Unlike lichens, mosses are true plants and have tiny leaves that turn green (or green-brown) and unfurl when wetted. Common soil crust mosses include *Bryum argenteum, B. caespiticium, Crossidium aberrans, Tortula plinthobia, Pterygoneurum ovatum,* and *Syntrichia ruralis.* The large thalloid liverworts *Athalamia hyalina* and *Riccia sorocarpa* can be fairly common. As elevation and available moisture increase, the lichen and moss flora are more diverse and approximate that found on the Colorado Plateau.

One of the interesting aspects of soil crusts is that regardless of soil type, climate, vegetation, or where they occur in the world, most of the same genera, and many of the same species, are found in soil crusts around the globe. Ubiquitous cyanobacterial and algal species include *Calothrix parietina, Hantzschia amphioxys, Microcoleus vaginatus, Nostoc commune, Pinnularia borealis, Schizothrix calcicola, Scytonema hofmannii,* and *Tolypothrix tenuis.* Some of the lichens found in all regions are *Catapyrenium squamulosum, Collema tenax, C. coccophorum, Heppia lutosa,* and *Psora decipiens.* Cosmopolitan mosses include *Bryum argenteum* and *Pterygoneurum ovatum.*

It is interesting to speculate why these species can occur in such seemingly disparate environments. The most likely explanation is that the soil surface is one of the most harsh environments in the world, especially in deserts, and only a few species can adapt to it. Temperatures can be both very hot (75°C) and very cold (−4°C), and any soil surface organism must be able to handle both extremes. What little rain falls leaves the soil surface quickly, through either evaporation or drainage.

Soil crust organisms must therefore be able to dry completely and quickly without much damage. They also need the ability to hydrate quickly without damage, as these organisms are metabolically active only when wet, and times of moisture are limited. In addition, lichens, mosses, and many species of cyanobacteria are immobile and thus cannot escape harmful ultraviolet rays. Most of these species produce sun-screening pigments that partially block these rays or alleviate the intracellular damage they cause. Mosses curl up when they dry, shading their more sensitive surfaces and exposing the underside of the leaves, where protective pig-ments are found. Larger cyanobacteria are relatively mobile and can leave the soil surface to seek protection at depth. However, not all species can adopt these strategies or can "afford" them. Therefore, it is likely that only a few types of organisms, and only a few species within those types, can survive these extreme conditions.

Biological crusts are, literally, a carpet of photosynthetic life, contributing organic matter to all the soils in which they occur. This organic matter is an important food source for other organisms that decompose plant litter and keep nutrients available to living plants. Cyanobacteria also convert atmospheric nitrogen into a form usable by vascular plants. This is a very important function, as most desert soils are very low in nitrogen, limiting the ecosystem's productivity. In addition to creating and adding new nutrients to soils, soil crust organisms secrete compounds that keep existing soil nutrients available to vascular plants. As a result, vascular plants growing in crusted soils often have higher levels of many essential nutrients than plants growing in areas without crusts.

Another important role these soil crusts play in arid and semiarid ecosystems is soil stabilization. This function is especially critical in desert ecosystems, where vascular plant cover is limited and large expanses of soil are unprotected from wind and water erosion. When moistened, cyanobacterial filaments, or fibers, move through the soils, leaving a trail of sticky mucilage behind. This material links soil particles together, creating larger particles that are more resistant to both wind and water erosion. The soil-binding action is not dependent on the presence of living filaments: layers of abandoned material, built up over long periods of time, can still be found clinging tenaciously to soil particles at depth.

TABLE 23.1. *Dry Borders Lichens and Mosses*

LICHENS

Acarospora schleicheri	*Peltigera rufescens*
	Peltula patellata
Catapyrenium lachneum	*Peltula richardsii*
Catapyrenium lacinulatum	
Catapyrenium squamulosum	*Psora cerebriformis*
Cladonia chlorophaea	*Psora crenata*
Cladonia fimbriata	*Psora decipiens*
Cladonia pocillum	*Psora icterica*
Cladonia pyxidata	*Psora pacifica*
Collema coccophorum	*Psora tuckermanii*
Collema tenax	
	Squamarina lentigera
Desmazieria sp.	
Diploschistes muscorum	*Thrombium epigaeum*
	Toninia ruginosa
Endocarpon pusillum	*Toninia sedifolia*
	Toninia tristis subsp. *asiae-centralis*
Fulgensia bracteata	
Fulgensia desertorum	MOSSES
Fulgensia subbracteata	*Bryum argenteum*
	Bryum caespiticium
Heppia adglutinata	
Heppia lutosa	*Crossidium aberrans*
Heppia despreauxii	*Crossidium erosum*
Leprocaulon microscopicum	*Funaria muehlenbergii*
Leptochidium albociliatum	
Leptogium californicum	*Grimmia laevigata*
Leptogium corniculatum	
Leptogium lichenoides	*Pterygoneurum ovatum*
Leptogium tenuissimum	
Leptogium teretiusculum	*Syntrichia ruralis*
Peltigera collina	*Tortula plinthobia*
Peltigera didactyla	
	Weissia controversa

The crusts serve other functions as well. One of the most important is how crusts influence levels of soil moisture. Their effect on the infiltration of rainwater is site-dependent, as factors such as soil texture and chemistry, soil surface roughness, crust species composition, slope and aspect, and landscape position also bear heavily on this process. Crusts can reduce water infiltration by filling soil pores or increase infiltration by roughening soil surfaces. Once water has entered the soil, crusts generally reduce evaporative losses. Crusts also are the heartbeat of desert biodiversity: the 100 or so species of cyanobacteria, mosses, lichens, and liverworts often greatly exceed the number of vascular plants and animals present at a site. And this is not even counting the species of fungi, bacteria, and microarthropods that are present as well.

Lots of things rely on soil crusts for food. Whether alive or dead, they make a tasty meal for protists (e.g., amoebae, ciliates, flagellates), nematodes and microarthropods (e.g., mites, tardigrades, isopods), macroarthropods (e.g., tenebrionid beetles, termites, ants), bacteria, and fungi. Whereas common soil fungi are found in all crust types, unique saprotrophic fungi are involved in the decomposition of lichens and bryophytes. There is also a synergy between bacteria, fungi, protozoa, and cyanobacteria. Grazing by protozoa stimulates cyanobacterial nitrogen fixation. The addition of heterotrophic bacteria and fungi to soils significantly increases cyanobacterial biomass. Bacteria and fungi release nutrients and scavenge cyanobacterial "wastes," including oxygen, thus enhancing cyanobacterial nitrogen fixation. In turn, the nitrogen provided by the cyanobacteria increases microbial decomposition activity.

You perhaps think we know a lot about soil crusts, but let me tell you the truth: we know very little. For instance, we know they fix nitrogen and carbon, but how much? When? Where does it go? We don't know yet. What happens to soil food webs and soil nutrient availability when you remove the lichens and mosses and are just left with cyanobacteria, as when a site is disturbed? Don't know. How can they live years and years and years without water, yet be instantly "on" when watered? Don't know. How do these organisms withstand the incredibly harsh conditions (talk about sunburn!) found on the desert soil surface? Don't know. What is going to happen to them with climate change, as patterns of precipitation and temperature change? Don't know. All that we don't know makes the small handful of things we *do* know look quite pitiful. In other words, we know almost nothing about the basic building block, the very foundation, of the entire desert ecosystem.

The Unraveling of It All

One thing we do know is that many human activities are incompatible with the presence and well-being of soil crusts. Most lichens, mosses, and many species of cyanobacteria are intolerant of being crushed, regardless of whether the crushing mechanism is tires, tanks, hooves, or Vibram soles. As a result, soils experiencing frequent and/or severe disturbance are dominated by a few hardy species of cyanobacteria rather than the rich diversity of cyanobacteria, algae, lichens, and mosses that would otherwise occupy that site.

The cyanobacterial fibers that confer such tensile strength to crusts are no match for the compressional stress placed on them by feet or machinery, especially when the crusts are dry and therefore brittle. Crushed crusts contribute less nitrogen and organic matter to the ecosystem. Impacted soils are left highly susceptible to both wind and water erosion. Raindrop erosion is increased, and overland water flows carry detached material away. This is especially a problem when the destruction is in a continuous strip, as with vehicular or bicycle tracks, and/or on slopes, where erosion channels are quickly formed. Wind blows pieces of the pulverized crust away; it also blows the underlying loose soil around, covering nearby crusts. Because crustal organisms need to photosynthesize, burial can mean death. When large sandy areas are impacted in dry periods, previously stable areas can become a series of moving sand dunes in a matter of only a few years.

Figure 23.3. *Typical desert soil crust. (Photo by Bill Broyles)*

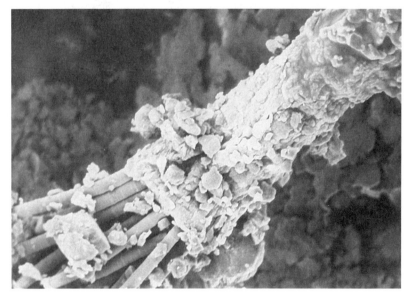

Figure 23.4. *Filamentous cyanobacteria migrating out of their sheaths. x950. (Photo courtesy Jayne Belnap)*

Recovery from disturbance depends on many site factors. Coarse-textured (e.g., sandy) soils recover more slowly than fine-textured soils (e.g., silt or clay). Large areas recover more slowly than small areas, as most colonization occurs from adjacent areas that have not been impacted. Places with greater precipitation or with winter rains, which evaporate more slowly than summer rains, recover more quickly than areas that receive less rain or receive it in summer. Unfortunately, this means that many areas in hot deserts recover very slowly or may not recover at all after severe disturbance. Recovery of cyanobacteria can occur on the order of decades, but under many circumstances lichens and mosses can take centuries to return. This makes it critical that we take care of the soil crusts around us, especially mosses and

Figure 23.5. Soil crust broken by wayward vehicle. (Photo by Bill Broyles)

DON'T BUST THE CRUST!

STAY ON TRAILS. PROTECT FRAGILE BIOLOGICAL SOIL CRUSTS

Figure 23.6. Don't bust the crust. (Courtesy Jayne Belnap)

lichens, because once they are lost, we may never see them again at that place.

So what would deserts be like without soil crusts? Very different than they are now—and boring. First, expect lots of loose sand, forming dunes and getting in your eyes and house. Second, expect a very different flora in those sandy areas: only a few highly specialized groups of plants can handle loose, blowing sand (see Chapter 17). And bugs and small things would be different too, as their ability to burrow and travel on surfaces is generally adapted to a certain level of soil stability. So help, please, to keep the desert a more interesting and lively place by protecting those little things that keep it all together. After all, it's the little things in life that count.

How Bob Was Named

Dear Ms. Belnap:

I just got back from Canyonlands [National Park]. It was beautiful. Thank you. I've visited many times over the past fifteen years, enough to watch the crusty desert soil have its name changed at least three times. Cryptogamic, microbiotic, cryptobiotic. What's the deal? Is this crust in the witness protection plan or something?

I understand that you're at least in part responsible for the name changes. Since the name is obviously not set in stone, I'd like to offer my suggestion. Let's face it. The crust is not grand like the rock formations or cute like the bunnies or beautiful like the flowering cacti. I'm sure it's fascinating to study, but in the whole scheme of things I'm afraid it's kind of ugly. Plus it lives with the danger that people who don't know better might step on it, the Rodney Dangerfield of crusts. It plays an important role, but it's hard for people to relate to.

Anthropomorphizing it is not a bad idea. In that same vein, we could give it a name that people could easily relate to, the kind of name their best friend might have; something short and sweet with instant name recognition. Drumroll please. How about this: Bob. Cryptobiotic crust is relatively easy to step on compared with Bob. I know what you're thinking: the name has to have a scientific bent. Don't worry! I've addressed that too. It's also an acronym for our "Bio-Organic Buddies." Can't you just hear the hikers saying, "Don't step on Bob! He's our buddy." It puts a human face on a crusty situation. If you have time, let me know what you think of my idea.

Sincerely,
Chris Keener
Denver, Colorado

Where to Find Out More

There are now multiple ways to find out more about soil crusts. For the less technical approach, there is a web page at www.soilcrust.org. This site has photos, information, and three thousand references. *Biological Soil Crusts: Structure, Function, and Management,* by J. Belnap and O. L. Lange, is a technical book published by Springer in 2003. There is also an excellent review paper by K. T. Harper and J. R. Marble, "A Role for Nonvascular Plants in Management of Arid and Semiarid Rangelands," in *Vegetation Science: Applications for Rangeland Analysis and Management,* edited by P. T. Tueller (Dordrecht: Kluwer Academic, 1988), pages 135–169.

Part Four

THE GULF
AND THE RIVER

Twenty-Four

Wine of the River

SANDY LANHAM

The Cessna wheels over a blowing whale, maybe the last of this long day. My passengers, both marine researchers from Mexico, peer down a wing at her. She glows electric blue and blows again. I twist the yoke. The horizon wobbles, then suddenly tilts more sharply. It slashes diagonally across my view. We are a spinning top about to topple. Green blue sideways, the world outside spins.

Pinacate Peak marches across the windshield and blows away. Hundred mile an hour winds, the speed of the airplane, scatter the horizon's images like raindrops. A line of golden sand streaks past right to left, then is flung into space. The Sierra San Pedro Mártir sweeps in, climbs the window, and spins off. Here comes the Pinacate again . . . pulling a chain of pinto mountains, all pinks and blue. The colors stream, spin off the window, off the airplane, and for all I know, off the planet too.

My world exists here, in the tight cabin of the airplane. The twirling sun flicks on and off.

Silvia Manzanilla, in the right-hand seat, bends farther out the open window. Her hair is a tangled cloud.

"Oh look!" she says. The blue whale gives one last blow, kicks up her tail, and dives.

The Cessna snaps to level, the horizon locks into place. Spinning ends. In front of us, the Sea of Cortez stretches a thousand miles of cool blue welcome.

Silvia shuts her notebook and then reaches into the back seat for a plastic bag.

"Would you like a cookie?" she asks.

The researchers on this flight are exploring the northern Gulf of California. They have long since settled into this week of flights. Their minds slip out the window and into the movie below. The ride is smooth, a magic carpet.

Fish leap, and their jumps ruffle the sea with a thousand whitecaps. Birds dive and explode in small splashes, then pop out to flap, wheel, and do it again. Whales cruise. Below us, one has a small calf. They cruise with a movement of muscles so fine-tuned that to us, there is no movement at all. The mother blows. Her tall spout is a punctuation mark to this week's statement of plenty.

Yesterday we discovered swarms of red krill, the tiny shrimplike creatures stuffed into squirming amoebas. Rivers of krill raced within their razor-edged borders. Paisleys swirled. To krill, life on the edge must be no life at all. A crusty paw of krill slid out from one pack. It appeared to grab the sea and wrench its quivering puddle up behind it, then again creeping across the sea like a snail. The waist of another pack cinched to almost nothing as its torso, then its head, mushroomed. I feared for its life.

In the morning flight, we had roared over the granddaddy of all packs. It exploded. Dozens of dolphins, hidden deep inside, rocketed straight to the surface and darted away. They sliced the krill in a starburst, like the tracers in fireworks. We startled, then laughed.

"Three o'clock, the other side of Consag. A blow!" Silvia's voice now rings in my headset.

Off the right wing, Consag Island spikes, a rock tooth iced with the guano of seabirds. Beyond it, a puff grows brighter, lingers, then fades. We head to a ripple left in the water, then see a sparkle off a wet back, and suddenly, dark forms are below, flowing in a dance of underwater shadows. A watery lens refracts the images. The shapes twirl, dissolve, then form again. A moonbeam seems to swirl a cape around them, so brilliantly white that for an instant, I want to fold myself in it and sleep.

The shapes rise.

Figure 24.1. *Silvia Manzanilla* (right) *and Sandy Lanham. (Photo by Carlos Navarro)*

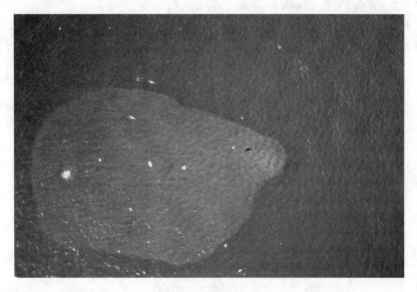

Figure 24.2. *Krill. (Photo by Carlos Navarro)*

The airplane stands on a wingtip, spinning in place. We look straight down. I pull hard on the yoke to keep us aloft. Two whales, each with a single white jaw, rise. Armless Buddhas, an activist once said. Benign creatures, I dutifully echoed. Now I know differently. Baleen plates are exposed during feeding. Monstrous teeth show in the giant suck of krill.

Three seconds more. We wait. Now!

The blue mirror shatters; fin whales break to the sky. They wear obscene grins.

Expelled water gushes through baleen, cascading down their sides. As they level off, I hear the pops of their jaw ligaments unhinging, from one thousand feet up and over the roar of the engine.

Not far off, another fin whale whips the entire length of her body like a shark's tail, propelling herself with a final burst of speed into a krill pack. Inside, she bends it an agonizing fifty degrees to shovel its entire length.

"Did you see that? Did you see!" Talk in the airplane's cabin now comes in staccato bursts.

Other years, whales had rolled to their sides, eyes up, examining our big yellow bird as it examined them. Today we are ignored. Even the breath of these whales does not have its predictable rhythm. Researchers use the height of blows, their shape, and number to judge a whale's species. Count the blows. One, two, three, dive. Fin whale! Today all bets are off. The breath of these whales comes in gasps, fueling the suck of krill.

We bank toward a circle of spinning fish. Three hundred golden bat rays, a species like manta rays, advance on it too. Their delta bodies are wingtip to wingtip, all pumping attack speed. All week we have noted extreme numbers of these rays, perhaps ten thousand or more. But this is new. We circle low. Giant mantas launch themselves airborne under us, black-and-white bodies tumbling through space and crashing back to the sea, musical cymbals in a score that now is Sousa.

The bat rays seem intent on piercing the fish pack like a Mongol horde. But in the last instant the rays maneuver into loose lines and bank, G-forcing around its ragged edge. Bait fish, vulnerable on the fish pack's fringe, may dodge into the safe nooks that magically appear, the black and open mouths of the rays. Or perhaps the rays vacuum something tinier, invisible to us at five hundred feet.

The spinning circle tightens. The knot holds.

"Has anyone seen this before? Do people know they do this?" Silvia is stunned. She locks her video camera on the sea. Its whir finally dies as she pulls in from the open window.

"Give me a GPS waypoint. Please." The demand is professional, crisp. She needs the position, the precise latitude and longitude, to record this event. She picks up her tape recorder's mic and speaks. The engine drones, fusing her words with its steady drumming like missed beats. Below, the sea is a blue prairie. We drift. Soon I am lost to other flights, to memory.

The airplane cruises over another vast prairie, a golden one, a hundred miles to the east. It is a milk run, from Tucson to Hermosillo. Another researcher sits beside me. He has sparkling eyes, the kind of man who loves to dance, a brave man, brave enough even to love his wife.

Exequiel Ezcurra turns to me and asks, "Why do you do this?"

The wide world rolls out in front of the airplane, the Sonoran Desert. A hawk plays on a rising bubble of air, then with a flick of his tail feathers is gone. This desert was once a forest of mesquite, palo verde, and ironwood trees, sheltering deer and other creatures so small . . . well, so small that a puppy could poke his nose at them. Now it is a sea of golden grass, an African pasture grass transplanted here for cows. It is a silent howl. Bulldozers growl at its edges, the native desert.

I work to protect what is left, I think, what I see every time the wheels leave the ground. But this answer is not quite honest, not good enough for someone like Exequiel. So I say nothing. He waits.

When I started Environmental Flying Services, I knew that the Mexicans had no money to pay for flights. So I would raise it in the United States. A nonprofit organization, someone said it is called. Requests to survey whales, track pronghorn antelope, and discover secret forests all poured in. The money did not. When it finally did come, it trickled. It was enough.

Over Benjamin Hill, Exequiel gazes at the African savanna that passes under our wings. Once I saw a herd of mule deer flee this new world for the shelter of the last remaining mesquite trees. In Hermosillo I once saw a raven with clipped wings sit in a box cage. His eyes were pinpricks of rage.

"Is it because you were bored?" Exequiel asks kindly. His eyes are deep pools. My answer finally registers, clinking into place.

"Yes," I say with a blush. I do it for me. He smiles.

Blue whales, blue crabs. I fly for all things, big and small. Even things with feet. In fact, I once saw pronghorn antelope. More than once, hundreds of times.

I survey them, sometimes in the Pinacate region, where the wind spills with the lava flows, cascading off volcanic peaks. The sky is thick with pterodactyls that do not fly, the earth with mammoths that do not thunder. Almost no one lives here. Sand dunes line up, ancient shorelines with changes of heart.

Figure 24.3. Sandy Lanham and her airplane Emily. (Photo by Kaye Craig)

We fly low, hugging the earth. Up the naked brown hills and down. Fly the line straight, slow the airspeed, check the compass, now turn . . . lazy, slow turn and fly the line straight, slow the airspeed, check the compass. Stretch an arm back and tug on the pant leg of José. He startles, his eyes swim, then he yawns. Flying for pronghorn is hours and hours of yawning nothing, seeing not a rabbit, not a coyote, seeing absolutely nothing. . . .

Then suddenly, in front of you, to the left! Movement catches your eye and quick, you look!

Nine pronghorn antelope shoot down an arroyo, velvet darts licking creosote air, going fast and, as you wheel over them, faster. Bags of bone pump, noses stretch, moon asses sail down the wash on a wave of dust and now rock muscles tighten, they leap . . . up . . . up . . . a steep scree bank, scrambling, pebbles rain like popcorn hail and . . . in the clear! Accelerating into the forever plains and this time meaning it . . . running, running, blowing, pushing the speeds of a cheetah, stretching a line of stick bodies across miles of sand until all you see is a line of speeding dust and then all you see is . . . nothing.

Your heart pounds and you wonder, what just happened? The trigger is the snap of a twig, a whiff of not-right, a cloud that drifts in front of the sun. A pronghorn antelope lives his entire life a twitch away from full speed. He is a genetic running machine.

I once saw pronghorn antelope, and the big yellow bird came screaming over at a hundred feet. I once saw pronghorn antelope not run.

We circled back.

Six pronghorn jerked like Mexican jumping beans on a hot grill. Three pogoed in circles. Then we saw it: a dead fawn lay at their feet, its legs stuck rigidly out. The pronghorn antelope were overriding a genetic command in order to stay with one of their young.

They were choosing.

Silvia finishes her dictation, and the tape recorder snaps off. Pulling her headset's microphone back down in place, she blows, testing, testing. Our Chief has returned.

In the slanting rays of a falling sun, Earth shows her stuff. Mountains flip on their sunset colors. Blue falls deeper into blue. The sand dunes to the north, El Gran Desierto, roll out eighty miles of golden light. On the sea the circus opens for the night. Fish splash in spinning carousels. Acrobat birds flip and dive. Rhinestones spill on blue satin as schools of sardines dart. Hundreds of dolphins leap in great running stitches, pulling wakes of sparkling thread. Some twirl underwater; wavy white bellies stroke the indigo deep with the light of glowsticks.

The Sonoran sun, that clenched fist of white light, is about done for the day. The sea's turn comes.

"Kiddies," she whispers. "All krill rise." The krill packs grow quickly in number and size. Puffs of whales soon mark them, like a beach full of clams squirting juice at low tide.

"I can't believe this flight. I just can't believe it," Silvia speaks. But of course, she can.

Silvia directs this project, part of her dissertation for Instituto de Ecología, UNAM. In 1984, when a report of a strange new porpoise wafted over the gulf and debates on its existence in the wild echoed in university halls, Silvia checked it out. She drove and mostly walked the remote beaches of the upper gulf, two hundred miles of bare-bones sand. She brought back one and a half fresh carcasses of the new species, called the vaquita, cradled in the bed of her pickup. Debate ceased.

One of her prizes had died in a gill net. Its suffocated body had been cut free by a fisherman's knife. Among the first few specimens ever collected, one held forensic evidence of a crime. Silvia, a researcher with an activist's heart, believes this can be changed. She is a believer.

"Heh! What's that?" A voice booms. It is Carlos Navarro, the big man wedged into the back seat, riding this week as second observer. He works for the Center for the Study of Deserts and Oceans in Puerto Peñasco. He is usually a quiet man.

He points to the west, where a cloudburst has centered over a krill pack. It rains intensely.

A few days ago Silvia and I had a fight. We had passed a sleek whale, smaller than a fin whale, stepping in shallow dives off the coast of San Felipe. Her slick footprints, circles left on the water's surface by the downward pull of her dives, dotted the sea.

"Sei whale," I said.

"No," Silvia answered, her eyes suddenly glued straight ahead. "I don't think so. It's a Bryde's whale." The battle buzzed for the rest of the flight, like a horsefly trapped in the cockpit. Carlos was silent. That night over margaritas, we turned to him.

"Clearly a Bryde's whale. I distinctly saw its three nose ridges." Sei whales have only one. Carlos is a man of immense, if sometimes hidden, knowledge. Stuffed now in the back seat, survival equipment and baggage up to his ears, he sits impacted as a wisdom tooth.

"Heads up, girls!" he says more urgently. "Ten o'clock. Two miles. It's raining harder."

I look at the pouring rain ahead, then at the sky. I am confused. I need to get my bearings. The Sierra San Pedro Mártir looms on the horizon, rising like a towering thunderstorm in northern Baja California. But there is not a cloud in the sky. Not one, ice blue, forever.

The krill, now just seconds away, rain harder.

"What is this?" A whisper comes over the intercom. It may even be my own.

We approach. Backlit by the sun, fireflies seem to glitter over the patch of krill, then all disappears. A giant paddle, banded in white, slices the surface of the water and then slides under. Ten seconds pass, the krill again go mad. Finally I see. The krill are leaping airborne, their tiny bodies flying up and plop-plopping down in a million raining splashes. The krill are raining on themselves.

I pull the Cessna away. No one wants to interrupt this, well, whatever this is. The raining dies, the krill disappear. Then suddenly reappear. It starts again, more furiously. Then a long flipper, banded in white like a stripe on a clown, slaps the water and a Minke whale follows, plowing to the sea's surface. Feeding on the krill from underneath, she comes up for air. As the krill go down.

This dance between whale and fleeing krill may have gone on for hours.

I once told a friend that I would give five years of my life to see this sea just once as it existed a hundred years ago. He scoffed and left the room; he wants to live in Los Angeles. Today my life must surely be shorter.

Unwinding like a retiring frigatebird, the Cessna descends to just above the sea. Racing with us are skiffs, holding fishermen happy about the day's catch, going home to a hot meal and a cold beer and a hope for the same tomorrow. A giant manta pumps next to one. No one bothers to mention it. But this manta will not be ignored. It squirts a fat red jet of excrement. We laugh.

It is the satisfied belch of the sea.

The Cessna has logged thousands of hours of flights over this sea. Pockets of intense activity are standard fare. So are hours of yawning nothing. But the airplane is always an intruder. When we cruise over sperm whales logging in the sun, they startle and sound. Hundreds of dolphins often wheel in shattered formation to flee us. Once a pod of pilot whales, those twenty-foot chunks of black muscle, formed a defensive line, shoulder to shoulder, to deliver a cross-species message: No!

The northern gulf's activity this day in May 1998 was both fierce and widespread, but the airplane flew behind a one-way mirror. Feeding, the gulf's species did not care.

Why this banquet now?

The Colorado River once wove its fabric through a zipperless border between the United States and Mexico. Dammed six decades ago, the river's water now rarely crosses a political divide sanctioned by the United States–Mexico Water Treaty of 1944. Dams built in the United States destroyed the river's natural flow. When the water was impounded and directed west, the Imperial and Mexicali deserts were transformed into farmland. The delta became a destroyed land.

Abundant runoff from the snow pack in the

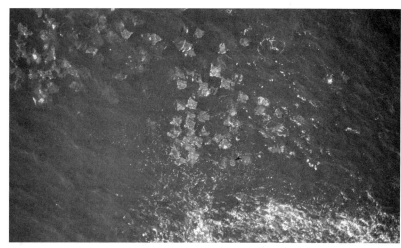

Sierra Nevada bestowed a blessing last year. The wet touch of El Niño did the same this year. Freshwater poured into the gulf from the Colorado River for the last two years. Was this fiesta a result of freshwater?

Mexican fishermen are sure that it is. They claim that the northern gulf's productivity died because of the blocking of the river's flow, beginning with the dedication of Hoover Dam in 1935. Opponents retort that at about the same time, the number of fishermen exploded. Gill nets began to weave a web across the gulf, like a net of moray eels. Overfishing, not the river, is the problem, they say.

Our flights are part of a project that seeks an answer. These researchers are looking into the effects of El Niño, including the flow of freshwater. Packed into the hard data of sea temperatures and salinity, fish capture rates, Landsat photos, and aerial sightings, the answer may reveal itself, just as our dolphins did from within the individual facts of krill.

Over Isla Montague in the delta, the Colorado River splits. We scan its canals for the black dots that would signal that the rare porpoise still lives and for green ones that would mark life's toehold in this destroyed and eerie land. The flat pan of the delta slides past us, kicking up pelicans, lifting as a hundred parts of one to impose a single, slow wingbeat on the emptiness.

The Colorado River delta was once the womb of the Sea of Cortez. Willows and cottonwoods lined its channels; tree roots snaked into mud. Wild nipa grass danced a foot-stomping jig of a million golden heads. Fry born in tangled shelters

Figure 24.5. *Flying the delta. (Photo by Carlos Navarro)*

grew to bite-size, then as fresh-faced graduates swarmed into the gulf. A wren's song would be heard first, then the bird would appear on a wet limb. The fiesta here made music.

On a river now dammed to a trickle, pockets of life suck on a drying breast.

We strain out the windows. The wind goes squirrelly, rocking us from side to side. We skim the most critical place of all, where in past years we found vaquita. The river below us moves its saltwater sludge out to sea. Bottlenose dolphins slice it with their tall, hooked dorsal fins. A string of pearls drapes them, then slowly transforms into a line of pelicans skimming the water.

For an hour, we search. The wind again shifts, now chopping us as it chops the water below.

But we find no vaquita, not one. No pug nose or flash of triangular fin. No humble, sweet nodding dives. No calf tucked to its mother's side. No proof that the vaquita still live. A mere five feet long, perhaps only six hundred vaquita remain.

No one knows. She is one of the most endangered cetaceans in the world and lives only here, in the northern gulf. Scientists say she may need the river to survive. The Yuma clapper rail, desert pupfish, and other endangered species may need it too.

"Maybe tomorrow," Silvia says, putting her notebook away. "I think there is hope."

Officials in the United States have a standard reply when faced with inquiries about releasing freshwater from the Colorado River: show us the scientific proof that freshwater relates to a productive northern gulf. These researchers, or others like them, might.

What will people do then? Given the same choice as the pronghorn, how will we choose?

To the north, a mound of sand lifts, kicked by a steel-toed boot of air off the delta's floor and into the ride of its life. It swirls, gathers strength, and now snakes across the emptiness, twirling high and ever higher. Sand will never make it to convection, I think. Grains of sand will never accelerate up forever, snapping their tiny chains with the pop-pops of a million freedoms. Gravity always wins back its golden grains.

I point this fact out to my academic, head-in-the-clouds, good friend Silvia.

She stiffens. Once again, her eyes lock straight ahead. "Look. People are not grains of sand."

This time I am right. Right? Then again, with a glance to Carlos . . . I could be wrong.

The Cessna banks to Puerto Peñasco and a landing, as the Sonoran sun slips into its sea.

Acknowledgments

An earlier version of this essay appeared in *Ocean Realm* (Winter 1998–99).

Twenty-Five

New Life for the Colorado River Delta

EDWARD P. GLENN AND PAMELA L. NAGLER

The Colorado River Delta has undergone a rebirth over the past twenty years. The riparian corridor, once choked with salt cedar, now supports a 100-km stretch in which cottonwood and willow trees have established amidst the salt cedar. Wildlife has returned. More than 350 species of birds have been documented in the delta. In spring at least 110 species of migratory landbirds migrate through the trees on their way to northern nesting areas. Cattails have returned to river backwaters, providing nesting sites for waterbirds. The first pair of nesting Yuma clapper rails to be seen on the Mexico stretch of river since dams were built were spotted in 2002. Mountain lions prowl the riverbanks.

Ciénega de Santa Clara, the largest marsh in the Sonoran Desert, is home to 6,000 nesting Yuma clapper rails as well as beaver, bald eagles, and numerous resident and migratory waterfowl. More than 300,000 shorebirds and 60,000 ducks and geese use the delta wetlands each year. Endangered desert pupfish by the tens of thousands swim warily in the Cerro Prieto salt ponds, making an occasional meal for gull-billed terns (themselves a threatened species) roosting on nearby soil mounds. Corvina and even totoaba have returned to the river's estuary. The shrimp catch at San Felipe has doubled since the 1980s.

Water in the Delta

This abundance is supported by water. The modern delta is supplied by three principal sources. First is the Colorado River itself. After dams were constructed, flows to the delta virtually stopped for forty-five years. First Lake Mead, behind Hoover Dam, and then Lake Powell, behind Glen Canyon Dam, each took twenty years to fill. During those years excess water in the watershed was simply stored behind the dams. Lake Powell reached capacity in 1981. Water flowed again to the delta, with a vengeance, in 1983. This El Niño year produced historic snowfall in the Rocky Mountains. Snowmelt in spring produced floods so large that the emergency spillways on Glen Canyon Dam were opened for the first time, and came close to failing. From 1983 to 1986 the delta was completely flooded below the agricultural fields. Low-lying fields were abandoned. A series of levees was built to contain future floods and channel them to the sea. Inadvertently, this construction created a protected natural area of 160,000 ha between the levees where settlement and agriculture were restricted because of flood danger.

Further water has flowed in each major El Niño event since 1983. The riparian corridor once again experiences a pulse-flow regime to wash salts from the riverbanks and allow the establishment of cottonwoods and willows. The beneficial effects of the 1983, 1993, and 1997–98 flood releases have been preserved in the stands of native trees they germinated along the river banks.

The second source of water is agricultural return flows from the United States and Mexico. About a third of the water used to irrigate fields in this region is recaptured in drain lines or ditches. This water is too salty for further human use and is sent to disposal. A steady stream of mildly saline groundwater pumped from the Wellton-Mohawk Irrigation District in the United States has created Ciénega de Santa Clara, a large cattail marsh on the eastern edge of the delta. On the western side of the delta, agricultural drain water from the Mexicali Valley flows into the Río Hardy to join the Colorado River about 70 km above the mouth of the river, creating a brackish perennial flow to the sea. This part of the river, a nursery area for shrimp and fish from the marine zone, supports vast thickets of saltbush and reeds along the shoreline and cattail marshes in the backwaters. Recently, we found a previously unknown set of wetlands

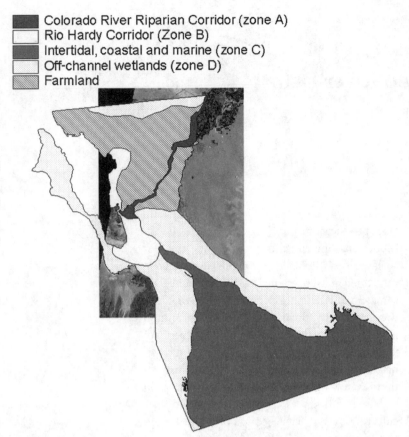

Colorado River Riparian Corridor (zone A)
Rio Hardy Corridor (Zone B)
Intertidal, coastal and marine (zone C)
Off-channel wetlands (zone D)
Farmland

Figure 25.1. Ecozones of the Colorado River delta, displayed on an ETM+ satellite image of the delta taken in May 2002. Zone A = riparian corridor; B = Río Hardy corridor; C = intertidal, coastal, and marine zone; D = off-channel wetlands; E = farmland.

supported by seepage from the All-American Canal, which carries Colorado River water along the border from Yuma to the Imperial Valley.

The third source of water is the sea. The upper Gulf of California is a funnel for the tides, creating a tidal amplitude of up to 10 m at the northern end, where the Colorado River enters. These tides run as far upriver as the junction with the Río Hardy, creating a vast intertidal area of mud, sand, and saltgrass beds, a feeding and nesting area for thousands of waterbirds. The tidewater is especially important when it is blended with river water. When the river runs, the intertidal portion of the river has low salinity and serves as a protected nursery area for fish fry and shrimp larvae, boosting the commercial catch of fish and shrimp in the following years. Doubtless the entire food web of the upper gulf benefits from river flows, in ways yet to be documented.

Ecozones of the Delta

We have divided the delta into five ecozones (Figure 25.1): (1) the Colorado River corridor, (2) the Río Hardy corridor, (3) the intertidal, coastal, and marine zone, (4) off-channel wetlands, and (5) farmland. Recently, an experts' workshop de-

tailed the conservation values, threats, and opportunities facing each zone (Glenn, Radtke et al. 2001). For the first time, large-scale vegetation and wildlife surveys are being conducted in the delta, and Minute 306 of the United States–Mexico Water Treaty recognizes the importance of the delta's wetland and riparian ecosystems. Ciénega de Santa Clara and the marine zone are protected in the Reserva de la Biosfera Alto Golfo de California y Delta del Río Colorado. All the delta ecosystems depend at least in part on human-managed water flows, and thus their continued existence depends on wise management decisions in the United States and Mexico. The key conservation issues facing each of the zones are outlined below. The unique regional flora of the delta and adjacent deserts and mountains is described in Felger (2000).

The Colorado River Riparian Corridor

The Colorado River as a perennial water source officially ends at Morelos Dam, at the international boundary between the United States and Mexico. By this point, all the U.S. water allotments have been withdrawn from the river, and at the dam, Mexico's 10 percent share of the river is diverted into Canal Central. The actual river, though, continues downstream 150 km to the sea, confined between flood-control levees but with enough room to spread over its banks when there is sufficient water. The first 100 km is a narrow riparian corridor that has been recolonized by native trees since pulse floods resumed (Figure 25.2). This is an extremely dynamic ecosystem. Tree studies conducted in 1998 showed that 70 percent of the trees were only five years old, started by the 1993 floods. Though young, these trees grew very fast and were 10 m tall with a diameter of 10 cm by the time of the survey. Most of the trees were willows, forming dense thickets along the river, with cottonwoods on the river's higher terrace.

A repeat survey in 2002 showed again that the most common age class was five-year-old trees—in this case, started by the El Niño releases of 1997–2000 (Nagler et al. 2005). Though still present, the older trees had been supplanted by a younger cohort. And there were plenty of new saplings along the riverbanks, started by 2001–2 releases of water, waiting to take their turn as the dominant age class. Osvel Hinojosa-Huerta has been collecting vegetation data and conducting bird surveys at 312 sites throughout the riparian corridor (Chapter 27, this volume). He finds that two things contribute most to high-quality bird habitat in this zone: the presence of native trees and the presence of water.

Two principal threats hang over this ecozone. First is the threat of channelization and vegetation clearing by management agencies. The International Boundary and Water Commission (IBWC) has proposed to dig a pilot channel through the Limitrophe region, capable of carrying all but the largest flow releases. This channel would mark the boundary between the United States and Mexico. IBWC has further proposed to clear vegetation along each side of the channel to increase the carrying capacity of the river between the levees. The Comisión Nacional del Agua (CNA) in Mexico plans to extend the channel and vegetation clearing farther downstream, to the junction with the Río Hardy. These plans, if implemented, would devastate the tree populations of the riparian zone, greatly reducing the value of the corridor as a bird migration route. Birds migrating up the Sonoran Coast are funneled into the delta, the neck of the funnel being the riparian zone. Hence this threat to the riparian zone is also a threat to the integrity of the Pacific Flyway.

The second threat is the lack of a guaranteed source of water. Because the riparian corridor is bounded by levees and is narrow, only modest flows are sufficient to flood the banks and germinate trees. We estimate that a spring flood of 100–200 m³/s of water delivered every four to five years is sufficient to germinate new cohorts of trees. Since 1981 much more water than that has actually reached the sea. We further estimate that an annual maintenance flow of 2 m³/s would provide permanent aquatic habitat that would benefit birds, insects, and other wildlife. This flow has been provided by "administrative spills"—water that is ordered by irrigation districts but not actually consumed. Plans have been made to try to capture both these sources for human use. Minute 306 may provide a mechanism to explicitly consider the impact of water management decisions on the ecosystems of the delta.

The Río Hardy Corridor

This former backup arm of the Colorado River flows from south of the Cerro Prieto geothermal ponds to the junction with the Colorado River near the tourist camp at La Mosqueda. Approxi-

Figure 25.2. Native trees have regenerated in the riparian corridor. (Photo by Pamela L. Nagler)

mately 30 km in length, it now carries irrigation return flows from the Mexicali Valley farms. The water is brackish (about 3–5 ppt salts), so few native trees grow along the banks. Nevertheless, the Río Hardy is an important corridor for shorebirds, waterbirds, and songbirds. When the Colorado River floods, the backwaters of the floodplain fill with water. They support wetlands, shallow ponds, and thousands of acres of saltbush and salt cedar. Water quality is the most serious conservation problem on the Río Hardy. In the absence of floods the main water source is irrigation return flows, which are not only high in total salts but may contain pesticide residues, heavy metals, selenium, and nitrates from fertilizers. Fortunately, none of these contaminants have seriously affected the health of the wildlife using the corridor, so far. The flushing flows of the Colorado River help keep contaminants below levels of risk for wildlife or humans. However, continued monitoring is needed to ensure the safety of this ecozone.

The Cerro Prieto salt ponds (Figure 25.3) are above the headwaters of Río Hardy. These manmade ponds receive spent geothermal water after it has been used (as steam) to generate electricity south of Mexicali. When the geothermal facility was first built, its wastewater was discharged into Río Hardy, but there were concerns about its possible toxicity to people and wildlife along the river. The water is discharged into a series of rectangular

ponds to cool and evaporate to solid salts. Ponds in the brackish salinity range are colonized by duckweed and periphyton, as well as pupfish by the thousands; they appear to be the only vertebrates present in the ponds. The soil removed to make the ponds was left in mounds around or in the ponds, providing protected roosting sites for a number of unique waterbirds. These man-made habitats are completely dependent on the operational decisions made by the managers of the geothermal facility. Fortunately, the managers are now aware of the ecological value of the ponds and mounds and are taking steps to preserve and enhance their wildlife value. Despite the strong mix of chemicals present in the ponds, no toxic accumulations have been found in their sediments or biota.

Intertidal and Marine Zones

The junction of the Colorado and Hardy rivers is the beginning of the intertidal zone, even though the Gulf of California is another 50 km down river. A water control structure at La Mosqueda releases Río Hardy agricultural drain water to the mainstem of the river, which mixes with seawater driven upriver by the tides. The river is perennial in this stretch and increases in both volume and salinity as it approaches Isla Montague at the mouth of the river. Shrimp and mullet, as well as bass, tilapia, and other freshwater fish, are caught as far north as the Cucupá fishing camps below La Mosqueda. The intertidal zone is a breeding area for marine species such as shrimp, corvina, and the endangered totoaba, a large, high-quality fish that was the basis for an early commercial fishery in the region. Kayaking down the river from the junction of the Río Hardy to the sea has become a popular activity, and when the Colorado is in flood, a tidal bore still forms, like the one that destroyed steamboats in the 1800s (see Nelson, this volume). In 1998

two fishermen drowned when "El Burro" swamped their pangas.

The vegetation of this zone is relatively simple. Common reed grows along the riverbanks, and cattail grows in areas of standing water away from the channel. The cattails come and go with the flood events on the river. Their tubers can survive through dry seasons and resprout when water returns. However, most of the floodplain below the junction of the Hardy and Colorado rivers is covered with a virtual monoculture of salt cedar from Asia, established in the early 1900s. Approximately 60,000 ha are dominated by this single plant, which grows in nearly impenetrable thickets. This may be the largest stand of salt cedar in the world, as in its native range it is controlled by insects. The role of this plant in the local ecoregion is unknown. Birds and mammals tend to be sparse in the thickets, yet they surely feed detritus into the estuary and marine zone, and the detrital food chain drives much of the marine zone's productivity.

Ironically, the intertidal part of the river supported much more aquatic habitat in the 1970s, before flood flows resumed, than it does today. The reason was a sandbar on the river, which prevented seawater from penetrating upriver and which backed up the Río Hardy waters above the dam. This sandbar was created by the action of the tides that pushed silt up the river to form a natural dam about 25 km from the river's mouth. The steady, slow flow of the Río Hardy spread over the floodplain north of the dam, creating 60,000 ha of wetland and riparian habitat instead of the salt cedar present there today.

What was the value of this habitat? The older Cucapás remember it as a vast marsh filled with fish. What were the risks? No one knows. In today's world we would worry about water quality, since the water source was agricultural return flows with the problems described above. A restoration project is under way to recreate some of this former habitat by damming a small portion of the intertidal zone below the fishing camps. The backwater thus created will allow fishermen to guide their pangas through the chokepoints on the river and out to the marine zone and will give a preview to conservation scientists of what a larger set of backwaters would be like.

The marine zone begins at Isla Montague. The island and adjacent shore are fringed with Palmer's saltgrass *(Distichlis palmeri),* found in the northern Gulf of California. Its large grain was a staple food of the Cucupás in the past, but without freshwater flow in the river, grain production is reduced (Felger, this volume, chapter 15). Nevertheless, the island is an important breeding and feeding ground for waterbirds. In the past the influence of the Colorado River on the Gulf of California extended as far south as the Midriff Islands (e.g., Isla Tiburón). Today, with much diminished flows, the influence is less. A logical dividing line would be the limit of the biosphere reserve—a line drawn across the gulf between San Felipe and Puerto Peñasco. This incorporates the home territory of two endangered marine species, the totoaba and the vaquita.

The biggest need for the intertidal and marine zone is more water: the question is, how much? The large flood events on the river are probably gone forever, or at least they will be very infrequent. Reduction in flows, and with it silt and nutrients, has undoubtedly had a negative impact on some components of the marine food web. For example, the vast cheniers of shell piled up on Isla Montague and along the western shoreline were left by a brackish-water clam that is scarcely present in the modern delta. On the other hand, some functions of the marine ecosystem have been revived by the modest flows of the past twenty years. A study of the annual San Felipe shrimp catch showed a positive influence of the river on the succeeding year's harvest (Galindo-Bect et al. 2000). Even a modest flow can double or triple the next year's catch. These small floods do not carry sufficient water, silt, or nutrients to affect the marine zone directly, but they reduce the salinity in the intertidal portion of the river to the point that predator fish cannot penetrate to the nursery areas of larval shrimp and fish fry, including totoaba and corvina, both of which have returned to the marine zone and estuary.

Some other threats to the marine zone may not be as urgent as they have seemed. Since the river's silt is now captured behind upstream dams, some observers fear that the delta will disappear due to accretion. The evidence of accretion is easy to find: stand on the banks at high tide and you will see large chunks of the riverbank calve away into the current. Tire tracks that marked a safe passage along the river a month ago may now suddenly disappear into the abyss. Yet this accretion is due to head cutting and occurs mainly at the more upstream end of the intertidal zone. Isla Montague and the surrounding shorelines are actually gaining land. The water at the mouth of the river is as brown as ever, owing to the resuspension of silt by the tides, and new silt is still added in the form of wind-blown dust from the desert. Furthermore, there is no evidence that pesticides and heavy metals are impacting the marine zone as feared.

Off-Channel Wetlands

This is a catchall designation for several important wetland groups that are not directly supported by water from the Colorado River. Some are natural, but most are supported by agricultural drain water or canal seepage. Their anthropogenic origins do not diminish their importance as wildlife habitats. Almost all the water that reaches the delta has passed through human hands, but it is no less the wet for that. Wildlife and vegetation studies conducted over the past ten years have shown that these wetlands are critical stopover and nesting areas on the Pacific Flyway, and local residents hunt, fish, and provide guiding services in them. Yet they are so little known to the outside world that few had official place-names before 1992.

Mexican and American scientists first noticed the Andrade Mesa wetlands (with about 3,500 ha in Mexico) while doing low-level, aerial vegetation mapping in the delta in 2002 (Figure 25.4). Some of the flights originated at the Mexicali airport, and the scientists noticed a large complex of wetlands nestled into low spots in the dunes just east of the airport. They occur along the southern escarpment of the Andrade Mesa dunes, at the northern edge of the agricultural fields in Mexico. They are fed by seepage from the All-American Canal. This unlined canal, an engineering marvel of its time, was completed in 1940 and carries up to 300 m³/s of water from the Colorado River to Imperial Valley, slicing through the dunes along the United States–Mexico border. About 2 percent of the water seeps under the dunes into Mexico, where some of it is recovered by pumps and used for irrigation while the rest supports the Andrade Mesa wetlands.

The wetlands were soon mapped and at least partly explored on foot, and they proved to support 43 species of birds, including rare and endangered species (Yuma clapper rail, long-billed savannah sparrow, gull-billed tern, possibly black

Figure 25.4. Andrade Mesa wetlands, supported by seepage from the All-American Canal. (Photo by Pamela L. Nagler)

rail). These wetlands have a simple hydrology. Seepage water from the canal surfaces in low spots in the dunes and percolates to a central evaporation pond, which can be quite saline. Around the pond are saltgrass beds, and around the saltgrass are stands of cattail. Covering the dunes are halophyte shrubs and honey mesquite trees, rooted into the water beneath. Although just now noticed by the outside world, these wetlands may date back a hundred years, when the first canal was cut across Andrade Mesa. The U.S. Bureau of Reclamation plans to line the canal to prevent seepage. Mexico and the United States have long been in dispute about this plan, which would eliminate the wetlands.

Ciénega de Santa Clara (Figure 25.5), at 4,200 ha, receives 85 percent of its water (about 110,000 acre-ft/yr) from the Wellton-Mohawk Irrigation District in the United States and the rest from local irrigation return flows. Both sources enter at the northern end, in separate canals, to create a dense cattail marsh at the spot where the main arm of the San Andreas Fault enters the sea. The ciénega was re-created in 1977, when the United States began sending brackish groundwater from Wellton-Mohawk to this spot in the delta via a 100-km concrete canal (the M.O.D.E., or Main Outlet Drain Extension, canal). Formerly this water was delivered to Mexico as part of its irrigation allotment, but it was so saline that it damaged the crops. The two countries negotiated Minute 242 of their water treaty, guaranteeing that water delivered to Mexico would be no more than 10 percent more saline than water at Imperial Dam in the United States. The U.S. Bureau of Reclamation built the Yuma Desalting Plant to attempt to salvage the saline water source, but it operated only briefly in 1993, at one-third capacity.

Meanwhile, twenty-five years of water delivery in the M.O.D.E. canal have turned the ciénega into a wetland jewel. A local *ejido* runs a tourist camp, and tours of the delta including the ciénega can be booked from Ajo, Arizona. The boundaries of the core zone of the Reserva de la Biosfera Alto Golfo de California y Delta del Río Colorado, established in 1992, were adjusted to include the ciénega in recognition of its outstanding wildlife values. The main threat to the ciénega is the Yuma Desalting Plant, which still sits in "ready standby" on the United States–Mexico border below Yuma. The state of Arizona is suing to resume operation.

El Indio wetlands are a similar but smaller set of marshes southwest of the ciénega. They are fed by a large drainage ditch that collects drain water from the San Luis agricultural area to the north. Associated with the marshes is a large, apparently permanent shallow lake, at Rancho San Rafael, choked with cattail and filled with waterfowl. As with the ciénega, the water sources feeding these wetlands are not secure. Despite their inclusion in the biosphere reserve, they do not receive official consideration in the water management decisions that affect their fate.

El Doctor wetlands are natural. They are a series of springs (*pozos*) that bubble up in the intertidal zone south of the ciénega. Most of them are just below the eastern escarpment of the delta, where it joins El Gran Desierto. Rainwater falling on the western flanks of the Sierra el Pinacate flows under the desert sand to emerge on the delta mudflats. The water is slightly salty and supports a bull's-eye pattern of plant growth. Freshwater forms such as cattails are nearest the center whereas more salt-tolerant plants ring the outer areas. We documented 22 species of aquatic plants growing in these marshes.

Although these wetlands are not vast in area, they are a long green line across barren desert, connecting the southeastern end of the delta with the coastal *esteros* to the south. Osvel Hinojosa-Huerta and Jaqueline García-Hernández are finding that they are extraordinarily important for supporting birds as they migrate up the Sonoran coast and through the delta on their way north (Chapter 27, this volume). In fact, this may be a major, but previously unrecognized, migration route for songbirds, so numerous are they in Hinojosa-Huerta and García-Hernández's mist nets. The wetlands are part of the biosphere reserve but have been degraded by heavy cattle grazing. The federal government of Mexico plans to construct a highway to link the towns of El Golfo and Puerto Peñasco, which would complete the Sonoran coastal highway and connect the delta to the rest of Mexico and the United States. Inevitably, El Golfo will grow, and there will be a temptation to install a well field along the Gran Desierto escarpment to recover for human use the freshwater that now feeds the wetlands. This would be the end of the El Doctor wetlands.

Protecting the New Green Lagoons

Aldo Leopold explored the delta with his brother in 1928. He described an endless series of green lagoons surrounded by forests filled with deer, coyote, and maybe even jaguars. Writing about his trip years later, he remarked that he never returned to the delta but was told that the green lagoons now grew melons, and he hoped they were the sweeter for that (Leopold 1949). We think he gave up on the delta too soon.

In our ten years of exploring the delta with our friends, we have experienced the same sense of discovery as earlier explorers. We've found new

Figure 25.5. *Ciénega de Santa Clara, largest marsh in the Sonoran Desert. (Photo by Pamela L. Nagler)*

wetlands, seen regenerated forests that no one knew existed, and made up place-names that are now on maps. We've been lost in the woods, stuck in the sand, suffered heat exhaustion. The first modern descent of the river from the last road crossing to the intertidal zone was undertaken during the El Niño flows of 1998. There is much less wild delta than there was a hundred years ago, but there is more than there was 25 years ago.

Although surrounded by 1.5 million people, the delta wildlands have a measure of protection provided by the surrounding levees and the biosphere reserve. It is true that the Colorado River supplies water for 22 million people and is over-appropriated. But less than 1 percent of the river flow is needed to support the delta ecosystems. That water consists of waste flows from agriculture and occasional flood flows that, so far, cannot be easily turned to human use. We think those who love nature still have time to enjoy the delta and to work to preserve it for the next generation of explorers.

Marine Fishes of the Upper Gulf Biosphere Reserve, Northern Gulf of California

Philip A. Hastings and Lloyd T. Findley

A book entitled *Dry Borders* does not immediately conjure up an image of fishes, let alone an image of hundreds of meter-long predatory ones churning the waters. One might not envision small, silvery fishes lining a wave-washed beach to bury their eggs in the sand either. Nonetheless, the northern Gulf of California counts among its inhabitants just such remarkable creatures, as well as a surprising array of other fishes. Fishes have played an important role in the economic development of the region and continue to fascinate and inspire those fortunate enough to visit the gulf and observe them firsthand. However, the marine region of the northern gulf has changed dramatically over the past several decades, and its fish communities are in danger of changing permanently; in fact, they have already begun to do so.

In June 1993 Mexico established the Reserva de la Biosfera del Alto Golfo de California y Delta del Río Colorado to protect the unique faunal assemblage of this region, with emphasis placed on two endemic and endangered species, the legendary totoaba and the vaquita, or Gulf of California harbor porpoise (Diario Oficial 1993). Total surface area of the reserve, including its marine portion and (greatly diminished) fresh- and brackish-water wetlands along with its adjacent desert lands, is 934,756 hectares, making it one of the largest biosphere reserves in Mexico. The reserve is divided into two areas (Figure 26.1). The nuclear, or core, zone *(zona nucleo)* includes the remaining wetlands of the lowermost Colorado River and the low mud islands and tidal channels of the river's now hypersaline estuary at the very head of the Gulf of California; its southern terminus is demarcated by a line connecting the fishing town of El Golfo de Santa Clara, Sonora, and the southern end of the Estero La Ramada, north of San Felipe, Baja California. Conservation of natural resources within the nuclear zone is purportedly complete, with no exploitative or extractive activities permitted. The second area, about 80 percent of the reserve and comprising mainly the marine waters and coastlines of the northernmost gulf, is a buffer zone *(zona de amortiguamiento)* extending southward of the nuclear zone to a line connecting Punta San Felipe (Punta Machorro), at the northern edge of the town of San Felipe, and Punta Pelícano (Punta Cholla, Roca del Toro), a few kilometers west-northwest of the town of Puerto Peñasco, Sonora. Certain kinds of regulated extractive activities (principally several types of fishing) are allowed within the buffer zone (INE 1995). Following an overview of the history of ichthyology in this extraordinary region, we present a summary of the marine fish fauna recorded from the biosphere reserve.

Ichthyology in the Northern Gulf of California

The study of fishes in the northern gulf had a relatively slow start. Though the deserts surrounding the gulf enjoyed a complex and storied history of scientific exploration, these same deserts effectively isolated the northern Gulf of California from early ichthyologists, most of whom apparently chose to forgo the rigors of the necessary overland expedition. Consequently, the early exploration of the northern gulf ichthyofauna was dominated by ship-based expeditions. Still, since the northern gulf was at the "end of the line," relatively few ships ventured as far north as the current biosphere reserve: there was no safe deepwater harbor or other major settlement in the region, and the conditions were often treacherous. Moreover, the southern and central portions of the gulf (e.g., Guaymas, Mazatlán, La Paz) were biologically fascinating and more accessible. Despite the deep regional knowledge of Native American peoples, such as the Cucapás (Cocopahs), Quechans (Yumas), Hia C'ed O'odham (Sand Papagos), and Comcáac (Seris), the northern Gulf of California remained a frontier to the science of ichthyology until relatively recent times.

The first European explorers who ventured into the extreme northern gulf were usually in search of pearls, gold, or the Strait of Anián, a mythical seawater passage to the East Indies and (later) to Alta California (Bowen 2000; Flint & Flint 2005; Lindsey 1983; Ness 1993). Most published accounts of their expeditions rarely if ever mention fishes. Instead, the few early explorers who reached the delta of the Colorado River typically commented on the environmental extremes of the region, such as the summer heat, great tidal ranges (amplitudes), tidal bores, vast tidal flats, and shifting and treacherous channels, as well as the apparent paucity of life on the surrounding barren lands (Moriarty 1965; Sykes 1937). One of the earliest to mention fishes was Lt. Joseph C. Ives, commissioned by the U.S. secretary of war to survey the lower Colorado River for its potential for steamboat traffic, in the hope of opening up an aquatic supply line to mining and military camps upriver (e.g., Fort Yuma). In 1857 Ives reported that a retired ferryman had settled on the western side of the river's delta at "Robinson's Landing," just north of Isla Montague, to make oil from "black fish" that spawned there, possibly a reference to the dark-colored totoaba (Sykes 1937; Thurston 1973). If so, a settlement for harvesting the once abundant totoaba heralded the key role this species was to play in the region's economic development as the impetus for the establishment of fishing camps (later to become towns) at Punta Peñasco, El Golfo de Santa Clara, and San Felipe (Bahre et al. 2000; Munro-Palacio 1994).

The first scientific collection of fishes supported by a research vessel was a short excursion in 1881 into the northern gulf by the U.S. Coast and Geodetic steamer *Hassler,* captained by Lt. Henry E. Nichols. One 23-inch-long corvina (Sciaenidae) obtained at San Felipe was described as *Cynoscion othonopterus* by Charles Henry Gilbert, soon to figure prominently in North American ichthyology, and his mentor and colleague, David Starr Jordan, widely recognized as the father of American ichthyology. On opening the stomach of this single specimen, they found a recently ingested anchovy (Engraulidae) and also described

Figure 26.1. The nuclear and buffer zones of the Reserva de la Biosfera del Alto Golfo de California y Delta del Río Colorado, northernmost Gulf of California. (Digitally prepared by N. Camacho)

it as a new species, *Stolephorus opercularis* Jordan & Gilbert, 1882, now considered a synonym of the common anchoveta, *Cetengraulis mysticetus* (Günther 1867).

The first extensive collection of fishes in the extreme northern gulf was made by scientists and crew aboard the U.S. Fish Commission steamer *Albatross* (Figure 26.2). This legendary research ship was assigned to the Pacific coast in 1888 to study its environment and marine life. In the spring of 1889 the ship embarked from San Francisco to explore the coasts of southern California and western Mexico (Allard 1999). The *Albatross* first entered the Gulf of California on March 11, 1889, and reached the area now included in the biosphere reserve near the northeasternmost corner of the gulf on March 25. Unfortunately, the ship did not linger in the northern gulf, passing Rocas Consag on March 27 on its way southward. While at anchor, the crew of the *Albatross* typically fished from the ship with hand lines, and off "Shoal Point," near the mouth of the Colorado River, they caught large numbers of "squeteague" (corvinas, *Cynoscion* species, family Sciaenidae) and "sea bass" (probably *Totoaba macdonaldi,* also a corvina-like sciaenid). So many fish were caught, in fact, that

Figure 26.2. *The U.S. Fish Commission steamer* Albatross, *1896.*

the ship's commander felt "obliged to put a stop to the fishing" (Tanner 1892:440). The crew also collected using seines and gillnets, but Commander Tanner complained that "sharks and dogfish [likely smoothhounds of the genus *Mustelus* and the Pacific sharpnose shark, *Rhizoprionodon longurio*] were found throughout the gulf in sufficient numbers to make gill-net fishing impracticable" (Tanner 1892:440). During this cruise the *Albatross* made 22 dredge or trawl stations in the northern gulf (above 29° N latitude), although only 10 (stations 3023 to 3032) were above 31° N latitude (Tanner 1892) and thus in the current biosphere reserve.

The chief naturalist on board the *Albatross* at this time was the aforementioned great ichthyologist Charles Henry Gilbert (Figure 26.3), about whom the U.S. commissioner of fish and fisheries had written to Commander Tanner, "You will find Professor Gilbert an exceedingly agreeable man . . . one of the most accomplished ichthyologists of the present time . . . an experienced and enthusiastic collector" (Dunn 1997:270). Gilbert oversaw the field collections and later described the fishes collected from this and other *Albatross* cruises from this time period (e.g., Gilbert 1890, 1892; Gilbert & Scofield 1898). Species still considered valid that were described by Gilbert based on specimens collected from within the current biosphere reserve include a bewildering array of fishes: the corvina-like totoaba, *Totoaba macdonaldi* (Gilbert, 1890) (Sciaenidae); the spotfin cusk-eel, *Ophidion galeoides* (Gilbert, 1890) (Ophidiidae); the Cortez pipefish, *Syngnathus carinatus* (Gilbert, 1892) (Syngnathidae); the pennant goby, *Bollmania ocellata* (Gilbert, 1892) (Gobiidae); the squirrel sand perch, *Diplectrum sciurus* (Gilbert, 1892) (Serranidae); and

the Cortez halibut, *Paralichthys aestuarius* (Gilbert & Scofield, 1898) (Paralichthyidae). In total, Gilbert described 20 new genera and 176 new species of fishes based on specimens collected during this gulf cruise and three other *Albatross* cruises off western North America (Dunn 1997), permanently establishing his place in the history of ichthyology of the eastern Pacific. In addition to the species described by Gilbert, the ocellated turbot, *Pleuronichthys ocellatus* (Starks & Thompson, 1910) (Pleuronectidae), and the Cortez stingray, *Urobatis maculatus* (Garman, 1913) (Urolophidae), were later described by others based on *Albatross* specimens collected in 1889 from the current biosphere reserve. The *Albatross* revisited the Gulf of California on other occasions, including an important cruise in 1911, but in this instance the ship turned back southward after passing Isla Ángel de La Guarda and thus did not enter the current biosphere reserve (Townsend 1916).

Relatively few other scientific vessels collected fishes in the extreme northern Gulf of California. One exception was the research yacht *Pawnee*, which visited the gulf in 1926 as part of a survey of fishes from Mexico to Panama for the private Bingham Oceanographic Collection of New York City (Moore & Boardman 1991). Charles Breder, of the New York Aquarium, reported on fishes from this cruise (Breder 1928a, b, c), describing as new *Urotrygon binghami* (Breder, 1928), now considered a synonym of the thorny stingray, *Urotrygon rogersi* (Jordan & Starks, 1895) (Urolophidae); the northern gulf anchovy, *Anchoa mundeoloides* (Breder, 1928) (Engraulidae); and a new genus of silversides in honor of Carl L. Hubbs, *Hubbsiella* (now considered a synonym of the grunion genus *Leuresthes*, Atherinopsidae), from specimens collected in the area of the current biosphere reserve. Subsequently, another anchovy, *Anchoviella parri* Hildebrand, 1943 (Engraulidae), was described from *Pawnee* specimens that had been collected at San Felipe in 1926. Interestingly, this mystery anchovy apparently has not since been collected, although Whitehead et al. (1988:324), based on the morphological characters provided by Hildebrand (1943), disputed its assignment to the genus *Anchoviella* and only briefly and rather enigmatically noted it as "an upper Gulf form of *A* [*nchoa*] *lucida*, perhaps a distinct species." Later Whitehead and Rodríguez-Sánchez (1995) evidently accepted it as a valid species, albeit again rather enigmatically, in that "*Anchoa parri*" appears as such in their identification key to tropical eastern Pacific anchovies (pages 1068–71) and its accompanying table of morphological characters, but they failed to include it in their list of species present in the area (page 1072) and in their treatment of 23 regional anchovy species (pages 1073–87). Unfortunately, the untimely death of Peter J. P. Whitehead, the world's foremost authority on the systematics of anchovies, prevented his resolution of the taxonomic status of the mystery anchovy.

During the latter half of the twentieth century, most ship-based collection records for fishes from the biosphere reserve were from the bycatch associated with the shrimp trawling industry. One species, the Cortez butterfish, *Peprilus ovatus* Horn, 1970 (Stromateidae), was described based on specimens taken from shrimp trawls off El Golfo de Santa Clara and elsewhere in the northern gulf.

The offshore, trawl-based shrimp fishery in the gulf began under Japanese influence around 1921 and was centered at Guaymas (Hedgpeth & Ricketts 1978) until the 1940s and 1950s, when the fishery expanded to all exploitable areas of the gulf. The number of trawlers increased rapidly through the following decades to a peak of about 1,400 in 1983, declined to 1,144 in 1997, then increased again to 1,470 in 2000 (García-Caudillo & Gómez-Palafox in prep.). Collections of bycatch fishes from such bottom trawlers in the northern gulf were made in the 1940s and 1950s under the direction of Carl L. Hubbs (Scripps Institution of Oceanography [SIO]) and Boyd W. Walker (University of California Los Angeles [UCLA]) and in the late 1960s and early 1970s under the auspices of Donald A. Thomson and John R. Hendrickson (University of Arizona). Published accounts and theses documenting bycatch fishes of the northern gulf include Berdegué 1956, Castro-Aguirre et al. 1970, Guevara-Escamilla 1974, Romero 1978, Pérez-Mellado & Findley 1985, and Nava-Romo 1994. These studies are particularly important because they provide the only quantitative estimates of the offshore fish fauna of the northern gulf.

Land-based exploration of the marine waters of the extreme northern gulf was relatively difficult, owing to the lack of good roads into the region and difficulty in collecting along the soft and shifting shoreline. A few early collections, however, near the fishing camps of San Felipe and Punta

Figure 26.3. Charles Henry Gilbert (1891), legendary collector and describer of Pacific coast fishes. (Photo courtesy of Indiana University Archives)

Peñasco, included specimens of species new to science, such as the gulf anchovy, *Anchoa helleri* (Hubbs, 1921) (Engraulidae), collected at San Felipe by Edmund Heller in 1921. Other shore collections using mainly beach seines and gillnets were made during the 1940s to 1960s primarily in the San Felipe area by SIO and UCLA personnel under the guidance of Hubbs and Walker, in the early 1960s by students at California State University Long Beach (CSULB) under the tutelage of Arthur S. Lockley, and somewhat later by students in the Marine Science Program at the University of Arizona under the direction of Thomson.

Thomson and his students began extensive studies of the biology of the northern gulf in 1964 (Thomson 1969). Their work, mainly on the Sonora side of the gulf, included a number of trips to El Golfo de Santa Clara, which led to a series of publications on the systematics, ecology, and behavior of the gulf grunion, *Leuresthes sardina*. Study of the rocky-shore fishes of the northern gulf by Thomson and his students was facilitated by establishment of field stations at Puerto Peñasco, first at a mostly open-air facility called Costa Azul and later at a more substantial installation located in the García House south of town, in the area known today as Las Conchas. A historically significant publication (Thomson & Lehner 1979), based on repeated quantitative samples from the extensive rocky tidepools near the field station (Figure 26.4), provides one of the earliest and indeed one of the only quantitative baselines for

Figure 26.4. *Station Beach reef at Puerto Peñasco, 1966, the site of extensive samples of reef-associated fishes analyzed by Thomson and Lehner (1979). Punta Peñasco is seen in the background. (Photo by D. A. Thomson)*

species abundance of reef fishes in the northern gulf. These and other collections of fishes from throughout the gulf formed the basis of a popular guide to the common fishes of the gulf (Thomson & McKibbin 1976) and of the well-known *Reef Fishes of the Sea of Cortez* (Thomson et al. 1979, 2000). One of the most common intertidal species, the Sonora blenny, *Malacoctenus gigas* Springer, 1959, which is endemic to the gulf, was described based on specimens from the Puerto Peñasco area.

During the late 1960s and into the 1980s a colleague of Thomson's at the University of Arizona, John R. Hendrickson, was deeply involved in its Marine Science Program and, along with several students, carried out investigations on the biology of Gulf of California sea turtles and fishes. Hendrickson conducted pioneering work on the reproductive biology of the totoaba and was the first to attempt its aquaculture (Flanagan & Hendrickson 1976; Hendrickson 1979). The deep concern he and his American and Mexican colleagues had for the fate of this giant fish eventually led to the totoaba's official designation as an endangered species by both Mexico and the United States, the first marine fish accorded that status.

Apart from some additional research on the totoaba (e.g., see Cisneros-Mata et al. 1995 and references therein), including laboratory-based studies on captive individuals (Morales-Ortiz 1999; Ortiz-Viveros 1999), the most recent years have seen a general decline in ichthyological collecting

and studies in the far northern gulf. However, observations on certain species continue to be made, principally by researchers at Mexican institutions such as the Ensenada campus of the Universidad Autónoma de Baja California (e.g., Gorgonio Ruiz-Campos and students) and, especially, the state of Sonora's Estación de Campo de El Golfo de Santa Clara of the Instituto del Medio Ambiente y del Desarrollo Sustentable del Estado de Sonora (IMADES). At the latter, important work on the northern-gulf endemic corvina, *Cynoscion othonopterus,* particularly its response to a relatively recently revived (but now apparently again declining) fishery, continues to be carried out by Martha Román-Rodríguez, assisted by her biologist husband, José Campoy-Favela, the administrative director of the biosphere reserve.

Fishes of the Alto Golfo Biosphere Reserve

We compiled a list of marine fish species recorded within the Alto Golfo Biosphere Reserve (see first checklist at end of this chapter) based on a database of all species of macrofauna known from the Gulf of California (Brusca et al. 2005; Findley et al. in press). Although the southern limit of the biosphere reserve's buffer zone extends from Punta San Felipe (Punta Machorro) to Punta Pelícano (Punta Cholla, Roca del Toro), just west-northwest of Punta Peñasco (Figure 26.1), we included all fishes taken in the vicinity of San Felipe, Baja California, and Puerto Peñasco, Sonora. This was deemed appropriate because older collection records commonly use the place-names *San Felipe* and *Puerto Peñasco* without precise details of locality. It also permitted us to take advantage of the extensive surveys of reef fishes done over several years at Station Beach (Figure 26.4), just east of Punta Peñasco (Thomson et al. 1979, 2000:Figure 3) by researchers from the University of Arizona (e.g., Thomson & Lehner 1979). Our species list is based on published systematic and other accounts of fishes from the region, unpublished records (e.g., Guevara-Escamilla 1974; Nava-Romo 1994), and surveys of holdings of natural history collections housing fishes from the region. Most important among these are the Scripps Institution of Oceanography (SIO) of the University of California San Diego, the University of California Los Angeles (UCLA), the University of Arizona (UAZ), and the Natural History Museum of Los Angeles

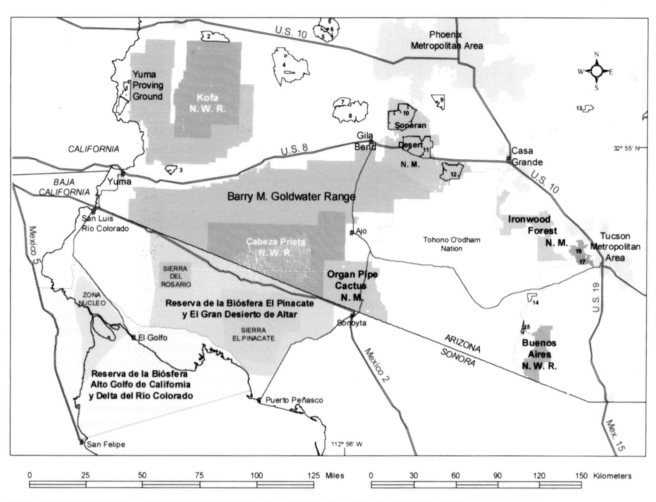

Map Legend

▢ Political Boundaries	Tohono O'odham Nation	═══ Interstate Highways
Urban Areas	Military Reservations	─── Secondary Highways
# Towns		

Reserva de la Biósfera El Pinacate y El Gran Desierto de Altar	U.S. National Monuments	U.S. Wilderness Areas
Zona Nucleo Sierra del Rosario	**16** Saguaro National Park (West)	
Zona Nucleo Sierra El Pinacate	**17** Tucson Mountain Park	
Reserva de la Biósfera Alto Golfo y Delta del Río Colorado	U.S. National Wildlife Refuges	
Zona Nucleo		

U.S. Wilderness Areas
1 Trigo Mountains Wilderness
2 New Water Mountains Wilderness
3 Muggins Mountains Wilderness
4 Eagle Tail Mountains Wilderness
5 Big Horn Mountains Wilderness
6 Hummingbird Springs Wilderness
7 Signal Mountain Wilderness
8 Woolsey Peak Wilderness
9 Sierra Estrella Wilderness
10 North Maricopa Mountains Wilderness
11 South Maricopa Mountains Wilderness
12 Table Top Mountains Wilderness
13 White Canyon Wilderness
14 Baboquivari Peak Wilderness
15 Coyote Mountains Wilderness

Digital coverages assembled from the following sources: Sonoran Desert N.M., Ironwood Forest N.M., and Wilderness Area boundaries from BLM-Phoenix (2001). ~ Tohono O'odham, Buenos Aires and Cabeza Prieta N.W.R., Organ Pipe Cactus N.M., Saguaro N.P., and Tucson Mountain Park boundaries: Pima County Land Information System (2000). ~ Other Arizona boundaries: Arizona Land Resource Information System (ALRIS). ~ Biósfera boundaries adapted from polygons provided by The Nature Conservancy-Tucson (refer to Marshall et al. 2000). ~ Major political boundaries and U.S. roads: ESRI U.S. datasets. ~ Mexico roads, Gulf of California boundary and Colorado River digitized from a Landsat-7 image of October 1999. ~ All coverages projected to UTM, datum NAD83, spheroid GRS1980. ~ Image processing and map preparation by K. Mauz, Arizona Remote Sensing Center, University of Arizona (September 2001).

Co.1. Dry Borders region of the Sonoran Desert with bio-reserve protected areas: Sonoran Desert National Monument, Cabeza Prieta National Wildlife Refuge, Barry M. Goldwater Range, Organ Pipe Cactus National Monument, Reserva de la Biosfera El Pinacate y Gran Desierto de Altar, and Reserva de la Biosfera del Alto Golfo de California y Delta del Río Colorado. (Map by Kathryn Mauz)

C0.2. Organ Pipe Cactus
National Monument.
(Photo © Jack Dykinga)

Co.3. Cabeza Prieta National Wildlife Refuge.
(Photo © Jack Dykinga)

C0.4. Reserva de la Biosfera El Pinacate y Gran Desierto de Altar. (Photo © Jack Dykinga)

C0.5. Sonoran Desert National Monument. (Photo © Jack Dykinga)

Co.6. Barry M. Goldwater
Range, Tinajas Altas.
(Photo © Jack Dykinga)

Co.7. Reserva de la Biosfera
Alto Golfo de California y
Delta del Río Colorado.
(Photo © Jack Dykinga)

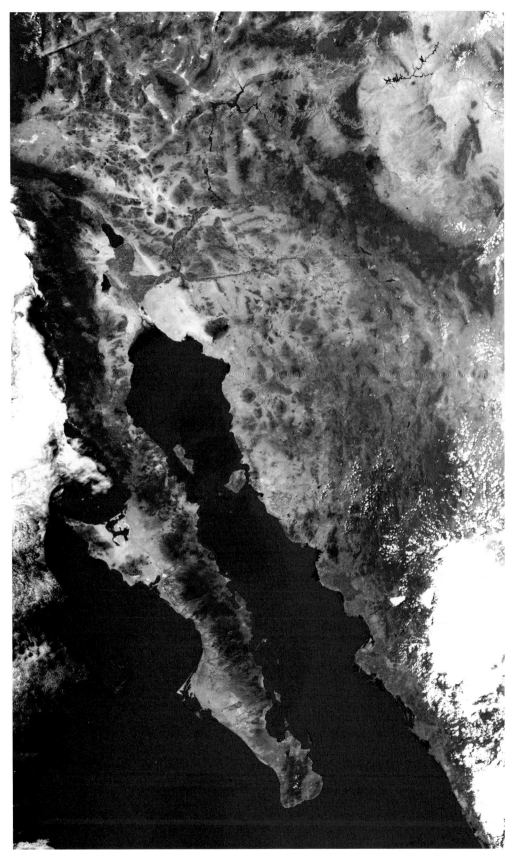

C2.1. Southwestern North America. False-color infrared image of Arizona, northwestern Sonora, and the Baja California peninsula acquired by the Advanced Very High Resolution Radiometer (AVHRR) on July 8, 1987, from an altitude of 833 km (518 mi) above the Earth. (© 2002 by K. C. Horstman)

0   30 mi

0   50 km

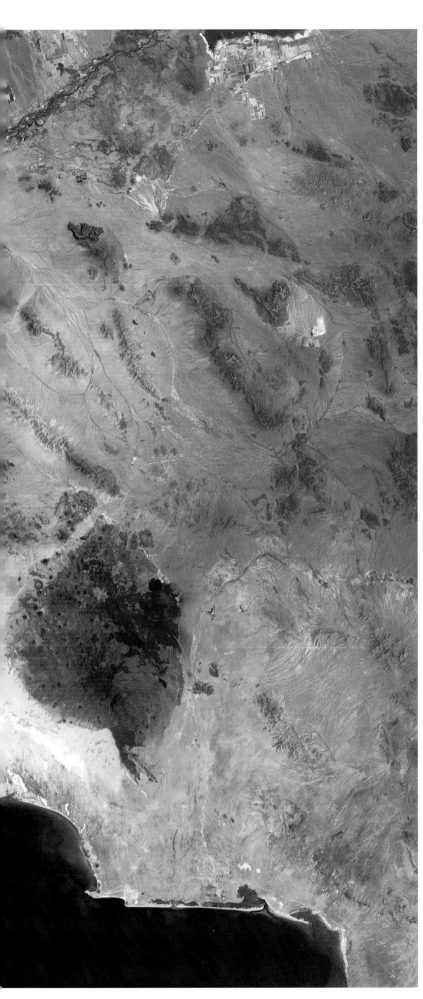

C2.2. Southwestern Arizona and adjacent regions. Mosaic of three visible-spectrum Landsat images acquired in the early 1990s from an orbital altitude of approximately 700 km (440 mi) above the Earth. The area shown is 259 km (161 mi) west to east and 217 km (135 mi) north to south. (© 2002 by K. C. Horstman)

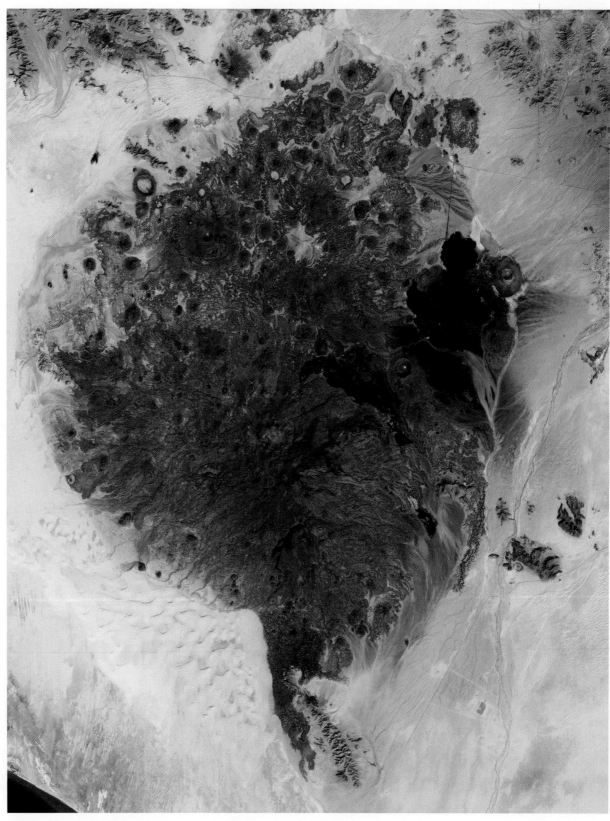

C2.3. Pinacate Volcanic Field. The volcanic field is the
dark region in this false-color infrared image acquired
in 1999 by Landsat 7. The image area is 51 km (32 mi)
west to east and 66 km (41 mi) north to south. (© 2002
by K. C. Horstman)

C2.4. Lower Colorado River delta. The yellow-tan region to the northeast is the Gran Desierto of Sonora, and the mountains of Baja California are visible in the west part of the image. Water appears blue, plants are shown as green, and blue streaks in the Gulf of California show suspended sediments carried by streams and tidal currents. Area covered by this image subset is 109 km (68 mi) west to east and 105 km (65 mi) north to south. (© 2002 by K. C. Horstman)

C15.25. Agavaceae. *Agave deserti.* Sierra Blanca. (Photo by Richard S. Felger)

C15.26. Agavaceae. *Hesperoyucca whipplei.* Sierra del Viejo. (Photo by Richard S. Felger)

C15.27. Amaranthaceae. *Amaranthus palmeri.* (Photo by Richard S. Felger)

C15.28. Cactaceae. *Opuntia engelmannii* var. *engelmannii.* (Photo by Richard S. Felger)

C15.29. Poaceae. *Distichlis palmeri.* Río Colorado delta. (Photo by Richard S. Felger)

C15.30. Saururaceae. *Anemopsis californica.* Laguna Prieta. (Photo by Mark Dimmitt)

C15.31. Solanaceae. *Lycium fremontii.* (Photo by Richard S. Felger)

C15.32. *Hyles lineata* larvae on *Pectis papposa.* (Photo by Dale S. Turner)

C17.18

C17.19

C17.20

C17.21

C17.23

C17.22

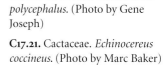

C17.24

C17.25

C17.18. Pteridaceae. *Notholaena standleyi.* (Photo by Kathryn Mauz)

C17.19. Asclepiadaceae. *Funastrum cynanchoides.* (Photo by Kathryn Mauz)

C17.20. Cactaceae. *Echinocactus polycephalus.* (Photo by Gene Joseph)

C17.21. Cactaceae. *Echinocereus coccineus.* (Photo by Marc Baker)

C17.22. Euphorbiaceae. *Euphorbia pediculifera.* (Photo by Kathryn Mauz)

C17.23. Nolinaceae. *Nolina bigelovii.* (Photo by Richard S. Felger)

C17.24. Simaroubaceae. *Castela emoryi.* (Photo by Kathryn Mauz)

C17.25. Zygophyllaceae. *Kallstroemia californica.* (Photo by Kathryn Mauz)

C18.1. Sonoran pronghorn (*Antilocapra americana sonoriensis*). (Photo by Robert S. Henry, Arizona Game and Fish Department)

C18.2. Kit fox (*Vulpes velox macrotis*). (Photo by Robert S. Henry, Arizona Game and Fish Department)

C18.3. Botta's pocket gopher (*Thomomys bottae albatus*). (Photo by Robert S. Henry, Arizona Game and Fish Department)

C18.4. Mountain lion (*Puma concolor*). (Photo by Robert S. Henry and Michael Sumner, Arizona Game and Fish Department)

C18.5. Bighorn sheep ram (*Ovis canadensis mexicana*). (Photo by Robert S. Henry, Arizona Game and Fish Department)

C18.6. Ringtails (*Bassariscus astutus*). (Photo by Paul and Joyce Berquist)

C18.7. Javelina with baby (*Pecari tajacu*). (Photo by Paul and Joyce Berquist)

C18.8. Coyotes (*Canis latrans*). (Photo by Paul and Joyce Berquist)

C19.5. Anna's hummingbird
(*Calypte anna*). (Photo by David
J. Griffin)

C19.6. Black-throated sparrow
(*Amphispiza bilineata*). (Photo
by David J. Griffin)

C19.7. Gambel's quail (*Callipepla
gambelii*). (Photo by David J.
Griffin)

C19.8. Western screech-owl
(*Otus kennicottii*). (Photo by
David J. Griffin)

C19.9. Ash-throated flycatcher
(*Myiarchus cinerascens*). (Photo
by David J. Griffin)

C19.10. Rock wren (*Salpinctes
obsoletus*). (Photo by David J.
Griffin)

C19.11. Cactus wren
(*Campylorhynchus bruneicapillus*).
(Photo by David J. Griffin)

C19.12. Hooded oriole (*Icterus
cucullatus*). (Photo by David J.
Griffin)

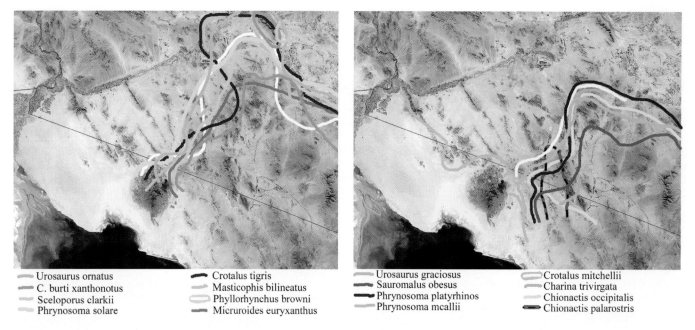

Urosaurus ornatus		Crotalus tigris
C. burti xanthonotus		Masticophis bilineatus
Sceloporus clarkii		Phyllorhynchus browni
Phrynosoma solare		Micruroides euryxanthus

Urosaurus graciosus		Crotalus mitchellii
Sauromalus obesus		Charina trivirgata
Phrynosoma platyrhinos		Chionactis occipitalis
Phrynosoma mcallii		Chionactis palarostris

C21.8. Range margins for 16 reptile species in the dry borderlands. Lines are eye-fit by overlay on Figure 12.7, with buffer added to compensate for paucity of records. *Left image* shows west and north (arid) margins of eight Arizona Upland species. *Right* portrays east and south margins of six Colorado-Mojave Desert species as they approach the Arizona Upland, plus *P. mcallii* (a Gran Desierto specialist) and *C. palarostris* (narrowly distributed in the area transitional between the two herpetofaunas).

C21.9. Species found in the Lower Colorado Valley. *Top:* western **shovel-nosed snake** (individual in Rosario Dunes), very abundant in sands. (Photo by P. C. Rosen) *Bottom:* **rosy boa** (here a Mexican rosy boa from the Puerto Blanco Mountains), found in rocky environments. (Photo by Cecil Schwalbe)

C21.10. Species found in the Arizona Upland. *Top:* **saddled leaf-nosed snake,** very abundant on loam. (Photo by Cecil Schwalbe) *Bottom:* **tiger rattlesnake,** basaltic-rhyolitic hills adjoining Valley of the Ajo. (Photo by P. C. Rosen)

C22.4. Sonoran Desert toad (*Bufo alvarius*). (Photo by Erik Enderson). **C22.5. Great Plains toad** (*Bufo cognatus*). (Photo by Erik Enderson). **C22.6. Green toad** (*Bufo debilis*). (Photo by Erik Enderson). **C22.7. Sonoran green toad** (*Bufo retiformis*). (Photo by Erik Enderson). **C22.8. Sonoran green toad** (*Bufo retiformis*). (Photo by Erik Enderson). **C22.9. Great Plains narrowmouth toad** (*Gastrophryne olivacea*). (Photo by Erik Enderson). **C22.10. Lowland burrowing treefrog** (*Pternohyla fodiens*). (Photo by Erik Enderson). **C22.11. Couch's spadefoot** (*Scaphiopus couchii*). (Photo by Erik Enderson).

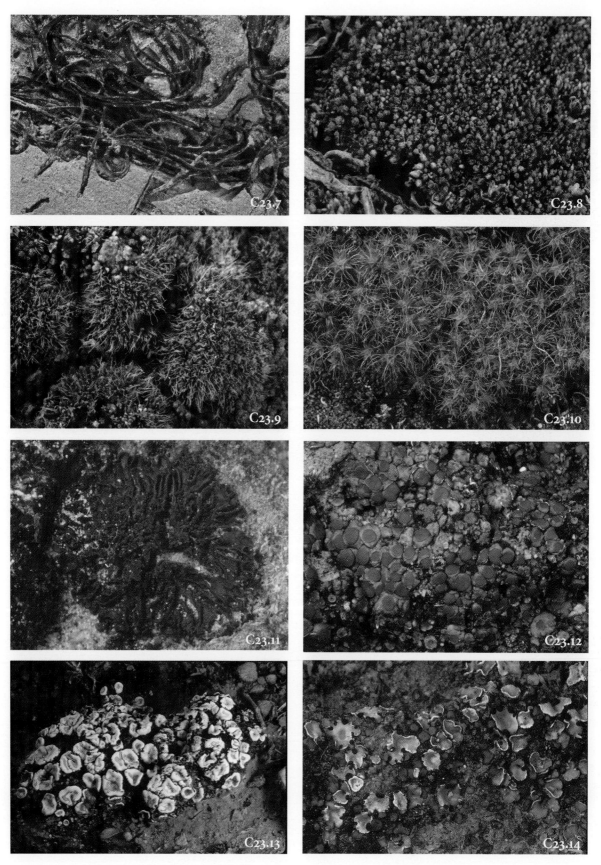

C23.7. *Nostoc commune* (cyanobacteria). **C23.8.** *Bryum argenteum* (moss). **C23.9.** *Pterygoneurum ovatum* (moss). **C23.10.** *Syntrichia ruralis* (moss). **C23.11.** *Collema tenax* (lichen). **C23.12.** *Peltula patellata* (lichen). **C23.13.** *Psora crenata* (lichen). **C23.14.** *Psora decipiens* (lichen). (All photos by Stephen Sharnoff)

C27.2. American white pelican (*Pelecanus erythrorhynchos*). (Photo by Paul and Joyce Berquist)

C27.3. Blue-footed booby (*Sula nebouxii*). (Photo by Paul and Joyce Berquist)

C27.4. Mallard (*Anas platyrhynchos*). (Photo by Paul and Joyce Berquist)

C27.5. Lesser yellowlegs (*Tringa flavipes*). (Photo by Paul and Joyce Berquist)

C27.6. Great blue heron (*Ardea herodias*). (Photo by Paul and Joyce Berquist)

C27.7. American bittern (*Botaurus lentiginosus*). (Photo by Paul and Joyce Berquist)

C27.8. Great egret (*Ardea alba*). (Photo by Paul and Joyce Berquist)

C27.9. Yuma clapper rail (*Rallus longirostris yumanensis*). (Photo by Yamilett Carillo)

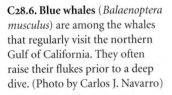

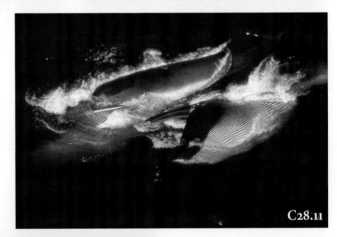

C28.6. Blue whales (*Balaenoptera musculus*) are among the whales that regularly visit the northern Gulf of California. They often raise their flukes prior to a deep dive. (Photo by Carlos J. Navarro)

C28.7. Algae bloom, upper Sea of Cortez, June 1998. (Photo by Carlos J. Navarro)

C28.8. Estuary, Adair Bay. (Photo by Carlos J. Navarro)

C28.9. Remnant vegetation, Colorado River, Mexico, 1997. (Photo by Carlos J. Navarro)

C28.10. Salt pan, Colorado River delta. (Photo by Carlos J. Navarro)

C28.11. Fin whales feeding. (Photo by Carlos J. Navarro)

C28.12. California sea lions. (Photo by Carlos J. Navarro)

C29.6. *Aphrodita sonorae* (Annelida: Polychaeta), dorsal view. One of the largest and most beautiful worms in the Sea of Cortez. Populations of this northern gulf endemic species have been decimated by offshore commercial shrimp trawling. (Photo by A. Kerstitch)

C29.7. The rare northern gulf endemic coral, *Astrangia sanfelipensis*, known only from two beachrock sites at San Felipe and Coloradito. (Photo by A. Kerstitch)

C29.8. The mysterious **acorn barnacle** *Balanus subalbidus*, attached to dead tree branches in Laguna Salada, which is dry in this photograph. (Photo by R. C. Brusca)

C29.9. *Heliaster kubiniji*, the **sunstar**. Once one of the most common animals, and top predators, in the littoral region of the northern gulf, this species experienced "double jeopardy" in the early 1980s, when a combination of overcollecting (mainly by or for tourists) and a strong 1983 El Niño event eliminated them from the entire northern gulf. Continued collection pressure has helped prevent this species from reestablishing itself in the northern gulf. (Photo by R. C. Brusca)

C29.10. Fiddler crab (*Uca princeps*). (Photo by Carlos J. Navarro)

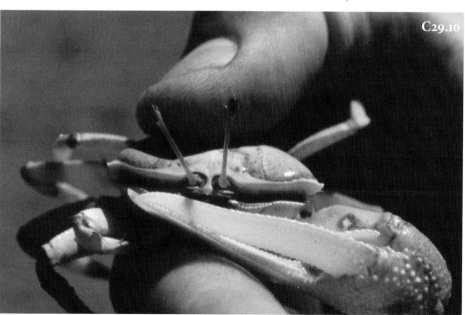

C30.9. Leatherback turtle hatchlings (*Dermochelys coriacea*). Leatherbacks have experienced a dramatic population crash in the Pacific in recent years. Some scientists believe nesting populations in this ocean basin will go extinct by the year 2020. (Photo by Kim Cliffton)

C30.9

C30.10. Stuffed hawksbill turtle (*Eretmochelys imbricata*), displayed in Guaymas, around 1985. Hawksbills, the source of the prized tortoiseshell of commerce, are now rare but still in demand for the attractive carapace. (Photo by Jeffrey A. Seminoff)

C30.10

C30.11. Olive ridley (*Lepidochelys olivacea*). The olive ridley is the most common nester in the Gulf of California. The species has made a dramatic recovery in recent years due to conservation legislation in Mexico. (Photo by Jeffrey A. Seminoff)

C30.12. Green turtle (*Chelonia mydas [=agassizii]*). Green turtles in the eastern Pacific have been the subject of taxonomic debate over the last decade: various scientists have supported both subspecies and full species status. (Photo by Wallace J. Nichols)

C30.13. Loggerhead (*Caretta caretta*). All loggerhead turtles in the eastern Pacific have nesting beach origins in the western Pacific, primarily if not exclusively in Japan. (Photo by Jeffrey A. Seminoff)

C30.11

C30.12

C30.13

County (LACM), but collections at the Guaymas Campus of the Instituto Tecnológico y de Estudios Superiores de Monterrey (ITESM), the Mazatlán Unit of the Centro de Investigación en Alimentación y Desarrollo (CIAD-MAZ), and the Ensenada campus of the Universidad Autónoma de Baja California (UABC) were also surveyed. Records of the freshwater fish fauna in the lowermost Colorado River, recently reviewed by W. L. Minckley (1999, 2002) and Mueller and Marsh (2002), are not included here.

A total of 260 species of marine fishes have been recorded from within the waters of the biosphere reserve. This represents 29 percent of the approximately 908 species so far recorded from the Gulf of California (defined as extending from the delta region southward to Cabo San Lucas, Baja California Sur, on the peninsular side, and Cabo Corrientes, Jalisco, on the mainland side) (Findley et al. in press). One striking result of this compilation is the relatively high number of cartilaginous fishes recorded in the extreme northern gulf. The sharks, rays, and chimaeras (class Chondrichthys) of the gulf number 88 species, 46 of which (52 percent) have been recorded from the waters of the biosphere reserve. This finding may be attributed in part to the relative mobility of most cartilaginous fishes, coupled with the ample availability of suitable habitats in the northern gulf, which is dominated by the soft substrates occupied by most rays and many sharks. Also, reduction and eventual cessation of Colorado River flow into the northern gulf since the termination of construction of Hoover Dam in 1935 has almost certainly increased the likelihood of occurrence of strictly marine pelagic species (e.g., thresher and shortfin mako sharks), which might not be expected to occur in the relatively low-salinity, estuarine waters of the historical northern gulf. Because the sharks and rays of the gulf have come under intense fishing pressure in recent years (e.g., Applegate et al. 1993), the biosphere reserve has the potential to serve as an important refuge for these relatively long-lived and low-fecundity species, especially if commercial fishing for them can be better regulated or, preferably, eliminated from the reserve's buffer zone. However, an even larger protected area may be warranted, given the mobility of many of them.

The rich diversity of sharks and rays in the biosphere reserve stands in contrast to the relative paucity of marine ray-finned ("bony") fishes (class Actinopterygii). Although more species of ray-finned fishes have been recorded in the reserve (214), this number represents only 26 percent of the 817 ray-finned fish species known from the gulf (Findley et al. in press). This is partly the result of the relatively cold winter surface-water temperatures of the northern gulf, which, coupled with the relative scarcity of hard substrates, limit the number of tropical reef fish species in the region (Thomson & Lehner 1979; Walker 1960).

The fish fauna occupying the marine waters of the biosphere reserve is a particularly complex mixture of biogeographic elements (Walker 1960). It includes a number of eurythermal species widespread in the eastern Pacific; a number of tropical species also found farther south in the tropical eastern Pacific; several "northern disjuncts" (e.g., Figure 26.5), or species found both in the northern gulf and along the outer coast of the Baja California peninsula and in southern California but which are absent from the southern gulf (Bernardi et al. 2003; Huang & Bernardi 2001; Present 1987; Walker 1960); and several species endemic to the Gulf of California (Findley et al. 1999; Findley et al. in press; Walker 1960).

One gulf endemic, the delta silverside, *Colpichthys hubbsi,* has the distinction of being the only species of fish known solely from the biosphere reserve. Specimens of this species were first collected by Carl Hubbs, who recognized it as an undescribed species distinct from the related false grunion, *Colpichthys regis.* Hubbs intended to describe it with his graduate student and later long-time colleague from UCLA, Boyd Walker. Based on its unique morphology, they planned to place the new species in a new monotypic genus. However, as sometimes happens, they never completed their study, and the species was later formally described by Ben Crabtree (1989), then a student at UCLA, who placed it in the genus *Colpichthys,* based on both morphological and genetic data, and named it in honor of Hubbs in recognition of his discovery of the species. The delta silverside has been recorded only from the delta region of the Colorado River southward to San Felipe on the western side of the gulf and southward to El Golfo de Santa Clara on the eastern side. Its current status is unknown, but its restricted historical distribution implies that its life history was intimately tied to the former extensive estuary of the

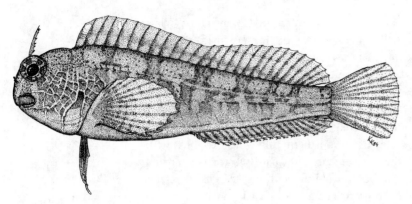

Figure 26.5. Hyposblennius gentilis, *the bay blenny, or* borracho de bahía, *family Blenniidae, a "northern disjunct" species, common on rocky reefs in the northern Gulf of California and in southern California. (Drawing by K. Kotrschal)*

Colorado River. Its numbers have undoubtedly declined since the cessation of flow from the river. Although we have been informed that Michael Horn and students at California State University Fullerton have recently collected and are studying a few specimens, the most recent published collections of *C. hubbsi* are from 1984 (Crabtree 1989), indicating that it persists in probably very low numbers in the biosphere reserve. Curiously, its presumed former abundance may have mirrored that of the delta clam, *Mulinia coloradoensis*, a species that was historically abundant in the delta's estuary but essentially absent just south of San Felipe; this clam was thought to be extinct until the recent discovery of a small remnant population at the mouth of the Colorado River channel (Rodriguez, Flessa, & Dettman 2001:Figure 4; Rodriguez, Flessa et al. 2001).

Ecological Components of the Fish Fauna of the Alto Golfo Biosphere Reserve

Soft-Bottom Fishes

The dominant ecological component of the Alto Golfo Biosphere Reserve ichthyofauna is associated with soft bottoms of sand and mud and includes representatives of several groups of fishes characteristic of both the continental shelf and shallow coastal bays and lagoons. Chief among them are the anchovies (Engraulidae), herrings (Clupeidae; Figure 26.6), New World silversides (Atherinopsidae), a variety of perciform fishes such as the corvinas and other croakers (Sciaenidae; Figure 26.7), the grunts (Haemulidae), and several groups of flatfishes or flounders (Pleuronectiformes). The dominance of soft-bottom fishes is not surprising given the fact that for millions of years the Colorado River deposited vast amounts of fine-

grained sediments in the northern Gulf of California. Consequently, most of the marine area of the biosphere reserve is sand and mud, both along the coastal margins and along the gently sloping continental shelf on the northern margin of the relatively shallow Wagner Deep, the gulf's northernmost tectonic basin. Suspended sediment from the historical and unregulated Colorado River would have made the waters of the biosphere reserve extremely turbid much of the time. Even today they are usually turbid, but mainly as the consequence of resuspended sediment stirred from the bottom by powerful tidal currents (Baba et al. 1991; Carriquiry & Sánchez 1999).

Because the northern gulf, unlike the central and southern gulf, has a relatively extensive continental shelf habitat, many gulf fishes typical of this habitat have been reported from the biosphere reserve. The northern gulf also is ideal habitat for commercially targeted penaeid shrimps and has been extensively exploited by shrimp trawlers operating there for several decades (Galindo-Bect et al. 2000; Magallón-Barajas 1987). Many of our records of fishes from the biosphere reserve are from surveys of the shrimp bycatch, or *acompañante del camarón* (e.g., Guevara-Escamilla 1974; Nava-Romo 1994; Pérez-Mellado & Findley 1985;). The current status of most of these species is unknown, but the populations of most are probably greatly reduced from repeated and nearly unrelenting trawling in the region (Engel & Kvitek 1998; Nava-Romo 1994; Watling & Norse 1998).

Historically, the salinity regime of the northern gulf must have been extremely complicated. Springtime flows from the Colorado River would have turned the entire northern gulf into an estuarine system dominated by a large salt wedge (Lavín & Sánchez 1999). Salinity of northern gulf surface waters probably increased during periods of reduced river flow from summer to winter, but even then, portions of the relatively enclosed northern gulf, especially the delta region, must have been essentially estuarine in character most or all of the time. Consequently, it is not surprising that fishes able to tolerate wide ranges in salinity dominated the northern gulf ichthyofauna (Walker 1960) (Figure 26.8). Currently, the waters of the biosphere reserve are not estuarine in nature but are typically more salty (Bray & Robles 1991) than open ocean water (approximately 35 ppt). This is because the normally hot, dry deserts surrounding the northern gulf promote a rate of evaporation of seawater that is much higher than the rate of freshwater replenishment (Lavín et al. 1998). For example, at Puerto Peñasco, evaporation exceeds precipitation by as much as 3.15 meters per year, resulting in a net flow of water from the open ocean into the southern gulf and thence northward (Bray & Robles 1991). In essence, the gulf now acts as a huge straw, sucking water from the open Pacific and conveying it into the atmosphere over the surrounding deserts.

Estuaries are well-known spawning, nursery, and refuge areas for many fishes, but this key brackish-water habitat is now essentially missing from the upper gulf. Although the now hypersaline coastal lagoons (esteros) there still serve as important spawning and nursery sites for many fishes and other organisms, the effects of this change in habitat on estuarine-dependent fishes and other biota of the northern gulf certainly must have been great, but for the most part it can only be guessed at. This uncertainty exists because we have no quantitative estimates of the biotic communities of the northern gulf before the cessation of Colorado River input and generally no reliable way to recreate an appropriate baseline (see Rodríguez, Flessa, & Dettman 2001 and Rodriguez, Flessa et al. 2001 for an exception).

As noted by Walker (1960), typically intertidal (littoral) fishes are uncommon in the extreme northern gulf, especially along sandy and muddy coastal areas. This is not surprising since the region experiences some of the largest tidal ranges known on the planet, with maxima of more than seven meters near the mouth of the Colorado River (Lavín et al. 1998; Maluf 1983; Matthews 1968; Roden 1964). Because the bottom gradient is very slight in the extreme northern gulf, these enormous tidal changes expose vast mud and sand flats that stretch seaward for up to five kilometers (Maluf 1983), conditions that few fish species can tolerate. Notable exceptions include species adapted to environmental extremes such as the mudsucker gobies (*Gillichthys* spp.), which can survive in the shallow, poorly oxygenated tidal channels or burrow into the mud during low tides (Barlow 1961, 1963; Todd & Ebeling 1966).

Reef Fishes

With the exceptions of rocky headlands at the southern margins of Puerto Peñasco and San

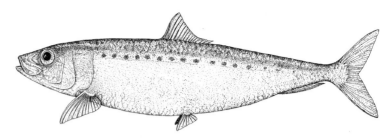

Figure 26.6. Sardinops caeruleus *(or* Sardinops sagax caeruleus*), the North Pacific sardine, or* sardina monterrey, *family Clupeidae, a commercially important pelagic herring common in the Alto Golfo Biosphere Reserve. (Drawing by T. Hansen)*

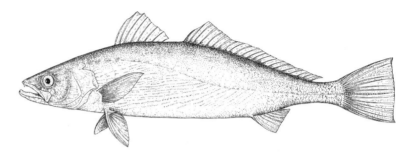

Figure 26.7. Cynoscion parvipinnis, *the shortfin corvina, or* corvina aleta corta, *family Sciaenidae, a popular foodfish common in the northern Gulf of California. (Drawing by T. Hansen)*

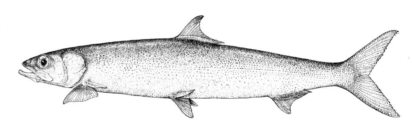

Felipe, the shoreline of the Alto Golfo Biosphere Reserve is almost exclusively sand or mud. Important rocky outcrops of volcanic and coquina (beachrock) origins include Punta Borrascoso at the northwestern corner of Bahía Adair (Figure 26.1), the northernmost rocky reef in the gulf (Thomson et al. 1979:Figure 2), and the areas around San Felipe and Puerto Peñasco (Figure 26.4). These areas harbor a relatively abundant, if not species-rich, reef-fish fauna (Thomson & Lehner 1979). However, another factor limiting reef-fish diversity in the northern gulf is the relatively cold winter temperatures of its surface waters, which can be lethal to tropical species (Heath 1967; Thomson & Lehner 1979; Walker 1960). Interestingly, a few hardy reef fishes reach their greatest abundance in the seemingly inhospitable northern gulf, including the aptly named Sonora goby, *Gobiosoma chiquita;* the Sonora blenny, *Malacoctenus gigas;* and the Sonora clingfish, *Tomicodon*

Figure 26.8. Elops affinis, *the* machete, *family Elopidae, one of the few marine fishes that historically frequented the lower Colorado River system, having been recorded far upriver in southwestern Arizona and in the Salton Sea of California. (Drawing by T. Hansen)*

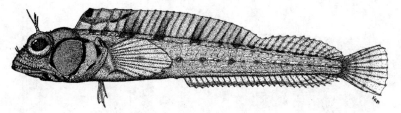

Figure 26.9. Acanthemblemaria crockeri, *the browncheek blenny, or tubícola cachetón, family Chaenopsidae, a Gulf of California endemic recorded from reefs at Isla San Jorge but not yet known to occur in the Alto Golfo Biosphere Reserve. (Drawing by K. Kotrschal)*

humeralis. Still, reef fishes make up a relatively small component here compared with more southerly regions of the gulf, where rocky reefs are dominant, winter temperatures are warmer, and reef fishes are significantly more diverse (Thomson et al. 1979, 2000).

A few species of reef fishes not known from the biosphere reserve have been recorded from the nearby Isla San Jorge, Sonora, and Rocas Consag, Baja California (see second checklist at end of chapter). Both of these rocky islands are outside the southern boundary of the current biosphere reserve but are under consideration for inclusion in an expanded reserve buffer zone. Although only 14 "new" species of fishes would be added to the fauna of the biosphere reserve (e.g., Figure 26.9), inclusion of these islands would protect more abundant and more diverse assemblages of reef-associated species than are present on the adjacent mainland reefs within the biosphere reserve (Thomson & Gilligan 1983).

Pelagic Fishes

A surprisingly large number of species of pelagic (open-water) fishes have been recorded from the Alto Golfo Biosphere Reserve. This diversity may be unnaturally high as a consequence of the reduced freshwater input to the northern gulf. Historically, species such as thresher sharks and sailfish were probably rarely if ever present in the low-salinity waters of the northern gulf. Because of the present-day relatively high salinity of the biosphere reserve's marine portion, virtually any pelagic fish species in the gulf may be an occasional visitor to the area.

A Comment on Freshwater Fishes

Nine species of native freshwater fishes are known from the main stream of the lower Colorado River, and eight have been recorded from the waters of the delta region (Minckley 1999, 2002; Mueller & Marsh 2002): four species of minnows (Cyprinidae), two species of suckers (Catostomidae), one species of pupfish (Cyprinodontidae) and one

species of livebearer (Poeciliidae). As a consequence of extensive human-induced changes to the region's physical and biological environment, all these fishes are now absent or extremely rare in the lower Colorado. Two that are present (bonytail, *Gila elegans,* and razorback sucker, *Xyrauchen texanus*) owe their sparse occurrence to recent restocking efforts. A third species, the amazingly adaptable but nonetheless endangered desert pupfish, *Cyprinodon macularius macularius,* persists in a few small isolated spring-fed ponds and irrigation ditches marginal to the regionally important Ciénega de Santa Clara wetland (where it also occurs) and in shallow ponds of residual waters of the Cerro Prieto Geothermal Station near the greatly reduced headwater of the Río Hardy, once the major tributary of the Colorado River in the delta region (Minckley et al. 2001; Varela-Romero et al. 2002; see also Glenn & Nagler, this volume). None of these marginal habitats lies within the nuclear (core) zone of the biosphere reserve. Sadly, in place of the native fish fauna is a bewildering array of 38 introduced fish species (Minckley 1999, 2002; Mueller & Marsh 2002), for "the Lower Colorado River has the dubious distinction of being among the few major rivers of the world with an entirely introduced fish fauna" (Mueller & Marsh 2002:2). Even one of the limited success stories, the occurrence of the desert pupfish in the Ciénega de Santa Clara (Glenn et al. 1992, 1996; Zengel & Glenn 1996), is threatened by increased demands for the limited freshwater that supplies this fragile wetland (Glenn et al. 2001; see also Glenn & Nagler, this volume). Indeed, "the future is grim for native fish in the Lower Colorado River" (Mueller & Marsh 2002:65).

Two Remarkable Fishes from the Alto Golfo Reserve

Totoaba

The best-known fish in the northern Gulf of California, and deservedly so, is the totoaba, *Totoaba macdonaldi,* a giant member of a speciose family of sandy-shore fishes (Sciaenidae) that thrives in estuarine conditions. This gulf endemic was one of the first species described from the region (as *Cynoscion macdonaldi*) by Charles Henry Gilbert in 1890, based on specimens collected near the mouth of the Colorado River aboard the *Albatross.* It is one of the largest fishes in the gulf (Figure 26.10) and was at one time a dominant member of the northern gulf ichthyofauna. In the original description Gilbert wrote:

> This species is very abundant along the entire eastern shore of the gulf of California, and congregates in great numbers near the mouth of the Colorado River. It enters the rivers and is found in shallow water near the shore, where it is easily approached and speared. At the head of the Gulf it is known as the sea basse, while in the vicinity of Guaymas it…goes by the native name of "Totuava." It does not seem to be known at La Paz, and was not seen by us on the western side of the gulf. Many specimens were taken by hand-lines at the head of the Gulf, the largest weighing 172 pounds. Large specimens were also seen at Guaymas and at the mouth of the Rio del Fuerte. (Gilbert 1890:65)

Much has since been written about this impressive fish, the largest member of a diverse, worldwide group of fishes, the drums, croakers, and corvinas of the family Sciaenidae, which includes many important food fishes. Although the abundance of this species has declined markedly, the ecological and historical importance of the totoaba in the northern gulf should not be underestimated. In the past, adults and large juveniles *(machorros)* must have played a key role as top trophic-level predators (e.g., Román-Rodríguez 1990). Eggs, larvae, and small juveniles, generated in vast numbers from the totoaba's massive spawning aggregations, which historically may have occurred from January to June (Flanagan & Hendrickson 1976), must have also been key components in the food web of the northern gulf. The totoaba fishery, expanding northward from Guaymas, was largely responsible for the initial settlement of San Felipe, Puerto Peñasco (Bahre et al. 2000; Huey 1953; Munro-Palacio 1994), and, later, El Golfo de Santa Clara in the delta region. Ironically, these fishing villages were established before the development of the infrastructure (refrigeration and paved roads) ideally needed to get whole fishes or their fillets to market (Figure 26.11). Totoaba, like most other sciaenids, bear a large gas bladder used to regulate buoyancy and to generate sounds via special "drumming" muscles in males (Fish & Mowbray 1970). These bladders from sciaenids were (and are) highly sought after, especially in the Far East, where they are used as stock for special soups. Called *buche* in Sonora, these bladders were the "pearls" of these marvelous

Figure 26.10. Totoaba macdonaldi *catch at San Felipe, 1938. (Photo provided by J. Seminoff)*

animals, attracting the attention of Asian traders and thus the attention of gulf fishermen. The early totoaba fishery exported only the *buches,* which, after removal from the fish, were dried and shipped to the Far East via the port of Guaymas. Some of the flesh was eaten locally, but most was simply discarded until mobile refrigeration made it possible to ship totoaba to markets in the southwestern United States, where demand grew quickly (Bahre et al. 2000; Chute 1928). The reported catches of totoaba peaked in 1938 and 1942 but then declined precipitously (Arvizu & Chávez 1972; Cisneros-Mata et al. 1995; Flanagan & Hendrickson 1976). This decline has been mainly at the hands of the intensive fishery, especially the effective gillnet fishery that operated during the totoaba reproductive season, as well as the high incidental mortality of juveniles in shrimp trawls (Barrera-Guevara 1990; Flanagan & Hendrickson 1976; Ortiz de Montellano 1987). In addition, the spawning

Figure 26.11. *Trucks being loaded with totoaba carcasses for transport to southern California, near San Felipe, 1926. (Photo by L. M. Huey)*

and nursery area of this species was radically altered by dam builders along the Colorado River. Even the brief flow from the Colorado River into the gulf during the relatively wet year of 1983 stimulated a significant recruitment pulse for the totoaba (Cisneros-Mata et al. 1995). All indications are that this long-lived and highly fecund species could recover if illegal fishing were to stop and if the environment of the northern gulf were returned, even sporadically, to its former "estuarine" conditions (Román-Rodríguez & Hammann 1997).

Because of the precipitous decline in the fishery, the Mexican government placed a total ban on the capture of totoaba in 1975. In 1976 it was placed on the endangered list of the Convention on International Trade in Endangered Species (CITES); in 1979 it was added to the U.S. Endangered Species list (Barrera-Guevara 1990; Lagomarsino 1991), where it remains (Musick et al. 2000). The marine portion of the Alto Golfo Biosphere Reserve was established in part to protect the totoaba and another gulf endemic species, the critically endangered vaquita, or Gulf of California harbor porpoise, *Phocoena sinus* (Flores-Skydancer & Turk Boyer 2002; Gallo-Reynoso 1998; Navarro, this volume; Rojas-Bracho & Taylor 1999; Vidal et al. 1999). The aquaculture work on totoaba begun by John Hendrickson has recently been brought to fruition with the successful laboratory rearing and spawning of this important fish by researchers led by Conal David True at the Ensenada campus of the Universidad Autónoma de Baja California, leading to restocking of small totoabas in the northern gulf. Enforcement of fishing restrictions within the biosphere reserve will remain a key feature in the recovery of this and other large species of sciaenids in the northern gulf ecosystem, such as the equally impressive Gulf corvina, *Cynoscion*

othonopterus. This species, about which we know relatively little, also appears to be in renewed decline (Cudney-Bueno & Turk Boyer 1998; Román-Rodríguez et al. 1998).

Gulf Grunion

A particularly remarkable intertidal visitor to beaches of the Alto Golfo Biosphere Reserve is the gulf grunion, *Leuresthes sardina,* a member of the New World silverside family Atherinopsidae. This is an extraordinary fish, magnificently adapted to the extreme environmental conditions of the northern gulf. What happens to gulf grunion during most of their lives as "normal" subtidal fishes is completely unknown. But, unlike the case for most gulf fishes, we know a great deal about their reproductive behavior because spawning occurs in the intertidal zone. At very predictable intervals in the spring and early summer along sandy beaches of the northern gulf such as those near El Golfo de Santa Clara, gulf grunion gather to engage in a most unusual spawning behavior, called a "grunion run" (Moffatt & Thomson 1975; Reynolds & Thomson 1974; Thomson & Muench 1976). Unlike their close relative, the California grunion, *L. tenuis,* which runs only at night, gulf grunion can run either during daylight hours or at night, depending on tidal conditions. Predictions of gulf grunion runs were included in the tide calendar for the northern Gulf of California (Thomson 2002) for a single year (1977), but the practice was stopped because of concerns about overexploitation of this vulnerable fish during its runs (D. A. Thomson, personal communication 2002).

A grunion run begins when hundreds to thousands of these fish closely approach the shore's surf line, an event signaled by congregating pelicans and seagulls feeding near the shore. The first direct sign of a run occurs when a few isolated males begin riding small waves shoreward onto the beach. Slowly, almost imperceptibly, the number of fish in the wave wash on the beach grows and swells until a ribbon of writhing, mostly male fish marks the receding tide line (Figure 26.12). Then the females, heavy with eggs, begin their dash onto shore, quickly burying the posterior part of their bodies in the wet sand with rapid and vigorous tail beats and depositing a small clutch of eggs a few centimeters under the surface. These nearly vertical females are at once encircled by one or sometimes two or three males, which release sperm that flows down the female's sides and fertilizes the eggs below (Figure 26.13). The females then dash back to the water while the males remain on the beach to spawn with other nearby females. This remarkable behavior, accomplished at the precise and propitious moment in the ebb and flow of northern gulf tides, ensures that the eggs will remain "safely" buried in moist sand for their developmental period of about two weeks. In the next tidal series, when the waves again reach that level of the beach, they moisten, expose, and agitate the eggs, stimulating them to hatch and launching the newborn larvae on the first stage of their otherwise unknown life in the gulf.

Grunion runs are still a common seasonal occurrence in the northern gulf, and small ones have been recorded even as far south as Bahía Bacochibampo at Guaymas. Unfortunately, we have little information on the historical distribution and abundance of this species and can only speculate that it, like other fishes characteristic of the northern gulf, may have suffered from the extreme changes in its environment. On the other hand, gulf grunion may be more abundant than they were historically, given the unfortunate population declines of such dominant piscivores of the northern gulf as the totoaba and related sciaenid fishes.

Figure 26.12. A daytime grunion run, El Golfo de Santa Clara, 1998. (Photo by D. A. Thomson)

Summary

Our survey of the literature and natural history collections for species of marine fishes recorded from the Alto Golfo Biosphere Reserve of the far-northern Gulf of California revealed a surprisingly large number of species. Although the reserve is relatively small and constitutes the most environmentally extreme part of the gulf, the 260 species recorded there represent approximately 29 percent of all fish species recorded from the entire Gulf of California. It should be noted that this list is necessarily inflated compared with the number of species that may be found in the reserve at any one time. Our list is based on the aggregate records for the entire history of scientific collecting in the gulf and includes many species not normally or only seasonally found there. Because the reserve is open to the remainder of the gulf, temporary occurrence there is possible for many other gulf fishes. Marine fishes are notoriously mobile, being able to disperse passively as eggs or larvae with ocean currents and in many cases actively as swimming juveniles or adults. Also, our list may not exactly reflect the species composition that occurs there today because the ecosystem of the northern gulf has been extensively altered via the cessation of flow from the Colorado River and the nearly relentless bottom trawling for shrimps over the past several decades. The impacts of these changes remain largely unknown, but it may be safely assumed that the fauna today is quite different from what it was even sixty years ago. Certainly the image of the commander of the *Albatross* putting an end to fishing at the mouth of the Colorado River because his crew had caught too many large fishes seems incredible today. The most hopeful signs for the future are the conservation measures already in place and those evolving as a consequence of the establishment of the Alto Golfo Biosphere Reserve, along with their strict enforcement. These measures are key components in the protection of the unique assemblage of fishes that characterizes the northern Gulf of California.

Acknowledgments

We thank Albert van der Heiden, Héctor Plascencia, Jorge Torre, J. Manuel Nava-Romo, Mauricia Pérez-Tello, Martha Román, José Campoy, Alejandro Robles, Juan Carlos Barrera, Carlos Navarro, Gorgonio Ruiz-Campos, and Cynthia Klepadlo for assistance in compiling records of fishes from the region. Kurt Kotrschal, Jeff Seminoff, and

Figure 26.13. *Spawning gulf grunion, or pejerrey sardina, Leuresthes sardina, during a night run, El Golfo de Santa Clara, 1985. Note erect female (near center) with encircling males. (Photo by D. A. Thomson)*

Donald Thomson provided illustrations and granted permission for their use. Nohemi Camacho digitally prepared Figure 26.1. We thank W. Linn Montgomery for reviewing and improving an earlier draft of this chapter. Funding for the Macrofauna Golfo database project was initially provided by the Mexican government's Comisión Nacional para el Conocimiento y Uso de la Biodiversidad (CONABIO) and by several other organizations via Conservation International's Región Golfo de California Program in Guaymas. The latter continues to support the project, for which we especially thank María de los Ángeles Carvajal and Alejandro Robles. Over the years Donald A. Thomson and the late John R. Hendrickson provided encouragement and numerous opportunities for us and many other researchers to explore the biology of the Gulf of California.

Annotated Checklist of Marine Fishes recorded in or immediately adjacent to the Alto Golfo Biosphere Reserve

Higher classification and common names follow Nelson et al. 2004. Habitats: P = pelagic; R = reefs; S = soft bottoms.

Class Chondrichthys – cartilaginous fishes
Heterodontiformes
    Heterodontidae – bullhead sharks; tiburones cornudos

Heterodontus francisci – horn shark; tiburón puerco	S
Heterodontus mexicanus – Mexican horn shark; tiburón perro	R,S
Orectolobiformes	
Rhincodontidae – whale sharks; tiburones ballena	
Rhincodon typus – whale shark; tiburón ballena	P
Carcharhiniformes	
Triakidae – hound sharks; cazones	
Mustelus californicus – gray smoothhound; cazón mamón	S
Mustelus henlei – brown smoothhound; cazón hilacho	S
Mustelus lunulatus – sicklefin smoothhound; cazón segador	S
Carcharhinidae – requiem sharks; tiburones gambusos	
Carcharhinus altimus – bignose shark; tiburón narizón	P
Carcharhinus brachyurus – narrowtooth shark; tiburón cobrizo	P
Carcharhinus falciformis – silky shark; tiburón piloto	P
Carcharhinus leucas – bull shark; tiburón toro	P,S
Carcharhinus limbatus – blacktip shark; tiburón volador	P
Carcharhinus obscurus – dusky shark; tiburón gambuso	P
Carcharhinus porosus – smalltail shark; tiburón poroso	P
Nasolamia velox – whitenose shark; tiburón coyotito	P
Negaprion brevirostris – lemon shark; tiburón limón	P,S
Rhizoprionodon longurio – Pacific sharpnose shark; cazón bironche	P,S
Sphyrnidae – hammerhead sharks; tiburones martillo	
Sphyrna lewini – scalloped hammerhead; cornuda común	P
Sphyrna mokarran – great hammerhead; cornuda gigante	P
Sphyrna tiburo – bonnethead; cornuda cabeza de pala	P,S
Sphyrna zygaena – smooth hammerhead; cornuda prieta	P
Lamniformes	
Alopiidae – thresher sharks; tiburones zorro	
Alopias pelagicus – pelagic thresher; zorro pelágico	P
Alopias superciliosus – bigeye thresher; tiburón zorro ojón	P

Alopias vulpinus – thresher shark; tiburón
zorro común P

Cetorhinidae – basking sharks; tiburones
peregrinos

Cetorhinus maximus (extirpated) –
basking shark; tiburón peregrino P

Lamnidae – mackerel sharks; jaquetones

Carcharodon carcharias – white shark;
tiburón blanco P

Isurus oxyrinchus – shortfin mako; mako P

Hexanchiformes

Hexanchidae – cow sharks; tiburones
cañabotas

Notorynchus cepedianus – broadnose
sevengill shark; tiburón pinto P,S

Squatiniformes

Squatinidae – angel sharks; angelotes

Squatina californica – Pacific angel shark;
angelote del Pacífico S

Torpediniformes

Narcinidae – electric rays; rayas eléctricas

Diplobatis ommata – bullseye electric ray;
raya eléctrica diana R,S

Narcine entemedor – giant electric ray;
raya eléctrica gigante S

Rajiiformes

Rhinobatidae – guitarfishes; guitarras

Rhinobatos leucorhynchus – whitesnout
guitarfish; guitarra trompa blanca S

Rhinobatos productus – shovelnose
guitarfish; guitarra viola S

Zapteryx exasperata – banded guitarfish;
guitarra rayada S

Rajidae – skates; rayas

Raja binoculata – big skate; raya bruja
gigante S

Dasyatidae – whiptail stingrays; rayas látigo

Dasyatis dipterura – diamond stingray;
raya látigo diamante S

Dasyatis longa – longtail stingray; raya
látigo largo S

Urolophidae – round stingrays; rayas
redondas

Urobatis concentricus – reef stingray;
raya redonda de arrecife R,S

Urobatis halleri – round stingray; raya
redonda común S

Urobatis maculatus – Cortez stingray;
raya redonda de Cortés S

Urotrygon aspidura – Panamic stingray;
raya redonda panámica S

Urotrygon chilensis – blotched stingray;
raya redonda moteada S

Urotrygon rogersi – thorny stingray;
raya redonda de púas S

Gymnuridae – butterfly rays; rayas mariposa

Gymnura marmorata – California butterfly ray; raya mariposa californiana S

Myliobatidae – eagle rays; águilas marinas

Myliobatis californica – bat ray; tecolote P,S

Rhinopteridae – cownose rays; rayas gavilán

Rhinoptera steindachneri – golden
cownose ray; gavilán dorado P

Mobulidae – mantas; mantas

Mobula munkiana – pygmy devil ray;
manta chica P

Class Actinopterygii – ray-finned fishes

Elopiformes

Elopidae – tenpounders; machetes

Elops affinis – machete; machete del
Pacífico P

Albuliformes

Albulidae – bonefishes; macabíes

Albula sp. – Cortez bonefish; macabí de
Cortés P,S

Anguilliformes

Muraenidae – morays; morenas

Gymnothorax castaneus – Panamic green
moray; morena verde panámica R

Gymnothorax equatorialis – spottail
moray; morena cola pintada S

Ophichthidae – snake eels; tiesos

Myrichthys tigrinus – tiger snake eel;
tieso tigre S

Myrophis vafer – Pacific worm eel; tieso
lombriz S

Ophichthus triserialis – Pacific snake eel;
tieso del Pacífico S

Ophichthus zophochir – yellow snake eel;
tieso amarillo S

Muraenesocidae – pike congers; congrios
picudos

Cynoponticus coniceps – conehead eel;
congrio espantoso S

Clupeiformes

Engraulidae – anchovies; anchoas

Anchoa helleri – gulf anchovy; anchoa
del golfo P

Anchoa ischana – sharpnose anchovy;
anchoa chicotera P

Anchoa lucida – bright anchovy; anchoa
ojitos P

Anchoa mundeoloides – northern gulf
anchovy; anchoa golfina P

Anchoa nasus – bignose anchovy; anchoa
trompuda P

Anchoa parri – mystery anchovy; anchoa
misteriosa P

Anchoa walkeri – persistent anchovy;
anchoa persistente P

Anchovia macrolepidota – bigscale anchovy; anchoveta escamuda — P

Cetengraulis mysticetus – anchoveta; anchoveta bocona — P

Clupeidae – herrings; sardinas

Dorosoma petenense (intoduced) – threadfin shad; sardina maya — P

Etrumeus teres – round herring; sardina japonesa — P

Harengula thrissina – flatiron herring; sardinita plumilla — P

Opisthonema libertate – deepbody thread herring; sardina crinuda — P

Sardinops caeruleus – Pacific sardine; sardina monterrey — P

Siluriformes

Ariidae – sea catfishes; bagres marinos

Ariopsis c.f. *guatemalensis* — S

Bagre panamensis – chihuil; bagre chihuil — S

Argentiformes

Argentinidae – argentines; argentinas

Argentina sialis – Pacific argentine; argentina del Pacífico — P,S

Aulopiformes

Synodontidae – lizardfishes; chiles

Synodus lucioceps – California lizardfish; chile lucio — S

Synodus scituliceps – lance lizardfish; chile arpón — S

Ophidiiformes

Ophidiidae – cusk-eels; brótulas y congriperlas

Lepophidium prorates – prowspine cusk-eel; congriperla cornuda — S

Ophidion galeoides – spotfin cusk-eel; congriperla adornada — S

Bythitidae – viviparous brotulas; brótulas vivíparas

Ogilbia spp. – several undescribed species of viviparous brotulas — R

Gadiformes

Moridae – codlings; moras y carboneros

Physiculus nematopus – charcoal codling; carbonero de fango — S

Merlucciidae – merlucciid hakes; merluzas

Merluccius angustimanus – Panama hake; merluza panameña — P,S

Merluccius hernandezi – Cortez hake; merluza de Cortés — P,S

Merluccius productus – Pacific hake; merluza norteña — P,S

Batrachoidiformes

Batrachoididae – toadfishes; peces sapos

Porichthys analis – darkedge midshipman; sapo de luto — S

Porichthys mimeticus – mimetic midshipman; sapo mimético — S

Lophiiformes

Antennariidae – frogfishes; ranisapos

Antennarius avalonis – roughjaw frogfish; ranisapo antenado — R

Ogcocephalidae – batfishes; murciélagos

Zalieutes elater – roundel batfish; murciélago biocelado — S

Mugiliformes

Mugilidae – mullets; lisas

Mugil cephalus – striped mullet; lisa rayada — P,S

Mugil curema – white mullet; lisa blanca — P,S

Atheriniformes

Atherinopsidae – New World silversides; charales y pejerreyes

Atherinops affinis – topsmelt; pejerrey pescadillo — P,S

Colpichthys hubbsi – delta silverside; pejerrey delta — P,S

Colpichthys regis – false grunion; pejerrey charal — P,S

Leuresthes sardina – gulf grunion; pejerrey sardina — P,S

Beloniformes

Belonidae – needlefishes; agujones

Ablennes hians – flat needlefish; agujón sable — P

Strongylura exilis – California needlefish; agujón californiano — P

Tylosurus crocodilus – houndfish; agujón lisero — P

Tylosurus pacificus – Pacific agujon; agujón del Pacífico — P

Exocoetidae – flyingfishes; voladores

Fodiator acutus – sharpchin flyingfish; volador picudo — P

Hemiramphidae – halfbeaks; pajaritos

Hyporhamphus naos – Pacific silverstripe halfbeak; pajarito del Pacífico — P

Hyporhamphus rosae – California halfbeak; pajarito californiano — P

Gasterosteiformes

Syngnathidae – pipefishes and seahorses; peces pipa y caballitos de mar

Cosmocampus arctus – snubnose pipefish; pez pipa chato — R,S

Hippocampus ingens – Pacific seahorse; caballito del Pacífico — S

Syngnathus auliscus – barred pipefish; pez pipa anillado — S

Syngnathus carinatus – Cortez pipefish; pez pipa de Cortés — S

Scorpaeniformes

Scorpaenidae – scorpionfishes; escorpiones y rocotes

    Scorpaena guttata – California scorpionfish; escorpión californiano   S

    Scorpaena mystes – stone scorpionfish; escorpión roquero   R

    Scorpaena sonorae – Sonora scorpionfish; escorpión de Sonora   S

Triglidae – searobins; vacas y rubios

    Prionotus ruscarius – rough searobin; vaca rasposa   S

    Prionotus stephanophrys – lumptail searobin; vaca voladora   S

Perciformes: Percoidei

Serranidae – sea basses and groupers; cabrillas y meros

    Cephalopholis panamensis – Panama graysby; cabrilla enjambre   R

    Diplectrum labarum – highfin sand perch; serrano espinudo   S

    Diplectrum macropoma – Mexican sand perch; serrano mexicano   S

    Diplectrum pacificum – Pacific sand perch; serrano cabaicucho   S

    Diplectrum sciurus – squirrel sand perch; serrano ardilla   S

    Epinephelus acanthistius – gulf coney; baqueta   R,S

    Epinephelus analogus – spotted cabrilla; cabrilla pinta   R

    Epinephelus niphobles – star-studded grouper; baqueta ploma   R

    Mycteroperca rosacea – leopard grouper; cabrilla sardinera   R

    Paralabrax maculatofasciatus – spotted sand bass; cabrilla de roca   S,R

    Rypticus nigripinnis – twice-spotted soapfish; jabonero doble punteado   R

Polyprionidae – wreckfishes; náufragos

    Stereolepis gigas – giant sea bass; pescara   R,S

Opistognathidae – jawfishes; bocones

    Opistognathus punctatus – finespotted jawfish; bocón punteado   S

Apogonidae – cardinalfishes; cardenales

    Apogon retrosella – barspot cardinalfish; cardenal de Cortés   R

Malacanthidae – tilefishes; blanquillos

    Caulolatilus affinis – Pacific golden-eyed tilefish; conejo   S

Coryphaenidae – dolphinfishes; dorados

    Coryphaena hippurus – dolphinfish; dorado   P

Carangidae – jacks; jureles y pámpanos

    Caranx caballus – green jack; jurel bonito   P

    Caranx caninus – Pacific crevalle jack; jurel toro   P

    Chloroscombrus orqueta – Pacific bumper; horqueta del Pacífico   P

    Oligoplites altus – longjaw leatherjack; piña bocona   P

    Oligoplites refulgens – shortjaw leatherjack; piña flaca   P

    Oligoplites saurus – leatherjack; piña sietecueros   P

    Selar crumenophthalmus – bigeye scad; charrito ojón   P

    Selene peruviana – Pacific moonfish; jorobado papelillo   P

    Trachinotus paitensis – paloma pompano; pámpano paloma   P

    Trachinotus rhodopus – gafftopsail pompano; pámpano fino   P

Lutjanidae – snappers; pargos y huachinangos

    Hoplopagrus guentherii – barred snapper; pargo coconaco   R

    Lutjanus argentiventris – amarillo snapper; pargo amarillo   R

    Lutjanus guttatus – spotted rose snapper; pargo lunarejo   R,S

    Lutjanus novemfasciatus – Pacific dog snapper; pargo prieto   R

Lobotidae – tripletails; dormilonas

    Lobotes pacificus – Pacific tripletail; dormilona del Pacífico   P

Gerreidae – mojarras; mojarras

    Eucinostomus currani – Pacific flagfin mojarra; mojarra tricolor   S

    Eucinostomus dowii – Pacific spotfin mojarra; mojarra manchita   S

    Eucinostomus entomelas – darkspot mojarra; mojarra mancha negra   S

    Eucinostomus gracilis – graceful mojarra; mojarra charrita   S

Haemulidae – grunts; burros y roncos

    Anisotremus davidsonii – sargo; sargo rayado   R,S

    Anisotremus interruptus – burrito grunt; burro bacoco   R,S

    Haemulon flaviguttatum – Cortez grunt; burro de Cortés   R

    Haemulon maculicauda – spottail grunt; burro rasposo   R

    Haemulon steindachneri – Latin grunt; burro latino   R,S

    Haemulopsis leuciscus – raucous grunt; ronco ruco   S

Haemulopsis nitidus – shining grunt; ronco brillante — S

Orthopristis reddingi – bronzestriped grunt; burrito rayado — S

Pomadasys panamensis – Panamic grunt; roncacho mapache — S

Xenistius californiensis – salema; salema — R,S

Sparidae – porgies; plumas

Calamus brachysomus – Pacific porgy; pluma marotilla — R,S

Polynemidae – threadfins; barbudos

Polydactylus approximans – blue bobo; barbudo seis barbas — S

Sciaenidae – drums and croakers; corvinas y berrugatas

Atractoscion nobilis – white seabass; corvina cabaicucho — S

Bairdiella icistia – bairdiella; ronco roncacho — S

Chielotrema saturnum – black croaker; corvinata negra — S

Cynoscion othonopterus – gulf covina; corvina golfina — S

Cynoscion parvipinnis – shortfin corvina; corvina aleta corta — S

Cynoscion reticulatus – striped corvina; corvina rayada — S

Cynoscion xanthulus – orangemouth corvina; corvina boquinaranja — S

Isopisthus remifer – bigeye corvina; corvina ojona — S

Larimus pacificus – Pacific drum; boquinete del Pacífico — S

Menticirrhus nasus – highfin kingfish; berrugato real — S

Menticirrhus panamensis – Panama kingfish; berrugato panameño — S

Menticirrhus undulatus – California corbina; berrugato californiano — S

Micropogonias altipinnis – golden croaker; chano sureño — S

Micropogonias megalops – gulf croaker; chano norteño — S

Ophioscion strabo – squint-eyed croaker; corvineta bizca — S

Pareques viola – rock croaker; payasito gungo — R

Totoaba macdonaldi – totoaba; totoaba — S

Umbrina roncador – yellowfin croaker; berrugata aleta amarilla — S

Mullidae – goatfishes; chivos

Pseudupeneus grandisquamis – bigscale goatfish; chivo escamudo — S

Pomacanthidae – angelfishes; ángeles

Pomacanthus zonipectus – Cortez angelfish; ángel de Cortés — R

Kyphosidae – sea chubs; chopas

Girella simplicidens – gulf opaleye; chopa ojo azul — R

Hermosilla azurea – zebraperch; chopa bonita — R

Kyphosus analogus – blue-bronze chub; chopa rayada — R

Kyphosus elegans – Cortez sea chub; chopa de Cortés — R

Perciformes: Labroidei

Pomacentridae – damselfishes; castañetas y jaquetas

Abudefduf troschelii – Panamic sergeant major; petaca banderita — R

Stegastes rectifraenum – Cortez damselfish; jaqueta de Cortés — R

Labridae – wrasses; doncellas y señoritas

Halichoeres chierchiae – wounded wrasse; señorita herida — R

Halichoeres dispilus – chameleon wrasse; señorita camaleón — R

Halichoeres nicholsi – spinster wrasse; señorita solterona — R

Halichoeres notospilus – banded wrasse; señorita listada — R

Halichoeres semicinctus – rock wrasse; señorita piedrera — R

Scaridae – parrotfishes; loros

Nicholsina denticulata – loosetooth parrotfish; pococho beriquete — R

Perciformes: Trachinoidei

Uranoscopidae – stargazers; miracielos

Astroscopus zephyreus – Pacific stargazer; miracielo perro — S

Perciformes: Blennioidei

Dactyloscopidae – sand stargazers; miraestrellas

Dactylagnus mundus – giant stargazer; miraestrellas gigante — S

Dactyloscopus lunaticus – moonstruck stargazer; miraestrellas lunática — S

Dactyloscopus pectoralis – whitesaddle stargazer; miraestrellas fisgona — S

Myxodagnus opercularis – dart stargazer; miraestrellas virote — S

Labrisomidae – labrisomid blennies; trambollos

Exerpes asper – sargassum blenny; trambollo sargacero — R

Labrisomus xanti – largemouth blenny; chalapo — R

Malacoctenus gigas – Sonora blenny; trambollo de Sonora R

Malacoctenus hubbsi – redside blenny; trambollo rojo R

Paraclinus sini – flapscale blenny; trambollito frondoso R

Chaenopsidae – tube blennies; trambollos tubícolas

Emblemaria hypacanthus – gulf signal blenny; tubícola flamante R

Emblemaria walkeri – elusive signal blenny; tubícola fugaz R

Blenniidae – combtooth blennies; borrachos

Hypsoblennius gentilis – bay blenny; borracho de bahía R,S

Hypsoblennius jenkinsi – mussel blenny; borracho mejillonero R,S

Perciformes: Gobiesocoidei

Gobiesocidae – clingfishes; chupapiedras

Gobiesox papillifer – bearded clingfish; chupapiedra barbona R

Gobiesox pinniger – tadpole clingfish; chupapiedra renacuajo R

Gobiesox schultzi – smoothlip clingfish; chupapiedra labioliso R

Pherallodiscus funebris – fraildisc clingfish; chupapiedra discofrágil R

Tomicodon boehlkei – Cortez clingfish; chupapiedra de Cortés R

Tomicodon humeralis – Sonora clingfish; chupapiedra de Sonora R

Tomicodon zebra – zebra clingfish; chupapiedra cebra R

Perciformes: Gobioidei

Eleotridae – sleepers; guavinas

Eleotris picta – spotted sleeper; guavina manchada S

Gobiidae – gobies; gobios

Aruma histrio – slow goby; gobio lento R

Bathygobius ramosus – Panamic frillfin; mapo panámico R

Bollmannia ocellata – pennant goby; gobio penacho S

Coryphopterus urospilus – redlight goby; gobio semáforo R,S

Ctenogobius sagittula – longtail goby; gobio aguzado S

Evermannia sp. – estero goby; gobio de estero S

Gillichthys mirabilis – longjaw mudsucker; chupalodo grande S

Gillichthys seta – shortjaw mudsucker; chupalodo chico S,R

Gobiosoma chiquita – Sonora goby; gobio chiquito R

Gobiosoma sp. – patchscale goby; gobio parche escamitas R

Gobulus crescentalis – crescent goby; gobio creciente R

Ilypnus gilberti – cheekspot goby; gobio mejilla manchada S

Ilypnus luculentus – bright goby; gobio brillante S

Lythrypnus dalli – bluebanded goby; gobio bonito R

Microgobius brevispinis – Balboa goby; gobio de Balboa S

Microgobius cyclolepis – roundscale goby; gobio escamas redondas S

Parrella ginsburgi – darkblotch goby; gobio lunarejo S

Quietula guaymasiae – Guaymas goby; gobio guaymense S

Quietula y-cauda – shadow goby; gobio sombreado S

Perciformes: Acanthuroidei

Ephippididae – spadefishes; peluqueros

Chaetodipterus zonatus – Pacific spadefish; chambo P

Perciformes: Scombroidei

Trichiuridae – cutlassfishes; sables

Trichiurus nitens – Pacific cutlassfish; sable del Pacífico S

Scombridae – mackerels; macarelas

Auxis thazard – frigate mackerel; melva P

Scomber japonicus – Pacific chub mackerel; macarela estornino P

Scomberomorus concolor – gulf sierra; sierra golfina P

Scomberomorus sierra – Pacific sierra; sierra del Pacífico P

Istiophoridae – billfishes; picudos

Istiophorus platypterus – sailfish; pez vela P

Makaira indica – black marlin; marlin negro P

Perciformes: Stromateoidei

Stromateidae – butterfishes; palometas

Peprilus ovatus – Cortez butterfish; palometa de Cortés P

Peprilus snyderi – salema butterfish; palometa salema P

Pleuronectiformes

Paralichthyidae – sand flounders; lenguados areneros

Ancyclopsetta dendritica – threespot sand flounder; lenguado tresojos S

Etropus crossotus – fringed flounder;
   lenguado ribete   S
Etropus peruvianus – Peruvian flounder;
   lenguado zapatilla   S
Hippoglossina bollmani – spotted flounder;
   lenguado pintado   S
Hippoglossina stomata – bigmouth sole;
   lenguado bocón   S
Paralichthys aestuarius – Cortez halibut;
   lenguado de Cortés   S
Paralichthys woolmani – dappled flounder;
   lenguado huarache   S
Syacium ovale – oval flounder; lenguado
   ovalado   S
Xystreurys liolepis – fantail sole; lenguado
   cola de abanico   S
Pleuronectidae – righteye flounders; platijas
Pleuronichthys guttulatus – diamond
   turbot; platija diamante   S
Pleuronichthys ocellatus – ocellated turbot;
   platija ocelada   S
Pleuronichthys verticalis – hornyhead
   turbot; platija cornuda   S
Achiridae – American soles; lenguados suelas
Achirus mazatlanus – Pacific lined sole;
   tepalcate   S
Cynoglossidae – tonguefishes; lenguas
Symphurus chabanaudi – darkcheek
   tonguefish; lengua cachete prieto   S
Symphurus elongatus – elongate
   tonguefish; lengua esbelta   S
Symphurus fasciolaris – banded
   tonguefish; lengua listada   S
Symphurus williamsi – yellow
   tonguefish; lengua amarillenta   S

Tetraodontiformes

Balistidae – triggerfishes; cochitos
Balistes polylepis – finescale triggerfish;
   cochi   R,S
Ostraciidae – boxfishes; peces cofre
Lactoria diaphana – spiny boxfish;
   cofre espinoso   P
Tetraodontidae – puffers; botetes
Sphoeroides annulatus – bullseye puffer;
   botete diana   S

Sphoeroides lispus – naked puffer;
   botete liso   S
Sphoeroides sechurae – Peruvian puffer;
   botete peruano   S

Fishes recorded from Rocas Consag (RC) and/or Isla San Jorge (ISJ) but not yet recorded in the Alto Golfo Biosphere Reserve

Serranidae – sea basses and groupers; cabrillas y meros
Serranus psittacinus – barred serrano; serrano guaseta: RC; ISJ
Pomacentridae – damselfishes; castañetas y jaquetas
Chromis atrilobata – scissortail chromis; castañeta cola de tijera: RC
Labridae – wrasses; doncellas y señoritas
Bodianus diplotaenia – Mexican hogfish; vieja mexicana: ISJ
Tripterygiidae – triplefins; tres aletas
Axoclinus nigricaudus – Cortez triplefin; tres aletas colinegra: RC; ISJ
Crocodilichthys gracilis – lizard triplefin; lagartija tres aletas: RC; ISJ
Labrisomidae – labrisomid blennies; trambollos
Labrisomus multiporosus – porehead blenny; trambollo cabeza porosa: ISJ
Malacoctenus tetranemus – throatspotted blenny; trambollo pintado: ISJ
Starksia spinipenis – phallic blenny; trambollito macho: RC
Xenomedea rhodopyga – redrump blenny; trambollito nalga roja: RC, ISJ
Chaenopsidae – tube blennies; trambollos tubícolas
Acanthemblemaria crockeri – browncheek blenny; tubícola cachetón: ISJ
Chaenopsis alepidota – orangethroat pikeblenny; tubícola lucio: ISJ
Coralliozetus micropes – zebraface blenny; tubícola cara de cebra: ISJ
Protemblemaria bicirrus – warthead blenny; tubícola tupido: RC, ISJ
Ptereleotridae – dartfishes; gobios dardos
Ptereleotris carinata – Panamic dartfish; gobio dardo panámico: RC

Twenty-Seven

Hovering Over the Alto Golfo:

The Status and Conservation of Birds from the Río Colorado to the Gran Desierto

OSVEL HINOJOSA-HUERTA, JAQUELINE GARCÍA-HERNÁNDEZ, YAMILETT CARILLO-GUERRERO, AND ENRIQUE ZAMORA-HERNÁNDEZ

As we paddle our way through the Ciénega de Santa Clara, the living sounds of the Green Lagoons surround us—*keks, brreets, wichitys*—warbling songs that rebound in the water and escape through the cattails, from above and beyond the marsh.

Such are the songs of life of the birds at the Alto Golfo, the birds that fly, soar, hover, and wade throughout the Colorado delta, the Colorado Desert in Baja, the Gran Desierto in Sonora, and the Sierra del Pinacate, traversing rivers, mountains, marshes, and the ever magnificent Gulf of California.

The admiration for birds has a long history in the Alto Golfo region. Deeply embedded in the native cultures of this country, the appreciation and respect for nature extends to bird species, which often symbolize mystical and mythological attributes and after which many places are named (Kniffen 1932; Williams 1973). For the native Cucapás along the Colorado and Hardy rivers, birds are more than cohabitants of the land; they are neighbors that share valuable understanding of the patterns of nature (Onesimo González, traditional chief of the Cucapá Tribe, El Mayor, Baja California, personal communication 2001).

Ever since the first European explorers reached the region, the Alto Golfo has been described as a land of fascination and contrasts, a hardy place full of natural wonders, and by several, one of the most desolate places in North America (Fradkin 1984; Leopold 1949; North 1910). The Alto Golfo is also the setting for multiple stories of ecosystem decay and species at risk, contrasting with surprising recoveries and amazing ecological restoration (Glenn et al. 1996, 2001; Hinojosa-Huerta et al. 2001a; Zengel et al. 1995, 1996).

This region is as well the home for more than 350 avian species and a temporal wintering or stopover site for thousands of migratory birds (see checklist at end of chapter). The multiplicity of biomes in the region creates a mosaic of habitat types in the transitions between deserts, riparian corridors, brackish marshes, extensive mudflats, and the sea (Felger et al. 1997). This diverse mosaic supports a complex array of bird communities; for example, one might see verdins *(Auriparus flaviceps)* building a nest and short-billed dowitchers *(Limnodromus scolopaceus)* probing the mud while a sora *(Porzana carolina)* is whining nearby, a mixed flock of wood-warblers (Parulidae) is foraging intensively, and a magnificent frigatebird *(Fregata magnificens)* is flying overhead. Unique environmental characteristics provide habitat for some endemic birds, such as the Yuma clapper rail *(Rallus longirostris yumanensis)* and the large-billed savannah sparrow *(Passerculus sandwichensis rostratus)*, which nest in the marshes and grasses of the Colorado delta. Each of the biomes within the Alto Golfo supports a characteristic avian community, contributing to the richness of the region's bird life.

As in most of the Sonoran Desert, five seasons mold bird life in the Alto Golfo: spring, dry summer, wet summer, fall, and winter (Dimmitt 2000). The floods of the Colorado, which historically occurred in spring and early summer, complement these seasonal patterns (Zamora-Arroyo et al. 2001). The life histories of birds intermingle with the seasons and periods of floods to shape the region's temporal patterns, and as the seasons progress, the composition of the avifauna changes dramatically.

The Setting

We concentrated our attention in the northernmost area of the Alto Golfo, including the delta of the Río Colorado and surrounding deserts in both Baja California and Sonora, the marine zone of the Alto Golfo from San Felipe, B.C., to Puerto

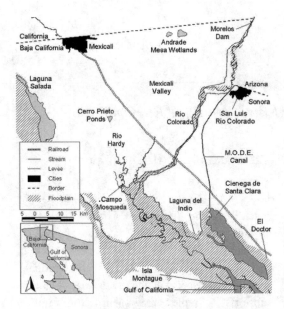

Peñasco, Sonora, and the Gran Desierto, Sierra del Pinacate, and Río Sonoyta (Figure 27.1).

These localities encompass distinct habitat types: riparian corridors dominated by cottonwoods *(Populus fremontii)* and willows *(Salix gooddingii)* in the Río Colorado, marshes dominated by emergent plants in the Río Hardy and Ciénega de Santa Clara, large stands of the exotic salt cedar *(Tamarix* spp.) in the confluence of the Hardy and Colorado rivers, vast mudflats near the mouth of the Colorado and Isla Montague, and the marine zone and rocky islands between Puerto Peñasco and San Felipe. Southeast of the Colorado River delta is a string of *pozos* along the desert escarpment, including El Doctor (Ezcurra et al. 1988). These *pozos* are tiny vegetated islands surrounded by a sea of sand in the Gran Desierto. Farther southeast lie the volcanic desert and sand dunes at El Pinacate, dominated by cacti and ironwood *(Olneya tesota);* the desert riparian corridor of the Río Sonoyta with a vegetation association of mesquite *(Prosopis* spp.) and palo verde *(Parkinsonia* spp.); the sandy and rocky coast between El Golfo de Santa Clara and Puerto Peñasco; and the estuaries at Bahía Adair, Estero Morúa, and Estero La Pinta, dominated by salt-tolerant plants.

A View from the Past

The Alto Golfo was one of the first regions to be visited by European explorers in the 1530s, yet it was one of the last places in North America to be fully mapped, described, and colonized (Hornaday 1908; Lumholtz 1990). This lack of attention meant little ecological disruption for birds, and until recently the entire region was a vast wilderness with barely a human footprint.

The remoteness of the region also meant a scarcity of biological surveys and descriptions of these biotic communities while still in pristine condition. Nevertheless, a few hardy naturalists, ornithologists, and explorers were brave and curious enough to venture into the deserts, beaches, and swamps of the Alto Golfo.

One of the first biologists to investigate this country was Edgar A. Mearns. From 1892 to 1895, while serving as surgeon of the International Boundary Survey, he conducted extensive surveys and collected more than 30,000 specimens for the U.S. National Museum along the United States–Mexico border (Mearns 1907). Mearns visited the Alto Golfo from December 1893 to May 1894, hiring Miguel, a young Cucapá, to help him with the collections and to serve as a guide. Mearns was impressed by the harshness of the desert, the critical value of the tinajas (natural water tanks), the heat, and the lushness of the Colorado River delta. He described the delta as a tropical tract dominated by unusually tall cottonwoods, abundant willows, and dense grassy marshes.

Mearns noted the delta's abundant avifauna: "The tide creeks and broad bays about our camp were swarming with waterfowl, which were nowhere else seen in so great abundance. Pelicans, cormorants, geese, ducks, cranes, herons, and small waders almost covered the shores and bays, the sky was lined with their ever changing geometrical figures, and the air resounded with their winnowing wing-strokes and clanging voices, not only during the day, but through most of the night" (1907:73). He also described how songbirds and other small birds abounded in the grassy savannahs, mesquite groves, and willow thickets.

William W. Price also visited the lower Colorado and Alto Golfo before the 1900s. He spent nearly a month between November and December 1898 observing birds in the region (Price 1899). Price found 91 species, of which he was most impressed by the American white pelicans *(Pelecanus erythrorhynchos),* describing them as extremely abundant along the lower river and the gulf, with hundreds of flocks "that would sometimes join in immense gatherings darkening the sky" (1899:90). He noted thousands of sandhill cranes *(Grus canadensis),* especially at Laguna Salada, and hundreds of zone-tailed hawks *(Buteo albonotatus)* hovering over a marsh wildfire, "undoubtedly to prey upon the abundant cotton rats and other rodents" (Price 1899:91). He found waterfowl to be common, with great numbers of brant *(Branta bernicla)* at Laguna Salada and Río Hardy. Of the songbirds, he found numerous Abert's towhees *(Pipilo aberti)* and Audubon's warblers *(Dendroica coronata)* in mesquite-willow thickets, dense marshlands, and arrowweed tracts.

A few years later the naturalists Edgar W. Nelson and Edgar A. Goldman visited the Baja California side of this region (Nelson 1921). Nelson led a year-long exploration (1905–6) of the peninsula for the Bureau of Biological Survey of the U.S. Department of Agriculture. During the expedition the two men carried out exhaustive surveys that resulted in detailed descriptions of the faunal districts of Baja California. Nelson himself did not visit the Colorado River delta during this expedition, but Goldman led a boat trip to the delta during the spring of 1905, accompanied by D. T. MacDougal, a botanist from the Carnegie Institution of Washington. They surveyed the Río Hardy, Sierra Cucapá, Cerro Prieto, and Río Nuevo during a period when most of the area was flooded. From the Colorado Desert, near San Felipe, Nelson listed 22 species, mainly desert birds, including desert thrashers *(Toxostoma* spp.), cactus wren *(Campylorhynchus brunneicapillus),* verdin, Abert's towhee, greater roadrunner *(Geococcyx californianus),* Gila woodpecker *(Melanerpes uropygialis),* and white-winged dove *(Zenaida asiatica).* He also noted the "vast numbers of waterfowl that resort to the delta of the Colorado" in winter (Nelson 1921:112).

W. T. Hornaday reported in detail the events and observations of a scientific expedition into the Pinacate during November 1908, in which he was joined by D. T. MacDougal, Godfrey Sykes, and J. M. Phillips (Hornaday 1907). The expedition traveled from Tucson to the Gulf of California, passing through the town of Sonoyta and over the river of the same name. Hornaday described the Río Sonoyta as a "little stream . . . with the desert coming down to its northern margin . . . on the southern bank, the oasis began and ran riot. . . . The other side was a perfect jungle of desert willows and other small trees" (1907:83). He commented that the bird life was greater and more interesting than they had expected during that time of year, and he made notes on a dozen species,

including red-tailed hawk *(Buteo jamaicensis),* bald eagle *(Haliaeetus leucocephalus),* golden eagle *(Aquila chrysaetos),* great horned owl *(Bubo virginianus),* phainopepla *(Phainopepla nitens),* cactus wren, and Gambel's quail *(Callipepla gambelii).* Noteworthy observations include an American coot *(Fulica americana)* and an American bittern *(Botaurus lentiginosus)* at the Río Sonoyta—waterbirds in one of the driest regions of North America. The expedition party marveled at the abundance and characteristics of cactus wren nests in the cholla cacti, the great numbers of quail and ravens, and the scarcity of roadrunners. The expedition's bird observations are not very detailed, however, as the group lacked optical equipment for the identification of small songbirds and hummingbirds and did not collect specimens.

In December 1909 the Norwegian naturalist Carl Lumholtz made his own explorations of the Río Sonoyta, the Pinacate, and the Colorado delta, studying both the natural and cultural landscape (Lumholtz 1990). He was assisted by three Mexicans and three Papago Indians. Lumholtz was deeply in love with the landscape of this region, writing: "The desert is radiant with good cheer, and the hardy, healthy looking plants and trees with their abundant flowers inspire courage. One feels in communion with nature. . . . Could I select the place where I should like best to die, my choice would be one such as this" (1990:307). Lumholtz was not a professional ornithologist, and thus his notes on the bird life are very general and pertain only to the most conspicuous and common species. Nevertheless, they provide valuable information from a little-studied region. At Río Sonoyta he noted the presence of American coots, a great egret *(Ardea alba),* several ducks, and a small flock of geese. In the Pinacate region Lumholtz commonly found northern mockingbirds *(Mimus polyglottos),* thrashers, hawks, falcons, and ravens; Gambel's quail and doves were abundant, especially near the tinajas; and he observed a black-tailed gnatcatcher *(Polioptila melanura)* nesting on a palo verde. In January 1910 he started a journey from the Pinacate to the Colorado delta. Along the way he visited Laguna Prieta, a salt lake with cattail *(Typha domingensis)* marshes where he noted the presence of seabirds but made no reference to their species or numbers. Later in January he arrived at the Colorado delta, passing through thickets of willows, mesquite, and arrowweed and along marshes covered with cattails and reeds (*Scirpus* spp.). In the delta Lumholtz noted throngs of shorebirds, gulls, and especially cranes.

A. J. van Rossem and Joseph Grinnell studied the birds of northwestern Mexico extensively during the 1920s and 1930s, concentrating on taxonomy and distribution and the classification and description of collected specimens, van Rossem (1945) in Sonora and Grinnell (1928) in Baja California. Their work still provides valuable baseline information for assessing changes in the region's avifauna, as it provides historic records of breeding, wintering, and transient species and subspecies at localities such as Río Hardy, Cerro Prieto, Rocas Consag, El Doctor, Puerto Peñasco, Isla San Jorge, and Río Colorado.

Southern California ornithologist Griffin Bancroft visited the Colorado River delta, the Colorado Desert of Baja California, and the Alto Golfo several times during the 1920s and 1930s (Bancroft 1922, 1926, 1932). Even though he was in awe of "the delta jungle within the desert country" (Bancroft 1926:209), he noted: "In Mexico perhaps one half the present farming acreage was until recently, willow associations of the Delta. Salvaged the jungle became an integral, indistinguishable portion of the major system, but the subjugation, the clearing, draining, leveling of swamps and thickets and tributaries, is one of the West's famous achievements. A river harnessed to obey, cement dams and waterworks with foundations resting on silt, lakes and canals coming or going at the word of command, an effective though unruly Slave of the Lamp" (Bancroft 1932:385).

During a winter hunting expedition Bancroft observed 30 species (Bancroft 1922). Most significant were fulvous whistling duck (*Dendrocygna bicolor*) and roseate spoonbill (*Ajaia ajaja*), both now extirpated from the delta. The most abundant birds were white-crowned sparrow (*Zonotrichia leucophrys*), Gambel's quail, Abert's towhee, mourning dove (*Zenaida macroura*), common ground-dove (*Columbina passerina*), and cactus wren. In the marshlands he noted sora and marsh wren (*Cistothorus palustris*).

Ten years later Bancroft approached the delta on board the *Least Petrel*, a small vessel. On his way he visited Rocas Consag, "a setting that approaches artistic perfection" (Bancroft 1932:373). Here Bancroft documented the nesting of the brown booby (*Sula leucogaster*), black storm-petrel

(*Oceanodroma melania*), least storm-petrel (*O. microsoma*), peregrine falcon (*Falco peregrinus*), Craveri's murrelet (*Synthliboramphus craveri*), and red-billed tropicbird (*Phaethon aethereus*). In the delta Bancroft stopped at Islas Montague and Gore to wait for "el burro," the tidal bore. At Montague, Bancroft discovered the nests of large-billed savannah sparrows. He also looked, unsuccessfully, for nests of Yuma clapper rails. Unlike other clapper rails, the local subspecies prefers freshwater or brackish inland ciénegas to intertidal marshes.

Bancroft recognized the importance of water in maintaining the delta ecosystem, noting that the variety of water sources resulted "in a multitude of local areas of diversified vegetation," supporting a rich avifauna (Bancroft 1926:209). Finally, he described in detail the uniqueness of the delta, its regional importance, and the delicate balance it supports in a border region: "Such is the delta, as fascinating, as puzzling, and as changeable as weather. Surrounded by desert and constantly fighting to preserve its identity, it is as unlike its immediate surroundings as adjoining countries well can be. Host to most of the desert birds, which seek out its arid phases as they find them here and there, still it has, from Caracaras on the north to Large-billed Sparrows on the south, its quota of birds which hereabouts do not make their homes elsewhere" (Bancroft 1926:210).

Aldo Leopold also visited the region, in a hunting trip during the 1920s (Leopold 1949). Disregarding recommendations by the locals to avoid the delta's perilous wilderness, he and his brother Carl headed for Rillito (close to today's Ciénega de Santa Clara). They stayed in this "weird and impressive" wetland system of the eastern Colorado delta for ten days, following quail, geese, deer, and *el tigre*, the jaguar. On October 26, 1922, the brothers unloaded at the bank of a "pretty little slough" where an abundance of shorebirds, cranes, spoonbills, kingfishers, ducks, cormorants, and quail welcomed them while geese flew overhead and the egrets on the willows "looked like a premature snow storm" (Leopold 1949:142). Leopold described how "dawn on the Delta was whistled in by Gambel's Quail . . . and when the sun peeped, it slanted across a hundred miles of lovely desolation, a vast flat bowl of wilderness rimmed by jagged peaks" (1949:141). At the point of the Mesa Arenosa, near Ejido Luis Encinas Johnson, Sonora, Leopold found the "green lagoons," which he described as "a series of pools, full of herons and lined with waving willows of the most delicate green; the water, bearing the reflections of the willows, is of a brilliant verdigris hue" (Leopold 1953:16).

Further exploration led the Leopold brothers to one of the historic channels of the river, in which "a verdant wall of mesquite and willow separated the channel from the thorny desert beyond. At each bend we saw egrets, each white statue matched by its white reflection. Fleets of cormorants drove their black prows in quest of skittering mullets; avocets, willets, and yellowlegs dozed one legged on the bars, mallards, widgeons, and teals sprang skyward in alarm" (Leopold 1949:142).

Years later Leopold recalled his expedition through the Colorado delta with nostalgia for a place that "has been made safe for cows and forever dull for adventurous hunters . . . as freedom from fear has arrived, but a glory has departed from the green lagoons" (1949:144).

Some of the species observed by Leopold have been extirpated from the delta, and most of the populations from the remnant species have declined. But dawn in the delta is still whistled in by quails, and the sun slants across miles of lovely desolation, flat wilderness, and jagged peaks. Hope still flies around the blue skies and resounds in the marshes of the delta. With our actions and decisions we can preserve the Green Lagoons for the enjoyment of the adventurous explorer within ourselves.

Changes in Avian Habitats and Communities

A century of human intervention has jeopardized the diversity of bird life and the ecological relationships in the Alto Golfo. Thirteen resident or breeding species of birds here are legally protected under Mexican laws (classified as endangered, threatened, or needing special protection), as well as seventeen others that use this area as stopover or wintering ground (Diario Oficial 2002; see checklist). Major causes for the declines in bird populations are habitat loss and fragmentation associated with water management practices, agricultural expansion, and tourism development, and the introduction of exotic species of plants and animals.

The loss of wetlands and riparian areas has been especially critical. Along the Río Sonoyta the surface water and groundwater are being depleted

by the growing human population in Puerto Peñasco and Sonoyta, and some tracts of the river have been invaded by salt cedar.

Tourism and urban development is threatening the fragile desert estuaries in Puerto Peñasco, and the introduction of exotic species of plants (especially salt cedar) and animals (mainly rats and feral cats) is a major conservation concern over the whole region, especially at islands such as San Jorge.

More than 80 percent of the natural areas in the Colorado River delta have disappeared as a result of water management practices in the watershed and agricultural expansion in the Mexicali Valley (Valdés-Casillas et al. 1998). Flows of the Colorado into the delta and Alto Golfo are irregular and scarce, and the brackish delta estuary of former times now has higher salinity than the sea (Glenn et al. 2001). Groundwater in the San Luis and Mexicali valleys has been overexploited, increasing the depth of the water table and negatively affecting the *pozos* and springs at the edge of the desert escarpment.

Most affected have been the bird species that depend on the native vegetation of the Colorado River delta. Populations have declined regionally, and four species have been extirpated locally.

Historically, the cottonwood-willow association was very common along the myriad of streams traversing the delta. This habitat type extended from the main channel in Yuma, west to the Río Nuevo, south to Cerro Prieto and Río Hardy, and east again to the Green Lagoons, at what we know now as the Ciénega de Santa Clara and El Doctor (Sykes 1937). The historic extension of the cottonwood-willow association is hard to estimate but probably was in the tens of thousands of hectares. Most of this area is now used for agriculture, or has become dry salt flats, or is dominated by the exotic-invasive salt cedar. Only about 1,100 hectares of this association remains in the delta, one of the largest such areas in the entire lower Colorado basin (Zamora-Arroyo et al. 2001).

Some of the riparian-dependent species of major concern are the southwestern willow flycatcher (*Empidonax traillii extimus*), western yellow-billed cuckoo (*Coccyzus americanus occidentalis*), and fulvous whistling-duck (*Dendrocygna bicolor*). These species formerly nested in the delta, but there are no recent records of breeding activity for any of them.

The southwestern willow flycatcher is an endangered subspecies whose populations have declined all over the southwestern United States and northwestern Mexico, mainly because of habitat loss associated with management of streams in the region (Unitt 1987). Current total population is estimated at 600 pairs (Sogge et al. 1997). Historic nesting records of southwestern willow flycatchers in the delta include Cerro Prieto and the mainstem of the river near Yuma (Sferra et al. 1997; Unitt 1987), but no breeding has been observed recently. However, the remnant riparian patches in the delta are an important part of the spring migration route of this species. In particular, willow flycatchers occupy backwater lagoons dominated by dense stands of native broadleaf trees as stopover sites on their way north (García-Hernández et al. 2001).

Populations of the western yellow-billed cuckoo have also declined over the past decades throughout western North America (Hughes 1999). In the United States the yellow-billed cuckoo is protected by the state Endangered Species Act in California and is considered a threatened species in Arizona and Utah. Currently, western populations of the species are candidates for protection under the federal Endangered Species Act (U.S. Fish and Wildlife Service 2001). Historically, this species was a common breeder in the riparian areas of the Río Colorado (Patten et al. 2001), with records near Cerro Prieto (Grinnell 1928), but today it has been almost extirpated from much of the lower Colorado (Rosenberg et al. 1991). A few individuals have been detected during the breeding season along the mainstem of the Colorado in areas dominated by cottonwoods (Osvel Hinojosa-Huerta, observation; Patten et al. 2001). No breeding has been confirmed yet, but some pairs may be attempting to nest in the regenerated riparian areas of the delta.

The fulvous whistling-duck was a common breeding resident before the 1930s (Bancroft 1922; van Rossem 1945), but no recent records have been reported (Patten et al. 2001). Likewise, the roseate spoonbill and sandhill crane were common winter visitors during the early 1900s (Bancroft 1922; Grinnell 1926, 1928; Murphy 1917) but have not been spotted in the region recently.

Populations of the large-billed savannah sparrow, an endemic subspecies that winters on the coast of southern California, have also been re-duced in the last few decades (Unitt 1984). These sparrows nest in the saltgrass areas of the delta. Their breeding grounds are now confined to a few spots in the Ciénega de Santa Clara, El Doctor, Isla Montague, Cerro Prieto, and the mouth of the Río Colorado (Mellink & Ferreira-Bartrina 2000; Molina and Garrett 2001).

The historic abundance of waterfowl in the Colorado delta region has become a matter of nostalgia and storytelling for local residents and visiting hunters. Hundreds of thousands of ducks and geese from at least 26 species used to visit the region in winter (Kramer & Migoya 1989). Habitat for wintering waterfowl has been reduced to a few thousand hectares during the dry years in the delta. Currently, waterfowl habitat at the Ciénega de Santa Clara and Río Hardy extends over 8,000 hectares. Estero Morúa, Estero Las Pintas, and Bahía Adair near Puerto Peñasco are also important stopover sites. In the 1990s, aerial winter surveys estimated nearly 50,000 individuals during wet years (1993–94) and just over 4,000 individuals during dry years (1995–96) (U.S. Fish and Wildlife Service 1993–96).

Despite these changes in avian habitats, many species still thrive in the region. Thousands of individuals of over a hundred species of Neotropical migratory songbirds stop at the revived cottonwood-willow areas of the Río Colorado, in the mesquite thickets of the Río Sonoyta, and on the strings of *pozos* along the eastern escarpment of the Sonoran Desert during spring migration (mid-March–mid-June). These islands of treestands surrounded by the desert and the sea form a migratory route for birds in their journeys between their wintering grounds in southern Mexico and Central America and their breeding grounds in the United States and Canada. The quality of stopover sites is key in defining the population trends of migratory songbirds (Moore 1998; Petit 1997). Thus the conservation of such sites in the Alto Golfo is critical for the preservation of Neotropical migratory songbirds.

The Alto Golfo also provides crucial stopover sites for migratory shorebirds, especially at Bahía Adair, the mouth of the Río Colorado, and the Ciénega de Santa Clara. Over 150,000 shorebirds from 32 species visit the delta every year (Mellink et al. 1997; Morrison et al. 1992). For this reason, the delta is part of the Western Hemisphere Shorebird Reserves Network (WHSRN 1993) and a Wetland of International Importance in the Ramsar Convention (Ramsar Convention Bureau 1998).

Marshbirds are also an important component of the avifauna of the region, especially at the Ciénega de Santa Clara, El Doctor, and Río Hardy. Six species of rails occur in these areas, and five regularly breed here. The Yuma clapper rail, an endemic subspecies of the lower Colorado and delta, endangered in the United States and threatened in Mexico, is very abundant. Over 3,000 pairs breed in the Ciénega de Santa Clara, probably more than 70 percent of the subspecies' total population (Hinojosa-Huerta et al. 2001a). Clapper rails have benefited from accidental management practices of agricultural drainage water that have restored cattail marshes in the ciénega and Río Hardy. Nevertheless, these practices are not standard, and since this water has not been allotted for the environment, it could be reclaimed. The habitat for the subspecies in the ciénega is maintained with agricultural runoff from the Wellton-Mohawk Valley in Arizona. This same water is slated to be desalted in Yuma and sold for human consumption. If that occurs, the marsh at the ciénega would be reduced drastically and the population of Yuma clapper rails could decline sharply.

California black rails *(Laterallus jamaicensis coturniculus)* also breed in this region, although in smaller numbers (Hinojosa-Huerta et al. 2001b). Probably there are fewer than 50 nesting pairs between El Doctor and the Ciénega de Santa Clara. Inland populations of the subspecies are very rare and have declined over the last three decades (Evens et al. 1991). In Mexico the subspecies is listed as endangered (Diario Oficial 2002), and in the United States it is considered threatened by the state of California and a species of concern by the U.S. Fish and Wildlife Service (California Department of Fish and Game 1999). Black rails were thought to be absent from this region because of widespread habitat degradation (Evens et al. 1991), but they were recently discovered (Piest and Campoy 1999). Black rails require shallow (3 cm or more) and stable water levels in marshes near upland vegetation, and thus available habitat is very scarce and sensitive to human activities. A local threat for the subspecies may be the presence of cattle in the most suitable areas at El Doctor and the Ciénega de Santa Clara, although the impact of cattle on the black rails has not been evaluated.

Officials from the Alto Golfo Biosphere Reserve; Ducks Unlimited de México, A.C. (DUMAC); and IMADES have been working to exclude cattle from the most sensitive areas of the marsh but have achieved limited results.

Leopold, Nelson, Lumholtz, Price, and Bancroft never saw rock doves *(Columba livia),* house sparrows *(Passer domesticus),* ring-necked pheasants *(Phasianus colchicus),* or European starlings *(Sturnus vulgaris)* in the Colorado River delta, yet these species are the most common sight today in the rural towns and agricultural areas of the Mexicali Valley. The colonization of the region by these exotic species is directly related to the habitat modifications introduced by human activities, but the impact on the native avifauna has not been studied in detail. These exotic species are not common in areas that have been regenerated or that maintain natural habitat features, so their impact on populations of native birds is likely still limited.

Some native species have expanded their ranges and increased their populations in western North America as human activity has grown. Most notorious are red-winged blackbirds *(Agelaius phoeniceus)* and brown-headed cowbirds *(Molothrus ater).* The effect of the expansion of these species has not been evaluated in the Alto Golfo. However, the impacts of cowbirds have been carefully evaluated in other riparian areas of the Sonoran Desert, where habitat fragmentation and intensified farming practices have increased the nest parasitism of cowbirds, causing population declines in riparian-dependent songbirds such as willow flycatchers and Bell's vireos *(Vireo bellii;* Sogge et al. 1997).

Bird Conservation in the Alto Golfo

Information on the status and population trends of avian species in the Alto Golfo is scarce. Thus management decisions for the conservation of birds and their habitats have lacked the support of robust scientific data. Nevertheless, government agencies and environmental organizations have achieved important conservation steps by protecting critical areas, based on requirements for focal species such as the Yuma clapper rail.

In 1993 the Mexican government established the Reserva de la Biosfera Alto Golfo de California y Delta del Río Colorado, designating the Ciénega de Santa Clara, El Doctor wetlands, Isla Montague, and mudflats in the Río Colorado mouth its core zone. This reserve now protects more than 70 percent of the breeding population of Yuma clapper rails and the largest breeding population of California black rails in Mexico. It also protects one of the most important stopover sites for Neotropical migratory passerines along western North America at El Doctor, an important breeding ground for waterbirds at Montague, and habitat for over 150,000 wintering shorebirds at the river mudflats. The Reserva de la Biosfera El Pinacate y Gran Desierto de Altar was established a year later, protecting critical stopover sites for migrant birds along desert riparian tracts of the Río Sonoyta, especially for warblers, hummingbirds, and raptors.

Even though these two reserves together encompass an area of 1.65 million hectares, important sites for birds still lack legal protection or conservation status. One of the most critical but unprotected bird sanctuaries is the riparian corridor of the Río Colorado in Sonora and Baja California, which provides habitat for migrant and resident songbirds. Also without protection are the adjacent wetlands of the Río Hardy, which represent one of the best opportunities for restoration in the lower Colorado basin and are one of the strongholds for the region's wintering waterfowl. Other important unprotected sites include Estero Morúa, Estero La Pinta, and the extended floodplain of the Río Sonoyta, lying just outside the limits of the two biosphere reserves. The region encompassed by these sites is also a stepping-stone in the migratory corridor of shorebirds, waterfowl, raptors, and more than 100 species of passerines, and a feeding ground for gulls, terns, and other seabirds.

All these unprotected areas face strong pressures: upstream water diversions, invasion of exotic species, flood-control activities and vegetation clearing, tourism and urban development, and wildfires. To overcome these threats, a binational partnership of environmental organizations, universities, and local communities is working to cover these conservation gaps. In the Colorado River delta the local organization AEURHYC (Environmental Association of Users of the Hardy and Colorado Rivers) is working with Pronatura Sonora, the Sonoran Institute, and the University of Arizona to restore marsh wetlands in the Río Hardy and to establish legal protection for critical sites of the riparian corridor. A common goal for the delta is to identify sources of water that could maintain and enhance existing riparian patches in the long term. In the meantime a binational team in partnership with local communities is working with landowners near the Río Hardy to restore marsh and mesquite bosque habitat types. The purpose of this project is to examine the response of native vegetation and wildlife to various restoration strategies and to develop ways to work within the existing legal and social framework of land and water rights for habitat enhancement.

Still, the region has many conservation needs. In the larger picture it is imperative that decision makers and the general public understand that habitat degradation and population declines in birds are the result of land and water management policies that were implemented on both sides of the border without regard for the environmental consequences. The letter of intent signed by the U.S. and Mexican governments for cooperation on sister reserves along the border and the joint declaration for the enhancement of wetlands of the Colorado River delta (Minute 306 of the United States–Mexico International Water Treaty of 1944) are only the first steps toward binational management of these shared ecosystems. A stronger binational dialogue is needed to fully protect the Alto Golfo.

A transboundary regional plan for water management and allocation of instream flows should be developed to maintain all remnant patches of riparian vegetation and wetlands. International guidelines need to be drafted by authorities and communities in both countries to ensure that such environmental flows will remain in the river and to secure the protection of existing important sites.

It is also critical to identify and implement nongovernmental strategies to protect habitat for birds, especially in private and *ejido* lands and in federal areas that could be used as a government concession and managed by local communities for environmental purposes. The implementation of conservation strategies lacks focus and loses its potential if we don't understand the status and trends of the targeted resources. Focal species and birds of concern should be identified for the different habitat types in the region, and these species should be carefully monitored over the long run. Binational cooperation, local participation, and a strong monitoring program with a robust scientific framework are the keys to implementing long-term conservation strategies to preserve the amazing avifauna of the Alto Golfo.

The admiration for birds has a long history in the Alto Golfo. And so we continue with the tradition, enjoying the company of our feathered friends along the running waters of the Río Colorado, under bright blue skies and brilliant green willows, hoping that this unique setting can be enhanced and maintained forever.

Acknowledgments

We thank Carlos Valdés-Casillas and Edward Glenn for introducing us to the Alto Golfo. We are especially grateful to Onésimo González, Mónica González, Javier Mosqueda, Don Jesús Mosqueda, Juan Butrón, José Juan Butrón, Mauricio Butrón, Miguel Cruz, Martha Román, José Campoy, and Miriam Lara for their hospitality and continuous help. Helena Iturribarría-Rojas, Gerardo Sánchez-Bon, and Juan José Rivera-Díaz have been brave and generous enough to join the Colorado Delta Field Crew: many thanks. Our work has been possible because of the wonderful help of Sacha Heath, Chris McCreedy, and Roy Churchwell (Point Reyes Bird Observatory); Robert Mesta (Sonoran Joint Venture); Bill Shaw and Bill Mannan (School of Renewable Natural Resources, University of Arizona); Meredith de la Garza and Raquel Castro (Pronatura Sonora); and the National Fish and Wildlife Foundation.

Checklist of the Birds of the Reserva de la Biosfera Alto Golfo de California y Delta del Río Colorado

The species accounts summarize current knowledge on the status of birds in the Alto Golfo, mostly based on the extensive review work done by Patten et al. (2001) in Baja California and by Russell & Monson (1998) in Sonora. We complemented the list with later sources and our own field observations. A list of records and observers is presented only if the species is casual or accidental in the region. We include only those species for which there is at least one definite record within the Alto Golfo. Localities are shown in Figure 27.1 and described in Chapter 39 of this volume.

All uncredited records and statements about status are based on our field observations. Observers' initials are as follows: ACF = Alejandra Calvo-Fonseca, EZH = Enrique Zamora-Hernández, HIR = Helena Iturribarría-Rojas, JGH = Jaqueline García-Hernández, MAG = Miguel Ángel Guevara, OHH = Osvel Hinojosa-Huerta, and YCG = Yamilett Carrillo-Guerrero. We also include records by Steve Ganley (S. Ganley, personal communication; available at http://www.primenet.com/~sganley), Kimball Garrett (K. Garrett, personal communication), and Richard A. Erickson (RAE).

The annotated checklist follows the taxonomic nomenclature and order of the seventh edition of the *Check-list of North American Birds* (American Ornithologists' Union 1998, including the changes made in the supplements to the check-list [Banks et al. 2004]). Subspecies is given only if it has relevance to legal status or protection in Mexico, as defined in the Norma Oficial Mexicana NOM-059-ECOL-2001 (Diario Oficial 2002). Names in Spanish follow Escalante et al. (1996). When a different common name is used in the region, the official name is given first, followed by the local name.

Designations for abundance and temporal status of birds are based on the categories in Patten et al. 2001 and Russell & Monson 1998. The designations for abundance are as follows: **common:** frequently encountered and/or in large numbers; **fairly common:** encountered in modest numbers; **uncommon:** present in the area but found infrequently; **rare:** seen only on occasion, but range lies within the Alto Golfo; **casual:** out of usual range but could be expected every other year; **accidental:** away from the normal range and not normally expected.

Designations for the temporal occurrence of birds in the Alto Golfo are as follows: **resident:** occurs during most of the year in the region; **visitor:** spends a few weeks to a few months in the region; **transient:** spends a short time (usually a few days) in the region during migration; **vagrant:** occurs sporadically in the region, which is out of its usual range.

ANSERIFORMES

ANATIDAE – DUCKS, GEESE, AND SWANS

Fulvous whistling-duck *(Dendrocygna bicolor)* – Pijiji canelo. Former breeding resident in Río Colorado (Bancroft 1922; van Rossem 1945) but no recent records. Postbreeding visitors from breeding grounds at Imperial Valley might occur in Río Colorado and Mexicali Valley (Patten et al. 2001).

Greater white-fronted goose *(Anser albifrons)* – Ganso careto mayor. Rare spring transient through the Colorado delta and coastal areas, more regular at Ciénega de Santa Clara. Formerly a regular and abundant winter visitor to Colorado delta (Saunders & Saunders 1981).

Snow goose *(Chen caerulescens)* – Ganso blanco. Fairly common winter visitor at Ciénega de Santa Clara and adjacent agricultural fields, although formerly much more abundant (Leopold 1989; Murphy 1917; Saunders & Saunders 1981).

Ross's goose *(Chen rossi)* – Ganso de Ross. Uncommon winter visitor at Ciénega de Santa Clara.

Brant *(Branta bernicla)* – Branta. Uncommon spring transient in northern gulf, Cerro Prieto, and Río Hardy. Casual summer (K. Garrett in Patten et al. 2001) and winter visitor at Cerro Prieto (Price 1899). *B. b. nigricans,* the subspecies that occurs in this region, is protected as threatened in Mexico (Diario Oficial 2002).

Canada goose *(Branta canadensis)* – Ganso canadiense. Common winter visitor at Ciénega de Santa Clara and adjacent agricultural fields, uncommon elsewhere. Although most Canada geese are *B. c. moffitti* (Saunders & Saunders 1981), there is one record of three individuals of the endangered Aleutian Canada goose *(B. c. leucopareia)* in the Colorado delta (Russell & Monson 1998).

Wood duck *(Aix sponsa)* – Pato arcoiris. Accidental vagrant, with only one recorded at the pond of the Bosque Zoológico de Mexicali on July 8, 2003 (RAE).

Gadwall *(Anas strepera)* – Pato pinto. Fairly common winter visitor at Ciénega de Santa Clara and Río Hardy. Fairly common transient elsewhere in the delta and along the coast.

Eurasian wigeon *(Anas penelope)* – Pato silbón. Casual winter visitor, with one record near Río Hardy (Ruiz-Campos & Rodríguez-Meraz 1997), one at Puerto Peñasco (Russell & Monson 1998), and one at Cerro Prieto (RAE, January 13, 2003).

American wigeon *(Anas americana)* – Pato chalcuán. Fairly common winter visitor and casual summer visitor in the Colorado delta; common transient through the coast.

Mallard *(Anas platyrhynchos)* – Pato de collar. Fairly common winter visitor in the Colorado delta and coast, most abundant at Ciénega de Santa Clara. Uncommon nonbreeding visitor in summer throughout delta. One confirmed breeding record (a recent fledgling observed) at the Limitrophe Zone of the Colorado River, on May 31, 2000 (data from Arizona Breeding Bird Atlas, September 2003, facilitated by Troy Corman, Arizona Game and Fish Department).

Blue-winged teal *(Anas discors)* – Cerceta aliazul. Regular but uncommon winter visitor and transient at Río Hardy and Ciénega de Santa Clara. Rare summer visitor at Río Colorado and Andrade Mesa wetlands (HIR and OHH).

Cinnamon teal *(Anas cyanoptera)* – Cerceta castaña. Uncommon breeder at Río Hardy, Río Colorado, and the Andrade Mesa wetlands (Hinojosa-Huerta, Nagler et al. 2002). Fairly common winter visitor at Ciénega de Santa Clara and common transient through the region.

Northern shoveler *(Anas clypeata)* – Pato cucharón norteño. Common winter visitor at Ciénega de Santa Clara and Río Hardy. Rare nonbreeding summer visitor.

Northern pintail *(Anas acuta)* – Pato golondrino norteño. Common winter visitor at Ciénega de Santa Clara and Río Hardy. Rare nonbreeding summer visitor, one record of 2 males and 1 female at Andrade Mesa wetlands on July 8, 2002 (Hinojosa-Huerta, Nagler et al. 2002).

Green-winged teal *(Anas crecca)* – Cerceta aliverde. Common winter visitor throughout the delta and coastal wetlands.

Canvasback *(Aythya valisineria)* – Pato coacoxtle. Uncommon winter visitor throughout the delta and coastal wetlands. Rare summer visitor at Ciénega de Santa Clara and Andrade Mesa wetlands (HIR).

Redhead *(Aythya americana)* – Pato cabecirrojo. Common winter visitor at Ciénega de Santa Clara and Río Hardy; common transient throughout coast. Rare summer visitor, with records at Cerro Prieto (Patten et al. 2001), Río Hardy (Ruiz-Campos & Rodríguez-Meraz 1997), and Andrade Mesa wetlands (Hinojosa-Huerta, Nagler et al. 2002). Breeding has not been documented.

Ring-necked duck *(Aythya collaris)* – Pato piquianillado. Rare winter visitor in drains and marshes of the Colorado delta and coastal wetlands.

Greater scaup *(Aythya marila)* – Pato-boludo mayor. Casual winter visitor, with only 4 records: two at Cerro Prieto (Grinnell 1928), one at Río Colorado (Patten et al. 2001), and one at Puerto Peñasco (Russell & Monson 1998).

Lesser scaup *(Aythya affinis)* – Pato-boludo menor. Fairly common winter visitor and transient in the delta and throughout coast.

Harlequin duck *(Histrionicus histrionicus)* – Pato arlequín. Casual winter visitor to Puerto Peñasco, with only 6 birds recorded (Kaufman & Witzeman 1979; Russell & Monson 1998).

Surf scoter *(Melanitta perspicillata)* – Negreta de marejada. Common winter visitor and spring transient in northern gulf, uncommon near shore.

White-winged scoter *(Melanitta fusca)* – Negreta aliblanca. Rare winter visitor in northern gulf and off Puerto Peñasco.

Long-tailed duck *(Clangula hyemalis)* – Pato colilargo. Casual spring vagrant in the northern gulf, with one recorded at San Felipe (Huey 1927) and another at Puerto Peñasco (Russell & Monson 1998).

Bufflehead *(Bucephala albeola)* – Pato monja. Uncommon winter visitor at Ciénega de Santa Clara and coastal wetlands.

Common goldeneye *(Bucephala clangula)* – Ojodorado común. Rare winter visitor in Colorado delta and coastal wetlands.

Hooded merganser *(Lophodytes cucullatus)* – Mergo de caperuza. Rare winter visitor along Río Hardy.

Common merganser *(Mergus merganser)* – Mergo mayor. Rare but sometimes numerous winter visitor and spring transient at Río Hardy, Río Colorado, Cerro Prieto, Ciénega de Santa Clara, and Puerto Peñasco.

Red-breasted merganser *(Mergus serrator)* – Mergo copetón. Common winter visitor in northern gulf, with greatest numbers near Puerto Peñasco (Russell & Monson 1998), uncommon in the delta. One summer record at the Río Hardy on July 7, 2003 (RAE).

Ruddy duck *(Oxyura jamaicensis)* – Pato tepalcate. Common winter visitor along Río Hardy and Ciénega de Santa Clara. Uncommon breeder at Río Hardy (OHH, YCG), Andrade Mesa wetlands (Hinojosa-Huerta, Nagler et al. 2002), and sewage ponds of Puerto Peñasco (Russell & Monson 1998).

GALLIFORMES

Odontophoridae – New World Quail

California quail *(Callipepla californica)* – Codorniz californiana. Fairly common breeding resident in Colorado Desert region of Baja California.

Gambel's quail *(Callipepla gambelii)* – Codorniz chiquiri. Common breeding resident throughout the region. Most abundant in Colorado delta.

GAVIIFORMES

Gaviidae – Loons

Red-throated loon *(Gavia stellata)* – Colimbo gorjirrojo. Rare winter visitor and spring transient in gulf and on coast of Puerto Peñasco.

Pacific loon *(Gavia pacifica)* – Colimbo ártico. Common winter visitor in gulf; rare in Colorado delta (Río Hardy and Cerro Prieto).

Common loon *(Gavia immer)* – Colimbo común. Common winter visitor and migrant (spring and fall) in the gulf. Casual summer visitor off Puerto Peñasco, Ciénega de Santa Clara, and Cerro Prieto.

Yellow-billed loon *(Gavia adamsii)* – Colimbo piquiamarillo. Casual summer vagrant, with only one recorded at Río Hardy (Simon & Simon 1974).

PODICIPEDIFORMES

Podicipedidae – Grebes

Least grebe *(Tachybaptus dominicus)* – Zambullidor menor. Casual summer vagrant; one recorded on Río Hardy at Campo Flores on May 17, 1999 (OHH). Species under special protection in Mexico (Diario Oficial 2002).

Pied-billed grebe *(Podilymbus podiceps)* – Zambullidor piquipinto. Fairly common breeding resident at Ciénega de Santa Clara, uncommon at Río Hardy and agricul-tural drains of the Mexicali Valley. Common transient and winter visitor elsewhere.

Horned grebe *(Podiceps auritas)* – Zambullidor cornudo. Rare winter visitor in gulf, Ciénega de Santa Clara, and Puerto Peñasco.

Eared grebe *(Podiceps nigricollis)* – Zambullidor orejudo. Common winter visitor throughout the region. Uncommon summer resident at Ciénega de Santa Clara and Cerro Prieto, but breeding activity has not been documented.

Western grebe *(Aechmophorus occidentalis)* – Achichilique piquiamarillo. Uncommon winter visitor throughout the region. Formerly a common breeding resident in Colorado delta, with records from the 1980s (Patten et al. 2001), but there are no recent breeding records.

Clark's grebe *(Aechmophorus clarkii)* – Achichilique piquinaranja. Uncommon winter visitor throughout the region, although in fewer numbers than western grebes. Probably was also a breeding resident in the Colorado delta (Patten et al. 2001).

PROCELLARIIFORMES

Diomedeidae – Albatrosses

Laysan albatross *(Phoebastria immutabilis)* – Albatros de Laysan. Rare spring visitor to the northern gulf and transient through the Mexicali Valley to the Salton Sea (Newcomer & Silber 1989; Patten et al. 2001). Protected as a threatened species in Mexico (Diario Oficial 2002).

Procellaridae – Shearwaters and Petrels

Northern fulmar *(Fulmarus glacialis)* – Fulmar norteño. Casual vagrant on the coast of Puerto Peñasco; only two individuals recorded (Russell & Lamm 1978).

Pink-footed shearwater *(Puffinus creatopus)* – Pardela patirrosada. Fairly common summer visitor to offshore regions of the northern gulf.

Sooty shearwater *(Puffinus griseus)* – Pardela gris. Common summer visitor offshore in the northern gulf.

Black-vented shearwater *(Puffinus opisthomelas)* – Pardela mexicana. Uncommon visitor to the northern gulf, with three records (August, September, and December) near the coast of Puerto Peñasco (Russell & Monson 1998).

Hydrobatidae – Storm-Petrels

Leach's storm-petrel *(Oceanodroma leucorhoa)* – Paíño de Leach. Rare summer visitor to northern gulf (Patten et al. 2001).

Black storm-petrel *(Oceanodroma melania)* – Paíño negro. Common resident in the gulf, probably breeds at Rocas Consag (Bancroft 1927; Patten et al. 2001). Common close to Sonoran shore during summer but rare during other seasons (Russell & Monson 1998). Protected as threatened in Mexico (Diario Oficial 2002).

Least storm-petrel *(Oceanodroma microsoma)* – Paíño mínimo. Common resident in the gulf. Reported breeding at Rocas Consag (Bancroft 1927) and probably still breeds there. Uncommon during spring near Puerto Peñasco (Russell & Monson 1998). Protected as threatened in Mexico (Diario Oficial 2002).

PELECANIFORMES

PHAETHONTIDAE – TROPICBIRDS

Red-billed tropicbird *(Phaethon aethereus)* – Rabijunco piquirrojo. Regular breeder at Isla San Jorge although uncommon near shore. Rare elsewhere in northern gulf. Three individuals were detected at Rocas Consag (Bancroft 1927; Patten et al. 2001) and one at the mouth of the Río Colorado (van Rossem & Hachisuka 1937). Former breeder inland at Puerto Peñasco (Russell & Monson 1998).

SULIDAE – BOOBIES AND GANNETS

Masked booby *(Sula dactylatra)* – Bobo enmascarado. Rare offshore in northern gulf. One record near Rocas Consag (Patten et al. 2001).

Blue-footed booby *(Sula nebouxii)* – Bobo pata azul. Fairly common perennial visitor to the northern gulf and mouth of Río Colorado. Most abundant in summer and fall, during postbreeding dispersal (Patten et al. 2001).

Brown booby *(Sula leucogaster)* – Bobo vientre-blanco. Fairly common perennial visitor to northern gulf and mouth of the Río Colorado (Dunning 1988; Mellink et al. 1997). Uncommon but regular near the Sonoran shore in summer (Russell & Monson 1998).

PELECANIDAE – PELICANS

American white pelican *(Pelecanus erythrorhynchos)* – Pelícano blanco americano. Fairly common winter and spring visitor in Colorado delta region. Uncommon summer visitor as nonbreeder. Rare elsewhere.

Brown pelican *(Pelecanus occidentalis)* – Pelícano café. Common perennial visitor throughout the coast and marine areas as a nonbreeder. Regular but uncommon summer visitor inland to Cerro Prieto and Río Hardy; rare during winter.

PHALACROCORACIDAE – CORMORANTS

Brandt's cormorant *(Phalacrocorax penicillatus)* – Cormorán de Brandt. Breeding at Isla San Jorge was observed for the first time in 1999 (Cervantes-Sanchez & Mellink 2001). Rare visitor elsewhere in the northern gulf (Russell & Monson 1998).

Double-crested cormorant *(Phalacrocorax auritus)* – Cormorán bicrestado. Common perennial nonbreeding visitor to the Colorado delta and coastal areas, with increased numbers between November and February.

FREGATIDAE – FRIGATEBIRDS

Magnificent frigatebird *(Fregata magnificens)* – Fragata magnífica. Uncommon postbreeding visitor (May–September) throughout coastal and marine areas. Rare at other months.

CICONIIFORMES

ARDEIDAE – HERONS AND BITTERNS

American bittern *(Botaurus lentiginosus)* – Torcomón. Uncommon winter visitor at the Ciénega de Santa Clara, rare at Río Hardy and associated drains.

Least bittern *(Ixobrychus exilis)* – Garcita de tular. Common breeding resident at Ciénega de Santa Clara; uncommon at Río Hardy, Río Colorado, and Andrade Mesa wetlands (Hinojosa-Huerta, Nagler et al. 2002).

Great blue heron *(Ardea herodias)* – Garzón cenizo. Common breeding resident at Colorado delta and coastal wetlands of the Sonoran shore.

Great egret *(Ardea alba)* – Garza blanca. Common breeding resident at Cerro Prieto, Río Hardy, and agricultural drains of the Mexicali Valley. Perennial nonbreeding visitor at other wetland areas.

Snowy egret *(Egretta thula)* – Garza nivea. Common local breeding resident at Isla Montague and Cerro Prieto (Molina & Garrett 2001; Palacios & Mellink 1992). Common visitor throughout the Colorado delta and coastal wetlands.

Little blue heron *(Egretta caerulea)* – Garceta azul. Rare summer visitor to coastal wetlands of Puerto Peñasco and probably the Colorado delta.

Tricolored heron *(Egretta tricolor)* – Garza tricolor. Rare summer vagrant in the Colorado delta, more regular at the Ciénega de Santa Clara. Nesting by two pairs observed in 2002 suggests that the species might be a rare breeder in the region (Mellink et al. 2002).

Reddish egret *(Egretta rufescens)* – Garza rojiza. Casual vagrant in the Colorado delta and coastal wetlands of Baja and Sonora and probably an occasional breeder at Isla Montague (Mellink et al. 2002). Species under special protection in Mexico (Diario Oficial 2002).

Cattle egret *(Bubulcus ibis)* – Garza ganadera. Common breeding resident in the Mexicali Valley. Colonized this region in the 1960s (Mora 1997). Uncommon breeder and transient on the coast of Sonora. Nine egrets were recorded in the Pinacate region in 1987 (Russell & Monson 1998).

Green heron *(Butorides virescens)* – Garza verde. Common breeding resident at Río Colorado, Río Hardy, and Ciénega de Santa Clara.

Black-crowned night heron *(Nycticorax nycticorax)* – Garza-nocturna coroninegra. Fairly common breeding resident throughout the Colorado delta. Uncommon visitor to the coastal wetlands of Puerto Peñasco.

Threskiornithidae – Ibises and Spoonbills

White ibis *(Eudocimus albus)* – Ibis blanco. Casual vagrant to Colorado delta and Sonoran coast. Seven birds were observed at the Ciénega de Santa Clara on March 11, 1999 (OHH).

White-faced ibis *(Plegadis chihi)* – Ibis cariblanco. Common winter visitor in the Mexicali Valley and Ciénega de Santa Clara. Common transient through the Sonoran coast. Probably breeds along Río Colorado and Ciénega de Santa Clara.

Roseate spoonbill *(Ajaia ajaja)* – Espátula rosada. Formerly an irregular but numerous winter visitor in the Colorado delta (Bancroft 1922; Grinnell 1926). There are no records since the 1920s.

Ciconiidae – Storks

Wood stork *(Mycteria americana)* – Cigüeña americana. Formerly a common postbreeding visitor but now is a rare visitor, with a few records along Río Colorado and Río Hardy (Mellink et al. 2002; Ruiz-Campos & Rodríguez-Meraz 1997). Species under special protection in Mexico (Diario Oficial 2002).

Cathartidae – New World Vultures

Black vulture *(Coragyps atratus)* – Zopilote negro. Rare visitor to Pinacate and Río Sonoyta region.

Turkey vulture *(Cathartes aura)* – Aura cabecirroja. Common perennial inland visitor throughout the region.

FALCONIFORMES

Accipitridae – Hawks, Kites, and Eagles

Osprey *(Pandion haliaetus)* – Águila pescadora. Uncommon breeding resident along Río Colorado and Puerto Peñasco. Fairly common nonbreeding resident throughout the delta and coastal areas.

White-tailed kite *(Elanus leucurus)* – Milano coliblanco. Fairly common breeding resident in Río Colorado and Mexicali Valley. Started to colonize the region in the late 1970s (Rosenberg et al. 1991).

Bald eagle *(Heliaeetus leucocephalus)* – Águila cabeciblanca. Uncommon winter visitor, with birds regularly visiting Ciénega de Santa Clara and Río Hardy each winter. Protected as an endangered species in Mexico (Diario Oficial 2002).

Northern harrier *(Circus cyaneus)* – Gavilán rastrero. Common winter visitor and transient throughout Colorado delta and coastal wetlands. More abundant at Ciénega de Santa Clara.

Sharp-shinned hawk *(Accipiter striatus)* – Gavilán pajarero. Uncommon winter visitor and transient in the Colorado delta region. Species under special protection in Mexico (Diario Oficial 2002).

Cooper's hawk *(Accipiter cooperi)* – Gavilán de Cooper. Uncommon winter visitor and transient throughout the delta and Sonoran coast. Species under special protection in Mexico (Diario Oficial 2002).

Harris' hawk *(Parabuteo unicinctus)* – Aguililla de Harris. Casual visitor to El Doctor and Puerto Peñasco, with only two recent records (Russell & Monson 1998). Reported as a common breeding resident before the 1930s (Grinnell 1928). Species under special protection in Mexico (Diario Oficial 2002).

Red-shouldered hawk *(Buteo lineatus)* – Aguililla pechirroja. Only two records, both of them juveniles, at Mexicali in January 1989 and December 1994 (Patten et al. 2001). Species under special protection in Mexico (Diario Oficial 2002).

Swainson's hawk *(Buteo swainsoni)* – Aguililla de Swainson. Uncommon winter visitor in the Colorado delta. Rare spring transient through Puerto Peñasco and the Colorado delta. One summer record near Algodones, B.C., July 7, 2003 (RAE). Species under special protection in Mexico (Diario Oficial 2002).

Zone-tailed hawk *(Buteo albonotatus)* – Aguililla aura. Uncommon winter visitor. Previously unrecorded in the region. In 2002 we observed two individuals on September 24, two on November 19, and three on December 19, all along the riparian corridor of the Río Colorado.

Red-tailed hawk *(Buteo jamaicensis)* – Aguililla coliroja. Common inland winter visitor and uncommon breeder throughout the region.

Ferruginous hawk *(Buteo regalis)* – Aguililla real. Uncommon but regular winter visitor, especially around Puerto Peñasco. Rare in Colorado delta. Species under special protection in Mexico (Diario Oficial 2002).

Golden eagle *(Aquila chrysaetos)* – Águila real. Casual visitor to Río Sonoyta (Sonoyta to Puerto Peñasco), with only three records (Russell & Monson 1998), and at Río Colorado, with only one record (JGH, July 2003). Species protected as threatened in Mexico (Diario Oficial 2002).

Falconidae – Falcons

Crested caracara *(Caracara plancus)* – Caracara común. Former rare winter visitor in the Colorado delta (Grinnell 1928; Stone & Rhoads 1905). Only one record at the coast near Puerto Peñasco, and breeding is presumed near Sonoyta (Russell & Monson 1998).

American kestrel *(Falco sparverius)* – Cernícalo americano. Common breeding resident in the Colorado delta. Presumed breeding near Sonoyta (Russell & Monson

1998). Common winter visitor and transient throughout the region.

Merlin *(Falco columbarius)* – Esmerejón. Rare winter visitor and transient in the Colorado delta, at Puerto Peñasco, and near Sonoyta.

Peregrine falcon *(Falco peregrinus)* – Halcón peregrino. Rare but regular winter visitor and transient in the Colorado delta and Puerto Peñasco. Probably breeds on Rocas Consag (Bancroft 1927). Species under special protection in Mexico (Diario Oficial 2002).

Prairie falcon *(Falco mexicanus)* – Halcón pradeño. Rare winter visitor and transient throughout the Colorado delta, Pinacate, Puerto Peñasco, and Río Sonoyta. Species protected as threatened in Mexico (Diario Oficial 2002).

GRUIFORMES

RALLIDAE – RAILS, GALLINULES, AND COOTS

California black rail *(Laterallus jamaicensis coturniculus)* – Polluela negra, ralito negro. Rare breeding resident at Ciénega de Santa Clara and El Doctor, with fewer than 50 pairs (Hinojosa-Huerta, Shaw & DeStefano 2001). Subspecies listed as endangered in Mexico (Diario Oficial 2002) and as a priority taxon for conservation in the United States (California Department of Fish and Game 1999). Single birds detected at Laguna del Indio (May 25, 2001), Río Hardy (May 30, 2001), Río Colorado (June 9, 2002), and a canal at Ejido Luis Encinas Johnson (June 13, 2002).

Yuma clapper rail *(Rallus longirostris yumanensis)* – Rascón picudo de Arizona, palmoteador de Yuma. Common breeding resident at Ciénega de Santa Clara, with an estimated population of over 6,000 individuals (Hinojosa-Huerta, DeStefano & Shaw 2001). Uncommon at other wetland sites, including Río Hardy, Río El Mayor, El Doctor, Río Colorado mainstem, All-American Canal marshes, and throughout agricultural drains in Mexicali Valley. Subspecies endemic to lower Colorado River and delta, listed as threatened in Mexico (Diario Oficial 2002) and endangered in the United States (Eddleman & Conway 1998).

Virginia rail *(Rallus limicola)* – Rascón limícola. Common breeding resident at Ciénega de Santa Clara and El Doctor, with numbers augmented by winter visitors. Rare breeder at Ríos Hardy and Colorado. Rare transient in Río Sonoyta and Puerto Peñasco region. Species under special protection in Mexico (Diario Oficial 2002).

Sora *(Porzana carolina)* – Polluela sora. Common winter visitor at Ciénega de Santa Clara, El Doctor, and Río Hardy, where it is a rare summer visitor and probably breeds. Uncommon transient in Río Sonoyta, Puerto Peñasco, and Río Colorado.

Common moorhen *(Gallinula chloropus)* – Gallineta común. Common breeding resident throughout marshes of the Colorado delta. Rare visitor to Puerto Peñasco and Río Sonoyta.

American coot *(Fulica americana)* – Gallareta americana. Common breeding resident throughout marshes of the Colorado delta, with numbers augmented by winter visitors. Common transient and winter visitor in Puerto Peñasco and Río Sonoyta.

GRUIDAE – CRANES

Sandhill crane *(Grus canadensis)* – Grulla canadiense. Formerly a common winter visitor in the Colorado delta (Leopold 1989; Murphy 1917; van Rossem 1945), but no records since the 1930s. Only two records elsewhere, at Río Sonoyta (Audubon 1906) and Puerto Peñasco (Russell & Monson 1998).

CHARADRIIFORMES

CHARADRIIDAE – PLOVERS

Black-bellied plover *(Pluvialis squatarola)* – Chorlo gris. Common transient and winter visitor at Ciénega de Santa Clara, at El Doctor, and throughout the coast. Uncommon summer visitor in the same areas.

Snowy plover *(Charadrius alexandrinus nivosus)* – Chorlito niveo. Uncommon breeding resident at El Doctor salt flats, Ciénega de Santa Clara, and Cerro Prieto ponds. Western populations have declined since the 1920s (Powell 1998), and species is listed as threatened in Mexico (Diario Oficial 2002) and endangered in the United States (Powell 1998).

Wilson's plover *(Charadrius wilsonia)* – Chorlito piquigrueso. Common breeding resident in coastal wetlands of Puerto Peñasco. Uncommon winter visitor at Ciénega de Santa Clara, El Doctor, and Isla Montague. Formerly bred at San Felipe (Patten et al. 2001).

Semipalmated plover *(Charadrius semipalmatus)* – Chorlito semipalmeado. Fairly common transient at Ciénega de Santa Clara, El Doctor, Río Colorado, and along the coast. Uncommon winter visitor in the Colorado delta.

Piping plover *(Charadrius melodus)* – Chorlito chiflador. Rare winter visitor and transient at Puerto Peñasco, but no records since 1982 (Russell & Monson 1998) and two at the Ciénega de Santa Clara (March 1999 and December 2004, OHH). Species listed as endangered in Mexico (Diario Oficial 2002).

Killdeer *(Charadrius vociferus)* – Chorlito tildío. Common breeding resident in Colorado delta, coastal areas, and Río Sonoyta.

Mountain plover *(Charadrius montanus)* – Chorlito llanero. Regular winter visitors between Puerto Peñasco, Sonoyta, and the Pinacate region (Russell & Monson 1998). May also winter in northern Mexicali Valley (Patten et al. 2001). Species protected as threatened in Mexico (Diario Oficial 2002).

Haematopodidae – Oystercatchers

American oystercatcher *(Haematopus palliatus)* – Ostrero americano. Uncommon perennial visitor to coastal areas of northern gulf. Breeds locally at Isla Montague (Peresbarbosa & Mellink 2001) and coastal wetlands of Puerto Peñasco region (Russell & Monson 1998).

Black oystercatcher *(Haematopus bachmani)* – Ostrero negro. Casual vagrant, with only three records from Puerto Peñasco (Russell & Monson 1998).

Recurvirostridae – Stilts and Avocets

Black-necked stilt *(Himantopus mexicanus)* – Candelero americano. Common breeding resident throughout Colorado delta and Mexicali Valley.

American avocet *(Recurvirostra americana)* – Avoceta americana. Common perennial visitor throughout Colorado delta, with greatest numbers registered at Laguna Salada, Cerro Prieto, and Ciénega de Santa Clara. Uncommon breeder at Ciénega de Santa Clara and Cerro Prieto. Common winter visitor and transient along coast.

Scolopacidae – Sandpipers and Phalaropes

Greater yellowlegs *(Tringa melanoleuca)* – Patamarilla mayor. Fairly common transient and winter visitor in the Colorado delta and through the coast.

Lesser yellowlegs *(Tringa flavipes)* – Patamarilla menor. Fairly common transient in fall and spring in the Colorado delta and throughout the coast; and uncommon winter visitor in Puerto Peñasco (Russell & Monson 1998) and the Colorado delta (Patten et al. 1993).

Solitary sandpiper *(Tringa solitaria)* – Playero solitario. Rare fall transient and winter visitor in Colorado delta, with only six records (Patten et al. 2001; RAE, September 2000; OHH, March 2002).

Willet *(Catoptrophorus semipalmatus)* – Playero pihuiui. Common transient and winter visitor in Colorado delta and coastal areas. Rare summer visitor in Peñasco and Colorado delta.

Wandering tattler *(Heteroscelus incanus)* – Playero vagabundo. Uncommon winter visitor and transient along coast of northern gulf. Casual in Colorado delta.

Spotted sandpiper *(Actitis macularia)* – Playero alzacolita. Fairly common transient and winter visitor in Colorado delta and coastal areas. Rare summer visitor in Colorado delta.

Whimbrel *(Numenius phaeopus)* – Zarapito trinador. Common winter visitor and transient in Mexicali Valley, Colorado delta, and coastal areas. A few individuals regularly summer in alfalfa fields of Mexicali Valley.

Long-billed curlew *(Numenius americanus)* – Zarapito picolargo. Common transient and winter visitor in Colorado delta and coastal areas.

Marbled godwit *(Limosa fedoa)* – Picopando canelo. Common transient and winter visitor, with major aggregations at Ciénega de Santa Clara and Puerto Peñasco. Regular uncommon summer visitor.

Ruddy turnstone *(Arenaria interpres)* – Vuelvepiedras rojizo. Fairly common transient and winter visitor at coastal areas of northern gulf. Casual at Cerro Prieto (Patten et al. 2001).

Black turnstone *(Arenaria melanocephala)* – Vuelvepiedras negro. Uncommon transient and winter visitor at coastal areas of northern gulf.

Surfbird *(Aprisa virgata)* – Playero de marejada. Common spring transient and uncommon winter visitor along shore of northern gulf.

Red knot *(Calidris canutus)* – Playero gordo. Fairly common, but sometimes numerous, transient and winter visitor on coast of northern gulf. Casual at Cerro Prieto.

Sanderling *(Calidris alba)* – Playero blanco. Common transient and winter visitor along coast, less abundant at Colorado delta.

Semipalmated sandpiper *(Calidris pusilla)* – Playerito semipalmeado. A rare transient along coast of the Gulf of California. Only three records, one near San Felipe (Wurster & Radamaker 1992) and two at Puerto Peñasco (Russell & Monson 1998).

Western sandpiper *(Calidris mauri)* – Playerito occidental. Common transient and winter visitor throughout Colorado delta and coastal areas.

Least sandpiper *(Calidris minutilla)* – Playerito mínimo. Common transient and winter visitor throughout Colorado delta and coastal areas, although less numerous than western sandpipers.

Baird's sandpiper *(Calidris bairdii)* – Playerito de Baird. Probably a rare fall transient, but only three records (Patten et al. 1993, 2001; Russell & Monson 1998).

Pectoral sandpiper *(Calidris melanotus)* – Playerito pectoral. Casual fall vagrant along coast; only two records (Gallucci 1981; Russell & Monson 1998).

Dunlin *(Calidris alpina)* – Playero dorsirojo. Fairly common transient winter visitor throughout Colorado delta and along coast.

Stilt sandpiper *(Calidris himantopus)* – Playero zancudo. Only two records, at Cerro Prieto (Patten et al. 2001) and Ciénega de Santa Clara (March 22, 2003; MAG, OHH), but probably an uncommon transient.

Short-billed dowitcher *(Limnodromus griseus)* – Costurero piquicorto. Common winter visitor and spring transient, fairly common fall transient. Most numerous at Ciénega de Santa Clara.

Long-billed dowitcher *(Limnodromus scolopaceus)* – Costurero piquilargo. Common transient and winter visitor at Colorado delta and along coast. Most abundant near El Golfo de Santa Clara.

Wilson's snipe *(Gallinago delicata)* – Agachona común. Uncommon transient and winter visitor at Colorado delta and coastal wetlands.

Wilson's phalarope *(Phalaropus tricolor)* – Falarapo de Wilson. Common transient along the coast and Colorado delta and can be numerous at Cerro Prieto. Casual winter visitor in northern gulf.

Red-necked phalarope *(Phalaropus lobatus)* – Falarapo cuellirrojo. Common transient throughout coast and Colorado delta. Aggregations of about 10,000 birds were documented at Cerro Prieto (Patten et al. 2001).

Red phalarope *(Phalaropus fulicaria)* – Falarapo piquigrueso. Casual transient and winter visitor. Only three records: one at San Felipe in 1926 (Huey 1927), a group of 30 at Puerto Peñasco in 1979, and a single bird at Peñasco on 1990 (Russell & Monson 1998).

LARIDAE – JAEGERS, GULLS, TERNS, AND SKIMMERS

Pomarine jaeger *(Stercorarius pomarinus)* – Salteador pomarino. Rare winter visitor and transient in northern gulf, with three records near San Felipe (Patten et al. 2001), one in the gulf (Wilbur 1987), and one at Puerto Peñasco (Russell & Monson 1998).

Parasitic jaeger *(Stercorarius parasiticus)* – Salteador parásito. Rare winter visitor and transient in northern gulf, with one inland record at Cerro Prieto, two records near San Felipe (Patten et al. 2001), and two at Puerto Peñasco (Russell & Monson 1998).

Long-tailed jaeger *(Stercorarius longicaudus)* – Salteador colilargo. Casual fall vagrant, recorded only at Cerro Prieto (Patten et al. 2001).

Laughing gull *(Larus atricilla)* – Gaviota reidora. Fairly common breeder at Isla Montague (Palacios & Mellink 1992) and Cerro Prieto (Molina & Garrett 2001). Fairly common summer and rare winter visitor throughout the region.

Franklin's gull *(Larus pipixcan)* – Gaviota de Franklin. Rare spring transient and casual summer visitor. Records at Cerro Prieto, San Felipe, Laguna Salada (Patten et al. 2001), Golfo de Santa Clara, and Puerto Peñasco (Russell & Monson 1998).

Bonaparte's gull *(Larus philadelphia)* – Gaviota de Bonaparte. Fairly common transient and winter visitor at Cerro Prieto, Ciénega de Santa Clara, and coastal areas.

Heermann's gull *(Larus heermanni)* – Gaviota de Heermann. Common perennial nonbreeding visitor to northern gulf. Species under special protection in Mexico (Diario Oficial 2002).

Mew gull *(Larus canus)* – Gaviota piquiamarilla. Only one record from 1994 Christmas Bird Count at Puerto Peñasco (S. Ganley). Patten et al. (2001) report it as a probably rare but regular winter visitor.

Ring-billed gull *(Larus delawarensis)* – Gaviota piquianillada. Common transient and winter visitor throughout the region, less numerous as a nonbreeding summer visitor, especially in Colorado delta.

California gull *(Larus californicus)* – Gaviota californiana. Common winter visitor and uncommon nonbreeding summer visitor.

Herring gull *(Larus argentatus)* – Gaviota plateada. Fairly common winter visitor. Sometimes numerous at Puerto Peñasco (Russell & Monson 1998).

Thayer's gull *(Larus thayeri)* – Gaviota de Thayer. Rare winter visitor to northern gulf, with only a few records near San Felipe and Cerro Prieto (RAE).

Lesser black-backed gull *(Larus fuscus)* – Gaviota dorsinegra menor. Casual winter vagrant, with only one record at Puerto Peñasco during a Christmas Bird Count (National Audubon Society 2002).

Yellow-footed gull *(Larus livens)* – Gaviota patamarilla. Common nonbreeding visitor year-round in northern gulf and along coast; common summer visitor and transient in Colorado delta. Species under special protection in Mexico (Diario Oficial 2002).

Western gull *(Larus occidentalis)* – Gaviota occidental. Rare but regular winter visitor in northern gulf, San Felipe, and Puerto Peñasco.

Glaucous-winged gull *(Larus glaucescens)* – Gaviota aliglauca. Rare winter visitor, with records from San Felipe (Huey 1927; Patten et al. 2001) and Puerto Peñasco (Russell & Monson 1998).

Glaucous gull *(Larus hyperboreus)* – Gaviota blanca. Rare and irregular winter visitor to northern gulf. Only six records, two from San Felipe (Patten et al. 2001) and four from Puerto Peñasco (Russell & Monson 1998).

Sabine's gull *(Xema sabini)* – Gaviota de Sabine. Casual fall transient, with only two records from Puerto Peñasco (Russell & Lamm 1978).

Black-legged kittiwake *(Rissa tridactyla)* – Gaviota pata negra. Casual winter vagrant, with only one record from Puerto Peñasco (Russell & Monson 1998).

Gull-billed tern *(Sterna nilotica vanrossemi)* – Gallito piquigrueso. Status of western subspecies *vanrossemi* uncertain but probably declining in numbers; this species is under consideration to be listed as endangered in the United States (Parnell et al. 1995). Common breeder at Isla Montague and Cerro Prieto ponds. Common visitor to Colorado mainstem, Río Hardy, canals, and drains as forager. These colonies, along with the Salton Sea population, are the stronghold in its northern range (Molina & Garrett 2001).

Caspian tern *(Sterna caspia)* – Golondrina-marina cáspica. Uncommon breeder at Cerro Prieto (Mellink et al. 2002; Molina & Garrett 2001); fairly common perennial visitor throughout Colorado delta and coastal areas.

Royal tern *(Sterna maxima)* – Golondrina-marina real. Fairly common but irregular breeder at Isla Montague (Palacios & Mellink 1993; Peresbarbosa & Mellink 2001); fairly common perennial visitor along coast.

Elegant tern *(Sterna elegans)* – Golondrina-marina elegante. Irregular breeder at Isla Montague (Peresbarbosa & Mellink 2001); fairly common nonbreeding visitor along coast. Species under special protection in Mexico (Diario Oficial 2002).

Common tern *(Sterna hirundo)* – Golondrina-marina común. Common transient and rare winter visitor, especially around Puerto Peñasco (Russell & Monson 1998), but also recorded at Cerro Prieto (Patten et al. 2001).

Forster's tern *(Sterna forsteri)* – Golondrina-marina de Forster. Uncommon breeder at Cerro Prieto (Molina & Garrett 2001). Common perennial visitor throughout the region.

Least tern *(Sterna antillarum)* – Golondrina-marina mínima. Uncommon breeder, with colonies at Isla Montague, El Doctor, and coastal wetlands north of San Felipe and Puerto Peñasco (Palacios & Mellink 1996). Uncommon spring and summer visitor at other wetland and coastal areas; casual fall transient and winter visitor along coast (Russell & Monson 1998). Species under special protection in Mexico (Diario Oficial 2002).

Black tern *(Chlidonias niger)* – Golondrina-marina negra. Common transient throughout Colorado delta and coast. Uncommon summer visitor at Andrade Mesa wetlands (Hinojosa-Huerta, Nagler et al. 2002).

Black skimmer *(Rhynchops niger)* – Rayador americano. Common breeder at Isla Montague (Peresbarbosa & Mellink 1994) and Cerro Prieto (Molina & Garrett 2001). Fairly common transient and winter visitor along coast, especially at El Golfo de Santa Clara and Puerto Peñasco.

ALCIDAE – AUKS, MURRES, AND PUFFINS

Craveri's murrelet *(Synthliboramphus craveri)* – Mérgulo de Craveri. Reported breeding at Rocas Consag by Bancroft (1927). Probably a resident on northern gulf (Patten et al. 2001). Species is listed as threatened in Mexico (Diario Oficial 2002).

COLUMBIFORMES

COLUMBIDAE – PIGEONS AND DOVES

White-winged dove *(Zenaida asiatica)* – Paloma aliblanca. Common breeding visitor throughout delta, more numerous in riparian corridor of the Colorado.

Mourning dove *(Zenaida macroura)* – Paloma huilota. Common breeding resident throughout the region.

Inca dove *(Columbina inca)* – Tórtola colilarga. Uncommon breeding resident in Colorado delta, Puerto Peñasco, and Río Sonoyta.

Common ground-dove *(Columbina passerina)* – Tórtola común. Common breeding resident at Río Colorado and Río Sonoyta.

Ruddy ground-dove *(Columbina talpacoti)* – Tórtola rojiza. Casual vagrant; only one record at Puerto Peñasco (Russell & Monson 1998).

CUCULIFORMES

CUCULIDAE – CUCKOOS AND ROADRUNNERS

Yellow-billed cuckoo *(Coccyzus americanus occidentalis)* – Cuco piquiamarillo. Western populations have declined drastically (Hughes 1999), and the subspecies has been almost extirpated from Colorado delta. Recent records during the breeding season (1 pair in July 1995 [Patten et al. 2001]; 1 bird in June 2000, 2 pairs in July 2001, 2 singing males in June 2002, and 6 singing males in 2003 [YCG, OHH, HIR, and EZH]) suggest that cuckoos might nest in the restored riparian patches of Río Colorado. The western subspecies is under consideration to be listed as endangered in the United States (U.S. Fish and Wildlife Service 2001).

Greater roadrunner *(Geococcyx californianus)* – Correcaminos mayor. Fairly common breeding resident in riparian and desertscrub areas.

STRIGIFORMES

TYTONIDAE – OWLS

Barn owl *(Tyto alba)* – Lechuza de campanario. Uncommon breeding resident throughout Colorado delta, Pinacate, and Puerto Peñasco.

STRIGIDAE – OWLS

Western screech-owl *(Otus kennicottii)* – Tecolote occidental. Formerly an abundant breeder along Río Colorado (Russell & Monson 1998), now an uncommon breeding resident. Rare breeding resident along Río Sonoyta and in Pinacate region.

Great horned owl *(Bubo virginianus)* – Búho cornudo. Fairly common breeding resident throughout the region.

Elf owl *(Micrathene whitneyi)* – Tecolotito enano. Probably was an uncommon breeder along Río Colorado (Wilbur 1987), but there are no recent records from the delta. Common summer resident near Sonoyta, where breeding is presumed (Russell & Monson 1998).

Burrowing owl *(Athene cunicularia)* – Búho llanero. Common breeding resident throughout Mexicali Valley, with an estimated population of 3,800 individuals

(Iturribarría-Rojas 2002), conforming the largest population in the Baja California peninsula (Palacios et al. 2000). Less abundant in winter. Uncommon breeder around Puerto Peñasco.

Long-eared owl *(Asio otus)* – Búho cornudo-caricafé. Casual winter visitor around San Felipe, Puerto Peñasco, and Pinacate region. Only four records for the region (Russell & Monson 1998; Patten et al. 2001; RAE, February 1998).

Short-eared owl *(Asio flammeus)* – Búho orejicorto. Rare winter visitor throughout delta and Puerto Peñasco. Species under special protection in Mexico (Diario Oficial 2002).

Northern saw-whet owl *(Aegolius acadicus)* – Tecolote-abetero norteño. Only one record: a freshly killed bird near Puerto Peñasco in November 1977 (Russell & Monson 1998).

CAPRIMULGIFORMES

CAPRIMULGIDAE – NIGHTHAWKS

Lesser nighthawk *(Chordeiles acutipennis)* – Chotacabras menor, tapacaminos. Common breeder and rare winter visitor throughout Colorado delta. Uncommon breeder at Río Sonoyta, Pinacate, and Puerto Peñasco.

Common poorwill *(Phalaenoptilus nuttallii)* – Pachacua norteña. Fairly common breeding resident along Río Colorado and Río Sonoyta; rare in Pinacate.

APODIFORMES

APODIDAE – SWIFTS

Vaux's swift *(Chaetura vauxi)* – Vencejo de Vaux. Common spring and uncommon fall transient throughout Colorado delta and along coast.

White-throated swift *(Aeronautes saxatalis)* – Vencejo gorjiblanco. Fairly common winter visitor throughout delta. One record at Pinacate; presumed breeding at Río Sonoyta (Russell & Monson 1998).

TROCHILIDAE – HUMMINGBIRDS

Black-chinned hummingbird *(Archilochus alexandri)* – Colibrí barbinegro. Uncommon transient and breeder along the Río Colorado.

Anna's hummingbird *(Calypte anna)* – Colibrí de Anna. Common transient through the region. Uncommon local resident and presumed breeder at Río Colorado (Patten et al. 2001).

Costa's hummingbird *(Calypte costae)* – Colibrí de Costa. Fairly common breeding resident in Colorado delta, Río Sonoyta, Pinacate, and Puerto Peñasco.

Calliope hummingbird *(Stellula calliope)* – Colibrí de Caliope. Rare spring transient at El Doctor and Río Sonoyta.

Rufous hummingbird *(Selasphorus rufus)* – Zumbador rufo. Uncommon spring and rare fall transient throughout the coast, Pinacate, and Colorado delta.

Allen's hummingbird *(Selasphorus sasin)* – Zumbador de Allen. Rare spring transient throughout the coast, Río Sonoyta, and Colorado delta, notably at El Doctor.

CORACIIFORMES

ALCEDINIDAE – KINGFISHERS

Belted kingfisher *(Ceryle alcyon)* – Martín-pescador norteño. Fairly common winter visitor and transient in Colorado delta, Puerto Peñasco, and Río Sonoyta.

Green kingfisher *(Chloroceryle americana)* – Martín-pescador verde. Only one record, near Puerto Peñasco (Russell & Monson 1998).

PICIFORMES

PICIDAE – WOODPECKERS

Gila woodpecker *(Melanerpes uropygialis)* – Carpintero de Gila. Common breeding resident along Río Colorado, Río Sonoyta, Pinacate, and Puerto Peñasco.

Yellow-bellied sapsucker *(Sphyrapicus varius)* – Chupasavia vientre amarillo. Casual winter vagrant, with only one record at Río Hardy (Patten et al. 1993). A hybrid between a yellow-bellied sapsucker and red-breasted sapsucker was banded at El Doctor on October 7, 2003 (ACF).

Red-naped sapsucker *(Sphyrapicus nuchalis)* – Chupasavia nuquiroja. Rare winter visitor along Colorado, Hardy, and Sonoyta rivers.

Red-breasted sapsucker *(Sphyrapicus ruber)* – Chupasavia pechirroja. Casual spring and winter vagrant, with only two spring records at El Doctor: one observed by K. Garrett and one banded on December 13, 2003 (HIR). A hybrid between a yellow-bellied sapsucker and red-breasted sapsucker was banded at El Doctor on October 7, 2003 (ACF).

Ladder-backed woodpecker *(Picoides scalaris)* – Carpintero listado. Common breeding resident along Río Colorado and in riparian and desertscrub areas of Río Sonoyta and Pinacate.

Northern flicker *(Colaptes auratus)* – Carpintero collarejo. Fairly common winter visitor throughout riparian areas and mesquite stands.

Gilded flicker *(Colaptes chrysoides)* – Carpintero collarejo desértico. Formerly an uncommon resident of the Hardy and Colorado rivers (Grinnell 1928), but no recent records. Presumed breeding along Río Sonoyta (Russell & Monson 1998).

PASSERIFORMES

Tyrannidae – Flycatchers

Olive-sided flycatcher *(Contopus cooperi)* – Pibí boreal. Uncommon spring transient throughout Colorado delta.

Western wood-pewee *(Contopus sordidulus)* – Pibí occidental. Common spring and fairly common fall transient in Colorado delta and along coast.

Alder flycatcher *(Empidonax alnorum)* – Mosquero pálido. Accidental spring transient. Only one record, at El Doctor on May 14, 2003 (OHH and HIR). The bird was captured, identified using wing and bill morphology measurements (Pyle 1997), and released.

Willow flycatcher *(Empidonax traillii)* – Mosquero saucero, papamoscas saucero. The endangered subspecies *E. t. extimus* formerly bred along the Río Colorado and Río Hardy (Unitt 1987). No breeding activity has been detected since 1928, despite extensive surveys from 1998 to 2004 (García-Hernández et al. 2001; Hinojosa-Huerta, García-Hernández & Shaw 2002; OHH and HIR, surveys 2003 and 2004). "Western" willow flycatchers *(E. t. adastus, E. t. brewsteri,* and *E. t. extimus)* are common migrants during spring (May–mid-June) and fall (August–early October), conspicuous at El Doctor and willow stands of Río Colorado.

Hammond's flycatcher *(Empidonax hammondii)* – Mosquero de Hammond. Uncommon spring transient throughout coast, El Doctor, and Río Colorado.

Gray flycatcher *(Empidonax wrightii)* – Mosquero gris. Uncommon spring and fall transient and rare winter visitor at El Doctor, Río Colorado, and Río Sonoyta.

Dusky flycatcher *(Empidonax oberholseri)* – Mosquero oscuro. Casual spring transient through El Doctor and Río Colorado. One bird banded at El Doctor on May 15, 2003 (OHH).

Pacific-slope flycatcher *(Empidonax difficilis)* – Mosquero occidental. The most abundant migrant flycatcher throughout the Colorado delta, especially in spring. Abundant at El Doctor from mid-March to mid-May.

Black phoebe *(Sayornis nigricans)* – Mosquero negro. Common breeding resident throughout Colorado delta and canals of the Mexicali Valley. Common transient and winter visitor along coastal scrub and Río Sonoyta.

Eastern phoebe *(Sayornis phoebe)* – Papamoscas fibí. Casual winter vagrant, with one record in Colorado Desert region of Baja California (Patten et al. 2001).

Say's phoebe *(Sayornis saya)* – Mosquero llanero. Common winter visitor, especially at Río Colorado, El Doctor, and Río Sonoyta. Presumed breeding in Colorado delta (Patten et al. 2001).

Vermilion flycatcher *(Pyrocephalus rubinus flammeus)* – Brasita, mosquero cardenal, pájaro bule, chapaturrín.

Fairly common breeding resident along riparian areas of Río Colorado, Río Hardy, and Laguna del Indio. Apparently was almost extirpated as a breeder in Colorado delta (Patten et al. 2001), but the local population has increased, most likely associated with revegetation of riparian areas in response to instream flows.

Ash-throated flycatcher *(Myiarchus cinerascens)* – Copetón gorjicenizo. Uncommon breeder along Río Colorado, Río Sonoyta, and desertscrub areas of San Felipe, Puerto Peñasco, and Pinacate. Common transient and rare winter visitor.

Brown-crested Flycatcher *(Myiarchus tyrannulus)* – Papamoscas tirano. Potential rare breeder along the Limitrophe Zone of the Colorado River, with few pairs observed in the area (data from Arizona Breeding Bird Atlas, September 2003, facilitated by Troy Corman, Arizona Game and Fish Department).

Tropical kingbird *(Tyrannus melancholicus)* – Tirano tropical. Casual winter vagrant, with only one recorded at Puerto Peñasco during the Christmas Bird Count of 2001 (National Audubon Society 2002).

Cassin's kingbird *(Tyrannus vociferans)* – Tirano de Cassin. Casual vagrant, with only four records: Pozo Salado (Patten et al. 2001), Puerto Peñasco (Russell & Monson 1998), Río Hardy (EZH and OHH), and El Golfo de Santa Clara (RAE, August 3, 1997).

Western kingbird *(Tyrannus verticalis)* – Tirano occidental. Common breeder throughout Colorado delta. Presumed breeder at Río Sonoyta (Russell & Monson 1998). Common transient through coastal desertscrub.

Eastern kingbird *(Tyrannus tyrannus)* – Tirano viajero. Casual vagrant, with only one recorded at Laguna Salada in June 1997 (Patten et al. 2001).

Laniidae – Shrikes

Loggerhead shrike *(Lanius ludovicianus)* – Lanio americano, alcaudón verdugo, verduguillo. Fairly common breeder and common winter visitor in desertscrub and riparian areas throughout the region.

Vireonidae – Vireos

White-eyed vireo *(Vireo griseus)* – Vireo ojiblanco. Accidental spring vagrant. Only one record, from El Doctor (K. Garrett).

Bell's vireo *(Vireo bellii)* – Vireo de Bell. Formerly was a common breeder along Río Colorado (Rosenberg et al. 1991), now a rare breeder in remnant riparian patches of the Colorado. Uncommon spring transient through El Doctor and Río Colorado.

Gray vireo *(Vireo vicinior)* – Vireo gris. Uncommon winter visitor and transient at coastal and lowland desertscrub areas of Río Sonoyta–Puerto Peñasco–Pinacate region (Bates 1992; Russell & Monson 1998). Only one record for San Felipe (Grinnell 1928).

Plumbeous vireo *(Vireo plumbeus)* – Vireo plomizo. Common transient and uncommon winter visitor at Río Colorado and El Doctor.

Cassin's vireo *(Vireo cassinii)* – Vireo de Cassin's. Rare winter visitor and transient at Río Colorado, El Doctor, Río Sonoyta, and Puerto Peñasco.

Hutton's vireo *(Vireo huttoni)* – Vireo reyezuelo. Rare transient and winter visitor at Río Sonoyta and El Doctor.

Warbling vireo *(Vireo gilvus)* – Vireo gorgojeador. Very abundant fall and spring transient at El Doctor, Río Colorado, and Río Sonoyta.

Red-eyed vireo *(Vireo olivaceus)* – Vireo ojirrojo. Accidental spring vagrant. Only one record, from El Doctor (K. Garrett).

Corvidae – Crows and jays

Clark's nutcracker *(Nucifraga columbiana)* – Cascanueces americano. The only record is of a skull found near Puerto Peñasco in 1972 (Russell & Monson 1998).

American crow *(Corvus brachyrhynchos)* – Cuervo americano. Casual winter vagrant along Río Colorado and Mexicali Valley, usually in large flocks.

Common raven *(Corvus corax)* – Cuervo grande. Fairly common breeding resident throughout the region.

Alaudidae – Larks

Horned lark *(Eremophila alpestris)* – Alondra cornuda. Fairly common breeding resident and common winter visitor throughout Colorado delta, Puerto Peñasco, and Río Sonoyta.

Hirundinidae – Swallows

Purple martin *(Progne subis)* – Martín azul. Rare spring transient through El Doctor, Ciénega de Santa Clara, and Puerto Peñasco.

Tree swallow *(Tachycineta bicolor)* – Golondrina arbolera. Common transient and winter visitor through Colorado delta, coastal areas, and Río Sonoyta.

Violet-green swallow *(Tachycineta thalassina)* – Golondrina cariblanca. Fairly common spring transient and uncommon winter visitor and fall transient through Colorado delta, coastal areas, and Río Sonoyta. Locally breeds along cliffs near Laguna Salada at least during wet years (Patten et al. 2001).

Northern rough-winged swallow *(Stelgidopteryx serripennis)* – Golondrina aliserrada norteña. Common transient through Colorado delta and coastal areas. Common breeder in the Mexicali Valley and Río Sonoyta.

Bank swallow *(Riparia riparia)* – Golondrina ribereña. Uncommon transient along Río Colorado, Ciénega de Santa Clara, El Doctor, and the coast.

Cliff swallow *(Petrochelidon pyrrhonota)* – Golondrina risquera. Common breeder under bridges in Río Colorado, Mexicali Valley, and Río Sonoyta. Common transient through delta and coastal areas.

Barn swallow *(Hirundo rustica)* – Golondrina ranchera. Common spring and fall transient through Río Colorado, Ciénega de Santa Clara, El Doctor, Río Sonoyta, and the coast.

Remizidae – Verdins

Verdin *(Auriparus flaviceps)* – Baloncillo. Common breeding resident throughout the region.

Sittidae – Nuthatches

Red-breasted nuthatch *(Sitta canadensis)* – Saltapalos canadiense. Casual spring vagrant, with only one record, at El Doctor (K. Garrett).

White-breasted nuthatch *(Sitta carolinensis)* – Saltapalos pechiblanco. Casual winter and spring vagrant, with only one recorded at Puerto Peñasco during the Christmas Bird Count of 2001 (National Audubon Society 2002) and one at Río Colorado on May 24, 2003 (HIR).

Certhiidae – Creepers

Brown creeper *(Certhia americana)* – Trepador americano. Casual winter visitor at Puerto Peñasco, with only two records (Russell & Monson 1998).

Troglodytidae – Wrens

Cactus wren *(Campylorhynchus brunneicapillus)* – Matraca desértica. Common breeding resident throughout the region.

Rock wren *(Salpinctes obsoletus)* – Saltapared roquero. Uncommon breeding resident at San Felipe, Sierra Cucapá, El Golfo de Santa Clara, and Puerto Peñasco (Patten et al. 2001; Russell & Monson 1998). Rare winter visitor throughout delta, Río Sonoyta, and Pinacate.

Canyon wren *(Catherpes mexicanus)* – Saltapared barranquero. Rare breeding resident at cliffs and small canyons around Río Sonoyta, Puerto Peñasco, and Pinacate. Rare winter visitor in rocky areas of Colorado Desert region of Baja California.

Bewick's wren *(Thryomanes bewickii)* – Saltapared de Bewick. Fairly common winter visitor throughout Colorado delta, coast, and Río Sonoyta.

House wren *(Troglodytes aedon)* – Saltapared continental norteño. Uncommon winter visitor and spring transient throughout the region.

Sedge wren *(Cistothorus platensis)* – Saltapared sabanero. Only one recorded, at El Doctor in December 1983 (Peter Pyle and Steve Howell in Russell & Monson 1998).

Marsh wren *(Cistothorus palustris)* – Saltapared pantanero. Common breeding resident at Ciénega de Santa

Clara, El Doctor, and agricultural drains of Mexicali Valley with emergent vegetation. Common winter visitor at Puerto Peñasco and Río Sonoyta.

REGULIDAE – KINGLETS

Ruby-crowned kinglet *(Regulus calendula)* – Reyezuelo sencillo. Common winter visitor throughout the region.

SYLVIIDAE – GNATCATCHERS

Blue-gray gnatcatcher *(Polioptila caerulea)* – Perlita grisilla. Fairly common winter visitor at Río Colorado, El Doctor, Río Sonoyta, and Puerto Peñasco.

California gnatcatcher *(Polioptila californica)* – Perlita californiana. Uncommon resident near south end of Bahía San Felipe (Mellink & Rea 1994).

Black-tailed gnatcatcher *(Polioptila melanura)* – Perlita colinegra. Common breeding resident at Río Colorado, El Doctor, Río Sonoyta, Pinacate, and Puerto Peñasco.

TURDIDAE – THRUSHES

Western bluebird *(Sialia mexicana)* – Azulejo gorji-azul. Rare and irregular winter visitor to Río Sonoyta (Russell & Monson 1998), Río Colorado, and San Felipe (Patten et al. 2001).

Mountain bluebird *(Sialia currucoides)* – Azulejo pálido. Rare and irregular winter visitor throughout the region.

Townsend's solitaire *(Myadestes townsendi)* – Clarín norteño. Rare winter visitor at Río Sonoyta.

Swainson's thrush *(Catharus ustulatus)* – Zorzalito de Swainson. Common spring and uncommon fall transient through El Doctor, Río Colorado, and coastal desertscrub.

Hermit thrush *(Catharus guttatus)* – Zorzalito coli-rrufo. Fairly common transient and winter visitor at El Doctor, Río Colorado, and Río Sonoyta.

American robin *(Turdus migratorius)* – Zorzal petir-rojo. Uncommon and irregular winter visitor throughout the region. One summer record at Mexicali on July 8, 2003 (RAE).

MIMIDAE – MOCKINGBIRDS AND THRASHERS

Gray catbird *(Dumetella carolinensis)* – Maullador gris. Accidental spring vagrant, with one individual banded at El Doctor on May 17, 2004, and recaptured on May 27, 2004, at the same site (HIR).

Northern mockingbird *(Mimus polyglottos)* – Cenzontle norteño. Common breeding resident throughout the region.

Sage thrasher *(Oreoscoptes montanus)* – Cuitlacoche de artemesia. Uncommon spring transient and winter visitor throughout the region.

Brown thrasher *(Toxostoma rufum)* – Cuitlacoche rojizo. Only one recorded, at Puerto Peñasco in 1981 (Russell & Monson 1998).

Bendire's thrasher *(Toxostoma bendirei)* – Cuitlacoche de Bendire. Uncommon winter visitor to Río Sonoyta–Pinacate region. Casual winter vagrant to Río Colorado, with only one record (Daniels et al. 1993).

Curve-billed thrasher *(Toxostoma curvirostre)* – Cuitlacoche piquicurvo. Uncommon breeding resident at Río Sonoyta, Pinacate, Puerto Peñasco, and El Golfo de Santa Clara.

Crissal thrasher *(Toxostoma crissale)* – Cuitlacoche crisal. Fairly common breeding resident at Río Colorado. Uncommon winter visitor to Pinacate and Río Sonoyta.

Le Conte's thrasher *(Toxostoma lecontei)* – Cuitlacoche pálido. Uncommon breeding resident in open desert-scrub regions.

MOTACILLIDAE – WAGTAILS AND PIPITS

American pipit *(Anthus rubescens)* – Bisbita ameri-cana. Common winter visitor throughout Colorado delta, coastal areas, and Río Sonoyta.

BOMBYCILLIDAE – WAXWINGS

Cedar waxwing *(Bombycilla cedrorum)* – Ampelis americano. Uncommon and irregular winter visitor to Río Colorado, Puerto Peñasco, and Río Sonoyta.

PTILOGONATIDAE – SILKY FLYCATCHERS

Phainopepla *(Phainopepla nitens)* – Capulinero negro. Fairly common breeding resident in remnant mesquite patches of Colorado delta, Río Sonoyta, and Pinacate.

PARULIDAE – WOOD-WARBLERS

Orange-crowned warbler *(Vermivora celata)* – Chipe corona-naranja. Common transient and winter visitor, most commonly found at El Doctor, Río Colorado, and Río Sonoyta.

Nashville warbler *(Vermivora ruficapilla)* – Chipe de Nashville. Common spring and uncommon fall transient at El Doctor, Río Colorado, and coastal areas of Río Sonoyta. Casual in winter, with only two records (Patten et al. 2001).

Lucy's warbler *(Vermivora luciae)* – Chipe de Lucy. Formerly a common breeder throughout Colorado delta (Russell & Monson 1998), but no recent records. Presumed breeding near Sonoyta (Russell & Monson 1998). Rare transient through Río Colorado and El Doctor.

Yellow warbler *(Dendroica petechia)* – Chipe amarillo. Formerly a common breeding resident in Colorado delta (Grinnell 1928; van Rossem 1945), now a rare summer visitor with unconfirmed breeding. Common transient through El Doctor, Río Colorado, and Río Sonoyta. Rare winter visitor, with only two records at

Puerto Peñasco (Russell & Monson 1998) and two at Mexicali (Patten et al. 2001; RAE, January 2003).

Cape May warbler *(Dendroica tigrina)* – Chipe atigrado. Accidental winter vagrant. Only one recorded, at Puerto Peñasco in December 1989 (David Stejskal in Russell & Monson 1998).

Black-throated blue warbler *(Dendroica caerulescens)* – Chipe azulnegro. Accidental fall vagrant. Only one recorded, at Río Sonoyta in October 1975 (Groschupf et al. 1988).

Yellow-rumped warbler *(Dendroica coronata)* – Chipe rabadilla amarilla. Common transient and winter resident in Colorado delta, Río Sonoyta, Pinacate, and coastal desertscrub.

Black-throated gray warbler *(Dendroica nigrescens)* – Chipe negrigris. Fairly common spring and uncommon fall transient through El Doctor, Río Colorado, and Puerto Peñasco.

Townsend's warbler *(Dendroica townsendi)* – Chipe de Townsend. Fairly common spring transient through coastal desertscrub, El Doctor, and Río Colorado. This species has been recorded three times during winter at Puerto Peñasco (Russell & Monson 1998).

Hermit warbler *(Dendroica occidentalis)* – Chipe cabeciamarillo. Uncommon spring transient through El Doctor and Río Colorado.

Yellow-throated warbler *(Dendroica dominica)* – Chipe garganta amarilla. Accidental spring vagrant. Only one recorded, at Quitovac (about 40 km southeast of Sonoyta) in May 1982 (Amadeo Rea in Russell & Monson 1998).

Prairie warbler *(Dendroica discolor)* – Chipe pradeño. Accidental fall vagrant. Only one observed, at El Doctor in October 1999 (van Riper et al. 1999).

Palm warbler *(Dendroica palmarum)* – Chipe playero. Accidental winter vagrant. Ten birds were observed at El Doctor in December 1983 (Peter Pyle and Steve Howell in Russell & Monson 1998), and three at Puerto Peñasco in December 1993 (Steve Ganley in Russell & Monson 1998).

American redstart *(Setophaga ruticilla)* – Pavito migratorio. Casual transient, with only one recorded at Sonoyta in November 1968 (R. Cunningham in Russell & Monson 1998) and two at El Doctor on September 17, 2002 (HIR), and September 26, 2003 (banded, ACF).

Ovenbird *(Seiurus aurocapillus)* – Chipe suelero. Accidental spring vagrant. Only one recorded, at El Doctor in May 2002 (OHH and EZH).

Northern waterthrush *(Seiurus noveboracensis)* – Chipe charquero. Accidental fall vagrant. Only one recorded (banded) at El Doctor on November 8, 2003 (ACF).

Macgillivray's warbler *(Oporornis tolmiei)* – Chipe de Tolmie. Fairly common spring and fall transient through coastal desertscrub, Río Sonoyta, El Doctor, and Río Colorado.

Common yellowthroat *(Geothlypis trichas)* – Mascarita común. Common breeding resident at Hardy and Colorado rivers, Ciénega de Santa Clara, and El Doctor. Common transient and winter visitor at Río Sonoyta and Puerto Peñasco.

Hooded warbler *(Wilsonia citrine)* – Chipe encapuchado. Accidental spring vagrant, with one individual banded at El Doctor on June 12, 2004 (HIR).

Wilson's warbler *(Wilsonia pusilla)* – Chipe de Wilson. The most abundant of the migrant warblers. Common spring and fall transient through coastal desertscrub, El Doctor, Río Sonoyta, and Río Colorado.

Canada warbler *(Wilsonia canadensis)* – Chipe de Canadá. Accidental spring vagrant, with one individual banded at El Doctor on May 27, 2004 (HIR).

Yellow-breasted chat *(Icteria virens)* – Gritón pechiamarillo. Uncommon breeder along Hardy and Colorado rivers. Uncommon spring and fall transient through coastal desertscrub, El Doctor, and Río Colorado.

THRAUPIDAE – TANAGERS

Summer tanager *(Piranga rubra)* – Tángara roja. Formerly a common breeder along the Hardy and Colorado rivers (Grinnell 1928; Miller et al. 1957), but no recent breeding activity has been documented. Only three recent records, a female at Río Hardy in April 1984 (Patten et al. 2001), a male at Río Colorado in September 1999 (van Riper et al. 1999), and a second-year male banded at the Río Colorado on May 26, 2004 (HIR).

Western tanager *(Piranga ludoviciana)* – Tángara occidental. Common spring and fall transient through coastal desertscrub, El Doctor, Río Sonoyta, and Río Colorado.

EMBERIZIDAE – TOWHEES, SPARROWS, AND LONGSPURS

Green-tailed towhee *(Pipilo chlorurus)* – Rascador coliverde. Uncommon transient and winter visitor along Río Colorado and Río Sonoyta.

Spotted towhee *(Pipilo maculates)* – Rascador pinto. Rare winter visitor at San Felipe (Patten et al. 2001), El Golfo de Santa Clara, Río Colorado (OHH), and Puerto Peñasco (Russell & Monson 1998).

Canyon towhee *(Pipilo fuscus)* – Rascador arroyero. Common resident along Río Sonoyta, where breeding is presumed (Russell & Monson 1998).

Abert's towhee *(Pipilo aberti)* – Rascador de Abert. Common breeding resident throughout Colorado delta, especially along Río Colorado.

Cassin's sparrow *(Aimophila cassinii)* – Zacatonero de Cassin. Casual spring vagrant. One recorded north of Puerto Peñasco (Russell & Monson 1998).

Rufous-crowned sparrow *(Aimophila ruficeps)* – Zacatonero corona rufa. Rare resident near Sonoyta, where breeding is presumed (Russell & Monson 1998).

Chipping sparrow *(Spizella passerina)* – Gorrión cejiblanco. Uncommon winter visitor and transient throughout Colorado delta, Puerto Peñasco, and Río Sonoyta.

Clay-colored sparrow *(Spizella pallida)* – Gorrión pálido. Casual transient. Only one bird recorded, at Puerto Peñasco (Russell & Monson 1998).

Brewer's sparrow *(Spizella breweri)* – Gorrión de Brewer. Common winter visitor throughout the region.

Vesper sparrow *(Pooecetes gramineus)* – Gorrión coliblanco. Uncommon winter visitor at Río Colorado and Río Sonoyta.

Lark sparrow *(Chondestes grammacus)* – Gorrión arlequín. Fairly common winter visitor to Colorado delta and Puerto Peñasco. Breeding may occur in Mexicali Valley (Patten et al. 2001).

Black-throated sparrow *(Amphispiza bilineata)* – Gorrión gorjinegro. Uncommon breeding resident in desertscrub areas, in both Colorado Desert region in Baja California (Patten et al. 2001) and Pinacate region in Sonora (Russell & Monson 1998).

Sage sparrow *(Amphispiza belli)* – Gorrión de artemesia. Fairly common winter visitor at coastal dunes, open creosotebush, and saltbush communities throughout the region (Russell & Monson 1998).

Lark bunting *(Calamospiza melanocorys)* – Gorrión alipálido. Rare winter visitor and spring transient, with three records near San Felipe (Patten et al. 2001) and four near Puerto Peñasco (Russell & Monson 1998).

Savannah sparrow *(Passerculus sandwichensis)* – Gorrión sabanero. Common winter visitor throughout the region. The large-billed savannah sparrow *(P. s. rostratus)* is a common breeder at Isla Montague, Cerro Prieto, Ciénega de Santa Clara, El Doctor, and coastal salt marshes, although it is threatened and declining (Mellink & Ferreira-Bartrina 2000). *P. s. rostratus* is under special protection in Mexico (Diario Oficial 2002).

Grasshopper sparrow *(Ammodramus savannarum)* – Gorrión chapulín. Casual winter vagrant, with one record north of San Felipe (Patten et al. 2001) and one north of Puerto Peñasco (Russell & Monson 1998).

Fox sparrow *(Passerella iliaca)* – Gorrión rascador. Casual winter visitor. Two records in Mexicali Valley (Patten et al. 2001) and one in Río Sonoyta (Russell & Monson 1998).

Song sparrow *(Melospiza melodia)* – Gorrión cantor. Common breeding resident throughout Colorado delta.

Lincoln's sparrow *(Melospiza lincolnii)* – Gorrión de Lincoln. Fairly common winter visitor to Colorado delta, coastal desertscrub, and Río Sonoyta.

Swamp sparrow *(Melospiza georgiana)* – Gorrión pantanero. Rare winter visitor along coastal marshes, Río Sonoyta, and Río Colorado.

White-throated sparrow *(Zonotrichia albicollis)* – Gorrión gorjiblanco. Casual winter visitor near Puerto Peñasco, with only one definite record (Russell & Monson 1998).

White-crowned sparrow *(Zonotrichia leucophrys)* – Gorrión coroniblanco. Common winter visitor and transient throughout the region.

Golden-crowned sparrow *(Zonotrichia atricapilla)* – Gorrión coronidorado. Rare winter visitor; one record at Mexicali (Patten et al. 2001) and another near Puerto Peñasco (Russell & Monson 1998).

Dark-eyed junco *(Junco hyemalis)* – Junco ojioscuro. Uncommon winter visitor at Colorado delta, Puerto Peñasco, and Río Sonoyta.

McCown's longspur *(Calcarius mccownii)* – Escribano de McCown. Accidental winter visitor, with four individuals observed on December 8, 2004, at the Mesa de Andrade dunes (OHH).

Chestnut-collared longspur *(Calcarius ornatus)* – Escribano cuellicastaño. Casual winter visitor, with a flock of more than 50 birds observed at Río Colorado in November 1994 (Patten et al. 2001) and a flock of 24 recorded at Puerto Peñasco in October 1976 (Russell & Monson 1998).

CARDINALIDAE – CARDINALS

Northern cardinal *(Cardinalis cardinalis)* – Cardenal norteño. Uncommon resident around Puerto Peñasco and Sonoyta, where breeding is presumed (Russell & Monson 1998). Only one record at Río Colorado, 6 km south of Morelos Dam (May 6, 2003; OHH).

Pyrrhuloxia *(Cardinalis sinuatus)* – Cardenal desértico. Rare summer resident around Puerto Peñasco and Sonoyta; breeding is presumed at the latter (Russell & Monson 1998).

Rose-breasted grosbeak *(Pheucticus ludovicianus)* – Picogordo pecho rosa. Casual spring vagrant, with three records at El Doctor (K. Garrett in April 1999; EZH on May 17, 2002; OHH on May 20, 2003; this last bird was captured, photographed, and released).

Black-headed grosbeak *(Pheucticus melanocephalus)* – Picogrueso tigrillo. Common spring and uncommon fall transient through El Doctor, Río Sonoyta, and Río Colorado.

Blue grosbeak *(Guiraca caerulea)* – Picogrueso azul. Common breeder along riparian areas of Río Colorado.

Lazuli bunting *(Passerina amoena)* – Colorín lazulita. Fairly common spring transient through coastal desert-scrub and El Doctor; uncommon throughout Mexicali Valley.

Indigo bunting *(Passerina cyanea)* – Colorín azul. Casual spring vagrant, with one recorded at El Doctor in April 2002 (OHH and EZH).

Painted bunting *(Passerina ciris)* – Colorín sietecolores. Accidental winter vagrant. One male was collected near Puerto Peñasco in December 1965 (Russell & Monson 1998).

ICTERIDAE – BLACKBIRDS

Red-winged blackbird *(Agelaius phoeniceus)* – Tordo sargento. Common breeding resident throughout Colorado delta. Common winter visitor at Puerto Peñasco and Río Sonoyta. The population of this species has increased over the last decades with the growth of agriculture in the region.

Eastern meadowlark *(Sturnella magna)* – Pradero común. Casual winter vagrant, with only three records from Puerto Peñasco (Russell & Monson 1998).

Western meadowlark *(Sturnella neglecta)* – Pradero occidental. Fairly common breeding resident, especially at El Doctor, Ciénega de Santa Clara, and alfalfa fields of Mexicali Valley. Common winter visitor throughout the region.

Yellow-headed blackbird *(Xanthocephalus xanthocephalus)* – Tordo cabeciamarillo. Fairly common breeding resident, especially at Ciénega de Santa Clara. Common winter visitor throughout the region.

Rusty blackbird *(Euphagus carolinus)* – Tordo canadiense. Accidental, with only one record near Puerto Peñasco (Russell & Monson 1998).

Brewer's blackbird *(Euphagus cyanocephalus)* – Tordo de Brewer. Common winter visitor throughout Colorado delta, Puerto Peñasco, and Río Sonoyta. Only two records of summer birds (Ruiz-Campos & Rodríguez-Meraz 1997).

Great-tailed grackle *(Quiscalus mexicanus)* – Zanate mayor. Common breeding resident throughout most of the region. Most abundant around agricultural fields and towns.

Bronzed cowbird *(Molothrus aeneus)* – Vaquero ojirojo. Rare summer resident, presumed breeding at Río Colorado and Puerto Peñasco. We observed displaying males at Río Colorado (April 2002, HIR), at Ejido Johnson near Ciénega de Santa Clara (May 2002, EZH), and at Ejido Pachuca near Morelos Dam (June 2003, OHH). Rare winter visitor, with 9 birds recorded in the Mexicali Valley on Jaunary 13, 2003 (RAE).

Brown-headed cowbird *(Molothus ater)* – Vaquero cabecicafé. Common breeding resident throughout Colorado delta, Puerto Peñasco, and Río Sonoyta, with numbers augmented in winter. Populations of this cowbird have increased with farming activity in the region.

Hooded oriole *(Icterus cucullatus)* – Bolsero cuculado. Fairly common breeder along riparian areas of Río Colorado. Presumed breeding near Sonoyta (Russell & Monson 1998).

Bullock's oriole *(Icterus bullockii)* – Bolsero de Bullock. Common breeder along Río Colorado. Common transient through Puerto Peñasco, Río Sonoyta, and El Doctor.

Baltimore oriole *(Icterus galbula)* – Bolsero de Baltimore. Accidental spring vagrant, with only one recorded (banded) at El Doctor on May 30, 2004 (HIR).

Scott's oriole *(Icterus parisorum)* – Bolsero tunero. Rare spring transient and winter visitor, and uncommon breeder around San Felipe and Colorado Desert region of Baja California (Patten et al. 2001).

FRINGILLIDAE – FINCHES

Purple finch *(Carpodacus purpureus)* – Fringílido purpúreo. Accidental winter vagrant, with only one bird recorded at the 1995 Christmas Bird Count of Puerto Peñasco (S. Ganley).

Cassin's finch *(Carpodacus cassinii)* – Fringílido de Cassin. Accidental winter vagrant. Only one record, from Puerto Peñasco in December 2001 (National Audubon Society 2002).

House finch *(Carpodacus mexicanus)* – Fringílido mexicano. Common breeding resident throughout the region.

Pine siskin *(Carduelis pinus)* – Dominico pinero. Rare and irregular winter visitor, with three records from Colorado delta region (Grinnell 1928; Patten et al. 1993; Ruiz-Campos & Rodríguez-Meraz 1997), one from Puerto Peñasco, and one from Sonoyta (Russell & Monson 1998).

Lesser goldfinch *(Carduelis psaltria)* – Dominico dorsioscuro. Fairly common winter visitor throughout the region and uncommon breeder along Río Colorado.

Lawrence's goldfinch *(Carduelis lawrencei)* – Dominico de Lawrence. Rare transient and casual winter visitor at Puerto Peñasco, Río Sonoyta, Río Hardy, Sierra Cucapá, and Sierra las Pintas (south of Sierra Cucapá), where it was recorded breeding only once (Patten et al. 2001).

American goldfinch *(Carduelis tristis)* – Dominico americano. Probably a rare winter visitor, with only two records: near La Ventana (Patten et al. 2001) and near Sonoyta (Russell & Monson 1998).

NON-NATIVE SPECIES

Ring-necked pheasant *(Phasianus colchicus)* – Faisán de collar. Common breeding resident in the Mexicali Valley.

Rock dove *(Columba livia)* – Paloma doméstica. Common breeding resident, even colonizing pipes through levee system of Río Colorado.

European starling *(Sturnus vulgaris)* – Estornino europeo. Common breeding resident around urban areas and farms. Reached the Mexicali Valley in the 1950s (Cardiff 1961).

House sparrow *(Passer domesticus)* – Gorrión doméstico. Common breeding resident throughout the region, especially around cities and towns. Probably reached the Mexicali Valley after 1910 (Patten et al. 2001).

Twenty-Eight

Aquatic Mammals of the Northern Sea of Cortez and Colorado River Delta

CARLOS J. NAVARRO-SERMENT

The waters that surround our boat, here in the northern Sea of Cortez, are cold and murky, and we can readily feel the force of the strong tidal current. There is something strange in the ambiance, as if some of the features in the whole landscape wouldn't quite fit: the wide, gently sloping shoreline left behind by the receding tide stands in contrast with the harsh rocky islet of Rocas Consag; the snowy peaks of the sierra San Pedro Mártir to the west, sharp and jagged compared with the sinuous sand dunes of the Gran Desierto to the north. This area of contrasts seems unlike anywhere else, as if gifted by a life of its own. And quite alive it is! Several meters away from us, a huge swarm of feeding creatures fills the air with their noises: brown pelicans plunge from the heights trying to catch a mouthful of shrimp-like krill while Heermann's gulls fly around them looking for a "leaking" pelican beak. Tiny eared grebes dive for a krill or two, hoping to avoid an unplanned inspection of a pelican's gular pouch. Adding to the confusion, a couple of fin whales loll languidly on their left sides synchronously, mouths wide open at the surface, scaring away the birds as they engulf tons of seawater with their distended throats. Closing their mouths, they look like huge balloons as they float for a couple seconds at the surface, filtering the krill from the water through comb-like baleen hanging from their palates. Yes, these waters feel alive!

The whole Sea of Cortez, also known as the Gulf of California or Mar de Cortés, is home to at least 30 species of marine mammals, including 26 cetaceans (whales, dolphins, and porpoises) and 4 pinnipeds (seals and sea lions). Its high levels of productivity, a result of strong, nutrient-rich upwellings and the diversity of its habitats, from shallow mudflats and estuaries to deep-water basins, make the Sea of Cortez one of the richest and most diverse areas of comparable size in the world in terms of marine mammals, home to 25 percent of the known species (Urbán et al. 2005; Vidal et al. 1993).

The upper end of the gulf, roughly from the Colorado River delta, in the corner where Sonora meets the Baja California peninsula and where the Reserva de la Biosfera Alto Golfo de California y Delta del Río Colorado is located, south to the chain of big, midriff islands—Tiburón, San Esteban, Ángel de la Guarda, and others—has its own set of oceanographic characteristics. These conditions reach their extreme in its northernmost area, shallower than the rest, with a dramatic annual flux in sea-surface temperature, from below 10°C (50°F) to more than 32°C (90°F) (Thomson et al. 2000). Salinity gradient, too, is extreme in this region, but with a peculiar twist: before drastic reductions in the flow of the Colorado River, the ocean water contained higher concentrations of salt as one moved farther from the river delta, but now that gradient has been reversed, with the northernmost portion of the gulf having the highest salinities of all (Carbajal et al. 1997; Thomson et al. 2000). The whole area is dominated by one of the biggest tidal ranges in the world, up to a maximum of about 7–10 m (23–33 ft), which generate currents of up to 3 m/second (10 ft/s) along channels (Carbajal et al. 1997) and expose huge mudflats, tide pools, and sandbars twice every day, creating a dynamic habitat for marine, intertidal, and coastal creatures, marine mammals included. Many animal species call this place of extremes home, using it as a feeding, spawning, nursery, or wintering grounds or even living here year round. The vaquita has become so closely adapted that it has become an endemic species, found nowhere else in the world. Here 11 cetacean species and one pinniped are regularly encountered, although 10 more cetaceans have been reported, for a total of 22 marine mammals that can be found in the extreme north of the gulf (Vidal et al. 1993). Two aquatic rodent species also live in the waters of the Colorado River delta, where the river otter used to do the same.

Those first fishermen who started following the huge, endemic *totoaba (Totoaba macdonaldi)* migration into the upper gulf during the winter months of the early 1920s, paddling and sailing from Guaymas, must have noticed the abundance of whales and dolphins there. Although focused on catching as many as possible of the big fish—up to 2 m (6.6 ft) long and more than 100 kg (220 lb)—they kept an eye on the many different mammals, even naming a few landmarks after them, such as Cerro de la Ballena, or Whale's Hill, at Puerto Peñasco and Punta Bufeo, or Orca's Point, south of San Felipe. Encounters between fishermen and cetaceans were abundant, as the two often met near the immense schools of fish. Totoaba used to congregate in huge schools during their annual migration to the northern end of the gulf for spawning, and sometimes groups of a thousand or more would trap schools of sardines or other small fish against the shore, thrashing the water into foam (Hastings & Findley, this volume). Dolphins, sea lions, and the occasional whale must have joined the meleé, looking for a meal for themselves. With the experienced eye of people used to nature, fishermen noticed that several different types were present, some that usually were far offshore and even one, the smallest, that they had not seen before. They called that little guy *vaquita*.

Species Accounts

The vaquita *(Phocoena sinus)* is the only true porpoise (belonging to the Phocoenidae family) found in Mexican waters; in fact, it has the most limited distribution of any marine cetacean, being restricted to the uppermost Gulf of California (Jaramillo-Legorreta et al. 1999; Silber et al. 1994; Vidal 1995; Vidal et al. 1993), in an area roughly defined as the region north of a line connecting Puertecitos in Baja California and Puerto Peñasco in Sonora. Unfortunately, the vaquita is in great danger of extinction (Rojas-Bracho & Taylor 1999; Urbán et al. 2005; Vidal 1995; Vidal et al. 1993).

The vaquita is among the smallest cetaceans, reaching a maximum of 1.5 m (4.95 ft) in length, with little or no beak, a short and somewhat stubby body, and a high dorsal fin. It has a dark gray cape

Figure 28.1. Vaquita. (Drawing by Carlos J. Navarro, courtesy of CEDO)

that gradually diffuses into a lighter tone on its sides; the throat and belly are white with pink tones. However, the vaquita's most distinctive coloration is a bold facial pattern that includes a black eye patch and black mouth contour.

The vaquita is a shy creature, not fond of getting close to boats; it is not easily seen and may be difficult to distinguish at sea from a small bottlenose dolphin by the inexperienced observer. It was unknown to science until March 18, 1950, when Ken Norris, of the University of California at Los Angeles, picked up a bleached skull from the beach north of San Felipe (Norris & McFarland 1958). This small cetacean is so scarce that its external appearance and coloration remained a mystery to scientists until 1985, when seven fresh specimens, caught incidentally during experimental fishing operations to assess the status of the totoaba, were examined (Brownell et al. 1987). The most recent attempt to calculate the vaquita's population took place in 1997, when only 567 individuals were estimated (Jaramillo-Legorreta et al. 1999). Of the world's marine cetaceans, only the Chinese river dolphin, or baiji *(Lipotes vexillifer),* may be more endangered. I clearly remember the first time I saw a live vaquita in the Colorado River delta. Close to a group of the much larger and more abundant bottlenose dolphins, two tiny porpoises swam erratically in the mud-colored waters, arching their backs as if rotating over an imaginary axis, briefly exposing their disproportionately high, triangular dorsal fins. They kept on busily chasing some fish or invertebrate prey while I marveled and felt privileged.

Vaquitas live in shallow waters, usually 20–35 m deep, and up to 40 km from shore (Gallo-Reynoso 1998; Vidal 1995). They may favor the clay and silt bottoms created by Colorado River discharges (Gallo-Reynoso 1998), feeding on at least 20 species of fishes and invertebrates associated

Figure 28.2. A young vaquita (Phocoena sinus) several weeks old still shows the white vertical stripes characteristic of many young cetaceans, a reminder of the curled position in which it grew while inside the uterus. (Photo by Carlos J. Navarro)

with soft bottoms (Findley et al. 1996; Pérez-Cortés 1996). Although this number of prey species may indicate that the vaquita is an opportunistic feeder (Rojas-Bracho & Taylor 1999), it can still be threatened by a change in the abundance or composition of prey species due to the reduction of Colorado River flow (Gallo-Reynoso 1998) or the area's extensive shrimp trawling (Nava-Romo 1995). The vaquita is also highly susceptible to gillnetting (Gallo-Reynoso 1998; Rojas-Bracho & Taylor 1999; Vidal 1995), a common fishing practice throughout the region and perhaps the greatest immediate danger to its survival (Urbán et al. 2005). Considering the extent of gillnetting in the gulf, it is remarkable that the vaquita has survived so long.

Far more easily seen than the vaquita because of its abundance, larger size, and showy manner, bottlenose dolphins, or *toninas (Tursiops truncatus)*, are present year round. The bottlenose dolphin, well known from television and marine parks, can reach up to 3.8 m (12.5 ft) in length and has a short, stubby beak and a tall, falcate dorsal fin. Its coloration consists of a number of gray tones, always darker in the back and lighter on the sides and belly. *Toninas* are usually heavily scarred from intraspecific play or fighting.

Traveling in either small groups or big aggregations of more than 500 individuals, this abundant and cosmopolitan species lives in both inshore and offshore waters (Leatherwood et al. 1988; Silber et al. 1994; Vidal et al. 1993). Highly acrobatic, they sometimes delight human observers with exuberant leaps and jumps, often while following boats. I remember vividly one such clown, who apparently found some hidden pleasure in soaking us as it splashed repeatedly right next to our boat.

Bottlenose dolphins feed on a wide variety of fishes and invertebrates and use many different strategies to catch their prey. In the Colorado River delta's shallow channels, I have seen them

many times launching themselves onshore, eating the small fish they have deliberately stranded before reentering the water.

Also present in the upper gulf is the long-beaked common dolphin *(Delphinus capensis)*, a species recently redescribed (Heyning & Perrin 1994) from warm temperate and tropical waters around the world, known as *cochito* by local fishermen. Smaller than the *tonina*, the long-beaked common dolphin measures up to 2.5 m (8.25 ft), with a more slender and streamlined figure and a distinctive color pattern in which the dark dorsal cape dips most deeply onto the sides at midbody. The resulting V-shaped saddle and the yellowish-tan zones on each side are useful for distinguishing this species at sea (Leatherwood and Reeves 1983). The long-beaked common dolphin is an offshore, pelagic species that preys mostly on small schooling fish such as sardines and anchovies. It often travels in big groups and is sometimes seen in aggregations of hundreds or thousands; in fact, it may be the most abundant cetacean in the Gulf of California (Vidal et al. 1993). In contrast, other offshore species such as the rough-toothed dolphin *(Steno bredanensis)* and striped dolphin *(Stenella coeruleoalba)* are not as common in the Sea of Cortez. Their presence in the northernmost portion is known only by single, stranded individuals on a beach near El Golfo de Santa Clara, Sonora, and near San Felipe, Baja California, respectively (Vidal et al. 1993). The rough-toothed dolphin resembles the bottlenose in size and color, but its long, slender beak grades into the melon, or "forehead," with no sharp demarcation, as in the former; a close inspection of its teeth reveals a series of vertical wrinkles from which this dolphin gets its common name (Leatherwood et al. 1988). Striped dolphins may confuse an inexperienced observer at sea, as this species' color pattern and general body shape are similar to those of the long-beaked common dolphin; however, it lacks the characteristic V-shaped saddle of the latter, having a distinctive light shoulder blaze extending back and up from the light lateral areas (Leatherwood et al. 1988). Like most delphinids, rough-toothed and striped dolphins eat small schooling fish and squid.

Another dolphin species, the Risso's *(Grampus griseus)*, may be present occasionally, as the stranding of five individuals at Punta Bufeo, 160 km south of San Felipe (Vidal et al. 1993), suggests, although its preference for waters deeper than 180 m (594 ft) (Leatherwood et al. 1988) makes its regular presence in the upper gulf unlikely. However, it is a cosmopolitan species that appears to be abundant in many parts of its range. This species' head, tapered but with a blunt beak, and extensive white scarring over a gray, robust body up to 4 m (13.2 ft) long are highly characteristic (Leatherwood & Reeves 1983).

A close relative and member of the same family as dolphins, the false killer whale, or *bufeo prieto (Pseudorca crassidens),* is a large and amusing oceanic predator of large fish, squid, and the occasional dolphin (Leatherwood et al. 1988). Measuring up to 6 m (19.8 ft) long and all black, it possesses one of the largest continuous ranges of any cetacean, from tropical to temperate seas around the world (Vidal et al. 1993). False killer whales are highly energetic and capable of great leaps into the air. Although I have been lucky enough to observe their antics around Rocas Consag, off San Felipe, this species seems to be less common in the northernmost Gulf of California than its unmistakable relative, the orca, or killer whale *(Orcinus orca),* the largest member of the dolphin family (Delphinidae). Locally known as *bufeo* or *bufeo mascarillo,* the killer whale is widely distributed throughout the Sea of Cortez, where it is neither abundant nor rare (Silber et al. 1994; Vidal et al. 1993), but its true status there remains unknown (Guerrero-Ruíz et al. 1998; Vidal et al. 1993). It is known, though, that at least some groups of killer whales photo-identified off California have been seen inside the gulf (Guerrero-Ruíz et al. 1998). This large predator, whose mature males reach up to 9 m (29.7 ft) in length, feeds on a wide array of creatures, from small schooling fish and seabirds to sharks and blue whales (Leatherwood et al. 1988); within the boundaries of the Alto Golfo Biosphere Reserve, killer whales have been observed chasing, killing, and eating a Bryde's whale *(Balaenoptera edeni)* (Silber et al. 1990). Fishermen from El Golfo de Santa Clara once described to me how a pod of *bufeos mascarillos* attacked a big totoaba school off Punta Borrascoso, Sonora: dozens of the 50–80-kg (110–176-lb) fish were sent into the air by the *bufeos'* strong blows and tail hits amidst a whitewater surface. After a while, when the whales were satiated and had dispersed, fishermen moved in and picked up the remains that floated around—totoaba carcasses cut in half!

Although most fishermen in the gulf and elsewhere are afraid of killer whales, documented attacks on boats are rare and have usually been provoked (Leatherwood et al. 1988). Nevertheless, it is both an eerie and marvelous feeling to see a full-grown orca male watching you, studying your every move, one meter away from your boat.

The short-finned pilot whale *(Globicephala macrorhynchus),* also known as *bufeo prieto* due to its basically all-black coloration, interrupted by a light gray saddle behind the dorsal fin, is another large (up to 7.2 m, or 23.8 ft) member of the dolphin family. Its distinctive thick, bulbous forehead and wide, low dorsal fin easily identify it. It is an abundant, oceanic, squid-eating species with a worldwide distribution (Leatherwood et al. 1988). Because of its preference for deep waters, this gregarious whale is not common in the northernmost Sea of Cortez, although strandings have been recorded as far north as Cholla Bay, near Puerto Peñasco, Sonora (Vidal et al. 1993).

Beaked whales, members of a different, poorly known family (Ziphiidae), are oceanic, deepdiving, and secretive cetaceans that seem to subsist primarily on squid. They are characterized by a dramatic reduction in dentition (number of teeth), as only the males of most species have a pair of exposed teeth (Leatherwood et al. 1988). But despite their small number of teeth, beaked whales seem to use them quite often against each other; many individuals, particularly males, of most species are heavily marked by white scars, possibly from territorial fighting (Heyning 1984). Due to the shallowness of the northern gulf, it is not a likely place for beaked whales, although the stranding of two Baird's beaked whales *(Berardius bairdii)* 25 km north of Puertecitos, Baja California, indicates that the species visits the area (Navarro-Serment and Manzanilla-Naim 1999). Characterized by a prominent forehead that gently slopes to a long, cylindrical beak, this largest of the beaked whales and second largest toothed whale (to almost 13 m, or 42.9 ft, in length), is a north Pacific species whose abundance, habits, and movements inside the Gulf of California are highly speculative. The same can be said about the only other beaked whale species known from the upper gulf, Cuvier's beaked whale *(Ziphius cavirostris),* a cosmopolitan species whose skeletal remains have been collected near San Felipe, Baja California, and throughout the gulf (Vidal et al. 1993). One of the better-known

members of the family, this species has a medium-size, robust body up to 7 m (23.1 ft) in length and a short beak. It develops a lighter coloration on its head and neck over a tan or light brown body with age; old males may appear entirely white from a distance (Leatherwood et al. 1988).

Also a deep diver, but a member of a different family (Physeteridae), the pygmy sperm whale *(Kogia breviceps)* closely resembles the general body shape of its bigger relative the sperm whale, with a blunt and square head, small lower jaw, and robust body. It is much smaller than its larger cousin, reaching a maximum of only 3.5 m (11.5 ft) in length. This species is not easily seen, as it is small, solitary, secretive, and generally an inhabitant of offshore waters. A cosmopolitan species of tropical and temperate latitudes, the pygmy sperm whale has been recorded in the upper gulf at San Felipe and Puerto Peñasco (Silber et al. 1994; Vidal et al. 1993). Though not documented in the area, the dwarf sperm whale *(K. sima)* is a slightly smaller (2.7 m, or 8.9 ft) similar species whose distribution and habits appear to resemble those of the pygmy sperm whale and may also be present in the upper gulf, as it has been seen close to the area in the Canal de Ballenas, Baja California (Vidal et al. 1993). Although not a showy species, dwarf sperm whales occasionally breach, clearly exposing their pink-colored bellies, as I have been lucky enough to observe off Carmen Island, in the southern Sea of Cortez. Both species prey almost exclusively on squid.

Their larger relative the sperm whale, or *cachalote (Physeter macrocephalus)*, needs little description for those familiar with Herman Melville's *Moby Dick;* its disproportionately large head over a long and thin lower jaw and the wrinkled body skin are unmistakable. Males are much larger than females, growing up to 18.3 m (60 ft) or possibly more. Deep-diving champions, sperm whales

have one of the most extensive distributions of any marine mammal, ranging from the equator to the edges of polar ice in all oceans. This species has been recorded throughout the Sea of Cortez, though mostly in the southern half owing to its preference for deep waters (Vidal et al. 1993). Groups of sperm whales have been seen off Puerto Peñasco and around Isla San Jorge, and some individuals have stranded at Las Conchas and La Cholla beaches. It is likely that *cachalote* groups occasionally travel that far north in the gulf following the movements of a favorite prey, the Humboldt squid *(Dosidicus gigas).*

Baleen whales are well represented within the boundaries of the Alto Golfo Biosphere Reserve, as seven of the twelve known species in the world are found there. Fin whales *(Balaenoptera physalus)* are the second largest whales, with individuals growing up to 27 m (89 ft) in the Southern Hemisphere, and are the most abundant of the baleen whales in the gulf, with sightings in all seasons and most months (Vidal et al. 1993). There is mounting evidence for a resident population of fin whales in the Sea of Cortez (Urbán et al. 2005; Vidal et al. 1993). At least some fin whales may be born in the upper gulf, as the finding of placentas on the beaches near Puerto Peñasco and the presence of very small individuals that I have photographed suggest. Fin whales are versatile feeders on small schooling fish and crustaceans (Leatherwood et al. 1988); watching from the air as two or three pairs of fin whales feed is a sight not easily forgotten. Moving in pairs, swimming synchronously as they roll over on their left sides, mouths wide open, and engulfing a near-solid krill "ball," they resemble a marine ballet (see Lanham, this volume).

Being the largest creatures ever (up to an unbelievable 33.3 m, or 110 ft, and 180,000 kg, or 400,000 lb), blue whales *(Balaenoptera musculus)* need lots of space and prefer deep, offshore waters, although sometimes this species too may approach the northern gulf's shoreline close enough to be seen from the coast. In fact, I may hold some kind of record for blue whale watching from my former bedroom on top of CEDO's tower in Puerto Peñasco!

Minke whales *(Balaenoptera acutorostrata)* are highly adaptable cetaceans and can be found in many different types of marine habitats (Leatherwood et al. 1988). The minke is one of the smallest, reaching up to 10.7 m (35 ft) in length, and one of the most widely distributed of the baleen whales. It is a sleek whale with a sharply pointed head and a tall, falcate dorsal fin; its body is dark gray above and white underneath, and it has a white band across the flippers characteristic of this species. Although abundant in many parts of its range and the target of the last whaling operations still in existence, it is not considered common in the Sea of Cortez. There are several records of its presence in the northern gulf, as indicated by the stranding of two individuals near El Golfo de Santa Clara, Sonora (Vidal et al. 1993).

Another species, the sei whale (Balaenoptera borealis), is much larger than the minke, measuring up to 19.5 m (64 ft). Its body is dark gray and is often covered by white oval scars, presumably the result of bites from a small, pelagic pair of species known as cookie-cutter sharks; a tall and erect dorsal fin is also characteristic. The sei whale is an infrequent visitor to the Gulf of California (Urbán et al. 2005; Vidal et al. 1993), but three of us—my dear friends Sandy Lanham and Silvia Manzanilla and myself—have been lucky enough to see them feeding on krill close to Rocas Consag, in the northern gulf (see Lanham, this volume).

Very similar to the sei, Bryde's whale (Balaenoptera edeni) is often hard to tell apart from it. Bryde's whale, though, is a far more abundant inhabitant of the Sea of Cortez. A little smaller than the sei, it grows up to 15.6 m (51 ft) in length and also possesses a tall, erect dorsal fin and dark body coloration. Its distinctive characteristic is three longitudinal ridges on top of the rostrum on most individuals. Bryde's whale is a tropical and warm temperate species distributed all over the gulf, especially during the summer (Silber et al. 1990; Silber et al. 1994; Vidal et al. 1993).

The humpback whale (Megaptera novaeangliae) is possibly the most photographed whale, and its robust body, reaching up to 17 m (56 ft), extremely long flippers, and head covered with rounded protuberances needs little description. A cosmopolitan species, it is also found throughout the gulf, particularly during winter months, although some individuals are thought to stay in the midriff area of the Sea of Cortez year round (Vidal et al. 1993). Individuals can be seen on occasion in the northern gulf, as I have around Rocas Consag.

Well known for their yearly migration between their north Pacific feeding grounds and the

Figure 28.4. Fin whales (Balaenoptera physalus) *are easily identified by the light color of their lower jaws, in contrast with their darker upper jaws. (Photo by Carlos J. Navarro)*

lagoons of Baja California Sur, where their young are born, many gray whales (Eschrichtius robustus) readily enter the gulf (Mellink & Orozco-Meyer 2002; Urbán et al. 2005; Vidal et al. 1993). The gray whale is a medium-size baleen whale with a maximum length of 15 m (49 ft); its mottled gray coloration and narrow head, with barnacles and lice growing in patches, and the absence of a dorsal fin make this species fairly unmistakable. It is a coastal species, and individuals are known to have entered the shallow channels of the Colorado River delta, where local fishermen sometimes call them cachalote.

The only pinniped in the northernmost Gulf of California, the abundant California sea lion (Zalophus californianus), locally known as lobo, is a well-known species that is often seen in zoos and oceanariums. It ranges along the coast and offshore islands from British Columbia to Banderas Bay, Mexico; a subspecies known as the Galapagos sea lion (Z. c. wollebaeki) is found at that archipelago. As with most sea lions, males grow much larger than females, weighing up to 390 kg (860 lb), compared with the 110 kg (240 lb) of females. California sea lions are widely distributed throughout the gulf, where 29 colonies have been identified (Aurioles 1988; Vidal et al. 1993). Some 83.5 percent of the species' population in the gulf is found from the midriff islands northward (Aurioles 1988). In the extreme north of the gulf, sea lions are limited by the scarcity of rocky islands where they may give birth to their young, and the only colonies in the area today are found at Rocas Consag and Isla San Jorge (see Felger, this volume, Chapter 15). As with most pinnipeds elsewhere in the world, California sea lions are subject to attack by killer whales and great white sharks (Carcharodon carcharias). Locally known as tiburón tonina, or bottlenose dolphin shark, because of the fact that, when landed, its tail adopts an horizontal posture

due to the long length of its lower lobe, resembling a dolphin's, the white shark is also an inhabitant of the waters of the Alto Golfo Biosphere Reserve. Fishermen from El Golfo de Santa Clara and other regions report that *lobo* remains are often found among the shark's stomach contents.

Other aquatic mammals have been found in the waters of the Colorado River delta, such as the northern river otter *(Lontra canadensis)*. Edgar A. Mearns collected this species in the late 1880s near the place where the international boundary crosses the Colorado River (Leopold 1959), and several specimens are known from the Colorado River in Arizona (Hoffmeister 1986). However, this species has presumably been extirpated from the delta, most likely by the reduction of the river's freshwater flow (Gallo-Reynoso 1997; Mellink et al. 1999).

Another aquatic mammal native to the Colorado River is the beaver *(Castor canadensis)*. Beaver, or *castor*, needs little description, as most of us are familiar with this large (875–1,175 mm, or 35–47 in) rodent of wood-eating habits and large, dorso-ventrally compressed, rounded tail. Although its numbers have decreased because of the severe reduction of the river's flow and the shrinking of formerly large stands of cotton-woods *(Populus fremontii)* and willows *(Salix gooddingii)* along its banks, beavers continue to live in the region, in the Valle de Mexicali and other delta sites (Mellink et al. 1999). Beaver population levels in the area are highly variable and dependent on extraordinary water releases in the Mexican portion of the Colorado River (Mellink & Luévano 1998).

Also present in the highly modified watercourses of the Colorado River delta today is the muskrat *(Ondatra zibethicus)*, although early accounts from the area fail to mention it (Pattie 1831 in Mellink 1995). Before the extensive dam construction and water diversions of the Colorado River, muskrat populations might have been small or patchy, possibly because of the frequent floods. However, this medium-size aquatic rodent (240–300 mm, or 16.8–21 in, of which a bit less than half belongs to the large, laterally compressed tail) is now widespread throughout the area, being found in many irrigation canals in the Valle de Mexicali (Leopold 1959; Mellink 1995; Mellink et al. 1999) and the Ciénega de Santa Clara, Sonora (Mellink et al. 1999). Somewhat similar in external appearance to the muskrat, but much bigger, is the *coypu,* or nutria *(Myocastor coypus),* a South American rodent introduced in several places, including the Sierra de Juárez, Baja California, although it doesn't seems to have become established there (Mellink et al. 1999). I am not aware of any records for this species in the delta, but it may be that individuals from the United States could become established in the Valle de Mexicali (Mellink et al. 1999).

Threats and Conservation

Habitat alteration due to the reduction of the freshwater flow of the Colorado River may pose a threat to endemic marine invertebrate and fish species, as well as the vaquita, because environmental conditions changed in many known and unknown ways after the extensive damming and diverting of the river, beginning early in the twentieth century (Carbajal et al. 1997; Cisneros et al. 1995). Salinity levels in the extreme north, for example, have increased owing to evaporation and lack of freshwater, turning the Colorado River delta, originally a positive estuarine system, into a negative one, meaning that formerly brackish areas are now hypersaline (Gallo-Reynoso 1998; Thomson et al. 2000). Dams and upstream diversions have dramatically reduced the natural flow of freshwater, silt, and nutrients to the Sea of Cortez, and except during unusually high flood years, almost no flow has reached the gulf since the early 1960s, when the Glen Canyon dam was completed (Morrison et al. 1996). The calculated flow that currently reaches the delta represents only 4 percent of the original discharges registered from 1910 to 1920 (Carbajal et al. 1997). The reduction of the freshwater discharges must have radically modified the hydrography and dynamics of the Colorado River delta and the northern part of the Gulf of California (Carbajal et al. 1997). Although primary productivity remains high in the northern gulf today and enough nutrients may still be present, trapped in interstitial water and liberated into the water column by delta erosion caused by tidal currents (Rojas-Bracho & Taylor 1999), it is hard for me to imagine that the area, in fact the entire Sea of Cortez, remains unaffected by the loss of an estimated average of 200 million tons per year of sediment and nutrients that the river used to carry into the gulf (Morrison et al. 1996). If productivity is high today, just imagine what it used to be!

Marine mammals are susceptible to dangers from many kinds of human activities. The increase in fishing and shipping poses the threats of reduction of prey species, boat collisions, underwater noises, and pollution. Although the available data do not indicate that hydrocarbon pesticides or other contaminants are currently a threat to cetaceans in the Gulf of California (Rojas-Bracho & Taylor 1999), die-offs of at least 425 individual marine mammals and 200 seabirds in the Alto Golfo between early January and mid-February 1995 were likely caused by the discharge of an unknown toxic substance into the water (Vidal & Gallo-Reynoso 1996) and constitute a reminder of the fragility of nature.

Although the number of shrimp trawlers has decreased in the area because of the collapse of shrimp fishing during the late 1980s and early 1990s, it has resulted in an influx of artisanal fishermen who operate from outboard motorboats, called *pangas* (Cudney-Bueno & Turk Boyer 1998). Also, the opening of new markets for fish species previously not exploited commercially, such as the chano *(Micropogonias megalops),* and the resurgence in 1993 of a strong fishery for the gulf corvina *(Cynoscion othonopterus),* a species that had not been fished commercially since the 1960s, motivated many inland people to move to such places as San Felipe and El Golfo de Santa Clara (Cudney-Bueno & Turk Boyer 1998). The risk of entanglement and suffocation that gill nets, the most common fishing device used by artisanal fishermen in the area, pose for cetaceans, particularly small coastal species like the vaquita, is well known (Gallo-Reynoso 1998; Rojas-Bracho & Taylor 1999; Urbán et al. 2005; Vidal 1995). Thus although the vaquita may be naturally rare (Rojas-Bracho & Taylor 1999), it was and still is being caught incidentally in gill nets, especially in the totoaba, shark, and mackerel fisheries (Rojas-Bracho & Taylor 1999; Vidal et al. 1993; Vidal 1995). At least 128 vaquitas were captured incidentally between 1985 and 1992, most in gill nets (Vidal 1995). Fortunately, illegal totoaba fishing is an uncommon practice today, but new regulations regarding fishing practices all over the vaquita's range and strong enforcement are urgently needed to stop or reduce the species' incidental capture by fishermen (Rojas-Bracho & Taylor 1999). In addition, new boundaries of the Alto Golfo Biosphere Reserve should be considered, as its present limits do not fully enclose the area where vaquitas concentrate (Gallo-Reynoso 1998; Jaramillo-Legorreta et al. 1999; Urbán et al. 2005). Every effort toward the conservation of this unique species should be pursued to prevent it from being the first cetacean ever to become extinct by human means.

The glassy surface of the water is barely disturbed by our boat's slow pace. As the sun quietly sets behind the Baja mountains, the northern gulf is tinted fiery red and a group of pelicans fly by, forming a perfect line. Far away, small ripples reveal a lonely giant, a whale shark, who unhurriedly swims just below the surface. Despite the beauty of the moment, my mind keeps thinking: too many nets, too many people with the need and the right to make a living, almost no freshwater flowing into the gulf... and then a single small, triangular dorsal fin breaks the surface and, rotating over an imaginary axis, disappears.

Marveling and feeling warm in my heart, I smile.

Acknowledgments

I thank the following people for what I have learned from them about the marine and river mammals of the northern gulf and with whom I have shared many joyful moments: Omar Vidal, Lloyd T. Findley, Peggy Turk Boyer, Richard Boyer, Sandy Lanham, Silvia Manzanilla-Naim, Felipe Maldonado, Juan Pablo Gallo-Reynoso, Peter A. Nelson, José Luis Carrillo, Samuel Gallardo, Eric Mellink, Flip Nicklin, Héctor Pérez-Cortéz, and Alberto Delgado-Estrella. Peter A. Nelson also reviewed the manuscript and provided many useful suggestions.

Checklist of the Aquatic Mammals of the Northern Sea of Cortez and Colorado River Delta

For each species, one or more English (E), Spanish (S), or local (L) common names are given, followed by its scientific name (italics), main habitat, and status. At least one conservation status is provided, after either the International Union for Conservation of Nature (IUCN; Reeves et al. 2003) or the Norma Oficial Mexicana NOM-059-ECOL-2001 (Mex.).

Order Cetacea (whales, dolphins, and porpoises)

Suborder Odontoceti (toothed whales)

Family Phocoenidae

Vaquita, Gulf of California porpoise (E), vaquita (S), *Phocoena sinus,* coastal waters, critically endangered (IUCN), endangered (Mex.).

Family Delphinidae

Common bottlenose dolphin (E), delfín nariz de botella (S), tonina (L), *Tursiops truncatus,* inshore and offshore waters, data deficient (IUCN), subject to special protection (Mex.).

Rough-toothed dolphin (E), delfín de dientes rugosos (S), *Steno bredanensis,* offshore waters, data deficient (IUCN), subject to special protection (Mex.).

Risso's dolphin (E), delfín de Risso (S), *Grampus griseus,* offshore waters, data deficient (IUCN), subject to special protection (Mex.).

Striped dolphin (E), delfín listado (S), *Stenella coeruleoalba,* offshore waters, lower-risk conservation-dependent (IUCN), subject to special protection (Mex.).

Long-beaked common dolphin (E), delfín común de rostro largo (S), cochito (L), *Delphinus capensis,* offshore waters, least concern (IUCN), subject to special protection (Mex.).

False killer whale (E), orca falsa (S), bufeo prieto (L), *Pseudorca crassidens,* offshore waters, least concern (IUCN), subject to special protection (Mex.).

Killer whale, orca (E), orca, ballena asesina (S), bufeo, bufeo mascarillo (L), *Orcinus orca,* inshore and offshore waters, lower-risk conservation-dependent (IUCN), subject to special protection (Mex.).

Short-finned pilot whale (E), ballena piloto, calderón de aletas cortas (S), bufeo prieto (L), *Globicephala macrorhynchus,* offshore waters, lower-risk conservation-dependent (IUCN), subject to special protection (Mex.).

Family Ziphiidae

Baird's beaked whale (E), ballena picuda de Baird, zifio de Baird (S), *Berardius bairdii,* offshore waters, lower-risk-conservation-dependent (IUCN), subject to special protection (Mex.).

Cuvier's beaked whale (E), ballena picuda de Cuvier, zifio de Cuvier (S), *Ziphius cavirostris,* offshore waters, data deficient (IUCN), subject to special protection (Mex.).

Family Physeteridae

Pygmy sperm whale (E), cachalote pigmeo (S), *Kogia breviceps,* offshore waters, least concern (IUCN), subject to special protection (Mex.).

Dwarf sperm whale (E), cachalote enano (S), *Kogia sima,* offshore waters, least concern (IUCN), subject to special protection (Mex.).

Sperm whale (E), cachalote (S), *Physeter macrocephalus,* offshore waters, vulnerable (IUCN), subject to special protection (Mex.).

Suborder Mysticeti (baleen whales)

Family Eschrichtidae

Gray whale (E), ballena gris (S), cachalote (L), *Eschrichtius robustus,* inshore waters, lower-risk conservation-dependent (IUCN), subject to special protection (Mex.).

Family Balaenopteridae

Humpback whale (E), ballena jorobada (S), *Megaptera novaeangliae,* inshore and offshore waters, vulnerable (IUCN), subject to special protection (Mex.).

Common minke whale (E), ballena minke común (S), ballenato (L), *Balaenoptera acutorostrata,* inshore and offshore waters, near threatened (IUCN), subject to special protection (Mex.).

Bryde's whale (E), ballena Bryde (S), *Balaenoptera edeni,* inshore and offshore waters, data deficient (IUCN), subject to special protection (Mex.).

Sei whale (E), ballena sei (S), *Balaenoptera borealis,* offshore waters, endangered (IUCN), subject to special protection (Mex.).

Fin whale (E), ballena de aleta, rorcual común (S), *Balaenoptera physalus,* inshore and offshore waters, endangered (IUCN), subject to special protection (Mex.).

Blue whale (E), ballena azul (S), *Balaenoptera musculus,* offshore waters, endangered (IUCN), subject to special protection (Mex.).

Order Carnivora

Family Otariidae (sea lions and fur seals)

California sea lion (E), lobo marino de California (S), lobo (L), *Zalophus californianus,* inshore waters, subject to special protection (Mex.).

Family Mustelidae (martens, otters, etc.)

Northern river otter (E), nutria de río norteña (S), *Lontra canadensis,* freshwater, extirpated (Mex.).

Order Rodentia

Family Muridae

Muskrat (E), rata almizclera (S), *Ondatra zibethicus,* freshwater, theatened (Mex.).

Family Castoridae

Beaver (E), castor (S), *Castor canadensis,* freshwater, endangered (Mex.).

Twenty-Nine

Invertebrate Biodiversity in the Northern Gulf of California

Richard C. Brusca

Discovering the Northern Gulf and Its Invertebrate Biodiversity

Earliest Discoveries

Probably for over 10,000 years Native Americans have traveled through the Sonoran Desert to visit or live on the shores of the northern Gulf of California (Sea of Cortez). Here they found a stunning diversity and abundance of shellfish and finfish, easily harvested during the twice-daily low tides, and sea turtles that could be captured in shallow waters. They also found fresh water in the Colorado, Sonoyta, and Concepción rivers and in the *pozos* (springs) that welled up through fissures in the soil, fed by groundwater originating as far away as modern-day Arizona (Figure 29.1). Along the coast of the Gran Desierto many of these pozos are surrounded by vast beds of crystallized salt, a commodity that further enhanced the value of visits to the upper gulf (Figure 29.2). Ancient shell middens at least two thousand to six thousand years old, and perhaps much older (Brusca 2004a; Ritter 1985, 1998), inform us that native people exploited coastal shellfish (molluscs and crustaceans) in the northern Gulf of California for food and jewelry, some of which was traded far and wide, reaching northern Arizona and California.[1] To these early collectors of the upper gulf's rich invertebrate biodiversity, the region must have been important beyond imagination. There was reliable freshwater and a predictable and inexhaustible food supply (and shells and salt for trading). And because of the high seasonal turnover of coastal life in the subtropical upper gulf, the seafood varied through the year (Brusca 1980b, 2002a, 2002b, 2004b; Brusca et al. 2001; Chapters 14 and 15, this volume).

Belief in a sea passage through North America, connecting the Atlantic and Pacific oceans (the fabled "Strait of Anian"), brought the first Europeans, led by Hernan Cortés, to the Gulf of California. Cortés made five explorations of the Pacific coast between 1527 and 1539, including a failed attempt to colonize Baja California in 1535 (Bowen 2000; Brusca 2004b). Cortés never saw the northernmost gulf, but assigned to his deputy, Francisco de Ulloa, the sailing expedition that reached the upper gulf in 1539. Thus Ulloa and his men were probably the first Europeans to set eyes on this region. Ulloa was also the first European to prove that the Baja California peninsula was not an island. Father Eusebio Francisco Kino (1645–1711) saw the upper gulf when he visited El Pinacate on his first trip in 1698, and again in 1706. On his second expedition to the Pinacate, from the top of the Sierra Pinacate, Kino saw the mouth of the Colorado River, and Baja was once again declared a peninsula, not an island. Just before his death, Kino drew a fairly accurate map of the Sea of Cortez, clearly indicating the Baja peninsula.[2]

Before the twentieth century, few European or U.S. explorers or naturalists spent time in the Gulf of California. One hundred and thirty-seven years after Kino's death Frederick Reigen, a Belgian citizen who lived in Mazatlán from 1848 to 1850, took up collecting molluscs in the gulf. Reigen amassed one of the largest collections of seashells of all time—14 tons of shells! The Reigen collection found its way to Liverpool, and from there it was partly dispersed. Much of it was published on by Philip Carpenter (Carpenter 1857; see Hendrickx & Toledano-Granados 1994).

Another early collector of marine invertebrates in the region was John Xantus (de Vesey), a controversial Hungarian hired by the U.S. Coast Survey as a tidal observer stationed at the tip of Baja California (April 1859 to mid-1861). Most of Xantus's collections are now at the Smithsonian Institution (e.g., Jordan & Gilbert 1882). From 1888 to 1894 the French chemical engineer Leon Diguet studied natural history while employed by the famous Boleo Mine in Santa Rosalía. Diguet made many collections, most of which ended up at the Museum d'Histoire Naturelle in Paris. Ten marine invertebrates from the gulf have been named in Diguet's honor (six crustaceans, three molluscs, and one polychaete). Many conspicuous land plants also bear his name, such as the giant barrel cactus of Isla Catalina *(Ferocactus diguetii)* and the bushy ocotillo of the southern gulf coast *(Fouquieria diguetii)*.

During the following three decades a few ichthyologists made collections of fishes at some readily accessible sites, notably Guaymas and Mazatlán, which were reported on mainly by David Starr Jordan and colleagues (e.g., Evermann & Jenkins 1891; Jordan 1895; see Chapter 26, this volume). Oceanographic data were recorded and some marine invertebrates were trawled by the U.S. Fish Commission steamer *Albatross* in the late 1880s and early 1890s, and again in 1911, and most of these specimens are also at the Smithsonian Institution (e.g., Gilbert 1892). Aside from a brief foray in 1889, the *Albatross* did not work in the northern gulf. However, from the *Albatross* expedition came the original description of a legendary fish, the totoaba *(Totoaba macdonaldi)*, described by C. H. Gilbert, the ship's chief naturalist. The chief invertebrate biologist on the *Albatross* expeditions was the malacologist Paul Bartsch.

Daniel Trembly MacDougal (first director of Tucson's Desert Botanical Laboratory, later of the Carnegie Institution of Washington, D.C.) and his party explored the Pinacate area in 1907, but only one member of the group reached the gulf coast, the "official geographer" Godfrey Sykes (Hornaday 1908). In 1909–10 Carl Lumholtz explored the Pinacate and the entire upper gulf coast of Sonora (Lumholtz 1912). Lumholtz not only spent time on the shores of the upper gulf; he visited the coastal pozos and salinas, writing, "Judging from the extraordinary springs I encountered on the shore of the salt deposit, Salina Grande, near the coast, there must be a large sheet of fresh water underneath most of that western coastal desert" (Lumholtz 1912:ix). The "sheet of water" Lumholtz referred to is a shallow water table that probably originates in what is now Pinacate Biosphere Reserve and Cabeza Prieta National Wildlife Refuge (Brusca 2004b; Ezcurra et al. 1988). Lumholtz eventually arrived on the beach at what is today El

Figure 29.1. Coastal pozos in the Gran Desierto, south of El Golfo de Santa Clara. (Photo by R. C. Brusca)

Figure 29.2. Coastal salinas in the Gran Desierto, south of El Golfo de Santa Clara. (Photo by R. C. Brusca)

Golfo de Santa Clara, finding it littered with giant branches and trunks of cottonwood and willow from the once great Colorado River riparian forests. Lumholtz's travel log notes that "the upper part of the Gulf abounds in fish" (1912:258), which he and his party, on occasion, took in great numbers by tossing sticks of dynamite into the water from the shoreline!

Lumholtz spent considerable time with the O'odham people and talked with leaders of their salt expeditions, a trek that used to take them from as far away as the Gila River in Arizona to the pozos, salinas, and shores of the upper gulf. Lumholtz met "El Doctor Pancho," one of the Sand Papago (Areneños), who was then living in the O'odham settlement at Quitobaquito. The Hia C'ed O'odham (Sand Papagos) are said to have been a hardy lot, living a nomadic lifestyle in the Gran Desierto. However, the fact that they had a reliable supply of fresh water from the scattered but known pozos and tinajas, as well as access to the rich biodiversity of the upper gulf (including an abundance of shellfish), suggests to me that their life might not have been so difficult. In addition to fish and crustaceans, they are known to have taken sea lions and at least some sea turtles along the coast, as well as foraging on small game and insects and on many coastal and inland plants of the region (Chapter 15, this volume), including the fabled "sandfood," or "root of the sands" (*Pholisma sonorae).*

Another of the earliest oceanographic expeditions to the Sea of Cortez was William Beebe's 1936 expedition under the auspices of the New York Zoological Society—the "*Zaca*," or "Templeton Crocker," expedition (*Zaca* was the ship, Templeton Crocker its owner). The *Zaca* expedition was, as typical of Beebe's expeditions, weak on science and heavy on Beebe's own brand of machismo. Beebe's narrative of the journey (*The Zaca Venture*, 1938) makes better reading for testosterone-laden sport fishermen than for those with a sincere interest in natural history. Nevertheless, the expedition produced a large number of invertebrate specimens that provided a source of taxonomic research material for several subsequent decades (by such great invertebrate zoologists as Jocelyn Crane, Steve Glassell, Fenner Chace, Aaron Treadwell, Elisabeth Deichmann, Fred Ziesenhenne, and Martin Burkenroad). Unlike most expeditions, Beebe made the decision to concentrate collecting efforts at just three localities: Bahía Inez, Cabo San Lucas and the adjoining Arena and Gorda banks, and Clarion Island. Thus the *Zaca* never reached the northern gulf. However, Beebe culled some cogent information about the Sea of Cortez in 1936. His interviews with Mexican fishermen indicated that upward of 20 million tuna and skipjack were being caught annually along the coast of northwestern Mexico, with no apparent diminution in their numbers over the years—testimony to the highly productive waters of the region. Beebe also encountered Japanese fishing boats in the gulf, probably some of the first Japanese penetrations into this sea, establishing a pattern that has persisted, episodically, ever since. Although Beebe was well aware of the beauty and diversity of life in the Sea of Cortez, he had an exploitative view of nature, and some of the most descriptive passages in his account describe shooting sharks and manta rays (with rifles and pistols) from the deck of the *Zaca* for "sport." The last line of his book reads, "At my next formal dinner, when the guests are absorbed in the delicacy of their green turtle soup, I will rejoice in the memory of the brooding turtles of Clarion Island."

John Steinbeck and Ed Ricketts Visit the Sea of Cortez

In 1940, four years after the *Zaca* expedition, modern marine biology in the Gulf of California had its birth with the remarkable pioneering expedition of Ed Ricketts and John Steinbeck aboard the *Western Flyer,* a purse seiner out of Monterey, California (Figure 29.3).[3] The biology (and philosophy) of that amazing voyage is chronicled in their 1941 book, *Sea of Cortez: A Leisurely Journal of Travel and Research* (also see Astro & Hayashi 1971; Beegel et al. 1997; Brusca 1993, 2004a; Hedgpeth 1978). It was this expedition that first documented, in an organized way, the seashore life of the gulf. Using funds from Steinbeck's successful writing career, the two men chartered the *Western Flyer* for a six-week expedition to the gulf.[4] The Ricketts-Steinbeck expedition just reached the upper gulf, its northernmost collecting sites being the Midriff Islands (Puerto Refugio, Isla Ángel de la Guarda, and Red Bluff Point, Isla Tiburón). Their landmark voyage had a profound impact, bringing the Sea of Cortez into the consciousness of both the American public and the scientific world. The expedition visited 24 sites and collected over 400 species of marine invertebrates (Table 29.1), 93 of which have found their way to the Smithsonian Institution and are today available in the collections of the National Museum of Natural History. For more than thirty years, their expedition report was the only place anyone could turn for a synoptic view of invertebrate life in the Sea of Cortez (Brusca 2004a).[5]

Since Steinbeck and Ricketts

Expeditions from Scripps Institution of Oceanography, the University of California at Los Angeles, Stanford University, the California Academy of Sciences (actually beginning as early as 1888), and the University of Southern California's Allan Hancock Foundation in the 1940s and 1950s ushered in an era of organized research effort in the gulf. The expeditions and taxonomic publications of the once glorious but now defunct Allan Hancock

Foundation stand above all others in documenting the biodiversity of the gulf (Brusca 1980a). Between 1942 and 1983 the Hancock Foundation publications on Pacific marine life produced an astonishing 22,469 pages of primarily invertebrate taxonomic text that stands as a watershed in marine biodiversity research (University of Southern California 1985).

Between 1958 and 1972 the Belvedere Scientific Fund of San Francisco also sponsored several investigations and publications on the Sea of Cortez. It was through the personal interest of Kenneth Bechtel (sponsor of the fund) and Lewis Wayne Walker (of the Arizona-Sonora Desert Museum) that the Isla Rasa Reserve was established in the gulf, and the Desert Museum continued funding the reserve (and Bernardo Villa's research) well into the 1970s. From 1960 to 1969 the San Diego Museum of Natural History operated the Vermilion Sea Field Station at Bahía de los Angeles, and in 1962 it undertook a major expedition in the gulf (funded, again, by the Belvedere Fund).

Despite all this previous work, when I arrived in the gulf in 1969, the only synoptic compilation of information on marine invertebrates was the Ricketts and Steinbeck volume (1941), and there

Figure 29.3. Ed Ricketts, circa 1938. (Photo courtesy Joel Hedgpeth)

were no keys to assist one in identifying the invertebrates of the region. I realized this after I began a two-year residence in Mexico working for the University of Arizona's Marine Biology Program. I quickly discovered that if I wanted students to know what they were looking at in gulf tidepools, I would have to write the keys myself. Thus it came to be that, in 1969, I gave up my lifestyle of chasing waves and Grateful Dead concerts in California and moved to Puerto Peñasco to live on the shores of the Sea of Cortez for two years. There I designed and built a small marine lab for the University of Arizona, made countless

TABLE 29.1. *Numbers of (named) invertebrate species/subspecies treated in the three synoptic compilations of Gulf of California invertebrates.*

PHYLUM	STEINBECK & RICKETTS 1941	BRUSCA 1980B	HENDRICKX ET AL. 2005
Porifera	14	22	86
Cnidaria	10	54	253
Ctenophora	0	2	4
Platyhelminthes (Turbellaria)	5	14	22
Nemertea	1	10	17
Sipuncula	6	9	11
Echiura	2	3	4
Annelida	48	137	718
Arthropoda: Crustacea	143	279	1,051
Arthropoda: Pycnogonida	0	9	15
Mollusca	113	262	2,193
Ectoprocta (Bryozoa)	14	110	169
Brachiopoda		3	5
Echinodermata	61	60	262
Chaetognatha	0	0	20
Hemichordata (enteropneusts)	2	3	3
Chordata, Urochordata (tunicates, appendicularians)	10	10	37
Chordata, Cephalochordata (lancelets)	1	0	1
TOTAL	430	987	4,871

field trips throughout the gulf, and shipped specimens of invertebrates to specialists around the world. Out of that emerged the first edition of *Common Intertidal Invertebrates of the Gulf of California* (Brusca 1973; 2d ed. 1980b). Much of those two years was spent exploring the shores of the gulf with J. Laurens Barnard, a good friend and colleague who was on loan from the Smithsonian Institution to the University of Arizona (Brusca 1993).

Since 1973, knowledge of the upper gulf and its biodiversity has increased substantially through research by scientists at the University of Arizona, Centro de Investigación Científica y de Educación Superior de Ensenada (CICESE), Universidad de Sonora (UNISON), Instituto Tecnológico y de Estudios Superiores de Monterrey (ITESM)–Campus Guaymas, Universidad Autónoma de Baja California Sur (UABCS), Centro de Investigaciones Biológicas del Noroeste (CIBNOR), Centro de Investigación en Alimentación y Desarrollo (CIAD), and the Facultad de Ciencias of the Universidad Nacional Autónoma de México (UNAM) as well as its Instituto de Ciencias del Mar y Limnología (ICML-UNAM) Mazatlán field station and Instituto de Biología (IB-UNAM). This body of work has resulted in many publications describing the flora, fauna, and environment of the region, much of it catalogued in Brusca et al. 2001, Brusca et al. 2004, Hendrickx et al. 2005, Schwartzlose et al. 1992, and Thomson et al. 2000. Today 5,970 species of animals (macrofauna) are known from the Sea of Cortez, 2,261 of them from the northern gulf. However, compared with knowledge about much of the world's coastline, exploration and documentation of the biodiversity of the Sea of Cortez, especially the northern gulf, is still in its early stages, and I estimate that more than half the gulf's invertebrate fauna remains undescribed, while the natural history of almost all species is still unknown.

The Northern Gulf of California: A Unique Oceanographic Region

The Sea of Cortez exists today because 5–10 million years ago a 1,800-km-long continental sliver attached itself to the eastern margin of the great Pacific Plate and peeled away from mainland Mexico to begin a slow journey northwestward. Today the southern half of this sliver comprises the Baja California peninsula, one of the most remote peninsulas in the world and exceeded in length only by the Malay and Kamchatka peninsulas. The gulf itself covers 258,593 km^2 (99,843 mi^2), has a coastline of 3,260 km, and spans over nine degrees of latitude, traversing the Tropic of Cancer in its southern reaches. The northern gulf, that area from (and including) the Midriff Islands to the delta of the Colorado River, covers about 60,000 km^2 (24,000 mi^2) of ocean surface and is a unique body of water in many ways. It lies in the driest part of the Sonoran Desert. The estimated mean evaporation rate for the northern gulf is 1.1 m/yr, while precipitation is only 4–8 cm/yr (Alvarez-Borrego 1983; Lavín et al. 1998). Because evaporation far exceeds freshwater input, the entire gulf is regarded as an "evaporation basin," and most of this deficit occurs in its northern part (Bray & Robles 1991). Lavín et al. (1998) regard the entire upper gulf (that region with a depth less than 100 m) as a "negative estuary" (a semi-enclosed embayment with little or no freshwater input and with decreasing salinities from the uppermost region toward the mouth). Salinities also have increased here in response to a dramatic reduction of freshwater (river) discharge over the past 70 years, the increase of saline agricultural drainage, and probably global warming (enhancing evaporation). Summer surface salinities reach 40 ppt in the various coastal *esteros* and inner areas of the Colorado River delta, whereas over deeper water in the northern gulf surface salinities are 35.3 to 37.2 ppt. The year-round salinity pump at the head of the gulf generates a pressure gradient that results in gravity currents that drive dense saline surface waters to the bottom—to depths of 30 m in the summer and 200 m in the winter (i.e., into the Wagner Basin, and out of the northern gulf by way of the Salsipuedes Basin and Channel). In the central and southern gulf, salinities are closer to typical oceanic waters (35.0 to 35.8 ppt) (on the oceanography of the central and southern gulf, see Alvarez-Borrego 1983; Bray & Robles 1991; Brusca 2004a).

The northern gulf is further distinguished by having some of the greatest tides in the world. The annual tidal range (amplitude) at San Felipe and Puerto Peñasco is about 7 m, and on the Colorado River delta at the head of the gulf it is nearly 10 m. Much of the low delta islands of Montague and Pelícano (= Isla Gore) is under water during high spring tides. In fact, most of the northern gulf itself (north of the Midriff Islands) is shallow, largely less than 100 m in depth, with the deepest areas reaching about 230 m in the small Wagner Basin and in the larger Dolphin Basin above Isla Ángel de la Guarda and extending into the deeper Salsipuedes Basin that separates the island from the peninsula (Alvarez-Borrego 1983; Brusca 2004a; Maluf 1983). Circulation in the upper Gulf of California has not been well studied, but limited evidence suggests it is primarily clockwise in the winter (October to April) and primarily counterclockwise in the summer (May to September).

Another important distinguishing feature of the northern gulf is its strong biseasonal hydrographic regime. Coastal seawater temperatures throughout the northern gulf are low in the winter, dropping to 8–12°C (equivalent to southern California's warm-temperate shores), but rising to 30°C or more in the summer (Brusca 1980b, 2004a; Brusca et al. 2005). Because of its cold winter water temperatures and associated temperate fauna, the northern gulf should be classified as a subtropical region, like the Gulf of Mexico coastal region in the United States.

Still another distinguishing feature of the northern gulf is its exceptionally high rates of primary productivity, comparable to those of the Bay of Bengal or the great upwelling areas off the west coasts of Baja California, Peru, and North Africa (Alvarez-Borrego 1983). High nutrient levels, shallow waters, abundant solar radiation, and strong tidal mixing combine to make the northern gulf one of the most productive marine regions in the world. Primary productivity in the northern gulf is two to three times greater than that of the open Atlantic or open Pacific at similar latitudes (Zeitzschel 1969). Nutrient levels and standing crops of both phytoplankton and zooplankton in the northern gulf are high year round and show little seasonality, although in recent years important sources of nutrients have probably been agricultural drainage and the release of ancient nutrients trapped in Colorado River sediments that are now eroding. Bray and Robles (1991) suggest that influx of cold deep water into the southern gulf brings nutrients into the Sea of Cortez and elevates productivity where it upwells, but it is not clear to what extent these nutrients reach the northern gulf. Large fishes, sea turtles, and at least twelve species of whales and dolphins, including the critically endangered vaquita porpoise, exploit the productive northern gulf waters. Suspension-feeding clams, crustaceans, and polychaete worms also occur in great abundance throughout this region.

Older estimates of oxygen concentrations in the northern gulf tended to be high, decreasing from about saturation values at the surface (5–6 ml/l) to about 1 ml/l at 300–500 m depth in the Dolphin Basin. However, almost no contemporary data exist for bottom conditions in this region. Although strong tidal currents in the northern gulf keep the water column well mixed, it seems almost certain that bottom areas chronically disturbed by the numerous shrimp trawlers (and accumulation of their discarded bycatch on the sea floor) experience hypoxia (less than 0.2 ml/l dissolved oxygen) or even anoxia (Pérez-Mellado & Findley 1985).

Invertebrate Biodiversity

Origins and Maintenance of Faunal Diversity

The flora and fauna that inhabit the northern gulf arrived there from diverse sources: tropical Central America, the Caribbean Sea (before the final closure of the Panama seaway about 3.2 million years ago), the temperate shores of California (during the 15–20 glacial periods that pushed cold waters south and into the gulf over the past two million years), and even across the vast stretch of the Pacific Ocean from the tropical West Pacific (Briggs 1974; Brusca 1980b, 2002b, 2004a; Brusca & Wallerstein 1979; Castro-Aguirre & Torres-Orozco 1993; Duque-Caro 1990; Rosenblatt 1967; Rosenblatt & Waples 1986; Thomson et al. 1979, 2000; Walker 1960). These various biotic sources have enriched the diversity of the gulf over the past three million years. During past glacial events, temperate "California species" were able to extend their ranges into the gulf as cold isotherms pushed below the tip of the Baja California peninsula, trapping these species in the northern gulf during subsequent warm interglacials. Most of these cold-water species disappeared from the gulf during the warm periods, such as seen today, but some were adaptable enough to survive as isolated populations in the uppermost gulf. Many of these now comprise the California–northern gulf disjunct temperate fauna, which includes species such as the long-fingered shrimp *(Betaeus longidactylus)* and the purse crab *(Randallia ornata)*. Still others appear to have undergone speciation events and probably now represent California/gulf sister-species pairs, although phylogenetic studies on invertebrates have not yet investigated this probability.

Invertebrate community composition at any given locality in the upper gulf comprises a reasonably predictable mix of species, combined with a much larger suite of "unpredictable" species, the unpredictability being driven by complex networks of interacting physical and biological factors. However, *relative* species diversity is predictable and largely a function of habitat and substrate type. Benthic (bottom-dwelling) invertebrate species diversity (i.e., species richness) is highest on rocky bottoms, relatively stable shores, and intertidal or shallow bottoms composed of softer sedimentary rocks such as sandstones or eroded volcanic tuffs and rhyolites. Benthic invertebrate diversity is lowest on beaches composed of smooth hard rocks such as granites and basalts and on unstable beaches of sand or cobble, the latter perhaps having the lowest (benthic) diversity of any coastal habitat. Areas that have a variety of substrate types harbor more species than do more homogeneous ones. *Esteros* (moderately hypersaline coastal lagoons, or "negative estuaries") are notably diverse areas, and these habitats provide important nursery and feeding grounds for the young of many coastal fish and shellfish species, including the majority of Mexico's commercial finfish and shrimp species (Glenn et al. 2005). There have been no comprehensive surveys of any *esteros,* or other wetlands, in the Gulf of California. Analysis of the Macrofauna Golfo Project database produced a list of 212 species of invertebrates from the mangrove lagoons of Baja California Sur (Whitmore et al. 2005). The islands of the gulf also harbor an extraordinarily high species diversity, and these areas serve as important refugia for species that have been extirpated on the mainland coast. In addition, these islands commonly harbor a fauna more typical of coastal communities hundreds of kilometers to the south.

Species diversity and composition are heavily influenced by seasonal oceanographic conditions in the northern gulf, where marked seasonal changes occur. The climate of the surrounding Sonoran Desert has a strong bearing on this shallow region, and as noted earlier, it experiences extreme seasonal variations in seawater temperatures. As a result, the northern gulf is essentially a warm-temperate marine environment during the winter but a tropical marine environment during the summer. The distinct seasonal species turnover in invertebrates and algae is striking, as tropical species disappear during the cold winters (e.g., *Gnathophyllum panamense, Ocypode occidentalis, Pentaceraster cumingi, Nidorellia armata*) and temperate species vanish during the warm summers (e.g., *Pachygrapsus crassipes, Aplysia californica, Betaeus longidactylus*). The central gulf shows far less seasonality in water temperatures, and the southern gulf shows almost no seasonality.

An Extraordinary Diversity

The accumulation of species diversity since the Sea of Cortez opened has produced one of the most biologically rich marine regions on earth. The benthic habitats and the pelagic waters of the gulf are famous for supporting high numbers of species and large population sizes among all marine taxa: invertebrates, fishes, marine mammals, sea turtles, and marine birds. At least 40 percent of Mexico's fisheries production comes from the gulf and 15 percent from the northern gulf alone (Brusca & Bryner 2004; Brusca et al. 2001; Cudney-Bueno 2000). In the northern gulf, remarkably high biodiversity occurs on the very limited intertidal beachrock ("coquina") formations that occur at just four sites: Puerto Peñasco and Punta Borrascosa in Sonora, and San Felipe and Coloradito in Baja California. These small, rare, eroding beachrock habitats harbor disproportionately high species diversity, giving them high priority for protection (Figure 29.4). High diversity is also found at Isla San Jorge and Rocas Consag, both of which serve as refugia and recruitment sources for the mainland shores. And exceptionally high biodiversity, including rich pelagic diversity (and abundance) driven by year-round upwelling, distinguishes the Midriff Islands. The offshore benthic region of the northern gulf formerly maintained a high species diversity and biomass. However, in subtidal areas that are susceptible to heavy bottom trawling (i.e., shallower than 100 m) much diversity has been lost over the past 50 years due to excessive disturbance (see below). Nevertheless, we have almost no empirical data on community composition and food web structure for the northern gulf's offshore benthic or pelagic habitats. One of the most pressing research needs is to achieve an understanding of benthic community structure in this region and a sense of how profound the effects of bottom trawling have actually been on this system.

Marine macrofaunal diversity in the Gulf of California is exceptionally high, comprising 5,965 named species: 4,852 invertebrates and 1,113 vertebrates (891 fishes; 222 nonfish vertebrates) (Brusca 2004a; Brusca et al. 2005; Hendrickx et al. 2005).[6] Owing to the presence of many undescribed invertebrate species, including many members of the planktonic and offshore communities, this total is estimated to be about half the actual animal diversity of the gulf (Table 29.2). Overall faunal diversity decreases gradually from the south to the north. In the northern gulf, in addition to the four beachrock formations noted above, Puerto Refugio (at the northern end of Isla Ángel de la Guarda) and the isolated Rocas Consag have long been recognized as "biodiversity hot spots."

Forty-seven percent of the gulf's macroinvertebrate species occur in the northern gulf (2,261 species), and 1,045 (18 percent of the gulf species) are known from the Reserva de la Biosfera Alto Golfo de California y Delta del Río Colorado (Table 29.3). In the northern gulf, molluscs (1,000 species), arthropods (509 species), and annelids (polychaetes) (287 species) are the most diverse phyla. Within the Mollusca the gastropods and bivalves stand out with 656 and 285 species, respectively. Among the Arthropoda the brachyuran crabs and amphipods are most diverse with 167 and 126 species, respectively. Of the invertebrate species known from the northern gulf, 128 (5.7 percent) are unique to this area (endemic).[7]

Examination of Table 29.3 reveals further interesting patterns of invertebrate biodiversity in the northern gulf. Even though no coral reefs occur in this region (indeed, the only true coral reef in the gulf is at Bahía Pulmo, near La Paz; Brusca & Thomson 1977), 17 species of corals occur in the northern gulf, making the coral diversity richer than that of sea anemones (12 species). Notably rich diversity also occurs among the gastropods (657 species), bivalves (285 species), polychaetes (285 species), true (brachyuran) crabs (167 species), echinoderms (138 species), ectoprocts (119 species), gammaridean amphipods (85 species), hydroids (60 species), isopods (41 species), tidepool (caridean) shrimps (40 species), chitons (38 species), hyperiidean amphipods (31 species), and porcelain crabs (29 species). Also notable is a single species

of marine earthworm (Annelida: Oligochaeta), *Bacescuella parvithecata,* which occurs rarely in the northern (and central) gulf. The 5 species of sea fans reported from the region are only a small percentage of the actual gorgonian diversity, and I have recorded at least 10 undescribed species from the northern gulf. Similarly, only a single species of jellyfish has been reported from the northern gulf, although I have recorded at least a half-dozen others in these waters. And the 9 species of tunicates reported from the northern gulf probably represent only 10 percent of the actual diversity of this region.

Among the 128 species of invertebrates endemic to the northern gulf are two elegant and giant aphroditid polychaetes *(Aphrodita mexicana, A. sonorae),* sometimes called "sea mice," both of which are now greatly reduced in numbers and threatened because of excessive bottom (shrimp) trawling (Figure 29.5). The beautiful coral *Astrangia sanfelipensis,* today known only from the San Felipe and Coloradito "coquina reefs," is also threatened by habitat destruction at those two upper gulf sites. In addition, seven species of pea crabs (Pinnotheridae) are endemic to the northern Gulf, as are two goneplacid crabs *(Glyptoplax consagae, Speocarcinus spinicarpus),* the cone snail *Conus angulatus* (previously considered a synonym of *C. regularis),* the scallop *Leptopecten palmeri,* the carpet anemone *Palythoa ignota,* the aggressive samurai hydroid *Samuraia tabularosa* (so far known only from a single site, Punta Pelícano, near Puerto Peñasco), and 11 species of sea slugs (Gastropoda: Nudibranchiata) including the beautiful giant black slug *Aplysia vaccaria.* Among the caridean shrimps are three species of the uncommon genus *Ambidexter* that are endemic to the northern gulf (in

Figure 29.4. Beachrock ("coquina") littoral habitat, one of the rarest habitats in the Sea of Cortez. Only four such coastal formations are known from the gulf, two in Sonora (Puerto Penasco, Punta Borrascosa) and two in Baja California (San Felipe, Coloradito). The Puerto Peñasco and San Felipe sites have been largely destroyed biologically, though they remain recoverable. (Photo by R. C. Brusca)

TABLE 29.2. *Known and predicted species diversity in major invertebrate groups in the entire Gulf of California.*

PHYLUM	NO. OF SPECIES RECORDED FROM GULF	NO. OF SPECIES PREDICTED TO OCCUR IN GULF
Porifera	**86**	**860**
Cnidaria	**253**	**526**
Hydrozoa	146	292
Anthozoa	102	204
Scyphozoa	5	30
Ctenophora	**4**	**20**
Platyhelminthes	**22**	**110**
Nemertea	**17**	**30**
Sipuncula	**11**	**22**
Echiura	**4**	**7**
Annelida	**717**	**820**
Oligochaeta	1	3
Polychaeta	715	816
Pogonophora	1	1
Arthropoda	**1,044**	**1,522**
Pycnogonida	15	45
Cirripedia	45	47
Copepoda	?	25
Ostracoda	?	25
Stomatopoda	28	33
Mysida	3	10
Amphipoda	232	464
Isopoda	81	110
Tanaidacea	2	20
Cumacea	8	20
Euphausiacea	14	20
Dendrobranchiata	26	42
Stenopodidea	2	4
Caridea	130	145
Astacidea	1	1
Thalassinidea	19	24
Palinura	8	9
Anomura	129	192
Brachyura	301	336
Mollusca	**2,196**	**2,590**
Monoplacophora	1	2
Polyplacophora	57	62
Gastropoda	1,532	1,630
Bivalvia	566	848
Scaphopoda	20	25
Cephalopoda	20	23
Bryozoa (Ectoprocta)	**169**	**338**
Brachiopoda	**5**	**7**
Echinodermata	**263**	**300**
Chaetognatha	**20**	**25**
Hemichordata	**2**	**5**
Chordata	**39**	**292**
Ascidia	17	250
Appendicularia	21	40
Cephalochordata	1	2
TOTAL	**4,852**	**7,474**

Note: Phylum names and species numbers are in boldface.

---

fact, these are the only members of this genus in the entire Sea of Cortez). A group of intertidal isopods also occurs as endemics in the northern gulf (e.g., *Synidotea francesae, Erichsonella cortezi, Colidotea findleyi, Mesanthura nubifera, Colanthura bruscai, Probopyrus pandalicola,* and *Schizobopyrina striata*). One of the many unsolved mysteries in the Sea of Cortez is the appearance of the Atlantic barnacle, *Balanus subalbidus,* in Laguna Salada during flood years. This barnacle has not been reported from anywhere in the Gulf of California or Pacific Ocean, yet in years when floodwaters from the Colorado delta and upper gulf invade the laguna, live *B. subalbidus* are found attached to the branches of dead (flooded) terrestrial trees and shrubs (Van Syoc 1992). Dead specimens are easily collected when the lakebed is dry.

Destruction of Biodiversity in the Northern Gulf

Before the 1960s, pressure on the northern gulf's environment was minimal, and anyone visiting the region would have witnessed a seemingly endless bounty of sea life, probably not differing substantially from the diversity encountered by indigenous people over past millennia. A walk in the intertidal zone during low tide revealed dozens of species of large-bodied invertebrates, especially echinoderms and molluscs. Common under most large rocks and boulders were large seastars (*Oreaster occidentalis, Nidorellia armata, Astropecten armatus, Pharia pyramidata, Linckia columbiae, Heliaster kubiniji, Astrometis sertulifera, Luidia columbia* and *L. phragma*), spectacular huge brittlestars (*Ophioderma teres* and *O. panamense, Ophiocoma aethiops* and *O. alexandri*), and large urchins (*Eucidaris thouarsii, Centrostephanus coronatus, Arbacia incisa, Lytechinus pictus, Echinometra vanbrunti*). Also common were large cucumbers, such as *Brandtothuria arenicola* and *B. impatiens, Fossothuria rigida,* and *Isostichopus fuscus.* Large molluscs that were equally common included many spectacular murexes, cones, olives, and cowries (e.g., *Haustellum elenesis, Hexaplex nigritus, Hexaplex princeps, Phyllonotus erythrostomus,* many species of *Conus*). There are no longer any sites on the northern gulf mainland where these large invertebrates exist in abundance in the intertidal zone. In fact, these spectacular large-bodied invertebrates have become rare or extirpated altogether from most of the mainland northern gulf's intertidal regions. The chocolate sea cucumber *(Isostichopus fuscus)* is now reduced to so few sites, because of overfishing, that it is federally listed in Mexico as a threatened species. Before the 1970s, sorting through a shrimp trawl was also an extraordinary experience, and in those days the bycatch provided a living library of the animal kingdom—a veritable textbook of invertebrate zoology. This too is no longer the case.

Beginning in the 1950s three factors began to have synergistic, negative impacts on the biodiversity of the northern (indeed, the entire) gulf. First was the establishment of Mexico's national fisheries program, which led to an overgrowth of fishing efforts and subsidized the exploitation of marine resources. Second was the realization that tourism held the potential to generate enormous income, which led to national and regional policies and practices that set a path toward wholesale destruction of coastal resources. And third has been the disruption of all the rivers that once flowed into the gulf, including all the once-perennial rivers of Sonora—among them the mighty Colorado River. Exacerbating these issues has been an explosive and unchecked population growth in the southwestern United States and northwestern Mexico.[8] These environmental challenges are reviewed in some detail in Brusca 2004a, Brusca & Bryner 2004, Brusca et al. 2001, and Brusca et al. 2005.

Fisheries

Today every fishery in the gulf is probably overfished (Brusca 2004a; Brusca et al. 2001; Brusca et al. 2005; Greenberg and Vélez-Ibáñez 1993; Musick et al. 2000; Sala et al. 2002; Sala et al. in press). In the northern gulf large serranids (groupers, *cabrillas*) and sciaenids (corvinas, *chanos*), some of which are endemic or nearly endemic to the gulf, are especially at risk. These species are sensitive to overharvesting because of their late maturity and formation of localized spawning aggregations. In addition, most sciaenids in the northern gulf require estuarine habitats once provided by the Colorado River delta for spawning and nursery grounds. The American Fisheries Society lists the gulf, especially its northern part, as one of five geographic "hot spots" in North America, where numerous fish species are at risk. Commercially valuable invertebrate species are facing the same fates, as population sizes of black murex

Figure 29.5. *Shrimp boats in Puerto Peñasco, Sonora. (Photo by R. C. Brusca)*

(Muricanthus nigritus), pink-mouth murex *(Hexaplex erythrostomus)*, chocolate sea cucumber *(Parastichopus fuscus)*, shrimps *(Penaeus* spp.), octopuses, and others have plummeted over the past decade.[9]

Industrial shrimp fishing exacts a harsh toll on the northern gulf's benthic environment (Figure 29.6). The ocean bottom in this region is estimated to be dragged by shrimp nets as frequently as four times per year (Brusca et al. 2001; García-Caudillo 1999; Pérez-Mellado & Findley 1985). Shrimp nets are indiscriminant killers, raking the sea floor like vacuum cleaners, trapping and killing everything in their path (Dayton et al. 2002; Engel & Kvitek 1998; Watling & Norse 1998). This high rate of bottom trawling has seriously damaged these fragile benthic habitats, and the nets capture an average of 10–30 kg bycatch per kilogram shrimp (depending on the time of year) in the northern gulf (Brusca 2004a; Brusca et al. 2005). The number of commercial shrimp trawlers in the gulf grew from 700 in 1970 to a high of 1,700 in 1989 and then decreased to 1,200 in 1999 (J. M. García-Caudillo & S. Carroll, personal communication 2001), despite warnings as early as the 1970s of a possible crisis resulting from overexploitation (e.g., Snyder-Conn & Brusca 1977). As of 2002, hundreds of shrimp boats were still

Figure 29.6. *Shrimp fishing bycatch being sent to a rendering plant for conversion into fertilizer and stock feed. (Photo by R. C. Brusca)*

working *within* the Alto Golfo Biosphere Reserve, and perhaps 1,000 small-scale fishers were using gill nets in the northern gulf. Catch per unit of effort has been declining for decades, but government subsidies continue to artificially sustain the overcapacity of the industrial fishing fleet. Without government subsidies the current level of commercial trawling would not be economically feasible. In fact, the economics of commercial shrimping shifted so much at the beginning of the twenty-first century that the number of bottom trawlers working out of the three main fishing ports in the northern gulf fell to just 130 boats (115 in Puerto Peñasco, 15 in San Felipe, and none in El Golfo de Santa Clara). Limited scientific and anecdotal information suggests that sweeping changes in benthic/demersal community structure have taken place over the past 50 years as a result of this disturbance, including an accelerating decrease in the diversity and biomass of the bycatch, possibly heralding a regional benthic/demersal ecosystem collapse (Brusca 2004a; Brusca et al. 2005). In the late 1960s, sorting through the bycatch of a shrimp trawl produced hundreds of species of invertebrates, in most known phyla. Today these same bottom trawl nets (in the northern gulf) capture primarily scavenging species (e.g., portunid crabs, skates, rays), and the diver-

sity of the past is gone. The destruction of the benthic ecosystem has disrupted the food web of the entire northern gulf, probably altering the pool of available prey for the endangered vaquita. Gill nets kill vaquita directly, at an estimated rate of 30 to 80 annually (D'Agrosa et al. 1995; Vidal 1995; see Navarro, this volume).

Commercial fishing boats using gill nets and long-lines overexploit offshore waters, and small boat *(panga)* fishers often take shrimp and finfish from estuaries and other coastal lagoons before they have reached reproductive maturity. Narco-traffickers using the Sea of Cortez to transport drugs from Mexico to the United States present a new and growing threat to biodiversity. They abandon or trade their *pangas* (skiffs) in the upper gulf in such high numbers that the local fishers have greatly increased their boat presence, and impact, in the region.

Tourism

In areas of heavy and increasing tourism in the northern gulf, such as Puerto Peñasco and San Felipe, littoral biodiversity is but a shadow of what it was just 20 years ago. Part of the tourism-driven loss comes from the hand collecting of animals by visitors and the trampling underfoot of fragile habitats exposed at low tide. But also important is the collection of large molluscs and echinoderms by residents for sale to tourists as curios or to local restaurants, where they are served in seafood cocktails (e.g., large bivalve and gastropod molluscs, octopuses). Today in the northern gulf these large-bodied species are found almost exclusively on island refugia or highly inaccessible stretches of the mainland coast, although many still occur in reduced numbers subtidally.

Increasing losses of coastal habitats due to encroaching housing and resort developments, poorly designed marinas, and aquaculture installations lacking environmental controls are threatening the rich *estero* habitats of the northern gulf that serve as critical spawning and nursery grounds for shrimp and other invertebrate and fish species (Glenn et al. 2005).[10] Loss of these wetlands also reduces important stopover sites for migratory birds. Mexico's planned "Nautical Ladder" (Escalera Náutica) proposes 23 marinas around both sides of the Baja California peninsula and south on the mainland all the way to Teacapán (Sinaloa). The marinas themselves will cause permanent loss of wetlands, and building the infrastructure required to connect them with roads and services will certainly also be damaging.

Rivers That Are No More

All the rivers that once reached the Gulf of California have been drastically altered or destroyed by overdraft and diversion, and none of the rivers of Sonora now reach the sea (i.e., Ríos Colorado, Sonoyta, Concepción, Magdalena-Asunción, San Ignacio, Sonora, Yaqui, Mayo, and Fuerte). Historically, the Colorado River carried an estimated 16.7 million acre-feet (maf) of water to the delta annually (Carriquiry & Sánchez 1999). In the nineteenth century, especially from 1850 to 1880, riverboats steamed from the Sea of Cortez up the lower Colorado/Gila River system into Arizona. Until completion of Hoover (Boulder) Dam in 1935, creating Lake Mead, freshwater from the Colorado River flowed into the northern gulf throughout the year, with great seasonal floods resulting from spring snow-pack melt in the Rocky Mountains. By the time Glen Canyon Dam was completed in 1962, input of Colorado River water to the delta and northern gulf had ceased. For 20 years after completion of Glen Canyon Dam, as Lake Powell filled, virtually no water from the river reached the sea. In 1968, flow readings at the southernmost measuring station on the river were discontinued, since there was nothing left to measure. Today 20 dams (58 if the Colorado River's tributaries are included) and thousands of kilometers of canals, levees, and dikes have converted the Colorado River into a highly controlled plumbing system in which every drop of water is carefully counted, managed, and fought over. The original water allocations, set in the 1920s, were based on Colorado River data from an unusually wet period, and the allocation assumed an average river flow of about 22 maf/year. Thus 17.5 maf/year of legal entitlements exist to the river's water. But the river's average flow over the last 500 years has actually been about 14 maf/year: there are more legal claims to the water than are possible to meet (Brusca & Bryner 2004; Brusca et al. 2001)! It is no wonder that today little water reaches the delta. In addition, most of the delta's wetlands have been converted into farmland. What was once 2 million acres of wetlands has been reduced to about 150,000 acres. Owing to the greatly reduced freshwater flow, the powerful tides of this region now overwhelm the

river channel. During spring tides, seawater creates an estuarine basin for 50–60 km upriver, averaging 2–8 km wide and 16 km wide at the mouth. This marine intrusion has killed most of the freshwater flora and fauna that used to live along the lowermost river corridor (e.g., Felger 2000).

Native ecosystems on the delta of the Colorado River have been under siege for many decades from urban and agricultural expansion and upstream water management decisions in the United States and Mexico. Many good reviews of this subject exist (e.g., Brusca & Bryner 2004; Brusca et al. 2001; Brusca et al. 2005; Glenn et al. 1996, 1999). Although the lower delta is part of the Alto Golfo Biosphere Reserve (Diario Oficial 1993; Morales-Abril 1994), the ecological future of the region remains critically threatened. The small remaining wetlands on the delta provide important habitat for shorebirds and migratory waterfowl and support the largest remaining populations of at least two endangered species, the desert pupfish and Yuma clapper rail (Glenn et al. 2005; see Hinojosa-Huerta et al., this volume). The indigenous Cucapá people still use the riparian zone of the delta for subsistence (see Williams, this volume). Since Lake Powell filled in 1981, occasional flood flows have again been reaching the delta, which has led to regeneration of some of the river floodplain. In addition, two important anthropogenic wetlands now exist on the delta, the 4,400-ha Ciénega de Santa Clara and the 15,000–20,000-ha Río Hardy wetland, which together contain most of the nonmarine aquatic habitat on the delta (Figure 29.7). In their natural state they were supported by the Colorado River flow, but they are now sustained by the disposal of brackish agricultural drainage water into the lower delta (plus occasional flood flows). There is no guarantee that these wetlands will continue to receive the secondary runoff water that now sustains them. And given climate predictions and possible reduction in Colorado River flows over coming decades, the threat to these critical habitats will only increase. As of 2004, there existed no published studies of the water quality or invertebrate fauna of these wetlands.

Before construction of Hoover Dam the annual sediment discharge from the Colorado River into the gulf was enormous, estimated to have ranged from 45 to 455 million metric tons/year. Accumulated river sediments on the delta are

Figure 29.7. The Ciénega de Santa Clara, on the Colorado delta. (Photo by R. C. Brusca)

thousands of feet thick. The entire northern gulf is considered the Colorado River Sedimentary Province. The name of the river itself, *Colorado,* is Spanish for a red or ruddy color. However, the reduction of freshwater input and sediment discharge since 1935 has modified the hydrography of the Colorado River delta/northern gulf system, initiating a regime of deltaic erosion. New deltaic deposition no longer takes place, and the entire delta is now exposed to the hydrodynamic forces of tides, currents, and storms, promoting resuspension, erosion of ancient river sediments, and the gradual export of sediments to the west and eventually out of the northern gulf. These changes are altering the littoral wetlands and biological equilibrium of the region. They are also destroying habitat for an estimated 340 species of marine invertebrates that inhabit the sand/mud benthic ecosystem of the delta region.

It is likely that the reduction of freshwater input into the northern gulf, in combination with other anthropogenic factors, has driven some species to (or nearly to) extinction. However, we have so few historical or baseline data for marine organisms of this region that extinctions (or local extirpations) would go unnoticed for commercially unimportant or otherwise little-known species. There has never been a comprehensive dedicated survey of the marine fauna of the northern gulf and Colorado River delta ecosystem.

The delta clam, *Mulinia coloradoensis,* was once one of the most abundant animals of the uppermost gulf. Windrows of its shells line the beaches of the delta and western shores of the northern gulf. This species was thought to be ex-

tinct until its recent rediscovery in small numbers near the mouth of the river (Kowalewski et al. 2000; Rodriguez et al. 2001). It has been speculated that the near demise of this clam is the result of decreased benthic productivity resulting from upstream diversion of the Colorado River's flow. However, there is no indication that nutrient levels (and hence productivity) have decreased significantly in the northern gulf, and nutrients that have been lost by depletion of riverine input may have been regained in the form of agricultural runoff and delta erosion (releasing ancient trapped nutrients). Hence the near extinction of this species may be linked to another, as yet unknown, factor related to reduction of freshwater input to the delta.

Freshwater input from the Colorado River is also important to the life history of commercial shrimps of the region. Commercial shrimp catches have been falling since the 1960s, owing to a combination of overfishing and loss of habitat for young. It has been estimated that an influx of just 250,000 acre-feet/year of Colorado River water would double shrimp production in the northern gulf (Galindo-Bect et al. 2000). The young of these shrimp use the shallow wetlands and *esteros* of the region, including the tidelands of the delta, as a nursery, migrating into these areas before their offshore planktonic larval phase. When the shrimp reach a juvenile or subadult stage, they migrate offshore once again. In combination with historical overfishing and capture of juveniles in shrimp nets, reduction of brackish estuarine habitat has likely driven the giant northern gulf endemic totoaba to near extinction as well. Continued absence of freshwater input could also seriously affect the endemic Palmer's saltgrass *(Distichlis palmeri),* which appears to need periodic freshwater flooding to germinate (Felger 2000). In addition, aquatic birds rely heavily on the gulf's coastal lagoons and wetlands, all of which are on the great western flyway (Glenn et al. 2005; see also Hinojosa-Huerte et al., this volume).

Rescuing Biodiversity

Since the mid-1980s a growing conservation movement has emerged in northwestern Mexico, led by such organizations as the Arizona-Sonora Desert Museum, the Sonoran Institute, CoBi (Comunidad y Biodiversidad), Conservation International, Pro*esteros,* Pronatura, Sierra Madre, World Wildlife Fund, CEDO (Centro Intercultural de Estudios de Desiertos y Océanos), and many smaller grass-roots organizations often associated with local communities and *ejidos*. These organizations are beginning to have a powerful influence on conservation in the northern gulf. Their participation was critical to the setting aside of the Reserva de la Biosfera Alto Golfo de California y Delta del Río Colorado; to the establishment of conservation priorities for the gulf and its islands; to the development, with artisanal fishers and indigenous people (e.g., Seris, Cucapás), of sustainable fisheries; and to the improvement, with state and federal governmental agencies, of protection of the marine and coastal environment. Over the past decade, as a result of the efforts of these groups, fisheries laws are tightening up, gillnetting is on the verge of becoming illegal, bottom trawling is becoming better regulated (soon to be banned, we hope), and high-visibility species such as totoaba and vaquita are attracting the attention of conservationists all over North America. Much of this conservation work is described in Brusca 2004a, Brusca & Bryner 2004, Brusca et al. 2001, and Brusca et al. 2005. New laws prohibit the use of gillnets with mesh sizes greater than six inches and the "destruction of the marine floor" (e.g., shrimp trawling) in all protected areas in the gulf, including the Alto Golfo Biosphere Reserve. These laws could go a long way toward reducing the incidental take of vaquita and sea turtles and protecting the sea floor, but it will be up to the federal government (PROFEPA, the enforcement arm of SEMARNAT) to enforce these laws (and fishers are protesting them). As for the Colorado River delta, however, it is unlikely that its ecological and water issues will be resolved until the debate reaches the U.S. and Mexican State Departments and executive offices. There are also many fundamental questions that remain unanswered regarding the upper gulf's ecosystems: What is the nature of the benthic/water column food web of the upper gulf, and how does energy flow through the system? How has this system been impacted by bottom (shrimp) trawlers over the past few decades? Where do the migratory waterfowl enter this food web and what do they feed on? Where are the key commercial and sport fish spawning and nursery grounds? How are commercial species such as shrimp affected by freshwater input (e.g., from the Colorado River)? How important are annual freshwater pulses from the Colorado River to the marine ecosystems?

Despite the considerable damage that has already been inflicted on northern gulf environments, and the many lingering threats, there is cause for optimism. If the conservation movement in the Sea of Cortez continues with its present momentum, new areas will be protected and all protections will be better enforced. Most urgent is to ban *all* bottom trawling in the northern gulf, to protect the four "coquina reefs" in the upper gulf, to improve enforcement of existing laws in protected areas, to increase public education, and to better understand the marine ecosystems of the upper gulf. Fortunately, one still can find island and coastal refugia, areas not easily accessible by road or large fishing boats, which serve as important shelters for species extirpated elsewhere in the northern gulf. Current discussions on a biodiversity action and sustainable management plan for the gulf, spearheaded by regional nongovernmental conservation organizations as well as several government agencies, are focusing on protection of the island refugia, but mainland coastal habitats need to be on their agenda as well.

Acknowledgments

Thanks to Wendy Moore, Tom Van Devender, Richard Felger, Bill Broyles, and Larry Marshall for critiquing this chapter. Thanks to Joel Hedgpeth and Dave Montgomery, who, 40 years ago, introduced me to the complex world of John Steinbeck and Ed Ricketts, and to Lindsey Haskin, who recently rekindled this lifelong interest.

Notes

1. Ancient peoples who exploited the northern gulf's rich coastal biodiversity left behind huge piles of shells, or middens. Some of these shell middens are more than a mile across, and some have depths of more than one meter. Estero Morua, near the town of Puerto Peñasco, is encircled by ten discrete shell middens covering about 50 percent of its shoreline, each containing tens of thousands of mollusc shells (comprising more than 30 species) and pottery from at least four distinct cultures. I have radiocarbon-dated (^{14}C) two food shells *(Cardita affinis* and *Hexaplex erythrostomus)* from two fire sites (ash layers) at Estero Morua at calibrated ages (Stuiver & Reimer 1993) of 1969 YrBP (radiocarbon age 2010 ± 55) and 2024 YrBP (radiocarbon age 2075 ± 40) (radiocarbon dates determined by the University of

Arizona/National Science Foundation Accelerator Mass Spectrometry Laboratory). The only remains from crab dining at Estero Morua are the large claws of the blue crab *(Callinectes bellicosus);* no remains of carapaces or walking legs have been found. In the past, Estero Morua received freshwater from the Sonoyta River, which used to empty into the Gulf of California via the eastern arm of the *estero* (at least during flood years), although this river has not reached the gulf with any regularity at least since the turn of the last century (a good turn-of-the-century map of the river can be found in Hornaday 1908). See Gifford 1946 and Foster 1975 for additional information on the middens of this *estero.*

2. The earliest map to show Baja California as a peninsula might have been the "chart series" of Battista Agnese (1538-48), probably capitalizing on Ulloa's 1539 discovery. It was also correctly depicted on Sebastian Cabot's 1544 map and of course the superlative maps of Mercator (1569) and Ortelius (1570: *Theatrum Orbis Terrarum).* However, the majority of the European maps produced before the early seventeenth century still depicted Baja California as an island, and it was the work of Padre Eusebio Kino that finally laid the issue to rest for European cartography.

3. Members of the expedition were Ed Ricketts, John Steinbeck, Carol Henning (the first of Steinbeck's three wives), Hall ("Tex") Travis (engineer), Anthony Berry (captain), Sparky Enea (Berry's brother-in-law), and Tiny Colleto (crewman). Spencer Tracy was supposed to go on the trip but got tied up on a motion picture. Steinbeck paid Berry $2,500 for the six-week charter of the *Western Flyer.* At least five species of invertebrates from the Sea of Cortez have been named in honor of Ed Ricketts: *Mysidium rickettsi* (a mysid), *Longiprostatum rickettsi* (a flatworm), *Isometridium rickettsi* (a sea anemone), *Palythoa rickettsi* (a zoanthid), *Adesia rickettsi* (a sea slug).

4. The northern gulf region extends from the marine-influenced Colorado River delta south to (and including) the Midriff Islands (las Islas del Cinturón), the largest being Islas Tiburón and Ángel de la Guarda, and to Bahía San Francisquito (Baja California) and Bahía Kino (Sonora). Within the northern gulf is the Reserva de la Biosfera Alto Golfo de California y Delta del Río Colorado, extending from the delta to a line running from Punta Pelícano (= Roca del Toro; the southern margin of Bahía Cholla and the larger Bahía Adair), Sonora, across the gulf to Punta El Machorro (= Punta San Felipe), at San Felipe.

5. Steinbeck grew up in the Salinas Valley of California and early on developed a strong fascination with the sea. In his youth he took a few classes at Stanford University, including a summer marine biology course at Hopkins Marine Station, in Monterey, California, in 1923. In part, it was his love of the sea that drove him to move to Pacific Grove (near Monterey) in 1929, the year his first book was published *(Cup of Gold),* thus setting the stage for his inevitable meeting with maverick marine biologist Ed Ricketts. *Cannery Row* (1945) was written after Steinbeck had moved to New York, shaken by the death of his long-time friend. The book was an exercise in grieving Ed's death and finding peace after the turbulent years Steinbeck had endured. "Doc," in *Cannery Row,* is Steinbeck's idealized image of Ed and the vehicle through which Steinbeck expresses his own (and presumably Ed's) philosophy of life, which celebrates the wisdom of experiencing life without preconception and the joy of savoring each moment as it occurs. As a natural followup to *Cannery Row,* Steinbeck went full circle with *East of Eden* (1952), also written in New York, which celebrates his own life growing up in the Salinas Valley, his family, and the fundamental human power to choose between good and evil, expressed also through the observation of tidepools in *The Log from the Sea of Cortez.*

6. Marine macrofauna is defined here as those animals 0.5 mm or larger in size, or easily visible to the naked eye (this excludes copepods and ostracods but includes all other nonmicroscopic animal species).

7. Overall invertebrate endemicity in the gulf is 16% (767 species). At the phylum level, the highest endemism occurs in Brachiopoda (80%), Ctenophora (50%), Platyhelminthes (41%), Echiura (25%), and Mollusca (21%). At lower taxonomic levels, highest endemism occurs among Anthozoa (34%), Polyplacophora (26%), Gastropoda (26%), and Cumacea (25%). However, these figures should be viewed with caution because many taxa are very poorly studied in the gulf and the tropical eastern Pacific in general (e.g., Brachiopoda, Cnidaria, Ctenophora, Platyhelminthes, Echiura, Cumacea, Tanaidacea, micromolluscs, Urochordata, Hemichordata).

8. Approximately 23 million people live in the lower Colorado River basin today, a population that is largely dependent on water from the Colorado River. By 2020 it is estimated that more than 38 million people will be living in this region. The population of the Sonoran Desert itself now exceeds 7 million and has experienced a sevenfold increase in the past 50 years, with a doubling between 1970 and 1990. This is the fastest growth and most massive land conversion in North America's history. Hermosillo (the capital of Sonora) grew by 116% during this period. There are no signs that this growth is tapering off.

9. Even marine algae are overharvested in northwestern Mexico (mainly along the Baja peninsula), a region that provides 10% of the world production of agarophytes. The most important commercial species is the red alga *Gelidium robustum,* harvested since 1945 but never regulated.

10. Much of the coastline of Sinaloa and southern Sonora has been carved up into aquaculture farms. Most of these are shrimp farms, and 95% (64 million pounds in 2000) of this farm-raised shrimp makes its way to the United States. About 90% of the world's aquaculture facilities are in developing nations, and they are essentially "slash-and-burn" in their approach: bulldozers tear out mangrove forests and other coastal habitats and replace them with fish or shrimp ponds. In concept, these coastal ponds are cheap and easy to construct; a pipe at one end of the pond pulls clean ocean water in, and a pipe at the other end spits water out, laden with shrimp (or fish) wastes, excess food, antibiotics, disease organisms, and parasites. Therein lies the next insult—not only is coastal habitat destroyed by the bulldozers, but the coastal waters themselves are polluted with the outfall. Inland, closed, nonpolluting systems are possible, but they are more expensive to build and operate.

TABLE 29.3. *Annotated list of macroinvertebrates known from the northern Gulf of California.*

TAXA	AUTHOR(S)	DISTRIBUTION IN GULF	HABITAT	DEPTH	RANGE (M)
PHYLUM PORIFERA (SPONGES)					
CALCAREA					
Leucosolenia cf. *irregularis*	Jenkin, 1908	NGC;CGC;SGC;BR	BEN;LIT	0	8
Leucetta losangelensis	(de Laubenfels, 1930)	NGC;CGC;SGC;BR;SWB	BEN;LIT	0	111
DEMOSPONGIAE					
?*Laxosuberites* ?*rugosus*	(Schmidt, 1868)	NGC	BEN;LIT	0	?
Acarnus erithacus	de Laubenfels, 1927	NGC;CGC;BR	BEN;LIT	0	700
Adocia ambrosia	Dickinson, 1945	NGC;CGC;BR	BEN;LIT	1	24
Adocia gellindra	(de Laubenfels, 1932)	NGC	BEN;LIT	0	?
Antho lithophenix	(de Laubenfels, 1927)	NGC;CGC	BEN;LIT	0	90
Anthosigmella varians	(Duchassaing & Michelotti, 1864)	NGC;CGC;BR	BEN;LIT	0	24
Aplysina sp. A		NGC;CGC;BR	BEN;LIT	0	100
Aulospongus cerebella	(Dickinson, 1945)	NGC	BEN	?	90
Axinella mexicana	de Laubenfels, 1935	NGC	BEN	6	140
Biemna rhadia	de Laubenfels, 1930	NGC	BEN	18	700
Chondrilla nucula	Schmidt, 1862	NGC;CGC;SGC;BR	BEN;LIT	0	5
Clathria pennata californiana	de Laubenfels, 1932	NGC;BR	BEN;LIT	0	51
Cliona celata	Grant, 1826	NGC;CGC;SGC;BR;SWB	BEN;LIT;PAR	0	120
Cliona cf. *chilensis*	Thiele, 1905	NGC;CGC;BR;SWB	BEN;LIT	0	46
Dragmacidon opisclera	de Laubenfels, 1935	NGC;CGC;SGC	BEN	10	137
Dysidea fragilis	(Montagu, 1814)	NGC;BR	BEN;LIT	0	640
Endectyon byle	(de Laubenfels, 1930)	NGC;CGC;SGC;SWB	BEN	3	396
Erylus discastera	Dickinson, 1945	NGC	BEN	?	140
Geodia japonica	(Sollas, 1888)	NGC	BEN	?	90
Geodia mesotriaena	Lendenfeld, 1910	NGC;CGC;SGC;SWB	BEN;LIT	0	369
Halichondria cf. *panicea*	(Pallas, 1766)	NGC;CGC;SGC	BEN;LIT	0	127
Haliclona cf. *bogarthi*	Hechtel, 1965	NGC;CGC;SGC;BR	BEN;LIT	0	16
Halisarca cf. *sacra*	de Laubenfels, 1930	NGC;CGC;SGC	BEN;LIT	0	?
Hymeniacidon adreissiformis	Dickinson, 1945	NGC;BR	BEN;LIT	0	?
Hymeniacidon rubiginosa	Thiele, 1905	NGC	BEN;LIT	0	?
Hymeniacidon sinapium	de Laubenfels, 1930	NGC;CGC;BR	BEN;LIT	0	103

TABLE 29.3 (CONT'D). *Annotated list of macroinvertebrates known from the northern Gulf of California.*

Species	Author				
Iophon pattersoni	(Bowerbank, 1866)	NGC;CGC;SGC	BEN	15	970
Laxosuberites cf. rugosus	(Schmidt, 1868)	NGC;CGC;SGC	BEN;LIT	0	?
Microtylostylifer partida	Dickinson, 1945	NGC	BEN	?	140
Mycale cf. fascifibula	(Topsent, 1904)	NGC	BEN	?	90
Myrmekioderma sp.		NGC;BR	BEN	?	?
Myxichela microtoxa	Dickinson, 1945	NGC	BEN	40	?
Pachastrella dilifera	de Laubenfels, 1934	NGC	BEN;LIT	0	250
Pachastrella multipora	Dickinson, 1945	NGC	BEN	20	90
Sphinctrella osculanigera	Dickinson, 1945	NGC	BEN	13	?
Sphinctrella tricornis	(Wilson, 1904)	NGC;CGC;SGC	BEN	364	693
Spirastrella coccinea	(Duchassaing & Michelotti, 1864)	NGC;CGC;3R	BEN;LIT	0	?
Stelletta clarella	de Laubenfels, 1930	NGC;CGC;3R	BEN;LIT	0	396
Stylissa ? oxeon	(Dickinson, 1945)	NGC	BEN	100	140
Suberites mineri	(de Laubenfels, 1935)	NGC;CGC	BEN;LIT	0	40
Terpios zeteki	(de Laubenfels, 1936)	NGC;CGC;SGC;BR	BEN;LIT	0	5
Tethya aurantia	(Pallas, 1766)	NGC;CGC;SGC;BR	BEN;LIT	0	440
Tetilla arb	(de Laubenfels, 1930)	NGC;CGC;SWB	BEN;LIT	0	150
Tetilla mutabilis	de Laubenfels, 1930	NGC	BEN	?	?

PHYLUM CNIDARIA (SEA ANEMONES, CORALS AND THEIR KIN)

ANTHOZOA
CERIANTIPATHARIA (CERIANTIPAHARIANS)

Botruanthus benedeni	(Torrey & Kleeberger, 1909)	NGC;CGC	BEN	?	?
Ceriantbus vas	McMurrich, 1893	NGC	BEN	?	80
Isarachnanthus panamensis	Carlgreen, 1924	NGC;BR	BEN;LIT	0	3
Pachycerianthus aestuari	(Torrey & Kleeberger, 1909)	NGC	BEN;LIT	0	1

HEXACORALLIA
ACTINIARIA (SEA ANEMONES)

Aiptasia californica	Carlgren, 1952	NGC;CGC;SGC;BR	BEN;LIT	0	3
Anthopleura dowii	Verrill, 1869	NGC;CGC;SGC;BR	BEN;LIT	0	3
Anthothoe carcinophila	(Verrill, 1869)	NGC;BR	COM	1	?
Anthothoe panamensis	(Verrill, 1869)	NGC	LIT	0	?
Bunodactis mexicana	Carlgren, 1951	NGC;CGC;BR	BEN;LIT;LACS	0	2
Bunodosoma californica	Carlgren, 1951	NGC;CGC;SGC;BR	BEN;LIT	0	3

TABLE 29.3 (CONT'D). *Annotated list of macroinvertebrates known from the northern Gulf of California.*

Calamactis praelongus	Carlgren,1951	NGC;CGC;BR	BEN;LIT;LACS	?	?
Calliactis polypus	(Verrill, 1869)	NGC;CGC;SGC;SWB	BEN;LIT;LACS	0	3
Diadumene leucolena	(Verrill, 1866)	NGC;BR	BEN;LIT;LACS	0	2
Phyllactis bradleyi	(Verrill, 1869)	NGC;CGC;BR	BEN;LIT	0	63
Phyllactis concinnata	(Drayton, in Dana, 1846)	NGC;CGC;SGC;BR	BEN;LIT	?	?
Telmatactis panamensis	Verrill, 1869	NGC;CGC;SGC	BEN;LIT	0	?
SCLERACTINIA (CORALS)					
Astrangia californica	Durham & Barnard,1952	NGC	BEN	29	?
Astrangia concepcionensis	Durham,1947	NGC;CGC;SGC;BR	BEN	0	73
Astrangia coronadoensis	Durham,1947	NGC;CGC	BEN	4	29
Astrangia cortezi	Durham & Barnard,1952	NGC	BEN	18	46
Astrangia haimei	Verrill, 1866	NGC;CGC;SGC;BR;SWB	BEN	0	83
Astrangia pedersenii	Verrill, 1870	NGC;CGC;SGC	BEN	7	11
Astrangia sanfelipensis	Durham & Barnard,1952	NGC;BR	BEN	4	?
Balanophyllia cedrosensis	Durham,1947	NGC;CGC	BEN	63	119
Dendrophyllia oldroydae	Oldroyd, 1924	NGC;CGC	BEN	121	576
Desmophyllum dianthus	(Esper, 1794)	NGC	BEN	32	2,460
Endopachys grayi	Milne Edwards & Haime, 1848	NGC;CGC;SGC	BEN	36	400
Heterocyathus aequicostatus	Milne Edwards & Haime, 1848	NGC;CGC;SGC	BEN	18	109
Paracyathus stearnsii	Verrill, 1869	NGC;CGC	BEN	0	360
Phyllangia consagensis	(Durham & Barnard,1952)	NGC;CGC;SGC;SWB	BEN	18	82
Porites panamensis	(Verrill, 1866)	NGC;CGC;SGC;BR;SWB	BEN;LIT	0	10
Porites sverdrupi	Durham,1947	NGC;CGC;SGC	BEN	15	28
Sphenotrochus hancocki	Durham & Barnard,1952	NGC	BEN	18	270
ZOANTHIDEA (ZOANTHIDS)					
Epizoanthus gabrieli	Carlgren,1951	NGC;CGC;SGC;BR	BEN;LIT	0	1
Palythoa ignota	Carlgren,1951	NGC;BR	BEN;LIT	0	1
Palythoa rickettsi	Carlgren,1951	NGC	BEN;LIT	0	5
OCTOCORALLIA					
GORGONACEA (SEA FANS AND SEA WHIPS)					
Eugorgia ampla	Verrill, 1864	NGC;BR	BEN	?	?
Eugorgia aurantiaca	(Verrill, 1864)	NGC;CGC;SGC;SWB	BEN;LIT	0	20

TABLE 29.3 (CONT'D). *Annotated list of macroinvertebrates known from the northern Gulf of California.*

Species	Authority	Distribution	Habitat		
Lophogorgia alba	Duchassaing & Michelotti, 1864	NGC;CGC;BR	BEN	?	?
Muricea californica	Aurivillius, 1931	NGC;CGC;SGC;BR;SWB	BEN	?	?
Pacifigorgia adamsi	(Verrill, 1868)	NGC;CGC;SGC;BR;SWB	BEN	?	?
PENNATULACEA (SEA PENS AND SEA PANSIES)					
Cavernularia darwinii	Hickson, 1921	NGC;CGC;SGC	BEN	100	150
Ptilosarcus ?undulatus	(Verrill, 1865)	NGC;CGC;SGC;SWB	BEN	5	?
Stylatula elongata	(Gabb, 1863)	NGC;CGC;SGC;BR	BEN;LACS	0	70
HYDROZOA (HYDOZOANS)					
CAPITATA					
Samuraia tabularasa	Mangin, 1991	NGC;CGC	BEN;LIT	0	1
CHONDROPHORA					
Porpita pacifica	Lesson, 1826	NGC;CGC;SGC;BR	PEL;FLOT;NEUS	N/A	
Physalia utriculis	La Martiniere, 1787	GCN;CGC;GCS;BR;SWB	PEL;FLOT;NEUS	N/A	
FILIFERA					
Janaria mirabilis	Stechow, 1921	NGC;CGC;SGC;BR;SWB	BEN;COM	7	137
HYDROIDA					
Aglaophenia diegensis	Torrey, 1902	NGC;CGC;SGC	BEN;LIT	0	243
Aglaophenia inconspicua	Torrey, 1902	NGC;BR	BEN;LIT	0	72
Aglaophenia pinguis	Fraser, 1938	NGC;CGC;SGC;SWB	BEN;LIT	0	135
Aglaophenia triplex	Fraser, 1948	NGC	BEN	21	24
Antennularia compacta	Fraser, 1938	NGC	BEN	18	37
Antennularia irregularis	Fraser, 1938	NGC	BEN	18	99
Antennularia reversa	Fraser, 1938	NGC	BEN	92	137
Antennularia septata	Fraser, 1938	NGC	BEN	37	137
Antennularia tetraseriata	Fraser, 1938	NGC;SWB	BEN	11	137
Bimeria gracilis	Clarke, 1876	NGC;CGC;SGC	BEN	0	450
Campanularia castellata	Fraser, 1925	NGC	BEN	37	128
Campanularia denticulata	Clarke, 1876	NGC;CGC;SGC;BR	BEN;LIT	0	66
Campanularia emarginata	Fraser, 1938	NGC;CGC;SWB	BEN	8	137
Campanularia bincksi	Alder, 1857	NGC	BEN	0	165
Campanulina forskalea	(Peron & LeSueur, 1809)	NGC;CGC	BEN	90	135
Clytia acutidentata	Fraser, 1938	NGC	BEN	0	82
Clytia edwardsi	(Nutting, 1901)	NGC;CGC	BEN	0	136

TABLE 29.3 (CONT'D). *Annotated list of macroinvertebrates known from the northern Gulf of California.*

Species	Authority					
Clytia irregularis	Fraser, 1938	NGC	BEN	9	136	
Clytia kincaidi	(Nutting, 1899)	NGC	BEN;LIT	0	126	
Clytia universitatis	Torrey, 1904	NGC;CGC;SGC;BR	BEN;LIT;COM	0	183	
Eudendrium carneum	Clarke, 1882	NGC;CGC;SGC	BEN	3	108	
Eudendrium eximium	Allman, 1877	NGC;BR	BEN;LIT	0	18	
Eudendrium ramosum	(Linnaeus, 1767)	NGC;CGC;SGC;BR	BEN;LIT	0	171	
Eudendrium tenellum	Allman, 1877	NGC;CGC;SWB	BEN;LIT	0	270	
Eudendrium tenue	A. Agassiz, 1865	NGC	BEN;LIT	0	137	
Filellum serpens	(Hassall, 1852)	NGC;CGC;SWB	BEN	18	165	
Gonothyraea gracilis	(Sars, 1851)	NGC;CGC;SGC;BR	BEN;LIT	0	165	
Halecium beani	(Johnston, 1838)	NGC;CGC;SGC	BEN	2	139	
Halecium bermudense	Congdon, 1907	NGC	BEN	82	108	
Halecium fasciculatum	Fraser, 1938	NGC	BEN	64	108	
Halecium flexum	Fraser, 1948	NGC	BEN	2	82	
Halecium gracile	Verrill, 1874	NGC	BEN	0	81	
Halecium insolens	Fraser, 1938	NGC;CGC;SGC	BEN	0	45	
Halecium nanum	Alder, 1859	NGC	BEN	14	82	
Halecium parvulum	Bale, 1888	NGC	BEN	18	64	
Halecium regulare	Fraser, 1938	NGC	BEN	18	81	
Halecium tenellum	Hincks, 1861	NGC;CGC	BEN	82	270	
Halecium tenue	Fraser, 1938	NGC	BEN	18	144	
Hebella calcarata	(A. Agassiz, 1865)	NGC;CGC;SGC	BEN	22	82	
Lafoea dumosa	(Fleming, 1828)	NGC	BEN	82	92	
Lafoea intermedia	Fraser, 1938	NGC;CGC;SGC	BEN	18	274	
Lictorella adhaerens	Fraser, 1938	NGC;CGC;SGC	BEN	81	216	
Lictorella convallaria	(Allman, 1877)	NGC;CGC;SWB	BEN	5	220	
Lictorella reflexa	Fraser, 1948	NGC;CGC;SWB	BEN	84	220	
Lictorella rigida	Fraser, 1948	NGC	BEN	84	139	
Lovenella producta	(Sars, 1873)	NGC;CGC	BEN	81	137	
Monostaechas quadridens	(McCrady, 1859)	NGC;CGC;SGC	BEN	5	92	
Obelia hyalina	Clarke, 1879	NGC;CGC;SGC;BR;SWB	BEN;LIT	0	63	
Obelia plicata	Hincks, 1869	NGC;CGC	BEN;LIT	0	270	
Pasya quadridentata	(Ellis & Solander, 1786)	NGC	BEN	9	46	

TABLE 29.3 (CONT'D). *Annotated list of macroinvertebrates known from the northern Gulf of California.*

Plumularia corrugata	Nutting, 1900	NGC;CGC	BEN	15	144
Plumularia lagenifera	Allman, 1885	NGC;CGC;SGC;SWB	BEN;LIT	0	270
Plumularia megalema	Fraser, 1948	NGC;CGC;SGC	BEN	33	137
Plumularia reversa	Fraser, 1948	NGC	BEN	36	117
Plumularia sinuosa	Fraser, 1938	NGC;CGC;SGC	EPIF;LIT	0	54
Scandia expansa	Fraser, 1938	NGC	BEN	11	165
Sertularella exilis	Fraser, 1938	NGC	BEN	81	139
Sertularella pedrensis	Torrey, 1904	NGC;CGC;SGC;SWB	BEN	9	165
Sertularella similis	Fraser, 1948	NGC	BEN	81	128
Sertularia cornicina	(McCrady, 1859)	NGC	BEN	108	82
Sertularia desmoides	Torrey, 1902	NGC	BEN;LIT	0	45
Sertularia exigua	Allman, 1877	NGC;CGC;SGC;SWB	BEN;LIT	0	102
Sertularia stabilis	Fraser, 1948	NGC	BEN	21	24
Sertularia stookeyi	Nutting, 1904	NGC;SWB	BEN;LIT	0	128
SIPHONOPHORA					
Dromalia alexandri	Bigelow, 1911	NGC;CGC;SGC	BEN;PEL	99	273
Physalia utriculus	La Martiniere, 1787	NGC;CGC;SGC;BR;SWB	PEL;FLOT;NEUS	?	?
SCYPHOZOA (JELLYFISHES)					
Stomalophus sp.	NA	NGC;BR	PEL	?	?
PHYLUM CTENOPHORA (COMB JELLIES)					
Pleurobrachia sp.	NA	NGC;CGC;SGC;BR	PEL	?	?
PHYLUM PLATYHELMINTHES (FLATWORMS)					
TURBELLARIA (FREE-LIVING FLATWORMS)					
Alleena mexicana	Hyman, 1953	NGC;CGC;SGC;BR	LIT;BEN	0	?
Alloioplana sandiegensis	(Boone, 1929)	NGC;CGC;BR	LIT;BEN	0	?
Longiprostatum rickettsi	Hyman, 1953	NGC	BEN;LIT	0	?
Marcusia ernesti	Hyman, 1953	NGC;CGC;SGC;BR	LIT;BEN	0	?
Ommatoplana levis	(Hyman, 1953)	NGC;BR	LIT;BEN	0	?
Ommatoplana mexicana	(Hyman, 1953)	NGC;CGC;BR	LIT;BEN	0	?
Prosthiostomum multicelis	Hyman, 1953	NGC;CGC;BR	LIT;BEN	0	?
Pseudoceros bajae	Hyman, 1953	NGC;CGC;SGC;BR	LIT;BEN	0	?
Pseudoceros mexicanus	Hyman, 1953	NGC;CGC;BR	LIT;BEN	0	2
Pseudostylochus burchami	(Heath & McGregor, 1912)	NGC;BR	BEN	20	70

TABLE 29.3 (CONT'D). *Annotated list of macroinvertebrates known from the northern Gulf of California.*

Species	Author				
Thysanozoon sp.		NGC;BR	LIT;BEN	0	2
Zygantroplana stylifera	Hyman, 1953	NGC	LIT;BEN	0	3

PHYLUM NEMERTEA (RIBBON WORMS)

Species	Author				
Baseodiscus delineatus	(Delle Chiaje, 1823–1829)	NGC;CGC;SGC;BR	BEN;LIT	0	1
Baseodiscus punnetti	(Coe, 1904)	NGC;BR	BEN;LIT	0	380
Carinoma mutabilis	Griffin, 1898	NGC	BEN;LIT	0	40
Cerebratulus lineolatus	Coe, 1905	NGC	BEN	0	70
Lineus flavescens	Coe, 1904	NGC;CGC;SGC;SWB	BEN;LIT	0	3
Lineus geniculatus	(Delle Chiaje, 1828)	NGC;CGC	BEN	0	30

PHYLUM MOLLUSCA (MOLLUSCS)

CEPHALOPODA (SQUIDS AND OCTOPUSES)

Species	Author				
Octopus alecto	Berry, 1953	NGC;CGC;SGC;BR	BEN;LIT;NER	0	155
Octopus bimaculatus	Verrill, 1883	NGC;CGC;SGC;BR	BEN;LIT;NER	0	55
Octopus digueti	Perrier & Rochebrune, 1894	NGC;CGC;SGC;BR	BEN;LIT;NER	0	?
Octopus fitchi	Berry, 1953	NGC;CGC;BR	BEN;LIT;NER	0	?
Octopus penicillifer	Berry, 1954	NGC;CGC;SGC	BEN	21	?

GASTROPODA (SNAILS AND SLUGS)
PROSOBRANCHIA
ARCHAEOGASTROPODA

Species	Author				
Anatoma keenae	(McLean, 1970)	NGC;CGC;SGC	?	73	146
Arene lurida	(Dall, 1913)	NGC;CGC	BEN;LIT;NER	0	30
Arene balboai	(Strong & Hertlein, 1939)	NGC;CGC;SGC;BR	BEN	5	37
Calliostoma gordanum	McLean, 1980	NGC;CGC;SGC	BEN	999	128
Calliostoma leanum	(C.B. Adams, 1852)	NGC	BEN;LIT	0	180
Calliostoma marshalli	Lowe, 1935	NGC;CGC;SGC;BR;SWB	BEN;LIT	0	35
Calliostoma mcleani	Shasky & Campbell, 1964	NGC;CGC	BEN;LIT	0	90
Calliostoma nepheloide	Dall, 1913	NGC;CGC;SGC;SWB	BEN	9	128
Calliostoma palmeri	Dall, 1871	NGC;CGC;BR	BEN;LIT	12	45
Diodora alta	(C.B. Adams, 1852)	NGC;CGC;SGC;BR	BEN	0	35
Diodora inaequalis	(Sowerby, 1835)	NGC;CGC;SGC;BR	BEN;LIT;NER	0	36
Diodora pusilla	Berry, 1959	NGC;CGC;BR	BEN	9	146
Diodora saturnalis	(Carpenter, 1864)	NGC;CGC;SGC;BR	BEN;LIT;LACS	0	35

TABLE 29.3 (CONT'D). *Annotated list of macroinvertebrates known from the northern Gulf of California.*

Species	Author				
Emarginula velascoensis	Shasky, 1961	NGC;CGC;SGC	?	73	550
Eulithidium cyclostoma	(Carpenter, 1864)	NGC;CGC;SGC	BEN	6	37
Eulithidium substriata	(Carpenter, 1864)	NGC;CGC;SGC	BEN;LIT;NER	0	?
Eulithidium variegata	(Carpenter, 1864)	NGC;CGC;SGC;BR;SWB	BEN;LIT;NER	0	35
Fissurella rubropicta	Pilsbry, 1890	NGC;CGC;SGC	BEN	35	?
Fissurellidea bimaculata	Dall, 1871	NGC;BR	?	?	?
Iothia lindbergi	McLean, 1985	NGC	BEN	?	183
Lottia acutapex	(Berry, 1960)	NGC;CGC;SGC;BR	BEN;LIT	0	20
Lottia atrata	(Carpenter, 1864)	NGC;CGC;SGC;BR;SWB	BEN;LIT;LACS	0	?
Lottia dalliana	(Pilsbry, 1891)	NGC;CGC;BR	BEN;LIT	0	?
Lottia stanfordiana	(Berry, 1957)	NGC;CGC;BR	BEN;LIT	0	?
Lottia strigatella	(Carpenter, 1864)	NGC;CGC;SGC	BEN;LIT	0	12
Lottia strongiana	(Hertlein, 1958)	NGC;CGC;SGC;BR	BEN;LIT;NER	0	20
Lottia turveri	(Hertlein & Strong, 1951)	NGC;CGC;BR	BEN;LIT	0	12
Lucapinella milleri	Berry, 1959	NGC;CGC;SGC;BR	BEN;LIT;NER	0	35
Macrarene californica californica	(Dall, 1908)	NGC;CGC;SGC	BEN	37	183
Macrarene farallonensis	(A. G. Smith, 1952)	NGC;CGC;SGC	BEN	64	137
Nerita funiculata	Menke, 1851	NGC;CGC;SGC;BR	BEN;LIT	0	41
Otolloria fricki	(Crosse, 1865)	NGC;CGC;SGC;BR	BEN	3	75
Parviturbo stearnsii	(Dall, 1918)	NGC;CGC;BR	BEN	3	41
Patelloida semirubida	(Dall, 1914)	NGC;CGC;SGC;BR	BEN;LIT;NER	0	35
Plesiothyreus malonei	(Vanatta, 1912)	NGC;CGC;SGC;BR	BEN	0	100
Rimula mexicana	Berry, 1969	NGC;CGC	BEN	30	80
Solariella peramabilis	Carpenter, 1864	NGC	?	?	183
Solariella triplostephanus	Dall, 1910	NGC;CGC;SGC;BR	BEN	12	55
Tectura ubiquita	(Lindberg & McLean, 1981)	NGC;CGC;SGC;SWB	BEN	0	5
Tegula corteziana	McLean, 1970	NGC;CGC;3R	BEN;LIT;NER	0	30
Tegula felipensis	McLean, 1970	NGC;BR	BEN;LIT;NER	0	?
Tegula globulus	(Carpenter, 1857)	NGC;CGC;SGC	BEN;LIT;NER	0	9
Tegula mariana	(Dall, 1919)	NGC;CGC;BR	BEN;LIT	0	20
Tegula rubroflammulata	(Koch in Philippi, 1843)	NGC;CGC;BR	BEN;LIT	0	114
Tegula rugosa	(A. Adams, 1853)	NGC;CGC;BR	BEN;LIT	0	?
Theodoxus luteofasciatus	(Miller, 1879)	NGC;CGC;BR	BEN;LIT;LACS	0	?
Titiscania limacina	(Bergh, 1875)	NGC;CGC;SGC;BR	BEN;LIT	0	?

TABLE 29.3 (CONT'D). *Annotated list of macroinvertebrates known from the northern Gulf of California.*

Species	Reference	Distribution	Habitat		
Turbo fluctuosus	Wood, 1828	NGC;CGC;SGC;BR	BEN;LIT;NER	0	40
Turbo mazatlanicus	Pilsbry & Lowe, 1932	NGC;CGC;SGC	BEN;LIT;NER	0	37
Turbo squamiger	Reeve, 1843	NGC;CGC	BEN	6	61
Turcica admirabilis	Berry, 1969	NGC;CGC;SGC	BEN	50	180
CAENOGASTROPODA					
Acanthina lugubris angelica	Oldroyd, 1918	NGC;CGC;SGC;BR;SWB	BEN;LIT	0	?
Acanthina lugubris lugubris	(Sowerby, 1822)	NGC;CGC;SGC	BEN;LIT	0	2
Acanthotrophon sorenseni	(Hertlein & Strong, 1951)	NGC;CGC;SGC	BEN	100	110
Acirsa cerralvoensis	(DuShane, 1970)	NGC;CGC;SGC	BEN	7	38
Aesopus sanctus	Dall, 1919	NGC;CGC;SGC	BEN	6	41
Agathotoma alcippe	(Dall, 1918)	NGC;CGC;BR	BEN;LIT	0	100
Agathotoma klasmidia	Shasky, 1971	NGC;CGC;SGC	BEN	20	40
Agatrix strongi	(Shasky, 1961)	NGC;CGC;SGC	BEN	37	200
Alaba interruptelineata	Pilsbry & Lowe, 1932	NGC;CGC	BEN	11	41
Alaba jeannettae	Bartsch, 1910	NGC;CGC;SGC	?	?	?
Alaba supralirata	Carpenter, 1857	NGC;CGC;SGC	BEN	9	35
Alleorus deprellus	Strong, 1938	NGC;CGC;BR	?	6	12
Alvania inconspicua	(C.B. Adams, 1852)	NGC;CGC	BEN	12	35
Anachis lillianae	Withney, 1978	NGC;CGC;SGC;BR	BEN	0	?
Anachis scalarina	(Sowerby, 1832)	NGC;CGC;SGC;BR	BEN;LIT	0	?
Anticlimax occidens	Pilsbry & Olsson, 1952	NGC;CGC;BR	BEN	12	37
Antillophos veraguensis	(Hinds, 1843)	NGC;CGC;SGC;BR	BEN;LIT	0	402
Aorotrema humboldti	(Hertlein & Strong, 1951)	NGC;CGC	BEN	18	35
Asperiscala canna	(Dall, 1919)	NGC;CGC;SGC;BR;SWB	BEN;LIT	0	?
Asperiscala elenense	(Sowerby, 1844)	NGC;CGC;SGC;SWB	BEN	0	?
Asperiscala gradata	(Sowerby, 1844)	NGC	BEN	0	?
Asperiscala buffmani	(DuShane & McLean, 1968)	NGC;CGC;BR	BEN;LIT	0	?
Asperiscala lowei	(Dall, 1906)	NGC;CGC	BEN;LIT	0	183
Asperiscala walkerianum	(Hertlein & Strong, 1951)	NGC;CGC;BR	BEN	0	23
Assiminea compacta	(Carpenter, 1864)	NGC;CGC;SGC	BEN;LIT;LACS	0	?
Attiliosa nodulosa	(A. Adams, 1855)	NGC;CGC;BR	BEN	0	80
Austrotrophon cerrosensis	(Dall, 1891)	NGC;CGC	BEN	100	183
Axelella campbelli	(Shasky, 1961)	NGC;CGC	BEN	18	91
Babelomurex costata	(Blainville, 1832)	NGC;CGC;SGC	BEN	0	41

TABLE 29.3 (CONT'D). *Annotated list of macroinvertebrates known from the northern Gulf of California.*

Species	Author	Distribution	Habitat		
Babelomurex hindsii	(Carpenter, 1857)	NGC;CGC;SGC	BEN;PAR	11	99
Bailya anomala	(Hinds, 1844)	NGC;CGC;SGC	BEN;LIT	0	15
Bellaspira acclivicosta	McLean & Poorman, 1970	NGC;CGC	BEN	20	40
Bellaspira melea	Dall, 1919	NGC;CGC	BEN	10	183
Bizetiella carmen	(Lowe, 1935)	NGC;CGC	BEN	12	118
Buchema granulosa	(Sowerby, 1834)	NGC;CGC;SGC	BEN	0	55
Caducifer biliratus	(Reeve, 1846)	NGC;CGC;SGC	BEN	2	146
Caecum elongatum	Carpenter, 1857	NGC;CGC;SGC	?	?	?
Caecum firmatum	C.B. Adams, 1852	NGC;CGC;SGC	BEN	11	27
Caecum limnetes	Long, 1972	NGC;BR	?	?	?
Caecum quadratum	Carpenter, 1857	NGC;CGC;SGC;BR	BEN	11	27
Calliclava aegina	(Dall, 1919)	NGC;CGC;SGC	BEN	15	30
Calliclava alcmene	(Dall, 1919)	NGC;CGC;SGC	BEN	35	70
Calliclava palmeri	(Dall, 1919)	NGC;CGC;SGC	BEN;LIT	0	20
Calyptraea conica	Broderip, 1834	NGC;CGC;SGC;SWB	BEN	5	183
Calyptraea mamillaris	Broderip, 1834	NGC;BR;SWB	BEN;LIT;LACS	0	81
Cancellaria cassidiformis	Sowerby, 1832	NGC;CGC;BR	BEN;LIT	0	37
Cancellaria bivetia jayana	Keen, 1958	NGC;BR	BEN	18	75
Cancellaria obesa	Sowerby, 1832	NGC;CGC	BEN;LIT	0	90
Cantharus macrospira	(Berry, 1957)	NGC;CGC;SGC;BR	BEN;LIT	0	81
Cantharus pallidus	(Broderip & Sowerby, 1829)	NGC;BR	BEN	0	73
Carinodrillia adonis	Pilsbry & Lowe, 1932	NGC;CGC;SGC	BEN	35	100
Carinodrillia dichroa	Pilsbry & Lowe, 1932	NGC;CGC	BEN	9	100
Carinodrillia halis	(Dall, 1919)	NGC;CGC;SGC	BEN	18	100
Carinodrillia hexagona	(Sowerby, 1834)	NGC;CGC;SGC;BR	BEN;LIT	0	40
Casmaria vibexmexicana	(Stearns, 1894)	NGC;CGC;SGC	BEN;LIT	0	22
Cerithidea californica mazatlanica	Carpenter, 1857	NGC;CGC;SGC	BEN;LIT;LACS	0	?
Cerithiopsis bristolae	Baker, Hanna & Strong, 1938	NGC;CGC;SGC	BEN	35	?
Cerithiopsis tuberculoides	Carpenter, 1857	NGC;CGC;SGC;BR	BEN	12	25
Cerithium maculosum	Kiener, 1841	NGC;CGC;SGC;BR;SWB	BEN;LIT	0	9
Cerithium stercusmuscarum	Valenciennes, 1833	NGC;CGC;SGC;SWB	BEN;LIT;LACS	0	12
Cerodrilla cybele	(Pilsbry & Lowe, 1932)	NGC;CGC;SGC	BEN	10	100
Cheilea cepacea	(Broderip, 1834)	NGC;CGC;BR	BEN;LIT	0	183

TABLE 29.3 (CONT'D.). *Annotated list of macroinvertebrates known from the northern Gulf of California.*

Cirsotrema togatum	(Hertlein & Strong, 1951)	NGG;CGC;SGC	BEN	18	100
Cirsotrema vulpinum	(Hinds, 1844)	NGG;CGC	BEN	9	100
Clathurella rigida	(Hinds, 1843)	NGG;CGC;SGC	BEN;LIT	0	35
Cochlespira cedonulli	(Reeve, 1843)	NGG;CGC;SGC	BEN	20	275
Cochliolepis cornis	Hertz, Myers & Gemmell, 1992	NGG; BR	BEN	0	25
Columbella aureomexicana	(Howard, 1963)	NGG;CGC;SGC;BR	BEN;LIT	0	40
Columbella strombiformis	Lamarck, 1822	NGG;CGC;SGC;BR	BEN;LIT	0	20
Compsodrillia albonodosa	(Carpenter, 1857)	NGG;CGC;SGC;BR	BEN;LIT	0	20
Compsodrillia alcestis	(Dall, 1919)	NGG;CGC;SGC	BEN	20	100
Compsodrillia duplicata	(Sowerby, 1834)	NGG;CGC	BEN	11	100
Compsodrillia baliplexa	(Dall, 1919)	NGG;CGC;SGC;BR;SWB	BEN	10	55
Compsodrillia opaca	McLean & Poorman, 1971	NGG;CGC;SGC	BEN	95	140
Compsodrillia thestia	(Dall, 1919)	NGG;CGC;BR	BEN	0	20
Conus brunneus	Wood, 1828	NGG;CGC;SGC;BR;SWB	BEN;LIT	0	20
Conus dalli	Stearns, 1873	NGG;CGC;SGC	BEN;LIT	0	15
Conus princeps	Linnaeus, 1758	NGG;CGC;BR	BEN;LIT	0	35
Conus lucidus	Wood, 1828	NGG;CGC;SGC;BR;SWB	BEN	0	41
Conus poormani	Berry, 1968	NGG;CGC;BR	BEN	55	165
Conus archon	Broderip, 1833	NGG;CGC;SGC	BEN	9	400
Conus regularis	Sowerby, 1833	NGG;CGC;SGC;BR;SWB	BEN;LIT	0	100
Conus perplexus	Sowerby, 1857	NGG;CGC;SGC;BR;SWB	BEN;LIT	0	73
Conus angulatus	A. Adams, 1854	NGG;BR	?	?	?
Conus tornatus	Sowerby, 1833 ex Broderip, MS	NGG;CGC;BR	BEN	0	57
Conus ximenes	Gray, 1839	NGG;CGC;SGC	BEN;LIT	0	90
Coralliophila macleani	Shasky, 1970	NGG;CGC;SGC;BR	BEN;LIT;PAR	0	30
Cosmioconcha palmeri	(Dall, 1913)	NGG;CGC;SGC;BR	BEN	9	108
Cosmioconcha pergracilis	(Dall, 1913)	NGG;SWB	BEN	27	106
Costoanachis berryi	(Shasky, 1970)	NGG;CGC;SGC	BEN	1	66
Costoanachis coronata	(Sowerby, 1832)	NGG;CGC;SGC;BR;SWB	BEN;LIT	0	72
Costoanachis hilli	(Pilsbry & Lowe, 1932)	NGG;CGC;SGC;BR	BEN;LIT	0	30
Costoanachis sanfelipensis	(Lowe, 1935)	NGG;BR	BEN;LIT	0	?
Costoanachis varia	(Sowerby, 1832)	NGG;CGC;BR	BEN;LIT	0	30
Costoanachis vexillum	(Reeve, 1858)	NGG;CGC;BR	BEN;LIT	0	?

TABLE 29.3 (CONT'D). *Annotated list of macroinvertebrates known from the northern Gulf of California.*

Species	Authority	Distribution	Habitat		
Cotonopsis birundo	(Gaskoin, 1852)	NGC;CGC;BR	BEN;LIT	2	236
Crassispira appressa	(Carpenter, 1864)	NGC;CGC;SGC	BEN;LIT	0	5
Crassispira bifurca	(E. A. Smith, 1888)	NGC;CGC;BR	BEN;LIT	0	35
Crassispira currini	McLean & Poorman, 1971	NGC;CGC;SGC	BEN;LIT	0	2
Crassispira discors	(Sowerby, 1834)	NGC;CGC;SGC	BEN;LIT	0	41
Crassispira incrassata	(Sowerby, 1834)	NGC;CGC;SGC;BR	BEN;LIT	0	35
Crassispira kluthi	E. K. Jordan, 1936	NGC;CGC;SGC;BR;SWB	BEN;LIT	0	50
Crassispira maura	(Sowerby, 1834)	NGC;CGC;SGC	BEN	0	60
Crassispira monilifera	(Carpenter, 1857)	NGC;CGC;SGC	BEN;LIT	0	?
Crassispira pluto	Pilsbry & Lowe, 1932	NGC;CGC;SGC;BR	BEN;LIT	0	72
Crassispira rustica	(Sowerby, 1834)	NGC;CGC	BEN;LIT	0	100
Crassispira tepocana	Dall, 1919	NGC;CGC	BEN	20	72
Crassispira unicolor	(Sowerby, 1834)	NGC;CGC;SGC;BR	BEN;LIT	0	45
Crassispira xanti	Hertlein & Strong, 1951	NGC;CGC;SGC	BEN	7	55
Crepidula excavata	(Broderip, 1834)	NGC;CGC;SGC;BR	BEN;LIT	0	100
Crepidula incurva	(Broderip, 1834)	NGC;CGC;SGC;BR	BEN;LIT	0	35
Crepidula lessonii	Broderip, 1834	NGC;CGC;SGC;BR	BEN;LIT	0	?
Crepidula onyx	Sowerby, 1824	NGC;CGC;SGC;BR	BEN	0	80
Crepidula striolata	Menke, 1851	NGC;CGC;SGC;BR	BEN;LIT	0	30
Crepidula uncata	Menke, 1847	NGC;CGC;SGC;BR	BEN;LIT;LACS	0	?
Crossata californica sonorana	(Berry, 1960)	NGC;CGC	BEN;PAR	0	178
Crucibulum concameratum	Reeve, 1859	NGC;CGC;SGC	BEN	9	81
Crucibulum lignarium	(Broderip, 1834)	NGC;CGC;SGC	BEN;LIT	0	100
Crucibulum monticulus	Berry, 1969	NGC;CGC;SGC	BEN	35	183
Crucibulum personatum	Keen, 1958	NGC;CGC;SGC;BR	BEN	12	50
Crucibulum scutellatum	(Wood, 1828)	NGC;CGC;BR	BEN;LIT	0	181
Crucibulum spinosum	(Sowerby, 1824)	NGC;CGC;BR	BEN;LIT;LACS	0	61
Cyclostremiscus bailyi	(Hertlein & Strong, 1951)	NGC;CGC;BR	BEN	22	24
Cyclostremiscus bifrontia	(Carpenter, 1857)	NGC;CGC;SGC	?	10	35
Cyclostremiscus janus	(C.B. Adams, 1852)	NGC;CGC;SGC	BEN	?	?
Cyclostremiscus parvus	(C.B. Adams, 1852)	NGC;CGC	BEN	11	35
Cyclostremiscus perparvus	(C.B. Adams, 1852)	NGC;BR	?	?	?
Cyclostremiscus psix	Pilsbry & Olsson, 1952	NGC;BR	BEN	0	?

TABLE 29.3 (CONT'D). *Annotated list of macroinvertebrates known from the northern Gulf of California.*

Cyclostremiscus salvatierrensis	Hertz, Myers & Gemmell, 1992	NGC;CGC;SGC	BEN	1	55
Cyclostremiscus spiceri	(Baker, Hanna & Strong, 1938)	NGC;CGC;BR	BEN	1	20
Cyclostremiscus tenuisculptus	(Carpenter, 1865)	NGC;CGC;SGC;BR	BEN;LIT;NER	0	?
Cyclostremiscus tricarinatus	(C.B. Adams, 1852)	NGC;CGC;BR	BEN	12	35
Cyclostremiscus trigonatus	(Carpenter, 1857)	NGC;CGC;SGC;BR	BEN	35	?
Cymatium corrugatum amictum	(Reeve, 1844)	NGC;CGC;SGC	BEN	30	118
Cymatium gibbosum	(Broderip, 1833)	NGC;CGC;SGC;BR	BEN;LIT	0	100
Cymatium parthenopeum keenae	(Beu, 1970)	NGC;CGC;SGC	BEN;LIT	0	100
Cymbula bratcherae	Cate, 1973	NGC;CGC;SGC;BR	?	?	?
Cyphoma emarginata	(Sowerby, 1830)	NGC;CGC;SGC;BR	BEN;PAR	11	118
Cypraea albuginosa	Gray, 1825	NGC;CGC;SGC	BEN	0	38
Cypraea annettae annettae	Dall, 1909	NGC;CGC;SGC;BR	BEN;LIT	0	38
Cypraea cervinetta	Kiener, 1843	NGC;CGC;BR	BEN;LIT	0	41
Cypraea isabellamexicana	Stearns, 1893	NGC;CGC;SGC	BEN	0	12
Cypraecassis coarctata	(Sowerby, 1825)	NGC;CGC;SGC;BR	BEN;LIT	0	41
Daphnella allemani	(Bartsch, 1931)	NGC;CGC	BEN;LIT	0	73
Daphnella bartschi	Dall, 1919	NGC;CGC;SGC;SWB	BEN	12	35
Daphnella mazatlanica	Pilsbry & Lowe, 1932	NGC;CGC;SGC;BR	BEN;LIT	0	40
Daphnella retusa	McLean & Poorman, 1971	NGC;CGC;SGC	BEN	12	100
Decipifus gracilis	McLean, 1959	NGC;CGC;SGC	BEN;LIT	2	2
Decipifus lyrta	(Baker, Hanna & Strong, 1938)	NGC;BR	BEN;LIT	0	3
Decipifus macleani	Keen, 1971	NGC;BR	BEN;LIT	0	20
Delonovolva aequalis	(Sowerby, 1832)	NGC;CGC;SGC;BR	BEN	4	100
Depressiscala polita	(Sowerby, 1844)	NGC	BEN;LIT	11	393
Dermomurex cunninghamae	(Berry, 1964)	NGC;CGC	BEN	18	100
Diastoma fastigiatum	(Carpenter, 1864)	NGC	BEN	20	30
Distorsio constricta	(Broderip, 1833)	NGC;CGC;SGC	BEN	2	118
Distorsio decussata	(Valenciennes, 1832)	NGC;CGC;SGC	BEN	11	99
Distorsio jenniernestae	Emerson & Piech, 1992	NGC;CGC;SGC	BEN;LIT	0	183
Distorsio minoruohnishii	Parth, 1989	NGC;CGC;SGC	BEN	15	165
Drillia acapulcana	(Hertlein & Strong, 1951)	NGC;CGC;SGC	BEN	20	72
Drillia aerope	(Dall, 1919)	NGC;CGC;SGC;SWB	BEN	20	100

TABLE 29.3 (CONT'D.). *Annotated list of macroinvertebrates known from the northern Gulf of California.*

Drillia berryi	McLean & Poorman, 1971	NGC;CGC;SGC	BEN	50	183
Drillia cunninghamae	McLean & Poorman, 1971	NGC;CGC;SGC	BEN	25	100
Drillia inornata	McLean & Poorman, 1971	NGC;CGC;SGC	BEN	50	100
Drillia roseola	(Hertlein & Strong, 1955)	NGC;CGC;SGC;BR	BEN	12	70
Drillia salvadorica	(Hertlein & Strong, 1951)	NGC;CGC;SGC	BEN	6	45
Drillia tumida	McLean & Poorman, 1971	NGC;CGC;SGC;BR;SWB	BEN	20	74
Elephantulum heptagonum	(Carpenter, 1857)	NGC;CGC;SGC	BEN	11	27
Elephantulum liratocinctum	(Carpenter, 1857)	NGC;CGC;BR	BEN	3	17
Enaeta cumingii	(Broderip, 1832)	NGC;CGC;SWB	BEN;LIT	0	49
Engina jugosa	(C.B. Adams, 1852)	NGC;CGC;SGC;BR	BEN	12	162
Engina solida	Dall, 1917	NGC;CGC;SGC	BEN	0	35
Episcynia bolivari	Pilsbry & Olsson, 1946	NGC;CGC;BR	BEN	12	35
Eualetes centiquadra	(Valenciennes, 1846)	NGC;CGC;BR	BEN	?	100
Euclathurella carissima	(Pilsbry & Lowe, 1932)	NGC;CGC;BR	BEN;LIT	0	10
Eulima recta	C.B. Adams, 1852	NGC;CGC;BR	BEN	12	?
Eulima townsendi	(Bartsch, 1917)	NGC;CGC	BEN	20	30
Eulimetta pagoda	Warén, 1992	NGC;CGC;SGC	BEN	3	44
Eulimostraca linearis	(Carpenter, 1857)	NGC;CGC;SGC	?	?	?
Eupleura muriciformis	(Broderip, 1833)	NGC;CGC;BR	BEN;LIT	0	180
Finella excurvata	(Carpenter, 1857)	NGC;CGC;SGC	BEN;LIT	0	18
Finella monicensis	(Bartsch, 1911)	NGC	?	?	?
Fusinus turris	(Valenciennes, 1832)	NGC	BEN;LIT	0	200
Fusinus cinereus	(Reeve, 1847)	NGC;CGC;SGC	BEN;LIT	0	35
Fusinus colpoicus	Dall, 1915	NGC;CGC;SGC	BEN	9	165
Fusinus consagensis	Poorman, 1981	NGC;BR	BEN	20	30
Fusinus dupetitthouarsi	(Kiener, 1840)	NGC;CGC;SGC;BR;SWB	BEN;LIT	0	200
Fusinus felipensis	Lowe, 1935	NGC;BR	BEN;LIT	0	?
Fusinus fredbakeri	Lowe, 1935	NGC;CGC;3R	BEN	12	104
Fusinus sonorae	Poorman, 1981	NGC;CGC	BEN	100	183
Fusiturricula armilda	(Dall, 1908)	NGC;CGC;SGC	BEN	35	280
Gemmula hindsiana	Berry, 1958	NGC;CGC;SGC;SWB	BEN	40	225
Globidrillia ferminiana	(Dall, 1919)	NGC	BEN	20	45
Globidrillia micans	(Hinds, 1843)	NGC;CGC;SGC;BR	BEN	10	30
Globidrillia strobbeeni	(Hertlein & Strong, 1951)	NGC;CGC;SGC	BEN	8	40

TABLE 29.3 (CONT'D). *Annotated list of macroinvertebrates known from the northern Gulf of California.*

Glyphostoma candida	(Hinds, 1843)	NGC;CGC;SGC;SWB	BEN	40	183
Glyphostoma neglecta	(Hinds, 1843)	NGC;CGC;BR	BEN	20	50
Glyphostoma thalassoma	(Dall, 1908)	NGC	BEN	70	183
Granulina margaritula	(Carpenter, 1857)	NGC;CGC;SGC;BR	BEN;LIT	0	110
Haustellum elenensis	(Dall, 1909)	NGC;CGC;BR	BEN;LIT	0	36
Hespererato columbella	(Menke, 1847)	NGC;CGC;SGC;BR	BEN;LIT	0	145
Hexaplex nigritus	(Philippi, 1845)	NGC;CGC;SGC;BR	BEN;LIT	0	60
Hexaplex princeps	(Broderip, 1833)	NGC;CGC;SGC	BEN	0	41
Hindsiclava andromeda	(Dall, 1919)	NGC;CGC;SGC	BEN	40	160
Hindsiclava militaris	(Reeve, 1843, ex Hinds, MS)	NGC;CGC;SGC	BEN	18	102
Hirtoscala reflexa	(Carpenter, 1856)	NGC;CGC;SGC;BR	BEN	9	41
Hirtoscala replicatum	(Sowerby, 1844)	NGC;CGC;SGC;BR	BEN	5	108
Hormospira maculosa	(Sowerby, 1834)	NGC;CGC;SGC;BR	BEN;LIT	0	117
Imaclava pilsbryi	Bartsch, 1950	NGC;CGC;SGC;BR	BEN	13	30
Imaclava unimaculata	(Sowerby, 1834)	NGC;CGC;SGC	BEN	10	80
Jenneria pustulata	(Lightfoot, 1786)	NGC;CGC;SGC;BR	BEN;LIT;PAR	0	40
Knefastia dalli	Bartsch, 1944	NGC;CGC;BR	BEN;LIT	0	80
Knefastia tuberculifera	(Broderip & Sowerby, 1829)	NGC;CGC;SGC;BR	BEN;LIT	0	88
Knefastia walkeri	Berry, 1958	NGC;CGC;SGC	BEN	18	102
Kurtzia aethra	(Dall, 1919)	NGC;CGC	BEN	20	70
Kurtzia arteaga	(Dall & Bartsch, 1910)	NGC;CGC;BR	BEN	20	100
Kurtzia granulatissima	(Mörch, 1860)	NGC;CGC;BR;SWB	BEN	11	40
Kurtziella antiochroa	(Pilsbry & Lowe, 1932)	NGC;CGC;BR	BEN	10	50
Kurtziella antipyrgus	(Pilsbry & Lowe, 1932)	NGC;CGC	BEN;LIT	20	100
Kurtziella cyrene	(Dall, 1919)	NGC;CGC;BR	BEN	10	70
Kurtziella plumbea	(Hinds, 1843)	NGC;CGC;SGC;BR	BEN	10	100
Kurtziella powelli	Shasky, 1971	NGC;BR	BEN;LIT	20	40
Kylix alcyone	(Dall, 1919)	NGC	BEN	?	139
Kylix becuba	(Dall, 1919)	NGC;CGC;SGC;BR	BEN	14	35
Kylix ianthe	(Dall, 1919)	NGC;CGC;SGC;BR	BEN	13	50
Kylix paziana	(Dall, 1919)	NGC;CGC;SGC	BEN	20	80
Kylix zacae	Hertlein & Strong, 1951	NGC;CGC	BEN	10	183
Lamellaria diegoensis	Dall, 1885	NGC;CGC;BR	BEN;LIT	0	139
Lamellaria inflata	(C.B. Adams, 1852)	NGC;CGC	BEN	0	35

TABLE 29.3 (CONT'D.). Annotated list of macroinvertebrates known from the northern Gulf of California.

Species	Author	Distribution	Habitat		
Lamellaria perspicua	(Linnaeus, 1758)	NGC;CGC;BR	BEN	0	1,287
Lapsigyrus mutans	(Carpenter, 1857)	NGC;CGC;SGC;BR	BEN	20	?
Latirus praestantior	Melvill, 1892	NGC;CGC;SGC	BEN	10	35
Liocerithium judithae	Keen, 1971	NGC;CGC;SGC;BR;SWB	BEN;LIT	0	?
Lioglyphostoma ericea	(Hinds, 1843)	NGC;CGC;SGC	BEN	40	183
Lirobarleeia albolirata	(Carpenter, 1864)	NGC;CGC;SGC	?	?	?
Lirobarleeia clarionensis	(Bartsch, 1911)	NGC;CGC	BEN	35	?
Lirobarleeia lirata	(Carpenter, 1857)	NGC;CGC;SGC	BEN	8	?
Littoraria aberrans	(Philippi, 1846)	NGC;BR	?	?	?
Littoraria rosewateri	Reid, 1999	NGC;CGC;SGC;BR;SWB	BEN;LIT	0	0
Lydiphnis cymatotropis	Pilsbry & Olsson, 1945	NGC;CGC;SGC	?	?	?
Maesiella maesae	McLean & Poorman, 1971	NGC;CGC	BEN	15	35
Malea ringens	(Swainson, 1822)	NGC;CGC;SGC;BR	BEN;LIT	0	53
Mancinella tuberculata	(Sowerby, 1835)	NGC;CGC;SGC;BR	BEN;LIT	0	?
Marseniopsis sharonae	(Willett, 1939)	NGC;BR	BEN	0	5
Melanella gibba	(de Folin, 1867)	NGC;CGC;BR	BEN	12	40
Melanella retexta	(Carpenter, 1857)	NGC;CGC;SGC	?	?	?
Melanella yod	(Carpenter, 1857)	NGC;CGC;SGC;BR	BEN	0	35
Melongena patula	(Broderip & Sowerby, 1829)	NGC;CGC;SGC;BR	BEN;LIT;LACS	0	2
Metaxia convexa	(Carpenter, 1857)	NGC;CGC;SGC;BR	BEN	2	40
Microdaphne trichodes	(Dall, 1919)	NGC;CGC;SGC;BR	BEN	0	146
Miraclathurella bicanalifera	(Sowerby, 1834)	NGC;CGC;SGC;BR	BEN	0	72
Mitra fultoni	E. A. Smith, 1892	NGC;CGC	BEN;LIT	0	90
Mitra tristis	Broderip, 1836	NGC;CGC;SGC;BR	BEN;LIT	0	20
Mitrella dorma	Baker, Hanna & Strong, 1938	NGC;CGC;SGC;BR	BEN	0	50
Mitrella granti	Lowe, 1935	NGC;CGC;BR	BEN	0	?
Mitrella millepunctata	(Carpenter, 1864)	NGC;CGC	BEN	0	35
Mitrella ocellata	(Gmelin, 1791)	NGC;CGC;SGC;BR	BEN	0	30
Mitromorpha mitriformis	(Shasky, 1961)	NGC;CGC;SGC	BEN	22	183
Mitromorpha baileyi	(McLean & Poorman, 1971)	NGC;CGC;SGC	BEN	20	60
Murexiella humilis	(Broderip, 1833)	NGC;CGC;SGC;BR	BEN;LIT	0	99
Murexiella mildredae	Poorman, 1980	NGC;CGC	BEN	100	183
Muricopsis zeteki	Hertlein & Strong, 1951	NGC;CGC;BR	BEN	3	27
Nannodiella fraternalis	(Dall, 1919)	NGC;CGC;SGC	BEN	11	70

TABLE 29.3 (CONT'D). *Annotated list of macroinvertebrates known from the northern Gulf of California.*

Species	Author				
Nannodiella nana	(Dall, 1919)	NGC;CGC	BEN	11	70
Nassarina belenae	Keen, 1971	NGC;CGC;SGC;BR	BEN	7	100
Nassarius brunneostoma	(Stearns, 1893)	NGC;CGC;SGC;BR	BEN;LIT	0	?
Nassarius cerritensis	(Arnold, 1903)	NGC;CGC	BEN	35	100
Nassarius guaymasensis	(Pilsbry & Lowe, 1932)	NGC;CGC;BR	BEN;LIT	0	100
Nassarius howardae	Chace, 1958	NGC;CGC;BR	BEN	18	276
Nassarius insculptus	(Carpenter, 1864)	NGC;CGC;SGC	BEN	20	135
Nassarius iodes	(Dall, 1917)	NGC;CGC;SGC;BR	BEN;LIT;LACS	0	18
Nassarius limacinus	(Dall, 1917)	NGC;CGC;SGC;BR	BEN;LIT	0	24
Nassarius nodicinctus	(A. Adams, 1852)	NGC;CGC;SGC;BR	BEN	18	97
Nassarius pagodus	(Reeve, 1844)	NGC;CGC;SWB	BEN	0	118
Nassarius shaskyi	McLean, 1970	NGC;CGC;SGC;SWB	BEN	18	100
Nassarius taeniolatus	(Philippi, 1845)	NGC;CGC;BR	BEN	10	40
Nassarius tiarula	(Kiener, 1841)	NGC;CGC;SGC;BR	BEN;LIT	0	2
Nassarius versicolor	(C.B. Adams, 1852)	NGC;CGC;SGC;BR;SWB	BEN;LIT	0	81
Natica broderipiana	Récluz, 1844	NGC;CGC;SGC;BR	BEN	2	118
Natica chemnitzii	Pfeiffer, 1840	NGC;CGC;BR;SWB	BEN;LIT	0	30
Natica lunaris	(Berry, 1964)	NGC;CGC;SGC;BR	BEN	13	46
Natica scethra	Dall, 1908	NGC;CGC	BEN;LIT	0	281
Neorapana muricata	(Broderip, 1832)	NGC;CGC	BEN;LIT	0	78
Neverita reclusiana	(Deshayes, 1839)	NGC;CGC;SGC;BR	BEN;LIT	0	50
Niso baueri	Emerson, 1965	NGC;CGC	BEN	35	80
Niso excolpa	Bartsch, 1917	NGC;CGC;BR	BEN	12	100
Niso hipolitensis	Bartsch, 1917	NGC;CGC	BEN	5	41
Niso lomana	Bartsch, 1917	NGC	BEN	9	183
Niso splendidula	(Sowerby, 1834)	NGC;CGC;SGC	BEN	10	110
Nitidiscala arcana	(Dushane, 1979)	NGC;BR	BEN;LIT	0	18
Nitidiscala durhamianum	(Hertlein & Strong, 1951)	NGC;BR	BEN	9	27
Nitidiscala hexagona	(Sowerby, 1844)	NGC;CGC;SGC;SWB	BEN;LIT	0	1
Nitidiscala bindsii	(Carpenter, 1856)	NGC;CGC;BR	BEN	0	198
Nodilittorina albicarinata	(McLean, 1970)	NGC;CGC;SGC;BR	BEN;LIT	0	?
Nodilittorina aspera	(Philippi, 1846)	NGC;CGC;SGC;BR;SWB	BEN;LIT	0	41
Nodilittorina modesta	(Philippi, 1846)	NGC;CGC;SGC	BEN;LIT	0	41
Oliva polpasta	Duclos, 1833	NGC;CGC;SWB	BEN	20	35

TABLE 29.3 (CONT'D). *Annotated list of macroinvertebrates known from the northern Gulf of California.*

Species	Author	Distribution	Habitat		
Oliva spicata spicata	(Röding, 1798)	NGC;CGC;SGC;BR	BEN;LIT	29	0
Oliva subangulata corteziana	Petuch & Sargent, 1986	NGC	BEN	?	20
Oliva undatella	Lamarck, 1811	NGC;CGC;SGC;SWB	BEN;LIT	29	0
Olivella dama	(Wood, 1828 ex Mawe MS)	NGC;CGC;SGC;BR	BEN;LIT	35	0
Olivella fletcberae	Berry, 1958	NGC;CGC;BR	BEN;LIT	41	0
Olivella gracilis	(Broderip & Sowerby, 1829)	NGC;CGC;SGC	BEN	41	12
Olivella sphoni	Burch & Campbell, 1963	NGC;CGC;SGC	BEN	37	4
Olivella steveni	Burch & Campbell, 1963	NGC;CGC;SGC;BR	BEN;LIT	37	0
Olivella zanoeta	(Duclos, 1835)	NGC;CGC;SGC;BR	BEN	49	10
Olivella zonalis	(Lamarck, 1811)	NGC;CGC;SGC	BEN;LIT	?	0
Opalia crenatoides	(Carpenter, 1864)	NGC;CGC;SGC	BEN	30	0
Opalia funiculata	(Carpenter, 1857)	NGC;CGC;SGC	BEN;LIT	30	0
Opalia sanjuanensis	(Lowe, 1932)	NGC;CGC;BR	BEN;LIT	36	0
Opalia spongiosa	Carpenter, 1864	NGC;CGC;SGC	BEN	72	16
Opeatostoma pseudodon	(Burrow, 1815)	NGC;CGC;SGC;BR	BEN;LIT	41	0
Parametaria dupontii	(Kiener, 1850)	NGC;CGC;SGC	BEN	40	0
Parvanachis gaskoini	(Carpenter, 1857)	NGC;CGC;SGC	BEN;LIT	?	0
Pascula ferruginosa	(Reeve, 1846)	NGC;CGC;BR	BEN;LIT	?	0
Persicula phrygia	(Sowerby, 1846)	NGC;SWB	BEN;LIT	20	0
Petaloconchus flavescens	Carpenter, 1857	NGC;CGC;SGC	?	?	?
Petaloconchus innumerabilis	Pilsbry & Olsson, 1935	NGC;CGC;SGC	BEN	?	35
Philbertia doris	Dall, 1919	NGC;CGC;SGC;BR	BEN	50	12
Phos dejanira	(Dall, 1919)	NGC;CGC;SGC;BR	BEN	33	12
Phos gaudens	Hinds, 1844	NGC;CGC;SGC;BR	BEN	110	18
Phyllonotus erythrostomus	(Swainson, 1831)	NGC;CGC;SGC;BR	BEN;LIT	100	0
Pilosabia pilosa	(Deshayes, 1832)	NGC;CGC;SGC;BR	BEN;LIT	180	0
Pilsbryspira bacchia	(Dall, 1919)	NGC;CGC;SGC;BR	BEN	35	0
Pilsbryspira nymphia	(Pilsbry & Lowe, 1932)	NGC;CGC;SGC;BR	BEN;LIT	6	0
Pleuroploca princeps	(Sowerby, 1825)	NGC;CGC;SGC;BR	BEN	41	3
Plicopurpura patula pansa	Gould, 1853	NGC;CGC;SGC;SWB	BEN;LIT	41	0
Polinices bifasciatus	(Griffith & Pidgeon, 1834)	NGC;CGC;BR;SWB	BEN;LIT	60	0
Polinices intemeratus	(Philippi, 1853)	NGC	BEN;LIT	333	0
Polinices uber	(Valenciennes, 1832)	NGC;CGC;SGC	BEN;LIT	100	0
Polystira nobilis	(Hinds, 1843)	NGC;CGC;SGC;BR	BEN	183	18
Polystira oxytropis	(Sowerby, 1834)	NGC;CGC;SGC	BEN	110	20

TABLE 29.3 (CONT'D). *Annotated list of macroinvertebrates known from the northern Gulf of California.*

Polystira picta	(Reeve, 1843)	BEN	NGC;CGC;SGC;BR	20	70
Pteropurpura erinaceoides	(Valenciennes, 1832)	BEN;LIT	NGC;CGC	0	88
Pteropurpura macroptera	(Deshayes, 1839)	BEN	NGC	?	183
Pterynotus pinniger	(Broderip, 1833)	BEN	NGC;CGC	11	82
Pyrgocythara danae	(Dall, 1919)	BEN	NGC;CGC;BR	10	30
Pyrgocythara emersoni	Shasky, 1971	BEN;LIT	NGC;CGC;BR	0	?
Pyrgocythara belena	(Dall, 1919)	BEN	NGC;CGC;SGC	11	40
Pyrgocythara melita	(Dall, 1919)	BEN	NGC;CGC;SGC;BR	20	40
Pyrgocythara phaethusa	(Dall, 1919)	BEN	NGC;CGC;BR	0	40
Pyrgocythara scammoni	(Dall, 1919)	BEN;LIT	NGC;CGC;BR;SWB	0	35
Pyrgospira obeliscus	(Reeve, 1843)	BEN	NGC;CGC;SGC;BR	20	90
Recluzia palmeri	(Dall, 1871)	?	NGC;CGC;SGC	?	?
Rhinocoryne humboldti	(Valenciennes, 1832)	BEN;LACS	NGC;CGC;BR	?	27
Rissoina burragei	Bartsch, 1915	?	NGC;CGC;BR	?	?
Rissoina clandestina	(C.B. Adams, 1852)	BEN	NGC;CGC	11	41
Rissoina stricta	Menke, 1850	BEN;LIT	NGC;CGC;SGC;SWB	0	?
Rissoina woodwardi	Carpenter, 1857	BEN	NGC;CGC;SGC;BR	35	?
Rissoina zeltneri	(De Folin, 1867)	?	NGC;CGC;SGC	11	41
Rissoina mexicana	Bartsch, 1915	BEN	NGC;CGC;SGC;BR	0	0
Sabinella shaskyi	Warén, 1992	BEN	NGC;CGC;SGC	5	45
Seila assimilata	(C.B. Adams, 1852)	BEN;LIT	NGC;CGC;SGC;BR	0	41
Seila kanoni	(de Folin, 1867)	BEN;LIT	NGC;CGC;SGC	0	41
Seila pulmoensis	DuShane & Draper, 1975	BEN;LIT	NGC;CGC;SGC;BR	0	41
Serpulorbis eruciformis	(Mörch, 1862)	?	NGC;BR	?	?
Sinnialena rufa	(Sowerby, 1832)	?	NGC;CGC;SGC;BR	11	27
Sincola gibberula	(Sowerby, 1832)	BEN;LIT	NGC;CGC;SGC;BR;SWB	0	183
Sinum grayi	(Deshayes, 1853)	BEN	NGC;CGC;SGC	25	160
Sinum sanctijohannis	(Pilsbry & Lowe, 1932)	BEN	NGC;CGC	18	165
Solariorbis ametabolus	Pilsbry & Olsson, 1952	BEN	NGC	2	18
Solariorbis annulatus	(Carpenter, 1857)	?	NGC;CGC;SGC;BR	?	?
Solariorbis carinatus	(Carpenter, 1857)	BEN	NGC;CGC;SGC	2	7
Solariorbis concinnus	(C.B. Adams, 1852)	?	NGC;CGC	9	18
Solariorbis cortezi	Myers, Hertz & Gemmell, 1991	BEN;LIT;NER	NGC;CGC	0	1
Solariorbis ditropis	Pilsbry & Olsson, 1952	BEN	NGC;CGC	35	?

TABLE 29.3 (CONT'D). *Annotated list of macroinvertebrates known from the northern Gulf of California.*

Solariorbis gibraleonis	Pilsbry & Olsson, 1952	NGC	?	?	?
Solariorbis bambachi	(Strong & Hertlein, 1939)	NGC;CGC;BR	BEN	12	35
Solariorbis hypolius	Pilsbry & Olsson, 1952	NGC;BR	?	?	?
Solariorbis minutus	(C.B. Adams, 1852)	NGC;CGC	BEN	35	?
Solariorbis regularis	(C.B. Adams, 1852)	NGC;CGC	BEN;LIT	0	?
Splendrillia bratcherae	McLean & Poorman, 1971	NGC;CGC	BEN	12	100
Steironepion tincta	(Carpenter, 1864)	NGC;CGC;SGC	BEN	11	41
Strictispira ericana	(Hertlein & Strong, 1951)	NGC;CGC;SGC	BEN	10	100
Strictispira stillmani	Shasky, 1971	NGC;CGC;SGC;BR	BEN;LIT	0	41
Strombina angularis	(Sowerby, 1832)	NGC;CGC;SGC	BEN	12	300
Strombina carmencita	Lowe, 1935	NGC;CGC;SGC	BEN	9	165
Strombus galeatus	Swainson, 1823	NGC;CGC;SGC;BR	BEN;LIT	0	41
Strombus gracilior	Sowerby, 1825	NGC;CGC;BR	BEN;LIT;LACS	0	48
Strombus granulatus	Swainson, 1822	NGC;CGC;SGC	BEN;LIT	0	75
Subcancilla attenuata	(Broderip, 1836)	NGC;CGC;SGC;BR	BEN	9	91
Subcancilla erythrogramma	(Tomlin, 1931)	NGC;CGC;SGC	BEN	0	165
Tectarius muricatus	(Linnaeus, 1758)	NGC;BR	?	?	?
Teinostoma ecuadorianum	Pilsbry & Olsson, 1941	NGC;CGC.BR	BEN	12	35
Teinostoma hemphilli	Strong & Hertlein, 1939	NGC;CGC;BR	BEN	11	35
Teinostoma berbertianum	Hertlein & Strong, 1951	NGC;CGC;BR;SWB	BEN	3	35
Teinostoma imperfectum	Pilsbry & Olsson, 1945	NGC;BR	?	?	?
Teinostoma politum politum	A. Adams, 1853	NGC;CGC;BR	BEN	0	15
Teinostoma politum ultimum	Pilsbry & Olsson, 1945	NGC;BR	BEN;LIT	0	1
Teinostoma amplectans	Carpenter, 1857	NGC;CGC;SGC;BR;SWB	BEN	12	?
Tenaturris merita	(Hinds, 1843)	NGC;CGC;BR	BEN;LIT	0	35
Terebra affinis	Gray, 1834	NGC	BEN;LIT	0	100
Terebra argosya	Olsson, 1971	NGC;CGC	?	0	41
Terebra armillata	Hinds, 1844	NGC;CGC;SGC;BR;SWB	BEN	1	110
Terebra berryi	Campbell, 1961	NGC;CGC;3R	BEN	2	37
Terebra brandi	Bratcher & Burch, 1970	NGC;CGC;SGC	BEN;LIT	0	76
Terebra bridgesi	Dall, 1908	NGC;CGC;3R	BEN;LIT	0	25
Terebra churea	Campbell, 1964	NGC;CGC;BR	BEN	1	108
Terebra corintoensis	Pilsbry & Lowe, 1932	NGC;CGC;BR	BEN;LIT	0	41
Terebra crenifera	Deshayes, 1859	NGC;CGC;SGC;BR	BEN;LIT	0	110

TABLE 29.3 (CONT'D). *Annotated list of macroinvertebrates known from the northern Gulf of California.*

Terebra elata	Hinds, 1844	NGC;SWB	BEN;LIT	0	90
Terebra glauca	Hinds, 1844	NGC;CGC;SGC	BEN;LIT	0	90
Terebra larvaeformis	Hinds, 1844	NGC;CGC;SGC;BR;SWB	BEN	5	73
Terebra ornata	Gray, 1834	NGC;CGC	BEN;LIT	0	85
Terebra petiveriana	Deshayes, 1857	NGC;CGC;BR	BEN;LIT	11	90
Terebra puncturosa	Berry, 1959	NGC;CGC;SWB	BEN;LIT	0	90
Terebra robusta	Hinds, 1844	NGC;CGC;SGC;SWB	BEN;LIT	0	110
Terebra roperi	Pilsbry & Lowe, 1932	NGC;CGC;SGC;BR;SWB	BEN	4	31
Terebra tuberculosa	Hinds, 1844	NGC;CGC;SGC;BR;SWB	BEN;LIT	0	100
Terebra variegata	Gray, 1834	NGC;CGC;SGC;BR;SWB	BEN;LIT	0	110
Thais kiosquiformis	(Duclos, 1832)	NGC;CGC;SGC;BR;SWB	BEN;LIT;LACS	0	?
Tiariturris spectabilis	Berry, 1958	NGC	BEN	35	90
Trachypollia lugubris	(C.B. Adams, 1852)	NGC;CGC;SGC	BEN	0	40
Trigonostoma goniostoma	(Sowerby, 1832)	NGC;CGC;BR	BEN;LIT	0	36
Trigonostoma bullatum	(Sowerby, 1832)	NGC;CGC;BR	BEN	21	82
Triphora excolpa	Bartsch, 1907	NGC;CGC;SGC;BR	BEN	11	41
Triphora bannai	Baker, 1926	NGC;CGC;SGC;BR	BEN	4	35
Tripsycha tripsycha	(Pilsbry & Lowe, 1932)	NGC;CGC;SGC;BR	BEN;LIT	0	40
Tripterotyphis lowei lowei	(Pilsbry, 1931)	NGC;CGC;SGC	BEN;LIT	0	150
Tritonoharpa siphonata	(Reeve, 1844)	NGC;CGC;SGC	BEN	18	180
Trivia californica californica	(Sowerby, 1832 ex Gray, MS)	NGC;CGC;SWB	?	?	?
Trivia campus	(Cate, 1979)	NGC;BR	?	?	?
Trivia elsiae	Howard & Sphon, 1960	NGC	?	?	?
Trivia myrae	Campbell, 1961	NGC;CGC;SGC;BR	BEN	18	146
Trivia solandri	(Sowerby, 1832 ex Gray, MS)	NGC;CGC;SGC;BR	BEN;LIT	0	35
Trophonopsis diazi	(Durham, 1942)	NGC	?	1573	1,720
Trophonopsis lorenzoensis	(Durham, 1942)	NGC	?	1573	1,720
Truncatella californica	Pfeiffer, 1857	NGC;BR;SWB	BEN;LIT	0	?
Turritella anactor	Berry, 1957	NGC;BR	BEN;LIT	0	49
Turritella clarionensis	Hertlein & Strong, 1951	NGC;CGC;SGC	BEN	27	100
Turritella gonostoma	Valenciennes, 1832	NGC;CGC;SGC;BR	BEN;LIT	0	2
Turritella leucostoma	Valenciennes, 1832	NGC;CGC;SGC;BR	BEN;LIT	0	50
Turritella mariana	Dall, 1908	NGC;CGC;SGC	BEN	22	150
Turritella nodulosa	King & Broderip, 1832	NGC;CGC;SGC;BR;SWB	BEN	4	170

TABLE 29.3 (CONT'D). Annotated list of macroinvertebrates known from the northern Gulf of California.

Turritella rubescens	Reeve, 1849	NGC;CGC;SGC	BEN	20	55
Turveria encopendema	Berry, 1956	NGC;CGC;BR	BEN;PAR;COM	?	?
Turveria pallida	Warén, 1992	NGC;CGC	BEN;COM	0	?
Typhisala clarki	(Keen & Campbell, 1964)	NGC;CGC;BR;SWB	BEN;LIT	0	99
Typhisopsis coronatus	(Broderip, 1833)	NGC;CGC;SWB	BEN	18	80
Vanikoro aperta	(Carpenter, 1864)	NGC;CGC;SGC	BEN	6	41
Vermetus contortus	(Carpenter, 1857)	NGC;CGC;SGC	BEN;LIT	0	?
Vermetus indentatus	(Carpenter, 1857)	NGC;CGC;SGC;BR	BEN;LIT	0	35
Vermicularia frisbeyae	McLean, 1970	NGC;CGC;SGC	BEN	12	110
Vitrinella ?naticoides	Carpenter, 1857	NGC;CGC;SGC;BR	?	?	?
Vitrinella dalli	(Bartsch, 1911)	NGC;CGC;BR	BEN	10	?
Vitrinella goniomphala	Pilsbry & Olsson, 1952	NGC;CGC;BR	?	?	?
Vitrinella subquadrata	Carpenter, 1857	NGC;CGC;SGC;BR	?	?	?
Vitrinella tiburonensis	Durham, 1942	NGC	?	393	?
Vitrinella zonitoides	Pilsbry & Olsson, 1952	NGC	?	?	?
Xenophora conchyliophora	(Born, 1780)	NGC;CGC;BR	BEN	18	635
Zanassarina anitae	(Campbell, 1961)	NGC;CGC;BR	BEN	0	100
Zanassarina atella	(Pilsbry & Lowe, 1932)	NGC;CGC	BEN	0	60
Zanassarina pammicra	(Pilsbry & Lowe, 1932)	NGC	BEN	?	?
Zebina preposterum	(Berry, 1958)	NGC;BR	?	?	?
Zonulispira grandimaculata	(C.B. Adams, 1852)	NGC;CGC;SGC;BR	BEN;LIT	0	35
HETEROBRANCHIA					
Architectonica nobilis	Röding, 1798	NGC;CGC;SGC;BR;SWB	BEN;LIT	0	183
Chrysallida oonisca	(Dall & Bartsch, 1909)	NGC;CGC;SGC	BEN	?	?
Chrysallida reigeni	(Carpenter, 1857)	NGC;CGC;SGC;BR	BEN	?	?
Chrysallida telescopium	(Carpenter, 1857)	NGC;CGC;SGC;BR	BEN	?	?
Chrysallida torrita	(Dall & Bartsch, 1909)	NGC;CGC;SGC	BEN	?	?
Discotectonica placentalis	(Hinds, 1844)	NGC;CGC;SGC;SWB	BEN	18	100
Evalea palmeri	(Bartsch, 1912)	NGC;BR	BEN	?	?
Heliacus mazatlanicus	Pilsbry & Lowe, 1932	NGC;CGC;SGC;BR	BEN	3	38
Heliacus planispira	Pilsbry & Lowe, 1932	NGC;CGC;SGC	BEN	36	?
Heliacus bicaniculatus	(Valenciennes, 1832)	NGC;CGC;SGC;BR	BEN	0	36
Herviera glirella	(Melvill & Standen, 1896)	NGC;CGC	?	8	37
Hoffmannola hansi	Marcus & Marcus, 1967	NGC;CGC;SGC	BEN;LIT	0	?

TABLE 29.3 (CONT'D.). *Annotated list of macroinvertebrates known from the northern Gulf of California.*

Iselica kochi	Strong & Hertlein, 1939	NGC;BR	BEN	5	15
Iselica ovoidea	(Gould, 1853)	NGC;CGC;SGC;BR	BEN	12	35
Miralda terebellum	(C.B. Adams, 1852)	NGC;CGC	BEN	12	41
Odostomia lacunata	Carpenter, 1857	NGC;CGC;SGC	BEN	35	?
Odostomia berrerae	Baker, Hanna & Strong, 1928	NGC;CGC	BEN	?	?
Odostomia convexa	Carpenter, 1857	NGC;CGC;SGC;BR	BEN	26	45
Odostomia gabrielensis	Baker, Hanna & Strong, 1928	NGC;CGC;BR	BEN	?	?
Odostomia excolpa	Bartsch, 1912	NGC;BR	BEN	?	?
Odostomia scalariformis	Carpenter, 1857	NGC;CGC;SGC	BEN	35	?
Onchidella binneyi	Stearns, 1893	NGC;CGC;BR	BEN;LIT	0	30
Onchidella hildae	(Hoffman, 1928)	NGC;BR	BEN;LIT	0	?
Peristichia bermosa	(Lowe, 1935)	NGC;CGC;BR	BEN	12	35
Pseudotorinia architae panamensis	Bartsch, 1918	NGC;CGC;SGC;BR	?	7	41
Pyramidella adamsi	Carpenter, 1864	NGC;CGC;BR	BEN;LIT	0	35
Pyramidella linearum	Pilsbry & Lowe, 1932	NGC;CGC;BR	BEN	18	37
Pyramidella panamensis	Dall & Bartsch, 1909	NGC;CGC;SGC;BR	BEN	18	91
Pyramidella mazatlanica	Dall & Bartsch, 1909	NGC;CGC;SGC	BEN	0	81
Pyramidella auricoma	Dall, 1889	NGC;CGC;SGC;BR	BEN	?	97
Turbonilla ceralva	Dall & Bartsch, 1909	NGC;CGC;BR	BEN	?	?
Turbonilla sinaloana	Strong, 1949	NGC;CGC;SGC	BEN	35	?
Turbonilla soniliana	Hertlein & Strong, 1951	NGC;CGC;BR	BEN	12	?
Turbonilla bannai	Strong, 1938	NGC;CGC;SGC	BEN	18	45
Turbonilla subangulata	(Carpenter, 1857)	NGC;CGC;SGC;BR	BEN	0	?
Turbonilla stenogyra	Dall & Bartsch, 1909	NGC;BR	BEN	?	?
Turbonilla kelseyi	Dall & Bartsch, 1909	NGC;CGC;SGC	BEN	35	35
Turbonilla paramoea	Dall & Bartsch, 1909	NGC	?	?	?
Turbonilla coyotensis	Baker, Hanna & Strong, 1928	NGC;CGC	BEN	20	40
Turbonilla sedillina	Dall & Bartsch, 1909	NGC;CGC;SGC	BEN	35	?
Turbonilla alarconi	Strong, 1949	NGC;CGC	BEN	?	?
Turbonilla peñascoensis	Lowe, 1935	NGC;CGC;BR	BEN	18	20
Turbonilla azteca	Baker, Hanna & Strong, 1928	NGC;CGC	BEN	2	6
Turbonilla francisquitana	Baker, Hanna & Strong, 1928	NGC	BEN	?	?
Turbonilla balidoma	Dall & Bartsch, 1909	NGC;CGC;SGC	BEN	12	?
Turbonilla bistias	Dall & Bartsch, 1909	NGC;CGC	BEN	35	38

TABLE 29.3 (CONT'D). *Annotated list of macroinvertebrates known from the northern Gulf of California.*

Species	Authority	Distribution	Habitat		
Turbonilla kaliwana	Strong, 1949	NGC	BEN	?	?
Turbonilla macbridei	Dall & Bartsch, 1909	NGC;CGC;BR	BEN	16	18
Turbonilla mayana	Baker, Hanna & Strong, 1928	NGC;BR	BEN	?	?
Turbonilla porteri	Baker, Hanna & Strong, 1928	NGC	BEN	?	?
Turbonilla sanctorum	Dall & Bartsch, 1909	NGC;CGC;BR	BEN	18	?
Turbonilla sealei	Strong & Hertlein, 1939	NGC;BR	BEN	5	15
Turbonilla gonzagensis	Baker, Hanna & Strong, 1928	NGC;CGC	BEN	?	?
Turbonilla pazana	Dall & Bartsch, 1909	NGC;CGC;BR	BEN	18	35
Turbonilla stylina	(Carpenter, 1865)	NGC;CGC;BR	?	?	?
Turbonilla excolpa	Dall & Bartsch, 1909	NGC;CGC;SGC;BR	BEN	?	?
OPISTHOBRANCHIA (SEA SLUGS)					
Acanthodoris pina	Marcus & Marcus, 1967	NGC;BR	BEN;LIT	0	?
Acanthodoris serpentinotus	Williams & Gosliner, 1979	NGC;BR	BEN;LIT	0	?
Acteocina angustior	Baker & Hanna, 1927	NGC;CGC;SGC;BR	BEN	3	40
Acteocina carinata	(Carpenter, 1857)	NGC;CGC;SGC;BR	BEN	2	45
Acteocina gonzagensis	(Baker & Hanna, 1927)	NGC	BEN	20	30
Acteocina inculta	(Gould & Carpenter, 1857)	NGC;CGC	BEN;LACS	?	?
Acteocina infrequens	(C.B. Adams, 1852)	NGC;CGC;SGC;BR;SWB	BEN;LACS	2	30
Acteocina tabogaensis	(Strong & Hertlein, 1939)	NGC;BR	BEN	18	34
Acteon panamensis	Dall, 1908	NGC	BEN	?	2,3,20
Aegires albopunctatus	MacFarland, 1905	NGC	BEN	0	18
Aeolidiella chromosoma	(Cockerell & Eliot, 1905)	NGC;CGC;BR	BEN;LIT	0	30
Ancula lentiginosa	Farmer & Sloan, 1964	NGC	BEN;LIT	0	?
Aplysia californica	Cooper, 1863	NGC;CGC;SGC;BR	BEN;LIT	0	30
Aplysia juliana	Quoy & Gaimard, 1832	NGC;CGC;BR	BEN	?	?
Aplysia parvula	Mörch, 1863	NGC;CGC;BR	BEN	0	?
Aplysia vaccaria	Winkler, 1955	NGC	BEN;LIT	0	?
Aplysiopsis smithi	(Marcus, 1961)	NGC;CGC	BEN	?	?
Armina californica	(Cooper, 1863)	NGC;CGC;SGC;BR	BEN;LIT	0	80
Atys casta	Carpenter, 1864	NGC;CGC;SGC	BEN	9	41
Bajaeolis bertschi	Gosliner & Behrens, 1986	NGC	?	?	?
Berthella stellata	(Risso, 1826)	NGC;CGC;BR	?	1	10
Berthellina engeli	Gardiner, 1936	NGC;CGC;BR	BEN;LIT	0	18
Bulla gouldiana	Pilsbry, 1895	NGC;CGC;SGC;BR	BEN;LIT;LACS	0	35

TABLE 29.3 (CONT'D.). *Annotated list of macroinvertebrates known from the northern Gulf of California.*

Bulla punctulata	A. Adams in Sowerby, 1850	NGC;CGC;SGC;SWB	BEN;LIT	0	35
Cadlina flavomaculata	MacFarland, 1905	NGC;BR	BEN;LIT	0	220
Cerberilla pungoarena	Collier & Farmer, 1964	NGC	BEN	?	?
Chromodoris norrisi	Farmer, 1963	NGC;CGC;SGC;BR	BEN;LIT	0	20
Connualevia marcusi	Collier & Farmer, 1964	NGC	BEN	?	?
Connualevia mizuna	Marcus & Marcus, 1967	NGC;BR	BEN	0	30
Cuthona longi	Behrens, 1985	NGC	BEN	3	?
Cylichna atahualpa	(Dall, 1908)	NGC	BEN	?	590
Cylichna fantasma	(Baker & Hanna, 1927)	NGC;CGC	BEN	9	30
Dendrodoris krebsii	(Mörch, 1863)	NGC;CGC;BR	BEN;LIT	0	5
Dendronotus nanus	Marcus & Marcus, 1967	NGC;BR	CST	4	?
Diaulula sandiegensis	(Cooper, 1863)	NGC;CGC;SGC;BR	BEN;LIT	0	37
Dirona picta	MacFarland in Cockerell & Eliot, 1905	NGC;BR	BEN;LIT	0	10
Discodoris mavis	Marcus & Marcus, 1967	NGC;BR	BEN	?	?
Dolabrifera dolabrifera	(Rang, 1828)	NGC;CGC;SGC;BR	BEN	0	?
Doriopsilla albopunctata	(Cooper, 1863)	NGC;BR	BEN;LIT	0	30
Doriopsilla gemela	Gosliner, Schaefer & Millen, 1999	NGC	BEN;LIT	0	9
Doriopsilla janaina	Marcus & Marcus, 1967	NGC	BEN;LIT	0	?
Doriopsilla rowena	Marcus & Marcus, 1967	NGC;CGC;SGC;BR	BEN	20	30
Doris pickensi	Marcus & Marcus, 1967	NGC;CGC;BR	BEN;LIT	0	?
Doto amyra	Marcus, 1961	NGC;BR	?	?	?
Doto lancei	Marcus & Marcus, 1967	NGC;CGC;BR	?	?	?
Elysia bedgpethi	Marcus, 1961	NGC;CGC	BEN	0	?
Embletonia gracilis	Risbec, 1928	NGC	?	?	?
Eubranchus cucullus	Behrens, 1985	NGC	BEN	0	?
Eubranchus rustyus	(Marcus, 1961)	NGC;BR	BEN;EPIF	0	?
Flabellina bertschi	Gosliner & Kuzirian, 1990	NGC;CGC;BR	BEN	0	22
Flabellina cynara	(Marcus & Marcus, 1967)	NGC;CGC;SGC;BR	BEN;LIT	0	72
Flabellina iodinea	(Cooper, 1863)	NGC;CGC;SGC;BR	BEN;LIT	0	39
Flabellina marcusorum	Gosliner & Kuzirian, 1990	NGC;CGC;SGC	BEN	10	22
Flabellina stohleri	Berstch & Ferreira, 1974	NGC	BEN;LIT	0	?
Glossodoris dalli	(Bergh, 1879)	NGC;CGC;SGC;BR;SWB	BEN;LIT	0	30

TABLE 29.3 (CONT'D). *Annotated list of macroinvertebrates known from the northern Gulf of California.*

Glossodoris sedna	(Marcus & Marcus, 1967)	NGC;CGC;SGC;BR	BEN;LIT	0	20
Haminoea virescens	(Sowerby, 1833)	NGC;CGC;BR	BEN;LIT;LACS	0	36
Haminoea angelensis	Baker & Hanna, 1927	NGC;CGC;BR	BEN	7	30
Hemissenda crassicornis	(Eschscholtz, in Rathke, 1831)	NGC;BR	BEN;LIT	0	37
Hermaea billae	Marcus & Marcus, 1967	NGC;BR	BEN	?	?
Histiomena convolvula	(Lance, 1962)	NGC;CGC;BR	BEN;LIT	0	30
Hypselodoris agassizii	(Bergh, 1894)	NGC;CGC;SGC;BR	BEN	0	3
Hypselodoris californiensis	(Bergh, 1879)	NGC;CGC;SGC;BR	BEN;LIT	0	31
Hypselodoris ghiselini	Bertsch, 1978	NGC;CGC;SGC;BR	BEN;LIT	0	4
Inuda luarna	Marcus & Marcus, 1967	NGC;BR	BEN;LIT	0	?
Janolus barbarensis	(Cooper, 1863)	NGC;CGC;BR	BEN;LIT	0	?
Laila cockerelli	MacFarland, 1905	NGC;CGC;SGC	BEN	0	34
Melibe leonina	(Gould, 1852)	NGC	BEN;LIT	0	37
Navanax inermis	(Cooper, 1863)	NGC;CGC;SGC;BR	BEN;LIT	0	30
Okenia angelensis	Lance, 1966	NGC	BEN;LIT	0	?
Phidiana hiltoni	(O'Donoghue, 1927)	NGC	BEN;LIT	0	220
Phyllaplysia padinae	Williams & Gosliner, 1973	NGC;CGC	?	?	?
Pleurobranchus areolatum	(Mörch, 1863)	NGC;CGC;3GC;BR	BEN;LIT	0	30
Polycera alabe	Collier & Farmer, 1964	NGC;CGC;3R	BEN	20	30
Polycera hedgpethi	Marcus, 1964	NGC;BR	BEN;LIT	0	30
Polycerella glandulosa	Behrens & Gosliner, 1988	NGC;CGC	BEN	0	20
Rostanga pulchra	MacFarland, 1905	NGC;BR	BEN;LIT	0	102
Spurilla major	(Eliot, 1903)	NGC	?	?	?
Stiliger cf. fuscata	(Gould, 1870)	NGC;BR	BEN	?	?
Stiliger fuscovittata	Lance, 1962	NGC	BEN	?	?
Stylocheilus longicauda	(Quoy & Gaimard, 1824)	NGC;CGC;SGC;BR	BEN;LIT;LACS	0	?
Sulcoretusa paziana	(Dall, 1919)	NGC;CGC;BR	BEN	22	40
Tambja eliora	(Marcus & Marcus, 1967)	NGC;CGC;SWB	BEN;LIT	0	30
Taringa aivica timia	Marcus & Marcus, 1967	NGC;BR	BEN	0	?
Tayuva ketos	Marcus & Marcus, 1967	NGC;CGC;SGC;BR	BEN;LIT	0	?
Tridachiella diomedea	(Bergh, 1894)	NGC;CGC	BEN;LIT	0	15
Tritonia pickensi	Marcus & Marcus, 1967	NGC;CGC;SGC;BR	BEN;LIT	0	?
Tyrinna evelinae	(Ernst Marcus, 1958)	NGC;CGC;ER	BEN;LIT	0	?
Volvulella cylindrica	(Carpenter, 1864)	NGC;CGC;ER	BEN	12	75

TABLE 29.3 (CONT'D). Annotated list of macroinvertebrates known from the northern Gulf of California.

Taxon	Authority					
Volvulella panamica	Dall, 1919	NGC;BR	BEN		11	41
PULMONATA (PULMONATE SNAILS)						
Marinula rhoadsi	Pilsbry, 1910	NGC;BR	BEN;LIT;LACS		0	?
Melampus olivaceus	Carpenter, 1857	NGC;CGC;SGC;BR	BEN;LIT;LACS		0	?
Melampus mousleyi	Berry, 1964	NGC;BR	BEN		20	30
Pedipes angulatus	C.B. Adams, 1852	NGC;CGC;BR	BEN		11	41
Sarnia mexicana	(Berry, 1964)	NGC	?		?	?
Williamia peltoides	(Carpenter, 1864)	NGC;CGC;SGC;BR	BEN;LIT		0	41
BIVALVIA (CLAMS AND THEIR KIN)						
Abra tepocana	Dall, 1915	NGC;BR	BEN;NER		18	26
Adrana exoptata	(Pilsbry & Lowe, 1932)	NGC;CGC;SGC;BR	BEN;NER		7	48
Adrana penascoensis	(Lowe, 1935)	NGC;CGC;SGC;BR	BEN;NER		18	30
Aligena cokeri	Dall, 1909	NGC;CGC;BR	BEN;LIT;NER		0	25
Aligena nucea	Dall, 1913	NGC;CGC;BR	BEN;LIT;NER		0	33
Aligena obliqua	Harry, 1969	NGC;CGC;SGC;BR	BEN;LIT;NER		0	18
Anadara adamsi	Olsson, 1961	NGC;CGC;SGC	BEN;NER		20	70
Anadara cepoides	(Reeve, 1844)	NGC;CGC	BEN;NER		18	84
Anadara concinna	(Sowerby, 1833)	NGC;CGC;SGC	BEN;NER		9	180
Anadara formosa	(Sowerby, 1833)	NGC;CGC;SGC	BEN;NER		8	122
Anadara multicostata	(Sowerby, 1833)	NGC;CGC;SGC;SWB	BEN;LIT;EPIF;NER		0	130
Anadara obesa	(Sowerby, 1833)	NGC;CGC;SGC	BEN;EPIF		10	112
Anadara reinharti	(Lowe, 1935)	NGC;CGC;SGC;BR	BEN;LIT;EPIF;NER		2	122
Anadara tuberculosa	(Sowerby, 1833)	NGC;CGC;SGC	BEN;LIT;EPIF;LACS		0	32
Anatina cyprinus	(Wood, 1828)	NGC;CGC	BEN;NER		20	50
Anomia adamas	Gray, 1850	NGC;CGC;SGC	BEN;LIT;NER		0	393
Anomia peruviana	d'Orbigny, 1846	NGC;CGC;SGC;BR	LIT;BEN;CST;EPIF		0	130
Arca mutabilis	(Sowerby, 1833)	NGC;CGC;SGC;SWB	BEN;LIT;CST;NER		0	82
Arca pacifica	(Sowerby, 1833)	NGC;CGC;SGC;BR;SWB	BEN;LIT;EPIF;LACS		0	150
Arcinella californica	(Dall, 1903)	NGC;CGC;SGC	BEN;NER		18	110
Arcopsis solida	(Sowerby, 1833)	NGC;CGC;SGC;BR	BEN;LIT;EPIF;NER		0	30
Argopecten circularis	(Sowerby, 1835)	NGC;CGC;SGC;BR;SWB	CST;BEN;NER		1	150
Asthenothaerus colpoica	(Dall, 1915)	NGC;CGC;SGC	BEN;LIT;NER		0	110
Asthenothaerus diegensis	(Dall, 1915)	NGC;CGC;SWB	BEN;LIT;NER		0	119
Asthenothaerus villosior	Carpenter, 1864	NGC;CGC;SGC;BR	BEN;LIT;NER		0	73

TABLE 29.3 (CONT'D). *Annotated list of macroinvertebrates known from the northern Gulf of California.*

Species	Author				
Atrina tuberculosa	(Sowerby, 1835)	NGC;CGC;BR	BEN;LIT;NER	0	23
Barbatia alternata	(Sowerby, 1833)	NGC;CGC;BR	BEN;LIT;NER	0	27
Barbatia gradata	(Broderip & Sowerby, 1829)	NGC;CGC;SGC;SWB	BEN;LIT;EPIF;NER	0	70
Barbatia lurida	(Sowerby, 1833)	NGC;CGC	BEN;LIT;NER	0	55
Barbatia reeveana	(d'Orbigny, 1846)	NGC;CGC;SGC	BEN;LIT;CST;LACS	0	120
Barnea subtruncata	(Sowerby, 1834)	NGC;CGC;BR	BEN;LIT;NER	0	30
Basterotia californica	Durham, 1950	NGC;CGC;SGC;BR	BEN;LIT	0	100
Basterotia panamica	Coan, 1999	NGC;CGC;SGC;BR	BEN;LIT	0	119
Basterotia peninsularis	(Jordan, 1936)	NGC;CGC;BR;SWB	BEN;LIT;NER	0	46
Basterotia quadrata	(Hinds, 1843)	NGC;CGC;BR	BEN;LIT	6	119
Basterotina rectangularis	Coan, 1999	NGC;CGC;SGC	BEN;LIT	6	119
Bornia chiclaya	Olsson, 1961	NGC;BR	BEN	?	?
Brachidontes adamsianus	(Dunker, 1857)	NGC;CGC;SGC	BEN;LIT;NER	0	1
Brachidontes semilaevis	(Menke, 1849)	NGC;CGC;SGC;BR	BEN;LIT;NER	0	31
Bushia phillipsi	Coan, 1990	NGC;CGC	BEN;NER	38	183
Cardiomya costata	(Sowerby, 1834)	NGC;CGC;SGC;BR;SWB	BEN;NER	4	84
Cardiomya didyma	(Hinds, 1843)	NGC;BR	BEN;NER	18	48
Cardiomya ecuadoriana	(Olsson, 1961)	NGC	BEN;NER	55	146
Cardiomya isolirata	Bernard, 1969	NGC;CGC	BEN;NER	55	183
Cardiomya lanieri	(Strong & Hertlein, 1937)	NGC;CGC;SGC	BEN;NER	15	238
Carditamera affinis	(Sowerby, 1833)	NGC;CGC;SGC;BR	BEN;LIT;NER	0	27
Cardites crassicostata	(Sowerby, 1825)	NGC;CGC;SGC	BEN;LIT;NER	0	55
Chama arcana	Bernard, 1976	NGC;CGC	BEN;LIT;NER	0	50
Chama buddiana	C.B. Adams, 1852	NGC;CGC;SGC;BR	BEN;LIT;NER	0	80
Chama echinata	Broderip, 1835	NGC;CGC;SGC;SWB	BEN;LIT;NER	0	25
Chama frondosa	Broderip, 1835	NGC;CGC;SGC;BR	BEN;LIT;EPIF;NER	0	32
Chama sordida	Broderip, 1835	NGC;CGC;SGC;BR	BEN;LIT;NER	0	82
Chama venosa	Reeve, 1847	NGC;CGC	BEN;LIT;NER	0	4
Chione californiensis	(Broderip, 1835)	NGC;CGC;SGC;BR	BEN;LIT;NER;LACS	0	80
Chione cortezi	(Carpenter, 1864)	NGC;CGC;BR;SWB	BEN;LIT;NER	0	1
Chione fluctifraga	(Sowerby, 1853)	NGC;CGC;SGC	BEN;LIT;NER	0	25
Chione mariae	(d'Orbigny, 1846)	NGC;CGC;SGC;BR	BEN;NER	9	180
Chione tumens	Verrill, 1870	NGC;CGC;SGC;SWB	BEN;LIT;NER	0	10
Chione undatella	(Sowerby, 1835)	NGC;CGC;SGC;BR	BEN;LIT;NER;LACS	0	90

TABLE 29.3 (CONT'D). *Annotated list of macroinvertebrates known from the northern Gulf of California.*

Species	Author				
Chionopsis amathusia	(Philippi, 1844)	NGC;CGC;SGC	BEN;NER	22	110
Chionopsis gnidia	(Broderip & Sowerby, 1829)	NGC;CGC;SGC;BR	BEN;LIT;NER	0	42
Chionopsis pulicaria	(Broderip, 1835)	NGC;CGC;SGC;BR	BEN;NER	9	92
Chionopsis purpurissata	Dall, 1902	NGC;CGC;SGC	BEN;NER	0	80
Chlamys lowei	(Hertlein, 1935)	NGC;CGC;SGC;SWB	BEN;NER	37	180
Codakia distinguenda	(Tryon, 1872)	NGC;CGC;SGC;BR;SWB	BEN;LIT;NER	0	47
Compsomyax subdiaphana	(Carpenter, 1864)	NGC;CGC;BR	BEN	7	23
Condylocardia digueti	Lamy, 1916	NGC;CGC;SGC	BEN;LIT;NER	0	40
Cooperella subdiaphana	(Carpenter, 1864)	NGC;CGC;BR	BEN;NER	7	72
Corbula ira	Dall, 1908	NGC;CGC	BEN;NER	47	330
Corbula luteola	Carpenter, 1864	NGC;CGC;SGC;SWB	BEN;LIT;NER	0	120
Corbula marmorata	Hinds, 1843	NGC;CGC;SGC;BR	BEN;NER	3	90
Corbula nasuta	Sowerby, 1833	NGC;CGC;SGC;BR;SWB	BEN;NER	3	90
Corbula speciosa	Reeve, 1843	NGC;CGC;SGC	BEN;NER	13	110
Crassinella pacifica	(C.B. Adams, 1852)	NGC;CGC;SGC;BR;SWB	BEN;NER	3	158
Crassinella varians	(Carpenter, 1857)	NGC;CGC;SGC;SWB	BEN;LIT;NER	1	1,720
Ctena mexicana	(Dall, 1901)	NGC;CGC;SGC;SWB	BEN;LIT;NER	0	80
Cumingia lamellosa	Sowerby, 1833	NGC;CGC;SGC	BEN;LIT;NER	0	25
Cumingia pacifica	(Dall, 1915)	NGC;CGC;BR	BEN;NER	22	90
Cyathodonta dubiosa	Dall, 1915	NGC;CGC	BEN;NER	13	183
Cyathodonta undulata	Conrad, 1849	NGC;CGC;SWB	BEN;LIT;NER	0	64
Cyclinella singleyi	Dall, 1902	NGC;CGC;SGC	BEN;LACS;NER	15	12
Cyclinella ulloana	Hertlein & Strong, 1948	NGC;CGC;SGC	BEN;NER	10	81
Cyclopecten catalinensis	(Willet, 1931)	NGC	BEN;NER	29	180
Cyclopecten exquisitus	Grau, 1959	NGC	BEN;NER	22	274
Cymatoica undulata	(Hanley, 1844)	NGC;CGC;BR	BEN;NER	7	100
Delectopecten zacae	(Hertlein, 1935)	NGC;CGC;SGC	BEN;NER	10	1,840
Dimya californiana	Berry, 1936	NGC;CGC	BEN;NER	84	1,227
Diplodonta inezensis	(Hertlein & Strong, 1947)	NGC;CGC	BEN;NER	11	64
Diplodonta orbella	(Gould, 1851)	NGC;CGC;BR	BEN;LIT;NER	0	110
Diplothyra curta	(Sowerby, 1834)	NGC;BR	BEN;LIT;NER	10	18
Divalinga eburnea	(Reeve, 1850)	NGC;CGC;SGC;SWB	BEN;LIT;NER	0	180
Donax caelatus caelatus	Carpenter, 1857	NGC;CGC;SGC	BEN;LIT;CST;NER	0	3
Donax californicus	Conrad, 1837	NGC;CGC;SGC;BR;SWB	BEN;LIT;LACS;NER	0	70

TABLE 29.3 (CONT'D.). *Annotated list of macroinvertebrates known from the northern Gulf of California.*

Species	Authority			Habitat	Distribution
Donax gracilis	Hanley, 1845	0	50	BEN;LIT;NER	NGC;CGC;SGC;SWB
Dosinia ponderosa	(Gray, 1838)	3	110	BEN;NER;LACS	NGC;CGC;SGC;BR
Ennucula colombiana	Dall, 1908	11	730	BEN;LIT;NER	NGC;CGC.BR
Ennucula linki	(Dall, 1916)	0	44	BEN;LIT;NER	NGC;CGC.BR
Ensis nitidus	(Clessin, 1888)	0	50	BEN;LIT;NER	NGC;BR;SWB
Ensis tropicalis	Hertlein & Strong, 1955	11	25	BEN;NER	NGC;BR
Ensitellops bertleini	Emerson & Puffer, 1957	9	100	BEN;LIT	NGC;CGC;SGC;BR
Entodesma lucasanum	(Bartsch & Rehder, 1939)	0	20	BEN;LIT;NER	NGC;CGC;SGC;BR
Entodesma pictum	(Sowerby, 1834)	3	35	BEN;NER	NGC;CGC;SGC;BR
Eucrassatella antillarum	(Reeve, 1842)	5	206	BEN;LIT;CST;EPIF	NGC;CGC;SGC
Eucrassatella gibbosa	Sowerby, 1832	5	110	BEN;EPIF;NER	NGC;CGC;SGC;BR;SWB
Fabella stearnsii	(Dall, 1899)	4	32	BEN;LIT	NGC;CGC;SWB
Flabellipecten sericeus	(Hinds, 1845)	13	183	BEN;LACS;NER	NGC;CGC;SGC
Fugleria illota	(Sowerby, 1833)	0	73	BEN;LIT;NER	NGC;CGC;SGC;BR
Galeommella peruviana	(Olsson, 1961)	0	15	BEN;LIT;NER	NGC;BR
Gari fucata	(Hinds, 1844)	5	140	BEN;NER	NGC;CGC;SGC;SWB
Gari helenae	Olsson, 1961	0	47	BEN;LIT;NER	NGC;CGC;BR
Gari maxima	(Deshayes, 1855)	0	1	BEN;LIT;NER	NGC;BR
Gastrochaena ovata	Sowerby, 1834	0	31	BEN;LIT;NER	NGC;CGC;SGC;BR
Globivenus fordii	(Yates, 1890)	10	70	BEN;NER	NGC
Globivenus isocardia	(Verrill, 1870)	0	110	BEN;LIT;NER	NGC;CGC;SGC
Glycymeris gigantea	(Reeve, 1843)	0	92	BEN;LIT;NER	NGC;CGC;SGC;BR;SWB
Glycymeris maculata	(Broderip, 1832)	0	84	BEN;LIT;NER	NGC;CGC;3R;SWB
Glycymeris septentrionalis	(Middendorff, 1849)	?	?	BEN;LIT;NER	NGC
Gregariella chenui	(Récluz, 1842)	30	90	BEN;LIT;NER	NGC;BR
Gregariella coralliophaga	(Gmelin, 1791)	4	100	BEN;NER	NGC;CGC;SGC;BR
Haliris aequacostata	(A. Howard, 1950)	165	190	BEN;NER	NGC
Halodakra subtrigona	(Carpenter, 1857)	0	41	BEN;LIT;NER	NGC;CGC;SGC;BR
Here excavata	(Carpenter, 1857)	5	110	BEN;NER	NGC;CGC;SGC
Heterodonax pacificus	(Conrad, 1837)	0	2	BEN;LIT;NER	NGC
Hiatella arctica	(Linnaeus, 1767)	0	800	BEN;LIT;NER	NGC;CGC;BR
Hyotissa hyotis	Linnaeus, 1758	2	25	BEN;NER	NGC;CGC
Isognomon janus	Carpenter, 1857	0	35	BEN;LIT;NER	NGC;CGC;SGC;BR
Isognomon recognitus	(Mabille, 1895)	0	10	BEN;LIT;NER	NGC;CGC;SGC;BR

TABLE 29.3 (CONT'D). Annotated list of macroinvertebrates known from the northern Gulf of California.

Species	Author				
Laevicardium elatum	(Sowerby, 1833)	NGC;CGC;SGC;BR	BEN;LIT;NER	0	65
Laevicardium elenense	(Sowerby, 1840)	NGC;CGC;SGC;BR;SWB	BEN;LIT;NER	0	161
Leiosolenus spatiosa	(Carpenter, 1857)	NGC;CGC;SGC;BR	BEN;LIT;NER	0	27
Lepton lediformis	Olsson, 1961	NGC	BEN	0	?
Leptopecten palmeri	(Dall, 1897)	NGC;BR	BEN;LIT;NER	0	100
Leptopecten velero	(Hertlein, 1935)	NGC;CGC	BEN;NER	5	100
Limaria orbignyi	(Lamy, 1930)	NGC;CGC;SGC;BR	BEN;LIT;NER	0	34
Limaria pacifica	(d'Orbigny, 1846)	NGC;CGC;SGC;BR	BEN;LIT;NER	0	?
Limatula similaris	(Dall, 1908)	NGC;CGC	BEN;NER	18	106
Linga cancellaris	(Philippi, 1846)	NGC;CGC;SGC	BEN;LIT;NER	0	100
Linga leucocymoides	(Lowe, 1935)	NGC;CGC;SGC	BEN;NER	18	110
Linga undatoides	(Hertlein & Strong, 1945)	NGC;CGC	BEN;LIT;NER	0	30
Lioberus salvadoricus	(Hertlein & Strong, 1946)	NGC;BR	BEN;NER	4	40
Lithophaga aristata	(Dillwyn, 1817)	NGC;CGC;SGC	BEN;LIT;NER	0	300
Lithophaga attenuata	(Deshayes, 1836)	NGC;CGC;SGC;BR	BEN;LIT;NER	0	30
Lithophaga plumula	(Hanley, 1844)	NGC;CGC;SGC	BEN;COM;NER	5	37
Lucina fenestrata	Hinds, 1845	NGC;CGC;SGC	BEN;NER	13	74
Lucina lampra	(Dall, 1901)	NGC;CGC;SGC;BR	BEN;LIT;NER	0	55
Lucina nutalli	Conrad, 1837	NGC;CGC;SGC;BR	BEN;NER	10	461
Lucinoma annulata	(Reeve, 1850)	NGC;CGC	BEN;NER	55	183
Lyonsia californica	Conrad, 1837	NGC;CGC;SGC	BEN;NER	4	97
Macoma carlottensis	Whiteaves, 1880	NGC	BEN;NER	5	1,550
Macoma elytrum	Keen, 1958	NGC;CGC;SGC;BR	BEN;NER	22	180
Macoma siliqua	(C.B. Adams, 1852)	NGC;CGC;SGC;BR	BEN;NER	20	180
Mactra dolabriformis	(Conrad, 1867)	NGC;CGC;SGC;BR	BEN;LIT;NER	0	28
Mayrakeena angelica	(Rochebrune, 1895)	NGC;CGC;BR	BEN;LIT;NER	0	35
Megapitaria aurantiaca	(Sowerby, 1831)	NGC;CGC;SGC	BEN;LIT;NER	0	30
Megapitaria squalida	(Sowerby, 1835)	NGC;CGC;SGC;BR	BEN;LIT;NER	0	180
Modiolus capax	(Conrad, 1837)	NGC;CGC;SGC;BR	BEN;LIT;NER	0	180
Modiolus rectus	(Conrad, 1837)	NGC;CGC;SGC	BEN;LIT;NER	0	45
Mulinia coloradoensis	Dall, 1894	NGC;BR	BEN;NER	9	92
Mysella compressa	(Dall, 1913)	NGC;CGC;BR	BEN;NER	0	64
Mysella grippi	(Dall, 1912)	NGC	BEN;NER	12	60
Mytella guyanensis	(Lamarck, 1819)	NGC;CGC;SGC;BR	BEN;LIT;NER	0	30

TABLE 29.3 (CONT'D.). Annotated list of macroinvertebrates known from the northern Gulf of California.

Species	Author				
Mytella strigata	(Hanley, 1843)	BEN;LACS;LIT;NER	NGC;CGC;SGC	0	2
Nemocardium annettae	(Dall, 1889)	BEN;LIT;NER	NGC;CGC;SGC;BR	0	64
Nemocardium pazianum	(Dall, 1916)	BEN;NER	NGC;CGC;SGC;BR	10	126
Nodipecten subnodosus	(Sowerby, 1835)	BEN;LIT;NER;LACS	NGC;CGC	0	110
Noetia reversa	(Sowerby, 1833)	BEN;EPIF;NER	NGC;CGC;SGC	15	92
Nucinella subdola	(Strong & Hertlein, 1937)	BEN;NER	NGC;CGC;SGC	3	46
Nucula declivis	Hinds, 1843	BEN;NER	NGC;CGC;SGC;BR	2	64
Nucula exigua	Sowerby, 1833	BEN;NER	NGC;CGC;SGC	11	1,900
Nucula schencki	Hertlein & Strong, 1940	BEN;NER	NGC	13	45
Nuculana costellata	(Sowerby, 1833)	BEN;NER	NGC;CGC;SGC;BR	15	64
Odontorhina cyclia	Berry, 1947	BEN;NER	NGC	11	1,886
Oppenheimopecten vogdesi	(Arnold, 1906)	BEN;LACS;NER	NGC;CGC;BR	0	220
Ostreola conchaphila	(Carpenter, 1857)	BEN;LIT;NER	NGC;CGC;SGC;BR	0	100
Pandora brevifrons	Sowerby, 1835	BEN;NER	NGC;BR	15	20
Pandora cornuta	C.B. Adams, 1852	BEN	NGC;CGC;BR	9	18
Pandora granulata	Dall, 1915	BEN;LIT;NER	NGC;CGC;BR	0	72
Pandora uncifera	Pilsbry & Lowe, 1932	BEN;LIT;NER	NGC;CGC;SGC	0	35
Panopea globosa	Dall, 1898	BEN;NER	NGC;CGC;SGC;BR	9	60
Papyridea aspersa	(Sowerby, 1833)	BEN;LIT;CST;NER	NGC;CGC;SGC;SWB	0	60
Parabyotissa quercinus	(Sowerby, 1871)	BEN	NGC;CGC;SGC;BR	0	?
Parvilucina approximata	(Dall, 1901)	BEN;LIT;NER	NGC;CGC;SGC	0	1,043
Parvilucina mazatlanica	(Carpenter, 1857)	BEN;LIT;NER	NGC;CGC;SGC	0	1,043
Periploma planiusculum	Sowerby, 1834	BEN;LIT;NER	NGC;CGC;SGC;BR	0	26
Periploma stearnsii	Dall, 1896	BEN;NER	NGC;CGC;SGC	14	44
Petricola lucasana	Hertlein & Strong, 1948	BEN;LIT;NER	NGC;CGC;SGC;BR	0	10
Petricola robusta	Sowerby, 1834	BEN;NER	NGC;CGC;SGC;BR	11	23
Phlyctiderma discrepans	(Carpenter, 1857)	BEN;NER	NGC;CGC;SGC	9	35
Pholas chiloensis	Molina, 1782	BEN;LIT;NER	NGC;CGC;BR	0	10
Pinna rugosa	Sowerby, 1835	BEN;LIT;NER	NGC;CGC;SGC;BR	0	12
Pitar concinnus	(Sowerby, 1835)	BEN;LIT;LACS;NER	NGC;CGC;SGC;BR;SWB	0	73
Pitar frizzelli	Hertlein & Strong, 1948	BEN;NER	NGC;CGC;SGC	35	110
Pitar belenae	Olsson, 1961	BEN;NER	NGC;CGC;BR	22	45
Pitar besperius	Berry, 1960	BEN;NER	NGC;CGC;SGC;BR	15	40
Pitar newcombianus	(Gabb, 1865)	BEN;LIT;NER	NGC;CGC;BR	0	220

TABLE 29.3 (CONT'D). *Annotated list of macroinvertebrates known from the northern Gulf of California.*

Pitar perfragilis	Pilsbry & Lowe, 1932	NGC;CGC	BEN;NER	14	183
Pitar pollicaris	(Carpenter, 1864)	NGC;CGC;SGC;BR	BEN;LIT;NER	0	20
Plicatula anomioides	Keen, 1958	NGC;CGC;SGC;BR	BEN;LIT;NER	0	29
Plicatula inezana	Durham, 1950	NGC;CGC	BEN;NER	45	140
Plicatula penicillata	Carpenter, 1857	NGC;CGC;SGC	BEN;NER	20	80
Pristes oblongus	Carpenter, 1864	NGC;BR	BEN;LIT;NER	0	2
Protothaca grata	(Say, 1831)	NGC;CGC;SGC;BR	BEN;LIT;NER	0	390
Psammotreta aurora	(Hanley, 1844)	NGC;CGC;SGC	BEN;NER	14	35
Psammotreta mazatlanica	(Deshayes, 1855)	NGC;CGC;SGC	BEN;NER	20	183
Psammotreta viridotincta	(Carpenter, 1856)	NGC;CGC	BEN;NER	10	30
Psephidia cymata	Dall, 1913	NGC;BR	BEN;NER	25	82
Pseudochama corrugata	(Broderip, 1835)	NGC;CGC;SGC	BEN;LIT;NER	0	5
Pseudochama janus	(Reeve, 1847)	NGC;BR	BEN;NER	10	47
Pseudochama panamensis	(Reeve, 1847)	NGC;CGC;SGC	BEN;LIT;NER	0	70
Pseudochama saavedrai	Hertlein & Strong, 1946	NGC;CGC;SGC;BR	BEN;LIT;NER	0	70
Pteria sterna	(Gould, 1851)	NGC;CGC;SGC;BR	BEN;LIT;NER	0	45
Pythinella sublaevis	(Carpenter, 1857)	NGC;CGC;SGC	BEN;NER	11	35
Raeta undulata	(Gould, 1851)	NGC;CGC;SGC;BR	BEN;LIT;NER	0	29
Rangia mendica	(Gould, 1851)	NGC;CGC;SGC;BR	BEN;LIT;NER	0	1
Rupellaria denticulata	(Sowerby, 1834)	NGC;CGC;SGC	BEN;LIT;NER	0	2
Saccella acrita	(Dall, 1908)	NGC;CGC;SGC;BR	BEN;NER	6	90
Saccella elenensis	(Sowerby, 1833)	NGC;CGC;BR	BEN;NER	4	180
Saccella impar	(Pilsbry & Lowe, 1932)	NGC;CGC;BR	BEN;NER	4	72
Saccostrea palmula	(Carpenter, 1857)	NGC;CGC;SGC;BR	BEN;LIT;COM;NER	0	36
Sanguinolaria tellinoides	Adams, A., 1850	NGC;CGC;SGC	BEN;LIT;CST;NER	0	10
Semele bicolor	(C.B. Adams, 1852)	NGC;CGC;SGC	BEN;LIT;NER	0	20
Semele californica	(Reeve, 1853)	NGC;CGC;SWB	BEN;LIT;NER	0	3
Semele craneana	Hertlein & Strong, 1949	NGC;CGC;SGC;BR	BEN;NER	32	110
Semele flavescens	(Gould, 1851)	NGC;CGC;SGC;BR;SWB	BEN;LIT;NER	0	5
Semele guaymasensis	Pilsbry & Lowe, 1932	NGC;CGC;SGC;BR	BEN;LIT;NER	0	110
Semele jamesi	Coan, 1988	NGC;CGC;SGC;SWB	BEN;NER	5	161
Semele jovis	(Reeve, 1853)	NGC;CGC;SGC;BR	BEN;LIT;NER	0	100
Semele lenticularis	(Sowerby, 1833)	NGC;CGC;SGC	BEN;LIT;NER	0	44
Semele rosea	(Sowerby, 1833)	NGC;CGC;SWB	BEN;LIT;NER	0	113

TABLE 29.3 (CONT'D.). *Annotated list of macroinvertebrates known from the northern Gulf of California.*

Semele rubropicta	Dall, 1871	NGC;CGC	BEN;LIT;NER	0	55
Semele venusta	(Reeve, 1853)	NGC;CGC;SGC	BEN;LIT;NER	10	183
Semele verrucosa pacifica	Dall, 1915	NGC;CGC;SGC;BR	BEN;LIT;NER	0	128
Septifer zeteki	Hertlein & Strong, 1946	NGC;CGC;BR	BEN;NER	3	90
Solecardia eburnea	Conrad, 1849	NGC;CGC;BR	BEN;LIT;NER	0	60
Solemya valvulus	Carpenter, 1864	NGC;CGC;SGC;BR	BEN;NER	2	400
Solen gemmelli	Cosel, 1992	NGC	BEN	0	?
Solen pfeifferi	Dunker, 1862	NGC;CGC;BR	BEN;NER	7	24
Solen rostriformis	Dunker, 1862	NGC;CGC;SGC;BR	BEN;LIT;NER	0	45
Spheniopsis frankbernardi	Coan, 1990	NGC;SWB	BEN;NER	13	91
Spondylus calcifer	Carpenter, 1857	NGC;CGC;SGC;BR	BEN;LIT;NER	0	55
Spondylus ursipes	Berry, 1959	NGC;CGC	BEN;NER	0	36
Strigilla cicercula	(Philippi, 1846)	NGC;CGC;SGC;BR	BEN;NER	0	90
Strigilla dichotoma	(Philippi, 1846)	NGC;CGC;SGC	BEN;NER	7	8
Strigilla serrata	Mörch, 1860	NGC;CGC;SGC;BR	BEN	?	?
Strophocardia megastropha	(Gray, 1825)	NGC;CGC;SGC	BEN;LIT;EPIF	0	100
Tagelus affinis	(C.B. Adams, 1852)	NGC;CGC;SGC	BEN;LIT;NER	0	73
Tagelus peruvianus	Pilsbry & Olsson, 1941	NGC;CGC	BEN;LIT;NER	0	2
Tagelus politus	(Carpenter, 1857)	NGC;CGC;SGC;BR	BEN;LIT;NER	0	180
Tellidora burneti	(Broderip & Sowerby, 1829)	NGC;CGC;SGC;BR	BEN;LIT;NER	0	29
Tellidorella cristulata	Berry, 1963	NGC	BEN;NER	27	110
Tellina amianta	Dall, 1900	NGC;CGC;SGC;BR	BEN;NER	3	72
Tellina brevirostris	Deshayes, 1855	NGC;CGC;SGC	BEN;NER	10	70
Tellina carpenteri	Dall, 1900	NGC;CGC;SGC;SWB	BEN;NER	1	500
Tellina coani	Keen, 1971	NGC;CGC;BR	BEN;LIT;NER	0	30
Tellina cumingii	Hanley, 1844	NGC;CGC;SGC;SWB	BEN;NER	3	73
Tellina hiberna	Hanley, 1844	NGC;CGC;SGC	BEN;NER	4	55
Tellina lyrica	Pilsbry & Lowe, 1932	NGC;CGC;SGC	BEN;NER	7	180
Tellina meropsis	Dall, 1900	NGC;CGC;SGC;BR	BEN;LIT;NER	0	180
Tellina pacifica	Dall, 1900	NGC;CGC	BEN;NER	7	180
Tellina pristiphora	Dall, 1900	NGC;CGC;SGC	BEN;NER	22	155
Tellina prora	Hanley, 1844	NGC;CGC;SGC;BR	BEN;NER	11	42
Tellina reclusa	Dall, 1900	NGC;CGC;SGC;BR	BEN;NER	5	70
Tellina recurvata	Hertlein & Strong, 1949	NGC;CGC;SGC	BEN;NER	9	72

Tellina rhynchoscuta	(Olsson, 1961)	NGC;CGC;SGC	BEN;LIT;NER	0	24
Tellina simulans	C.B. Adams, 1852	NGC;CGC;SGC	BEN;LIT;NER	0	180
Tellina ulloana	Hertlein, 1968	NGC;BR;SWB	BEN;NER	22	48
Tellina virgo	Hanley, 1844	NGC;CGC;SGC;SWB	BEN;LIT;NER	0	15
Temnoconcha cognata	(C.B. Adams, 1852)	NGC;CGC;SGC	BEN;NER	8	77
Thracia bereniceae	Coan, 1990	NGC;CGC;SGC;BR	BEN;LIT;NER	0	46
Thracia curta	Conrad, 1837	NGC;CGC;SGC	BEN;LIT;NER	0	48
Timoclea squamosa	(Carpenter, 1857)	NGC;CGC;SGC;BR	BEN;NER	3	50
Tivela argentina	(Sowerby, 1835)	NGC;CGC;SGC;BR	BEN;NER	13	23
Tivela byronensis	(Gray, 1838)	NGC;CGC;SGC;BR	BEN;NER	0	90
Trachycardium biangulata	(Broderip & Sowerby, 1829)	NGC;CGC;SGC	BEN;LIT;NER	0	161
Trachycardium consors	(Sowerby, 1833)	NGC;CGC;SGC	BEN;LIT;NER	0	100
Trachycardium panamense	(Sowerby, 1833)	NGC;CGC;BR	BEN;LIT;NER	0	65
Trachycardium procerum	(Sowerby, 1833)	NGC;CGC;SGC	BEN;LIT;NER	0	92
Trachycardium senticosum	(Sowerby, 1833)	NGC;CGC;SGC;BR	BEN;LIT;NER	0	72
Transennella humilis	(Carpenter, 1857)	NGC;CGC;SGC	BEN;LIT;NER	0	24
Trigoniocardia granifera	(Broderip & Sowerby, 1829)	NGC;CGC;SGC;SWB	BEN;LIT;NER	1	65
Tryphomyax mexicanus	(Berry, 1959)	NGC;CGC;SGC;BR	BEN;NER	5	37
Tucetona multicostata	(Sowerby, 1833)	NGC;CGC;SGC	BEN;NER	40	90
Undulostrea megodon	(Hanley, 1846)	NGC;CGC;SGC;BR	BEN;NER	27	180
Verticordia ornata	(d'Orbigny, 1846)	NGC;CGC;SGC	BEN;NER	18	168
Vesicomya suavis	Dall, 1913	NGC	BEN	?	1,345
POLYPLACOPHORA (CHITONS)					
Acanthochitona angelica	Dall, 1919	NGC;CGC;SGC	BEN;LIT	9	50
Acanthochitona avicula	(Carpenter, 1866)	NGC;CGC;SGC;BR;SWB	BEN;CST	2	60
Acanthochitona exquisita	(Pilsbry, 1893)	NGC;CGC;SGC	BEN;LIT;NER	0	2
Acanthochitona hirudiniformis	Sowerby, 1832	NGC	BEN;LIT;CST	0	41
Callistochiton elenensis	(Sowerby, 1832)	NGC;CGC;SGC;BR	BEN;LIT;NER	0	90
Callistochiton palmulatus	Dall, 1879 ex Carpenter MS	NGC	BEN	40	60
Chaetopleura euryplax	Berry, 1945	NGC;CGC;SWB	BEN;LIT;NER	0	2
Chaetopleura mixta	(Dall, 1919)	NGC;CGC;SGC;BR	BEN;LIT;NER	0	162
Chaetopleura shyana	Ferreira, 1983	NGC;CGC	BEN;LIT;NER	0	5
Chaetopleura unilineata	Leloup, 1954	NGC;CGC;SGC;BR	BEN	0	90
Hanleyella oldroydi	(Dall, 1919)	NGC	BEN	120	170

TABLE 29.3 (CONT'D.). *Annotated list of macroinvertebrates known from the northern Gulf of California.*

Ischnochiton carolianus	Ferreira, 1984	NGC;CGC	BEN	61	182
Ischnochiton chaceorum	Kaas & van Belle, 1990	NGC;BR	BEN;LIT;NER	0	1
Ischnochiton guatemalensis	(Thiele, 1910)	NGC;CGC;BR;SWB	BEN;LIT;NER	0	12
Ischnochiton tridentatus	(Pilsbry, 1893)	NGC;CGC;SGC;BR	BEN;LIT;NER	0	30
Lepidochitona beanii	(Carpenter, 1857)	NGC;CGC;SGC;BR	BEN;LIT;NER	0	230
Lepidochitona laurae	(Berry, 1963)	NGC	BEN;NER	10	90
Lepidochitona lirulata	(Berry, 1963)	NGC;CGC;BR	BEN;LIT;NER	0	1
Lepidozona clathrata	(Reeve, 1847)	NGC;CGC;SGC;BR	BEN;LIT;NER	0	10
Lepidozona crockeri	(Willett, 1951)	NGC;CGC;SGC	BEN;LIT;NER	0	109
Lepidozona formosa	Ferreira, 1974	NGC;CGC;SGC	BEN;LIT;NER	5	60
Lepidozona laurae	Ferreira, 1985	NGC;CGC	BEN	60	183
Lepidozona pectinulata	(Pilsbry, 1893, ex Carpenter)	NGC;SWB	BEN;LIT	0	40
Lepidozona serrata	(Carpenter, 1864)	NGC;CGC;SGC;BR;SWB	BEN;LIT;NER	0	15
Lepidozona sirenkoi	Kaas & van Belle, 1990	NGC;BR	BEN;LIT;NER	0	1
Lepidozona skoglundi	(Ferreira, 1986)	NGC;CGC;SGC;BR	BEN	6	15
Lepidozona stohleri	Ferreira, 1985	NGC;CGC	BEN	12	60
Lepidozona subtilis	Berry, 1956	NGC;CGC;BR	BEN	2	3
Lepidozona tenuicostata	Kaas & van Belle, 1990	NGC;BR	BEN;LIT;NER	0	1
Leptochiton nexus	Carpenter, 1864	NGC	LIT;BEN;CST	12	144
Leptochiton rugatus	(Pilsbry, 1892)	NGC;CGC;SWB	LIT	0	458
Nuttallina crossota	Berry, 1956	NGC;CGC;BR	BEN;LIT;NER	0	1
Placiphorella hanselmani	Clark, 1994	NGC;CGC;BR	BEN;LIT;NER	0	39
Stenoplax boogii	(Haddon, 1886)	NGC;CGC;SGC	BEN;LIT;NER	0	64
Stenoplax circumsenta	Berry, 1956	NGC;CGC	BEN;LIT;NER	0	72
Stenoplax limaciformis	(Sowerby, 1832)	NGC;CGC;SGC;BR	BEN;LIT;NER	0	41
Stenoplax magdalenensis	(Hinds, 1845)	NGC;CGC;SGC;BR;SWB	BEN;LIT;NER	0	?
Stenoplax sonorana	(Berry, 1956)	NGC;CGC;3R	BEN;LIT;NER	0	?
SCAPHOPODA (TUSK SHELLS)					
Cadulus austinclarki	Emerson, 1951	NGC;CGC;SGC	BEN;NER	2	405
Dentalium neohexagonum	Sharp & Pilsbry, 1897	NGC;BR	BEN;NER	1	256
Dentalium oerstedii oerstedii	Mörch, 1860	NGC;CGC;SGC;BR	BEN;NER	4	145
Dentalium pretiosum berryi	Smith & Gordon, 1948	NGC	BEN;NER	37	298
Dentalium quadrangulare	Sowerby, 1832	NGC;CGC;SGC;BR	BEN;NER	5	73
Dentalium sectum	Deshayes, 1826	NGC;CGC	BEN;NER	0	9

TABLE 29.3 (CONT'D). *Annotated list of macroinvertebrates known from the northern Gulf of California.*

Dentalium vallicolens	Raymond, 1904	NGC	BEN;NER	5	477
Fustiaria innumerabilis	(Pilsbry & Sharp, 1897)	NGC;CGC;SGC	BEN;NER	11	165
Gadila fusiformis	(Pilsbry & Sharp, 1898)	NGC;CGC;SGC	BEN;NER	7	365
Gadila perpusilla	(Sowerby, 1832)	NGC;CGC;SGC;BR	BEN;NER	11	3,450
Graptacme inversum	(Deshayes, 1826)	NGC;CGC;BR;SWB	BEN;NER	13	37
Graptacme semipolita	(Broderip & Sowerby, 1829)	NGC;CGC;SGC	BEN;NER	2	75
Laevidentalium splendidum	(Sowerby, 1832)	NGC;CGC;SGC;BR	BEN;NER	2	110
Siphonodentalium quadrifissatum	(Pilsbry & Sharp, 1898)	NGC;CGC;SGC;BR	BEN;NER	4	365
Tesseracme bancocki	(Emerson, 1956)	NGC;CGC;SGC;BR	BEN;NER	15	42

PHYLUM SIPUNCULA (PEANUT WORMS)

Apionsoma misakianum	(Ikeda, 1904)	NGC;CGC;SGC;BR	BEN;LIT;COM	0	5
Phascolosoma agassizii	Keferstein, 1866	NGC;CGC;SGC;BR;SWB	BEN;LIT	0	1
Phascolosoma perlucens	Baird, 1868	NGC;CGC;BR	BEN;LIT	0	3
Sipunculus nudus	Linnaeus, 1766	NGC;CGC;SGC;BR;SWB	BEN;LIT;LACS	0	1
Themiste hennahi	Gray, 1828	NGC;CGC;BR	BEN;LIT	0	1

PHYLUM ECHIURA (SPOON WORMS)

Ochetostoma edax	Fisher, 1946	NGC;CGC;SGC	LIT; BEN	0	?
Thalassema steinbecki	Fisher, 1946	NGC;CGC;SGC	BEN	18	300

PHYLUM ANNELIDA (SEGMENTED WORMS)

OLIGOCHAETA (EARTHWORMS)

Bacescuella parvithecata	Erséus, 1978	NGC;CGC;BR	BEN;LIT	0	0

POLYCHAETA (POLYCHAETES)

Acoetes pacifica	(Treadwell, 1914)	NGC;CGC	BEN	10	640
Acrocirrus crassifilis	Moore, 1923	NGC	BEN	354	505
Acrocirrus incisa	Kudenov, 1975	NGC;BR	BEN;LIT	0	?
Aglaophamus dicirris	Hartman, 1950	NGC;CGC;SGC;BR;SWB	BEN;LIT	0	200
Aglaophamus fossae	Fauchald, 1972	NGC	BEN	864	1,395
Aglaophamus lyrochaetus	(Fauvel, 1902)	NGC;CGC;BR	BEN;LIT	0	100
Amaeana occidentalis	(Hartman, 1944)	NGC;CGC	BEN;LIT	0	200
Amphicteis scaphobranchiata	Moore, 1906	NGC;CGC;SGC;BR	BENLIT	0	1,188
Anaitides mucosa	(Oersted, 1843)	NGC	BEN	57	200
Anaitides williamsi	Hartman, 1936	NGC;CGC;SGC	BEN;LIT	0	?
Ancistargis hamata	(Hartman, 1960)	NGC;CGC;SGC	BEN;LIT	0	0

TABLE 29.3 (CONT'D). *Annotated list of macroinvertebrates known from the northern Gulf of California*

Species	Reference	Region	Habitat		
Anobothrus bimaculatus	Fauchald, 1972	NGC;CGC	BEN;OCE	720	1,620
Anotomastus gordiodes	(Moore, 1909)	NGC	BEN;LIT	0	200
Aphrodita mexicana	Kudenov, 1975	NGC;BR	BEN	29	39
Aphrodita sonorae	Kudenov, 1975	NGC;BR	BEN	36	?
Apoprionospio dayi	Foster, 1969	NGC;BR	BEN;LIT	3	200
Apoprionospio pygmaea	(Hartman, 1961)	NGC;CGC;SGC;BR	BEN;LIT	21	200
Arabella iricolor	(Montagu, 1804)	NGC;CGC;SGC;BR;SWB	BEN;LIT	2	90
Arabella mutans	(Chamberlin, 1919)	NGC;CGC;SGC	BEN	2	36
Arabella semimaculata	(Moore, 1911)	NGC;CGC;SGC	BEN	2	83
Arenicola glasselli	Berkeley & Berkeley, 1939	NGC;BR	BEN	?	?
Aricidea fragilis	Webster, 1879	NGC;CGC;SGC;BR	BEN;LIT	28	106
Aricidea pacifica	Hartman, 1944	NGC;CGC;SGC;BR	BEN;LIT	0	?
Aricidea simplex	Day, 1963	NGC;CGC;SGC;BR	BEN;LIT	35	1,072
Armandia brevis	Moore, 1906	NGC;CGC;SGC	BEN;LIT	0	100
Armandia intermedia	Fauvel, 1902	NGC;CGC;SGC	BEN;LIT	0	104
Asabellides lineata	(Berkeley & Berkeley, 1943)	NGC;CGC;SGC	BEN	45	102
Asychis disparidentata	(Moore, 1904)	NGC	BEN	83	1,409
Axiothella rubrocincta	(Johnson, 1901)	NGC;CGC;SGC;BR	BEN;LIT	0	200
Bhawania goodei	Webster, 1884	NGC;CGC;ER	BEN;LIT	0	80
Bispira monroi	(Hartman, 1961)	NGC;BR	BEN;LIT	0	?
Boccardia anophthalma	(Rioja, 1962)	NGC;BR	BEN;COM	15	22
Boccardia tricuspa	(Hartman, 1939)	NGC;BR	BEN;LIT;COM	0	15
Brada villosa	(Rathke, 1843)	NGC	BEN;LIT	0	2,000
Brania limbata	(Claparède, 1868)	NGC	BEN;LIT	0	?
Capitella capitata	(Fabricius, 1780)	NGC;CGC;SGC	BEN;LIT;LACS	0	1
Capitita ambiseta	Hartman, 1947	NGC	BEN;LIT	0	200
Carazziella calafia	Blake, 1979	NGC	BEN;LIT	0	37
Caulleriella alata	(Southern, 1914)	NGC;CGC;SGC	BEN;LIT	0	200
Caulleriella hamata	(Hartman, 1948)	NGC;CGC;SGC	BEN	?	100
Ceratocephale oculata	Banse, 1977	NGC;CGC;SGC;BR	BEN;LIT	22	106
Ceratocephale pacifica	Hartman, 1960	NGC;CGC	BEN	840	2,545
Ceratonereis singularis	Treadwell, 1929	NGC;CGC;SGC	BEN;LIT	0	?
Ceratonereis tentaculata	Kinberg, 1866	NGC;CGC;SGC	BEN	7	72
Chaetopterus variopedatus	(Renier, 1804)	NGC;CGC;BR	BEN;LIT	0	27

TABLE 29.3 (CONT'D). *Annotated list of macroinvertebrates known from the northern Gulf of California.*

Species	Author, year				
Chaetozone corona	Berkeley & Berkeley, 1941	NGC;CGC;SGC	BEN;LIT	4	119
Chloeia entypa	Chamberlin, 1919	NGC;CGC;SGC;BR;SWB	BEN;LIT	0	118
Chloeia viridis	Schmarda, 1861	NGC;CGC;SGC;BR;SWB	BEN	9	270
Chone mollis	(Bush, 1904)	NGC;CGC;SGC;BR	BEN;LIT;LAGS	0	?
Chrysopetalum occidentale	Johnson, 1897	NGC;CGC;BR	BEN;LIT	0	?
Cirriformia luxuriosa	(Moore, 1904)	NGC;CGC;SGC;BR	BEN;LIT	0	18
Cirriformia spirabrancha	(Moore, 1904)	NGC;CGC;SGC	BEN;LIT	0	78
Cossura candida	Hartman, 1955	NGC;CGC;SGC	BEN	12	2,440
Dasybranchus lumbricoides	(Grube, 1878)	NGC;CGC;SGC	BEN	30	207
Dasybranchus parplatyceps	Kudenov, 1975	NGC;CGC	BEN;LIT	0	?
Dasybranchus platyceps	Hartman, 1947	NGC	BEN;LIT	0	?
Decamastus nudus	Thomassin, 1970	NGC;CGC;SGC	BEN;LIT	26	114
Diopatra neotridens	Hartman, 1944	NGC;CGC;SGC;BR;SWB	BEN	8	100
Diopatra obliqua	Hartman, 1944	NGC;CGC;SGC;BR;SWB	BEN	3	45
Diopatra ornata	Moore, 1911	NGC;CGC;SGC;SWB	BEN	10	90
Diopatra papillata	Fauchald, 1968	NGC	BEN	72	108
Diopatra splendidissima	Kinberg, 1857	NGC;CGC;SGC;SWB	BEN;LIT	0	117
Diopatra tridentata	Hartman, 1944	NGC;CGC;SGC;BR;SWB	BEN	9	207
Dispio uncinata	Hartman, 1951	NGC;CGC	BEN;LIT	0	106
Dorvillea annulata	(Moore, 1906)	NGC;CGC;SGC	BEN	72	260
Dorvillea cerasina	(Ehlers, 1901)	NGC;CGC;SGC	BEN;LIT;COM	0	27
Drilonereis falcata	Moore, 1911	NGC;CGC;SGC;BR;SWB	BEN	29	2,500
Drilonereis nuda	Moore, 1909	NGC	BEN	5	144
Eclysippe vanelli	(Fauvel, 1936)	NGC;CGC;SGC	BEN	15	313
Eteone dilatae	Hartman, 1936	NGC	BEN;LIT	0	200
Euarche tubifex	Ehlers, 1887	NGC;BR	BEN	13	450
Eulalia mexicana	Fauchald, 1972	NGC	BEN	720	770
Eulalia myriacyclum	(Schmarda, 1861)	NGC;CGC;SGC;BR	BEN;LIT	0	?
Eumida sanguinea	(Oersted, 1843)	NGC;CGC;SGC	BEN;LIT	0	200
Eumida uschakovi	Kudenov, 1979	NGC;BR	BEN;LIT	0	?
Eunice afra	Peters, 1854	NGC;CGC;SGC;BR;SWB	BEN;LIT	0	?
Eunice antennata	(Savigny, 1820)	NGC;CGC;SGC;BR;SWB	BEN;LIT	0	270
Eunice aphroditois	(Pallas, 1788)	NGC;CGC;SGC;BR	BEN;LIT	0	36
Eunice cariboea	Grube, 1856	NGC;CGC;SGC;BR	BEN;LIT	0	36

Species	Author				
Eunice filamentosa	Grube, 1856	NGC;CGC;SGC;BR	BEN;LIT	0	40
Eunice mexicana	Fauchald, 1970	NGC;CGC;SGC;SWB	BEN	14	108
Eunice sonorae	Fauchald, 1970	NGC;CGC;SGC	BEN;LIT	0	?
Eunice vittata	(delle Chiaje, 1828)	NGC;CGC;SGC;SWB	BEN;LIT	1	200
Eunice vittatopsis	Fauchald, 1970	NGC;CGC.SGC;BR	BEN;LIT	0	33
Eunice websteri	Fauchald, 1969	NGC;CGC.SGC	BEN	10	100
Eupomatus recurvispina	(Rioja, 1941)	NGC;CGC:.BR	BEN;LIT	0	?
Eurythoe complanata complanata	(Pallas,1766)	NGC;CGC;SGC;BR;SWB	BEN;EPIF	0	108
Exogone lourei	Berkeley & Berkeley, 1938	NGC;CGC;SGC	BEN;LIT	0	200
Fabricinuda limnicola	(Hartman, 1951)	NGC;CGC;SGC	BEN;LIT	0	?
Glycera americana	Leidy, 1855	NGC;CGC;SGC;BR;SWB	BEN;LIT	0	309
Glycera convoluta	Keferstein, 1862	NGC;CGC;SGC;BR	BEN;LIT	0	47
Glycera dibranchiata	Ehlers, 1868	NGC;CGC;SGC;BR;SWB	BEN;LIT	0	1,139
Glycera longippinis	Grube, 1878	NGC;BR	BEN	32	60
Glycera oxycephala	Ehlers, 1887	NGC;CGC;BR	BEN;LIT	0	705
Glycera papillosa	Grube, 1857	NGC	BEN;LIT	33	35
Glycera profundi	Chamberlin, 1919	NGC;CGC	BEN	1020	2560
Glycera robusta	Ehlers, 1868	NGC;CGC	BEN;LIT	0	298
Glycera sphyrabrancha	Schmarda, 1861	NGC;CGC;BR	BEN;LIT	30	49
Glycera tesselata	Grube, 1863	NGC;CGC;SGC;BR;SWB	BEN;LIT	5	1,386
Glycinde armigera	Moore, 1911	NGC;CGC;SGC;SWB	BEN	18	1,197
Glycinde polygnatha	Hartman, 1950	NGC;CGC;SGC	BEN;LIT	0	122
Glycinde solitaria	(Webster, 1879)	NGC;BR	BEN	60	60
Goniada acicula	Hartman, 1940	NGC;CGC;SGC	BEN	5	72
Goniada littorea	Hartman, 1950	NGC	BEN;LIT	0	?
Goniadella gracilis	(Verril, 1873)	NGC	BEN;LIT	0	34
Grubeulepis mexicana	(Berkeley & Berkeley, 1939)	NGC;CGC;SGC	BEN;LIT;CST	0	50
Gyptis arenicolus glabrus	Hartman, 1961	NGC	BEN	37	660
Halosydna brevisetosa	Kinberg, 1855	NGC;CGC;SGC;BR	BEN;LIT;COM	0	522
Halosydna glabra	Hartman, 1939	NGC;CGC;SGC	BEN;LIT	0	21
Halosydna johnsoni	(Darboux, 1899)	NGC;CGC;SGC;BR	BEN;LIT	0	21
Haploscoloplos elongatus	(Johnson, 1901)	NGC;CGC;SGC	BEN;LIT	0	293
Harmothoe hirsuta	Johnson, 1897	NGC;CGC;SGC	BEN;LIT	0	8
Hesione intertexta	Grube, 1878	NGC;CGC;SGC;BR	BEN;LIT;CST	0	45

TABLE 29.3 (CONT'D). *Annotated list of macroinvertebrates known from the northern Gulf of California.*

Species	Author	Region	Habitat		
Hyalinoecia juvenalis	Moore, 1911	NGC;CGC;SGC;SWB	BEN	9	405
Hydroides crucigera	Morch, 1863	NGC;CGC;SGC;BR	BEN;LIT	0	?
Idanthyrsus armatopsis	Fauchald, 1972	NGC	BEN	1227	1,386
Isolda pulchella	Müller, 1858	NGC;CGC;SGC	BEN	10	50
Kinbergonuphis microcephala	(Hartman, 1944)	NGC;CGC;SGC;BR	BEN;LIT	0	27
Kinbergonuphis pulchra	(Fauchald, 1980)	NGC;CGC;SGC;BR	BEN;EPIF	0	50
Kinbergonuphis vermillionensis	(Fauchald, 1968)	NGC	BEN;LIT	0	126
Kinbergonuphis virgata	(Fauchald, 1980)	NGC	BEN;LIT	0	68
Laborostratus zaragozensis	Hernández & Solís, 1998	NGC;BR	BEN;PAR	30	34
Langerhansia heterochaeta	(Moore, 1909)	NGC	BEN;LIT	0	720
Laonice cirrata	(Sars, 1851)	NGC;CGC;SGC;BR	BEN;LIT	0	200
Leiocapitella glabra	Hartman, 1947	NGC;CGC	BEN	36	100
Leitoscoloplos mexicanus	(Fauchald, 1972)	NGC	BEN	1360	1,400
Leitoscoloplos pugettensis	(Pettibone, 1957)	NGC	BEN;LIT	0	163
Lepidasthenia gigas	(Johnson, 1897)	NGC;CGC;SGC;BR	BEN;LIT;COM	0	50
Lepidonotus purpureus	Potts, 1910	NGC	BEN;LIT	0	72
Lepidonotus squamatus	(Linnaeus, 1767)	NGC;CGC;SGC	BEN;LIT	?	1,410
Lepidonotus versicolor	Ehlers, 1901	NGC;CGC;SGC	BEN;LIT	0	297
Lopadorhynchus krohnii	(Claparède, 1870)	NGC;CGC;SGC	PEL	?	?
Lumbrineris crassidentata	Fauchald, 1970	NGC;CGC;SGC;BR	BEN;LIT	0	2,520
Lumbrineris erecta	(Moore, 1904)	NGC;CGC;SGC	BEN;LIT	0	43
Lumbrineris index	Moore, 1911	NGC	BEN	30	1,267
Lumbrineris januarii	(Grube, 1878)	NGC;CGC	BEN	23	54
Lumbrineris lagunae	Fauchald, 1970	NGC;CGC;SGC	BEN	9	1,197
Lumbrineris latreilli	Audouin & M. Edwards, 1834	NGC;CGC;SGC;SWB	BEN;LIT	0	2,376
Lumbrineris limicola	Hartman, 1944	NGC;CGC;SGC	BEN	11	105
Lumbrineris minima	Hartman, 1944	NGC	BEN;LIT	0	?
Lumbrineris penascensis	Fauchald, 1970	NGC;BR	BEN;LIT	0	?
Lumbrineris platylobata	Fauchald, 1970	NGC;CGC;SGC	BEN;LIT	0	30
Lumbrineris simplicis	Hartman, 1959	NGC	BEN;LIT	0	?
Lumbrineris tetraura	(Schmarda, 1861)	NGC;CGC;SGC;BR	BEN;LIT	0	72
Lumbrineris zonata	(Johnson, 1901)	NGC;CGC;BR	BEN;LIT	0	80
Lysidice ninetta	Audouin & M. Edwards, 1833	NGC;CGC;SGC;SWB	BEN;LIT	0	108
Lysippe aff. mexicana	Fauchald, 1972	NGC;CGC;SGC;BR	BEN	19	2,439

TABLE 29.3 (CONT'D). Annotated list of macroinvertebrates known from the northern Gulf of California.

Species	Authority				
Magelona californica	Hartman, 1944	NGC;CGC;SGC;BR	BEN;LIT	0	1,458
Maldane cristata	Treadwell, 1923	NGC;CGC;SGC	BEN	579	2,763
Maldane sarsi	Malmgren, 1865	NGC;CGC;SGC;BR	BEN;LIT	0	3,537
Malmgrenia hartmanae	Kudenov, 1975	NGC;BR	BEN;COM	40	40
Marphysa aenea	(Blanchard, 1849)	NGC;CGC;SGC;SWB	BEN;LIT	0	22
Marphysa angelensis	Fauchald, 1970	NGC;CGC;SGC	BEN	20	40
Marphysa sanguinea	(Montagu, 1815)	NGC;CGC;SGC;BR;SWB	BEN;LIT	0	200
Mediomastus californiensis	Hartman, 1944	NGC;CGC;SGC	BEN;LIT	1	517
Megalomma pigmentum	Reish, 1963	NGC;CGC;SGC	BEN;LIT;LACS	0	45
Megalomma splendida	(Moore, 1905)	NGC;CGC;SGC;BR	BEN	?	200
Mesochaetopterus alipes	Monro, 1928	NGC;BR	BEN	2	?
Mesochaetopterus mexicanus	Kudenov, 1975	NGC;BR	BEN	2	?
Microphthalmus riojai	Reish, 1968	NGC	BEN	?	?
Mooreonuphis cirrata	(Hartman, 1944)	NGC	BEN	20	40
Mooreonuphis nebulosa	(Moore, 1911)	NGC;CGC;GC;SWB	BEN	12	309
Myxicola infundibulum	(Renier, 1804)	NGC;BR	BEN;LIT	0	71
Naineris dendritica	(Kinberg, 1867)	NGC;CGC;SGC	BEN;LIT	0	10
Neanthes caudata	(delle Chiaje, 1828)	NGC;CGC;SGC;BR	BEN;LIT	0	21
Neanthes cortezi	Kudenov, 1979	NGC;BR	BEN;LIT	0	?
Neanthes micromma	Harper, 1979	NGC;CGC;SGC;BR	BEN;LIT	28	79
Neanthes pelagica	Linnaeus, 1761	NGC;CGC;SGC	BEN;LIT	0	100
Neanthes succinea	(Frey & Leuckart, 1847)	NGC;CGC;SGC	BEN;LIT	0	?
Nematonereis unicornis	(Grube, 1840)	NGC	BEN;LIT	0	?
Neoleprea californica	(Moore, 1904)	NGC;BR	BEN;LIT	0	200
Nephtys bilobatus	Kudenov, 1975	NGC	BEN	?	?
Nephtys capensis	Day, 1953	NGC	BEN;LIT	0	30
Nephtys magellanica	Augener, 1912	NGC;CGC;SGC	BEN;LIT	0	135
Nephtys panamensis	Monro, 1928	NGC;CGC;SGC;BR	BEN;LIT	0	108
Nephtys picta	Ehlers, 1868	NGC	BEN;LIT	20	50
Nephtys squamosa	Ehlers, 1887	NGC;CGC;SGC;BR	BEN;LIT	0	216
Nereis eugeniae	(Kinberg, 1866)	NGC;CGC	BEN;LIT	0	500
Nereis procera	Ehlers, 1868	NGC	BEN	9	1,944
Nereis riisei	Grube, 1857	NGC;CGC;SGC	BEN;LIT	5	99
Nereis zonata	Malmgren, 1867	NGC	BEN;LIT	0	255

TABLE 29.3 (CONT'D). Annotated list of macroinvertebrates known from the northern Gulf of California.

Species	Author	Distribution	Habitat		
Nicon moniloceras	(Hartman, 1940)	NGC	BEN;LIT	198	0
Ninoe dolicognatha	Rioja, 1941	NGC;CGC;SGC;BR	BEN;LIT	?	0
Ninoe foliosa	Fauchald, 1972	NGC	BEN	1,355	216
Notocirrus californiensis	Hartman, 1944	NGC;BR	BEN	104	14
Notomastus americanus	Day, 1973	NGC;CGC;SGC	BEN	100	30
Notomastus hemipodus	Hartman, 1947	NGC;CGC;SGC;BR	BEN;LIT	120	0
Notomastus latericeus	Sars, 1850	NGC;CGC;SGC	BEN;LIT	4,360	0
Notomastus lineatus	Claparède, 1870	NGC;CGC;SGC;SWB	BEN;LIT	298	0
Notomastus lobatus	Hartman, 1947	NGC;CGC;SGC;BR	BEN	527	52
Notomastus sonorae	Kudenov, 1975	NGC;CGC;BR	BEN;LIT	?	0
Notomastus tenuis	Moore, 1909	NGC;CGC;SGC;BR	BEN;LIT	2,520	0
Notopygos ornata	Grube, 1856	NGC;CGC;SGC;BR;SWB	BEN;LIT	126	0
Odontosyllis phosphorea	Moore, 1909	NGC;CGC;SGC	BEN;LIT	21	0
Oenone fulgida	(Savigny, 1818)	NGC;CGC;SGC;BR	BEN;LIT	40	0
Onuphis vexillaria	Moore, 1911	NGC;CGC;SGC;BR	BEN	1,980	14
Onuphis zebra	Berkeley & Berkeley, 1939	NGC;CGC;SGC	BEN	36	0
Ophelina acuminata	Oersted, 1843	NGC;CGC;SGC;BR	BEN;LIT	5,000	10
Ophiodromus pugettensis	(Johnson, 1901)	NGC;CGC;SGC;BR	BEN;LIT	?	0
Orbinia johnsoni	(Moore, 1909)	NGC	BEN;LIT	14	0
Orbinia riseri	(Pettibone, 1957)	NGC;CGC;SGC	BEN;LIT	160	0
Owenia collaris	Hartman, 1955	NGC;CGC;SGC;BR	BEN	2,000	31
Owenia fusiformis	delle Chiaje, 1844	NGC	BEN	?	1
Paleanotus bellis	(Johnson, 1897)	NGC	BEN;LIT	?	0
Palola paloloides	(Moore, 1909)	NGC;CGC;SGC;BR	BEN;LIT	165	0
Palola siciliensis	(Grube, 1840)	NGC;CGC;SGC;BR;SWB	BEN;LIT	33	0
Paradoneis lyra	(Southern, 1914)	NGC;CGC;SGC	BEN	2,160	20
Paranaites polynoides	(Moore, 1909)	NGC	BEN	2,480	?
Parandalia fauveli	(Berkeley & Berkeley, 1941)	NGC;CGC;SGC	BEN;LIT	107	0
Paraprionospio pinnata	(Ehlers, 1901)	NGC;CGC;SGC;BR	BEN;LIT	2,000	0
Pareurythoe californica	(Johnson, 1897)	NGC;CGC	BEN;LIT	?	0
Pectinaria hartmanae	Reish, 1968	NGC	BEN	?	?
Pelagobia longicirrata	Greeff, 1879	NGC;CGC;SGC	PEL	?	?
Perinereis elenacasoi	Rioja, 1947	NGC;CGC;SGC;BR	BEN;LIT	?	0
Perinereis monterea	(Chamberlin, 1918)	NGC;CGC;SGC;BR;SWB	BEN;LIT	?	0

Species	Author, year	Region	Habitat		
Perinereis osoriotafalli	León González & Solis, 1998	NGC;CGC;SGC;BR	BEN;LIT	0	0
Petaloproctus borealis	Ardwidsson, 1907	NGC;BR	BEN;LIT	30	1,680
Phalacrophorus pictus	Greeff, 1879	NGC;CGC;SGC	PEL	?	?
Pherusa neopapillata	(Hartman, 1961)	NGC;CGC;SGC	BEN;LIT	0	556
Phyllochaetopterus limicolus	Hartman, 1960	NGC;CGC	BEN	119	1,910
Phyllodoce tuberculosa	Kudenov, 1975	NGC;BR	BEN;LIT	0	?
Phylo felix	Kinberg, 1866	NGC	BEN	7	99
Phylo nudus	(Moore, 1911)	NGC	BEN	?	590
Pionosyllis gigantea	Moore, 1908	NGC	BEN	122	198
Piromis americana	(Monro, 1928)	NGC	BEN;LIT	0	32
Piromis arenosus	Kinberg, 1867	NGC;BR	BEN;LIT	0	30
Pista cristata	(Muller, 1776)	NGC;CGC,SGC	BEN;LIT	0	82
Pista elongata	Moore, 1909	NGC;CGC	BEN;LIT	0	21
Platynereis bicanaliculata	(Baird, 1863)	NGC;CGC,SGC;BR;SWB	BEN;LIT	0	1,620
Platynereis dumerilii	(Audouin & M. Edwards, 1833)	NGC	BEN;LIT	0	200
Poecilochaetus johnsoni	Hartman, 1939	NGC;CGC;SGC	BEN;LIT	15	2,300
Polycirrus californicus	Moore, 1909	NGC	BEN;LIT	0	2,000
Polydora barbilla	Blake, 1980	NGC;BR	BEN;COM	15	15
Polydora convexa	Blake & Woodwick, 1972	NGC	BEN;COM	15	15
Polydora giardi	Mesnil, 1896	NGC;CGC;BR	BEN;LIT;COM	0	180
Polydora heterochaeta	Rioja, 1939	NGC	BEN;LACS	0	?
Polydora nuchalis	Woodwick, 1953	NGC;BR	BEN;LIT;LACS	0	?
Polydora socialis	(Schmarda, 1861)	NGC;CGC;SGC;BR	BEN;LIT;LACS;COM	0	68
Polydora websteri	Hartman, 1943	NGC;CGC;SGC;BR	BEN;COM	15	30
Polyodontes frons	Hartman, 1939	NGC	BEN	13	293
Polyodontes oculeus	(Treadwell, 1901)	NGC;CGC;SGC;BR	BEN	7	36
Polyophthalmus pictus	(Dujardin, 1839)	NGC;CGC;SGC	BEN;LIT	0	9
Pontogenia laeviseta	Hartman, 1939	NGC;CGC;SGC	BEN	18	144
Prionospio bocki	Söderström, 1920	NGC	BEN;LIT	0	104
Prionospio cirrifera	(Wirén, 1883)	NGC;CGC;SGC	BEN	1	1,775
Prionospio ehlersi	Fauvel, 1928	NGC;CGC;SGC	BEN	29	1,700
Prionospio heterobranchia heterobranchia	Moore, 1907	NGC;CGC;SGC	BEN	0	102
Prionospio multibranchiata	Berkeley, 1927	NGC	BEN;LIT	0	104

TABLE 29.3 (CONT'D). *Annotated list of macroinvertebrates known from the northern Gulf of California.*

Prionospio steenstrupi	Malmgren, 1867	NGC;CGC;SGC;BR	BEN;LIT	0	1,500
Protodorvillea gracilis	(Hartman, 1938)	NGC;CGC;SGC	BEN;LIT	0	117
Protula tubularia balboensis	Monro, 1933	NGC;BR	BEN;LIT	0	?
Sabellides manriquei	Salazar-Vallejo, 1996	NGC	BEN	46	380
Sagitella kowalewskii	Wagner, 1872	NGC;CGC;SGC	PEL	0	2,000
Scalibregma inflatum	Rathke, 1843	NGC;CGC;SGC	BEN	36	2,250
Scionella japonica	Moore, 1903	NGC;CGC	BEN;LIT	102	1,620
Scolelepis acuta	(Treadwell, 1914)	NGC	BEN;LIT	0	?
Scolelepis maculata	(Hartman, 1961)	NGC;BR	BEN;LIT	0	?
Scolelepis pigmentata	Reish, 1959	NGC	BEN	?	2,000
Scolelepis ?chevalieri	(Fauvel, 1901)	NGC;BR	BEN;LIT	0	?
Scoloplos acmeceps	Chamberlin, 1919	NGC;CGC;SGC	BEN;LIT	0	200
Scoloplos texana	Maciolek & Holland, 1978	NGC	BEN	1	90
Sigambra bassi	(Hartman, 1947)	NGC;CGC;SGC	BEN;LIT	0	74
Spiochaetopterus costarum costarum	Claparède, 1870	NGC;CGC;SGC;BR	BEN;LIT	1	90
Spiochaetopterus costarum monroi	Gitay, 1969	NGC;BR	BEN;LIT	0	?
Spiophanes bombyx	(Claparède, 1870)	NGC;CGC;SGC;BR	BEN;LIT	0	2,000
Spiophanes missionensis	Hartman, 1941	NGC;CGC;SGC;BR	BEN;LIT	0	300
Sthenelanella uniformis	Moore, 1910	NGC	BEN;LIT	0	320
Streblosoma crassibranchia	Treadwell, 1914	NGC	BEN;LIT	0	475
Streblosoma longifilis	Rioja, 1962	NGC;CGC;SGC;BR	BEN	22	22
Syllidia liniata	Hartmann-Schroder, 1962	NGC;CGC	BEN	?	?
Syllis elongata	(Johnson, 1901)	NGC;CGC;SGC;BR	BEN;LIT	0	66
Thalenessa lewisii	(Berkeley & Berkeley, 1939)	NGC;CGC;SGC	BEN	5	57
Tharyx monilaris	Hartman, 1960	NGC;CGC;SGC;SWB	BEN	6	3,060
Tharyx multifilis	Moore, 1909	NGC;CGC;SGC;SWB	BEN	255	2,390
Tharyx parvus	Berkeley, 1929	NGC;CGC;SGC	BEN	35	78
Tharyx tesselata	Hartman, 1960	NGC;CGC;SGC	BEN;LIT	0	70
Thelepus hamatus	Moore, 1905	NGC	BEN;LIT	83	1,386
Thormora johnstoni	(Kinberg, 1855)	NGC;CGC;SGC	BEN;LIT	0	270
Tomopteris elegans	Chun, 1887	NGC;CGC;SGC	PEL	?	?
Tomopteris planktonis	Apstein, 1900	NGC;CGC;SGC	PEL	?	?
Travisia fusiformis	Kudenov, 1975	NGC;BR	BEN;LIT	0	?
Travisia gigas	Hartman, 1938	NGC;CGC;SGC	BEN;LIT	0	?

TABLE 29.3 (CONT'D). *Annotated list of macroinvertebrates known from the northern Gulf of California.*

Travisia hobsonae	Santos, 1977	NGC	BEN;LIT	10	106
Typhloscolex mulleri	Busch, 1851	NGC;CGC;SGC	PEL	0	2,000
Typosyllis fasciata	(Malmgren, 1867)	NGC;BR	BEN;LIT	0	?

PHYLUM ARTHROPODA (ARTHROPODS)

CRUSTACEA (CRUSTACEANS)
  MALACOSTRACA
    EUMALACOSTRACA
      EUCARIDA
        DECAPODA (CRABS, SHRIMPS, CRAYFISHES, AND LOBSTERS)
          DENDROBRANCHIATA (COMMERCIAL SHRIMPS)

Farfantepenaeus californiensis	(Holmes, 1900)	NGC;CGC;SGC;BR;SWB	BEN;LIT;NER	2	180
Litopenaeus stylirostris	(Stimpson, 1874)	NGC;CGC;SGC	BEN;LIT;NER	5	45
Metapenaeopsis beebei	(Burkenroad, 1938)	NGC;CGC;SGC	BEN;LIT;NER	5	91
Metapenaeopsis mineri	(Burkenroad, 1934)	NGC;CGC;SGC;BR;SWB	BEN;LIT;NER	3	115
Rimapenaeus pacificus	(Burkenroad, 1934)	NGC;CGC;SGC;BR	BEN;LIT;NER	12	45
Sicyonia aliaffinis	(Burkenroad, 1934)	NGC;CGC;SGC;BR;SWB	BEN;LIT;NER	4	242
Sicyonia disdorsalis	(Burkenroad, 1934)	NGC;CGC;SGC;BR;SWB	BEN;LIT;NER	5	139
Sicyonia disedwardsi	(Burkenroad, 1934)	NGC;CGC;SGC;BR;SWB	BEN;LIT;NER	5	249
Sicyonia disparri	(Burkenroad, 1934)	NGC;CGC;SGC	BEN;LIT;NER	0	82
Sicyonia ingentis	(Burkenroad, 1938)	NGC;CGC;SGC;BR;SWB	BEN;LIT;NER	5	307
Sicyonia martini	Pérez Farfante & Booth, 1981	NGC;CGC;SGC;SWB	BEN;LIT;NER	9	242
Sicyonia penicillata	Lockington, 1879	NGC;CGC;SGC;BR;SWB	BEN;LIT;NER	1	180
Sicyonia picta	Faxon, 1893	NGC;CGC;SGC;BR;SWB	BEN;LIT;NER	16	400
Solenocera mutator	Burkenroad, 1938	NGC;CGC;SGC;BR;SWB	BEN;LIT;NER	2	380

          PLEOCYEMATA
            ANOMURA
              GALATHEIDAE (GALATHEIDS)

Janetogalathea californiensis	(Benedict, 1902)	NGC;CGC	BEN;NER	87	3,998
Munida mexicana	Benedict, 1902	NGC;CGC;SGC;SWB	BEN;NER	16	145
Munida tenella	Benedict, 1902	NGC;CGC;SGC	BEN;NER	27	130
Pleuroncodes planipes	Stimpson, 1860	NGC;CGC;SGC	BEN;PEL;NER;OCE	48	3,000

              PORCELLANIDAE (PORCELAIN CRABS)

Euceramus transversilineatus	(Lockington, 1878)	NGC;CGC;SGC;BR;SWB	BEN;NER	3	63
Heteroporcellana corbicola	(Haig, 1960)	NGC;BR	BEN;COM;NER	18	45

TABLE 29.3 (CONT'D). *Annotated list of macroinvertebrates known from the northern Gulf of California.*

Species	Author (year)	Distribution	Ecology		
Megalobrachium erosum	(Glassell, 1936)	NGC;CGC;SGC;SWB	BEN;NER	9	45
Megalobrachium sinuimanus	(Lockington, 1878)	NGC;CGC;SGC	BEN;LIT;COM	0	5
Megalobrachium smithi	(Glassell, 1936)	NGC;CGC;BR	BEN;LIT;COM	0	5
Megalobrachium tuberculipes	(Lockington, 1878)	NGC;CGC;SGC;BR;SWB	LIT;BEN;COM;NE	2	18
Minyocerus kirki	Glassell, 1938	NGC;CGC;SGC;BR	BEN;COM;NER	0	24
Pachycheles calculosus	Haig, 1960	NGC;CGC;SGC;BR	LIT;BEN;COM;NE	0	7
Pachycheles marcortezensis	Glassell, 1936	NGC;CGC;SGC;SWB	BEN;COM;NER	3	82
Pachycheles panamensis	Faxon, 1893	NGC;CGC;SGC;SWB	LIT;BEN;COM;NE	0	7
Pachycheles setimanus	(Lockington, 1878)	NGC;CGC;SGC;BR	BEN;LIT;NER	0	50
Petrolisthes armatus	(Gibbes, 1850)	NGC;CGC;SGC;BR	LIT;BEN;LACS;NER	0	18
Petrolisthes crenulatus	Lockington, 1878	NGC;CGC;SGC;BR;SWB	LIT;BEN;COM;NE	2	27
Petrolisthes edwardsii	(de Saussure, 1853)	NGC;CGC;SGC;BR;SWB	LIT;BEN;COM;NE	0	40
Petrolisthes galapagensis	Haig, 1960	NGC;CGC	BEN;LIT;COM	0	1
Petrolisthes gracilis	Stimpson, 1859	NGC;CGC;SGC;BR;SWB	LIT;BEN;COM;NE	18	45
Petrolisthes hirtipes	Lockington, 1878	NGC;CGC;SGC;BR;SWB	LIT;BEN;COM;NE	9	40
Petrolisthes hirtispinosus	Lockington, 1878	NGC;CGC;SGC;BR	LIT;BEN;COM;NE	1	40
Petrolisthes lewisi	(Glassell, 1936)	NGC;CGC;SGC	BEN;LIT	0	6
Petrolisthes nigrunguiculatus	Glassell, 1936	NGC;CGC;SGC	BEN;LIT	0	1
Petrolisthes sanfelipensis	Glassell, 1936	NGC;CGC;SGC;BR;SWB	BEN;LIT;NER	0	50
Petrolisthes schmitti	Glassell, 1936	NGC;CGC;BR	BEN;LIT	0	1
Petrolisthes tiburonensis	Glassell, 1936	NGC;CGC;BR	BEN;LIT	0	1
Polyonyx nitidus	Lockington, 1878	NGC;CGC;SGC	BEN;COM;NER	6	48
Polyonyx quadriungulatus	Glassell, 1935	NGC;CGC;SGC;BR	BEN;COM	3	47
Porcellana cancrisocialis	Glassell, 1936	NGC;CGC;SGC;BR;SWB	LIT;BEN;COM;NE	0	115
Porcellana hancocki	Glassell, 1938	NGC;CGC;SGC	BEN;NER	45	103
Porcellana paguriconviva	Glassell, 1936	NGC;CGC;SGC;BR;SWB	LIT;BEN;COM;NER	0	90
Ulloaia perpusillia	Glassell, 1938	NGC;CGC;SGC;BR	BEN;COM;NER	0	15
HIPPOIDEA (MOLE AND SAND CRABS)					
Albunea lucasia	(de Saussure, 1853)	NGC;CGC;SGC	BEN;LIT;NER	0	45
Emerita analoga	(Stimpson, 1857)	NGC;CGC;SWB	BEN;LIT	0	1
Emerita rathbunae	Schmitt, 1935	NGC;CGC;SGC	BEN;LIT	0	1
Lepidopa californica	Efford, 1971	NGC;CGC	BEN;LIT;NER	0	152
Lepidopa esposa	Efford, 1971	NGC;CGC;SGC;BR	BEN;LIT;NER	0	2
Lepidopa mearnsi	Benedict, 1903	NGC;CGC;SGC;BR	BEN;LIT;NER	0	2

TABLE 29.3 (CONT'D). Annotated list of macroinvertebrates known from the northern Gulf of California.

PAGUROIDEA (HERMIT CRABS)

Species	Author				
Calcinus californiensis	Bouvier, 1898	NGG;CGC;3GC;BR;SWB	BEN;LIT	0	7
Clibanarius albidigitus	Nobili, 1901	NGG;CGC;3GC;BR	BEN;LIT;LACS	0	2
Clibanarius digueti	Bouvier, 1898	NGG;CGC;3GC;BR;SWB	BEN;LIT	0	1
Clibanarius panamensis	Stimpson, 1859	NGG;CGC;3GC;BR;SWB	BEN;LIT;LACS	0	3
Coenobita compressus	H. Milne Edwards, 1837	NGG;CGC;3GC;SWB	BEN;CST	0	1
Dardanus sinistripes	(Stimpson, 1859)	NGG;CGC;3GC;SWB	BEN;NER	9	110
Enallopaguropsis guatemoci	(Glassell, 1937)	NGG;CGC;3GC	BEN;NER	20	270
Enallopagurus spinicarpus	(Glassell, 1938)	NGG;CGC;3GC	BEN;NER	16	146
Iridopagurus occidentalis	(Faxon, 1893)	NGG;CGC;3GC	BEN;NER	55	120
Manucomplanus cervicornis	(Benedict, 1892)	NGG;CGC;3GC	BEN;NER	54	200
Manucomplanus varians	(Benedict, 1892)	NGG;CGC;3GC;BR;SWB	BEN;NER	11	183
Pagurixus anabuacus	Glassell, 1938	NGG;CGC;3GC;BR	BEN;LIT	0	18
Pagurixus bakeri	Holmes, 1900	NGG;CGC;3GC;BR;SWB	BEN;NER	40	232
Paguristes praedator	Glassell, 1937	NGG;CGC;3GC;BR;SWB	BEN;NER	40	155
Paguristes sanguinimanus	Glassell, 1938	NGG;CGC;3GC;BR	BEN;LIT	0	24
Pagurus albus	(Benedict, 1892)	NGG;CGC;3GC;BR	BEN;NER	5	30
Pagurus arenisaxatilis	Harvey & McLaughlin, 1991	NGG;CGC;3R	BEN;LIT	0	6
Pagurus benedicti	(Bouvier, 1898)	NGG;CGC;3GC;BR;SWB	BEN;NER	2	84
Pagurus gladius	(Benedict, 1892)	NGG;CGC;3GC;BR;SWB	BEN;NER	33	111
Pagurus lepidus	(Bouvier, 1898)	NGG;CGC;3GC;BR;SWB	BEN;LIT	1	40
Pagurus smithi	(Benedict, 1892)	NGG;CGC;3GC;BR;SWB	BEN;NER	33	111
Petrochirus californiensis	Bouvier, 1895	NGG;CGC;3GC;BR;SWB	BEN;NER	0	110
Phimochirus californiensis	(Benedict, 1892)	NGG;CGC;3GC;BR;SWB	BEN;NER	2	129
Phimochirus roseus	(Benedict, 1892)	NGG;CGC;3GC;BR;SWB	BEN;LIT	1	8
Pylopagurus longicarpus	Walton, 1954	NGC;BR	BEN;NER	44	110
Tomopagurus purpuratus	(Benedict, 1892)	NGG;CGC;3GC	BEN;NER	27	90

BRACHYURA ("TRUE" CRABS)

Species	Author				
Ala cornuta	(Stimpson, 1860)	NGG;CGC;3GC;BR	BEN;LIT;COM;EPIF	0	22
Arenaeus mexicanus	(Gerstaecker, 1856)	NGG;CGC;3GC;SWB	BEN;LACS;NER	0	80
Austinotheres angelicus	(Lockington, 1877)	NGG;CGC;BR	BEN;COM;NER	?	?
Bathyrhombila furcata	Hendrickx, 1998	NGG;CGC	BEN	55	644
Calappa convexa	de Saussure, 1853	NGG;CGC;3GC;BR;SWB	BEN;NER	3	75
Calappa saussurei	Rathbun, 1898	NGG;CGC;3GC;SWB	BEN;COM;NER	1	274

TABLE 29.3 (CONT'D). *Annotated list of macroinvertebrates known from the northern Gulf of California.*

Species	Authority				
Callinectes arcuatus	Ordway, 1863	NGC;CGC;SGC;BR;SWB	BEN;LACS;NER	0	75
Callinectes bellicosus	(Stimpson, 1859)	NGC;CGC;SGC;BR;SWB	BEN;LACS	0	20
Calyptraeotheres granti	(Glassell, 1933)	NGC;CGC;SGC;BR;SWB	BEN;LIT;COM	0	1
Cancer amphioetus	Rathbun, 1898	NGC;CGC;SGC;BR;SWB	BEN;NER	8	380
Cataleptodius occidentalis	(Stimpson, 1871)	NGC;CGC;SGC;BR;SWB	BEN;LIT;LACS	0	1
Chacellus pacificus	Hendrickx, 1989	NGC;CGC;SGC	BEN;NER	56	103
Chasmocarcinus latipes	Rathbun, 1898	NGC;CGC;SGC;SWB	BEN;NER	27	114
Collodes tenuirostris	Rathbun, 1893	NGC;CGC;SGC;BR;SWB	BEN;NER	6	365
Collodes tumidus	Rathbun, 1898	NGC;CGC;SGC;SWB	BEN;NER	20	128
Cronius ruber	(Lamarck, 1818)	NGC;CGC;SGC;BR;SWB	LIT;BEN;NER	0	60
Cryptodromiopsis sarraburei	(Rathbun, 1910)	NGC;CGC;SGC;BR;SWB	BEN;COM;NER	0	110
Cryptopodia bassleri	Rathbun, 1925	NGC;CGC;SGC;SWB	BEN;NER	3	81
Cyclograpsus escondidensis	Rathbun, 1933	NGC;CGC	BEN;LIT	0	1
Cycloxanthops vittatus	(Stimpson, 1860)	NGC;CGC;SGC	BEN;LIT;COM	0	55
Cyrtoplax panamensis	Ziesenhenne, 1940	NGC;CGC;SGC;BR	BEN;LIT	0	128
Daira americana	Stimpson, 1860	NGC;CGC;SGC	BEN;LIT;COM	0	5
Deilocerus hendrickxi	Tavares, 1993	NGC	BEN;NER	162	175
Deilocerus laminatus	Rathbun, 1935	NGC	BEN;NER	65	82
Dissodactylus lockingtoni	Glassell, 1935	NGC;BR	BEN;COM;NER	1	?
Dissodactylus nitidus	Smith, 1870	NGC;CGC;BR;SWB	BEN;COM;NER	1	10
Dissodactylus xantusi	Glassell, 1936	NGC;CGC;SGC;BR	BEN;COM;NER	1	?
Ebalia cristata	Rathbun, 1898	NGC;CGC;SGC	BEN;NER	66	146
Ebalia magdalenensis	Rathbun, 1933	NGC;CGC;BR;SWB	BEN;NER	3	33
Epialtoides paradigmus	Garth, 1958	NGC;CGC;SGC;BR	BEN;LIT	0	24
Epialtus minimus	Lockington, 1877	NGC;CGC;SGC;BR	LIT;BEN;COM;NE	0	31
Erileptus spinosus	Rathbun, 1893	NGC;CGC;SGC;BR	BEN;NER	5	549
Eriphia squamata	Stimpson, 1859	NGC;CGC;SGC;BR;SWB	BEN;LIT;COM	0	1
Ethusa lata	Rathbun, 1893	NGC;CGC;SGC;BR;SWB	BEN;NER	3	180
Ethusa panamensis	Finnegan, 1931	NGC;CGC;SGC	BEN;NER	2	45
Eucinetops lucasi	Stimpson, 1860	NGC;CGC;SGC;BR	BEN;LIT;EPIF;COM	0	1
Eucinetops panamensis	Rathbun, 1923	NGC;CGC;SGC	BEN;LIT	0	1
Euphylax robustus	A. Milne Edwards, 1874	NGC;CGC;SGC;BR	BEN;NER	10	75
Euprognatha bifida	Rathbun, 1893	NGC;CGC;SGC;SWB	BEN;NER	2	175
Eurypanopeus confragosus	Rathbun, 1933	NGC;CGC;SGC;BR	BEN;LIT;LACS	0	1

TABLE 29.3 (CONT'D). *Annotated list of macroinvertebrates known from the northern Gulf of California.*

Species	Author			Supralittoral	
Eurypanopeus ovatus	(Benedict & Rathbun, 1891)	NGC;CGC;SGC;BR	BEN;LIT	0	1
Eurypanopeus planissimus	(Stimpson, 1860)	NGC;CGC;SGC;SWB	BEN;LIT	0	1
Eurypanopeus planus	(Smith, 1869)	NGC;CGC;SGC	BEN;LIT	0	1
Eurytium affine	(Streets & Kingsley, 1879)	NGC;CGC;SGC;BR;SWB	BEN;LIT;LACS	0	1
Eurytium albidigitum	Rathbun, 1933	NGC;CGC;SGC;BR	BEN;LIT;LACS	0	1
Fabia carvachoi	Campos, 1986	NGC;BR	BEN;LIT;COM	0	?
Gecarcinus quadratus	de Saussure, 1853	NGC;CGC;SGC;BR	BEN;LACS;CST		
Geograpsus lividus	(H. Milne Edwards, 1837)	NGC;CGC;SGC	BEN;LIT	0	?
Glyptoplax consagae	Hendrickx, 1990	NGC;BR	BEN;NER	28	?
Glyptoxantbus meandricus	(Lockington, 1877)	NGC;CGC;SGC;BR	BEN;LIT	0	4
Goetice americanus	Rathbun, 1923	NGC;CGC	BEN;LIT	0	1
Gonopanope areolata	(Rathbun, 1898)	NGC;CGC;SGC;BR	BEN;NER	18	53
Gonopanope nitida	(Rathbun, 1898)	NGC;CGC;SGC	BEN;NER	13	20
Grapsus grapsus	(Linnaeus, 1758)	NGC;CGC;SGC;SWB	BEN;LIT	0	?
Hemigrapsus nudus	(Dana, 1851)	NGC	BEN;LIT	0	?
Hemigrapsus oregonensis	(Dana, 1851)	NGC;BR	BEN;LIT	0	?
Hemus finneganae	Garth, 1958	NGC;CGC;SGC	BEN;NER	1	59
Hepatus kossmanni	Neumann, 1878	NGC;CGC;SGC;BR;SWB	BEN;NER	3	75
Hepatus lineatus	Rathbun, 1898	NGC;CGC;SGC;BR;SWB	BEN;NER	1	185
Herbstia camptacantha	(Stimpson, 1871)	NGC;CGC;SGC	BEN;LIT;COM	0	69
Herbstia pubescens	Stimpson, 1871	NGC;CGC	BEN;LIT;COM	0	10
Heteractaea lunata	(H. Milne Edwards & Lucas, 1843)	NGC;CGC;SGC	BEN;LIT;COM	0	5
Heterocrypta macrobrachia	Stimpson, 1871	NGC;CGC;SGC;BR;SWB	BEN;NER	21	92
Hexapanopeus orcutti	Rathbun, 1930	NGC;CGC;SGC;BR	LIT;BEN;NER	0	28
Hexapanopeus rubicundus	Rathbun, 1933	NGC;CGC;BR	BEN;LIT	0	1
Hypoconcha lowei	Rathbun, 1933	NGC;BR	BEN;NER	13	100
Hypoconcha panamensis	Smith, 1869	NGC;CGC;SGC;BR	BEN;NER	2	180
Iliacantba schmitti	Rathbun, 1935	NGC;CGC;SGC;SWB	BEN;NER	16	275
Inachoides laevis	Stimpson, 1860	NGC;CGC;SGC;BR;SWB	LIT;EPIF;BEN;NER	3	102
Juxtafabia muliniarum	Rathbun, 1918	NGC;CGC;BR	BEN;COM;NER	?	?
Kraussia americana	Garth, 1939	NGC;CGC;SGC	BEN;NER	7	72
Leiolambrus punctatissimus	(Owen, 1839)	NGC;CGC;SGC;SWB	BEN;NER	22	98
Leucosilia jurinei	(de Saussure, 1853)	NGC;CGC;SGC	BEN;NER	0	17

TABLE 29.3 (CONT'D.). *Annotated list of macroinvertebrates known from the northern Gulf of California.*

Species	Author, year	Distribution	Habitat		
Libinia mexicana	Rathbun, 1892	NGC;CGC;SGC;BR	BEN;NER	15	72
Lipaesthesius leeanus	Rathbun, 1898	NGC;CGC;SGC	BEN;NER	7	73
Lissa aurivilliusi	Rathbun, 1898	NGC;CGC;SGC;SWB	BEN;NER	3	128
Lithadia cumingii	Bell, 1855	NGC;CGC;SGC;BR;SWB	BEN;NER	3	93
Lophopanopeus frontalis	(Rathbun, 1893)	NGC;CGC;SGC;BR	BEN;LIT	0	8
Malacoplax californiensis	(Lockington, 1877)	NGC;CGC;SGC;BR	LIT;BEN;LACS;NER	1	114
Medaeus pelagius	(Glassell, 1936)	NGC;CGC;SGC;BR;SWB	BEN;NER	23	91
Mesorhoea belli	(A. Milne Edwards, 1878)	NGC;CGC;SGC;BR;SWB	BEN;NER	11	110
Microphrys branchialis	Rathbun, 1898	NGC;CGC;SGC;SWB	BEN;NER	9	90
Microphrys platysoma	(Stimpson, 1860)	NGC;CGC;SGC;BR	ARCO;COM;LIT;BEN;NER	0	73
Mithrax denticulatus	Bell, 1835	NGC;CGC;SGC	ARCO;COM;LIT;BEN;NER	0	24
Mithrax sinensis	Rathbun, 1892	NGC;CGC;SGC	BEN;NER	0	100
Nanocassiope polita	(Rathbun, 1893)	NGC;CGC;SGC;SWB	BEN	5	275
Neopanope peterseni	Glassell, 1933	NGC;CGC	BEN;LIT	0	1
Notolopas lamellatus	Stimpson, 1871	NGC;CGC;SGC;BR	BEN;NER	1	100
Notosceles ecuadoriensis	(Rathbun, 1935)	NGC;CGC;SGC	BEN;NER	55	114
Ocypode occidentalis	Stimpson, 1860	NGC;CGC;SGC	BEN;LIT;LACS	0	1
Oediplax granulata	Rathbun, 1893	NGC;CGC;SGC;BR	BEN;NER	22	80
Opisthopus transversus	Rathbun, 1893	NGC;BR;SWB	BEN;LIT;COM	0	91
Orthotheres unguifalcula	(Glassell, 1936)	NGC;BR	BEN;LIT	0	1
Osachila levis	Rathbun, 1898	NGC;CGC;SGC	BEN;NER	22	110
Pachygrapsus crassipes	Randall, 1839	NGC;CGC;BR;SWB	BEN;LIT	0	1
Pachygrapsus transversus	(Gibbes, 1850)	NGC;CGC;SGC;SWB	BEN;LIT;LACS;COM	0	1
Palicus fragilis	(Rathbun, 1893)	NGC;CGC;SGC	BEN;COM;NER	35	270
Palicus lucasii	Rathbun, 1898	NGC;CGC;SGC	BEN;COM;NER	9	110
Palicus zonata	(Rathbun, 1893)	NGC;CGC;SGC;SWB	BEN;NER	15	73
Panopeus diversus	Rathbun, 1933	NGC;BR	?	?	?
Panopeus purpureus	Lockington, 1877	NGC;CGC;SGC;BR;SWB	BEN;LIT;LACS	0	1
Panoplax mundata	Glassell, 1935	NGC;CGC;SGC;BR	BEN;NER	13	35
Paractaea sulcata	(Stimpson, 1860)	NGC;CGC;SGC	BEN;COM;NER	5	30
Paradasygyius depressus	(Bell, 1835)	NGC;CGC;SGC;BR	BEN;NER	9	146
Parapinnixa nitida	(Lockington, 1877)	NGC;CGC;BR;SWB	BEN;LIT;COM	0	42
Parthenope excavata	(Stimpson, 1871)	NGC;CGC;SGC	BEN;NER	3	54
Pelia tumida	(Lockington, 1877)	NGC;CGC;SGC;BR;SWB	BEN;LIT	0	128

TABLE 29.3 (CONT'D). *Annotated list of macroinvertebrates known from the northern Gulf of California.*

Persephona subovata	(Rathbun, 1893)	NGC;CGC;SGC	BEN;NER	36	95
Persephona townsendi	(Rathbun, 1893)	NGC;CGC;SGC;BR	BEN;NER	3	104
Pilumnoides rotundus	Garth, 1940	NGC;CGC;BR	BEN;COM;NER	18	300
Pilumnus gonzalensis	Rathbun, 1893	NGC;CGC;SGC;BR	BEN;LIT	0	5
Pilumnus limosus	Smith, 1869	NGC;CGC;SGC;BR	BEN;LIT	0	55
Pilumnus spinohirsutus	(Lockington, 1877)	NGC;SWB	BEN;LIT	0	34
Pilumnus tectus	Rathbun, 1933	NGC;BR	BEN;LIT	0	1
Pilumnus townsendi	Rathbun, 1923	NGC;CGC;SGC;BR;SWB	BEN;LIT;COM;NER	2	90
Pinnaxodes gigas	Green, 1992	NGC;CGC;BR	BEN;LIT	20	?
Pinnixa abbotti	Glassell, 1935	NGC;BR	?	?	?
Pinnixa felipensis	Glassell, 1935	NGC;BR	?	?	?
Pinnixa fusca	Glassell, 1935	NGC;BR	?	?	?
Pinnixa huffmani	Glassell, 1935	NGC;BR	BEN;COM	?	?
Pinnixa pembertoni	Glassell, 1935	NGC;CGC;SGC;BR	LIT;BEN;COM	0	11
Pinnixa plectrophoros	Glassell, 1935	NGC;BR	BEN;LIT;COM	0	1
Pinnixa tomentosa	Lockington, 1877	NGC;BR	BEN;COM;NER	18	121
Pinnixa transversalis	(H. Milne Edwards & Lucas, 1844)	NGC;CGC;SGC;BR	BEN;COM;NER	0	128
Pinnotheres orcutti	Rathbun, 1918	NGC;CGC;SGC;BR	BEN;NER	32	37
Pitho picteti	(de Saussure, 1853)	NGC;CGC;SGC;SWB	LIT;EPIF;BEN;NER	0	82
Pitho sexdentata	Bell, 1835	NGC;CGC;SGC	BEN;LIT	0	36
Platypodiella rotundata	(Stimpson, 1860)	NGC;CGC;SGC;SWB	BEN;LIT;COM	0	1
Podochela bemphilli	(Lockington, 1877)	NGC;CGC;SGC;SWB	BEN;NER	0	166
Podochela latimanus	(Rathbun, 1893)	NGC;CGC;SGC;BR	BEN;LIT	0	67
Podochela lobifrons	Rathbun, 1893	NGC;CGC;SGC	BEN;NER	33	230
Podochela vestita	(Stimpson, 1871)	NGC;CGC;SGC;BR;SWB	BEN;NER	3	55
Portunus iridescens	(Rathbun, 1893)	NGC;CGC;SGC;SWB	BEN;NER	27	241
Portunus xantusii minimus	Rathbun, 1898	NGC;CGC;SGC;BR;SWB	BEN;NER	0	241
Pyromaia tuberculata	(Lockington, 1877)	NGC;CGC;SGC;BR;SWB	BEN;NER	0	412
Quadrella nitida	Smith, 1869	NGC;CGC;SGC	BEN;COM;NER	45	150
Randallia americana	(Rathbun, 1893)	NGC;CGC;SGC;BR	BEN;NER	18	175
Randallia ornata	(Randall, 1839)	NGC;CGC;SWB	BEN;NER	10	185
Ranilia angustata	Stimpson, 1860	NGC;CGC;SGC	BEN;NER	18	?
Raninoides benedicti	Rathbun, 1935	NGC;CGC;SGC;BR	BEN;NER	3	103

TABLE 29.3 (CONT'D). *Annotated list of macroinvertebrates known from the northern Gulf of California.*

Raymondia clavapedata	(Glassell, 1935)	NGC;BR;SWB	BEN;LIT;COM	0	27
Sesarma sulcatum	Smith, 1870	NGC;CGC;SGC;SWB	BEN;LIT;LACS	0	?
Solenolambrus arcuatus	Stimpson, 1871	NGC;CGC;SGC	BEN;COM;NER	2	110
Speloeophorus digueti	(Bouvier, 1898)	NGC;CGC;SGC;BR	BEN;NER	24	114
Speloeophorus schmitti	Glassell, 1935	NGC;BR	BEN;LIT	0	1
Speocarcinus granulimanus	Rathbun, 1893	NGC;CGC;SGC;BR	BEN;NER	7	102
Speocarcinus spinicarpus	Guinot, 1969	NGC;BR	BEN;NER	9	73
Sphenocarcinus agassizi	Rathbun, 1893	NGC;CGC;SGC	BEN;NER	55	165
Stenocionops angusta	(Lockington, 1877)	NGC;CGC;SGC;BR;SWB	BEN;NER	0	55
Stenocionops beebei	Glassell, 1936	NGC;CGC;SGC;BR;SWB	BEN;NER	27	110
Stenocionops ovata	(Bell, 1835)	NGC;CGC;SGC;SWB	BEN;COM;EPIF;NE	15	275
Stenorhynchus debilis	(Smith, 1871)	NGC;CGC;SGC;BR;SWB	BEN;NER	0	154
Symethis garthi	Goeke, 1980	NGC;CGC;SGC	BEN;NER	9	55
Teleophrys cristulipes	Stimpson, 1860	NGC;CGC;SGC;SWB	BEN;COM;NER	0	128
Tetragrapsus jouyi	(Rathbun, 1893)	NGC;CGC;SGC;BR	BEN;LIT	0	1
Thoe sulcata sulcata	Stimpson, 1860	NGC;CGC;SGC	BEN;COM;LIT	0	5
Thyrolambrus glasselli	Garth, 1958	NGC;CGC;SGC;SWB	BEN;COM;NER	3	70
Trizocarcinus dentatus	(Rathbun, 1893)	NGC;CGC;SGC;BR	BEN;NER	27	139
Tumidotheres margarita	(Smith, 1869)	NGC;CGC	BEN;COM;NER	1	?
Uca crenulata coloradensis	(Rathbun, 1893)	NGC;CGC;BR	BEN;LIT;LACS	0	1
Uca crenulata crenulata	(Lockington, 1877)	NGC;CGC;SGC;BR;SWB	BEN;LIT;LACS	0	1
Uca latimanus	(Rathbun, 1893)	NGC;CGC;SGC;BR	BEN;LIT;LACS	0	1
Uca musica musica	Rathbun, 1914	NGC;CGC;SGC;BR;SWB	BEN;LIT;LACS	0	1
Uca princeps monilifera	Rathbun, 1914	NGC;CGC;BR	BEN;LIT;LACS	0	1
Uca princeps princeps	(Smith, 1870)	NGC;CGC;SGC	BEN;LIT;LACS	0	1
Ublias ellipticus	Stimpson, 1871	NGC;CGC	BEN;LIT;COM	0	1
Xanthodius sternberghii	Stimpson, 1859	NGC;CGC;SGC;BR;SWB	BEN;LIT	0	1
CARIDEA (TIDEPOOL SHRIMP)					
Alpheus bellimanus	Lockington, 1877	NGC;CGC;SGC	BEN;NER	0	300
Alpheus felgenhaueri	Kim & Abele, 1988	NGC;CGC;SGC	BEN;LIT	0	1
Alpheus floridanus	Kingsley, 1878	NGC;CGC;SGC	BEN;LIT;COM	0	37
Alpheus bebes	Kim & Abele, 1988	NGC;CGC;SGC	BEN;COM;NER	0	74
Alpheus byeyoungae	Kim & Abele, 1988	NGC;CGC;SGC	BEN;LIT;COM	0	1
Alpheus normanni	Kingsley, 1878	NGC;CGC;SGC;BR	BEN;NER	2	73

TABLE 29.3 (CONT'D). *Annotated list of macroinvertebrates known from the northern Gulf of California.*

Species	Author	Region	Habitat		
Alpheus sulcatus	Kingsley, 1878	NGC;CGC;SGC;SWB	BEN;LIT;COM	0	1
Alpheus umbo	Kim & Abele, 1988	NGC;CGC;SGC	BEN;LIT;COM	0	1
Alpheus villus	Kim & Abele, 1988	NGC	BEN;LIT;COM	0	6
Ambidexter panamensis	Abele, 1972	NGC;BR	BEN;LIT	0	1
Ambidexter swifti	Abele, 1972	NGC;BR	BEN;NER	0	70
Ambidexter symmetricus	Manning & Chace, 1971	NGC	BEN;LIT	0	1
Automate dolichognatha	de Man, 1888	NGC;CGC;SGC	BEN;NER	0	100
Betaeus longidactylus	Lockington, 1877	NGC;BR	BEN;LIT	0	1
Gnathophyllum panamense	Faxon, 1893	NGC;CGC;SGC;BR	BEN;LIT;COM	0	20
Hippolyte californiensis	Holmes, 1895	NGC;CGC	BEN;LIT	0	10
Hippolyte williamsi	Schmitt, 1924	NGC;BR	BEN;LIT	0	10
Latreutes antiborealis	Holthuis, 1952	NGC;CGC;SGC;BR;SWB	BEN;LIT	4	46
Leptochela serratorbita	Bate, 1888	NGC;CGC;SGC	LIT;BEN;NER	20	110
Lucifer typus	H. Milne Edwards, 1837	NGC;CGC;SGC;SWB	PEL;OCE	200	730
Lysmata californica	(Stimpson, 1866)	NGC;CGC;SGC;SWB	BEN;LIT	0	33
Neocrangon zacae	(Chace, 1937)	NGC	BEN;LIT	9	37
Neopontonides dentiger	Holthuis, 1951	NGC;CGC;SGC	BEN;NER	1	66
Palaemon ritteri	Holmes, 1895	NGC;CGC;SGC;BR;SWB	BEN;LIT	0	40
Palaemonella holmesi	(Nobili, 1907)	NGC;CGC;SGC;BR;SWB	BEN;COM;NER	2	90
Pasiphaea americana	Faxon, 1893	NGC;CGC;SGC;SWB	PEL;OCE;NER	150	1,000
Pasiphaea pacifica	Rathbun, 1902	NGC;CGC	PEL;OCE	75	730
Periclimenes infraspinis	(Rathbun, 1902)	NGC;CGC;SGC;BR	BEN;COM;NER	0	150
Periclimenes lucasi	Chace, 1937	NGC;CGC;SGC;BR	BEN;NER	0	90
Plesionika beebei	Chace, 1937	NGC;CGC;SGC;SWB	PEL;BEN;NER;OCE	73	914
Pontonia longispina	Holthuis, 1951	NGC;CGC	BEN;LIT	0	1
Pontonia pinnae	Lockington, 1878	NGC;CGC;SGC;BR	BEN;LIT	0	4
Processa peruviana	Wicksten, 1983	NGC;CGC;SGC;BR;SWB	BEN;NER	26	180
Processa pippinnae	Wicksten & Méndez, 1985	NGC;CGC	PEL;NER;OCE	150	644
Sergestes halia	Faxon, 1893	NGC;CGC;SGC;SWB	PEL;OCE	200	1,617
Synalpheus digueti	Coutière, 1909	NGC;CGC	BEN;LIT;COM	0	10
Synalpheus goodie occidentalis	Coutière, 1909	NGC;CGC;SGC	BEN;COM	20	40
Synalpheus lockingtoni	Coutière, 1909	NGC;CGC;SGC;BR;SWB	BEN;LIT;COM	0	8
Synalpheus sanjosei	Coutière, 1909	NGC;CGC;BR;SWB	BEN;LIT	0	20

TABLE 29.3 (CONT'D). *Annotated list of macroinvertebrates known from the northern Gulf of California.*

Species	Author				
Synalpheus townsendi mexicanus	Coutière, 1909	NGC;CGC;SGC	BEN;LIT;COM	0	35
Thor algicola	Wicksten, 1987	NGC;CGC;SGC;BR	BEN;LIT	0	25
Typton serratus	Holthuis, 1951	NGC;CGC	BEN;LIT;COM	1	5
PALINURA (SPINY LOBSTER AND SLIPPER LOBSTER)					
Evibacus princeps	Smith, 1869	NGC;CGC;SGC;BR	BEN;NER	10	90
Panulirus inflatus	(Bouvier, 1895)	NGC;CGC;SGC	BEN;LIT	1	30
THALASSINIDEA (MUD SHRIMP AND GHOST SHRIMP)					
Acanthaxius caespitosa	(Squires, 1979)	NGC;CGC;SGC	BEN;NER	72	200
Axiopsis baronai	Squires, 1977	NGC;BR	BEN;LIT	5	9
Callianassa uncinata	Milne-Edwards	NGC;CGC;SGC;BR	BEN;LIT	0	0
Calocarides quinqueseriatus	(Rathbun, 1902)	NGC;CGC;SGC	BEN	293	1,780
Neaxius vivesi	(Bouvier, 1895)	NGC;CGC;SGC;BR;SWB	BEN;LIT;COM	0	4
Upogebia burkenroadi	Williams, 1986	NGC	?	?	?
Upogebia dawsoni	Williams, 1986	NGC;CGC;SGC;BR	BEN;LACS;NER	0	2
Upogebia jonesi	Williams, 1986	NGC;BR	BEN;LIT;NER	0	72
Upogebia thistlei	Williams, 1986	NGC;CGC;SGC;BR	BEN;LIT;LACS	0	2
EUPHAUSIACEA (EUPHAUSIDS)					
Euphausia lamelligera	Hansen, 1911	NGC;CGC;SGC;SWB	PEL;OCE;NER	100	500
Nematoscelis difficilis	Hansen, 1911	NGC;CGC;SGC;SWB	PEL;OCE;NER	0	450
Nyctiphanes simplex	Hansen, 1911	NGC;CGC;SGC;BR;SWB	PEL;OCE;NER	0	300
PERACARIDA					
AMPHIPODA					
CAPRELLIDEA (SKELETON SHRIMP AND WHALE LICE)					
Cyamus balaenopterae	Barnard, 1931	NGC;CGC;SGC;SWB	COM	0	?
Cyamus boopis	Lütken, 1870	NGC;CGC;SGC;SWB	COM	0	?
Cyamus catodontis	Margolis, 1954	NGC;CGC;SGC;SWB	COM	0	?
Cyamus erraticus	Roussel de Vauzème, 1834	NGC;CGC;SGC;SWB	COM	0	?
Cyamus orcini	Leung, 1970	NGC;CGC;SGC;SWB	COM	0	?
Cyamus ovalis	Roussel de Vauzème, 1834	NGC;CGC;SGC;SWB	COM	0	?
Isocyamus delphinii	(Guérin-Méneville, 1837)	NGC;CGC;SGC;SWB	COM	0	?
Neocyamus physeteris	(Pouchet, 1888)	NGC;CGC;SGC;SWB	COM	0	?
Syncyamus chelipes	(Costa, 1866)	NGC;CGC;SGC;SWB	COM	0	?
Syncyamus pseudorcae	(Bowman, 1955)	NGC;CGC;SGC;SWB	COM	0	?

GAMMARIDEA (COMMON AMPHIPODS)

Acuminodeutopus periculosus	Barnard, 1969	NGC;BR	BEN	0	38
Ampelisca agassizi	(Judd, 1896)	NGC;CGC	BEN	5	195
Ampelisca cristata	Holmes, 1908	NGC;CGC;5GC;BR	BEN	6	152
Ampelisca bancocki	Barnard, 1954	NGC;CGC;5GC	BEN	9	157
Ampelisca lobata	Holmes, 1908	NGC;CGC;5GC	BEN	0	183
Ampelisca mexicana	Barnard, 1954	NGC;CGC;5GC	BEN	4	73
Ampelisca milleri	Barnard, 1954	NGC;CGC;5GC	BEN	15	187
Ampelisca pugetica	Stimpson, 1864	NGC;CGC;5GC;SWB	BEN	9	487
Ampelisca romigi	Barnard, 1954	NGC;CGC;5GC	BEN	1	504
Ampelisca schellenbergi	Shoemaker, 1933	NGC;CGC	BEN	0	46
Amphideutopus oculatus	Barnard, 1959	NGC	BEN	1	162
Amphilochus neapolitanus	Della Valle, 1893	NGC	BEN	0	80
Amphitoe plumulosa	Shoemaker, 1938	NGC;CGC;5GC	BEN	0	18
Amphitoe pollex	Kunkel, 1910	NGC;CGC	BEN	0	2
Amphitoe ramondi	Audouin, 1826	NGC;CGC;SWB	BEN	0	2
Amphitoe tea	Barnard, 1965	NGC	BEN	0	67
Anamixis ?yarrega	(Barnard, 1974)	NGC;CGC;3R	BEN	0	8
Argissa hamatipes	(Norman, 1869)	NGC	BEN	4	1,096
Batea conductor	(Barnard, 1969)	NGC	BEN	?	?
Batea coyoa	Barnard, 1969	NGC	BEN	9	37
Batea rectangulata	Shoemaker, 1925	NGC;CGC	BEN	0	40
Batea susurrator	Barnard, 1969	NGC;CGC	BEN	0	37
Bemlos macromanus	Shoemaker, 1925	NGC;CGC;5GC	BEN	0	9
Bemlos tebuecos	(Barnard, 1979)	NGC;CGC;5GC;BR	BEN	0	1
Cornudilla cornuta	(Barnard, 1969)	NGC	BEN	19	46
Corophium baconi	Shoemaker, 1934	NGC;CGC;5GC;BR	BEN	0	55
Corophium uenoi	Stephensen, 1932	NGC	BEN;LIT;LACS	0	24
Dissiminassa dissimilis	(Stout, 1913)	NGC;CGC;5GC;BR	BEN	0	73
Elasmopus bampo	Barnard, 1979	NGC;CGC;5GC;BR	BEN	0	2
Elasmopus serricatus	Barnard, 1979	NGC;CGC;5GC;BR	BEN	0	2
Elasmopus tiburoni	Barnard, 1979	NGC;CGC;3R	BEN	0	2
Eobrolgus spinosus	(Holmes, 1905)	NGC;CGC;3R	BEN	0	73
Ericthonius brasiliensis	(Dana, 1853)	NGC;CGC;5GC;BR	LIT; BEN	0	171

TABLE 29.3 (CONT'D). Annotated list of macroinvertebrates known from the northern Gulf of California.

Species	Reference				
Eudevenopus metagracilis	(Barnard, 1964)	NGC	BEN	0	47
Foxiphalus apache	Barnard & Barnard, 1982	NGC	BEN	0	53
Foxiphalus cognatus	(Barnard, 1960)	NGC;CGC	BEN	0	325
Foxiphalus golfensis	Barnard & Barnard, 1982	NGC;CGC;SGC	BEN	0	91
Gammaropsis thompsoni	(Walker, 1898)	NGC;SWB	BEN	1	27
Gammaropsis tonichi	(Barnard, 1969)	NGC;CGC;SGC;BR	BEN	9	16
Garosyrrhoe disjuncta	Barnard, 1969	NGC	BEN	0	24
Gitanopsis baciroa	Barnard, 1979	NGC;CGC;SGC;BR	BEN	0	1
Gitanopsis pusilloides	Shoemaker, 1942	NGC;SWB	BEN	0	20
Heterophoxus oculatus	(Holmes, 1908)	NGC	BEN	2	1,785
Hippomedon ?propinquus	Sars, 1895	NGC	BEN	15	30
Hyale californica	Barnard, 1979	NGC	BEN	0	2
Hyale yaqui	Barnard, 1979	NGC;CGC;SGC;BR	BEN	0	7
Jassa falcata	(Montagu, 1808)	NGC	BEN	7	18
Jassa slatteryi	Conlan, 1990	NGC;BR	EPIF; BEN	0	40
Leucothoe alata	Barnard, 1959	NGC;CGC;SGC	BEN	0	24
Liljeborgia marcinabrio	Barnard, 1969	NGC	BEN	46	?
Listriella melanica lazaris	Barnard, 1969	NGC	BEN	2	44
Macronassa macromerus	(Shoemaker, 1916)	NGC;CGC;SGC	BEN	0	1
Maera diffidentia	(Barnard, 1969)	NGC	BEN	0	24
Maera reishi	Barnard, 1979	NGC;CGC	BEN	0	6
Megaluropus falciformis	Barnard, 1969	NGC	BEN	2	108
Megaluropus visendus	Barnard, 1969	NGC	BEN	2	17
Melita sulca	(Stout, 1913)	NGC;CGC;SGC;BR	BEN	0	101
Microjassa macrocoxa	Shoemaker, 1942	NGC;CGC;SGC;SWB	BEN	0	38
Monoculodes hartmanae	Barnard, 1962	NGC	BEN	2	146
Monoculodes nyei	Shoemaker, 1933	NGC;BR	BEN	0	1
Nasageneia nasa	(Barnard, 1969)	NGC;CGC;SGC;BR	BEN	0	1
Neomegamphopus roosevelti	Shoemaker, 1942	NGC;CGC;SGC;SWB	BEN	11	42
Orchomene magdalenensis	(Shoemaker, 1942)	NGC;SWB	BEN	2	46
Pachynus barnardi	Hurley, 1963	NGC	BEN	12	183
Paramicrodeutopus schmitti	(Shoemaker, 1942)	NGC;CGC;SGC;SWB	BEN	0	221
Parapleustes commensalis	Shoemaker, 1952	NGC	BEN;PAR	9	?
Pariphinotus escabrosus	(Barnard, 1969)	NGC;CGC;SGC;BR	BEN	0	16

Photis ?bifurcata	Barnard, 1962	NGC	BEN	11	93
Photis brevipes	Shoemaker, 1942	NGC;SWB	BEN	0	135
Photis californica	Stout, 1913	NGC	BEN	10	139
Photis elephantis	Barnard, 1962	NGC;CGC;SGC;BR	BEN	0	6
Podocerus brasiliensis	(Dana, 1853)	NGC;CGC;SGC	BEN	0	24
Podocerus fulanus	Barnard, 1962	NGC;CGC;SGC;BR	BEN	0	42
Polycheria osborni	Calman, 1898	NGC;CGC;SGC	BEN	0	1
Posophotis seri	Barnard, 1979	NGC;BR	BEN	0	6
Rhachotropis luculenta	Barnard, 1969	NGC	BEN	38	46
Rhepoxynius epistomus	(Shoemaker, 1938)	NGC;CGC;SGC	BEN	0	182
Rhepoxynius gemmatus	(Barnard, 1969)	NGC	BEN	2	9
Rhepoxynius tridentatus	(Barnard, 1954)	NGC	BEN	0	38
Rildardanus tros	Barnard, 1969	NGC	BEN	9	16
Rudilemboides stenopropodus	Barnard, 1959	NGC	BEN	0	68
Synchelidium rectipalmum	Mills, 1962	NGC	BEN	0	100
Tiburonella viscana	(Barnard, 1964)	NGC	BEN	0	27
Urristes entalladurus	Barnard, 1963	NGC	BEN	2	38
Zoedeutopus cinaloanus	Barnard, 1979	NGC;CGC:BR	BEN	0	1
HYPERIIDEA (PELAGIC/HYPERIID AMPHIPODS)					
Cranocephalus scleroticus	(Streets, 1878)	NGC	PEL	?	?
Eupronoe armata	Claus, 1879	NGC;CGC;SGC	PEL	25	350
Eupronoe maculata	Claus, 1879	NGC;CGC;SGC	PEL	0	550
Eupronoe minuta	Claus, 1879	NGC;CGC;SGC	PEL	0	2,900
Euthamneus rostratus	(Bovallius, 1887)	NGC;CGC;SGC	PEL	18	55
Glossocephalus milneedwardsi	Bovallius, 1887	NGC;CGC;SGC;BR	PEL	25	75
Hyperia leptura	Bowman, 1973	NGC;SWB	PEL	?	?
Hyperietta luzoni	(Stebbing, 1888)	NGC;CGC;SGC	PEL	25	1,087
Hyperietta stebbingi	Bowman, 1973	NGC;CGC;SGC;SWB	PEL	25	2,400
Hyperietta stephenseni	Bowman, 1973	NGC;CGC;SGC	PEL	25	600
Hyperietta vosseleri	(Stebbing, 1904)	NGC;CGC;SGC;SWB	PEL	100	2,330
Hyperoche medusarum	(Kröyer, 1838)	NGC;CGC;SGC	PEL	?	?
Lestrigonus bengalensis	Giles, 1887	NGC;CGC;SGC;BR	PEL;NER	25	2,245
Lestrigonus shoemakeri	Bowman, 1973	NGC;CGC;SGC;BR	PEL	25	695
Lycaea pulex	Marion, 1874	NGC;CGC;SGC;BR	PEL	?	?

TABLE 29.3 (CONT'D.). *Annotated list of macroinvertebrates known from the northern Gulf of California.*

Lycaea serrata	Claus, 1879	NGC;CGC;SGC	PEL	?	?
Oxycephalus clausi	Bovallius 1887	NGC;CGC;SGC;BR	PEL	0	600
Oxycephalus piscator	H. Milne-Edwards, 1830	NGC;CGC;SGC	PEL	0	100
Parascelus edwardsi	Claus, 1879	NGC;CGC;SGC;BR	PEL	?	?
Phronima dunbari	Shih, 1991	NGC;CGC;SGC;SWB	PEL	?	?
Platyscelus serratulus	Stebbing, 1888	NGC;CGC;SGC	PEL	0	2,650
Primno brevidens	Bowman, 1978	NGC;CGC;SGC	PEL	140	2,400
Rhabdosoma minor	Fage, 1954	NGC;CGC;SGC	PEL	?	?
Rhabdosoma whitei	Bate, 1862	NGC;CGC;SGC	PEL	0	600
Scina borealis	(Sars, 1883)	NGC;CGC;SGC	PEL	50	3,000
Simorhynchotus antennarius	(Claus, 1871)	NGC;CGC;SGC;BR	PEL	25	50
Streetsia challengeri	Stebbing, 1888	NGC;CGC;SGC	PEL	0	2,340
Tetrathyrus arafurae	Stebbing, 1888	NGC;CGC;SGC	PEL	850	975
Tetrathyrus forcipatus	Claus, 1879	NGC;CGC;SGC	PEL	0	1,800
Tetrathyrus pulchellus	Barnard, 1930	NGC;CGC;SGC	PEL	?	?
Vibilia wolterecki	Behning, 1939	NGC;CGC;SGC;SWB	PEL	100	1,000
CUMACEA (CUMACEANS)					
Campylaspis rubromaculata	Lie, 1969	NGC	BEN	?	?
Cyclaspis nubila	Zimmer, 1936	NGC	BEN; LIT	0	80
Diastylis calderoni	Donath-Hernández, 1988	NGC;BR	?	?	?
Leptocuma forsmani	Zimmer, 1943	NGC;BR;SWB	BEN; LIT	0	13
Oxyurostylis pacifica	Zimmer, 1936	NGC	BEN	3	170
Oxyurostylis tertia	Zimmer, 1943	NGC	BEN	8	?
ISOPODA (ISOPODS) **ANTHURIDEA**					
Califanthura squamosissima	(Menzies, 1951)	NGC;CGC;SGC;BR;SWB	BEN;LIT	0	142
Colanthura bruscai	Poore, 1984	NGC;BR	BEN;LIT	0	27
Cortezura penascoensis	Schultz, 1977	NGC;CGC;SGC;BR	BEN;LIT	0	45
Mesanthura nubifera	Wagele, 1984	NGC	BEN;LIT	0	?
Mesanthura occidentalis	Menzies & Barnard, 1959	NGC;CGC	BEN;LIT	0	55
Paranthura elegans	Menzies, 1951	NGC;CGC;SGC;BR	BEN;LIT	0	55
Paranthura longitelson	Wagele, 1984	NGC;CGC	BEN;LIT	0	3

TABLE 29.3 (CONT'D). *Annotated list of macroinvertebrates known from the northern Gulf of California.*

ASELLOTA

Uromunna ubiquita	(Menzies, 1952)	NGC;CGC;BR	?	0	35

EPICARIDEA

Probopyrus pandalicola	(Packard, 1879)	NGC	?	?	?
Schizobopyrina striata	Nierstrasz & Brender à Brandis, 1929	NGC	BEN;LIT	0	?

FLABELLIFERA

Ancinus granulatus	Holmes & Gay, 1909	NGC;CGC;SGC;BR	?	0	29
Ceratothoa gilberti	(Richardson, 1904)	NGC;CGC;SGC;BR	BEN;PAR	?	?
Cirolana neilbrucei	Brusca, Wetzer, & France, 1995	NGC;CGC;SGC	BEN;LIT	0	36
Cirolana parva	Hansen, 1890	NGC;CGC;SGC;BR	BEN;LIT	0	145
Cymothoa exigua	Schioedte & Meinert, 1884	NGC;CGC;SGC;BR;SWB	BEN;PAR	2	120
Eurhusa menziesi	(Brusca, 1981)	NGC;CGC;SGC;SWB	BEN;LIT;PAR	0	457
Eurhusa vulgaris	(Stimpson, 1857)	NGC;CGC;SGC;BR;SWB	BEN;PAR	1	311
Eurydice caudata	Richardson, 1899	NGC;CGC;SGC;BR;SWB	LIT;BEN;PEL	0	170
Excirolana braziliensis	Richardson, 1912	NGC;CGC;SGC;BR	LIT;CST;BEN	0	16
Excirolana mayana	(Ives, 1891)	NGC;CGC;SGC;BR;SWB	LIT;BEN	0	16
Excorallana bruscai	Delaney, 1984	NGC;CGC;SGC;BR	LIT;BEN	0	55
Excorallana houstoni	Delaney, 1984	NGC;CGC;SGC	BEN;LIT	0	18
Excorallana tricornis occidentalis	Richardson, 1905	NGC;CGC;SGC;BR;SWB	BEN;LIT;COM	0	138
Excorallana truncata	(Richardson, 1899)	NGC;CGC;BR	LIT;BEN	0	183
Heteroserolis carinata	(Lockington, 1877)	NGC;CGC;SGC	BEN	0	114
Livoneca bowmani	Brusca, 1981	NGC;CGC;SGC;BR;SWB	BEN;PAR	14	80
Natatolana californiensis	(Schultz, 1966)	NGC;CGC;SGC	LIT;COM;BEN	40	2,000
Natatolana carlenae	Brusca, Wetzer, & France, 1995	NGC;CGC;SGC;BR	BEN	15	1,168
Nerocila acuminata	Schioedte & Meinert, 1881	NGC;CGC;SGC;BR;SWB	BEN;PAR;LACS	1	103
Paracerceis sculpta	(Holmes, 1904)	NGC;CGC;SGC;BR;SWB	BEN;LIT;COM	0	68
Rocinela belliceps	(Stimpson, 1864)	NGC;CGC;SGC	BEN;PAR	265	284
Rocinela signata	Schioedte & Meinert, 1879	NGC;CGC;SGC;BR	BEN;PAR;LIT	0	73

ONISCIDEA (TERRESTRIAL ISOPODS)

Ligia baudiniana	Milne-Edwards, 1840	NGC;CGC;SGC	BEN;LIT	0	?
Tylos punctatus	Holmes & Gay, 1909	NGC;CGC;SGC;SWB	BEN;LIT	0	?

VALVIFERA

Cleantioides occidentalis	(Richardson, 1899)	NGC;CGC;BR	BEN;LIT	0	50

TABLE 29.3 (CONT'D). *Annotated list of macroinvertebrates known from the northern Gulf of California.*

Species	Authority	Distribution	Habitat		
Colidotea findleyi	Brusca & Wallerstein, 1977	NGC;BR	BEN;LIT;EPIF	0	27
Erichsonella cortezi	Brusca & Wallerstein, 1977	NGC;BR	BEN;LIT;EPIF	0	?
Eusymmerus antennatus	Richardson, 1899	NGC;CGC;SGC;BR;SWB	BEN;LIT;LACS	0	20
Idotea metallica	Bosc, 1802	NGC;CGC;SGC	FLOT;NEUS;NER	ON FLOAT- ING ALGAE	
TANAIDACEA (TANAIDS)					
Neastacilla californica	(Boone, 1918)	NGC;CGC;SGC;BR	BEN;LIT	0	99
Synidotea francesae	Brusca, 1983	NGC;BR	BEN;LIT	0	?
Parapseudes latifrons	(Grube, 1864)	NGC;CGC;SGC	BEN	0	18
HOPLOCARIDA, STOMATOPODA (MANTIS SHRIMPS)					
Alachosquilla digueti	(Coutière, 1905)	NGC;CGC;SGC	BEN;LIT;COM;NER	0	54
Eurysquilla veleronis	(Schmitt, 1940)	NGC;CGC;SGC	BEN;NER	29	91
Hemisquilla ensigera californiensis	Stephenson, 1967	NGC;CGC;SGC	BEN;NER	33	106
Meiosquilla dawsoni	Manning, 1970	NGC;BR	BEN;LIT	0	25
Nannosquilla canica	Manning & Reaka, 1979	NGC;CGC;SGC	BEN;LIT;NER	5	33
Neogonodactylus stanschi	(Schmitt, 1940)	NGC;CGC;SGC;SWB	BEN;LIT;NER	0	17
Squilla bigelowi	Schmitt, 1940	NGC;CGC;SGC;BR	BEN;NER	6	150
Squilla tiburonensis	Schmitt, 1940	NGC;CGC;SGC	BEN;NER	15	112
MAXILLOPODA					
CIRRIPEDIA, PEDUNCULATA (STALKED BARNACLES)					
Arcoscalpellum californicum	(Pilsbry, 1907)	NGC;SWB	BEN	18	400
Octolasmis californiana	Newman, 1960	NGC, CGC, SGC	BEN;PAR	?	?
CIRRIPEDIA, SESSILIA (ACORN BARNACLES)					
Arossia panamensis eyerdami	(Henry, 1960)	NGC;CGC	BEN;COM;LIT	0	85
Balanus improvisus	Darwin, 1854	NGC;CGC;SGC;BR	BEN;COM;EPIF;LACS;LIT	0	36
Balanus inexpectatus	Pilsbry, 1916	NGC;CGC;SGC;BR;SWB	BEN;LACS;LIT	0	?
Balanus parkeri	Zullo, 1967	NGC;CGC	BEN;COM	25	36
Balanus trigonus	Darwin, 1854	NGC;CGC;SGC;SWB	BEN;COM;PEL	0	450
Chelonibia testudinaria	(Linnaeus, 1757)	NGC;CGC;SGC	BEN;COM;PEL	?	?
Chthamalus anisopoma	Pilsbry, 1916	NGC;CGC;SGC	COM;BEN;LIT	0	?
Conopea galeata	(Linnaeus, 1771)	NGC;CGC;SGC;BR	BEN;COM	0	90
Hexacreusia durhami	(Zullo, 1961)	NGC;CGC;SGC;BR	BEN;COM;CST	1	3
Membranobalanus robinae	Van Syoc, 1988	NGC;CGC	BEN;COM;LIT	?	?

TABLE 29.3 (CONT'D). Annotated list of macroinvertebrates known from the northern Gulf of California.

Paraconcavus mexicanus	(Henry, 1941)	NGC;CGC;SGC;BR;SWB	BEN;LACS;LIT;COM	0	73
Tetraclita rubescens	Darwin, 1854	NGC;CGC.SGC;SWB	BEN;LIT	0	?
Tetraclita stalactifera confinis	Pilsbry, 1916	NGC;CGC.SGC	BEN;LIT	0	?
PYCNOGONIDA (SEA SPIDERS)					
Ammothella spinifera	Cole, 1904	NGC;CGC:SGC;BR	LIT;BEN;COM;NER	0	3
Anoplodactylus erectus	Cole, 1904	NGC;BR	BEN;NER	3	171
Anoplodactylus robustus	Hilton, 1939	NGC;BR	BEN;NER	18	45
Anoplodactylus viridintestinalis	(Cole, 1904)	NGC;BR	BEN;LIT;NER	0	999
Nymphon lituus	Child, 1979	NGC;CGC;BR	BEN;LIT;NER	0	9
Nymphon pixellae	Scott, 1942	NGC;CGC;BR	BEN;NER	18	330
Nymphopsis duodorsospinosa	Hilton, 1942	NGC;CGC;BR	BEN;LIT;NER	0	45
Pygnogonum stearnsi	Ives, 1892	NGC;CGC;BR	BEN;EPIF	0	999
Tanystylum intermedium	Cole, 1904	NGC;BR	BEN;COM;LIT;NER	0	9
Tanystylum oculospinosum	Hilton, 1942	NGC;CGC;SWB	BEN;LIT;NER	0	46

PHYLUM BRACHIOPODA (LAMP SHELLS)

Glottidia palmeri	Dall, 1871	NGC;BR	BEN	15	15
Glottidia sp.		NGC;BR	BEN; LIT	0	?

PHYLUM ECTOPROCTA (BRYOZOA) (BRYOZOANS)

GYMNOLAEMATA
CHEILOSTOMATA

Aetea anguina	(Linnaeus, 1758)	NGC;CGC	BEN	0	40
Aetea ligulata	Busk, 1852	NGC;CGC;SGC;SWB	BEN	12	72
Aetea recta	Hincks, 1862	NGC;CGC	BEN	0	144
Aimulosia palliolata	(Canu & Bassler, 1928)	NGC;CGC;SGC	BEN	6	180
Alderina smitti	Osburn, 1950	NGC;CGC;SGC	BEN	0	108
Anexechona ancorata	Osburn, 1950	NGC;CGC;SGC;SWB	BEN	4	90
Antropora claustracrassa	(Canu & Bassler, 1930)	NGC;CGC;SGC	BEN	2	180
Antropora tincta	(Hastings, 1930)	NGC;CGC;SGC	BEN	0	140
Aplousina flum	(Jullien & Calvet, 1903)	NGC;CGC	BEN	18	118
Arthropoma circinata	(MacGillivray, 1869)	NGC;CGC	BEN	36	81
Bellulopora bellula	(Osburn, 1950)	NGC;CGC;SWB	BEN	25	108
Bugula californica	Robertson, 1905	NGC;CGC;SGC;BR	BEN	0	57
Bugula longirostrata	Robertson, 1905	NGC;CGC	BEN	18	208

TABLE 29.3 (CONT'D). *Annotated list of macroinvertebrates known from the northern Gulf of California.*

Bugula minima	(Waters, 1909)	NGC	BEN	54	90
Bugula neritina	(Linnaeus, 1758)	NGC;CGC;SGC	BEN	1	72
Celleporaria brunnea	(Hincks, 1884)	NGC;CGC;SGC	BEN	0	83
Celleporaria quadrispinosa	(Canu & Bassler, 1930)	NGC;CGC;SGC	BEN	0	142
Celleporella hyalina	(Linnaeus, 1758)	NGC	BEN	30	32
Chaperiopsis condylata	(Canu & Bassler, 1930)	NGC;CGC	BEN	1	180
Chaperiopsis patula	(Hincks, 1881)	NGC;CGC;SGC	BEN	5	90
Cleidochasma contracta	(Waters, 1899)	NGC;CGC;SGC	BEN	2	72
Cleidochasma porcellana	(Busk, 1860)	NGC;CGC;SGC	BEN	1	81
Conopeum commensale	Kirkpatrick & Metzelaar, 1922	NGC;CGC;BR;SWB	BEN	4	81
Copidozoum protectum	(Hincks, 1884)	NGC	BEN	0	54
Copidozoum tenuirostre	(Hincks, 1880)	NGC;CGC;SGC	BEN	0	126
Crepidacantha poissoni	(Audouin, 1826)	NGC;CGC;SGC	BEN	18	129
Cribilaria radiata	(Moll, 1803)	NGC;CGC;SGC	BEN	1	244
Cyclicopora longipora	(MacGillivray, 1882)	NGC;CGC	BEN	72	108
Cycloperiella rosacea	Osburn, 1947	NGC;CGC;SGC	BEN	2	108
Dakaria sertata	Canu & Bassler, 1930	NGC;CGC;SGC	BEN	4	108
Discoporella umbellata	(Defrance, 1823)	NGC;CGC;SGC	BEN	13	180
Electra crustulenta	(Pallas, 1766)	NGC;CGC	BEN	9	81
Escharella major	(Hincks, 1884)	NGC;CGC	BEN	25	243
Fenestrulina malusi	(Audouin, 1826)	NGC;CGC	BEN	25	180
Floridina antiqua	(Smitt, 1873)	NGC;CGC;SGC	BEN	13	100
Gemelliporidra aculeata	Canu & Bassler, 1928	NGC	BEN	30	34
Hemismittoidea osburni	Soule & Soule, 1973	NGC;CGC;SGC	BEN	30	72
Hippaliosina rostrigera	(Smitt, 1873)	NGC;CGC;SGC	BEN	18	72
Hippodiplosia insculpta	(Hincks, 1882)	NGC;CGC;SGC	BEN	4	230
Hippomonavella longirostrata	(Hincks, 1883)	NGC;CGC	BEN	2	180
Hippopetraliella magna	(d'Orbigny, 1852)	NGC;CGC	BEN	18	54
Hippopleurifera mucronata	(Smitt, 1873)	NGC;CGC;SGC	BEN	0	239
Hippopodina californica	Osburn, 1952	NGC;CGC	BEN	21	235
Hippoporella gorgonensis	Hastings, 1930	NGC;CGC;SGC	BEN	0	147
Hippothoa distans	MacGillivray, 1869	NGC;CGC;SGC	BEN	2	72
Hippothoa expansa	Dawson, 1859	NGC;CGC	BEN	18	56
Lagenicella lacunosa	Bassler, 1934	NGC;CGC;SGC	BEN	0	180

TABLE 29.3 (CONT'D.). *Annotated list of macroinvertebrates known from the northern Gulf of California.*

Species	Author	Distribution	Habitat		
Lagenicella marginata	(Canu & Bassler, 1930)	NGC	BEN	2	140
Lagenicella mexicana	(Osburn, 1952)	NGC;CGC;SGC	BEN	25	72
Lagenicella punctulata	(Gabb & Horn, 1862)	NGC;CGC;SGC	BEN	1	90
Lagenicella spinulosa	(Hincks, 1884)	NGC;CGC;SGC	BEN	2	8
Mamillopora cupula	Smitt, 1873	NGC;CGC;SGC	BEN	18	109
Membranipora savarti	(Audouin, 1826)	NGC;CGC;SGC	BEN	13	76
Membranipora tenuis	Desor, 1848	NGC;CGC;SGC;BR	BEN	0	6
Membranipora tuberculata	(Bosc, 1802)	NGC;CGC;SGC	BEN	0	9
Membraniporella aragoi pacifica	Osburn, 1950	NGC;CGC;SGC	BEN	4	180
Micropora coriacea inarmata	Soule, 1959	NGC;CGC;SGC	BEN	2	81
Microporella ciliata	(Pallas, 1766)	NGC;CGC;SGC	BEN	0	72
Microporella cribosa	Osburn, 1952	NGC	BEN	36	72
Microporella gibbosula	Canu & Bassler, 1930	NGC;CGC;SGC	BEN	4	140
Mollia patellaria	(Moll, 1803)	NGC;BR	BEN	0	40
Odontoporella adpressa	(Busk, 1854)	NGC;CGC;SGC	BEN	1	72
Parasmittina californica	(Robertson, 1908)	NGC;CGC;SGC	BEN	23	270
Parasmittina crosslandi	(Hastings, 1930)	NGC;CGC;SGC	BEN	1	180
Parasmittina fraseri	Osburn, 1952	NGC;CGC;SGC	BEN	5	108
Parasmittina triangularis	Soule & Soule, 1973	NGC;CGC;SGC	BEN	1	80
Parasmittina trispinosa	(Johnston, 1825)	NGC;CGC;SGC	BEN	18	81
Phidolopora labiata	(Gabb & Horn, 1862)	NGC;CGC	BEN	25	90
Porella porifera	(Hincks, 1884)	NGC;CGC;SGC	BEN	1	180
Porella rogickae	Soule, 1961	NGC;CGC;SGC	BEN	12	72
Reginella mucronata	(Canu & Bassler, 1923)	NGC;CGC	BEN	2	217
Reptadenella hymanae	Soule, 1961	NGC;CGC;SGC	BEN	0	45
Reptadenella violacea	(Johnston, 1847)	NGC;CGC;SGC	BEN	2	225
Reteporellina bilabiata	Osburn, 1952	NGC;CGC;SGC;SWB	BEN	25	83
Retevirgula lata	Osburn, 1950	NGC;CGC	BEN	9	54
Retevirgula tubulata	(Hastings, 1930)	NGC;CGC;SGC	BEN	0	144
Rhynchozoon grandicella	Canu & Bassler, 1923	NGC;CGC	BEN	18	83
Rhynchozoon rostratum	(Busk, 1855)	NGC;CGC;SGC	BEN	1	72
Schizomavella auriculata	(Hassall, 1842)	NGC;CGC	BEN	4	72
Schizoporella cornuta	(Gabb & Horn, 1862)	NGC;CGC;SGC	BEN	4	180
Schizoporella inarmata	(Hincks, 1884)	NGC;CGC;SGC;BR	BEN	0	102

TABLE 29.3 (CONT'D). *Annotated list of macroinvertebrates known from the northern Gulf of California.*

Schizoporella trichotoma	Waters, 1918	NGC;CGC	BEN	9	180
Scrupocellaria bertholetti	(Audouin, 1826)	NGC;CGC;SGC	BEN	0	180
Scrupocellaria bertholetti tenuirostris	Osburn, 1950	NGC;CGC;SGC	BEN	1	6
Scrupocellaria mexicana	Osburn, 1950	NGC;CGC;SGC;SWB	BEN	23	81
Scrupocellaria varians	Hincks, 1882	NGC;CGC	BEN	72	248
Sessibugula translucens	Osburn, 1950	NGC	BEN	9	108
Smittina landsborovi	(Johnston, 1847)	NGC;CGC	BEN	23	90
Smittina maccullochae	Osburn, 1952	NGC;CGC	BEN	4	90
Smittoidea prolifica	Osburn, 1952	NGC;CGC	BEN	28	81
Stephanosella vitrea	Osburn, 1952	NGC;CGC	BEN	9	97
Stylopoma informata	(Lonsdale, 1845)	NGC;CGC;SGC	BEN	0	72
Stylopoma spongites	(Pallas, 1766)	NGC;CGC;SGC	?	?	?
Synnotum aegyptiacum	(Audouin, 1826)	NGC;CGC;BR	BEN	0	81
Thalamoporella californica	(Levinsen, 1909)	NGC;CGC;BR	BEN	0	44
Thalamoporella gothica	(Busk, 1856)	NGC;CGC;SGC	BEN	0	10
Trematooecia hexagonalis	(Canu & Bassler, 1930)	NGC;CGC;SGC	BEN	2	135
Tremogasterina granulata magnipora	Soule, 1969	NGC;CGC;SGC	BEN	9	83
Trypostega venusta	(Norman, 1864)	NGC;CGC;SGC	BEN	4	180
Uscia mexicana	Banta, 1969	NGC	?	?	?
Watersipora cucullata	(Busk, 1854)	NGC;CGC;SGC	BEN	4	72
CTENOSTOMATA					
Amathia distans	Busk, 1886	NGC;CGC	BEN	22	72
Buskia socialis	(Hincks, 1877)	NGC;CGC;SWB	BEN	23	57
Penetrantia densa	Silén, 1946	NGC;CGC;SGC	BEN	0	33
Walkeria tuberosa	Heller, 1867	NGC;CGC	BEN	25	32
STENOLAEMATA CYCLOSTOMATA					
Aidanosagitta neglecta	(Aida, 1897)	NGC;CGC;SGC;SWB	OCE;PEL;NER	0	200
Crisia operculata	Robertson, 1910	NGC;CGC;SGC	BEN	0	81
Crisia serrulata	Osburn, 1953	NGC	BEN	37	117
Crisulipora occidentalis	Robertson, 1910	NGC	BEN	0	54
Disporella californica	(d'Orbigny, 1853)	NGC;CGC;SGC;SWB	BEN	0	138
Escharina vulgaris	(Moll, 1803)	NGC;CGC	BEN	2	81
Fasciculipora pacifica	Osburn, 1953	NGC;CGC;SGC;BR	BEN	0	42

Species	Author	Distribution	Habitat		
Ferosagitta robusta	(Doncaster, 1903)	NGC;CGC;SGC;SWB	OCE;PEL;NER	0	200
Filicrisia franciscana	(Robertson, 1910)	NGC;CGC	BEN	2	90
Flaccisagitta enflata	(Grassi, 1881)	NGC;CGC;SGC;SWB	OCE;NER;PEL	0	320
Lichenopora buskiana	Canu & Bassler, 1928	NGC;CGC;BR	BEN	0	14
Lichenopora novae-zelandiae	(Busk, 1875)	NGC;CGC;SGC	BEN	0	81
Mesosagitta decipiens	(Fowler, 1905)	NGC;CGC;SGC;SWB	OCE;PEL;NER	20	2,650
Mesosagitta minima	(Grassi, 1881)	NGC;CGC;SGC;SWB	OCE;PEL;NER	0	590
Parasagitta euneritica	(Alvariño, 1961)	NGC;CGC;SGC;BR;SWB	OCE;PEL;NER	0	350
Plagioecia sarniensis	(Norman, 1864)	NGC	BEN	0	34
Serratosagitta pacifica	(Tokioka, 1940)	NGC;CGC;SGC;SWB	OCE;PEL;NER	0	350
Stomatopora granulata	(Milne Edwards, 1838)	NGC;CGC;SGC	BEN	2	72
Tubulipora flexuosa	(Pourtales, 1867)	NGC;CGC	BEN	36	95
Tubulipora pacifica	Robertson, 1910	NGC;CGC	BEN	0	57
Tubulipora tuba	(Gabb & Horn, 1862)	NGC;BR	BEN	18	210

PHYLUM ECHINODERMATA (ECHINODERMS)

ASTEROIDEA (SEASTARS)

Species	Author	Distribution	Habitat		
Amphiaster insignis	Verrill, 1868	NGC;CGC;SGC;SWB	BEN;LIT	0	128
Asterina miniata	(Brandt, 1835)	NGC;CGC;SGC;SWB	BEN;LIT	0	302
Asteropsis carinifera	(Lamarck, 1816)	NGC;CGC	BEN;LIT	0	36
Astrometis sertulifera	(Xantus, 1860)	NGC;CGC;SGC;BR	BEN;LIT	0	156
Astropecten armatus	Gray, 1840	NGC;CGC;SGC;BR;SWB	BEN;LIT	0	302
Astropecten ornatissimus	Fisher, 1906	NGC;CGC;SGC	BEN	9	366
Astropecten verrilli	de Loriol, 1899	NGC;CGC;SGC	BEN	2	488
Echinaster parvispinus	A.H. Clark, 1916	NGC;SWB	BEN	18	29
Echinaster tenuispina	Verrill, 1871	NGC;CGC;SGC;BR;SWB	BEN;LIT	0	73
Heliaster kubiniji	Xantus, 1860	NGC;CGC;SGC;BR;SWB	BEN;LIT	0	10
Henricia aspera	Fisher, 1906	NGC	BEN	18	572
Henricia clarki	Fisher, 1910	NGC;CGC;SGC	BEN	27	1,503
Leptychaster stellatus	Ziesenhenne, 1942	NGC;CGC	BEN	40	86
Linckia columbiae	Gray, 1840	NGC;CGC;SGC;BR;SWB	BEN;LIT	0	156
Linckia guildingii	Gray, 1840	NGC;CGC;SGC;SWB	BEN;LIT	0	20
Luidia armata	Ludwig, 1905	NGC;SWB	BEN	15	284
Luidia bellona	Lutken, 1864	NGC;CGC;SGC;SWB	BEN	4	201

TABLE 29.3 (CONT'D). *Annotated list of macroinvertebrates known from the northern Gulf of California.*

Luidia columbia	(Gray, 1840)	NGC;CGC;SGC;BR;SWB	BEN;LIT	0	220
Luidia foliolata	Grube, 1865	NGC;CGC;SGC	BEN;LIT	0	476
Luidia phragma	H.L. Clark, 1910	NGC;CGC;BR;SWB	BEN;LIT	0	137
Mithrodia bradleyi	Verrill, 1867	NGC;CGC;SGC	BEN;LIT	0	50
Narcissia gracilis gracilis	A.H. Clark, 1916	NGC;CGC;SGC	BEN;LIT	0	128
Nidorellia armata	(Gray, 1840)	NGC;CGC;SGC;BR;SWB	BEN;LIT	0	73
Odontaster crassus	Fisher, 1905	NGC	BEN	27	595
Pentaceraster cumingi	(Gray, 1840)	NGC;CGC;SGC;SWB	BEN;LIT	0	183
Pharia pyramidata	(Gray, 1840)	NGC;CGC;SGC;SWB	BEN;LIT	0	139
Phataria unifascialis	(Gray, 1840)	NGC;CGC;SGC;BR;SWB	BEN;LIT	0	50
Pseudarchaster pusillus	Fisher, 1905	NGC	BEN	99	1,326
Sclerasterias heteropaes	Fisher, 1924	NGC;CGC	BEN	18	457
Tethyaster canaliculatus	(A.H. Clark, 1916)	NGC;CGC;SGC;BR	BEN	6	178
OPHIUROIDEA (BRITTLESTARS)					
Amphichondrius laevis	Ziesenhenne, 1940	NGC;CGC;SGC	BEN	4	280
Amphiodia occidentalis	(Lyman, 1860)	NGC;CGC	BEN;LIT	0	367
Amphiodia psara	H.L. Clark, 1935	NGC	BEN	12	161
Amphioplus strongyloplax	(H.L. Clark, 1911)	NGC	BEN	4	1,408
Amphipholis geminata	(Le Conte, 1851)	NGC;CGC;BR	BEN;LIT	0	82
Amphipholis perplexa	(Nielsen, 1932)	NGC;CGC;SGC;SWB	BEN	0	143
Amphipholis platydisca	Nielsen, 1932	NGC;CGC;SGC;BR;SWB	BEN;LIT	0	137
Amphipholis puntarenae	(Lutken, 1856)	NGC	BEN	0	508
Amphipholis squamata	(Delle Chiaje, 1828)	NGC;CGC;SWB	BEN	0	823
Amphiura arcystata	H.L. Clark, 1911	NGC;CGC;SGC	BEN	6	849
Amphiura diomedeae	Lutken & Mortensen, 1899	NGC;CGC;SGC	BEN	44	3,017
Asterocaneum spinosum	(Lyman, 1875)	NGC;CGC;SGC;BR	BEN	4	183
Diopederma danianum	(Verrill, 1867)	NGC;CGC;SGC	BEN	7	137
Dougaloplus amphacanthus	(McClendon, 1909)	NGC;CGC	BEN	9	1,646
Hemipholis gracilis	Verrill, 1867	NGC;BR	BEN	?	?
Ophiacantha phragma	Ziesenhenne, 1940	NGC;CGC;SGC	BEN	13	644
Ophiacantha quadrispina	H.L. Clark, 1917	NGC;CGC;SGC	BEN	183	549
Ophiactis savignyi	(Muller & Troschel, 1842)	NGC;CGC;SGC;BR;SWB	BEN;LIT	0	128
Ophiactis simplex	(Le Conte, 1851)	NGC;CGC;SGC;BR;SWB	BEN;LIT	0	302
Ophiocnida californica	Ziesenhenne, 1940	NGC;CGC;SGC	BEN	6	302

TABLE 29.3 (CONT'D). *Annotated list of macroinvertebrates known from the northern Gulf of California.*

Species	Authority	Distribution	Habitat		
Ophiocnida hispida	(Le Conte, 1851)	NGC;CGC;SGC	BEN	0	794
Ophiocoma aethiops	Lutken, 1859	NGC;CGC;SGC;BR;SWB	BEN;LIT	0	30
Ophiocoma alexandri	Lyman, 1860	NGC;CGC;SGC;BR;SWB	BEN;LIT	0	70
Ophioderma panamense	Lutken, 1859	NGC;CGC;SGC;BR;SWB	BEN;LIT	0	20
Ophioderma teres	(Lyman, 1860)	NGC;CGC;SGC;BR	BEN;LIT	0	54
Ophioderma variegatum	Lutken, 1856	NGC;CGC;SGC;SWB	BEN;LIT	0	110
Ophiolepis crassa	Nielsen, 1932	NGC;CGC;SGC;SWB	BEN	6	230
Ophiolepis variegata	Lutken, 1856	NGC;CGC;SGC;BR	BEN;LIT	0	110
Ophionereis annulata	(Le Conte, 1851)	NGC;CGC;SGC;BR;SWB	BEN;LIT	0	229
Ophionereis eurybrachiplax	H.L. Clark, 1911	NGC	BEN	0	457
Ophionereis perplexa	Ziesenhenne, 1940	NGC;CGC;3R	BEN;LIT	0	73
Ophiopaepale diplax	(Nielsen, 1932)	NGC;CGC;SGC;SWB	BEN;LIT	0	230
Ophiopholis bakeri	McClendon, 1909	NGC;CGC	BEN	9	1,006
Ophiopholis longispina	H.L. Clark, 1911	NGC	BEN	51	1,746
Ophiophragmus marginatus	(Lutken, 1859)	NGC;CGC;SGC;BR	BEN;LIT	0	134
Ophiophragmus tabogensis	Nielsen, 1932	NGC;CGC;SGC	BEN;LIT	0	128
Ophiophthalmus normani	(Lyman, 1879)	NGC;CGC;SGC	BEN	51	2,600
Ophioplinthaca granifera	(Lutken & Mortensen, 1899)	NGC;CGC;SGC	BEN	267	2,086
Ophiopsila californica	A.H. Clark, 1921	NGC;CGC;SGC	BEN	33	201
Ophiostigma tenue	Lutken, 1856	NGC;CGC;SGC;SWB	BEN	4	101
Ophiothrix galapagensis	Lutken & Mortensen, 1899	NGC;CGC;SGC	BEN;LIT	0	549
Ophiothrix spiculata	Le Conte, 1851	NGC;CGC;SGC;BR;SWB	BEN;LIT	0	2,059
Ophiura luetkeni	(Lyman, 1860)	NGC;CGC;SGC	BEN	0	1,097
Ophiuroconis bispinosa	Ziesenhenne, 1937	NGC;CGC;SGC	BEN	4	143
ECHINOIDEA (SEA URCHINS, SAND DOLLARS, SEA BISQUITS)					
Agassizia scrobiculata	Valenciennes, 1846	NGC;CGC;SGC;BR;SWB	BEN;LIT	0	220
Allocentrotus fragilis	(Jackson, 1912)	NGC;CGC;SGC	BEN	50	1,200
Aporocidaris milleri	(A. Agassiz, 1898)	NGC;CGC;SGC;SWB	BEN	300	3,937
Arbacia incisa	(A. Agassiz, 1863)	NGC;CGC;SGC;BR;SWB	BEN;LIT	0	52
Astropyga pulvinata	(Lamarck, 1816)	NGC;CGC;SGC;SWB	BEN;LIT	0	90
Brisaster latifrons	(A. Agassiz, 1898)	NGC;CGC;SGC;BR	BEN	9	2,817
Brissopsis columbaris	A. Agassiz, 1898	NGC;CGC;SGC	BEN	899	1,271
Brissopsis pacifica	(A. Agassiz, 1898)	NGC;CGC;SGC;SWB	BEN	9	2,379
Brissus obesus	Verrill, 1867	NGC;CGC;SGC;BR;SWB	BEN;LIT	0	240

TABLE 29.3 (CONT'D). Annotated list of macroinvertebrates known from the northern Gulf of California.

Species	Authority	Distribution	Habitat		
Centrostephanus coronatus	(Verrill, 1867)	NGC;CGC;SGC;BR;SWB	BEN;LIT	0	125
Clypeaster europacificus	H.L. Clark, 1914	NGC;CGC;SGC	BEN;LIT	0	402
Clypeaster ochrus	H.L. Clark, 1914	NGC;CGC;SGC;BR	BEN;LIT	0	162
Clypeaster rotundus	(A. Agassiz, 1863)	NGC;CGC;SGC;BR;SWB	BEN;LIT	0	91
Clypeaster speciosus	Verrill, 1870	NGC;CGC;BR;SWB	BEN;LIT	0	128
Diadema mexicanum	A. Agassiz, 1863	NGC;CGC;SGC;BR	BEN;LIT	0	113
Echinometra oblonga	(Blainville, 1825)	NGC;CGC;SGC	BEN;LIT	0	34
Echinometra vanbrunti	A. Agassiz, 1863	NGC;CGC;SGC;BR;SWB	BEN;LIT	0	106
Encope grandis	L. Agassiz, 1841	NGC;CGC;SGC;BR;SWB	BEN;LIT	0	120
Encope micropora	L. Agassiz, 1841	NGC;CGC;SGC;BR;SWB	BEN;LIT	0	82
Encope perspectiva	L. Agassiz, 1841	NGC;CGC;SGC	BEN	15	27
Eucidaris thouarsii	(Valenciennes, 1846)	NGC;CGC;SGC;BR;SWB	BEN;LIT	0	150
Hesperocidaris asteriscus	H.L. Clark, 1948	NGC;CGC;SGC	BEN	2	183
Hesperocidaris perplexa	(H.L. Clark, 1907)	NGC;CGC;SGC	BEN	13	1,500
Lovenia cordiformis	A. Agassiz, 1872	NGC;CGC;SGC;BR;SWB	BEN;LIT	0	201
Lytechinus pictus	(Verrill, 1867)	NGC;CGC;SGC	BEN;LIT	0	300
Mellita grantii	Mortensen, 1948	NGC;CGC;SGC;BR	LIT;LACS	0	6
Mellita longifissa	Michelin, 1858	NGC;CGC;SGC;BR;SWB	BEN;LIT	0	60
Meoma grandis	Gray, 1851	NGC;CGC;SGC;SWB	BEN;LIT	0	200
Metalia nobilis	Verrill, 1867	NGC;CGC;SGC;BR	BEN;LIT	0	18
Moira atropos clotho	(Michelin, 1855)	NGC;CGC;SGC;BR	BEN;LIT	0	160
Nacospatangus depressus	H.L. Clark, 1917	NGC;CGC	BEN	5	302
Plagiobrissus pacificus	H.L. Clark, 1940	NGC;CGC;SGC	BEN	6	137
Spatangus californicus	H.L. Clark, 1917	NGC;CGC;SGC	BEN	10	644
Strongylocentrotus purpuratus	(Stimpson, 1857)	NGC;CGC	BEN;LIT	0	161
Tripneustes depressus	A. Agassiz, 1863	NGC;CGC;SGC	BEN;LIT	0	73
HOLOTHUROIDEA (SEA CUCUMBERS)					
Apentamera lepra	Deichmann, 1941	NGC;CGC	BEN	55	91
Athyone glasselli	(Deichmann, 1936)	NGC;CGC;BR	BEN;LIT	0	6
Chiridota aponocrita	H.L. Clark, 1920	NGC;CGC;SGC;BR	LIT	0	?
Cucumaria chilensis	Ludwig, 1875	NGC	BEN	32	163
Epitomapta tabogae	Heding, 1928	NGC;CGC;SGC;BR	LIT	0	?
Euapta godeffroyi	(Semper, 1868)	NGC;CGC;SGC;BR	BEN;LIT	0	31
Holothuria arenicola	Semper, 1868	NGC;CGC;SGC;BR	BEN;LIT	0	9

Holothuria dificilis	Semper, 1868	NGC;CGC;SGC	BEN;LIT	0	70
Holothuria gyrifer	(Selenka, 1867)	NGC;CGC;SGC;SWB	BEN;LIT	0	7
Holothuria impatiens	(Forskaal, 1775)	NGC;CGC;SGC;BR;SWB	BEN;LIT	0	11
Holothuria inhabilis	Selenka, 1867	NGC;CGC;SGC	BEN;LIT	1	203
Holothuria lubrica	Selenka, 1867	NGC;CGC;SGC;BR;SWB	BEN;LIT	0	55
Holothuria paraprinceps	Deichmann, 1937	NGC;CGC;SGC;BR	BEN;LIT	0	90
Holothuria rigida	(Selenka, 1867)	NGC;CGC;SGC;BR;SWB	BEN;LIT	0	18
Holothuria theeli	(Deichmann, 1938)	NGC;CGC	BEN;LIT	0	55
Holothuria zacae	Deichmann, 1937	NGC;CGC;SGC	BEN;LIT	0	220
Isostichopus fuscus	(Ludwig, 1875)	NGC;CGC;SGC;BR	BEN;LIT	0	39
Lissothuria bancocki	(Deichmann, 1941)	NGC;CGC	BEN	5	302
Lissothuria ornata	Verrill, 1867	NGC;CGC;SGC	BEN	0	36
Neothyone gibbosa	Deichmann, 1941	NGC;CGC;SGC;BR	BEN;LIT	0	6
Neothyone panamensis	(Ludwig, 1887)	NGC	BEN;LIT	0	3
Parastichopus californicus	(Stimpson, 1857)	NGC	BEN;LIT	0	180
Parastichopus parvimensis	(H.L. Clark, 1913)	NGC	BEN	36	?
Pentamera chierchia	(Ludwig, 1887)	NGC;CGC;BR	BEN;LIT	0	78
Pseudocnus californicus	(Semper, 1868)	NGC;CGC;SGC;SWB	BEN;LIT	0	190
Psolus diomedeae	Ludwig, 1894	NGC;CGC	BEN	13	302
Thyone parafusus	Deichmann, 1941	NGC;CGC	BEN;LIT	0	70
Thyonella mexicana	(Deichmann, 1941)	NGC;CGC;SGC;BR	BEN	18	65

PHYLUM CHAETOGNATHA (ARROW WORMS)

Aidanosagitta neglecta	(Aida, 1897)	NGC;CG;SG;SWB	OCE;PEL;NER	0	200
Ferosagitta robusta	(Doncaster, 1903)	NG;CG;SG;SWB	OCE;PEL;NER	0	200
Flaccisagitta enflata	(Grassi, 1881)	NG;CG;SG;SWB	OCE;NER; PEL	0	320
Mesosagitta decipiens	(Fowler, 1905)	NG;CG;SG;SWB	OCE;PEL;NER	20	2650
Mesosagitta minima	(Grassi, 1881)	NG;CG;SG;SWB	OCE;PEL;NER	0	590
Parasagitta euneritica	(Alvariño, 1961)	NG;CG;SG;3R;SWB	OCE;PEL;NER	0	350
Serratosagitta pacifica	(Tokioka, 1940)	NG;CG;SG;SWB	OCE;PEL;NER	0	350

PHYLUM HEMICHORDATA
ENTEROPNEUSTA (ACORN WORMS)

Saccoglossus sp.		NGC	BEN;LIT	0	0

TABLE 29.3 (CONT'D). Annotated list of macroinvertebrates known from the northern Gulf of California.

PHYLUM CHORDATA (CHORDATES)

UROCHORDATA (TUNICATES)
ASCIDIACEA (SEA SQUIRTS)

Archidistoma pachecae	(Van Name, 1945)	NGC;CGC	?	?	?
Ascidia ceratodes	(Huntsman, 1912)	NGC	BEN;NER	18	54
Ascidia sydneiensis protecta	Van Name, 1945	NGC;CGC	BEN;COM	?	46
Cystodytes dellechiajei	(Della Valle, 1877)	NGC;CGC	BEN;LIT;NER	0	720
Didemnum carnulentum	Ritter & Forsyth, 1917	NGC;CGC;SGC	BEN;LIT;NER	1	27
Eudistoma mexicanum	Van Name, 1945	NGC	?	32	?
Polyclinum laxum	Van Name, 1945	NGC;CGC;BR	BEN;COM	?	?
Polyclinum vasculosum	Pizon, 1908	NGC;BR	BEN	?	?

CEPHALOCHORDATA (LANCELETS)

Branchiostoma californiense		NGC;CGC, SGC	BEN	0	2

Notes: Species/subspecies names are followed by author and date of description (in parentheses if the species has been subsequently transferred to a genus different from the original assignment), distribution in gulf, general habitat, shallowest known occurrence, and deepest known occurrence (in meters). Higher taxa are in uppercase; species are listed alphabetically in their higher taxa.

The northern gulf extends from the Colorado River delta southward to (and includes) the Midriff Islands (the largest being Islas Tiburón and Ángel de la Guarda). The central gulf ranges from the southern edge of the Midriff Islands to Guaymas (Sonora) and to Punta Coyote (Baja California Sur). The southern gulf extends southward to Cabo Corrientes, Jalisco, on the mainland, and to Cabo San Lucas on the Baja California peninsula.

Codes: NGC, Northern Gulf of California; CGC, Central Gulf of California; SGC, Southern Gulf of California; BR, Alto Golfo Biosphere Reserve; SWB, Southwest Baja California (Cabo San Lucas to the northern limit of Bahía Magdalena); BEN, benthic; LIT, fundamentally a littoral species (intertidal and in some cases extending into the subtidal); NER, neritic; OCE, oceanic; NEUS, neustonic; COM, commensal with another animal; PAR, parasitic; EPIF, epiphytic (living on algae or halophytic angiosperms); LACS, living in coastal lagoons and esteros; CST, coastal.

Thirty

Sea Turtles of the Alto Golfo:
A Struggle for Survival

Jeffrey A. Seminoff and Wallace J. Nichols

They told us that sea turtles had all but vanished in the Gulf of California. And who were we to know better—after all, we were speaking to a pair of researchers who had over sixty combined years of experience, and the only evidence of sea turtles we gulf neophytes had seen up to that point were sun-bleached shell fragments, stuffed turtles hanging on restaurant walls, and the occasional carcass half-buried in the sand. As new graduate students, we were excited about meeting with our adviser, Donald Thomson, and famous sea turtle biologist John Hendrickson to discuss our prospective studies. As it turned out, however, both were skeptical of our research plans, pointing out that the years of hunting and accidental capture by nets and hooks had caused local sea turtle populations to decline so sharply that staking our graduate careers on these endangered species was simply too risky. Nonetheless, after careful consideration, a strong dose of stubbornness, and encouragement from friends like Richard Felger and Bill Calder, we went for it.

By the time we initiated our project, two years had passed since President Carlos Salinas de Gortari's 1990 decree outlawing the consumption or use of all sea turtle products in Mexico (Diario Oficial 1990). Many believe that this legislation was a decade late, but few would argue against its necessity. Sea turtles, particularly the green turtle, were being openly caught, transported, sold, and eaten throughout northwestern Mexico. Yet despite these pressures, sea turtles were clinging to existence in the Gulf of California.

Our first travels in the Alto Golfo were to such areas as El Golfo de Santa Clara, San Felipe, Bahía Adair, and Puerto Peñasco. As we came to discover, our research was just as much a journey into the cultural depths of our host country as it was a scientific endeavor. There were strong traditions of sea turtle use in virtually all the communities lining the gulf. People relied on sea turtles not only for sustenance but also for cultural identity, medicinal cures, and economic solvency.

Sea Turtles and Indigenous Peoples of the Alto Golfo

To the southwest from atop Sykes Crater in the Pinacate Biosphere Reserve one can see the distant Sonoran desert landscape blend into the gulf's Bahía Adair. This area is part of the Alto Golfo, a biogeographically distinct zone of the Gulf of California stretching southward from the Colorado River delta to just north of Bahía San Luis Gonzaga on the Baja California peninsula and slightly south of Puerto Peñasco along the Sonoran coast. Like the surrounding desert regions, this arid landscape has a rich history of indigenous presence.

Native cultures were closely tied to the Alto Golfo's marine and freshwater ecosystems, benefiting from the abundance of natural resources for both food and nonfood uses. Indigenous groups included the Cucapás, who inhabited the delta region and lower reaches of the Río Colorado; the Hia C'ed O'odham, who often made use of marine resources along the Alto Golfo's Sonoran coast; the seafaring Seris, farther south along the Sonora coast; and the Cochimís, along the northern Baja California coast. Sea turtles naturally occurred within the marine and/or aquatic range of each of these cultures and in some cases played a key role in their traditions and practices (e.g., Aschmann 1966; Felger & Moser 1985).

The Seris, or Comcáac, are renowned for their strong cultural and spiritual link to sea turtles (Felger et al. 1976; Felger & Moser 1985; Nabhan 2003). Today they live primarily in the villages of Punta Chueca and El Desemboque, north of Bahía Kino, but their territory once stretched from Guaymas northward to at least Puerto Lobos, and the Seris have names for places as far north as the Colorado

River (Felger & Moser 1985; Moser 1963; also see Chapter 39, this volume). In historic times a group of Seri ancestors known as the Xiica Hai Iic Coii ("those who are toward the wind") occupied the northern part of the overall Seri territory, north of Punta Tepopa. Also known as the Tepocas or Salineros, these or other Seris sometimes ventured or even lived as far north as the Alto Golfo region (Moser 1963; Mary Beck Moser, personal communication 2003). Seri knowledge of sea turtles was unparalleled among indigenous cultures in North America, and although there has been a gradual loss of traditional knowledge with the passing of the elder generations, the Seris continue to identify strongly with these marine creatures (Felger et al. 2005; Nabhan 2003; Seminoff et al. 2005).

Aquatic ecosystems were also a cultural foundation for the Cucapás, only in their case it was the fresh, brackish, and seawater environments of the Río Colorado. During historic times when the Colorado was the dynamic freshwater ecosystem of legends past, the vastness of its delta created a giant aquatic corridor into the interior of the Sonoran Desert. Although we don't know what role sea turtles played in Cucapá culture, certainly this indigenous tribe was aware of their presence. Sea turtles were known to occur near the Cucapá village of El Mayor, some 80 km from the gulf proper (Richard Felger & Amadeo Rea, unpublished data). Moreover, during a field trip in 2002 to the Colorado delta Richard Felger was told by local fisher Miguel Ángel Romo Bustón that sea turtles were once fairly common in the river. Señor Bustón commented that today he sees only two or three per year in the delta (Richard Felger, unpublished notes).

Southwest from the delta along Baja California's gulf coast, it appears that sea turtles, at least the hawksbill, were also used by the region's indigenous inhabitants. During his voyage to the Colorado delta in 1539, Francisco de Ulloa, leading three ships sent by Cortés to explore the region, encountered people near San Luiz Gonzaga (probably Cochimís). He later wrote: "They had a little enclosure of woven grass without any cover over the top, where they lodged, ten or twelve paces from the sea. We found inside no sort of bread or anything resembling it, nor another food except fish, of which they had some which they killed with well-twisted cords that had thick hooks made

of tortoise shell bent in fire" (Wagner 1929). Such hooks have been documented for other indigenous cultures (Frazier 2003), but this is the only mention of tortoiseshell hooks in the Gulf of California. Moreover, aside from pictographs resembling sea turtles that we have seen in the region, it is the only evidence of sea turtle use by the Cochimís, a group of people who have long been culturally extinct (Aschmann 1966).

Sea turtles have been a part of the marine landscape of the northern gulf through the centuries, and reliance on them continues today with local Mexican cultures. However, whereas the Seris and Cochimís were relatively small groups that even in times of maximal catch had little impact on sea turtle populations, local Mexican communities, because of their sheer numbers and a high demand for sea turtle products, have extracted sea turtles at an unparalleled rate. As a result of their utility through the ages, sea turtle populations have paid a heavy price.

The Alto Golfo and Sea Turtle Life History

Sea turtles are remarkable in the variety of broadly separated localities that individuals inhabit over the course of their lives. From hatchling to adult, these animals undergo ontogenic shifts in habitat use that encompass nesting beaches, juvenile developmental habitats, migratory corridors, and adult foraging grounds. On emergence, hatchlings depart the nesting beach to begin the oceanic phase of their life cycle, perhaps floating passively for a year or more in major current systems (gyres) that serve as open-ocean developmental grounds (Carr 1987). While offshore, small turtles commonly associate with rafts of flotsam and jetsam, which offer protection from predators and provide food (Carr & Meylan 1980; Nichols et al. 2001). Most turtles eventually move into coastal developmental habitats rich in food resources where they forage and grow until maturity (Musick & Limpus 1997; Seminoff, Resendiz et al. 2002; Seminoff, Resendiz, & Nichols 2002). Depending on the species, age to maturity may be between 10 and 50 years; ridleys and leatherbacks are the fastest to mature, and green turtles the slowest (Chaloupka & Musick 1997). On maturity, sea turtles carry out breeding migrations that take them from foraging grounds in areas such as the Alto Golfo to their natal nesting beaches. These migrations are undertaken

TABLE 30.1. *Accounts of sea turtle nesting in the Alto Golfo.*

DATE	SPECIES	EVIDENCE	LOCATION	SOURCE
1911	unknown	nesting female	delta region	Townsend 1916
1960s	leatherback	hatchlings	San Felipe	Caldwell 1962; W. J. Nichols, unpubl. notes
November 1961	olive ridley	8 hatchlings	Puerto Peñasco	H. Jones, UAZ Collection
October 1965	olive ridley	2 hatchlings	Puerto Peñasco	M. C. Truett, UAZ Collection
October 1995	olive ridley	77 hatchlings	Puerto Peñasco	Boyer 1995
November 1996	olive ridley	75 hatchlings	Playa Encanto, Puerto Peñasco	P. Turk Boyer, pers. comm.; Navarro 1997
October 2000	olive ridley	5 hatchlings	Playa Las Conchas, Puerto Peñasco	P. Turk Boyer, pers. comm.
2000	olive ridley	turtle tracks	Playa Rueben, San Felipe	P. Turk Boyer, pers. comm.
2000	olive ridley	turtle tracks	Playa El Burro, El Golfo de Santa Clara	P. Turk Boyer, pers. comm.

every few years by both males and females and often span thousands of kilometers (Nichols et al. 1999; Nichols, Bird, & García 2000; Nichols 2003; Seminoff, Alvarado et al. 2002).

Sea turtle nesting in the Alto Golfo has been reported on occasion (Table 30.1, Figure 30.1), yet the region has probably never been a particularly important area for such activity, instead being essential as a foraging area for both juvenile and adult sea turtles. The earliest report of nesting in the region comes from a trip into the Gulf of California in 1911 by the *Albatross,* sponsored by the New York Zoological Society (see Hastings & Findley, this volume). On that trip Charles Townsend (1916:445) noted, "Turtles are said to abound near the mouth of the Río Colorado where their eggs are deposited in the sand. The inhabitants of the Peninsula seem to have no difficulty in obtaining a supply of them." Although this passage appeared in the context of the green turtle, it is not certain that this is the species Townsend was discussing. Large green turtles with shelled eggs have reportedly been captured by fishermen in Bahía de los Angeles (Caldwell 1962; Nichols & Seminoff, unpublished data), and our friend Juan de la Cruz, a fisher from Juncalito, has claimed to see *tortugas prietas* nesting on the island of Monserrate. To date, however, there have been no substantiated reports of this species nesting anywhere in the gulf.

We believe that leatherbacks and olive ridleys are probably the only two sea turtle species that nest in the Gulf of California. Both regularly nest in the cape region of Baja California Sur (Fritts et al. 1982; Olguin-Mena 1990) and near Mazatlán, Sinaloa (Seminoff 1994), but accounts of nesting farther north in the gulf are less common. Caldwell (1962) tells of a hotel proprietor in San Felipe who had seen leatherback hatchlings nearby in July 1962. A fisherman echoed this report when he told one of us (WJN) of leatherbacks nesting on beaches north of San Felipe in the 1960s. Similarly, Edward Moser was once told by the Seris that hatchlings had been seen in the Infiernillo Channel (Richard Felger, unpublished data). Although the presence of hatchlings does not provide concrete evidence of nesting in the area, such accounts, coupled with the fact that leatherbacks grow beyond hatchling size in a matter of weeks (Witham & Futch 1977), suggest that these small turtles originated nearby.

The olive ridley is by far the most common nester in the gulf. Ridley nests have been observed in areas such as Punta Chivato, Baja California Sur (W. Nichols, unpublished data), and near the towns of Bahía Kino (Seminoff & Nichols, unpublished data) and Bahía de los Angeles (Resendiz & Seminoff, unpublished data) in Sonora and Baja California, respectively. Moreover, Caldwell (1962) recounts a story of sea turtle eggs being dug up and consumed near the town of Bahía Gonzaga.

Figure 30.1. *Selected sea turtle nesting areas in the eastern Pacific. Inset: Locations of solitary nesting reports for olive ridley and leatherback turtles in the upper Gulf of California. The loggerhead turtle is present in the eastern Pacific but does not nest in the region.*

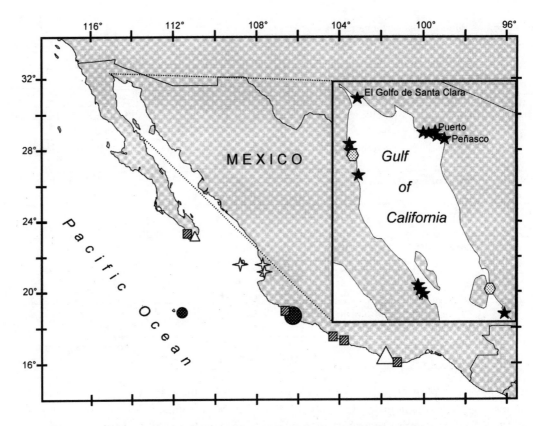

★ solitary olive ridley nest reported in the Gulf of California

⬡ solitary leatherback nest reported in the Gulf of California

✦ hawksbill nesting reported (Nayarit, Jalisco, and Islas Marias)

▨ leatherback rookery

△ minor olive ridley rookery (Baja California Peninsula)

● minor green turtle rookery (Revillagigedos Islands)

⬤ major green turtle rookery (Michoacán)

△ Mexico's largest olive ridley rookery (Escobilla, Oaxaca)

Based on the small size of the eggs, Caldwell reasoned that they were from *Chelonia, Lepidochelys,* or *Caretta.* However, since we now know that the closest *Caretta* nesting beach is in Japan, it stands to reason that these eggs were from one of the other two, most likely *Lepidochelys.* Even today fishermen often confuse the green turtle with the olive ridley turtle. Interestingly, these reports are consistent with indigenous knowledge: the Seris described the olive ridley as the only sea turtle that possessed eggs on capture (Felger et al. 2005).

Olive ridley nesting has been reported in the Alto Golfo on multiple occasions (Table 30.1). The earliest accounts come by the way of 10 hatchling specimens that are currently in the University of Arizona's herpetological collection: 8 were collected in November 1961 midway between Puerto Peñasco and Cholla Bay by Harry Jones (UAZ 28112–UAZ 28119) and 2 in October 1965 near Cholla Bay by Mary C. "Sandy" Truett (UAZ 28120–UAZ 28121). More recently, in October 1995, Boyer (1995) reported that two fishermen encountered some 70 hatchlings scurrying to the water on Playa Bonita near Puerto Peñasco. After biologists from the Centro Intercultural de Estudios del Desiertos y Océanos (CEDO) arrived, an additional 7 hatchlings were found. Since then, hatchlings have been found at Playa Encanto in November 1996 (75 hatchlings) and Las Conchas beach in October 2000 (5 hatchlings). In addition, turtle tracks (most likely from olive ridleys) were spotted in 2000 at Playa Rueben north of San Felipe and at Playa El Burro near El Golfo de Santa Clara (Navarro 1997; Peggy Turk Boyer, unpublished notes). These were only solitary nests, but because females typically deposit several clutches within a season, it is likely that additional nests were laid.

The reports summarized here likely represent only a minuscule fraction of the actual number of nesting events in the Alto Golfo; nevertheless, the greatest importance of this region for sea turtles, even the olive ridley, is as a feeding area. Benthic habitats host diverse assemblages of marine algae and invertebrates (Brusca 1980, this volume; Norris 1975), both of which are important components in the diets of sea turtles. In addition, offshore waters hold a variety of gelatinous prey. Species such as the green turtle and hawksbill maintain residency in specific coastal habitats, remaining in these areas for extended periods while foraging on benthic resources (Seminoff, Resendiz, & Nichols 2002). Others such as the leatherback roam offshore waters in search of salps and sea jellies.

Species Accounts of Sea Turtles in the Alto Golfo

Six of the world's seven sea turtle species nest on the shores of Mexico and forage in the coastal and offshore waters. For this reason, Mexico is often considered the sea turtle capital of the world. Five species are present in the Gulf of California: the leatherback, hawksbill, olive ridley, green turtle, and loggerhead. All have a circumglobal distribution except the olive ridley, which is found primarily in the eastern Pacific, Indian, and southwestern Atlantic oceans. There is evidence that all five occurred in the Alto Golfo region (Table 30.2).

Leatherback (Dermochelys coriacea)

The leatherback is one of the most remarkable larger vertebrates living in the world's oceans. Locally called *siete filos* or *laúd*, it is the sole member of the family Dermochelyidae, an ancient lineage dating back over 100 million years. The leatherback is the largest of the extant sea turtles, attaining a shell length of over 2 m and a weight of up to 800 kg (Pritchard & Trebbau 1984). With its flexible leathery shell, lack of epidermal scales, and teardrop-shaped body, the leatherback appears perfectly adapted for a life at sea (Figure 30.2a, b). The species possesses dorsal and ventral keels (on the dorsum it possesses seven keels, hence the name *siete filos*) that enable it to move through the water with maximum efficiency. Not surprisingly, leatherbacks have a more pelagic existence than any other species, living off the abundant sea jellies and other gelatinous megaplankton that associate with the deep scattering layer in offshore waters (Eckert et al. 1989). Their large size provides for considerable thermal inertia, which prevents excessive cooling and overheating. This endotherm-like thermoregulation, termed *gigantothermy* (Paladino et al. 1990), enables leatherbacks to access abundant food resources in cold pelagic waters that other sea turtle species avoid.

Leatherback nesting occurs along the Pacific coast from Mexico to Costa Rica and in the cape region of Baja California probably near Todos Santos. In the eastern Pacific, foraging occurs from Chile to Alaska and in the Gulf of California. According to Seri knowledge, leatherbacks have never been particularly common in the central gulf (Felger & Moser 1985), and accounts in the Alto Golfo are few and far between. The first evidence of nonhatchlings in the Alto Golfo was provided when Caldwell (1962) wrote about a leatherback that was captured and killed near San Felipe in the summer of 1961. Stranded leatherbacks have since been found near El Golfo in July 1970 (Richard Felger, unpublished data) and March 1975 (Cliffton, Felger, & Nabhan in Cliffton et al. 1982) and near Puertocitos in November 1980 (Bryan Brown, personal communication, in Cliffton et al. 1982). More recently, a leatherback measuring over 1.5 m in length was captured by fishermen near El Golfo in 1991 (Carlos Navarro, personal communication 1994). During our research we have seen two carapaces of leatherbacks in Puerto Peñasco, one at a private residence and the second at CEDO.

Perhaps the most intriguing account of leatherback presence in the Alto Golfo comes from ongoing research by Peter Dutton, Scott Eckert, and Scott Benson off the coast of California. Since 1999 this team has captured over 30 leatherbacks near Monterey Bay and released them with satellite transmitters. In October 2002 an adult male was captured and released, and by May 2003 it had gone around the tip of Baja and all the way to the Alto Golfo, where it remained for several months before the signal was lost (Dutton et al., unpublished data). Remarkably, genetic analysis has established that this turtle originated from nesting beaches in southeast Asia (Peter Dutton, unpublished data).

There are oral history accounts of Seris finding hatchlings emerging from nests at least twice

TABLE 30.2. *Synopsis of the biology of sea turtles from the Alto Golfo.*

Common Name (English, Spanish)	Latin Name	Distinguishing Characteristics	Diet	Foraging Areas in Eastern Pacific	Nesting Areas in Eastern Pacific and Alto Golfo	Status in Gulf of California	IUCN Listing	Primary Threats
Leatherback, *tortuga laúd, siete filos*	*Dermochelys coriacea*	Largest living sea turtle; length ≥ 2 m; weight to 800 kg; leathery shell, teardrop-shaped body; 7 dorsal ridges	Sea jellies, cyphophores, salps	Tropical and temperate pelagic zones from Alaska to Chile	BC Cape region to southern Mexico; rare in AG	Pacific populations have crashed; rare in gulf	Critically endangered	Egg collection, incidental capture in longline and drift-net fisheries
Hawksbill, *tortuga carey*	*Eretmochelys imbricata*	Length to 90 cm; weight to 100 kg; hawklike beak; overlapping carapace plates; serrated shell margin	Sponges, invertebrates	Coral reefs and rocky habitats from Baja to Peru	Nayarit, Jalisco; Islas Marías; no nesting in AG	Rare in gulf	Critically endangered	Tortoiseshell trade, egg collection
Olive ridley, *tortuga golfina*	*Lepidochelys olivacea*	Smallest sea turtle; length to 70 cm; weight to 60 kg	Invertebrates (crustaceans, molluscs)	Benthic and pelagic habitats from Baja to Peru	BC Cape region to southern Mexico; uncommon in AG	Common off central Mexico; uncommon in gulf	Endangered	Egg collection; incidental capture in longline, purse seine, and trawl fisheries
Green turtle, East Pacific green turtle, black turtle, *tortuga prieta, tortuga negra*	*Chelonia mydas*	Most common turtle in gulf; length to 100 cm; weight to 200 kg; scissorlike beak	Seagrass, marine algae, invertebrates (sponges, sea jellies, crustaceans, molluscs)	Coastal bays, lagoons, and estuaries from California to Chile	Michoacán and Revillagigedo Islands; no confirmed nesting in Gulf of California	Most common sea turtle Gulf of California; common in AG	Endangered	Illegal hunting, egg collection, incidental capture in set-net and shrimp-trawl fisheries
Loggerhead, *caguama, tortuga perica, tortuga amarilla, tortuga javelina*	*Caretta caretta*	Length to 95 cm; weight to 180 kg; very broad skull	Invertebrates (especially pelagic red crabs, molluscs)	Benthic and pelagic habitats of Pacific coast of Baja and Gulf of California	No nesting in eastern Pacific	Uncommon in gulf, rare in AG	Endangered	Illegal hunting, incidental capture in longline, drift-net, and set-net fisheries

during the mid-twentieth century. The hatchlings were found as they were heading to the sea, not as small turtles in the sea (Richard Felger, unpublished data; also see Nabhan 2003). Similarly, Edward Moser and Richard Felger were told by the Seris that hatchlings had been seen in the Infiernillo Channel (Richard Felger, unpublished data). Although the presence of hatchlings does not provide concrete evidence of nesting in the area, such accounts coupled with the fact that leatherbacks grow beyond hatchling size in a matter of weeks (Witham & Futch 1977) suggest that these small turtles originated nearby.

Today leatherback turtles are in serious decline in the Pacific Ocean. Because they live the majority of their lives in pelagic zones, leatherbacks are particularly susceptible to impacts from high-seas longline and drift-net fisheries (Eckert & Sarti 1997). Bycatch in these commercial fisheries coupled with the adverse effects of decades of egg poaching have decimated populations throughout the Pacific (Spotila et al. 2000). These declines are particularly evident in the western Pacific Ocean, where the nesting colony in Terengganu, Malaysia (once the Pacific's largest rookery), has vanished. The situation is very similar in the eastern Pacific: at Llano Grande, the largest nesting colony along the Pacific coast of Mexico and a site where more than 2,000 nests were deposited annually in the early 1990s, less than 10 females nested during the 2002–2003 nesting season (Ana Barragán, personal communication 2003). At Mexiquillo, the second largest rookery in Mexico, the population has dropped from over 1,000 females in the 1980s to less than 5 during the 2002–2003 nesting season (Laura Sarti, personal communication 2003). Leatherback populations in the Pacific Ocean have declined to the extent that some researchers estimate that this species will become extinct in the Pacific within the next two decades (Spotila et al. 2000). Its conservation status in the Atlantic is quite different, as many nesting rookeries have recovered in recent years (e.g., Dutton et al. 2003).

Hawksbill Turtle (Eretmochelys imbricata)

At seafood restaurants in coastal towns such as Puerto Peñasco, El Golfo de Santa Clara, and San Felipe a shellacked hawksbill carapace hanging on the wall is a familiar sight. Hawksbills, like all other sea turtles except the leatherback, are in the

Figure 30.2a. Leatherback turtle, dorsal view. (Drawing by Thomas D. McFarland)

Figure 30.2b. Leatherback turtle, ventral view. (Drawing by Thomas D. McFarland)

family Cheloniidae, a group that is found in the fossil record as far back as 50 million years ago. This species reaches 90 cm in length and 100 kg in weight and gets its name from its unusual hawk-like beak (Figure 30.3). This morphology appears functionally beneficial for a spongivorous diet: hawksbills eat sponges almost exclusively (Witzell 1983). They forage along rocky shores and coral reefs and are tied to tropical waters more than any other sea turtle species.

Locally known as *carey*, hawksbills are best described by the imbricate, coffee- and caramel-colored scutes on the carapace and plastron, especially during juvenile and subadult life stages. The beauty and workability of these keratinous plates, known as *tortoiseshell, carey, penca,* or *bekko,* has caused the hawksbill turtle to be the target of an

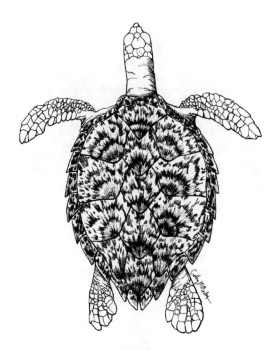

exhaustive harvest for artisanal uses (Groombridge & Luxmoore 1989). The material is fashioned into combs, pendants, and fine jewelry. In addition to the value of hawksbills for these handcrafted pieces, stuffed turtles or carapaces hung above a doorway are thought to bring good luck to a home. These nonconsumptive uses, coupled with the harvest of eggs, juveniles, and adults for food, have caused hawksbill populations to plummet worldwide.

The hawksbill is the only sea turtle species present in the eastern Pacific for which we know of no large nesting congregations. Cornelius (1982) reported infrequent nesting along the Pacific coast of Central America. In Mexico a large population was reported in the 1950s and 1960s from the Tres Marías Islands, which may have been a major breeding ground (Parsons 1962). By the 1980s, however, no major hawksbill nesting rookeries remained in the eastern Pacific (Cliffton et al. 1982). Hawksbill turtles continue to nest, albeit rarely, along the Pacific coast of Mexico. Accounts of sporadic nesting in the Mexican coastal states of Jalisco and Nayarit indicate potential nesting beach origins within 1,000 km of the Alto Golfo (Raquel Briseño, personal communication 2001). Closer to home, adult-sized hawksbills are common near Cabo Pulmo in the Cape region, and there is speculation that the species may nest in the area on occasion, although it has gone undetected so far (Melissa Paxton, personal communication 2003).

Hawksbill turtles were once common throughout much of the gulf (Cliffton et al. 1982). Seri elders explain that large hawksbills were abundant as recently as the 1950s in their territory (Felger & Moser 1985); however, even during the epoch of great sea turtle abundance, hawksbills were apparently uncommon in the Alto Golfo. In 1765, for example, the Spanish missionary Padre Norberto Ducrue (O'Crouley 1774, translated in Aschmann 1966:45) noted after a voyage of several months throughout the gulf that hawksbills, although present in southern waters, were not found in the northern gulf: "There are turtles in great abundance in both seas but the one with the transparent shell known as *Carey* exists only in the southern extremity on the Pacific side, and in the Gulf is found up to latitude 27 1/2° N. In areas farther to the north it is not found, either in the Pacific or in the Gulf."

According to our information, however, it appears that this species is at least occasionally present in the Alto Golfo. One of us (JAS) has seen tortoiseshell jewelry for sale by street vendors in Puerto Peñasco as recently as 1998. When asked, the vendor volunteered that the material was from a turtle caught locally. In addition, during his research on the artisanal fisheries of the Alto Golfo in the 1990s, Richard Cudney, a graduate student at the University of Arizona, found a piece of tortoiseshell in the sand along the Wellton-Mohawk (M.O.D.E.) canal, close to the Ciénega de Santa Clara (Richard Cudney, personal communication 2002).

Despite the tremendous declines of hawksbill turtles in the Gulf of California, impacts on the species continue (Seminoff et al. 2003). Fishermen unanimously report that if a hawksbill turtle is captured, it is never returned to the ocean. As a result, hawksbills are critically endangered in the eastern Pacific (Meylan & Donnelly 1999). It is clear that their recovery will require conservation efforts that focus not only on the subsistence harvesting of these beautiful animals but also on the culture that propels their value for the tortoiseshell industry and souvenir trade.

Olive Ridley (Lepidochelys olivacea)

The olive ridley is the most common sea turtle in the eastern Pacific Ocean and also the smallest, topping out at 70 cm in length and 60 kg in weight (Figure 30.4a, b). Inhabiting both neritic and pelagic habitats of the eastern Pacific (Kopitsky et al. 2005), ridleys forage on a variety of invertebrates. Whereas we have captured olive ridleys feeding in waters as shallow as 3 m in the gulf, Bob Pitman (1990; personal communication 2002) has reported seeing hundreds if not thousands of ridleys in pelagic waters hundreds of miles from the Mexican coast during his numerous cruises on the NOAA vessel *David Star Jordan*.

Seri knowledge suggests that olive ridleys were fairly common in the central gulf before the 1960s but have since become rare (Felger & Moser 1985). Aside from the scattered accounts of nesting already described, little is known of their distribution in the Alto Golfo.

Olive ridleys are called *golfinas* throughout Mexico and have received considerable attention recently owing to the recovery of some nesting populations along the Pacific coast (Márquez et al. 1998). For instance, at the largest rookery, in Escobilla, Oaxaca, olive ridleys were nearly wiped out because of decades of egg harvest and killing of adults for meat and leather products. However, since the passing of the 1990 moratorium, this population has rebounded to what many believe is pre-exploitation abundance: more than 400,000 turtles nested during an *arribada* (a mass nesting event) in 2001 (Rene Márquez, personal communication 2002). This is one of the greatest success stories in the history of sea turtle conservation and is perhaps the best example of how conservation legislation such as the 1990 closure of legal sea turtle fisheries in Mexico can pave the way for population recovery.

Green Turtle (Chelonia mydas)

The population of green turtles in the eastern Pacific (also called east Pacific green turtles or black turtles) has been the subject of considerable taxonomic debate. Some scientists believe it should be afforded full specific status as *Chelonia agassizii* (Pritchard 1999), but others argue that it is at most a subspecies of the pantropical green turtle (i.e., *Chelonia mydas agassizii*) and perhaps nothing more than a unique population (Karl & Bowen 1999). This is a archetypical debate between systematists and geneticists. Regardless of the disagreement, there is no doubt that green turtles in the eastern Pacific and Gulf of California are an

Figure 30.4a. Ridley turtle, dorsal view. (Drawing by Thomas D. McFarland)

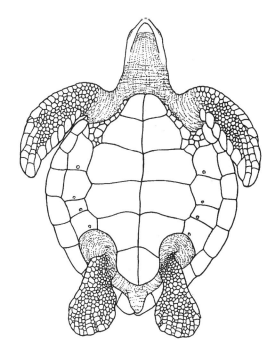

Figure 30.4b. Ridley turtle, ventral view. (Drawing by Thomas D. McFarland)

important component of the coastal ecosystem, regional economy, and cultural heritage.

Green turtles occur in coastal waters of the eastern Pacific from southern California to Chile, where they forage along islands and in coastal bays, estuaries, and lagoons. Their diet has been described as primarily herbivorous, consisting of marine algae and seagrass with occasional mangrove leaves (López-Mendilaharsu 2002; Seminoff, Resendiz, & Nichols 2002). In addition, green

Figure 30.5a. Green turtle, dorsal view. (Drawing by Thomas D. McFarland)

Figure 30.5b. Green turtle, ventral view. (Drawing by Thomas D. McFarland)

turtles in this region consume larger portions of animal matter than *Chelonia* in other parts of the world (Bjorndal 1997; López-Mendilaharsu et al. 2003; Seminoff et al. 2000). Locally known as *tortugas negras* or *tortugas prietas,* green turtles may attain a shell length of slightly over a meter and weigh up to 200 kg (Figure 30.5a, b).

The temperate waters of the central and upper Gulf of California create an environment that is thermally challenging for green turtles during winter months: it is not uncommon for water temperatures to drop below 15°C. In response, green turtles become sluggish and sometimes exhibit overwintering torpor (Felger et al. 1976), a behavior so unusual that even the most novice of sea turtle biologists have heard of the famed "hibernating turtles" from the gulf. Unfortunately, this behavior facilitated large-scale har-

vests of torpid turtles during the 1960s and 1970s (Felger et al. 1976), a practice that continues today in many areas (Seminoff, observation).

Green turtles are by far the most abundant sea turtle in the Gulf of California. They originate from rookeries in Michoacán and the Revillagigedos Islands (Peter Dutton, unpublished data; Nichols 2003). The initial connection came from tag returns reported by Cliffton et al. (1982). An additional scientific link came from an adult female captured in 1985 near Piedra San Bernabé in the northern gulf with flipper tags applied in April 1984 in Michoacán, a site more than 1,750 km to the south (Alvarado & Figueroa 1992; Figueroa et al. 1993). Nesting beach–foraging area links have since been established through satellite telemetry (Nichols et al. 1999), genetics (Peter Dutton, unpublished data; Nichols 2003), and additional flipper tag recoveries (Seminoff, Alvarado et al. 2002).

Accounts in the Alto Golfo date back to at least 1889, according to Townsend (1916:445), who wrote that green turtles "are plentiful in the Gulf of California, and the *Albatross* obtained specimens in the vicinity of Willard Bay, on the Peninsula near the head of the Gulf in 1889." Today green turtles are regularly present at Puerto Peñasco near the long cochina reef that runs the length of beach south of town. Turtles are often caught in entanglement nets used to catch *Mobula* rays at the El Borrascoso reef and outside La Cholla (Richard Cudney, unpublished data). The species is mostly observed during winter months but appears to reside in the area between at least July and February (Richard Cudney, personal communication). To the west, green turtles are present in the vicinity of San Felipe, where a number of discarded carapaces have been recovered (Nichols, unpublished data). Moreover, the aforementioned accounts of sea turtles in the Colorado River are most likely green turtle sightings.

Despite their relative abundance in the Alto Golfo, there is little doubt that the current green turtle population is orders of magnitude smaller than that of decades past. This crash is due primarily to past and present harvests of turtles for food and oil but also to incidental capture in marine fisheries operations. If we have any hope of recovering this population, it is imperative that hunting of green turtles in neritic habitats of the Alto Golfo is stopped and that fisheries are managed so as to reduce if not eliminate all incidental sea turtle bycatch.

Loggerhead Turtle (Caretta caretta)

The loggerhead is an enigmatic species in the eastern Pacific Ocean. This turtle can be found in foraging habitats along the Pacific coast of the Baja California peninsula and in the Gulf of California, but the closest nesting beaches are across the Pacific in Japan and Australia. After years of speculation, the first link between these foraging and nesting populations came in the early 1990s via genetic analysis (Bowen et al. 1995). Direct evidence has since been gathered through the recovery of a flipper-tagged turtle in Japan that was initially released in Baja California (Resendiz et al. 1998) and through satellite telemetry of the famed loggerhead named Adelita, released in Baja and tracked as she swam back to Japan, a journey that spanned 11,500 km and took 368 days between August 1996 and August 1997 (Nichols, Resendiz et al. 2000). The trans-Pacific movements of loggerheads are one of the most amazing examples of animal migration. Interestingly, after spending years foraging in the eastern Pacific, once loggerheads return to their natal Japanese nesting beaches for reproduction, they remain in the western Pacific for the remainder of their life cycle.

Loggerheads in the gulf reach a maximum of 95 cm in length and 180 kg in weight, although the vast majority of individuals are substantially smaller than this, averaging 62 cm in length (Seminoff et al. 2004) (Figure 30.6a, b). There are a variety of names for this species in northwestern Mexico, including *tortuga caguama*, *tortuga javelina*, *tortuga perica*, and *tortuga amarilla*. The species forages throughout benthic and pelagic regions of the central eastern Pacific, mainly along the west coast of the Baja California peninsula and the Gulf of California. Its diet consists of invertebrates (crustaceans, molluscs), especially the pelagic red crab *(Pleuroncodes planipes)* (Nichols 2003). Loggerheads are seen regularly in foraging habitats in the central gulf (Seminoff 2000; Seminoff et al. 2004), but their distribution in the Alto Golfo is poorly known. To date, only two loggerheads have been documented in the Alto Golfo: one that was taken near San Felipe (Shaw 1947) and one that was landed near Puerto Peñasco and is at the University of Arizona Herpetological Collection (see Rosen, this volume).

Figure 30.6a. Loggerhead turtle, dorsal view. (Drawing by Thomas D. McFarland)

Figure 30.6b. Loggerhead turtle, ventral view. (Drawing by Thomas D. McFarland)

Loggerhead abundance in the Pacific is declining rapidly. Like leatherbacks, loggerheads are heavily impacted by commercial longline and drift-net fisheries as they move across the Pacific Ocean. However, unlike leatherbacks, loggerhead turtles face additional threats of entanglement in nearshore artisanal set-net fisheries as they enter Baja California waters (Gardner & Nichols 1999; Hoyt Peckham, unpublished data). Despite almost complete protection of nesting beaches, nesting abundance of loggerheads in Japan has fallen dramatically in the last decade. Without immediate broad-based conservation measures focusing on bycatch reduction, we fear that the loggerhead turtle will follow the path of the Pacific leatherback.

Local Fisheries and the Decline of Sea Turtles

The Gulf of California has long been considered a sea turtle hot spot in the eastern Pacific Ocean. Renowned for its diversity of marine habitats and abundance of algae, seagrass, and invertebrate food resources, this region once hosted abundant sea turtle populations. In recent decades, however, the numbers have dwindled, partly due to incidental fisheries impacts but primarily due to the unabated exploitation of turtles in foraging areas throughout the region.

Commercial and Subsistence Hunting

For nearly a century, humans have commercially harvested sea turtles from areas along the Baja California peninsula (Agler 1913; Averett 1920). Because of the extreme abundance of these creatures, the catch rates of earlier times are virtually unimaginable today. During the earliest years harvest was heavier in the southern portions of the peninsula, but by the 1920s, sites in the northern gulf were increasingly targeted. In the 1920s J. A. Craig (1926:167) described sea turtle hunting (presumably the green turtle) in San Felipe: "During the spring months there are numbers of large sea turtles caught at San Felipe. Most of them are harpooned, although a few are taken alive and shipped out to Los Angeles or San Diego. These turtles are very rich in fat and the principal object of their capture is to secure this oil. The turtles are cut up and the flesh and fat placed in large pans filled with water. The fat is then boiled out and allowed to separate from the water. After being cooled, it has about the consistency of soft lard, and is light yellow in color. It is packed in five-gallon oil cans and sold for a good price to druggists. The turtle meat remaining is salted and dried in the sun and used for food."

At that time many turtles were also purchased by distributors from Calexico. Turtles were loaded onto the beds of large trucks and shipped north. From San Felipe to Calexico it is 135 miles over the dry floodplains bordering the Colorado River. Most of the road was level but very rough; in some places it followed the course laid by the pioneers who first navigated the area in pack trains. Flooding of the river sometimes stopped passage, and on more than one occasion transporters were marooned on elevated crests waiting for the muddy water to subside (Craig 1926). On a good day it would take about twelve hours or more to travel the dirt roads from San Felipe to Calexico. The heartiness of the turtles would allow for safe arrival even days after being loaded onto the trucks.

In addition to the San Felipe–Calexico turtle exportation route, sea turtles were shipped from Puerto Peñasco across the border to small towns in Arizona. Robert "Bob" Lenon (personal communication to Bill Broyles, 1998) explained that in the 1930s "there was a 24-hour cafe in downtown Gila Bend run for many years by an old German with the name of Jake Miller (probably Mueller until World War I). He used to import big sea turtles from Rocky Point and concoct a hearty turtle soup therefrom, but was soon forced to quit. Too much of the carcass had to be discarded. 'One hundred percent waste,' he avowed, and when my dad questioned him about those figures, Jake replied, 'Ya, even more than that!'"

Green turtles were abundant throughout the gulf, and the population supported a lucrative fishery for decades (Carr 1961). Speaking of the Bahía de los Angeles hunting, David Caldwell (1963:147) wrote, "I saw over 500 landed in a 3-week summer period in 1962 at Los Angeles Bay alone, and a comparable number, considering fishing effort, per week in winter." Extraction was so heavy that during their investigations of green turtles, Caldwell and Caldwell (1962) coined this species the "black steer" of the Gulf of California. Heavy harvest rates continued through the 1970s, but by the early 1980s sea turtle populations in the gulf had crashed (Figure 30.7). As a result, fishing cooperatives disbanded throughout the peninsula. Nevertheless, many fishermen continued to harvest what few turtles they could on their own, selling them to independent buyers.

Although protected by strong laws in Mexico and the United States as well as international treaties, sea turtles, particularly green turtles, continue to be captured and sold. This activity is illegal and difficult to quantify, but there is no doubt that it continues today, as the culture of turtle meat consumption remains strong in many social circles of Mexico and the United States (Felger et al. 2005). Money drives the illegal exploitation, and it is not uncommon for a single large green turtle to fetch upward of US$1,000 on the black market that supplies the demand in urban centers such as Ensenada, Tijuana, Hermosillo, San Diego, Tucson, and Phoenix. In contrast, turtle meat may be sold for less than the price of chicken or beef (about US$2–3/lb in 2005) in the communities in which they are landed (Wallace Nichols, unpublished data). With the combined financial and cultural incentives it is not difficult to understand why people continue to hunt sea turtles illegally.

An Economy Built on Shrimp

At the harbors and boat-storage areas of Puerto Peñasco and San Felipe it is hard to miss the sight of dozens of rusting, dry-docked shrimp trawlers, their abundance telling of the region's once-lucrative fishery. Shrimp trawling in the Alto Golfo was the cornerstone of the local fisheries-based economy and, as in many places in the world, has been detrimental to the survival of sea turtles. The main targets of the gulf shrimping industry are the brown shrimp, *Penaeus californiensis,* and the blue shrimp, *P. stylirostris,* but trawling practices also catch a variety of nontarget species.

To make their catch, shrimp trawlers drag their large nets on the sea floor, and these benthic substrates include areas where sea turtles go to feed or rest. With up to four nets working for hours on end, a single vessel scours a path of up to sixty miles in a day (A. Kerstitch, personal communication 1997). Unfortunately, the vastness of the area increases the chances of turtle capture, and the long tow times ensure that when trapped, turtles will drown. Although all species are subject to the impacts from shrimp trawling in the Alto Golfo, the green turtle is most affected: we have encountered dead green turtles on numerous occasions along the shores of San Felipe and Puerto Peñasco (Seminoff & Nichols, unpublished data). With few exceptions, our observations have coincided with the shrimp season; lights drifting back and forth across the sea's midnight horizon signal the presence of shrimp trawlers.

In addition to trawling activity, a drift-net fishery continues in the Alto Golfo (Cudney-Bueno & Turk Boyer 1998). Like shrimp nets, drift nets indiscriminately capture a variety of marine organisms, including the highly endangered

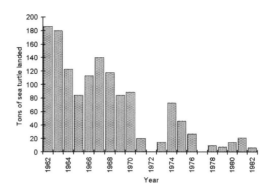

Figure 30.7. Tons of sea turtle landed in Bahía de los Angeles, 1962–1982.

vaquita (Vidal 1993; see Navarro, this volume) as well as sea turtles. Although recent efforts to close drift-net fisheries have been unsuccessful, it is apparent that the use of nets must be controlled or completely eliminated in the Alto Golfo to prevent local turtle populations from declining even further.

Sea Turtle Survival and Conservation in Mexico

Sea turtle populations in the Gulf of California have declined substantially from former levels. Leatherbacks and hawksbills are currently listed as critically endangered, green turtles and loggerheads are listed as endangered, and the olive ridley is listed as vulnerable in the World Conservation Union (IUCN) Red Data Book (Hilton-Taylor 2000). All are included in Appendix 1 of the Convention on International Trade in Endangered Species of Wild Fauna and Flora (CITES).

Over the last three decades a variety of conservation activities have been undertaken to ensure the survival of all sea turtles in Mexico. In 1966, on-the-ground conservation began in the form of nesting beach protection at several of the primary sea turtle nesting areas along the Pacific coast of Mexico (Seminoff 1994). In 1979 green turtle nesting beaches in Michoacán, the most important for the species in Mexico, were finally afforded protection (Figueroa et al. 1993). Additional efforts to protect this species came in 1990 when the Mexican government declared a moratorium on the harvest and trade of sea turtles in Mexico (Diario Oficial 1990). Although not common enough, there are encouraging signs and reasons for hope. For example, between 2001 through 2005 green turtle nesting seasons in Michoacán, researchers reported the largest nesting abundance since the early 1980s (Javier Alvarado, personal communication 2003). Moreover, for the first time there

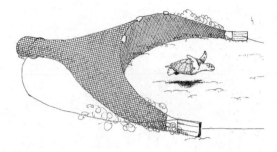

Figure 30.8. A turtle about to be captured in a trawling net lacking a turtle excluder device (TED). Although some nets deployed in the Alto Golfo had TEDs as early as 1997, their use was not mandated by law until December 1999 (Diario Oficial 1999). (Drawing by Todd Steiner)

have been publicized cases in which turtle poachers have been sentenced to jail terms in Baja and Sonora (Nichols & Safina 2004; Luis Fuego, personal communication).

In response to the tremendous sea turtle mortality caused by trawling activity, governments around the world began to mandate the use of turtle excluder devices (TEDs), contraptions that are fitted into shrimp nets to enable turtles to escape before being trapped (Figure 30.8). The use of TEDs has been effective in reducing sea turtle mortality in many shrimping areas. Along the Pacific coast of Mexico an Official Norm of Emergency first established the use of TEDs in March 1996, and the devices were mandated for permanent use in December 1999 (Diario Oficial 1999). Nevertheless, although these steps were promising advances in the conservation of sea turtles, implementation of TEDs has not yet been fully accepted by the local shrimping fleets.

After many years of conservation effort some sea turtle populations in the Gulf of California may be making a slow return. Because these species mature late and grow slowly, however, such efforts must be long-term. In response to the problems of illegal poaching, we must focus on ways to slow the take of turtles. One of the solutions is increased enforcement of existing laws along with the implementation of grass-roots conservation activities such as community-based enforcement (Delgado & Nichols 2005; Nichols, Bird, & García 2000; Seminoff et al. 2005). This will require a concerted effort on the part of enforcement officers and conservationists to address both supply and demand of sea turtles as well as the cultural context in which sea turtle conservation issues are embedded. Marine protected areas, such as the Alto Golfo Biosphere Reserve, can provide the necessary framework for management efforts and legal mechanisms. Considering all the recent advances and pending conservation plans, we are cautiously optimistic that we will witness during our lifetime the restoration of sea turtle populations in the Alto Golfo.

Acknowledgments

We thank Donald Thomson, Cecil Schwalbe, and Richard Felger for their tremendous motivation and guidance. Jennifer Gilmore and Dana Nichols have supported us throughout our travels in Mexico and continue to inspire us today. We extend special thanks to Peggy Turk Boyer, Richard Cudney, Richard Felger, and Phil Rosen for providing information on sea turtle presence and to Cathy Moser Marlett, Thomas McFarland, and Todd Steiner for artwork included in this chapter. Components of our sea turtle research in the Gulf of California have been supported by the Archie Carr Center for Sea Turtle Research, Blue Ocean Institute, Earthwatch Institute, National Marine Fisheries Service, PADI Foundation, ProPenínsula, Wallace Research Foundation, WildCoast, and the University of Arizona. Our research was authorized by the Secretaría de Medio Ambiente, Recursos Naturales, y Pesca and the Secretaría de Medio Ambiente y Recursos Naturales. Lastly, we thank the government of Mexico for providing us with the opportunity to study sea turtles in the Gulf of California over the last two decades.

Thirty-One

In Search of *El Burro,* the Tidal Bore of the Río Colorado Delta

Steve Nelson

S everal times each month, on days around the new and full moon, a wall of water surges up the estuary of the Colorado River at the head of the highest incoming tides. This curious phenomenon, known to science as a tidal bore and to local Cucapá Indian and Mexican fishermen as *el burro,* occurs in a setting of magnificent isolation, often unobserved by humans.

Most eyewitness accounts of *el burro* date from the nineteenth century, during the brief era of commercial steamboat navigation on the river. Upstream impoundment and diversion of Colorado River water during the twentieth century reduced the river's flow, diminishing the size and force of the bore. During the driest years of the 1960s and 1970s, some speculated that the bore, like the river itself, might be a thing of the past. But *el burro* reappeared in the 1980s when river water once again reached the sea, and it remains an important and recurring feature of the estuary.

This chapter is a review of historical accounts of *el burro,* combined with some of my own observations. These accounts reveal details of the bore's behavior and characteristics and provide insight into changing channel and estuary conditions over time.

Tidal Bores

The precise number of rivers worldwide having tidal bores is not known. The Tidal Bore Research Society lists 55 known bores on every continent except Antarctica. The mightiest bore occurs on the Qianjiang River, near Hangzhou, China. This great bore reaches a height of over 30 ft (9.1 m) and a speed of 17 mph (27 km/hr) (Tricker 1964). The Amazon River bore, called the *pororoca,* is sometimes 25 ft (7.6 m) high and sweeps several hundred miles up the river's many channels. Major North American bores include the Petitcodiac River bore in New Brunswick and the bores of the

Turnagain Arm and Knik Arm near Anchorage, Alaska (Lynch 1982).

Two conditions must be met for a tidal bore to form in a coastal river. Tides of the adjoining sea must be exceptionally high: a range of 20 ft (6.1 m) between high and low water is usually required. The river must also be shallow with a gently sloping bottom and a broad, funnel-shaped estuary (Chanson 2001; Lynch 1982).

A bore is most likely to form at the time of the spring tides, which are the two tides of highest range each month. The spring tides occur shortly after the full and new phases of the moon, when the sun and moon pull together to produce the greatest extremes. A bore is unlikely to appear on neap tides, which occur on the quarter phases of the moon when the sun and moon pull at right angles to one another, minimizing the tide range.

All factors needed to produce powerful bores are present at the head of the Gulf of California (Figure 31.1). Spring tides range up to 30 ft (9.1 m). North of Puerto Peñasco and San Felipe the gulf quickly narrows toward the three mouths of the river, funneling the powerful incoming tide into the river channel. At the top of Isla Montague the mouths converge into a single channel that crosses a mudflat plain having a surface gradient of only 10 in/mi (15.7 cm/km) in the first 23 mi (37 km) (Thompson 1968). As tidal water surges into the river channel, it encounters friction from the shallow bottom and opposing current of the river, which steepens it into a wave or series of waves. Where the water is shallow enough, the upper water spills over and the wave breaks into a bore (Clancy 1968).

Early Observations

The first European known to experience a Colorado River bore was Hernando de Alarcón, who entered the estuary with three ships on August 26,

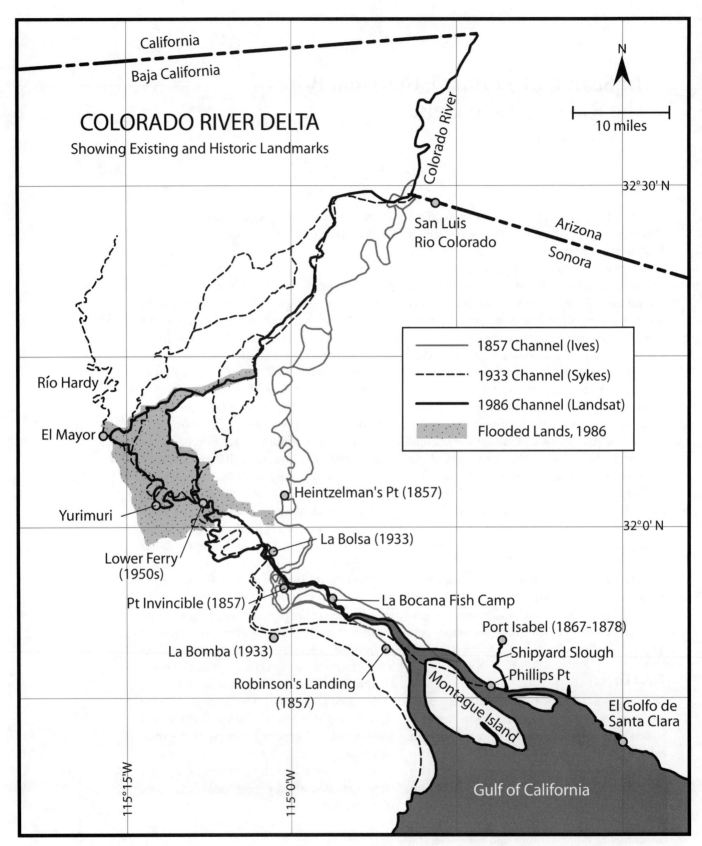

Figure 31.1. *The Colorado River delta: prominent historical and contemporary landmarks and the alignments of the main river channels in 1857 (from Ives 1861), 1933 (from Sykes 1937), and 1986 (based on Landsat imagery and my field observations). (Map by Diane Boyer and Peter Griffiths)*

1540, in support of the Coronado expedition. As the tide ebbed fiercely, the fleet ran aground on the river's sandy bottom, and then the powerful ebb current welled up and rushed over the deck of Alarcón's flagship. Alarcón wrote, "If a great surge of the sea had not come and driven our ship right up and given her leave, as it were, to breathe awhile, we had there been drowned" (Freeman 1923). This account is very unusual in that Alarcón credits the bore with rescuing his ship. As we will see, *el burro* is more often cited as a destructive force.

In July 1826 retired British navy lieutenant Robert William Hale Hardy entered the river with the private 25-ton schooner *Bruja,* seeking to replenish his food supply from the Indians. On July 22 Hardy observed a small bore, "boiling up full eighteen inches above the surface, and roaring like the rapids of Canada." His observation of an 18-in (45.7-cm) bore is about what would be expected on July 22, which was four days past spring tide, as the sun and moon were moving out of the alignment that created the biggest tides and bores. During the following week, while Hardy and his ship sat aground on a mid-channel bar, he reported no bores (Hardy 1977).

James Ohio Pattie descended the Colorado in January 1828 with a beaver-trapping party that included his father. On January 18 the trappers made camp on the lower river shortly after detecting a tidal influence in the river current. Pattie's father took the first watch and sounded the alarm when he heard the approach of a rushing noise, which he took for a rainstorm. The group stopped its hurried preparations for rain as the bore approached in the light of an almost-full moon. Pattie recounted: "We landsmen from the interior, and unaccustomed to such movements of water, stood contemplating with astonishment the rush of the tide coming in from the sea, in conflict with the current of the river. At the point of conflict there arose a high ridge of water, over which came the sea current, combing down like water over a milldam" (Pattie 1930). The river quickly rose to cover the campsite in 3 ft (0.9 m) of water. The bore forced the trappers to abandon their trip down the river and strike out overland toward the Pacific coast.

U.S. army lieutenant George Derby entered the estuary in late December 1850 with the schooner *Invincible.* Derby's objective was to determine the

feasibility of the Colorado as a route of supply for an army post (eventually known as Fort Yuma) to be established near the junction with the Gila. Derby first saw a tidal bore near Point Invincible on January 2, 1851, the day of the new moon. About 4 ft (1.2 m) in height, it extended all the way across the river channel: "This huge comber moved steadily onward, occasionally breaking as it rushed over the shoals of Gull and Pelican islands; passing the vessel, which it swung around on its course, it continued up the river. This phenomenon was of daily occurrence until about the time of the neap tides, and shows the truth of Hardy's assertion, 'there is no such thing as slack-water in the river Colorado'" (Derby 1852).

Note that Derby says the wave broke only when it encountered shallow water. When the slope of the shallow bottom is less than 3 degrees, as in the Colorado River estuary, a bore will develop into a spilling breaker. When the wave starts to spill, the ratio of water depth to wave height is about 1.2 to 1 (Fox 1983). The bore observed by Derby would have spilled when the water depth was $4 \times 1.2 = 4.8$ ft (1.5 m) or less. Elsewhere the bore was a smooth, nonbreaking undular wave similar to the one pictured in Figure 31.2.

The combined assessment of Derby and Major Samuel Heintzelman, commander of the Yuma post, convinced private parties that the river was feasible for navigation (Leavitt 1943). The first steamboat entered service between the estuary and Fort Yuma in 1852. In 1857 the army dispatched Lt. Joseph C. Ives to determine the upriver head of navigation. Instead of ascending the river in one of the private boats already operating, Ives elected to bring his own prefabricated steamboat for assembly at Robinson's Landing near Isla Montague in the estuary. The prefabricated boat was arguably a waste of taxpayers' money, but the month-long assembly period gave Ives plenty of time to observe and document the workings of the tides. It also gave his cartographer, Baron F. W. von Engloffstein, the time needed to precisely map the river's mouth and lower channels (Krygier 1997). Ives first witnessed the bore by the light of a full moon on November 30, 1857:

> About nine o'clock, while the tide was still running out rapidly, we heard, from the direction of the Gulf, a deep booming sound, like the noise of a distant waterfall. Every moment it became louder

Figure 31.2. Southeasterly view of el burro *on October 12, 1985, passing the Tide Pole site. The waves are moving upstream from right to left. Note that the lead wave is breaking only in the shallow water near the east (Sonoran) bank of the river. The bank is prominently visible near the breaking lead wave but has nearly disappeared under flood waters by the end of the wave set. The downstream channel in the middle background is already full to overflowing. (Photo by Steve Nelson)*

and nearer, and in half an hour a great wave, several feet in height, could be distinctly seen, flashing and sparkling in the moonlight, extending from one bank to the other, and advancing swiftly upon us. While it was only a few hundred yards distant, the ebb tide continued to flow by at a rate of three miles an hour. A point of land and an exposed bar close under our lee broke the wave into several long swells, and as these met the ebb the broad sheet around us boiled up and foamed like the surface of a cauldron, and then, with scarcely a moment of slack water, the whole went whirling by in the opposite direction. In a few moments the low rollers had passed the island and united again in a single bank of water, which swept up the narrow channel with the thunder of a cataract. At a turn not far distant it disappeared from view, but for a long time, in the stillness of the night, the roaring of the huge mass could be heard reverberating among the windings of the river, till at last it became faint and lost in the distance. (Ives 1861:28)

Note that the bore was already well developed when it passed Ives's location just above Isla Montague. Later observers reported the zone of *el burro*'s genesis to be about 8 mi (13 km) downstream from Robinson's Landing, midway along the east side of Isla Montague near Phillips Point (Sykes 1937; Leigh 1941). Although there are no reports of bores forming on the remote west side of Isla Montague, it seems likely that they develop there as well.

Godfrey Sykes made his first downriver voyage to the gulf in late 1890 (Sykes 1891–1892, 1893–1902, 1903; see D. Boyer, this volume, chapter 13). He learned about "the great tidal-bore, or 'burro,' as it was known to the Mexicans along the border settlements" (Sykes 1944:214), from river steamboat captain Jack Mellon. Following Captain Mellon's advice, he and companion Charles McLean tied off their sailboat to a mid-channel snag and awaited the bore. They were "suddenly involved in chaos, with a maelstrom of swirling water all around us," but successfully rode out the bore's passage and made it to the gulf the following morning (Sykes 1944:215).

Sykes's account indicates that the bore's Mexican name, *el burro,* was in common usage by 1890. The name was probably derived from the expression *burro de agua,* which in Mexico and Caribbean countries refers to a large wave of water (*Harper-Collins Unabridged Spanish Dictionary,* 5th ed., s.v. "burro de agua").

Hazard to Navigation

The bore claimed a number of vessels during the years of commercial navigation on the lower river. The schooner *Victoria* was lost on her maiden voyage in the mid-1860s (variously reported as 1864 or 1867). After arriving at the mouth of the river with a load of lumber, the captain dropped anchor, apparently unaware of the extreme tides at that location. According to Sykes (1937), the *Victoria*'s back was broken as she settled onto the bar with the receding tide. Hendricks (1990) reported that the ship came to rest on the fluke of her anchor, holing her badly. The bore then broke up the damaged ship and scattered her cargo throughout the lower delta. No lives were lost.

In 1874 the river steamboat *Nina Tilden* was retired to a mooring in Shipyard Slough near Port Isabel, a staging area in the estuary where cargo was transferred from oceangoing to river vessels. Caught by an exceptionally heavy bore, the vessel broke her moorings, got caught broadside, and rolled over, blocking the channel until she was scrapped (Leavitt 1943; Lingenfelter 1978; Sykes 1937).

The 36-ton steamer (also sometimes referred to as a gas-powered motor launch) *Topolobampo* was lost to *el burro* in 1922. Accounts of this incident are contradictory, but according to news reports appearing in the *Calexico (California) Chronicle* on November 20 and 21, 1922, the accident occurred in the moonless early morning hours of November 19. The captain brought the ship 20 mi (32 km) up the river to the tiny seaport of La Bomba, apparently without regard for tidal conditions. The ship ran aground shortly before midnight and was struck by a bore that was reportedly 15 to 20 ft (4.6–6.1 m) high, which lifted the boat "high on its crest from the middle." The vessel broke in two under the strain and then capsized.

Many of the 125 persons on board (migrant laborers, their families, and crew) were pitched into the churning waters, and only 36 survived.

A number of variations of the *Topolobampo* story are encountered in the literature. Waters (1946) wrote that the disaster happened on a full moon, which does not square with the November 19 date. Other accounts place the incident in the month of September 1921 or 1922, with a loss of about 130 lives (Gordon 1924; Sykes 1937). There is no indication that more than one ship was lost during this period, and it is likely that all accounts refer to the same event. I am inclined to place the most weight on the contemporary newspaper accounts and to accept that the incident occurred on November 19, 1922, with the loss of 85 lives.

Although the bore was undoubtedly a large one, the height of the wave reported by the *Chronicle* is questionable. The bore apparently took people on the ship by surprise, and it would have been difficult to judge its height accurately in the pitch-black night. Hendricks (1990) speculated that bore waves up to 15 ft (4.6 m) high could have been produced during the great floods that occurred in pre-dam days. Such waves would be consistent with those produced on high-flow rivers such as the Amazon. Flows of up to 150,000 cubic feet per second (cfs) or (4,250 m^3/sec) occurred during the historic June flood (Sykes 1937), but the grounding of the *Topolobampo* at low tide indicates that the river was not in flood on November 19, 1922. Captains generally avoided the delta during major floods (Leavitt 1943), which may account for the lack of reliable reports of such great waves.

Twentieth-Century Changes

The twentieth century brought major changes to the estuary, some natural and some human-caused. These changes disrupted the balance between river flow and tidal forces, thereby modifying the behavior of *el burro*. The first change was a natural westward shift in the river's channel. Throughout the second half of the nineteenth century the river below Yuma followed a relatively direct course to the sea, along the eastern side of the delta near the Sonoran Mesa (Figure 31.1). The untamed river flooded each spring, each time depositing suspended sediments onto its banks. Deposition over time gradually aggraded, or raised, the channel above the level of the lands to the west. In 1909 the river broke out of this raised channel to flow westward into an indistinct and ever-changing network of sloughs. The river gave up much of its sediment load as it wandered sluggishly though the maze. Most of the resulting clarified water eventually found its way into the Río Hardy, which became the main channel to tidewater. Sykes (1937) attributed the deepening of the Hardy channel to tidal action. It is also probable that the increased flow of clarified water scoured and back-cut the channel, extending the head of tidewater further upstream. By the early 1930s a well-defined and unobstructed tidal channel extended inland more than 40 mi (64 km) from the river's mouth (Sykes 1937). *El burro* could now travel up this deep channel well into the Río Hardy wetlands.

With the closure of Hoover Dam in 1935, the seasonal flooding that once sustained the delta stopped completely for six years as Lake Mead filled. Although some floods occurred between 1941 and the completion of Glen Canyon Dam in 1963, they were much smaller than in pre-dam days (Luecke et al. 1999). Despite the reduced flow, *el burro* continued to be seen in the 1940s and 1950s. Viewing a bore from the Sonoran shore in late 1940, Leigh (1941) reported, "Its crest, a wall of white water about four and a half feet high, seemed to stretch away for miles." He reported the bore to be eroding the riverbanks in many places and expressed concern that its unrestrained power might actually breach the low crest of land separating the gulf from the Imperial Valley (Leigh 1941). In October 1953 Mose and Estelle Daniels reported extensive tidal flooding in the farmlands of the lower delta. Encamped on a small bluff near La Corvina, about 12 mi (19 km) above La Bomba, they saw both midday and midnight bores during their three-day stay (Daniels & Daniels 1954).

Releases into Mexico virtually ceased after Glen Canyon Dam was closed in 1963. From that time until Lake Powell filled in 1980, very little freshwater reached the delta (Luecke et al. 1999). During this period the tides were free to work on the intertidal channel without the influence of river flow. Instead of cutting through to the Imperial Valley as some had feared, the tides gradually plugged the channel. A sandbar obstruction that prevented the passage of small power boats had been reported in the lower river channel as early as 1956 (Kira 2000). By 1972, when its presence was noted on an aerial photo, the bar had sealed off the channel completely. In 1979 the Secretaría de Agricultura y Recursos Hidráulicos (SARH) of Mexico reported that the sandbar began about 7 mi (11 km) below the confluence with the Río Hardy and extended downstream another 18 mi (29 km) to a point about 14 mi (23 km) above Isla Montague. It rose to a height of 6 ft (1.8 m) above the normal river channel bottom, with 5 mi (8 km) of its top above the water surface. The channel downstream from the sandbar was now a slough. At all but the highest spring tides the river was completely cut off from the sea (Bureau of Reclamation 1975; U.S. Army Corps of Engineers 1982).

The bar obstructing the channel was built by the same tidal forces that maintain a tidal berm along the riverbanks and coastal margins of the mudflats. The local tidal regime is such that the lowest low tide of the day directly precedes the highest high (Figure 31.3). This type of tide typically floods faster than it ebbs, producing strong incoming currents that pick up bottom sediments and deposit them in coastal shoal water areas during high water slack (Thompson 1968). When present, *el burro* enhances the process. Advancing bore waves accentuate bottom scour and transport sediments upstream to be deposited in intertidal zones (Chanson 2001). As a result, the shores of the estuary and the coastal margins of the mudflats are slightly elevated in a broad berm. The flowing river maintains a breach in the berm through which its waters reach the sea. After the river's flow was curtailed at midcentury, tidal action first obstructed the channel with a bar and eventually closed the coastal berm across the channel, cutting the river off from the gulf.

The River Returns, 1983

Releases of freshwater into Mexico resumed after Lake Powell filled in 1980. In 1983 runoff from an unusually heavy Rocky Mountain winter snow pack passed down through the full reservoirs and crossed the international boundary (Martin 1989). When this water encountered the tidal berm, it flooded the intertidal mudflats and created a vast area of interconnected freshwater lakes and marshes (Figure 31.4). Another heavy winter in the Rockies kept the water coming in 1984. During this time I was living and working in El Centro, California, where the flooding was big news. In October 1984 two friends and I decided to charter a plane and see it for ourselves. The magnitude of the flooding was awe-inspiring. The entire delta

was under water, from the northern levees almost to San Felipe and from the Laguna Salada to the Ciénega de Santa Clara. Water from this huge delta wetland overtopped the coastal berm in many small channels. Erosion was cutting each little channel back upstream, gradually breaching the berm and slowly draining the flooded lands. Some of these channels drained directly into the gulf, but most flowed into the old river estuary.

In late November 1984 I paddled a kayak from Yurimuri, on the lower Río Hardy, across the flooded lands, through one of the breaches in the tidal berm, and down the estuary to El Golfo, Sonora. It was the first of a series of recreational kayak and power-boat trips I was to make in the delta over the next three years. My primary interest was in monitoring the development of a new tidewater channel. By February 1987, just before high river flows were curtailed, the new channel had reached the site of the old Lower Ferry, which became tidal again after being cut off from the sea for a quarter century.

I first saw *el burro* on October 12, 1985, while flying over the delta with friends from the Arizona Historical Society (Figure 31.2). We were scouting a new route through the flooded wilderness below in preparation for a paddle trip from the International Boundary to El Golfo. Our overflight fell on the new moon, with a predicted tide range of 19.5 ft (5.9 m) at Puerto Peñasco and perhaps 30 ft (9 m) at the mouth of the river below us. About 8 mi (13 km) above Isla Montague we spotted a closely spaced set of a dozen waves moving rapidly upstream. The initial wave appeared to be 4 or 5 ft (1.2–1.5 m) high, with each succeeding wave a little smaller than the one before. A small motorboat, or *panga*, raced upriver just ahead of the advancing waves. The *panga* driver was a local fisherman, wise in the ways of *el burro*. Halfway through an s-shaped double bend in the channel, he turned to face the oncoming bore from the inside of the bend.

As the bore approached the first bend, the perfect wave pattern broke up. Although its structure became confused, the tide rushed around the bend with undiminished speed, quickly covering the exposed mud bars along the inside bank. A large breaking wave appeared opposite the waiting *panga* but did not reach over to the boat's protected location. The *panga* swirled in the eddies as the channel quickly filled with water but never

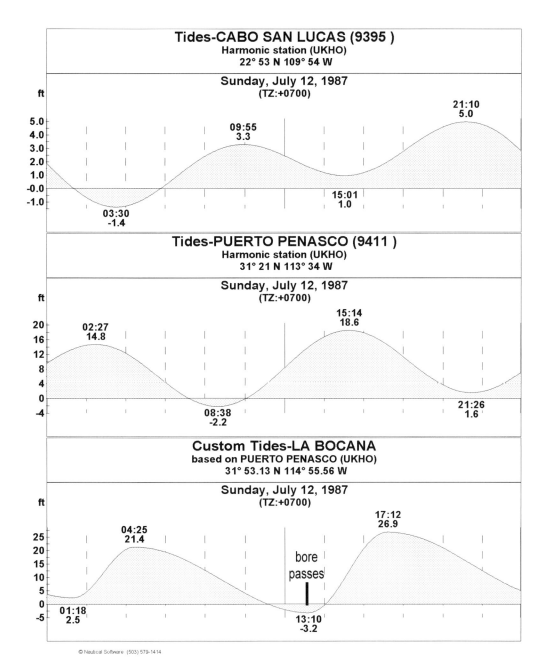

Figure 31.3. *Tide prediction graphs for Cabo San Lucas, Puerto Peñasco, and La Bocana for July 12, 1987. Note the different height scales on the left of each graph. Times of tidal events for La Bocana are based on the author's observations. The tidal range for La Bocana is an estimate based on historic data from Thompson 1968. The tide graphs were generated by* Tides and Currents Pro for Windows *from Nobeltec Nautical Software.*

appeared to be in any danger. Soon the regular series of a dozen waves re-formed just upstream of the second bend, to continue upriver as before. The fishermen, now riding a fast upstream current in the rapidly rising water behind *el burro,* began to fish as our plane turned back toward the river's mouth. There was no bore when we paddled through the area a week later on the quarter moon. It would be more than a year before I had an opportunity to see *el burro* from river level.

Seeking dry places to camp, I avoided the bore on most boating trips. But others were descending the river with the specific objective of seeing *el burro.* Bill Moody and a group of friends

from Yuma, Arizona, paddled from Yurimuri to El Golfo in late February 1986. On the night of February 23 the group camped on high ground on a bend in the river 8.3 mi (13.4 km) above Isla Montague and watched a bore by the light of the full moon. It passed their location at 12:05 a.m. MST (Bill Moody, personal communication 1986). A month later Charles Bowden and Bill Broyles observed both midday and midnight bores during a paddle from Yuma to El Golfo. Bowden reported the midday bore to be about 5 ft (1.5 m) high (Bowden 1987).

On a boat trip down the river in May 1986 I found a number of new fish camps in the lower

Figure 31.4. *Landsat 5 satellite image of the Colorado River delta on June 9, 1984. Colorado River water is trapped behind the coastal tidal berm and plug in the river channel, flooding a vast area of intertidal mudflats and Río Hardy wetlands. Small overflow channels are cutting back through the tidal berm at more than twenty points, gradually draining the flooded lands.*

Image labels: flooded lands (lakes and marshes); tidal berm; Gulf of California

estuary. A refrigerator truck was parked at one of them! The flooded area had now receded enough to allow the local fishermen to drive almost to the mouth of the river. This was exciting news: I decided to return by truck to get a closer look at the bore. It was a trip I would repeat eight times over the next two years in the company of good friends who in addition to companionship provided important logistical and photographic support.

Observations at La Bocana, 1986–1988

After some exploration along the levee system that protects delta farmland, we eventually found an informal fishermen's truck track that provided access to a fish camp called La Bocana, which had recently been established on the Sonoran bank 11.3 mi (18.3 km) upriver from Isla Montague. The truck track closely paralleled the riverbank for a mile and a half (2.4 km) above La Bocana. We soon found several other excellent bore viewpoints downstream from the fish camp. The most important site was located 8.8 mi (14.1 km) above Isla Montague, where someone had placed a graduated tide-gauging pole in a stand of Indian wheat (Palmer's saltgrass, *Distichlis palmeri*) fronting a straight reach of the river that often produced nicely formed bores. The Tide Pole (which has since washed into the river channel) became the first stop on each bore-watching trip, unless it was

cut off by muddy conditions resulting from the previous night's high tide. Farther to the northwest another track accessed an upper observation point near the historic location of La Bolsa, 21.2 mi (34.2 km) above Isla Montague.

Several tide prediction tools from various U.S. and Mexican sources were used to plan our trips. The closest tide information readily available was for Puerto Peñasco, so it became the basis of our predictions. Tide range values and predicted times of tidal events appearing in this chapter were standardized using the MAR V0.5 harmonic tide prediction software program developed by Juan Ignacio Gonzáles of El Centro de Investigación Científica y de Educación Superior de Ensenada, Baja California (CICESE).

The best days for a bore-watching trip are those having the greatest tide range. Bill Moody and party had observed a bore on a tide with a range of 20.1 ft (6.1 m) at Puerto Peñasco, but did the range have to be that big? On our first trip (October 18–19, 1986) we observed no bore on a midday tide with a range of 15.0 ft (4.6 m) and a very small bore on a midnight tide having a range of 17.9 ft (5.5 m). Afterward we limited trips to days when the Puerto Peñasco range was predicted to be 19.0 ft (5.8 m) or greater.

Returning on February 27, 1987, we learned that a 19-ft range could produce a very impressive bore. The previous evening's high tide left the mud flats too wet for us to reach the Tide Pole, so we observed the bore from a bend in the river 1.1 mi (1.8 km) upstream. At 12:50 p.m. MST a glint of light down near the Tide Pole caught my eye. It was *el burro!* The wave looked big and menacing: in places it broke over the top of the west bank. A cloud of wheeling gulls and terns advanced with it. For a few moments, the wave disappeared behind a downstream bend, and all we could see of its progress was the avian cloud. The bore passed us at exactly 1:00 p.m. MST. As waves reverberated back and forth in the bend, the birds paused to hover and dive in the chaos of churning muddy water. Frenzied birds (Figure 31.5) accompanied all the bores we observed before a drop in river flow after the end of March 1987. We continued to see bores after the flow dropped, but few birds accompanied them.

The tide prediction graphs in Figure 31.3 illustrate the relationship between tide phases and the bore. Tides on the west coast of North America are mixed, having unequal highs and lows each day (Cabo San Lucas graph). In the northern gulf (Puerto Peñasco and La Bocana graphs) the lower low water immediately precedes the higher high water, producing powerful flood tides. In the open sea the periods of the flood and ebb are nearly equal, but in the narrow channel of the estuary at La Bocana the period of the flood becomes shorter and the ebb longer.

The bore is the abrupt arrival of the flood tide, and its passage occurs at the moment of low tide. Low water at La Bocana occurs about four and a half hours after the low at Puerto Peñasco. Low tide at La Bolsa, 10.1 mi (16.3 km) above La Bocana, occurs about an hour and fifteen minutes later. The time of the bore's passage was fairly consistent at individual points, ranging from +4:17 to +4:26 at the Tide Pole (three observations), +4:24 to +4:40 at La Bocana (two observations), and +5:34 to +5:36 at La Bolsa (two observations). I feel reasonably confident in advising anyone interested in seeing *el burro* to be in place at La Bocana no later than four hours after the Puerto Peñasco low.

Environmental factors affect the time of a bore's arrival. It should arrive earlier when strong winds blow inland from the sea (in the case of the Colorado River, south or southeast winds blowing up the gulf), when freshwater flow is present, channels are well scoured, and barometric pressure is low. Factors tending to delay its arrival include strong winds blowing away from land (in this case, north or northwest winds blowing down the gulf), an absence of freshwater, unscoured or meandering channels, and high barometric pressure (Rowbotham 1983).

Although no measurements of wave heights were made, the bores were noticeably smaller following the reduction in river flow after March 1987. From October 1986 through February 1987 the volume of water coming into Mexico at the Southern International Boundary averaged around 10,000 cfs (283 m³/sec). After early March, flows at the International Boundary were generally less than 900 cfs (25 m³/sec), sometimes dropping to very low levels, although the full effect of this reduction was not seen in the lower estuary until after the end of March. Bores occurring through March 1987 produced breaking waves estimated

Figure 31.5. El burro *on March 29, 1987, viewed from the Tide Pole site. The bore is advancing from left to right. Note that the wave (estimated to be 4–5 ft high) is breaking along both banks of the river but not in the deeper water of midchannel. Circling gulls and terns are looking for food churned up by the wave. (Photo by Lynn Anderson)*

to be 4 to 5 ft (1.2–1.5 m) high along the margins of the channel in shallow water (Figure 31.5). Waves in the deeper water of midchannel showed less tendency to break and were generally not as high. Bores after March 1987 generally produced breaking waves 2 to 3 ft (0.6–0.9 m) high. The smaller waves tended to break across a wider portion of the channel because of shallower conditions (Figure 31.6). An exception to this general rule occurred on August 9, 1987, when *el burro* was nearly as large as its pre-March predecessors, probably enhanced by strong southeasterly winds that blew all day long. The importance of river flow was driven home when I revisited La Bocana on April 25, 2002, when no freshwater at all was flowing into Mexico. Despite a Puerto Peñasco tide range of over 20 ft (6.1 m), only a tiny and intermittent bore appeared.

El burro's upstream speed is impressive. On several occasions we paced it with a truck for about a mile along the straight reach above La Bocana fish camp (Figure 31.7). In each case the truck's speedometer registered about 12 mph (19 km/hr). More precise estimates were derived by recording the time of passage between the Tide Pole and La Bocana Bend, where the truck track left the river above the fish camp. The March 29 bore (Figure 31.3) covered the 3.9 mi (6.2 km) between these points in 21 minutes (11.1 mph, 17.9 km/hr), while the June 13 bore took 22 minutes (10.6 mph, 17.1 km/hr). The higher the wave and the deeper the water, the faster *el burro* moves. The faster March 29 bore was the bigger of the

Figure 31.6. El burro *on May 14, 1987, viewed from the Tide Pole site. Note that this bore, which occurred after a substantial reduction in freshwater flow, is breaking across the entire channel—an indication of shallow conditions. (Photo by Phil Ashworth)*

Figure 31.7. El burro *on May 14, 1987, above La Bocana fish camp. This bore is typical of the smaller bores (wave heights of 2–3 ft) observed after the reduction in river flow in March 1987. (Photo by Phil Ashworth)*

served farther downstream. The larger of the two, that of August 9, averaged 9.1 mph (14.6 km/hr) between La Bocana and La Bolsa, whereas the smaller bore of April 16 averaged 8.4 mph (13.5 km/hr) over the same distance.

Throughout history, and despite many changes to the delta over the past century, *el burro* has roared up the estuary for several days each fortnight, sometimes scouring out and sometimes filling in the river's channel. It continues to this day, smaller at times when the river is dry or nearly so, and finding some of its old power and strength when the river returns or when abnormally large tides and southeast winds cooperate. This unique and enduring part of the estuarine environment plays an important role in shaping the intertidal wetlands. Were it easier to see, it would be popularly regarded as one of the region's natural wonders. Those fortunate enough to see it will never forget the experience.

Acknowledgments

The following people assisted in the research for this chapter by generously sharing their time, skills, and information over the past 18 years: Rick André, Bill Broyles, Don Bufkin, Bob Callahan, Richard Felger, Al Goff, Steve Hayden, Bill Hendricks, Sandy Lanham, Andy Masich, and Anita Williams. Bob Webb reviewed a preliminary draft and provided many helpful suggestions. Special thanks to Lynn Anderson and Phil Ashworth for providing the excellent photos of *el burro* and to Diane Boyer and Peter Griffiths, who prepared the map appearing as Figure 31.1. Diane Boyer also provided access to journals and maps prepared by her great-grandfather, Godfrey Sykes. Finally, I would like to thank all the many good friends who joined me in memorable adventures in search of *el burro*.

Tide range values and predicted times of tidal events appearing in this chapter were calculated using the MAR V0.5 harmonic tide prediction software program developed by Juan Ignacio Gonzáles of El Centro de Investigación Científica y de Educación Superior de Ensenada, Baja California (CICESE). This software produces tide predictions and solar and lunar ephemeral data up to two years into the future and also has a historical prediction capability extending back 500 years. For twentieth-century tides, predictions were also

two, and there was more freshwater in the channel that day. Increased freshwater river flow also tends to increase the speed of a bore, because of increased depth, although this is partially offset by the force of the flow against which the bore must run (Tricker 1964; Rowbotham 1983).

On August 9, 1987, and April 16, 1988, we tracked bores as far upstream as La Bolsa, 10.1 mi (16.3 km) above La Bocana. La Bolsa is about 15 mi (24 km) downstream from the old Lower Ferry location where large bores were reported in the 1950s. Both bores we observed were much diminished by the time they reached La Bolsa and were clearly moving much more slowly than when obrun using the *Tides and Currents Pro for Windows,* version 2.5, software program with licensed United Kingdom Hydrographic Office (UKHO) data. The CICESE data generally predicts a slightly greater (4% on average) tide range for Puerto Peñasco than UKHO. Predicted times for tidal events correlated closely (±15 min) between the two prediction tools. The tide graphs used in Figure 31.3 were generated by *Tides and Currents Pro for Windows* from Nobeltec Nautical Software, (503) 579–1414.

The website of the Tidal Bore Research Society is http://tidal-bore.tripod.com/index.html.

Part Five

CONSERVATION

Sonoran Desert National Park

STEWART L. UDALL

I grew up in the country, up on the Colorado Plateau. When you grow up in a small farming community and you raise your own food, you're living close to the land, close to animals. We worked with horses all the time. So when I practiced law in Tucson after World War II, I was attracted to the Sonoran Desert. I remember taking my boys when they were five and six onto Pusch Ridge just north of Tucson, and we had a very exciting time because we spooked a desert big horn sheep, and he jumped down close in front of us. Then later, before I was a congressman, some friends and I did a hike up to Baboquivari. We did it from the Tohono O'odham side, and that was a wonderful experience. You couldn't live in Tucson then and live as we did and not have a tremendous appreciation for this very wonderful desert.

I had friends in Tucson who were "classic" conservationists of the old school, and I used to do hikes with them. I remember going up to Mount Wrightson. Again, I took my kids on these trips, and we talked on those walks about the conservation movement, the conservation tradition, and of course its beginning, nearly a hundred years ago now, with the conservation movement of President Theodore Roosevelt, a president leading it, Gifford Pinchot and others, the Sierra Club and John Muir and so on. We talked about those things, and of course I did a lot of reading, too. So, I came to the job of congressman and secretary of the interior with a pretty strong awareness of conservation values.

We had a tremendous run in the 1960s of expanding the national park system—national seashores, four new national parks, one in the Cascades, another Canyonlands in Utah. It was a period when there was strong support in Congress, bipartisan support, for these park projects, and I was able, therefore, all during the 1960s, to

not only entertain ideas from members of Congress but to originate things.

The idea of a Sonoran Desert National Park, I guess I have to claim some credit for that. In the last year that I was secretary, which was President Johnson's final year, as it turned out, I proposed a series of national monuments that would be created by the president signing a proclamation. There were two or three huge ones in Alaska; I proposed the enlargement of two national monuments: Arches and Capitol Reef in Utah. Those I made with a recommendation that the president expand Capitol Reef boundaries into BLM land and make it four times larger. Simultaneously, I made a recommendation that Congress make it a national park, because only Congress can create national parks.

The final one that I put in, I did because I thought it was a wonderful idea, but I also did it to show my bona fides that I wasn't picking on other states by asking the president to create monuments. This proposal would combine Organ Pipe Cactus National Monument with the Cabeza Prieta, and it would give you something over a million acres [1.2 million acres] of a national park right on the international boundary, in what is the real heart of the Sonoran Desert.

There probably would have been some lively discussion. Friends of mine, who were wildlifers and who loved the Cabeza Prieta Wildlife Refuge, didn't like it, so it turned out later. But this idea didn't surface; that's the way national monument proposals are. We didn't broadcast it; it didn't receive a lot of publicity. I wondered afterward whether Senator Hayden, then in his last term, would have been for it. But I didn't talk to people, and it didn't emerge as a big public dispute. I simply was proposing to the president of the United States that as he left office, as other presidents have done, that he sign national monument

533

proclamations creating new national monuments in Alaska, Utah, and in Arizona.

I had talked to the national park people at high levels, and as I recall they brought in the superintendent from Organ Pipe Cactus, and there were discussions—after all, international boundaries and state lines have no meaning when you are talking about huge natural areas. They pointed out to me that the area where organ pipe cactus grew extended into Mexico. I know we talked about the Pinacate as a remarkable geographic area in Mexico. I think there were preliminary talks of an international park then, not so much with government officials but by conservationists in Sonora. But I have to say, in all honesty, the government of Mexico at that time didn't seem to have a very high priority of having national parks jointly with the United States on the border.

The international boundary is so artificial. This was to be a huge new international park, the Sonoran Desert Park, since the Sonoran Desert stretched off into Mexico, and there were some wonderful areas there. Of course it was arid, there were very few roads, and it was protected; that surely, as I recall, was part of our discussion. But the idea of an international park, the U.S. and Mexico, was kind of a dream at that point. We didn't get down to practical cases.

I did outdoor trips with Lady Bird Johnson, the president's wife, and we did a two-day float in the Big Bend, on the river. I don't recall whether Mexican officials joined us, but there was a lot of talk, at that time, about that as another area that could be, in effect, a joint national park. Well, we were already doing this in a couple of cases with Canada, where on the international border we had park lands that were jointly administered in a compatible way.

You have to remember, the president didn't do what I had recommended. I thought of it later, and I was talking to someone a while back, that it would have been done, but I couldn't get Lyndon Johnson, as president, to be Lyndon Johnson. He balked at this, and he balked at the ones in Alaska. He did the two in Utah, to his credit, but he was the one that opposed it. As far as I know, he didn't talk to Senator Hayden and he didn't talk to others. But he rejected the big proposals and did the small proposals. Of course, at that point the idea died. It got some publicity at that point, and the next I heard was in the late 1970s and 1980s when I moved back to Arizona, and there were people in Tucson and there were conservation groups that began studying and looking at this, but now we had this new element, that there were people that they could talk to in the Mexican government and across the border. There were books published that were wonderful. One gave you this big picture of what a magnificent thing this would be to have a Sonoran Desert National Park, that could have been over two million acres, stretching on both sides of the border about equally. I just thought that was a marvelous idea.

It's a very complicated story. Articles were written about it, and I could refer you to them. There's a professor that wrote a study, and she looked at my oral history—and the lawyer that worked for President Johnson—it's kind of a mystery. You know Johnson—he liked to think big, he liked to do things big—so I had the Park Service prepare a wonderful book with photographs, a huge one, and we presented it to him. Then, at the end, I wanted to show him that most of the presidents since Teddy Roosevelt had exercised the power under the Antiquities Act of creating national monuments. Well, not all of them had, but most of them had, and who was one of the ones that really wielded the pen and did big things in his last weeks? Herbert Hoover. Herbert Hoover did Death Valley National Monument in California and Glacier Bay in Alaska, a total of four million acres.

What I was proposing to President Johnson was seven million acres—that would have been a record, in terms of acreage, and I just said it right out for him, "Mr. President, if four million acres was just about right for Herbert Hoover, seven million is right for Lyndon Johnson." But he didn't . . . he balked, and I don't know exactly why. He was having his lawyers and other people talk to me. There were some other things that were under way. We had a break, a very sharp break, the last month that I was in office. We'd gotten along very well, and he, for reasons that I'll never understand, he didn't do it. And he waited until ten o'clock in the morning of his last day in office, two hours before he went to the inauguration of Richard Nixon, that's when he finally made his decisions, and it was a strange thing. I'll have to write about it sometime. President Johnson did these two wonderful things in Utah, but they were probably about 400,000 acres, not seven million. He rejected the big ones.

Was there any resistance to the Sonoran Desert National Park plan from military people with regard to this plan? We're talking about 28 years ago [1969]; the answer is "no" because, number one, this didn't receive a lot of publicity and, number two, I was not proposing that we take that military gunnery range or bombing range associated with Luke Field. They named it after Senator Goldwater; I don't know if he wanted it or not. But, that is part of the Sonoran Desert. Ultimately, when they no longer use it, that too could be part of this international park. They might have opposed it if they knew about it, but I don't think they knew because it didn't get all that much publicity. This fight between President Johnson that was going on behind the veil, as it were . . . but if I had been proposing to take part of the gunnery range, I would have had to have gone to the secretary of defense and I'm sure they would have opposed it.

I have been encouraged from all that I have heard that there are discussions on both sides and that there are Mexican officials and citizens who see this as a wonderful thing to do together. I think the United States and Mexico are on a track now, with the new trade agreement and everything, of merging our societies and our values and so on. I think to have the kind of relationship we ought to want to have in the future, we ought to have the Mexican border be like the Canadian border where it's not a matter of contention, but where we work on joint things with mutual respect. I think for that reason, having an international park concept pushed forward could be a bond between the two countries, showing that we share the same values.

The environmental/ecological movement has grown, and it has gained international adherence, especially with the biosphere reserve idea, sponsored through the United Nations. These arbitrary international boundaries that are drawn all over the world are not related to ecological values or conservation values. I think the nations of the world see a common interest in preserving parts of the biosphere as parks, or preserving the biosphere as a whole, with regard to global warming, for example. I think this is a whole new change that has come about in the last 20 years, and I think it is very welcome. This Sonoran Desert Park could be an example that other nations could imitate, doing on a large scale, not something small but on a large scale, where you have a geographic area that is a common desert that two nations own.

If you proposed something of this scale today and it was in effect put out for public comments,

I'm sure that in Arizona—I don't know about Mexico—there would be very lively discussions. There might be heated opposition. Now fortunately the Cabeza Prieta is a wildlife refuge—there are no cattle there, no other intruding interests—and so the opposition I would think would not be too heavy or too large. But as the nation saw last September [1996], President Clinton created the Escalante–Grand Staircase National Monument in Utah, 1.7 million acres, larger than the Arizona one President Johnson turned down that I proposed to him. If you recall, this didn't get into the press until two or three weeks before it was done, and this is a great power that presidents have. They don't have to hold public hearings; maybe they should. In that case it was quietly proposed to the president, he took some soundings, but the public didn't know until about three weeks before it was done that it was being considered. That's one of the peculiarities of the power given to the president under the Antiquities Act of 1906, and of course President Teddy Roosevelt used it to preserve the Grand Canyon itself.

The Sonoran Desert National Park was like Clinton did in 1996 in Utah. I didn't put the idea out publicly; therefore I didn't have to muster support. I had to convince the president of the United States to use the power that he had, and of course that power extends only over publicly owned land. Organ Pipe was public—it had been created—and the Cabeza Prieta was a national wildlife refuge, so the president had the power to do it. I wasn't in a situation where I had to get the Audubon Society or other groups pushing and making a lot of noise. In fact, I was a bit fearful that if we had too much publicity, that the president might decline, because, say, "It sounds like the people in Arizona or the people in the Southwest don't want this; why are you proposing it, Mr. Udall?"

When it comes to land policies, conservation policies, urban livability, a lot of communities have a lot more to say about their future, and are saying it. I think Santa Fe in 1997 is a very good example, where you have a mountain ordinance to protect and stop development in the mountains and things of that kind. There are different kinds of communities, though, and it's hard to get action in Phoenix and Los Angeles or such huge communities now. In smaller communities a will to preserve or conserve can be developed, and if a little money is needed, it can be appropriated, and this is now being done in many places. Then we have some of the most wonderful work I know of today [being] done by the Nature Conservancy in Arizona. What they, a private organization, have done in the last 25 years is a wonderful thing. We are seeing the same thing here in Santa Fe with our little Santa Fe Conservancy.

I think we are building good relations with our neighboring countries, with which we share immense, long borders. There has been a lot of contention with Mexico, but I'm delighted to see a lot of it dying down. There's still a lot of problems. Some of them are environmental, but I think the sooner the two nations agree on conservation practices and agree on joint projects, the faster it will move along. The Canadians used to tell me that in terms of conservation concepts, "we lag behind you 20 years," and I see signs that Mexico too is catching up, and that encourages me.

Acknowledgments

From a taped interview by Jack Loeffler, Santa Fe, New Mexico, May 3, 1997. Transcribed by Luke Evans; coordinated by Gary Paul Nabhan. The full interview is archived with the Stewart Lee Udall Papers, Special Collections, University of Arizona Library, Tucson.

Thirty-Three

Conservation and Landscape Transformation in Northwestern Mexico

Alberto Búrquez and Angelina Martínez-Yrízar

Mexico is the fourth richest area in the world in terms of biodiversity (Challenger 1998; Flores & Geréz 1988; Mittermeier & Goettsch Mittermeier 1992). Efforts to set up nature reserves in Mexico have had three major periods: the beginning of the twentieth century, the mid-1930s, and from the 1980s onward. The early attempts were oriented toward protecting dense, tall temperate forests; at the time, tropical lowlands and drylands were considered more abundant and less valuable ecosystems. Despite the great emphasis given to temperate and more recently to wet lowland tropical forests, the largest share of the richness of Mexican species is in the drylands, which cover about 70 percent of the country and have a high degree of endemism (Rzedowski 1991a). Yet drylands have received little recognition as areas of high biodiversity, and until recently, limited efforts were made to protect them (Flores & Geréz 1988; Janzen 1988).

Protection of the environment in Mexico began at about the same time as in the United States. In 1876 Desierto de los Leones was the first protected area decreed to safeguard a small portion of the extensive pine and fir forests of central Mexico. Afterward the Mexican government attempted to copy, without much success, the structure of the National Park Service of the United States. The main emphasis was on preserving small areas considered national monuments. These were set aside mainly for recreation rather than for management or protection of biological diversity. This first reserve system added only nine areas in the 58 years following the establishment of the Desierto de los Leones reserve (Anaya et al. 1992).

In the late 1930s the director of Flora and Fauna, Miguel Angel de Quevedo, single-handedly launched an intense lobbying effort to protect natural areas in Mexico. He was a visionary concerned with the conservation of natural resources of immediate use such as forests, the protection of up-river basins from erosion, and the establishment of large wildlife ranges. As a result, about 800,000 ha distributed over 17 Mexican states were protected (Colosio 1993). However, these reserves were not part of a national development strategy and never received funds for management. Many reserves had, and still have, land ownership problems, and they were repeatedly used as land banks for future development (Anaya et al. 1992; INE/CONABIO 1995). Despite the long history of reserve designation in Mexico, until 1936 there was not a single protected area in Sonora, and by 1994 there was still no area in the state attaining minimum international management standards of protection, a striking contrast with its neighbor across the international border, which has an extensive reserve system dating back many decades.

In this chapter we describe the present extent and history of the reserves in northwestern Mexico and discuss the major threats to the region. As the largest changes in the landscape have occurred in the continental rather than the peninsular environments, and most of the northwestern border of Mexico occurs in Sonora, we concentrate our attention on this Mexican state.

Extant Reserves in Northwestern Mexico

The landscape of northwestern Mexico encompasses a wide range of biomes, including most of the major Mexican vegetation types (Brown 1982; Brown and Lowe 1980; Búrquez et al. 1992; Gentry 1942; Marshall 1957; Rzedowski 1978; White 1948). Sonora by itself is a major reservoir of what Rzedowski (1991a, b) calls the "genuinely Mexican species," species that have differentiated mainly in the arid and semiarid zones of northern Mexico. The Sonoran vascular flora is estimated to include about 5,000 species (Felger et al. 2001; Rzedowski 1991a). This figure represents about 20 percent of the Mexican flora in an area that is less than 10 percent of the country, which has an estimated national total of about 22,000 known species (Rzedowski 1991a). Even more striking figures are found for the fauna, which encompasses a rich, poorly known assemblage of species with Neo-tropical and Neartic affinities for almost every major taxon (Felger & Wilson 1995). Baja California holds numerous endemic species and is the only area in Mexico with extensive chaparral communities (Challenger 1998).

The dominant feature of northwestern Mexico is the Sonoran Desert. As defined by Shreve (1951), it covers a wide range of environments, from extremely xeric to relatively mesic. The former are readily recognized by the scant plant cover and severe climatic constraints. However, much of the desert owes its diversity to diffuse transitions into varied thornscrub and tropical deciduous forests (Búrquez 1997; Búrquez et al. 1999; Martínez-Yrízar et al. 2000). The desert also has oases that arise from seeps and artesian springs in deep canyons, and forests that once flourished in the great desert river deltas (Felger 1999, 2000; Yetman & Búrquez 1996). Toward the east the great Sierra Madre Occidental harbors, at different elevations, tropical deciduous forests, oak woodlands, pine-oak forests, and conifer forests (Búrquez et al. 1992; Felger & Johnson 1995), and on the shores of the Gulf of California, wetlands add to Sonora's overall diversity, including the northernmost mangrove swamps on the continent (Felger & Moser 1985; Felger et al. 2001). The great biodiversity found in Sonora and the peninsula of Baja California is primarily caused by the uneven distribution of precipitation, surface water, and climate, along with marked variation in topography, geological substrates, and soils (Brown 1982; Búrquez et al. 1999; Wiggins 1980).

In spite of the biological and habitat richness of northwestern Mexico, nature reserves were not decreed until 1936–39 (Vargas et al. 2000). During this period five areas were set aside in Sonora: (1) Arroyo de Nogales, near Nogales, (2) Sierras Los Ajos, Buenos Aires y La Púrica, southeast of Cananea, (3) Cajón del Diablo, southwest of Hermosillo, (4) Zona Protectora Forestal de la Ciudad de Hermosillo, and (5) Bavispe, near the town of Bavispe (Figure 33.1). This last reserve added new areas to the already decreed Sierras Los Ajos, Buenos Aires y La Púrica. These actions protected

about 282,000 ha, or approximately 1.5 percent of the state (Table 33.1), mainly pine and oak forests, although some portions of the Sonoran Desert were protected by Cajón del Diablo and Zona Protectora Forestal de la Ciudad de Hermosillo.

The first reserve in Baja California was decreed in 1928; it was a faraway island in the Pacific, Isla Guadalupe, with a unique vegetation and fauna (e.g., Moran 1996). The national park Sierra de San Pedro Mártir was established in 1947, and in 1962 the Constitución de 1857 reserve brought protection to about 5,000 ha of pine-oak and chaparral communities. One year later the sixth reserve in Sonora was set aside: Isla Tiburón. On paper the protected areas of Sonora amounted to about 403,000 ha (2.2% of the state) and those in Baja California only 103,000 ha (1.4% of the state). No reserves were decreed in Baja California Sur until 1972, when Complejo Lagunar Ojo de Liebre was set aside for the protection of the gray whale (Vargas, Escobar, & del Angel 2000). In 1978 a new edict added the midriff islands (Islas del Golfo) to the Isla Tiburón reserve, increasing the protected area by nearly 150,000 ha. A year later, about 30,000 ha in the magnificent Sierra El Pinacate were protected as a wildlife refuge in Sonora (Table 33.1; Búrquez & Castillo 1994).

In 1980 a large expanse of Sonoran Desert ecosystems was protected by the wildlife refuge Valle de los Cirios in Baja California (2,521,776 ha). By then the edicts protecting the environs of Nogales and Hermosillo had been long ignored. These early-protected areas near major towns were being devoured by city growth and development. The rest were protected only by their isolation. However, they did not escape logging (the high sierras), cattle ranching (all reserves, excluding the gulf islands), the introduction of large, wild herbivores (African antelopes on the mainland; bighorns on Isla Tiburón), and the overexploitation of fisheries (gulf islands).

A new era of reserve designation was initiated in 1988 when a prominent desert area in Baja California Sur was established: Reserva de la Biosfera El Vizcaíno. Its implementation gave hopes of real protection to the largest tract of Sonoran Desert so far decreed—2,546,790 ha (Ortega & Arriaga 1991). Work by Instituto de Ecología, Universidad Nacional Autónoma de México (UNAM), and Centro Ecológico de Sonora led to the establishment of the Reserva de la Biosfera El Pinacate

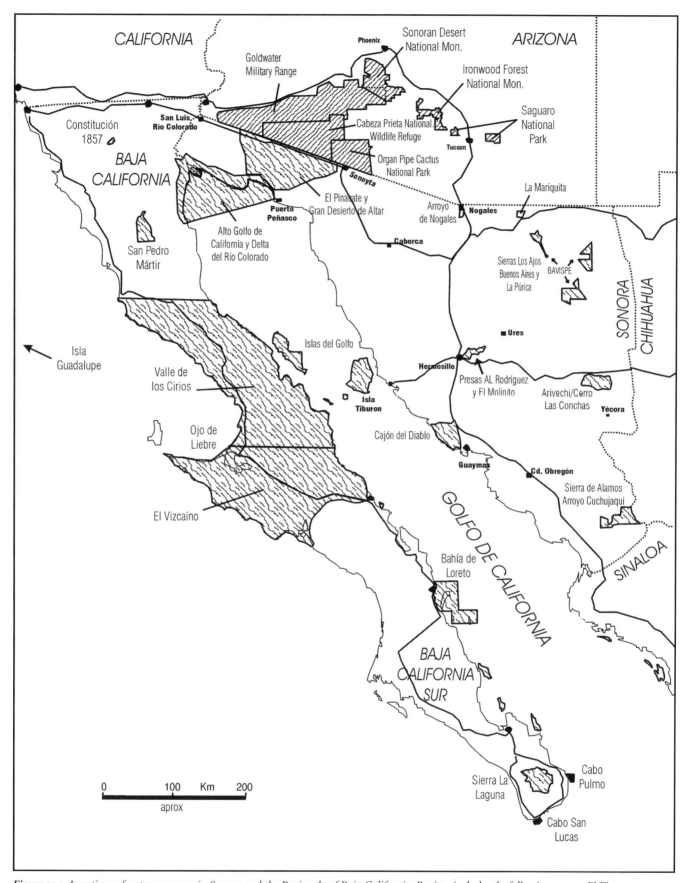

Figure 33.1. *Locations of nature reserves in Sonora and the Peninsula of Baja California. Bavispe includes the following ranges: El Tigre, Juriquipa/Pilares, Las Iglesitas, Los Ajos, Buenos Aires y La Púrica, and La Madera. The Barry M. Goldwater Range, Cabeza Prieta National Wildlife Refuge, and the Sonoran Desert, Ironwood Forest, and Organ Pipe Cactus national monuments are indicated to show the possible extent of a United States–Mexico international Sonoran Desert reserve. Data from official decrees in* Diario Oficial de la Nación, Benítez & Loa 1996, *and unpublished reports from Centro Ecológico de Sonora; data for reserves in the U.S. from World Wide Web (www) sites of the National Park Service, U.S. Fish and Wildlife Service, and Bureau of Land Management.*

TABLE 33.1. *Extant nature reserves in northwestern Mexico, by order of creation.*

RESERVE	STATUS	LOCATION	YEAR CREATED	MAIN ECOSYSTEM	AREA (HA)
Isla Guadalupe	Reserva Especial de la Biosfera	Pacific BC	1928	Desertscrub, pine-oak forest, and numerous endemic spp.	25,000
Arroyo de Nogales	Zona Protectora Forestal[a]	Northern S	1936	Oak woodlands/desert grassland/riparian	8,650
Sierras Los Ajos, Buenos Aires y La Púrica	Reserva Forestal Nacional[b]	NES	1936	Oak-pine forest	21,494
Cajón del Diablo	Reserva de Caza[c,d]	Central coast S	1937	Sonoran Desert	50,000
Ciudad de Hermosillo	Zona Protectora Forestal[a,c]	Central S	1938	Sonoran Desert/riparian	17,250
Bavispe	Reserva Forestal Nacional y Refugio de la Fauna Silvestre[c]	NES	1939	Oak-pine forest	184,770
Sierra de San Pedro Mártir	Parque Nacional	Northern BC	1947	Pine forest, fir forest, chaparral	72,911
Constitución de 1857	Parque Nacional	BC	1962	Oak-pine, chaparral	5,009
Isla Tiburón	Zona de Reserva Natural y Refugio de la Fauna Silvestre[d,e]	Gulf of California	1963	Sonoran Desert	120,756
Complejo Lagunar Ojo de Liebre	Reserva de la Biosfera	BCS	1972	Insular and marine	60,343
Islas del Golfo de California	Zona de Reserva y Refugio de Aves Migratorias	Gulf of California	1978	Sonoran Desert/marine	150,000
Sierra El Pinacate	Reserva Forestal y Refugio de la Fauna Silvestre[f]	NW S	1979	Sonoran Desert	28,660
Valle de los Cirios	Area de protección de flora y fauna	Central BC	1980	Sonoran Desert	2,521,776
El Vizcaíno	Reserva de la Biosfera	BC	1988	Sonoran Desert	2,546,790
Reserva del Centro Ecológico de Sonora	Endowment to the state park[a,g]	Central S	1988	Sonoran Desert	CA. 1,000
El Pinacate y Gran Desierto de Altar	Reserva de la Biosfera	NW S	1993	Sonoran Desert	714,557
Alto Golfo de California y Delta del Río Colorado	Reserva de la Biosfera	NW S and NE BC	1993	Sonoran Desert/marine	934,756
Presas Abelardo L. Rodríguez/El Molinito	Zona sujeta a conservación ecológica[g]	Central S	1994	Sonoran Desert/wetlands	28,000
Sierra La Laguna	Reserva de la Biosfera	Southern BCS	1994	Desertscrub, pine forest, tropical deciduous forest	112,437
Sierra de Alamos– Río Cuchujaqui	Area de Protección de Flora y Fauna Silvestre y Acuática	Southern S	1996	Tropical deciduous forest/ pine-oak forest	92,889
Cabo Pulmo	Parque Nacional	Southern BCS	1995	Coral reef	7,111
Bahía de Loreto	Parque Nacional	BCS	1996	Mangrove, dunes, desert	206,581
Cabo San Lucas	Area de Protección de Flora y Fauna	Southern BCS	2000	marine	3,996
Arivechi–Cerro Las Conchas	Zona sujeta a conservación ecológica[g]	Eastern S	2000	Sonoran Desert	72,300

Notes: Total area of Sonora is 18,543,100 ha; Baja California, 7,160,200 ha; and Baja California Sur, 7,142,000 ha. S = Sonora; BC = Baja California; BCS = Baja California Sur. Locations are shown in Figure 33.1. [a]*Unofficially appropriated for urban and rural development.* [b]*In 1939 included within Reserva Forestal Nacional y Refugio de Fauna Silvestre Bavispe.* [c]*Not formally delimited. The area is approximate.* [d]*Reserva Especial de la Biosfera from 1989.* [e]*In 1978 included within the Islas del Golfo de California designation.* [f]*In 1994 included within Reserva de la Biosfera El Pinacate y Gran Desierto de Altar.* [g]*State of Sonora decree.*

y Gran Desierto de Altar in 1993 (Table 33.1). This reserve, together with El Vizcaíno and Valle de los Cirios, included the most pristine areas of the Sonoran Desert. At the same time, another biosphere reserve, proposed by a consortium of Mexican institutions, was decreed: Reserva de la Biosfera Alto Golfo de California y Delta del Río Colorado. It is mainly marine, with approximately 70 percent of its area in the sea, but includes critical land areas in the delta and along the coast.

Recent additions of protected land are the Presas Abelardo L. Rodríguez y El Molinito (Del Castillo 1994) and the Sierra de Alamos–Río Cuchujaqui. The former includes two artificial impoundments and the highly disturbed riverside of the Río Sonora near Hermosillo, and the latter provides a measure of protection for diverse tropical deciduous and oak forests in southern Sonora. The state government designated Arivechi–Cerro Las Conchas a wildlife refuge in 2000, the latest official addition to the nature reserve system of Sonora. In Baja California Sur several reserves were also proclaimed in the 1990s: Bahía de Loreto, Cabo Pulmo, and Cabo San Lucas to protect mainly marine environments, and Sierra La Laguna, an isolated sierra at the tip of the peninsula, to safeguard thornscrub, tropical deciduous forests, and pine-oak forests (Table 33.1).

Today about 1,500,000 ha, or 8 percent, of land in the state of Sonora has some form of protection; in both Baja California (the northern state) and Baja California Sur nearly 37 percent of the area is protected (ca. 2,700,000 ha each). These figures do not include reserves lost to city development or marine areas. Through the Comisión Nacional de Áreas Naturales Protegidas (CONANP) the federal government is increasing its efforts to operate the reserves formally. Nevertheless, the allocation of funds is still precarious and some reserves have no protection other than that given by the edicts and their natural isolation.

Planned Reserves in Sonora

In addition to the Secretaría del Medio Ambiente y Recursos Naturales (SEMARNAT, the federal environmental agency), institutions such as UNAM, state universities, the Comisión Nacional para el Conocimiento y Uso de la Biodiversidad (CONABIO), several state-level agencies, and many nongovernmental organizations (NGOs) are working on selecting and studying high-priority areas

for protection in Mexico. For Sonora, the Centro Ecológico de Sonora and CONABIO (Arriaga et al. 2000; Benítez & Loa 1996), with the aid of NGOs and academic institutions, have proposed areas of high priority for conservation in various parts of the state (Table 33.2). If decreed, important portions of the Sonoran Desert, Gulf of California marine environment, and sky islands in the Sierra Madre Occidental will receive protection and more adequate management.

Proposed reserves such as Sierra San Luis, Sierra La Mariquita, Sierra El Tigre, Mesa El Campanero, and Sierra Mazatán are sky islands with oak, pine-oak, and pine forests. They also include portions of desert grasslands and small areas of foothills thornscrub. During 1997–98 an area of 2,196 ha in Sierra La Mariquita, northeastern Sonora, was endowed to the Instituto Nacional de Astrofísica, Optica y Electrónica (INAOE) to guarantee optimal conditions for scientific research at the Observatorio Astrofísico Guillermo Haro (Estévez 1999). This area has been included in the projected Reserva Mavavi, an extension of the Ajos-Bavispe reserve, proposed by the Instituto Nacional de Ecología (INE) and SEMARNAT. The proposal calls for an increase in area from the present 185,000 ha to 780,000 ha. It would include the basin of the Río San Pedro, a tributary of the Gila River, as well as Sierra Los Ajos, Buenos Aires, La Púrica, and La Mariquita mountains. The area collects about 50 percent of the Río Sonora basin precipitation and provides the main water supply for Hermosillo, the state capital (J. L. Guerra Limón, Los Ajos reserve director, personal communication 2003). It is also renowned for its biodiversity, connectivity with southern tropical ecosystems, and mineral reserves. If decreed, it will encourage the protection of the Sonoran sky islands, a complement to the protected areas in the mountains of Arizona. However, the proposal has not yet been approved, and it is strongly resisted by the mining lobby, which has steered the opinion of peasants *(ejidatarios)* and small landowners.

Coastal environments are considered in the proposed reserves of Las Bocas, Bahía de Lobos, Estero El Soldado, Cajón del Diablo y Cañón El Nacapule, and Sierra Bacha. These reserves also include considerable portions of Sonoran Desert or, as in the cases of Bahía de Lobos and Las Bocas, coastal thornscrub (Búrquez et al. 1999; Friedman

TABLE 33.2. *Proposed nature reserves in Sonora, Mexico.*

RESERVE	LOCATION	MAIN ECOSYSTEM
Reserves Not Yet Decreed		
Las Bocas	Huatabampo	Coastal thornscrub, coastal wetlands
Bahía de Lobos	Guaymas	Coastal thornscrub, coastal wetlands
Estero El Soldado	Guaymas	Sonoran Desert, coastal wetlands
Sierra Bacha	Pitiquito	Sonoran Desert
Bahía San Jorge	Caborca	Sonoran Desert, coastal wetlands
Sierra El Viejo	Caborca	Sonoran Desert, foothills thornscrub
Trincheras	Trincheras	Sonoran Desert
Sierra Libre	La Colorada/Hermosillo/ Guaymas	Sonoran Desert, foothills thornscrub, tropical deciduous forest
Sierra Bacatete	Guaymas/Cajeme	Sonoran Desert, foothills thornscrub, tropical deciduous forest
San Javier/Tepoca	San Javier/Yécora/Onavas	Riparian, foothills thornscrub, tropical deciduous forest
Soyopa/Sahuaripa	Soyopa/Sahuaripa	Riparian, foothills thornscrub, tropical deciduous forest
Mazocahui/Puerta del Sol	Ures/Baviácora	Riparian, foothills thornscrub, tropical deciduous forest
Sierra San Luis	Agua Prieta	Desert grassland, oak-pine forest
Mesa El Campanero/Arroyo El Reparo	Yécora	Pine-oak forest, tropical deciduous forest, highland wetlands
El Carrizo	Benjamin Hill/Trincheras/ Opodepe/Carbó	Sonoran Desert, desert grassland
Sierra de Mazatán	Mazatán/Ures	Sonoran Desert, foothills thornscrub, oak woodland
Cerro Agualurca/Centro Ecológico de Sonora	Hermosillo	Sonoran Desert, foothills thornscrub
Santuario del Aguila Calva	Sahuaripa/Soyopa	Foothills thornscrub, tropical deciduous forest
Reserves Already Decreed but with a New Proposal in Progress		
Cajón del Diablo, Cañón El Nacapule	Hermosillo and Guaymas	Sonoran Desert, foothills thornscrub, tropical deciduous forest, marine
Islas Tiburón y San Esteban	Gulf of California	Sonoran Desert, foothills thornscrub, marine
Mavavi: Sierras Los Ajos, Buenos Aires y La Púrica, including El Tigre, Huachineras, and La Mariquita	NE Sonora	Oak-pine forest, desert grassland, highland wetlands

Notes: *Location is the municipality where most of each reserve is found. Locations are illustrated in Figure 33.1.*

1996). Mesa El Campanero y Arroyo El Reparo, the area between San Javier and Tepoca, and Soyopa and Sahuaripa are proposed reserves protecting riparian habitats, foothills thornscrub, and the most northern tropical deciduous forests on the continent (Table 33.2). Until recently, tropical deciduous forests have been one of the least protected biomes of Mexico (Trejo & Dirzo 2000), and they are among the most endangered major tropical ecosystems (Janzen 1988). Soyopa and Sahuaripa have also been recognized as important breeding areas for the endangered bald eagle (Guadalupe Morales, personal communication 2002).

Other planned reserves that include substantial portions of Sonoran Desert are located at Sierra Libre, Sierra Bacatete, Sierra El Viejo, Rancho El Carrizo, Sierra Mazatán, Trincheras, and Cerro Agualurca. The already mentioned area of Cajón del Diablo y Cañón El Nacapule, located in Gentry's Guaymas Monadnock (Gentry 1949), has a wealth of endemics and disjunct tropical taxa shared with Baja California and the Sierra Madre foothills along Mexico's Pacific coast (Búrquez et al. 1999; Felger 1999; Turner et al. 1995). Sierra Libre, Puerta del Sol/Mazocahui, and Sierra Bacatete are similar cases, virtually unexplored biologically but known to have a rich disjunct tropical flora as well as remains of Seri, Opata, and Yaqui cultures (see Yetman & Búrquez 1996). Trincheras is famous for its prehistoric agricultural terraces and other features. Sierra El Viejo, near Caborca, has remarkable transitions of several Sonoran Desert subdivisions and probably the northwesternmost extension of foothills thornscrub (Brown & Lowe 1980). Here substantial numbers of desert bighorn sheep *(Ovis canadensis mexicana)* are still found (Medellín et al. 2005). The only population of boojum tree *(Fouquieria columnaris)* on the mainland is located in Sierra Bacha, along the coast south of Puerto Libertad (Felger & Moser 1985; Hastings & Turner 1965). In this pristine area of the Central Gulf Coast subdivision of the Sonoran Desert there are also populations of desert bighorn and archaeological features and artifacts of the Seri culture. South of Benjamin Hill in the northern desert grasslands is Rancho El Carrizo, where the only remaining natural populations of masked bobwhite *(Colinus virginianus ridgwayi)* are found (Garza-Salazar et al. 1992). It also supports fine examples of the desert grassland–shrubland con-

tinuum of the Plains of Sonora subdivision (Búrquez et al. 1998). These reserves would protect a gradient harboring notable transitions in vegetation, from marine environments to coastal wetlands and from Sonoran Desert to coniferous forests. They would also add distinct units of the Sonoran Desert to the already existing reserves of El Pinacate y Gran Desierto de Altar and Alto Golfo de California y Delta del Río Colorado, as well as to the special microcosms of the protected Islas del Golfo de California and Cajón del Diablo.

Human Impacts on the Sonoran Desert Region

The growth and decline of large-scale agriculture, extensive and intensive cattle ranching, the damming and silting of rivers, indiscriminate logging, and fisheries overexploitation are some of the human activities that have affected the landscape and resources of the region (Stoleson et al. 2005).

Agriculture

Historically, most of the settlements in Sonora were on the western edge of the Sierra Madre Occidental and in the Madrean foothills. Precolumbian agriculture was common along the river margins, sometimes with sophisticated irrigation systems (Camou 1991; Moreno 1992). In historical times agricultural development in the desert was confined to small areas with a shallow water table, but nonetheless by the end of the nineteenth century it had seriously affected riparian habitats (Bahre 1991; Camou 1991).

After many years of low rates of population increase, growth in Sonora accelerated rapidly in the twentieth century, mainly because of the development of large-scale agriculture in the coastal plains (Stoleson et al. 2005). In the late 1940s the vast aquifers of the Río Concepción, Río Sonora, and Río Mátape basins began to be appropriated. The Río Mayo and Río Yaqui deltas were not extensively altered until the construction of dams upriver between the 1940s and 1960s. The resulting reservoirs stimulated further population growth through the generation of electricity and the rapid expansion of agriculture. By the late 1970s the delta regions and their associated alluvial plains were almost entirely converted to field crops. Thus within a few years huge expanses of natural vegetation had been cleared. The vast mesquite forests of the Llanos de San Juan Bautista, in the deltaic plains of the Río Sonora, disappeared with the colonization of the Costa de Hermosillo irrigation district (Felger & Lowe 1976). The progressive salinization of the aquifer and the increasing cost of water extraction have caused a decrease in the land devoted to crop production. From the original 150,000 ha cleared for agriculture, only about 70,000 ha remain operative, and the rest is derelict land. The nonsustainable operation of this district, the ever-lowering water table (dropping up to 1 m yr^{-1}), and the faltering local economy are documented by Moreno (1994, 2000).

In the Río Yaqui and Río Mayo deltas' coastal plains, nearly one million ha of mesquite, cottonwood, and willow riparian forests and coastal thornscrub disappeared after dams upriver started to operate. These rivers followed the same path of vegetation eradication as that of the Colorado after the construction of Hoover Dam (Felger 2000; Glenn et al. 1992). Today both irrigation districts face serious environmental problems because of poor drainage, salinization, and toxic levels of pesticides and fertilizers (Celis 1992).

Cattle Ranching

Compared with agriculture, cattle raising has a relatively brief history in the drylands of North America. By the sixteenth century, Precolumbian agricultural towns along the fertile foothills of the Sierra Madre and major desert rivers, as well as hunter-gatherer societies in the desert, had attained a precarious equilibrium with their use of resources. This equilibrium was broken when cattle were introduced by the Europeans as a new form of land use. Cattle created a major source of conflict between the new pastoralists and the indigenous agriculturists—cattle did not respect boundaries, particularly those of unfenced crops (Camou 1991; Doode & Pérez 1994; Moreno 1992). It also affected hunter-gatherer societies, whose members considered cattle a rich source of animal protein roaming the common land, ready and easy to harvest (Felger & Moser 1985; Thompson 1989). Until the last century only localized areas of desertscrub were used for cattle raising. Because of constant raids by Native Americans, cattle were confined to small areas, which often were overgrazed. By the end of the nineteenth century the organization of the large "haciendas" allowed extensive exploitation of the arid lands. Large cattle

herds transformed the natural balance between desert grasslands and desertscrub, contributing to the so-called invasion of mesquite and thornscrub (Archer 1989, 1994; Bahre 1991; Búrquez et al. 1998; Hastings & Turner 1965; Johnston 1963). During the Mexican Revolution cattle stocks diminished drastically (Machado 1981), allowing some recovery of the rangelands. However, the cattle industry regained momentum, mainly in northern Mexico, transforming large expanses of semiarid and arid lands (Barral 1988; Búrquez et al. 1998; Ezcurra & Montaña 1988).

The introduction of Indo-African buffelgrass (*Pennisetum ciliare*) in the 1960s, promoted by the USDA Soil Conservation Service (Cox et al. 1988; Johnson & Navarro 1992), altered large expanses of the Sonoran drylands beyond recognition. Buffelgrass, which increases the range productivity of cattle forage by about three times (Hanselka & Johnson 1991), is planted after the desertscrub and thornscrub are stripped away. Unfortunately, this process eradicates desert perennials that provide winter and spring forage when buffelgrass is dormant. The replacement of native perennials coupled with overstocking of cattle led to a perceived higher occurrence of drought, despite the fact that rainfall patterns have not changed appreciably in this century. It is paradoxical that the desert has historically been devoted to cattle raising, the most water-demanding land use. To produce 1 kg of beef in the desert requires 100,000–200,000 kg of water, whereas most other crops can yield the same amount of energy with only 500–2,000 kg water. Broiler chickens, a source of high-quality protein, need only about 4 percent of the water used by beef per kilogram of protein produced (Pimentel et al. 1997).

After a few years buffelgrass productivity decreases, and prescribed fires are needed to increase soil fertility and stop the return of some desert and thornscrub species. In addition, there is enough fuel accumulation in the form of indigestible stubble to allow extensive natural burning. Since Sonoran Desert plant species are not fire-adapted, a cycle of decreasing biodiversity begins, converting the rich desert into a species-poor grassland (Búrquez et al. 1998, 2002). Paired samples with and without buffelgrass show an order of magnitude decrease in species numbers and a fourfold decrease in standing crop biomass (maximum of 5 tons per ha above-ground standing crop in buffelgrass vs. 20 tons per ha in natural desertscrub; Búrquez et al. 2002). Central Sonora, particularly the Plains of Sonora desert subdivision, has been the most severely affected area, with about one million ha already cleared for pasture (Búrquez et al. 2002; Johnson & Navarro 1992) and a government call for as much as 6 million additional ha. Adventive buffelgrass is now expanding its range through repeated natural burning of the desertscrub and is present throughout Sonora at elevations below 1,000 m (Búrquez et al. 2002; Cox et al. 1988; Yetman & Búrquez 1994).

Given the government subsidies to establish exotic grasslands, to maintain large cattle herds, and to support marginal cattle ranching, the desert and thornscrub in Sonora will probably be replaced in the near term by ecosystems with significantly lower species diversity and reduced structural complexity, unless control measures are implemented.

Mesquite Logging, Charcoal Production, and Clearings

The largest production of legal hardwood legumes for charcoal is in the districts of Hermosillo, Guaymas, Puerto Peñasco, Sonoyta, and San Luis Río Colorado. These areas have historically accounted for more than half the mesquite extraction in Sonora (in 1985, for example, 74,700 out of a total of 135,300 m³; INEGI 1990). Former mesquite forests have disappeared at an alarming rate because of demand for charcoal in Sonoran and North American markets. The establishment of clearings for buffelgrass is closely related to charcoal production. The woody remains from clearings are piled in long *chorizos* (sausages), forming strips of dead vegetation that are later sorted for fuelwood and charcoal. Populations of ironwood *(Olneya tesota),* among the oldest plants in the Sonoran Desert, have shifted toward smaller sizes because of illegal logging for charcoal, *desmontes* (clearings), and the gathering of wood for sculpture or carvings (Búrquez & Quintana 1994; Nabhan & Plotkin 1994). Old-growth ironwood is a major community structuring element of the southern Sonoran Desert, allowing the persistence of many species and forming true islands of diversity under its canopy (Búrquez & Quintana 1994; Tewksbury & Petrovich 1994). Any reduction in this particular habitat can threaten populations

with low numbers, such as queen of the night cactus (*Peniocereus striatus;* Nabhan & Suzán 1994), or species with low rates of recruitment, such as columnar cacti and ironwood itself (Búrquez & Quintana 1994).

Mining and Urban Development

Mining and cement works generate extensive landscape alteration, depriving the land of its natural vegetation cover, accelerating erosion, polluting rivers with toxic wastes, and producing large clouds of airborne particles. Traditionally, the environmental impacts of digging, leaching, and smelting operations have not been acknowledged. Vegetation rehabilitation and restoration with native species at the end of operation is negligible. The economic importance of mining is increasing exponentially in Sonora, now Mexico's leading mineral producer, so such alteration of the environment is likely to continue.

Urban centers in the desert also have grown exponentially, placing stress on scant water supplies. Deep-well water extraction and water diversion from rivers, coupled with effluent discharges from city sewage, are rapidly affecting water distribution and quality. The reduction of the natural cover of phreatophytes that depended on the underground aquifer has promoted erosion and increased the quantity of aerosols. Industry has grown in both the borderlands and the interior of the state with the installation of numerous maquiladora assembly lines for the United States market (Lara 1992). Maquiladoras have overtaxed the water resources available for development in the major cities, exacerbating environmental damage. Toxic wastes generated by the maquiladoras and mining industry are often mishandled or casually discharged, causing not only severe damage to natural ecosystems but also serious human health problems (Denman 1992; INEGI 1993; Moreno-Vázquez 1991).

Hermosillo is following the development model of Phoenix, its counterpart in Arizona. Chronically short of water, it is home to about one-fourth the Sonoran population. Government initiatives have called for large-scale water projects, ranging from the plan to connect the Río Yaqui to the Río Sonora basin to supply water for population and industrial growth to the building of massive desalination projects (Búrquez &

Martínez-Yrízar 2000). Apart from the enormous construction costs, these projects may decrease energy generation by diminishing water availability for the dams upriver or require large investments in energy to desalinate. Alternative actions such as increasing city water-use efficiency have been only superficially analyzed, reflecting the current pattern of government development projects that consistently omit environmental concerns (Joseph 1993; Ortíz 1993).

Urban development has also taken its toll on Sonora's nature reserves. Three of the reserves have already disappeared through the ignorance and complacency of local authorities. The edicts protecting the Arroyo de Nogales and Zona Protectora Forestal de Hermosillo were ignored, and these areas were appropriated for urban growth. In 1996 the reserve by which the Centro Ecológico de Sonora had been endowed by a former governor was cleared to promote urban development. Ironically, the impact assessment to effect this land-use change was furnished by the same Centro Ecológico de Sonora (now Instituto del Medio Ambiente y Desarrollo Sustentable del Estado de Sonora, or IMADES), a Sonoran government agency. This case reflects the tenuous status of many nature reserves in Mexico during the 1990s (see, e.g., Otero & Consejo 1992 and Jardel et al. 1992 regarding the problems faced by other Mexican reserves).

Desert Coastal Wetlands, Rivers, and Fisheries

The Sonoran Desert has an intimate relationship with the Gulf of California and the Pacific Ocean. Humidity from the ocean streams into the desert during the monsoon thunderstorms. Cold currents in the Pacific create unique communities based on dew deposition in the west side of the peninsula, and within the gulf a narrow strip of desertscrub and the coastal thornscrub in southern Sonora are directly influenced by dew deposition, salt spray, and sand movement. In turn, the coastal wetlands and continental platform are enriched by the load of sediments and organic matter carried by arroyos and rivers (see Felger & Lowe 1976).

Fisheries in the Gulf of California have decreased markedly in recent decades. Steinbeck and Ricketts (1951) wrote passionately about the ongoing destruction of the Gulf of California by trawler fishing boats. Little has transpired since that time to address these prescient concerns. Recently, some attempts have been made to preserve the productivity of the gulf, without a great deal of success: the Alto Golfo reserve is now fully operating and the site of substantial research, but fishermen have curtailed most efforts to bring about a sustainable use of upper gulf resources (see Brusca, Turk Boyer, and Hastings & Findley, this volume; Bergman 2002). Upriver dams have stopped the annual floods rich in nutrients and have blocked, by virtue of the lack of water in the estuaries, the entrance of many marine species that used river deltas as spawning areas. The effects of such changes are evident today. The totoaba (*Totoaba macdonaldi)*, once so abundant that it supported a large fishery, now is listed as endangered, along with the small vaquita porpoise *(Phocoena sinus)*, also endemic to the upper gulf (Hastings & Findley, and Navarro, this volume). Sea turtles, formerly abundant (Clifton et al. 1982; Felger et al. 1976; Felger & Moser 1985), are also listed as endangered and legally protected (Felger et al. 2005; Navarro, Seminoff & Nichols, and Turk Boyer, this volume). The shrimp fishery has suffered serious decline, and the sardine fishery is following suit (Doode et al. 1992). Along with overexploitation, a major role has been played by the damming of the large rivers that feed the gulf: the Colorado, the Mayo, and the Yaqui. Before construction of Hoover Dam, the Colorado alone carried an annual average of 180 million tons of sediments past Yuma, Arizona (Fradkin 1981). Today only during periods of extraordinary runoff does fresh water from the Colorado reach the sea, and when these rare waters enter the gulf, they are laced with pesticides and fertilizers (Bergman 2002). This case is repeated on a smaller scale with the Río Yaqui and Río Mayo (Celis 1992). There is little hope that fresh water will flow again into the gulf unless high-level agreements are reached between governments. In the Río Fuerte, in northern Sinaloa, another huge dam—Luis Donaldo Colosio—was completed at Huites. It provides water for development of the relatively pristine coastal thornscrub of southern Sonora and northern Sinaloa.

The transformation of coastal wetlands for aquaculture and tourism has affected the growth of fisheries by diminishing precious habitat used by many fish species for breeding. This is the case at Estero Puerto Peñasco, in the upper gulf; Estero

La Cruz, near Bahía Kino; Estero Bacochibampo, Estero El Soldado, Estero El Rancho, Bahía San Carlos, and Bahía Empalme in the Guaymas region; and many others farther south, including the large inlet of Agiabampo. Most of these estuaries have been buried or drowned by land reclamation, destruction of the mangrove vegetation, and the construction of ponds for shrimp and oyster production.

Conclusions

The development of Sonora, and most of northern Mexico, has relied on extensive rather than intensive use of the land. Widespread cattle ranching has extirpated large areas of the natural vegetation cover, promoted erosion, and introduced exotic species that are now fully naturalized. These changes compromise the tenuous ecological balance by creating new competitors and new ecosystem dynamics, mainly the fire-grass cycle. For its part, large-scale agriculture in the desert relies on the nonsustainable use of groundwater and fossil fuels and on ever-silting dams, pesticides, and fertilizers.

The exploitation of minerals and industrial development have not been matched by strong measures to protect the environment. Especially lacking is the establishment of large nature reserves. The need for preserving natural areas has clashed with the desires of government and investors to develop large-scale mining, water-use projects, coastal tourism, fisheries, cattle ranching, and agriculture. The importance of nature reserves in preserving biodiversity, protecting upriver basins from erosion, providing recreation, keeping hydrological systems in balance, and reducing health risks have been only cursorily taken into account in government programs (Búrquez & Martínez-Yrízar 2000).

The lack of coordination between government agencies creates conflicts that directly affect the value of resources within a given community. For example, the development of marinas in desert coastal wetlands eradicates mangrove swamps, affecting in turn their recreational value and the population dynamics of marine species that use them as recruitment grounds. These wetlands are also silted and polluted by upstream erosion caused by agricultural drainage, mining, and cattle ranching. Efforts to preserve the Sonoran Desert are feeble and underfunded when compared with investments promoting the development of industry, mining, agriculture, cattle ranching, and tourism. Protected natural areas are a major component in the resolution of these conflicting interests because they provide sites where natural processes ameliorate the human use of areas nearby. Natural areas are no longer protected by their isolation, simply because there are no longer isolated places anywhere.

Acknowledgments

Preliminary versions of this chapter were reviewed by Mario Cirett, Richard S. Felger, Robert H. Robichaux, David L. Venable, and David Yetman. Samuel Ocaña, former governor of Sonora and past director of Centro Ecológico de Sonora, allowed the review of unpublished proposals for planned reserves in Sonora. Help from him and his staff, especially Armando Aparicio, Carlos Castillo, Florentino Garza, Martín Haro, Cristina Meléndez, Guadalupe Morales, and Iván Parra, is greatly appreciated. This chapter was supported by funds from CONACyT project 0080-N9106, DGAPA-UNAM project IN212894, and CONABIO project H-122 grants to AB.

Thirty-Four

Growing a Conservation Community:

The CEDO Story

PEGGY J. TURK BOYER

I t is one hundred degrees and rising in the Tucson desert as I begin to write this account. The saguaros are beginning to bloom. I'm anxious to return to our home on the shores of the northern Gulf of California at Puerto Peñasco, Sonora, where I first discovered the gulf and its *gente*. I began my studies there as a University of Arizona biology student, and for my graduate work I spent a lot of time on my knees observing the unicorn snail, *Acanthina angelica.*

This small snail is a master of the dynamic northern gulf rocky intertidal habitat, where its food supply is in constant flux. On the outer edge of its shell the snail has an elongated spine that it uses to pry open its barnacle prey. It feeds on two barnacle species, the small acorn barnacle *(Cthamalus anisopoma)* of the middle intertidal rocks and the larger thatched barnacle *(Tetraclita stalactifera),* which lives a bit higher in the upper middle intertidal zone. The snail feeds most efficiently when the length of the spine fits the size of the barnacle. Long-spined snails are often found among the larger barnacle species whereas the smaller-spined individuals feed among the small species. When storms sweep through the region, disturbed sediments scour the rocks and destroy large patches of the barnacles. As barnacle abundance varies, the unicorn snail can change the length of its spine to enable it to feed efficiently on the most abundant barnacle. If large barnacles are in short supply, a long-spined snail can deposit shell around the spine and make it short again (Yensen 1979).

Meanwhile, the barnacles of the northern gulf are not defenseless against this onslaught. Natural selection has favored a mechanism to enable them to handle the voracious snails. If a unicorn snail crawls over a young, developing acorn barnacle, leaving traces of a chemical trigger, the barnacle will develop a bent-over shape, and its aperture will not face upward, where it is accessible to the snail's spine (Lively 1986). This strategy increases the barnacle's survival in a predation-stressed environment. Bent-over barnacles cannot produce as many eggs as the typical form; hence both forms persist in the population (Lively 1986). Such is the way of the northern gulf. Individual snails and barnacles adapt rapidly to changing physical and biological conditions.

When I first visited Puerto Peñasco in 1975, professors John Hendrickson and Don Thomson of the University of Arizona's Ecology and Evolutionary Biology Department headed a thriving marine biology program. They and their students conducted field activities out of a small beach house in Puerto Peñasco owned by a gentleman named José Garcia. The Garcia House sat beside an experimental shrimp mariculture enterprise, just east of Punta Peñasco, that was operated jointly by the University of Arizona's Environmental Research Lab (ERL) and the Centro de Investigación en Ciencia y Tecnología of the Universidad de Sonora (CICTUS).

Carl Hodges, ERL's first director and founder of the affiliated nonprofit Desert Development Foundation (DDF), and CICTUS director Xico Murrieta understood the importance of basic marine science, so they began making plans to support and expand the University of Arizona marine program. They envisioned a new organization called the Institute for Deserts and Oceans, or IDO. It would operate out of a new facility located in the Las Conchas housing development east of the shrimp labs and would be supported with profits from the shrimp mariculture commercial enterprise. Nicholas Yensen was hired as the first director in 1978. After a successful fundraising campaign led by Blake Brophy, Yensen was able to convert the unfinished Las Conchas recreation center and office building into a simple but functional biological field station. He received a grant to travel the world in search of halophytes, salt-tolerant plants that were being raised at Puerto Peñasco using the effluent from the shrimp farm. These plants showed commercial promise for coastal desert regions, where freshwater is scarce.

Prior to his departure Yensen hired *un servidor* (yours truly) as the facility's first resident biologist. Under the auspices of DDF, in 1980 I invited the researchers and classes that were using the Garcia House to use the new field station at *el castillo,* the name locals and visitors used to refer to this Greek monastic-style building. Later it would be named Edificio Agustín Cortés, after a partner in the Las Conchas housing development and promoter of the United States–Mexico shrimp partnership. In my spare time I conducted my master's thesis research on the formation of breeding clusters in long- and short-spined unicorn snails (Turk 1981).

It soon became clear that there were communication problems among the partners of the shrimp operation. After several years of unsuccessful lobbying to allow aquaculture shrimp to be sold outside Mexico's national system of cooperatives that managed all naturally harvested shrimp, the shrimp farm sponsors decided to maximize profits by moving operations to Hawaii. When they began to ship the project's prime reproducing shrimp to the Hawaiian facility, the Mexican partners called in the *federales* to stop them. The U.S. partners took offense, and the enterprise—a potential world leader in shrimp mariculture—came to an abrupt end. Ironically, the Hawaiian operation didn't succeed either.

The dream and the source of funding for the Institute for Deserts and Oceans dissolved with that partnership. While I finished my graduate studies, I stayed on as the resident biologist in a beautiful, empty castle with no electricity, little water, and a very shaky future. But a new partnership was already forming. In 1979, on my first trip to *el castillo,* I had met Rick Boyer, an enthusiastic educator and renaissance man. He had come down to Puerto Peñasco to visit his brother, Edward, who was helping me teach a class and was working on his marine biology degree at the University of Arizona (Boyer 1987). Rick, an English literature major, was on sabbatical from his job as director of a high school in Alabama. With his love of nature and science and his many talents,

Figure 34.1. The long-spined unicorn snail (Acanthina angelica) *spines its large barnacle prey* (Tetraclita stalatifera) *of the rocky intertidal zone at Puerto Peñasco. (Photo courtesy of CEDO)*

Figure 34.2. CEDO directors Rick Boyer and Peggy Turk Boyer as newlyweds, November 30, 1985. (Photo courtesy of CEDO)

Rick stayed and soon became the facility's first volunteer. He also assisted ERL and DDF with their experimental halophyte research, which was relocated to the fields near the castle after the shrimp partnership dissolved in 1980.

As more classes and researchers began using the facilities as a field base for studies of the northern gulf's intertidal inhabitants, our knowledge of the region grew and our financial base solidified with the revenues generated from these visiting U.S. academic groups. Though the future was still uncertain, two challenges held our attention: (1) to deliver this growing body of natural history into the hands of the local community and (2) to erase the bitter feelings that lingered over the loss of the shrimp mariculture business.

Figure 34.3. *The tides expose a vast, rocky intertidal zone in front of the CEDO field station, Puerto Peñasco, beckoning marine researchers from far and wide. (Photo courtesy of CEDO)*

Olivia and Dario Beltrán were hired to help clean and maintain the field station that was also my home. Their visits every few days were welcome opportunities to speak Spanish, which I had first learned as a child in Mississippi. Mrs. Mora, a Cuban refugee, had taught Spanish at my elementary school, and I fell in love with the sound and feel of it—*las palabras y sus ritmos son música al oido.* As an eight-year-old I also became fascinated with the Sonoran Desert and created a model of it for a science fair project. The world was coming full circle. The Beltráns soon adopted me into their family, and after growing up with seven brothers and sisters, I felt right at home.

Our ranks at *el castillo* grew when Felipe Maldonado, skipper of the University of Arizona's research vessel, *La Sirena,* moved the boat and his family to Puerto Peñasco from Guaymas to more easily serve university classes and researchers. They lived with me at *el castillo* for a few months when they first arrived, and since that time I have watched Felipe's children and grandchildren grow up. I would use the telephone at the home of Agustín Cortés, and he often invited me for coffee and lunch with his family. Agustín introduced me to other prominent members of the community. I grew and they grew as they incorporated me into their families and we shared our cultures.

The community was fascinated by our microscopes and buckets. We were novelties, and they were willing to join in the fun. It was easy to find ways to contribute at La Casa de Cultura in Puerto Peñasco. We invited our talented American friends and family to do a photo exhibit and a rock concert (the "Oceanliners" were a big hit). We taught

English classes, inviting students to play soccer with our nephews and nieces and to sing our favorite folk tunes ("You Are My Sunshine" was popular in both English and Spanish). These folks became keenly interested as we began to share information about the natural history of the gulf. They had many experiences to share, and so we grew together in our understanding of each other and nature.

From 1983 to 1985 we taught short courses in marine ecology, meteorology, and marine mammals (Turk et al. 1986) at a local high school (Centro de Estudios Técnologicos del Mar, or CETMAR) that specialized in the more technical aspects of marine resource exploitation. When American high school students who were visiting from Tucson offered to donate seven Commodore Vic computers, CETMAR built itself a computer lab and we taught courses in basic programming, contributing wherever we could.

Our affiliation with the American side of the shrimp-farming fiasco didn't seem to matter to those who were sincere in their desire to contribute to their community's education. The closest of these friends—Guillermo Munro, Lorenzo Cuadras, Minerva Nuñez, Fernando Gonzales, Fausto Soto, Carlos Flores, and Lili Chersin—would in 1987 become the founding members of the Mexican board of directors of el Centro Intercultural de Estudios de Desiertos y Océanos, or CEDO. They would support and guide the building of a unique intercultural model for community-based conservation. We saw the gulf with a scientist's eye; they were focused on the economic perspective. We both saw it as a way of life: we lived here, worked here, and played here. It was our home, and we cared deeply about the gulf and its environmental well-being. With this group, from the beginning there was no "them" or "us"—just "we."

We often encountered U.S. tourists during our intertidal explorations, and they too showed an eagerness to learn more about the area and our studies. We offered talks to interested groups and passers-by, and through word of mouth we grew into a tourist center. In 1984 a 55-foot fin whale (*Balaenoptera physalus*) carcass washed ashore at the mouth of the remote Estero La Pinta, and we invited a group of visiting students from a University of Arizona oceanography class to help us collect it. With knives in hand and young male bravado to spare, we cut away at the ripe flesh, separating it from the bones, letting the tides work on it for a week at a time, and finally brought it back to the center to soak in Biz, an enzyme-activated laundry detergent, which removed its pungent oils. We then prepared it as a landmark public exhibit for our center and the community.

Flood tides bring many marine mammal carcasses to the uppermost gulf (Maldonado et al. 1984). Several vaquita specimens washed ashore in the early 1980s, and we were there to retrieve them (Magatagan et al. 1983). Not much had been learned about this porpoise since its discovery in 1958, so these specimens stimulated a renewed interest among the scientific community. Our field station became a center for vaquita studies.

In January 1984 we received notice of a possible live vaquita in the harbor. "It's a small animal with a square-shaped, blunt snout," we were told. If fishermen were identifying and reporting a vaquita, our education programs must be working! When we arrived at the scene, we found a group of fishermen attempting to lift a six-foot-long slippery, scratched-up mammal up the oily, rocky slopes of the harbor. To lend a hand we pulled out a blanket and made a sling and then rushed it to the old shrimp labs, where we knew there were some large tanks being maintained by the Universidad de Sonora. It was a strange experience for us to hold such a desperate animal, but it must have been even stranger for this sea creature to spend its last moments flying down the road in our pickup truck. We later identified it as a rare pygmy sperm whale *(Kogia breviceps)* (Vidal et al. 1987b).

In 1984 I joined a research cruise in the northern gulf led by Lloyd Findley, then of the Instituto Tecnológico de Estudios Superiores de Monterrey, Campus Guaymas. We set out to document the marine mammals of the region. During that trip Alejandro Robles and I shared a turn of observation duty while offshore of Rocas Consag. With binoculars in hand we both froze when we saw a blunt snout peek out of the water. It rolled forward, exposing its back, and then a disproportionately large, triangular dorsal fin appeared. The animal stayed on the surface a mere 30 seconds before slipping back into the water, exposing no fluke. It would not surface again. We confirmed it as the Gulf of California porpoise *(Phocoena sinus)*—a vaquita!

This shared experience became the foundation of many years of friendship and collabora-

Figure 34.4. *Puerto Peñasco community leaders, CEDO board members, and painters Fernando Gonzalez* (left) *and David Hoyos depict nature and the environment at city hall. (Photo courtesy of CEDO)*

Figure 34.5. *CEDO biologist Peggy Turk Boyer discovers a fin whale* (Balaenoptera physalus) *washed ashore upside-down in front of CEDO. (Photo courtesy of CEDO)*

tion with Alejandro and another colleague, Luis Bourillón. Alejandro would become director of Conservation International's Mexican programs and eventually all its Latin American programs. In these positions and in his appreciation of the value of building conservation from the community up

Figure 34.6. *Young Francisco Maldonado mourns the pygmy sperm whale* (Kogia breviceps) *that stranded in the Puerto Peñasco harbor. (Photo courtesy of CEDO)*

Figure 34.7. *Biologists Luis Bourillón, Karlos Garaté, and Peggy Turk Boyer take a break from their observations of marine mammals onboard a research cruise in the northern Gulf of California. (Photo courtesy of CEDO)*

as CEDO was doing, Alejandro would be instrumental in linking CEDO with the broader Mexican conservation community and with funding opportunities. Luis would eventually establish a nonprofit organization known as Comunidad y Biodiversidad (COBI) at Guaymas, Sonora, which would model CEDO's community-based approach in promoting conservation in the gulf.

A live vaquita calf was brought to us in 1994 by vacationing researchers from the Arizona Game and Fish Department who had learned about vaquita at the CEDO talks (Boyer 1994). The vaquita had washed up alone in the surf just east of CEDO and north of Isla San Jorge. After

several unsuccessful attempts to lead it back into the sea, the researchers decided to bring it to CEDO. Since the umbilicus was still attached, we estimated it to be only hours old. We immediately put the little porpoise into a small tank and for the next two hours gathered materials and information about how to care for it. Without its mother, however, the newborn was doomed. Its last moments were like those of the pygmy sperm whale—spasms interspersed with dead calm, release of a milky substance from the blowhole, and then the heart-wrenching stillness of death.

The researchers who found the infant vaquita had observed fishermen using gill nets offshore in the direction of Isla San Jorge. By the mid-1990s the threat that these nets posed to vaquita had been well documented. In 1985 experimental gill nets set in El Golfo de Santa Clara to study the totoaba population had caught seven vaquitas. This bycatch alarmed the scientific community, and research to document the mortality caused by these nets intensified. CEDO conducted the first survey of fishermen at Puerto Peñasco. Based on their recall of captures and what we learned about their fishing activities, and using what was known about vaquita distribution, we estimated 32 vaquitas captures per year for the upper gulf gill-net fisheries (Turk Boyer & Silber 1994). This figure stimulated researchers and students at the Instituto Tecnológico del Estudios Superiores de Monterrey to scrutinize mortality at El Golfo de Santa Clara, where vaquitas were being caught regularly. During one year of intense, continuous effort the researchers recorded 39 captures at El Golfo alone (D'Agrosa et al. 1995). Soon the vaquita was widely recognized as one of the most endangered marine cetaceans in the world, and its restricted range in the northernmost Gulf of California became more evident (Vidal 1995).

Scientists think the vaquita of the northern gulf derives from a population of Burmeister's porpoises *(Phocoena spinipinnis)* that today live off the east and west coasts of South America (Brownell 1982). These porpoises are typically cold-water creatures, and it is thought that a population became trapped in the northern gulf during a warming trend following a period of glaciation. The vaquita that lives here today has several features that distinguish it from its southern relative and perhaps allow it to handle the warmer temperatures typical of northern gulf summers. A

Figure 34.8. Biologist Silvia Manzanilla takes a first look at a vaquita. (Photo courtesy of CEDO)

taller dorsal fin, larger pectoral fins, and smaller body size may be adaptations for keeping cool.

The vaquita is endangered and may not survive. Gill nets, so well designed for use where the currents are strong, as in the northern gulf, have proliferated, along with fishermen, *pangas,* and outboard motors. Today we estimate that over 1,000 *pangas* (small fiberglass boats equipped with outboard motors and a variety of types of fishing gear) are working in the upper gulf (Turk Boyer & Flores-Skydancer 2002). Gill nets were first used to exploit the totoaba *(Totoaba macdonaldi),* and as that fishery collapsed and the totoaba became the first marine fish to be listed as endangered (1979 in the United States; 1993 in Mexico), the nets were used for sharks and other species. This method may eventually even replace the bottom-trawling technique used by industrial shrimpers. All gill nets capture vaquita, and calculations based on the current population estimate of 567 animals (Jaramillo-L. et al. 1999) tell us that human-caused mortality must remain below 0.2 vaquita deaths per year for the species to recover (Rojas-Bracho & Jaramillo 2002).

Trying to ensure a future for the vaquita has been a central theme at CEDO. In 1996 we initiated a community action program that involved small-scale fishermen in the process of documenting their fishing practices and their ideas for management (Cudney-Bueno & Turk Boyer 1998). Fishermen expressed concern about vaquita and their declining fisheries, and some were eager to work with us. We began research to develop sustainable fisheries with commercial divers who harvest benthic molluscs (Cudney-Bueno 2000, 2001), and with others we monitored their willingness to change their fishing practices or find alternative livelihoods (Turk Boyer & Flores-Skydancer 2002). The dialogue continues with the production of publications on vaquita for both fishermen and decision makers (Flores-Skydancer & Turk Boyer 2002; Turk Boyer 2001); publication of a regional newspaper, *Voces del Mar y del Desierto,* on the biosphere reserves (Turk Boyer, ed. 2001); and development of new fishing guidelines within the Alto Golfo Biosphere Reserve, using what we have learned from fishermen (Programa de Conservación y Manejo Reserva de la Biosfera Alto Golfo de California y Delta del Río Colorado, in prep.). We're holding our breaths to see if management will be implemented in time to save the vaquita.

While we worked feverishly on behalf of the vaquita, the tides continued their eternal ebbs and flows, exposing and then covering vast intertidal expanses of shoreline twice a day, beckoning researchers from far and wide. In the early 1980s the common intertidal invertebrate and fish species were being described and their ranges documented (Brusca 1980; Thomson et al. 1979; Thomson & McKibbin 1976), but that was really only a beginning. Only half the total number of species have been described (Brusca 2002). Marine algae from the region were documented but not studied extensively (Dawson 1966; Norris 1975). In the next decade, however, gulf research would bloom.

For example, one group of visiting researchers honed in on the symbiotic relationship between an alga and a tunicate. The alga *Prochloron didemni* had been discovered in the central Gulf of California (Lewin 1977), causing much excitement since it seemed to have descended from a hypothesized ancestor of the chloroplast. It contained photosynthetic pigments and chloroplasts structured like those in the Chlorophyta (green algae), but it maintained the primitive prokaryotic cell structure of the Cyanophyta (blue-green algae), linking these two groups. This discovery led to the creation of a new algal division, the Prochlorophyta! Further studies of the symbiosis between the tunicate and the alga at Puerto Peñasco, the northern limit of *Prochloron,* showed that the seasonal abundance of each species was not synchronized (McCourt et al. 1984). It was proposed that facultative symbioses—relationships that aren't required for survival—would tend to evolve in highly seasonal and unpredictable environments such as the northern gulf. In this case such a symbiosis allows the tunicate to adapt independently to changing environmental conditions (Michaels 1983).

Early studies of the Gulf of California sunstar *Heliaster kubinijii* in the northern gulf rocky intertidal zones gave origin to the keystone predator concept. Marine ecologist Robert Paine (1966) proposed that the sunstar helps keep populations of various species such as barnacles, mussels, and snails in check by preying on them all; thus the presence of the predator maintains diversity. Subsequent studies by Ed Boyer at Puerto Peñasco, however, formulated a slightly different role for the sunstar. After a decade of unusually warm sea temperatures in the 1970s caused massive sunstar die-offs, the species almost disappeared from the Gulf of California intertidal zones (Dungan et al. 1982). Boyer's comparison of species diversity before and after the sunstar's disappearance showed little change. He proposed that the sunstar's role is more like one leg of a table: when the leg was removed, the table (diversity) wobbled a bit but didn't collapse. Several predatory snails also appear to keep the prey species in check, functioning as additional legs on the table (Boyer 1987). This diverse intertidal community with multiple predators was able to remain stable despite the sunstar's disappearance.

To support such studies, we at CEDO made a commitment to monitor climate, which included taking daily readings of onshore sea temperatures in front of the field station. This would add to the 20 years of similar sea temperature data that had been taken at the shrimp labs, 5 km to the west (Turk Boyer et al. 2004). In collaboration with John Hendrickson we also initiated a monitoring program for the common rocky intertidal organisms in front of CEDO. These data document the normal patterns of abundance and distribution (Turk Boyer et al. 1986), and further analyses may reveal effects of seasons, El Niño or La Niña events, or global climate change.

We found ourselves functioning as the region's environmental "eyes and ears," learning to distinguish normal patterns from unusual phenomena. In addition to recovering vaquita specimens and the pygmy sperm whale, we observed nesting olive ridley sea turtles (Boyer 1995; Navarro 1997), photographed dinoflagellate blooms, investigated die-offs of loons and pelicans, and recorded countless other observations. In early September 2002, for example, masses of dying pelicans were observed during an El Niño event, a die-off most likely caused by lack of food (Turk Boyer & Boyer 1991).

In November 1985 Rick Boyer and I were married. Our honeymoon is recorded as a gap in the weather data series. It was clear that the activities at *el castillo* needed a more formal commitment, a new identity, legal status, and financial structure. In the winter of 1986–87, with the blessing of our parent organization (DDF), we invited friends and colleagues from Puerto Peñasco and Tucson to help create two nonprofit organizations, one in Mexico and one in the United States, each with its own board of directors. The two organizations would share a single mission and the same name—el Centro Intercultural de Estudios de Desiertos y Océanos, A.C., or the Intercultural Center for the Study of Deserts and Oceans, Inc. The term *intercultural* was used, as opposed to *international,* because, as board member Guillermo Munro noted, "We should reach beyond national perspectives and focus on intercultural cooperation" (personal communication 1987).

The first formal project of this newly formed organization—*CEDO News/Noticias del CEDO,* a bilingual natural history newsletter on the northern gulf and surrounding Sonoran Desert—was published in 1987 and would serve to disseminate these scientific findings and programs to an international community of stakeholders. It was followed in 1988 by the creation of a community forum to identify environmental issues and work together to solve local problems. Many successful community campaigns (11 annual events and running) came out of this forum, each one adapted to the state of the community and the messages and activities that were needed at the time. The first campaign included a radio show, talks and field trips for schoolchildren, a junior ecologist program, and a clean-up day with almost ten thousand people (approximately one-third of the town's population) out picking up trash (Turk Boyer & Boyer 1990). The city's sparkle after this clean-up was obvious. People were amazed and extremely proud of what they were able to accomplish by working together. It was this event that marked the beginning of an environmental movement for which the Puerto Peñasco community became known throughout Mexico and the United States.

There were a few setbacks along the way. As we learned to work in the community, we had to deal with some of the hard feelings left over from the shrimp-farm days, accusing headlines by a yellow journalist, and a run-in with a xenophobic mayor and his police squad at a CEDO fiesta. But bit by bit, CEDO grew. And the community has grown to depend on CEDO, seeking our opinion and aid in solving local environmental problems. A well-informed public is demanding, however, and limited resources and growing stresses on local environmental health challenge our ability to provide all the information needed.

A proposed biosphere reserve, the Reserva de la Biosfera Alto Golfo de California y Delta del

Figure 34.9. *Researchers Rick McCourt and Becky Simmons bring specimens of* Sargassum, *tunicates, and symbiotic* Prochloron *to CEDO for a closer look. (Photo courtesy of CEDO)*

Río Colorado, offered an opportunity to protect both biodiversity and fisheries. In the early 1990s, ecological crises grew along with economic ones: high bycatch associated with shrimp trawling (Nava-Romo 1994; Rivera Montijo & Turk Boyer 1992) was threatening benthic communities; shrimp production had plummeted (Hoyos 1991); totoaba populations were endangered; and vaquita were being caught at an alarming rate in gill nets employed by *panga* fishermen. CEDO helped the industrial fishermen view the proposed reserve as a place to protect and manage the shrimp's spawning grounds and as a way to ensure their future use of these resources. They agreed to give it a try, and by signing onto the proposal for its establishment they provided the government the local support needed to establish the reserve. Several years later a CEDO study of small-scale fishing activities and a community action program began involving small-scale fishermen in the reserve as well.

During the hillside ceremony at Cerro Prieto dedicating the biosphere reserve, Alejandro Robles congratulated the many people and organizations involved in its creation, "but especially the fishermen. The fishermen," he said, "are aware of the problems with their fisheries. It is an enormous sacrifice for them to reduce or change the activities that sustain them in order to guarantee the sustainability of the natural resources and the fishing industry itself" (Robles 1993).

As optimistic as we all were about the opportunity the new reserve presented for conservation in the upper gulf, permanent improvements were slow to unfold. A decade would go by before new research findings, a united conservation community, strategic plans, open dialogues with some fishermen, and a renewed political will would converge to spur the government into action. At the beginning of the 2002–3 shrimping season an emergency law was enacted banning trawling and eliminating many of the larger gill nets from the biosphere reserve. Industrial fishermen opposing the ban staged two protests at Puerto Peñasco that caught international attention and effectively pressured the government to negotiate a compromise, ending the ban within a month.

The first of these protests occurred at CEDO. A week of television media bombardment featuring CEDO staff talking about vaquita and reporters blaming trawlers for killing vaquita infuriated the local shrimp trawlers. They knew they were not the principal cause of vaquita mortality—it was gill nets. We at CEDO knew this as well, but the reporters got it wrong. Elimination of trawling would reduce impacts on the ecosystem and fisheries but only indirectly protect vaquita. These actions and misrepresentations in the name of vaquita confounded an already confused and struggling shrimping industry.

On the morning of October 15, 2002, a group of 75 wives of fishermen and shrimpers marched to CEDO for an explanation. As they approached, cries of "La Peggy! La Peggy!" could be heard over the hum of shrimp boats that were idling offshore, ready to storm the reserve in protest. Helicopters circled overhead. Children and reporters wandered in and out of the CEDO courtyard while protesters outside shouted their concerns to CEDO board members. Board members were not eager for me to confront this angry group, but eventually a contingent of women entered requesting that I address the crowd. Face to face, as they pleaded and began asking me specific questions, I agreed to answer them, but only if we focused on the facts. The crowd gathered inside to listen.

I explained that CEDO's work in the decade from 1993 to 2003 had, for good reason, focused on small-scale fisheries. We knew these fisheries were more directly related to vaquita mortality, and we didn't have the resources to work with shrimp trawlers, too. Also about this time the

shrimp industry underwent a major reorganization that led to more regional control and decision making by the Camara Nacional de la Industria Pesquera (CANAIPES).

I told the protesters that we were sorry we had not been able to continue working with them. I offered to help by collecting data and analyzing it if they were seriously interested in improving management of the resources, although we would need their financial support to hire additional staff to take this on. I also talked about protected areas as one of the mechanisms proposed by scientists for management of marine resources and about some of the exciting evidence being gathered by fishermen right here at Puerto Peñasco showing that reserves can help fisheries.

Several hours of these discussions seemed to satisfy many of the protesters, and things calmed down. Eventually, a fisherman proclaimed, "She can't help us [change the government's decision]; it is time to go."

A few days later, on October 19, fishermen staged another protest, this time blocking the highway leading north of Puerto Peñasco, holding thousands of tourists captive and preventing others from entering Puerto Peñasco. For more than 30 hours the town was in turmoil, and no one could reason with the shrimpers. People in the tourism business who tried to dissuade the protesters were accused of not supporting their fishing community: "You're either with us or against us," they were told. The situation came very close to erupting into violence. The best and the worst of our two cultures were pitted against each other. On the one hand, community members brought water, food, and friendship to the waiting tourists; taxis offered services to and from the blockade; venders sold food; on the other, fishermen stood by with bats in hand to prevent people from crossing their barricade. Some tourists waited in the long line of cars, anxious to get home; others shouted obscenities, showing their obnoxious "American" colors; meanwhile, many were elated about being "forced" to spend yet another day on the beautiful beaches of Puerto Peñasco.

When word reached the highest levels of government in the United States and in Mexico, negotiations with local fishermen began. A compromise was arranged that would permit the local fleets to trawl in the Alto Golfo Biosphere Reserve for a few months, but future trawling would require fishermen to present an environmental impact study to show that trawling does not destroy the benthic ecosystem. Fishermen bought some time, and negotiations continue, but only with the local shrimp fleet. Few shrimpers from communities outside the biosphere reserve would be allowed to trawl in the area. Stakeholders have grouped and regrouped, dividing and uniting on the issues in different ways. Gill-net fishermen and trawlers at Puerto Peñasco are joining together to present a united view to the government, though traditionally they have fought for fishing rights in shallow coastal waters. Election-year politics brought fisheries issues to the fore at local and state levels. The national offices of the secretary of the environment and the fisheries department are battling over jurisdiction of fisheries in protected areas; and environmental groups, a bit weary, are forming coalitions and redefining strategies. A new coalition of fishermen, conservationists, and the primary commercializer of shrimp (Ocean Garden), offers hope for reducing conflicts and promise for progress. Many issues are yet to be resolved, and the future of the upper gulf ecosystem hangs in the balance.

Meanwhile, as summertime rolls in and the monsoons begin to build and release their moisture over the Sonoran Desert, magnificent black *tijeritas* (frigatebirds) ride the skyways to the northern gulf. A look underwater at this time of year reveals schools of anchovies. The *sierra* soon follow (as well as restaurant signs advertising fresh *sierra* and ceviche). Feeding frenzies of resident bottle-nosed dolphins gather offshore at Puerto Peñasco. Portuguese man-of-wars join this northward parade, as perhaps the best indicator of the monsoon's arrival. Taking the cue, we abandon daily swims. Each man-of-war is a hydroid colony whose water-colored gas bag allows it to float and drift with the currents of the open sea. In Spanish they are called *aguas malas.* Armed with long fishing tentacles laden with nematocysts (stinging cells) that have a venom as powerful as cobra poison, they bring "bad water" to the seashore. The monsoon winds used to wash *Janthina,* a pelagic snail, and *Porpita,* another hydroid, ashore, but they seem less common nowadays.

Offshore of Puerto Peñasco the warm summer months also mark the time for formation of breeding clusters of the black murex snail, *Hexaplex (Muricanthus) nigritus.* This predatory snail feeds on abundant mussels and other molluscs and probably plays a keystone role in maintaining biodiversity on subtidal patch reefs of the northern gulf.

In 1993 commercial hookah divers from Puerto Peñasco collected over 600 tons of the black murex snail, which is easy to gather in these breeding aggregations. The meat is sold in local markets for seafood. Six years later the catch was a mere 90 tons (Cudney 2000). In 1996 the divers approached CEDO's fisheries project coordinator, Richard Cudney, with their concern about the decline of the murex and the future of this fishery. Richard responded by studying the fishery and the snail's natural history (Cudney-Bueno 2000). We shared these research results with the divers and together made a commitment to monitor the resources and design management initiatives.

The divers' first actions were to close the snail fishing season during the summer breeding peak (2001) and to close their prime fishing grounds at Isla San Jorge, 20 miles offshore of Puerto Peñasco, for one year (November 2000 to October 2001). The government has now recognized a formal season closure for the snail. In the summer of 2001 divers did surveys of murex and scallop (another species they harvest) at the island, and they were encouraged by what they saw. In their "temporary reserve," abundance and size-classes of both species increased. This success motivated them to establish several more "reserves" or "no-take" zones and to continue monitoring them. We then helped the divers set up controlled experiments to compare their no-take areas with areas where they continue to fish. While the divers monitored their fisheries, Cudney and other researchers studied the effects of these actions on other components of biodiversity so that we might gain a better understanding of the overall benefit of such reserves on biodiversity as well as fisheries. Cudney also studied the socioeconomic parameters that led to cooperative actions like those the divers demonstrated. The divers believed in what they were seeing, and this kept them engaged and committed to these de facto reserves. In 2004, when word spread of the high productivity of these reserves, interlopers from farther south came to reap the benefits. Unwilling to watch others benefit at their expense, the Puerto Peñasco divers soon followed suit. Today divers want to revive the "no take" areas, and we are working with them to design permanent means to control access.

These CEDO efforts build on similar ones that are being promoted by COBI with fishermen at Bahía de Kino and Isla San Pedro Mártir, the most oceanic of the gulf's islands (see *CEDO News*, Spring 2006). These experiences are teaching us how to use the tools of science to effectively involve communities in the management of resources.

Research in the northern gulf has shown that the rocky reefs of this region are among the gulf's biodiversity treasures. Their protection as biodiversity hotspots is critical. Commercial fishing, sportfishing, recreational activities, and the general degradation of coastal ecosystems due to tourist developments and changes in water flow from the Colorado River are exerting growing pressures on the region. Mini-reserves like those created by the divers may emerge as the best model for sustainable use of resources for these and other habitats throughout the gulf. The promise of a future lies in identifying the most critical of these habitats and informing and involving stakeholders—fishermen, researchers, and the government—in research and management.

At this writing CEDO has been part of the Puerto Peñasco and gulf conservation community for over 25 years, the estimated maximum age of a vaquita. And just as the unicorn snail grows long or short spines to adapt to changing food supplies, CEDO's multidisciplinary approach and dual nature as a bicultural organization has enabled it to respond to the changing needs of stakeholders in two cultures. With tides, species, economics, and politics in constant flux and often at odds, CEDO has maintained its course with a consistent non-political, rational, and inclusive voice. We have brought information to the government and stakeholders so that both can understand the issues, and when they are ready and the time is right, we try to provide opportunities to design sustainable ways to use resources. We are developing living models, example by example, in solid waste disposal, water conservation, ecotourism, building with recycled materials, fisheries management, and conservation of biodiversity.

CEDO's conservation momentum is one that evolved from an intuitive sense that the knowledge of nature offers us truths that transcend cultures and disciplines and that can guide us. The keepers of that knowledge are not necessarily from big places and lofty institutions. The local harvesters who labor at the net, enjoy the sunsets, and battle the waves and surf also have important stories and truths to tell. Being with them is important; listening is important; sitting together at the kitchen table or in the boardroom is important; following through with their initiatives as well as your own is important; working together as a team is important; speaking other languages is important; making information available to all is important; looking at the whole picture is important; taking the time to be a member of the community and its families and growing together is important. Using all the tools available is necessary.

The Sonoran Desert borderlands and its desert sea seem to attract a unique breed of human, a breed that seeks the limits, the ebb and flow of tides, flash floods, 115° summers, magnificent sunsets, challenges, chaos. These borderlands are rich in the cultural traditions of the O'odham, the Cucapá, Mexico, and the U.S. Biologists and ecologists are drawn here as well, to unlock the secrets of its rhythms and its less predictable changes. All these diverse human experiences and ways of knowing are at our fingertips, ready to be used as tools for designing a future. Protected areas, biosphere reserves, and conservation communities and organizations have sprouted north and south of the border. Today they are converging to create a collective vision for our desert and sea: solar energy, recycled water, construction of earthships and straw-bale houses, the Colorado River flowing to the sea, shrimp *(camarónes)* forever, many vaquita, totoaba galore, southwestern willow flycatchers *(papamosca saucero)*, Sonoran pronghorn *(berrendos)*, flat-tailed horned lizards *(chamaleón del desierto de Altar)* and pristine dunes, rufous hummingbirds *(colibrí rufus)*, ironwood *(palo fierro)*, and saguaros in bloom.

Acknowledgments

This chapter is dedicated to John Hendrickson, University of Arizona professor and world-renowned marine biologist, who passed away on September 6, 2002. Doc Hendrickson's passion for science, the oceans, the Gulf of California, storytelling, his students, and life helped energize this process of growing a conservation community. His last words to me, during CEDO's 20th anniversary fiesta, were, "Peggy, I like the way you've done this thing."

I also thank the community of Puerto Peñasco for embracing my family and the CEDO family, for weathering the good times and the bad with us as a family does, and for believing in us and growing with us.

My husband, Rick Boyer, wrote me the following poem shortly after we met:

El Elegante

Southern stars full rising moon
A picnic at sunset we started at noon
Cactus and crystals
     Wind from the crater
A quiet consumed us as we lay there
No birds no people no planes
     Only sky
And a world below us all open to the eye
I grew in love in that place
Taught and touched by what
     Was in your face
Along the rim where we walked
In each other's arms while we talked
My horizons widened my hopes
     My heart
Leapt up knowing that this was
     But a start.

Figure 34.10. John Hendrickson aboard the University of Arizona's research vessel Adventyr, *preparing the setline for a deepwater trap deployed on the bottom of the Wagner Deep, northern Gulf of California, July 1973. (Photo by L. T. Findley)*

Cooperation Across Borders

A Brief History of Sonoran Desert Conservation Beyond Boundaries

Wendy Laird Benner, Joaquin Murrieta-Saldivar, and John Shepard

The spirit of Carbunco was present in the early spring of 1995 when citizens of the Sonoran Desert gathered for the Celebration of Desert Cultures in Caborca, Sonora. This ecoregional conference was a benchmark for the integration of communities, managers of protected areas, Native Americans, and the biodiversity of the Sonoran Desert. One of the memorable outcomes of the conference, sponsored by the International Sonoran Desert Alliance, was creation of the *Sonoran People's Tapestry* by fiber artist Ann Keuper (Figure 35.1). Its fabrics represent the spiritual, biological, and social elements that weave together humanity and nature, creating the culture of the Sonoran Desert.

Participants in the conference were asked to bring symbols representing their sense of "home" in the desert, any object whatsoever that expressed their spiritual ties to nature. Someone brought feathers of birds from all corners of the bioregion. A Tohono O'odham teacher brought the start of a basket woven from yucca fibers and reflected, "We encourage our children to carry on our traditions and culture.... Working on basketry teaches us patience." Others brought a saguaro "boot," a seashell, corn kernels, a petroglyph replica, a railroad spike from Puerto Peñasco, minerals from Caborca, Cocopah beadwork, hair from a coyote, a travel tag, an audiotape of stories (see Table 35.1 for a complete list of objects). Artist Keuper watched and listened and closed her eyes, imagining the desert world and sensing things unseen. Then she went to work and wove the symbols into the tapestry, which now travels to communities throughout the region, continuing to share the story of diversity, collaboration, and love for the desert landscape.

The tapestry is like the plans that governments must weave to protect the land, its people, its plants and animals, and its soul. In November 1996 Arizona governor Fife Symington joined Sonora governor Manlio Fabio Beltrones in declaring support for a new conservation initiative to protect the Sonoran Desert. The governors specifically endorsed the creation of a binational network of Sonoran Desert biosphere reserves to coordinate resource management, facilitate scientific research, and guide economic development activities that are compatible with conservation efforts in the region. In May 1997 U.S. secretary of interior Bruce Babbitt and Mexican secretary of environment Julia Carabias signed a letter of intent pledging to work jointly in protecting natural areas along the United States–Mexico border with special priority given to the Sonoran Desert. Both initiatives reflect a growing recognition that efforts to preserve the fragile Sonoran Desert ecosystem cannot be limited by the international border. They also represent important milestones in efforts to promote cooperative management of the desert's cultural and natural resources among government agencies, local residents, and nongovernmental organizations.

The governors proposed a network of biosphere reserves to address significant challenges to the region's ongoing conservation efforts. Despite the fact that approximately 3.8 million acres on both sides of the border have been accorded various levels of protection, this region of the Sonoran Desert falls under the jurisdiction of more than a dozen federal, state, and local agencies, guided by differing and often conflicting priorities. Among U.S. federal agencies, the National Park Service, Fish and Wildlife Service, Bureau of Land Management, Marine Corps, and Air Force manage lands in the region. Similarly, in Mexico SEMARNAT (Secretaría del Medio Ambiente, Recursos, Naturales), the federal environmental agency, and state and municipal agencies share administrative responsibilities. As Harold Smith, former superintendent of Organ Pipe Cactus National Monument,

560

Figure 35.1. Sonoran People's Tapestry, *by Ann Keuper. Approx. 50 × 60 in. The tapestry is an artistic metaphor for community, cooperation, strength, innovation, and diversity. The weaving was conceived to encourage cross-cultural awareness and understanding among the diverse ethnic groups that live in the Sonoran Desert. (Photo courtesy of Matilda Essig)*

aptly notes, "It's one landscape, but there are a lot of boundaries and lines and jurisdictions out here, all of which can become zones of conflict" *(Earth Times 1996)*.

This seemingly intractable problem makes the proposed network of biosphere reserves both timely and relevant to conservation in the Sonoran Desert. Whether the proposal is formally adopted remains to be seen, but it is a transboundary collaboration, occurring at an informal level among local community leaders, resource managers, conservation groups, and business owners who have fostered an innovative alliance to protect the desert.

It is this partnership, spanning nations, cultures, and jurisdictions, that offers the greatest promise for preserving a large area of the Sonoran Desert. To understand its unique qualities requires delving into a bit of history to acknowledge the early vision and contributions of many individuals and organizations. In this way we also hope to underscore that involving local communities and diverse interest groups is critical for the conservation of the desert.

The idea that preserving the Sonoran Desert would require a bold and new approach dates back more than 30 years, when then U.S. secretary of the interior Stewart Udall proposed creation of a single binational protected area. Up through the early 1970s, various proposals to establish international parks were put forward but never implemented. It was not until 1976, when Organ Pipe Cactus National Monument was designated a biosphere reserve by the National Park Service and recognized by the United Nations Education, Scientific and Cultural Organization (UNESCO), that the foundation was laid for cross-border cooperation.

Unlike other protected areas, biosphere reserves operate within a larger landscape, one that incorporates the concerns of adjacent communities and land management units. An underlying principle of such reserves is that local residents can play a constructive role in protecting natural

TABLE 35.1. *Ingredients of Sonoran People's Tapestry.*

Twisted wire found in desert around Caborca

Old horse bit

Canvas with Caborca dirt and paint

U.S. Forest Service kerchief

Horseshoe

Chilean yarn weaving

Red, worn kerchief

1994 National M.E.ch.A Conference Poster, Arizona State University, red, black and white

Dried lizard

Horsehair from "Dark Beauty"

Cassia pods

Natural brown and white cotton

Mountain yucca

Beargrass

Liz's brown hair

Mesquite root bark from an area bulldozed for development in Tucson

Orange coral

Shells of many ocean species

Devil's claws

Sun-bleached devil's claw

Folklórico/Southwest School of Music and Dance shirt

Grapevine from brandy vineyards of Caborca

Javelina jawbone

Unidentified bone

Taller de Artes Plasticas, "Oasis," Caborca (leather, cholla skeleton with eyes)

Blue and orange archaeologist's flagging tape

Car rental paper, Flores Burruel family, Caborca

Babu bubblegum wrappers

Heart-shaped lollipop wrapper

Old purple glass from Bisbee dump

AlkaSeltzer wrapper

Cocopah beaded necklace and earrings

Cocopah beaded turtle from the west reservation near Somerton, Arizona

Tiny peyote-stitch beadwork ring

Small flat fish

Disney buttons

Caborca button

Tercera Conferencia Annual Certificate U.S. Youth from Ajo

Wheat from Caborca

Old fork

Snake remains and vertebrae

Bound sage

Fishbones

19 rocks from mining area of Cananea

Wendy Laird's statement at the end of the conference: "We are a border people and we are becoming one with all this diversity"

Old harmonica case

Assorted crab claws

Cottonwood leaves from Yaqui Deer Dance

Braided white horsehair with beads

Clamshell

Tohono O'odham basket weaving begun at conference

Peyote Church pin from Tohono O'odham shaman who blessed the weaving

Old spoon

Corn

3 plastic figures of cowboys and Indians

Unknown bone

Coral growing from shell

Park ranger's hat

Rattlesnake skin

Military macaw feather

Lilac-crowned Amazon finch feather

Yucca needle and braided fiber

Black hair of relative who died of cancer

Black-and-white portrait of infant Tohono O'odham girl Andrea Isabel

Triggerfish and unknown fishbones

Pottery shards found at Agua Blanca Ranch, Avra Valley, Arizona

Fax paper packaging

US $1 bill

Nicaraguan centavos

Top of old bottle

Coral

Sponge

Lava

Rusted hook

Key from the Mexican sculptor and muralist Nereo de la Peña

Seri ironwood dolphin

Truck keychain

Beaded ring

Handmade copper plate

Well-traveled luggage tag

National Park Service patch

Immature Harris's hawk feather

Unknown pelvis bone

Petroglyph medallion

Saguaro "boot"

Railroad spike

Tucson map cover

Mesquite pods

Acorn woodpecker feathers

Owl feather

resources and that these conservation efforts can also improve economic conditions and local quality of life. Cooperation among scientists, land managers, and local residents is encouraged. Furthermore, cooperation and networking among biosphere reserves is actively promoted through UNESCO's Man and the Biosphere program.

Soon after Organ Pipe Cactus National Monument was declared a biosphere reserve, Mexico established biosphere reserves as a protected-area option. The state of Sonora responded by studying the volcanic craters of the Pinacate and the waters and delta of the upper Gulf of California for possible nomination as biosphere reserves. In 1993 the Mexican government approved the state's petitions, creating El Pinacate y Gran Desierto de Altar and El Golfo de California y Delta del Río Colorado biosphere reserves. UNESCO subsequently recognized them as internationally significant biosphere reserves.

"The creation of these two biosphere reserves reflected a real change in conservation policy for Mexico," notes María Elena Barajas, former director of the state of Sonora's Department of Ecology. "Both areas are finally getting the protection they deserve" (personal communication 1996).

Almost concurrent with efforts to establish biosphere reserves in Mexico, a diverse group of people began meeting to share their knowledge about the Sonoran Desert and to discuss ways to protect it. "There were lots of discussions percolating," recalls Carlos Nagel, president of the now-dissolved organization Friends of PRONATURA, a U.S. sister group to the Mexican conservation organization PRONATURA, A.C. "The Arizona-Mexico Commission had just established an environmental committee. There was a continuing symposium on the Gulf of California, and a small group of us had begun supporting a ranger to work in the Pinacate" (personal communication 1996).

In 1988, energized by the growing interest in the region, Friends of PRONATURA and members of the Arizona-Mexico Commission co-sponsored a symposium on the Pinacate held in Hermosillo, Sonora. The symposium brought together scientists, nongovernmental organizations, local residents, and—for the first time—members of the Tohono O'odham Nation, whose homelands encompass 2.8 million acres of the desert.

For the Hia C'ed clan of the Tohono O'odham, their participation held special meaning. "All American Indians consider their homeland to be critical to their continued physical existence, much less the maintenance of their culture and identity," explained Mike Flores to those attending the symposium. "The Hia-Ced O'odham are no different.... They consider the Pinacate to be the location of their creation and further consider it to be the home of I'itoi, the one who accomplished their creation" (personal communication 1995). The O'odham expressed a strong desire to participate in future activities affecting the Pinacate.

Participants of the symposium in Hermosillo recognized the need to build better relationships across borders and to increase local awareness about the unique qualities of the region. The group agreed to explore the possibility of holding a larger public forum modeled after Arizona's Town Hall meetings to promote dialogue among residents of the Sonoran Desert. Friends of PRONATURA, with the help of the Sonoran Institute, a conservation organization established in 1991 to promote community stewardship of the desert, took the lead in organizing the gathering.

The first of what was to be three regional town-hall meetings was held in Ajo, Arizona, in 1992. More than 200 people attended, including local residents, business leaders, members of the O'odham Nation, and federal, state, and county representatives. As a result of the enthusiasm and interest generated at the gathering, a core group of individuals began to meet to consider establishing a formal entity that would foster communication and cooperation among stakeholders in the Sonoran Desert. The group agreed to form an alliance of representatives from the United States, Mexico, and Tohono O'odham Nation called the International Sonoran Desert Alliance (ISDA).

In the years since ISDA incorporated as a nonprofit organization, it has worked to promote dialogue, cooperation, and environmental stewardship among communities of the Sonoran Desert. ISDA has developed multicultural educational curricula on the desert environment, initiated community youth environmental improvement projects, established a regional resource center, and coordinated an exchange program among indigenous groups in the United States and Mexico.

Along with the Sonoran Institute, ISDA in 1995 convened a series of smaller community meetings to identify local environmental and economic development priorities. One outcome of these meetings was the creation of a regional working group to assess the feasibility of setting up training, certification, and marketing programs for ecotourism in the Sonoran Desert. These efforts translated into the establishment of La Ruta de Sonora Ecotourism Association. La Ruta is a hybrid: a nongovernmental organization and business-oriented enterprise that promotes a philosophy of responsible and ethical tourism for the region and provides opportunities for its residents to generate new sources of income from sustainable business ventures and services. The Sonoran Desert's natural resources, diverse cultures, traditions, and customs are richly valuable assets that support this emerging conservation industry. La Ruta believes that providing incentives and opportunities that require preserving and protecting these resources and values will foster an ethic of community-based conservation and development for the Sonoran Desert.

"These latest activities are really significant," notes Carlos Yruretagoyena, a former president of ISDA, "because they merge the interests of local communities and biosphere reserves. Community leaders are concerned about people making a living in the desert. Biosphere reserve managers want to promote sustainable use of local resources. Now both groups will have a chance to pursue these mutually desirable goals" (personal communication 1997).

Through its projects, ISDA has consistently sought to strengthen ties among biosphere reserves, other protected areas in the region, and nearby communities. Members of ISDA have made numerous public presentations to introduce the biosphere reserves to local residents. ISDA has invited managers of protected areas to speak at meetings and conferences and has sponsored activities that bring community leaders, students, and others to the reserves. The result is that biosphere reserve managers now participate in a wide range of community forums, and local residents assist reserve staffs with their activities.

Members of ISDA also have helped strengthen biosphere reserves as research institutions, securing funds to purchase computer equipment, provide staff training, and establish communication links between reserves. Having laid a strong foundation for cooperation in the region, ISDA and its partners set out to formalize these partnerships, which led them to propose the Binational Network of Sonoran Desert Biosphere Reserves (Chester 2001). Although the network would not impose any new mandates on current management practices on either public or private land, it would contribute to cooperation, understanding, and dialogue among management agencies and local residents. The 3.8-million-acre network would represent one of the largest contiguous protected areas in any desert in the entire world.

"I see a lot of opportunities for working closely together," explains Howard Ness, director of the National Park Service's Office of Mexican Affairs. "The tangible benefits will include joint research, ecological monitoring and restoration, visitor management, and law enforcement. The ultimate beneficiary, of course, will be the desert and the people who live there" (personal communication 1996).

In August 1996 ISDA, the Sonoran Institute, the Arizona-Sonora Desert Museum, and the National Park Service convened a meeting of resource managers, government officials, community leaders, and members of the O'odham Nation to discuss how to ensure that the network would be formally established. A plan of action was outlined, with the governors' declaration being an initial objective. A memorandum of understanding was drafted among U.S. resource management agencies, and ISDA continued working in collaboration with resource managers from the states of Sonora and Baja California to discuss opportunities for cooperation. Out of these efforts the Sonoran Desert Ecosystem Partnership was crafted as a permanent forum to discuss and resolve large-scale conservation issues shared by residents and protected-area managers in the Sonoran Desert ecoregion.

Through this spirit of partnership and collaborative approaches toward conservation at an ecoregional level, an effort was put together with the Nature Conservancy (TNC), the Sonoran Institute (SI), and Instituto del Medioambiente y Desarrollo Sustentable del Estado de Sonora (IMADES) to jointly develop an ecoregional analysis of conservation priorities for the Sonoran Desert. The identification of biodiversity hot spots in the Sonoran Desert and the process of gathering experts to share their knowledge, passion, and understandings of this unique desert were two of the top priorities. This process did not stop at the biophysical components. Efforts continue to tie in the human dimension that daily interacts with nature.

At the same time that this analysis was conducted (1998–2000), an artistic and tangible approach was begun to acknowledge the shared responsibilities and trust of the 1997 letter of intent signed by SEMARNAT and DOI. A brochure was developed emphasizing the importance of international management and friendship for the conservation of the Sonoran Desert.

Community conservation through economic development is the new vision for the Sonoran Desert border region. Carlos Nagel stresses, "If we improve the quality of life of our communities with responsible economic development, the environment will also benefit from these actions" (personal communication 2001).

The International Conference on Biodiversity and Society, organized by UNESCO and Columbia University in May 2001 in New York, touted the importance of collaboration and partnerships. The Sonoran Desert was recognized as a valuable model that fuses cultural diversity, biological diversity, and conflict jurisdictions and evaluates the trade-offs between society and nature so the human footprint has less impact on the environment. The existence of protected areas and the recognition of human populations in the desert is the right step toward an ecoregional planning that integrates the welfare of people and nature in the same goal.

The ongoing conservation efforts in the Sonoran Desert ultimately reflect an emerging global trend in conservation. In a partnership described as "community stewardship," local residents join with protected-area managers to preserve natural resources and ensure that economic development is compatible with local conservation efforts. Both in their scope and in their tangible conservation benefits, these efforts hold great promise for achieving the ideals of the biosphere reserve concept. "The importance of these ideals is that they change people's perceptions and attitudes towards the place, without changing much in the landscape" (Murrieta-Saldivar 2000:16).

Acknowledgments

We dedicate this chapter to the memory of Héctor Abrego: El, que siempre saludaba con un fuerte apretón de manos y una amable sonrisa típica del Desierto Sonorense. Héctor, a career employee with the Bureau of Land Management in Arizona, was a great supporter of ISDA and provided significant guidance for its initiatives.

In addition to individuals quoted in this chapter, we acknowledge the following people who have made important contributions toward conservation of the Sonoran Desert and the development of the proposed Binational Network of Sonoran Desert Conservation Areas: Juan Carlos Barrera, director, World Wildlife Fund—Sonora; Dean Bibles, chair, U.S. Man and Biosphere Program; Alberto Búrquez, Institute of Ecology, Universidad Nacional Autónoma de México; Carlos Castillo, director, Pinacate Biosphere Reserve; Steve Cornelius, Sonoran Institute, Sonoran Desert Ecoregion Program; Lorraine Eiler, Hia C'ed O'odham Nation; Exequiel Ezcurra, president, Instituto Nacional de Ecología, SEMARNAT; Isabel Granillo, former director, La Ruta de Sonora Ecotourism Association; Joe Joaquin, Tohono O'odham Nation; Beau McClure, special assistant, International Programs, Bureau of Land Management; Gary Nabhan, former director of science, Arizona-Sonora Desert Museum; Luther Propst, executive director, Sonoran Institute; Robert Schumacher, former manager, Cabeza Prieta National Wildlife Refuge; and Joe Wilder, director, Southwest Center, University of Arizona. Finally, we acknowledge the residents and leaders of the communities of the Sonoran Desert who have participated in these conservation efforts.

Thirty-Six

Vertebrates of the Lower Río Colorado:

What Can Be Done?

Eric Mellink

Conservation and management of the biota of the Río Colorado delta is the focus of much debate. The controversy stems from the fact that both the delta's environmental problems and some solutions to them deal with water from the river, water that is currently used to irrigate crops and provide for the necessities of urban dwellers far away, in other watersheds. I am not a specialist on human conflict solutions, and my intention here is to provide a brief overview of the recent history of the vertebrates associated with the Mexican portion of the Río Colorado, concluding with some thoughts on how biological conservation in this area might be addressed.

Human Activities in the Mexican Portion of the Delta of the Río Colorado

Early human occupants of the delta, ancestors of the Cucapás (or Cocopahs, as they are referred to in English) and of other Yuman groups, seem to have reached the area from the north between 3,000 and 2,000 years ago (Williams 1983). They lived by gathering, fishing, trapping, hunting, and eventually some farming, for which they built rudimentary irrigation systems in the delta. They complemented their diet with *biznagas* (barrel cacti) and agaves (century plants) gathered in the high desert (Kelly 1977). The population grew to many thousands, as documented by Hernando de Alarcón in 1540 and by Francisco de Escobar in 1604–5 (Williams 1983). Despite the relatively large population, the negative impacts of the hunting-gathering activities on the biota were probably negligible, and the presence of farmed patches surely benefited the local fauna (see Nabhan et al. 1982).

In 1539, fewer than 50 years after Europeans "discovered" the Americas, Francisco de Ulloa reached the delta but did not explore it. The following year, Hernando de Alarcón reached the area by boat and Melchior Díaz traveled by land

to meet him. Between then and the late eighteenth century there were only two visits to the area: by Juan de Oñate in 1604 (with Francisco de Escobar as a record keeper) and by Eusebio Francisco Kino in 1702. Toward the end of the eighteenth century a number of visitors came: Ferdinand Consag (1746), Francisco Garcés (1771–76), Juan Bautista de Anza (1774, 1775), Pedro Fagés and José Velásquez (1785), and Joaquín de Arrillaga (1796), and then in the nineteenth century Robert William Hale Hardy (1826), the last the only one with no religious interests. Except for Garcés, who visited the area several times and became known to the Cucapás, these explorers had a rather ephemeral presence and no lasting impact in the area.

Toward the end of the eighteenth century the area served as a refuge for Indians escaping the influence and control of the missionaries in northern Baja California and as a hideout in which to slaughter and eat the cattle stolen from the missions (Gómez Estrada 2000). Neither of these activities seems to have had any impact on the environment, unless escaped cattle led to the establishment of feral populations. Given that their robbers probably guarded them very tightly, this does not seem likely.

After this period, impact from non-Indian activities began to have a tangible effect. Beaver trappers arrived (Davis 1982; Mearns 1907), and one, James Ohio Pattie, even trapped in the Mexican portion of the Colorado (Pattie 1831). Trapping caused the extirpation of beavers from many areas, reducing their overall numbers (Grinnell 1914; Nelson 1921; Weber 1970). More important, since it led to the loss of beaver dams, it promoted an increase in the downriver transport of sediments (Dobyns 1978, 1981). Thus the large amounts of sediments recorded in the river by Sykes (1937b) reflected a major anomaly rather than the normal conditions that had dominated prior to beaver trapping. Augmented amounts of sediments might have increased the frequency of shifts in the river course within the delta. However, whether the loss of beaver pools or the augmented levels of sediments and river shifts had notable impacts on the delta's vertebrates is not known.

The impact on the delta increased rapidly after 1848 when the beaver trappers were followed by hordes of adventurers rushing to their destiny in the northern California gold fields. To protect those using the southern Arizona-California route, the U.S. government built Fort Yuma in 1849. After an 1850 exploration by George Derby, commercial navigation from San Francisco, along the Gulf of California and culminating in Fort Yuma, was established to overcome the difficulties of land travel between California and Arizona. Though sailboats were used for the oceanic voyage, steamboats made the trip between the mouth of the Colorado and Yuma. Lumber to power them could not have come from anywhere but the delta.

Eventually, railroad transportation replaced water transport, but even when navigation slowed and became restricted to the U.S. side of the river, lumber to power the boats was sometimes hauled from the lower delta (Sykes 1937b). Not only were trees used to power the steamboats, but at this time forage was gathered and baled for use in Fort Yuma and Arizona City (illegally, and by an American; Gómez Estrada 2000). However, the extensive forests of fast-growing riparian trees precluded any major impact on the delta's habitat from this lumber cutting (Felger 2000). Likewise, local grass communities were probably not affected by their use as forage.

Farming in the delta by non-Indians began a couple of decades later. Along the Mexican portion of the river, land parcels were allotted to entrepreneurs, and Colonia Lerdo was established in 1874 (Sánchez Ramírez 1990). Among the commercial activities was the extraction of thousands of tons of *cáñamo silvestre* (wild hemp, *Sesbania exaltata;* Felger 2000). For three years, large amounts of *cáñamo* were obtained. Nature then imposed itself with a shift in the Río Colorado's course that inundated Colonia Lerdo, damaged the machinery, and thwarted the operation (Gómez Estrada 2000). Modern farming began in the U.S. portion of the delta in 1901 and in the Mexican portion in 1909. The first dam, Laguna Dam, was built in 1907. In the beginning, small amounts of water were

diverted, so the overall habitat modification was limited.

Throughout the late nineteenth and early twentieth centuries ranchers used the area for cattle grazing. They did not clear huge tracts or stock large numbers of animals, but at the failure of Colonia Lerdo, Berkshire pigs that were part of the enterprise established feral populations (Sánchez Ramírez 1990; Sykes 1937b) and became game for the Cucapás (Williams 1983). It is likely that some cattle and horses escaped and became feral as well. Also during this time it became fashionable to adorn women's hats with the nuptial feathers of white egrets. This fad caused the decrease of egret populations all over the world, including in the delta of the Río Colorado (Mellink 2000). Although agriculture and water diversion were minor in the early twentieth century, by 1933 restrictions on the free flow of water had already caused a notable drying in the delta (Sykes 1937a).

Sportsmen and scientists were not necessarily aware of these impacts, and they all praised the Río Colorado delta for its wealth of wildlife (for a superb version, see Leopold 1949 and 1953, and for an academic's report, Murphy 1917). Interestingly, although the intention of most visitors was to hunt, some made the long trip to Volcano Lake to get mud treatments for health purposes.

The construction of Hoover Dam in 1935 marked the beginning of the final assault on the delta's landscape. The transformation reached such spectacular levels that the delta currently has very little resemblance to what it was a century ago. Several authors aptly describe the history of agriculture in the region (see, e.g., Gómez Estrada 2000; Hendricks 1996; Kerig 2001; and Sánchez Ramírez 1990), so I do not describe it here.

Specific Impact of Human Activities

The wide-scale agricultural transformation of the area dramatically altered the delta's biological integrity; as Minckley (1982:78) states, "The lower Río Colorado…[has]…one of the most highly modified channels in western North America. The most characteristic feature of aquatic habitats in arid zones, extreme variability in time and space, has been suppressed." Minckley also notes that the extent of wetland habitat has been greatly reduced, almost disappearing at times.

Only a few wetland areas exist today, including those associated with the Ciénega del Doctor, the Río Hardy, and the Ciénega de Santa Clara (Glenn et al. 1996). The Ciénega del Doctor is fueled by artesian springs that lie along the Cerro Prieto fault, on the eastern side of the delta. Despite its small size, it is rich in plant species (Ezcurra et al. 1988; Felger 2000; Zengel et al. 1995). Other wetlands in the area include irrigation canals and agricultural drainages, as well as ephemeral wetlands produced by irrigation water spillover and tailwaters.

The Ciénega del Río Hardy was a large wetland fed by water from the Río Hardy and the Colorado. However, large volumes of water discharged during the mid-1980s eroded the natural dam that created this wetland, leading to its drainage (J. M. Payne, personal communication 1995). Currently, some riparian forest is in the processes of recovering in the area (see Glenn & Nagler, this volume). The Ciénega de Santa Clara, the largest wetland in the Mexican portion of the delta, was created and is currently fed by brackish agricultural drainwater from Arizona (Glenn et al. 1992, 1996) and thus is very vulnerable to changes in the flow and quality of this water (Zengel et al. 1995).

The extensive changes in habitat have affected the animals that live in the delta. The most obvious impact derives from the areal reduction of wetlands and riparian habitats. Such reduction has directly caused decreases (or even extirpation) in a number of native species (see Leopold 1959; Mellink & Ferreira 2000; Mellink & Luévano 1998; Patten et al. 2001; Rodriguez et al. 2001; Rosenberg et al. 1991 and references therein). The populations of ten species of fishes have been severely depleted in the lower Colorado, and the Sonoran Desert toad *(Bufo alvarius)*, lowland leopard frog *(Rana yavapaiensis)*, Sonoran mud turtle *(Kinosternon sonoriensis)*, checkered garter snake *(Thamnophis marcianus)*, beaver *(Castor canadensis)*, and river otter *(Lutra canadensis)* have disappeared or declined, or are likely to have declined, as a result of wetland reduction. Decreases in the availability of riparian habitat has caused the reduction or elimination of several nesting birds, including the fulvous whistling-duck *(Dendrocygna bicolor)*, southwestern willow flycatcher *(Empidonax traillii extimus)*, crissal thrasher *(Toxostoma crissale coloradense)*, large-billed savannah sparrow *(Passerculus sandwichensis rostratus)*, and various species of herons and egrets. Additionally, the degrada-

tion of former habitat types resulted in the eradication of the jaguar *(Panthera onca)*. Plowing of desert areas may have reduced populations of the flat-tailed horned lizard *(Phrynosoma mcallii)*, and the lack of freshwater reaching the sea has affected estuarine species such as the Colorado delta clam *(Mulinia coloradoensis)*, a number of fishes, and according to many, the endangered vaquita porpoise *(Phocoena sinus)* (see Brusca; Hastings & Findley; and Navarro, this volume).

It is also very likely that marsh bird populations were greatly reduced as a result of the delta's changes. The creation of the Ciénega de Santa Clara offered some amelioration, for it provided favorable habitat for some species such as the endangered Yuma clapper rail *(Rallus longirostris yumanensis)* and the black rail *(Laterallus jamaicensis)*. Although the Yuma clapper rail occurs widely in the delta, the ciénega is its only real stronghold (Hinojosa-Huerta et al. 2001; see Hinojosa-Huerta et al., this volume).

Not all species have been negatively impacted, however, and the local populations of some native species may actually have increased in number, probably because of an areal increase in shrubby field-edge habitat, which provides more food. A tentative list of populations likely to have increased in number (besides those species considered "agricultural pests") includes the Great Plains toad *(Bufo cognatus)*, Woodhouse toad *(B. woodhousii)*, tree lizard *(Urosaurus ornatus)*, Sonoran gopher snake *(Pituophis melanoleucus affinis)*, white-faced ibis *(Plegadis chihi)*, muskrat *(Ondatra zibheticus)*, and cotton rat *(Sigmodon hispidus eremicus)* (see Grismer 1994, 2002; Mellink 1995). The likelihood that the cotton rat has increased in the Mexican portion of the Colorado merits investigation, as the weed-free farming in the adjacent United States has raised concerns about its status there (Ohmart et al. 1988; Williams 1986).

Other species native to northwestern Mexico and the southwestern United States colonized the delta of the Río Colorado after agricultural development led to the creation of migration corridors. Those species that are confirmed on this list of newcomers, or that are at least good candidates, are the northern cardinal *(Cardinalis cardinalis)*, Anna's hummingbird *(Calypte anna)*, indigo bunting *(Passerina cyanea)*, bronzed cowbird *(Molothrus aeneus)*, inca ground-dove *(Columbina inca)*, and brown-crested flycatcher *(Myarchus tyrannu-*

lus). Although not all these species have been recorded in the Mexican portion of the delta, that is likely due to the paucity in survey effort as opposed to a lack of habitat use (see Hinojosa-Huerta et al., this volume). The laughing gull *(Larus atricilla)* and black skimmer *(Rynchops niger)* may also represent recent arrivals. The cattle egret *(Bubulcus ibis)* is a special case, for it reached America from Africa, presumably riding a storm in the 1880s, and has since dispersed widely.

Finally, humans have intentionally or accidentally introduced species that were released either directly to the delta or to neighboring areas from which they were able to reach the delta on their own. In addition to many species of agriculture-related plants (crops, ornamentals, and weeds) and domestic and commensal vertebrates (European starlings, house sparrows, rock doves, domestic animals, rats and mice), humans have introduced insects (notably European bees, *Apis mellifera;* perhaps already the Argentine ant, *Linepithema humile)* and birds such as the ring-necked pheasant *(Phasianus colchicus),* which was introduced intentionally to the area as a game species.

The wetlands have been particularly abused in this regard. At the turn of the twentieth century the carp *(Cyprinus carpio)* had already been introduced to the lower Colorado (Dill 1944; Gilbert & Scofield 1898). By 1942 there were already 11 introduced fishes (Dill 1944), and by the late 1980s there could have been as many as 26 species of alien fishes in the area (Mueller & Marsh 2002; Ohmart et al. 1988; see Hastings & Findley, this volume). Other introduced species in the wetlands include the Asian clam *(Corbicula fluminea),* paper floater mussel *(Anodonta imbecillus),* crayfish *(Procambarus,* probably *P. clarki),* freshwater shrimp *(Palaemonetes paludosus),* bullfrog *(Rana catesbeiana),* Rio Grande leopard frog *(R. berlandieri),* tiger salamander *(Ambystoma tigrinum),* soft-shelled turtle *(Apalone spinifera),* painted turtle *(Chrysemy picta),* and although it is no longer there, American alligator *(Alligator mississippiensis).*

My Thoughts

Given the extensive modifications that have occurred in terms of the available habitat and the species that comprise the local communities, I do not think it is realistic to pretend to conserve the original biological communities of the delta. True,

most of the species that originally inhabited the delta are still there, but the communities no longer exist in their original form. It would be difficult to argue that current communities are even similar to those that predominated before the extensive and cumulative modifications occurred.

The delta habitats have disappeared because of the lack of running water, and adding decent amounts of flowing water would create wetlands resembling those that existed before the abuse of the delta and containing many of their biotic members. However, simply adding water to the delta will not restore the original conditions as long as the newcomers remain within the biological communities. But getting rid of all the newcomers is not attainable.

This does not mean that the delta is a lost cause or that it is not worthwhile to focus on it for biological conservation. Indeed, it is very worthwhile. First, we can "use" the delta to conserve particular species or subspecies that are under threat of extinction because of our abuse of the area. Although single-species focus is becoming politically incorrect, this might be one of our more profitable, at least in the short term, actions for biological conservation in the delta.

Second, we can create biotic communities that resemble the original ones as closely as possible rather than aim to restore them to their original state. This implies not only the allocation of good-quality water to the area but also the eradication or population control of the introduced species that have the most negative impact. The amounts of water needed are quite modest, less than a twelfth of Mexico's allocation of Río Colorado's flow (Varady et al. 2001). In this creation of wetlands, I have three comments.

First, let's think about the conceptual framing of the communities to be created. This might seem silly: of course, most of us would say, the original habitats should be used as models. But what do we mean by *original habitats*? Those that were present before Indian people arrived? Before the Europeans got here? After that but before the dams were built? The great hunting period of the 1940s–60s? Certainly, our knowledge is not sufficient to partition it this finely, except for the case of before and after the dams were constructed.

Such an exercise to define a model for the proposed habitat creation might seem superficial. However, I bring it up because I have heard the expression *conservation of the delta* used with different ideas in mind. For example, some people advocate the creation of riparian forests for songbirds, wetlands to attract waterfowl for hunting purposes, and marshes for rails. None of these scenarios considers beavers or cotton rats. Even more divergent opinions, proposed by conservation managers in a flier distributed about a decade ago, suggested that the soft-shelled turtle should be considered threatened—a peculiar perception of biological conservation, since it is an introduced species! On the other hand, I have also heard the opinion that introduced fish should not be removed since they have become a functional part of the wetlands where they occur. Agreeing on a habitat model will attune the players and reduce frictions as conservation actions progress.

Second, let's not put all our eggs (if we can get the hen to lay!) in one basket. Much of the effort directed toward biological conservation in the delta is focused on the Ciénega de Santa Clara. I agree that we should care about this wetland, but we should not neglect to establish several other wetlands and connecting riparian habitats. We should not even neglect developing connections between small patches of wetland within agricultural areas.

Third, let's not trade research for action. Most of the species that we know or suspect to have been affected by the changes in the delta, including those that have decreased and those that have increased, should be carefully studied to determine their status. Ecological processes in these modified communities are prime targets for research. Even the implementation of management actions can set the stage for careful and insightful ecological research. Although much research can be carried out in the delta in the absence of environmental management, the latter should not be done without the former.

We cannot protect the native habitats of the delta of the Río Colorado, since they are no longer there, nor can we hope to restore them completely. However, there is plenty of room for meaningful biological management in the delta. How far can we go? It will depend on how much water, money, expertise, and devotion we can gather. It will not be easy, as multiple parties will be competing for the same water and funds, but any successes we achieve will be worth the effort.

Acknowledgments

Sharon Herzka provided insightful comments: thank you very much.

Thirty-Seven

Last Call:

Leaving Something Behind

CHARLES BOWDEN

It is a matter of honor even though I never gave my word. Seventeen years ago, I stood at a counter in Organ Pipe Cactus National Monument, a little-visited backwater of the national park system on the Mexican line in southern Arizona. Julian Hayden, then about seventy, was leaning forward and speaking to a young woman. Hayden had rolled into Arizona on a motorcycle in the 1920s when the roads where dirt and the only way to cool the air was wait for winter. He knew more about the deserts of southwestern Arizona and northwestern Mexico than any other man alive. He was a lean man, almost fatally handsome, and that day he was all but charming the pants off a young woman working for the park service. When we left, he explained to me that she was a descendant of Don Alberto Celaya and I was stunned.

You have to know the bloodlines here to have some notion. In the first decade of this century, a pleasantly crazed Norwegian named Carl Lumholtz came into the country, and in the tiny village of Sonoyta on the edge of the great desert Lumholtz hired a boy named Alberto Celaya to guide him into a vast wilderness that eventually became his book of the place, something he called *New Trails in Mexico*. On that wandering with burros into the thousands of square miles of waterless desert, Lumholtz stumbled into the world of Juan Caravajales, thought at the time to be the last Sand Papago living on the native ground. And then in 1912 Caravajales quit the desert and it became empty of so much as a footprint. In the 1950s Hayden started wandering the place, and Celaya as an old man became his teacher. At Papago Tanks, Hayden found Caravajales' old camp—a woven mat for a bed, some food and ollas (clay water jugs)—left as if he departed the night before and would soon be back. In the low rainfall—zero to three inches a year—things have a way of staying the same here. The wind moves the soil and so there is no stratigraphy. A bone tossed aside a thousand years ago will rest next to a cigarette butt. Hayden found early man sites that go back into a cauldron of debate—ten thousand years? twenty thousand years? a hundred thousand years?

When Hayden entered the country, the game knew naught of man, and once a badger waddled up and sniffed his boot and then ambled off again. I've lain on the hard ground and had bighorn sheep walk by fifteen feet away and treat me for what I am—an ungainly but apparently harmless biped. And so when Hayden flirted with the young woman of the family Celaya, he touched a chord of knowing this unknown ground that stretched back all of the twentieth century, a kind of lineage of desert rats.

So we went into that country, my first time, into a place on the Mexican site of volcanic craters and vast lavas and old intaglios left by earlier lovers and abandoned camps from back of the beyond and sleeping circles, low rock enclosures to block the wind, and old stone hammers and total silence. The tongues of lava licked north across the line into the United States where yet more emptiness loomed, a tract of five thousand square miles without a house, a person, a cow, or a voice. Hayden was leery of me and my scribbling pen.

I remember when it all changed. It was dusk, we'd been sipping mescal, and I sprawled on the ground listening to the big emptiness when suddenly Hayden was looming over me and snorted, "I don't give a damn what you write." I was in. And the better part of me never came back. Julian and I became friends. The desert and I became lovers. That's the beginning of it, and now that I've bounced down some hard years, I know it will never end for me. I've got personal ties. Hundreds of miles of walking where there are no trails, and damn little water. A friend buried in the emptiness in a simple hole so that he can watch what he loved forever. I think of my friend a lot. He always figured to come back as a vulture, and when I see

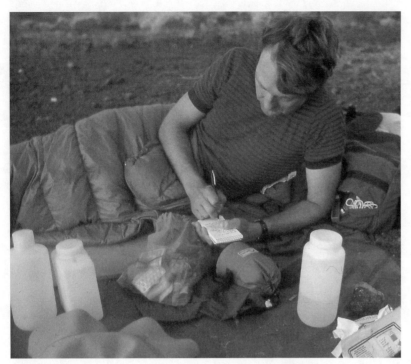

Figure 37.1. Charles Bowden deep in the Pinacate, 1984. (Photo by Bill Broyles)

a buzzard wheeling overhead now I always smile to myself. Julian himself once took me to a knoll out there where he'd scattered the ashes of two premier desert rats—Malcolm Rogers and later Ronald Ives. And now Julian is gone, passing away peacefully in his eighty-seventh year, his head no doubt filled with the dirt and heat and silence of a thousand camps he'd made.

A few years or so ago, a friend of mine and one of Julian's prize students in desert rathood, a man named Bill Broyles, came to me and said, "We've got to do something." So we sat in my backyard and he spelled it out. That's where this matter of honor came in and the power of the vow I never recalled taking. We sputtered an hour or so and set on this notion: we'd create a five-thousand-square-mile national park on the U.S. side, a dab of ground big enough to swallow the Grand Canyon and Yosemite together. We'd build it out of three chunks of federal land—Organ Pipe, the Cabeza Prieta National Wildlife Refuge, and the Barry Goldwater Gunnery Range. Firing would continue on the Gunnery Range until an epidemic of peace broke out or the military changed its training methods to the world of laser beams. No matter. Parks are forever, and we could wait out the needs of the gods of war. All we wanted was to protect the ground now. And forever. We'd call it the Sonoran Desert National Park, and it would be the last stronghold in our nation for silence,

for the rare Sonoran pronghorn, for botanical originality such as the elephant tree, and for the haunting scale of bigness that was the making of the American people, the sense that things were much too large to be conquered or ever owned by the likes of us. We would create a reserve for the soul as we, as a people, hurl ourselves into another millennium. The place would link up with the desert on the Mexican side, that volcanic wonderland that the republic of Mexico has already made a federal reserve. And this desert would in turn embrace the protected zone of the upper Gulf of California. When we stared at the map sitting in my yard, we realized we were looking at the biggest potential zone of silence and space and life left in the Western Hemisphere south of the Arctic. And we knew in fact and in our bones, this natural bounty was already starting to disappear as the six billion *Homo sapiens* on this mobbed planet finally turned even to this hard desert in their desperate search for escape from the ugly machine world they'd fashioned. It was a handshake deal out there in the yard under my mesquite tree, and now the thing is rolling, sound, and better for you than a fistful of vitamins.

I remember being out once with Julian on an early-man site. The ground was littered with hammers and choppers and you could all but hear the scream of the dying game, the smack of the stone busting up the bones for marrow. Sleeping circles fashioned of stone a millennium or two or more before dotted the ground. I curled up in one to feel the bodies of the ancient ones. The site stood on the lip of a crater, one named after Don Alberto Celaya, Julian's mentor in the long ago. Ives and Rogers' shades watched us from a nearby hill where their ashes had been scattered. I all but expected a woolly mammoth to lurch into view. I could look north and know that the desert swept clean and free well into the United States and that I might walk sixty miles and be alone every inch of the way.

Julian said, "Come here," and I obediently trotted after him. He led me into the creosote and soft sands and then he stopped and kicked something with his foot. I looked down and saw a metate, an old grinding stone of green and white flecked rock. The thing gleamed up at me like an emerald. He said, "I'm leaving this here."

And then we said nothing. I understood. Just as once I dropped down into the sacred cave of I'itoi up under a volcanic peak and found a prayer stick left by some other pilgrim a century or a thousand years before and I looked at it a moment, and then shoved it deeper into a rock crevice so it would stay there forever. Just as my friend Broyles once wandered up a canyon in the Sierra Pintas and found two perfect ollas sitting out in the open, and left them there forever. Just as proper folk tossed my late friend Edward Abbey into a hole in this country and left him there to become a vulture.

Once I walked two hundred miles across this ground and nothing happened but the beat of my heart. Once I sat in the June heat for a week, the temperature in the afternoon banging between 115 and 120, and watched a family of vultures day by day disassemble a dead coyote. Each day the vultures would take a break and line up like penguins at a slimy rock waterhole and one by one drink. We lived together for days without a cross word between us.

So that's what I'm going to do before I die. Help create this park, and the word *park* is just a buzz of sound to contain these memories and to make damn sure this place that does not need me or you or give a damn about us stretches out, untouched, into this thing we call the future. It'll be a weird park. Hardly a road. Hardly a prayer of water. Frightening in the scale of its empty valleys and lonely peaks. And silent. I can't scant this matter of silence. The periodic blast of jets on the gunnery range during training days does not really make a dent into this puddle of stillness. Once I stood in the middle of the Tule Desert in June and the rains had failed for so very long and there were no insects and the birds in midday hid in the brush and left the sky empty. I must have been thirty or forty miles in any direction from another human being. Suddenly, I could hear this gurgling sound and behind the gurgles I detected this faint thumping. I snapped alert, looked around for the intruder into my domain. Then I fell into an understanding. I was hearing the blood coursing through my veins, the beat of my heart. That's what I mean when I use the word *silence,* a level of quiet the cemeteries only hear about through rumor. I know a guy who now and then wanders this country and he once told me, "If you are out there and you find another person out there, you feel violated."

I mentioned to him that my friend Bill Broyles liked to scamper about out there. The man looked

Figure 37.2. Charles Bowden and Julian Hayden, Pinacate, 1984. (Photo by Bill Broyles)

at me and flared, "I've come across his spoor." It's that kind of country.

It's beautiful, has its checklist of biological treasures and endangered this and that. There are turgid scientific papers measuring its flesh and bones. And I know with this park a bunch of damn rules will come and I will hate every goddamn rule. No matter. It's gotta be made safe from us before I die or I'm gonna go to my grave one pissed-off rat.

For the next few years, I'm going to be giving speeches, pressing the flesh in congressional offices, and late at night sitting in my yard cursing all the details. But I'm going to help get it done. And when I'm dead, I'm going to be out there. Out there with Ed Abbey and Julian Hayden and Ronald Ives and Malcolm Rogers and early Americans and bighorn sheep and pronghorn and elephant trees and searing heat and hard rock. And silence. And it does not matter whether they toss my body in the local cemetery or burn it to ash. I'll be out there. After that first time, I never left. The desert is with me. It scowls, washes my face with its furnace breath, and at night pounds my head with a billion stars hanging down like ornaments. It doesn't give a damn about me. Or you, for that matter. That's not why I'm doing it.

I give a damn about it.

I gave my word. I just can't remember when. Or why.

Acknowledgments

An earlier version of this essay appeared in *Esquire,* December 1999.

Part Six

PLACE-NAMES

Thirty-Eight

Changing Place-Names in the Pinacate

Julian D. Hayden

Identification of places from names and descriptions found in the journals of earlier travelers is sometimes difficult. As the regional common tongue in the Southwest changed from Indian to Spanish to frontier English to "civilized" English, so did place-names change. Some names have been transliterated into Spanish and preserved, such as (Papago) Ali'chukson, which became Tucson; others have been forgotten and renamed by later settlers, often several times. The vigorous and uninhibited language of the frontier named many places after their obvious resemblances to parts of human or animal anatomy, usually sexual, and these have eventually been "Comstocked." Walker Butte, the volcanic plug north of Coolidge, Arizona, was to the Pima Indians a reminder of the wolf's virility and was so named. The early whites renamed the butte after the lactatory mechanism of an Indian woman, and lately it was renamed Walker's Butte, to the edification of the old-timers, who recall when a spade was a spade. Similarly, a frontiersman would be baffled by reference to the Castle Dome Mountains of western Arizona, for the desert rat knew them as the S-H Mountains, a clear description of their likeness to a utilitarian structure common to most pioneer backyards. As an exception, the Grand Tetons of Wyoming preserved their frontier name, perhaps because French is a "cultured" language, or perhaps because the unacceptable usually sounds better in another language and becomes permissible, even romantic.

These comments are pertinent to the attempts in late years to retrace the path of Dr. Carl Lumholtz, the Norwegian geographer, in the forbidding, arid and difficult volcanic mass of the Sierra Pinacate, in the Gran Desierto de Altar of northwestern Sonora, Mexico. Dr. Lumholtz, it will be recalled, traveled the region in 1910 on horseback and published an account of his travels, with a sketch map, in *New Trails in Mexico*. The Pinacate had been visited in 1698 by Padre Kino, who named the mountain Cerro de Santa Clara and referred to an Indian village of Suvuk, on the southeast side and now lost. William T. Hornaday, accompanying Godfrey Sykes and Dr. Daniel T. MacDougal, the party leader, partially explored the Pinacate in 1907, as described by him in *Camp-Fires on Desert and Lava*. Since that time, until 1956, visitors have been few and generally not inclined to memorialize their travels in books. The Mexican inhabitants of Sonoyta, base of operations for both the Hornaday party and Lumholtz, knew little of the mountains, and Don Alberto Celaya of Sonoyta, who had guided Lumholtz, remarked in 1960 that as late as 1930 not six Mexicans in Sonoyta had heard of the Cerro Colorado, a landmark cone east of the Pinacate, let alone seen it.

In 1954–58 the opening of Mexican Highway No. 2, from Sonoyta to San Luis R.C. along the international border, made access to the Pinacate relatively easy; both Mexican woodcutters and North American students of the desert entered it, the former tracing a network of truck trails into the lavas, the latter often attempting to follow both Lumholtz's and Hornaday's maps. Tinajas de los Pápagos, or Tinajas del Indio, or Papago Tanks, were easy to identify, being the only waterhole on the north end of the mountain and on one of the main trails to California. Confusion arose when the search for Lumholtz's Tinaja de los Chivos and Tinaja del Tule was begun, and many trips on foot and by jeep were made in trying to locate these tanks. A tank in the approximate location of Tinaja de los Chivos was found by William Woodin of Tucson in 1960, but it turned out to be that named Tinaja del Tule by Hornaday, and the "Tinaja del Tule" upstream from T. de los Chivos, mentioned but not visited by Lumholtz, could not be found at all.

577

Figure 38.1. *Filiberto "El Viejito" Pérez, near Tinaja de los Chivos, about 1969. (Photo by James T. Gutmann)*

In and after 1956 José Navarro of San Luis R.C. made several trips into the Pinacate, accompanying Filiberto Pérez, "El Viejito," also of San Luis, visiting several tanks on the southwest slope. El Viejito (the Little Old One) had been prospecting for some 45 years there, on the west side, in search of the mother lode of a piece of gold-bearing float he had found as a youth, and he knew the country well. In 1961 José Navarro guided the writer to these tanks, visiting first "Tinaja del Bote," a temporary tank near the junction of lava and dunes near Lumholtz's Indian Camp, or Sunset Camp. El Viejito had named this tank "Bote," or "Bucket," tank, from a handmade galvanized-iron bucket that was cached in the cliffs nearby, bearing the date of galvanizing, 1893. Here tules were growing in the silt bar forming the downstream wall of the

tank. Below Tinaja del Bote the clear Indian trail described by Lumholtz was intersected and was followed uphill to the tank known to El Viejito and Navarro as "Tinaja de los Chivos." This tank had obviously been frequented in the past by Mexican hunters and was the tank Woodin had reached in 1960, Hornaday's "Tinaja del Tule." El Viejito had also shown Navarro, who showed the writer, another tank several kilometers from "Chivos," which he had named Tinaja del Huarache, or Sandal Tank, a most impressively situated permanent tank, probably not seen by more than a couple of parties since Indian times.

The confusing identification of "Chivos" seemed now a simple matter of deduction. Since Hornaday's guide of 1907 had apparently never been to Tinaja del Tule but was going on information received, perhaps from Indians, he could not be relied upon for positive identification of the tank. He had clearly intended to take Hornaday's party to the approximate location of Tinaja del Bote before turning into the mountain proper but had been ordered by MacDougal to proceed directly toward the peaks before making his southing. When by the greatest of good fortune the party practically fell into a tank, it was accepted as Tinaja del Tule and was so figured in Hornaday's book. (The illustration of the central pool at Tule is wrongly captioned; it is of the central pool at Papago Tanks. See *Camp-Fires on Desert and Lava,* page 239a.)

On the other hand, Lumholtz's "Chivos," according to his sketch map, was in the same location. This writer deduced, then, that Tinaja del Tule proper was what El Viejito had named "Tinaja del Bote," because of the tules seen growing there, and that "Tinaja del Tule" was in reality Lumholtz's Tinaja de los Chivos. This deduction was supported by El Viejito's having named the tank "Chivos," and everyone interested seemed satisfied; by a series of mischances, photos of "Chivos" were not shown to Don Alberto Celaya, then nearing his final illness, for identification.

In the winter of 1963–64, Woodin, camped at "Tinaja de los Chivos," encountered a party of Mexican prospectors who showed him a permanent tank of great size, downstream from "Chivos," and said that they had named this hitherto unknown tank "Tinaja de San Carlos" after the name saint of a prospector. Woodin described it to this writer, who visited it in April of 1964. This "Tinaja de San

Carlos" was almost impossible to find, hidden deep in an arroyo with vertical walls, and it was not surprising that it had not been seen by El Viejito and others, including the writer, who had walked near it earlier.

A survey of this new tank and its surroundings showed extensive Indian occupation, very few pieces of pre-1917 glass, and three tin cans, well-rusted, one post-1944 and two post-1956, probably left at the same time. Obviously, this tank had been visited by few persons since Indian times.

Comparison of the tank's situation with that of Tinaja de los Chivos, as described by Lumholtz, solved the mystery of Chivos and Tule. This newly found "Tinaja de San Carlos" is the Tinaja de los Chivos of Lumholtz, corresponding to his description in all respects, while Tinaja del Tule, known correctly by Hornaday's guide and recently as "Chivos," lay in the proper position as reported by Lumholtz, who had not visited it (see Table 38.1).

No doubt the true Tinaja de los Chivos will now be known as Tinaja de San Carlos, and Tinaja del Tule as Tinaja de los Chivos, while Tinaja del Bote thus far remains unnamed on the maps, and Tinaja del Huarache, to compound the confusion, has been renamed "Pyramid Camp" by recent American visitors.

The differing Spanish and English names of the tank last mentioned illustrate a common situation in this part of the Sonoran desert. Lumholtz gave the name Paso de Juana, after a New York friend of his named Jane, to a pass in the Sierra

Figure 38.2. Julian Hayden, Pinacate, 1956. (Photo by Paul H. Ezell)

Tuseral northwest of the Pinacate, a name not known to the Mexicans, who call it El Puerto. The local term, Choclo Duro, or patent leather shoe, is applied to a difficult dune area where the shoe was found, well known to all Mexican travelers on the old Sonoyta–San Luis trail; it is not known at all to Americans. The dune expanse west of Choclo Duro, north of the crater named by Hornaday MacDougal Crater (which has no local name other than El Gran Depresión), is known as Los Diputados, after the legislators who died there of thirst in 1945 when their car broke down.

The permanent tanks on the east side of the Pinacate, once known to the Indians as Moitjútjupo

TABLE 38.1. *Comparison of tinaja names.*

Hornaday	Lumholtz	El Viejito	Sykes	Other
T. del Indio	T. de los Pápagos		Papago Tanks	Papago Tanks
		T. del Bote		
T. del Tule	T. del Tule	T. de los Chivos		T. de los Chivos
	T. de los Chivos			T. de San Carlos
		T. del Huarache		Pyramid Camp
		Volcán de Chichi	Moon Crater	Volcán de Chichi
	T. de Emilia		T. de Emilia	T. de Palo Verde?

("many pools"), and to the present-day Mexicans as Tinajas de Palo Verde, are recognized by Americans as Tinajas de Emilia, after Lumholtz, who gave them his aunt's name, Emily. The tanks south of Tinajas de Emilia, for which Lumholtz used the local names of Tinaja del Cuervo, Pinto, and Galletal, probably cannot now be identified with accuracy, since the old-timers among the Mexicans have passed away. To return to the southwest curve of the Pinacate, the Indian name of Hótunikat (Sunset Camp), referred to by Lumholtz as applying to a village site at the junction of lava and dunes, lies next to a crater named Moon Crater in 1956 by Glenton Sykes of Tucson. This crater was known to El Viejito and Navarro as Volcán de Chichi, a descriptive and very earthy term that will probably last among the Mexicans in the region.

This problem of polylingual names is a very real one. While custom dictates the continued use of the first name to appear in print, it might be advisable to list all the various names of a place in publications relating to the area. Certainly an American suffering from thirst, asking a woodcutter in the Pinacate for the location of Tinaja de Emilia or Pyramid Camp, might become even more desiccated before finding his way to water.

Thirty-Nine

Our Grand Desert:

A Gazetteer for Northwestern Sonora, Southwestern Arizona, and Northeastern Baja California

Bill Broyles, Luke Evans, Richard Stephen Felger, and Gary Paul Nabhan

> The purpose of the desert is to walk through, and think.
> — *Travis Edmonson (2001)*

Since you're busy today, we won't load your seat cushion and coffee mug into the van. We won't see how far we can drive or how many stops we can make. But we would like to take you on an armchair tour of our favorite places in northwestern Sonora, southwestern Arizona, and even a few in northeastern Baja California. This is the cactus coast, the *gran despoblado,* Brer Jackrabbit's cactus patch, the center of the desert rat universe. If you like sand in your shoes, warm handshakes, a hint of mystery, cactus flowers, and grand openness, then you'll love this region as much as we do.

In the second century A.D. Claudius Ptolemy assembled some eight thousand place-names of the known world in a gazetteer he titled *Geographia.* Nearly two thousand years later, it's time to round up what we know of our region's desert places, so that socially and scientifically we can better understand where we're at, what we have, and where we're going. The names given here clarify our optimistic borderland, our special frontier, our geography of tomorrow. They are used by residents and historians, by scientists and students, by planners and managers, by outdoor workers and armchair explorers. These names resound richly to those who already know them.

Place-names are important on several levels. They reveal human and natural histories, give us handles for geography, allow comparisons of scientific collections, incite our curiosity, and fuel our spirit of adventure. They applaud the *antepasados* who came before us and accent our human preoccupation with water: over forty percent of the place-names in this arid region are associated with sources of freshwater.

This gazetteer is designed to assist you in locating and interpreting place-names mentioned elsewhere in this book, as well as in the pages and on the lips of those who cherish this region. It is a map reader's companion. Julian Hayden (Chapter 38, this volume) encourages us to list and clarify the various names of places, lest we go astray literally and metaphorically. Issac Taylor (1898:4) warned, "The vitality of a name is lost when the meaning is no longer generally understood." We hope to energize vitality. Ronald Ives (1964:32) noted that "recent field studies have shown a great confusion of names and locations." We aim to reduce confusion.

We hope that this gathering will enhance our mutual understanding and sharpen our shared vision of this unique borderland ecosystem, for our future is here in this desert.

Dilemmas

Despite their practicality, place-names sometimes create complications. This gazetteer contains hundreds of names, but some are not wearing well. The name Squaw Tits, for example, offends some people but has been on the USGS maps since 1950. Bryan (1925:225) referred to this feature as Double Butte, although its O'odham name, Vipi Do'ag ('breasts mountain'), predates Bryan's descriptive name. We pondered using the publication of this gazetteer as an opportunity to tout Bryan's label, but we see our role as reporters, not revisionists or reformers. Similar dilemmas affect other places in the nation and state (e.g., Squaw Peak, Shit House Mountains, Dead Mexican Creek, Niggerhead Mountain, Dead Indian Canyon, Gringo Gulch, Big Dick Canyon). As public attitudes and tolerance change, as synonyms are born and others fade from use, and as future generations view their places more clearly and sensitively, such dilemmas will be resolved democratically.

The incremental nature of the formal naming process will certainly temper any sudden tendency to change. Five washes near Gila Bend—Cemetery, Citrus Valley, Evans, Hacker, and West Quilotosa—illustrate this process. The names have some informal, local currency, and in 2001 when the town of Gila Bend needed referents for a flood-control project, the town council proposed these names (Turner 2001). However, as of 2003 only Citrus Valley Wash and West Quilotosa Wash have been accepted by the Arizona State Board of Geographic and Historic Names. Cemetery Wash was rejected because an arroyo near Wickenburg (70 miles away) bears the same name; the names Evans (no relation to our coauthor) and Hacker were rejected because persons must have been deceased for a minimum of five years to have a place named for them. These names were rejected on simple policy grounds and carried little in the way of cultural controversy. The board has invited new proposals for the unaccepted names (Arizona State Board on Geographic and Historic Names Minutes, July 11 and October 30, 2001; Julie Hoff, personal communication). Proposed or existing names that strike at human emotions certainly make such processes even more difficult. Clearly, naming is not the cut-and-dried business it may initially appear. For a complete treatment of the official policies and procedures of naming, see Orth & Payne 1997.

Another issue affecting place-names in this region is the U.S. Board of Geographic Names policy against assigning names to previously unnamed features within wilderness areas. While the majority of lands covered in this gazetteer fall outside congressionally designated wilderness, one of the region's strongest appeals is its wildness and lack of human impact. There is something mysterious and beautiful about a region with few named features, an appeal many of our readers undoubtedly share. Aldo Leopold (1966) asked, "Of what avail are forty freedoms without a blank spot on the map?" He also warned us that such blank spots are shrinking and, once lost, cannot be restored. The desire to pepper wild places with names goes against the grain of wilderness, where "man himself is a visitor who does not remain" (*Wilderness Act,* 16 U.S.C. 1131).

Place-names lie on the landscape alongside the other detritus of human wanderings. While more innocuous than tire tracks, tin cans, and prospect holes, names on a map can detract from the mystery of a place. Too, place-names can innocently draw unneeded attention to a place. Certainly, far more people have climbed Cabeza Prieta Peak than have climbed the true (but unnamed) highpoint of the Cabeza Prieta Mountains, four miles to the north. And for some reason, Paradise Canyon seems a much more appealing destination when viewed on a map than, say, the equally beautiful but unnamed canyon immediately to the south. Fortunately, most spaces don't need names to be memorable and meaningful and are far more amenable to personal, private nicknames than public, published labels.

For these and other reasons, we refrain from suggesting additional names of deserving people we have known (or wish we had known). An Ed Abbey Peak would certainly have a place here, as would a Charles Sheldon Tinaja or a Julian Hayden Crater (although Hayden himself declined Chuck Wood's nomination; see Caravajales Crater). We also considered suggesting plant or animal names; we have Saguaro Gap, but no barrel cactus, bursage, or brittlebush represented. We have Packrat Hill, Sheep Peak and Sheep Mountain, and Antelope Tank, but no places named for rattlers, turkey vultures, or badgers (except for an O'odham translation). In the end we declined the role of nominator. If a place requires or merits a name, it will earn it.

Organization and Layout

The information for each site or locality is organized in the following manner: (1) place-name (area); (2) type of feature, and its relationship to a larger or wider geographic feature; (3) brief human or natural history; (4) origin or derivation of the name if known to us, with translations from other languages noted by single quotation marks; for synonyms or other names known to have been used, the equal (=) sign means "also known as" or "the same as"; (5) coordinates, in degrees (NAD 1927); and (6) elevation, usually meters in Mexico, feet in the United States.

The names are listed alphabetically, by major word (for example, "Tinaja de Anna" precedes "Tinaja Batamote"); variant, limited, or former names are typically mentioned under the entry for the modern name or the name that is most commonly used. Elevations and coordinates for mountain ranges are usually given for their summits. Expansive features (towns, bays, plains, etc.) are typically located by their approximate centers. Unless noted, coordinates for linear features (valleys, canyons, streams, etc.) are located at their mouths. See *The National Gazetteer of the United States of America: Arizona 1986,* pp. x–xi (United States Geological Survey 1987), for a fuller description of cartographic conventions. Latitudes and longitudes given here are as accurate as the published or plotted sources allow and are not intended for navigation or legal descriptions.

Since the very concept of bio-reserve looks beyond political boundaries, entries are mingled and spill beyond the linear confines of legal and administrative boundaries. We have tried to gather most place-names within these special administrative areas, and we include some selected names outside their boundaries and realize the need for a comprehensive gazetteer of the surrounding region, especially the lower Colorado River valley. Four 1:250,000 maps (Mexicali, Puerto Peñasco, San Felipe, and Los Vidrios or Ajo) provide an overview of the region and remind us to avoid the "white map syndrome" of letting national or management borderlines confine our scientific, personal, or political horizons (Nagel 1992).

Mexican and United States cartographers published these maps using NAD 1927 datum, and we maintain that convention, so readers who prefer their coordinates in UTMs, NAD 1983, or some other format or datum will need to make that conversion. We apologize for the intermix of metric and English elevations from cartographic sources, but conversion introduces unneeded ambiguity and error. Generally, we have converted linear distances to provide kilometers south of the border and miles north of the international line. For the convenience of our readers, conversion formulas are provided at the beginning of the gazetteer.

Although this index is extensive, no gazetteer is ever truly finished. For example, Mexico has announced it will begin construction of the long-proposed coastal highway through the Alto Golfo biosphere reserve and we can expect new communities and resorts along the route. New names will follow. And for example, as this edition goes to press, we are still following leads on the derivations of Espanto Mountain, Haley Hills, and Rainbow Valley, among others. Someone out there knows—but it isn't us, yet. We predict that before the ink dries on this edition, someone will call

with the message, "Everybody knows how Espanto got its name. Back in the year…" We welcome your calls, additions, and corrections (in care of the University of Utah Press, or the University of Arizona Southwest Center, Tucson AZ 85721–0185). This second edition includes many refinements and additional entries beyond the first edition (Broyles et al. 1997). We fully expect and earnestly invite readers to provide additional information and documents that will enrich future editions.

Methodology

Information in this gazetteer was gathered through modern and historic maps, historical accounts, journals, field notes, interviews, and other sources. We have drawn from a wealth of "gray" literature, which may be available only regionally in the university, historical society, and agency archives of Arizona and Sonora. Besides citations in the bibliography, sources include maps by Mexico's Instituto Nacional de Estadística, Geografía, e Informática and the United States Geological Survey (USGS). Personal communications appear as first and last names of informants, with no date given.

The USGS has published maps of this area for more than one hundred years. We consulted all known editions and series of USGS maps, including 60, 30, and 15 minute series (all now out of print), as well as the modern and more familiar 7.5 minute series. Over the years, many place-names, locales, roads, or other features have "dropped off" USGS maps, while others, of course, have been added. In cases where historic place-names no longer appear on modern maps, we plotted these features by interpolation as accurately as the historic sources would allow. We also used many other historic and modern maps available to us, some official, some not.

Many named locales never appeared on maps, and still others existed in areas that have subsequently undergone dramatic change (the Colorado River delta, for example) and are impossible to precisely locate since they have effectively been erased from the landscape. These places are known to us through oral histories, field journals, surveys, historic accounts, historic maps, and other sources. When we are unable to precisely locate these features, we provide coordinates preceded by the phrase *vicinity of.* In some cases, the locations of features are so vaguely known that we are unable to provide any coordinates. Further research and investigation may enable refinements.

We do not distinguish between names officially accepted by the U.S. Board of Geographical Names and unofficial names. Many of the place-names in this gazetteer are well known in this region but lack official recognition at either the state or federal level.

In the first edition of this gazetteer (Broyles et al. 1997), most coordinates were derived using paper maps, agency sources, and global positioning systems (GPS). Since then, improvements in mapping software and other technologies have enabled us to derive the same information more precisely. For this edition, most coordinates for U.S. entries were plotted using DeLorme 3-D Topo-Quads mapping software based on USGS 7.5 minute topographic maps, providing an accuracy of ±50 feet (15 m) or better for most locations. Technology currently available to us limits this capability for many entries in Mexico, so those remain largely unchanged from the first edition. We hope emerging technologies will remedy those limitations for future editions. Locations for many Mexican places are from the nomenclator on the backs of recent 1:50,000 topographic maps. Other coordinates are plotted from maps or read from hand-held GPS units at the actual geographical sites.

Coordinates for cemeteries, archaeological sites, sacred sites, and other sensitive areas are omitted. If you have knowledge of these areas, please respect them with utmost reverence and refrain from visiting them. Even prehistoric sites may remain sacred and religiously significant for a number of modern people. Inconspicuous as well as obvious Native American sites or areas may have been highly important by providing residence, farming, hunting, gathering, burial, ceremony, travel, grazing, water, medicine, communication, art, or tool and craft uses, but they remain integral to the *himdag* (way of life) in a continuum and are never "abandoned" or just "temporary" (Doyel & Eiler 2003:17, 22).

For tinajas, tanks, and stock ponds, we use *perennial* to mean usually holding water throughout the year, if replenished by the region's bi-seasonal precipitation; *intermittent* sources retain water from one to six months, and *ephemeral* sources for less than a month (Brown et al. 1983; Brown & Johnson 1983). It is worth noting that in this true desert there seem to be no absolutely per-

manent freshwater sources: well pumps malfunction, long-term droughts cancel springs and mock usually reliable tinajas, and even the mighty Colorado River occasionally runs dry at its mouth.

Visitors to desert waterholes around the world understand how precious water is. Wildlife and humans may need to drink it, so use it only in emergencies. Treat it as if your own life depended on it, for someday it might. Camp more than one-quarter mile away from waterholes and never bathe or swim in them. Never rely on finding water at any waterhole listed in this gazetteer.

Readers should note that by convention the USGS uses neither possessives (as in Major's Tank or Wall's Well) nor accents (as in Díaz Spire or José Juan Hill), but in Mexico, cartographers do. Several styles of spelling place-names in Mexico are currently practiced (Alberto Búrquez, personal communication). Almada (1990) prefers dropping capitals on general categories of geographic features; for example, río Sonoyta or golfo de California. Some maps produced in Mexico capitalize all letters of a place-name, for example, SAN LUIS or RANCHO LOS VIDRIOS. It is especially bewildering trying to determine when to capitalize the first letter of definite articles in place-names; it's Volcán La Luna but Tinaja de los Pápagos. Some authors commonly capitalize all first letters of names except "de" or "del," as in Cerro El Chivo or Sierra de La Salada. Others in Mexico favor dropping the geographic feature entirely, for example, La Luna (dropping Volcán) or Los Alacranes (dropping Sierra). We use a fuller and more traditional style.

For Native American terms, we try to use the current orthographies adopted by tribes in the region, but we note how the term was earlier transcribed on maps or in explorers' accounts. Whenever possible, we give literal translations to further enrich our images of this land. Modern Tohono and Hia C'ed (= Hia-ced, Hia c-ed, Hia Ced) O'odham orthography was developed by linguists Albert Alvarez and Kenneth Hale (1970), adopted by the Tohono O'odham Nation as its official language, and explained in Ofelia Zepeda's *Papago Grammar* (1983). Here, however, the allophone **v** is used instead of **w,** since the sound is more frequently used by Hia C'ed O'odham in common speech. The linguistic marks for O'odham words include some symbols not found in common fonts, such as the diacritical ˀ, a glottal stop that is sometimes rendered ' (as in 'A'li), and ' is what we use in *Dry Borders.* The O'odham place-names come from interviews and study conducted by Gary Nabhan and Jacquie Kahn on behalf of the Hia-ced O'odham Alliance, which has graciously consented to share the information here because it does not betray sacred sites or cemeteries. Although most names have been verified with several native speakers, the number of elders with traditional knowledge is dwindling, so a few names have been shared with us by only one source. Unless otherwise noted, most of our historic transcriptions come from Lumholtz 1912. Preferred spellings are listed first. Fuller renderings of O'odham, Cucapá, Quechan (Yuman), and Maricopa names and geography would be lengthy and worthy studies unto themselves (compare Aporta 2003).

Come along. The desert awaits.

Acknowledgments

A host of people graciously shared their immense knowledge of this region, including Howard Aitken, John Annerino, Carlos Armendariz, Don Belknap, Fillman Bell, Oscar Bell, Peggy Turk Boyer, George Bryant, Alberto Búrquez, Charles Cameron, Lorey Cachora, Roger DiRosa, Lorraine Eiler, Exequiel Ezcurra, Don Fedock, Karl W. Flessa, Bernard "Bunny" Fontana, Isabel Granillo, David Griffin, Al Guenther, John Gunn, Jim Gutmann, Rich Hanson, Annita Harlan, Tom Harlan, Julian D. Hayden, Hank Hays, Bill Henry, Bob Henry, Steve Henry, Winnie Conley Henry, Julie Hoff, Letty Bender Hofstra, Mike Holt, Perry Duane "P. D." Holt, Steve Holt, Richard Homes, Bill Hoy, Joseph Jordan, Jacquie Kahn, Charles Ketchem, Joe Kinney, Paul Krausman, Peter Kresan, Sandy Lanham, John S. Laird, Bob Lenon, Jim Malusa, Joe McCraw, Anita Bender McGee, Robert McLemore, Michelle "Scout" Monroe, Gale Monson, John Morgart, George Morrison, Mary Beck Moser, Betty Hocker Moser, Carolina Navarro, Steve Nelson, Alton Netherlin, Dexter Oliver, David Ortiz-Reyna, Tom Potter, Bonnie Price, Lee Price, Tony Ramón, Amadeo Rea, Karen Reichhardt, David Roberson, Margaret Ross, Jim Runyan, Sue Rutman, Bob Schumacher, Joan E. Scott, Francisco "Chulpo" Shunie, Norman Simmons, Ed C. Smith, Glenton Sykes, Ed Tuffly, Beverly Turner, Tim Turner, Dan Urquidez, Fernando Valentine, Mel Vasquez, Anita Alvarez Williams, Michael F. Wilson, and Jon Young. Staff members of the Arizona Game and Fish Department, U.S. Border Patrol, Bureau of Land Management, National Park Service, Fish and Wildlife Service, U.S. Air Force, and U.S. Marine Corps also supplied information. Numerous staff members at the University of Arizona Main Library in Tucson, the Arizona State Archives in Phoenix, and the map archives of the U.S. Geological Survey in Reston, Virginia, were especially helpful.

All photographs are by Bill Broyles unless otherwise noted.

We especially thank David Shaul for updating the O'odham spellings and translations.

Luke Evans thanks Bill Broyles and Richard Felger for inviting him on this journey. He also thanks his wife, Jeanne Wade-Evans, for her patience during his long hours at the map table.

Richard Felger thanks the Wallace Research Foundation for support during this project.

Gary Nabhan, aided by Jacquie Kahn, gratefully acknowledges the assistance and encouragement of Hia C'ed O'odham and Tohono O'odham leaders and elders.

Bill Broyles thanks the University of Arizona's Southwest Center for assisting his spoken-history research of the region and its place-names.

Finally, we gratefully and admiringly acknowledge the fundamental work of Barnes (1935), Granger (1960, 1983), Hoy (1993), Irish (1972), and Walker & Bufkin (1986).

Abbreviations

AG = Reserva de la Biosfera Alto Golfo y Delta del Río Colorado
CP = Cabeza Prieta National Wildlife Refuge
GR = Barry M. Goldwater Range
OP = Organ Pipe Cactus National Monument
PI = Reserva de la Biosfera El Pinacate y El Gran Desierto de Altar
SD = Sonoran Desert National Monument
AGFD = Arizona Game and Fish Department
BC = Baja California
BCS = Baja California Sur
BLM = U.S. Bureau of Land Management
BM = surveyors' bench mark
Co. = county
FWS = U.S. Fish and Wildlife Service
NPS = U.S. National Park Service
SPRR = Southern Pacific Railroad
TON = Tohono O'odham Nation
USGS = U.S. Geological Survey

Conversions of measurement:

one kilometer = 0.62 miles

one mile = 1.61 kilometers

one meter = 3.28 feet

one foot = 0.3 meters

one square kilometer = 100 hectares = 0.386 square miles

one square mile = 259 hectares = 2.590 square kilometers

one hectare = 2.471 acres

one acre = 0.4047 hectares

At 32°00′00″N latitude, 113°00′00″W longitude (about 4 miles NNE of Quitobaquito, or about at the center of the Dry Borders region):

1 second of latitude = 30.8 meters/101.1 feet

1 minute of latitude = 1,848 meters/6,063 feet/1.15 statute miles

1 degree of latitude = 110,887 meters/363,802 feet/68.9 statute miles

1 second of longitude = 26.25 meters/86 feet

1 minute of longitude = 1,575 meters/5,167 feet/0.98 statute miles

1 degree of longitude = 94,493 meters/310,017 feet/58.72 statute miles

Reminder: coordinates are shown in NAD 1927.

A

A-1 Basin (CP). A canyon basin in central Cabeza Prieta Mountains, 3.7 mi N of Cabeza Prieta Peak. Named by Huyson "Jim" Johnson of CP staff because it was an excellent-looking place, and A-1 was synonymous with "first-rate," as in "A-1 Pilsner Beer" and "A-1 Sauce." 32°20′37″N, 113°48′14″W. 1,240 ft.

'A'al Ṣon-t-am Do'ag (PI? OP?). A mountain between Quitobaquito and Sonoyta. O'odham for 'baby root mountain' (Bell et al. 1980). Precise location unknown. ='A'al Sondam Do'ag.

'A'al Vaipia (OP). Major springs in southwestern corner of Organ Pipe Cactus National Monument. Hia C'ed O'odham for 'little springs' or 'little waters'. =Quitobaquito.

'A'al Vaipia Do'ag (OP). See Quitobaquito Hills.

Abra Plain, La (OP). A broad valley and watershed sloping SW from the Puerto Blanco Mountains to the Sonoyta River. An isolated population of *Lycium californicum,* a dwarf wolfberry shrub, grows here near the Sonora border. *Abra* is Spanish for an 'opening', 'valley', or 'plain'; perhaps named for adjacent "puerto blanco" opening (see Puerto Blanco Mountains), or it may signify a plain, which would redundantly label this area Plain Plain (Bill Hoy) and would rank it with other double names like Rillito River and Picacho Peak. 31°57′18″N, 112°56′02″W. 1,050–1,700 ft.

Acañig (GR). Mountain somewhere E of Black Gap between Gila Bend and Ajo (Fillman Bell). O'odham for 'back cracker', indicating very rough terrain.

Acuña Tinajas (OP). Several intermittent tinajas 1 mi SW of Kino Peak in Bates Mountains (Brown et al. 1983). Likely named for an early settler with surname Acuña. 32°05′53″N, 112°56′48″W. 2,020 ft.

Acuña Valley (OP). Acuña cactus *(Echinomastus erectocentrus* var. *acunensis)* derives its name from this, its type locality (see Paredes Aguilar et al. 2000). =Acuña Canyon. Mouth at 32°05′30″N, 112°57′10″W. 1,600 ft.

Acuña Well (OP). A well dug by hand in early 1900s (Greene 1977). 32°03′31″N, 112°56′21″W. 1,490 ft.

Adair Bay (AG). See Bahía Adair.

Adobe Pass (CP). A smugglers' trail across S Growler Mountains, angling toward Adobe Well. 31°12′26″N, 112°59′50″W. 2,130 ft.

Adobe Windmill and Well (CP). Well and tank developed for livestock but now used only by wildlife; about 9 mi SW of Ajo, in southern stretch of Daniels Arroyo. It is the only working remnant of Adobe Wells or Seven Wells, drilled by Bobby Cameron in 1939. John Cameron told son Bobby to drill here while other cowhands went off to round up some cattle, and by their return later in the day, water was flowing from a depth of 25 ft. Reportedly, delicious watermelons were raised here. A prehistoric hand-dug well may have preceded this well (Oscar Bell, Charles Cameron). Cameron family had an adobe ranch house nearby, namesake of the wells. 32°16′26″N, 112°58′03″W. 1,621 ft.

Adonde (Yuma Co.). A stage station and railroad watering stop and station 2.5 mi WSW of Wellton. The SPRR reached here late in 1878, and soon the new station had a 50,000-gallon water tank, "a temporary platform for delivery of freight, barber shop, two saloons, one hotel, telegraph with a lady operator, Chinese wash house, railroad office and one butcher shop," although the hotel was really a rail car, and within a few months it became the "hotel" at Texas Hill (Devine 2004:143). A few Hia C'ed O'odham lived here along the Southern Pacific line in 1915. Spanish for 'where' or interrogative 'to where?'. Mammalogist Edgar Mearns collected extensively here in 1894 during the U.S.-Mexico Boundary Survey. 32°39′42″N, 114°11′30″W. 219 ft.

Agua Dulce (PI). Shallow river pools on Río Sonoyta 8 km WSW of Quitobaquito; Lumholtz (1912:196) reported "growth of mezquites at either side and streams of running water appearing at intervals, the last time at Agua Dulce." Spanish for 'fresh (sweet) water', in contrast to the next appearance of the river at Agua Salada ('salty water') 5 km downstream. =Ikus S-gakĭ, O'odham for 'dried-out cloth or clothing', and historically

Figure 39.1. Adobe Well namesake, 1989. (All photos by Bill Broyles unless otherwise noted)

transcribed Ikuskaatsh, =Ikus Gakx. Vicinity of 31°56′N, 113°06′W. 270 m.

Agua Dulce Mountains (CP). Granitic mountain arc with three main sections in SE corner of CP. Named for pools on Sonoyta River S of the range. =Sierra del Ojo on some older maps; *ojo (del agua)* is Spanish for 'spring'. Also called Sonoyta Mountains by some, but not to be confused with Sonoyta Hills in OP. Summit (Quitovaguita BM) at 32°01′32″N, 113°08′41″W. 2,850 ft.

Agua Dulce Pass (CP). An ancient trail through a gap in the range, 0.8 mi ESE of Agua Dulce summit. This pass has an isolated population of the rare yellow-spined prickly pear *(Opuntia engelmannii* var. *flavispina),* perhaps planted by Native Americans (see Felger, this volume, chapter 15). 32°01′25″N, 113°07′54″W. 1,640 ft.

Agua Dulce Pronghorn Catchment (CP). Water development in Deer Hollow, 4 mi E of Papago Well. Collection dams direct runoff to 11,000-gallon underground storage tank and wildlife drinker. Built in 2003 at site of Antelope Tank to serve Sonoran pronghorn, it supplanted an earlier parabolic-saucer catchment (=Antelope Saucer, Antelope Catchment) at the same location. 32°06′02″N, 113°12′52″W. 1,075 ft.

Agua Dulce Spring (CP). One of few known springs in the region. This fracture spring sits in a canyon on SE slopes of the Agua Dulce Mountains. A late-summer storm in 1987 scoured and rearranged the canyon bottom, severely diminishing the spring's flow. Comparative photos show that the spring as we once knew it is now overlain by tons of rock and sediment. The spring now flows less than 5 gallons per day; historically, it flowed up to 50 gallons per day. 32°01′21″N, 113°08′31″W. 2,050 ft.

Agua Dulce Tank (CP). A small dam and intermittent waterhole in 1989 constructed about 100 m downstream from Agua Dulce Spring. Artificial game waters in CP and western GR are described and discussed by Broyles (1997). 32°01′17″N, 113°08′28″W. 1,900 ft.

Agua Salada (PI). Intermittent pools on Río Sonoyta about 5 km downstream (SW) of Agua Dulce; 10 km SW of Quitobaquito. 2.4 km upstream of Los Pozitos, where sand scooped out of the Sonoyta River permitted travelers to reach water. Like Agua Dulce, this place was settled in the late 1800s by Hia C'ed O'odham who moved away from tinajas that had dried up or been appropriated by cattlemen (Clotts 1915). Because of evaporation and stagnation, the puddled water here was brackish and inferior but was consumed when necessary. White alkali salt covers portions of the ground and riverbed. Spanish for 'salty water'. =On Ṣu:dagĭ, historically transcribed Onokshóotak, O'odham for 'salt water'. 31°55′30″N, 113°08′00″W. 260 m.

Aguaje de los Alquives (GR). Tinaja S of Gila River. May =Dripping Springs, although Bryan (1925:415) and Lenon (1987) argue convincingly that Alquives is Baker Tanks. Many early explorers, padres, and soldiers passed by here; see Bolton 1936, Bryan 1925, Hartmann 1989, Ives 1989, and Lenon 1987. =Algibes, name used by O'odham. Spanish for 'watering place of the cisterns'.

Aguajita Spring (OP). A small but permanent spring in Aguajita Wash several meters N of the international

Figure 39.2. *Agua Dulce Spring, 1984.*

may be named in allusion to their similarly pinnacled skylines, which for some people evoke eagle tails. =Sierra del Aguila. North summit (32°38′46″N, 113°20′28″W) stands 1,800 ft, and southern summit is 1,715 ft.

Ahpar (GR). See Tinajas Altas Mountains. Quechan for 'tail-end mountains', since they are the southernmost of the Gila Mountain group. =Yua Pad.

Ajo (Pima Co.). An unincorporated copper-mining town in western Pima County. In discussion of the town of Ajo, Zepeda (1985:23–24) relates that "Ajo (a:sos) 'garlic' was of course named by the Spanish people. Mr. [Miguel] Velasco spoke of a mountain that was very steep and rocky. On this mountain many wild garlic plants grew, and so they called the place Ajo, 'garlic.' He says that this mountain is no longer there; it is now a hole in the ground." This ajo is likely to be *Allium macropetalum,* a small, native onion that has a garlic-like flavor, rather than *Hesperocallis undulata,* the onion-like ajo lily, which would not be common on mountain slopes.

Two other derivations have been proposed. Some contend that Ajo is derived from the ajo lily (which local O'odham also call *a:sos*) that grows in sandy desert valleys near the town. Dobyns contends that the town derived its name from the O'odham term *o'ohon* (historically transcribed *au'auho*) for the red oxides and green carbonates used as mineral dyes for facepaint (Dobyns 1955; Hoy 1970).

The copper outcrops at Ajo were used prehistorically, and O'odham showed these minerals to an 1853 American expedition that included Tom Childs Sr. and Peter Brady, who reported rediscovering ore here and were instrumental in opening larger mining operations. Big-time copper mining began in 1911 but ended in 1983 (Reynolds 1996; Rickard 1996). The Ajo smelter including landmark smokestack were dismantled in 1995–96. The name generically includes former settlements of Gibson, Clarkston, Mexican Town, Ajo Indian Village (=Indian Town), and Old Ajo. Near or at old waterholes and village of Moik Vahia (=Moivavi, O'odham for 'many wells' or 'soft wells'), which once stood where the open-pit mine is now. 2000 population: 3,705. 32°22′25″N, 112°51′41″W. 1,751 ft.

Ajo Mine (CP). Group of adits and prospects in Agua Dulce Mountains along road to Bassarisc Tank. Not to be confused with major copper mine at town of Ajo. The property was worked by Mr. T. J. Jones between 1915 and 1920, and the ore was carried to Papago Well, where it was processed by an *arresta* [*sic; arrastra,* milling wheel]. According to Jones, the prior owner, Mr. Malone, made the mine break even, but "Mr. Malone was a barber, not a miner, and he did quite a lot of useless work" (quoted in Miller 1979:73). Numerous other prospects and workings are also in the area. 32°04′20″N, 113°12′49″W. 1,230 ft.

border, about 1.8 mi E of Quitobaquito. In 1988 cattails *(Typha)* reappeared here after lying dormant for at least 20 years, when a massive web of cattail rhizomes was exposed by a flood that removed overlying rubble (see Felger et al. 1992). Spanish for 'small waterhole'. 31°56′22″N, 113°00′38″W. 1,100 ft. See Papalote, El (Sonora), a truck stop 0.3 mi S on the same arroyo.

Aguajita Wash (OP). Major drainage for La Abra Plain to Sonoyta River. Source at 32°01′28″N, 112°54′33″W. 1,910 ft.

Aguila Mountains (GR). Mountain range 12 mi SE of Dateland. Its northern half is a sloping basaltic plateau called Malpais Hill (Bryan 1925), but not to be confused with another Malpais Hill E of here. Its southern half is rugged rhyolite and andesite eroded into fantastic shapes. Associated with Eagle Tanks, one of its two primary tinajas. Spanish for 'eagle'. Not to be confused with Eagle Tail Mountains 45 mi to the N, although both

Ajo Mountains (OP). Major mountain range straddling the eastern boundary of OP and western boundary of Tohono O'odham Reservation. These block-faulted volcanics of the Basin and Range formed in the mid-Tertiary orogeny, 36–17 million years ago. The higher elevations support many "sky island" relict plants that were more widespread in Pleistocene times, before the latest advent of the Sonoran Desert (Betancourt et al. 1990; see Van Devender, this volume); these include *Juniperus coahuilensis, Morus microphylla, Quercus turbinella,* and *Vaquelinia californica.* The Hia C'ed O'odham collected chiltipines *(Capsicum annuum* var. *aviculare),* the farthest northwest range of this Neotropical species, and wild teparies *(Phaseolus acutifolius).* See Hoy 1994 for an account of an 1840–41 military expedition in the range. The names of adjoining Sierra de Santa Rosa and Sierra la Nariz to the south have been extended to this range on many older maps. The range has also held at least a dozen other variant names. Official name is Ajo Range, but today Ajo Mountains is a far more common label. Summit is Mount Ajo; =Santa Rosa Peak, Ajo Peak. 32°01′36″N, 112°41′23″W. 4,808 ft.

Also **Ajo Mountain Drive,** a scenic roadway loop built in 1953 from Highway 85 to the W base of these mountains.

Ajo Peak (Pima Co.). A sharply pointed peak 4 mi SW of Ajo in Little Ajo Mountains. Known also as Peñasco Peak; not to be confused with Mount Ajo. =S-vepegĭ Mo'okam, O'odham for 'reddish head'; To:lo Vi:pidoḍ Weco, for 'bull testicles underneath'; Huevos de Toro, Spanish for 'bull testicles'. 32°20′06″N, 112°54′24″W. 2,617 ft. Southern neighbor of North Ajo Peak; 32°20′53″N, 112°54′52″W. 2,776 ft.

Akimel (Sonora). An O'odham settlement about 1 mi downstream of Mexican settlement of Sonoyta. Historically transcribed Akimuri, O'odham for 'river' or 'running wash'. =El Pueblo.

Alamo Canyon (OP). A large canyon on the western slope of the Ajo Mountains. Spanish for 'cottonwood tree' *(Populus fremontii).* =Tres Alamos Canyon. "When I was in that country this was known as Tres Alamos" (Nichol 1948). North, middle, and south forks converge to form one canyon, hence 'three alamos'. Mouth at 32°04′18″N, 112°43′39″W. 2,260 ft.

Alamo Wash (OP). This arroyo drains Alamo Canyon and eventually merges with Cherioni Wash at 32°07′29″N, 112°52′36″W. 1,490 ft.

Alamo Well (OP). Well dug at the mouth of Alamo Canyon by William Miller before 1910. The Miller family purchased the well from settlers named Powell and Hubsteader; later it belonged to Ruben Daniels and then the Robert Gray family. =Grays Ranch, Alamo Ranch.

Figure 39.3. Aguila Mountains.

Figure 39.4. Ajo, mural.

The Grays, being from Texas, simply called it the Alamo (Sue Rutman). 32°03′59″N, 112°42′51″W. 2,390 ft.

Albino (GR). A camp or rest stop shown on maps of latter nineteenth century along west branch of El Camino del Diablo, between Tinajas Altas and Fortuna Mine. Its attraction—grass for livestock? water or shade for travelers? guidepost?—is unclear. Vicinity of northern Butler Mountains. Spanish for 'albino,' perhaps light-colored rock. A candidate location is S tip of Vopoki Ridge at 32°26′20″N, 114°15′36″W. 1,028 ft.

Possibly Albina, Spanish for 'salt marsh,' such as the small, seasonal wet area just N of Butler Mountains and near washes draining Davis Plain (Howard Aitken). This spot does comply roughly with the old maps. =Davis Lagoon. 32°25′19″N, 114°14′34″W. 875 ft.

When viewed from the international boundary, a ridge locally known as White Face is a distinctive landmark near Fortuna Mine (Howard Aitken), but location does not match Albino. White Face is at 32°31′44″N, 114°19′20″W. 920 ft.

Algodones Dunes (California). A large field of wind-blown sand dunes between Yuma and the Salton Sea. The field, about 7 mi wide and 44 mi long, was a barrier to early travelers, and building a road across the dunes was arduous (Rube 1996). The geology of these dunes is discussed by Greeley et al. (1978), Smith (1970), and Kresan (this volume). The name is a corruption of Halchidhoma, the name of a tribe that lived there when Venegas passed that way in 1759; *algodon*, Spanish for 'cotton', is the result (Gudde 1998). 32°57′ N, 115°06′ W. 550 ft.

’Alĭ Jek (TON). See Menager's Dam.

’Alĭ Ke:k Ce:k (Yuma Co.) O'odham name for a mountain and good waterhole near Wellton and S of Antelope Hill. Probably =Baker Tanks. O'odham for 'piggyback mountain'. =’Alĭ Ge:k Cu:k, ’Alĭ Ge:k Ce:ki. Historically transcribed Ali Guk Ktchuki, literally 'little one put on something standing' or 'where baby fell' (Alĭ I-geṣk Ke:k) (Fillman Bell).

Ali Wau Pass (OP). Gap between Ajo and Santa Rosa mountains used by prehistoric and historic travelers. Tohono O'odham for 'small cliff' *(ali vavĭ, ali waw),* of which there are many in the pass. =Gusano Pass (Spanish for 'worm' or 'caterpillar'). 31°54′13″N, 112°37′10″W. 2,046 ft.

Almejas, Las (AG) Two different beaches in upper Gulf of California, one on eastern shore (31°41′30″N, 114°31′00″W) near El Golfo and other on western shore N of San Felipe (31°06′N, 114°52′W), which now includes playas Blanca, del Sol, Hawaii, Unión, Paraíso, La Ponderosa, and Grande. Spanish for 'the clams'.

Alto Golfo Biosphere Reserve (Sonora, BC). See Reserva de la Biosfera Alto Golfo y Delta del Río Colorado.

American Slough (Yuma Co.). One of a series of lagoons, sloughs, and backwaters that occupied abandoned meander bends and marshes of the Colorado River before flood control and agricultural development. Now drained and replaced by agricultural fields and orange orchards. 1.5 mi W of present-day Somerton. 32°35′48″N, 114°43′55″W. 105 ft.

Andrade Mesa wetlands (BC). At least six wetland areas along the All-America Canal in the Andrade Mesa dunes S of canal or along S escarpment of the dunes. The wetlands are formed by seepage from the canal and have become important habitat for migratory birds and other wildlife. They include marshes, playas, and vegetated dunes. They vary in area from 3,025 ha to 111 ha and total about 6,200 ha (Hinojosa-Huerta et al. 2002). The area is 8–15 mi W of Yuma at S end of Algodones Dunes. See Glenn & Nagler, this volume; Hinojosa-Huerta, this volume. Two of the lagoons are at 32°37′00″N, 115°06′58″W, and 32°37′51″N, 115°07′02″W. Elevations are about 50 m.

Antelope Bridge (Yuma Co.). Old bridge across Gila River, adjacent to Antelope Hill. Prior to the bridge's construction in the early 1920s, the road route between Phoenix and Yuma came through here from Hyder, Norton, and Roll. This was a treacherous crossing, with a major ford involved, or at least a very wide bed of sand, difficult for the underpowered vehicles of the time (Ross 1923). 32°42′47″N, 114°00′55″W. 268 ft.

Antelope Hill (Yuma Co.). Butte S of Gila River and 4 mi W of Tacna. Named by Lt. Nathaniel Michler for a herd of pronghorn seen in vicinity (Emory 1859). It was an important prehistoric campsite and metate quarry, as shown by numerous metates and pestles formerly found there and by its role in spoken histories of regional tribes, such as the Quechan (Lorey Cachora). Its Tertiary red, arkosic sandstone was ideal for grindstone production. Unfortunately, the Arizona Department of Transportation and the Bureau of Reclamation are destroying numerous archaeological features while quarrying fill for canal banks and roadways (see Schneider 1993; Schneider & Altschul 2000). Hia C'ed O'odham consider it a dangerous mountain. =Vi:ji Do'ag, Wi:ji Do'ag (O'odham for 'furless hill', 'hairless hill', or 'bare hill'; or casually translated 'elephant hill'); Cerro del Metate (named by Fray Francisco Garcés in 1768); Cerro de Santa Cecelia (by Garcés in 1775 [Granger 1983]). An Hia C'ed O'odham village, once located "under" the hill, was called Miakam, 'the near one' (Bell et al. 1980). =Antelope Peak (Fourr 2004:36). 32°42′14″N, 114°00′54″W. 815 ft.

Antelope Hill Station (Yuma Co.). Way station on the Butterfield Overland Stage route, established in 1859. After the demise of the stage, name was changed to Tacna. When Tacna was moved 4 mi E to its present location, name was changed to Noah. See Tacna. 32°41′06″N, 114°01′17″W. 329 ft.

Antelope Hills (CP). Small range N of Papago Well. Named by CP staff for endangered Sonoran pronghorn *(Antilocapra americana sonoriensis).* Summit at 32°11′54″N, 113°16′42″W. 1,533 ft.

Antelope Peak (SD). Conical peak in NW portion of Table Top Wilderness. Presumably named for endangered Sonoran pronghorn *(Antilocapra americana sonoriensis)* that used to range as far east as SD. Their range in the U.S. has now shrunk to portions of the CP, GR, and OP (Thompson-Olais 1994), and their long-term viability is very much in question. 32°47′53″N, 112°10′25″W. 3,117 ft.

Antelope Tank (CP) Waterhole bulldozed in former charco at Deer Hollow in northern Agua Dulce Mountains, 4 mi E of Papago Well. This represo was dug about 1957 but is unreliable source of water since a flood breached its dam. Built to serve Sonoran pronghorn known to live in vicinity, but they seldom drink water (Thompson-Olais 1994). A *charco* is a clay-bottomed natural depression that holds runoff intermittently; a *represo* is an excavated and dammed charco, also called stock tank or mud tank (Bryan 1925). =Antelope Represo, Antelope Represa. See Agua Dulce Pronghorn Catchment. 32°06′03″N, 113°12′53″W. 1,080 ft.

Araby (Yuma Co.). Railroad siding and former section house near Yuma. "The name may have been derived from the fact that the surrounding country resembles an Arabian desert" (Granger 1960:368). 32°40′33″N, 114°31′16″W. 212 ft.

Arch Canyon (OP). Canyon in Ajo Mountains with double natural rock arch in metamorphic rock. Drains NW from Mount Ajo. Larger arch is 90 ft wide by 36 ft tall. Park Service rangers occasionally are asked, "How many undiscovered arches are in the monument?" Mouth at 32°02′26″N, 112°42′42″W. 2,600 ft.

Arizona. A state in the American Southwest. It was admitted to the U.S. on February 14, 1912, and for many years was the youngest of 48 states. Its capital is Phoenix. Area is 114,006 mi² (295,276 ha). Population 4,669,000 in 2000. Until the 1853 Gadsden Purchase, Arizona's lands S of the Gila River lay in Mexico; these included OP, CP, SD, and GR (Walker & Bufkin 1986). Formerly, many scholars believed that "Arizona" derived from O'odham Ali Son Aki, for 'wash of small springs', Ali Shondag for 'place at the spring', or Ali Ṣonak, for 'place at the little spring or place of the little mountain base' (Garate 1999; Granger 1983; David Shaul). However, recent research strongly suggests that "Arizona" is Basque for 'the good oak trees' *(aris onak* or *ariz onak)*, which meshes with the context of Basque miners working the fabled *planchas de plata* lode 18 mi SW of Nogales, Arizona (Garate 1999, 2005).

Arizona Highway 84. Old highway that ran from Casa Grande to Gila Bend; paved in 1934. This route was a shortcut for travelers on U.S. Highway 80, the main southern conduit between the east and west coasts. Highway 84 bypassed Phoenix and was the more direct route between Tucson and Gila Bend. The road was superseded by I-8 in the early 1960s, but significant portions of the old roadbed remain, though they are no longer in use. The best example is at Freeman, where the old roadbed passes in front of the ruined service station. Another station, Big Horn, also served travelers on Highway 84 but closed before the advent of I-8 (see McGee & Hofstra, this volume).

Arizona Highway 85. Highway S from Buckeye through Gila Bend, Ajo, and OP to Lukeville. It continues as Mexico Highway 8 to Puerto Peñasco. The portion between Buckeye and Gila Bend was built and paved in 1955, bypassing old U.S. 80 (see U.S. Highway 80). =Lukeville Highway, Bankhead Highway, Buckeye Road, Gila Bend Road, Tucson Highway, Ajo-Sonoyta Highway.

Figure 39.5. Antelope Peak. (Photo by Dale S. Turner)

Arizona Highway 86. Highway between Why and Tucson through the Tohono O'odham Nation and its capital, Sells. =Tucson Highway, Ajo Way, Ajo-Tucson Highway.

Armenta Well (OP). Two now-dry wells near confluence of Kuakatch Wash and Cuerda de Leña in northern OP. Abraham Armenta homesteaded here in 1930, but according to Hia C'ed O'odham oral history, he was allowed to use the *ak-ciñ* (dry-farm) field by Darby Well residents, who had farmed here much longer. Near Armenta's Place, a farmstead. 32°11′19″N, 112°49′47″W. 1,590 ft.

Arroyo. Spanish for 'dry wash' or 'ephemeral river'.

Arroyo Diablo (AG). One grand but relatively unknown feature in the region is this serpentine slough 10 km W of Bahía Ometepec (Thompson 1968). It is readily visible from space-shuttle photos of the Río Colorado delta but virtually inaccessible by land or water because of treacherous mud. "It is a very, very subtle feature that would stand out only during certain times of the tide. The maps make it look like a permanently wet feature, but it is not. The topographic relief in that part of the delta is on the order of a few centimeters at most. I'm almost certain that the feature is not an old river bed, but is in fact, a tidal slough" (Karl W. Flessa). It spans nearly 30 km and is associated with a number of salt flats. Spanish for 'devil arroyo', but no name is in common currency. 31°40′, 114°56′. Sea level.

Arroyo Palo Fierro (Sonora). This arroyo, 32 km SW of Sonoyta, curves around N end of Sierra San Francisco, then parallels Mexico Highway 8 westward, and joins Río Sonoyta 2 km S of Ejido Nayarit. Spanish for 'ironwood tree' *(Olneya tesota),* whose wood seems as hard and heavy as *fierro* (iron). 31°43′00″N, 113°11′30″W. 160–300 m.

Arroyo la Tinaja (PI). Large wash that runs SW through Tinajas de los Pápagos. It originates on N slopes of Pinacate Mountains, 8 km SE of Sykes Crater, and occasionally flows W through gap in Sierra Extraña before dissipating in the sands 2 km W of Pozo Nuevo. =Arroyo de los Pápagos. Passes Tinajas de los Pápagos at 31°54′59″N, 113°36′17″W. 60–400 m.

Arroyo Tule (PI). See Tinaja del Tule.

A'ud (CP). An O'odham agave-gathering site and pothole NW of Ajo, near Charlie Bell Well. Historically transcribed A'oot, referring to *Agave deserti*.

Avalon (Yuma Co.). See Ivalon.

Avik Amook To'or (GR) See Tinajas Altas Mountains, Gila Mountains.

Aztec (Yuma Co.). A telegraph station with a well 9 mi E of Dateland. It was built in 1881 along the Southern Pacific Railroad and lent its name to the Aztec Hills. In the 1930s Aztec had a gas station, cabins, and café run by the Elkins family; Ma Elkins was rated the best cook between Yuma and Gila Bend. The Elkinses' ramada was immense (60 to 80 ft on a side), with room for lots of cars under it: "Shade is valuable for desert businesses" (Bob Lenon). In 2000 a large feedlot was constructed immediately S of the site. 32°49′24″N, 113°26′43″W. 495 ft.

Aztec Hills (GR). A small range of mountains astride N boundary of GR and 4 mi E of Dateland on I-8. 32°47′41″N, 113°29′04″W. Summit 1,180 ft.

B

Babcock (AG). Proposed town in Colorado delta, 19 mi NW of Isla Montague. Working with Gen. Guillermo Andrade, the Colorado River Land Company at one time owned over 850,000 acres of the delta and approached a number of potential investors to develop towns, a port, and agriculture there. In 1891 the company offered to sell land to "Elisha S. Babcock, the San Diego promoter who developed Coronado [at San Diego, California]" (Hendricks 1967:170). The name Babcock appears on a 1907 USGS map but not on Sykes's maps of that period. See Port Otis. Vicinity 31°57′10″N, 115°04′58″W. (Steve Nelson).

Badilla Crater (PI). Volcanic maar crater 4 km E of Crater MacDougal. Named for Alfredo Badilla Martínez of Sonoyta, where in mid-twentieth century he served as hunting guide, game warden, and *comisario* (Bill Hoy). When working as manager of a gold mine owned by Bernard Gillespie, Badilla informed Gillespie, "You are being sued again." The boss raved and demanded to know why *he* was being sued. Badilla replied, "Because, Señor, you are the only bastard around with any money" (MacPherson 1973:72). =Cráter Badilla, Badilla Maar Crater, Volcán Tinajita. Commonly misspelled Badillo. 31°58′16″N, 113°34′29″W. 280 m.

Bahía. Spanish for 'bay'.

Bahía Adair (AG). This bay at northern end of Gulf of California is 40 km across and 16 km wide and runs W from Punta Cholla near Puerto Peñasco to Punta Borrascoso. It is characterized by a shallow, sandy bottom and extensive mudflats along the shore. The tidally inundated wetlands include halophytic shore plants such as *Allenrolfea occidentalis, Batis maritima, Distichlis palmeri, Frankenia salina, Monanthochloë littoralis, Salicornia subterminalis, Suaeda esteroa,* and the endemic *Suaeda puertopenascoa.* The bay constitutes an important marine spawning and feeding ground, where Hia C'ed O'odham formerly harvested plentiful shoreline sea foods, gathered salt, and learned sacred songs (Childs 1954; Felger, this volume, Chapter 15).

Named Adair Bay by British lieutenant Robert William Hale Hardy (1829:320), probably for John Adair (1655–1722). Hardy's mission was to survey the upper Gulf of California for pearls and fisheries. Adair was a Scottish cartographer who established standards of surveying excellence in producing a classic set of charts, *Description of the Sea-coast and Islands of Scotland, With Large and Exact Maps, for the Use of Seamen* (Stephen & Lee 1917). =Adair Bay. Occasionally misspelled Aduar. 31°35′N, 113°55′W.

Bahía de la Cholla (Sonora). Bay 8 km WNW of Puerto Peñasco. Since the mid-twentieth century a tourist camp on southern beach has grown into a sprawling vacation village called Cholla Bay. Bay is a favorite haunt of tidepool watchers and conchologists. A study of the bay's sedimentary history can be found in Fürsich & Flessa 1987. Land E of bay is undergoing massive development of tourist facilities, which will radically change the local biology. Named for an expansive stand of low-growing teddybear cholla *(Cylindropuntia bigelovii).* =Playa La Cholla, Cholla Bay. 31°21′40″N, 113°36′40″W.

Bahía Punta Peñasco (Sonora). Bay W of Punta Peñasco and Puerto Peñasco. 31°19′N, 113°35′W. Sea level.

Bahía San Felipe (BC). See San Felipe.

Baja California (BC). The northern of the two Mexican states on the peninsula. Its capital is Mexicali. 69,984 km². =Baja California Norte.

Baja California Sur (BCS). The southern of the two Mexican states on the Baja California peninsula; it lies S of the 28th parallel. The capital is La Paz.

Baja California peninsula. Peninsula on SW corner of North America. Separates Gulf of California from Pacific Ocean. It consists of the Mexican states of Baja California Sur and Baja California (Norte). =Lower California. The American state of California was known as Alta California (Upper California). In the sixteenth and seventeenth centuries, geographers heatedly debated whether this was an island or a peninsula (Sykes 1915b). The gulf and the peninsula also figured prominently in the search for a direct sailing route from Europe to China via the mythical Straits of Anian (Sykes 1915a).

Baker Mine (OP). Abandoned mine shaft in Puerto Blanco Mountains NW of Senita Basin. Named for Charles Baker, who worked this site and others in the late 1800s. See Baker Peaks. 31°58′49″N, 112°52′20″W. 1,900 ft.

Baker Peaks (GR). Several distinctive conical, shale peaks 4 mi SW of Tacna. Named for Charles Baker, who established a ranch at Baker Tanks about 1870; at one time he drove stagecoaches to Tucson and later he was murdered. He also had been a hard-rock miner who worked claims in the Puerto Blanco Mountains (Bill Hoy). =Baker Butte, Poso Peak, Poso Butte. May =ʼAlĭ Ge:k Ce:ki. 32°38′36″N, 113°59′49″W. 1,415 ft.

Baker Tanks (GR). A series of six intermittent to perennial natural tinajas in conglomerate bedrock immediately SW of Baker Peaks. Focal point for prehistoric peoples. May be labeled La Tinaja or Tinaxa on Padre Kino's 1701 map (in Ives 1989); in contradiction of Bolton (1936), Kino shows a range of mountains W of La Tinaja, which might not be the case if La Tinaja were Dripping Springs. See Aguaje de los Alquives. A well drilled here early in twentieth century is now abandoned. Scenes of a forgettable movie called *Black Day, Blue Night* were filmed here in 1995. The plot was billed as a "crime thriller" with a mysterious hitchhiker picked up by two women in the desert, but few critics bothered to review it. =La Poza, Los Pozos; =ʼAlĭ Ge:k Ce:ki, see ʼAlĭ Ke:k Ce:k. 32°37′26″N, 114°00′32″W. 524 ft.

Bambarria, La (PI). See Sierra Blanca.

Ban Hi:nk (Pima Co.). See Why. O'odham for 'coyote howls'.

Bandeja Well (Pima Co.). Windmill and line shack 10 mi S of Ajo, 0.4 mi SW of Lime Hill and on side arroyo to Cuerda de Leña. Properly, Bandejas Well, since name means 'pots and pans', after a vaquero living there who was noted for his cooking utensils (Charles Cameron). 32°13′23″N, 112°55′19″W. 1,560 ft.

Banera Tinaja (OP). Intermittent tinaja in low hills separating Bates and Puerto Blanco mountains. May =Earls Tinaja, though Brown et al. (1983) note that OP files provide a different location for Earls Tinaja. 32°03′20″N, 112°54′24″W. 1,1610 ft.

Barajita Tinajas (TON). Several tinajas in canyon on E slope of Ajo Mountains, including seep-fed Barajita No. 4, one of the two perennial tinajas in the range. Vicinity of 32°04′36″N, 112°41′04″W. 3,000 ft.

Figure 39.6. Baker Tanks.

Barajita Valley (TON). Flat valley E of Ajo Mountains. Spanish for 'small deck of cards'. 32°03′20″N, 112°36′20″W. 2,150–2,300 ft.

Barajita Well (TON). Well and stock tank on E flank of Ajo Mountains. 32°04′37″N, 112°40′15″W. 2,380 ft.

Bassarisc Tank (CP) Artificial waterhole for wildlife in western Agua Dulce Mountains. Completed in 1961, it is an adit with a shade ramada built over the entrance in an attempt to reduce evaporation. The ecological consequences and effectiveness of such developed waters are under discussion (Broyles 1995). Named for a ringtail *(Bassariscus astutus)* family seen in vicinity. An extensive thicket of teddybear cholla *(Cylindropuntia bigelovii)* stands SW of this tank. 32°04′08″N. 113°12′00″W. 1,300 ft.

Batamote (PI). Hills, arroyo, arroyo crossing, and tinaja where Río Sonoyta cuts through low hills midway between Sonoyta and Puerto Peñasco. Name also applied synonymously to the southern reach of the Río Sonoyta, an area that Ives (1989) labeled archaeologically sterile. Spanish for the shrub *Baccharis salicifolia* (seep willow). =Sikol Veco Vahia, Sikol Ce:po Vahia; historically transcribed Sicobutobabia (a name recorded by Kino and Salvatierra [Ives 1989]); Hia C'ed O'odham for 'round tinaja spring'. The twin bridges, Puentes Cuates, where Mexico Highway 8 crosses Arroyo Batamote, are at 31°40′35″N, 113°18′00″W. 125 m.

Batamote Hills (PI). Three hills composed of mid-Tertiary volcanic rock, 3 to 10 km NE of Batamote Crossing. The basalt has an age of 14 million years (Lynch 1981). A colony of organ pipe cactus *(Stenocereus thurberi)* grows on the east-facing slopes (Felger 2000). The Batamote drainage occupies a prominent gap between two of these hills. The highest point (31°43′35″N, 113°14′10″W) is identified as Cerro Tecolote on the Los Norteños topographical map and is shown on

Lumholtz's (1912) map as Batamote. =Cerros Bata-mote, Colinas Batamote. San Pedro microwave station is at the 380-m summit; =Microondas Batamote. See Tinaja Batamote.

Batamote Mountains (Pima Co.). Basaltic mountains 7 mi NE of Ajo. Extinct volcanic source for area's basalt dating to Laramide orogeny. Named for *Baccharis salicifolia* (seep willow) found in area. Summit (BM Papago) 32°28′06″N, 112°44′23″W. 3,202 ft.

Batamote Mountains Catchments (GR, Pima Co.). Wildlife water catchments and guzzler troughs in Bata-mote Mountains, numbered chronologically.

Number 1 (Pima Co.). =AGFD #575. 1.9 mi SSE of Coffeepot Mountain. 32°27′27″N, 112°36′20″W. 2,590 ft.

Number 2 (Pima Co.). =AGFD #576. 3 mi N of Burro Gap. 32°26′50″N, 112°40′55″W. 2,030 ft.

Number 3 (Pima Co.). =AGFD #577. 2.1 mi WNW of Coffeepot Mountain. 32°29′26″N, 112°39′20″W. 2,070 ft.

Number 4 (GR). =AGFD #674. On N flank of Batamote Mountains, 2.1 mi NNW of Batamote Mountains summit. 32°29′41″N, 112°45′20″W. 1,680 ft.

Batamote Well (Pima Co.). A well along Tenmile Wash at W tip of Batamote Mountains, =Ten Mile Well. First dug about 1917 atop a perched water table. 32°29′24″N, 112°52′23″W. 1,340 ft.

Bates Mountains (OP). This spectacular mountain mass in NW part of OP is composed of mid-Tertiary basalt and latite. Named for a settler at Bates Well. As late as 1918 this range was considered part of Growler Mountains. =Bates Range. Summit is Kino Peak (BM Tesmo) at 32°06′34″N, 112°57′17″W. 3,197 ft.

Bates Pass (OP). Prominent pass in large north-south-running canyon immediately E of Kino Peak. An ancient trail travels through this pass to Bates Well and is still used by illegal immigrants and smugglers. As recently as 2003 visitors to the pass found the path extremely beaten, with still-warm campfires, discarded clothing, and large amounts of trash along the route (see Anner-ino 1999). 32°06′36″N, 112°56′45″W. 1,800 ft.

Bates Pass Tinaja (OP). Intermittent tinaja 0.7 mi E of Kino Peak. =Centipede Tank. 32°06′36″N, 112°56′38″W. 1,840 ft.

Bates Well (OP). Windmill, small ranch house, corrals, and line shack at N end of Bates Mountains. Well was hand-dug by W. B. Bates around 1886 and passed through a succession of ranching owners including Ruben Daniels, the McDaniels brothers, and Henry Gray. Bryan (1925:418) notes that to local Mexicans it was 'El Viet' (the Bate), because they could not twist their tongues to say 'Bates'. To the O'odham it was Juñ Kaija, meaning 'to have a lot of columnar cactus fruit or seeds caked up'; historically transcribed Tjunikáatto, 'where there

are dry cactus fruit seeds thick on the ground'; =Ju:ñi Ka:c, Jun Kaij, Jooynekajk. Some Hia C'ed O'odham claim that the name of this important settlement thus refers to burnt seeds tossed on the ground while organ pipe cactus jam is being made; others interpret it as 'saguaro seed cakes'. Organ pipe cactus are not espe-cially abundant at the site. =Growler Wells, Growler Pass, The Bates, Bates Spring Well (though today there are no known springs in the area), Rube Daniels' Place (Clotts 1915; Sue Rutman). 32°10′10″N, 112°56′59″W. 1,355 ft.

Bean Pass (CP). Gap in northern Sierra Pinta, 9.6 mi NW of Heart Tank. Named for numerous *Sebastiania bilocularis* (a Mexican jumping bean shrub, formerly called *Sapium biloculare*) by refuge's Gale Monson and Jim Johnson while on resource reconnaissance trip in March 1956 aboard horses Chief and Buzz. 32°22′48″N, 113°38′00″W. 1,160 ft.

Bee Spring (OP). Tiny seep 1 mi S of Ali Wau Pass on W flank of Sierra de Santa Rosa. Brown et al. (1983) state that the seep was first found in 1972 and has a flow rate of about one drop every 5–10 seconds. It is not known if the seep is permanent. Only in the driest of regions would such a miniscule water supply even be noted. 31°54′54″N, 112°38′14. 2,000 ft.

Bell BM (CP). Horizontal control bench mark in Growler Valley along Camino del Diablo. 32°07′06″N, 113°06′39″W. 1,063 ft.

Bell Mine (CP). Abandoned mine on N flank of Agua Dulce Mountains. Once owned by Charlie Bell, this early 1950s claim showed traces of gold and copper but never produced commercially. 32°02′40″N, 113°09′53″W. 1,460 ft.

Bell Pass (CP). Gap trending NE through eastern Agua Dulce Mountains. Named for nearby Bell Mine and its discoverer, Charlie Bell. 32°02′47″N, 113°10′40″W. 1,440 ft.

Bender Spring (GR). A fracture spring 0.2 mi NE of Squaw Tit. Before 1925 it was enlarged with a hand-dug pit 10 ft deep; today it is silted in. =Indian Spring; High Lonesome Spring; Sand Tank Mountains Pothole #2; AGFD #794. 32°40′58″N, 112°22′29″W. 3,100 ft.

Bender Wash (SD, GR). Arroyo on N side of Javelina Mountain in Sand Tank Mountains. Plants here include large stands of the small, leafless *Castela emoryi*, one of Arizona's three crucifixion-thorn trees. Ormal Allen Bender and his family operated the Buzzard X Ranch in this area in the 1920s (Hafford 1993; McGee & Hofstra, this volume). The ranch was so named because the brand looked like a buzzard over an 'X'. Joins Sand Tank Wash at 32°53′52″N, 112°40′27″W. 850 ft.

Betty Lee Mine (GR). Abandoned mining operation on E side of Copper Mountains. Extensive workings, with 700-ft-deep shaft connecting to 2,000 ft of adits on seven levels. In 1931 equipment at the site consisted of a gasoline hoist, an assay office, and several buildings, with a pothole developed into a cistern (Wilson 1933). The mine changed ownership numerous times. =Arizona Consolidated Mining Company, Frisco & Ella J. Mines, Swenson Mine, Copple & McIntosh Mine, Linden Mine. 32°30′28″N, 113°59′39″W. 1,400 ft.

Betty Lee Tank (GR). Waterhole developed 1956 from remains of an older cistern near Betty Lee Mine. =Betty Lee Cistern, AGFD #200. 32°30′03″N, 113°58′37″W. 1,180 ft.

Big Horn Reservoir (SD). Large, breached stock tank in S Maricopa Mountains, 2.7 mi NE of Big Horn Station. 32°53′15″N, 112°21′32″W. 1,940 ft.

Big Horn Station and **Big Horn Road** (SD). Big Horn Station, 20 mi E of Gila Bend, was a homestead, gas station, and proposed townsite along old Arizona State Route 84 before the construction of I-8. Now abandoned, it was associated with the Bender family (see McGee & Hofstra, this volume). Big Horn Road leads S from I-8 into Sand Tank Mountains. See Bender Wash. =Buzzard X Ranch. Station at 32°51′33″N, 112°23′31″W. 1,722 ft.

Big Pass (GR, CP). Wide gap between Buck Peak and Copper Mountains. Counterpart to Little Pass, 5 mi to SE. 32°26′00″N, 113°57′14″W. 900 ft.

Big Tank (SD). Livestock tank in N Vekol Valley, E of Maricopa Mountains. More properly, this is Big Bruce Tank, as compared with nearby Little Bruce Tank, dug in the same period by O. K. "Red" Bruce for the Conley family. Big Tank is a little bigger and holds water longer (Winnie Conley Henry). =Big Bruce Tank. 32°55′42″N, 112°15′32″W. 1,590 ft.

Big Wash (SD). Large wash emerging from W side of Maricopa Mountains and draining into Gila River. Appears on numerous older maps, but name has fallen from use. Precise location unknown.

Black Bottom Tank (GR). A water catchment constructed in 1972 in Sauceda Mountains for wildlife, about 3.7 mi NW of Hat Mountain. Named for the naturally stained rock bottom below the waterline. 32°40′12″N, 112°47′13″W. 1,640 ft.

Black Butte (GR). Descriptive name for landmark on N side of Sauceda Mountains, 6 mi NE of Hat Mountain. 32°42′36″N, 112°40′45″W. 1,720 ft. See Butte Tank.

Black Gap (GR). Pass where Arizona Highway 85 runs between basaltic Sauceda Mountains and granitic White Hills. A railroad siding by the same name was once here as well. May =Gogokǐ, O'odham for 'to be full of prints' or 'peeling mountain'. 32°45′09″N, 112°49′26″W. 1,045 ft.

Black Gap Well (GR). Drilled well along Tucson, Cornelia, & Gila Bend Railroad. W of Sauceda Mountains. 32°42′49″N, 112°50′01″W. 1,057 ft.

Black Mountain (SD). Volcanic mountain 2.8 mi WSW of Table Top Mountains. 32°44′23″N, 112°10′17″W. 3,306 ft.

Black Mountain (Pima Co.). Basalt mountain 3 mi SSE of Ajo. High point of Little Ajo Mountains. =Darby Mountain; Koʼokomaḍkam, O'odham for 'belonging to blue palo verde', which is abundant in the arroyos around the mountain's base. 32°19′25″N, 112°50′32″W. 3,008 ft.

Black Mountain Catchments (Pima Co.). These four artificial waterholes S and W of Ajo were constructed between 1954 and 1966 for wildlife.

   Number 1 (Pima Co.). =AGFD #392. 2.9 mi S of Black Mountain. 32°16′51″N, 112°50′25″W. 1,689 ft.

   Number 2 (Pima Co.). =AGFD #393. 0.4 mi SW of Eberling Tank. 32°15′03″N, 112°49′32″W. 1,620 ft.

   Number 3 (Pima Co.). =AGFD #394. 0.6 mi S of John the Baptist. 32°15′01″N, 112°53′36″W. 1,610 ft.

   Number 4 (Pima Co.). =AGFD #673. 0.8 mi WSW of Ajo Peak. 32°19′48″N, 112°55′06″W. 1,900 ft.

Black Mountain Well (SD). Well in Vekol Valley 2.2 mi SW of Black Mountain. 32°42′53″N, 112°11′44″W. 2,088 ft.

Black Tank Well (GR). Well on N bajada of Crater Range, 5.3 mi NW of Midway. 32°40′22″N, 112°55′43″W. 975 ft.

Black Tanks (GR). A series of eight plunge-pool tinajas in NE part of Crater Range. Prehistoric peoples used the area, and modern ranchers dammed two of the larger potholes to water cattle. Along old route from Ajo to Gila Bend or Sentinel. May =Gila Tanks, as noted in George Kippen's 1854–58 diary (Hoy 1995). =AGFD #813. 32°37′42″N, 112°57′44″W. 1,100 ft.

Blaisdell (Yuma Co.). Railroad siding and former settlement on NW side of Gila Mountains. Blaisdell was the jumping-off point for the Fortuna Mine and points south during the mine's heyday, and a water pipeline ran 12 mi to the mine from a well here. Named for Hiram W. Blaisdell, who supervised construction of two canals in the area in 1888. 32°42′51″N, 114°25′29″W. 180 ft.

Blankenship Well and **Ranch** (OP). A ranch with well and watering trough for livestock just N of international boundary, 4.5 mi ESE of Lukeville. Built about 1914 by Lon Blankenship and his sons Lon Jr. and Joe; they called it Rattlesnake Ranch. The Henry Gray family bought it in 1919 and renamed it Dos Lomitas, for the two hills immediately W of the ranch; when one of his sons asked him why the change from Rattlesnake, Robert L. Gray replied, "'Cause, by God, I wanted to!" (Bill Hoy). House and sheds made from discarded railroad ties. =Grays Ranch, though this name has been applied to at least two other locales associated with the Gray family. =Dos Lomitas Well. 31°51′30″N, 112°44′24″W. 1,429 ft.

Figure 39.7. Black Tanks.

Blindman Butte (GR). Small butte 11 mi SSW of Gila Bend and 0.2 mi E of Arizona Highway 85. 32°48′13″N, 112°47′19″W. 1,074 ft.

Blue Plateau (SD). Flattish basalt-capped summit ridge in NW part of Sand Tank Mountains. Reportedly has bluish tinge when seen from a distance, and "some days it looks absolutely purple at sunset" (Duane Holt). 32°47′31″N, 112°32′38″. 2,910 ft.

Bluebird Mine Well (CP). Abandoned well that served Bluebird Mine in southern Growler Mountains, 0.8 mi W of Scarface Mountain. Developed by Sam Clark; named for bluebird seen there by Robert Temple and Elmer Montgomery, who worked the claim (Bill Hoy). Lazuli buntings, western bluebirds, and mountain bluebirds have been reported in CP. 32°12′20″N, 112°56′51″W. 1,610 ft.

BM (USA, throughout region). =Bench mark; a surveyor's horizontal control mark or point atop unnamed summits. Surveyors prefer 3–6-letter words for bench marks. For example, BM Cholla in northern Granite Mountains is named for jumping cholla (*Cylindropuntia fulgida*) and teddybear cholla (*C. bigelovii*) that are abundant in the area.

BM Simmons is a 2,200-ft peak in southern Sierra Pinta (CP), named for Norman M. Simmons, manager of CP in mid-1960s, expert on desert bighorn sheep, and friend of the surveyors. Later Simmons served on the original UNESCO committee that created the Man in the Biosphere concept. U.S. topographic features are seldom named for living persons.

BM Monson is point 2477 (2,477 ft) in southern Mohawk Mountains. Gale Monson was Simmons's boss in U.S. Fish and Wildlife Service, which manages CP. Monson was instrumental in preventing federal government from giving CP to the Arizona State Land Department and Arizona Game and Fish Department in mid-1950s.

BM Charley [*sic*] in the Growler Mountains was named for Charlie Bell, close friend of Tom Childs (see Charlie Bell Well).

BM Bat is for Batamote, point 1886 (1,886 ft) in southern mountains of the same name.

Bob Curtis Tank (Pima Co.). A water catchment in northern Sikort Chuapo Mountains, 15 mi E of Ajo and 2.3 mi S of Coffeepot Mountain. Built in 1993 and named for a Wisconsin hunter who financially supported water developments for wildlife. =AGFD #1040. 32°26′54″N, 112°37′35″W. 2,940 ft.

Boca. Spanish for 'mouth', here of a bay, passage, or river.

Boca el Abrigo, Boca la Baja, and **Boca de Enmedio** (AG). See Isla Montague.

Boca la Bolsa (AG). Mouth to Estero la Ramada, 26 km NNW of San Felipe. Spanish for 'mouth of the pocket', such as a bay. 31°15′41″N, 114°53′09″W. Sea level.

Bocana, La (AG). Fishing camp near La Bocana Bend of Colorado River. Spanish for 'mouth' of a river. The camp is 31°53′51″N, 114°56′16″W. 10 ft. The bend is at 31°54′54″N, 114°56′47″W (Steve Nelson).

Bomba, La (AG). Abandoned seaport in Colorado River delta, E of N tip of Sierra de las Pintas. "The 'city' of La Bomba, the 'seaport' of this section of Mexico, with two small steamers a week, consists of seven small buildings, including a radio station, and at the time of our visit boasted five inhabitants and seven automobiles and trucks. The 'port' is a slushy, crumbling river bank. . . . The freight brought in is mostly liquor for the border towns while fish are shipped south. The 'city' is flooded about 6 inches deep every new moon, we were told, and at times of high water in the river it is cut off for weeks at a time. It is soon to be linked with Mexicali by Government-built railroad, much of the grading has been done, but it can never be much of a port" (Gordon 1924:98). Vicinity 31°50′31N, 115°01′38″W. 3 m (Steve Nelson).

Bonillas Cone (PI). Volcanic cone 1 km SE of Pinacate Peak. Named for Ygnacio S. Bonillas Jr., mining engineer, who wrote the first scholarly piece on Pinacate geology (Bonillas 1910; Lynch & Gutmann 1987). He was an active field man and apparently noted many of the Pinacate calderas considerably earlier than 1900 (Ives 1964). Bonillas was born February 1, 1858, in San Ignacio, Sonora, and died in Nogales, Arizona, on January

31, 1944, one day short of his 86th birthday. In between, this son of a blacksmith grew up in Tucson, where he attended the first public school in the territory (founded in 1871 by Gov. Anson P. Safford) and where an elementary school is named for him. To pay for his school books, he worked directly for Gov. Safford, blacking his boots, feeding his mules, and sweeping his office (Tucson was Arizona Territory's capital from 1867 to 1877). Bonillas graduated from Massachusetts Institute of Technology in 1884 and opened assay offices in Tombstone and Hermosillo. Later he served as a mining engineer; elementary teacher; engineering instructor at the University of Arizona; businessman; prefect and mayor of Magdalena, Sonora; mayor of Nogales, Sonora; and Mexico's ambassador to U.S. during World War I; he was hailed as "the savior of Mexico" for his work to prevent U.S. from declaring war on Mexico in 1917; and in 1920 he was the front-running candidate for president of Mexico before the assassination of his friend and mentor President Venustiano Carranza (*Arizona Daily Star* 1931, 1942, 1944; *Tucson Citizen* 1954). 31°45′51″N, 113°29′38″W. 1,060 m.

Bonita Well (OP). Well dug in 1937 for livestock on Aguajita Wash 5 mi NW of Quitobaquito Springs. Spanish for 'pretty'. =Rancho Bonito. 32°00′32″N, 112°58′28″W. 1,355 ft.

Booth Hills (SD). Small group of hills on far E side of SD, 5.1 mi S of Mobile. Probably named for Edwin C. Booth, who in 1935 homesteaded 320 acres in N half of section 26, immediately SE of the hills. 32°58′44″N, 112°14′58″W. 2,216 ft.

Borrego Canyon (GR). Major canyon in southern Tinajas Altas Mountains. The only place in Arizona where long-lobed four o'clock (*Mirabilis tenuiloba*) has been found (Felger 1993, 2000). Mouth at 32°17′58″N, 114°02′25″W. 1,240 ft.

Borrego Tank (GR). Natural tinaja in Borrego Canyon, southern Tinajas Altas Mountains, 1.7 mi S of Tinajas Altas. It was modified with a dam in 1988, and its water is intermittent. Spanish for 'sheep' or 'lamb', here desert bighorn sheep (*Ovis canadensis mexicana*). Almost named Queen of the Night Tank, for a *Peniocereus greggii* that struggles to grow here. =AGFD #962. 32°17′07″N, 114°03′03″W. 1,590 ft.

Bosque (Maricopa Co.). A railroad stop and small settlement on the Southern Pacific Railroad established in 1895 for the shipping of ironwood and mesquite for the Phoenix Wood and Coal Company. The cutting was done on government land, and the U.S. government sued the company, which was made to pay 25 cents per acre for "cutting timber on public lands" (Granger 1960: 177). Local Gila Bend figure Thomas H. Farley (1898–1989) was born in Bosque, where the SPRR had com-

Figure 39.8. Borrego *Tank.*

pany homes at one time. Farley was friends with author Earl Stanley Gardner and with actor Andy Devine, who gave Tom a pair of white burros that became Tom's trademark (*Gila Bend Sun* 1999; see Mesquite Well). Spanish for 'forest grove', apparently alluding to once plentiful trees in this area, now greatly diminished. 32°58′22″N, 112°33′45″W. 1,065 ft.

Bosque Siding (SD). Modern railroad siding 2.7 mi downslope from original settlement. In mid-twentieth century railroad tank cars filled with drinking water were parked here for Gila Bend residents, since local water was brackish and water imported from Maricopa wells was quite good (John Laird). Associated with La Palma Corral, where cattle were penned before shipment by rail. La Palma did have a palm tree, probably supported by overflow from watering troughs. W end of siding at 32°57′55″N, 112°36′32″W. 950 ft.

Bosque Well (SD). Well and corral 0.5 mi S of Bosque Siding. 32°57′41″N, 112°35′47″W. 991 ft.

Boulder Canyon (OP). Deep canyon choked with boulders on W side of Ajo Mountains. 1 mi NW of Ajo Peak. Mouth at 32°01′57″N, 112°42′35″W. 2,800 ft.

Bryan Mountains (CP). Narrow granitic range S from Mohawk Mountains. Named for geologist Kirk Bryan (see Bryan 1925). They were considered part of the Mohawk Mountains before they were renamed by E. D. Wilson (1931). In his geologic map of southern Yuma County (1933), Wilson depicted the Mohawks as ending at the pass where Game Tank now lies. Everything south of that point was part of the Bryan Mountains, including the small hills now called the Antelope Hills (N of Papago Well). For some unexplained reason, the Bryans "shrank" when the official mapmakers arrived in the 1960s. =Mohawk Mountains. 32°18′26″N, 113°22′43″W. 1,794 ft.

Buchan (SD). Railroad siding and former settlement on SPRR midway between Estrella and Mobile. Appears

Figure 39.9. Buckhorn
Tank.

on numerous older maps. 33°02′47″N, 112°18′19″W.
1,370 ft.

Buck Mountain Tank (CP). Waterhole constructed
during 1949 1.3 mi WNW of Buck Peak. Name occasionally has drifted from original Buck Mountain Tank
appellation to =Buck Peak Tank; also =Buck Mountains Tank. 32°23′07″N, 113°54′57″W. 1,240 ft.

Buck Mountains (CP). See Buck Peak.

Buck Peak (CP). Gneiss and schist mountain in NW
corner of CP. The name predates 1918. Though officially
part of the Cabeza Prieta Mountains, some consider it
a separate range, and the name Buck Mountains occasionally appears in reports and maps, as does Buck Peak
Mountains. Wilson (1931) mistakenly believed Buck
Peak to be the high point of the Cabeza Prieta Mountains; that point is actually 4.7 mi SE. *Buck* was colloquial term for a desert bighorn ram; reportedly, many
were seen on this mountain, though few are seen today.
Summit is at BM Buck, 32°22′56″N, 113°53′38″W. 2,629 ft.

Buckhorn Tank (CP). Adit blasted in southern Cabeza
Prieta Mountains as a waterhole for wildlife in 1948. A
natural but intermittent tinaja preceded development
and was used by prehistoric people. 3 mi W of Tule
Well. Name denotes enduring horns from skeletons of
desert bighorn sheep. After a week's stay at this place,
Ann Zwinger (1993:154) wrote, "Easy landscapes stifle
me.... I prefer the absences and big empties.... I prefer
the raw edges and the unfinished hems of the desert
landscape." 32°14′08″N, 113°47′57″W. 1,410 ft.

Also **Buckhorn Pass** (CP). Small pass west of Buckhorn Tank. 32°14′08″N, 113°48′09″W. 1,420 ft.

Bull Pasture (OP). Elevated basin on W slope of Ajo
Mountains, 0.8 mi S of Ajo Peak. Noted for seasonally
abundant grasses, so cattle were pastured here, hence
the name. Historically, intermittent water was had at
Bull Pasture Spring, but today the spring is unfound,
though USGS maps depict a spring at 32°00′57″N,
112°41′28″W (3,180 ft). Several fine tinajas are in the
basin, including East Arroyo Tinaja, Spring Arroyo Tinajas, and West Arroyo Tinajas (Brown & Johnson 1983;
Brown et al. 1983). Many botanical collections have
been made here, including wild tepary bean (Nabhan &
Felger 1978) and one of a few populations of the hybrid
Agave × *ajoensis* (formerly *Agave schottii* var. *treleasei*),
a sterile hybrid between *Agave deserti* and *Agave schottii*
(Hodgson 1999; see Chapter 17, this volume). 32°00′53″N,
112°41′35″W. 3,245 ft.

Buried Range (PI). See Sierra Enterrada.

Burro Gap (Pima Co.). Road and trail where Tenmile
Wash passes westward through Batamote Mountains,
10 mi E of Ajo. 32°24′15″N, 112°41′19″W. 1,830 ft.

Burro Spring (GR). Intermittent spring in Sand Tank
Mountains, 0.8 mi ESE of Dragon's Teeth pinnacles.
Feral burros pawed the sand to reach water here (Duane
Holt). =Sand Tank Mountains Pothole #1; AGFD #635.
32°38′11″N, 112°24′29″W. 2,440 ft.

Burro Spring (OP). A small spring in Quitobaquito
Hills, 0.6 mi N of Quitobaquito Springs. At one time
wild burros roamed this area. It supports a small population of the native reedgrass, or carrizo (*Phragmites
australis;* Felger et al. 1992). 31°57′12″N, 113°01′11″W.
1,160 ft.

Butler Mountains (GR). A small, very arid, granitic
range 4 mi W of Tinajas Altas Mountains and S of
Vopoki Ridge. Its base is partially buried by drifting
sands. Important packrat fossil-midden study site (Van
Devender 1990). Named by geologist E. D. Wilson
(1931) for Gurdon Montague Butler, dean of College of
Mines at University of Arizona (1915–40) and director
of Arizona Bureau of Mines (1918–40). =Las Cuevitas
(Spanish for 'little caves') on some older maps in recognition of the many wind-eroded caves (tafoni) in the
granitic rock (Barney 1943); sometimes misspelled Las
Quavitas. Summit is BM Lech (for Lechuguilla Desert,
though it is in Yuma Desert) at 32°22′34″N, 114°12′23″W.
1,169 ft.

Butte Tank (GR). Represo 0.5 mi E of Black Butte.
32°42′21″N, 112°40′02″W. 1,405 ft.

Butterfield Pass (SD). Gap in central Maricopa Mountains where the Butterfield Overland Stage route crossed
the Maricopa Divide. The route was established in 1857
by John Butterfield, with the principal purpose of

transporting mail between St. Louis and San Francisco. The trip along the southern route took 25 days, and conditions for passengers were primitive. Stops along the trail were only to change horses and drivers, and good meals were provided once per day. Coaches ran twice per week, and passengers could wait for the next coach, but sleeping accommodations usually consisted of blankets on the floor and a meal of beans, beef, and biscuits. Completion of the Southern Pacific Railroad in the 1870s ended the stage service. A popular jeep trail now follows the old route through the pass and the heart of SD (Aleshire 2004).

Butterfield Pass was called Puerto de los Cocomaricopas by Francisco Garcés, with the D'Anza expedition in 1775. He also named Sierra Maricopa in honor of the tribe, though Kroeber & Fontana (1986:34) remind us that "the Maricopa were not originally a 'tribe' in the formal sense of the word." Instead, they were an amalgam of at least five Yuman groups. =Pima Pass. 32°02′49″N, 112°28′06″W. 1,734 ft.

C

Caailipolaacoj (Sonora, AG? PI?). Dry lake bed N of Puerto Peñasco. Seri for 'laguna salada' (Mary Beck Moser). Precise location unknown.

Cabeza Prieta Mountains (CP). A major range composed of geologically complex basalts and granites from both Laramide and mid-Tertiary orogenies. Regional geology is discussed and dated in Shafiqullah et al. 1980. Area noted for desert bighorn sheep. Gaillard calls these the Tule Mountains (International Boundary Commission 1898), and Mearns (1907:19) calls them the Granite Mountains. Some older maps label them the Devil Hills, a name now relegated to a series of small hills NE of the main range. High point is unnamed BM Cabeza (32°20′59″N, 113°49′26″W. 2,830 ft), but most distinctive peak is basalt-capped landmark of **Cabeza Prieta Peak** (=Cerro de la Cabeza Prieta, Sierra de la Cabeza Prieta, Spanish for 'black or dark head' and likely derived from O'odham name S-cuk Mo'o, for 'black head'), at 32°17′21″N, 113°48′28″W. 2,559 ft.

Cabeza Prieta National Wildlife Refuge (=CP). Federal wildlife and wilderness area covering 860,010 acres (3,480 km²). It is the third largest refuge and the largest refuge wilderness area in the lower 48 states. It was established in 1939 (as Cabeza Prieta Game Range) to protect wildlife, especially desert bighorn and Sonoran pronghorn, and is administered by the U.S. Fish and Wildlife Service. It was redesignated Cabeza Prieta National Wildlife Refuge in 1975. The refuge is bounded by Sonora to the S. It occupies the SE corner of Yuma County and SW corner of Pima County, Arizona. A preliminary flora was published by N. Simmons (1966) and substantially revised by Felger et al. (this volume, Chapter 17). Its precipitation is highly variable (Comrie

Figure 39.10. Cabeza Prieta Peak.

& Broyles 1998, 2002). Its cultural history is discussed in Ahlstrom et al. 2001 and its geology in H. Simmons (1965). Abbey (1984) and Peacock (1986, 2006) narrate hikes across the refuge.

Several times the Fish and Wildlife Service has considered relinquishing the refuge and disposing of this desert jewel but has been thwarted by alert citizens (e.g., Carhart 1955). Airspace over CP is restricted and controlled by the military. Legal boundary descriptions can be found in Executive Order 8038 (January 25, 1939). Originally, it was proposed to be part of a large (3.5 to 6 million acres) protected area between the Colorado River and Arizona Highway 85; CP, OP, and the Kofa National Wildlife Refuge are remnants of that visionary plan. For a short period in 1975 the refuge included the Tinajas Altas Mountains, but a legislative snafu reversed this protective acquisition. =Cabeza Prieta Wildlife Range, Cabeza Prieta Game Range. Refuge headquarters is in Ajo at 32°23′10″N, 112°52′19″W. 1,772 ft.

Cabeza Prieta Pass (CP). A primitive trail through the mountains 2 mi NW of Cabeza Prieta Tanks. 32°18′52″N, 113°49′25″W. 1,510 ft.

Cabeza Prieta Tanks (CP) Usually perennial tinajas in central Cabeza Prieta Mountains, 1.2 mi N of Cabeza Prieta Peak. The deepest of 6 main pools is 73 in. Perhaps also known as Agua Escondido (Spanish for 'hidden water') since the tinajas lie in inconspicuous side canyon. The natural tinajas hold about 17,000 gallons when full (Broyles 1996a). One of few known localities in Arizona for *Eucnide rupestris,* a strange, glassy-spined rock plant in family Loasaceae. =Cuk Mo'okam Ce:po; historically transcribed ˢTjukomókamtjúupo, O'odham for 'tinajas below the black head'. An important camp for millennia, it may have been inhabited by Native Americans into the twentieth century (Lumholtz 1912: 324, 397). For fuller prehistory of entire region, see Ahlstrom et al. 2001; Broyles et al., this volume, Chap-

Figure 39.11. Cabeza Prieta Tanks.

ter 14; Fontana 1974; McGuire & Schiffer 1982. 32°18′29″N, 113°48′11″W. 1,540 ft.

A waterhole developed in 1962 in the S fork of the same canyon is called Sheep Hollow Tank. 32°18′27″N, 113°48′09″W. 1,530 ft.

Cactus Flat (PI). Sandy flat about 3 km E of Pinacate Junction and N of Playa Díaz; 51 km W of Sonoyta and S of Mexico Highway 2. Seven species of cacti have been found growing here among the creosotebushes and galleta grass on this open plain: *Carnegiea gigantea, Echinocereus engelmannii, Ferocactus wislizeni, Cylindropuntia arbuscula, C. fulgida, C. ramosissima,* and *Grusonia kunzei.* Five more cactus species grow nearby. Cacti, especially the saguaro, often begin life in sheltered sites beneath large legumes such as palo verde and ironwood, which serve as nurse plants. However, larger desert shrubs or trees are absent here, so the large and perennial galleta grass *(Hilaria rigida)* is the most frequent nurse plant (Felger 2000). 31°58′N, 113°19′W. 200 m.

Caesar Tank (GR). Stock pond 5.4 mi NW of Maricopa Peak in Sand Tank Mountains. 32°48′26″N, 112°26′44″W. 1,880 ft.

Café Álamo (PI). Small café and store along S side of Mexico Highway 2, 49.3 km W of Sonoyta and about 2 km E of Pinacate Junction. 31°59′27″N, 113°19′37″W. 220 m.

Café el Oasis (PI). A small restaurant along Mexico Highway 2, 35 km W of Sonoyta. 31°58′N, 113°11′W. 300 m.

Café El Trece (PI). Small café along south side of Mexico Highway 2, 13 km WNW of Sonoyta. Spanish for 'thirteen', same as site's kilometer post. 31°55′30″N, 112°58′29″W. 340 m.

Cajón del Diablo (CP). Small canyon between low ranges W of Tule Tank where older roadbed of Camino del Diablo once passed. This short portion of the ancient route was bypassed in the late 1940s when the roadbed for the current *camino* was bladed by government agents. The older route may have passed through here to gain access to several intermittent tinajas just off the trail, as well as feed for livestock in the form of big galleta grass *(Hilaria rigida),* which is relatively abundant in the canyon. A modern FWS administrative trail now passes through here en route to Cabeza Prieta Tanks and Wellton. Cajón is Spanish for 'narrow canyon'. 32°13′41″N, 113°48′21″W. 1,220 ft.

California. American coastal state created 1850, famed for gold rush of 1849. 158,869 mi² (411,470 ha). Motto is "Eureka, I have found it." Capital is Sacramento. Population 32,268,000 in 2000.

Californias, The. The state of California together with the Baja California peninsula. Named for mythical land called California ruled by fictional Queen Calafre, in 1383 Portuguese text by Vasco Lobeira (Sykes 1915c). Other early names include New Granada, Quivera, Axa, Totonteac, and New Albion. After the 1700s the mainland was called Nuevo California and the peninsula was Antigua California (Crosby 1994).

Camel Skeleton (CP). Mammalogist Edgar Mearns (1907:19), who collected and camped at this location on the Camino Diablo N of Boundary Monument 181 in February 1894, found a camel skeleton here. Starting in 1856, the U.S Army and Lt. Edward F. Beale brought camels to serve as pack and riding animals in the arid American West. Other camels were shipped privately to work in mines and on freight lines. The camels were very capable, but their soft feet didn't fare well on rocky ground or in mines, so most were turned loose. Feral camels—adaptable and prolific—were seen throughout southwestern Arizona, including Sonoyta, Ajo, Maricopa Wells, and the Gila River, until 1931. Camel meat became popular in mining camps, including Gunsight. Over 400 were captured along the Gila River and sent to a circus in Australia (Boyd 1995; Smith 1935). Both dromedaries (from North Africa and Turkey) and Bactrian (from western China) were imported, but Mearns apparently did not classify his find. Vicinity of 32°06′44″N, 113°30′44″W. 800 ft.

Camelback Mountain (Pima Co.). This ridge 1 mi SW of Ajo resembles the hump of a dromedary. Feral camels from 1860s U.S. Army and mining operations multiplied and their descendants roamed SW Arizona; some reportedly served as food in Gunsight mining camp ca. 1890, and the last one was reported near Sonoyta in 1931, so the name came easily. Three mountains once formed Ajo's southern skyline, but two of them—Oklahoma and Arkansas—have been removed to make room for the mine pit; only Camelback remains. Cross near summit is 1926 monument to John C. Greenway, general manager of New Cornelia Copper Co. =A-Mountain (for whitewashed Ajo "A"). 32°21′52″N, 112°52′40″W. 2,573 ft.

Camerons Stock Tank (Pima Co.). Large livestock represo just outside eastern CP boundary; 9 mi SSW of Ajo and 1 mi W of John the Baptist Mountains. Dug on a tributary to Cuerda de Leña by John Cameron family in mid-twentieth century, it holds about 14 acre-ft when full. Good place to observe birds. 32°15′04″N, 112°59′49″W. 1,680 ft.

Camerons Tank (Pima Co.). Livestock represo on Rio Cornez, 5 mi SE of Ajo and 0.2 mi S of Arizona Highway 85. Named for John Cameron family. 32°19′47″N, 112°47′10″W. 1,625 ft.

Camino del Diablo, El (CP, GR). The infamous ancient route from Sonoyta to Yuma. It crosses the northern part of the Pinacate region, runs through CP to Tinajas Altas, and ends at the Gila River. Route was taken by Padre Eusebio Kino in 1699; by settlers from Mexico going to San Diego, Los Angeles, and San Francisco areas; and by many forty-niners to the California goldfields. The first motorcar trip across it was in 1915 by Raphael Pumpelly (1918), and it remains a primitive road. See Broyles 1993; Bryan 1925; Hartmann 1989; McGee 1901; Sykes 1931, 1951. Spanish for 'road of the devil'. Commonly called the Devil's Highway.

The origin of the name is a puzzle. Gaillard (1896), the International Boundary Commission (1898), and McGee (1901) mention that the road between Agua Dulce and Yuma was called El Camino del Diablo, but McGee in 1901 still refers to it primarily as the Old Yuma Trail, and Lumholtz (1912:197) notes, "Many recent authorities speak of this part of the trail as the *Camino del Diablo,* but nobody in Sonoita knows it under that name." =The Devil's Highway, Sonora Trail, Sonoyta-Yuma Trail, Yuma-Caborca Trail, Camino del Muerto, Old Yuma Trail. Kuldell's 1918 map calls it "Old Camino Real."

Incidentally, despite his early work in this region, the area's only geographical name personally involving W. J. McGee is Klotho's Temple in the Muggins Mountains, N of the Gila River. It was named in 1900 by De Lancey Gill for McGee's daughter, Klotho (McGee 1915), and derives from the mythic Clotho, one of the Three Fates (Granger 1983).

Hogner (1938) presents an interesting travelogue of camping along El Camino. Summers (1937) paints a fictionalized account of Padre Kino along the route.

Camp Grip (CP). A U.S. Border Patrol outpost along El Camino del Diablo about 3 mi W of Papago Well. The camp, a 4,000-ft^2 modular building with generators, parking pads, and heliport, is temporary but has every camping convenience except a washing machine, because it would use too much water. Agents are stationed here to respond quickly, especially for search-and-rescue missions in the heat of summer, when there are two groups of people trying to evade the Border Patrol: "the ones who were rescued and the ones who will need to be rescued" (Robert McLemore). Installed in 2002 after 14 undocumented aliens died near the Granite Mountains and named for the need to "get a grip" on the smuggling problems between Bates Well and Tule Well. =Camp Vidrios, Camp Oasis, Paradise, Desert Eden, and expletives. Agents also are stationed at Bates Well. After 2001 the Border Patrol was reorganized and renamed U.S. Customs and Border Protection (CBP), under the Department of Homeland Security (DHS). Vicinity 32°05′N, 113°20′W. 800 ft.

Campo. Spanish for camp, tourist or trailer park, farm or ranch, temporary settlement.

Campo, El (AG). Local name for scientific collection site on edge of Ciénega de Santa Clara. See Hunter's Camp (AG). 32°01′22″N, 114°54′57″W. Just above sea level.

Campo Don Abel (AG). One of the northernmost tourist camps along the beach N of San Felipe. A collection of houses and trailers managed by Ramon Soberanes. When asked who the site was named for, he said "un hombre" (Karl Flessa; Rodriguez et al. 2001). 31°11′N, 114°53′W. 2 m.

Campo Mosqueda (BC). A tourist camp established in the 1970s on Río Hardy. It is named for the Mosqueda family, owners of the camp. Founder Jesús Mosqueda and one of his sons, Javier, have been leaders in community-based conservation and restoration efforts in the Colorado River delta and along Río Hardy. On their private lands they started the first reforestation effort in the area, helping create the local environmental association AEURHYC (Asociación Ecológica de Usuarios de los Ríos Hardy y Colorado—Ecological Association of Users of the Hardy and Colorado Rivers), and promoting ecotourism and sustainable economic activities (Osvel Hinojosa-Huerta). 32°09′24″N, 115°16′36″W. 20 m.

Campo Rojo (PI). Campsite 4 km E of Pinacate Peak and at S foot of a red volcanic butte. Long a favorite

Figure 39.12. *Carnegie Peak.*

camping place at end of a jeep road and beginning of easiest approach to Pinacate summit. Also a favorite photo point for senita cactus *(Pachycereus schottii)* and elephant trees *(Bursera microphylla)* against ragged lava backdrop. N of Emilia Tanks. =Emilia Camp, Hunter's Camp, Palo Verde Camp, Red Cone Camp. 31°46′30″N, 113°26′50″W. 420 m.

Campo el Zanjón (AG). Fishing camp along W bank of a wide, deep channel of Río Colorado, 11 km SW of Luis Encinas Johnson. Spanish for 'deep ditch'. Vicinity of 31°56′N, 115°02′W. 5 m.

Canal de Descarga R. Sánchez Toboada (Sonora). See Wellton-Mohawk Main Outlet Drain Extension.

Canyon Diablo (Maricopa Co.). See Tenmile Wash.

Capitán, El (Sonora). Cluster of small, rugged peaks 40 km ESE of San Luís Río Colorado. Distinctive landmarks in otherwise flat desert lands. The peaks are composed of limestone and slate, with jasper and quartz pebbles strewn across adjacent flats. A limestone kiln, fueled by thousands of discarded automobile tires, provided lime for masonry construction in San Luis R.C. in mid-twentieth century. Named by Lumholtz (1912:243). See Zumbador, El. =Cerro Sumbador, Cerro Zumbado; Boundary Hills. 32°18′11″N, 114°22′40″W. 220 m.

Caravajales Crater (PI). Shallow volcanic crater 10 km SW of MacDougal Crater. Its rim rises about 18 m above sandy plain, and diameter is 366 m (May 1973). Named for Juan Caravajales, an Hia C'ed O'odham who lived and farmed in area. He was made famous by Lumholtz, though Caravajales died not alone in the Gran Desierto dunes as reported (Lumholtz 1912) but among relatives in Wellton, Arizona (Bell et al. 1980). =Cráter Caravajales, Hayden Crater (per Wood 1972: 36, but Julian Hayden had already christened it Caravajales in his notes and scoffed at having something named for himself). 31°54′43″N, 113°41′34″E. 100 m.

Caravajales Flat (PI). Seasonally verdant flat 2 km SW of Tinajas de los Pápagos; named for Juan Caravajales by Julian Hayden. =Argemone Flat, after seasonally profuse *Argemone gracilenta* (prickly poppy). 31°54′N, 113°36′W. 200 m.

Cardigan Mine (Pima Co.). Large grouping of prospects, adits, and shafts lying on and around Pinnacle Peak and higher reaches of Darby Wash in the Little Ajo Mountains. The Ajo Scenic Loop Drive travels through the heart of this property. 32°21′15″N, 112°53′14″W. 2,080 ft.

Cardigan Peak (Pima Co.). A summit in Little Ajo Mountains 2.5 mi W of Ajo. Named for a prospector. The Hia C'ed O'odham contract this name into Cargan Do'ag (Cardigan Mountain) and use it as a key landmark. =S-mu'umk, O'odham for 'many sharp points'. 32°21′52″N, 112°54′33″W. 2,922 ft.

Cardigan Well (Pima Co.). Former settlement 3 mi SW of Ajo. See Corrigan.

Carnegie Peak (PI). Second highest peak in the Sierra Pinacate, 1.2 km east of Pinacate Peak. Peak and ridge are on rim of eroded, much larger Volcán de Santa Clara. Its cinder slopes are near the angle of repose. Its age is estimated at 38,000 years ± 8,000 (Gutmann et al. 2000). Named by Hornaday (1908) for philanthropist Andrew Carnegie, sponsor of Desert Botanical Laboratory in Tucson. =Santa Clara, Santa Brigida (names by Kino: Bolton 1919). 31°46′23″N, 113°29′08″W. 1,130 m (about 3,708 ft).

Carrizal, El (Sonora). One of Padre Kino's campsites on Río Sonoyta, about 10 km WSW of Quitobaquito, midway between Agua Dulce and Agua Salada (Ives 1989). Spanish for 'place of the carrizo' *(Phragmites australis),* the native reedgrass, which is still found in the area (Felger 2000).

On February 17, 1699, Padre Eusebio Kino and his party camped "en un carrizal que hace el arroyo" [in a stand of carrizo that is situated in the arroyo] "about 25 miles" westward from Sonoyta (Burrus 1971:230, 291). Kino named this place Los Carrizales. Today a grove of carrizo, standing in several large patches, grows along the E bank of the river at the base of an alkaline bajada of Sierra de Los Tanques, apparently at the site of a seep or spring. This grove is about 5 km upstream from where Ives (1989) maps Kino's Los Carrizales. No other carrizo is known from the Río Sonoyta (Felger 2000). =Ko'okomatk Ki:kam, O'odham for 'one(s) living among the carrizo'; historically transcribed Coamaquidam. A short distance upstream from Agua Dulce. About 31°56′N, 113°07′W. 280 m.

Castle Rock (OP). A castle-like pinnacle in Ajo Mountains on the ridge between Grass Canyon and Alamo

Canyon. To some viewers it looks more like a hammer head (Sue Rutman). 32°05'23N", 112°43'33"W. 3,250 ft.

Celaya Crater (PI). A broad volcanic crater 24 km N of Pinacate Peak; 914 m in diameter and 88 m deep. Named, perhaps by Jahns (1959), in honor of Alberto Celaya (1885–1962), long-time resident of Sonoyta, guide and friend of scholars Carl Lumholtz, Richard Jahns, Ronald Ives, and Julian Hayden (Ives 1962; see Hayden, this volume, Chapter 8). =Cráter Celaya, Celaya Maar Crater, Volcán los Vidrios. 31°59'01"N, 113°26'46"W. 260 m.

Cement Tank (OP). A concrete dam and stock tank 1 mi WSW of Diaz Spire. Built in 1918 by Lon Blankenship. 31°58'05"N, 112°41'17"W. 1,980 ft.

Cemetery Wash (GR, Maricopa Co.). Arroyo passing SW corner of Gila Bend Pioneer Cemetery and immediately W of Highway 85 and I-8 interchange. 1 mi of its channel lies within GR. Name formally proposed July 2, 2001, by Gila Bend town council but declined by Arizona state officials because it duplicates previously named Cemetery Wash near Wickenburg, Arizona. Crosses Gila Bend to Ajo rail line at 32°55'52"N, 112°43'28"W. 750 ft.

Cerdán, Ejido (Sonora). See Ejido Aquiles Serdán.

Cerro. Spanish for 'hill'.

Cerro el Aguila (PI). Small sierra 3 km SW of MacDougal Crater. 31°57'35"N, 113°39'23"W. 340 m.

Cerro Blanco (OP). Light-colored, granitic hill in extreme SW corner of OP. *Agave deserti* and *Dudleya arizonica* are found here (Felger 2000). Spanish for 'white hill'. 31°57'47"N, 113°04'45"W. 1,094 ft.

Cerro Borrego (BC). Peak 46 km S of Mexicali in Sierra Mayor. Presumably named for *borrego cimarrón* (Spanish for 'wild sheep' or 'bighorn sheep', here the peninsular subspecies, *Ovis canadensis cremnobates*). 32°12'32"N, 115°25'08"W. 660 m.

Cerro del Borrego (BC). Mountain 60 km NW of San Felipe, in Sierra San Felipe. Stands just N of Valle Borrego. =Cerro el Arrajal. 31°21'59"N, 115°16'24"W. 1,360 m.

Cerro el Chivo (PI). Cinder cone in southwestern part of Pinacate volcanic field; 11 km W of Pinacate Peak. Spanish for 'goat', or colloquially, 'bighorn sheep'. =Chivos Cone, Chivos Butte. 31°46'09"N, 113°37'03"W. 340 m.

Cerro Cipriano (Sonora). An eastern peak in Sierra Cipriano, 13 km SW of Sonoyta. 31°55'57"N, 112°59'08"W. 820 m.

Cerro Colorado (PI). Large, isolated tuff cone at NE side of Pinacate region, 25 km NE of Pinacate Peak. Named for the reddish rock; its colors are especially vivid at sunset. The name predated the Carnegie expedition of 1907: "That was 'Cerro Colorado,' so Mr. Mil-

ton said, otherwise known as 'Red Hill'" (Hornaday 1908:139). Lumholtz (1912:203) reports it is "light in color, almost pinkish, hence its name Cerro Colorado, with deep furrows from the top down and with an air of recent formation about it." Cerro Colorado evidently is at least 27,000 years old, ±6,000 years (Gutmann et al. 2000). Spanish for 'red hill'. =Volcán Colorado, Cráter Colorado, Cerro Colorado Crater. 750 m maximum diameter. 31°55'02"N, 113°18'02"W. 220 m at top of southern rim.

Cerro los Cuates (PI). Twin volcanic cones in W Pinacate lava, 6 km N of Sierra Extraña. Spanish for 'twins'. 31°54'N, 113°41'W. 190 m.

Cerro el Halcón (PI). Cinder cone 3.5 km N of Cráter de La Luna. Named by Glenton Sykes in 1956 for a hawk nest near summit (Glenton Sykes). One such nest once stood over 4 ft tall but was vandalized. Wreckage from a small plane sabotaged in early 1980s lies on its W flank. Spanish for 'falcon'. =Cerro el Falcon [sic], Hawk Butte; Cerro la Cueva, presumably after a lava-tube cave at its base. 31°47'30"N, 113°41'10"W. 160 m.

Cerro el Huérfano (Sonora). Butte 13 km W of Quitobaquito at bend of Río Sonoyta; 1.2 km SW of boundary marker 173. Named 'orphan' since it stands apart from its parent, Sierra de la Salada. One map misplaces it within Sierra de la Salada, S of border monument 175. In 1918 Rancho de López was just E of Cerro Huérfano, along the Río Sonoyta. 31°57'05"N, 113°04'55"W. 340 m.

Cerro Kino (PI). Very steep volcanic cone lying 3 km W of Tinajas de los Pápagos and on N side of Arroyo del Papago (see Arroyo la Tinaja). The main trail from the tinajas to the dunes passes its base. It contains an erosion cave that Juan Caravajales used for shelter, including his bed and fireplace. Named by Hayden (1966), who argued that Kino, Manje, and Salvatierra had climbed the cone in April 1701 at sunset to view the sea and say mass (1998:34). 31°54'52"N, 113°38'07"W. 300 m.

Cerro Lágrimas de Apache (AG). Hill 1 km E of Mexico Highway 5, midway between Mexicali and San Felipe. Spanish for 'Apache tears'. 31°39'16"N, 115°03'26"W. 200 m.

Cerro la Lava (PI). Microwave communications relay station tower 2 km S of Mexico Highway 2 and 2.5 km N of Rancho Guadalupe Victoria. The turnoff to La Lava is also the Pinacate Biosphere entrance to MacDougal and Sykes craters. = Microondas la Lava. 32°01'57"N, 113°34'08"W. 340 m.

Cerro el Machorro (AG). See Punta el Machorro.

Cerro el Mayo (PI). Volcanic cone 18 km NE of Pinacate Peak and 2 km N of Tecolote Cone. Named for University of Arizona geology professor Evans B. Mayo (rhymes with "day-o") in 1960s. =Mayo Cone. 31°53'42"N, 113°21'54"W. 360 m.

Figure 39.13. *Cerro la Silla.*

Cerro los Ojos (PI). A peak in southern Tuseral Mountains. Spanish for 'eyes', 'springs', or 'window rocks'. 32°05′42″N, 113°41′06″W. 580 m.

Cerro la Pastora (PI). See Pyramid Peak. =Cerro la Pastoria.

Cerro Pinto (PI). Granitic mountain 10 km S of Tinajas Altas and 2 km S of Mexico Highway 2. Named by Lumholtz for its "different, very dark color" (1912:311). It is the westernmost of the steep granitic mountains W of the Pinacate volcanic field along Mexico Highway 2. This extremely arid mountain is the only known locality in Sonora for *Tidestromia suffruticosa* (Felger 2000). May =Republic Mountain (Sheldon 1993). See Sahuaro, El; Joyita, La. A road leads to the microwave tower atop the N end at 32°13′45″N, 114°03′10″W. 600 m.

Cerro Prieto (PI). Small basalt ridge 1 km S of Río Sonoyta and 14 km WNW of Sonoyta. 31°53′19″N, 112°59′49″W. 420 m.

Cerro Prieto (Sonora). Volcanic hill on the coast 12 km NW of Puerto Peñasco on E side of Bahía Adair. 31°23′31″N, 113°36′20″W. 120 m.

Cerro la Silla (PI). Basalt butte 21 km W of Los Vidrios, N of Mexico Highway 2, and 3.6 km NNW of Cerro la Lava microondas. Spanish for 'chair' or 'saddle'. 32°03′45″N, 113°33′03″W. 480 m.

Distinct from Sierra la Silla, Cerro la Silla, and La Silla microondas (microwave towers), which are 27 km SSE of Sonoyta and 6.5 km NNW of Quitovac.

Cerro Sombrero (PI). Cinder cone 24 km SW of Pinacate Peak. =Sombrero Cone. Possibly at 31°41′30″N, 113°37′30″W. 180 m.

Cerro Tecolote (PI). Cinder cone 4.8 km NE of Cráter Elegante. Spanish for 'owl'; a great horned owl *(Bubo virginianus)* nest was found on the cone. Tecolote campground is between Cerro Tecolote and Cerro Mayo. Gutmann et al. (2000:37) estimate the age of Tecolote at

27,000 (±6,000) years and note that it appears to be much younger and little modified by erosion; they caution that "on cones that appear so young, scars made by people on the landscape of this Biosphere Reserve are virtually permanent on a human timescale." =Tecolote Cone. 31°52′44″N, 113°21′35″W. 360 m.

Ceṣoñ Vahia (CP). See Sheep Tank. Also used by English-speaking cowboys for Charlie Bell Well (Sheep Well). =Ceṣoiñ Vahia.

Ceumĭ Ke:k (PI). See Tinaja Suvuk.

Chappell Well (GR). Abandoned well 7 mi SW of Wellton. Dug prior to 1920 by former Yuma County sheriff James "Chapo" Chappell. According to Bryan (1925: 206), it was used for watering cattle for one season and then abandoned. Precise location uncertain but would have been on Gila Mountains bajada 2 or 3 mi NE of Dripping Springs.

Charlie Bell Pass and **Charlie Bell Road** (CP). Pass through Growler Mountains on dirt road from Ajo to Charlie Bell Well. Today's dirt road through the pass follows prehistoric human trail and was bladed by Pima County Highway Department in 1930s. Pass at 32°23′37″N, 113°05′06″W. 1,486 ft.

Charlie Bell Well (CP). Windmill, storage tank, and trough W of Charlie Bell Pass at base of Growler Mountains. Site had a spring or seep in prehistoric times. Rediscovered by Charles Edgar Bell about 1928. Bell was a close friend of pioneer ranchers and businessmen Tom Childs Jr. and John Cameron. Among his varied careers, Bell was a peace officer, auto mechanic, and rancher, raising livestock at this well, including Angora goats. O'odham cowboys frequented this site for decades. Well was hand-dug to about 30 ft in 1930s. =Sheep Well; Ceṣoñ Vahia, O'odham for 'sheep well' or 'sheep tank'. 32°23′05″N, 113°06′07″W. 1,120 ft.

Cherioni Wash (OP). Arroyo that drains southern Valley of the Ajo. Lent name to the Cherioni Soil Series, the dominant soils formed from lava flows and on basalt mesa tops; they are shallow, very cobbly, fine sandy loam, high in lime and underlain by hardpan (Johnson 1997). Joins Cuerda de Leña at 32°09′32″N, 112°55′15″W (1,398 ft) to form Growler Wash.

Cherioni Well (OP). Two defunct wells 5 mi E of Kino Peak. One was drilled by Ruben Daniels in 1916 on Cherioni Wash along the old Ajo-Sonoita Road near junction of Alamo Wash. It was nearly always dry. Named for cherioni, or soapberry tree *(Sapindus drummondii)*, whose fruits were used for laundry soap; however, the name *cherioni* lacks currency in Sonora. According to Bryan (1925:182), Daniels chose the site "because of the presence of a large cherioni tree. In this instance the tree indicated water at shallow depth, but not in sufficient quantity to be valuable." =Daniels Well. Vicinity of 32°07′29″N, 112°52′33″W. 1,490 ft. A second well, known locally as The Cherion [*sic*], was dug in early 1930s for John Cameron's cattle (Bill Hoy). Vicinity of 32°06′16″N, 112°55′32″W. 1,500 ft.

Chia Canyon (CP). A canyon on E side of Sierra Pinta, 2 mi ESE of Heart Tank. Plentiful with fragrant desert lavender shrubs (*Hyptis emoryi)* but named for its mint-family relative, desert chia (*Salvia columbariae).* Mouth at 32°15′40″N, 113°30′48″W. 1,120 ft.

Chico Shunie Arroyo (CP). Arroyo flowing westward from North Ajo and Ajo peaks to Daniels Arroyo. Mouth at 32°19′07″N, 113°00′41″W. 1,500 ft.

Chico Shunie Hills (CP). Hills 6 mi SW of Ajo. Site of San Antonio mica mine. 32°17′57″N, 112°56′47″W. 2,144 ft.

Chico Shunie Temporal (CP). A dry-farming site that relied on seasonal rainfall or flooding, 5 mi WSW of Chico Shunie Well. From Spanish for 'temporary', 'weather', 'storm', 'rainy spell'. 32°18′21″N, 113°00′39″W. 1,540 ft.

Chico Shunie Well (CP). Several hand-dug wells in eastern CP, 6 mi SW of Ajo. Water level was at 45 ft about 1995. Francisco "Chico" Shunie (Cico Suni), an Hia C'ed O'odham born at Quitobaquito, worked as a cowboy and was a pascola dancer (Bowden 1987). Spoken histories date the establishment of this village before 1909 (Bell et al. 1980), and several Hia C'ed O'odham families had lived here before creation of CP in 1939. Son Francisco "Chulpo" Shunie lived there until his death on or about May 31, 1999. Also spelled Chico Suni. =Ciko Su:ni, C:ko Șoñ, Garcia Well. 32°19′42″N, 112°56′03″W. 1,792 ft.

Childs (Pima Co.). Settlement and railroad siding 5.5 mi N of Ajo at site of Phelps Dodge well that serves Ajo and Phelps Dodge mine. See Tucson, Cornelia, & Gila Bend Railroad, which began service in 1916. See Childs Valley. 32°27′15″N, 112°50′31″W. 1,430 ft.

Childs Mountain (CP). Basalt mountain with pronounced benches, 5 mi NW of Ajo. Named for Tom Childs, Sr. or Jr., both long-time Ajo residents. Summit has communications and radar facilities (locally known as the Golf Ball). During Korean War the U.S. Air Force built family houses at E base of mountain and built dormitories, post exchange, offices, and recreation facilities (including a swimming pool) on a terrace midway to summit. Despite these amenities, the post was rumored to have an exceptionally high desertion rate. Removal of the base buildings was completed spring 1996 and new radar dome installed. The mountain's O'odham name, Kavaḍk Me:k, means 'burnt shield', alluding either to a historic incident in which Quechan warriors looking for Maricopa enemies were pacified and symbolically burned one of their war shields or to

Figure 39.14. Charlie Bell Well, 1986.

its flat, blackened profile (Fillman & Oscar Bell). =Radar Hill. 32°25′56″N, 112°56′43″W. 2,862 ft.

Childs Mountain Tank (CP). A 2,000-gallon fiberglass catchment for hauled water for wildlife. 0.6 mi NE of summit. 32°26′23″N, 112°56′18″W. 2,280 ft.

Childs Tank (GR). Tinaja in Crater Range reported by early explorers and surveyors. May =Crater Tank. Its precise location is unknown but may be in vicinity of 32°36′N, 113°01′W.

Childs Valley (GR). Valley along Tenmile Wash N of Ajo. Thomas Childs Sr. joined a gold rush to California in 1856 and remained in Arizona along the Gila River and around Ajo. He helped launch the copper mines at Ajo and later established cattle ranches (Hoy 1999). His son, Tom Childs Jr. (1870–1951), had ranches at Ten Mile Well (Childs Ranch), Hotshot Well, and Green Gate Well (Childs 1954; Van Valkenburgh 1945). 32°34′17″N, 113°03′35″W. 1,300 ft.

Chimney Peak (SD). Prominent, guiding landmark along Butterfield Trail in Maricopa Mountains, N of Happy Camp and about 5 mi NNW of Estrella siding. Descriptive name appearing on maps from latter nineteenth century through early twentieth century but not on recent USGS maps. =Chimneys. Location not established, but on one 1884 map it is within T4S, R2W. Not the same as Chimney Rock, about 15 mi N of Yuma along Colorado River (Bartlett 1965:159). And probably not the same as "Chimney," as shown on a 1932 map by John F. Compton, who refers to an undetermined watering stop in vicinity of Enid railroad siding, between Gila Bend and Maricopa Wells (Hackbarth 1995).

Chinaman Flat (CP). Small valley 2 mi N of Agua Dulce Mountains and 1 mi E of Sheep Mountain. Its soil was a tempting place to try farming and ranching. Several defunct wells are in area. Name reportedly from Chinese immigrants who wished to farm area; another version says they were smuggled into country and then murdered here. In mid-twentieth century Jim Havins ran cattle here from his line camp at Papago Well. 32°07′21″N, 113°11′41″W. 1,020 ft.

Chinero, El (AG). Isolated hill on western shore of Gulf of California along Mexico Highway 5, 56 km N of San Felipe, in Llano el Chinero. Distinctive landmark, perhaps used by smugglers of Chinese immigrants into U.S. in late nineteenth and early twentieth centuries (Fradkin 1995). Local legend says that during the gold rush of 1849 a shipload of Chinese were set ashore near here and told the goldfields were nearby, but the immigrants perished in the inhospitable, waterless desert (Anita Alvarez Williams). 31°30′N, 115°01′W. 224 m.

Also **Llano el Chinero** (AG, BC). Wide bajada surrounding El Chinero hill, between Sierra Las Pintas and Sierra San Felipe. From about 300 m to sea level.

Chiulikam (TON). Historic Tohono O'odham village. See Sauceda. =Chiuli, Chiuli Kam, Pozo Colorado, Salcilla, Sauceda, Sauceda Well, Saucida, Saucito, Suwuki Vaya, Tschiulikam, Vokivaxia. 32°34′24N, 112°31′13″W. 2,095 ft.

Cholla, Pozo la (Sonora). See Pozo la Cholla.

Cholla Bay (Sonora). See Bahía de la Cholla.

Cholla Pass (CP). Gap through low hills 2 mi N of Agua Dulce Mountains. Endowed with a dense stand of five cholla species, predominantly jumping cholla (*Cylindropuntia fulgida*) and teddybear cholla (*C. bigelovii*). 32°06′40″N, 113°10′52″W. 1,060 ft.

Christmas Pass (CP). Pass around NW end of Drift Hills. Prospector Dan Drift and his daughter built this primitive roadway along a rocky arroyo so they could more easily drive to Wellton for supplies; they finished it on a Christmas Day in 1930s. See Drift Hills. 32°16′38″N, 113°41′35″W. 1,001 ft.

Ciénega del Indio (AG). Wetlands formed by discharge of agricultural drainage water from the San Luis Valley, S of the fields into the mudflats. Located W of Ciénega de Santa Clara and E of Río Colorado, they include shallow wetlands grown over with salt cedar, cattails, and common reed, plus a large, permanent pond at the southern end. The entire area, including the pond, supports large numbers of resident and migratory water-

fowl, including the endangered Yuma clapper rail. Fish abound, including desert pupfish in backwater saline pools, and game fish such as bass in the canals. Local guides take hunters into the wetlands during duck season. The area is in the Alto Golfo Biosphere Reserve, and IMADES has conducted several restoration projects there. =Laguna del Indio. Pond at 115°02′09″W, 32°00′14″N.

Ciénega de Santa Clara (AG). Major freshwater wetland in eastern Río Colorado delta. Here freshwater from springs and the Río Colorado joins agricultural wastewater discharge from the Wellton-Mohawk Main Outlet Drain Extension, forming a crucial biological haven rich in wildlife and plant life. It is poetically known as the Green Lagoon (Leopold 1966). This important ecological area, about 4,400 ha in extent, is vulnerable to desiccating fluctuations and noxious quality of incoming water (Felger 2000; Glenn et al. 1992, 1996; Malusa 1993). See Hunters Camp (AG) and Campo, El (AG). Also spelled *ciénaga;* Spanish for 'hundred waters' or 'hundred springs'; also 'swamp'. 32°02′16″N, 114°53′42″W. Slightly above sea level.

Ciko Su:ni (CP). See Chico Shunie Well.

Cinder Mountain (GR). Isolated volcanic cinder cone 12 mi N of Crater Range. May =Rock Peak. 32°47′28″N, 113°01′01″W. 982 ft.

Cipriano Hills (OP). This basalt range and extinct volcano S of Bates Mountains was a major source of regional lava. Named for Cipriano Ortega, reformed bandit and later owner of Santo Domingo settlement along Río Sonoyta (Hoy 1990). 32°02′12″N, 112°58′39″W. 2,604 ft.

Cipriano Pass (GR). A pass that separates Tinajas Altas Mountains from Gila Mountains; 2 mi NW of Raven Butte. Reportedly named for Cipriano Ortega, who may have driven cattle through this gap. Used by smugglers. =Smuggler Pass; Cerro Prieto Pass. 32°25′35″N, 114°09′34″W. 1,000 ft.

Cipriano Pass (OP). A gap in the southern Cipriano Hills, 3 mi N of Quitobaquito. 31°59′18″N, 113°01′07″W. 1,320 ft.

Cipriano, Represo (Sonora). See Represo Cipriano.

Cipriano Tanks (GR). Two developed water tanks in a canyon of southern Gila Mountains, 1.3 mi N of Cipriano Pass. Several natural tinajas are in the area. =Cipriano Pass Tank; AGFD #881. 32°26′23″N, 114°09′16″W. 1,200 ft.

Cipriano Well (OP). A hand-dug well 4 mi N of Quitobaquito. Used by Cipriano Ortega in late 1800s for his cattle grazing in lower Growler and Mohawk valleys. Clotts (1915) reports a corral, watering trough, and five wikiups where "the Indians of Quitobaquito sometimes live." =El Pozo, Henrys Well (for Henry Gray). 32°00′06″N, 113°01′34″W. 1,270 ft.

Not to be confused with another Cipriano Well (=El Pozo de Cipriano) 16 km SW of Sonoyta; see Sierra Cipriano.

Cipriano Well (Sonora). Well along Mexico Highway 2, 16 km SW of Sonoyta. =El Pozo de Cipriano. Presumably named for Cipriano Ortega, who ran cattle in this region in the late nineteenth century. 31°47′21″N, 112°59′08″W. 420 m.

Citrus Valley Wash (GR, Maricopa Co.). Arroyo that passes 4.7 mi W of Gila Bend. Name proposed July 2, 2001, by Gila Bend town council. The wash runs just E of Citrus Valley Road and into Citrus Valley region along the Gila River. Crosses I-8 at 32°56′00″N, 112°47′36″W. 720 ft.

Clark Gold Mine (OP). Group of shafts and adits NW of Growler Pass. Perhaps named for Sam Clark (see Clarkston), who established a townsite E of Ajo for miners as alternative to living in the company-owned town. Quite a few notable locals took a try at mining, ranching, or just about any other activity that might have raised extra cash. 32°11′17″N, 112°56′00″W. 1,500 ft.

Clarkston (Pima Co.). See Ajo. In 1915 Sam Clark laid out a townsite just east of the Ajo townsite developed by the New Cornelia Copper Co. Clarkston may have had as many as 1,200 residents before 1920. Clark's application for a post office was rejected because other places already used the name, so residents pushed to name it after then-president Woodrow Wilson. That too was rejected, but the letters of his name were rearranged to form 'Rowood', and the post office was established in 1918. Later, portions of Clarkston/Rowood were abandoned to make room for mining activities or were subsumed within Ajo. Two major fires in 1931 doomed the remaining town (Rickard 1996; Reynolds 1996). =Clarkstown, Clark's Addition. Known among local O'odham as Kalaks, a phonic derivation from Clark's. Former site at 32°22′00″N, 112°50′21″W. 1,710 ft.

Cloverleaf Crater (PI). See Molina Crater. This descriptive name was the one initially used by Hornaday (1908: 188), who later changed it to Molina.

Coffeepot Mountain (Pima Co.). Distinctive landmark 16 mi NE of Ajo. Named for vague resemblance to old-fashioned coffeepot used on wood-burning stoves. By local tradition hikers carry coffee to the summit to drink while enjoying the view. 32°28′56″N, 112°37′17″W. 3,466 ft.

Coffeepot Well (Pima Co.). A now-dry well 1.5 mi W of Coffeepot Mountain. 32°28′57″N, 112°38′34″W. 2,140 ft.

Coledon (SD). Abandoned railroad siding 2 mi downslope from Bosque on SPRR. Named for a railroad engineer, its name was shortened to Cole around 1900 to fa-

cilitate telegraphing (Granger 1983). The site fell into disuse prior to 1920. 32°57′36″N, 112°38′00″W. 890 ft.

Colfred (Yuma Co.). Railroad siding along SPRR 3 mi E of Tacna. Name taken from title and first name of Colonel Fred Crocker, treasurer of Southern Pacific Railroad in 1881. 32°42′17″N, 113°54′03″W. 331 ft.

Colfred Airport (Yuma Co.). Abandoned airfield S of Colfred, it was once a military training and emergency landing strip. 32°41′25″N, 113°52′35″W. 345 ft.

Colinas Batamote. See Batamote.

Colonia. Mexican *colonias* are settlements where members live on the land but may work elsewhere; they differ from *ejidos,* whose members must work the "homestead." Also used to denote a community subdivision.

Colonia Díaz (Sonora). Agricultural settlement on former meander of Río Colorado, 48 km SW of boundary marker 205 at San Luis R.C., possibly S of Ledón and on E bank of old channel. It thrived in late nineteenth and early twentieth centuries. It was one of Edgar Mearns's (1907) collection localities in the delta region of the Río Colorado. Because of the Río Colorado's shifting channel and few permanent reference points, much work remains to pinpoint old settlements and sites. Likely named for Porfirio Díaz, president of Mexico 1877–1880 and 1884–1911. Possibly vicinity of 31°11′N, 115°10′W. 14 m.

Colonia Lerdo (AG). Late nineteenth- and early twentieth-century farming settlement on the Sonora side of Río Colorado delta. The main settlement was named Ciudád Lerdo, and the collective name of the group of tracts was Colonia Lerdo (Bowen 2000; Hendricks 1967, 1971; Serafín 1992).

"Aside from an occasional Cocopah ranchería there was little sign of life on the lower river until... Lerdo Landing eighty miles above the mouth. Here on a mesa just east of the river sat Colonia Lerdo, a pleasant little town with eucalyptus-lined streets and some seventy inhabitants. The colony was started in June 1873 by San Francisco capitalist Thomas H. Blythe and Mexican Gen. Guillermo Andrade, who dreamed of building an agricultural empire on the lower Colorado, harvesting the wild hemp [*Sesbania*] . . . that abounded in the bottomlands. The colonists also experimented with growing cotton and raised small patches of corn and vegetables for their own use" (Lingenfelter 1978: 60). This hemp is a giant annual legume (*Sesbania herbacea*) and should not be confused with other kinds of hemp plants. Blythe later launched another river settlement that bears his name in California. In April 1889 Edward Palmer spent three days collecting specimens from the vicinity of Lerdo (see Felger 2000; MacDougal 1904; McVaugh 1956; Vasey & Rose 1890).

Based on maps (Kelly 1977; Sykes 1937) and other information, Colonia Lerdo probably was 9 km S of modern-day Riíto, on SW corner of Mesa de Andrade. Ciudád Lerdo was destroyed by a flood in about 1876 (Hendricks 1967). Named for Mexico's president Sebastián Lerdo de Tejada (1872–76), who signed over the federal land titles to the Compañía de Colorado land corporation in 1874 (Hendricks 1967). A road from Yuma to Colonia Lerdo was completed in 1878. E of Luis Encinas Johnson. =Matakan. Vicinity of 32°04′30″N, 114°57′45″W. 15 m elevation.

Colorado Desert (California, BC, Arizona? Sonora?). A vaguely defined, confusing designation for a western portion of the Sonoran Desert. Originally described by William P. Blake as the Salton Sea region (Blake 1855; Cecil-Stephens 1891; MacDougal 1908b), it incorporated the desert lands west of the Colorado River, south of the Mojave Desert, and north of the Gulf of California. At that time the Sonoran Desert had not been defined (Shreve 1951). Conklin (1878:73) distinguishes between the Colorado River basin and the Colorado Desert, which "lies wholly in California." Although he titled his book *The Wonders of the Colorado Desert,* James (1906:xxviii) found the word 'Colorado' very misleading (since it has nothing to do with the state of Colorado) and "the use of the name is to be deplored, though Professor Blake is deserving of the thanks of the world of intelligent readers and students for giving this section of the great Sonoranian [*sic*] Desert a name which positively identifies it." Walter T. Swingle suggested using the name Salton Basin (James 1906). Its geology is discussed in Norris 1995, and James (1906) describes other facets.

In the last half-century the term Colorado Desert has become confused with the Lower Colorado River Valley vegetation community of the Sonora Desert. Some authors limit "Colorado Desert" to the Sonoran Desert that extends into California (Dimmitt 2000); others apply the name to "a vast area stretching from the Coachella Valley around Palm Springs, California almost to Phoenix, Arizona, 250 miles eastward. From Needles, California, it extends southward into northern Sonora and Baja California, Mexico" (Stewart 1993:iv). Shreve (1951:124) noted that "the arm of the Sonoran Desert which extends into southeastern California . . . is often ambiguously called the 'Colorado Desert.'" Turner (1994) and Rosen (this volume) discuss the validity of separate categories for the Sonoran Desert, Colorado Desert, and Mojave Desert biomes.

Colorado River (AG). This major North American river empties into the Gulf of California, though in most recent years there has not been sufficient flow to sustain a river channel clear to the gulf. The Mexican portion of the river is called Río Colorado, and the portion N of the international border is labeled Colorado River. Named for the red sediment that once colored its waters and emptied into the Gulf of California, sometimes

poetically called the Vermillion Sea. Even the Seri Indians, who lived far S of the river's mouth, called it "the red river" (Felger & Moser 1985). =Hasoj Cheel (Mary Beck Moser).

The Río Colorado has been notoriously difficult to map because its channel changed with annual floods (see Derby 1969; Hardy 1829; Sykes 1937). Today it is heavily dammed and diverted for irrigation, industrial, and household uses. Once having a permanent flow navigable by steamboats, the Mexican portion of the river is now dry except during brief flood periods, e.g., 1983–84 and 1992. See Fletcher 1997 for a recent trip down the length of the river.

By one estimate the delta was at least three times more biologically productive before dam construction began on the river in 1905 (Kowalewski & Flessa 1995, 1996). An estimated 200 to 400 species of plants have been extirpated from the delta (Ezcurra et al. 1988). This flora was scarcely studied before the delta dried up and salinized. The cottonwood and willow forests are mostly gone from the Mexican side of the river, and very little remains N of the border. The remnant pockets of wetland vegetation in the delta region deserve vigorous protection, and some degree of restoration is possible (Glenn et al. 1996; see Glenn & Nagler, this volume).

Because of extreme tidal range (to 10 m; 32 ft), the river had a tremendous tidal bore (*el burro;* see Nelson, this volume). As a startled James Ohio Pattie described in 1827, "Our camp was inundated from the river. We, landsmen from the interior, and unaccustomed to such movements of water, stood contemplating with astonishment the rush of the tide coming in from the sea, in conflict with the current of the river. At the point of conflict rose a high ridge of water, over which came the sea current, combing down like water over a milldam" (Pattie 1930:241).

Steamboats carried passengers and cargo on the river from 1854 until the Southern Pacific Railroad reached Yuma in 1877. These boats burned wood, so riverside trees were felled and stacked at woodlots along the route. The steamers could travel about 50 km per day before stopping for the night and refueling. Woodlots were established at Port Famine (Sonora), about 100 mi below Yuma; the Gridiron (Sonora), 83 mi from Yuma; Ogden's Landing (Sonora), 55 mi from Yuma; Hualapai Smith's woodlot (Sonora), 45 mi from Yuma; and (John) Pedrick's lot (Arizona), 31 mi below Yuma (Sykes 1937; Lingenfelter 1978). See Ogden's Landing.

Before dams and diversion canals were constructed on the river for vast agricultural fields beginning in the early 1900s, the Colorado River flooded annually. Its 1903–1934 peak spring flows of 3,986,000 acre-feet for June averaged six times the average ebb of 482,900 acre feet in December (Kelly 1977; see Sykes 1937). Such flows maintained a significant riparian gallery forest along the river's braided and oxbowed course. These overstory trees included cottonwood, willow, and mesquite (Brown 1994; Sykes 1937). The wood from these trees fueled steamboats (Lingenfelter 1978), but most were cleared for domestic fuel, construction, and farmland, and the remainder died while the river died. A hint of this forest can be seen in Imperial National Wildlife Refuge, N of Yuma. Now invasive tamarix is the dominant streamside shrub.

The river corridor was also rich in wildlife. Leopold reported deer and jaguars in the river's delta; later he lamented, "I am told the green lagoons now raise cantaloupes. . . . Man always kills the things he loves, and so we the pioneers have killed our wilderness. Some say we had to. Be that as it may, I am glad I shall never be young without wild country to be young in. Of what avail are forty freedoms without a blank spot on the map?" (Leopold 1966:157–158).

=Colorado River; Río de Tizón, by Melchior Díaz in sixteenth century, after seeing Cucapás carry firebrands or torches; *tizón* is Spanish for 'torch'. The "red river" name may derive from either Yuman or O'Odham terms with the same meaning, e.g., Vegi Akimel, O'odham for 'reddish running water' (Fillman Bell). See Lingenfelter 1978, Sykes 1937, and Yates & Marshall 1974. See also Williams, this volume. The river's ultimate source is glacier-fed at Knapsack Col, a mountain pass in the Wind River Range of west-central Wyoming (43°09′16″N, 108°39′39″W, 12,240 ft). From there the river traverses 1,741 mi to its mouth on the Gulf of California at 31°48′30″N, 114°49′00″W.

Combat Village (GR). Simulated town with railroad yard and tank positions built in 1980s as training aid for military aviators. On E side of Copper Mountains, NE of Betty Lee Mine. 32°30′52″N, 113°57′42″W. 980 ft.

Cones, The (OP). Informal, descriptive name for cluster of conical rocks along trail between Bull Pasture and Ajo Peak. They are a favorite subject for photographers. 32°00′54″N, 112°41′11″W. 3,565 ft.

Conley Tank (SD). Stock tank 3.5 mi E of Butterfield Pass and 0.5 mi N of old Butterfield Stage route. In 1901 Samuel R. Conley homesteaded 160 acres along the Gila River SW of Liberty, Arizona (section 10 of T1S, R3W), and in 1923 Richard H. Conley earned title to 40 acres in the same section. The Conley family came from Oregon, ran cattle in the Vekol Valley, and lived in Liberty (Winnie Conley Henry). 33°03′59″N, 112°24′45″W. 1,455 ft.

Conley Well (Maricopa Co.). Well in N Vekol Valley 4 mi E of Maricopa Mountains. 32°53′58″N, 112°15′35″W. 1,631 ft.

Consag Rocks (AG). See Rocas Consag.

Copper Canyon (Pima Co.). Arroyo through Little Ajo Mountains, 4 mi W of Ajo. Named for minor outcrops of copper. Mouth at 32°22′14″N, 112°57′02″W. 1,685 ft.

Copper Mine Mountain (OP). Small hill pierced by prospect tunnel in NE part of OP. =Copper Hill, Copper Mountain, Copper Mountain Mine. 32°05′46″N, 112°45′01″W. 2,200 ft.

Copper Mountains (GR). A granitic range 10 mi SSW of Tacna in western GR. It teased prospectors with copper "color" but never fulfilled their dreams. Labeled Antelope Hills on several older maps. Unnamed summit (0.8 mi SE of Coyote Peak) is at 32°29′52″N, 113°59′46″W. 2,888 ft.

Cornelia Arroyo (Pima Co.). A dry wash rambling through Ajo. New Cornelia was the name of Col. John C. Greenway's copper company; he chose the name when in 1911 he bought out the Cornelia Copper Company, owned by A. J. Shotwell and John R. Boddie. Cornelia was the name of Boddie's first wife (Reynolds 1996). 1,560 ft.

Corner Well (CP). Defunct well at extreme SE corner of CP at OP boundary, 4 mi WNW of Quitobaquito. Drilled in 1955 by Jim Havins and also known as Needmore Well, since his ranch always needed more rain, water, feed, and money. 31°57′43″N, 113°05′04″W. 1,000 ft.

Cornez, Rio (Pima Co.). Arroyo draining N Valley of the Ajo. This place-name has enjoyed a high degree of mobility over the years; in the 1920s the name was applied to both Tenmile Wash and lower Sikort Chuapo Wash. By the 1960s it had disappeared entirely from maps of the area, only to reappear in the 1990s in a completely different location, this time originating in the Pozo Redondo Mountains 3 mi E of Why and emptying into Darby Arroyo 3.2 mi N of Arizona Highway 85. =Sikol Ce:po, Sikort Chuapo Wash, Tenmile Wash, Childs Wash, Rio Cornez Wash, Rio Tenmile Wash. Joins Darby Arroyo at 32°22′40″N, 112°47′25″W. 1,580 ft.

Corrigan (Pima Co.). Former O'odham village 2 mi SW of Ajo. It was a small village at an abandoned mine with a well, and in 1915 it had three houses and twelve residents (Clotts 1915). Its exact location is unknown. It may have been swallowed by the New Cornelia Mine or its associated tailings. Bryan (1925:334) referred to it as Corrigan Well, though this name may also have been applied to a different site (see Cardigan Well). Possibly =Vav O'la Do'ag or Vav Olas Do'ag ('rounded rocks'; =Locomotive Peak). See Thomas (1991), who reported a settlement with fields in this vicinity.

Cotton Center (Maricopa Co.). Small farming crossroads on Arizona Highway 80 eleven mi N of Gila Bend and 2 mi W of SD. Cotton is the primary agricultural product of the Gila River Valley, and its irrigation is the principal consumer of ground and surface water. The area's first modern cotton crop was harvested in 1923. 33°05'13"N, 112°39'59"W. 712 ft.

Cougar Canyon (GR). Canyon in Sauceda Mountains draining N to Sauceda Wash from N slopes of Tom Thumb. When predator bounties were in effect, a number of cougars (*Felis concolor*, =*Puma c.*) were trapped here in the 1950s by Lynn Cool and friends in the belief that the populations of cattle, deer, and javelina would increase (Duane Holt). Mountain lions still inhabit this region. Mouth at 32°35'02"N, 112°34'53"W. 1,960 ft.

County Line Hill (CP). Hill at junction of Yuma and Pima county lines at international boundary marker 178. 32°02'20"N, 113°19'59"W. 911 ft.

Coyote Peak (GR). A high peak in Copper Mountains. 32°30'44"N, 114°00'20"W. 2,808 ft.

Coyote Peak Tanks (GR). Three intermittent tinajas 0.8 mi NW of Coyote Peak. Two were enlarged with dams in 1984 as waterholes for wildlife. =Coyote Peak Potholes; AGFD #893. 32°31'07"N, 114°00'37"W. 1,620 ft.

Coyote Tinaja (GR). Intermittent tinaja 13 mi N of Ajo, in E Crater Range. Coyotes paw holes in sand-filled tinajas in order to reach water. 32°33'03"N, 112°52'03"W. 1,240 ft.

Coyote Wash (GR). Major arroyo draining Lechuguilla Desert northward to Gila River, though it seldom flows that far. Terminal end greatly modified by channelization and agricultural diversions south of Gila River. Wilson (1933:17) notes that Coyote Wash was prone to dramatic flooding following major rain events: "A recent example of the surprisingly torrential character of such occasional storms occurred during February, 1931, when serious floods from the south, in Coyote Wash, swept away part of the town of Wellton, together with several neighboring stretches of railroad and highway, and drowned one person." The channelization noted above presumably has remedied the flooding problem. In 2005 Coyote Wash condominiums, golf course, and RV park are being built N of GR boundary. Meets Gila River at 32°41'32"N, 114°11'12"W. 200 ft.

Coyote Water (GR). A waterhole on Coyote Wash 4 mi NE from Tinajas Altas. Bryan (1925:422) writes that Coyote Water "lies in the axial stream of the valley, which is a channel filled with coarse sand about 100 feet wide and with soft banks about 3 feet high. The sand lies in great waves, which indicates the way in which the sand moves downstream during floods. The water remains in a cavity or scour depression in the hardpan that underlies the sand of the channel and is obtained by digging about 4 ft. A wooden signboard and the marks of coyote or human digging will guide the traveler in finding the exact spot. The water is small in amount and not very permanent and has a bad taste. The taste

seems to be due to decaying plant roots." =Pozo de en Medio (used by Kino and Garcés [Bryan 1925; Ives 1965]), =Zacate Duro (Bryan 1925). 32°19'59"N, 113°59'23"W. 960 ft.

Cráter Elegante (PI). See Elegante Crater.

Cráter Elena (PI). A small tuff cone SW of Celaya Crater. Named by geologist Dan Lynch (1981:iii), perhaps for his wife, Elaine, whom, with several other friends, he "shamelessly pressed ... into service as sherpas to lug rocks down the mountain" during his field research in Sierra Pinacate. 31°57'39"N, 113°28'23'W. 400 m.

Cráter Grande (PI). See Sykes Crater.

Cráter de la Luna (PI). See Moon Crater.

Crater Range (GR). Mountain range N of Childs Valley and 12 mi NNW of Ajo. Its roughly eroded lavas include a basin that resembles a lunar crater. U.S. Air Force trains pilots to drop bombs and shoot air-to-ground cannons N, S, and SW of Crater Range. =Crater Mountains, The Crater; Ge Huḍa Do'ag, O'odham for 'big middle mountains' (a name also applied to Kofa Mountains, 85 mi NW of here) (Bell et al. 1980). 32°36'47"N, 113°01'38"W. 1,838 ft.

Cráter Trébol (PI). See Molina Crater.

Cráter Verdugo (PI). See MacDougal Crater.

Cruz de memoria (regional). Memorial wayside crosses commemorating the site of a fatality, usually from an auto accident. These are private place-markers in personal histories, e.g., auto wrecks, plane crashes, exposure (see Griffith 1992). Many of these crosses are annually redecorated with flowers and memorabilia on Día de los Muertos (All Soul's Day), November 2. In 1896 Capt. David D. Gaillard, surveyor of the international boundary, counted 115 stone crosses and rude wooden markers for travelers who succumbed along El Camino del Diablo; he estimated a total of at least 400 (Gaillard 1896). Well-known graves along El Camino del Diablo include the Grave of Eight (=Circle of 8) and Nameer's 1871 cross (possibly N. A. Meer, though we have yet to find his or her name in historic documents).

Travelers occasionally note memorials in the form of wooden crosses, heaped grave rocks, melted candles, plastic flowers, and petroglyphic inscriptions. For example, a mile W of Aztec overpass on I-8 is a white metal cross in remembrance of Louis Cochran, Arizona's first highway patrol officer to die in the line of duty; a drunk driver from California rear-ended Cochran's patrol car on old U.S. Highway 80 in 1958. The authors have helped lay to rest the ashes of several friends in this grand desert and, like untold others, attach private names (e.g., "Dave's Dunes" and "Ed's Lookout") and deep sentiment to otherwise insignificant and unnamed places. The ashes of archaeologist Malcolm J. Rogers, geographer

Ronald L. Ives, and archaeologist Julian D. Hayden are scattered atop the same nameless hill in the Pinacate. And the grave of Spanish soldier Melchior Díaz likely is somewhere SE of Sonoyta (Ives 1989).

We're reminded of Lumholtz (1912:307), who amid profuse wildflowers near Tinajas Altas reflected on his life, writing: "Could I select the place where I should like best to die, my choice would be one such as this. I hope at least it may not fall my lot to pass away in New York, where I might be embalmed before I was dead and where it costs so much to die that I might not leave enough to defray the expenses of a funeral." And we think of Olga Smith (1956:247–248), who realized, "It wouldn't be bad to die out here…[where] death did not seem the frightening transition it did in the city.… You could simply go to sleep under that ironwood tree over there, and with the shining stillness around you, go on through all eternity feeling the sun and the wind and the warmth of life about you."

Modern travel remains risky, especially for the unwary and unprepared. See Annerino 1999 for a map of recorded fatalities of walkers, especially those trying to avoid official ports of entry into the United States. Also see Spilken's (1983) fictionalized account of death in the desert.

Locations of public, tribal, private, family, and single gravesites are omitted in this gazetteer. Rest in peace (R.I.P.). Descanse en paz (D.E.P.).

Cuerda de Leña (Pima Co.). Large arroyo 8 mi SE of Ajo, renowned for its stands of mesquite and ironwood. Drains southern Valley of the Ajo. Spanish for 'cord of firewood'. Joins with Cherioni Wash 2 mi E of Bates Well to form Growler Wash at 32°09′32″N, 112°55′15″W. 1,390 ft.

Cuevitas, Las (GR). See Butler Mountains.

Cuk Do'ag (Yuma Co.). See Texas Hill.

D

Daniels Arroyo (CP). Valley and large arroyo draining land E of Growler Mountains. Named for Ruben "Rube" Daniels, who settled in area about 1905. Flows N. =Adobe Wash. Joins Growler Wash at 32°30′05″N, 113°16′26″W. 670 ft.

Daniels Well (OP). Well dug by Ruben Daniels around 1915 along Growler Wash at Bates Well. =Daniells Well, Denialls Spring Well. 32°09′57″N, 112°57′06″W. 1,340 ft.

Another **Daniels Well** (OP) was about 6 mi SE of Bates Well, along old Ajo-Sonoyta road. In 1918 it was 75 ft deep with 67 ft of water. May =Cherioni Well. Vicinity of 32°06′16″N, 112°55′32″W. 1,500 ft.

Darby Arroyo (Pima Co.). Drains land S of Ajo into Sikort Chuapo Wash, with their confluence at 32°23′36″N, 112°47′51″W. 1,560 ft.

Darby Wells (Pima Co.). Two older wells and former Hia C'ed O'odham settlement 2 mi S of Ajo. Established by Ortega and Garcia families of Hia C'ed O'odham descent but named for an early 1900s settler named Darby, perhaps William E. Darby. The Hia C'ed O'odham had as many as eight homes, fields, and a church here. =Vo'o Ṣoñ ('pond at the mountain base'); Do'ag We:co ('village under the mountain', a descriptive name used for several places in this region, e.g., Kaka). 32°20′15″N, 112°51′00″W. 1,800 ft.

Dart Tank (GR). A man-made game tank in southeastern Gila Mountains, 6 mi SE of Sheep Mountain. Built in 1995 and named for a nearby silver tow dart used by the military for air-to-air gunnery practice. 32°28′18″N, 114°10′37″W. 1,015 ft.

Dateland (Yuma Co.). Travelers' stop and settlement along SPRR and U.S. Highway 80 (now I-8). Excellent well water prompted Mrs. William Harrison to plant a grove of date palms *(Phoenix dactylifera)* here about 1930. She was a noted patron of natural history studies in southern California. The O'odham call dates *cukuḍ ṣoṣa,* likening them to the regurgitated pellets of the great horned owl (Rea 1997). 32°47′58″N, 113°32′23″W. 434 ft.

Dateland Airfield (Yuma Co.). Former military training site built during World War II, now a civilian field. =Dateland Air Force Auxiliary Field. 32°48′31″N, 113°31′38″W. 449 ft.

Davidson Canyon (CP). Canyon in Davidson Hills of western Agua Dulce Mountains. Named for Bill Davidson, head watchman for Phelps Dodge Mining Company, who surveyed a route after 1920 through this canyon for a proposed rail line to the Gulf of California for the company. The line from Ajo to Bahía San Jorge was never built (Hendricks 1971). A rough, old auto road to Mexico passed through here. A small population of senita cactus (*Pachycereus schottii*) occurs here, only a few of which occur naturally in the U.S. outside OP. =Davis Canyon, a misnomer. Mouth at 32°02′14″N, 113°15′31″W. 900 ft.

Davidson Hills (CP). Low hills 0.5 mi S of Papago Well, among Agua Dulce Mountains. Named for Bill Davidson, head watchman for Phelps Dodge Mining Co. 32°05′11″N, 113°16′55″W. 1,256 ft.

Davis Lagoon (GR). See Albino.

Davis Plain (GR). Sandy plain between Butler and Tinajas Altas mountains. It slopes gently to SW. Region is so arid that ephemeral streams carry scant sediment, so plain is aggrading instead of eroding. Named for geologist W. M. Davis (see Davis 1930) by Wilson (1931:228). Ironwood and mesquite are widespread along the washes and runnels, although many of these trees died during the severe drought of 2003–2004. Informally known as Woodcutter Flats after unsanctioned wood gathering along border (see Nabhan & Carr 1994). 32°26′15″N, 114°13′27″W. 900 ft.

Deadman Gap (GR). Pass through eastern Crater Range. Around 1913 a prospector died here of thirst and was buried nearby. Railroad and old Gila Bend–Ajo highway goes through this gap. 32°31′37″N, 112°50′54″W. 1,262 ft. Bryan (1925) places Deadman Gap 11 mi N of this location.

Deer Hollow (CP). Saguaro and mesquite forest along arroyo 1 mi S of Sheep Mountain. Refuge staff named it for mule deer, which are common here. 32°05′44″N, 113°12′49″W. 1,080 ft.

Delossa (Maricopa Co.). Abandoned railroad siding on SPRR about 3 mi W of Sentinel. Named for the De la Ossa family, well-known ranching family around the headwaters of the Santa Cruz River, in Santa Cruz County, Arizona (Granger 1960). Barnes (1935:126) calls it Delesa, "origin unknown." Precise location unknown. About 600 ft.

Desert Station (SD). =Happy Camp. Way station on the Butterfield Overland Stage route, W of Butterfield Pass in central Maricopa Mountains. Established in 1858, the station was about 11 mi E of the station at Gila Ranch. This and Desert Well Station were the two stops on the previously waterless trail and wagon road crossing the Forty Mile Desert between Maricopa Wells and Gila Bend (John Laird; Hackbarth 1995). In 1877 H. M.

Thompson and R. W. Masters hauled water in barrels by wagon from the Gila River to fill a cistern. By 1879 W. F. Thompson had a well and store there (Granger 1983).

Conklin (1878:208, 211) reports, "At this station water was brought 15 miles across as desolate a waste as one could imagine. A charge of 25¢ a head was made for watering horses. It was originally one dollar but for some reason reduced recently.... Contrary to the name [Happy Camp] ..., this spot is a dreary one." On the trip he also describes making a bed from manger straw gathered in the corral; eating custard, biscuits, beefsteaks, frijoles, boiled chicken on toast, ham, and potatoes, and drinking coffee black because there was no milk or sugar; sitting at a table made of planks laid between sawhorses; and paying special attention to secure the horses and mules in a brush corral so the passengers would not be left afoot. Yet he loved the adventure. "'Happy Camp,' like many of the 'Hotels of the Desert,' is nothing more than a camping spot, and combines all the vicissitudes as well as the ecstatic diversities of life on a frontier" (Conklin 1878:212). He used quotation marks around the name, implying an unofficial moniker. 33°01′50″N, 112°29′59″W. 1,440 ft.

Desert Well Station (SD). Water stop on Butterfield Stage route, 5 mi W of Mobile on E bank of the West Prong of Waterman Wash. Near North Tank. 33°04′01″N, 112°21′28″W. 1,340 ft. Several other places in Arizona and the Southwest also bear this name or variations (e.g., Desert Wells).

Desierto del Altar. See Gran Desierto, El.

Devil Hills (CP). Small group of stark hills 3 mi W from N end of Sierra Pinta. These names appear on late-1800s maps and apparently precede naming of the much larger Cabeza Prieta Mountains, leading to conjecture that their former name was Devil Hills and that the name El Camino del Diablo derived from Devil Hills. =Diablo Hills. 32°23′43″N, 114°43′35″W. 1,100 ft.

Diablo Canyon (OP). Canyon slicing through Diablo Mountains and draining northward. It has a rich plant life. =Canyon Diablo. Mouth at 32°00′50″N, 112°43′42″W. 2,240 ft.

Diablo Mountains (OP). Small but spectacular and rugged range immediately W of Ajo Mountains. Formed by a massive block of rhyolite faulted off the main Ajo Range. Spanish for 'devil'. Name seems to include not only the mountain associated with Diablo Canyon but also the long mountain of Tillotson Peak, running NNW from Diablo Canyon to Arizona Highway 85 (Tim Tibbitts). It could be argued without embarrassment that the Tillotson segment merits its own name or that both are really just part of the Ajo Mountains. If Tillotson Peak is included with Diablo Mountains, then it is the summit, at 32°01′33″N, 112°45′04″W. 3,374 ft. The summit of the Diablo Canyon block, unnamed, is at 32°00′15″N, 112°42′58″W. 3,372 ft.

Diablo Tinaja (OP). Natural pool in upper reach of Diablo Canyon; intermittent and very sheltered. 32°00′43″N, 112°43′21″W. 2,450 ft.

Diaz Crater (CP). A very shallow crater, probably a tuff ring, just N of El Camino del Diablo in Pinacate lava field. Named by William K. Hartmann and Dale Cruickshank for explorer Melchior Díaz, whose expedition passed near Sierra Pinacate in 1540 (Hartmann 1989; Wood 1972). 32°06′33″N, 113°28′42″W. 760 ft.

Diaz Pass (OP, TON). Pass and trail across Ajo Range, used by smugglers, 0.8 mi S of Diaz Peak. Named by Jon Young in 2000 for its proximity to Diaz Peak and Diaz Spire. After 2002 also called Mota Pass (Spanish for marijuana). 31°57′03″N, 112°39′28″W. 2,630 ft.

Diaz Peak (OP). High point of southern Ajo Mountains. Neighbor of Diaz Spire; both are extinct volcanoes and sources for much of the volcanic rock in the Ajo Range. Named for Capt. Melchior Díaz of 1540 Coronado expedition. Named by William Supernaugh: "I named it after Díaz . . . , the mapper who . . . was the first white man to penetrate this part of the country" (Supernaugh 1975:11). 31°58′05″N, 112°39′38″W. 4,024 ft.

Diaz Peak Tinaja (OP). Intermittent tinaja on NW slope of Diaz Spire. 31°58′17″N, 112°40′40″W. 2,400 ft.

Díaz, Playa (PI). See Playa Díaz.

Diaz Spire (OP). Pinnacle 0.5 mi W of Diaz Peak. 31°58′14″N, 112°40′14″W. 3,892 ft.

Diputados, Los (PI). Treacherous, soft sand on the early motor route between Sonoyta and San Luis R.C., 81 km W of Sonoyta. Named for several legislators ('delegates') stranded here in 1945 when their car got stuck in the sand (Barrios-Matrecito 1988); accounts vary on whether they survived or died. SW of Cerro La Silla, in vicinity of El Solito. 240 m.

Do'ag We:co (TON). See Kaka, Darby Wells.

Doctor, Estación el (AG). See Estación el Doctor.

Dome (Yuma Co.). Abandoned settlement at N end of Gila Mountains, 25 mi E of Yuma. It was founded in 1858 as Gila City with the discovery of placer gold, but the strike played out by 1872. Browne (1950:77) reports that by 1864 Gila City was reduced to "three chimneys and a coyote."

It was a Butterfield Stage stop and later a railroad siding. The name Dome was given to the station and siding because it was the shipping point for the Castle Dome and other mines 20 mi NE. Several Hia C'ed O'odham families settled here after coming to work the mines of the Gila River placers and the lodes in the Castle Dome Mountains (Bell et al. 1980) and remained for more than a century. Two former settlements have

been destroyed by mining and farming. Near the early historic villages of San Pedro and San Pablo visited by Kino; both O'odham and Yuman were spoken here. =Hi:lo (O'odham from Spanish *hilo,* 'thread'); Dome Sand Papago Village; Gila City. See Gila River. 32°45′17″N, 114°21′39″W. 191 ft.

Dominy Potholes (GR). Two intermittent potholes enhanced in 1982 for wildlife in a west-draining canyon of Mohawk Mountains. 1.5 mi SE of Mohawk summit BM 2775. Named for hunter Wade Dominy of Yuma. =AGFD #862. 32°34′19″N, 113°37′54″W. 1,060 ft.

Don Diego Tanks (GR). Four perennial to intermittent tinajas in narrow canyon of southern half of Aguila Mountains. 1.6 mi S of BM Eagle 1800. Used by prehistoric residents and historic travelers going between Yuma and Ajo. Named for Louis Jaeger, nineteenth-century Yuma businessman and wagonmaster who drove this route; he was affectionately known as Don Diego. =S-hia Tamke, Hia C'ed O'odham for 'urine laying' or 'fool's tank'; Tinaja del Don Diego, Don Diego Tank, AGFD #803. 32°37′15″N, 113°20′19″W. 940 ft.

Don Tank (SD). Stock tank on bajada of NE Maricopa Mountains. 33°08′26″N, 112°25′31″W. 1,280 ft.

Dos Apóstoles (PI). Twin volcanic buttes on southern fringe of Pinacate lava flow, about 13 km S of Pinacate Peak, where the dunes meet the lava. Named by Julian Hayden and Ann Woodin. =Two Apostles. Possibly at 31°39′N, 113°28′W. 255 m.

Dos Lomitas (OP). Two small hills just N of international boundary, 4.5 mi ESE of Lukeville. Spanish for 'two hills'. See Blankenship Well. 31°51′56″N, 112°45′17″W. 1,542 ft.

Dos Lomitas Stock Tank (OP). Formerly large stock tank NE of Dos Lomitas. Now breached and silted in, it may have held water to a depth of 6 ft and covered several acres (Brown et al. 1983). 31°52′16″N, 112°45′38″W. 1,420 ft.

Dos Playas (CP). Internally drained, twin playas in southern Mohawk Valley, 7 mi NW of Papago Well. Reportedly 250–300 acres each but seldom holding standing water in recent years. Barren when dry. 32°11′36″N, 113°20′20″W. 810 ft.

Double Butte (GR). See Squaw Tits.

Double Peak (TON). Distinctive pair of peaks in Vaiva Hills, 7.6 mi E of Table Top Mountains and 1 mi outside far SE border of SD. 32°45′07″N, 111°59′38″W. 2,268 ft.

Dowling (OP). A ranchstead and well along the international border 1 mi W of Lukeville; the well was dug by Pat Dowling about 1900. At one time the official international border crossing was here. Earliest name for this place was Edward Dunbar's Store, which was established

Figure 39.16. Dos Playas.

by 1857 and presumably also had a well (Bill Hoy). =Dowling Ranch. 31°53′15″N, 112°50′08″W. 1,400 ft.

Dowling Wash (OP, Sonora). Large wash running adjacent to Dowling Ranch site. Heads in U.S. at 31°54′51″N, 112°49′48″W (1,530 ft.) and drains into Sonoyta River about 1 mi E of where Mexico Highway 8 crosses the river.

Drag Road (GR). Trails maintained by the U.S. Border Patrol for tracking persons and vehicles illegally crossing the international border. Among the names used are Culver Drag (for Clair Culver, retired Border Patrol pilot); Granite Drag (along the W side of Granite Mountains); Hobbs Drag (after agent Kenneth Hobbs from Sonora, Texas, who built it, winter of 1967–1968); Lower Drag (lowest or southernmost, =Camino del Diablo); Military Road (passes near a military radar site at Baker Peaks); Mohawk Drag (which abuts Mohawk Mountains); Taint Road ("It ain't the East Mohawk Drag and 'taint the Culver Drag" [Bob McLemore]); Tractor Road (because it was initially cleared by a tractor pulling a grader blade); Unknown Road (an unknown person graded a road to his homesite S of Wellton); and Vidrios Drag (graded in early 1970s and named for illegal traffic coming from Los Vidrios). Border Patrol has nicknames for some local landmarks, such as Busters Pole (an intersection where agent Walter "Buster" Hummel drove over a three-foot-tall well casing while chasing a smuggler, and his patrol vehicle became hopelessly hooked to the pipe; however, on foot he still managed to apprehend the smuggler, the smuggler's truck, and 20 undocumented aliens); the Golf Ball (the water tank at the American Motors facility S of Wellton); and the Burned Bus (a school bus on an old target range W of Aguila Mountains on GR).

Dragons Tooth (GR). Distinctive pinnacles in Sand Tank Mountains 3 mi SW of Squaw Tit. More accurately, should be Dragon's Teeth and was originally so called (Duane Holt). 32°38′30″N, 112°25′13″W. 3,483 ft.

Dragons Tooth Tank (GR). Wildlife water catchment constructed in 1987, 0.5 mi W of tallest Dragons Tooth. =Dragons Tooth Catchment; AGFD #961. 32°38′36″N, 112°25′42″W. 2,810 ft.

Drift Hills (CP). Small range 5 mi NE of Tule Well. World War I U.S. Army veteran Dan Drift prospected these hills in 1930s and 1940s. He had a camp on their SW side and lived part of the time in Wellton, where he served as a scoutmaster. Drift's mines in the area were named the Dart & Kart, Banjo, and Tillie Pat. See Christmas Pass. 32°15′25″N, 113°40′19″W. 1,427 ft.

Drift Well (CP). A hand-dug, shallow well at Drift's camp; it is now caved in. 32°15′31″N, 113°41′04″W. 1,030.

Dripping Springs (GR). Seeps and tinajas, two of them permanent and two intermittent in eastern Gila Mountains, 11 mi SW of Wellton. Used prehistorically. A dam, built in 1955 on largest tinaja, pipes water to storage tanks and a trough for wildlife. Bolton (1936) debatably places Kino's La Tinaja here; if so, may =Aguaje de los Alquives, Algibes. =AGFD #235. 32°34′39″N, 114°16′39″W. 800 ft.

Dripping Springs (OP). Perennial natural spring and tinaja on N side of Puerto Blanco Mountains. Array of plants includes the legume shrub *Coursetia glandulosa* and the yellow monkey-flower *Mimulus guttatus* in the snapdragon family. Flows up to 2 gallons per minute from a fracture seep into a secluded pool. Used prehistorically and by historic travelers between Ajo and Sonoyta. One of the northernmost localities for *Rothschildia cinta,* the silkmoth whose cocoons are used for pascola rattles by Hia C'ed O'odham and Yaquis. 32°01′26″N, 112°53′29″W. 2,060 ft.

Dripping Springs Mine (OP). Abandoned mining operation 0.5 mi SW of Dripping Springs. 32°01′08″N, 112°53′52″W. 1,820 ft.

Dunn's Well (Pima Co.). Defunct well 3 mi NW of Ajo. Dunn was the rancher who drilled it, apparently between 1910 and 1950. 32°23′48″N, 112°54′29″W. 1,660 ft.

E

Eagle Canyon (CP). Steep canyon on E slope of Sierra Pinta, 2.5 mi SE of Heart Tank. Named for golden eagles *(Aquila chrysaetos)* seen there. Mouth at 32°15′37″N, 113°30′25″W. 1,090 ft.

Eagle Eye Pass (OP). Rise in the road where Arizona Highway 85 crosses the Diablo Mountains about milepost 66. Name suggested by first OP superintendent, Bill Supernaugh, because pass offered an eagle's-eye view of the monument (Sue Rutman). =Eagle Pass. 32°05′03″N, W112°46′40″W. 1,990 ft.

Eagle Tank (CP). This small tinaja in Eagle Canyon on E side of Sierra Pinta was tunneled in 1957 to make a larger, perennial water tank for wildlife. Site had been used prehistorically by humans. 32°15′02″N, 113°30′54″W. 1,450 ft.

Eagle Tanks (GR). Series of perennial to intermittent tinajas in narrow canyon of southern Aguila (=Eagle) Mountains, 1.9 mi SSE of BM Eagle 1800. Used prehistorically. In modern times served as stop on Jaeger Wagon Road between Mohawk and Ajo. A watering hole popular with prospectors, and at least one moonshine operation reportedly flourished here during Prohibition. Small dam built on lowest tank by AGFD. =Jaeger Tanks, Yeager Tanks; Eagle Tank; Aguila Mountains Pothole; AGFD #634; Vepegĭ Ce:po, historically transcribed Wupu'k Jiapaw, O'odham for 'red tinaja' or 'red cave'. 32°37′17″N, 113°19′37″W. 900 ft.

East Arroyo Tinaja (OP). Tinaja in Bull Pasture, Ajo Mountains. 32°00′53″N, 112°41′40″W. 3,050 ft.

East Pass (GR). Seemingly misnamed pass through *western* third of Crater Range. David Griffin speculates that it is the eastern of two passes that loop through the western Crater Range, the other being **West Pass** (4.5 mi W of East Pass). Labeled Cornez Pass on 1934 USGS Sentinel map, presumably for nearby Tenmile Wash, which in those days was known as Rio Cornez. 32°37′09″N, 113°04′42″W. 1,025 ft.

Easy Pass (CP). Name given by Tom Harlan to gap in southern O'Neill Hills through which the old route of the Camino del Diablo once passed on the way to Las Playas. From Easy Pass a straight line of vegetation growing in the former ruts of the old road can be seen and followed W toward the western end of Las Playas, where the old route meets the modern Camino at 32°05′34″N, 113°26′56″W (680 ft).

Instead of coming W from Ajo, Bates Well, and Papago Well as the modern Camino does, the old Camino came WNW from Agua Dulce on the Sonoyta River. It crossed the international border between monuments 177 and 178 in the vicinity of BM 812 (32°01′28″N, 113°17′12″W) and made a beeline for Easy Pass and Las Playas. Harlan gave the pass its name because it was the easiest and most direct route through the O'Neill Hills in the direction of Las Playas. This was the route followed by McGee (1901) and others. The modern route from Ajo was probably not established until the late 1800s with the establishment of Bates and Papago Wells (see Jaeger Wagon Road). It is likely that the older route fell into disuse in the early 1900s, though portions of it are mapped on the 1965 USGS O'Neill Hills 15′ map. Easy Pass is at 32°04′02″N, 113°22′18″W. 720 ft.

Eberling Tank (Pima Co.). Large represo on Cuerda de Leña 4.5 mi SSW of Ajo. Developed by the Eberling family for livestock about 1940, possibly at site of a natural charco. 32°15′17″N, 112°49′11″W. 1,620 ft.

Also **Little Eberling Tank** (Pima Co.), a smaller stock tank 1.2 mi to NE. 32°16′09″N, 112°48′38″W. 1,640 ft.

Figure 39.17. Dripping Springs, GR.

Figure 39.18. Eagle Tank, CP.

Figure 39.19. *Elegante Crater.*

Ejido. Comparable to a communal homestead, where residents could own 2.5 ha as long as they worked it.

Ejido Aquiles Serdán (Sonora). Agricultural settlement along Mexico Highway 2, about 55 km ESE of San Luis R.C. Situated along a major archaic geologic fault known as Mojave-Sonora Megashear, which epochs ago rivaled the San Andreas Fault in extent and magnitude (Stewart et al. 1990). Several modern faults in the San Andreas complex (the Algodones, Chinero, San Andreas, San Jacinto, Cocopah, and Laguna Salada faults, among others) are geologically active in the Río Colorado valley W of here. Serdán (b. 1877) was a revolutionary in Puebla, Puebla; he was killed in 1910 by government soldiers (Moreno 1960). =Ejido Aquiles Cérdan. 32°20′25″N, 114°18′42″W. 162 m.

Ejido Carlos Salinas de Gotari (AG). See Estación Gustavo Sotelo.

Ejido Cerro Colorado (PI). Three farming ejidos along Río Sonoyta, 15, 17, and 27 km W of Sonoyta, respectively. Número Uno: 31°54′46″N, 112°59′29″W; 340 m. Número Dos: 31°55′09″N, 113°00′45″W; 320 m. Número Tres: 31°56′04″N, 113°07′04″W; 280 m.

Ejido Durango (BC). Agricultural community in the lower Río Colorado delta between Río Hardy and Río Pescadores, 45 km SE of Mexicali and 8 km SE of Sierra Cucapá. Perhaps settled by immigrants from Mexican state of Durango. 32°11′29″N, 115°14′58″W. 11 m.

Ejido Felipe Ángeles (PI). Ejido immediately S of Los Vidrios, on S side of Mexico Highway 2. It offers roadside tire repair and the small Café Meraz. 32°01′24″N, 113°25′17″W. 220 m.

Ejido Joaquín Amaro (PI). Ejido located near western edge of PI, along Mexico Highway 2 and adjacent to Aquiles Serdán. Revolutionary and army officer Joaquín Amaro Domínguez was an ally of Alvaro Obregón and Plutarco Elías Calles against government of Venustiano Carranza; later secretary of national defense and director of National Military College. About 32°20′N, 114°20′W. 150 m.

Ejido Luis Encinas Johnson (AG). Farming settlement on Mesa de Andrade in Río Colorado delta, 16 km S of Riíto. =Ejido Luis Encinas Jhonson. 32°03′35″N, 114°57′30″W. 10 m.

Ejido Morelia (Sonora). Agricultural settlement along Río Sonoyta 7 km NW of Sonoyta. Named for the Mexican state of the same name. 31°53′20″N, 112°55′00″W. 360 m.

Ejido Nayarit (Sonora). Small settlement at Batamote crossing of Río Sonoyta on the SE side of Mexico Highway 8, across the highway from Ejido los Norteños. Founded in late 1970s, presumably by immigrants from the Mexican state of Nayarit. 31°37′55″N, 113°18′10″W. 160 m.

Ejido los Norteños (Sonora). Small agricultural community, founded in the 1970s, 1 km W of Batamote crossing; see Ejido Nayarit. Spanish for 'the northerners'. 31°38′00″N, 113°18′20″W. 160 m.

Ejido Oveido Mota (Sonora). An agricultural community in delta of Río Colorado, 15 km SSW of Riíto and 1 km W of Canal Zacatecas. It is above the salinized portion of the delta. Alberto Oveido Mota (1882–1955) was a physician who taught, wrote, held public office, and ran a medical school in Michoacán. 32°01′20″N, 114°58′58″W. 5 m.

Another Oveido Mota is shown on maps as an isolated dwelling 7 km W of the ejido. 32°01′15″N, 115°04′03″W. 5 m.

Elegante Crater (PI). Great maar crater 13 km NE of Pinacate Peak. Named by Lumholtz (1912) for its elegance, it is the largest of the Pinacate craters, 1,460 m wide and 243 m deep. Cracks in the small playa in the lowest portion of the crater floor may indicate continuing subsidence. See Gutmann 1976. =Cráter Elegante, Volcán El Elegante. 31°50′44″N, 113°23′28″W. Rim is 320 m; floor 80 m.

Emilia Camp (PI). See Campo Rojo.

Espanto Mountain (SD). Small mountain on NE edge of SD, 3.3. mi NW of Mobile. Name does not appear on early maps or on 1951 USGS 15′ topo; in 2003 the name was unknown to half a dozen long-time residents of Mobile area. Spanish for 'fright' or 'terror', though it can also mean 'ghost'. 33°05′07″N, 112°18′57″W. 1,835 ft.

Estación. Spanish for 'station', here camps for railroad workers who maintained track sections. =*cuadrilla del tramo.*

Estación el Doctor (Sonora). Settlement and railroad stop on Sonora Mesa along Sonora Highway 40. About

40 km NW of El Golfo de Santa Clara and near the Río Colorado. Important freshwater pozos, well, and wetlands 1 km W in bed of Río Colorado (Felger 2000; Glenn & Nagler, this volume). =El Doctor. Spanish for 'doctor'; there must be more to the story, but we're waiting to hear it. 31°57′30″N, 114°44′30″W. 14 m.

Estación Gustavo Sotelo (AG). Abandoned railroad maintenance station with a row of concrete houses, workshops, and a few immense salt cedar trees *(Tamarix aphylla)* planted in the lonely vastness of the Gran Desierto, at km post 207. Named in honor of one of the four civil engineers who helped build the railroad across the Gran Desierto and died of thirst when their truck bogged in heavy sand in July 1937 (Barrios-Matrecito 1988; Munro, this volume). They were lauded as Mexican heroes, memorialized in Niño Martini's 1964 novel *El Muro y la Trocha* and the movie *Viento Negro,* and remembered in four of these gandy dancer stations. In the late 1980s the station was renamed Ejido Carlos Salinas de Gotari (after Mexico's president at that time), but by 2003 all dwellings were falling into ruin.

This site apparently has become either a perpetuated error or one of those cryptic copyright signatures of cartographers, who frequently mislay this trackside settlement 10–16 km northward in the midst of giant dunes; even the illustrious *National Geographic Society Atlas* purposely misplaces it. 31°33′30″N, 113°42′25″W. 8 m.

Estación López Collada (AG). Remote railroad maintenance station in the dunes of the Gran Desierto NW of Puerto Peñasco, at km post 174. In 2003 only one house was occupied. Named in honor of civil engineer Jorge López Collada, "Jefe de una Brigada, quien pereció en el desierto de Altar en cumplimiento de su deber, mientras se ejecutaban las obras del Ferrocarril de Sonora y Baja California" (Almada 1952:435). López Collada and three fellow workers died of thirst in the dunes of the Gran Desierto in July 1937 (Barrios-Matrecito 1988; Munro, this volume). See Estación Gustavo Sotelo, Estación Sánchez Islas, and Estación Torres. In the early 1950s Bahía Adair was renamed Bahía Collada, a name still occasionally seen on period maps. 31°43′00″N, 113°59′00″W. 10 m.

Estación Sánchez Islas (AG). Abandoned railroad maintenance station at km 129, 10 km NNE of El Golfo. See Estación Gustavo Sotelo, Estación López Collada, Estación Torres. 31°45′41″N, 114°27′29″W. 123 m.

Estación Torres (AG). Railroad maintenance settlement at km post 141, 98 km W of Puerto Peñasco. 9 km to E stands a white obelisk (about 18 m tall) dedicated in 1975 to honor the four civil engineers who died of thirst while surveying the roadway at km post 150. They were Jorge López Collada, Gustavo Sotelo, José Sánchez Islas, and Jesús Torres Burciaga, for whom this settlement was named. 31°44′50″N, 114°19′25″W. 55 m.

Figure 39.20. *Estación El Doctor, 1985.*

Figure 39.21. *Estación López Collada, 1985.*

Estero. Spanish for 'estuary', 'tidal marsh', 'marine wetland'. Esteros are crucial habitat for young fish, shorebirds, and wetland plants. Because of high evaporation rates and shallowness, the region's esteros may be even saltier than seawater.

Estero Cerro Prieto (AG). A tidal marsh extending along the coast 2–6 km NNW of Cerro Prieto. The estero mouth is at 31°25′31″N, 113°39′38″W. Sea level.

Estero Chayo (AG). A shallow, intermittent waterway separating Isla Montague and Isla Gore. Spanish for 'dunce' or 'silly fool', possibly since this apparent but dead-end passage deceives boatmen. 31°40′N, 114°41′W. Sea level.

Estero las Lisas (AG). Tidal marsh 40 km NW of Puerto Peñasco; 6 km S of López Collada. Spanish for 'mullet', a schooling fish that feeds in sandy, shallow estuaries and bays. =Estero del Tule. 31°37′10″N, 113°58′00″W at estero mouth. Sea level.

Estero Morúa (Sonora). Large tidal marsh E of Puerto Peñasco. Named for the gentleman who acquired the property on the eastern side of the mouth, probably during the ejido reform period; his family still manages the property (Peggy Turk Boyer). 31°17′N, 113°26′W at estero mouth. Sea level.

Estero Ometepec (AG). Estuary and now-silted circular bay 5 km wide, between San Felipe and Río Colorado delta. Named for an 1873 exploring party's steamer, the *Ometepes* [*sic*]. See Sykes 1937. See Salinas Ometepec. =Bahía Ometepec. 31°22′N, 114°55′W. Sea level.

Estero Peñasco (Sonora). Tidal marsh at Puerto Peñasco. This wetland habitat was destroyed when the modern harbor was built in the 1970s. 31°18′00″N, 113°32′30″W. Sea level.

Estero la Ramada (AG). Estuary between San Felipe and Colorado delta. Presumably named for a beachside ramada for *vagabundo* (vagabond, itinerant) fishermen or tourists. 31°17′N, 114°54′W. Sea level.

Estes Canyon (OP). A spectacular canyon in central Ajo Mountains; its E wall culminates in Ajo Peak. Named for a settler who tried to raise livestock here about 1915. Mouth at 32°01′10″N, 112°32′34″W. 2,400 ft.

Estes Canyon Tinajas (OP). Two intermittent tinajas, both located in same streamcourse. First is at 32°00′57″N, 112°41′40″W (2,880 ft), at the base of a 100-ft ephemeral waterfall; second is 150 ft upstream at 2,980 ft.

Estrella (SD). Railroad siding and former settlement on SPRR in pass through central Maricopa Mountains. The eastbound railroad grade from Gila Bend to Estrella was one of the steepest on the line, so it was built on the Maricopa Divide with a large curve to reduce the slope. Trains required as many as four helper engines, and Estrella had a wye so they could turn around and return to Gila Bend. Named for Sierra Estrella 18 mi NNE. =Estrella Hill. 32°59′51″N, 112°25′25″W. 1,520 ft.

Estufa Tinaja (OP). See Tinaja Estufa.

Evans Wash (GR, Maricopa Co.). Arroyo S of Gila Bend and E of Arizona Highway 85. Name officially proposed July 2, 2001, by Gila Bend town council for Tom Evans, who had lived in Gila Bend since the 1960s and owned property near the wash; name denied by Arizona state officials because living persons cannot be nominated. Joins Cemetery Wash at the railroad bridge. 32°55′52″N, 112°43′28″W. 750 ft.

Evelyn Charco (Pima Co.). Stock tank 0.6 mi SW of Why. 32°15′35″N, 112°44′54″W. 1,770 ft.

Ewe Tank (GR). Subterranean fiberglass water tank built in 1995 in northern Tinajas Altas Mountains, 2 mi S of Raven Butte. 'Ewe' for female desert bighorn sheep here. 32°22′05″N, 114°06′04″W. 1,240 ft.

F

Falcón, Cerro el (PI). See Cerro el Halcón.

Feather Tail Mountain (SD). Local name for outlier of Sand Tank Mountains N of I-8, 12 mi E of Gila Bend. From 'the feather tail end' or 'tip', as in "where the Sand Tank Mountains feather out" (John Laird). =Feather Tail Mountains, Feathertails. 32°55′00″N, 112°34′08″W. 2,062 ft (BM Mitch).

Ferrocarril Sonora-Baja (Sonora, BC). Rail line from Mexicali to Benjamin Hill, connecting Sonora and Baja California. It was begun in 1936, and the golden spike was driven April 7, 1948. A western point near Mexicali was km 0, and Benjamin Hill was km 537 (Barrios-Matrecito 1988). Although the mud and flooding of the Río Colorado made construction difficult across the delta, the stretch from Fuentes Brotantes (km 69, near Riíto and Ejido Mesa Rica) to Puerto Peñasco was the most challenging to build because of extensive drifting sand (Ives 1949; Verdugo-Fimbres 1985). See Estación Gustavo Sotelo, Estación López Collada, Estación Sánchez Islas, and Estación Torres.

Filibusters Camp (Yuma Co.). Site 5 mi E of Wellton from which in 1856 Henry A. Crabb led an ill-fated expedition into Sonora to unseat Governor Gándara in favor of Crabb's friend, Pesqueira. Crabb and 100 of his men were captured near Caborca and killed, and Crabb's head was sent to Mexico City as proof of his demise. The Butterfield Overland Stage line established a station here in 1858 but abandoned it the following year in favor of a station 1.8 mi E called Antelope Hill (see Tacna). 32°40′50″N, 114°03′20″W. 300 ft.

Forgotten Canyon (OP). A small, dead-end canyon just N of the international border in the Sierra de Santa Rosa. The canyon is wild and remote, appearing that all that had once been there before was forgotten, and a park ranger once had difficulty finding his way out of the canyon, but that story has been "forgotten," too. Name dates from about 1999, but appears in law enforcement logs and maps (Jon Young). Mouth at N 31°50′44″N, 112°37′30″W. 1,700 ft.

Fortuna (Yuma Co.). Former railroad siding and settlement, now an outlying suburb of Yuma. Siding was also known as Ming Spur, for Frank Ming, mayor of Yuma in the 1920s. =Ninemile Station, as it was 9 mi from large SPRR complex at Yuma. 32°41′28″N, 114°27′05″W. 200 ft.

Fortuna Mine (GR). Major gold mine in N Gila Mountains. Operating intermittently from 1893 to 1926, the mine employed 80–100 men during its peak. Workings consisted of two shafts, one 1,100 feet deep, the other 359 feet deep, with much lateral work at various levels (Miller 1979; Wilson 1933). Lends name to Fortuna Wash and community of Fortuna along I-8 east of Yuma. 32°33′06″N, 114°19′47″W. 760 ft.

Fortuna Wash (GR, Yuma Co.). Arroyo on W side of Gila Mountains which ephemerally flows NW to Gila River. Named after Fortuna Mine. Joins Gila River at 32°43′22″N, 114°27′36″W. 150 ft.

Forty Mile Desert (SD). A travelers' shortcut between Maricopa and Gila Bend. Because the route was waterless and about 40–45 mi long, it became known as the Forty Mile Desert. The route reduced the trip from Tucson to Yuma by 80 mi, bypassing the arching northern bend of the Gila River through the Salt River Valley.

Undoubtedly traveled by Native Americans prior to advent of Europeans. The last major battle between American Indian tribes occurred at Maricopa Wells when a war party of Quechan and Mohave Indians crossed the Forty Mile Desert to attack the Maricopas in 1857 (Kroeber & Fontana 1986). The route was used and mapped by Padre Kino in 1699 (Bolton 1936). Starting at Tucson in 1775, Juan Bautista D'Anza crossed the desert with 240 people, 165 pack mules, 340 saddle animals, and 302 head of beef. Along the way they lost cattle, mules, and horses but gained a few souls when wives traveling with their husbands gave birth along the trail. When they arrived in San Francisco on March 27, 1776, five months later, they were the first civilian settlers of the city. The route was followed by the Kearny expedition and by the Mormon Battalion during the Mexican War of 1846. Thousands of argonauts used the route in 1849–50 on their way to the California gold fields.

The route was dry and seasonally hot. John Russell Bartlett (1965:211), who crossed it in June 1852, reported, "As there was no water the whole distance, the journey must be made in one march without stopping." His pack train went at night and traversed the 45 mi in 13 hours. Near exhaustion, they reached the banks of the Gila River, where they found water and pasture for the mules, while the men "creeping under some mesquite bushes soon fell asleep, rest being more desirable than food."

At times segments of the route were called the D'Anza Trail (now D'Anza National Historic Trail), Gila Trail, Mormon Battalion Trail, Mormon Trail, Leach's Wagon Road, Southern Route of the Overland Mail Trail, Butterfield Stage Line route, Old Emigrant Trail, and probably a few other synonyms. See Bartlett 1965, Cozzens 1988, Evans 1945, Harris 1960, and Reid 1935.

Freeman (SD). Former service station and ranchstead in Vekol Valley next to old Arizona Highway 84. Operated in 1950s by Harold S. Freeman and his wife; called Freeman's Roll In. The restrooms were an outhouse on the other side of the highway. Now a ruin S of I-8, 23 mi ESE of Gila Bend. 32°50′46″N, 112°17′46″W. 1,777 ft.

Figure 39.22. Fortuna Mine (Wilson 1933).

Freeman Interchange (SD). Interchange off I-8, 23 mi ESE of Gila Bend. Provides access to Sand Tank Mountains and lower E side of SD. 32°50′57″N, 112°19′07″W. 1,837 ft.

Freeman Mine (PI). See Tezontle Mine.

Frontera Canyon (GR). Canyon in southern Tinajas Altas Mountains. It trends NW from vicinity of El Sahuaro (along Highway 2 in Mexico) toward high point in the range. Crosses the international boundary, hence name 'frontera', coined by group of hikers in 1997 (Gayle Hartmann). Tree beargrass *(Nolina bigelovii)* grows to heights of 5 m here; one fallen specimen measured 6 m (Felger 2000). Mouth at 32°15′02″N, 114°01′31″W. 1,100 ft.

Fuentes Brotantes (Sonora). See Mesa Rica.

G

Gachado Ranch and **Well** (OP). Well, trough, and line shack along international border, 2 mi E of Lukeville. A sometimes-artesian spring here served prehistoric peoples. The modern well was dug before 1920. *Agachado* is Spanish for 'stooped' or 'bent' and here honors a uniquely crooked mesquite tree *(Prosopis velutina)*. 31°52′18″N, 112°47′13″W. 1,391 ft.

Gachado Wash (OP, Sonora). Wash running immediately W of Gachado Ranch and Well, crossing international boundary at 31°52′13″N, 112°47′23″W. 1,380 ft.

Gael (Yuma Co.). See Tacna.

Game Tanks (GR). Two water catchments developed for wildlife along spine of Mohawk Mountains. Both were built in 1982. Though both catchments are referred to by this name, Number 2 is the more accessible and well known, and the name is more often associated with it.

Number 1 (GR). 1.6 mi SE of Mohawk Mountains summit (BM 2775). =AGFD #863, Mohawk Catchment #1. 32°34′22″N, 113°37′43″W; 1,250 ft.

Number 2 (GR). Located in Game Tank Pass, a low gap 3.2 mi SE of Mohawk Mountains summit (BM

Figure 39.23. *Game Tank Number 2.*

2775). =AGFD #864, Mohawk Catchment #2. 32°33′50″N, 113°36′29″W. 800 ft.

Gap Butte (GR). Northernmost outlier of Growler Mountains, 8.1 mi NNW of Growler Peak. So named on USGS 1930 Sentinel map. It is unclear to what gap the name refers. The name appears to have fallen from use. =BM Paisano (Spanish for 'roadrunner' or 'fellow countryman or countrywoman'). 32°31′00″N, 113°09′29″W. 2,063 ft.

Gap Tank (SD). Stock tank 2.1 mi WNW of Gap Well. 33°01′00″N, 112°34′05″W. 1,070 ft.

Gap Well (SD). Well on W bajada of Maricopa Mountains 2.5 mi SW of Desert Station. Located 0.5 mi S of Butterfield Stage route in gap between two low hills. 33°00′26″N, 112°38′59″W. 1,188 ft.

Garcia Well (GR). Abandoned stock-watering well on the old Ajo-Stoval wagon road, 9 mi S of Dateland. Also a name once applied to Chico Shunie Well. 32°39′51″N, 113°34′05″W. 390 ft.

Ge Huḍa Do'ag (GR). See Crater Range.

Ge Huduns (CP). See Sheep Peak.

Geology Divide Tank (GR). Wildlife water catchment in Gila Mountains built in 1999, 2.6 mi SE of Sheep Mountain. Underground storage tank holds 10,000 gallons and is distributed in a 2,000-gallon walk-in trough. Named for nearby geologic contact that divides the Gila Mountains: Mesozoic gneiss and schist in N and granite in S. 32°30′12″N, 114°12′12″W. 980 ft.

Getz Well (SD). Cattle well 17 mi ESE of Gila Bend, named for the Marion and Polly Getzwiller ranching family. Known as "Getz," Marion (1916–2004) was born in Benson, Arizona, and was a charter member of the Professional Rodeo Cowboys Association; his special-

ties were calf roping, bull dogging, and team roping (*Gila Bend Sun* 2004c). 32°52′16″N, 112°26′53″W. 1,553 ft.

Gibson (Pima Co.). A townsite started just N of Ajo community about 1916 by Matthew Ellsworth Gibson and his wife, Laura. Gibson had its own utility company and chamber of commerce (Rickard 1996). Today it is a neighborhood of greater Ajo, with much of it renamed Ajo Heights. 32°22′54″N, 112°52′27″W. 1,810 ft.

Gibson Arroyo (Pima Co.). Arroyo on W side of Ajo. Named for founder of town of Gibson. Meets Tenmile Wash at 32°27′48″N, 112°50′29″W. 1,410 ft.

Gila Bend (Maricopa Co.). Town 3 mi S of the once-perennial Gila River, which bends westward here; at junction of Arizona Highway 85 and I-8. Prehistoric peoples congregated here; some built a walled village, Forteliza, or Fortified Hill, on a butte N of Gila Bend. Historic travelers followed the natural route along river here or cut directly eastward across the Forty Mile Desert to Maricopa Wells. This waterless jaunt prompted nineteenth-century tourist Charles D. Poston to pen:

> "Arrived at last at Gila Bend
> Our river journey comes to end.
> 'Tis wise to stop here, wheels to tauter
> To rest and fill the cans with water."
> (Barnes 1988:176)

The Butterfield Overland Stage established a station here in 1858 called Gila Ranch. Gila Bend was later an important watering point on the Southern Pacific Railroad, which arrived April 1, 1879.

Site may have been called Tezotal, a Maricopa Indian ranchería that had many ironwood trees and possibly lent its name to ironwood tree nomenclature, *Olneya tesota*. However, in Sonora *tesota* refers to cat-claw acacia *(Acacia greggii)*. Several O'odham villages are associated with the Gila Bend area, and their locations are vaguely known. Si:l Me:k (=Silimok) generally is shown 3 mi N of town, though Lumholtz (1912) places it 18 mi N. The correct name of Gila Bend village may be Tahi (mislabeled Si:l Me:k by the Bureau of Indian Affairs [King 1961]).

In the 1870s, when the Southern Pacific Railroad was being constructed across southern Arizona, the route "passed through the area of Gila Bend, where for as long as is known, the O'odham from Chuilikam [Chiulikam] had gathered food and sometimes planted crops. It apparently was never a permanent settlement, but when the railroad was being built, many O'odham moved to Gila Bend and remained there while the men worked on construction of the railroad bed" (Erickson 2003:88–89). Many of them stayed.

The current O'odham village of San Lucy was established as a separate reservation by President Chester Arthur in 1882 but is now one of the Tohono O'odham

Nation districts. =Si:l Me:k; Hi:la Vi:ñ Ceksanĭ, from 'Gila Bend outskirts' or 'borderline' (Saxton et al. 1983). Also =Akma·t, the Cocopah name for Gila Bend; and Opas Oidag, the O'odham name for where the Maricopa Indians formerly lived at Gila Bend. Other nearby villages include Tesota Ranchería, =Second Village; U'upaḍ Oidag (historically spelled Uhupat Oidak, Uupatoitak, meaning 'catclaw acacia fields'), 3 mi N of Gila Bend; Kui Vo'o, 10 mi NW of Gila Bend along the river, =Kui Vo'i, Kueva, Kuivo, meaning 'mesquite lying down' or 'west'; and Ranchería del Pelón.

In 1879 the railroad hired 150 Cocopah workers to supplement the Chinese laborers. The Cocopahs brought their families, who lived 2.5 mi outside Gila Bend. When the line reached Maricopa, they quit and went home.

Theba Ranch was about 10 mi W of Gila Bend along the railroad. The former settlement of San Diego was a few miles W of Gila Bend, on S bank of Gila River opposite El Tutto.

San Martín was W of Gila Bend but E of San Diego (Castetter & Bell 1951). Others, S-hewelig ('windy place') and Howij Dak ('banana yucca sitting'), are neighborhoods of Gila Bend.

Gila Bend and the territory southward were part of Mexico until the Gadsden Purchase of 1853, so plants collected here before then are labeled "Sonora, Mexico;" thus desert holly (*Atriplex hymenelytra*) was erroneously listed as found in NW Sonora (Felger 2000; Shreve & Wiggins 1964; Turner et al. 1995).

Bob Lenon reports that in the 1930s "there was a 24-hour cafe in downtown Gila Bend run for many years by an old German with the name of Jake Miller (probably Mueller until World War I). He used to import big sea turtles from Rocky Point and concoct a hearty turtle soup therefrom, but was soon forced to quit. Too much of the carcass had to be discarded. 'One hundred percent waste,' he avowed, and when my dad questioned him about those figures, Jake replied, 'Ya, even more than that!'"

Shortened to Gila in 1925 for convenience of railroad telegraphers but later reinstated as Gila Bend. Kupel (1999) summarizes the town's history.

2000 population: 1,980. 32°56'50"N, 112°42'56"W. 736 ft.

Gila Bend Auxiliary Field (GR). Active U.S. Air Force installation 4 mi S of Gila Bend. It opened during World War II as a training base for pilots. 32°53'10"N, 112°43'38"W. 854 ft.

Gila Bend Plains (Maricopa Co., GR, SD). Flat, open valley extending N from the Sauceda Mountains to the floodplain of the Gila River (Bryan 1925:216). Bounded on E by Sand Tank and Maricopa mountains and on W by Sentinel Plain. The name has largely fallen from use. 32°55'N, 112°41'W. 800 ft.

Figure 39.24. Gila Mountains.

Gila Bend–Pozo Blanco Road (GR, TON). Historic trail between Gila Bend and Pozo Blanco (a winter *ranchería* at S end of Sierra Blanca and N of Quijotoa Mountains). It ran through Chiulikam and Stoa Pitk (Ahlstrom 2000; Ahlstrom et al. 2001; Bryan 1925). Pozo Blanco (TON; =Stoa Vaya) is at 32°10'29"N, 112°13'37"W. 2,440 ft.

Gila City (Yuma Co.). See Dome.

Gila Mountains (GR). Large range in western GR 15 mi E of Yuma, extending SE from Gila River to Tinajas Altas Mountains. Gila River is displaced around their northern end. The mountains N of the river (now called the Laguna Mountains) were called Sierra de la Gila in 1854 by Lt. N. Michler. The name became Gila Mountains and Gila City Mountains when limited to the portion S of the Gila River. Gila Mountains are a relatively barren range of Mesozoic gneiss and schist in N and granite in S. =Sierra San Albino, Fortuna Range.

Range served as a division between Yuman tribes and Hia C'ed O'odham, with a shared village on northern tip. =Avik Amook To'or; Mokwintaorv, Quechan for 'fleecy blanket (of) clouds straddling rocks', because from the vicinity of Yuma, Quechans often saw fleecy clouds perched above the range during the summer rainy season, even when Yuma itself received no rain (George Bryant). The name Gila may come from a Mohave term meaning 'division' or 'boundary (between tribes)' (Fillman Bell). Summit is Sheep Mountain, 32°31'59"N, 114°14'01"W. 3,156 ft.

Gila River (Arizona). Formerly a major tributary to Colorado River but now greatly diminished by diversion for irrigation and domestic uses. Flows W from Gila Mountains of New Mexico to its mouth at Yuma. See Hi:lo. =Haa Si:il, Yuman for 'salty water' (Lorey Cachora); Onk Akimel, O'odham for 'salty river' (Fillman Bell); Akee-mull, Apache de Xila, Brazo de

Miraflores, Hah-quah-sa-eel, Hela, Jila, Río Azul, Río de las Balsas, Río del los Apóstoles, Río Gila, Río del Nombre Jesús, and Zila River. Confluence with Colorado is at 32°43′11″N, 114°33′15″W. 120 ft.

Gila Tanks (GR). A watering stop for travelers between Ajo and Gila Bend in 1850s (Kippin Diary in Hoy 1995). Probably =Black Tanks (Hoy 1995).

Gila Trail (Yuma Co., Maricopa Co., Pinal Co.). Pioneer route from Maricopa across the Forty Mile Desert to Gila Bend, then along Gila River from Gila Bend to Yuma. Routes from Texas and Chihuahua joined near Maricopa Wells. Gila Trail was favored because it generally had water and pasturage, but 49ers headed to California ran a gauntlet of hostile Apaches. See *Arizona Highways* 1984, Browne 1950, Etter 1998, Faulk 1973, and Harris 1960. See Forty Mile Desert.

Gillespie Dam (Maricopa Co.) Dam built in 1921 by the Gillespie Land and Irrigation Company on the Gila River, 20 mi N of Gila Bend. Frank A. Gillespie, who made a fortune in the Oklahoma oil fields (Gypsey Oil Company) and other enterprises, came to Arizona looking to develop land and farms. He picked up land and ideas from Samuel M. Webb, who had developed and irrigated farmlands along the lower Gila River starting about 1915. Frank, who had a ranch at Arlington, Arizona, assigned his son Bernard to run the Arizona operations, which at one time included 120,000 acres of arable land (MacPherson 1973). Development included the dam and 44 mi of canals. Eventually, upstream users and dams—Roosevelt Dam on the Salt River (1911) and Coolidge Dam on the Gila River (1930)—intercepted much of the flow, rendering the lower river intermittent and Gillespie Dam ineffective and forcing farmers to pump from the aquifer. The Gila River Pimas suffered a similar fate (DeJong 2003; Ezell 1994). 33°13′45″N, 112°46′06″W. 780 ft.

Gillespie Ranch (Maricopa Co.). Adobe mansion built by Bernard Gillespie (b. 1894) still stands. It included an airstrip and horse-racing track. Gillespie was rich, eccentric, and loyal to his friends (MacPherson 1973). His parties are still talked about. Ranch animals included monkeys and a mule painted to look like a zebra. Gillespie flew his own airplane (accounts differ on whether he had a pilot's license) and had a sport-fishing boat on the Gulf of California. Later in life he owned a gold mine in the Sierra Pinta, Sonora, and tried to develop 10,000 acres of beachfront property on the N shore of Bahía San Jorge east of Puerto Peñasco. See Theba. =Gila River Ranch, Paloma Ranch. 32°54′51″N, 112°53′33″W. 732 ft.

Glynns Falls (GR). Ephemeral waterfall on W side of Mohawk Mountains, about 0.35 mi W of summit BM 2775. It remains unclear for whom the falls were named.

=Glinns Falls, Glenns Falls. 32°35′16″N, 113°39′05″W. 1,800 ft.

Goldwater Range, Barry M. (Maricopa, Pima, and Yuma cos.). 1.7 million-acre Air Force and Marine Corps aerial training range established early in 1941. Formerly known as Luke Air Force Range but in 1986 renamed in honor of Arizona's long-time senator, Barry Goldwater. In 1941 Goldwater, then an officer in the Army Air Corps and working under the command of Lt. Col. Ennis C. Whitehead, served here and helped establish the range's boundaries. The range was inactive between 1946 and 1952 (Homburg et al. 1994), which explains a surge of attempts during those years to prospect and ranch this land (e.g., Monreal Well, Papago Indian Chief Mine). See Felger et al., this volume, Chapter 1. Legal boundary descriptions are in Federal Register Document 87–9191 (April 17, 1987).

As of 2001 the eastern range (1,042,163 acres) is managed by the U.S. Air Force, with headquarters at Luke Air Force Base, west of Phoenix.

The western range (691,758 acres) is managed by the U.S. Marine Corps, Yuma Marine Corps Air Station, Yuma.

Resources and environmental issues are covered in Brickler et al. 1986 and Hall et al. 2001.

=Barry M. Goldwater Military Range, Barry M. Goldwater Air Force Range, Luke Air Force Range, Luke Gunnery Range, Luke-Williams Air Force Range, Williams Military Reservation.

Golfo de Santa Clara, El (AG). Beachside fishing and tourist village on Gulf of California near SE corner of the Río Colorado delta. The town is the S terminus of Sonora Highway 40 from San Luis R.C. Usually referred to simply as El Golfo, it had about 5,000 inhabitants in 2004 (José Campoy). Vegetation on the nearby high dunes has been devastated by weekend tourists' use of recreational off-road vehicles; effects of off-roading and recovery strategies are discussed in Webb & Wilshire 1983. Mesa Arenosa to NE rises more than 100 m above beach. 31°41′10″N, 114°29′55″W. 3–10 m.

Gore Island (AG). See Isla Gore.

Gran Desierto, El (PI, Sonora). The great sand desert of northwestern Sonora, especially the moving dunes; sometimes used to include the entire region of northwestern Sonora. This largest (5,500 km²) sand sea (erg) in North America has a variety of eolian dune forms, including star dunes (see Blount & Lancaster 1990; Davis et al. 1990; Lancaster et al. 1987; McKee 1979; Kresan, this volume). It has a special flora (Felger 1980, 2000). Former home of the Areneños, Soba, or So'obmakam O'odham (Papagos). =Altar Desert, Gran Desierto del Altar. Named for the Distrito de Altar, a political subdivision that subsumes the grand western desert and was named for the town of Altar, Sonora, and for Río

Altar, a main tributary of district's largest watershed. "Altar...was named by Father Kino because it was near a little mountain which he thought resembled an altar" (Barnes 1988:16, citing letter from Frank C. Lockwood). Granger (1983:14) reports, "In 1693 when Fr. Eusebio Kino and Juan Mateo Manje stopped at the place where the [then nameless] Altar River disappeared into the sand, Kino dubbed the spot El Altar." However, Roca (1967:115 and n. 146) reminds us that the town was established as a presidio (garrison for troops) about 1753–1755, after the Pima uprising of 1751. Centered at 32°00′N, 114°30′W.

Granite Cap Peak (GR). See Red Top Mountain.

Granite Mountains (CP). A range of "hungry granite" 25 mi W of Ajo which proved barren of profitable minerals. This remote and seldom visited range provided the setting for a mystery novel of a lost desert civilization in the book *The Burning Sky* (Duncan 1966). Some early maps confused or combined this range with the Aguila Mountains immediately to the north. Bryan (1925:194) indicates that prospectors called the small outlying mountain on the NW end of the range Sierra del Diablo, or Devils Hills, though we can find no other reference to that name and suspect it was misplaced from Devil Hills at the NW corner of Sierra Pinta. Summit is BM Granite at 32°25′40″N, 113°18′26″W. 2,490 ft.

Granite Pass Tank (CP). A concrete-box waterhole developed for wildlife in 1951 on SE end of Granite Mountains. Despite the name, no pass crosses the mountains here. 32°19′02″N, 113°15′24″W. 1,060 ft.

Granite Spur (Yuma Co.). Abandoned railroad siding on SPRR, 2 mi E of Dome. Serviced mines and farms in area prior to 1930. 32°43′54″N, 114°21′02″W. 194 ft.

Grass Canyon (OP). Canyon on NW end of Ajo Mountains, 4.5 mi NNW of Ajo Peak. Named for "abundant grasses" that grow there (Sue Rutman). Mouth at 32°05′50″N, 112°43′03″W. 2,400 ft.

Greasewood Pass (CP). A gap across the international line between basalt mesas of the Tule Mountains (Malpais), and between border monuments 186 and 187 (see Humphrey 1987). Informal but inaccurate misnomer for creosotebush *(Larrea divaricata)*, which grows here and throughout the Sonoran Desert. 32°11′25″N, 113°49′02″W. 1,080 ft.

Green Gate Well and **Ranch** (GR). This well, 8 mi SW of Gila Bend, supplied water to the descriptively named Green Gate Ranch, owned at one time by Tom Childs Jr. 32°51′13″N, 112°48′17″W. 860 ft.

Grey Fox Mines (Yuma Co.). Group of mines at extreme N tip of Gila Mountains. Named for gray fox *(Urocyon cinereoargenteus)*, common here. 32°44′56″N, 114°23′39″W. 260 ft.

Grijalva Ranch (PI). See Rancho Guadalupe Victoria.

Growler (Yuma Co.). A busy place-name. Former Hia C'ed O'odham village 2 mi N of Mohawk Mountains, on N bank of Gila River. Also a station on SPRR. May =To:b Do'ag ('twisted neck') village. Situated 4 mi NW of mouth of San Cristobal Wash, which at one time was called Growler Wash. Now a railroad siding, it may have been synonymous with Norton. 32°48′55″N, 113°47′55″W. 322 ft.

Growler Canyon (OP). Canyon immediately E of Bates Well in gap through northernmost Bates Mountains. Mouth at 32°10′05″N, 112°56′24″W. 1,360 ft.

Growler Mountains (CP, OP). A large basaltic range 10 mi W of Ajo. It was named for John Growler, who prospected the area before 1880. Growler Mine (OP) was at S end of the range. As late as 1918 the name applied also to Bates Mountains. Summit is BM Gro in southern part of range at 32°14′35″N, 113°01′39″W. 3,293 ft.

Growler Pass (OP). Pass between Growler and Bates mountains, 1.5 mi NE of Bates Well. 32°10′55″N, 112°55′35″W. 1,487 ft.

Growler Peak (CP). A summit 1.4 mi N of Charlie Bell Pass. 32°24′37″N, 113°06′02″W. 3,027 ft.

Growler Valley (OP, CP, GR). Extensive valley bordered on E by Bates and Growler mountains and on W by Agua Dulce and Granite mountains. 32°25′05″N, 113°12′20″W. 1,100 ft.

Growler Wash (OP, CP). Major arroyo draining NW OP and central CP. Formed by confluence of Cuerda de Leña and Cherioni Wash, just east of Growler Canyon. =Bates Wash, Growler Creek, San Cristobal Wash. Joins San Cristobal Wash NW of Granite Mountains at 32°32′35″N, 113°26′16″W; 515 ft. Heads at 32°09′32″N, 112°55′15″W; 1,390 ft.

Figure 39.25. Granite Pass Tank.

Figure 39.26. *Halfway Tank.*

Gulf of California (Sonora, BC, BCS). The Pacific Ocean gulf between mainland Mexico and the Baja California peninsula. It is biologically rich and diverse but vulnerable to abuse and neglect. See Búrquez & Martinez 1992, Case et al. 2002. Because of oceanic pollution elsewhere, the gulf is becoming an increasingly important whale nursery (Sandy Lanham; Beatty 1996). =Golfo de California, Vermillion Sea; Mar de Cortez, Mar de Cortés, Sea of Cortez (after Spanish conquistador Hernán Cortés).

Gunsight Hills (TON, OP). Grouping of hills and broken terrain lying S of Arizona Highway 86 at N end of Ajo Mountains. Named for nearby ridge's resemblance to a gun sight on a rifle barrel. Highest peak is home to the Gunsight Mine, a complex of abandoned shafts and adits first located in 1878. The small mining community once located here was called Allen City, named for John Brackett "Pie" Allen (1818–1899), a storekeeper known for his good pies. Allen apparently ran stores in numerous mining camps in territorial Arizona, as his name appears in the histories of other mining towns (Granger 1960). 32°12′01″N, 112°41′04″W. 2,622 ft.

Gunsight Pass (TON). A wide gap in the Gunsight Hills 1 mi SW of the abandoned mine complex. 32°11′10″N, 112°42′36″W. 1,960 ft.

Gunsight Ranch (TON). See Schuchuli.

Gunsight Valley (TON). A narrow valley between the Pozo Redondo Mountains and the Gunsight Hills. 32°13′23″N, 112°40′58″W. 1,980 ft at Schuchuli.

Gunsight Wash (TON). Arroyo intermittently flowing westward past Schuchuli. It parallels Arizona Highway 86 between Gunsight Hills and Pozo Redondo Mountains. Joins Cuerda de Leña Wash at 32°14′45″N, 112°49′35″W. 1,600 ft.

Gustavo Sotelo, Estación (AG). See Estación Gustavo Sotelo.

Gutmann's Cone (PI). Volcanic cone on SE cliffs of Elegante Crater. Named for volcanologist James T. Gutmann by Dan Lynch (1981:84). Gutmann, Wesleyan University professor emeritus, has studied Pinacate geology for nearly four decades. See Bezy et al. 2000; Gutmann 1976, 2002; Gutmann & Prival 1996, 2000. 31°50′33″N, 113°23′06″W. 360 m.

H

H. E. Hill (GR). See High Explosive Hill.

Haa Si:il (Yuma Co., Maricopa Co.). See Gila River.

Hacker Wash (GR, Maricopa Co.). Arroyo S of Gila Bend and E of Arizona Highway 85; tributary to Cemetery Wash. Name officially proposed July 2, 2001, by Gila Bend town council for Harold Hacker (died March 9, 1999), an electrician who lived in Gila Bend for 45 years and owned property adjacent to the wash; declined by Arizona state officials because nominees must be deceased at least five years. Crosses Gila Bend to Ajo rail line at 32°55′08″N, 112°43′53″W. 770 ft.

Haley Hills (Maricopa Co., Pinal Co.). Dispersed group of hills 6.1 mi SE of Mobile and 1.6 mi E of SD boundary. Name appears on 1948 USGS 15′ topo map but not on maps of 1930s. 32°59′00″N, 112°12′30″W. 1,988 ft.

Half White Mountain (Yuma Co.). Hill 5 mi SE of Dateland, in Aztec Hills. Descriptive name. 32°46′52″N, 113°27′05″W. 620 ft.

Smaller hill 0.1 mi N is White Mountain, a jasper mine. 32°46′57″N, 113°27′04″W. 580 ft.

Halfway Corral (SD). Abandoned corral in Sand Tank Mountains located midway between Ninemile Well and Johnson Well. 32°46′11″N, 112°31′31″W. 1,723 ft.

Halfway Tank (CP). This constructed wildlife waterhole in NW Cabeza Prieta Mountains was built in 1948 "halfway" between Cabeza Prieta Tanks and Buck Mountain Tank. The valley east of this tank supports an extensive stand of teddybear cholla (*Cylindropuntia bigelovii*). 32°20′19″N, 113°51′40″W. 1,440 ft.

Halliwill Tank (GR). Water catchment built for wildlife in 1986 and named for a former Marine Corps officer and Yuma area sportsman who devoted his time to taking children with disabilities on outings to camp and fish. Located 2 mi SSE of Aguila Mountains at low twin-knobbed hill in Childs Valley, the tank was rebuilt in 1995 after an Air Force 500-pound practice bomb scored a direct hit in December 1994. =Halliwill Catchment; AGFD #936. 32°34′43″N, 113°15′47″W. 800 ft.

Happy Camp (SD). See Desert Station.

Hardy, Río (BC). See Río Hardy.

Hasoj Cheel (AG). =Colorado River. Seri for 'red river' (Mary Beck Moser).

Hat Mountain (GR). Distinctive hat-like butte in central Sauceda Mountains. Its flat top is a layer of erosion-resistant basalt. Photo of it in Lumholtz (1912:32b) was mislabeled. =Tea Kettle Mountain (counterpart to Coffeepot Mountain), Table Top (distinct from SD), Flat Top. Summit at BM Dome, 32°38′08″N, 112°44′29″W. 2,854 ft.

Havañi Kos (PI). See Tinaja del Cuervo. =Havanikosh.

Hazen Tank (SD). Stock tank on N bajada of Sheep Mountain, 2.3 mi NNE of Hazen Well. 33°09′00″N, 112°33′39″W. 1,260 ft.

Hazen Well (SD). Well in Maricopa Mountains in Margies Cove, 2.9 mi SSE of Margies Peak. The Hazen family is based in Buckeye, Arizona. 33°07′19″N, 112°34′54″W. 1,098 ft.

Heart Tank (CP). Natural perennial tinaja on W slope of Sierra Pinta, 0.7 mi NW of summit BM Pinta (2,950 ft). May be Padre Kino's Aguaje de la Luna, which he visited and gratefully used in 1699. Long used by people, it was named for its heart shape when full (see photo in Bolton 1936:411a), before a modern dam slightly raised and distorted the lip of the pool. Several intermittent tinajas are in the vicinity. =Pinto Tank on older maps; Aguaje de la Luna (Spanish for 'waterhole of the moon'), Tinaja de Corazón, Tinaja del Corazón. 32°16′01″N, 113°33′08″W. 1,310 ft.

Heintzelman Point (AG). Low bluff and river bend at head of tidewater in Río Colorado, 32 km above mouth. Named for Samuel Peter Heintzelman, soldier at Fort Yuma and later owner of Colorado Ferry Company in 1850s. =Punta Heintzelman. 32°02′55″N, 115°00′35″W. 10 m.

Hell-for-Sure Pass (OP). One of several smuggling routes entering Ali Wua Pass in Sierra de Santa Rosa. Named in 2000 by park ranger Jon Young, who crossed it on a summer day approaching 117° and high humidity. The steep, rocky climb from the south was "Hell-for-Sure" (Jon Young). N 31°54′05″N, 112°37′46″W. 2,210 ft.

Hiatikomalik (PI). See Sierra del Rosario.

Hiatitváxia (AG). See Pozo Caballo.

Hickiwan (TON). A dispersed village 22 mi E of Ajo. A long-time center for cattle ranching in the western part of the reservation; its farmlands have been curtailed by invasive grasses and cockleburs. Before 1875 this was a major village but in a different location (King 1961); the custom of moving place-names when the people of a village move leads to some confusion of locations and an overlap of names. O'odham for 'hair cut short'; 'rough', 'ridged'; 'rough mountain'. =Hikiwoñ; Pirigua, Perigua; Jiquibo, Hikibon, Hikivo, Hikuwan, Hikjovn; Kokuli;

Figure 39.27. Heart Tank.

Milpitas. May =San Geronimo, Tachitoa. 32°22′08″N, 112°28′29″W. 2,185 ft.

Hickiwan Peak (TON). Hill 1 mi SE of Hickiwan. 32°21′24″N, 112°28′02″W. 2,580 ft.

Hickiwan Valley (TON). Broad valley along Hickiwan Wash (Arroyo). =Perigua Valley. 32°16′04″N, 112°28′18″W. 2,200 ft at Hickiwan.

Hickiwan Wash (TON). Arroyo flowing S from Sauceda Mountains, past town of Hickiwan, and into San Simon Wash. 32°11′13″N, 112°22′42″W. 2,180 ft at Hickiwan.

Hidden Gorge Tinajas (OP). Four intermittent tinajas 0.9 mi SE of Kino Peak in Bates Mountains. 32°06′13″N, 112°56′25″W. 1,890 ft.

Hidden Valley Mountains (SD, Pinal Co.). Small group of mountains W of Hidden Valley and SE of Mobile. Local name for what are now called Booth Hills and Haley Hills on topo maps (Joe Kinney, Joseph Jordan).

High Explosive (H. E.) Hill (GR). Target zone for air-to-ground munitions in central GR, midway between Growler Mountains and Aguila Mountains, in a military zone known as South Tac (South Tactical Range). 32°32′15″N, 113°14′13″W. 884 ft.

At least two other GR target zones also bear name High Explosive Hill. One in East Tac is E of Pottebaum

Tank, in vicinity of 32°43′53″N, 112°34′17″W. 1,682 ft. Another is also in South Tac about 2 mi SW of East Pass.

High Tanks (GR). See Tinajas Altas.

Hi:lo (Yuma Co.). A mountain and a former Hia C'ed O'odham village near Dome on the Gila River. Derived from Spanish for 'thread', O'odham for 'thread', or Yuman for 'boundary'. Perhaps derived from Quechan word meaning 'salty water'. Possible source of name Gila. The Gila River was named by Padre Kino in 1701, after visiting this vicinity and calling the river Río Grande de Hyla. Fillman Bell reports that this river was a territorial boundary between tribes to the north and those to the south, so the thread metaphor may indicate both a wending river and a gentle barrier.

Hitjuupo (PI). See Tinajas de los Pápagos.

Hoa Murk (TON). A village 13 mi SE of Ajo. Traditionally, the O'odham lived in several villages, depending on seasons and conditions. For example, this village is 2 mi S of Sikort Chuapo and 3 mi N of Gunsight, and people moved between these and other villages depending on available rangeland for their cattle, rainfall for their fields, and harvest seasons for native plants. O'odham for 'burned basket'. =Hua Me:k (preferred spelling), Hoa Muerta, Pozo Ben, Roamine's Field. 32°16′48″N, 112°40′01″W. 1,960 ft.

Hocker Well (OP). Well 2.2 mi WNW of Quitobaquito and N of bend in Río Sonoyta. Named for Ike Hocker, who in early twentieth century drilled it for Tom Childs. Later Hocker and his family lived there for a while. 31°57′14″N, 113°03′21″W. 981 ft.

Hog Hole (Maricopa Co.). Stock tank immediately outside extreme NW corner of SD. Misnomer for javelina *(Pecari tajacu)*. 33°13′01″N, 112°37′54″W. 950 ft.

Hog Tank (SD). An intermittent stock tank in Vekol Valley, 4 mi ESE of Johnson Ranch. Dug by rancher Les Bender in the 1920s and named for hog-sized javelina; at one time he and his family operated Big Horn Station, Johnson Ranch, and Vekol Ranch (Letty Bender Hofstra and Anita Bender McGee; see McGee & Hofstra, this volume). 32°41′57″N, 112°17′30″W. 2,175 ft.

Holt Tank (GR). Small dam and water catchment in Sauceda Mountains, 2.5 mi N of Hat Mountain. Built in 1971 for wildlife and named for outdoorsman Perry Duane "P. D." Holt of Gila Bend. =Holt's Hole; AGFD #789. 32°40′15″N, 112°44′23″W. 1,720 ft.

Hombres Tank (CP). Natural tinaja in eastern Growler Mountains. Prehistoric pictographs of five human figures give its name. 32°26′34″N, 113°04′49″W. 1,800 ft.

Hornaday Mountains (PI). This small granitic range, 26 km NNW of Pinacate Peak, borders the NW margin of the Pinacate volcanic shield. Named for naturalist

William T. Hornaday (Hornaday 1908). A Pleistocene flora of these mountains is known from fossil plant remnants recovered in ancient packrat middens (Van Devender et al. 1990). On some maps =Sierrita el Temporal, a name unknown locally. 31°59′55″N, 113°37′38″W. 440 m.

Horseshoe Bend (AG). Historically important channel curve on Río Colorado. Type locality for *Distichlis palmeri* (nipa, an important native grain used by Cocopahs; see Felger 2000; Felger, chapter 15, this volume; Williams, this volume). 31°57′30″N, 115°07′30″W. 10 m.

Horseshoe Pass (OP, TON). A pass and trail across Ajo Range, used by smugglers, 2.0 mi SE of Diaz Peak. Named by park rangers about 1999 for its evenly and deeply curved shape when seen from the south (Jon Young). 31°56′28″N, 112°38′49″W. 2,650 ft.

Hot Shot Tank (Pima Co.). Stock tank immediately SE of Hot Shot Well site. 32°21′06″N, 112°46′53″W. 1,600 ft.

Hot Shot Well (Pima Co.). Abandoned ranch, well, and Prohibition-era speakeasy 4 mi ESE of Ajo. Established by Tom Childs Jr. The water was slightly thermic so perhaps gave a "hot shot," though it also meant a fast freight train or a conspicuous, talented person. =Childs Ranch, Hotcha or Hacha, Hatca; Vo'o S-a:nag, O'odham for 'reservoir with desert broom plants'. 32°21′09″N, 112°47′03″W. 1,610 ft.

Hótunikat (PI). See Tinaja de los Chivos.

House Finch Tinaja (OP). Small, intermittent tinaja located on E slope of Pinkley Peak. Reported in OP files (Brown et al. 1983:34) at vicinity of 32°00′15″N, 112°50′58″W. 2,000 ft.

Howij Dak (Maricopa Co.). Former O'odham village near, or a neighborhood in, Gila Bend. O'odham for 'banana yucca sitting' *(Yucca baccata)*. See Gila Bend.

Huerfano Hill (GR). Isolated volcanic cone on S edge of Sentinel Plain, 5.3 mi S of Sentinel. Spanish for 'orphan'. 32°47′00″N, 113°13′17″W. 735 ft.

Hummingbird Canyon (CP). Steep canyon on E side of Sierra Pinta, 1 mi E of Heart Tank. Named for seasonally bountiful hummingbirds that relish the flowers of chuparosa *(Justicia californica)* here. Mouth at 32°16′28″N, 113°31′00″W. 1,100 ft.

Hunters Camp (AG). Local name for an outpost on northwestern edge of Ciénega de Santa Clara in Río Colorado delta. In 1994, fish samples at this site confirmed the presence of endangered desert pupfish *(Cyprinodon macularius)* (Zengel et al. 1996). Once widespread throughout the West, this and other pupfish are now restricted to small pockets in their former ranges. 32°02′11″N, 114°54′50″W. Above sea level.

Hunters Camp (PI). See Campo Rojo.

Husigam (Pima Co.) An O'odham agave-gathering site somewhere W of Ajo. Possibly name is from O'odham *usabkam,* elephant tree *(Bursera microphylla),* which grows in the Growler and Granite mountains.

I

'Iattomkam Ce:po (GR?). A tinaja used by Hia C'ed O'odham on their walking journeys between Dome and Quitobaquito (Bell et al. 1980). =Tinaja de Manteras (meaning unknown but possibly related to rumored Mentira Tank). Precise location unknown but may refer to Eagle or Don Diego tanks, which lie along one route. O'odham for 'liar's tank'. ='Iadamkam Ce:po.

I'itoi's Cave (PI). This lava tube in Sierra Pinacate is an Hia C'ed O'odham holy place of emergence. According to one version, there once was a great flood on the land. I'itoi, creator of the O'odham, was saved by floating in a jar made of creosotebush lac. While the flood receded, he landed on Pinacate Peak. There he and his collaborator, Coyote, created many living things, including people, who multiplied too fast and made problems. So I'itoi waved his arms, caused another great flood, and stayed in the Pinacate for four hundred years. When the land dried, I'itoi returned north with his people, the O'odham, who chased away others living on their land. These events are celebrated in the Vi:gida (=Vi'igita, Vigida, Vigita, Vikita) ceremony (Valentine 1994), which was moved from the Pinacate to Quitovac by the O'odham's Areneño descendants (Van Valkenburgh 1945; Hayden 1987). Another I'itoi's Cave is located at the W base of Baboquivari Peak SW of Tucson. Both Pinacate Peak and Baboquivari Peak play prominent roles in O'odham sacred beliefs. Many other O'odham holy places and shrines are scattered throughout the region. Please respect all holy sites with utmost reverence and refrain from visiting them. Even prehistoric sites may be sacred and religiously significant for a number of modern people.

I'itoi's Cone (PI). Cinder cone 13 km E of Pinacate Peak and 6 km SE of Elegante Crater. Named for O'odham deity. Ives (1964) wrote that pitahaya (organ pipe cactus) grew on its summit, but when his friend Julian Hayden went there a few years later, he found none and brought the absence to Ives's attention. Ives, who sometimes floated ideas to see if anyone was listening, enjoyed the challenge and replied, "But you looked, didn't you!" (Julian Hayden). =Iitoi's Castle. 31°48′50″N, 113°22′44W. 340 m.

I'itoi Mo'o (Pima Co.). See Montezuma's Head.

Ikuskaatsh (PI). See Agua Dulce.

Indian Butte (SD). Small hill, 4 mi NNE of Table Top Mountains. 32°48′21″N, 112°05′50″W. 2,316 ft.

Indian Town (Pima Co.). See Ajo.

Indian Well (GR). Defunct well and corral along Growler Wash 1.5 mi N of Granite Mountains. 32°31′16″N, 113°18′48″W. 635 ft.

Ingalls Lagoon (Yuma Co.). One of many lagoons, sloughs, and backwaters that once occupied abandoned meander bends and marshes of the Colorado River. Named for Frank S. Ingalls, who came to Yuma in 1883 to take charge of the Yuma Territorial Prison. Ingalls was an early advocate of irrigated agriculture in the Yuma area. Apparently his efforts were successful—the lagoon that bore his name has long since been drained and replaced with agricultural fields and orange orchards. 2 mi N of present-day Somerton. 32°37′32″N, 114°43′05″W. 102 ft.

Interstate Highway 8 (I-8). U.S. Interstate Highway 8, N of GR and through S portion of SD. It generally parallels the Gila River's S bank between Yuma and Gila Bend. From Gila Bend the route travels E between the Maricopa and Sand Tank mountains to Casa Grande. Supplanted old U.S. Highway 80 and Arizona Highway 84.

Isla. Spanish for 'island'.

Isla Gore (AG). This low mudflat island at mouth of Río Colorado is inundated by extreme spring tides. Separated from Isla Montague by Estero Chayo. Vegetated with maritime halophytes, including *Distichlis palmeri* and *Cressa truxillensis.* When the Río Colorado regularly flowed to the sea, the 9-m (30-ft) tidal range here produced a tidal bore that occasionally sank river vessels and rendered riverbanks uninhabitable. Because of the forces of current and tide on sand and mud, this and the other delta islands are notoriously capricious in shape and location; for cartographers and navigators, they are more concept than place; for intrepid boaters who go ashore, they are memorable exercises in floundering in bottomless mud and up slippery banks.

Named by Hardy (1829) for Sir John Gore (1772–1836), a vice-admiral in the British navy who had an illustrious career; he also married the eldest daughter of Admiral Sir George Montagu (see Isla Montague) and evidently was a captain or friend of Hardy (Stephen & Lee 1917). Spelled Goree by Ives (1861). 31°42′50″N, 114°41′19″W. 3 m.

Isla Montague (AG). Large silt island in mouth of Río Colorado. It is inundated by extreme spring tides. Named by Lt. Hardy (1829) for Admiral Sir George Montagu (the proper spelling), his patron and friend. Montagu was "one of the most worthy characters in the navy, and one who at all times proved himself a most zealous and deserving officer" (Ralfe 1828:26; see Stephen & Lee 1917). 31°44′39″N, 114°45′53″W. 8 m (Steve Nelson).

Islas Montague, Gore, and Pelícano form four mouths *(bocas)* for Río Colorado; from W to E these are Boca la Baja (after its proximity to Baja California), Estero Chayo (Spanish for 'dunce estuary'), Boca de

Figure 39.28. Isla Pinta.

Enmedio (Spanish for 'middle' or 'halfway'), and Boca el Abrigo (Spanish for 'shelter' or 'cover'). These islands support dense saltscrub, including *Distichlis palmeri*, used for grain by the Cucapás (Felger 2000; Felger, this volume, Chapter 15).

Isla Pelícano (AG). Mudflat island at mouth of Colorado River, E of Isla Gore. Intermittently covered by tides. Spanish for 'pelican'. Not to be confused with two sandbars named Pelican Island and Gull Island by Lt. George H. Derby, in Río Colorado channel S of Point Invincible (Derby 1969). 31°45'05"N, 114°40'05"W. Sea level.

Isla Pinta (CP). Two granite outliers or "islands" off W "shore" of Sierra Pinta, 4.5 mi NW of Heart Tank. Should be Islas Pintas. Name from Sierra Pinta. 32°19'55"N, 113°36'49"W. 2,007 ft.

Isla Sacatosa (AG). Long, low-lying ridge of near-shore seashells about 33 mi N of San Felipe. The accumulation of shells is formed by erosion of seaward mudflats

and accompanying landward transport of shells. Technically, it is a *chenier,* currently forming because of the cessation of delivery of sediment to the delta. The study of cheniers offers important evidence for the extent, history, and effects of freshwater flow from the Colorado River into its estuary at the head of the Gulf of California (Rodriguez et al. 2001). Standing about 30 m wide and 3 m above the surrounding mudflats, Isla Sacatosa is an island during most tides and only rarely (perhaps once or twice a year) covered at extreme high tide. A local fisherman reports that the island's name—*sacatosa*—comes from the Spanish name for the grass *Distichlis palmeri*, which grows on the island (Karl Flessa). 31°30'6"N, 114°51'29"W. Intertidal.

Isla Vega (AG). A series of shelly bars or small islands rather than a single chenier island. R. W. Thompson (1968) suggests that these islands began to form after the completion of Hoover Dam cut off the sediment supply to the delta. See Isla Sacatosa; Rodriguez et al. 2001. Usually covered by spring high tides and has little to no vegetation (Karl Flessa). Name comes from "Vega Island," used by Thompson (1968:113). In Spanish, Vega can be a surname or can mean 'fertile lowland' or 'water meadow'. Local fishermen refer it as Las Isletas. 31°22'1"N, 114°51'39"W. Intertidal.

Islas San Jorge (Gulf of California, Sonora). Group of three small, rocky islands 41 km SE of Puerto Peñasco. An important seabird colony and breeding ground, especially for brown boobies *(Sula leucogaster)*, double-crested cormorants *(Phalacrocorax auritius)*, Brandt's cormorants *(Phalacrocorax penicillatus)*, Heerman's gulls *(Larus heermani)*, red-billed tropicbirds *(Phaethon aetherus)*, and Craveri's murrelets *(Synthliboramphus craveri)*. Mexican fishing bats *(Myotis vivesi)* also live on the island. Like other gulf islands, San Jorge was mined for guano in the mid-1800s, peaking in 1861 (Donlon 2003).

Inadvertently introduced by guano miners, non-native Norway, black, and Polynesian rats *(Rattus* spp.) preyed on bird eggs and birds, threatening the bird populations. Innovations in rodenticide have allowed target-species eradication of rats from the islands (Donlon et al. 2002). The sole plant species is *Chenopodium murale*, which is not native to the New World. There are no other mammals or reptiles. For the importance of the marine habitat, see Brusca, this volume, and Hastings & Findley, this volume.

All gulf islands have federal protection of terrestrial flora and fauna. Local fishermen are experimenting with and evaluating options for protecting the marine resources surrounding the island, such as establishing no-take zones or perhaps someday setting it aside as a biosphere reserve (see Boyer, this volume, Chapter 34; Hastings & Findley, this volume, Chapter 26).

Figure 39.29. Islas San Jorge. (Photo by Carlos Navarro)

Named by Lt. Robert William Hale Hardy of the British Royal Navy in 1826 (1829:304–305): "At two we saw a white island.... This land is composed of four small islands, about one hundred yards wide, and extending in a straight line about two thousand. As they do not appear on any charts, which have all been constructed on conjecture, I gave them the name of George's Islands, in honour of His Majesty George the Fourth." Hardy's fourth island is an intertidal reef.

Lighthouse stands on summit at 31°00′36″N, 113°14′38″W (WGS84). 236 ft.

Isletas, Las (AG). See Isla Vega. Spanish for 'the little islands'.

Ivalon (Yuma Co.). Old railroad siding and locale on Southern Pacific Railroad immediately E of Yuma and W of Araby. Today this is East Yard of railroad complex. "Ivalon was just a name" (Granger 1960:222). = Avalon. 32°41′14″N, 113°35′41″W. 215 ft.

Ives Flow (PI). The largest and southernmost lava flow in the Pinacate volcanic field, between Sierra Blanca and Pinacate Peak and covering more than 75 km². Composition of its lava is different from that of other Pinacate flows. Named by Dan Lynch (1981) for Ronald Lorenz Ives, historian and geographer who first visited region in 1932, on foot (see Ives 1989). Center is approximately 31°41′N, 113°28′W. 100 to 700 m.

J

Jack in the Pulpit (GR). "A most remarkable pinnacle of volcanic rock" (Bryan 1925:225) in NW Sand Tank Mountains, 17 mi SE of Gila Bend. This high butte is an eroded remnant of the ridge's topmost lava bed. It reminds some people of a preacher in a pulpit above the congregation (remember Orson Welles in the 1956 movie *Moby Dick*). 32°45′02″N, 112°32′45″W. 2,638 ft.

Jacks Well (CP). Well drilled in 1967 by Johnny Childs near Daniels Arroyo, 2.5 mi NE of Charlie Bell Pass in Growler Mountains. Named for CP employee C. "Jack" Garrett. 32°24′50″N, 113°03′00″W. 1,275 ft.

Jacksons Hole Tinaja (OP). This intermittent, bedrock tinaja 1.8 mi N of Dripping Springs in Puerto Blanco Mountains is located out in the valley. It is 5 ft deep and site of much prehistoric and historic use. Named for Earl Jackson, former director of Southwest Parks and Monuments Association, who liked to watch birds here (Bill Hoy). 32°02′58″N, 112°53′53″W. 1,700 ft.

Jaeger Wagon Road (GR, CP). Old freight trail from Ajo to Yuma. When the copper mine at Ajo opened after the Gadsden Purchase in 1854, Louis J. F. Jaeger pioneered two wagon roads to carry goods from Yuma to Ajo and to return with ore, which was shipped down the Colorado River by steamer and then on to Wales for smelting. The southern route roughly follows the mod-

Figure 39.30. Javelina Mountain. (Photo by Dale S. Turner)

ern road from Ajo to Bates Well and then to Las Playas, where it tied into El Camino del Diablo. The northern route followed the Gila Trail from Yuma to Don Diego Tanks and then SE to Ajo. A third route, possibly used by Jaeger, went past Cabeza Prieta Tanks. See Beattie 1928, Hargett 1967, Hoy 1995, Irwin ca. 1970. = Yeager, Iaeger. From German *Jäger*, 'hunter' or 'rifleman'.

Jarapeña, Volcán (PI). See Volcán Jarapeña.

Javelina Mountain (SD). Massive individual mountain within the Sand Tank range, 20 mi SE of Gila Bend. Its summit, Maricopa Peak, is the high point of the Sand Tank Mountains. Populations of Pleistocene relict plants, such as *Juniperus coahuilensis* and *Quercus turbinella*, occur here. Largely composed of gneiss and schist. Javelinas (collared peccaries, *Pecari tajacu*) are relative newcomers to this part of the desert (Davis 2001; Sowls 1997). 32°45′08″N, 112°22′45″W. 4,084 ft.

Javelina Tank (GR). Livestock tank 4 mi E of Hat Mountain in Sauceda Mountains. 32°37′31″N, 112°40′24″W. 1,790 ft.

Javelina Tinajas (OP). Series of three intermittent plunge-pool tinajas downstream from Wild Horse Tank, 1.5 mi E of Tillotson Peak. 32°01′19″N, 112°44′11″W. 2,275 ft.

Javelina Well (SD). Now-dry well 2 mi N of Maricopa Peak, developed by the Bender family in 1919 (Homburg et al. 1994). 32°46′55″N, 112°22′47″W. 2,240 ft.

Jiyi-jho'ag (Yuma Co.). See Wellton.

John the Baptist Mountains (Pima Co.). Basalt hills 7 mi S of Ajo. Named for John C. Butala, a hermit who had a cabin on E side of this range. He died in 1961. Likely nicknamed John the Baptist because of puns on his name or his appearance as a wild-eyed, wild-haired, ascetic prophet (Peaden 1978). 32°15′24″N, 112°54′21″W. 2,161 ft.

Figure 39.31. Jose Juan Tank.

Johnson Well (GR). Former ranch, cattle tank, and well, 3 mi S of Maricopa Peak. Developed by the Clements family about 1912 and later run by Oliver Johnson and then the Bender family. Later sold to Louis Johnson and partners, who included actor John Wayne (Letty Bender Hofstra and Anita Bender McGee; see also Chapter 7, this volume). =Clements Well, Johnsons Ranch. May =Stout's Well. 32°42′44″N, 112°21′23″W. 2,475 ft.

Jolla Wash, La (GR, PI). Arroyo 5 mi SE of Tinajas Altas. It originates just S of Coyote Wash, rounds the N end of Sierra de la Lechuguilla, crosses the international border, flows infrequently past La Joyita truck stop along Mexico Highway 2, and dies in the Gran Desierto sand sea. Spanish for 'jewel'; perhaps from *hoya*, Spanish for 'basin' or 'riverbed'. =La Joya. Source at 32°15′10″N, 113°56′42″W. 1,060 ft.

Jose Juan Hill (OP). Small hill 0.8 miles E of Jose Juan Tank. Contains a small outcrop of limestone on its north slope, one of only a few in this region. 32°05′10″N, 113°04′58″W. 1,248 ft.

Jose Juan Tank (CP). Site of prehistoric charco and *akciñ* farming area on San Cristobal Wash in Growler Valley, 24 mi SW of Ajo. Ranchers deepened the charco and added a small dam; in 1956 CP staff greatly enlarged the stock tank for use by wildlife. Pond is now intermittent here. Named for José Juan Orosco, an Hia C'ed O'odham hunting guide and medicine man who lived in vicinity. Seasonally, this represo supports rich wetland flora, some of which are not known elsewhere in the refuge, e.g., *Verbena bracteata.* 32°05′14″N, 113°05′51″W. 1,090 ft.

Joyita, La (PI). Truck stop and restaurant on Mexico Highway 2. It is 1.2 km NW of Cerro Pinto and 3.4 km W of El Sahuaro. A well was dug here in 1931 to serve travelers on the primitive Sonoyta–San Luis trail. Likely named (Spanish for 'little jewel') after nearby La Jolla Wash or La Joya Vieja ('old jewel', perhaps 'old pit') mining prospect in W Sierra del Viejo. 32°14′30″N, 114°03′45″W. 260 m.

Juñ Kaij (OP). See Bates Well.

Juniper Tank (GR). Catchment dam built in 1987 for wildlife, 1.2 mi WSW of Squaw Tit in Sand Tank Mountains. Possibly named for relict juniper (*Juniperus coahuilensis*) growing in area. =AGFD 949. 32°40′17″N, 112°23′50″W. 3,750 ft.

K

Ka:do:di Do'ag (TON). A mountain with unusual marble-like pebbles, 20 mi E of Ajo, between S-toha Bidga (Stoa Pitk) and Coffeepot Well. O'odham tossed marbles to forecast events or to select gambling partners. From O'odham *ga to:di* ('marble'; 'marble mountain'). 32°29′32″N, 112°32′44″W. 3,124 ft.

Kaka (TON). One of the oldest Tohono O'odham settlements (King 1961), this village is 33 mi NW of Ajo. Hia C'ed O'odham formerly visited Tohono O'odham here. See McGuire & Mayro 1978. O'odham for 'cleared fields'. =Do'ag We:co, 'under the mountain' (a name also used for Darby Wells). 32°30′42″N, 112°19′07″W. 2,255 ft.

Kaka Valley (TON). Valley in NW Tohono O'odham Nation. 32°34′05″N, 112°12′11″W. 2,035 ft.

Kaka Wash (TON). Arroyo beginning in GR and running E through village of Kaka. Joins Kohatk Wash at 32°34′35″N, 112°12′07″W. 2,015 ft.

Kalilville (Pima Co.). Store and settlement operated by Lebanese Syde Kalil and his family from 1924 to 1950 at the border where Lukeville is now. =Kaliltown. 31°52′50″N, 112°49′01″W. 1,400 ft.

Kim (Yuma Co.). Old railroad siding on Southern Pacific Railroad 2.4 mi E of Mohawk Pass. Named by SPRR president Epes Randolph for his Chinese cook, Kim. Apparently, Kim had never seen his "town," which consisted of only a single-track siding on a rather austere bajada of the Mohawk Mountains, so Randolph arranged for him to be dropped off and picked up by the next train. When Kim was asked what he thought of his town, he replied, "Fine! Fine! Lots of room to grow!" (Granger 1960:377). 32°44′05″N, 113°42′06″W. 399 ft.

Kino Crater (PI). A volcanic crater 15 m deep, about halfway between Badilla and Celaya craters, 18 km N of Pinacate Peak. Named for Jesuit missionary and explorer Padre Eusebio Kino. =Cráter Kino. 31°58′59″N, 113°30′32″W. 300 m.

Kino Pass (OP). The pass between Bates Well and Acuña Valley, E of Kino Peak. =Keno Pass. 32°06'36"N, 112°56'45"W. 1,810 ft.

Kino Peak (OP). Summit and eroded neck of extinct volcano that formed the Bates Mountains. Named in honor of Padre Kino. 32°06'34"N, 112°57'17"W. 3,197 ft.

Kino Tinajas (OP). Series of 6 small intermittent tinajas reportedly 1.5 mi NW of Kino Peak. May be in vicinity of 32°07'27"N, 112°57'47"W, 1,600 ft, but Brown et al. (1983) believe this location was inaccurately reported in OP files.

Kinter (Yuma Co.). Active railroad siding on Southern Pacific Railroad 2.4 mi W of Dome. If, as historians believe, Hernando Alarcón ascended the Gila River, the vicinity of Kinter may be the place where he turned back in September 1540 on his second trip inland from the Colorado delta. At the same place, Melchior Díaz later found the tree bearing the inscription, "Alarcón reached this point. At the foot of this tree there are letters" (Flint & Flint 2005). The nearby McPhaul bridge is named for Harry McPhaul, who had a copper prospect and marble claims at the N end of Gila Mountains (Wilson 1933). 32°45'24"N, 114°23'35"W. 180 ft.

Kohatk Wash (GR, TON). Arroyo beginning in SE Sand Tank Mountains and running into Tohono O'odham Nation. Named for an O'odham dialect group intermediate between Pima and Papago. =Kohaḍk, Kuhaḍk. Joins Santa Rosa Wash at 32°37'01"N, 111°55'50"N. 1,510 ft. The confluence is in Lake St. Clair, the intermittent impoundment created by Tat Momolikot Dam.

Ko'okomaḍk-kam (Pima Co.). A mountain near Darby Well. Perhaps =Black Mountain. O'odham for 'place of the blue palo verde'.

Kuakatch village and **Kuakatch Pass** (Pima Co., TON). Village and gap where wash cuts through N end of Ajo Mountains, adjacent to OP. Village at 32°08'17"N, 112°39'41"W. 2,129 ft. Pass at 32°07'46"N, 112°39'01"W. 2,160 ft.

Kuakatch Wash (OP). Major arroyo at N end of Ajo Mountains. See Walls Well. =Kuagĭ Ka:c, Ku:kack, Kw:kadc. O'odham for 'end of the mountain'. Joins Cuerda de Leña Wash at 32°11'05"N, 112°53'41"W. 1,450 ft.

Kui Vo'i (Maricopa Co.). Former O'odham settlement near Gila Bend. =Kui Vo'o, Kuivo, Kuevo. O'odham for 'mesquite tree lying down' or 'driftwood lying down'. See Gila Bend.

Kusvo To:b Do'ag (Yuma Co.). Mountain and spring near O'odham settlement at Mohawk and Mohawk Mountains. O'odham for 'twisted-neck mountain', perhaps the landmark northern summit pinnacle, which is labeled Mohawk Peak on some maps (1,975 ft). Village

Figure 39.32. *Kino Peak.*

just N of mountain was called To:b Do'ag ('neck mountain'). =Goosawa Toaptoak. See Growler.

L

Lacewell Pass (TON). U.S. Customs Service name for smugglers' pass in southern Sierra de Santa Rosa, 2 mi NW of international boundary monument 162. 31°50'18"N, 112°35'13"W. 1,840 ft.

Lago Díaz. See Playa Díaz.

Laguna. Spanish for 'lagoon', 'small lake', or 'tidal marsh'.

Laguna Diablo (BC). See Sierra San Pedro Mártir.

Laguna del Indio (AG). See Ciénega del Indio.

Laguna Prieta (Sonora). An intermittent lake 25 km SE of San Luis R.C. About 700 m by 1000 m if full, it has a shallow water table and small, vegetated pools of brackish water at the margins of its barren salt pan. It is surrounded by low, shifting dunes. The water level has apparently dropped since pumping of groundwater in nearby areas to N began in mid-twentieth century. Cucapás once farmed corn and tepary beans here, and Hia C'ed O'odham visited here, conferring the name Vapk, 'reeds'. See Ezcurra et al. 1988; Felger 2000; Hayden, this volume, Chapter 8; Lumholtz 1912.

When he visited here in 1750, Jesuit missionary Jacobo Sedelmayr reported, "We found water and a big canebrake among the dunes. It was about three arquebus shots long and formed a lagoon where there are pools of water all year long. The water is sweet where it comes out but it gets a little salty away from the source. There is pasturage around the water" (Matson & Fontana 1996:30). Sedelmayr named it San Juan Nepomuzeno (Saint John Nepomuck).

Spanish for 'dark lake'. =Vapk (O'odham for 'bullrush', *Scirpus* spp. [Rea 1997]). 32°18'30"N, 114°33'25"W. 40 m.

Laguna Salada (BC). A large, internally drained but usually dry lakebed basin (playa) 24 km SW of Mexicali. This alkali flat, between Sierra de los Cucapá and Sierra Juárez, joins the vast expanse of tidal salt flats that extend between these ranges to the gulf. It is nearly 100 km long and over 20 km wide. Fradkin (1995:335) reports that "it filled, at least partially, six times between 1884 and 1928." See Williams, this volume. Spanish for 'salty lake', appropriate since extreme evaporation precipitates salts. =Macuata Basin, Laguna Macuata, Laguna Muquata (from *ha wi mǝk,* Cocopah for 'water on the other side of the mountain' [Kelly 1977:40]); Jaeger (1958) contends that it may mean 'Indian', 'yellow', 'yellow place', or 'yellow water' and at one time was called Río Amarillo (Spanish for 'Yellow River'); Pattie's Basin. 32°22′N, 115°35′W. 5 m below sea level.

Laja, La (PI). See Tezontle Cone.

Lake Ajo (Pima Co.). Sewage treatment pond on E side of Ajo and NW base of tailings piles. Noted for sightings of shore- and waterbirds; stopover on flyway. For example, a flock of about 50 white pelicans rested there in October 2003 (*Ajo Copper News,* October 8, 2003). 32°23′12N, 112°51′07″W. 1,680 ft.

Lamb Tank (GR). Subterranean water tank built for wildlife in 1995 in S Tinajas Altas Mountains, at mouth of Surveyors Canyon. Named for young bighorn sheep. 32°16′26″N, 114°01′36″W. 1,200 ft.

Lechuguilla Tank (Sonora). Reported by Lumholtz (1912:239) as natural, intermittent tinaja in canyon on SW side of Sierra Lechuguilla. Used for watering cattle on the long drive from Sonoyta to San Luis R.C. Its precise location is unknown.

Lechuguilla Valley, or **Lechuguilla Desert** (GR). The arid valley-plain between the Cabeza Prieta and Tinaja Altas mountains. It is drained by Coyote Wash to the N and La Jolla Wash to the S. *Lechuguilla* is a generic Spanish name for agave, here *Agave deserti.* 32°28′08″N, 114°04′27″W. 500–1,300 ft.

LeSage (Yuma Co.). A small farming community and tourist facility in late 1920s, about 7 mi W of Aztec and 1 mi ENE of Dateland at Musina siding. It was founded by and named for Frenchman Pierre Lesage (the correct spelling); it burned down about 1931 (Barnes 1935; Granger 1983; Bob Lenon). About 32°47′44″N, 113°32′25″W. 445 ft.

Lerdo. See Colonia Lerdo.

Lewis Well (Pima Co.). Well along Gunsight Wash 0.3 mi E of Arizona Highway 85. It served travelers and livestock on Ajo-Tucson road in early twentieth century. 32°14′16″N, 112°44′39″W. 1,810 ft.

Ligurta (Yuma Co.). Tourist facilities on I-8, eight mi W of Wellton. Derivation of name unknown, but Granger

(1960) speculates that it may come from Spanish *lagarto,* 'lizard'. =Fossil Point. 32°40′28″N, 114°17′47″W. 234 ft.

Ligurta Wash (Yuma Co.). Arroyo draining NE Gila Mountains, including the eastern branch of Woodcutters Canyon and Sheep Mountain. To reach the Gila River, it crosses the Wellton-Mohawk Canal by means of a siphon. Ligurta Wash is not named on topo maps, but the Arizona Highway Department places it 2.5 mi E of Ligurta, where it crosses I-8 at 32°39′33″N, 114°15′06″W. 265 ft.

Lime Hill (Pima Co.). Hill 4 mi N of Bates Well. A source of marble mined for lime flux, once used in Ajo mine furnaces. The mines on the hill are named Growler Mica Mine and Phelps-Dodge Limestone. 32°13′39″N, 112°55′30″W. 1,840 ft.

Lisas, Estero las (AG). See Estero las Lisas.

Little Ajo Mountains (Pima Co., CP). Small range S and W of Ajo. Summit is Black Mountain. 32°19′25″N, 112°50′32″W. 3,008 ft.

Little Bruce Tank (SD). A stock tank 8.5 mi S of Mobile. Dug by O. K. "Red" Bruce for the Conley family (Winnie Conley Henry). Bruce also drove a water truck and operated heavy equipment in the Gila Bend area. 1.3 mi WNW of Big [Bruce] Tank. 32°56′03″N, 112°16′48W. 1,630 ft.

Little Eberling Tank (Pima Co.). See Eberling Tank.

Little Pass (CP). Narrow gap between Cabeza Prieta Mountains and Buck Peak; counterpart to Big Pass, 5 mi to the NW. 32°21′03″N, 113°53′28″W. 1,240 ft.

Little Rainbow Valley (SD, Maricopa Co.). Valley W of Rainbow Valley, between Buckeye Hills on N and Maricopa Mountains on S. It is drained by Rainbow Wash. 33°15′18″N, 112°34′18″W. 1,000 ft.

Little Table Top (TON). Flat-topped mountain 3.7 mi S of big Table Top Mountains. 32°42′09″N, 112°08′30″W. 3,097 ft.

Little Tenmile Wash (OP). Wash draining Puerto Blanco Mountains and La Abra Plain, eventually joining Sonoyta River E of Santo Domingo. Crosses international border 1.2 mi W of monument 170 at 31°55′21″N, 112°57′24″W. 1,190 ft.

Little Tule Tank (CP). Small rock tank 4 mi W of Ajo in streambed of Copper Canyon. It was built by Boy Scouts in 1961 and holds water for only a short time. 32°21′39″N, 112°55′58″W. 1,800 ft.

Little Tule Well (CP). Well and windmill in Copper Canyon, 5 mi W of Ajo. Originally dug about 1913 by Thomas Childs for cattle, it now serves wildlife. Called Tule Well on some old maps. 32°22′14″N, 112°57′02″W. 1,685 ft.

Locomotive Rock (Pima Co.). Distinctive conglomerate rock formation whose silhouette from certain directions resembles a small, old-time railroad locomotive with flared smokestack. 3 mi S of Ajo. =Locomotive Peak; see Vav Ola Do'ag. 32°19′31″N, 112°52′07″W. 2,107 ft.

Lookout Mountain (GR). A summit 3 mi E of Black Gap in NW Sauceda Mountains and 2 mi SW of Lookout Well. Presumably named for a lookout tower on the aerial-gunnery range. 32°44′35″N, 112°46′28″W. 2,681 ft.

Lookout Well (GR). Drilled well N of Sauceda Mountains, near a target lookout tower in aerial-gunnery range. 12 mi S of Gila Bend. 32°45′42″N, 112°44′39″W. 1,122 ft.

Looseboom Tank (Yuma Co.). Tinaja in northern Mohawk Mountains, N of I-8 and near Mohawk Peak. Precise location unknown. Possibly in vicinity of 32°45′08″N, 113°45′12″W. 580 ft.

López Collada, Estación (AG). See Estación López Collada.

Lord Will Mine (GR). Small group of adits and shafts on E side of Mohawk Mountains, 6.1 mi N of Monreal Well. Worked by Don, Phil, and John Childs during 1950s and 1960s. 32°27′01″N, 113°27′59″W. 820 ft.

Los Vidrios (PI). See Vidrios, Los.

Lost. . . . We have no coordinates for the region's legendary Lost Bell, Lost B-17, Lost Jabonero Mine (Soapmaker's Mine), Lost Mission, Lost Placer Gold, Lost Spanish Rifles, Lost Valley, Lost Wagon Train, or Lost Mentira Tank (a rumored tinaja somewhere near northern Growler Mountains or western Childs Mountain: *mentira* is Spanish for 'lie', since few people believe that it could be where it is [Lee Price]).

Lost Cabin Mine (OP). Small mine group in northern Sonoyta Mountains, 4.2 mi NW of Lukeville. 31°56′14″N, 112°50′39″W. 1,680 ft.

Lost City (CP). Extensive prehistoric campsite in Growler Valley, eastern CP, 18 mi SW of Ajo. Never a city with walls, it was a stopover on salt- and shell-gathering trips to Gulf of California. Now a treeless, silty flat; presumably, the vegetation was different or more lush when area was used as a campsite. 1,000 ft.

Lost Horse Peak (SD). Lone hill, 1.5 mi S of I-8 and 6.5 mi NNE of Maricopa Peak. Story behind the name would be worth hearing; names given to the wandering horse by the stranded cowboy would probably be rejected by cartographers. 32°49′54″N, 112°18′39″W. 2,175 ft.

Lost Horse Tank (SD). Stock pond (represo) 0.6 mi SSW of I-8's Freeman Road interchange. Presumably named for neighboring Lost Horse Peak, or vice versa. 32°50′32″N, 112°19′24″W. 1,820 ft.

Lower Well (CP). Abandoned livestock well and corral 9 mi WSW of Ajo on Daniels Arroyo. Possibly 'lower' or downstream from Adobe Wells and Windmill, where the Cameron family ran cattle. =West Well. 32°19′48″N, 113°01′08″W. 1,470 ft.

Luke Air Force Range (=GR). Previous name of Goldwater Range. Named for Frank Luke, World War I ace pilot (see Lukeville).

Lukeville (Pima Co.). Settlement and U.S. Customs station on international border N of Sonoyta. Founded by Charles Luke and named for himself or his son, World War I flying ace Frank Luke Jr., who was killed in action September 29, 1918. Frank was credited with destroying 11 enemy balloons and 4 airplanes (Franzi & Luke 1998; Hall 1928). He had worked at the Ajo mine, and his family owned this townsite. East of former border crossing at Dowling, where Jeff Milton (see Milton Mine) once had his office. =Gringo Pass, currently owned by Alfred "Al" Gay; *gringo* is an ethnic slur. =Kaliltown or Kalilville, owned by Syde Kalil from 1924 to 1950. 31°52′50″N, 112°49′01″W. 1,410 ft.

Luke-Williams Airfields (GR). Assortment of triangular-shaped airfields scattered at strategic locations across the eastern Goldwater Range. Most were built during World War II or the 1950s. None are active landing fields but instead serve as emergency landing fields or as target areas. Numerous other fields were constructed on the GR over the years; some were simple dirt strips that were later abandoned, while others were turned over to civilian uses.

　　Luke Number 7 (GR). In Childs Valley 7 mi N of Childs Mountain. =Williams Number 1. 32°31′57″N, 112°56′08″W. 1,210 ft.

　　Luke Number 8 (GR). N of Crater Mountains, 2.4 mi SSW of Midway. =Williams Number 2. 32°36′09″N, 112°52′10″W. 1,146 ft.

　　Luke Number 9 (GR). N of Crater Mountains, 2 mi NNW of Midway. =Williams Number 3. 32°39′33″N, 112°51′55″W. 1,100 ft.

　　Luke Number 10 (GR). W of Sauceda Mountains, 3.1 mi SSW of Black Gap. =Williams Number 4. 32°43′05″N, 112°50′49″W. 1,025 ft.

　　Luke Number 11 (GR). On N border of GR, 7 mi NW of Black Gap. =Williams Number 5. 32°49′25″N, 112°54′52″W. 802 ft.

　　Williams Number 6 (GR). N of White Hills, 7.6 mi SW of Gila Bend. 32°52′38″N, 112°48′32″W. 807 ft.

Lumholtz Tanks (PI). Tinajas somewhere S of Manje Cone. They were named by Ives (1964) for Carl Lumholtz (see Lumholtz 1912). These tinajas are not apparent today; possibly they filled with sand after rancher installed a concrete dam (Jim Gutmann). Perhaps vicinity of 31°53′N, 113°27′W. 300–400 m.

Lynchberg (PI). The Lynchberg *kipuka*—an island of older rock surrounded by younger lava—is the top of a granite peak that was almost buried by the Ives Flow in the southeastern Pinacate volcanic field. It is located more than 2 km N of Sierra Blanca. Recorded in 1993 by William D. "Bill" Peachey and C. T. "Tom" Bethard, it was a late discovery in Pinacate geology because its 23-m length is nearly hidden by pahoehoe lavas that had almost overtopped it from three directions. Name proposed by Peachey and Bethard in honor of Pinacate volcanologist Daniel Lynch, and secondarily for Lynchberg, Tennessee, where Jack Daniels "field solvent" is manufactured (Bill Peachey). 31°38′18″N, 113°29′11″W. 174 m.

M

MacDougal Crater (PI). Large maar crater in NW part of the Pinacate volcanic field, 1,100 m wide and 130 m deep, 26 km NW of Pinacate Peak. Relatively inaccessible floor provided a unique habitat for Turner's elegant study demonstrating the dynamic nature of vegetation change even in a very arid desert (Turner 1990; Turner et al. 2003). Named for Dr. Daniel Trembly MacDougal by Hornaday (1908). MacDougal founded the Carnegie Desert Laboratory on Tumamoc Hill in Tucson (McGinnies 1981) and was editor of *Plant World* journal (later known as *Ecology*). The lab is still a world leader in plant research and ecology. See Cerro Kino. =La Gran Depresión; Cráter MacDougal; Cráter Verdugo, Volcán El Verdugo, likely a misnomer and corruption of similar-sounding MacDougal, although *verdugo* (Spanish for 'executioner' or 'whip') is a common surname. 31°58′32″N, 113°37′35″W. 220 m at the crater rim.

MacDougal Pass (PI). Sandy gap through E side of Sierra Hornaday, 4 km SW of the present Rancho Victoria Guadalupe. The Hornaday (1908) expedition took its wagons through this long, sandy corridor between the lavas and the dunes from the border to MacDougal Crater. The present road to MacDougal Crater goes through another gap E of MacDougal Pass. 31°59′17″N, 113°36′16″W. 230 m.

Maggies Nipple (CP). Distinctive formation on ridgeline in Cabeza Prieta Mountains, 0.9 mi ENE from Halfway Tank. 32°20′36″N, 113°50′46″W. 2,400 ft.

Majors Tank (GR). Enhanced tinaja in a central canyon of the Copper Mountains, 0.5 mi WSW of Betty Lee Tank. Built in 1983, it holds water intermittently. Named for Orville "Major" Townsend, a heavy equipment operator and crew leader for Arizona Game and Fish Department (see Carr 1994:230); he worked on a number of waterhole development projects, and while sitting around the campfire one evening, the crew on this project voted to call it Major's Tank (Don Belknap).

USGS drops apostrophes from place-names. =Major Tank; AGFD #865. 32°29′55″N, 113°59′06″W. 1,200 ft.

Malpais Hill (GR). Lone basalt hill 27 mi SW of Gila Bend. Not the same as northern half of Aguila Mountains, which sometimes are labeled Malpais. Spanish for 'badlands', usually lava. 32°42′31″N, 113°04′35″W. 856 ft.

Manje Cone (PI). Volcanic cone 16 km NNE of Cráter Elegante. Named for soldier Juan Mateo Manje, a Spanish lieutenant detailed to accompany Padre Kino through the area in 1699. See Karns 1954. The precise location of Manje Cone merits further work (Jim Gutmann). Vicinity 31°54′N, 113°26′W. 500 m.

Margies Cove (SD). Central basin or valley within the Maricopa Mountains, 3.4 mi S of Margies Peak. Named for Margie Baker Woods. She and her husband, Desmund, assumed management of the Cactus Lodge, aka Lena's Place—a popular restaurant and nightclub near Cotton Center on Old Highway 80—from his parents, Lena and Jack Woods. When Arizona Highway 85 was built and paved in 1955, they moved the business to about milepost 134 on the new highway. They named it the Cosmo, but patrons joked that "Drinks cos' mo' at the Cosmo than the next place." Margie and Desmund loved to wander the nearby desert and cook over campfire coals, so he put a jeep trail into the mountains, now a hiking trail known as Margies Cove Trail (John Laird, Winnie Conley Henry). Reportedly, Margie's grave is in these mountains; the Cosmo is but a memory. 33°06′59″N, 112°34′32″W. 1,150 ft.

Margies Peak (SD). Prominent summit in N portion of Maricopa Mountains, 6.1 mi NE of Cotton Center. 33°09′33″N, 112°36′19″W. 2,493 ft.

Maricopa County. Arizona government administrative subdivision that covers northeastern GR and most of SD. County seat is Phoenix. Named for Maricopa Indians who lived along Gila River.

Maricopa Mountains (SD). Major mountain range N of GR and 36 mi SW of Phoenix, composed largely of Precambrian granites and gneiss. In the late 1980s it was a candidate site for the Superconducting Super Collider (SSC), which would have ringed the range with a 90-km-circumference tunnel to shoot 20TeV beams of protons and attempt to discover the Higgs boson and the LSP, the lightest supersymetric particle, revealing a mirror universe to our own. The project was awarded to Texas, where it died in 1993 for lack of funding. The name Maricopa Mountains used to apply to a much larger group of mountains. During the 1800s the Sierra Estrellas were considered part of the Maricopas, and before 1920 what are now called the Sand Tank Mountains also bore the name. That may explain why the summit of the Sand Tanks is called Maricopa Peak. Today the Maricopas are relegated to that portion of the former chain that lies N of I-8 but SW of Sierra Estrella. High point is unnamed summit at 3,272 ft in S portion of the range. 32°56′51″N, 112°23′32″W. 3,272 ft.

Also **North Maricopa Mountains Wilderness** (SD). Encompasses the N third of Maricopa Mountains. Created in 1990, it covers 63,200 acres and is managed by the Bureau of Land Management. It was incorporated into SD in 2001.

Also **South Maricopa Mountains Wilderness** (SD). Covers a 13-mi length of the Maricopa Mountains immediately N of I-8. Created in 1990, it covers 60,100 acres and is managed by the Bureau of Land Management. It was incorporated into SD in 2001.

Maricopa Mountains Catchments (SD, Maricopa Co.). Wildlife water catchments and guzzler troughs in the Maricopa Mountains, numbered chronologically.

Number 1 (SD). =AGFD #443. 1.7 mi ESE of Margies Peak. 33°09′15″N, 112°34′39″W. 1,245 ft.

Number 2 (SD). =AGFD #444. 0.2 mi SSW of Hazen Well. 33°07′10″N, 112°34′59″W. 1,110 ft.

Number 3 (SD). =AGFD #445. 2.4 mi SE of Hazen Well. 33°06′07″N, 112°32′52″W. 1,400 ft.

Number 4 (SD). =AGFD #446. 4.5 mi ESE of Margies Peak. 33°08′00″N, 112°32′01″W. 1,380 ft.

Number 5 (SD). =AGFD #447. 3.7 mi NE of Margies Peak. 33°11′10″N, 112°33′04″W. 1,370 ft.

Number 6 (SD). =AGFD #448. 2.0 mi NE of Margies Peak. 33°10′52″N, 112°35′02″W. 1,190 ft.

Number 7 (SD). =AGFD #449. 3.4 mi SSW of Margies Peak. 33°06′48″N, 112°37′31″W. 900 ft.

Number 8 (SD). =AGFD #450. 6.3 mi S of Margies Peak. 33°04′04″N, 112°36′34″W. 900 ft.

Number 9 (SD). =AGFD #451. 1.3 mi SW of Butterfield Pass. 33°02′12″N, 112°29′30″W. 1,520 ft.

Number 10 (SD). =AGFD #452. 3.2 mi W of Desert Station. 33°01′32″N, 112°33′17″W. 1,120 ft.

Number 11 (SD). =AGFD #453. 7.2 mi NW of Espanto Mountain. 33°09′02″N, 112°25′53″W. 1,220 ft.

Number 12 (SD). =AGFD #454. 3.5 mi NE of Butterfield Pass. 33°04′52″N, 112°24′48″W. 1,480 ft.

Number 13 (SD). =AGFD #707. 4.1 mi NNE of Big Horn. 32°54′31″N, 112°21′33″W. 2,120 ft.

Number 14 (SD). =AGFD #708. 4.6 mi NNW of Big Horn. 32°55′21″N, 112°25′04″W. 1,800 ft.

Maricopa Peak (SD). Summit of Javelina Mountain and high point of Sand Tank Mountains, 23 mi ESE of Gila Bend. Likely derived its name because the Sand Tank Mountains were once considered part of the Maricopa Mountains. Maricopa Peak would have been the high point of that range. Today the Maricopa Mountains are considered a separate range to the N of I-8, and the Sand Tank Mountains have their own status. 32°45′08″N, 112°22′45″W. 4,084 ft.

Maricopa Road (SD, Maricopa). Arizona Highway 238 from Maricopa to Gila Bend. It roughly parallels the railway. Paved in 2001 through unfenced, open rangeland, it soon earned the nickname "Dead Cow Road" (Tim Turner). Fenced in 2004.

Martinez Mine (OP). Mine group at N end of Sonoyta Mountains, 1.5 miles SE of Senita Basin. Named for part-time prospector J. A. C. Martinez, a store clerk in the "gent's furnishings" of the Ajo co-op and later in Charles Luke's Palace Commercial Company in Lukeville (Hoy 1970). 31°56′56″N, 112°50′50″W. 1,829 ft.

Mayo, Cerro el (PI). See Cerro el Mayo.

Mayor, El (BC). Traditional Cucapá settlement on Río Hardy, 8 km above confluence with Río Colorado and near Sierra del Mayor. Spanish for 'major', 'chief', 'larger', 'older'. =Campo Río Mayor Solano (Spanish for 'east wind'); La Carpa (Spanish for 'carp' fish). 32°08′04″N, 115°16′59″W. 10 m.

McCray Well (Maricopa Co.). Well and corral on a S fork of Bender Wash, 8 mi SE of Gila Bend. 32°53′01″N, 112°35′54″W. 1,053 ft.

McMillan Mine (CP). Abandoned prospect tunnels in N Cabeza Prieta Mountains 0.4 mi NE of Buck Peak Tank. 32°23′19″N, 113°54′40″W. 1,420 ft.

Médanos (Sonora). See Mesa Rica. A farm 3 km NNE of Riíto also goes by this name.

Menagers Dam and **Menagers Lake** (TON). Earthen and rock dam across narrow gap between Sierra de la Nariz and Cerritos de la Angostura, in far southwestern corner of Tohono O'odham reservation. Built in early twentieth century by settler Joseph Menager to catch runoff from several arroyos that drain La Quituni Valley and Ali Chuk Valley; it was projected to be 180 ft long, 30 ft tall, and hold 15,000 acre-ft (Clotts 1915). Hia C'ed O'odham descendants there formerly made baskets of limberbush fiber rather than of nolina and yucca. =ʼAlĭ Jeg, ʼAlĭ jek, Aljek; Alĭ Chuk (O'odham for 'little opening'); Angostura Dam (Spanish for 'narrows'). 31°49′06″N, 112°32′41″W. 1,742 ft.

Mesa. Spanish for 'table land' or 'flat highland'.

Mesa de Andrade (AG). A sandy mesa above Río Colorado floodplain, 54 km S of San Luis R.C. and 5 km SW of Riíto. Detached from Mesa de Sonora by a former channel of the river. Named for land baron and promoter Guillermo Andrade, who capitalized on federally disposed *terrenos baldíos* ('idle or unused lands') to develop farmlands, villages, utilities, roads, and irrigation canals in Mexicali Valley and the delta between 1874 and 1905 (Hendricks 1967). =Colonia Lerdo Mesa. 32°05′N, 114°57′W. 8 m.

Not to be confused with the border-crossing town of Andrade (named for same person), 5 mi W of Yuma, in California.

Mesa Arenosa (AG). Coastal mesa between El Golfo and Bahía Adair. This arching mesa, on the N wall of the San Jacinto fault, is composed of Tertiary and younger Río Colorado deltaic sediments. The uplifted mesa slopes inland NE, so it drains into the dunes of the Gran Desierto. Its seaward bluff is heavily eroded, creating "badlands" NE of El Golfo and exposing notable fossil beds containing saltwater invertebrates as well as freshwater and terrestrial vertebrates. Vegetation on the mesa is low, sparse, and devoid of trees and cacti, except an occasional forlorn teddybear cholla (*Cylindropuntia bigelovii*), but sometimes includes expanses of spring wildflowers. 31°39′40″N, 114°24′30″W. 50–160 m.

Mesa de Malpais (PI). Flat-topped, basalt mesa between Sierra Viejo and Sierra Tuseral. About 6 km long and 3 km wide, it is a distinctive, triangular feature on satellite photos of area. 32°08′51″N, 113°52′43″W. 400 m.

Mesa Rica (Sonora). Railroad section settlement and division point at the western edge of the Gran Desierto dunes, 5 km SE of Riíto. It is km post 69 on the rail line. See Munro, this volume. =Fuentes Brotantes (Spanish for 'flowing wells'), Médanos (Spanish for 'dunes'). 32°08′06″N, 114°55′24″W. 10 m.

Mesa de San Luis (Sonora). The sandy plateau at NW margin of the Gran Desierto, S of international border. It is the northerly portion of Mesa de Sonora. At its western margin the mesa rises abruptly to form the eastern limit of the Río Colorado delta. Named for city of San Luis Río Colorado. 32°23′N, 114°48′W. 35 m.

Mesa de Sonora (Sonora). The eastern bluff above Río Colorado floodplain, from San Luis Río Colorado to El Golfo. It apparently includes Mesa de San Luis and is north of Mesa Arenoso. =Sonora Mesa.

Mesa Wash (SD, TON). Major wash on Tohono O'odham Nation, draining SE portion of Table Top Wilderness. Joins Santa Rosa Wash at 32°42′41″N, 111°55′22″W. 1,430 ft.

Mesquital (GR). A portion of Growler Wash running between the Granite and Aguila mountains (Bryan 1925:202). Bryan believed this mesquite bosque was the only favorable location in the region for raising livestock, since "mesquite beans would furnish a reliable stock food." This area was crossed by the old Tucson-Yuma road (Jaeger Wagon Road), which had more travel in those days and so may have been a name known to travelers. Today it is part of an active bombing range near Red Point and is seldom visited, so the name has fallen into disuse. In vicinity of 32°31′18″N, 113°20′00″W. 620 ft.

Mesquite Well (SD). A well in Sand Tank Mountains, 17 mi SE of Gila Bend. Before development in early 1900s, there was a rock tank and seep at the base of ephemeral waterfalls in the lava. Tom Farley's family homesteaded here and built a rock cabin in the 1940s. They had lived in Bosque, where Tom's father worked for the railroad, but his mother didn't like train noise, so the family moved to Mesquite Well (*Gila Bend Sun* 1999, 2004a, b, d). About 1953 Tom's wife was killed by lightning while they were sitting on the front porch of the cabin; he was not struck (John Laird). =Mesquite Springs, AGFD #433. 32°49′21″N, 112°28′07″W. 1,786 ft.

Mexico Highway 2 (PI, Sonora). The northernmost highway across Mexico, and only one connecting Baja California with mainland. In the 1930s much of the road between Sonoyta and San Luis R.C. was a treacherous single-track trail through rough lava and shifting sand dunes. Local drivers who knew the ways of the desert (*choferes del desierto*) hired out their cars and drove passengers and cargo across this perilous route, but many novices and tourists perished. When two cars met head-on in the sandy portion, the men would lift one of the vehicles and move it out of the road while one car passed, and then the men picked up the other car and put it back on the road. If there were not enough men to move the vehicle, they waited for another vehicle and more manpower (Barrios-Matrecito 1988; Julian Hayden). The Sonoyta–San Luis Highway portion was graded during World War II but not paved until 1953–1955. At one time it was named Albelardo L. Rodriguez Military Highway, after a Sonoran governor (Bill Hoy). Along this route Peter Matthiessen (1989) set an eerie tale about the last wolf bounty hunter in the Southwest, and Hayden (1998:27) photographed what he thought was a wolf track in 1973, but no wolves are verified from this region.

Mexico Highway 5 (BC). Highway between Mexicali and San Felipe along western edge of AG, forming its western boundary.

Mexico Highway 8 (Sonora). Highway between Sonoyta and Puerto Peñasco. One of the first paved highways in Sonora, it was finished during World War II for military reasons. In places it forms the eastern boundary of PI.

Miakam (Yuma Co.). See Antelope Hill.

Microondas la Lava (PI). See Cerro la Lava.

Middle Tank (SD). Stock tank E of Maricopa Mountains and 4.2 mi E of Estrella. 33°00′07″N, 112°20′41″W. 1,510 ft.

Midway (GR). Railroad siding on Tucson, Cornelia, & Gila Bend Railroad, halfway between Gila Bend and Ajo. 32°37′57″N, 112°51′08″W. 1,160 ft.

Midway Station (Maricopa Co.) Long-abandoned settlement and way station along old U.S. 80, 9.2 mi E of Sentinel. Not a railroad station, as the SPRR ran about 0.8 miles S of here. 32°53′26″N, 113°03′32″W. 839 ft.

Midway Wash (GR). Arroyo between Sauceda Mountains and Crater Range. Heads NW of Coffeepot Mountain and dissipates at a "mesquital" (shown on some maps), which here is a bosque not of mesquites but primarily of foothill palo verde *(Parkinsonia microphylla)* N of Crater Range (David Griffin). Named Midway since at Arizona Highway 85 crossing it is roughly midway between Gila Bend and Ajo. Crossing at 32°34′53″N, 112°52′23′W. 1,163 ft.

Milton Mine (OP). Mine group located on S flank of Puerto Blanco Mountains 2 mi W of Senita Basin. Owned by Jefferson "Jeff" Davis Milton, frontier lawman and guide to the William Hornaday expedition to the Pinacate Mountains in 1907. Milton was "the most interesting man in Sonoyta, or for that matter a hundred miles around" (Hornaday 1908:98). See Haley 1948. Nevertheless, relations between Milton and certain members of the Hornaday party were somewhat strained, partly because of Hornaday's East Coast aristocratic view of western frontiersmen but also because Hornaday laid claim to being the first to climb Pinacate Peak, which Milton had clearly climbed well before the expedition (Hartmann 1989:105). Of course, neither Hornaday nor Milton could lay true claim to the summit; Padre Eusebio Kino had climbed the peak in 1698, and undoubtedly countless Indian travelers had climbed the summit even earlier. Mine at 31°58′08″N, 112°53′22″W. 1,625 ft.

Mina del Desierto (PI). Mining prospect and tourist stop on Mexico Highway 2, 2.5 km W of Paso de Juana (Paso del Águila) in Sierra Nina. The prospects (silver and copper) are 5 km NE of the highway stop. Stop is at 32°06′55″N, 113°46′30″W. 290 m.

Mina Triángula (PI). Cinder mine along Mexico Highway 2, 2 km WNW of Los Vidrios. As of 1997 it was the only licensed cinder *(morusa)* mine in PI; it is in the buffer zone. Spanish for 'triangle'. 32°02′00″N, 113°26′23″W. 220 m.

Mine. We list many mines in this gazetteer, but usually only those with some notoriety or those named on maps. This region, however, is pocked with the diggings and blastings of many a person who tried to get rich from this largely barren land. Very few even made a living of it, much less became wealthy. A reading of the named claims and mines in the region divulges some of the emotions people must have felt over the years while scratching in this desert ground. Some felt hope (Lord Will, Esperanza, Golden Dream, Golden King). Others expressed gratitude (Thanksgiving Mine). A few may have succumbed to wishful thinking (Showers of Platinum, Showers of Silver, Golden Pheasant, High Grade). Maybe others sought enlightenment (Guiding Star Mine); a few expressed delight (Surprise, Golden Wonder), while others fell into despair (Last Chance), but most were probably confronted with a taste of reality (Poor Man, Old Soak, Long Lost).

For a more thorough inventory of the region's mines and claims, see Miller 1979 and Wilson 1933, as well as the records of the BLM, FWS, NPS, and other agencies charged with managing these lands. For a wonderful account of prospecting life in this area in the good old days, see Smith 1956.

Mobile (Maricopa Co.). Community 3 mi E of SD. Name commonly but mistakenly thought to have been applied by settlers or former slaves from Mobile, Alabama, but section house for Southern Pacific Railroad and hotel for train passengers were known as Mobile as early as 1916, before any influx of homesteaders. First homesteader was Edison Lung, an Anglo American who worked for the SPRR at Mobile and then stayed instead of accepting a transfer to Yuma. He and his wife, Elsie, established residence in 1921 and received their 320-acre homestead patent in 1925. In 1929 other homesteaders—mostly blacks—came to the area from Oklahoma or Texas, frequently by way of Phoenix. The community grew until the 1940s, but "cheap agriculture turned out to be an impossibility" due to scant capital for development and lack of reliable water (Swanson 1992:15). In 1966 Phoenix educator William Warren brought 55 black families to Mobile and settled them in a new subdivision called Tangier Acres, later adding Warren Acres. The community turned to hog farming as the town's industry, but in 1970 4,000 pigs had to be destroyed because of cholera, ending the pig-farming era. "Mobile never was a self-sufficient community" (Swanson 1992:40). 33°03′19″N, 112°16′16″W. 1,320 ft.

Mobile Valley (SD, Maricopa Co.). Valley extending S of Mobile and W of Booth Hills. 33°03′29″N, 112°15′16″W. 1,300 ft.

Mohawk (Yuma Co.). This name has been applied to at least three separate settlements near N end of Mohawk Mountains. The first was an 1857 Butterfield Overland Stage station and then town at N end of the range. With the laying of the railroad in 1880, the name was transposed to Mohawk Station in Mohawk Pass (=Mohawk Summit) where the line tops a low mountain pass. The name seems to have been bestowed by an unknown New York settler who brought place-names from his home state. This site reported the highest average monthly temperature in Arizona with 110.9°F maxima for July (Sellers & Hill 1974:24, 330–331).

Probably never an easy place to live, especially in the early days. In 1872 a man named John Killbright committed suicide when he took poison and jumped into a well (Annerino 1999). In the 1930s the station was run by Jim "Mesquite Jim" Renner, who was "an excellent shade-tree mechanic" (Bob Lenon). Also, Chrystoval, a third site to SE, confusingly carried the name Mohawk for a few years. 32°43′42″N, 113°45′14″W. 545 ft.

Figure 39.33. Mohawk Dunes.

Figure 39.34. Mohawk Mountains.

Mohawk Dunes (GR). Relatively stable eolian sand dunes extending 15 mi along W side of Mohawk Mountains and 2 mi out from range. During years of favorable rains these dunes may offer a spectacular display of spring wildflowers (Felger et al. 2003); among the 78 species of plants on the dunes are several of special conservation concern, such as *Cryptantha ganderi* and Schott's wire lettuce *(Stephanomeria schottii),* which was rediscovered 100 years after being first collected (Lehto 1979). These dunes support an isolated population of the Colorado desert fringe-toed lizard *(Uma notata)* and several other sand-adapted reptiles (Turner 1998). See Annerino 1996; Bowden 1994; Bowers 1982, 1984, 1986. 32°34′52″N, 113°43′23″W. 380–680 ft.

Mohawk Mountains (GR). Rugged and stark schist mountains with typical Basin and Range NW trend. Contains unusually few named features. =Big Horn Mountains (after desert bighorn sheep) on some older maps, but not the same as Big Horn Mountains 80 mi

NW of Gila Bend. May =Lomas Negras ('black hills') on R. J. Hinton's 1878 map of Arizona, though Hinton does show a "Mohawk Mountain" and the Lomas Negras name would be more appropriate for Growler Mountains, which are not named on his map. Before the 1930s the Bryan Mountains were also considered part of the Mohawk Mountains. =Big Horn Mountains, Lomas Negro [sic], Mohawk Range. Summit is BM Mohawk, 11 mi SSE of Mohawk Pass. 32°35′22″N, 113°38′49″W. 2,775 ft.

Mohawk Mountains Catchments (GR). See Game Tanks, South Mohawk Tank.

Mohawk Pass (Yuma Co.). Low pass where modern I-8 and railroad traverse the Mohawk Mountains. High point for railroad is called Mohawk Summit, even after it was "daylighted" (downcut) about 30 ft to make the grade easier (Bob Lenon). =Mohawk Gap; the Gap. 32°43′51″N, 113°44′48″W. 527 ft.

Mohawk Peak (Yuma Co.). A summit in Mohawk Mountains, N of Mohawk Pass. It is not the range's high point but is by far its most prominent and distinctive landmark. A 1918 map labels this northern summit Mohawk Mountain. See Kusvo To:b Do'ag. 32°45′05″N, 113°45′39″W. 1,975 ft.

Mohawk Playa (GR). Small ephemeral lakebed between Mohawk Mountains and Mohawk Dunes, 6.8 mi S of Mohawk Pass. Following exceptional rains, the usually barren flat is sometimes covered with herbaceous plants sprouting from deep perennial roots, and cottonwood seedlings *(Populus fremontii)* may even sprout, though they soon wither and die once the water is gone (Felger et al. 2003). 32°47′36″N, 113°44′28″W. 475 ft.

Mohawk Valley (CP, GR). Broad creosotebush plain W of Mohawk and Bryan mountains and E of Sierra Pinta and Copper Mountains. Runoff flows NW in braided but unnamed washes in central valley and usually percolates below surface before reaching Mohawk Dunes. Clotts (1915:57) describes it as "broad and smooth, with much grass. There are no roads and no habitations." Today the vegetation is much more restrained and the climate seemingly more arid. The valley portion N of I-8 is sometimes referred to as Roll Valley because of its proximity to the small agricultural community of Roll, named for John H. Roll, who settled this area around 1925. 32°25′06″N, 113°33′23″W. 300–1,000 ft.

Mohawk Valley Catchment (CP). Parabolic saucer catchment 2.8 mi NW of Dos Playas. Installed in late 1980s to serve Sonoran pronghorn, it was removed in early 1990s after it was determined that pronghorn were not using it. One of region's shortest-lived places. Site at 32°13′30″N, 113°22′09″W. 880 ft.

Mohawk Wash (CP). Arroyo between Sierra Pinta and Cabeza Prieta Mountains. Ironically, Mohawk Wash announces itself most forcefully in Tule Desert, not the Mohawk Valley. Though it enters Mohawk Valley N of Point of the Pintas, it usually dies in the sands W of Mohawk Dunes around 32°31′17″N, 113°41′22″W (575 ft).

Another segment is mapped crossing I-8 at 32°42′16″N, 113°52′52″W (319 ft), but this wash originates in the N Cabeza Prieta Mountains and is hydrologically unrelated to the other, larger wash of the same name.

Moitjútjupo (PI). See Tinajas de Emilia.

Moivavi (Pima Co.). Former Hia C'ed O'odham settlement at Ajo and still an important meeting site. O'odham for 'many wells' or 'soft wells'. =Indian Town; Mui Vavia, Mu'i Wawia, Moik Vahia.

Moivayi (TON, Maricopa Co.). A village site in southern Sand Tank Mountains. An intermittent spring and well are nearby. Traditional summer village for residents of Kaka. 32°33′52″N, 112°27′34″W. 2,380 ft.

The name (=Moik Vahia) also is used for Ajo Indian Village (see Ajo). O'odham for 'soft wells' or 'many wells'.

Mokwintaorv (GR) See Tinajas Altas Mountains, Gila Mountains.

Molina Crater (PI). A small, three-lobed maar crater 1 km SE of MacDougal Crater. Together the sections resemble a clover leaf 150 m wide and 30 m deep. Each section has its own small playa. Site of 1970 Apollo 14 astronaut training in preparation for lunar mission. Olegario Molina was Mexico's *secretario de fomento* in 1908 when William T. Hornaday needed permits to hunt and travel in the Pinacate. =Volcán El Trébol, Cráter Trébol (Spanish for 'clover leaf'); Cloverleaf Crater, Cráter Molina. 31°57′42″N, 113°36′45″W. 200 m at crater rim.

Monreal Well (CP). Abandoned well and ranchito in gap between Bryan and Mohawk mountains, 32 mi W of Ajo. Storekeeper Angel Zapata Monreal of Ajo tried to ranch at this site but failed. He was told that prehistoric peoples camped here because the water table was high, so he drilled a well, starting about 1950, and erected an extensive corral and rough buildings, including a bomb shelter for security in case the military strafed him during its gunnery practice on Goldwater Range. The Air Force evicted him because he lacked permission to be on the land. In 1950s the arroyo on E margin of ranch had exceptionally large blue palo verdes (*Parkinsonia florida*; Gale Monson), now in decline. 32°22′49″N, 113°24′23″W. 740 ft.

Montague Island (AG). See Isla Montague.

Montezuma's Head (OP). Distinctive promontory resembling a head atop a torso, on NW side of Ajo Mountains, 6.5 mi N of Ajo Peak. Montezuma is synonym for an O'odham deity (see Badamo 1995).

Figure 39.35. *Mohawk Valley Catchment.*

Figure 39.36. *Monreal Well, Ranch, and bomb shelter, about 1990.*

=I'itoi Mo'o ('I'itoi's head'); La Monja ('the nun'); La Mona ('the monkey'). 32°06′53″N, 112°42′19″W. 3,634 ft.

Monument 198 Hill (GR). Small hill in Yuma Desert on international boundary upon which boundary monument 198 stands. A 1930 USGS reconnaissance map called these minor outcroppings the Sand Hills. 32°22′40″N, 114°25′37″W. 476 ft.

Monument Bluff (CP). Volcanic butte in Pinacate lava. International boundary monument 181 is located 0.5 mi S of here. 32°06′05″N, 113°30′45″W. 1,009 ft.

Moon Crater (PI). Maar crater 18 km W of Pinacate Peak at the SW side of the Pinacate volcanic field, bordered by dune fields; 26 m deep, 450 m wide. A volcanic cone rises from the central crater floor. Eolian dune sand is filling the crater, and a small ephemeral playa occupies the lowest portion of the crater floor. A large wash running along the west side of the crater supports xeroriparian vegetation dominated by arborescent legumes:

ironwood *(Olneya tesota),* blue palo verde *(Parkinsonia florida),* mesquite *(Prosopis glandulosa),* and smoke tree *(Psorothamnus spinosus).* The name Moon was applied in 1956 by Glenton Sykes (Ives 1964) because he thought the landscape looked lunar and he needed an impromptu name to give the group he was guiding (Glenton Sykes). =Cráter de la Luna, Volcán la Luna (Spanish for 'moon'); Volcán de Chichi, or Cráter Chichi (Spanish for 'female breast', in reference to the central cone). 31°45′14″N, 113°41′10″W. 100 m.

Mountain Well (SD). Well in N Maricopa Mountains, 1.7 mi SE of Margies Peak. 33°08′41″N, 112°34′53″W. 1,174 ft.

Muddy Spring (OP). A small, intermittent seep 0.4 mi NW of Quitobaquito that seldom has standing water. 31°57′00″N, 113°01′17″W. 1,140 ft.

Municipio (Mexico). Mexican administrative subdivision comparable to a U.S. county. As politics and demographies change, municipio boundaries may be changed or new municipios created. Currently, municipios in NW Sonora include Puerto Peñasco, San Luis Río Colorado, and General Plutarco Elías Calles (Sonoyta).

Murtegshóotak (AG). See Salina, La.

Musina (Yuma Co.). Settlement and possible railroad siding in vicinity of Dateland. The name appears on numerous maps (Lumholtz 1912), but definitive records of its history remain elusive.

N

Naia's (SD). Small roadside gas station and café 12 mi E of Gila Bend, along N side of Highway 84 at southern end of Feather Tail Mountain. Named for the woman who operated it when Highway 84 was yet unpaved (before 1934) until after World War II. She had no well so hitchhiked to town to fill water jugs. She specialized in selling tins of cure-all salve. Reportedly was the eastern widow of a rich man, but presently we don't even know if Naia was her first name or last (John Laird). Another gas station was in the vicinity at one time. =Naia's Place. Vicinity of 32°54′24″N, 112°34′W. About 1,180 ft.

Natural Tank (GR). Small ephemeral tinaja in NW Aguila Mountains, 1.2 mi NW of summit. It is with reason that no one bothered to name this pothole. 32°39′38″N, 113°21′09″W. 1,000 ft.

Nayarit, Ejido (Sonora). See Ejido Nayarit.

Needle Peak (TON). Conspicuous summit 7 mi E of Table Top Mountains and 4.5 mi S of I-8. Part of a group of hills called the Vaiva Hills (=Vaiwa), O'odham for 'cocklebur', probably *Xanthium strumarium,* a common weed in cultivated fields (Rea 1997). 32°45′55″N, 112°00′20″W. 2,062 ft.

Nicholsbergs (PI). Three kipukas on W side of Sierra Blanca near S end of Ives Lava Flow. A kipuka is an island of older rock, here granite, surrounded by younger lava. Two of the granite exposures are less than 1 m tall, but the top of the lava around each of them is more than 4 m higher. They were observed in 1993 by William D. "Bill" Peachey and C. T. "Tom" Bethard as examples of seldom described inflationary lava. This lava originates as a thin flow, and as it cools, a skin is formed, allowing it to thicken in place and "inflate" while molten lava continues to flow into it and forces the upper surface to rise (Bill Peachey). Name proposed by Peachey and Bethard in memory of well-known photographer Edward Tattnall "Tad" Nichols IV (1911–2000), who served as cinematographer for the Harvard expedition to Volcán Paricutín, Mexico, in 1943. He also took many images of the Pinacate and the Sonoran Desert (see Tad Nichols, this volume). 31°34′36″N, 113°28′13″W. 76 m.

Ninemile Well (Maricopa Co.). A well 9 mi SE of Gila Bend. 32°51′10″N, 112°39′17″W. 980 ft.

Noah (Yuma Co.). See Tacna.

No Name Canyon and **Pass** (OP). No Name Canyon and Pass, in Sierra de Santa Rosa, originally carried the name of a U.S. Customs patrol officer who suffered heat exhaustion in 1998 while tracking smugglers. He became dehydrated and delusional but made his way back to a road, where he was assisted by park rangers. It was agreed that the pass needed a name, but the officer asked that his name not be linked to it while he remains on active duty (Jon Young). Canyon mouth at N 31°51′55″N, 112°37′19″W, 1,710 ft.; pass at 31°51′16″N, 112°35′51″W. 2,310 ft.

North Ajo Peak (Pima Co.). See Ajo Peak.

North Alamo Junction Tinajas (OP). Series of intermittent tinajas in N fork of Alamo Canyon in Ajo Mountains. 32°04′34″N, 112°42′51″W. 2,660 ft.

North Alamo Tinaja (OP). Intermittent tinaja 1.5 mi NNE of Alamo Well in N fork of Alamo Canyon in Ajo Mountains. 32°05′09″N, 112°42′20″W. 3,250 ft.

North Gila Tank (GR). Water catchment in N Gila Mountains, 4.1 mi NNW of Dripping Spring and 2.3 mi SSE of Telegraph Pass. Built in 1999. Harvested water is stored in 5,000-gallon subterranean tank and distributed in 2,000-gallon walk-in trough. 32°37′52″N, 114°18′31″W. 620 ft.

North Pinta Tank (CP). A waterhole developed in 1951 in northern Sierra Pinta, 8 mi NW of Heart Tank. 32°21′27″N, 113°38′00″W. 1,040 ft.

North Table Top Mountains (Maricopa Co.). Northern extension of the Table Top Mountains, north of

I-8. Summit is BM Harn. 32°53′04″N, 112°10′34″W. 2,664 ft.

North Table Top Mountains Catchment (Maricopa Co.). Wildlife water catchment 4.6 mi N of Antelope Peak and N of I-8. =AGFD #706; North Table Top Mountains #1. 32°51′53″N, 112°10′11″W. 1,985 ft.

North Tank (SD). Stock tank on West Prong Waterman Wash, 6.6 mi E of Butterfield Pass. =Northwest Tank. 33°03′55″N, 112°21′23″W. 1,340 ft.

North Tank Well (SD). Well 1.3 mi E of North Tank. 33°03′39″N, 112°20′04″W. 1,345 ft.

Norton (Yuma Co.). Long-abandoned settlement at N end of Mohawk Mountains at Gila River. Named for postmaster Charles G. Norton, who was also a miner and engineer who built the first irrigation canal in Wellton. Granger (1983) suggests Norton may have been synonymous with Growler, which was immediately adjacent. Ross (1923:162) reports that Norton was at one time a place of some importance when early irrigation was in progress along the Gila River. When Ross visited, irrigated farming had not yet recovered from the devastating flood of 1891, when most settlers were forced out. He describes the road west of here as "desolate in the extreme. Old fences, dry irrigation ditches, and cleared fields that still show the marks of the plow testify to much farming activity in the past." Subsequent levee building has largely controlled the usually dry Gila River, allowing farming to return. Norton's 1920 population was 38. 32°48′38″N, 113°47′53″W. 314 ft.

O

Oasis, El (BC). Abandoned tourist stop along Mexico Highway 5 on western edge of AG. Near Range Hill NE of Sierra las Pintas. 31°48′55″N, 115°7′37″W. 30 m.

Oasis, El (PI). Tourist and truck stop 18 km NE of Puerto Peñasco on Mexico Highway 8. A small grove of shady tamarisk trees (*Tamarix aphylla*) enticed travelers on torrid days. Wells 4 km E of here in vicinity of Colonia Ortíz Garza at one time supplied most of the freshwater for Puerto Peñasco. =Pozo Camargo. 31°28′30″′N, 113°26′20″W. 50 m.

Oasis, Café el (PI). See Café el Oasis.

Ocapos (SD). See Shawmut.

Ogden's Landing (Sonora). Cargo transfer point on Río Colorado during steamboat days, 64 km by river S of the Colorado's confluence with the Gila; vicinity 13 km S of modern San Luis R.C. It was distinguished by a white sandbank and provided a convenient—and dry—landing for river ferry cargo and passengers (Sykes 1937). Named for Dr. Richard L. Ogden, part owner of a river ferry company with Samuel P. Heintzelman in the nineteenth century. Vicinity of 32°23′04″N, 114°50′53″W. 30 m (Steve Nelson).

Okie Well (GR). Dry and abandoned well in Childs Valley, 2 mi N of Growler Mountains. 32°34′05″N, 113°08′14″W. 905 ft.

Olla Tinaja (OP). Natural ephemeral tinaja 1 mi SE of Tillotson Peak. Spanish for 'pot' or 'kettle', in this region usually referring to a clay or glass jug or pot for carrying water. 32°00′46″N, 112°44′21″W. 2,200 ft.

Ometepec (AG). See Estero Ometepec.

O'Neill Hills (CP). Small granitic mountains 2 mi W of Agua Dulce Mountains. Older maps considered them part of the Agua Dulce Mountains. 32°05′08″N, 113°21′26″W. 1,200 ft.

O'Neill's Grave (CP). Last resting place of David O'Neill, a prospector whose "burros wandered away from camp in a storm, and after searching for them at least a day he died with his head in a mud hole" (Hartmann 1989:113). Buried near where he died in 1916, his grave is at O'Neill Pass along the Camino del Diablo. By one report, the two men who buried O'Neill were friends of his, prospectors by trade, and rugged, practical frontiersmen. They divvied up O'Neill's valuables and then covered him with dirt and rocks. A couple weeks later they ran out of tobacco and remembered that they had buried O'Neill's tobacco with him. They returned to the grave and retrieved the tobacco pouch, one reporting that it "chawed just as good as if it had been in my pocket all them two weeks" (Nichol 1939:67). Gravesite has been plundered at least three times since then without reward. 32°05′49″N, 113°21′10″W. 783 ft.

O'ogam Da:k (Pima Co.). See Ten Mile Ranch.

Orca Island (AG). A long, slightly vegetated, chenier ridge of seashells just S of Isla Vega. Named by marine biologist Donald Thomson for killer whales (*Orcinus orca*) (Karl Flessa). See Isla Sacatosa. 31°20′1″N, 114°52′50″W. Intertidal.

Organ Pipe Cactus National Monument (=OP). Established as a national monument in 1937, in western Pima County, it embraces 330,687 acres, much of it designated wilderness. It is administered by the U.S. National Park Service and is part of the worldwide UNESCO Biosphere Reserve system. The flora is described by Bowers (1980) and Felger et al. (1992 and this volume, Chapter 17). Named for organ pipe cactus, *Stenocereus thurberi*. See Abbey 1973 and Broyles 1996b. Legal boundary descriptions can be found in Presidential Proclamation No. 2232 (April 13, 1937). Its geology is discussed by Bezy et al. (2000). An alternative proposed site for the monument was 36 mi² in the Artesia Mountains S of Sells.

Informally called Organ Pipe and abbreviated ORPI or OPCNM, the full name seems awkward. "Because of the restricted connotations of 'Organ Pipe Cactus National Monument', it seems to me desirable, whenever

Figure 39.37. O'Neill's grave.

it becomes possible . . . that the name be changed to one more descriptive of the broader purposes of the area. Such designations as 'Sonoran Desert N.M.', 'Gila-Sonoran Desert N.M.' or even 'Sonoran N.M.', 'Gila-Sonoran N.M.'. Others may be more suitable. The above suggestions including the word 'Sonoran' serve to indicate the continuity of the area with the state of Sonora, Mexico, and also to call attention to 'Life Zone (Merriam)' represented. I believe the term 'Desert N.M.' has been suggested by the Gila Bend Chamber of Commerce. . . . The importance of the area is such that I would favor its ultimate designation as a National Park" (Weese [NPS executive at regional office] 1941).

NPS headquarters, visitor center, and research center are 5 mi N of Sonoyta. They appear in citations of plant collections and wildlife observations. The visitor center is named for park ranger Kristopher William "Kris" Eggle (b. August 15, 1973), who was murdered near Gachado Ranch on August 9, 2002, by a drug cartel hitman fleeing Mexican authorities. The headquarters is at 31°57′17″N, 112°48′01″W. 1,670 ft.

Ormall Tank (GR). Stock pond 3.5 mi ENE of Maricopa Peak. Named for Ormal (preferred spelling per Hafford 1993) Allen Bender, early rancher in this area. See McGee & Hofstra, this volume. 32°45′50″N, 112°18′40″W. 2,147 ft.

Ortega's Represo (Sonora). See Represo Cipriano.

Owl (Yuma Co.). Former gas station and settlement along highway and railroad at NW end of Mohawk Mountains, 2.5 mi WSW of Mohawk Pass. Now a magnet for junked vehicles. =Owl Station; originally Mohawk Inn. 32°43′18″N, 114°47′31″W. 440 ft.

Owl Wash (Yuma Co.). This arroyo runs from NW Mohawk Mountains past Owl to Gila River. Confluence with Gila River at 32°45′40″N, 113°48′58″W. 295 ft.

P

Pack Rat Hill (CP). Low hills forming a western outlier of Little Ajo Mountains, 8 mi W of Ajo. The packrats here are white-throated woodrats *(Neotoma albigula),* which build thorny nests of cholla joints in crevices and under bushes. 32°22′48″N, 113°00′18″W. 1,540 ft.

Padditt Well (GR). Abandoned well on Tenmile Wash at W end of Crater Range, 29 mi NW of Ajo. Corruption of Pettit, a family that had grazing allotment here. 32°40′48″N, 113°10′41″W. 746 ft.

Painted Rock Reservoir (Maricopa Co.). Artificial lake on Gila River. Dam is 19.2 mi NW of Gila Bend. Named for Painted Rock Mountains, which hold spectacular petroglyph displays of animals, people, and other figures (see Bartlett 1965:chap. 29). A bit of a misnomer, since most of the rock art consists of incised petroglyphs, not painted pictographs. The dam creating the reservoir was completed in 1959 and flooded numerous archaeological sites and settlements important to Native Americans. Formerly a state park, now run by BLM. See Si:l Me:k. Spillway at 33°04′40″N, 113°00′31″W. 661 ft.

Paisley Tinaja (OP). Intermittent tinaja in North Alamo Canyon. Named for tank's crescent-like shape, which at certain levels is similar to a paisley design. 32°04′24″N, 112°42′50″W. 2,540 ft.

Palo Verde Camp (OP). A 1930s cowboy line camp in NW corner of OP. Named for palo verde trees *(Parkinsonia florida* and *P. microphylla),* with photosynthetic green bark as well as in seasonal leaves. Spanish for 'green stick' or 'green wood'. 32°12′02″N, 113°04′02″W. 1,086 ft.

Palo Verde Camp (PI). See Campo Rojo.

Papago Indian Chief Mine (GR). Abandoned copper mine and prospects 3 mi W of Javelina Mountain. It was explored before 1920 and may have produced some copper, gold, and silver (Homburg et al. 1994). At one time it served as a well or cistern. 32°46′12″N, 112°29′56″W. 1,870 ft.

Papago Mountain (CP). Mountain 2 mi E of Papago Well in western Agua Dulce Mountains. The Tohono O'odham tribe has dropped the name Papago (see Tohono O'odham Nation). =Papago Hill. 32°05′32″N, 113°15′08″W. 2,141 ft.

Papago Wash (CP). Large wash running E to W immediately S of Papago Well. Roughly parallels Camino del Diablo from Papago Well, through O'Neill Pass, to Las Playas. Passes Papago Well at 32°05′53″N, 113°17′11″W. 900 ft.

Papago Well (CP). Well at W end of Agua Dulce Mountains. Drilled prior to 1909 to serve operations and crew at nearby Papago Mine and Legal Tender Mine at Papago Mountain. The claims were worked "in the late 1800s and early 1900s, but only a few tons of hand-picked gold-silver-copper ore were shipped" (Keith 1974:7). The name was first applied to "an old mine shaft 100 feet deep at the N.W. end of the Agua Dulce Mountains" (Clotts 1915:72). Later the well served Jim Havins's cattle outfit. In a wild, extensive show of sheet erosion, a 7-in cloudburst September 16–17, 1946, flooded the Havins ranch house. In another storm, April 23, 1955, Havins's cabin had 18 in of water inside and the flow in the adjacent arroyo was one-half mi wide with an estimated rate of 25,000 cfs. In August 1972 a flash flood would have washed away a truck-mounted drill rig at work deepening the well if it hadn't been attached to the drill string and deeply anchored inside the well (CPNWR Annual Reports). This site should not be confused with Tinajas de los Pápagos 22 mi SW in Mexico.

Bryan (1925:335) reports, "There was in 1920 a tripod and pulley erected over the well. Water was obtained by means of a steel cable drawn through a pulley and attached to a sand pump, the sand pump being lowered to water at a depth of 235 feet, filled through a valve at the bottom, and pulled out by attaching the cable to an automobile. A single horse or two men could pull out the sand pump when full, but it is doubtful if a man alone could obtain water." Several other wells drilled in vicinity were dry. 32°05′56″N, 113°17′11″W. 909 ft.

Papaguería. Spanish colonial name for those lands occupied by O'odham in southwestern Arizona and northwestern Sonora, extending roughly from the Altar and Avra valleys W of Tucson to the Gila Mountains E of Yuma, and from the Gila River S to the Gulf of California and the Magdalena, Concepción, and Altar rivers (Bernard Fontana; MacDougal 1908a; Officer et al. 1996). It is part of Pimería Alta.

Papalote, El (Sonora). Restaurant and truck stop along Mexico Highway 2, 18 km W of Sonoyta and 0.5 km S of Aguajita Spring along Aguajita Wash. A small grove of desert tree-caper *(Atamisquia emarginata)* grows at the international boundary N of El Papalote but in 2005 is imperiled by U.S. Department of Homeland Security operations. Spanish for 'windmill'. 31°56′18″N, 113°00′44″W. 325 m.

Paradise Canyon (CP). Rugged canyon on E side of Sierra Pinta, 3.5 mi SE of Heart Tank. CP staff thought it was a veritable paradise of wildlife and plants. Mouth at 32°15′11″N, 113°29′41″W. 1,060 ft.

Paradise Well (GR). Well and silted represo in southeastern Sand Tank Mountains 8 mi SSE of Maricopa Peak. 32°38′42″N, 112°21′06″W. 2,608 ft.

Parra Tank (CP). A washed-out represo on Growler Wash. Dug before 1950 with a horse and fresno scraper by Benjamin Parra and his son Manuel for livestock at the site of a natural charco. Mislocated and misspelled on one map as Perre Tank. 4 mi NW of NW corner of OP. 32°13′47″N, 113°09′00″W. 947 ft.

Paso del Águila (PI). Pass between Sierra Nina and Sierra Tuseral and location of a prehistoric foot trail and now Mexico Highway 2; the western of two gaps between these sierras. The name derives from an eagle-shaped rock perched on the granite skyline. Truck stop and restaurant here is El Águila. Spanish for 'eagle'. May or may not =Paso de Juana. "Where these two ranges approach each other there are two passes, formed by a small intervening mountain; the western pass is the narrower, and I named the eastern, which is quite beautiful, Paso De Juana, for my friend, Mrs. David [Jane] Lydig" (Lumholtz 1912:237); from Old French for 'Joan'; Juana is Spanish for 'Jane'. =El Puerto. 32°06′N, 113°45′W. 320 m.

Paso de Juana (PI). See Paso del Águila.

Pastizal de Efímeras (PI). Silt flats NE of Sierra Blanca. These are barren and dry playa-like flats except in wettest of times when there can be seasonally dense growth of ephemeral grasses and other short-lived annuals. Similar flats are S of Sierra Blanca. Thin fluvisol (soils periodically flooded by surface waters) and underlying salt pans (evaporite deposits) permit only shallow-rooted ephemeral plants and an occasional cholla (Ezcurra 1984; Felger 2000:572). Spanish for 'ephemeral grassland'. Vicinity of 31°33′N, 113°27′W. 80 m.

Peanut Hill (GR). Low volcanic hill in GR South Tactical Range, 1 km SSE of H. E. Hill. Used by biologists to observe Sonoran pronghorn and military spotters to observe munitions strikes on H. E. Hill. Daniels Arroyo swings northward around its N end; summit furnishes expansive view of Childs Valley and mountains surrounding it. On maps it appears peanut-shaped. 32°31′25″N, 113°13′52″W. 937 ft.

Pedregal, El (PI). Abandoned ejido along Mexico Highway 2, 2 km E of Sierra Viejo. Spanish for 'rocky ground'. 32°07′12″N, 113°51′07″W. 260 m.

Pedrera, La (AG). Hill just E of Mexico Highway 5, midway between Mexicali and San Felipe. Spanish for 'quarry' or 'stone pit'. 31°40′31″N, 115°03′47″W. 220 m.

Pembroke (Yuma Co.). Abandoned railroad station and well on SPRR, 1.7 mi W of Owl. The well here was insufficient to meet the railroad's needs, so the station was eliminated in favor of Owl. 32°43′01″N, 113°49′12″W. 391 ft.

Peñasco Peak (Pima Co.). See Ajo Peak.

Phillips Buttes (PI). Volcanic cliffs forming NW end of Sykes Crater. "Mr. Sykes and Dr. MacDougal have very appropriately named the red lava peaks surrounding Sykes Crater in honor of Mr. John M. Phillips, and they appear on the map as Phillips Buttes" (Hornaday 1908: 193). Phillips was a conservationist and friend of William T. Hornaday; together they were instrumental in establishing game laws and wildlife preserves in Mexico, Canada, and United States (see Hornaday 1931). The buttes may include the cone 1.8 km NW of Sykes Crater (James Gutmann). 31°56′47″N, 113°34′30″W. 420 m.

Phillips Point (AG). Point NW of Isla Pelícano; 1.3 nautical miles W of entrance to Puerto Isabel Slough (=Shipyard Slough). Black Beacon was on this point; White Beacon was at entrance of Puerto Isabel Slough (Narraganset Map 1875). =Punta Phillips. 31°46′12″N, 114°41′55″W (Steve Nelson).

Picacho del Diablo (BC). See Sierra San Pedro Mártir.

Piedra (Maricopa Co.). Active railroad siding and former settlement on SPRR between Sentinel and Theba, 14.8 mi W of Gila Bend. Spanish for 'stone'. Piedra lies on E edge of Sentinel lava field and is surrounded by volcanic rocks. Formerly =Painted Rock. 32°54′17″N, 112°59′05″W. 725 ft.

Pilot Knob (California). Distinctive landmark on W bank of Colorado River. So named because it served as a distant guidepost for frontier travelers crossing the open desert or navigating the Colorado River. =Avikwalál (Quechan), Güicolala (see Forbes 1965), Sierra Culaya (Emory 1859). 32°43′54″N, 114°44′57″W. 874 ft.

Pima County. Arizona governmental subdivision including entire OP and eastern GR and CP. County seat is Tucson. Named for riverine Pima Indians (Akimel O'odham).

Pimería Alta. Spanish colonial government name for northern homelands of Piman-speaking people in southwestern Arizona and northwestern Sonora. It was distinct from the lands of southern Pimans—Pimería Baja—and separated by territories of the Opatas and others (Officer et al. 1996; Spicer 1962). See Papaguería.

Pimería Well (GR). Abandoned well 6.5 mi SW of Dateland, along San Cristobal Wash. It was a "deep well drilled by the Pimería Land Co. in an ambitious attempt to irrigate" the San Cristobal Valley (Bryan 1925:361). Misspelled Pimoria on one map and Primera on another. 32°42′44″N, 113°36′31″W. 367 ft.

Pinacate, El, or **Pinacate volcanic field** (PI). The dominating shield volcano in central Gran Desierto. Its lava may derive from a mantle upwelling, like islands of Hawaii but unlike the other volcanoes in this region, which were created by subduction of the Farallon continental plate under the North American plate during Laramide and mid-Tertiary times. Known dates of Pinacate lavas are Pleistocene (1.7 ± 0.4 million to 12 ± 4 thousand years ago), but the underlying lava must be older and younger lava (Holocene age) may be present (James Gutmann). It includes lava flows, cones, craters,

and the main mountain mass. The flows cover approximately 2,000 km² in NW Sonora and about 15 mi² in Arizona. In Sonora this volcanic field is known as El Pinacate. The mountainous portion is often referred to as the Sierra Pinacate or Volcán Santa Clara. Portion in U.S. is the Pinacate lava flow. See Bowden 1984; Hartmann 1989; Hayden 1976, 1980, 1998; Hornaday 1908; Ives 1989; Lumholtz 1912; Lynch 1981, 1982; and *Simposio de Investigación sobre la Zona Ecológica de El Pinacate* 1988. Videographers Eduardo Gómez Limón and Guillermo Munro have filmed and produced several television shows featuring El Pinacate. For a fanciful visit to region, see Esquer 1928. Now protected as core area *(zona nucleo)* of Reserva de la Biosfera El Pinacate y El Gran Desierto de Altar.

Plant life is discussed by Felger (2000) and Ezcurra (1984, this volume). Ezcurra (1984:97) contends that "the main climatic difference between the Lower Colorado Valley Subdivision of the Sonora Desert and the Arizona Uplands Subdivision is in the frequency and regularity of rainfall rather than in the proportion of summer and winter rains."

Name is derived from Nahuatl *pinacatl*, 'beetle'; in NW Sonora *pinacate* is used for large, black stink beetles in genus *Eleodes* (e.g., *E. armata*). =S-cuk Do'ag, O'odham for 'black mountain'. See Pinacate Peak. Summit at 31°46′25″N, 113°25′55″W. 1,206 m.

Pinacate Biosphere Reserve (PI). See Reserva de la Biosfera El Pinacate y El Gran Desierto de Altar.

Pinacate Junction (PI). A major road entrance into Pinacate region and an important botanical collection point, 51 km W of Sonoyta. It is at the junction of Mexico Highway 2 and the road S to the Tezontle cinder mine and Cráter Elegante. Water accumulates at the edge of a small playa, in part enlarged by construction of the highway. Forrest Shreve apparently collected at this site in 1936. Plants occurring here include *Amaranthus crassipes, Eriochloa aristata, Eryngium nasturtiifolium, Euphorbia albomarginata, E. trachysperma, Guara parviflora, Leptochloa viscida, Marsilea vestita,* and *Teucrium cubense* (Felger 2000), which thrive with intermittently standing water. =Los Vidrios entrance to Pinacate Biosphere. 31°59′50″N, 113°21′W. 215 m.

Pinacate Lava Flow, Pinacate Valley (CP). Name on current USGS maps for the portion of Pinacate lava field that extends into U.S. in vicinity of Monument Bluff. Pinacate Valley is a misnomer since the flow is elevated above the surrounding Pinta Sands and Tule Desert and is not a valley. More accurately called Pinacate Lava Flow on earlier USGS maps. 32°06′44″N, 113°30′42″W. 750 ft.

Pinacate Peak (PI). Highest point in the Pinacate region, the summit of Volcán Santa Clara. On October 9, 1698, the intrepid Jesuit padre Eusebio Kino and his party were the first Europeans to ascend this peak. On November 5, 1706, Kino again climbed the peak and reported, "We saw very plainly the connection of this our land with that of the west" (Burrus 1971:156). Kino used this information to fuel his claim that Baja California is a peninsula and not an island, important because it would permit supply of peninsular missions by land from the mainland instead of the perilous sea voyage across the Gulf of California (see Bolton 1936; Hartmann 1989). Cartographers had forgotten that Hernando de Alarcón had proved this in 1540 (Roca 1967).

Cliffs on N side of the peak (ca. 31°45′35″N, 113°29′50″W. 1,080 m) support a small area of chaparral-like vegetation, mostly of Pleistocene relicts (Felger 2000; Van Devender et al. 1990).

Saint Clare (1194–1253) was founder of the Franciscan order of Poor Clares. =Volcán Santa Clara; S-cuk Do'ag; historically transcribed Schuk Toak, O'odham for 'black mountain'. 31°46′20″N, 113°29′54″W. Summit elevation variously reported, but 1,206 m (about 3,957 ft) is used officially.

Pinal County. Arizona governmental subdivision including part of SD. Seat is Florence. Named possibly derived from Pinal Apache Indians or from pine groves in mountainous areas on the county's E side (Granger 1960).

Pinkley Peak (OP). Vivid summit of Puerto Blanco Mountains, 9 mi NNW of Lukeville. Named by monument superintendent William Supernaugh for Frank Pinkley, popular and effective early superintendent of several southwestern parks and monuments during their formative and expansive years in 1920s and 1930s (Jewell 1959); Pinkley was known fondly as "The Boss." "Everything was unnamed down there [in the monument]. . . . Frank Pinkley died shortly after I went down there," so Supernaugh named it after him (Supernaugh 1975:10). Peak has the only known U.S. population of the lavender-flowered shrub *Solanum hindsianum*, which is common in nearby Sonora. 32°00′16″N, 112°51′27″W. 3,146 ft.

Pinkley Tank (OP). Intermittent tinaja on SE side of Pinkley Peak. =Government Tank. 31°59′57″N, 112°51′04″W. 2,100 ft.

Pinnacle Peak (Pima Co.). Descriptive name for peak in Little Ajo Mountains, 1.7 mi SW of Ajo. 32°21′07″N, 112°52′54″W. 2,523 ft.

Pinta Playa (CP). Internally drained playa at SW end of Sierra Pinta, 8 mi SSE of Heart Tank. Rainfall runoff is trapped between the Pinta Sands and Pinacate lava flow, forming shallow, ephemeral pond about 250 acres in size. 32°09′08″N, 113°29′46″W. 750 ft.

Pinta Sands (CP). Low eolian dunes and sand flats along Arizona-Sonora border at S end of Sierra Pinta. About 20 mi² (52 km²) in extent, they form a collar around far

Figure 39.38. Pinacate Peak, (left) and Carnegie Peak (right).

northern end of Pinacate lava field. A single monsoon storm in mid-September 1991 dumped more than 6.3 in of rain on the western Pinta Sands, causing severe erosion of the Camino Diablo, which acted like a river channel. In places the Camino was downcut to depths of 8 ft. The actual amount of rain is unknown because the rain gauge overflowed (Bill Broyles, unpublished data; see Comrie & Broyles 1998). 32°07′46″N, 113°33′41″W. 750 ft.

Pirigua (TON). See Hickiwan.

Pistol Pass (GR). Pass in Sauceda Mountains 2.5 mi NW of Tom Thumb. Named for Albert H. "Pistol" Stout IV (1950–2003), whose father and grandfather ranched here in early to mid-twentieth century. They pumped water from Tom Thumb Well through 30–40 mi of pipe to outlying concrete cattle troughs, as well as establishing or grading many of the area's roads. Pistol worked on these projects and as a cowboy. At one time a homemade sign at the pass read "Pistol Pete's Pass" (Duane Holt). 32°33′50″N, 112°36′34″W. 2,240 ft.

Pitahaya Canyon (OP). A canyon in northern Ajo Mountains, immediately S of Montezuma's Head. Name comes from Spanish *pitahaya*, 'organ pipe cactus', which grows here; applied by Andrew A. "Nic" Nichol while collecting plants in the canyon. "Pitahay [*sic*] Canyon was named by a Mexican I took there with me the first trip, back some time in 1926" (Nichol 1948). Mouth at 32°07′00″N, 112°42′43″W. 2,200 ft.

Platt Well (GR, SD). Two wells near Gila Bend are named for Henry Platt, who built them in 1950s. He came from St. Johns, Arizona, and leased the Vekol grazing allotment. One, now dry, is in the GR on Quilotosa Wash 20 mi SE of Gila Bend, S of Sand Tank Mountains. 32°40′46″N, 112°33′25″W. 1,720 ft.

The second is in SD, 5 mi ESE of Gila Bend, immediately S of I-8. 32°54′51″N, 112°37′22″W. 973 ft.

Playa. Spanish for 'beach' or 'dry lake bed'.

Playa Díaz (PI). Large, usually dry lakebed immediately NW of Cerro Colorado. Pinacate Junction is at the NW margin of the playa. =Lago Díaz, Playa Cerro Colorado. 31°56′20″N, 113°19′10″W. 190 m.

Playa Encanto (Sonora). Beach resort with vacation homes along the strand of coastal dunes at SE side of Estero Morúa, 10 km SE of Puerto Peñasco. There is a substantial population of coastal sand verbena (*Abronia maritima*) on the seaward slopes of the dunes (Felger 2000). Spanish for 'charming beach' or 'delightful beach'. 31°16′25″N, 113°47′00″W. 3 m.

Playa Hermosa (Sonora). Sandy beach and tourist resort extending W from Puerto Peñasco 6 km to Punta Pelícano (Pelican Point), N of Bahía Puerto Peñasco. Spanish for 'beautiful beach'. =Playa Arenosa ('sandy beach'). 31°20′N, 113°55′W. Above sea level.

Playa los Vidrios Viejos (PI). Playa with vertisol soil at Rancho Los Vidrios Viejos. 31°51′21″N, 113°13′18″W. 210 m. See Rancho los Vidrios Viejos.

Playas, Las (CP). Expansive, internally drained playa along El Camino del Diablo, 2.5 mi SSW of southern tip of Sierra Pinta. This watershed formerly drained into Río Sonoyta (as did Pinta Playa and Dos Playas) but was dammed by Pinacate lava flow. Bryan (1925: 419) reports, "This playa is a mesquite-bordered flat of mud-cracked clay about two miles in diameter in which water remains for a few days after a rain." Currently, this playa is still a bosque of stunted mesquite. Pumpelly (1918) recounts being saved from thirst here by a summer thunderstorm, and Bryan (1925:419) reminds us that "all the ancient routes from Sonoita to Yuma came through las Playas because there was a good possibility of finding water there and because of the presence of horse feed."

Rains and runoff occasionally leave standing water, turning the road into a quagmire but enabling several species of toads to breed here and encouraging more than 40 species of plants to grow. Many of the plant species are not seen in other habitats, and two of the annuals—*Euphorbia spathulata* and *Sibara virginica*—are not known anywhere else in the Sonoran Desert. 32°04′50″N, 113°26′06″W. 680 ft.

Plug Tank (SD). Stock tank 7.3 mi E of Margies Peak. 33°09′34″N, 112°28′46″W. 1,330 ft.

Point Invincible (AG). Low mudbank on N shore of Río Colorado, 14 km upriver from Isla Montague. Named for the schooner of U.S. Army lieutenant George H. Derby, who explored the river in 1850–51 to ascertain a supply route to Fort Yuma. =Punta Invencible. 31°54′46″N, 115°00′34″W. 10 m.

Other nearby points and reaches include Arnold's Island, Arnold's Reach, Charles Point, Green Hithe

Point, Halfway Reach, Howard's Point (31°55′58″N, 115°0′58″W), Newburgh Point, Peter Point, Robinson Point, Sea Reach, Smokey Coast, and Thomas's Island (Derby 1969; Hardy 1829); these names are little used today, especially since the river is no longer navigable.

Point of the Pintas (GR). Northern tip of Sierra Pinta. Also remnants of long-abandoned ranch with hand-dug well W of the point; it may have been line camp for former Yuma County sheriff James "Chapo" Chappell, who ran cattle S of Tacna. 32°25′00″N, 113°39′31″W. 1,272 ft.

Port Otis (AG). Proposed seaport in Colorado River delta about 8 mi SE of Puerto Isabel (Hendricks 1971). In the early 1900s Gen. Harrison Gray Otis, publisher of the *Los Angeles Times*, served on the board of the Colorado River Land Company, which promoted development and agriculture on the delta. Port Otis, first proposed in 1882, was to be the ocean terminus of the Mexicali and Gulf Railroad. This port was part of much larger plans that envisioned a railroad bringing coal from Grand Junction, Colorado, through the Grand Canyon, to the Gulf of California for shipment to cities on the Pacific coast; in 1889–1890 Robert Stanton (1965) surveyed a rail route through the Grand Canyon, but the subsequent discovery of oil in California doomed the coal shipments. Extreme tides, bottomless mud, and a meandering river channel would have made construction of Port Otis very difficult. The port was never built; instead, the railroad was built to Puerto Peñasco. See Babcock; Mesa de Andrade. Platted midway between Shipyard Slough and Santa Clara Slough, N of Isla Gore. Vicinity 31°45′51″N, 114°37′48″W.

Pottebaum Tank (GR). Represo for livestock, 17 mi SE of Gila Bend, between Quilotosa Wash and Sand Tank Mountains. Named for Henry Pottebaum, who built it before 1950 (John Laird). 32°43′55″N, 112°35′04″W. 1,525 ft.

Poverty Flat Tank (Maricopa Co.). Stock tank in N Vekol Valley, 1.5 mi E of Booth Hills. Name may refer to poor rangeland there for livestock or proximity to the impoverished nearby community of Mobile (Winnie Conley Henry). 32°58′22″N, 112°13′25″W. 1,460 ft.

Powers Well (OP). A dry well, 150 ft deep, dug in 1917 by Fred Powers, who had "expected to graze cattle in the Mohawk [now Growler] Valley" (Clotts 1915:75). About 6 mi S of Bates Well and on W side of Bates Mountains along road to Quitobaquito. 32°06′33″N, 113°00′32″W. 1,315 ft.

Poyner Water (SD). Water tank for livestock, 2.3 mi E of Cotton Center. 33°04′47″N, 112°37′41″W. 810 ft.

Pozitos, Los (PI). Ephemeral wells along Río Sonoyta where impervious dikes push subterranean flow toward the surface. Reportedly, shallow holes could be dug here to find water. Salt crusts dapple the banks. Roughly 17 km SW of Quitobaquito and downstream from Agua Salada. Vicinity 31°54′N, 113°11′W. 240 m.

Pozo. Spanish for 'well' or 'spring'. =poso. Some Mexican geographers suggest using *pozo* for a drilled or dug well, and *poza* for a waterhole, pool, natural spring, or artesian well, but names in this region do not yet follow that convention (see *Diccionario de la Real Academia*). We have not attempted to locate or describe all the coastal pozos recorded by May (1973).

Pozo Caballo (AG). Freshwater artesian spring along Bahía Adair coast in a salt flat, midway between Estación López Collada and La Salina. Spanish for 'horse spring', after naturally salt-preserved carcass of a horse nearby. =Hia C'eḍ Vavia; historically transcribed Hiatitváxia, O'odham for 'spring or well in the sand dunes'. Vicinity of 31°37′N, 114°00′N.

Pozo la Cholla (Sonora). Freshwater artesian spring exposed at low tides on a northern beach of Bahía de la Cholla or northwestern Bahía Adair, possibly near Estero Cerro Prieto. =Ha:namĭ C'eḍ Vahia; Lumholtz (1912:395) reports: "La Choya, Camp. In Papago, Hanammétjurtivaxia (*Hánam*, choya, a very spiny cactus of the opuntia genus which grows in abundance here; *métjurti* was interpreted to me as indicating 'in', 'near'; *váxia*, well, waterhole, spring).... This camp is a few yards from the beach, and fresh water is found in a hole that has been dug ten feet deep." The cholla here is *Cylindropuntia bigelovii*. =Pozo la Choya.

Pozo de en Medio (GR). See Coyote Water.

Pozo Nuevo (OP). Well and windmill 1 mi W of Cipriano Hills and 5 mi N of Quitobaquito. First dug in 1908, it later served as a line camp for the Gray family ranch. Spanish for 'new well'. =José Juan Orosco Well. 32°01′01″N, 113°02′00″W. 1,260 ft.

Pozo Redondo (TON). Tinaja and Tohono O'odham ranchería about 12 mi ESE of Ajo. A dug well was here before 1910 (King 1961). Spanish for 'round well' but probably named for a family: José María Redondo, a rancher, businessman, and politician in the region in late nineteenth century, had cattle here; his brother Jesús once had 2,000 head of cattle based at this well and even built a steam pump to provide them with well water in redwood troughs a hundred yards long; he built a mesquite-fence corral the size of a city block (Haley 1948). Bryan (1925:423) states that "the well was dug by a man named Redondo, whose descendants now live in Yuma. Redondo unfortunately overstocked the range, and his cattle had to be removed." For more on the Redondo family, see Winsor 1954 and Masich n.d.
    =Sikol Vahia, Sikol Ce:po, Sikort Chuapo; historically transcribed Sikorttjúupo ('round waterhole in the rock'); Bryan (1925:423) contends that the name is

Figure 39.39. A pozo along the coast.

"doubtless a reference to Redondo" brothers. 32°18′53″N, 112°40′19″W. 1,904 ft.

Pozo Redondo Mountains (Pima Co., TON). Low mountains 8 mi ESE of Ajo and immediately W of Pozo Redondo. −Gunsight Mountains. Summit is BM Childs. 32°18′45″N, 112°42′56″W. 3,097 ft.

Pozo Redondo Valley (TON). Narrow valley of Sikort Chuapo Wash, which intermittently flows northward past Pozo Redondo, between Pozo Redondo Mountains and Sikort Chuapo Mountains, 11 mi E of Ajo. 32°18′53″N, 112°40′19″W. 1,900 ft.

Pozo Salado (CP). A capped well at SW base of Childs Mountain, 5.7 mi NW of Ajo. Heavily mineralized water gave its name. Water reportedly found at depth of 16 ft in 1920s. Spanish for 'saline well'. =Salt Well. 32°24′10″N, 112°56′17″W. 1,560 ft.

Pozo Salado (OP). Well and cattle trough built in 1940 by Robert Gray, 8 mi WNW of Lukeville and 5 mi E of Quitobaquito. =Salt Well. 31°55′35″N, 112°56′23″W. 1,250 ft.

Pozo Tres Ojitos (AG). Small freshwater pozos in a salt flat along N side of the railroad, 18 km by sandy road W from Estación Gustavo Sotelo. One of Padre Kino's campsites, and described by Manje as 'three springs' of water named Cubo Cuasibabia (Burrus 1971:503). Vicinity of 31°38′N, 113°50′W. 20 m.

Pozos de San Miguel, Los (GR). Sandy waterhole where Wellton Hills force Coyote Wash subsurface flow toward the surface. Indigenous peoples reportedly dug shallow wells here, as did Padre Kino's party and later travelers (Ives 1989). The Fages expedition of 1781 "arrived [October 24] at the place called [Pozos] de San Miguel, where there was a pool of excellent water in abundance. The pool must have been about twenty yards long, two or three yards wide in places, and two yards deep. There was scarcely any pasture" (Ives 1989:193). More recently,

Figure 39.40. *Puerto Peñasco, old town, about 1988.*

Ives (1965:2) reports, "They are still useful if you have a lot of energy and a good shovel." Site imprecisely known today, but probably about 6 mi S of Wellton, vicinity 32°35′33″N, 114°06′42″W. 460 ft. =Los Pozos.

Presa. Spanish for 'dam' or 'impoundment'.

Presa Derivadora (Sonora). Dam 1.5 km E of Sonoyta on Río Sonoyta. Built in 1951, it impounds a small lake that is the largest freshwater pond in NW Sonora E of the Río Colorado. *Presa* is Spanish for 'dam' or 'impoundment'; *derivadora* here means deriving water from a source or spring. =Presa Divisidora (Spanish for 'divider', as for irrigation ditches). 31°51′33″N, 112°49′59″W. 395 m.

Puentes Cuates (Sonora). Arroyo crossed by double bridge on Mexico Highway 2, 7 km W of Mina del Desierto. Arroyo runs southward E of Sierra del Viejo and dissipates into sands of Gran Desierto. Spanish for 'twin bridges' and now used for the arroyo itself. 32°07′40″N, 113°50′50″W. 260 m. Also a name for twin bridges at Batamote on Mexico Highway 8 (Sonora).

Puerto. Spanish for 'port' or 'pass'.

Puerto Blanco Drive (OP). A scenic roadway W from OP headquarters around Puerto Blanco Mountains and returning by way of Quitobaquito. 31°53′37″N, 112°48′41″W. 1,440 ft.

Puerto Blanco Mountains (OP). Impressive range in central OP, 7 mi NNW of Lukeville. Named for a pass through light-colored tuff; Spanish for 'white pass'. =Dripping Springs Mountains. Summit is Pinkley Peak at 32°00′16″N, 112°51′27″W. 3,145 ft.

Puerto Blanco Pass (OP). Gap in Puerto Blanco Mountains. 32°01′24″N, 112°53′32″W. 2,180 ft.

Puerto Blanco Tinaja (OP). Largest known natural tinaja in Puerto Blanco Mountains, 1.2 mi SE of Dripping Springs. It is 4 ft deep and holds water intermittently. 32°01′02″N, 112°52′27″W. 2,100 ft.

Puerto Isabel (AG). Former steamboat landing, shipyard, and small port on Shipyard Slough, between the mouth of the Río Colorado and the Santa Clara Slough. Named for the schooner *Isabel,* which ventured into the slough in 1865 to transfer cargo. This small American settlement on Mexican soil, active 1867–1877, was established by the Colorado Steam Navigation Company as its shipyard, complete with dry dock. A steamer route from San Francisco connected with riverboats here. Edward Palmer collected plant specimens here, including the type collection of *Wislizenia palmeri,* a small shrub in the caper family (Felger 2000). See Childers 1966, Dolley 1957, Lingenfelter 1978, McVaugh 1956, and Sykes 1976. =Puerta Isabel; Puerto Otis. Vicinity of 31°48′W, 114°41′10″W, 10 km W from E shore.

Puerto Peñasco (Sonora). This fishing village, founded in early 1920s, is a rapidly growing town supported increasingly by tourism, eco-tourism, and U.S. retirees. Its shrimp industry has declined in recent years. The railroad station is at km post 237. The town's history is chronicled in Guillermo Munro's multipart series in Centro Intercultural de Estudios de Desiertos y Océanos' *Noticias del CEDO;* and the region's flavor is captured in Munro's (1992) *Las Voces Vienen del Mar.* See Ives 1950 and Verdugo-Fimbres 1985. Estimated 1996 population: 34,000. =Ge Su:dagĭ (Hia C'ed O'odham for 'big water'). The Hia C'ed O'odham called Hermosillo, Sonora, To:ta Waippia or To:ta Vaipa (White Wells) and Caborca, Sonora, Kawulk (Little Hill). Spanish for 'bluff port' or 'rocky port.' =Rocky Point (its original written name [Hardy 1829:310]). 31°18′05″N, 113°32′55″W. 10 m.

Punta. Spanish for 'point' or 'headland'.

Punta Borrascosa (AG). This sandy point with a defunct lighthouse, on the shore ESE of La Salina, marks the western lip of Bahía Adair. According to local fishermen, there is a reef offshore. Spanish for 'stormy point'. =El Borrascoso. 31°29′32″N, 114°01′42″W.

Punta Gordo (AG). Broad headland point S of La Salina and 15 km ESE of El Tornillal. Spanish for 'fat point' or 'big point'. 31°30′N, 114°10′W. 30 m.

Punta Machorro (AG). Sand point 6 km SE of El Golfo at head of Gulf of California. Spanish for 'totoaba point'. Totoaba *(Totoaba macdonaldi)* is a croaker-family fish that can grow to 2 m and 135 kg. It was once a prized sport and commercial fish, but its numbers have declined precipitously due to loss of habitat and overfishing. It is now legally protected, although poaching and pollution continue (see Hastings & Findley, this volume). 31°39′00″N, 114°26′55″W. Sea level.

Punta el Machorro (AG). Two buttes 2 km N of San Felipe on W coast of Gulf of California. =Cerro el Machorro. 31°02′30″N, 114°49′00″W. 300 m.

Punta Pelícano (Sonora). Small granitic peninsula at the S end of Bahía de la Cholla. Spanish for 'pelican point'. =Roca del Toro (Spanish for 'bull rock', by extension male sea lion). 31°21′N, 113°38′W. 100 m.

Punta Peñasco (Sonora). Landmark volcanic hill at Puerto Peñasco. Originally named Rocky Point by Lt. R. W. H. Hardy (1829:310): "We passed Rocky Point, for so I named it." 31°17′55″N, 113°32′47″W. 50 m.

Pyramid Peak (PI). A cinder cone surrounded by dunes 3.5 km NW of MacDougal Crater (see Ives 1964). Resembles an Egyptian pyramid surrounded by drifting sands. Not associated with Pyramid Tank. =Cerro la Pastora; mislabeled Pastoria on 1:50,000 topo map. Pastora is Spanish for 'shepherdess' and the common name for plantago (here *Plantago ovata*), a very good forage (Alberto Búrquez). 31°59′37″N, 113°40′16″W. 350 m.

Pyramid Tank (PI). See Tinaja Huarache.

Q

Quilotosa Wash (GR). Arroyo between Sauceda and Sand Tank mountains, draining to the Gila River. Means 'place of the greens', from Spanish *quelite*, 'greens, vegetables', and *–osa*, 'place of'. *Quelite* is generic for several species of annual plants, such as *Amaranth palmeri* and *Portulaca oleracea*. As recently as 2003, townsfolk of Gila Bend gathered salad greens from a place on the wash near town (Mel Vasquez). Mouth at 32°59′31″N, 112°45′26″W. 620 ft.

Quilotosa Well (GR). Abandoned well on Quilotosa Wash, 2.6 mi SSW of Gila Bend. It was associated with the Stout family. =Stouts Well, a name applied to this and another well in the area. 32°54′56″N, 112°44′27″W. 780 ft.

Quitobaquito (OP). Springs and oasis along the U.S.-Mexico border 13 mi W of Sonoyta. Perhaps the name derives from the Spanish for 'little Quitovac' (Hoy 1969). 'A'al Vaipia ('little spring' or 'little water') is the Hia C'ed O'odham name for Quitobaquito. In 1698 and 1699 the Jesuit explorer-missionary Padre Eusebio Kino visited the settlement of 'A'al Waippia and called it San Sergio. During the mid-1800s Mexican settlers began moving into the area. The first Anglo Americans began to settle in the area after the Gadsden Purchase in 1854. About 1860 Andrew Dorsey built a dam and ditches to hold and distribute the spring water. In 1887 the Orozco family, who were Hia C'ed O'odham, settled at Quitobaquito, remaining until 1957, when Jim Orozco's holdings were bought by the U.S. Park Service (Hoy 1970).

Since ancient times travelers to the region rested here. The water and gentle shade was a welcome respite on the route westward from Sonoyta along the infamous Camino del Diablo. The list of botanists who collected

Figure 39.41. Punta Borrascosa lighthouse, about 2000.

specimens at Quitobaquito reads like a who's who of southwestern botany, beginning with Arthur Schott in 1855 (Felger 2000).

Crops were grown at Quitobaquito even before Kino's visit in the late seventeenth century. Oral history accounts from the late nineteenth century and first half of the twentieth describe the region and tell of a number of crops grown there (Bell et al. 1980; Hoy 1969, 1970; Zepeda 1985). The flora and ethnobotany are described by Felger et al. (1992). Also see Bennett & Kunzmann 1989; Greene 1977; and Hoy 1969, 1970. The spring provides a setting for literary fiction by Nelson (1984, 1991). A hill or mountain NW of here was known to O'odham as Vainomi Do'ag. =′A'al Vaipia, 'A'al Waippia'; San Serguio de Bacapa, San Sergio; Quitovaquita. 31°56′40″N, 113°01′04″W. 1,100 ft.

Also, S-Cecpoḍk or Cecpoḍ (Sonora) was the settlement and fields now S of the international border. Sopolk or Sopoḍk (OP) was name of the older village near Quitobaquito Hills and was historically transcribed Sapadk, O'odham for 'flat', and called Flat Village (Bell et al. 1980).

Quitobaquito Hills (OP). These low hills N of Quitobaquito Springs are geologically complex granite, schist, and gneiss, with an overthrust fault (Tosdal et al. 1990). =′A'al Vaipia Do'ag; Sierra de Quitobaquita. 31°59′28″N, 113°01′42″W. 1,887 ft.

Quitovac (Sonora). Important Tohono O'odham and Hia C'ed O'odham settlement and oasis about 40 km SE of Sonoyta, S of Mexico Highway 2. Site of Vi'igita and site of paleological monument proposed by Sonoran archaeologists to honor importance of Pleistocene fauna fossilized here (e.g., mammoth bones and teeth). These fossils contributed to O'odham legend of the Ne: big monster, which lived in the pools and sometimes devoured people (Ives 1989; Nabhan 1982). The entire site is now doomed by a Canadian gold mining company. See Lumholtz 1912, Nabhan et al. 1982. =San Luis Beltran del Bacapa; Vak, Vapk (O'odham for 'bullrush', *Scirpus* spp.[Rea 1997], *Scirpus americanus* in this case [see Chapter 17, this volume]). 31°30′59″N, 112°45′11″W. 420 m.

R

Railroad. See Ferrocarril Sonora-Baja; Southern Pacific Railroad; Tucson, Cornelia, & Gila Bend Railroad.

Rainbow Hills (PI). Colorful lava hills and ridges forming E end of Sykes Crater. Named by W. T. Hornaday for a friend's memorable sighting of four desert bighorn rams silhouetted on the skyline here with a rainbow arching overhead; a painting by Carl Rungius of this scene was the color frontispiece for original *Camp-Fires on Desert and Lava* (Hornaday 1908). 31°56′12″N, 113°33′24″W. 460 m.

Rainbow Valley (SD, Maricopa Co.). Broad valley surrounding NE corner of SD. Bounded by Maricopa Mountains on W and Sierra Estrella on E. "The reason for the name has not been learned" (Granger 1983:511). A small farming community in the valley is sometimes called by the same name. =Jornada de las Estrellas, Hall Valley. See Little Rainbow Valley. 33°10′34″N, 112°21′56″W. 1,100 ft.

Rainbow Wash (Maricopa Co.) Arroyo in Rainbow Valley, draining N Maricopa Mountains and S Buckeye Hills. Joins Gila River at 33°10′50″N, 112°42′52″W. 710 ft.

Raleigh Well (SD). Now-dry well NW of Javelina Mountain. Built by Charles Raleigh, who later founded a cooking utensil company. 32°46′57″N, 112°26′28″W. 2,066 ft.

Rancho Bonito (OP). See Bonita Well.

Rancho Guadalupe Victoria (PI). Cattle ranch 10 km S of Mexico Highway 2 and 3 km S of La Lava microwave tower. Many tourists pass through it along the road to MacDougal Crater and Tinajas de los Pápagos; its vaqueros have been noted for their hospitality and their desert lore (see Broyles 1982). Originally called Colonia Cuauhtémoc ('eagle that falls'), after the last of the Aztec kings, born 1496, who was beheaded by Hernán Cortés in 1525 for resisting Spanish rule. Ranch was established in the early 1950s by Juan Bermúdez

and his brother Enrique (see Vidrios, Los); in 1964 the ranch was taken over by Jesús María Grijalva and is now owned by Luis and Benjamín Grijalva Cañeda. Water level in well is at 720 ft and warm (Charles Conner). Guadalupe Victoria was the first president of the Republic of Mexico (1824–1829). =La Pila (Spanish for 'water trough'), Colonia Cuauhtémoc, Grijalva Ranch. 32°00′35″N, 113°34′21″W. 210 m.

Rancho Pozo Nuevo (PI). A forlorn ranchito 1.3 km SW of Sierra Extraña. Trapped between sand dunes and lava flows, it sits in a silt flat that is sometimes used as an illicit airstrip. Julian Hayden reports that it was developed in 1960s by Luis Grijalva after he assumed Rancho Guadalupe Victoria 25 km to the NE. At Pozo Nuevo he found good water and ran cattle. It was later bought by Pedro Barba and Goyo Gonzales. Water level in well was 180 ft below the surface in 2002 (Charles Conner). Spanish for 'new well ranch'. 31°49′30″N, 113°43′00″W. 80 m.

Rancho los Vidrios Viejos (PI). Ranch and represo used by Alberto Celaya, among others. 8 km SE of Cerro Colorado. =Los Vidrios Viejos. 31°51′41″N, 113°14′07″W. 210 m. See Playa los Vidrios Viejos (PI).

Range Hill (BC). Distinctive white cliff at N end of Sierra las Pintas, used as navigational landmark on early mariner maps of the delta. 24 mi W of Phillips Point (Sykes 1907 map [Williams, this volume, Figure 11.1]; Narragansett Map 1875). =Promontorio. Vicinity of 31°51′N, 115°08′W. 813 ft.

Rasmussen Mine (CP). Group of shallow exploratory diggings from 1950s in SE O'Neill Hills, 1.6 mi S of O'Neill Pass. Probably for Charles Rasmussen of Ajo. 32°04′24″N, 113°20′53″W. 800 ft.

Rat Gap (GR). Pass in southern Mohawk Mountains, 6.5 mi SE of BM Mohawk 2775. Prevailing SW winds move sands from Mohawk Dunes NE through this gap. Named for kangaroo rats (*Dipodomys* spp.) whose burrows made travel by jeep or foot difficult here (Ed Tuffly). 32°31′19″W, 113°34′29″W. 630 ft.

Raven Butte (GR). Distinctive basaltic butte E of Tinajas Altas Mountains. Possibly named for its raven-black color, but the USGS Board of Geographic Names implausibly states that it was named for the large number of relatively tame ravens found there in the early 1900s. Many animals in this region never encounter humans so can appear tame or unafraid when first encountered. =Cerro Prieta. 32°24′15″N, 114°06′33″W. 1,773 ft.

Raven Butte Tank (GR). Intermittent tinajas near butte, used prehistorically and historically. The tank appears in two different locations on older and newer USGS maps, but neither depiction is accurate. A 1913 photograph of the tank appears in Sheldon 1993:26, but that specific location remains elusive. Shown on map as at 32°24′19″N, 114°07′09″W. 1,030 ft.

Red Cone (PI). Distinctive red volcanic cone 4 km E of Carnegie Peak. See Campo Rojo. 31°46′38″N, 113°26′48″W. 520 m.

Red Cone Camp (PI). See Campo Rojo.

Red Cross Mine (GR). Mine on E side of Mohawk Mountains, 5 mi S of I-8. Worked sporadically from about 1910 to 1941 and originally owned by G. W. Norton (see Norton). Wilson (1933) reports that in 1910 it produced one railroad car of silver ore valued at $10,000. 32°40′28″N, 113°41′28″W. 660 ft.

Red Point (GR). Reddish hill in target zone for live-fire Air Force exercises between Granite and Aguila mountains. See High Explosive (H. E.) Hill. 32°32′26″N, 113°17′48″W. 1,183 ft.

Red Tank Tinajas (OP). Three intermittent tinajas in bedrock 2 mi NNE of Senita Basin. =Red Tail Tanks Tinajas. 31°58′35″N, 112°50′43″W. 1,850 ft.

Red Tanks Well (OP). Abandoned well 3 mi W of OP headquarters. Named for nearby Red Tanks tinajas, it was dug by Ralph Gray about 1932 for cattle. 31°58′56″N, 112°50′24″W. 1,860 ft.

Red Top Mountain (GR). Reddish granite-topped peak in Gila Mountains, 1 mi W of Dripping Springs. =Granite Cap Peak (Bryan 1925). 32°34′41″N, 114°17′48″W. 2,196 ft.

Red Top Wash (GR, Yuma Co.). A large arroyo draining the Red Top Mountain and Dripping Springs area of northeastern Gila Mountains. It crosses the Wellton-Mohawk Canal over a flume. This wash is a good place to see smoke trees *(Psorothamnus spinosus).* =Little Wash. Meets Gila River 7.7 mi W of Wellton at 32°40′50″N, 114°16′25″W. 190 ft.

Redtail Tank (CP). Represo along Growler Wash. It was built in 1956 after Jose Juan Tank was finished but is now partially bypassed by ever-wandering channels. Named for a red-tailed hawk *(Buteo jamaicensis)* seen in a mesquite spar the day refuge staff was surveying the tank; this species still frequents the area. 32°14′51″N, 113°09′58″W. 916 ft.

Renner Barite Mine (Yuma Co.). Group of claims on W side of Mohawk Mountains about 1 mi NW of Mohawk Station. Claims were originally located by G. W. Norton in 1902 but later transferred to Jason Renner and Charles Sam. Some 18 carloads of barite were shipped from the mine between 1929 and 1930 (Miller 1979). 32°44′20″N, 113°45′49″W. 580 ft.

Represo Cipriano (PI). Dam across arroyo near El Camino del Diablo, 0.5 mi SW of U.S.-Mexico boundary marker 179. An east-west rock dam between two basaltic hills, apparently built to contain water draining

Figure 39.42. Raven Butte.

to Las Playas to the NW. Double row of cut and laid basaltic rocks. According to legend around Sonoyta, it was built by Cipriano Ortega and his brother Bartolo, possibly about 1887. In theory it would hold water and served not only as a stock tank but as an ambush station for the Ortega gang (Hoy 1970). The Carnegie party stopped their horses at the "Represa Tank" in 1907 (Hornaday 1908:350). The dam has long been breached at its W end. Intermittent water in charco pools near dam; on March 4, 1992, the shallow muddy water was writhing with tadpole shrimp *(Triops* sp.; Felger 2000). Seasonally supports *Marsilea vestita,* a fern relative with a leaf resembling a four-leaf clover. Area shows signs of prehistoric usage. *Represo, represa* is Spanish for 'mud tank', 'stock tank'. =Ortega's Represo; La Represa. 32°02′47″N, 113°22′57″W. 215 m.

Reserva de la Biosfera Alto Golfo y Delta del Río Colorado (=AG, Sonora, BC). A Mexican national biosphere reserve protecting the upper Golfo de California, coastal land, and Río Colorado delta. Created in 1993, it contains 942,270 ha, including a 160,620-ha nucleus. See Boyer 1996; Búrquez & Martínez, this volume; Felger et al., this volume, Chapter 1. Boundary descriptions can be found in Ocaña-García 1993. The railway forms the reserve's northern boundary. *Biosfera,* without the accent, is now more commonly used, but *Biósfera* appears in some older maps and publications.

Reserva de la Biosfera El Pinacate y El Gran Desierto de Altar (=PI, Sonora). A 714,656-ha Mexican national biosphere reserve W of Mexico Highway 8. It has two core areas, one of 41,392 ha protecting most of the Sierra del Rosario, and another of 228,113 ha centered on Pinacate Peak (Búrquez & Castillo 1994; Felger et al., this volume, Chapter 1). Boundary descriptions can be found in Búrquez & Castillo 1993; Búrquez & Martínez, this volume; Felger et al., this volume, Chapter 1. It was preceded by Parque Nacional El Pinacate. Its geology is discussed in Bezy et al. 2000. The railway forms the reserve's southern boundary.

Riíto (Sonora). Agricultural settlement near the Río Colorado at intersection of Sonora Highway 40 and Chihuahua-Pacífico railroad (see Ferrocarril Sonora-Baja), 42 km SSW of San Luis R.C. May derive name from Rillito (Spanish for 'little river'). =Riíto Salado, an easterly side channel of Río Colorado near here (Lumholtz 1912:248). =Nuevo Michoacán (a coastal state in southern Mexico). 32°09′56″N, 114°57′25″W. 20 m.

Numerous agricultural settlements N of Riíto fill the Río Colorado valley and its extensive floodplains. A series of dams now control fluctuations in the Colorado's flow, but the low volume and poor quality of the river's water are decried by users along lower Río Colorado (e.g., Casillas 1992; Fradkin 1995; Glenn & Nagler, this volume; Reisner 1986).

Rincon Spring (OP). See Williams Spring.

Río. Spanish for 'river'.

Río Colorado (AG). See Colorado River.

Río Hardy (BC). This tributary of the Río Colorado on W side of the delta drains valley SE of Mexicali, now an agricultural center. Named for his family by Lt. Hardy (1829:383), who explored area. =Hardy River. Mouth at 32°04′50″N, 115°13′00″W. Less than 10 m.

Edgar Mearns collected in the area E of Hardy-Colorado confluence and wrote, "The tide creeks and broad bays about our camp were swarming with waterfowl, which were nowhere else seen in so great abundance. Pelicans, cormorants, geese, ducks, cranes, herons, and small waders almost covered the shores and bays; the sky was lined with their ever-changing geometrical figures, and the air resounded with their winnowing wing-strokes and clanging voices, not only during the day, but through most of the night" (1907:128–129).

Río el Mayor (BC). The westernmost delta drainage-way and a tributary to Río Hardy, which it joins 1.5 km N of El Mayor. To protect farmlands, Canal Grebel now intercepts much of eastward runoff from Sierra Mayor that Río Hardy does not capture. 32°08′38″N, 115°17′04″W. 20 m.

Río Pescaderos (BC). Tributary to Río Hardy, joining at settlement El Mayor. It drains agricultural lands SE of Mexicali. Spanish for 'fish sellers'. =Río Pescadero. Confluence with Río Colorado at 32°08′N, 115°17′W. 10 m.

Río Pescadores (BC). Former tributary to Río Hardy, joining it about 5 km W of Río Pescaderos. It is now cut off from the Hardy. Spanish for 'fishermen'. 32°13′36″N, 115°17′15″W. 5 m.

Another river in the northern delta adds to the confusion of near-homonyms: Río Paredones (BC) forms a westward channel of Río Colorado entering

Volcano Lake. Allied with New River and Alamo River, it was a conduit for the flood of 1905, which diverted water from the Colorado River to the Salton Sink in California, thereby re-creating the Salton Sea (Sykes 1937). *Paredones* is Spanish for 'thick walls', here dikes, berms, and high banks, and the name was in use before 1900 (Chittenden 1901:199).

Río Sonoyta (Sonora, PI). Rising from springs just E of Sonoyta, this intermittent stream flows westward from the town and then abruptly southward along the E side of Pinacate region. Ultimately, when carrying rare surges of flooding, it ends at Estero Morúa on the Gulf of California. Its watershed may originate near Cajilon, N of the Quijotoa Mountains of Arizona, but its ultimate headwater needs clarification (see Ives 1989).

Near Sonoyta the meager, intermittent surface flow, along with its associated riparian vegetation, is diminishing due to extensive groundwater pumping for local agriculture since the 1970s. A flood on the night of August 6, 1891, initiated disastrous arroyo cutting, which lowered the water table. Soon afterward a series of ciénegas at Sonoyta dried up, and the village was relocated downstream to its present site (Lumholtz 1912). Wood-cutting, irrigation, and cattle grazing probably contributed to the erosion and demise of the ciénegas. We can only imagine the wetland life that once flourished here.

Pools near Sonoyta hold freshwater fish, including the native but endangered desert pupfish *(Cyprinodon macularis* subsp. *eremus)*. Willows *(Salix gooddingii)*, seep willow *(Bacharris salicifolia)*, and other wetland plants grow along the river. In many reaches, salt cedar *(Tamarix ramosissima)* now forms a dense corridor along the banks, presumably replacing and diminishing the native vegetation. Lower stretch between Batamote and seashore is relatively sterile archaeologically (Ives 1989) and without wetland vegetation.

In geologic times the river flowed westward around the Pinacate shield and emptied into Bahía Adair, until successive lava flows blocked its channel and forced it southward (Gutmann & Prival 1996; Jahns 1959), but Lynch (1981) disagrees. The region's maar craters arc along the river's former route; surface water was required for their creation (Gutmann 2002).

=Río Sonoita, Sonoyta River, Sonoyta Creek; Papago River. Flows through town of Sonoyta at 31°51′16″N, 113°03′47″W. 400 m. Mouth at 31°16′N, 113°19′W.

Ripoff Canyon (GR). Foot trail and pass through Gila Mountains, 1.5 mi SSE of Sheep Mountain. West of the pass the canyon is fairly gentle terrain; east of the pass it presents rocky and treacherous footing. Named in early 1980s by Border Patrol pilot David Roberson because undocumented aliens were using the canyon to bypass the Hobbs Drag Road and thereby ripping off (cheating) the Border Patrol (Joe McCraw). =Rip-off Canyon. 32°30′45″N, 114°13′15″W. 1,380 ft.

Roberson Tinajas (GR). Twin tinajas in a canyon that runs N along upper spine of Gila Mountains, 6 mi SW of Sheep Mountain. Named for U.S. Border Patrol pilot David F. Roberson of Yuma, who located them in the 1980s. 32°26′56″N, 114°10′41″W. 1,600 ft.

Robinsons Landing (AG). A "small frame building resting on the tops of piles about four feet above the ground" (Ives 1861:27). Built by riverboat captain David C. Robinson near mouth of Colorado River on west bank before 1858, it served as transfer port and way-point for early river travelers and cargo boats. "The owner and builder had been a mate of a vessel plying to the mouth of the river; believing that he could do a profitable business by taking blackfish [totoaba] and making oil, he had established his hermit-like retreat by the side of a little gully to which he had noticed the fish were in the habit of resorting" (Ives 1861:27). Robinson also had heard rumors that a ship bearing a large amount of gold for Count Rousset de Boulbon's expedition had sunk a few miles upriver. See also Lingenfelter 1978. 10 mi upstream from mouth of the Colorado River and about 2 mi above Unwin Point. 31°49′24″N, 114°51′15″W (Ives 1861).

Rocas Consag (Gulf of California, BC). Rocks and reef in Golfo de California, 30 km NE of San Felipe. The pinnacles lack any beach or vascular plants; reefs and treacherous rip currents make boating hazardous here. From a distance these guano-covered rocks resemble the sail of a ship. Although it is not currently within AG, Hastings & Findley (this volume) make a compelling case for adding it to the biosphere reserve.

Named for Father Ferdinand Konsák (Consag), who made an adventurous journey along Baja California's eastern coast by dugout canoe in 1746 (Crosby 1994; Sykes 1937). =Ship Rock, Clarence Island (by Hardy 1829, for Duke of Clarence, Lord High Admiral of England). 31°06′30″N, 114°29′W. 286 ft.

Rock Tank (GR). Ephemeral tinaja in NW Aguila Mountains, 2.5 mi NW of Aguila Mountains summit. 32°40′11″N, 113°22′25″W. 725 ft.

Rocky Point (GR). Abandoned railroad siding on Tucson, Cornelia, & Gila Bend Railroad, 0.5 mi N of Deadman Gap. 32°32′03″N, 112°50′50″W. 1,250 ft.

Rocky Point (Sonora). See Puerto Peñasco.

Romero Fields (PI). See Sierra Suvuk, Tinaja Suvuk.

Round Butte (SD). Rounded lava-escarpment butte in central Sand Tank Mountains, 2.5 mi ESE of Blue Plateau. 32°47′15″N, 112°30′05″W. 2,443 ft.

Rowood (Pima Co.). Former townsite E of modern Ajo (Rickard 1996). Name from a rearrangement of the first

Figure 39.43. Río Sonoyta at Sierra de los Tanques, about 1985.

Figure 39.44. Río Sonoyta at Batamote bridge, December 1982.

name of President Woodrow Wilson (term 1913–1921). See Ajo, Clarkston, Gibson. 32°22′05″N, 112°50′43″W. 1,714 ft.

Ruhen Monument (Sonora). See Sonoyta.

Rustler Canyon (OP). A large, secluded canyon in Ajo Mountains, S of Bull Pasture, 2.5 mi SSE of Ajo Peak, and N of Sweetwater Pass. Canyon curves around hill labeled BM 3075. Rustled cattle were sometimes hidden in this canyon. Mouth at 32°00′09″N, 112°39′54″W. 2,400 ft.

Rustler Canyon Tinajas (OP). Series of intermittent and ephemeral tinajas in Rustler Canyon. The tinajas occur in the stream channel from 2,560 ft to 2,750 ft. 32°00′28″N, 112°40′09″W.

Ryan Tank (GR). Tinaja in the Wellton Hills noted by Kirk Bryan (1925:203). The precise location of this tinaja is unknown, but the Wellton Hills were a favorite

Figure 39.45. *Rocas Consag. (Photo by Carlos Navarro)*

exploration area for prospectors at the time of Bryan's survey, and they would have known the locations of any tinajas in this small group of hills.

Ryans Canyon (GR). Canyon and arroyo in Sauceda Mountains, beginning about 0.5 mi SE of Tom Thumb pinnacle. Mouth at 32°35′11″N, 112°42′35″W. 1,740 ft.

S

Saguaro Gap (CP). Pass through southern Granite Mountains, 1.5 mi S of Granite Pass Tank. Named for numerous saguaros *(Carnegiea gigantea)* in area. 32°17′57″N, 113°15′43″W. 930 ft.

Saguaro Gap Well (CP). Abandoned well SE of Granite Mountains. It was built about 1951 by Alton Netherlin, an Ajo attorney who wanted to supplement his income by ranching. Poor water curtailed his efforts. 32°17′06″N, 113°13′32″W. 837 ft.

Sahuaro, El (PI). Truck stop on Mexico Highway 2, 3.4 km ESE of La Joyita and 2 km E of Cerro Pinto microondas tower. May =Rancho Pozo de Doña Victoria. 32°13′45″N, 114°01′50″W. 290 m.

Sahuaro Pass, El (GR). Pass on international boundary between Tinajas Altas Mountains and Sierra Lechuguilla, 4.5 mi SSE of Tinajas Altas and W of marker 190. N from El Sahuaro truck stop. =High Tanks Gate, a misnomer, since there is no gate here, nor even a fence. 32°15′08″N, 114°01′04″W. 1,100 ft.

Salazaria Wash (CP). Arroyo and canyon in eastern Tuseral (Tule) Mountains, 4 mi SE of Tule Well. Informally named by Annita Harlan for plentiful *Salazaria mexicana* (bladder sage), which was named to honor

José Salazar y Larregui, who headed the Mexican contingent of the international boundary survey of 1854 (Emory 1859).

From that same enterprise, William H. Emory, who led the American team of surveyors and scientists, is remembered with *Castela emoryi* (a crucifixion thorn), Arthur Schott with *Pachycereus schottii* (senita cactus), Josiah Gregg with *Peniocereus greggii* (night-blooming cereus), and George Thurber with *Stenocereus thurberi* (organ pipe cactus). George Engelmann and Asa Gray, the men who processed many of their collections, are remembered with *Opuntia engelmannii* (prickly pear) and *Krameria grayi* (white ratany), among others. Mouth at 32°11′42″N, 113°42′18″W. 1,000 ft.

Salina. Spanish for 'salt flat'.

Salina, La (AG). Grand salt basin 25 km SSW of López Collada. This long, narrow salt flat near Bahía Adair is surrounded by dunes except for former seaway to the S. A series of pozos, or pools, dots its margin. Lumholtz (1912:395) called it Salina Grande, describing it as "a large salt deposit forty miles east of the mouth of Colorado River, three miles from the coast. On the flat, north-western shore are sixteen fresh-water springs." The vegetation, flora, and hydrology are described by Ezcurra et al. (1988) and Felger (2000). =Meḍ g Ṣu:daġĭ, Memelig Sudagi; historically transcribed Murtegshóotak, O'odham for 'running water' or 'the water is flowing.' 31°31′N, 114°07′W. Less than 5 m.

Also **La Salina** (AG). A tiny settlement at the SE side of La Salina salt flat; its industry is commercial mining of salt from adjacent brine flats. 31°30′N, 114°08′W. 10 m.

Salina del Pinacate (AG). Salt flats 4 km SE of López Collada and at the head of Estero de las Lisas, in NW corner of Bahía Adair. Salt was harvested prehistorically for use and trade far inland; also commercially mined in modern times (see Ezcurra et al. 1988). This was a principal place for O'odham salt gathering. =On or Óno (O'odham for 'salt') or Ka:v Onkam ('badger's salt'), and historically transcribed Kavonoka. Vicinity 31°40′N, 113°56′W. Near sea level.

Salinas Ometepec (AG). Salt flats 37 km N of San Felipe. Commercially mined. Associated with Ejido Industrial Año de Juárez. See Estero Ometepec. 31°25′N, 114°59′W.

Salt Well (CP). Abandoned well in Growler Valley. It was drilled in 1952 by Alton Netherlin for livestock, but its water was too salty for use. 32°23′05″N, 113°11′42″W. 755 ft.

Salvatierra Cone (PI). A minor volcanic crater or cone 12 km NNE of Pinacate Peak and 7 km NW of Elegante Crater. Named by Ronald Ives in honor of the Jesuit missionary Juan María de Salvatierra, close friend of

Figure 39.46. La Salina.

Padre Kino. Ives admired these peripatetic explorers; his jeep was named El Peregrino, Spanish for 'pilgrim' and also the nickname of Sebastián Tarabal, an Indian who guided Capt. Juan Bautista de Anza and Fray Francisco Garcés across the desert to Yuma (Ives 1984, 1989). 31°52′34″N, 113°27′23″W. 510 m.

San Antonio Mine (CP). Mica mine in Chico Shunie Hills, 7 mi SW of Ajo. The mine claim at this site remains the only private inholding within CP. Although the FWS has offered numerous times to purchase the claim, the owners have declined. =Sunshine Mica Mine, Pumice Corporation of Arizona, Ballestreras Mine. 32°18′25″N, 112°57′02″W. 1,960 ft.

San Cristobal Valley (CP, GR). Lengthy valley originating E of Agua Dulce Mountains and running NW between Granite/Aguila mountains on E and Bryan/ Mohawk mountains on W to the Gila River. Named for religious settlement Christvale (=Chrystoval), founded in 1882, which tried to irrigate desert NE of Mohawk Mountains. In 1911 the site's name was shortened to Stoval to facilitate telegraphy (Granger 1960). Formerly considered a NW extension of Mohawk Valley. =San Cristobal Desert, San Cristobal Plain. 32°25′05″N, 113°23′06″W. 310–850 ft.

San Cristobal Wash (CP, GR). Arroyo that drains San Cristobal Valley. Joins Growler Wash SW of Aguila Mountains, and together they nominally merge with Gila River at N end of Mohawk Mountains; actually, their waters generally dissipate in silt flats 10 mi S of Dateland. Mouth at 32°47′07″N, 113°44′30″W. 310 ft.

San Felipe (BC). The northernmost town on the Baja California shore of the Gulf of California, 100 km S of Río Colorado delta and 193 km S of Mexicali. Originally a *vagabundo* fishing village, it is now a tourist mecca. Bajada W of town is Llano el Moreno ('brown plain'). Named for one of the saints Philip. 31°02′30″N, 114°50′00″W. 10 m.

Also **Bahía San Felipe** (BC). Bay immediately E of town.

San Luis (Yuma Co.). Twin city of San Luis Río Colorado, Sonora. Immediately north of the international border and port of entry, it serves commerce and agriculture. O'odham name was Gege Who Kihm ('wildcat village'). 2000 population: 15,322, up from 5,643 estimated in 1994. 32°29′06″N, 114°46′54″W. 136 ft.

San Luis Río Colorado (Sonora). Fast-growing city in the NW corner of Sonora, adjacent to E bank of Río Colorado. Known as San Luis R.C. to distinguish it from younger sister-city of San Luis, Arizona. A hub of transportation and agriculture founded 1906. Formerly Rancho Andrade (founded by Cipriano Domínguez) and renamed for "fiesta el Día de San Luis" (Serafín 1992). Estimated 1996 population: 123,090. 32°29′06″N, 114°46′54″W. 40 m.

San Pedro Mártir, Sierra (BC). See Sierra San Pedro Mártir.

Sánchez Islas, Estación (AG). See Estación Sánchez Islas.

Sand Tank Mountains (GR, SD). This extensive mountain range 11 mi SE of Gila Bend is noted for plateaus, pinnacles, canyons, and lavas. Features outstanding stands of saguaros and other desert plant life. Named by Kirk Bryan in 1920 for the Sand Tanks tinajas. Before then the Sand Tanks were considered a southern extension of the Maricopa Mountains. Alternately, some maps considered them a northern extension of the Sauceda Mountains. =Maricopa Mountains, Maricopa Range, Sauceda Mountains. Summit is Maricopa Peak. See Javelina Mountain. 32°45′08″N, 112°22′45″W. 4,084 ft.

Sand Tank Mountains Catchments (GR, SD). Wildlife water catchments and guzzler troughs in Sand Tank Mountains, numbered chronologically.

Number 1 (SD). =AGFD #396. 3.8 mi SW of Big Horn. 32°49′17″N, 112°25′43″W. 1,820 ft.

Number 2 (SD). =AGFD #397. On N flank of Squaw Tits, 4.8 mi W of Big Horn. Vicinity of 32°51′11″N, 112°28′27″W. 1,800 ft.

Number 3 (SD). =AGFD #499. 0.7 mi ESE of Bender Spring. 32°40′43″N, 112°21′53″W. 2,770 ft.

Figure 39.47. *Santo Domingo, 1907 (Hornaday 1908).*

Number 4 (SD). =AGFD #500. 3.8 mi SSE of Johnson Well. 32°39′45″N, 112°19′47″W. 2,490 ft.

Number 5 (SD). =AGFD #501. 1.0 mi SW of Johnson Well. 32°42′01″N, 112°21′54″W. 2,580 ft.

Number 6 (GR). =AGFD #502. 2.2 mi ESE of Maricopa Peak. 32°44′35″N, 112°20′33″W. 2,380 ft.

Number 7 (GR). =AGFD #637. 2.7 mi WSW of Dragons Tooth. 32°37′38″N, 112°27′48″W. 2,110 ft.

Number 8 (GR). =AGFD #638. 2.2 mi NW of Dragons Tooth. 32°39′57″N, 112°27′25″W. 2,180 ft.

Number 9 (GR). =AGFD #792. 1.6 mi NW of Papago Indian Chief Mine. 32°47′12″N, 112°31′02″W. 1,800 ft.

See also Bender Spring, Burro Spring, Dragons Tooth Tank, Mesquite Well.

Sand Tank Wash (GR, SD). Arroyo flowing NW toward Gila River from Javelina Mountain. Joins Gila River at 32°59′16″N, 112°43′04″W. 650 ft.

Sand Tank Well (GR). Corral and well drilled 600 ft W of original Sand Tanks. Dug prior to 1920 by Guido (=Jim?) Gatlin, who worked for a rancher named Clements; well was 75 ft deep with water at 60 ft. 32°44′58″N, 112°26′33″W. 2,360 ft.

Sand Tanks (SD). Sand-filled rock tinajas in large arroyo 20 mi SE of Gila Bend, at SW base of Javelina Mountain. These tinajas are plunge pools in tuffaceous conglomerate in a channel of Sand Tank Wash 30 ft deep and 50 ft wide. The upper pool, usually sand-filled, is about 20 ft wide by 40 ft long; lower pool is 4 ft by 6 ft. These were the only reliable sources of water in the range until wells were dug and drilled, most in the 1920s. Cattle were watered at Sand Tanks when driven NW from Stout's Well (see Johnson Well) to Gila Bend. Named for mountain range. Vicinity of 32°44′58″N, 112°26′33″W. 2,600 ft.

Santa Clara Slough (AG). Tidal slough on eastern edge of Río Colorado delta, 11 km NW of El Golfo de Santa Clara. The muddy banks are largely held together by mats of nipa *(Distichlis palmeri)*. =Estero Santa Clara. Its upper end =Rillito Salada and ties into Ciénega de Santa Clara. Mouth at 31°45′N, 114°35′W. Sea level.

Santa Rosa Peak (OP). See Ajo Mountains.

Santo Domingo (PI). Former hacienda on Río Sonoyta 12 km W (downstream) of Sonoyta. Developed by the infamous and later respected Cipriano Ortega, this feudal ranching and farming hacienda had its heyday 1870–1904 (Hornaday 1908; Hoy 1970, 1990). Now site of namesake modern-day ejido. Saint Dominic (ca. 1170–1221) founded the Dominicans; ironically, his order was the first to abandon manual labor. =Ejido Santo Domingo. 31°53′43″N, 112°57′35″W. 340 m.

Sargent's Point (AG). Promontory on western shore at head of Gulf of California, named by Lt. R. W. H. Hardy (1829) on his exploratory trip aboard ship *Bruja* in 1827. 31°41′08″N, 114°48′23″W. 3 m.

Sauceda (TON). Former Tohono O'odham winter ranchería, 20 mi NE of Ajo. Lumholtz (1912:384) called it the "main ranch of north-western Papaguería" with 50–70 houses and several springs and wells. Spanish for 'place of the willow grove'. =Saucita; O'odham name is Ce'ulkam or Cíuligam, 'where willow grows', historically transcribed Tshiulikami, Chiulikam, or 9 other variant names. 32°34′20″N, 112°31′10″W. 2,092 ft.

Also associated with the Sauceda village complex are S-Vegĭ Vahia or Wegi Wahi, historically transcribed Vokiváxia, O'odham for 'red well'; and Pozo Colorado, Spanish for 'red well'.

Sauceda Cave Pothole (GR). An artificial tinaja developed in 1974 for wildlife in Sauceda Mountains, 2.3 mi WNW of Hat Mountain. Mistakenly labeled Thanksgiving Day Tank on USGS Midway 7.5′ topo map (1986,

1996). =AGFD #675; Sauceda Mountains Pothole. See Sauceda Mountain catchments. 32°38′55″N, 112°46′42″W. 1,440 ft.

Sauceda Mountains (GR, TON). Wondrous volcanic range 16 mi S of Gila Bend. Was one of three primary sources of obsidian for ancient peoples in this region (Shackley 2005). See Sauceda. A 1930 USGS map divides the Saucedas into west and east halves, though those names are no longer used. 32°55′36″N, 112°39′11″W. 4,118.

Sauceda Mountains Catchments (GR). Wildlife water catchments and guzzler troughs in Sauceda Mountains, numbered chronologically.

Number 1 (GR). =AGFD #578. 1.9 mi SSE of Lookout Mountain. 32°43′04″N, 112°45′46″W. 1,270 ft.

Number 2 (GR). =AGFD #579. 1.5 mi W of Pistol Pass. 32°33′42″N, 112°38′04″W. 2,150 ft.

Number 3 (GR). =AGFD #580. 0.8 mi S of Tom Thumb. 32°31′17″N, 112°35′12″W. 2,420 ft.

Number 4 (GR). =AGFD #581. 1.8 mi NW of Pistol Pass. 32°34′58″N, 112°37′49″W. 2,140 ft.

Number 5 (GR). =AGFD #582. 0.5 mi E of Pistol Pass. 32°33′40″N, 112°36′04″W. 2,160 ft.

Number 6 (GR). =AGFD #583. 3.6 mi W of Pistol Pass. 32°33′23″N, 112°40′17. 2,078 ft.

Number 7 (GR). =AGFD #584. 2.5 mi WSW of Tom Thumb. 32°31′18″N, 112°37′30″W. 2,240 ft.

Number 8 (GR). =AGFD #585. 2.0 mi SE of Hat Mountain. 32°37′07″N, 112°42′45″W. 1,800 ft.

See also Black Bottom Tank, Holt Tank, Sauceda Cave Pothole (Sauceda Mountains Pothole), Thanksgiving Day Tank.

Sauceda Wash (GR). One of several major washes draining Sand Tank and Sauceda mountains N to the Gila River. Mouth at 32°59′17″N, 112°46′28″W. 610 ft.

Scarface Mountain (CP). Pocked peak at SE end of Growler Mountains, 3 mi NNE of Bates Well. 32°12′25″N, 112°56′07″W. 2,546 ft.

Schuchuli (TON). An O'odham village located 1 mi N of the Gunsight Mine. Once known as Haynes Well, probably dug before 1900. As goats were raised here, it was sometimes called Goat Ranch. Around 1925 a man named John Blair owned it, so the name became Blair Ranch. =Gunsight Ranch. Today the settlement is known as Schuchuli, Schuchuligk ('sure a lot of chickens', =S-cuculig), or Siswatk, Sisalatuk ('goat ranch'). See King 1961. Noted for its statue of Saint Francis and for being the first solar-powered Sonoran Desert village. 32°13′08″N, 112°41′01″W. 1,980 ft.

S-cuk Mo'o (CP). See Cabeza Prieta Mountains.

Sección 121 (AG). Abandoned railroad maintenance camp at km post 121 on Chihuahua-Pacífico line between Mexicali and Puerto Peñasco, 12 km N of El Golfo. =Sección K(ilometer) Ciento Veintiuno. 31°47′50″N, 114°31′25″W. 130 m.

Senita Basin (OP). Valley between Puerto Blanco Mountains and Sonoyta Mountains. It shelters the largest stand in U.S. of senita cactus (*Pachycereus schottii,* =Lophocereus schottii). 6 mi NW of Lukeville. 31°57′37″N, 112°51′26″W. 1,700 ft.

Senita Pass (OP). Low pass in Puerto Blanco Mountains, 0.9 mi SE of Senita Basin and 0.25 mi NE of Martinez Mine. 31°57′07″N, 112°50′43″W. 1,760 ft.

Senita Tank (CP). Waterhole in an adit on S edge of Drift Hills. It was built in 1957 for desert bighorn sheep, but they have seldom used it. "The [first bighorn] ram seen at Sinita Tank July 11 [1961] was down inside the dry tank when the observer [Gale Monson] reached the lip of the tank. The ram rushed up out of the hole on a 50° slope and then went straight up over the wall in front of the hole without seeming effort—a feat that must be seen to be believed. From the amount of sign in the area, he apparently has been making the [dry] artificial cave of Sinita Tank his home for some time, at least two weeks, and during this time undoubtedly went without water" (CP file report). Tank was named for a senita cactus (*Pachycereus schottii*) growing in vicinity; it represents northernmost range of species. =Sinita Tank. 32°15′24″N, 113°40′31″W. 1,060 ft.

Sentinel (Maricopa Co.). Railroad settlement along Southern Pacific Railroad and I-8, 30 mi W of Gila Bend. Named for nearby Sentinel Peak (4.5 mi ENE; 1,077 ft), which "stood out in the distance like a sentinel of the desert" (Barnes 1935:397). Listed as an Hia C'ed O'odham settlement by Jones (1969); families living here were hired locally and regionally for seasonal farm work. 32°51′34″N, 113°12′36″W. 695 ft.

Sentinel Plain (Maricopa Co.). Low but expansive sheet of lava deposited 4–8 million years ago, 25 mi WSW of Gila Bend. It extends roughly in a 10-mi radius from Sentinel Peak and can be viewed from Sentinel rest area on I-8. See Lynch 1982. Bryan (1925:217, 408) refers to the area S of here as "The Great Plain," though we know of no other use of that name. =Stanwix Flats, Tartron Flats, Sentinel Lava Plain. 32°56′45″N, 113°15′26″W. Average elevation 700 ft.

Sentinel Wash (Maricopa Co.). Arroyo draining N portion of Sentinel Plain. Joins Gila River at 32°56′16″N, 113°19′12″W. 440 ft.

Serdán, Ejido Aquiles (Sonora). See Ejido Aquiles Serdán.

Shawmut (SD). Active railroad siding on Southern Pacific Railroad, 16.7 mi E of Gila Bend. Formerly named Ocapos, which was a reversal of the first two letters of the words Southern Pacific Company. During construction of the railway a large camp of Chinese laborers encamped here (Devine 2004). 32°59′48″N, 112°30′37″W. 1,250 ft.

Figure 39.48. *Sierra Blanca.*

Sheep Hollow Tank (CP). See Cabeza Prieta Tanks.

Sheep Mountain (CP). Mountain 4 mi ENE of Papago Well, in northern Agua Dulce Mountains. Named for a solitary desert bighorn ram that lived on the mountain. =Sierra Borrego. 32°06′58″N, 113°13′10″W. 1,977 ft.

Sheep Mountain (GR). Summit of Gila Mountains, 11 mi SSW of Wellton. Named for desert bighorn sheep *(Ovis canadensis mexicana)* in area. 32°31′59″N, 114°14′01″W. 3,156 ft.

Sheep Mountain (SD). Prominent ridge in N Maricopa Mountains, 5.5 mi SE of Margies Peak. Named for desert bighorn sheep. 33°06′42″N, 112°31′48″W. 2,493 ft.

Sheep Mountain Tank (GR). Dam and fiberglass tanks 0.5 mi NW of Sheep Mountain; built in 1995 for wildlife. 32°32′17″N, 114°14′31″W. 1,660 ft.

Sheep Peak (CP). Pinnacle in northern Growler Mountains, 1.8 mi NW of Charlie Bell Well. Visible from as far away as I-8. =Sheep Tank Peak, Sheep Shit Peak; Ge Huduns, O'odham for 'big steep hill'. 32°24′16″N, 113°07′18″W. 2,217 ft.

Sheep Tank (CP). Twin natural, intermittent tinajas NE of Sheep Peak in Growler Mountains. Reportedly named prior to 1900 for dead bighorn found here after two bandits fleeing holdup in Phoenix poisoned this waterhole with strychnine to kill the posse chasing them. The bandits, James Kerrick (=Carrick, Kerrig) and Lee Bentley, were shot by the posse, who discovered the scheme and did not drink the water (O'Neal 1987). =Ceṣoiñ Vahia, O'odham for 'sheep tank', though this name sometimes is applied also to Charlie Bell Well. 32°27′08″N, 113°06′19″W. 1,340 ft.

Sheep Tank (GR). Defunct water catchment in canyon on E side of Vopoki Ridge and 3.6 mi SW of Sheep Mountain. 32°30′09″N, 114°16′58″W. 1,160 ft.

S-hewelig (Maricopa Co.). See Gila Bend.

S-hia Tamke (GR). Waterhole on W side of Aguila Mountains, possibly =Don Diego Tanks; S-hia Tampk, Siat'tamph (O'odham for 'urine laying' or 'fool's tank'). See Don Diego Tanks.

Shipyard Slough (AG). Tidal estuary on E side of Río Colorado delta, 15 km NW of El Golfo de Santa Clara. A ship repair and construction yard was built here in 1865 on the slough's upper reach to utilize the extreme tidal fluctuations to dry-dock vessels; see Puerto Isabel and Lingenfelter 1978. Mouth at 31°45′31″N, 114°40′45″W. Sea level.

Sierra. Spanish for 'mountain range'.

Sierra de los Alacranes (Sonora). See Sierra del Viejo.

Sierra Arida (CP). This subdivision of the Cabeza Prieta Mountains 3 mi E of Tule Well was not named until the mid-1960s. Many other significant places in the region still lack names. Spanish for 'arid mountain'. 32°13′52″N, 113°40′35″W. 1,770 ft.

Sierra Blanca (PI). This granitic mountain range 16 km SE of Pinacate Peak is surrounded on the N by lava flows and on the S by dunes. Larry May (1973) recorded a weather station reading of 134°F (57°C) on S side of range in late June 1971. Lumholtz (1912:279) reports it is called Sierra Blanca, "which, as its name implies, is of a very light granite color; the Indians too, in their language, call it the 'white range.'" =La Bambarria (Spanish for 'idiot' or 'fool', though its application here is unclear); Toa Komalik, O'odham for 'whitish thin place'; historically transcribed Tóakomalik, loosely translated as 'where it is thin and flat' (Mathiot 1963) or 'white'. 31°34′30″N, 113°26′50″W. 460 m.

Misapplied on one map to Sierra Extraña. Name shared with another Sierra Blanca (TON) 25 mi E of Why and 7 mi WNW of Quijotoa.

Sierra El Choclo Duro (PI). Name for section of nearly impassable sand on trail between Sonoyta and San Luis R.C. Now applied to lava butte 12 km NW of Pinacate microondas tower (=La Lava) and 24 km W of Los Vidrios. This butte is in the southern extension of what are called the Tuseral or Tule Mountains. *Choclo duro* is Spanish for 'patent leather shoe'; one purportedly was found there by travelers in 1920s or 1930s. 32°06′00″N, 113°38′55″W. 520 m.

Sierra Cipriano (Sonora). Granitic mountains 7 km SW of Sonoyta and on E side of Mexico Highway 8. This outlier of the 53-million-year-old Gunnery Range Granite was named for Cipriano Ortega (see Santo Domingo). A number of plants found on this mountain occur no farther west in northwestern Sonora, e.g., *Dodonea viscosa* and *Delphinium scaposum* (Felger 2000). 31°45′55″N, 113°14′24″W. 900 m.

Sierra Cubabi (Sonora). A large granitic mountain 8 km S of Sonoyta and on the NE side of Mexico Highway 2.

Godfrey Sykes climbed to its top in 1907 to ascertain its height. Western extent of white-tailed deer *(Odocoileus virginianus)*; generally, deer W of Arizona Highway 85 and Mexico Highway 8 are mule deer *(Odocoileus hemionus)*. A population of Sonoran rosewood *(Vauquelinia californica* subsp. *sonorensis)* in the Sierra Cubabi is the only documented record for the state of Sonora, although an observation of *Vaquelinia* in the Sierra del Viejo near Caborca may be this subspecies (Felger et al. 2001). Village of Cubabi is 4 km E of mountains. =Cobabi Mountains. Ka:v Vavia (=Kov Vavia, Kov Vahia, Cobabi) is O'odham for 'badger's well'. 32°33′03″N, 112°52′03″W. 1,330 m.

Sierra de los Cucapá (BC). Mountain range 16 km S of Mexicali. It forms E wall of Laguna Salada basin. Geothermic zone on its eastern pediment at Cerro Prieto is noted for bubbling mudpots and a geothermal plant. Range also features palm oases, sulfur mines, and several tinajas, including Pozo Coyote and Agua de las Mujeres. Summit is Dos Picos: Cerro Nuevo is the northern one, and Cerro Pescadores the southern and slightly higher.

This range, named for Cucapá Indians who live in delta region of Río Colorado, serves as a *zona indígena.* Between 1890 and 1900 the tribe had four bands: the Mat Skrui and Hwanyak, who lived primarily in the delta, and the Wi Ahwir and Kwakwarsh, who lived nearer to and in the sierra. Before the river was dammed, the Cucapás subsisted on agriculture, gathering, hunting, and fishing in cycles coinciding with the annual flooding of the Río Colorado, which on average crested in June at nearly 4 million acre-feet for the month (Kelly 1977; Williams 1983).

Southern end of range is separately labeled Sierra Mayor; N end is Cerro Centinela along international border. =Sierra de los Cocopahs, Cocopa Mountains, Sierra Cucapá. 32°22′34″N, 115°27′23″W. 1,060 m.

Sierra Enterrada (PI). Small granitic mountain SW of the Pinacate volcanic shield, 27 km WNW of Pinacate Peak. Surrounded and partially buried by windblown sand dunes. Exceptionally photogenic. Spanish for 'buried'. =Buried Range. 31°49′40″N, 113°47′05″W. 180 m.

Sierra Estrella (Maricopa Co., Pinal Co., Gila River Indian Reservation). Large mountain range on E side of Rainbow Valley and 9 mi NE of SD. Bryan (1925:221) gives his impression of this spectacular range: "Much of the topography and scenery is as rugged, wild, and grand as any found in the United States or Alaska." Despite being in Phoenix's backyard, the range remains remarkably free of human visitation, largely due to its rugged and extremely arid nature (see Annerino 1996).

Spanish for 'star', "as the white spot in forehead of a horse" (Barnes 1935:148). We have yet to find a definitive derivation but note two plausible theories. First,

the range has "a quartz peak which is snow white, and I have seen it shine like a star when illuminated by the sun or full moon" (John Gunn). Quartz Peak (4,052 ft) is about 0.5 mi W of Butterfly Mountain. Second, by foot, horseback, or stagecoach, the trip across the Forty Mile Desert from Maricopa Wells to Gila Bend usually was made at night to avoid the heat; some called it Jornada de las Estrellas, Spanish for 'journey of the stars'. The mountain range is near the starting point of that journey westward, or near the destination end if one is traveling eastward. The name Sierra de los [*sic*] Estrellas was in use by 1854 (Bailey 1963:83).

Conklin (1878:218) observes, "At Maricopa Wells there is an oblong isolated mountain range—known as Sa-de-la-Estrellas—one end of which shows a most beautiful and perfect profile of the old historic chief of the Aztecs, Montezuma—so recognized by the tribes of the country." Conklin joked that personally he thought the rocky profile looked more like George Washington than Montezuma.

The range has had several names. In 1775 Friar Francisco Garcés named the mountains Sierra de San Joseph de Cumars. The Akimel O'odham (Pima Indians) called the range Kómadk, Kamatuk, or Komatke, meaning 'flat', 'thick', or 'broad'. Kómadk is plural of 'ko'okmadki', which also means 'blue palo verde' (Rea 1997: 162). Sierra Estrella figures prominently in traditional River Piman culture (Rea 1997). After 1851 the name Maricopa Mountains also was used, while the Maricopa Indians called them 'We-al-hus'. Unnamed summit at 33°16′24″N, 112°16′48″W. 4,512 ft.

Sierra Extraña (PI). Granitic mountain at western margin of Pinacate lava shield, 20 km WNW of Pinacate Peak. Labeled the Strange Range by Hornaday (1908) because its color and form seem peculiarly out of place in this lava field. Spanish for 'strange'. Mislabeled Sierra Blanca on one map. 31°50′45″N, 113°41′25″W. 200 m.

Sierra Juárez (BC). Large and spectacular mountains forming W wall of Laguna Salada basin, 48 km SW of Mexicali. Range forms the E plateau of peninsular cordillera and has several peaks over 1,500 m. Some maps apply name Sierra de las Tinajas to the range's SE portion. Named for Benito Pablo Juárez, president of Mexico 1857–1872.

Botanically rich canyon oases on E escarpment support groves of native blue palm *(Brahea armata)* and desert fan palm *(Washingtonia filifera)*. From N to S, range's canyons are named Cañón de las Palmas Azules, Palmas de Cantú, Cañón de los Tanques, Cañón del Tajo, Cañón del Carrizo, Cañón de Guadalupe, Cañón la Mora, Cañón Palomar, Cañón Santa Isabel, and Cañón de Agua Caliente. The sierra is exceptionally rich archaeologically. Contains Parque Nacional Constitución de 1857, and *zonas indígenas* (comparable to U.S. Indian reservations) for Pai Pai Santa Catarina, Pai Pai Jumau, and Jumau Cochimi native peoples. Summit is Cerro la Campaña (Spanish for 'bell' or 'lookout') at 32°09′N, 115°59′W. 1,869 m.

Sierra Lechuguilla (PI, GR). Granitic mountain N of Sierra del Viejo and Mexico Highway 2, 30 mi SSE of Wellton. The main mass is in Sonora but extends into Arizona. *Lechuguilla* is a generic Spanish name for agave, here *Agave deserti*. Although the name predates 1918, the sierra has been considered by some to be a southern part of Tinajas Altas Mountains; =Sierra Tinajas Altas. Summit at 32°12′27″N, 113°57′14″W. 720 m.

Sierra el Mayor (BC). Mountains W of Río Colorado delta and 60 km SSE of Mexicali. Summit El Mayor is at 32°05′21″N, 115°18′27″W. 940 m; 3,159 ft.

Other summits include Cerro el Macho (Spanish for 'pillar', 'abutment', or 'manly'), Cerro el Águila (Spanish for 'eagle'; 700 m), Cerro el Coyote (520 m), Cerro el Metate (640 m), Cerro Peludo (Spanish for 'hairy' or 'shaggy'), and Cerro la Garza (Spanish for 'heron' or perhaps a surname).

Sierra Nina (Sonora). Steep granitic mountain S of Mexico Highway 2, 38 km NW of Pinacate Peak. Lumholtz (1912:237) named it for "my friend, Mrs. [Nina] John Gray, of Boston." From Nina, mythic goddess of the sea depths; it is not Niña. =Sierra del Águila. 32°05′35″N, 113°45′20″W. 630 m.

Sierra Pinacate (PI). See Pinacate, El; Pinacate Peak.

Sierra Pinta (CP). A major mountain range in CP. Named for its two-tone appearance: N half is blond granite, southern half is black gneiss. It represents the classical horst and graben geology of Basin and Range Province. Spanish for 'speckled' or 'painted'. =Pinto Range, Sierra Pintada. Summit is BM Pinta at 32°15′47″N, 113°32′31″W. 2,950 ft.

Sierra Pinta (Sonora). Granitic range 40 km ENE of Puerto Peñasco. Site of active and historic gold mining (see MacPherson 1973). 31°25′00″N, 113°05′10″W. 580 m.

Sierra de Pintas (BC). Colorful mountains 35 km W of Río Colorado delta. Ruin of La Fortuna Mine is famous attraction. See Range Hill. =Sierra Pinta, Sierra de las Pintas. 31°35′N, 115°10′W. 800 m.

Sierra del Rosario (PI). This extremely arid and isolated granitic range was named by Lumholtz (1912:243, 311) for its resemblance to a string of rosary beads strung across the dunes, though he notes that the name already had some currency. Surrounded by eolian dunes of the Gran Desierto, this range comprises a series of saw-toothed peaks with their bases buried by sand and alluvium. The range covers approximately 78 km² including its ramparts, and supports a flora of at least 111 species (Felger 1982, 2000). At one time desert bighorn sheep lived in the range, but likely they are now extir-

pated (Sheldon 1993). May (1973) reports a rainless episode here of at least 34 months. =Hia C'eḍ Komalk, historically transcribed Hiatikomalik, O'odham for 'mountain crest in the sand'. Summit at 32°05′25″N, 114°12′20″W. 562 m.

Sierra de la Salada (PI). Small mountains 11 km W of Quitobaquito, between Sierra de los Tanques and Agua Dulce Mountains, NW of Río Sonoyta. The main route of the old Camino del Diablo left the Río Sonoyta at the southern end of these mountains and then angled northwestward toward the vicinity of border monument 177. 31°58′00″N, 113°09′30″W. 460 m.

Sierra San Felipe (BC). Several groups of mountains W and NW of San Felipe. Its summits include Cerro Juan (3,369 ft) and Cerro Kino (4,290 ft; 31°00′N, 114°58′W).

Sierra San Francisco (Sonora). A granite range 32 km SW of Sonoyta and midway to Puerto Peñasco; E of Mexico Highway 8. It features a prominent tinaja and significant prehistoric petroglyphs. Jesuit missionary Francisco Xavier (1506–1551) was Padre Kino's patron saint. 31°38′05″N, 113°07′20″W. 810 m.

Sierra San Pedro Mártir (BC). Enormous and enchanting mountain range 40 km W of San Felipe but visible from most of northern Gulf of California. Backbone of Baja California. Occasionally appears as mirages and loomings to viewers on E shore of gulf (Ives 1989). Named for Mission San Pedro Mártir de Verona, established by Dominicans in 1794. Saint Peter Martyr (1206–1252) was born in Verona, Italy, joined the Dominicans, was appointed inquisitor of Lombardy, and was killed by Catharists.

This exceptionally rugged escarpment descends severely toward the Gulf of California. A series of canyons open to the east and include (from N to S) Cañón Esperanza (Spanish for 'hope'), Cañón el Diablito ('little devil'), Arroyo el Diablo ('devil'), Cañón Providencia ('providence'), Cañón del Cajón ('narrow canyon'), Cañada de En Medio ('middle'), El Barroso ('muddy' or 'reddish'), Arroyo Huatamote, Cañón Algodón ('cotton'), La Gringa (pejorative for 'American woman'), Arroyo Agua Caliente ('hot water'), El Berrendo ('pronghorn'), Cañón Parral ('grapevine arbor'), Arroyo Matomí, Arroyo Ames, and Arroyo el Volcán (Anita Alvarez Williams). Contains Parque Nacional Sierra San Pedro Mártir and is a candidate area for UNESCO biosphere reserve (Minnich et al. 1997; see Búrquez & Martínez, this volume). Kiliwa Indians have homeland in Arroyo León, one of the canyons. For adventure here, sample Annerino 1993, Clyde 1975, and O'Bryon 1989.

Summit is **Picacho del Diablo** (BC) at 31°02′30″N, 115°26′30″W. About 3,000 m (10,154 ft). =Cerro de la Encantada (Spanish for 'enchanted').

Also **Laguna Diablo** (BC). An alkali basin at eastern foot of the range. Spanish for 'devil's lake'.

Sierra Santa Clara (PI). See Pinacate Peak.

Sierra de Santa Rosa (OP). Small range at far SE corner of OP along border. Recent USGS maps include it as part of the Ajo Mountains. Alternately, name was once applied to the entire Ajo Range. Santa Rosa de Lima (1586–1617) was the first saint of the Americas. Summit for this smaller range is unnamed peak at 31°53′28″N, 112°37′19″W. 2,921 ft. It is not Santa Rosa Peak.

Sierra Suvuk (PI). Small range 14 km E of Sierra Pinacate. S-Vegĭ (O'odham for 'red'; Lumholtz 1912:393). Summit, E of Tinaja Suvuk, is at 31°45′37″N, 113°21′01″W. 300 m. The Romero floodwater agricultural field called Suvuk, where wheat was cultivated as recently as 1995, is 2 km SW of Sierra Suvuk.

Sierra de los Tanques (PI). Low but sprawling granitic mountains and hills 19 km W of Sonoyta, S of Mexico Highway 2 and W of Mexico Highway 8. Spanish for 'tanks' or 'ponds'. 31°52′30″N, 113°04′10″W. 595 m.

Sierra Tuseral (CP, PI). Rugged granitic and gneiss mountains N of Mexico Highway 2 and extending into CP. Spanish for 'rat hole', possibly for profuse and profound kangaroo rat (*Dipodomys* spp.; common Spanish name *tuso;* also pocket gopher, *Thomomys, tuza*) dens in sands SE of the range (see Lumholtz 1912). The Arizona portion also called Tule Mountains. On some Mexican maps called Sierra del Choclo Duro.

See Tule Mountains and Sierra El Choclo Duro. These ranges may all be synonymous; the issue needs clarification. Tuseral was name locally provided to Lumholtz (1912) and used by Tinker (1978), who had been in the area since the 1930s. Sheldon (1993) knew Tuseral and Tule as two distinct ranges in 1913. However, Gaillard calls both ranges Tule Mountains (International Boundary Commission 1898). Wilson (1933: 160) reports that "the Mexican portion of the range is called Sierra de Tuseral." =Sierra de Tuseral. Mexican summit (higher) is at 32°07′11″N, 113°42′25″W, 810 m; U.S. summit is at BM Tule, 32°10′28″N, 113°43′15″W, 2,307 ft.

Sierra del Viejo (Sonora). Range along S side of Mexico Highway 2, 50 km NW of Pinacate Peak. The largest of the steep, granitic, or crystalline rock mountains W of the Pinacate volcanic field, it is about 20 km long and 3 km wide. The north-facing slope supports an isolated, relict population of *Yucca whipplei* (Turner et al. 1995) as well as desert sumac (*Rhus kearneyi),* desert beargrass (*Nolina bigelovii),* and desert agave (*Agave deserti*). See Felger 2000.

The name Sierra del Viejo was used by Lumholtz (1912:300 and maps), but it may have been known by that name before his visit. Julian Hayden reports that

Figure 39.49. *Sierra del Rosario.*

this name was also used by Don Alberto Celaya and Miguel Ahumada. Ahumada was a mechanic who, in mid-1950s, salvaged dozens of abandoned autos out of the Gran Desierto. Spanish for 'the old one'. =Sierra Viejo; Sierra de los Alacranes ('mountains of the scorpions') on some maps but not so known locally; El Viejo Hombre (Roosevelt 1920). Not to be confused with Sierra del Viejo 40 km SSW of Caborca, Sonora. Summit is at 32°07′51″N, 113°54′29″W. 790 m.

Sierrita el Temporal (PI). See Hornaday Mountains.

Sikol Vahia (Pima Co.). See Pozo Redondo.

Sikort Chuapo (TON). See Pozo Redondo.

Sikort Chuapo Mountains (Pima Co.). Volcanic mountains 12 mi E of Ajo. =Sikol Ce:po, O'odham for 'round well' (see Pozo Redondo). Unnamed summit is at 32°22′07″N, 112°34′46″W. 3,603 ft.

Sikort Chuapo Wash (Pima Co.). Arroyo that originates in Gunsight Hills and runs E of Ajo to join Tenmile Wash near Childs. In 1920s Tenmile Wash and lower Sikort Chuapo Wash were mapped as Rio Cornez. =Sikol Ce:po. Confluence at 32°27′17″N, 112°49′45″W. 1,430 ft.

Si:l Me:k (Maricopa Co.). Former O'odham settlement along Gila River 15–18 mi N of Gila Bend. It was in floodplain of Painted Rocks Reservoir, so families moved away in 1965; may also have been temporarily abandoned before 1910 (King 1961). King also reports some confusion distinguishing Si:l Me:k and Tahi (see Gila Bend). Si:l is O'odham from Spanish *silla,* 'saddle'; O'odham for 'burnt' or 'dead saddle'. =Sil Muk, Sil Murk, Silimok. 32°59′08″N, 112°43′49″W. 660 ft.

Silla, La (PI). See Cerro la Silla.

Silver Star Canyon (CP). Canyon in Cabeza Prieta Mountains about 7 mi NNW of Cabeza Prieta Peak. Named for unproven Silver Star Mine prospect. Mouth at 32°23′32″N, 113°51′06″W. 1,080 ft.

Siovi Shuatak (TON). Summer ranchería on E side of Ajo Range, 4 mi E of Diaz Peak. S-I'orĭ Ṣu:dag is O'odham for 'sweet water'. 31°57′02″N, 112°35′38″W. 2,140 ft.

Siovi Shuatak Pass (TON). Pass through E side of Ajo Range, 1.5 mi NE of Diaz Peak and 1.5 mi ENE of Sweetwater Pass. 31°58′59″N, 112°38′30″W. 2,380 ft.

Siovi Shuatak Wash (TON). Arroyo draining E side of Ajo Range, eventually emptying into Menagers Lake at 31°49′16″N, 112°32′41″W. 1,740 ft.

Slit Rock (OP). Interesting cleft in rock on ridge in Santa Rosa Mountains, 12.5 mi ESE of Lukeville. 31°49′20″N, 112°36′39″W. 2,250 ft.

Slovan Well (GR). Former cattle well near intersection of Midway Wash and Tucson, Cornelia, & Gila Bend railway, 13 mi N of Ajo. 32°33′28″N, 112°51′13″W. 1,210 ft.

Smith Mine (GR). Abandoned mining claim in SW Copper Mountains, featured in *Gold on the Desert,* by Olga Wright Smith. She said of the remote and fierce Lechuguilla Desert: "I walked in the garden often these last days, preferably alone, and looked lovingly at my clumps of brittleweed, my fine beds of desert holly, my borders of paper daisies and desert marigolds. Fresh, after the autumn rains, the plants seemed to be putting forth their best efforts, now that I would be walking among them no more. Here, tended by unseen hands, grew plants equal to any in a botanical garden. They seemed to flourish for me alone, just as the birds seem to sing for me alone. There was no one else to see them, just as there was no one else to hear the birds sing" (Smith 1956:246).

Her plants probably were *Encelia farinosa, Ambrosia ilicifolia, Psilostrophe cooperi,* and *Baileya pleniradiata.* =Last Chance Mine, Copper Coin Mine, Pedestal and Everhandy Mine, Smith Bannard Mine. 32°29′12″N, 114°00′31″W. 1,020 ft.

Smoke Tree Wash (CP). Arroyo in eastern Cabeza Prieta Mountains, named for abundant smoke trees *(Psorothamnus spinosus).* Originates 2 mi S of Cabeza Prieta Peak and runs E to Mohawk Wash in mid–Tule Desert. Mouth at 32°21′40″N, 113°40′02″W. 840 ft.

Smuggler Pass (GR). See Cipriano Pass.

Smugglers Pass (CP). See Temporal Pass.

Smurr (Maricopa Co.). Active siding and former settlement on Southern Pacific Railroad, 3.2 mi W of Gila Bend. Formerly located 1 mi E of present location. Name derivation unknown. 32°55′43″N, 112°49′14″W. 728 ft.

S-mu'umk (Pima Co.). See Cardigan Peak.

Snake Pit Tinaja (OP). A secluded tinaja 1.5 m deep in North Alamo Canyon of Ajo Mountains. The steep sides of this tinaja occasionally trap animals, including snakes (see Fowlie 1965:68). 32°04′40″N, 112°42′30″W. 2,800 ft.

Sneed Ranch (Pima Co.). Ranchstead 4 mi NW of Ajo. Sneed family squatted there in 1926, and Nancy Sneed applied for a homestead in 1936; it is now owned by Lee and Bonnie Price (Bonnie Price). Nearby BM Sneed was for Sneed's ranch. 32°24′43″N, 112°54′28″W. 1,560 ft.

Soda, La (AG). Salt flats with several freshwater artesian pozos that support a miniature, fragile wetland flora including *Cyperus laevigatus, Distichlis spicata,* and *Nitrophila occidentalis.* Soda refers to trona (a form of calcium carbonate) and halite (table salt) found here; "the absence of sulfate salts on these flats supports the hypothesis that the origin of the salts is not marine" but rather from the continental freshwater aquifer (Ezcurra et al. 1988:41). About 20 km SE of López Collada. May =Jegda, O'odham for 'clearing'; historically transcribed Tjútjaka. 31°37′N, 113°49′W. Near sea level.

Solito, El (PI). Minor trail junction S from Mexico Highway 2 to Pozo Nuevo in western Pinacate, 20 km WNW of Los Vidrios. For a short time in late 1970s a person was living in a discarded vehicle here. Spanish for 'little lonely one' or 'loner'. 32°03′19″N, 113°37′43″W. 240 m.

Somerton (Yuma Co.). Agricultural town 7 mi SSW of Yuma. Founded in 1898 and named for Indiana hometown of Capt. A. D. Yocum. Center for Cocopah (=Cucapá) East Reservation and West Reservation. After the Cocopahs in U.S. were displaced by settlers and farms along the Colorado River, they were allotted these small reservations. Just E of town was at one time a small Hia C'ed O'odham camp where O'odham, Cocopahs, and Quechans traded. =Samt, its Cocopah name (Crawford 1989). 2000 population: 7,266. 32°35′48″N, 114°42′32″W. 101 ft.

Sonora. A state in northwestern Mexico; capital is Hermosillo. See Ortega-Noriega & del Río (1985) and Yetman (1996). 2000 population: 2,213,370.

In 1764 Juan Nentvig (1980:3) wrote, "It appears that this region was named Sonora from the beginning.... Although I know nothing of the etymology or origin of the name Sonora, I do not believe I am deceiving myself in being inclined to think it may have been suggested by her great wealth, the news of which swept sonorously across New Spain and into Europe."

The derivation runs deeper and is related to the Mexican place-names of Senora, Señora, Sonora, Arroyo de Señora, and Río Sonora. In 1540 Captain Tristán de Luna y Arellano moved his settlement to a valley which the Indians called Senora. "In the 1540s, a settlement, an area, a river, and a valley all went by an indigenous name recorded as Senora by members of the [Coronado] expedition to Tierra Nueva. The name was transmuted by the Spaniards into Señora and has become Sonora in more recent times.... The ruins of the town of Señora... may lie beneath Baviácora or Aconchi along the Río Sonora..." (Flint & Flint 2005:603, also page 393). From 'sonot,' Ópata for 'reed,' probably *Phragmites australis* (David Yetman).

Sonora Highway 40 (Sonora). Highway from San Luis Río Colorado to El Golfo de Santa Clara.

Sonora Mesa (Sonora). See Mesa de Sonora.

Sonoran Desert (Arizona, Sonora, BC, BCS). An aridlands biotic community and one of the four major North American deserts (Sonoran, Chihuahuan, Mojave, and Great Basin). By consensus, it is the Sonoran Desertscrub Biome. Approximately 100,000 mi^2 (260,000 km^2) in size, it supports over 2,000 plant and 550 vertebrate species (Dimmitt 2000).

Edward Cope (1873:32–36) proposed Sonoran as the name of this biotic province; Hobart Smith (1939:18) suggested Arizonian. Forrest Shreve, a botanist and ecologist at the Desert Botanical Laboratory in Tucson, wrote the classic and defining work on the Sonoran Desert and its subcommunities during the last year of his life as his health was failing (Bowers 1988). He used the word 'Sonoran' "for the area because it has long been employed in the physiographic and biological literature in nearly the same sense, because more of the area lies in the Mexican state of Sonora than in any other state, and finally because of its brevity and convenience" (1951:2).

Shreve (1951) elegantly described seven major vegetational regions in the Sonoran Desert, providing nomenclature, boundaries, and concepts that we use today. Two of Shreve's communities include the areas of northwestern Sonora, southwestern Arizona, and northeastern Baja California covered by studies in this volume. The lower elevations are within the Lower Colorado River Valley region and form the heart of the Sonoran Desert. The higher elevations in the Dry Borders region are in the Arizona Uplands (see Felger 2000; Rosen, this volume). Shreve also delineated Central Gulf Coast, Plains of Sonora, Vizcaino, and Magdalena Plain; his seventh subdivision, Foothills of Sonora, has been redefined in sequence by Felger (1966), Felger & Lowe (1976), Turner & Brown (1994), and Búrquez et al. (1999) as thornscrub.

This desert region has been described, conceived, and defined by Cope (1873), Harshberger (1911), Sanders (1921), Dice & Blossom (1937), Burt (1938), Dice (1939, 1943), Smith (1939), Shreve (1951), and Brown (1994) in sequence. James (1906:xxviii, xxix) used the name Sonoranian Desert and noted, "There is no authority yet who has divided them [the Mojave and Sonoran deserts], or said where one begins and the other ends." Dimmitt (2000) notes that the boundaries remain under discussion with revisions possible; for example, some biogeographers would exclude Baja California while others would include the entire Mojave Desert as part of the Sonoran Desert.

Possibly the best of a variety of definitions of *desert* is Dimmitt's (2000:10): "A desert is a biological community in which most of the indigenous plants and animals are adapted to chronic aridity and periodic, extreme droughts, and in which these conditions are necessary to maintain the community's structure."

Some aspects of Sonoran Desert climate and weather are discussed in Adams & Comrie 1997, Brazel & Evans 1984, Sellers & Hill 1974, and Smith 1986. General geology can be found in Lynch 1989, Menges & Pearthree 1989, and Tosdal et al. 1989. The environmental and biological challenges threatening the Sonoran Desert are many; see Nabhan & Holdsworth (1998), Marshall et al. (2000), and Cornelius (1998) for a sampling. Laird (1998) gives a good introduction to the region's literature. See Bowden & Dykinga 1992 and Broyles 2003.

Sonoran Desert National Monument (=SD). Protected area established in 2001 by Presidential Proclamation 7397 (*Federal Register* 66, no. 14 [January 22, 2001]: 7354–7358). Its 496,337 acres incorporate the Maricopa Mountains, the Table Top Mountains, and the NE section of the Sand Tank Mountains, as well as adjacent areas. Resource inventories and reports include Felger et al., this volume, Chapter 1; Gunn 2000; Shumaker 2000; and Turner et al. 2000. Hunt (1998) describes some of the hiking trails and natural history.

Sonoran Desert National Park (OP, CP). A national park proposed in 1966 by U.S. secretary of interior Stewart Udall and Arizona congressman Morris K. Udall. It would have combined OP with CP in the U.S., encouraged creation of a Pinacate Park in Mexico, and co-managed them as an international park (*Sonoran Desert National Park, Arizona: A Proposal* 1966).

Frank Gehlbach, Baylor University professor of biology and environmental studies, writes: "Above all, I support a Gran Desierto International Park, connecting Organ Pipe Cactus and Cabeza Prieta preserves with the Gila and Tinajas Altas ranges in Arizona and the extraordinary wilderness southward, the Desierto de Altar. This oft-mentioned but untried wildland would be North America's greatest desert museum, at least twelve thousand square miles in extent, matched only by the Sierra Madre in its vastness" (Gehlbach 1981:277).

Recently re-proposed to include OP and CP within a national park; designate OP, CP, PI, and AG as sister parks, modeled after Waterton-Glacier International Peace Park; and establish GR as a national preserve co-managed by U.S. Department of Defense and National Park Service. See Bowden, this volume; Broyles et al. 2001; Dollar 2000; Martínez del Rio & Broyles 2000; McGivney 1998, 2001.

Ironically, in 1935 Roger Toll and others in the U.S. Interior Department proposed setting aside 5 million acres in SW Arizona as a national monument. It would have included what we now call OP, CP, GR, Kofa National Wildlife Refuge, and adjoining lands.

Sonoyta (Sonora). Agricultural and commercial community on the Río Sonoyta, 3 km SW of Lukeville. Includes Sonoyta Viejo and Sonoyta Nuevo. One of oldest settlements in the region. From prehistoric times until the 1980s the economy was primarily agricultural. Padre Kino arrived in 1698 and introduced cattle and new crops. A series of ciénegas (swamps) at Sonoyta dried up in the aftermath of a flood on the night of August 6, 1891. Extensive arroyo cutting followed the flood, and the village of Sonoyta was relocated downstream to its present location (Ives 1989; Lumholtz 1912). Lumholtz (1912) devoted a chapter to Sonoyta, titled "A Charming Place." See Akimel. In 1921 the Arizona & Sonora Railroad Company had a concession to build a line from Puerto Peñasco to Sonoyta, and presumably on to Gila Bend, where it would tie into the main SPRR line (Hendricks 1971). It could have taken ore from the Ajo mines to distant smelters by sea and given the U.S. a de facto seaport on the Gulf of California. This railroad was never built.

=Sonoýta, Sonoita, Şon, Kavolk Şon; historically transcribed Kavortkson, O'odham for 'at the foot of the rounded hill'. Originally called Şon Oidag or Sonoidac (O'odham for 'spring fields' or 'fields at the rock base'); later San Marcelo de Sonoidag (Ives 1989). Seat of Municipio General Plutarco Elías Calles (Mexico's president 1924–28; see Moreno 1960). Estimated 1990 population: 10,000. 31°51′46″N, 112°50′55″W. 400m.

The Ruhen Monument, site of the Jesuit Mission of San Marcelo de Sonoydag just E of modern Sonoyta, is at 31°51′29″N, 112°50′02″W. Padre Enrique Ruhen was martyred here in 1751 during an O'odham and Pima uprising against the Catholic church and Spanish crown (Ives 1989).

Sonoyta Mountains (Sonora, OP). Low mountains 2 mi W of Lukeville. They are the eroded remnant of an 8-mi^2 granite pluton. 31°56′38″N, 112°50′59″W. 2,313 ft.

Sonoyta, Río (Sonora, PI). See Río Sonoyta.

Sonoyta Valley (OP, Sonora). Broad valley lying between the Ajo Range/Sierra de Santa Rosa on the E and the Puerto Blanco/Sonoyta Mountains on the W. In Mexico this name is applied only to the upper portion of the Río Sonoyta. =Sonoyta Plain. 31°54′01″N, 112°42′27″W. 1,600 ft.

Sopodk (OP). See Quitobaquito. =Sapadk.

South Alamo Tinaja (OP). A very secluded intermittent tinaja, 6 ft deep, in S fork of Alamo Canyon, Ajo Range. 32°03′04″N, 112°41′55″W. 3,100 ft.

South Bend (Maricopa Co.). Camp with water, shade, and pasturage at W edge of Forty Mile Desert where the Butterfield Trail meets the Gila River. Shown on some nineteenth-century maps as being where the big bend of the Gila River turned W toward Yuma. Vicinity

of 33°00′N, 112°41′30″W. 650 ft. Another camp, North Bend, was near the confluence of the Hassayampa and Gila rivers near modern Arlington.

South Copper Mountains Tank (GR). Catchment and underground storage tanks for wildlife water on S end of Copper Mountains, built in 1998, 4.2 mi SSE from Coyote Peak and 2 mi NNW from Big Pass. Water collected from 2 gabion dams is stored in a buried 10,000-gallon storage tank and distributed from a 2,000-gallon walk-in trough. 32°27′36″N, 113°58′13″W. 1,060 ft.

South Mohawk Tank (GR). Water catchment in southern Mohawk Mountains, 5.1 mi NW of Monreal Well and 0.7 mi N of CP boundary. Built in 2001. =Mohawk Number 3. 32°25′41″N, 113°28′23″W. 1,000 ft.

South Vekol Well (SD). Well and corral 6.3 mi W of Table Top Mountains. 32°44′15″N, 112°13′50″W. 1,945 ft.

Southern Pacific Railroad (Arizona, California). Major railway passing through Tucson, Gila Bend, and Yuma. It reached Yuma in 1877 from the west. The story behind the project is one of intriguing politics, tycoons and bribery, and creative engineering set against the backdrop of the Civil War and its aftermath, a state hungry for development, and a nation demanding a second transcontinental rail line (Devine 2004). A second line was later built from Phoenix to Wellton. The Southern Pacific Railroad (SPRR) was acquired by the Union Pacific Railroad in 1996, eliminating SPRR as a corporate entity. In this gazetteer, however, we continue to refer to the line as the SPRR, since most people know it by that name, which still appears on nearly all existing maps.

Spains Well (GR). Abandoned well on San Cristobal Wash 12 mi S of Dateland. Name from a pioneer Wellton family. May =Va:pag-gam. 32°37′25″N, 113°30′57″W. 425 ft.

Sphinx, The (OP). Informal name for a rock outcrop along trail between Bull Pasture and Ajo Peak, Ajo Range. It resembles the mysterious Egyptian monument at Giza. Its "head" is at 32°00′37″N, 112°41′23″W. 3,669 ft.

Spook Canyon (GR). An unusually deep, narrow, and shaded gorge W through Vopoki Ridge in S Gila Mountains. Blowing night winds sometimes create eerie, spooky sounds. Apparently, the enclosed headland of Davis Plain has captured wind-driven sands or erosional sediments and raised ground level to height that a major arroyo has been diverted westward through the incised canyon instead of draining southward along the E side of Vopoki Ridge. Mouth at 32°28′47″N, 114°17′03″W. 780 ft.

Spook Tank (GR). An intermittent tinaja at head of Spook Canyon; known to U.S. Border Patrol as Spook Tank. Following rains, several seeps may flow in the canyon downstream where topo map shows a tinaja at about

32°29′01″N, 114°16′49″W. 980 ft., but these sand-bottom depressions are ephemeral at best. May =Agua Escondida noted by D'Anza (Ives 1965); map =S. A. Tank (San Albino Tank?). 32°29′12″N, 114°16′34″W. 1,000 ft.

Spring Arroyo (OP). Wash in Ajo Range that runs through Bull Spring Pasture. Mouth at 32°00′55″N, 112°41′40″W. 3,020 ft.

Spring Arroyo Tinajas (OP). A series of perennial to intermittent tinajas in the lower channel of Spring Arroyo. The deepest is 8.5 ft. 32°00′56″N, 112°41′39″W. 3,030 ft.

Squaw Tit (GR). Lava-capped butte in southeastern Sand Tank Mountains, 5 mi S of Maricopa Peak. Though surrounded by mesas and cliffs, it derives its descriptive appellation from E face. Today such names will win awards neither for political correctness nor for spelling. Lavas are over 2,000 ft thick here (Bryan 1925). =Squawtit Peak; Vipi Do'ag, O'odham for 'breast mountain'. 32°40′37″N, 112°22′38″W. 4,021 ft.

Squaw Tits (SDS). Double-summited lava butte at N end of Sand Tank Mountains, 16 mi SE of Gila Bend and conspicuous from I-8. =Double Butte (Bryan 1925: 225); Vipi Do'ag, O'odham for 'breast mountain'. In O'odham legend, men "unlucky" with women should make a pilgrimage here, climb the twin peaks to wrap a ribbon around the summits, and then "fool around with them" to bring luck in courting women; our storyteller didn't designate a comparable landmark for "unlucky" maidens. 32°50′55″N, 112°28′31″W. 2,478 ft.

Stamps Well (GR). Mr. Stamp tried his hand at ranching, and he ran water wagons to 1920s Ajo households. He also owned the honeywagon that hauled sewage out of town. Three abandoned wells near or on the Sentinel Plain bear his name. One is 14 mi E of Dateland and 2 mi E of Tenmile Wash at 32°46′27″N, 113°18′02″W; 566 ft. The others are on the Sentinel Plain at 32°48′26″N, 113°07′33″W; 680 ft; and 32°48′39″N, 113°07′29″W; 678 ft.

Stanwix (Maricopa Co.). Stagecoach station established in 1858 on S bank of the Gila River, about 15 mi E of Texas Hill. It was a lively frontier outpost: Arizona pioneer, rancher, and politician King Woosley lived here (Fourr 2004; Goff 1981); Sherod Hunter and his Confederate troops stopped here in 1862 (Finch 1996). Operated by Uncle Billy Fourr at one time; he reports a number of murders along the stage and wagon route between Yuma and Maricopa (Fourr 2004). =Stanwixs Station, Stanwix Hall, Stanwix Ranch, Stanwicks, Stanwick Station, The Dutchman's Place, (Henry) Grinnel Station. Vicinity 32°56′N, 113°22′W. 450 ft.

By 1880 the railroad had supplanted the stage line, so the name was appropriated for a siding on the Southern Pacific Railroad, 8.25 mi E of Aztec and 4–5 mi SE of old Stanwix. 32°50′23″N, 113°19′20″W. 554 ft.

Figure 39.50. Spook Canyon.

Stanwix Flats (Maricopa Co.). A subdivision of the Sentinel Plain, generally considered that part of the plain N of I-8. See Sentinel Plain and Tartron Flat. 32°52′04″N, 113°19′15″W. 535 ft.

Station Beach (Sonora). Section of beach E of Puerto Peñasco. Classroom, study site, and collection point for Gulf of California scientists and students (see Boyer, this volume, Chapter 34; Hastings & Findley, this volume). The tradition began when University of Arizona students used José García's beach-front house as a dormitory and laboratory for a summer field school. It was located next to the university's shrimp laboratory. Named by marine biologist Donald A. Thomson, fondly also known as DAT. 31°17′43″N, 113°31′46″W. 6 m.

Stemwinder Mine (CP). Abandoned mine group and hand-dug well on northernmost salient of Buck Peak, 1.5 mi NNE of Buck Peak Tank and McMillan Mine. The hill on which these mines are located is referred to by Miller (1979) as "Copper Hill," though that name appears in no other records. The "guzzler" depicted on modern USGS maps is actually a cistern, long since cracked and unable to hold water. 32°24′20″N, 113°55′36″W. 1,060 ft.

Stinson Peak (GR, TON). Twin summits on southeastern GR boundary, 1.7 mi NE of Coffeepot Mountain. One peak is in GR, and the other is in Tohono O'odham Nation. Taller summit is 32°30′48″N, 112°34′20″W. 2,720 ft.

Stoa Pitk (TON). Summer ranchería in western reservation; potholes and plunge pools are nearby. Tom Childs ran cattle here in the early part of the twentieth century. During World War II the village leader, Pia Machita (Juan Julia Caccido), was jailed for urging young men of the village not to register for the draft (King 1961). See McGuire & Mayro 1978. O'odham for 'white clay in place'; White Mud Village (Bell et al. 1980). =S-toha Biḍk, S-toha Bit-ag; S-toha Bidga; Toa Biḍ (with dot below the d [ḍ] ='clay'; without the dot ='shit'), Totabit, and at least 6 other variants. 32°29′16″N, 112°31′05″W. 2,064 ft.

Stone Wall Mine (CP). Mine and prospects in S Agua Dulce Mountains, 1.1 mi W of Agua Dulce Spring. Claim belonged to Jack Ricks, who also made moonshine at various hideouts during Prohibition (see Wild Horse Tank, Tinaja Estufa). =Merry Widow, Ricks Mine, Sheep View. 32°01′16″N, 113°09′41″W. 1,760 ft.

Stouts Well (GR). Two wells S and SE of Gila Bend. Albert H. Stout, who came to the region about 1879, built several hotels in Gila Bend, the first in 1906. The first well attributed to Stout is 2.6 mi SSE of Gila Bend on Quilotosa Wash at 32°54′56″N, 112°44′27″W (780 ft). =Quilotosa Well. The other is described by Bryan (1925) as being about 25 mi SE from Gila Bend. In 1917 it was 74 ft deep with water at 24 ft and was owned by James Gatlin. Formerly good and permanent water. Site vaguely known today; may be same as or close to Johnson Well. Stout also had several wells near Dateland.

Stoval (Yuma Co.). Active Southern Pacific railroad siding next to I-8, 6 mi SW of Dateland. Stoval became one of several U.S. Army Air Force training fields in area during World War II; the abandoned field is 1.8 mi S of the siding at 32°44′20″N, 113°37′32″W (361 ft). Name derived from former settlement of Christoval near Texas Hill stage station along Gila River. It was founded as a religious commune about 1882 after railroad was completed in 1880. The railroad began using the name for the siding around 1911, shortening it to Stoval to facilitate telegraphing. =Christvale; Grinnel Station. See San Cristobal Valley. 32°45′54″N, 113°37′17″W. 400 ft.

Sunday Pass (CP). Pass through northern Sierra Pinta, 3 mi N of Heart Tank. Named by CP staff when they rode horseback over pass on a Sunday while surveying plants and animals. Route of an ancient foot trail. 32°18′35″N, 113°33′55″W. 1,260 ft.

Sunset Camp (PI). Ancient campsite SW of Tinaja de los Chivos. It was a major Hia C'ed O'odham ranchería and occasional site of Vikita ceremony (see Fontana 1987; Hayden 1987). =Hudunk, historically transcribed as Hótunikat, O'odham for 'westward camp' or 'sunset camp'. 100 m.

Surprise Canyon (CP). Canyon in central Cabeza Prieta Mountains, 2.5 mi N of Cabeza Prieta Peak. A member of the CP staff surmounted a ridge and was "surprised" to see such a glorious canyon there. Mouth at 32°19′26″N, 113°47′08″W. 1,240 ft.

Surveyors Canyon (GR). Canyon in S Tinajas Altas Mountains, 1.9 mi NNW of international boundary monument 190. Mouth at 32°16′30″N, 114°01′38″W. 1,160 ft.

Surveyors Tank (GR). Intermittent tinaja in Surveyors Canyon used in 1890s by surveyors of international boundary (International Boundary Commission 1898), in southern Tinajas Altas Mountains 3.5 mi SSE of Tinajas Altas. May =Engineers Tank. Shown on USGS 7.5 map at 32°16′20″N, 114°02′00″W; 1,360 ft. A tank can be found there, but this site does not completely fulfill historic descriptions (see Sheldon 1993:25, 91).

Suvuk (PI). See Sierra Suvuk, Tinaja Suvuk.

Sweetwater (TON). Ranchería on E side of Ajo Range. = S-I'ovĭ Ṣu:dag, S-i'ovi Ṣudagi, historically transcribed Siovi Shuatak, 'sweet water'. =Siovi Shuatak; Cochibo, Cochivo, Cochiba Well, Cochibo Well; Con Quien; Coons Can Well; Manuels Well. 31°57′36″N, 112°34′42″W. 2,080 ft.

Sweetwater Pass (OP). Gap in southern Ajo Mountains, 1.7 mi N of Diaz Peak. Important pass for seasonal O'odham migrations to gather saguaro and organ pipe fruit. 31°59′21″N, 112°39′29″W. 2,523 ft.

Sykes Crater (PI). Marvelous crater in northwestern Sierra Pinacate, 19 km NW of Pinacate Peak. The crater has a rim-to-rim diameter of 700 m and depth of 220 m. Named for Godfrey Sykes (Hornaday 1908), it is the second deepest of the Pinacate craters. Formerly frequented by desert bighorn sheep, whose numbers have apparently dwindled. The crater supports nearly 100 species of plants (Felger 2000). It was visited by geologist Y. S. Bonillas in 1882 (Bonillas 1910; Ives 1989). =Cráter de Sykes, Sykes Maar Crater; Cráter Grande, Volcán Grande. Shown by rarely used name Volcán Romo on Volcán El Elegante 1:50,000 map; presumably for Chico Romo, a Sonoyta rancher in early twentieth century who ran cattle and contraband from Sonoyta to San Luis R.C. (Bill Hoy); in 1918 a Rancho Romo was 5 km WNW of Sonoyta. 31°56′23″N, 113°34′06″W. 400 m at the rim.

T

Table Top (SD). The summit of Table Top Mountains.

Table Top Mountains (SD). Mountain range 23.4 mi WSW of Casa Grande. Distinctive flat-topped twin summits are a notable landmark in the region and high point of SD. The N summit is the higher. The summit plateau is capped by lava over Tertiary-age conglomerate and Oracle Granite bedrock; parts of the range are Precambrian metamorphic and granitic rocks, including Pinal Schist (Chronic 1995; Mauz, this volume). For a short time in the 1940s, the name was applied to what is now Stanfield, a small community 12.8 to the NE. =Flat Top, Table Rock. 32°45′12″N, 112°07′29″W. 4,373 ft.

Table Top Mountains Catchments (SD, Pinal Co.). Wildlife water catchments and guzzler troughs in Table Top Mountains, numbered chronologically.

Number 1 (SD). =AGFD #554. 3.4 mi NNE of Table Top. 32°47′41″N, 112°05′55″W. 2,140 ft.

Number 2 (SD). =AGFD #555. 3.3 mi WNW of Table Top. 32°46′30″N, 112°10′30″W. 2,320 ft.

Number 3 (SD). =AGFD #691. 2.0 mi E of Table Top. 32°44′50″N, 112°05′26″W. 2,300 ft.

Number 4 (SD). =AGFD #705. 2.9 mi W of Table Top. 32°45′00″N, 112°10′25″W. 2,240 ft.

See also North Table Top Mountains Catchment.

Table Top Valley (SD, Maricopa Co., Pinal Co.). Name once applied to N Vekol Valley, to W and N of Table Top Mountains, but has fallen from use. 32°41′54″N, 112°09′00″W. 2,100 ft.

Table Top Wilderness (SD). This congressionally designated wilderness area encompasses the bulk of the Table Top Mountains. Created in 1990, it covers 34,400 acres and is managed by the Bureau of Land Management. It was incorporated into the national monument in 2001.

Tacna (Yuma Co.). Agricultural community between I-8 and Gila River, 11 mi E of Wellton. Tacna has a somewhat complicated place-name history since it has been moved twice, and both locations have held three different names. The original Tacna was formerly situated 4 mi W of the present town, and it had supplanted an even older Butterfield Stage station named Antelope Hill (32°41′06″N, 114°01′17″W, 329 ft). There Max B. Noah set up a shade-tree gas station and later a townsite and roadside menagerie. Noah invented a tall tale about the name deriving from a seventeenth-century Greek priest named Tachnopolis who had converted local Indians, but the name Tacna was already a railroad siding before Noah's arrival. He billed the place as Tacna-by-the-Sea, though it was opposite the railroad siding with no water in sight, and his restaurant was called Noah's Ark.

About 1927 modern Tacna was moved to Ralph's Mill, a service station and café run by Joe E. Ralph. He built a mock Dutch windmill to attract customers (Granger 1983; Bob Lenon). Ralph's Mill was originally a railroad siding named Gael, for Robert Gael, who owned and operated a pumping plant and well nearby. Later Ralph's Mill was owned by Roy Kelland. 2000 population: 555. =New Tacna; Tachna. The original Tacna is now known as Noah. Currently (or at least until the next roadside entrepreneur comes along), Tacna is at 32°41′49″N, 113°57′09″W. 349 ft.

Figure 39.51. Table Top Mountains. (Photo by Dale S. Turner)

Tapón, El (PI). Major arroyo running W from Pinacate Peak. Spanish for 'tarpaulin' or 'lid'. Ramón Bojórquez once considered erecting a canvas-tarp diversion dam on a side channel of this arroyo to divert seasonal runoff for farming fields (Julian Hayden). Crosses jeep trail from Tinajas de los Pápagos to Cráter de la Luna at 31°52′N, 113°38′W. 150 m.

Tartron (Maricopa Co.). Abandoned siding on Southern Pacific Railroad, 7 mi E of Sentinel. =Tartion. 32°52′44″N, 113°05′57″W. 728 ft.

Tartron Flat (GR, Maricopa Co.). A subdivision of the Sentinel Plain, generally considered the E part of the plain S of I-8. See Sentinel Plain and Stanwix Flats. 32°52′14″N, 113°05′05″W. 730 ft.

Tavasci Mine (GR). Mine on W side of Mohawk Mountains, 6 mi S of Mohawk. More a testament to determination and dedication than to wealth and prosperity, its 300-ft tunnel was dug over a period of about 35 years by G. E. Tavasci, beginning around 1895. No significant production was recorded. =Victoria Mine, Clara Mine, Susie & Betty Mine. 32°39′26″N, 113°42′38″W. 710 ft.

Tecolote Cone (PI). See Cerro Tecolote.

Teddy Bear Pass (OP). Low gap between 2 hills along Ajo Mountain Loop Drive, 2.5 mi E of OP visitor center. Named for the dense stand here of teddybear cholla (*Cylindropuntia bigelovii*), which propagate from fallen stem segments. 31°57′40″N, 112°45′44″W. 1,760 ft.

Telegraph Pass (Yuma Co.). Pass on I-8 across northern Gila Mountains, 2 mi W of Ligurta. Name dates to original telegraph system along railroad in late 1870s; modern communications towers have replaced the telegraph line. 32°39′38″N, 114°19′35″W. 790 ft.

Temporal Pass (CP). Pass through Growler Mountains, 12 mi SW of Ajo. Named for its proximity to

Chico Shunie Temporal, it was a backdoor trail for smugglers importing moonshine into Ajo during Prohibition. See Chico Shunie Temporal. =Temporary Pass, Smugglers Pass. 32°16′51″N, 113°02′19″W. 1,980 ft.

Ten Mile Hill (OP). A small hill in La Abra Plain, just N of international boundary marker 171 (1,257 ft). So called because it is about 10 mi W of Highway 85 via the S Puerto Blanco Drive (Sue Rutman). 31°55′40″N, 112°58′15″W. 1,320 ft.

Ten Mile Ranch (Pima Co.). Ranch founded by Tom Childs Jr. on Tenmile Wash in early 1900s, SW corner of Batamote Mountains. The well had water at 62 ft in 1915. Childs's wife, Martha Garcia, was Hia C'ed O'odham, so this ranch became a hub of cross-cultural activities. The Childses not only raised their own thirteen children but adopted others and frequently had dozens of guests at the dinner table. See Childs Valley. =Childs Ranch (though this name also applies to Hotshot Well); Tenmile Ranch; O'ogam Dak, O'odham for 'seep willow sitting'. 32°29′23″N, 112°52′19″W. 1,340 ft.

Also **Ten Mile Well** (Pima Co.). Well at Childs's Ten Mile Ranch. =Batamote Well; Tenmile Well. 1,340 ft.

Tenmile Wash (GR). Arroyo draining Childs Valley to Gila River. So named because it is 10 mi N of Ajo at Arizona Highway 85. Wide wash lined by many trees, especially desert willow (*Chilopsis linearis*), as well as palo verdes, mesquites, and some enormous ironwoods. In 1920s Tenmile Wash and lower Sikort Chuapo Wash were mapped as Rio Cornez. =Rio Cornez Wash, Childs Wash, Ten Mile Wash, Rio Ten Mile Wash. Final 4 mi occasionally flows through Canyon Diablo (not =Diablo Canyon in OP; Spanish for 'devil') to join Gila River at 32°52′09″N, 113°28′29″W. 395 ft.

Tepee Butte (CP). Descriptive name for butte in eastern CP, 8 mi SW of Ajo. Interesting application since indigenous peoples of this region did not live in tepees. Instead, they made *ki* houses of brush and mud; erected huts and ramadas of tree branches, grass, hides, and sticks; lived in rock shelters; or slept in the open. 32°18′57″N, 112°58′57″W. 1,936 ft.

Texas Hill (Yuma Co.). Prominent landmark N of Gila River in San Cristobal Valley, 9 mi NW of Dateland. Important petroglyph site and former hot springs frequented by O'odham and Quechan travelers. J. A. McGann of Sentinel reported that O'odham used to come "all the way up from Mexico to take baths in the hot springs around the hill." A stage station near this hill was known as Grinnel Station (see Stanwix), then Texas Hill Station about 1870. The Texas connection may have come from Texan emigrants who were reportedly killed in the vicinity, or from Texans who ran cattle here in 1860s (Granger 1983). See Stoval. =Cuk Do'ag,

O'odham for 'black mountain'. 32°49′53″N, 113°41′33″W. 780 ft.

Tezontle Cone (PI). Volcanic cone and commercial cinder mine 18 km NE of Pinacate Peak. Tezontle is a Nahuatl name for 'volcanic cinders' or 'lapilli'. =La Laja (for 'slabs of lava'), La Morusa, Freeman Mine (for John Freeman, who operated it in the 1970s), or Materiales Tezontle. La Laja is a very young cinder cone about 12,000 years old, ±4,000 years (Gutmann et al. 2000). 31°55′45″N, 113°20′55″W. 300 m.

Thanksgiving Day Tank (GR). Tinaja and wildlife water catchment in Sauceda Mountains built in 1971, 1.8 mi NNW of Hat Mountain. Named by Duane Holt for Gila Bend Sportsman's Club annual campouts here, where for 10 to 15 consecutive years turkeys were pit-roasted on Thanksgiving Day (Duane Holt). Mislabeled on USGS Midway 7.5′ topo map (1986, 1996); the tank is actually 1.5 mi NE of the point depicted (see Sauceda Cave Pothole). =AGFD #778. 32°39′27″N, 112°45′23″W. 1,780 ft.

Thanksgiving Mine (CP). Mine in Tule Mountains, 3.7 mi SE of Tule Well. Appears as unnamed adit on USGS Sierra Arida map. Workings from 1940s consist of a 40-foot adit through a narrow vein of silver ore. Production unknown. 32°10′50″N, 113°42′52″W. 1,260 ft.

Theba (Maricopa Co.). Active railroad siding on Southern Pacific Railroad, 8.8 mi W of Gila Bend. Bernard Gillespie's ranch was at Theba, as well as a grocery store. At one time the lettuce crates had labels reading Queen of Theba. The derivation is a mystery. 32°55′11″N, 112°53′30″W. 725 ft.

Thompson Tank (GR). Steel water catchment 3.2 mi S of Aguila Mountains summit. Named for Floyd Thompson, game management agent with U.S. Fish and Wildlife Service; he showed the site to Arizona Game and Fish Department, which built the catchment in 1963 but gave it only a number (636) and not a name. The name later appeared on USGS maps, apparently nominated unofficially, unbeknown to the department (Don Belknap). =Águila Mountains Catchment #1. 32°36′04″N, 113°19′51″W. 820 ft.

Tiger Cage Stock Tank (OP). Formerly a steel stock tank 0.6 mi N of OP headquarters. Name derived from cattle holding pens, long ago removed, at the site. Gray family ranch hands considered the pens small and dangerous to enter when cattle were inside, so the site was dubbed the "tiger cage" (Brown et al. 1983:48). 31°57′47″N, 112°48′11″W. 1,700 ft.

Tiller Well (CP). Well drilled in 2003 to provide water for an experimental food-enhancement field for imperiled Sonoran pronghorn. Also supplies nearby drinking trough. East of Daniels Arroyo and 463 ft deep. Named

Figure 39.52. *Tinaja de los Chivos.*

for Don Tiller, CP manager 1997–2001. 32°23′28″N, 113°02′42″W. 1,326 ft.

Tillotson Peak (OP). Highest point of Diablo Mountains, 3.5 mi W of Mount Ajo. See discussion at Diablo Mountains. Named for Minor R. Tillotson, a National Park Service regional director. 32°01′33″N, 112°45′04″W. 3,374 ft.

Tinaja(s). Spanish for 'bedrock pool', 'waterhole', 'natural tank'; *ce:po* in O'odham.

Tinaja de Anna (PI). Intermittent tinaja on southern edge of Pinacate lava flow. Named for writer Ann Woodin; chapters of her book *Home Is the Desert* narrate her family's adventures in the Sierra Pinacate. She concludes her book: "A home is not just a house; it is the natural world around it, and with both his feet well rooted in this a child can look out with confidence to the world of man. Each will then have its proper meaning and proportion. Our home is the desert, and from it will come identity, solace and, yes, Joy, above all, Joy" (Woodin 1964:247). Vicinity 31°42′N, 113°34′W. 160 m.

Tinaja Batamote (PI). A waterhole that forms intermittently behind a sand berm on E side of Río Sonoyta (Ives 1989); called a tinaja but may really be a charco (a natural, mud tank). 31°42′00″N, 113°17′15″W. 150 m.

Tinaja Bojórquez (PI). Large but intermittent tinaja in W Pinacate lavas, about 16 km NW of Pinacate Peak. Named for Ramón Bojórquez, who ranched here in 1960s. 31°49′50″N, 113°36′39″W. 250 m.

Tinaja del Bote (PI). Natural intermittent tinaja in arroyo bottom, 2 km N of Cráter de La Luna. Spanish for 'tin can' or 'bucket'. 31°46′55″N, 113°40′45″W. 90 m.

Tinaja de Carlina (PI). Tinaja near Campo Rojo and 5 km ENE of Pinacate Peak. Ives (1989) believed it was perennial and named it for childhood friend Carleen Maley Hutchins, an expert on violins (see Hutchins 1962). Vicinity of 31°47′N, 113°28′W. 500 m.

Tinaja de los Chivos (PI). A deep, bedrock waterhole at the SW side of the Pinacate lava shield, 9 km WSW of Pinacate Peak. The water often lasts all year. Maximum water depth in the largest tinaja is nearly 4 m. Colloquial Spanish for 'bighorn sheep'. =Tinaja de San Carlos, patron saint of woodcutters. Near Huḍunig, O'odham for 'sunset' or 'west camp'. Historically transcribed Hótunikat, 'sunset place' or 'westward-facing camp'. One trail from Chivos leads to Sunset Camp; another leads to Tinajas de Emilia (Lumholtz 1912). Kino's El Tupo (=Ce:po) likely was here or in vicinity (Ives 1989). 31°44′54″N, 113°36′21″W. 250 m.

Tinaja del Cuervo (PI). A usually perennial tinaja 11 km SE of Pinacate Peak. Spanish for 'raven'. =Havañĭ Koṣ, historically transcribed Havanikosh, O'odham for 'raven's nest'. 31°40′28″N, 113°26′06″W. 180 m.

Tinaja Estufa (OP). Two intermittent tinajas in Bates Mountains, 0.8 mi SE of Kino Peak. Probably supplied water for Jack Ricks's moonshine still during Prohibition. Spanish for 'stove', after a stovepipe that protrudes from a nearby cave where Ricks lived. 32°06′26″N, 112°56′28. 1,900 ft.

Tinaja de Galletal (PI). Tinaja on edge of lava flow about 13 km SE of Pinacate Peak. Named for extensive stand of galleta grass *(Hilaria rigida)*. Vicinity of Vasai Cucu-gam. Vicinity of 31°43′N, 113°25′W. About 200 m.

Tinaja Huarache (PI). A bedrock waterhole 6 km W of Pinacate Peak, on SW side of the Pinacate lava shield.

Figure 39.53. *Tinaja del Cuervo.*

Figure 39.54. *Tinaja Huarache.*

Also called Pyramid Tank for a triangle-shaped hill nearby. Deepest of the Pinacate tinajas, with maximum water depth over 4 m (Broyles 1996a). Spanish for 'sandal'. 31°45′39″N, 113°34′42″W. 380 m.

Tinaja del Indio (PI). See Tinajas de los Pápagos.

Tinaja Romero (PI). Natural and enhanced intermittent tinaja 8 km SW of Suvuk. Its modern discovery could be a chapter in an outdoorsman's handbook: Sr. Antonio Romero of Puerto Peñasco "had emptied his canteen while hunting [and] was spared considerable discomfort and danger by observing the flight of doves to a tinaja, where he found water" (Hayden 1972:82). This tinaja had been used prehistorically by Hohokam and later by O'odham on trips to the Gulf of California to gather salt and seashells (see Hayden 1972). Spanish surname for 'pilgrim'. =Tinaja de los Romeros; Tanque de los Víboras (Spanish for 'tank of the rattlesnakes'), after a petroglyph there of a snake standing upright on its tail. 31°42′52″N, 113°24′21″W. 180 m.

Tinaja Suvuk (PI). Intermittent tinaja at W base of Sierra Suvuk in a side arroyo, not the main N/S channel. There are two pitahayas *(Stenocereus thurberi)* and several senitas *(Pachycereus schottii)* in the arroyo. Hia C'ed O'odham camped here and cultivated tepary beans, maize, and squashes; Lumholtz (1912:330) reports that it was their sole agricultural site. Later the Romero family had a *temporal* (dry farm) nearby, growing tepary beans *(Phaseolus acutifolius)* and other crops. S-Vegi (O'odham for 'red'; Lumholtz 1912:393). See Nabhan 1985. =Ceumĭ Ke:k, O'odham for 'senita cactus standing'; historically transcribed Tjúumikux, 'where the senita stands'. 31°45′46″N, 113°21′38″W. 90 m.

Tinaja del Tule (PI). Large bedrock pool in a canyon bottom, 9 km W of Pinacate Peak. Maximum water depth of largest, upper pool is about 3.6 m (Broyles 1996a) and is usually perennial but dries up during years of extreme drought (Julian Hayden). Spanish for 'cattails'. 31°46′10″N, 113°35′52″W. 260 m.

Also **Arroyo Tule** (PI). Deep, basalt-lined arroyo or canyon extending 2 km S downstream from the large, upper tinaja.

Tinajas Altas (GR). These are the most significant tinajas in the region.

Permanent water made these large tinajas "renowned in the pioneer history of the district," according to Lumholtz (1912:239, 396), though he was displeased in January 1910 to find "pieces of cast-off clothing, rusty tin cans, and other cheerless marks of human occupancy."

Nine sets of intermittent and perennial pools that hold at least 22,000 gallons when full. An arroyo from a hanging valley in these granitic mountains downcuts steeply through joint fractures to scour and pluck a staircase of pools. Long a prehistoric campsite. A good place to see *Rhus kearneyi* and *Nolina bigelovii.* See Tad Nichols, this volume. Its archaeology is discussed in Hartmann & Thurtle 2001.

Setting of Robinson Jeffers's poem "The Dead Men's Child," which includes lines "his life / Ran smooth because he had nothing *future* about him. / Men do not stumble on bones mostly but on seeds." =High Tanks;

Tinachas Altas; 'O'ovak or 'O' Voopod ('where the arrows were shot'). Lumholtz reports legend that two O'odham shot arrows from opposite sides of the mountain's spine. One man's arrows cleared the mountain; the other's fell short and made holes in the mountains which became tinajas. Fillman Bell asserts that 'O'ovak means 'a drawing hole' or 'place where moisture is gathered'. Also historically transcribed Oo'oo'woopa ('where the arrows lie down'). 32°18′42″N, 114°03′00″W. 1,180 ft.

Tinajas Altas Mountains (GR). Granitic range between Gila Mountains and Cerro Pinto in Sonora. =Ahpar/ Yua Pad, Yuman for 'tail-end mountains'; Avik Amook To'or/Mokwintaorv. See Gila Mountains. Summit is 32°16′24″N, 114°02′45″W. 2,764 ft.

Tinajas Altas Pass (GR). Gap in Tinajas Altas Mountains 1.1 mi NW of Tinajas Altas. 32°19′19″N, 114°03′48″W. 1,129 ft.

Tinajas de Emilia (PI). Set of intermittent to perennial tinajas 4 km ESE of Pinacate Peak and S of Campo Rojo. =Mu'i Cecpo, Muij Cecpo, Moik Cecpo; historically transcribed Moitjútjupo, O'odham for 'many' or 'soft pools' (tinajas); but Lumholtz (1912:204,397) renamed it "Las Tinajas de Emilia for my friend, Miss Emily Beebee of Boston." According to Don Alberto Celaya, the local name was Tinajas de Palos Verdes (Julian Hayden). 31°45′43″N, 113°27′06″W. 400 m.

Tinajas de los Pápagos (PI). This series of large bedrock tinajas on Arroyo la Tinaja is one of the few usually reliable waterholes in the Pinacate region, although in years of extreme drought it has gone dry (Julian Hayden). Its deepest pool is about 2.6 m, but when all pools are full, it holds in the range of 680,000 liters (about 180,000 gallons) (Broyles 1996a). It was a main camp for the Hia C'ed O'odham (=Sand Papago. Childs 1954; Lumholtz 1912; Van Valkenburgh 1945).

Julian Hayden reports that in early 1960s cowboys from Rancho Victoria built dams on several of the tinajas to increase water storage. They also built an Ópata-style hut of ocotillo wands, saguaro ribs, and sacaton grass; it had several rooms. The present one-room block house was built for Alejandro Bojórquez and his fiancée; she came to visit before the wedding, looked at it and the surrounding wilderness, and went straight back to San Luis. He lived there alone for a while. Name Tinaja del Indio may be for Juan Caravajales, who in early twentieth century also lived here alone (Lumholtz 1912).

Until the mid-1970s several large blue palo verde trees (*Parkinsonia florida*) stood along the arroyo where it exits the lava flow. These provided welcome shade near scarce water. Misreported in a Tucson paper that local cowboys felled the trees for firewood; this report became an unfounded parable about killing what we love best and need most, since palo verdes burn with little heat and great smoke.

Figure 39.55. Tinaja del Tule.

Figure 39.56. Tinajas Altas Mountains.

Hurricane Katherine blew down several venerable trees in September 1963 and had regional effects (Brazel & Evans 1984; Smith 1986). A storm in July 1982 caused extreme flooding and washed out an archaeological site that had been uneroded for the last 600 years (Julian Hayden). Overgrazing may have contributed to the flooding. See Sheldon (1993:57) for a photo of flash flooding here in 1915.

At least four novels pivot their plots around these tinajas: Jeanne Williams's *A Lady Bought with Rifles,* Louis L'Amour's *Kid Rodelo* and *Last Stand at Papago Wells,* and Zane Grey's *Desert Gold.*

=Tinaja del Indio, Tinajas de los Indios, Papago Tanks; Hia Ce:po, Hia C'ed O'odham for 'urine pool' or

Figure 39.57. *Tinajas de los Pápagos.*

'sandy tank', historically transcribed Hitjuupo. Lumholtz (1912:396) says this name refers "to imaginary spoliation by the departed." 31°54′59″N, 113°36′15″W. 220 m.

Tjúumikux (PI). See Tinaja Suvuk.

Toa Pit (TON). =Totopitk. See Stoa Pitk.

Tóakomalik (PI). See Sierra Blanca.

To:b Do'ag (Yuma Co.). See Growler; Kusvo To:b Do'ag.

Tohono O'odham Nation (Pima, Maricopa, and Pinal cos.). Designated in 1916, it is the second largest Native American reservation in U.S., with 2,774,536 acres extending from Tucson to Gila Bend. Population in 1994 was estimated at 8,697, with many more members living elsewhere (*Vista* 1996). Capital in Sells (=Artesa, Indian Oasis). It has eleven districts: Baboquivari, Chukut Kuk, Gu Achi, Gu Vo, Hickiwan, Pisinimo, San Lucy, San Xavier, Sells, Schuk Toak, Sif Oidak. A number of ranchos in northern Sonora are Tohono O'odham settlements. =Papago Indian Reservation. See Clotts (1915, 1917) for districts and villages before 1916.

Formerly known as Papago, an uncomplimentary Spanish name for Tohono O'odham and Hia C'ed (=Hia-ced, Hia C-ed, Hia Ced) O'odham groups of Piman Indians. Papago was possibly derived from Babawǐ O'odham (Papavi O'odham) or Bawǐ Ku'amdam (Pavi Kuamdam) for 'tepary bean eaters' and is similar to the Seri name for O'odham (*hapai,* 'tepary eaters'). First Hispanicized as Papabotas in seventeenth century. See Fontana 1983 and 1989 and Zepeda 1995.

The Hia C'ed O'odham Alliance, whose members have strong ties to Darby Wells, south of Ajo, is working to regain rights to their former homeland and to establish their own reservation. In 1996 they bought back from BLM 20 acres of their traditional homeland near Ajo (Allen 1996). See Darby Wells. In 2005 the Tohono O'odham Nation purchased 640 acres SE of

Why for $1.5 million; the tribal council may designate this parcel, formerly known as Roberts Ranch, as its twelfth district and a homeland for the Hia C'ed O'odham (*Ajo Copper News* 2005; Medrano 2005).

Tom Thumb (GR). Butte in southeastern Sauceda Mountains, 9 mi SE of Hat Mountain. Name from a Hans Christian Andersen fairy tale that featured Thumbelina and other miniature people. Charles Stratton (1838–1883), who stood 40 in tall (33 in by another account), weighed 70 pounds, and toured with P. T. Barnum's circus, was called General Tom Thumb. 32°32′00″N, 112°35′04″N. 3,058 ft.

Tom Thumb Well (GR). Well in Cougar Canyon 1.1 mi E of Pistol Pass in Sauceda Mountains. See Pistol Pass. 32°33′39″N, 112°35′22″W. 2,095 ft.

Tony Tank (GR). Dry well on Growler Wash 2.8 mi E of northernmost point of Granite Mountains. 32°30′02″N, 113°16′20″W. 680 ft.

Tordillo Mountain (CP). Two-toned granitic butte capped with basalt in far SW Cabeza Prieta Mountains along El Camino del Diablo, 4 mi SW of Cabeza Prieta Peak. Spanish for 'dappled' or 'gray'. =Tordilla Mountain. 32°15′58″N, 113°52′15″W. 2,170 ft.

Tornillal, El (AG). Freshwater pozo on beach below bluffs of Mesa Arenosa, 12 km SE of El Golfo. Spanish for 'screwbean' mesquite trees (*Prosopis pubescens*) growing in a narrow canyon eroded into the crumbly seaward cliffs. It is the only natural waterhole between La Salina and El Golfo; Lumholtz (1912) reports that bitter, brackish water could be obtained by digging at the canyon's mouth. Formerly an Hia C'ed O'odham camp, now a tourist camp. =Totṣagi Ṣu:dagǐ, O'odham for 'foamy water'; historically transcribed Totshakshootaki. 31°33′30″N, 114°18′00″W. 3 m.

Torres, Estación (AG). See Estación Torres.

Totṣagi Ṣu:dagǐ (AG). See Tornillal, El.

Tres Alamos Canyon. (OP). See Alamo Canyon.

Tres Ojitos, Pozo (AG). See Pozo Tres Ojitos.

Tshiulikami (TON). See Sauceda.

Tucson, Cornelia, & Gila Bend Railroad (Pima Co., Maricopa Co.). Spur line built in 1916 from Ajo to Gila Bend for carrying refined copper from the Ajo mine to the Southern Pacific mainline. For a number of years the caboose for these shipments carried passengers, and many local people fondly remember celebrating birthdays and special occasions aboard the train. The opening scenes of an otherwise barren movie *The Man Who Loved Cat Dancing* (1973) were shot on this route and near White Tanks. When the Ajo mine ceased operations in 1984, the line shut down, but in the 1990s occasional trains carried salvage minerals and equipment from the Ajo mine.

Tule, Tinaja del (Pl). See Tinaja del Tule.

Tule Desert (CP). Wide valley between Sierra Pinta and Cabeza Prieta Mountains. Extends to S end of Sierra Pinta and Las Playas. It is ironic that such a hot, arid valley is named after tules, or cattails *(Typha dominguensis);* however, the name derives from Tule Tank in Tule Mountains to the W.

The valley's watershed is split 3 mi E of Christmas Pass at the 930-ft contour. In years of lesser precipitation, soil in this divide becomes exceptionally dry and plant mortality rises dramatically, even among creosotebushes, so the area resembles a sterile zone pocked with abandoned rodent burrows. Drainage to SE approaches Pinta Playa, but channel is no longer distinct; to NW it goes into Mohawk Wash and disappears in sands W of Mohawk Dunes. Divide is at 32°16′37″N, 113°38′24″W. 926 ft.

Tule Lagoon (Yuma Co.). Slough that once occupied an abandoned meander bend of the Colorado River. Long since drained and replaced with agricultural fields and orange orchards, it appears on numerous maps from the early 1900s. 4.3 mi NNE of present day Somerton. 32°39′17″N, 114°41′02″W. 115 ft.

Tule Mountains (CP). Range 2 mi S of Tule Well, extending across international boundary. Confusion and possible synonymy with Sierra Tuseral; see discussion in Granger 1960, 1983. A 1918 map groups the Cabeza Prieta Mountains and the Tuseral Mountains under the name Tule Mountains. According to Wilson (1933:160), "the Mexican portion of the range is called the Sierra de Tuseral." =Sierra Tuseral, Sierra Choclo Duro. Portion 5 mi SW of Tule Well is a basalt mesa; =Mesa del Malpais. Mexican summit (higher) is at 32°07′11″N, 113°42′25″W; 810 m. U.S. summit is at BM Tule, 32°10′28″N, 113°43′15″W; 2,307 ft.

Tule Pass (CP). Broad pass into interior of Tule Mountains, 1.5 mi S of Tule Well. Before development of Tule Well the Camino del Diablo used to pass through here and head directly west toward Tule Tank. Around 1900 a wooden signboard here instructed travelers, "Go back [to Tule Well] and fill your canteen" (McGee 1901). Long abandoned, it is likely the road through the pass fell into disuse following the redevelopment of Tule Well in the 1940s, since there was no longer a need for travelers to make a beeline for the possible water at Tule Tank (Gale Monson). The route today is faint but easy to follow on foot. See Broyles 1982 for an account of one man's journey through this pass. 32°12′16″N, 113°44′42″W. 1,240 ft.

Tule Tank (CP). A natural tinaja of prehistoric and historic importance, 3 mi W of Tule Well. It was a water stop on El Camino del Diablo. Bryan (1925:337) reports that it "is 1,600 feet . . . up a narrow canyon. It consists of

Figure 39.58. Tule Tank.

a rock basin about 6 ft. in diameter at base of dry falls and is usually full of sand. Water is found in the sand for some time after rains. Not permanent." =Uḍuvhag-gam, Uḍuvag-gam, 'Uḍuvak, or Otoxakam (O'odham for 'where there is cattail'); Hispanicized as Utevak. Spanish for 'cattail' that probably historically grew here. 32°13′35″N, 113°47′45″W. 1,240 ft.

Not to be confused with Tinaja del Tule in Sierra Pinacate.

Tule Well (CP). Several historic wells at far southern end of Cabeza Prieta Mountains, a day's journey E of Tinajas Altas by foot or horseback. The earliest well was dug sometime "during the early [eighteen] 'sixties'. . . [when] an enterprising Mexican dug two wells near the road, in the Tule Mountains, built a small adobe house, and occupied it with his family for two years for the purpose of selling water to travelers" (International Boundary Commission 1898:24), but little if anything came of this enterprise. The rumor persists that he was killed by someone who had greater thirst than money, but the International Boundary Commission report (1898:24) contends that "the deaths from thirst along this route became so frequent that the road was soon abandoned." In 1917 Bryan (1925) recorded its water temperature as 69°F; the well was 35 ft deep (27.3 ft to water) and delivered 500 gallons/day of foul-tasting liquid. Area may have had a groundwater seep in mid-1800s; alkali salts still whiten the surface here. Formerly

Figure 39.59. *Tule Well, 1990.*

there were cattails here (Gale Monson); =Uḍuvhag Vahia, Uduvak Vahia, O'odham for 'cattail well'. Some nineteenth-century maps label a site in this vicinity "Corral," possibly referring to Tule Well or maybe Cajón del Diablo.

Now site has an adobe hut, built in 1989 to replace dilapidated line shack used in 1940s by Bureau of Animal Industry while patrolling border against stray cattle that might carry hoof-and-mouth disease. 32°13′34″N, 113°44′56″W. 1,174 ft.

Tuseral, Sierra (CP, PI). See Sierra Tuseral.

Tuseral Tank (CP). An artificial waterhole 2.5 mi S of Tule Well, on N side of Tuseral Mountains (shown as Tule Mountains on some maps). Tank was built in 1948 for wildlife. 32°11′14″N, 113°44′50″W. 1,340 ft.

Twin Peaks (OP). Dual summits just W of OP headquarters and 5.5 mi N of Lukeville. One proposal would have named them for James Gadsden, secretary of state who negotiated Gadsden Purchase, but descriptive name has stuck. The western and taller summit is sometimes called West Twin Peak. 31°57′39″N, 112°49′08″W. 2,615 ft.

Twin Tanks (SD). Stock tank 7 mi E of Estrella. 32°59′39″N, 112°18′10″W. 1,475 ft.

Two Apostles (PI). See Dos Apóstoles.

U

'Uḍuvag-gam (CP). See Tule Tank.

Uḍuvak Vahia (CP). See Tule Well.

Unwin Point (AG). Point on mainland BC shore opposite NW corner of Isla Montague. Possibly named for a friend of Lt. Hardy (1829:324, 383). Vicinity of 31°48′37″N, 114°01′01″W (Steve Nelson).

U.S. Highway 80. The predecessor of U.S. Interstate Highway 8, this highway served as the major southern conduit for travel between the E and W coasts of the U.S. before the construction of Interstates 8 and 10. The original route ran between Savannah, Georgia, and San Diego, California. With the completion of I-8 in the late 1960s, Highway 80's roadbed was either abandoned or became secondary roads alongside the freeway and through towns. A good example of the old roadbed can be found at Mohawk Pass, as well as the main streets through Gila Bend and Wellton. Called a variety of names along stretches through western Arizona, including Yuma–Gila Bend Road, Bankhead Highway, Yuma Road, Old Spanish Trail.

V

Vainomĭ Do'ag (OP). A desolate mountain somewhere NW of Quitobaquito. O'odham for 'iron mountain'. =Winum Do'ag.

Vaiva Hills (TON). Group of hills 7.9 mi ESE of Table Top Mountains. From *vaivel*, O'odham for 'cocklebur', *Xanthium strumarium,* a common weed in disturbed soils and cultivated fields (Rea 1997). 32°43′00″N, 111°59′44″W. 2,561 ft.

Vak or **Vapk** (Sonora). See Laguna Prieta, Quitovac.

Valentine Well (Pima Co.). Livestock well 4 mi S of Ajo, developed by Cameron family, which has ranched this area for almost a century. Bobby Cameron finished the well on a Valentine's Day in 1941–43. 32°19′13″N, 112°53′11″W. 1,880 ft.

Valle de San Felipe (BC). Dry lake bed (Laguna Diablo) at foot of Sierra San Pedro Mártir, 25 km W of town. =San Felipe Valley. Portion to N is called Valle Santa Clara. 31°02′N, 115°14′W. 500 m.

Valley of the Ajo (OP). Broad valley and watershed draining northeastern OP and extending to base of Batamote Mountains N of Ajo. 32°19′53″N, 112°47′06″W. 1,400–2,200 ft.

Va:pag-gam (GR). See Spains Well.

Vasai Cucu-gam (PI). Former O'odham village on SSE flank of Pinacate Peak, in vicinity of Tinaja Galletal and Tinaja Cuervo. =San José de Ramos of Kino (Ives 1989); Vaṣai Cu:ckam, Vaṣai Cuckum; historically transcribed Basoitutgam, O'odham for 'dark-colored grass' or 'grass standing'.

Vatopi Ki: (Yuma Co.). An island-like knoll and village in the Gila River floodplain possibly 1 mi NE of Antelope Hill. O'odham for 'fish house'. =Watopi Ki. Vicinity of 32°43′N, 114°01′W. About 300 ft.

Vatto Ki: (Sonora). A waterhole somewhere between Quitovac and Sonoyta, used by O'odham. =Batequi, O'odham for 'ramada house'.

Vav Olas Do'ag (Pima Co.). Place near Cardigan Peak and Ajo. Historically transcribed Wauaw'awlag, O'odham for 'rounded rocks'. =Vavĭ Olas Do'ag. Possibly =Loco-motive Rock.

Vekol Interchange (SD). Interchange off I-8, 9.6 mi NW of Table Top Mountains. Provides access to Table Top Wilderness and southern Vekol Valley.

Vekol Valley (SD, Maricopa Co.). Major valley between Sand Tank and Table Top mountains. Noted for patches of Sonoran savannah grassland, old but perennial repre-sos, and a variety of animals (see Enderson & Bezy, this volume). Geologically, the valley is a sediment-filled structural trough bounded by block-faulted mountains. The basin fill is at least 3,000 ft deep, with the water table ranging from 270 to 430 ft. Subsurface flow moves toward the Gila River between the northern-most Table Top Mountains and Booth Hills. An exper-iment to judge recharge of the aquifer from surface flow documented water movement from the surface to the water table at 330 ft in just five days, much faster than previous estimates. However, the moisture con-tent of the saturated soil above the water table returned to pre-experiment levels in about 20 days (Marie & Hollett 1996). Named for nearby Vekol Mine; from Piman *viikol*, 'great-grandparent'. 32°50′31″N, 112°15′16″W. 1,600 ft.

Vekol Wash (SD). Major arroyo draining Vekol Valley. Meets Santa Cruz Wash at 33°11′17″N, 112°08′20″W. 1,050 ft.

Venegas Pass (CP). Low pass through Tuseral Moun-tains, 0.7 mi E of border monument 186. 32°10′49″N, 113°47′05″W. 1,120 ft.

Venegas Prospects (CP). Group of mines and prospects 3.2 mi SSE of Tule Tank. Most significant attraction at the site is not the prospects themselves but the elabo-rate trail system leading up the mountain and connect-ing the various workings, suggesting that more effort was made to engineer and construct the trails than was expended on actual mining. The mine showed minor evidence of calcite, gypsum, and copper. =Santa Clara 1–8. 32°11′01″N, 113°46′32″W. 1,700 ft.

Ventana, La (BC). Rest stop and vista in easternmost ridge of Sierra de Pintas along Mexico Highway 5, 90 km N of San Felipe. Overlooks delta of Río Colorado. Spanish for 'window'. 31°44′25″N, 115°04′10″W. 20 m.

Vepegĭ Ce:po (GR). Waterhole on E side of Aguila Mountains; possibly =Eagle Tanks. O'odham for 'red tinaja', historically transcribed Wu'pu'k Jiapaw.

Vepegĭ S-mo'okad (Pima Co.). Two peaks above Cardi-gan Well, with a field beneath. Possibly =Ajo Peak and North Ajo Peak. O'odham for 'red(-haired) peaks popped up'.

Verdugo, Cráter el (PI). See MacDougal Crater.

Figure 39.60. Los Vidrios, 1984.

Victoria Mine (OP). Mine group in Sonoyta Moun-tains, 3.6 mi NNW of Lukeville. 31°55′47″N, 112°50′13″W. 1,660 ft.

Vidrios, Los (PI). Truck stop and restaurant on Mexico Highway 2, 57 km W of Sonoyta. Established in 1953 as a little ocotillo *jacal* (hut) for refreshments *(refrescos)*. Don Juan Bermúdez, who had a store at San Luis R.C., bought it shortly after it opened. He built and ran the restaurant, gas station, and small motel from 1956 until his health failed in the mid-1980s. It was also the family home, with children and pet parrots forming part of the scene. During this time Los Vidrios served as the unofficial cultural and information center for El Pina-cate, and for a number of years it was the only reliable place for meals and gas between Sonoyta and San Luis R.C. The ceiling was made of large pine slabs with the bark intact, hauled from the Sierra San Pedro Mártir. Fresh tortillas, enchiladas, frijoles, and cold beer were much appreciated, especially after days of dusty field-work and camping. Following Don Juan's death in 1985, the family sold Los Vidrios and the magic passed with its founder.

Spanish for 'broken glass' or 'glassy'. Name may come from bits of naturally occurring crystals found on lava flows, resembling broken glass to early explor-ers (Lynch 1981). Alternatively, according to Julian Hay-den, it was named for massive obsidians near Rancho los Vidrios, 25 km to the SE. Los Vidrios was one of 3 primary sources of obsidian in this region; the others were Sauceda Mountains and San Felipe (Shackley 2005). 32°01′36″N, 113°25′13″W. 220 m.

Vipi Do'ag (Maricopa Co.). See Squaw Tits.

Volcán Colorado (PI). See Cerro Colorado.

Volcán El Elegante (PI). See Elegante Crater.

Volcán Jarapeña (PI). Breached volcanic cone in far NW Pinacate lava field, 14 km W of MacDougal Crater. It is surrounded by sand. An enigmatic name. 31°59′06″N, 113°46′16″W. 340 m.

Volcán de La Luna (PI). See Moon Crater.

Volcán Romo (PI). See Sykes Crater.

Volcán Santa Clara (PI). See El Pinacate, Pinacate Peak.

Volcán La Tinajita (PI). See Badilla Crater. Spanish for 'volcano of the little waterhole'.

Volcán El Trébol. (PI). See Molina Crater.

Volcán El Verdugo (PI). See MacDougal Crater.

Volcán los Vidrios (PI). See Celaya Crater.

Vopaikam (GR). Historic O'odham field W of Aguila Mountains and near Vepegi Ce:po. It was an Hia C'ed O'odham *ak-ciñ* (temporal field) where San Cristobal Wash dies before reaching the Gila River. Possibly near Spains Well, 12 mi S of Dateland. May coincide with a large annual playa in the San Cristobal Wash that supported grasses and intermittent water in the 1920s (George Morrison). O'odham for 'place with a ditch'. =Wapagain.

Vopoki Ridge (GR). Jagged ridge in far southwestern Gila Mountains. Name alludes to the ridge's "serrated crest, which resembles the Papago symbol for lightning" (Wilson 1931:224). =Vepegĭ, O'odham for 'lightning' or 'electrical charge', but named by Wilson, not O'odham. 32°30′39″N, 114°17′40″W. 1,920 ft.

W

Wagner Basin (AG). An ocean-floor basin 60 km E of San Felipe. It is the northernmost rift trough in the Gulf of California. 31°02′N, 114°12′W. 200 m below sea level.

Walls Well (Pima Co.). Tohono O'odham ranchería and well at N end of Ajo Mountains, near Ku:kadc. Named for mine claimant Frederick Wall. The well was dug after 1880 and became a frequent stopover for travelers between Tucson and Sonoyta. It was a popular botanical collection site: D. T. MacDougal collected seep willow (*Baccharis salicifolia*) in 1907, and A. A. Nichols collected screwbean (*Prosopis pubescens*) here in 1939 (see Chapter 17, this volume). Screwbean no longer grows here. Groundwater pumping for mining and ranching provided sufficient surface water for many wetland plants that have long since disappeared from the site. Bryan (1925) reported that the well had water 19 ft below the surface but admonished travelers, "Bring your own bucket." =Pozo de Federico; Kuagĭ Ka:c, Ku:

kadc, historically transcribed Kuakatch, Kóokatsh, O'odham for 'mountain crest'. 32°08′17″N, 112°39′44″N. 2,129 ft.

Waterfall Tinajas (OP). Four intermittent tinajas in S fork of Alamo Canyon, Ajo Mountains. They range from 2 to 6 ft deep. The lowest one is sometimes referred to as Alcove Tinaja. 32°03′26″N, 112°42′31″W. 2,600 ft.

Waterman Wash (SD, Maricopa Co.). Arroyo draining Rainbow Valley. Named for Col. Waterman (first name unknown), who in 1888 explored Buckeye and Arlington areas for potential irrigation canals—an appropriate task for a man with his name (Granger 1983). Joins Gila River at 33°20′45″N, 112°31′00″W. 860 ft.

Also **West Prong Waterman Wash** (SD, Maricopa Co.). A branch of Waterman Wash draining Maricopa Mountains. =Waterman Wash. Joins Waterman Wash at 33°10′33″N, 112°21′58″W. 1,135 ft.

Wegi Wahia (TON). Village, corrals, and two wells 3 mi N of S-toha Bidga. O'odham for 'red wells'. =Vokivajea, Vokvajea, Vokiváxia; Poso Colorado; Red Well; near Moivayi and may =Sauceda (King 1961). 32°30′30″N, 112°26′W. Part of the Sauceda settlement complex.

Well That Johnny Dug (GR). This now-dry well was drilled by Johnny Childs, 4.5 mi S of Hat Mountain. 32°34′20″N, 112°45′10″W. 1,510 ft.

Wellton (Yuma Co.). Settlement named for several good wells drilled here when the Southern Pacific Railroad came through in 1877. 1 mi N of I-8; 30 mi E of Yuma. =Welltown; Jiyi-jho'ag; Miakam (Bell et al. 1980). 2000 population: 1,829, up from 1,569 estimated in 1994. 32°40′25″N, 114°08′29″W. 245 ft.

Wellton Hills (GR). Small hills 6 mi S of Wellton. They separate Lechuguilla Desert from Gila River Valley. 32°34′22″N, 114°08′11″W. 1,192 ft.

Wellton-Mohawk Main Outlet Drain Extension (M.O.D.E) (Yuma Co., AG, Sonora). Wellton-Mohawk drainage canal discharging expended irrigation water from fields in lower Gila River Valley to the Rio Colorado delta. The water carries away leached salts and field chemicals. For the history and politics of this project, see Ward 1999, 2003. During the 1980s and 1990s the Ciénega de Santa Clara became greatly enlarged where water emptied from the M.O.D.E. canal, and a number of environmental and conservation benefits followed (Glenn et al. 1992, 1996; Glenn & Nagler, this volume; Zengel & Glenn 1996). =Canal de Descarga R. Sánchez Toboada. Crosses international boundary at San Luis at 32°29′14″N, 114°47′23″W. 88 ft. The terminus is about 10 km SW of Riíto, at 32°03′26″N, 114°53′56″W.

West Arroyo Tinajas (OP). Series of intermittent tinajas up to 6 ft deep, in Bull Pasture of Ajo Mountains. 32°00′57″N, 112°41′49″W. 3,020 ft.

West Pass (GR). A gap and road through W Crater Range. A range fire here in spring 2005 burned several thousand acres, including trees along Tenmile Wash. 32°09′05″N, 113°08′20″W. 800 ft.

West Quilotosa Wash (GR, Maricopa Co.). A minor western fork of Quilotosa Wash, W of Gila Bend. Runs between Quilotosa Wash and Sauceda Wash. Name proposed July 2, 2001, by Gila Bend town council and officially adopted by Arizona officials. See Quilotosa Wash. Crosses Highway 85 at 32°53′02″N, 112°45′06″W. 840 ft.

West Tank (Maricopa Co.). Stock tank in Rainbow Valley 8.1 mi ENE of Margies Peak. 33°11′56″N, 112°28′21″W. 1,210 ft.

What Fo Canyon (CP). Canyon in northern Sierra Pinta 13 mi NW of Heart Tank. Named by Gale Monson and Jim Johnson of CP staff who preferred riding or walking in the desert to any place on Earth. Although nondescript the canyon is delightful, so they asked in mock bewilderment, "What's this canyon good fo'?" Mouth at 32°23′35″N, 113°38′24″W. 880 ft.

White Face (GR). See Albino.

White Hills (GR). Small group of hills and western outlier of Sauceda Mountains W of Arizona Highway 85, 12 mi S of Gila Bend. Its light-colored rock is granite and schist. 32°47′42″N, 112°50′44″W. 1,811 ft.

White Hills (SD). Small group of hills 5 mi ENE of Maricopa Peak. 32°46′16″N, 112°17′47″W. 2,649 ft.

White Mountain (Yuma Co.). See Half White Mountain.

White Tank (SD). Pair of stock ponds (represos) 4 mi E of Maricopa Peak. Likely named for White Hills. Older, eastern tank built by Les Bender in 1930s served well until a new owner tried to deepen it, ripping out the clay bottom; it held water only intermittently after that (Letty Bender Hofstra & Anita Bender McGee). 32°45′21″N, 112°18′16″W. 2,143 ft.

White Tanks (GR). Natural, intermittent tinajas at E end of Crater Range. 32°31′33″N, 112°49′39″W. 1,300 ft.

White Well (GR). Now-dry well in San Cristobal Valley, 14 mi S of Dateland. Dug by Wesley White sometime before 1923. =White's Well. 32°35′40″N, 113°32′30″W. 480 ft.

Why (Pima Co.). Unincorporated settlement at Y-junction of Arizona highways 85 and 86, 10 mi SE of Ajo. Reportedly a common question: "Why live here?" as well as pun on highway "wye." "Why" used since about 1965. Henry Dobyns notes that O'odham word for deer is homonym *huawi;* desert mule deer do inhabit this area. Coyote Howls mobile home park is English equivalent of historic O'odham name Ban Hi:nk (Margaret Ross). Home of the existential Why Wash laundry and

Figure 39.61. White *Tanks.*

the Why Not Travel Store. =Rocky Point Junction. 32°15′55″N, 112°44′20″W. 1,784 ft.

Wi:jĭ Do'ag (Yuma Co.). See Antelope Hill.

Wild Horse Tank (OP). Two major tinajas at N end of Diablo Mountains, 2 mi W of Ajo Peak. Used by prehistoric peoples and dammed during 1930s by Henry Gray for livestock. During Prohibition, Jack Ricks, Boots Burnham, and Newt Meadows operated a moonshine whiskey still here and in nearby Diablo Canyon (Greene 1977). 32°01′18″N, 112°43′35″W. 2,380 ft.

Williams Spring (OP). A series of seeps 1 mi NW of Quitobaquito. Named for Frank Williams, who in 1916–1920 irrigated a small alfalfa field here with water from the spring (Felger et al. 1992; Greene 1977; Hoy 1970). =Rincon Spring. 31°57′30″N, 113°01′26″W. 1,090 ft.

Woodcutters Canyon (GR). Canyon extending eastward from Fortuna Mine through Gila Mountains, exiting these mountains 0.6 mi S of Dripping Springs. Not actually a proper canyon, since it drains both ways and does not have a true source; more accurately a pass, especially since a route travels through it. Miners used it to transport native woods (especially ironwood and mesquite) gathered in mountains and in Lechuguilla Valley; the wood was used primarily for mine furnaces and kitchen fires. Western mouth near Fortuna Mine, 32°33′31″N, 114°19′31″W. 920 ft. Eastern mouth near Dripping Springs, 32°34′21″N, 114°16′13″W. 800 ft.

X

Xuksíl (BC). Historic Quechan village near present-day Algodones (aka Vicente Guerrero). When Garcés visited there in 1775, he renamed it El Llanto, Spanish for 'lamentation' (Forbes 1965). It was on the W bank of the Colorado River, across from San Pablo. In 1849 a ferry operated here. Vicinity of 32°42′55″N, 114°43′45″W. 130 ft.

Y

Yodaville (GR). A simulated village for urban combat training 15 miles SE of Yuma. Built in 1999, its 167 buildings are made of over 23,000 surplus cluster-bomb containers (stacked like Lego blocks) and wood, with artificial trees, infrastructure, vehicles, and soccer field. Designed to facilitate practice of close ground support by Marine Corps aircraft, it is a highly dangerous live-fire area, with hazards from bullets, practice bombs, unexploded ordinance, and lasers. Named for Major Floyd Usry, who proposed the concept after serving in the 1993 hostilities in Somalia. His radio call sign was Yoda, presumably after the *Star Wars* character (Shaffer 1999).

Youngker Tank (Maricopa Co.). Stock pond in Rainbow Valley 2 mi NE of SD. In 1932 Benjamin F. Youngker homesteaded 240 acres west of Buckeye, Arizona. In 1957 he and others in the family expanded their ranch and farm operations into Rainbow Valley. 33°12′12″N, 112°25′39″W. 1,100 ft.

Yuma (Yuma Co.) Major agricultural, tourist, military, commercial, and retirement city on the Colorado River in SW Arizona, just below confluence with the Gila River. Seat of Yuma County. Name may be Spanish for 'smoke' *(umo)* and former name for Quechan Indians, who periodically burned their fields; name Yuma first used by Padre Kino in 1690s; Cahuilla word *yu-mu* and Tohono O'odham word *yu-mi* for Quechan (Bee 1983) likely were derived from the Spanish Yuma (Donald Bahr, Bernard Fontana, David Shaul). See Forbes 1965, Granger 1960, Martin 1954, Westover 1966.

Fort Yuma was established in 1851 on the California side of the Colorado River to protect strategic "Yuma Crossing" from hostile Indians and, during the Civil War, Confederates. Fort Yuma was considered the hottest post in the country. The post surgeon reported that his watch "felt like a hot boiled egg in my pocket," and the parade ground was so hot that—though he could not personally vouch for the story—"a dog would run on three legs across it, barking with pain at every step." Gen. George C. Thomas, one of the post's early commanders, told of the veteran who in death had found hell so cool after the Yuma heat that "he returned to the barracks to requisition a few blankets as protection against the devilish chill" (California State Military Museum 2005). The post was abandoned in 1885.

Old Yuma is remembered for its ferry across the Colorado River, Indian mission, and territorial prison. Modern Yuma has the Marine Corps Air Station, agriculture, and seasonal residents. Area has the least frost of any Arizona locale. Major crops include cotton, alfalfa, onions, melons, citrus, and lettuce. Some touted crops—jojoba, flax, sugar beets, castor beans, sesame, and pistachios (Talbot 1996)—proved to be failures in the fields

or marketplace. Movies made in the vicinity include *Four Feathers* (1929), *Another Dawn* (1937), *The Desert Fox* (1951), *Flight of the Phoenix* (1966), and *The Getaway* (1994).

Ross (1923:164) reported Yuma as a "wide-awake, flourishing town, with several hotels, numerous stores and ice plants, electric light and power, and gas for cooking and heating." He also gave population numbers: 1910, 2,914; 1920, 4,237. He attributed the jump between 1910 and 1920 to the development of irrigated agriculture. That trend has not abated; Yuma was the third fastest growing area in the U.S. for the period 1990–2000, with a growth rate of 49.7%. Its 1990 population was 54,966. In 2000 it was 77,515, with a total of 160,026 in the metro area.

Vicinity of two Spanish colonial missions with pueblos: Purísima Concepción and San Pedro y San Pablo de Bicuñer (Bancroft 1889; Forbes 1965). =Colorado City (before 1858), Arizona (1858–63), Arizona City (1863–73), Yuma after 1873 (Walker & Bufkin 1986). 32°43′32″N, 114°37′13″W. 150 ft.

Yuma Auxiliary Airfields (GR, Yuma Co.) Three historic military airfields in the Yuma Desert. None were active landing fields but instead served as emergency landing fields or as target areas.

Yuma Number 1. (Yuma Co.). Now covered by subdivisions, this airfield was S of I-8, 7 mi W of Telegraph Pass. 32°39′19″N, 114°26′36″N. 299 ft.

Yuma Number 2. (GR). In center of Yuma Desert, 12.9 mi WSW of Telegraph Pass. 32°33′02″N, 114°30′18″W. 266 ft.

Yuma Number 4. (Yuma Co.). In Yuma Desert 6 mi ENE of San Luis. = Rolle Airfield. 32°30′59″N, 114°41′11″W. 164 ft.

Yuma County (Arizona). Governmental subdivision overlying western CP and GR. Seat in Yuma. Named for Quechan (=Yuma) Indians historically living along Colorado River.

Yuma Desert (GR). Broad area of sand and dunes between Tinajas Altas Mountains and Colorado River. Primary habitat of flat-tailed horned lizard *(Phrynosoma platyrhinos)*. Site of a live bombing range for U.S. Marine Corps. 32°30′33″N, 114°27′34″W. 140–700 ft.

Yurimuri (BC). Tourist camp along Río Hardy. Campers come to hunt, fish, and water-ski (Jim Griffin). One developer, who envisioned a Venice of the West, dredged canals and planned to sell river-front lots (Fradkin 1995). The floods of 1983 and 1993 wiped out many of the cabins and travel trailers. Home to a few Cucupá families. The name may derive from Cucupá word for cowpea or black-eyed pea, but the name and source of the pea merit further investigation (Anita Alvarez Williams). The black-eyed bean *(yorimuni, orimuni)* here is said to be named from the Mayo language, with *yori* meaning 'white' and *muni* meaning 'bean' (Castetter & Bell 1951); Gentry (1965) says that in Mayo *yori* means 'outsider' or 'foreigner', which indicates the bean was an introduced species. = Yorimuri, Yorimuni. 32°2'0"N, 115°12'11"W. 8 m.

Z

Zaaj Cooxapoj (Sonora, AG?). A white cliff near Puerto Peñasco. Seri for 'white cliff' (Mary Beck Moser). Precise location unknown.

Zumbador, El (Sonora). Treacherously soft, sandy stretch of road that stranded auto travelers in moving dunes *(médanos undulados)* before the road was paved. Along Mexico Highway 2, about 59 km E of San Luis Río Colorado. Doolittle's 1939 map locates its center about 6.5 km SE of boundary marker 198 and shows it as an obstacle 8 km long by 5 km wide that forced the primitive road to arc southward around it. It is at southern end of Yuma Desert. A sketchy 1942 USGS topo map of Yuma places El Zumbador about 5 km *S* of El Capitan and shows the former Santa Ana–Tijuana "highway" running about 10 km S of the border and its current alignment. Name also applied to an arroyo here, perhaps the one 2 km W of Ejido Ignacio Zaragoza and 12 km W of La Joyita. These dunes may hum or sing during sandstorms (see Haff 1986; Nori et al. 1997). Spanish for 'hummer', 'buzzer', or 'hummingbird'. Vicinity 32°17'50"N, 114°11'55"W. 210 m.

Zumbador, Cerro el (PI). See El Capitán.

We're glad you joined us. Que tenga un buen viaje.

References

1. Six Grand Reserves, One Grand Desert

Abouhaidar, F. 1992. Influence of livestock grazing on saguaro seedling establishment. In *Proceedings of the Symposium on Research in Saguaro National Monument,* January 23–24, 1991, edited by C. P. Stone & E. S. Bellantoni, pp. 57–61. Globe, Arizona: Southwest Parks and Monuments Association.

Aguilar-Rosas, L. E., R. Aguilar-Rosas, L. E. Mateo-Cid, & A. C. Mendoza-Gonzalez. 2002. Marine algae from the Gulf of Santa Clara, Sonora, Mexico. *Hydrobiologia* 477:231–238.

Annerino, John. 1999. *Dead in Their Tracks: Crossing America's Desert Borderlands.* New York: Four Walls Eight Windows.

Arizona Colorado River Commission. 1937. Night letter to President Franklin D. Roosevelt and others, August 4. Hayden Collection. Arizona State University Library, Tempe.

Arizona State Parks Board. 1985. Memorandum of Understanding with Cabeza Prieta National Wildlife Refuge: Natural Area Register, October 25, and Registered Natural Areas report, December 3. Phoenix.

Artz, Matthew C. 1989. Impacts of linear corridors on perennial vegetation in the east Mojave Desert: Implications for environmental management and planning. *Natural Areas Journal* 9:117–129.

Barbour, M., & N. L. Christensen. 1993. Vegetation. In *Flora of North America,* edited by Flora of North America Editorial Committee, 1:97–131. New York: Oxford University Press.

Belnap, Jayne. 1995. Surface disturbances: Their role in accelerating desertification. *Environmental Monitoring and Assessment* 37:39–57.

Bennett, P. S., & M. R. Kunzman. 1989. *A History of the Quitobaquito Resource Management Area, Organ Pipe Cactus National Monument, Arizona.* Technical Report No. 26. Tucson: Cooperative National Park Resource Studies Unit, University of Arizona.

Berry, Kristin H. 1980. A review of the effects of off-road vehicles on birds and other vertebrates. Workshop Proceedings, Management of Western Forests and Grasslands for Nongame Birds. February 11–14, Salt Lake City.

Bierregaard, R. O., T. E. Lovejoy, V. Kapos, A. A. dos Santos, & R. W. Hutchings. 1992. The dynamics of tropical rainforest fragments. *Bioscience* 42: 859–866.

Bleich, V. C., J. D. Wehausen, & S. A. Hol. 1990. Desert-dwelling mountain sheep: Conservation implications of a naturally fragmented distribution. *Conservation Biology* 4:383–390.

Bowers, J. E. 1980. Flora of Organ Pipe Cactus National Monument. *Journal of the Arizona-Nevada Academy of Science* 15:1–11, 33–47.

Brooks, Mathew L. 1999. Alien annual grasses and fire in the Mohave Desert. *Madroño* 46:13–19.

Brown, B. T., & R. R. Johnson. 1983. The distribution of bedrock depressions (tinajas) as sources of surface water in Organ Pipe Cactus National Monument, Arizona. *Journal of the Arizona-Nevada Academy of Science* 18:61–68.

Brown, David E., editor. 1982. Biotic communities of the American Southwest—United States and Mexico. *Desert Plants* 4:3–341.

Brown, D. E., & R. A. Minnich. 1986. Fire and creosote bush scrub of the western Sonoran Desert, California. *American Midland Naturalist* 116:411–422.

Brown, J. H. 1971. Mammals on mountaintops: Non-equilibrium insular biogeography. *American Naturalist* 105:467–478.

Broyles, Bill. 1993. El Gran Despoblado Park. Letter to Gayle Hartmann, Anita Williams et al., December 24. Copy in author's files.

———. 1995. Desert wildlife water developments: Questioning use in the Southwest. *Wildlife Society Bulletin* 23:663–675.

———. 1996. Surface water resources of ancient peoples of western Papaguería of the North American south-west. *Journal of Arid Environments* 33: 483–495.

———. 2004. The desert sisters. *Earth Island Journal* 19(3):35–38.

———. 2006. *Sunshot: Peril and Wonder in the Gran Desierto.* Tucson: University of Arizona Press.

Broyles, Bill, & Tricia L. Cutler. 1999. Effect of surface water on desert bighorn sheep in the Cabeza Prieta National Wildlife Refuge, southwestern Arizona. *Wildlife Society Bulletin* 27:1082–1088.

Broyles, Bill, Richard S. Felger, & Charles Bowden. 2001. The Sonoran corridor. Pages 244–267 in *The Gulf of California: A World Apart* [Spanish edition: *El Golfo de California: Un Mundo Aparte*]. Patricio Robles-Gil, Exequiel Ezcurra, & Eric Mellink, editors. Mexico City: Pegaso-Agrupación Sierra Madre.

Brusca, Richard C., Erin Kimrey, & Wendy Moore, editors. 2004. *A Seashore Guide to the Northern Gulf of California.* Tucson: Arizona-Sonora Desert Museum.

Buchmann, Stephen L., & Gary Paul Nabhan. 1996. *The Forgotten Pollinators.* Washington, D.C.: Island Press.

Bureau of Land Management. 1985. *Draft Resources Management Plan. Environmental Impact Statement for the Lower Gila South RMP/EIS Area.* Phoenix.

———. 1988. *Environmental Assessment Final AZ-027-7-21 and Lower Gila South RMP Monitoring Plan.* Phoenix.

———. 1995. *Maricopa Complex Wilderness Management Plan, Environmental Assessment, and Decision Record.* Phoenix.

———. 2001. *Bureau of Land Management, Arizona: National Landscape Conservation System.* Phoenix.

———. 2002. Santa Rosa and San Jacinto Mountains National Monument Fact Sheet. Palm Springs. www.blm.gov.palmsprings/fact_sheet.

Burnham, Frederick T. 1928. *Scouting on Two Continents.* Garden City, New York: Doubleday, Doran.

Búrquez, Alberto. 1998. Historical summary of the formation of the Biosphere Reserve El Pinacate y El Gran Desierto de Altar. In *The Sierra Pinacate,* by Julian D. Hayden, pp. 74–75. Tucson: University of Arizona Press.

Búrquez, A., & C. Castillo. 1994. Reserva de la Biosfera, El Pinacate y Gran Desierto de Altar: Entorno biológico y social. *Estudios Sociales* 5:9–64.

Carmony, Neil B., & David E. Brown. 1993. Epilogue. In *The Wilderness of the Southwest: Charles Sheldon's Quest for Desert Bighorn Sheep and Adventures with the Havasupai and Seri Indians,* edited by Neil B. Carmony & David E. Brown, pp. 193–204. Salt Lake City: University of Utah Press.

Cartron, Jean-Luc E., Gerardo Ceballos, & Richard S. Felger, editors. 2005. *Biodiversity, Ecosystems, and Conservation in Northern Mexico.* New York: Oxford University Press.

Chester, Charles C. 2006. *Conservation across Borders: Biodiversity in an Interdependent World.* Washington, D.C.: Island Press.

Comrie, Andrew C., & Bill Broyles. 2001. Variability and spatial modeling of fine-scale precipitation data for the Sonoran Desert of south-west Arizona. *Journal of Arid Environments* 50:573–592.

Cox, George W. 1998. *Cryptogamic Crusts.* Educational Bulletin 97–4 and 98–1. Spring Valley, California: Desert Protective Council.

D'Antonio, C. M., & P. M. Vitousek. 1992. Biological invasions by exotic grasses, the grass/fire cycle, and global change. *Annual Review of Ecology and Systematics* 3:63–87.

Davis, John H. 1957. *A Study of Conservation Objectives Relating to Its Establishment, Boundary Adjustments, and Private Interest in the Area.* National Park Service Report, November. Organ Pipe Cactus National Monument Library.

Davis, Tony. 1999. Push is on for huge national park to preserve southwest Ariz. desert. *Arizona Daily Star,* March 9, 1A, 9A.

Demaray, A. E. 1936. Letter to U.S. Senator Carl Hayden, September 26. Hayden Collection, Box 505, Folder 1. Arizona State University Library, Tempe.

Department of Defense. 1996. *DoD Instruction 4715.3: Environmental Conservation Program.* May 3. Washington, D.C.

Dimmitt, Mark. 2000. Biomes and communities of the Sonoran Desert region. In *A Natural History of the Sonoran Desert,* edited by Steven J. Phillips & Patricia Wentworth Comus, pp. 3–18. Tucson: Arizona-Sonora Desert Museum; Berkeley: University of California Press.

Dunbar, C. C. 1935. Letter from the Yuma County Chamber of Commerce to Senator Carl Hayden, June 27. Hayden Collection, Box 607, Folder 1. Arizona State University Library, Tempe.

Dunstan, C. E., & B. J. Fox. 1996. The effects of fragmentation and disturbance of rainforest on ground-dwelling small mammals on the Robertson Plateau, New South Wales, Australia. *Journal of Biogeography* 23:187–201.

Ecosystem Approach Memorandum. 1995. Memorandum of Understanding to Foster the Ecosystem Approach between the Council of Environmental Quality, Department of Agriculture, Department of the Army, Department of Defense, Department of Energy, Department of Housing and Urban Development, Department of Interior, Department of Justice, Department of Labor, Department of State, Department of Transportation, Environmental Protection Agency, and Office of Science and Technology Policy. December 15. Washington, D.C.

Eden, Jim. 1956. A history of Organ Pipe Cactus National Monument. Manuscript, Organ Pipe Cactus National Monument Library.

Espinoza Avalos, J. 1993. Macroalgas marinas del Golfo de California. In *Biodiversidad Marina y Costera de México,* edited by S. I. Salazar-Valejo & N. E. González, pp. 328–357. Mexico City: CONBIO y CIQRO México.

Esque, Todd C., Alberto Búrquez M., Cecil R. Schwalbe, Thomas R. Van Devender, Pamela J. Anning, & Michelle J. Nijhuis. 2002. Fire ecology of the Sonoran Desert tortoise. In *The Sonoran Desert Tortoise: Natural History Biology, and Conservation,* edited by Thomas R. Van Devender, pp. 313–333. Tucson: University of Arizona Press.

Esque, Todd C., & Cecil R. Schwalbe. 2002. Alien annual grasses and their relationships to fire and biotic changes in Sonoran Desertscrub. In *Invasive Exotic Species in the Sonoran Region,* edited by Barbara Tellman, pp. 164–194. Tucson: University of Arizona Press.

Ezcurra, E., M. Equihua, & J. López-Portillo. 1987. The desert vegetation of El Pinacate, Sonora, Mexico. *Vegetatio* 71:49–60.

Ezcurra, E., R. S. Felger, A. Russell, & M. Equihua. 1988. Fresh water islands in a desert sand sea: The hydrology, flora, and phytogeography of the Gran Desierto oases of northwestern Mexico. *Desert Plants* 9:35–44, 55–63.

Ezcurra, E., & V. Rodrígues. 1986. Rainfall patterns in the Gran Desierto, Sonora, Mexico. *Journal of Arid Environments* 10:13–28.

Federal Aviation Administration. 1998. *Final Environmental Assessment for Childs Mountain/Cabeza Prieta National Wildlife Refuge Air Route Surveillance Radar, Ajo, Arizona.* Contract No. DTFA08–93-Y-02833. Golden, Colorado: Research Management Consultants.

Felger, Richard S. 1980. Vegetation and flora of the Gran Desierto, Sonora. *Desert Plants* 2(2):87–114.

———. 1990. *Non-native Plants of Organ Pipe Cactus National Monument.* Technical Report No. 31. Tucson: Cooperative National Park Resource Studies Unit, University of Arizona.

———. 2000. *Flora of the Gran Desierto and Río Colorado of Northwestern Sonora.* Tucson: University of Arizona Press.

Felger, R. S., D. S. Turner, & M. F. Wilson. 2003. Flora and vegetation of the Mohawk Dunes, Arizona. *Sida* 20:1153–1185.

Felger, R. S., P. L. Warren, S. A. Anderson, & G. P. Nabhan. 1992. Vascular plants of a desert oasis: Flora and ethnobotany of Quitobaquito, Organ Pipe Cactus National Monument, Arizona. *Proceedings of the San Diego Society of Natural History* 8:1–39.

Fish and Wildlife Service. 1998. *Final Programmatic Environmental Assessment for the Future Management of Cabeza Prieta National Wildlife Refuge and Draft Comprehensive Conservation Plan.* Albuquerque.

Fleischner, Thomas L. 1994. Ecological costs of livestock grazing in western North America. *Conservation Biology* 8:629–644.

Foreman, Dave. 2004. *Rewilding North America: A Vision for Conservation in the 21st Century.* Washington, D.C.: Island Press.

Forman, Richard T. T., Daniel Sperling, John A. Bissonette, Anthony P. Clevenger, & 10 others. 2003. *Road Ecology: Science and Solutions.* Washington, D.C.: Island Press.

Gehlbach, Frederick R. 1981. *Mountain Islands and Desert Seas.* College Station: Texas A&M University Press.

Gibbons, Junius. 1937. Telegram to President Franklin D. Roosevelt and others, August 5. Hayden Collection. Arizona State University Library, Tempe.

Glenn, E. P., R. S. Felger, A. Búrquez, & D. S. Turner. 1992. Cienega de Santa Clara: Endangered wetland in the Colorado River Delta, Sonora, Mexico. *Natural Resources Journal* 32:817–24.

Glenn, E. P., C. Lee, R. Felger, & S. Zengel. 1996. Water management impacts on the wetlands of the Colorado River Delta, Mexico. *Conservation Biology* 10:1175–1186.

Goodman, Sherry W. 1994. Memorandum from S. W. Goodman, Deputy Under Secretary of Defense (Environmental Security) to Assistant Secretaries of the Army, Navy, and Air Force. Implementation of Ecosystem Management in the Department of Defense. August 8. Washington, D.C.

Greenway, Isabella. 1934. Letter to Gladstone MacKenzie, February 14. Greenway Collection MS 311, Box 34, Folder 432. Arizona Historical Society, Tucson.

Gunn, John. 2000. *An Assessment of the Desirability to Change the Future Management of Natural Resources in "Areas 1" and "9" Located in the Sand Tank Mountains and Sentinel Plain, Maricopa County, Arizona.* Mesa, Arizona: Southwest Natural Resource Management Consultants.

Gutmann, James T., Brent D. Turrin, & John C. Dohrenwend. 2000. Basaltic rocks from the Pinacate Volcanic Field yield notably young ^{40}Ar/^{39}Ar ages. *EOS, Transactions, American Geophysical Union* 81:33, 37.

Hall, John A., Pat Comer, Anne Gondor, Rob Marshall, & Stephanie Weinstein. 2001. *Conservation Elements of and a Biodiversity Management Framework for the Barry M. Goldwater Range, Arizona.* Tucson: Nature Conservancy.

Hardin, Garrett. 1968. The tragedy of the commons. *Science* 162:1243–1248.

Hartmann, William K. 1989. *Desert Heart.* Tucson: Fisher Books.

Hayden, Carl. 1936. Letter to A. E. Demaray, Associate Director, National Park Service, September 23. Hayden Collection, Box 505, Folder 1. Arizona State University Library, Tempe.

Homburg, Jeffery A., Jeffery H. Altschul, & Rein Vanderpot. 1994. *Intermontane Settlement Trends in the Eastern Papaguería.* Technical Series No. 37. Tucson: Statistical Research.

Hornaday, William T. 1906. *Camp-Fires in the Canadian Rockies.* New York: Charles Scribner's Sons. Reprint. New York: Arno Press, 1967.

———. 1908. *Camp-Fires on Desert and Lava.* New York: Charles Scribner's Sons. Reprint. Tucson: University of Arizona Press, 1983.

———. 1913. *Our Vanishing Wildlife: Its Extermination and Preservation.* New York: New York Zoological Society.

———. 1931. *Thirty Years War for Wild Life.* Stamford, Connecticut: Permanent Wild Life Protection Fund.

INRMP. 2003. Draft Environmental Impact Statement. *Barry M. Goldwater Range, Proposed Integrated Natural Resources Management Plan,* volumes 1 and 2. Phoenix: Luke Air Force Base.

INRMP Community Report. 2003. Draft Environmental Impact Statement. *Barry M. Goldwater*

Range, Proposed Integrated Natural Resources Management Plan. Phoenix: Luke Air Force Base.

Jones, Susan C., & William L. Nutting. 1989. Foraging ecology of subterranean termites in the Sonoran Desert. In *Special Biotic Relationships in the Arid Southwest,* edited by Justin O. Schmidt, pp. 79–106. Albuquerque: University of New Mexico Press.

Krausman, Paul R., Andrew V. Sandoval, & Richard C. Etchberger. 1999. Natural history of desert bighorn sheep. In *Mountain Sheep of North America,* edited by Raul Valdez & Paul R. Krausman, pp. 139–191. Tucson: University of Arizona Press.

Leslie, M., G. K. Meffe, J. L. Hardesty, & D. L. Adams. 1996. *Conserving Biodiversity on Military Lands: A Handbook for Natural Resources Managers.* Arlington, Virginia: Nature Conservancy.

Lingenfelter, R. E. 1978. *Steamboats on the Colorado River.* Tucson: University of Arizona Press.

Louw, Gideon N., & Mary K. Seely. 1982. *Ecology of Desert Organisms.* New York: John Wiley & Sons.

Ludwig, J. A. 1987. Primary productivity in arid lands: Myths and realities. *Journal of Arid Environments* 13:1–7.

Lumholtz, C. 1912. *New Trails in Mexico.* New York: Scribner. Reprint. Glorieta, New Mexico: Rio Grande Press, 1971.

Lynch, Daniel James. 1981. Genesis and geochronology of alkaline volcanism in the Pinacate Volcanic Field, northwestern Sonora, Mexico. Ph.D. dissertation, University of Arizona.

MacKay, William P. 1991. The role of ants and termites in desert communities. In *The Ecology of Desert Communities,* edited by Gary A. Polis, pp. 113–150. Tucson: University of Arizona Press.

Mackenzie, Gladstone. 1935. Letter from the Pima County Board of Supervisors to Senator Carl Hayden, February 7. Hayden Collection, Box 607, Folder 1. Arizona State University Library, Tempe.

Marshall, Rob, Susan Anderson, Michael Batcher, Pat Comer, Steve Cornelius, Robin Cox, Anne Gondor, Dave Gori, John Humke, Rafaela Paredes Aguilar, Iva E. Parra, & Sabra Schwartz. 2000. *An Ecological Analysis of Conservation Priorities in the Sonoran Desert Ecoregion.* Tucson: Nature Conservancy, IMADES, and Sonoran Institute.

May, L. A. 1973. Resources reconnaissance of the Gran Desierto region, northwestern Sonora, Mexico. Master's thesis, University of Arizona.

McAuliffe, Joseph R. 1995. The aftermath of wildfire in the Sonoran Desert. *Sonoran Quarterly* 49(3):4–8.

———. 2004. It's even drier in this dry land. *Sonoran Quarterly* 58(4):8–9.

McAuliffe, Joe, Erik Hamerlynck, & Travis Huxman. 2003. Ecologists study impacts of drought in the desert. *Sonoran Quarterly* 57(4):5–9.

McCourt, Richard M. 1983. Zonation and phenology of three species of *Sargassum* in the intertidal zone of the Northern Gulf of California. Ph.D. dissertation, University of Arizona.

McDougall, W. B. 1935. Letter to Walter P. Taylor, University of Arizona. Record Unit 7176, Box 31, Folder 3, U.S. Fish and Wildlife Service Field Reports. Smithsonian Institution Archives.

McLaughlin, S. P. & J. E. Bowers. 1982. Effects of fire on a Sonoran desert community. *Ecology* 63:246–248.

Meffe, Gary K., C. Ronald Carroll, and contributors. 1997. *Principles of Conservation Biology.* 2d edition. Sunderland, Massachusetts: Sinauer Associates.

Morales-Abril, G. 1994. Reserva de la Biosfera Alto Golfo de California y Delta del Río Colorado. *Ecologica* 3:26–27. (Hermosillo, Sonora)

Moreno, José Luis, editor. 1992. *Ecología, Recursos Naturales y Medio Ambiente en Sonora.* Hermosillo: Proambiente, State of Sonora, and Colegio de Sonora.

Morrison, P. H., H. M. Smith IV, & S. D. Snetsinger. 2003. *The Natural Communities and Ecological Condition of the Sonoran Desert National Monument and Adjacent Areas.* Winthrop, Washington: Pacific Biodiversity Institute.

Nabhan, G. P., F. Flores, F. Valentine, C. Nagel, H. Smith, H. Ness, B. McClure, & W. Laird. 1995. Completion of the Sonoran Desert Biosphere Network along the U.S./Mexico Border. Proposal presented at the UNESCO International Biosphere Conference, Seville, Spain, March 19–24.

Nabhan, Gary Paul, and Andrew R. Holdsworth. 1998. *State of the Desert Biome: Uniqueness, Biodiversity, Threats, and the Adequacy of Protection in the Sonoran Bioregion.* Tucson: Wildlands Project.

Nagel, Carlos. 1988. *Report on Treaties, Agreements, and Accords Affecting Natural Resource Management at Organ Pipe Cactus National Monument.* Cooperative National Park Resources Studies Unit Report No. 8. Tucson: University of Arizona and National Park Service.

Newmark, W. D. 1995. Extinction of mammal populations in western North American national parks. *Conservation Biology* 9:512–526.

———. 1996. Insularization of Tanzanian parks and the local extinction of large mammals. *Conservation Biology* 1:159–164.

Nixon, Richard M. 1972. Use of off-road vehicles on the public lands. Executive Order 11644, February 8. Washington, D.C.

Norris, J. N. 1975. Marine algae of the northern Gulf of California. Ph.D. dissertation, University of California, Santa Barbara.

Notice of Intent. 2000. Notice of Intent to Prepare an Environmental Impact Statement (EIS) for the Barry M. Goldwater Range's Integrated Natural Resources Management Plan. *Federal Register* 65, no. 141 (July 21): 45361.

NPS-OIA. 2004. *The NPS Sister Parks Initiative.* Washington, D.C.: National Park Service, Office of International Affairs. www.nps.gov/oia/topics/sister.

O'Leary, J. F., & R. A. Minnich. 1981. Postfire recovery of creosote bush scrub vegetation in the Western Colorado Desert. *Madroño* 28:61–66.

Phillips, John C. 1931. Remarks on the necessity for special protection to mountain sheep in Arizona—with suggestions for reserves devoted to this purpose. Manuscript, July. Record Unit 7176, Box 28, Folder 10, U.S. Fish and Wildlife Service Field Reports. Smithsonian Institution Archives.

Pierson, Elizabeth A., & Raymond M. Turner. 1998. An 85-year study of saguaro *(Carnegiea gigantea)* demography. *Ecology* 79:2676–2693.

Pinkley, Frank. 1935a. *Proposed Monuments.* Southwestern Monuments Annual Report. Casa Grande, Arizona: National Park Service.

———. 1935b. Letter to Roger W. Toll and Report on Proposed Kofa Mountains National Monument by Robert H. Rose. Record Unit 7176, Box 31, Folder 1, U.S. Fish and Wildlife Service. Smithsonian Institution Archives.

Pitt, Jennifer. 2001. Can we restore the Colorado River delta? *Journal of Arid Environments* 49:211–220.

Pitt, Jennifer, Chris W. Fitzer, & Lisa Force. 2002. New water for the Colorado River: Economic and environmental considerations for replacing the bypass flow. *University of Denver Water Law Review* 6(1): 68–86.

Polis, Gary A., editor. 1991. *The Ecology of Desert Communities.* Tucson: University of Arizona Press.

Presidential Proclamation 7397. 2001. Sonoran Desert National Monument. *Federal Register* 66, no. 14 (January 22): 7354–7358.

Ramamoorthy, T. B., R. Bye, A. Lot, & J. Fa. 1993. *Biological Diversity of Mexico: Origins and Distribution.* New York: Oxford University Press.

Robichaux, Robert H. 1999. *Ecology of Sonoran Desert Plants and Plant Communities.* Tucson: University of Arizona Press.

Rogers, G. F., & M. K. Vint. 1987. Winter precipitation and fire in the Sonoran Desert. *Journal of Arid Environments* 13:47–52.

Rosen, P. C., & C. H. Lowe. 1994. Highway mortality of snakes in the Sonoran Desert of southern Arizona. *Conservation Biology* 68:143–148.

Russo, John P. 1956. *The Desert Bighorn Sheep in Arizona.* Phoenix: Arizona Game and Fish Department.

Rutman, Susan. 1995. An assessment of wildland fire at Organ Pipe Cactus National Monument. On file, Organ Pipe Cactus National Monument.

Saxton, Edward H. 1978. Saving the desert bighorn. *Desert Magazine* (March): 16–18.

Schmidt, Justin O., editor. 1989. *Special Biotic Relationships in the Arid Southwest.* Albuquerque: University of New Mexico Press.

Sheridan, D. 1979. *Off-Road Vehicles on Public Lands.* Council on Environmental Quality. Washington, D.C.: U.S. Government Printing Office.

Shreve, Forrest. 1951. *Vegetation of the Sonoran Desert.* Carnegie Institution of Washington Publication No. 591. Reprinted as part 1 of Forrest Shreve & I. L. Wiggins, *Flora and Vegetation of the Sonoran Desert.* Stanford: Stanford University Press, 1964.

Shumaker, Jon M. 2000. *A Class 1 Cultural Resources Overview of the Proposed Sonoran Desert National Monument, Maricopa and Pinal Counties, Arizona.* Report for Sonoran Desert National Park Friends, Tucson.

Simmons, N. M. 1966. Flora of the Cabeza Prieta Game Range. *Arizona Academy of Science* 4:93–104.

Simms, W. H. 1938. Minutes: Arizona Scout Committee for Preservation of the Bighorn Sheep, February 3. Roosevelt Council of Boy Scouts of America, Phoenix.

Smith, E. L., editor. 1976. *Proposed Natural Areas in Arizona: A Summary.* Report from Arizona Academy of Science to Office of Economic Planning and Development, Office of the Governor, State of Arizona.

Sonoran Desert National Park Friends. 1999. *A Citizen's Proposal.* Brochure. Tucson.

Sowell, John. 2001. *Desert Ecology: An Introduction to Life in the Southwest.* Salt Lake City: University of Utah Press.

Steenbergh, Warren F., & Charles H. Lowe. 1977. *Ecology of the Saguaro: II. Reproduction, Germination, Establishment, Growth, and Survival of the Young Plant.* National Park Service Scientific Monograph Series No. 8. Washington, D.C.: U.S. Government Printing Office.

Stoleson, Scott H., Richard S. Felger, Gerardo Ceballos, Carol Raish, Michael F. Wilson, & Alberto Búrquez. 2005. Recent history of natural resource use and population growth in northern Mexico. In *Biodiversity, Ecosystems, and Conservation in Northern Mexico,* edited by Jean-Luc E. Cartron, Gerardo Ceballos, & Richard S. Felger, pp. 52–86. New York: Oxford University Press.

Sullivan, B. K., R. W. Bowker, K. B. Malmos, & E. W. A. Gergus. 1996. Arizona distribution of three Sonoran anurans: *Bufo retiformis, Gastrophryne olivacea,* and *Pternohyla fodiens. Great Basin Naturalist* 56:38–47.

Swetnam, Thomas W. 1990. Fire history and climate in the southwestern United States. In *Proceedings—Effects of Fire in Management of Southwestern Natural Resources, 15–17 Nov. 1988, Tucson, Arizona,* J. S. Drammes, technical coordinator, pp. 6–17. USDA Forest Service General Technical Report RM-191.

Sykes, G. 1937. *The Colorado Delta.* Carnegie Institution of Washington Publication No. 460. Washington, D.C.

Székely, Alberto, Luis Octavio Martínez Morales, Mark J. Spalding, & Dominique Cartron. 2005. Mexico's legal and institutional framework for the conservation of biodiversity and ecosystems. In *Biodiversity, Ecosystems, and Conservation in Northern Mexico,* edited by Jean-Luc E. Cartron, Gerardo Ceballos, & Richard S. Felger, pp. 87–106. New York: Oxford University Press.

Taylor, Walter P. 1935a. Memorandum on Proposed Game Preserves in Western Arizona, with Illustrations. Biological Survey report, January 10 and 14. Record Unit 7176, Box 30, Folder 16, U.S. Fish and Wildlife Service. Smithsonian Institution Archives.

———. 1935b. Report on Proposed Cabeza Prieta Wildlife Refuge, Arizona, November 19. Record Unit 7176, Box 30, Folder 17, U.S. Fish and Wildlife Service. Smithsonian Institution Archives.

Thompson-Olais, Laura. 1994. *Sonoran Pronghorn Recovery Plan Revision.* Albuquerque: U.S. Fish and Wildlife Service.

Trombulak, Stephen C., & Christopher A. Frissell. 2000. Review of ecological effects of roads on terrestrial and aquatic communities. *Conservation Biology* 14(1):18–30.

Tunnicliff, B., S. K. Brickler et al. (Natural Resources Planning Team). 1986. *Natural Resources Management Plan for Luke Air Force Range.* School of Renewable Natural Resources, College of Agriculture. Tucson: University of Arizona.

Turner, Dale S., Richard S. Felger, Kathryn Mauz, Carianne S. Funicelli, Tom Van Devender, & Jim Malusa. 2000. *Biological Resources of the Proposed Sonoran Desert National Monument, Arizona.* Tucson: Drylands Institute.

Turner, Dale S., & Carianne S. Funicelli. 2004. Demographic changes and epidermal browning in two protected populations of saguaro cactus *(Carnegiea gigantea). Desert Plants* 20(1):16–23.

Turner, Raymond M. 1990. Long-term vegetation change at a fully protected Sonoran Desert site. *Ecology* 71:464–477.

Varady, Robert, Andrea Kaus, Robert Merideth, & Katherine Hankins. 2003. *. . . to the Sea of Cortés: Nature, Water, Culture, and Livelihood in the Lower Colorado River: A Digest.* Tucson: Udall Center for Studies in Public Policy.

Varela-Romero, Alejandro, Gorgonio Ruiz-Campos, Luz María Yépiz-Velázquez, & Jorge Alaníz-García. 2002. Distribution, habitat, and conservation status of desert pupfish *(Cyprindon macularius)* in the Lower Colorado River Basin. *Fish Biology and Fisheries* 12:157–165.

Watkins, T. H. 1990. *Righteous Pilgrim: The Life and Times of Harold L. Ickes, 1874–1952.* New York: Henry Holt.

Webb, Robert H., & Howard G. Wilshire. 1983. *Environmental Effects of Off-Road Vehicles: Impacts and Management in Arid Regions.* New York: Springer-Verlag.

Weiner, Tim. 2003. Americans stake claims in Baja land rush. *New York Times,* October 26.

Wirt, E. B., & P. A. Holm. 1997. *Climatic Effects on Survival and Reproduction of the Desert Tortoise (Gopherus agassizii) in the Maricopa Mountains, Arizona.* Arizona Game and Fish Department Heritage Grant, IIPAM-I92035. Phoenix.

Wolf, B. O., & C. Martínez del Rio. 2000. Use of saguaro fruit by white-winged doves: Isotopic evidence of a tight ecological association. *Oecologia* 124:536–543.

Woo, Huikheng, Edward Glenn, Richard C. Brusca, & Rick McCourt. 2004. Algae. In *A Seashore Guide to the Northern Gulf of California,* edited by Richard C. Brusca, Erin Kimrey, & Wendy Moore, pp. 133–145. Tucson: Arizona-Sonora Desert Museum.

Yetman, David. 1994. Direct from the Director: El Gran Despoblado Park. *Vermillion Flycatcher* (Tucson Audubon Society), February, 3.

2. Remote Sensing of the Arid Borderland

Bagnold, R. A. 1941. *The Physics of Blown Sand and Desert Dunes.* London: Chapman and Hall.

Donnelly, M. F. 1975. Geology of the Sierra del Pinacate Volcanic Field, northern Sonora, Mexico, and southern Arizona, U.S.A. Ph.D. dissertation, Stanford University.

Hunt, G. R., J. W. Salisbury, & C. J. Lenhoff. 1971. Visible and near-infrared spectra of minerals and rocks: III. Oxides and hydroxides. *Modern Geology* 2:195–205.

McKee, E. D. 1974. Paleozoic rocks of Grand Canyon. In *Geology of Northern Arizona with Notes on Archaeology and Paleoclimate, Part 1, Regional Studies,* pp. 119–154. Proceedings of the Rocky Mountain Section meeting. Boulder, Colorado: Geological Society of America.

3. A Geologic Tour of the Dry Borders Region

Aragón-Noriega, E. A., & L. E. Calderón-Aguilera. 2000. Does damming of the Colorado River affect the nursery area of blue shrimp *Litopenaeus stylirostris* (Decapoda: Penaeidae) in the upper Gulf of California? *Revista de Biología Tropical* 48: 867–871.

Breed, C. S., J. E. McCauley, W. J. Breed, C. K. McCauley, & A. S. Cotera. 1984. Eolian (wind-formed) landscapes. In *Landscapes of Arizona: The Geological Story,* edited by T. L. Smiley, J. D. Nations, T. L. Péwé, & J. P. Schafer, pp. 359–413. New York: University Press of America.

Carriquiry, J. D., & A. Sánchez. 1999. Sedimentation in the Colorado River delta and Upper Gulf of California after nearly a century of discharge loss. *Marine Geology* 158:125–145.

Carruth, R. L. 1993. *Hydrogeology of the Quitobaquito Springs and La Abra Plain Area, Arizona, and Sonora, Mexico.* U.S. Geological Survey Water Resources Investigations Open-File Report. Tucson.

Davis, O. K., editor. 1990. Quaternary geology of Bahía Adair and the Gran Desierto region, field trip guide: Deserts—past and future evolution. *IGCP* 252:31.

Dixon, D. W. 1966. Geology of the New Cornelia Mine, Ajo, Arizona. In *Geology of the Porphyry Copper Deposits, Southwestern North America,* edited by S. R. Titley & C. L. Hicks, pp. 123–132. Tucson: University of Arizona Press.

Ezcurra, E., R. S. Felger, A. D. Russell, & M. Equihua, M. 1988. Freshwater islands in a desert sand sea: The hydrology, flora, and phytogeography of the Gran Desierto oases of northwestern Mexico. *Desert Plants* 9(2):35–44.

Felger, R. S. 2000. *Flora of the Gran Desierto and Río Colorado of Northwestern Mexico.* Tucson: University of Arizona Press.

Felger, R. S., P. L. Warren, L. S. Anderson, & G. P. Nabhan. 1992. Vascular plants of a desert oasis: Flora and ethnobotany of Quitobaquito, Organ Pipe Cactus National Monument, Arizona. *Proceedings of the San Diego Society of Natural History* 8(June): 1–39.

Flessa, K. W. 2002. Conservation paleontology. *American Paleontologist* 10(2):2–5.

Flessa, K. W., A. H. Cutler, & K. H. Meldahl. 1993. Time and taphonomy: Quantitative estimates of time-averaging and stratigraphic disorder in a shallow marine habitat. *Paleobiology* 19(2):266–286.

Galindo-Bect, M. S., E. P. Glenn, H. M. Page, K. Fitzsimmons, L. A. Galindo-Bect, J. M. Hernández-Ayon, R. L. Petty, J. García-Hernández, & D. Moore. 2000. Penaeid shrimp landings in the upper Gulf of California in relation to Colorado River freshwater discharge. *Fisheries Bulletin* 98:222–225.

García Hernández, J., K. A. King, A. L. Velasco, E. Shumilin, M. A. Mora, & E. P. Glenn. 2001. Selenium, selected inorganic elements, and organochlorine pesticides in bottom material and biota from the Colorado River Delta. *Journal of Arid Environments* 49:65–89.

Glenn, E. P, R. S. Felger, A. Búrquez, & D. S. Turner. 1992. Ciénega de Santa Clara: Endangered wetland in the Colorado River delta, Sonora, Mexico. *Natural Resources Journal of the University of New Mexico School of Law* 32:817–824.

Glenn, E. P., F. Zamora-Arroyo, P. L. Nagler, M. Briggs, W. Shaw, & K. Flessa. 2001. Ecology and conservation biology of the Colorado River delta, Mexico. *Journal of Arid Environments* 49:5–15.

Haxel, G. B., R. M. Tosdal, D. J. May, & J. E. Wright. 1984. Latest Cretaceous and early Tertiary orogenesis in south-central Arizona: Thrust faulting, regional metamorphism, and granitic plutonism. *Geological Society of America Bulletin* 95:631–653.

Kowalewski, M. 1996. Taphonomy of a living fossil: The lingulide brachiopod *Glottidia palmeri* Dall from Baja California, Mexico. *Palacios* 11:244–265.

Kowalewski, M., G. E. Avila-Serrano, K. W. Flessa, & G. A. Goodfriend. 2000. Dead delta's former productivity: Two trillion shells at the mouth of the Colorado River. *Geology* 28: 1059–1062.

Kowalewski, M., K. W. Flessa, & J. A. Aggen. 1994. Taphofacies analysis of recent shelly cheniers (beach ridges), northeastern Baja California, Mexico. *FACIES* 31:209–242.

Lancaster, N. 1989. The dynamics of star dunes: An example from the Gran Desierto, Mexico. *Sedimentology* 36:273–289.

Lavín, M. F., & S. Sánchez. 1999. On how the Colorado River affected the hydrography of the upper Gulf of California. *Continental Shelf Research* 19:1545–1560.

Lindsay, E. H. 1984. Late Cenozoic mammals from northwestern Mexico. *Journal of Vertebrate Paleontology* 4(2):208–215.

Lonsdale, P. 1989. Geology and tectonic history of the Gulf of California. In *The Geology of North America,* vol. N, *The Eastern Pacific Ocean and Hawaii,* pp. 499–521. Boulder, Colorado: Geological Society of America.

May, L. A. 1973. Resources reconnaissance of the Gran Desierto region, northwestern Sonora, Mexico. Master's thesis, University of Arizona.

Mueller, K. J., & T. K. Rockwell. 1995. Late Quaternary activity of the Laguna Salada fault in northern Baja California, Mexico. *Geological Society of America Bulletin* 107(1):8–18.

Rodriguez, C. A., K. W. Flessa, & D. L. Dettman. 2001. Effects of upstream diversion of Colorado River water on the estuarine bivalve mollusc *Mulinia coloradoensis. Conservation Biology* 15:249–258.

Schmidt, N. 1990. Plate tectonics and the Gulf of California region. *Arizona Geology* 20(2):1–4.

Shafiqullah, M., P. E. Damon, D. J. Lynch, S. J. Reynolds, W. A. Rehrig, & R. H. Raymond. 1980. K-Ar geochronology and geologic history of southwestern Arizona and adjacent areas. In *Studies in Western Arizona,* edited by J. P. Jenney & C. Stone, pp. 201–243. Digest No. 12. Tucson: Arizona Geological Society.

Sharp, R. P. 1994. *A Field Guide to Southern California.* 3d. ed. Dubuque, Iowa: Kendall Hunt.

Spencer, J. E., S. M. Richard, S. J. Reynolds, R. J. Miller, M. Shafiqullah, W. G. Gilbert, & M. J. Grubensky. 1995. Spatial and temporal relationships between mid-Tertiary magmatism and extension in southwestern Arizona. *Journal of Geophysical Research* 100(B7):10, 321–351.

Stock, J. M., A. B. Martin, F. V. Suárez, & M. M. Miller. 1991. Miocene to Holocene extensional tectonics and volcanic stratigraphy of northeastern Baja California, Mexico. In *Geological Excursions in Southern California and Mexico: Guidebook for the Geological Society of America Annual Meeting,* edited by M. Walawender & B. Hanan, pp. 45–67. Boulder, Colorado: Geological Society of America.

Sykes, G. 1937. *The Colorado River.* American Geographical Society Special Publication No. 19. New York: Kennikat Press.

Thompson, R. W. 1968. Tidal flat sedimentation on the Colorado River delta, northwestern Gulf of California. *Geological Society of America Memoir* No. 107. Boulder, Colorado.

Titley, S. R. 1981. Geologic and geotectonic setting of porphyry copper deposits in the southern cordillera. In *Relations of Tectonics to Ore Deposits in the Southern Cordillera,* edited by W. R. Dickinson &

W. D. Payne, pp. 79–97. Digest No. 12. Tucson: Arizona Geological Society.

Tosdal, R. M., G. B. Haxel, & J. E. Wright. 1989. Jurassic geology of the Sonoran Desert region, southern Arizona, southeastern California, and northernmost Sonora: Construction of a continental-margin magmatic arc. In *Geologic Evolution of Arizona,* edited by J. P. Jenney & S. J. Reynolds, pp. 397–434. Special Paper No. 17. Tucson: Arizona Geological Society.

Van Devender, T. R., T. L. Burgess, R. S. Felger, & R. M. Turner. 1990. Holocene vegetation of the Hornaday Mountains of northwestern Sonora, Mexico. *Proceedings of the San Diego Society of Natural History* 2:1–19.

3. Additional References

Brown, J. L. 1992. Interpretive geologic map of Mt. Ajo quadrangle, Organ Pipe Cactus National Monument, Arizona. Open File Report 92–93. Denver: U.S. Geological Survey and National Park Service.

Damon, P. E., D. J. Lynch, & M. Shafiqullah. 1984. Cenozoic landscape development in the Basin and Range province of Arizona. In *Landscapes of Arizona: The Geological Story,* edited by T. L. Smiley, J. D. Nations, T. L. Péwé, & J. P. Schafer, pp. 175–206. New York: University Press of America.

Davis, O. K., A. H. Cutler, K. H. Meldah, M. R. Palacios-Fest, J. F. Schreiber Jr., B. E. Lock, L. J. Williams, N. Lancaster, C. A. Shaw, & S. M. Sinitiere. 1990. Quaternary and environmental geology of the northeastern Gulf of California. In *Geologic Excursions Through the Sonoran Desert Region, Arizona and Sonora,* edited by G. E. Gehrels & J. E. Spencer, pp. 136–154. Special Paper No. 7. Tucson: Arizona Geological Survey.

Dokka, R. K., & R. H. Merriam. 1979. Tectonic evolution of the main gulf escarpment, NE Baja California, Mexico. In *Baja California Geology Field Guides and Papers,* edited by P. L. Abbott & R. G. Gastil, pp. 139–152. Geological Society of America Annual Meeting Field Trip Guidebook. Boulder, Colorado: Geological Society of America.

Fradkin, P. L. 1981. *A River No More: The Colorado River and the West.* New York: Knopf.

Gastil, R. G., et al. 1975. *Reconnaissance Geology of the State of Baja California.* Memoir No. 140. Boulder, Colorado: Geological Society of America.

Hartmann, W. K. 1989. *Desert Heart: Chronicles of the Sonoran Desert.* Tucson: Fisher Books.

Lynch, D. J. 1989. Neogene volcanism in Arizona: The recognizable volcanoes. In *Geologic Evolution of Arizona,* edited by J. P. Jenney & S. J. Reynolds, pp. 681–700. Digest No. 17. Tucson: Arizona Geological Society.

———. 1991. Pinacate's largest lava flow. *CEDO News* 4(1):1–13.

Lynch, D. J., & J. T. Gutmann. 1987. Volcanic structures and alkaline rocks in the Pinacate volcanic field of Sonora, Mexico. In *Geologic Diversity of Arizona and Its Margins: Excursions to Choice Areas: Field Trip Guidebook for 100th Geological Society of America Annual Meeting,* pp. 309–322. Special Paper No. 5. Tucson: Arizona Bureau of Geology and Mineral Technology.

Montgomery, E. L., & J. W. Harshbarger. 1989. Arizona hydrogeology and water supply. In *Geologic Evolution of Arizona,* edited by J. P. Jenney & S. J. Reynolds, pp. 827–840. Digest No. 17. Tucson: Arizona Geological Society.

Morán-Zenteno, D. 1994. The geology of the Mexican Republic. *American Association of Petroleum Geologists Studies in Geology* 39:5–33.

Reisner, M. 1986. *Cadillac Desert.* New York: Penguin Books.

Reisner, M., & S. Bates. 1990. *Overtapped Oasis: Reform or Revolution for Western Water?* Washington, D.C.: Island Press.

Steinbeck, J. 1975. *The Log from the Sea of Cortez.* New York: Viking Press.

Tosdal, R. M., T. H. Anderson, G. B. Haxel, D. J. May, & J. E. Wright. 1990. Highlights of Jurassic, Late Cretaceous to Early Tertiary, and Middle Tertiary Tectonics, south-central Arizona and north-central Sonora. In *Arizona Geological Survey Special Paper No. 7,* edited by G. Gehrels & J. Spencer, pp. 76–88. Tucson: Arizona Geological Survey.

Tucker, W. C. 1980. Tectonic Geomorphology of the Luke Air Force Range, Arizona. In *Studies in Western Arizona,* edited by J. P. Jenney & C. Stone, pp. 63–87. Digest No. 14. Tucson: Arizona Geological Society.

4. Airing Out the Desert Basement: The Physical Geography of the Sonoran Desert National Monument

Behrensmeyer, A. K., J. D. Damuth, W. A. DiMichele, R. Potts, H. D. Sues, & S. L. Wing, editors. 1992. *Terrestrial Ecosystems Through Time.* Chicago: University of Chicago Press.

Bryan, K. 1922. *Erosion and Sedimentation in the Papago Country, Arizona.* U.S. Geological Survey Bulletin No. 730-B. Washington, D.C.: U.S. Government Printing Office.

———. 1925. *The Papago Country, Arizona: A Geographic, Geologic, and Hydrologic Reconnaissance with a Guide to Desert Watering Places.* U.S. Geological Survey Water Supply Paper No. 499. Washington, D.C.: U.S. Government Printing Office.

Christenson, G. E., & C. R. Purcell. 1985. Correlation and age of Quaternary alluvial-fan sequences, Basin and Range province, southwestern United States. In *Soils and Quaternary Geology of the Southwestern United States,* edited by D. L. Weide, pp. 115–122. Special Paper No. 203. Boulder, Colorado: Geological Society of America.

Cunningham, D., E. DeWitt, G. Haxel, S. J. Reynolds, & J. E. Spencer. 1987. Geologic map of the Maricopa Mountains, central Arizona. 1 sheet, scale 1:62,500. Open File Report 87–4. Tucson: Arizona Geological Survey.

Demsey, K. A. 1989. Geologic map of Quaternary and upper Tertiary alluvium in the Phoenix South 30′ × 60′ Quadrangle, Arizona. Open File Report 89–7. Tucson: Arizona Geological Survey. 1 sheet, scale 1:100,000.

Dockter, R. D., & W. J. Keith. 1978. Reconnaissance geologic map of Vekol Mountain Quadrangle, Arizona. U.S.G.S. Miscellaneous Field Studies Map MF-931. Reston, Virginia: U.S. Geological Survey. 1 sheet, scale 1:62,500.

Eberly, L. D., & T. B. Stanley, Jr. 1978. Cenozoic stratigraphy and geologic history of southwestern Arizona. *Geological Society of America Bulletin* 89: 921–940.

Huckleberry, G. 1997. Rates of Holocene soil formation in south-central Arizona. Open File Report 97–7. Tucson: Arizona Geological Survey.

Matlock, D. T. 1983. Simulative models for the analysis of ground-water flow in Vekol Valley, the Waterman Wash area, and the Bosque area, Maricopa and Pinal Counties, Arizona. Master's thesis, University of Arizona.

McConnell, R. L. 1972. The Apache Group (Proterozoic) of central Arizona, with special reference to the paleoecology of the Mescal Formation. Ph.D. dissertation, University of California, Santa Barbara.

Morrison, R. B. 1985. Pliocene/Quaternary geology, geomorphology, and tectonics of Arizona. In *Soils and Quaternary Geology of the Southwestern United States,* edited by D. L. Weide, pp. 123–146. Special Paper 203. Boulder, Colorado: Geological Society of America.

Pendall, E. 1994. Surficial geology, soils, and vegetation patterns of the Table Top Mountain Area, Pinal and Maricopa Counties, Arizona. Open File Report 94–22. Tucson: Arizona Geological Survey. 37 pp. + 1 sheet, scale 1:24,000.

Peterson, J. A., R. M. Tosdal, & M. I. Hornberger. 1987. Geologic map of the Table Top Wilderness Study Area, Pinal and Maricopa Counties, Arizona. U.S.G.S. Miscellaneous Field Studies Map MF-1951. Reston, Virginia: U.S. Geological Survey. 1 sheet, scale 1:24,000.

Reynolds, S. J., & S. J. Skotnicki. 1993. Geologic map of the Phoenix South 30′ × 60′ Quadrangle, central Arizona. Open File Report 93–18. Tucson: Arizona Geological Survey. 1 sheet, scale 1:100,000.

Shakel, D. W., L. T. Silver, & P. E. Damon. 1977. Observations of the history of the gneissic core complex, Santa Catalina Mountains, southern Arizona. *Geological Society of America Abstracts with Programs* 9:1169–1170.

Shride, A. F. 1967. *Younger Precambrian Geology in Southern Arizona.* U.S. Geological Survey Professional Paper No. 566. Washington, D.C.: U.S. Government Printing Office.

5. Confessions of a Repeat Photographer

Bowers, Janice E., Robert H. Webb, & Renée J. Rondeau. 1995. Longevity, recruitment and mortality of desert plants in Grand Canyon, Arizona, USA. *Journal of Vegetation Science* 6:551–564.

Bull, William B. 1974. Playa processes in the volcanic craters of the Sierra Pinacate, Sonora, Mexico. *Zeitschrift für Geomorphologie,* neue Folge, Supplementum Band 20:117–129.

Goldberg, Deborah E., & Raymond M. Turner. 1986. Vegetation change and plant demography in permanent plots in the Sonoran Desert. *Ecology* 67: 695–712.

Hattersley-Smith, G. 1966. The symposium on glacier mapping. *Canadian Journal of Earth Sciences* 3(6): 737–743.

Hornaday, William T. 1908. *Camp-Fires on Desert and Lava.* New York: Charles Scribner's Sons.

Lumholtz, Carl. 1912. *New Trails in Mexico.* New York: Charles Scribner's Sons.

Shantz, Homer L., & Billie L. Turner. 1958. *Photographic Documentation of Vegetational Changes in Africa over a Third of a Century.* College of Agriculture Report No. 169. Tucson: University of Arizona.

Turner, Raymond M. 1963. Growth in four species of Sonoran Desert trees. *Ecology* 44(4):760–765.

———. 1990. Long-term vegetation change at a fully protected Sonoran Desert site. *Ecology* 71(2): 464–477.

6. Ice Ages in the Sonoran Desert: Pinyon Pines and Joshua Trees in the Dry Borders Region

Anderson, R. S., & T. R. Van Devender 1991. Comparison of pollen and macrofossils in packrat *(Neotoma)* middens: A chronological sequence from the Waterman Mountains, southern Arizona, U.S.A. *Review of Paleobotany and Palynology* 68:1–28.

———. 1995. Vegetation history and paleoclimates of the coastal lowlands of Sonora, Mexico—Pollen records from packrat middens. *Journal of Arid Environments* 30:295–306.

Betancourt, J. L., T. R. Van Devender, & P. S. Martin, editors. 1990. *Packrat Middens: The Last 40,000 Years of Biotic Change.* Tucson: University of Arizona Press.

Brakenridge, G. R. 1978. Evidence for a cold, dry full-glacial climate in the American Southwest. *Quaternary Research* 9:22–40.

Bryson, R. A., & W. Wendland. 1967. Tentative climatic patterns for some late glacial and post-glacial episodes in central North America. In *Life, Land, and Water,* edited by S. J. Meyer-Oakes, pp. 271–298. Winnipeg: University of Manitoba Press.

Clements, F. E. 1936. Nature and structure of the climax. *Journal of Ecology* 24:252–284.

Felger, R. S. 2000. *Flora of the Gran Desierto and Río Colorado of Northwestern Mexico*. Tucson: University of Arizona Press.

Galloway, R. W. 1983. Full-glacial climate in the southwestern United States. *Annals of the Association of Geographers* 60:245–256.

Gleason, H. A. 1939. The individualistic concept of the plant association. *American Midland Naturalist* 21:92–110.

Hall, W. E., T. R. Van Devender, & C. A. Olson. 1988. Late Quaternary arthropod remains from Sonoran Desert packrat middens. *Quaternary Research* 29:1–18.

———. 1989. Late Quaternary and modern arthropods from the Ajo Mountains of southwestern Arizona. *Pan-Pacific Entomologist* 65:322–347.

———. 1990. Late Quaternary and modern arthropods from the Puerto Blanco Mountains, Organ Pipe Cactus National Monument, southwestern Arizona. In *Packrat Middens: The Last 40,000 Years of Biotic Change*, edited by J. L. Betancourt, T. R. Van Devender, & P. S. Martin, pp. 363–379. Tucson: University of Arizona Press.

Hansen, R. M. 1980. Shasta ground sloth food habits, Rampart Cave, Arizona. *Paleobiology* 4:302–319.

Hornaday, W. T. 1908. *Camp-Fires on Desert and Lava*. New York: Charles Scribner's Sons.

Hunter, K. L., J. L. Betancourt, B. R. Riddle, T. R. Van Devender, K. L. Cole, & W. G. Spaulding. 2001. Ploidy race distributions since the last glacial maximum in the North American desert shrub, *Larrea tridentata*. *Global Ecology and Biogeography* 10:521–533.

Lanner, R. M., & T. R. Van Devender. 1998. The recent history of pines in the American Southwest. In *The Ecology and Biogeography of Pinus*, edited by D. M. Richardson, pp. 171–182. Cambridge: Cambridge University Press.

Lindsay, E. H. 1984. Late Cenozoic mammals from northwestern Mexico. *Journal of Vertebrate Paleontology* 4:208–215.

Long, A., R. M. Hansen, & P. S. Martin. 1974. Extinction of the Shasta ground sloth. *Geological Society of America Bulletin* 85:1843–1848.

Martin, P. S. 1963. *The Last 10,000 Years*. Tucson: University of Arizona Press.

———. 1984. Pleistocene overkill: The global model. In *Quaternary Extinctions*, edited by P. S. Martin & R. G. Klein, pp. 345–403. Tucson: University of Arizona Press.

McAuliffe, J. R., & T. R. Van Devender. 1998. A 22,000-year record of vegetation and climate change in the north-central Sonoran Desert. *Palaeogeography, Palaeoclimatology, Palaeobotany* 141:253–275.

Mead, J. I., & A. M. Phillips III. 1981. The late Pleistocene and Holocene fauna and flora of Vulture Cave, Grand Canyon, Arizona. *Southwestern Naturalist* 26:257–288.

Mead, J. I., E. L. Roth, T. R. Van Devender, & D. W. Steadman. 1984. The late Wisconsin vertebrate fauna from Deadman Cave, southern Arizona. *Transactions of the San Diego Society of Natural History* 20:247–276.

Mead, J. I., & T. R. Van Devender. 1981. Late Holocene diet of *Bassariscus astutus* in the Grand Canyon, Arizona. *Journal of Mammalogy* 62:439–442.

———. 1991. Late Quaternary *Chaenaxis tuba* (Pupillidae) from the Sonoran Desert, south-central Arizona. *The Veliger* 34:259–263.

Peñalba, M. C., & T. R. Van Devender. 1998. Cambios de vegetación y clima en Baja California, México, durante los últimos 20,000 años. *Geología del Noroeste* 2:21–23.

Porter, S. C. 1989. Some geological implications of average Quaternary glacial conditions. *Quaternary Research* 32:245–261.

Rhode, D. 2002. Early Holocene juniper woodland and chaparral taxa in the central Baja California Peninsula, Mexico. *Quaternary Research* 57:102–108.

Sankey, J. T., T. R. Van Devender, & W. H. Clark. 2001. Late Holocene plants, Cataviña, Baja California, Mexico. *Southwestern Naturalist* 46:1–7.

Shaw, C. A., and H. G. McDonald. 1987. First record of giant anteater (Xenartha, Myrmecophagidae) in North America. *Science* 26:186–188.

Shreve, F. 1915. *The Vegetation of a Desert Mountain Range as Conditioned by Climatic Factors*. Carnegie Institute of Washington Publication No. 217. Washington, D.C.

———. 1937. Thirty years of change in desert vegetation. *Ecology* 18:463–478.

Snyder, C. T., & W. B. Langbein. 1962. The Pleistocene lake in Spring Valley, Nevada, and its climatic implications. *Journal of Geophysical Research* 67:2385–2394.

Spilman, T. J. 1976. A new species of fossil *Ptinus* from fossil wood rat nests in California and Arizona (Coleoptera, Ptinidae), with a postscript on the definition of a fossil. *Coleopterists Bulletin* 30:239–244.

Turner, R. M., J. E. Bowers, & T. L. Burgess. 1995. *Sonoran Desert Plants: An Ecological Atlas*. Tucson: University of Arizona Press.

Turner, R. M., & D. E. Brown. 1982. Sonoran desertscrub. *Desert Plants* 4:181–221.

Van Devender, T. R. 1990a. Late Quaternary vegetation and climate of the Chihuahuan Desert, United States and Mexico. In *Packrat Middens: The Last 40,000 Years of Biotic Change*, edited by J. L. Betancourt, T. R. Van Devender, & P. S. Martin, pp. 104–133. Tucson: University of Arizona Press.

———. 1990b. Late Quaternary vegetation and climate of the Sonoran Desert, United States and Mexico. In *Packrat Middens: The Last 40,000 Years of Biotic Change*, edited by J. L. Betancourt, T. R. Van Devender, & P. S. Martin, pp. 134–165. Tucson: University of Arizona Press.

———. 2001. Deep history and biogeography of *La Frontera*. In *Vegetation and Flora of La Frontera: Vegetation Change along the United States–Mexican*

Boundary, edited by G. L. Webster & C. J. Bahre, pp. 56–83. Albuquerque: University of New Mexico Press.

———. 2002. Cenozoic environments and the evolution of the gopher tortoises (genus *Gopherus*). In *The Sonoran Desert Tortoise: Natural History, Biology, and Conservation,* edited by T. R. Van Devender, pp. 29–51. Tucson: University of Arizona Press.

Van Devender, T. R., & G. L. Bradley. 1990. Late Quaternary mammals from the Chihuahuan Desert: Paleoecology and latitudinal gradients. In *Packrat Middens: The Last 40,000 Years of Biotic Change,* edited by J. L. Betancourt, T. R. Van Devender, & P. S. Martin, pp. 350–362. Tucson: University of Arizona Press.

Van Devender, T. R., T. L. Burgess, R. S. Felger, & R. M. Turner. 1990. Holocene vegetation of the Hornaday Mountains of northwestern Sonora, Mexico. *Proceedings of the San Diego Natural History Museum* 2:1–19.

Van Devender, T. R., T. L. Burgess, J. C. Piper, & R. M. Turner. 1994. Paleoclimatic implications of Holocene plant remains from the Sierra Bacha, Sonora, Mexico. *Quaternary Research* 41:99–108.

Van Devender, T. R., & W. E. Hall. 1994. Holocene arthropods from the Sierra Bacha, Sonora, Mexico, with emphasis on beetles. *Coleopterists Bulletin* 48:30–50.

Van Devender, T. R., & J. I. Mead. 1978. Early Holocene and late Pleistocene amphibians and reptiles in Sonoran Desert packrat middens. *Copeia* 1978:464–475.

Van Devender, T. R., J. I. Mead, & K. L. Cole. 1983. Late Quaternary mammals from Sonoran Desert packrat middens. *Journal of Mammalogy* 64:173–180.

Van Devender, T. R., J. I. Mead, & A. M. Rea. 1991. Late Quaternary plants and vertebrates from Picacho Peak, Arizona, with emphasis on *Scaphiopus hammondi* (western spadefoot). *Southwestern Naturalist* 36:302–314.

Van Devender, T. R., A. M. Rea, & W. E. Hall. 1991. Faunal analysis of late Quaternary vertebrates from Organ Pipe Cactus National Monument, southwestern Arizona. *Southwestern Naturalist* 36:94–106.

Van Devender, T. R., A. M. Rea, & M. L. Smith. 1985. The Sangamon interglacial vertebrate fauna from Rancho La Brisca, Sonora. *Transactions of the San Diego Society of Natural History* 21:23–55.

Wells, P. V. 1964. Late Pleistocene vegetation and degree of pluvial climatic change in the Chihuahuan Desert. *Science* 153:970–975.

Wells, P. V., & R. Berger. 1967. Late Pleistocene history of coniferous woodland in the Mojave Desert. *Science* 155:1640–1647.

Wells, P. V., & J. H. Hunziker. 1976. Origin of the creosotebush (*Larrea*) deserts of southwestern United States. *Annals of the Missouri Botanical Garden* 63:883–961.

Wells, P. V., & C. D. Jorgenson. 1964. Pleistocene woodrat middens and climatic change in the Mojave Desert: A record of juniper woodlands. *Science* 143:1171–1174.

Winograd, I. J., J. M. Landwehr, K. R. Ludwig, T. B. Coplen, & A. C. Riggs. 1997. Duration and structure of the past four interglaciations. *Quaternary Research* 48:141–154.

Yang, T. W. 1970. Major chromosomal races of *Larrea divaricata* in North America. *Journal of the Arizona-Nevada Academy of Science* 6:41–45.

7. Growing Up at the Big Horn: Suggested Reading

Hafford, William. 1993. When yesterday was new. *Arizona Highways,* November, 4–9.

McGee, Anita Bender. 1985. The ranch. *Arizona Republic,* August 4.

8. A Trip to Laguna Prieta

Bahr, Donald, Juan Smith, Julian D. Hayden, & William Smith Allison. 1994. *The Short, Swift Time of the Gods on Earth: The Hohokam Chronicles.* Berkeley: University of California Press.

Broyles, Bill. 1988. Desert archaeology: An interview with Paul H. Ezell, 1913–1988. *Journal of the Southwest* 30:398–449.

Ezcurra, Exequiel, Richard S. Felger, Ann D. Russell, & M. Equihua. 1988. Freshwater islands in a desert sand sea: The hydrology, flora, and phytogeography of the Gran Desierto oases of northwestern Mexico. *Desert Plants* 9:35–44, 55–63.

Ezell, Paul H. 1954. An archaeological survey of northwestern Papaguería. *Kiva* 19(2–4):1–26.

———. 1991. The Arenenos (Sand Papago): An interview with Alberto Celaya, 1951. In *Ethnology of Northwest Mexico: Spanish Borderlands Sourcebooks,* 6:400–405, edited by Randall H. McGuire. New York: Garland.

———. 1994. Plants without water: The Pima-Maricopa experience. *Journal of the Southwest* 36:315–392.

Felger, R. S. 2000. *Flora of the Gran Desierto and Río Colorado of Northwestern Mexico.* Tucson: University of Arizona Press.

Fontana, Bernard L. 1988. On Paul Ezell. *Journal of the Southwest* 30:390–397.

Hayden, Julian D. 1965. Fragile-pattern areas. *American Antiquity* 31:272–276.

———. 1967. Summary of the prehistory and history of the Sierra Pinacate, Sonora, Mexico. *American Antiquity* 34:335–344.

———. 1985. Sierra Pinacate. In *Camera, Spade, and Pen: An Inside View of Southwestern Archaeology,* edited by Marc Gaede & Marnie Gaede, pp. 145–152. Tucson: University of Arizona Press.

———. 1987. The Vikita ceremony of the Papago, 1936–1945. *Journal of the Southwest* 29:273–324ff.

Hornaday, William T. 1908. *Camp-Fires on Desert and Lava.* New York: Charles Scribner's Sons. Reprint. Tucson: University of Arizona Press, 1983.

Ives, Ronald L. 1962. In memory: Alberto Celaya. *Explorers Journal* 40(2):91–92.

———. 1963. Alberto Celaya, 1885–1962. *Kiva* 28(3): 21–22.

———. 1964. *The Pinacate Region, Sonora, Mexico.* California Academy of Sciences Occasional Paper 47. San Francisco.

———. 1989. *Land of Lava, Ash, and Sand.* Tucson: Arizona Historical Society.

Lumholtz, Carl. 1912. *New Trails in Mexico.* London: T. Fisher Unwin. Reprint. Tucson: University of Arizona Press, 1990.

———. 1921. My life of exploration. *Natural History* 21(3):224–243.

9. Afield with Desert Scientists

Benson, Lyman, & Robert A. Darrow. 1981. *Trees and Shrubs of the Southwestern Deserts.* Tucson: University of Arizona Press.

Bowers, Janice Emily. 1988. *A Sense of Place: The Life and Work of Forrest Shreve.* Tucson: University of Arizona Press.

Davis, William A., & Stephen M. Russell. 1979. *Birds in Southeastern Arizona.* Tucson: Tucson Audubon Society.

Gentry, Howard Scott. 1982. *Agaves of Continental North America.* Tucson: University of Arizona Press.

Hornaday, William T. 1908. *Camp-Fires on Desert and Lava.* New York: Charles Scribner's Sons. Reprint. Tucson: University of Arizona Press, 1983.

Humphrey, Robert R. 1974. *The Boojum and Its Home.* Tucson: University of Arizona Press.

Lowe, Charles H., editor. 1964. *The Vertebrates of Arizona.* Tucson: University of Arizona Press.

Mallery, T. D. 1936. Rainfall records for the Sonoran Desert. *Ecology* 17:110–121, 212–215.

McGinnies, William G. 1981. *Discovering the Desert.* Tucson: University of Arizona Press.

McKee, Edwin D. 1979. *A Study of Global Sand Seas.* Professional Paper No. 1052. Washington, D.C.: U.S. Geological Survey.

Monson, Gale, & Lowell Sumner. 1980. *The Desert Bighorn.* Tucson: University of Arizona Press.

Nichols, Tad. 1999. *Glen Canyon: Images of a Lost World.* Santa Fe: Museum of New Mexico Press.

Phillips, Allan, Joe Marshall, & Gale Monson. 1983. *The Birds of Arizona.* Tucson: University of Arizona Press.

Shreve, Forrest, & Ira L. Wiggins. 1964. *Vegetation and Flora of the Sonoran Desert.* 2 vols. Stanford: Stanford University Press.

Sykes, Godfrey. 1927. The Camino del Diablo, with notes on a journey in 1925. *Geographical Review* 17:62–74.

———. 1931. Rainfall investigations in Arizona and Sonora by means of long-period rain gauges. *Geographical Review* 21:229–233.

———. 1951. Summer journey on the Devil's Road. *Desert Magazine* 14(6):5–6.

Turnage, William V., & T. D. Mallery. 1941. *An Analysis of Rainfall in the Sonoran Desert and Adjacent Territory.* Carnegie Institution of Washington Publication No. 529. Washington, D.C.

Turner, Raymond M., Janice E. Bowers, & Tony L. Burgess. 1995. *Sonoran Desert Plants: An Ecological Atlas.* Tucson: University of Arizona Press.

Turner, Raymond M., Robert H. Webb, Janice E. Bowers, & James Rodney Hastings. 2003. *The Changing Mile Revisited.* Tucson: University of Arizona Press.

10. El Viento Negro: A Saga of the Sonora–Baja California Railroad

Barrios Matrecito, Valdemar. 1988. *Por las Rutas del Desierto.* Hermosillo: Government of the State of Sonora Publications.

Munro Palacios, Guillermo. 1994. *Las Voces Vienen del Mar.* Hermosillo: Sonoran Institute of Culture, Government of the State of Sonora.

Valdéz Huerta, Daniel. 1979. *Historia del Ferrocarril en Baja California.* Mexico City: Costa Amic Editores.

Verdugo Fimbres, María Isabel. 1985. *Presente y Pasado: Historia del Municipio de Puerto Peñasco.* Hermosillo: Secretary of Education and Culture of the Government of Sonora, INAH-SEP.

Viento Negro. 1964. Directed by Servando González. Starring David Reynosa, José Eliás Moreno, Eleazar "Chelela" García, Enrique Lizaldo, and Fernando Ciangherotti. Screenplay by Rafael García Travesí and Servando González. Based on the novel *El Muro y la Trocha,* by Niño Martini Yanco (1964).

11. Sing the River

Bergman, Charles. 2002. *Red Delta: Fighting for Life at the End of the Colorado River.* Golden, Colorado: Fulcrum.

Briggs, Mark K., & Steve Cornelius. 1997. *Opportunities for Ecological Improvement Along the Lower Colorado River and Delta.* Final Report. Prepared for Defenders of Wildlife, Washington, D.C., and National Park Service, U.S./Mexico Affairs Office, Las Cruces, New Mexico, July. Tucson: Sonoran Institute.

Burke, Adam. 2001. Lessons for the Colorado. *High Country News* 33(18):12.

Carrier, Jim, & Jim Richardson. 1991. The Colorado: A river drained. *National Geographic* 179(6): 2–34.

———. 1992. *The Colorado: A River at Risk.* Englewood, Colorado: Westcliff.

Castetter, Edward F., & Willis H. Bell. 1951. *Yuman Indian Agriculture.* Albuquerque: University of New Mexico Press.

Chittenden, Newton H. 1901. Among the Cocopahs. *Land of Sunshine* 14:196–204.

Clark, Jo, Michael Clinton, Paul Cunningham, David H. Getches, Jose Luis Lopezgamez, Melissa Hathaway, Luis Octavio Martinez Morales, Beatrice Bogada, Jaime Palafox, & Carlos Valdes-Casillas. 2001. *Immediate Options for Augmenting Water Flows to the Colorado River Delta in Mexico.* Report presented to the David and Lucile Packard Foundation.

Cohen, Michael. 2001. Delta in a delicate balance. *Americas,* September, 36–43.

Davis, Tony, & Michael P. Berman. 2001. Healing the Gila. *High Country News,* October 22, 20.

Felger, Richard Stephen. 2000. *Flora of the Gran Desierto and Río Colorado of Northwestern Mexico.* Tucson: University of Arizona Press.

Fletcher, Colin. 1997. *River: One Man's Journey on the Colorado, Source to Sea.* New York: Knopf.

Forbes, Jack D. 1960. *Warriors of the Colorado: The Yuman and Quechan Nation and Their Neighbors.* Norman: University of Oklahoma Press.

Glenn, Edward P., R. S. Felger, A. Búrquez & D. S. Turner. 1992. Cienega de Santa Clara: Endangered wetland in the Colorado River delta. *Natural Resources Journal* 32(4):817–24.

Glenn, Edward P., Christopher Lee, R. S. Felger, & Scott Zengel. 1996. The Colorado River is not dead, but needs management. *Conservation Biology* 10: 1175–1186.

Glennon, Robert Jerome, & Peter W. Culp. 2002. The last green lagoon: How and why the Bush administration should save the Colorado River delta. *Ecology Law Quarterly,* October, 903.

Hanscom, Greg. 2001. Bringing back the bosque: Pueblo tribes take the lead in restoring the Rio Grande's riverside forest. *High Country News* 33(22):1, 10–12.

Huseman, Ben W. 1995. *Wild River, Timeless Canyons: Balduin Molhausen's Watercolors of the Colorado.* Fort Worth: Amon Carter Museum; Tucson: University of Arizona Press.

Kelly, William H. 1977. *Cocopa Ethnography.* Anthropological Papers of the University of Arizona No. 29. Tucson: University of Arizona Press.

Knowland, Smokey, & Family. 1985. *River Love: The Colorado River.* Garden Grove, California: Litho Graphics.

Kuhn, James E. 1997. *Guide to the Birds of the Imperial Valley.* Self-published foldout pamphlet.

Lingenfelter, Richard E. 1978. *Steamboats on the Colorado River, 1852–1916.* Tucson: University of Arizona Press.

Magagnini, Stephen. 2003. On their land, tribes' law is the last word. *Kumeyaay Daily News* (electronic newspaper). April 6. Reprinted from *Sacramento Bee.*

McKee, Edwin D., Richard F. Wilson, William J. Breed, & Carol S. Breed. 1967. *Evolution of the Colorado River in Arizona.* Flagstaff, Arizona: Northland Press.

Morrison, Jason I., Sandra L. Postel, & Peter H. Gleik. 1996. *The Sustainable Use of Water in the Lower Colorado River Basin: A Joint Report of the Pacific Institute for Studies in Development, Environment, and Security and the Global Water Policy Project Prepared with the Support of the United Nations Environment Programme and the Turner Foundation.* Oakland: Pacific Institute.

Nelson, Melissa, & Philip M. Klasky. 2001. The power of song in the protection of Native lands. *Orion Afield* 5(4):22–25.

Porter, Eliot. 1968. *Down the Colorado: John Wesley Powell's Diary of the First Trip Through the Grand Canyon, 1896.* New York: Promontory Press, with Chanticleer Press.

Porter, Eliot, & David Brower, editors. 1966. *The Place No One Knew.* San Francisco: Sierra Club.

Postel, Sandra. 1993. *Last Oasis.* Washington, D.C.: Worldwatch Institute.

———. 1995. Where have all the rivers gone. *World Watch,* May/June, 9–19.

———. 1996. *Dividing the Waters: Food Security, Ecosystem Health, and the New Politics of Scarcity.* Washington, D.C.: Worldwatch Institute.

———. 1999. *Pillar of Sand: Can the Irrigation Miracle Last?* New York: W. W. Norton.

Summerhayes, Martha. 1979. *Vanished Arizona.* Lincoln: University of Nebraska Press. Originally published 1908.

Sykes, Godfrey. 1914. *Geographical Features of the Cahuilla Basin.* Carnegie Institution of Washington Publication No. 193, pp. 13–20. Washington, D.C.

———. 1915. The reclamation of a desert. *Geographic Journal* 46:447–457.

———. 1926. The delta and estuary of the Colorado River. *Geographic Revue* 16:232–255.

———. 1937. *The Colorado Delta.* Washington, D.C.: Carnegie Institution.

Teter, Betsy. 2001. Can stories save a river? *Orion Afield* 5(4):14–15.

Vasey, George. 1889. New or little known plants— *Uniola palmeri. Garden and Forest* 2:401–402.

Williams, Anita Alvarez de. 1975. *Travelers Among the Cucapá.* Los Angeles: Dawson's Book Shop.

———. 1983. Cocopa. In *Southwest,* edited by Alfonso Ortiz, pp. 99–112. Handbook of North American Indians, vol. 10, William C. Sturtevant, general editor. Washington, D.C.: Smithsonian Institution.

Yates, Richard, & Mary Marshall. 1974. *The Lower Colorado River: A Bibliography.* Yuma: Arizona Western College.

Yensen, Susana Bojórquez de. 1984. The nutritional value of a halophytic plant: *Distichlis palmeri* (Vasey) Fassett. Master's thesis, University of Arizona.

Zwinger, Ann H. 1995. *Downcanyon: A Naturalist Explores the Colorado River Through the Grand Canyon.* Tucson: University of Arizona Press.

13. Godfrey Sykes and the *Hilda*

Anderson, Michael F. 1998. *Living at the Edge: Explorers, Exploiters, and Settlers of the Grand Canyon*

Region. Grand Canyon, Arizona: Grand Canyon Association.

Arizona Enterprise (Florence). 1890a. Around the world: Two Arizona cowboys will make the journey. November 22, p. 3.

———. 1890b. Daring navigators: The young men who left Needles to sail round the world. December 6, p. 2.

———. 1891. Sykes and McLean: Disastrous ending of their voyage. February 21, p. 1.

Arizona Journal Miner (Prescott). 1891. Untitled article. December 21, p. 3.

Arizona Sentinel (Yuma). 1890a. Local Notes. November 29, p. 3.

———. 1890b. Untitled article. December 20, p. 3.

———. 1891. Local Notes. February 14, p. 3.

Coconino Sun (Flagstaff). 1892. Local Brevities. April 14, p. 3.

———. 1893. Local Brevities. August 10, p. 3.

———. 1894. Local Brevities. August 9, p. 7.

———. 1895. Here and There. June 20, p. 2.

———. 1900. Brief Locals. July 21, p. 9.

———. 1903. Lost in the Colorado. August 8, p. 1.

Dill, David B. 1987. Terror on the Hassayampa: The Walnut Grove Dam Disaster of 1890. *Journal of Arizona History* 28(3):283–306.

Flagstaff Democrat. 1896. Town Talk. September 14, p. 5.

Giclas, Henry L. 1985. Stanley Sykes. *Journal of Arizona History* 26(2):203–226.

Hornaday, William T. 1908. *Camp-Fires on Desert and Lava*. New York: Charles Scribner's Sons.

MacDougal, Daniel T. 1906. The delta of the Rio Colorado. *Bulletin of the American Geographical Society* 38(1):1–16.

———. 1914. *The Salton Sea: A Study of the Geography, the Geology, the Floristics, and the Ecology of a Desert Basin*. Carnegie Institution of Washington Publication No. 193. Washington, D.C.

Sykes, Emma Walmisley. 1898. Unpublished diary. In possession of the Sykes family.

Sykes, Glenton. 1982. The naming of the boojum. *Journal of Arizona History* 23(4):351–356.

Sykes, Godfrey G. 1891–92. Unpublished diary: "Sch *Hilda*." In possession of the Sykes family.

———. 1893–1902. Unpublished diary. Microfilm. Huntington Library, San Marino, California.

———. 1903. Unpublished daily diary. In possession of the Sykes family.

———. 1927. The Camino del Diablo, with notes on a journey in 1925. *Geographical Review* 17(1):62–74.

———. 1931. Rainfall investigations in Arizona and Sonora by means of long-period rain gauges. *Geographical Review* 21(2):229–233.

———. 1937. *The Colorado Delta*. American Geographical Society Special Publication No. 19. Baltimore: Carnegie Institution of Washington and the American Geographical Society of New York.

———. 1944. *A Westerly Trend*. Tucson: Arizona Pioneers Historical Society.

14. Native Peoples of the Dry Borders Region

Adolph, E. F., & associates. 1947. *Physiology of Man in the Desert*. London: Interscience.

Ahlstrom, Richard V. N., editor. 1998. *Living in the Western Papaguería: An Archaeological Overview of the Barry M. Goldwater Air Force Range in Southwestern Arizona*. SWCA Cultural Resource Report No. 98–186. Tucson: ARCADIS Geraghty and Miller Environmental Services and SWCA Environmental Consultants.

———, editor. 2001. *A Cultural Resources Overview and Assessment for the Cabeza Prieta National Wildlife Refuge*. Report No. 01–24. Tucson: SWCA Environmental Consultants.

Ajo Copper News. 2005. Tohono O'odham may form district for Hia Ced. February 25, 1.

Allen, Paul L. 1996. Indians get fraction of land back. *Tucson Citizen*, October 15, 1A, 5A.

Altschul, Jeffrey H., editor. 1995. The Archaic-Formative Transition in the Tucson Basin. Special issue, *Kiva* 60(4):457–650.

Altschul, Jeffrey H., & Bruce A. Jones. 1989. *A Cultural Resources Sample Survey of Operation Zones, Barry M. Goldwater Range, Marine Corps Air Station, Yuma Arizona*. Technical Series No. 24. Tucson: Statistical Research.

Altschul, Jeffrey H., & Adrianne G. Rankin. In press. *Fragile Patterns: Perspectives on Western Papaguería Archaeology*. Tucson: Statistical Research and University of Arizona Press.

Andrews, John P., & Todd W. Bostwick. 2000. *Desert Farmers at the River's Edge: The Hohokam and Pueblo Grande*. Phoenix: Pueblo Grande Museum.

Bailey, L. R. 1973. *Indian Slave Trade in the Southwest*. Los Angeles: Westernlore Press.

Barstad, Janet. 1999. *Hohokam Pottery*. Tucson: Western National Parks Association.

Basso, Keith H., editor. 1971. *Western Apache Raiding and Warfare: From the Notes of Grenville Goodwin*. Tucson: University of Arizona Press.

Bayman, James M., & Manuel R. Palacios. 2002. *Water Storage in a Hohokam Reservoir at Organ Pipe Cactus National Monument*. Final report to Southwest Parks and Monuments Association [now Western National Parks Association], Tucson.

Bean, Lowell John. 1978. Cahuilla. In *California*, edited by Robert F. Heizer, pp. 575–587. Handbook of North American Indians, vol. 8, William C. Sturtevant, general editor. Washington, D.C.: Smithsonian Institution.

Bean, Lowell John, & Charles R. Smith. 1978. Gabrielino. In *California*, edited by Robert F. Heizer, pp. 538–549. Handbook of North American Indians, vol. 8, William C. Sturtevant, general editor. Washington, D.C.: Smithsonian Institution.

Bee, Robert L. 1983. Quechan. In *Southwest*, edited by Alfonso Ortiz, pp. 86–98. Handbook of North American Indians, vol. 10, William C. Sturtevant, general editor. Washington, D.C.: Smithsonian Institution.

Bell, Fillman, Keith M. Anderson, & Yvonne G. Stewart. 1980. *The Quitobaquito Cemetery and Its History.* Tucson: National Park Service, Western Archeological Center.

Blackburn, Thomas C., & Lowell John Bean. 1978. Kitanemuk. In *California,* edited by Robert F. Heizer, pp. 564–569. Handbook of North American Indians, vol. 8, William C. Sturtevant, general editor. Washington, D.C.: Smithsonian Institution.

Bowen, Thomas. 1976. *Seri Prehistory: The Archaeology of the Central Coast of Sonora, Mexico.* Anthropological Papers of the University of Arizona No. 27. Tucson: University of Arizona Press.

———. 2000. *Unknown Island: Seri Indians, Europeans, and San Esteban Island in the Gulf of California.* Albuquerque: University of New Mexico Press; Tucson: University of Arizona Southwest Center.

Brott, Clark W. 1966. How stones became tools and weapons. In *Ancient Hunters of the Far West,* by Malcolm J. Rogers, edited by Richard F. Pourade, pp. 139–193. San Diego: Union-Tribune.

Browne, J. Ross. 1950. *A Tour Through Arizona, 1864, or Adventures in the Apache Country.* Tucson: Arizona Silhouettes.

Broyles, Bill. 1996. Surface water resources for prehistoric peoples in western Papaguería of the North American south-west. *Journal of Arid Environments* 33:483–495.

Brugge, David M. 1983. Navajo prehistory and history to 1850. In *Southwest,* edited by Alfonso Ortiz, pp. 489–501. Handbook of North American Indians, vol. 10, William C. Sturtevant, general editor. Washington, D.C.: Smithsonian Institution.

Bryan, Kirk. 1925. *The Papago Country, Arizona: A Geographic, Geologic, and Hydrologic Reconnaissance with a Guide to Desert Watering Places.* Water-Supply Paper No. 499. Washington, D.C.: U.S. Geological Survey.

Castetter, Edward F., & Willis H. Bell. 1942. *Pima and Papago Indian Agriculture.* Albuquerque: University of New Mexico Press.

———. 1951. *Yuman Indian Agriculture: Primitive Subsistence on the Lower Colorado and Gila Rivers.* Albuquerque: University of New Mexico Press.

Childs, Thomas. 1954. Sketch of the "Sand Papago." *Kiva* 19(2–4):27–39.

Coues, Elliott. 1900. *On the Trail of a Spanish Pioneer: The Diary and Itinerary of Francisco Garcés.* 2 vols. New York: F. P. Harper.

Crosswhite, Frank. 1981. Desert plants, habitat, and agriculture in relation to the major pattern of cultural differentiation in the O'odham people of the Sonoran Desert. *Desert Plants* 3(2):47–76.

Diamond, Jared. 1999. *Guns, Germs, and Steel: The Fates of Human Societies.* New York: W. W. Norton.

Dillehay, Thomas D. 2000. *The Settlement of the Americas: A New Prehistory.* New York: Basic Books.

Doyel, David E., & Lorraine Marquez Eiler. 2003. *Hia C'ed O'odham Traditional Cultural Places on the Barry M. Goldwater Range, Southwestern Arizona.* Estrella Cultural Research Paper No. 7. Project F02604–98-M-V015, Luke Air Force Base Range Management Office. Phoenix.

Eiler, Lorraine Marquez, & David E. Doyel. In press. The extinct tribe. In *Fragile Patterns: Perspectives on Western Papaguería Archaeology.* Tucson: Statistical Research and University of Arizona Press.

Erickson, Winston P. 2003. *Sharing the Desert: The Tohono O'odham in History.* Tucson: University of Arizona Press.

Ezell, Paul H. 1954. An archaeological survey in northwestern Papaguería. *Kiva* 19(2):1–26.

———. 1961. *The Hispanic Acculturation of the Gila River Pimas.* Memoir 90, American Anthropological Association. *American Anthropologist* 63(5).

———. 1963. *The Maricopas: An Identification from Documentary Sources.* Anthropological Papers of the University of Arizona No. 6. Tucson: University of Arizona Press.

———. 1983. History of the Pima. In *Southwest,* edited by Alfonso Ortiz, pp. 149–160. Handbook of North American Indians, vol. 10, William C. Sturtevant, general editor. Washington, D.C.: Smithsonian Institution.

———. 1991. The Areneños (Sand Papago)—Interview with Alberto Celaya [1953]. In *Spanish Borderlands Sourcebooks: Ethnology of Northwest Mexico,* 6, edited by Randall H. McGuire, pp. 400–407. New York: Garland.

———. 1994. Plants without water: The Pima-Maricopa experience. Annotated by Bernard L. Fontana. *Journal of the Southwest* 36(4):315–392. Based on Paul H. Ezell and Richard L. Carrico, *Plants Without Water: The Pima-Maricopa Experience.* Washington, D.C.: Indian Claims Commission, 1974.

Ezzo, Joseph A., & Jeffrey H. Altschul, editors. 1993. *Glyphs and Quarries of the Lower Colorado River Valley: The Results of Five Cultural Resource Surveys.* Technical Series No. 44. Tucson: Statistical Research.

Ezzo, Joseph A., & William L. Deaver. 1998. *Watering the Desert: Late Archaic Farming at the Costello-King Site.* Technical Series No. 68. Tucson: Statistical Research.

Fagan, Brian. 2000. *The Little Ice Age: How Climate Made History, 1300–1850.* New York: Basic Books.

Felger, Richard S. 1977. Mesquite in Indian cultures of southwestern North America. In *Mesquite: Its Biology in Two Desert Scrub Ecosystems,* edited by B. B. Simpson, pp. 150–176. Stroudsburg, Pennsylvania: Dowden, Hutchinson, & Ross.

———. 1980. Vegetation and flora of the Gran Desierto, Sonora, Mexico. *Desert Plants* 2(2):87–114.

———. 2000. *Flora of the Gran Desierto and Río Colorado of Northwestern Mexico.* Tucson: University of Arizona Press.

Felger, Richard Stephen, & Mary Beck Moser. 1985. *People of the Desert and Sea: Ethnobotany of the Seri Indians.* Tucson: University of Arizona Press.

Felger, Richard S., Peter L. Warren, L. Susan Anderson, & Gary P. Nabhan. 1992. Vascular plants of a desert oasis: Flora and ethnobotany of Quitobaquito, Organ Pipe Cactus National Monument, Arizona. *Proceedings of the San Diego Society of Natural History* 8:1–39.

Ferg, Alan, & William D. Peachey. 1998. An atlatl from the Sierra Pinacate. *Kiva* 64:175–200.

Ferguson, T. J. 1997. *Hopi Reconnaissance of the Carlota Copper Project: Ethnohistoric Overview and Cultural Concerns.* Draft report submitted to SWCA, Inc., Environmental Consultants, Tucson.

Ferguson, T. J., Chip Colwell-Chanthaphong, & Roger Anyon. 2004. One valley, many histories: Tohono O'odham, Hopi, Zuni, and Western Apache history in the San Pedro valley. *Archaeology Southwest* 18(1):1–14.

Flint, Richard, & Shirley Flint. 2005. *Documents of the Coronado Expedition, 1539–1542: They Were Not Familiar with His Majesty, Nor Did They Wish to Be His Subjects.* Dallas: Southern Methodist University Press.

Fontana, Bernard L. 1965. An archaeological survey of the Cabeza Prieta Game Range, Arizona. Ms. on file, Arizona State Museum Library, University of Arizona, Tucson.

———. 1974. Man in arid lands: The Piman Indians of the Sonoran Desert. In *Desert Biology,* edited by G. W. Brown, Jr., 2:489–528. New York: Academic Press.

———. 1983a. Pima and Papago: Introduction. In *Southwest,* edited by Alfonso Ortiz, pp. 125–136. Handbook of North American Indians, vol. 10, William C. Sturtevant, general editor. Washington, D.C.: Smithsonian Institution.

———. 1983b. History of the Papago. In *Southwest,* edited by Alfonso Ortiz, pp. 137–148. Handbook of North American Indians, vol. 10, William C. Sturtevant, general editor. Washington, D.C.: Smithsonian Institution.

———. 1989. *Of Earth and Little Rain: The Papago Indians.* Tucson: University of Arizona Press.

———. 1999. *A Guide to Contemporary Southwest Indians.* Tucson: Southwest Parks and Monuments Association.

Forbes, Jack D. 1965. *Warriors of the Colorado: The Yumas of the Quechan Nation and Their Neighbors.* Norman: University of Oklahoma Press.

Ford, Richard I. 1983. Inter-Indian exchange in the Southwest. In *Southwest,* edited by Alfonso Ortiz, pp. 711–722. Handbook of North American Indians, vol. 10, William C. Sturtevant, general editor. Washington, D.C.: Smithsonian Institution.

Gifford, E. W. 1931. *The Kamia of Imperial Valley.* Bureau of American Ethnology Bulletin No. 97. Washington, D.C.: U.S. Government Printing Office.

———. 1933. *The Cocopah.* University of California Publications in American Archaeology and Ethnography 31:257–334. Berkeley.

———. 1936. Northeastern and Western Yavapai. *Publications in American Archaeology and Ethnology* 34(4):247–354.

———. 1946. Archaeology in the Puerto Peñasco region, Sonora. *American Antiquity* 11(4): 214–221.

Goodwin, Grenville. 1942. *Social Organization of the Western Apache.* Chicago: University of Chicago Press.

Graybill, Donald A., David A. Gregory, Gary S. Funkhouser, & Fred L. Nials. In press. Long-term streamflow reconstructions, river channel morphology, and aboriginal irrigation systems along the Salt and Gila River. In *Environmental Change and Human Adaptation in the Ancient Southwest,* edited by David E. Doyel & Jeffrey S. Dean. Salt Lake City: University of Utah Press.

Greenleaf, J. Cameron. 1975. A fortified hill site near Gila Bend, Arizona. *Kiva* 40:213–282.

Hackenberg, Robert A. 1983. Pima and Papago ecological adaptations. In *Southwest,* edited by Alfonso Ortiz, pp. 161–177. Handbook of North American Indians, vol. 10, William C. Sturtevant, general editor. Washington, D.C.: Smithsonian Institution.

Hale, Kenneth, & David Harris. 1979. Historical linguistics and archaeology. In *Southwest,* edited by Alfonso Ortiz, pp. 170–177. Handbook of North American Indians, vol. 9, William C. Sturtevant, general editor. Washington, D.C.: Smithsonian Institution.

Hartmann, Gayle Harrison, & Mary Charlotte Thurtle. 2001. The archaeology of Tinajas Altas, a desert waterhole in southwestern Arizona. *Kiva* 66(4): 489–518.

Hartmann, William K. 1989. *Desert Heart: Chronicles of the Sonoran Desert.* Tucson: Fisher Books.

Harwell, Henry, O. Marsh, & C. S. Kelly. 1983. Maricopa. In *Southwest,* edited by Alfonso Ortiz, pp. 71–85. Handbook of North American Indians, vol. 10, William C. Sturtevant, general editor. Washington, D.C.: Smithsonian Institution.

Haury, Emil W. 1975. *The Stratigraphy and Archaeology of Ventana Cave.* Tucson: University of Arizona Press.

———. 1976. *The Hohokam: Desert Farmers and Craftsmen.* Tucson: University of Arizona Press.

Hayden, Julian D. 1965. Fragile-pattern areas. *American Antiquity* 31(2):272–276.

———. 1967. A summary prehistory and history of the Sierra Pinacate, Sonora. *American Antiquity* 32(3):335–344.

———. 1969. Gyratory crushers of the Sierra Pinacate, Sonora. *American Antiquity* 34(2):154–161.

———. 1972. Hohokam petroglyphs of the Sierra Pinacate, Sonora, and the Hohokam shell expeditions. *Kiva* 37:74–84.

———. 1976. Pre-Altithermal archaeology in the Sierra Pinacate, Sonora, Mexico. *American Antiquity* 41:274–289.

———. 1982. Ground figures of the Sierra Pinacate, Sonora, Mexico. In *Hohokam and Patayan: Prehistory of Southwestern Arizona,* edited by Randall H. McGuire & Michael B. Schiffer, pp. 581–588. New York: Academic Press.

———. 1985. Food animal cremations of the Sierra Pinacate, Sonora, Mexico. *Kiva* 50(4):237–248.

———. 1998. *The Sierra Pinacate.* Tucson: Southwest Center and University of Arizona Press.

Heilen, Michael P. 2004. Julian Hayden's Malpais model: A pre-Clovis claim from the American Southwest. *Kiva* 69(3):305–311.

Heizer, Robert F. 1978. Trade and trails. In *California,* edited by Robert F. Heizer, pp. 690–693. Handbook of North American Indians, vol. 8, William C. Sturtevant, general editor. Washington, D.C.: Smithsonian Institution.

Hendricks, William O. 1967. Guillermo Andrade and land development on the Mexican Colorado River delta. Ph.D. dissertation, University of Southern California.

———. 1971. Port Otis. In *Brand Book II,* pp. 172–185. San Diego: San Diego Corral of the Westerners.

Hill, Matthew, & J. S. Bruder. 2000. *Farmers and Foragers or Cultivators and Collectors: Opportunistic Occupation in the Interior Desert of Western Papaguería.* Dames & Moore Research Paper No. 57. Phoenix.

Hoover, J. W. 1941. Cerros de Trincheras of the Arizona Papagueria. *Geographical Review* 31:228–239.

Huckell, Bruce B. 1984. The Paleo-Indian and Archaic occupation of the Tucson basin: An overview. *Kiva* 49:133–145.

Ives, Ronald L. 1961. The quest of the blue shells. *Arizoniana* [now *Journal of Arizona History*] 2 (Spring): 3–7.

———. 1965. Population of the Pinacate region. *Kiva* 31:37–45.

Johnson, Alfred E. 1963. The Trincheras culture of northern Sonora. *American Antiquity* 29:174–186.

Jorgensen, Joseph G. 1983. Comparative traditional economics and ecological adaptations. In *Southwest,* edited by Alfonso Ortiz, pp. 684–710. Handbook of North American Indians, vol. 10, William C. Sturtevant, general editor. Washington, D.C.: Smithsonian Institution.

Kelly, William H. 1977. *Cocopa Ethnography.* Anthropological Papers of the University of Arizona No. 29. Tucson: University of Arizona Press.

Khera, Sigrid, & Patricia S. Mariella. 1983. Yavapai. In *Southwest,* edited by Alfonso Ortiz, pp. 38–54. Handbook of North American Indians, vol. 10, William C. Sturtevant, general editor. Washington, D.C.: Smithsonian Institution.

Kockelman, William J. 1983. Management concepts. In *Environmental Effects of Off-Road Vehicles: Impacts and Management in Arid Regions,* edited by Robert H. Webb & Howard G. Wilshire, pp. 399–446. New York: Springer-Verlag.

Kroeber, Clifton B., & Bernard L. Fontana. 1986. *Massacre on the Gila: An Account of the Last Major Battle Between American Indians, with Reflections on the Origin of War.* Tucson: University of Arizona Press.

Lumholtz, Carl. 1912. *New Trails in Mexico.* London: T. Fisher Unwin. Reprint. Tucson: University of Arizona Press, 1990.

Luomala, Katharine. 1978. Tipai-Ipai. In *California,* edited by Robert F. Heizer, pp. 592–609. Handbook of North American Indians, vol. 8, William C. Sturtevant, general editor. Washington, D.C.: Smithsonian Institution.

Lyons, Patrick D. 2003. *Ancestral Hopi Migrations.* Tucson: University of Arizona Press.

MacDougal, Daniel T. 1907. The desert basins of the Colorado River. *Bulletin of the American Geographical Society* 39:705–729.

Madsen, David B., editor. 2004. *Entering America: Northeast Asia and Beringia Before the Last Glacial Maximum.* Salt Lake City: University of Utah Press.

Martí, Julio César Montané. 1995. *Francisco de Ulloa: Explorador de ilusiones.* Hermosillo: Universidad de Sonora.

Martin, Paul S., & Richard G. Klein, editors. 1984. *Quaternary Extinctions: A Prehistoric Revolution.* Tucson: University of Arizona Press.

Masse, W. Bruce. 1980. *Excavations at Gu Achi: A Reappraisal of Hohokam Settlement and Subsistence in the Arizona Papagueria.* Western Archeological Center Publications in Anthropology No. 12. Tucson: National Park Service.

———. 1991. The quest for subsistence sufficiency and civilization in the Sonoran Desert. In *Chaco and Hohokam: Prehistoric Regional Systems in the Southwest,* edited by Patricia L. Crown & W. James Judge, pp. 195–223. Santa Fe: School of American Research Press.

———. In press. Elder Brother's creations. In *Fragile Patterns: Perspectives on Western Papaguería Archaeology,* edited by Jeffrey H. Altschul & Adrianne G. Rankin. Tucson: Statistical Research and University of Arizona Press.

Masse, W. Bruce, & Fred Espenak. In press. Sky as environment: Solar eclipses and Hohokam culture change. In *Environmental Change and Human Adaptation in the Ancient Southwest,* edited by David E. Doyel & Jeffrey S. Dean. Salt Lake City: University of Utah Press.

Masse, W. Bruce, & Adrianne G. Rankin. 1996. *Draft Recommended Guidelines for the Management of Cultural Resources in the Western Papaguería.* Phoenix: Western Papaguería Cultural Resources Workshop Planning Committee, Luke Air Force Base.

———. In press. The once and future Western Papaguería Cultural Resources Workshop. *Fragile Patterns: Perspectives on Western Papaguería Archaeology,* edited by Jeffrey H. Altschul &

Adrianne G. Rankin. Tucson: Statistical Research and University of Arizona Press.

McClellan, Carole, & Lawrence Vogler. 1977. *An Archaeological Assessment of the Luke Air Force Range Located in Southwestern Arizona.* Arizona State Museum Archaeological Series No. 113. Tucson.

McGuire, Randall H. 1982a. Environmental background. In *Hohokam and Patayan: Prehistory of Southwestern Arizona,* edited by Randall H. McGuire & Michael B. Schiffer, pp. 13–56. New York: Academic Press.

———. 1982b. Ethnographic studies. In *Hohokam and Patayan: Prehistory of Southwestern Arizona,* edited by Randall H. McGuire & Michael B. Schiffer, pp. 57–99. New York: Academic Press.

———. 1982c. A history of archaeological research. In *Hohokam and Patayan: Prehistory of Southwestern Arizona,* edited by Randall H. McGuire & Michael B. Schiffer, pp. 101–152. New York: Academic Press.

———. 1982d. Problems in culture history. In *Hohokam and Patayan: Prehistory of Southwestern Arizona,* edited by Randall H. McGuire & Michael B. Schiffer, pp. 153–222. New York: Academic Press.

McGuire, Randall H., & Michael B. Schiffer, editors. 1982. *Hohokam and Patayan: Prehistory of Southwestern Arizona.* New York: Academic Press.

McGuire, Randall H., & María Elisa Villalpando C. 1993. *An Archaeological Survey of the Altar Valley, Sonora, Mexico.* Arizona State Museum Archaeological Series No. 184. Tucson.

Medrano, Lourdes. 2005. Place to call home: O'odham help their landless kin carve out a tiny homeland. *Arizona Daily Star,* February 6, 1A, 15A.

Meigs, Peveril. 1939. *The Kiliwa Indians of Lower California.* Ibero-Americana No. 15. Berkeley: University of California Press.

Mitchell, Douglas R., & M. Steven Shackley. 1995. Classic Period Hohokam obsidian studies in southern Arizona. *Journal of Field Archaeology* 22: 291–304.

Nabhan, Gary Paul, Wendy Hodgson, & Frances Fellows. 1989. A meager living on lava and sand? Hia Ced O'odham food resources and habitat diversity in oral and documentary histories. *Journal of the Southwest* 31(4):508–533.

Opler, Morris E. 1983. The Apachean culture pattern and its origin. In *Southwest,* edited by Alfonso Ortiz, pp. 368–392. Handbook of North American Indians, vol. 10, William C. Sturtevant, general editor. Washington, D.C.: Smithsonian Institution.

Owen, Roger C. 1969. Contemporary ethnography of Baja California, Mexico. In *Ethnology,* edited by Evon Z. Vogt, pp. 871–878. Handbook of Middle American Indians, vol. 8. Austin: University of Texas Press.

Rankin, Adrianne G. 1995. *Archaeological Survey at Organ Pipe Cactus National Monument, Southwestern Arizona, 1989–1991.* Tucson: National Park Service, Western Archeological and Conservation Center.

Rea, Amadeo M. 1997. *At the Desert's Green Edge: An Ethnobotany of the Gila River Pima.* Tucson: University of Arizona Press.

———. 1998. *Folk Mammalogy of the Northern Pimans.* Tucson: University of Arizona Press.

Reid, Jefferson, & Stephanie Whittlesey. 1997. *The Archaeology of Ancient Arizona.* Tucson: University of Arizona Press.

Rogers, Malcolm. 1939. *Early Lithic Industries of the Lower Basin of the Colorado River and Adjacent Desert Areas.* San Diego Museum Papers No. 3. San Diego.

Schiffer, Michael B. 1982. Hohokam chronology: An essay on history and method. In *Hohokam and Patayan: Prehistory of Southwestern Arizona,* edited by Randall H. McGuire & Michael B. Schiffer, pp. 299–344. New York: Academic Press.

Schmidt-Nielsen, Knut. 1964. *Desert Animals: Physiological Problems of Heat and Water.* New York: Oxford University Press.

Schneider, Joan S. 1993. Antelope Hill: A cultural resources inventory and inquiry into prehistoric milling implement quarrying and production behaviors along the lower Gila River, Yuma County, Arizona. In *Glyphs and Quarries of the Lower Colorado River Valley: The Results of Five Cultural Resource Surveys,* edited by Joseph E. Ezzo & Jeffrey Altschul, pp. i–79 (Part 1). Technical Series No. 44. Tucson: Statistical Research.

Schneider, Joan S., & Jeffrey H. Altschul. 2000. *Of Stones and Spirits: Pursuing the Past of Antelope Hill.* Technical Series No. 76. Tucson: Statistical Research.

Shackley, M. Steven. 2005. *Obsidian: Geology and Archaeology in the North American Southwest.* Tucson: University of Arizona Press.

Shackley, M. Steven, & David B. Tucker. 2001. Limited prehistoric procurement of Sand Tank obsidian, southwestern Arizona. *Kiva* 66(3):345–374.

Sheldon, Charles. 1993. *The Wilderness of the Southwest: Charles Sheldon's Quest for Desert Bighorn Sheep and Adventures with the Havasupai and Seri Indians.* Edited by Neil B. Carmony & David E. Brown. Salt Lake City: University of Utah Press.

Simmons, Norman M. 1969. Heat stress and bighorn behavior in the Cabeza Prieta Game Range, Arizona. *Desert Bighorn Council Transactions* 13:55–63.

Southworth, C. H. 1914. From the Pima calendar stick, 1839–1913. Transcribed by James H. Jones, Jr. Ms. on file, Arizona State Museum, Tucson.

Spier, Leslie. 1933. *Yuman Tribes of the Gila River.* Chicago: University of Chicago Press.

Stewart, Kenneth M. 1983. Mohave. In *Southwest,* edited by Alfonso Ortiz, pp. 55–70. Handbook of North American Indians, vol. 10, William C. Sturtevant, general editor. Washington, D.C.: Smithsonian Institution.

Stone, Connie L. 1986. *Deceptive Desolation: Prehistory of the Sonoran Desert in West Central Arizona.* Cultural Resource Series Monograph No. 1. Phoenix: Bureau of Land Management.

—————. 1991. *The Linear Oasis: Managing Cultural Resources Along the Lower Colorado River.* Cultural Resource Series Monograph No. 6. Phoenix: Bureau of Land Management.

Teague, Lynn S. 1993. Prehistory and the traditions of the O'odham and Hopi. *Kiva* 58:435–454.

Thomas, Robert K. 1991. West of the Papago Indian Reservation, south of the Gila River, and the problem of Sand Papago identity. In *Ethnology of Northwest Mexico: A Sourcebook,* edited by Randall H. McGuire, pp. 357–399. New York: Garland. Originally published 1953.

Tower, Donald B. 1945. The use of marine mollusca and their value in reconstructing prehistoric trade routes in the American Southwest. *Papers of the Excavators' Club* 2(3):i–56ff.

Underhill, Ruth Murray. 1938a. *Singing for Power.* New York: Ballantine Books.

—————. 1938b. A Papago calendar record. *University of New Mexico Bulletin* 322 (March 1): 3–66.

—————. 1946. *Papago Indian Religion.* New York: Columbia University Press.

Van Devender, Thomas R. 1990. Late Quaternary vegetation and climate of the Sonoran Desert, United States and Mexico. In *Packrat Middens: The Last 40,000 Years of Biotic Change,* edited by Julio L. Betancourt, Thomas R. Van Devender, & Paul S. Martin, pp. 134–165. Tucson: University of Arizona Press.

Van Keuren, Scott, Susan L. Stinson, & David R. Abbott. 1997. Specialized production of Hohokam plain ware ceramics in the lower Salt River Valley. *Kiva* 63:155–175.

Waters, Michael R. 1982. The lowland Patayan ceramic tradition. In *Hohokam and Patayan: Prehistory of Southwestern Arizona,* edited by Randall H. McGuire & Michael B. Schiffer, pp. 275–297.New York: Academic Press.

—————. 1992. *Principles of Geoarchaeology: A North American Perspective.* Tucson: University of Arizona Press.

Whitely, Peter M. 2002. Archaeology and Oral Tradition: The Scientific Importance of Dialogue. *American Antiquity* 67:405–415.

Whittlesey, Stephanie M. 1994. Culture history overview of the Papaguería. In *Intermontane Settlement Trends in the Eastern Papaguería: Cultural Resources Sample Survey in the Northeastern Barry M. Goldwater Range, Maricopa County, Arizona,* edited by Jeffrey A. Homburg, Jeffrey H. Altschul, & Rein Vanderpot, pp. 26–37. Technical Series No. 37. Tucson: Statistical Research.

Whittlesey, Stephanie M., Richard Ciolek-Torrello, & Matthew A. Sterner. 1994. *Southern Arizona: The Last 12,000 Years. A Cultural-Historical Overview for the Western Army National Guard Aviation Training Site.* Technical Series No. 48. Tucson: Statistical Research.

Williams, Anita Alvarez de. 1974. *The Cocopah People.* Phoenix: Indian Tribal Series.

—————. 1975. *Travelers Among the Cucupá.* Los Angeles: Dawson's Book Shop.

—————. 1983. Cocopa. In *Southwest,* edited by Alfonso Ortiz, pp. 99–112. Handbook of North American Indians, vol. 10, William C. Sturtevant, general editor. Washington, D.C.: Smithsonian Institution.

—————. 2004. *Primeros Pobladores de la Baja California.* Mexicali: Instituto Nacional de Antropología.

Zepeda, Ofelia. 1985. *The Sand Papago Oral History Project.* Tucson: National Park Service, Western Archeological and Conservation Center.

15. Living Resources at the Center of the Sonoran Desert: Regional Uses of Plants and Animals by Native Americans

Adorno, R., & P. Pautz. 1999. *Álvar Núñez Cabeza de Vaca: His Account, His Life, and the Expedition of Pánfilo de Narváez.* 3 vols. Lincoln: University of Nebraska Press.

Andrews, J. P., & T. W. Bostwick. 1997. *Desert Farmers at the River's Edge: The Hohokam and Pueblo Grande.* Phoenix: Parks, Recreation and Library Department, Pueblo Grande Museum and Cultural Park.

Aschmann, H. 1959. *The Central Desert of Baja California: Demography and Ecology.* Ibero-America No. 42. Berkeley: University of California Press.

Bailey, L. R., editor. 1963. *Survey of a Route on the 32nd Parallel for the Texas Western Railroad, 1854: The A. B. Gray Report and Including the Reminiscences of Peter R. Brady Who Accompanied the Expedition.* Los Angeles: Westernlore Press.

Baegert, J. 1952. *Observations in Lower California.* Berkeley: University of California Press.

Barco, M. del 1980. *The Natural History of Baja California.* Translated by E. Tiscareno. Los Angeles: Dawson's Book Shop.

Barrows, D. 1900. *The Ethno-botany of the Coahuilla Indians of Southern California.* Chicago: University of Chicago Press.

Bean, L. J., & K. S. Saubel. 1972. *Temalpakh: Cahuilla Indian Knowledge and Usage of Plants.* Banning, California: Malki Museum.

Bell, F., K. M. Anderson, & Y. G. Stewart. 1980. *The Quitobaquito Cemetery and Its History.* Tucson: National Park Service, Western Archeological Center.

Bell, W. H., & E. F. Castetter. 1937. *The Utilization of Mesquite and Screwbean by the Aborigines in the American Southwest.* Bulletin No. 314. Albuquerque: University of New Mexico.

—————. 1941. *The Utilization of Yucca, Sotol, and Beargrass by the Aborigines in the American Southwest.* Bulletin No. 372. Albuquerque: University of New Mexico.

Bohrer, V. 1970. Ethnobotanical aspects of Snaketown, a Hohokam village in southern Arizona. *American Antiquity* 35:413–430.

Bolton, H. E. 1919. *Kino's Historical Memoir of Pimería Alta: A Contemporary Account of the Beginnings of*

California, Sonora, and Arizona. 2 vols. Cleveland: Arthur H. Clark.

———. 1930. *Anza's California Expeditions.* 5 vols. Berkeley: University of California Press.

———. 1949. *Coronado, Knight of Pueblos and Plains.* New York: Whittlesey House.

Bourke, J. G. 1889. Notes on the Cosmogony and Theogony of the Mohave Indians of the Rio Colorado, Arizona. *Journal of American Folk Lore* 2: 169–189.

Bowen, T. 1986. Survey in the Gran Desierto, NW Sonora, Mexico. Unpublished field notes.

———. 2000. *Unknown Island: Seri Indians, Europeans, and San Esteban Island in the Gulf of California.* Albuquerque: University of New Mexico Press.

Boyd, E. J. 1995. *Noble Brutes: Camels on the American Frontier.* Plano, Texas: Wordware.

Bradley, R. J. E. 1995. The Role of Casas Grandes in prehistoric shell exchange networks within the Southwest. Ph.D. dissertation, Arizona State University.

Brand, D. D. 1988. The honeybee in New Spain and Mexico. *Journal of Cultural Geography* 9:71–82.

Brusca, R. C. 2004. A history of discovery in the Upper Gulf of California. In *A Seashore Guide to the Northern Gulf of California,* edited by R. C. Brusca, E. Kimry, & W. Mooer, pp. 9–24. Tucson: Arizona-Sonora Desert Museum.

Burrus, E. J. 1954. *Kino Reports to Headquarters: Correspondence of Eusabio F. Kino, S.J., from New Spain with Rome.* Rome: Institutum Historicum Societatis Jesu.

———. 1971. *Kino and Manje: Explorers of Sonora and Arizona.* Rome: Jesuit Historical Institute.

Castetter, E. F. 1935. *Uncultivated Native Plants Used as Sources of Food.* Ethnobiological Studies in the American Southwest, I. University of New Mexico Bulletin, Biological Series 4(1). Albuquerque.

Castetter, E. F., & W. H. Bell. 1937. *The Aboriginal Utilization of the Tall Cacti in the American Southwest.* Ethnobiological Studies in the American Southwest, IV. University of New Mexico Bulletin, Biological Series 5(1). Albuquerque.

———. 1941. *The Utilization of Yucca, Sotol, and Beargrass by the Aborigines in the American Southwest.* Ethnobiological Studies in the American Southwest, VII. University of New Mexico Bulletin, Biological Series 5(5). Albuquerque.

———. 1942. *Pima and Papago Indian Agriculture.* Albuquerque: University of New Mexico Press.

———. 1951. *Yuman Indian Agriculture.* Albuquerque: University of New Mexico Press.

Castetter, E. F., W. H. Bell, & A. R. Grove. 1938. *The Early Utilization and the Distribution of Agave in the American Southwest.* Ethnobiological Studies in the American Southwest, VI. University of New Mexico Bulletin, Biological Series 5(4). Albuquerque.

Castetter, E., & R. Underhill. 1935. *The Ethnobiology of the Papago Indians.* Ethnobiological Studies in the American Southwest, II. University of New Mexico Bulletin, Biological Series 4(3). Albuquerque.

Chestnut, V. 1902. Plants used by the Indians of Mendocino County. *Contributions from the United States National Herbarium* 7:295–408.

Childs, T., with H. F. Dobyns. 1954. Sketch of the "Sand Indians." *Kiva* 19:27–39.

Chittenden, N. H. 1901. Among the Cocopahs. *Land of Sunshine* 14:196–204.

Cleland, J. H., A. York, & A. Johnson. 2000. The tides of history: modeling Native American use of recessional shorelines. KEA Environmental, San Diego, California, ESRI User Conference (online). *http://gis.esri.com/library/userconf/proco0/professional/papers/PAP377/p377.htm* (accessed 1 February 2004).

Clotts, H. V. 1917. *History of the Papago Indians and History of Irrigation, Papago Indian Reservation, Arizona.* Washington, D.C.: Department of the Interior, United States Indian Service.

Coues, E. 1900. *On the Trail of a Spanish Pioneer… Frances Garcés.* 2 vols. New York: Harper.

Coville, F. 1892. The Panamint Indians of California. *American Anthropologist* 5:351–361.

Crawford, J. M. 1989. *Cocopa Dictionary.* Berkeley: University of California Press.

Crosswhite, F. S. 1980. The annual saguaro harvest and crop cycle of the Papago, with reference to ecology and symbolism. *Desert Plants* 2:2–61.

Cudney Bueno, R. 2000. Management and conservation of benthic resources harvested by small-scale Hookah divers in the Northern Gulf of California, Mexico: The black murex snail fishery. Master's thesis, University of Arizona.

Cudney-Bueno, R. 2001. Co-management of the hookah diving fisheries. *CEDO News* 9(2):12–19, 42.

———. 2004. Reproductive ecology of the black murex snail, *Hexaplex nigritus* (Philips) in the Northern Gulf of California, Mexico: Implications for management and conservation. In *Proceedings of the Gulf of California Conference 2004,* June 13–15, 2004, pp. 92–93. Tucson.

Culpeper, N. 1652. *Culpeper's Complete Herbal.* Reprint. London: W. Foulsham, 1975.

Curtin, L. S. M. 1949. *By the Prophet of the Earth.* Santa Fe: San Vicente Foundation.

D'Antoni, H. L., & O. T. Solbrig. 1977. Algarrobos in South American cultures past and present. In *Mesquite: Its Biology in Two Desert Scrub Ecosystems,* edited by B. B. Simpson, pp. 189–199. Stroudsburg, Pennsylvania: Dowden, Hutchinson, and Ross.

Densmore, F. 1922. Field-work among the Yuma, Cocopa, and Yaqui Indians. *Smithsonian Institution, Explorations and Field-work, Miscellaneous Collections* 74(5):147–153.

Drucker, P. 1937. *Culture Element Distributions: V, Southern California.* University of California Anthological Records 1(1). Berkeley.

———. 1941. *Culture Element Distributions: XVII, Yuman-Piman.* University of California Anthological Records 6(3). Berkeley.

Ebeling, W. 1986. *Handbook of Indian Foods and Fibers of Arid America.* Berkeley: University of California Press.

Edmonds, J. M., & J. A. Chweya. 1997. *Black Nightshades: Solanum nigrum L. and Related Species: Promoting the Conservation and Use of Underutilized and Neglected Crops.* Handbook No. 15. Rome: Plant Genetic Research Institute.

Euler, R. C., & V. H. Jones. 1956. Hermetic sealing as a technique for food preservation among the Indians of the American Southwest. *Proceedings of the American Philosophical Society* 100:87–99.

Ezell, P. 1937. Shell work of the prehistoric Southwest. *Kiva* 3:10–12.

Felger, R. S. 1977. Mesquite in Indian cultures of southwestern North America. In *Mesquite: Its Biology in Two Desert Scrub Ecosystems,* edited by B. B. Simpson, pp. 150–176. Stroudsburg, Pennsylvania: Dowden, Hutchinson, and Ross.

———. 1979. Ancient crops for the twenty-first century. In *New Agricultural Crops,* edited by G. Ritchie, pp. 5–20. AAAS Selected Symposium No. 38. Boulder, Colorado: Westview Press.

——— 2000. *Flora of the Gran Desierto and Río Colorado of Northwestern Mexico.* Tucson: University of Arizona Press.

———. 2002. Sinaloa shootout. In *Backcountry Pilot: Flying Adventures with Ike Russell,* edited by T. Bowen, pp. 2–14. Tucson: University of Arizona Press.

Felger, R. S., M. B. Johnson, & M. F. Wilson. 2001. *Trees of Sonora, Mexico.* New York: Oxford University Press.

Felger, R. S., & E. Joyal. 1999. The Palms (Arecaceae) of Sonora, Mexico. *Aliso* 18:1–18.

Felger, R. S., & M. B. Moser. 1985. *People of the Desert and Sea: Ethnobotany of the Seri Indians.* Tucson: University of Arizona Press.

Felger, R. S., M. B. Moser, & E. W. Moser. 1983. The desert tortoise in Seri Indian culture. In *Desert Tortoise Council: Proceedings of 1981 Symposium,* pp. 113–120. Long Beach, California: Desert Tortoise Council.

Felger, R. S., & G. P. Nabhan. 1978. Agroecosystem diversity: A model from the Sonoran Desert. Pages 128–149 In *Social and Technological Management in Dry Lands,* edited by N. L. Gonzalez, pp. 128–149. AAAS Selected Symposium No. 10. Westview Press: Boulder, Colorado.

Felger, R. S., D. S. Turner, & M. F. Wilson. 2003. Flora and vegetation of the Mohawk Dunes, Arizona. *Sida* 20:1153–1185.

Felger, R. S., P. L. Warren, L. S. Anderson, & G. P. Nabhan. 1992. *Vascular Plants of a Desert Oasis: Flora and Ethnobotany of Quitobaquito, Organ Pipe Cactus National Monument, Arizona.* Proceedings of the San Diego Society of Natural History, No. 8. San Diego.

Flint, R., & S. Flint. 2005. *Documents of the Coronado Expedition, 1539–1542: They Were Not Familiar with His Majesty, Nor Did They Wish to Be His Subjects.* Dallas: Southern Methodist University Press.

Follett, W. I. 1957. Fish remains from aboriginal sites in the Punta Peñasco Region of Sonora, Mexico. *Transactions of the San Diego Society of Natural History* 12(14):279–286.

Fontana, B. L. 1965. An archeological survey of the Cabeza Prieta Game Refuge, Arizona. Ms. on file, Arizona State Museum, University of Arizona, Tucson.

———. 1974. Man in Arid Lands: The Piman Indians of the Sonoran Desert. In *Desert Biology,* edited by G. W. Brown, Jr., 2:489–528. New York: Academic Press.

Fontana, H. M., & B. L. Fontana. 2000. *Trails to Tiburón: The 1894 and 1895 Field Diaries of W J McGee.* Tucson: University of Arizona Press.

Ford, R. I. 1983. Inter-Indian exchange in the Southwest. In *Southwest,* edited by Alfonso Ortiz, pp. 711–722. Handbook of North American Indians, vol. 10, William C. Sturtevant, general editor. Washington, D.C.: Smithsonian Institution.

Forde, C. D. 1931. Ethnography of the Yuma Indians. University of California Publications in American Archaeology and Ethnology 28(4). Berkeley.

Foster, J. W. 1975. Shell middens, paleoecology, and prehistory: The case from Estero Morua, Sonora, Mexico. *Kiva* 41:185–194.

Foster, M. S., & D. R. Mitchell. 2000. *An Archaeological Reconnaissance Survey of the Puerto Peñasco Area, Sonora, Mexico.* Phoenix: SWCA Environmental Consultants.

Gasser, R. 1982. Hohokam use of desert foods. *Desert Plants* 34:216–234.

Gasser, R., & S. Kwiatkowski. 1991. Regional signatures of Hohokam plant use. *Kiva* 56:207–226.

Gentry, H. S. 1942. *Rio Mayo Plants: A Study of the Flora and Vegetation of the Valley of the Rio Mayo, Sonora.* Carnegie Institution of Washington Publication No. 527. Washington, D.C.

———. 1963. *The Warihio Indians of Sonora-Chihuahua: An Ethnographic Survey.* Bureau of American Ethnology Bulletin No. 186. Washington, D.C.: U.S. Government Printing Office.

———. 1982. *Agaves of Continental North America.* Tucson: University of Arizona Press.

Gifford, E. W. 1931. *The Kamia of Imperial Valley.* Bureau of American Ethnology Bulletin 97. Washington, D.C.: U.S. Government Printing Office.

———. 1933. *The Cocopah.* University of California Publications in American Archaeology and Ethnography 31:257–334. Berkeley.

———. 1936. *Northeastern and Western Yavapai.* University of California Publications in American Archaeology and Ethnography 34:247–345. Berkeley.

———. 1946. Archaeology in the Punta Peñasco region, Sonora. *American Antiquity* 11:215–221.

Gilbert, C. H. 1890. Scientific results of explorations by the U.S. Fish Commission steamer *Albatross.*

XII. A preliminary report on the Pacific coast of North America during the year 1889, with descriptions of twelve new genera and ninety-two new species. *Proceedings of the U.S. National Museum* 13:49–126.

Glenn, E. P. 1987. Relationship between cation accumulation and water content of salt-tolerant grasses and a sedge. *Plant Cell and Environment* 10:205–212.

Gould, F. W., M. A. Ali, & D. E. Fairbrothers. 1972. A revision of *Echinochloa* in the United States. *American Midland Naturalist* 87:36–59.

Greenhouse, R., R. Gasser, & J. Gish. 1981. Cholla bud roasting pits: An ethnoarchaeological example. *Kiva* 46:227–242.

Hardy, R. W. H. 1829. *Travels in the interior of Mexico in 1825, 1826, 1827, and 1828.* London: Colburn & Beatley. Reprint. Glorieta, New Mexico: Rio Grande Press, 1977.

Haury, E. W. 1975. Shell. In *Excavations at Snaketown,* pp. 135–153. Tucson: University of Arizona Press. Reprint of H. S. Gladwin, E. W. Haury, E. B. Styles, & N. Gladwin, Medallion Papers XXV, Globe, Arizona: Gila Pueblo, 1938.

———. 1976. *The Hohokam: Desert Farmers and Craftsmen; Excavations at Snaketown, 1964–1965.* Tucson: University of Arizona Press.

Havard, V. 1895. Food plants of the North American Indians. *Bulletin of the Torrey Botanic Club* 22:98–123.

Hayden, J. D. 1969. Gyratory crushers of the Sierra Pinacate, Sonora. *American Antiquity* 34:154–161.

———. 1972. Hohokam petroglyphs of the Sierra Pinacate, Sonora, and the Hohokam shell expeditions. *Kiva* 37:74–83.

———. 1985. Food animal cremations of the Sierra Pinacate, Sonora, Mexico. *Kiva* 50:237–248.

———. 1987. The Vikita ceremony of the Papago, 1936–45. *Journal of the Southwest* 29:273–324.

Heintzelman, S. P. 1857. Report of July, 1853. In *Indian Affairs on the Pacific,* U.S. House of Representatives, 34th Congress, 3d session, House Executive Document No. 76, pp. 34–54. Washington, D.C.: U.S. Government Printing Office.

Heizer, R. 1945. Honey-dew "sugar" in western North America. *The Masterkey* 19:140–145.

Henshilwood, Christopher, Peter Nilssen, & John Parkington. 1994. Mussel drying and food storage in the Late Holocene, SW Cape, South Africa. *Journal of Field Archaeology* 21:103–109.

Hodgson, W. C. 2001. *Food Plants of the Sonoran Desert.* Tucson: University of Arizona Press.

Hrdlička, A. 1908. Physiological and medical observations among the Indians of the southwestern United States and northern Mexico. *Bureau of American Ethnology Bulletin* 34:1–266.

Hunn, E. 1999. Size as limiting the recognition of biodiversity in folkbiological classifications: One of four factors governing the cultural recognition of biological taxa. In *Folkbiology,* edited by D. L. Medin & S. Atran, pp. 47–69. Cambridge, Massachusetts: MIT Press.

Ives, R. L. 1961. The quest of the blue shells. *Arizoniana* 2 (Spring): 3–7.

Jernigan, E. W. 1978. *Jewelry of the Prehistoric Southwest.* Albuquerque: University of New Mexico Press.

Jöel, J. 1976. Some Paipai accounts of food gathering. *Journal of California Anthropology* 3:58–71.

Jones, V. 1945. Use of honey-dew as food by Indians. *The Masterkey* 19:145–149.

Kay, M. A. 1996. *Healing with Plants in the American and Mexican West.* Tucson: University of Arizona Press.

Kearney, T. H., & R. H. Peebles. 1960. *Arizona Flora.* 2d ed., with supplement by J. T. Howell & E. McClintock. Berkeley: University of California Press.

Kelly, W. H. 1949. Cocopa attitudes and practices with respect to death and mourning. *Southwestern Journal of Anthropology* 5(2):151–164.

———. 1977. *Cocopa Ethnography.* Anthropological Papers of the University of Arizona No. 29. Tucson: University of Arizona Press.

Kingsbury, J. M. 1964. *Poisonous Plants of the United States and Canada.* Englewood Cliffs, New Jersey: Prentice-Hall.

Kirk, D. R. 1970. *Wild Edible Plants of Western North America.* Happy Camp, California: Naturegraph.

Kniffen, F. B. 1931. *Lower California Studies III: The Primitive Cultural Landscape of the Colorado Delta.* University of California Publications in Geography 5(2). Berkeley.

Kroeber, A. L. 1941. *Culture Element Distribution, XV: Salt, Dogs, Tobacco.* Anthropological Records, Vol. 6, No. 1. Berkeley: University of California.

Kroeber, C. B., & B. L. Fontana. 1986. *Massacre on the Gila: An Account of the Last Major Battle Between American Indians, with Reflections on the Origin of War.* Tucson: University of Arizona Press.

Lumholtz, C. 1912. *New Trails in Mexico.* London: T. Fisher Unwin. Reprint. Tucson: University of Arizona Press, 1990.

MacDougal, D. T. 1906. The delta of the Rio Colorado. *Bulletin of the American Geographical Society* 38:1–16.

Manje, J. M. 1954. *Unknown Arizona and Sonora, 1693–1721: Luz de Tierra Incógnito.* Translated by Harry J. Karns. Tucson: Arizona Silhouettes.

Marmaduke, W. S., & R. J. Martynec, editors. 1993. *Shell Town and the Hind Site: A Study of Two Hohokam Craftsmen Communities in Southwestern Arizona.* Flagstaff: Northland Research.

May, L. A. 1973. Resource reconnaissance of the Gran Desierto region, northwestern Sonora, Mexico. Master's thesis, University of Arizona.

McGuire, R. H. 1982. Ethnographic studies. In *Hohokam and Patayan: Prehistory of Southwestern Arizona,* edited by R. H. McGuire & M. B. Schiffer, pp. 57–99. New York: Academic Press.

McGuire, R. H., & M. B. Schiffer, editors. 1982. *Hohokam and Patayan: Prehistory of Southwestern Arizona.* New York: Academic Press.

Mearns, E. A. 1892–93. Field Books, Mexican Boundary Survey, vol. 3. On file, U.S. National Herbarium, library, Natural History Museum, Smithsonian Institution, Washington, D.C.

Meigs, P. 1939. *The Kiliwa Indians of Lower California.* Ibero-Americana No. 15. Berkeley: University of California Press.

Mellink, E. 1995. Status of the muskrat in the Valle de Mexicali and Delta del Rio Colorado, Mexico. *California Fish and Game* 81:33–38.

Merrick, L. C., & D. M. Bates. 1989. Classification and nomenclature of *Cucurbita argyrosperma. Baileya* 23:94–102.

Michael, P. W. 2003. *Echinochloa* P. Beauv. In *Flora of North America,* edited by M. E. Barkworth, K. M. Capels, S. Long, & M. B. Piep, 25:390–403. New York: Oxford University Press.

Michler, N. 1987. From the 111th meridian of longitude to the Pacific Ocean. In *Report on the United States and Mexican Boundary Survey,* vol. 1, part 1, by W. H. Emory, pp. 101–125. Austin: Texas State Historical Association. Reprint of Emory, 1859, Executive Documents of the House of Representatives, No. 135, 34th Congress, 1st session.

Minnich, R. A. 1987. The distribution of forest trees in northern Baja California, Mexico. *Madroño* 34: 98–127.

Mitch, L. W. 1972. The saguaro—A history. *Cactus and Succulent Journal* 44:118–129.

Mitchell, D. R., & M. S. Foster. 2000. Hohokam shell middens along the Sea of Cortez, Puerto Peñasco, Sonora, Mexico. *Journal of Archaeology* 27–41.

Moerman, D. E. 1998. *Native American Ethnobotany.* Portland, Oregon: Timber Press.

Mueller, G. A., & P. C. Marsh. 2002. *Lost, a Desert River and Its Native Fishes: A Historical Perspective of the Lower Colorado River.* U.S. Geological Survey, Biological Resources Division, Information and Technology Report USGS/BRD/ITR–2002–0010:1–69. Denver: U.S. Government Printing Office.

Nabhan, G. P. 1978. Chiltepines! Wild spice of the American Southwest. *El Palacio* 84:30.

———. 1982. *The Desert Smells Like Rain: A Naturalist in Papago Indian County.* San Francisco: North Point Press.

———. 1985. *Gathering the Desert.* Tucson: University of Arizona Press.

———. 2002. When desert tortoises talk, Indians listen. In *The Sonoran Desert Tortoise,* edited by T. R. Van Devender, pp. 355–375. Tucson: University of Arizona Press.

Nabhan, G. P., J. Berry, & C. Weber. 1979. Legumes in Papago-Pima Indian diet and ecological niche. *Kiva* 44:173–190.

Nabhan, G. P., & J. M. J. de Wet. 1984. *Panicum sonorum* in Sonoran Desert agriculture. *Economic Botany* 38:65–82.

Nabhan, G. P., & R. S. Felger. 1978. Teparies in southwestern North America. *Economic Botany* 32:2–19.

Nabhan, G. P., W. Hodgson, & F. Fellows. 1989. A meager living on lava and sand? Hia Ced O'odham food resources and habitat diversity in oral and documentary histories. *Journal of the Southwest* 31:508–533.

Nabhan, G. P., & A. Rea. 1987. Plant domestication and folk-biological change: The Upper Piman/devil's claw example. *American Anthropologist* 89:57–73.

Nabhan, G. P., A. M. Rea, K. L. Reichhardt, E. Mellink, & C. F. Hutchinson. 1982. Papago influences on habitat and biotic diversity: Quitovac oasis ethnoecology. *Journal of Ethnobiology* 2:124–143.

Nabhan, G. P., A. Whiting, H. Dobyns, R. Hevly, & R. Euler. 1981. Devil's claw domestication: Evidence from southwestern Indian fields. *Journal of Ethnobiology* 1:135–164.

Nakashima, E. 1916. Notes on the totuava (*Cynoscion macdonaldi* Gilbert). *Copeia* 37:85–86.

Navarro S., C. 2003a. *Crocodylus acutus* in Sonora, México. *Crocodile Specialist Group Newsletter, IUCN/The World Conservation Union—Species Survival Commission* 22(1):21.

———. 2003b. Abundance, habitat use, and conservation of the American crocodile in Sinaloa. *Crocodile Specialist Group Newsletter, IUCN/The World Conservation Union—Species Survival Commission* 22(2):22–23.

Nelson, E. W. 1921. *Lower California and Its Natural Resources.* Memoirs of the National Academy of Sciences No. 16. Washington, D.C.

Nelson, R. S. 1991. *Hohokam Marine Shell Exchange and Artifacts.* Archaeological Series No. 179. Tucson: Arizona State Museum.

Owen, R. 1963. The use of plants and non-magical technique in curing illness among the Paipai, Santa Catarina, Baja California, México. *América Indígena* 23:319–345.

Palmer, E. 1870. Fish-hooks of the Mohave Indians. *American Naturalist* 12:403.

———. 1871. Food products of the North American Indians. In *Report of the Commissioner of Agriculture for the Year 1870,* pp. 404–428. Washington, D.C.: Government Printing Office.

———. 1878. Plants used by the Indians of the United States. *American Naturalist* 12:593–606, 646–655.

Paredes Aguilar, R., T. R. Van Devender, & R. S. Felger. 2000. *Las Cactáceas de Sonora: Su Diversidad, Uso y Conservación.* Tucson: Arizona-Sonora Desert Museum Press.

Pattie, J. O. 1988. *Personal Narrative of James O. Pattie.* Edited by Richard Batman. Missoula, Montana: Mountain Press.

Pennington, C. 1963. *The Tarahumara of Mexico: Their Environment and Material Culture.* Salt Lake City: University of Utah Press.

Pinkava, D. J. 2003. Vascular Plants of Arizona: Cactaceae. Part 6. *Opuntia* P. Miller. *Journal of the Arizona-Nevada Academy of Science* 35:137–150.

Rea, A. M. 1981. Resource utilization and food taboos of Sonoran Desert peoples. *Journal of Ethnobiology* 1:69–83.

———. 1983. *Once a River: Bird Life and Habitat Changes on the Middle Gila.* Tucson: University of Arizona Press.

———. 1997. *At the Desert's Green Edge: An Ethnobotany of the Gila River Pima.* Tucson: University of Arizona Press.

———. 1998. *Folk Mammalogy of the Northern Pimans.* Tucson: University of Arizona Press.

———. In press. *Wings in the Desert: A Folk Ornithology of the Northern Pimans.* Tucson: University of Arizona Press.

Ritter, E. W. 1985. Investigations of archaeological variability in northeastern Baja California Sur, Mexico. In *The Archaeology of West and Northwest Mesoamerica,* edited by M. S. Foster & P. C. Weigand, pp. 393–418. Boulder: Westview Press.

———. 1998. Investigations of prehistoric behavioral ecology and culture change within the Bahia de los Angeles Region, Baja California. *Pacific Coast Archeological Society Quarterly* 34(3):9–43.

Rosenthal, E. H. 1977. Sierra Pinacate percussion-flaked shell tool manufacture. *Journal of Field Archaeology* 4:372–375.

Russell, F. 1908. *The Pima Indians.* Annual Report, Bureau of American Ethnology 26:3–389. Washington, D.C.

Schaefer, J. 1994. The challenge of archeological research in the Colorado Desert: Recent approaches and discoveries. *Journal of California and Great Basin Anthropology* 16:60–80.

Sheldon, C. 1979. *The Wilderness of Desert Bighorn and Seri Indians.* Edited by D. E. Brown, P. M. Webb, & N. B. Carmony. Phoenix: Arizona Desert Bighorn Sheep Society.

Shreve, F. 1951. *Vegetation of the Sonoran Desert.* Carnegie Institution of Washington Publication No. 591. Washington, D.C. Reprinted as Part 1 of *Vegetation and Flora of the Sonoran Desert,* by F. Shreve & I. L. Wiggins. Stanford: Stanford University Press, 1964.

Spier, L. 1933. *Yuman Tribes of the Gila River.* Chicago: University of Chicago Press.

Standley, P. 1923. *Trees and Shrubs of Mexico.* Contributions from the U.S. National Herbarium 23(3). Washington, D.C.: U.S. Government Printing Office.

Thomas, R. K. 1991. Papago land use west of the Papago Indian Reservation, south of the Gila River, and the problem of Sand Papago identity—Interviews [1953]. In *Ethnology of Northwest Mexico: A Sourcebook,* edited by R. H. McGuire, pp. 357–399. New York: Garland. Originally published 1953.

Thomson, D. A., L. T. Findley, & A. N. Kirstitch. 2000. *Reef Fishes of the Sea of Cortez.* Austin: University of Texas Press.

Train, P., J. R. Hendrichs, & W. A. Archer. 1957. *Medicinal Uses of Plants by Indian Tribes in Nevada.*

Lawrence, Massachusetts: Quarterman Publications. Originally published in 1941 by the U.S. Department of Agriculture, Washington, D.C.

Treutlein, T. 1945. The Relation of Filippe Segesser [1737]. *Ibero-Americana* 27(3):139–188.

Trippel, E. J. 1889. The Yuma Indians. *Overland Monthly,* 2d series, 13:561–584; 14:1–11.

Turner, R. M., J. E. Bowers, & T. L. Burgess. 1995. *Sonoran Desert Plants: An Ecological Atlas.* Tucson: University of Arizona Press.

Underhill, R. 1946. *Papago Indian Religion.* New York: Columbia University Press.

Uphof, J. C. T. 1968. *Dictionary of Economic Plants.* New York: J. Cramer.

Van Valkenburgh, R. 1945. Tom Childs (interview notes). Ms. on file, Amerind Foundation, Dragoon, Arizona.

Vargas, V. D. 2004. Shell ornaments, power, and the rise of the Cerro de Trincheras. In *Surveying the Archaeology of Northwest Mexico,* edited by G. E. Newell & E. Gallaga, pp. 65–76. Salt Lake City: University of Utah Press.

Vasey, G. 1889. New or little known plants. *Garden and Forest* 2:401–403.

Vasey, G., & J. N. Rose. 1890. List of plants collected by Dr. Edward Palmer in Lower California in 1889. *Contributions from the United States National Herbarium* 1:9–28.

Villalpando, M. E. 1997. La tradición Trincheras y los grupos costeros del Desierto Sonorense. In *Prehistory of the Borderlands: Recent Research in the Archaeology of Northern Mexico and the Southern Southwest,* edited by J. Carpenter & G. Sanchez, pp. 95–112. Archaeological Series No. 186. Tucson: Arizona State Museum, University of Arizona.

Waselkov, G. A. 1987. Shellfish gathering and shell midden archaeology. In *Advances in Archaeological Method and Theory,* edited by M. B. Schiffer, pp. 93–210. New York: Academic Press.

Watson, S. 1889. Contributions to American Botany. Upon a collection of plants made by Dr. Edward Palmer in 1887, about Guaymas, Mexico, at Muleje and Los Angeles Bay in Lower California, and on the island of San Pedro Martin in the Gulf of California. *Proceedings of the American Academy of Arts and Sciences* 24:36–82.

Weiss, A. 1994. The impact of nutritional change on the emergence of diabetes in two Tipai Cochimí communities in Baja California. Ph.D. dissertation, University of California, Irvine.

Wiggins, I. L. 1964. Flora of the Sonoran Desert. Part 2 of *Vegetation and Flora of the Sonoran Desert,* by F. Shreve & I. L. Wiggins, pp. 189–1740. Stanford: Stanford University Press.

Wilke, P. J. 1978. *Late Prehistoric Human Ecology at Lake Cahuilla, Coachella Valley, California.* Contributions of the University of California Archaeological Facility No. 38. Berkeley.

Wilke, P. J., M. DeDecker, & L. Dawson. 1979. *Dicoria canescens* Torr. & Gray: An aboriginal food plant in the arid West. *Journal of California and Great Basin Anthropology* 1:188–192.

Williams, A. 1974. *The Cocopah People.* Phoenix: Indian Tribal Series.

———. 1975. *Travelers Among the Cucapá.* Los Angeles: Dawson's Book Shop.

———. 1983. Cocopa. In *Southwest,* edited by Alfonso Ortiz, pp. 99–112. Handbook of North American Indians, vol. 10, William C. Sturtevant, general editor. Washington, D.C.: Smithsonian Institution.

———. 1987. Environment and edible flora of the Cocopa. *Environment Southwest* 519:22–27.

Woodward, A. 1936. A shell bracelet manufactury. *American Antiquity* 2:117–125.

Yanovsky, E. 1936. *Food Plants of the North American Indians.* U.S. Department of Agriculture Miscellaneous Publications No. 237. Washington, D.C.: U.S. Government Printing Office.

Yatskievych, G. 1985. Notes on the biology of the Lennoaceae. *Cactus and Succulent Journal* (U.S.) 57:73–79.

Yensen, N. P. 2001. *Halófitas del Golfo de California y Sus Usos (Halophytes of the Gulf of California and Their Uses).* Hermosillo: Universidad de Sonora.

Yensen, S. B., & C. W. Weber. 1986. Composition of *Distichlis palmeri* grain, a saltgrass. *Journal of Food Science* 51:1089–1090.

———. 1987. Protein quality of *Distichlis palmeri* grain, a saltgrass. *Nutrition Reports International* 35:963–972.

Yetman, D., & R. S. Felger. 2002. Ethnoflora of the Guarijíos. In *Guarijíos of the Sierra Madre: The Hidden People of Northwestern Mexico,* edited by D. Yetman, pp. 174–230. Albuquerque: University of New Mexico Press.

Zepeda, O. 1985. *The Sand Papago Oral History Project.* Tucson: National Park Service, Division of Archeology, Western Archeological and Conservation Center.

Zigmond, M. L. 1981. *Kawaiisu Ethnobotany.* Salt Lake City: University of Utah Press.

Zuloaga, F. O., & O. Morrone. 1996. Revisión de las especies americanas de *Panicum* subgénero *Panicum* sección *Panicum* (Poaceae: Panicoideae: Paniceae). *Annals of the Missouri Botanical Garden* 83:200–280.

16. A Botanist's View of the Center of the Universe

Benson, L., & R. A. Darrow. 1981. *Trees and Shrubs of the Southwestern Deserts.* 3d ed. Tucson: University of Arizona Press.

Burkart, A. 1976. A monograph of the genus *Prosopis* (Leguminosae subfam. Mimosoideae). *Journal of the Arnold Arboretum* 57:219–49, 450–525.

Búrquez, A., M. Miller, & A. Martínez-Yrízar. 2002. Mexican grasslands, thornscrub, and the transformation of the Sonoran Desert by invasive exotic buffelgrass *(Pennisetum ciliare).* In *Invasive Exotic Species in the Sonoran Region,* edited by B. Tellman, pp. 126–146. Tucson: University of Arizona Press.

Burrus, E. J. 1971. *Kino and Manje, Explorers of Sonora and Arizona: Their Vision of the Future, a Study of Their Expeditions and Plans.* St. Louis: Jesuit Historical Institute.

Dimmitt, M. A. 1987. The hybrid palo verde 'Desert Museum': A new, superior tree for desert landscape. *Desert Plants* 8:99–103.

Felger, R. S. 1977. Mesquite in Indian cultures of southwestern North America. In *Mesquite: Its Biology in Two Desert Scrub Ecosystems,* edited by B. B. Simpson, pp. 150–176. Stroudsburg, Pennsylvania: Dowden, Hutchinson, and Ross.

———. 1990. Mesquite, a world food crop. *Aridus* 2(1):1–3.

———. 1992. Reflections on a desert legume trinity. *Aridus* 4(4):1–5,7.

———. 2000. *Flora of the Gran Desierto and Río Colorado of Northwestern Mexico.* Tucson: University of Arizona Press.

Felger, R. S., & M. B. Moser. 1985. *People of the Desert and Sea: Ethnobotany of the Seri Indians.* Tucson: University of Arizona Press.

Felger, R. S., P. L. Warren, L. S. Anderson, & G. P. Nabhan. 1992. *Vascular Plants of a Desert Oasis: Flora and Ethnobotany of Quitobaquito, Organ Pipe Cactus National Monument, Arizona.* Proceedings of the San Diego Society of Natural History, No. 8. San Diego.

Hartmann, W. K. 1989. *Desert Heart.* Tucson: Fisher Books.

Hawkins, J. A., L. White Olascoaga, C. E. Hughes, J.-L. R. Contreras Jiménez, & P. Mercado Ruaro. 1999. Investigation and documentation of hybridization between *Parkinsonia aculeata* and *Cercidium praecox* (Leguminosae: Caesalpinioidea). *Plant Systematics and Evolution* 216:49–68.

Hodgson, W. C. 2001. *Food plants of the Sonoran Desert.* Tucson: University of Arizona Press.

Jahns, R. H. 1959. Collapse depressions of the Pinacate Volcanic Field, Sonora, Mexico. *Arizona Geological Society Guidebook II,* 165–184. Tucson: Arizona Geological Society.

Johnston, M. C. 1962. The North American mesquites *Prosopis* sect. *Algarobia* (Leguminosae). *Brittonia* 14:72–90.

Kearney, T. H., & R. H. Peebles. 1960. *Arizona Flora.* 2d ed. With supplement by J. T. Howell & E. McClintock. Berkeley: University of California Press.

Lavin, M. 1988. *Systematics of Coursetia (Leguminosae-Papilionoideae).* Systematic Botany Monographs No. 21. Ann Arbor, Michigan.

Lavin, M., & M. Sousa S. 1995. *Phylogenetic Systematics and Biogeography of the Tribe Robinieae (Leguminosae).* Systematic Botany Monographs No. 45. Ann Arbor, Michigan.

Lynch, D. J. 1981. Genesis and geochronology of alkaline volcanism in the Pinacate Volcanic Field, northwestern Sonora, Mexico. Ph.D. dissertation. University of Arizona.

Nabhan, G. P., & J. L. Carr, eds. 1994. *Ironwood: An Ecological and Cultural Keystone on the Sonoran Desert.* Occasional Paper No. 1. Washington, D.C.: Conservation International.

Rea, A. 1997. *At the Desert's Green Edge: An Ethnobotany of the Gila River Pima.* Tucson: University of Arizona Press.

Rzedowski, J., & G. Calderón de Rzedowski. 1988. Análisis de la distribución geográfica del complejo *Prosopis* (Leguminosae, Mimosoideae) en Norteamérica. *Acta Botanica Mexicana* 3:7–19.

Shreve, F. 1964. *Vegetation of the Sonoran Desert,* Part I. In *Vegetation and Flora of the Sonoran Desert,* by F. Shreve & I. L. Wiggins, vols. 1 and 2. Stanford: Stanford University Press.

Turner, R. 1990. Long-term vegetation change at a fully protected Sonoran Desert site. *Ecology* 71:464–477.

17. Botanical Diversity of Southwestern Arizona and Northwestern Sonora

Alvarez, A., & K. Hale. 1970. Toward a manual of Papago grammar: Some phonological terms. *International Journal of American Linguistics* 36:83–97.

Barbour, M., & N. L. Christensen. 1993. Vegetation. In *Flora of North America* 1:97–131. New York: Oxford University Press.

Barneby, R. C. 1964. *Atlas of North American* Astragalus. Memoirs of the New York Botanical Garden, vol. 13. New York.

Benson, L., & R. A. Darrow. 1945. *A Manual of Southwestern Desert Trees and Shrubs.* University of Arizona Bulletin 15, no. 2. Tucson: University of Arizona.

———. 1981. *Trees and Shrubs of the Southwestern Deserts.* 3d ed. Tucson: University of Arizona Press.

BLM. 1988. *Environmental assessment final AZ-027-7-21 and Lower Gila South RMP Monitoring Plan.* Phoenix District Office, Bureau of Land Management.

Bowers, J. E. 1980. Flora of Organ Pipe Cactus National Monument. *Journal of the Arizona-Nevada Academy of Science* 15:1–11, 33–47.

Brown, D. E. 1978. The vegetation and occurrence of chaparral and woodland flora on isolated mountains with the Sonoran and Mohave deserts in Arizona. *Journal of the Arizona-Nevada Academy of Science* 13:7–12.

———, editor. 1982. Biotic communities of the American Southwest—United States and Mexico. *Desert Plants* 4:3–341.

Búrquez, A., & C. Castillo. 1994. Reserva de la Biósfera, El Pinacate y Gran Desierto de Altar: Entorno biológico y social. *Estudios Sociales* 5:9–64.

Castetter, E. F., & W. H. Bell. 1951. *Yuman Indian Agriculture.* Albuquerque: University of New Mexico Press.

Comrie, A. C., & B. Broyles. 2002. Variability and spatial modeling of fine-scale precipitation data for the Sonoran Desert of south-west Arizona. *Journal of Arid Environments* 50:573–592.

Cronquist, A. 1981. *An Integrated System of Classification of the Flowering Plants.* New York: Columbia University Press.

Ezcurra, E., M. Equihua, & J. López-Portillo. 1987. The desert vegetation of El Pinacate, Sonora, Mexico. *Vegetatio* 71:49–60.

Ezcurra, E., R. S. Felger, A. Russell, & M. Equihua. 1988. Fresh water islands in a desert sand sea: The hydrology, flora, and phytogeography of the Gran Desierto oases of northwestern Mexico. *Desert Plants* 9:35–44, 55–63.

Ezcurra, E., & V. Rodrígues. 1986. Rainfall patterns in the Gran Desierto, Sonora, Mexico. *Journal of Arid Environments* 10:13–28.

Felger, R. S. 1980. Vegetation and flora of the Gran Desierto, Sonora, Mexico. *Desert Plants* 2:87–114.

———. 1990. *Non-native Plants of Organ Pipe Cactus National Monument.* Technical Report No. 31. Tucson: Cooperative National Park Resource Studies Unit, University of Arizona.

———. 2000. *Flora of the Gran Desierto and Río Colorado of Northwestern Mexico.* Tucson: University of Arizona Press.

Felger, R. S., M. B. Johnson, & M. F. Wilson. 2001. *Trees of Sonora, Mexico.* New York: Oxford University Press.

Felger, R. S., D. S. Turner, & M. F. Wilson. 2003. Flora and vegetation of the Mohawk Dunes, Arizona. *Sida* 20:1153–1185.

Felger, R. S., P. L. Warren, S. A. Anderson, & G. P. Nabhan. 1992. Vascular plants of a desert oasis: Flora and ethnobotany of Quitobaquito, Organ Pipe Cactus National Monument, Arizona. *Proceedings of the San Diego Society of Natural History* 8:1–39.

Felger R. S., M. Wilson, B. Broyles, & G. P. Nabhan. 1997. The binational Sonoran Desert biosphere network and its plant life. *Journal of the Southwest* 39:411–560.

Glenn, E. P., R. S. Felger, A. Búrquez, & D. S. Turner. 1992. Ciénega de Santa Clara: Endangered wetland in the Colorado River delta, Sonora, Mexico. *Natural Resources Journal* 32:817–824.

Glenn, E. P., C. Lee, R. Felger, & S. Zengel. 1996. Effects of water management on the wetlands of the Colorado River delta, Mexico. *Conservation Biology* 1175–1186.

Goodpaster, C., & J. E. Bowers. 2004. *Best Spring Ever: Why EL Niño Makes the Desert Bloom.* Sacramento: California Native Plant Society Press.

Hayden, J. 1997. Changing place names in the Pinacate. *Journal of the Southwest* 39:697–702.

Hickman, J. C., editor. 1993. *The Jepson Manual.* Berkeley: University of California Press.

Holmgren, P. K., N. H. Holmgren, & L. C. Barnett. 1990. *Index Herbariorum.* Part 1: The herbaria of the world. 8th ed. New York: New York Botanical Garden. Also at *http://www.nybg.org/bsci/ih/ih.html* (accessed February 2004).

Kearney, T. H., & R. H. Peebles. 1960. *Arizona Flora.* 2d ed. With supplement by J. T. Howell & E. McClintock. Berkeley: University of California Press.

Kelly, W. H. 1977. *Cocopa Ethnography.* Anthropological Papers of the University of Arizona No. 29. Tucson: University of Arizona Press.

Mabry, T. J., J. H. Hunziker, & D. R. DiFeo. 1977. *Creosote Bush: Biology and Chemistry of* Larrea *in New World Deserts.* Stroudsburg, Pennsylvania: Dowden, Hutchinson, & Ross.

Malusa, J. 2003a. *Vegetation of the BLM Lands Near Ajo, Arizona.* Report submitted to Chief of Resources Management, Organ Pipe Cactus National Monument, under cooperative agreement CA860197006-W02. Available as GIS coverage for ArcView and ArcGIS, Organ Pipe Cactus National Monument, 10 Organ Pipe Drive, Ajo, AZ 85321–9626.

———. 2003b. *Vegetation of the Cabeza Prieta National Wildlife Refuge, Arizona.* Report submitted to Chief of Resources Management, Organ Pipe Cactus National Monument, under cooperative agreement CA860197006-W02. Available as GIS coverage for ArcView and ArcGIS, Organ Pipe Cactus National Monument, 10 Organ Pipe Drive, Ajo, AZ 85321-9626.

Mathiot, M. 1973, 1976. *A Dictionary of Papago Usage.* Language Science Monographs vol. 8, nos. 1 and 2. Bloomington: Indiana University Press.

May, L. A. 1973. Resource reconnaissance of the Gran Desierto. Master's thesis, University of Arizona.

McLaughlin, S. P., & J. E. Bowers. 1999. Diversity and affinities of the flora of the Sonoran floristic province. In *Ecology of Sonoran Desert Plants and Plant Communities,* edited by R. H. Robichaux, pp. 12–35. Tucson: University of Arizona Press.

Morrison, P. H., H. M. Smith IV, & S. D. Snetsinger. 2003. *The Natural Communities and Ecological Condition of the Sonoran Desert National Monument and Adjacent Areas.* Winthrop, Washington: Pacific Biodiversity Institute.

Nabhan, G. P. 1983. Papago fields: An arid lands ethnobotany and agricultural ecology. Ph.D. dissertation, University of Arizona.

Nabhan, G. P., W. Hodgson, & F. Fellows. 1989. A meager living on lava and sand? Hia Ced O'odham food resources and habitat diversity in oral and documentary histories. *Journal of the Southwest* 31:508–533.

National Register of Big Trees. 1996. *American Forests.* Washington, D.C.

Pendall, E. 1994. Surficial geology, soils, and vegetation patterns of the Table Top Mountain area, Pinal and Maricopa Counties, Arizona. Open File Report No. 94–22. Tucson: Arizona Geological Survey.

Ramamoorthy, T. B., R. Bye, A. Lot, & J. Fa. 1993. *Biological Diversity of Mexico: Origins and Distribution.* New York: Oxford University Press.

Reichenbacher, F. W. 1990. Tumamoc globeberry studies in Arizona and Sonora, Mexico. Final report prepared for the U.S.D.I.–Bureau of Reclamation, Phoenix.

Rose, J. N., & P. C. Standley. 1912. Report on a collection of plants from the Pinacate region of Sonora. *Contributions from the United States National Herbarium* 16:5–20.

Saxton, D., L. Saxton, & S. Enos. 1983. *Dictionary, Papago and Pima to English, English to Papago and Pima.* 2d ed. Edited by R. L. Cherry. Tucson: University of Arizona Press.

Shreve, F. 1951. *Vegetation of the Sonoran Desert.* Carnegie Institution of Washington Publication No. 591. Washington, D.C.

Simmons, N. M. 1966. Flora of the Cabeza Prieta Game Range. *Arizona Academy of Science* 4: 93–104.

Turner, R. M. 1990. Long-term vegetation change at a fully protected Sonoran Desert site. *Ecology* 71: 464–477.

Turner, R. M., J. E. Bowers, & T. L. Burgess. 1995. *Sonoran Desert Plants: An Ecological Atlas.* Tucson: University of Arizona Press.

Van Devender, T. R., T. L. Burgess, R. S. Felger, & R. M. Turner. 1990. Holocene vegetation of the Hornaday Mountains of northwestern Sonora, Mexico. *Proceedings of the San Diego Society of Natural History* 2:1–19.

Venable, D. L., & C. E. Pake. 1999. Population ecology of Sonoran Desert annual plants. In *Ecology of Sonoran Desert Plants and Plant Communities,* edited by R. H. Robichaux, pp. 115–142. Tucson: University of Arizona Press.

Warren, P. L., B. K. Mortenson, B. D. Treadwell, J. E. Bowers, & K. L. Reichhardt. 1981. *Vegetation of Organ Pipe Cactus National Monument.* Technical Report No. 8. Tucson: Cooperative National Park Resource Studies Unit, University of Arizona.

Watson, M. C., & W. R. Ferren, Jr. 1991. A new species of *Suaeda* (Chenopodiaceae) from coastal northwestern Sonora, Mexico. *Madroño* 38:30–36.

Wiggins, I. L. 1964. *Flora of the Sonoran Desert.* Part 2 of *Vegetation and Flora of the Sonoran Desert,* by F. Shreve & I. L. Wiggins, pp. 189–1740. Stanford: Stanford University Press.

———. 1980. *Flora of Baja California.* Stanford: Stanford University Press.

Wilson, M. F., L. Leigh, & R. S. Felger. 2002. Invasive exotic plants in the Sonoran Desert. In *Invasive Exotic Species in the Sonoran Region,* edited by B. Tellman, pp. 81–90. Tucson: University of Arizona Press.

Zengel, S. A., & E. P. Glenn. 1996. Presence of the endangered desert pupfish (*Cyprinodon macularius,* Cyprinidontidae) in Cienega de Santa Clara, Mexico, following an extensive marsh dry-down. *Southwestern Naturalist* 41:73–78.

18. Mammals of the Sonoran Desert Borderland Reserves

Arizona Game and Fish Department. 2002. Jaguar photographed in southern Arizona. *Arizona Wildlife Views* 45–2:2.

Bright, J. L., & J. J. Hervert. 2005. *Sonoran Pronghorn 2004 Aerial Survey Summary.* Nongame and Endangered Wildlife Program Technical Report No. 240. Phoenix: Arizona Game and Fish Department.

Bright, J. L., & J. J. Hervert. 2006. Sonoran Pronghorn 2004 Mexico Aerial Survey Summary. Nongame and Endangered Wildlife Program Technical Report No. 241. Phoenix: Arizona Game and Fish Department.

Brown, D. E., & R. S. Henry. 1981. On relict occurrences of white-tailed deer within the Sonoran Desert in Arizona. *Southwestern Naturalist* 26: 147–152.

Brown, D. E., & C. A. López González. 2000. Jaguarundi (*Herpailurus yagouaroundi* Geoffroy 1803) not in Arizona or Sonora. *Journal of the Arizona-Nevada Academy of Science* 33(1):1–3.

Cockrum, E. L. 1960. *The Recent Mammals of Arizona: Their Taxonomy and Distribution.* Tucson: University of Arizona Press.

————. 1981. *Bat Populations and Habitats at the Organ Pipe Cactus National Monument.* Technical Report No. 7. Tucson: Cooperative National Park Resources Studies Unit, University of Arizona.

Cockrum, E. L., & Y. Petryszyn. 1986. *Mammals of the Organ Pipe Cactus National Monument.* Special Report No. 5. Tucson: Cooperative National Park Resources Studies Unit, University of Arizona.

————. 1992. *Mammals of the Southwestern United States and Northwestern Mexico.* Tucson: Treasure Chest Publications.

Dalton, V. M., & D. C. Dalton. 1994. Mine/bat survey: Eastern and western sections, Barry M. Goldwater Air Force Range. Report prepared for Luke Air Force Natural Resources Program, 58SG/CEVN, Luke Air Force Base, Arizona.

Golightly, R. T., Jr. 1981. The comparative energetics of two desert canids: The *coyote (Canis latrans)* and the kit fox *(Vulpes macrotis).* Ph.D. dissertation, Arizona State University.

Grinnell, J. 1914. An account of the mammals and birds of the lower Colorado valley. *University of California Publications in Zoology* 12:51–294.

Henry, R. S., & L. K. Sowls. 1980. *White-Tailed Deer of the Organ Pipe Cactus National Monument, Arizona.* Technical Report No. 6. Tucson: Cooperative National Park Resources Studies Unit, University of Arizona.

Hoffmeister, D. F. 1986. *Mammals of Arizona.* Tucson: University of Arizona Press.

Hornaday, W. T. 1908. *Camp-Fires on Desert and Lava.* New York: Charles Scribner's Sons.

Huey, L. M. 1942. A vertebrate faunal survey of the Organ Pipe Cactus National Monument, Arizona. *Transactions of the San Diego Society of Natural History* 9:353–375.

Instituto Nacional de Ecología. n.d. Listado de fauna silvestre. Reserva de la Biosfera El Pinacate y Gran Desierto de Altar. Hermosillo, Sonora.

Leopold, A. 1966. *A Sand County Almanac with Essays on Conservation from Round River.* New York: Oxford University Press.

Mearns, E. A. 1907. *Mammals of the Mexican Boundary of the United States.* U.S. National Museum Bulletin No. 56. Washington, D.C.: Government Printing Office.

Mellink, E. 1995. Status of the muskrat in the Valle de Mexicali and Delta del Rio Colorado, Mexico. *California Fish and Game* 81(1):33–38.

Mellink, E., J. Luevano, & J. Domínguez. 1999. *Mamíferos de la Península de Baja California.* Centro de Investigación Científica y de Educación Superior de Ensenada, Baja California, Mexico.

Pattie, J. O. 1988. *Personal Narratives of James O. Pattie.* Edited by R. Batman. Missoula, Montana: Mountain Press.

Petryszyn, Y., & S. Russ. 1996. Nocturnal rodent population densities and distribution at Organ Pipe Cactus National Monument, Arizona. Technical Report No. 52. Tucson: National Biological Service, Cooperative Park Studies Unit, University of Arizona.

Roman, M., & J. Campoy. 1998. Listado de mamíferos en Alto Golfo de California y delta del Río Colorado. Reserva de la Biosfera Alto Golfo de California y Delta del Río Colorado, San Luis Río Colorado, Sonora, Mexico.

Sheldon, C. 1979. *The Wilderness of Desert Bighorns and Seri Indians.* Edited by D. E. Brown, P. M. Webb, & N. B. Carmony. Phoenix: Arizona Desert Bighorn Sheep Society.

Sowls, L. K. 1997. *Javelinas and Other Peccaries: Their Biology, Management, and Use.* College Station: Texas A&M University Press.

U.S. Department of the Interior, National Park Service. 1997. Final general management plan/development concept plans/environmental impact statement, Organ Pipe Cactus National Monument, Pima County, Arizona. Ajo, Arizona.

U.S. Department of the Interior, U.S. Fish and Wildlife Service. 1998. Final programmatic environmental assessment for the future management of Cabeza Prieta NWR and draft comprehensive conservation plan objectives. Appendix A. Albuquerque, New Mexico.

Wilson, D. E., & D. M. Reeder, editors. 1993. *Mammal Species of the World.* Washington, D.C.: Smithsonian Institution Press.

Zoellick, B. W., N. S. Smith, & R. S. Henry. 1989. Habitat use and movements of desert kit foxes in western Arizona. *Journal of Wildlife Management* 53: 955–961.

19. Birds of Arizona's Southwestern Borderland

American Ornithologists' Union. 1998. *Check-list of North American Birds.* 7th ed. Lawrence, Kansas: Allen Press.

Andrews, Bob, Bob Righter, & Mike Carter. 1992. A proposed format for local bird checklists. *Colorado Field Ornithologists Journal* 26(1):12–18. Jamestown, North Dakota: Northern Prairie Wildlife Research Center Home Page. *http://www.npwrc.usgs.gov/resource/othrdata/chekbird/format.htm* (version 15 November 2000).

Arizona Game and Fish Department. 2002. *Arizona Breeding Bird Atlas.* Phoenix: Arizona Game and Fish Department, Non-Game Branch. Data tables and notes on species provided to D. J. Griffin by Cathy Wise and Troy Corman.

Austin, George T., & E. Linwood Smith. 1974. Use of burrows by brown towhees and black-throated sparrows. *Auk* 91:167.

Beck, Benjamin B., Christopher W. Engen, & Peter W. Gelfand. 1973. Behavior and activity cycles of Gambel's quail and raptorial birds at a Sonoran desert waterhole. *The Condor* 75:466–470.

Bibles, Brent, & Lisa K. Harris. 1999. Neotropical migratory bird monitoring program Barry M. Goldwater Air Force Range, Arizona. Final Report prepared for: Environmental Science, Management and Technical Section, U.S. Dept. of the Air Force, 56 FE/RMO/ESMT, 14185 W. Falcon St., Luke AFB, AZ 85309–1149. Contract No. FQ4887 F02604 97MS177.

Cutler, Patricia L. 1996. Wildlife use of two artificial water developments on the Cabeza Prieta National Wildlife Refuge, southwestern Arizona. Master's thesis, University of Arizona.

Cutler, Tricia L., & Michael L. Morrison. 1998. Habitat use by small vertebrates at two water developments in southwestern Arizona. *Southwest Naturalist* 43(2):155–162.

Cutler, Tricia L., Michael L. Morrison, & David J. Griffin. 1996. Final report: Wildlife use of Jose Juan Tank and Red Tail Tank, Cabeza Prieta National Wildlife Refuge, Southwestern Arizona. U.S. Department of Defense, Contract N68711-93-LT-3026.

Dimmitt, Mark A. 1999. Biomes and communities of the Sonoran Desert region. In *A Natural History of the Sonoran Desert,* edited by Steven J. Phillips and Patricia Wentworth Comus, pp. 3–18. Berkeley: University of California Press.

Department of Defense. n.d. Checklist of birds, Barry M. Goldwater Air Force Range. Jamestown, North Dakota: Northern Prairie Wildlife Research Center Home Page. *http://www.npwrc.usgs.gov/resource/othrdata/chekbird/r2/barrgold.htm* (version 27 June 2000).

Ehrlich, Paul, David S. Dobkin, & David Wheye. 1988. *The Birder's Handbook: A Field Guide to the Natural History of North American Birds.* New York: Simon & Schuster.

Ganley, Steve. 2001a. The 101st Audubon Christmas Bird Count: Sierra Pinta, Cabeza Prieta NWR, Arizona. *American Birds.* (Results for years 1997–2001 are accessible online at *www.birdsource.org;* older records [1955–93] are on file at Cabeza Prieta NWR.)

———. 2001b. The 101st Audubon Christmas Bird Count: Ajo–Cabeza Prieta NWR, Arizona. *American Birds.* (Results for years 1998–2001 are accessible online at *www.birdsource.org.*)

Gould, Patrick J. 1961. Territorial relationships between cardinals and pyrrhuloxias. *The Condor* 63: 246–256.

Groschupf, Kathleen D., Bryan T. Brown, & R. Roy Johnson. 1988. *An Annotated Checklist of the Birds of Organ Pipe Cactus National Monument, Arizona.* Tucson: Cooperative National Park Research Studies Unit, University of Arizona.

Gubanich, Alan. 1966. Avian utilization of desert waterholes. Master's thesis, University of Arizona.

Hall, J. A., P. Comer, A. Gondor, R. Marshall, & S. Weinstein. 2001. *Conservation Elements of and a Biodiversity Management Framework for the Barry M. Goldwater Range, Arizona.* Tucson: Nature Conservancy of Arizona.

Hardy, Paul C. 1997. Habitat selection by elf owls and western screech-owls in the Sonoran Desert. Master's thesis, University of Arizona.

Hardy, Paul C., Tiffany Abeloe, Robert X. Barry, & Michael L. Morrison. 1998. Abundance and habitat associations of common poorwills in the Sonoran Desert. *Southwestern Naturalist* 43:234–241.

Hardy, Paul C., Robert X. Barry, & Michael L. Morrison. 1999. Abundance and habitat associations of elf owls and western screech-owls in the Sonoran Desert. *Southwestern Naturalist* 44:311–323.

Hardy, Paul C., David J. Griffin, Amy J. Kuenzi, & Michael L. Morrison. 2003. Habitat use and abundance of passage Neotropical migrants in the Sonoran Desert. *Western North American Naturalist* 64(1):59–71.

Hardy, Paul C., & Michael L. Morrison. 2000. Factors affecting the detection of elf owls and western screech-owls. *Wildlife Society Bulletin* 28:333–342.

———. 2001. Nest site selection by elf owls in the Sonoran Desert. *Wilson Bulletin* 113:23–32.

———. 2003. Nest site selection by western screech-owls in the Sonoran Desert. *Western North American Naturalist* 63(4):533–537.

Hensley, M. Max. 1954. Ecological relations of the breeding bird population of the desert biome in Arizona. *Ecological Monographs* 24(2):185–207.

———. 1959. Notes on the nesting of selected species of birds of the Sonoran Desert. *Wilson Bulletin* 71: 86–92.

Huey, Laurence M. 1936. Notes from Maricopa County, Arizona. *The Condor* 38:172.

———. 1942. A vertebrate faunal survey of the Organ Pipe Cactus National Monument, Arizona. *San Diego Society of Natural History Transactions* 32: 353–376.

MacArthur, Robert H. 1958. Population ecology of some warblers of northeastern coniferous forests. *Ecology* 39:599–619.

Monson, Gale. 1936. Bird notes from the Papago Indian Reservation, southern Arizona. *The Condor* 38:175–176.

———. 1965. The Arizona desert. In *The Birdwatcher's America*, edited by O. S. Pettingill, Jr., pp. 304–311. New York: McGraw-Hill.

Monson, Gale, & Allan R. Phillips. 1981. *Annotated Checklist of the Birds of Arizona*. Tucson: University of Arizona Press.

Moore, Frank R., Sidney A. Gauthreaux, Jr., Paul Kerlinger, & Theodore R. Simons. 1993. Stopover habitat: Management implications and guidelines. In *Status and Management of Neotropical Migratory Birds: 1992 September 21–25*, edited by Deborah M. Finch & Paul W. Stangel, pp. 58–69. Gen. Tech. Rep. No. RM-229. Fort Collins, Colorado: U.S. Department of Agriculture, Forest Service, Rocky Mountain Forest and Range Experiment Station.

Moore, Frank R., & Theodore R. Simons. 1992. Habitat suitability and stopover ecology of Neotropical landbird migrants. In *Ecology and Conservation of Neotropical Migrant Landbirds*, edited by J. M. Hagen & D. W. Johnston, pp. 345–355. Washington, D.C.: Smithsonian Institution Press.

Morrison, Michael L., Paul C. Hardy, David J. Griffin, & Amy J. Kuenzi. 1996. *Neotropical Migratory Bird Monitoring Program, Barry M. Goldwater Air Force Range, Arizona. Final Report*. Legacy Resource Management Program Project No. 950796. Natural and Cultural Resource Management and Environmental Impact Analysis Section, U.S. Department of the Air Force, 56 CES/CEVN, Luke Air Force Base, Arizona.

National Geographic Society. 2003. *Field Guide to the Birds of North America*. 3d ed. Washington, D.C.

Ohmart, Robert D., & Bertin W. Anderson. 1982. North American desert riparian ecosystems. In *Reference Handbook on the Deserts of North America*, edited by G. L. Bender, pp. 433–474. Westport, Connecticut: Greenwood Press.

Parker, Kathleen C. 1986. Partitioning of foraging space and nest sites in a desert shrubland bird community. *American Midland Naturalist* 115(2): 255–267.

Phillips, Allan R. 1940. Edgar Alexander Mearns (1856–1916), pioneer northern Arizona naturalist. *Plateau* 13(1):1–5.

Phillips, Allan R., Joe Marshall, & Gale Monson. 1964. *The Birds of Arizona*. Tucson: University of Arizona Press.

Phillips, Allan R., & Warren M. Pulich. 1948. Nesting birds of the Ajo Mountains region, Arizona. *The Condor* 50:271–272.

Rappole, John H. 2000. *Birds of the Southwest: Arizona, New Mexico, Southern California, and Southern Nevada*. College Station: Texas A&M University Press.

Rea, Amadeo M. 1983. *Once a River: Bird Life and Habitat Changes on the Middle Gila*. Tucson: University of Arizona Press.

Russell, Steven M., & Gale Monson. 1998. *The Birds of Sonora*. Tucson: University of Arizona Press.

Sibley, David Allen. 2000. *National Audubon Society, The Sibley Guide to Birds*. New York: Alfred A. Knopf.

Smyth, Michael, & George A. Bartholomew. 1966. The water economy of the black-throated sparrow and the rock wren. *The Condor* 68:447–458.

Sutton, George Miksch, & Allan R. Phillips. 1942. June bird life of the Papago Indian Reservation, Arizona. *The Condor* 44:57–65.

Turner, D. S., R. S. Felger, K. Mauz, C. S. Funicelli, T. Van Devender, & J. Malusa. 2000. *Biological Resources of the Proposed Sonoran Desert National Monument, Arizona*. Tucson: Drylands Institute.

Unitt, Phillip. 1984. *The Birds of San Diego County*. Memoir No. 13. San Diego: San Diego Society of Natural History.

U.S. Fish & Wildlife Service. 1991. Birds of Cabeza Prieta National Wildlife Refuge. Jamestown, North Dakota: Northern Prairie Wildlife Research Center Home Page *http://www.npwrc.usgs.gov/resource/ othrdata/chekbird/r2/cabeza.htm* (version 1995).

Vander Wall, Stephen B., & James A. MacMahon. 1984. Avian distribution patterns along a Sonoran desert bajada. *Journal of Arid Environments* 7:59–74.

Witzeman, Janet L., Salome R. Demaree, & Eleanor L. Radke. 1997. *Birds of Phoenix and Maricopa County, Arizona*. 2d ed. Phoenix: Maricopa Audubon Society.

20. Long-nosed Bats and White-winged Doves: Travels and Tribulations of Two Migrant Pollinators

Able, K. P. 1999. *Gathering of Angels: Migrating Birds and Their Ecology*. Ithaca, New York: Comstock Books.

Alcock, J. 1993. *The Masked Bobwhite Rides Again*. Tucson: University of Arizona Press.

Berthold, P. 1993. *Bird Migration: A General Survey*. New York: Oxford University Press.

Brown, D. E. 1989. *Arizona Game Birds*. Tucson: University of Arizona Press.

Buchmann, S. L., & G. P. Nabhan. 1996. *The Forgotten Pollinators*. Covelo, California: Island Press.

Fleming, T. H., & V. J Soza. 1994. Effects of nectarivorous and frugivorous mammals on reproductive success of plants. *Journal of Mammalogy* 75:845–851.

Fleming, T. H., M. D. Tuttle, & M. A. Horner. 1996. Pollination biology and the relative importance of nocturnal and diurnal pollinators in three species of Sonoran Desert columnar cacti. *Southwestern Naturalist* 41:257–269.

Kearns, C. A., D. W. Inouye, & N. M. Waser. 1998. Endangered mutualisms: The conservation of plant-pollinator interactions. *Annual Review of Ecology and Systematics* 29:83–112.

Martínez del Rio, C., B. Wolf, & R. A. Haughey. 2004. Saguaros and white-winged doves: The natural history of an uneasy partnership. In *Conserving*

Migratory Pollinators and Nectar Corridors in Western North America, edited by Gary Paul Nabhan, pp. 122–143. Tucson: University of Arizona Press.

Morse, D. H. 1971. The insectivorous bird as an adaptive strategy. *Annual Review of Ecology and Systematics* 2:177–200.

Rojas-Martínez, A., A. Valiente-Banuet, M. C. Arizmendi, A. Alcanatara-Eguren, & H. T. Arita (1999). Seasonal distribution of the long-nosed bat *(Leptonycteris curasoae)* in North America: Does a generalized migration pattern really exist? *Journal of Biogeography* 26:1065–1077.

Wilkinson, G. S., & T. H. Fleming. 1996. Migration and evolution of lesser long-nosed bats, *Leptonycteris curasoae,* inferred from mitochondrial DNA. *Molecular Ecology* 5:329–339.

Wolf, B. O., & C. Martinez del Rio. 2000. Use of saguaro fruit by white-winged doves: Isotopic evidence of a tight ecological association. *Oecologia* 124:536–543.

21. Reptiles and Amphibians of Arid Southwestern Arizona and Northwestern Sonora

Allred, D. M., D. E. Beck, & C. D. Jorgensen. 1963. Biotic communities of the Nevada Test Site. *Brigham Young University Science Bulletin,* Biological Series II:1–52.

Asplund, K. K., & C. H. Lowe. 1964. Reproductive cycle of the iguanid lizards *Urosaurus ornatus* and *Uta stansburiana* in southeastern Arizona. *Journal of Morphology* 115:27–34.

Averill-Murray, R. C., A. P. Woodman, & J. M. Howland. 2002. Population ecology of the Sonoran Desert tortoise in Arizona. In *The Sonoran Desert Tortoise: Natural History, Biology, and Conservation,* edited by T. R. Van Devender, pp. 109–134. Tucson: University of Arizona Press and Arizona-Sonora Desert Museum.

Banta, B. H. 1962. A preliminary account of the herpetofauna of the Saline Valley Hydrologic Basin, Inyo County, California. *Wasmann Journal of Biology* 20:161–251.

Betancourt, J. L., T. R. Van Devender, & P. S. Martin, editors. 1990. *Packrat Middens: The Last 40,000 Years of Biotic Change.* Tucson: University of Arizona Press.

Brown, D. E. 1994. Sonoran Savannah Grassland. In *Biotic Communities, Southwestern United States and Northwestern Mexico,* 2d ed., edited by D. E. Brown, pp. 137–141. Salt Lake City: University of Utah Press.

———, editor. 1994. *Biotic Communities, Southwestern United States and Northwestern Mexico.* 2d ed. Salt Lake City: University of Utah Press.

Brown, D. E., & C. H. Lowe. 1980. *Biotic Communities of the Southwest.* Map. General Technical Report RM-78. Fort Collins, Colorado: USDA Forest Service.

Brown, D. E., C. H. Lowe, & J. F. Hausler. 1977. Southwestern riparian communities: their biotic importance and management in Arizona. In *Importance, Preservation, and Management of Riparian Habitat,* edited by R. R. Johnson & D. A. Jones, pp. 201–211. General Technical Report RM-43. Fort Collins, Colorado: USDA Forest Service, Rocky Mountain Forest and Range Experiment Station.

Brown, T. K., & K. A. Nagy. 1995. Herpetological surveys and physiological studies of the western portion of Fort Irwin NTC. Unpublished final report to Fort Irwin, Project 96.5. *http://www.mojave-data.gov/irwin/documents.php.*

Burger, W. L., & M. M. Hensley. 1949. Notes on a collection of reptiles and amphibians from northwestern Sonora. *Natural History Miscellanea* 35:1–6.

Bury, R. B. 1977. Structure and composition of Mojave Desert reptile communities determined with a removal method. In *Herpetological Communities,* edited by N. J. Scott, Jr., pp. 135–142. Wildlife Research Report No. 13. U.S. Fish and Wildlife Service. Fort Collins, Colorado.

Bury, R. B., C. T. Esque, L. A. DeFalco, & P. A. Medica. 1994. Distribution, habitat use, and protection of the desert tortoise in the eastern Mojave Desert. In *Biology of North American Tortoises,* edited by R. B. Bury & D. J. Germano, pp. 57–72. Fish and Wildlife Research No. 13. Washington, D.C.: U.S. Department of the Interior, National Biological Survey.

Camp, C. L. 1916. Notes on the local distribution and habits of the amphibians and reptiles of southeastern California in the vicinity of the Turtle Mountains. *University of California Publications in Zoology* 12:17:503–544.

Clarkson, R. W., & J. C. deVos. 1986. The bullfrog, *Rana catesbeiana* Shaw, in the lower Colorado River, Arizona-California. *Journal of Herpetology* 20:42–49.

Cochran, C., M. Dimmitt, H. Lawler, P. Siminski, & D. Thayer. 1990. A Pinacate adventure. *Sonorensis* 10(3):2–13.

Crother, B. I. 2003. Scientific and standard English names of amphibians and reptiles of North America North of Mexico: Update. *Herpetological Review* 34:196–203.

de Queiroz, A., & H. M. Smith. 1996. *Thamnophis eques* (Mexican garter snake): Geographic distribution. *Herpetological Review* 27:155.

Duellman, W. E., & C. H. Lowe, Jr. 1953. A new lizard of the genus *Cnemidophorus* from Arizona. *Chicago Academy of Sciences, Natural History Miscellanea* 120:1–8.

Emory, W. H. 1848. *Notes of a Military Reconnaissance from Fort Leavenworth, in Missouri, to San Diego, in California, Including Parts of the Arkansas, Del Norte, and Gila Rivers.* 30th Congress, 1st session. Executive Document No. 41. Washington, D.C.: Wendell and Van Benthuysen.

———. 1856–59. *Report on the United States and Mexico Boundary Survey, Made under the Direction of* the *Secretary of the Interior.* 2 vols. Washington, D.C.: House of Representatives, Cornelius Wendell, Printer.

Felger, R. S. 2000. *Flora of the Gran Desierto and Río Colorado of Northwestern Mexico.* Tucson: University of Arizona Press.

Felger, R. S., & M. B. Moser. 1985. *People of the Desert and Sea: Ethnobotany of the Seri Indians.* Tucson: University of Arizona Press.

Foreman, L. D., editor. 1997. Flat-tailed horned lizard rangewide management strategy. Prepared by the Flat-tailed Horned Lizard Working Group of Interagency Coordinating Committee. Riverside, California: BLM.

Funk, R. S. 1967. A new colubrid snake of the genus *Chionactis* from Arizona. *Southwestern Naturalist* 12:180–188.

Germano, D. J., R. B. Bury, C. T. Esque, T. H. Fritts, & P. A. Medica. 1994. Range and habitats of the desert tortoise. Pages 73–84 In *Biology of North American Tortoises,* edited by R. B. Bury & D. J. Germano, pp. 73–84. Fish and Wildlife Research No. 13. Washington, D.C.: U.S. Department of the Interior, National Biological Survey.

Gloyd, H. K. 1937. A herpetological consideration of faunal areas in southern Arizona. *Bulletin of the Chicago Academy of Sciences* 5:79–139.

Gonzáles-Romero, A., & S. Alvarez-Cárdenas. 1989. Herpetofauna de la región del Pinacate, Sonora, México: Un inventario. *Southwestern Naturalist* 34:519–526.

Gonzáles-Romero, A., A. Ortega, & R. Barbault. 1989. Habitat partitioning and spatial organization in a lizard community of the Sonoran Desert, Mexico. *Amphibia-Reptilia* 10:1–11.

Greene, H. W., & C. A. Luke. 1996. Amphibian and reptile diversity in the east Mojave Desert. In *Proceedings of the East Mohave Desert Symposium, 7–8 November 1992, University of California, Riverside,* edited by C. Luke, J. André, & M. Herring, pp. 53–58. Technical Reports, No. 10. Los Angeles: Natural History Museum of Los Angeles County.

Grismer, L. L. 2002. *Amphibians and Reptiles of Baja California.* Berkeley: University of California Press.

Hastings, J. R., & R. M. Turner. 1965. *The Changing Mile: An Ecological Study of Vegetation Changes with Time in the Lower Mile of an Arid and Semiarid Region.* Tucson: University of Arizona Press.

Hendrickson, D. A., & W. L. Minckley. 1985. Cienegas—Vanishing climax communities of the American Southwest. *Desert Plants* 6:131–175.

Hensley, M. M. 1950. Results of a herpetological reconnaissance in extreme southwestern Arizona and adjacent Sonora, with a description of a new subspecies of the Sonoran whipsnake, *Masticophis bilineatus. Transactions of the Kansas Academy of Science* 53:270–288.

Hoffmeister, D. F. 1986. *Mammals of Arizona.* Tucson: University of Arizona Press.

Huey, L. H. 1942. A vertebrae faunal survey of the Organ Pipe Cactus National Monument, Arizona. *Transactions of the San Diego Society of Natural History* 9(32):353–376.

Iverson, J. B. 1978. Distributional problems of the genus *Kinosternon* in the American Southwest. *Copeia* 1978:476–479.

Kluge, A. G. 1993. *Calabaria* and the phylogeny of erycine snakes. *Zoological Journal of the Linnean Society* 107:293–351.

Lamb, T., & A. M. McLuckie. 2002. Genetic differences among geographic races of the desert tortoise. In *The Sonoran Desert Tortoise: Natural History, Biology, and Conservation,* edited by T. R. Van Devender, pp. 67–85. Tucson: University of Arizona Press and Arizona-Sonora Desert Museum.

Leviton, A. E., R. H. Gibbs, E. Heal, & C. E. Dawson. 1985. Standards in herpetology and ichthyology: Part 1. Standard symbolic codes for institutional resource collections in herpetology and ichthyology. *Copeia* 1985:802–832.

Linsdale, J. M. 1940. Amphibians and reptiles in Nevada. *Proceedings of the American Academy of Arts and Sciences* 73:197–257.

Lowe, C. H. 1968. Fauna of desert environments. In *An Inventory of Geographical Research on Desert Environments,* edited by W. G. McGinnies, B. J. Goldman, & P. Paylore, pp. 567–645. Tucson: Office of Arid Land Studies, University of Arizona.

———. 1989. *The Riparianness of a Desert Herpetofauna.* Proceedings of the California Riparian Systems Conference, USDA Forest Service General Technical Report PSW-110. Berkeley: Pacific Southwest Forest and Range Experiment Station.

———, editor. 1964. *The Vertebrates of Arizona.* Tucson: University of Arizona Press.

Lowe, C. H., C. R. Schwalbe, & T. B. Johnson. 1986. *The Venomous Reptiles of Arizona.* Phoenix: Arizona Game and Fish Department.

Luckenbach, R. A. 1982. Ecology and management of the desert tortoise *(Gopherus agassizii)* in California. In *North American Tortoises: Conservation and Ecology,* edited by R. B. Bury, pp. 1–37. Wildlife Research Report No. 12. Washington, D.C.: U.S. Department of Interior, Fish and Wildlife Service.

MacDougal, D. T. 1908. *Botanical Features of North American Deserts.* Carnegie Institution of Washington Publication No. 99. Washington, D.C.

Mardt, C. R., K. R. Beaman, P. C. Rosen, & P. A. Holm. 2001. *Chionactis occipitalis* (Hallowell): Western shovel-nosed snake. *Catalogue of American Amphibians and Reptiles* 731:1–12.

May, L. A. 1973. Resource reconnaissance of the Gran Desierto. Master's thesis, University of Arizona.

———. 1976. Fauna de vertebrados de la región del Gran Desierto, Sonora, México. *Anales del Instituto Biología, Universidad Nacional Autónoma de México, Serie Zoológico* 47:143–182.

McAuliffe, J. R. 1997. Rangeland water developments: Conservation solution or illusion? In *Environmen-*

tal, Economic, and Legal Issues Related to Rangeland Water Developments, Proceedings of a symposium on environmental, economic, and legal issues related to rangeland water developments, 13–15 November 1997, Tempe, Arizona, Center for the Study of Law, Science, and Technology, Arizona State University, pp. 310–359. Tempe: Arizona State University.

McCord, R. D. 2002. Fossil history and evolution of the gopher tortoises (genus *Gopherus*). In *The Sonoran Desert Tortoise: Natural History, Biology, and Conservation,* edited by T. R. Van Devender, pp. 52–66. Tucson: University of Arizona Press and Arizona-Sonora Desert Museum.

McGuire, J. A. 1996. Phylogenetic systematics of crotaphytid lizards (Reptilia: Iguania: Crotaphytidae). *Bulletin of the Carnegie Museum of Natural History* 32:iv–143.

Mearns, E. A. 1907. *Mammals of the Mexican Boundary of the United States.* Bulletin No. 56. Washington, D.C.: U.S. National Museum.

Minckley, W. L. 1973. *Fishes of Arizona.* Phoenix: Arizona Game and Fish Department.

———. 1999. Frederic Morton Chamberlain's 1904 survey of Arizona fishes. *Journal of the Southwest* 41:177–237.

Morafka, D. J. 1996. Amphibian and reptile study of twenty sites in the southern and eastern portion of the National Training Center, Fort Irwin, California. Unpublished final report to Fort Irwin, Project 96.4. *http://www.mojavedata.gov/irwin/documents.php.*

Mueller, G. A., & P. C. Marsh. 2002. *Lost: A Desert River and Its Native Fishes; A Historical Perspective of the Lower Colorado River.* Information and Technology Report USGS/BRD/ITR-2002-0010. Denver: Government Printing Office.

Nabhan, G. P. 2003. *Singing the Turtles to Sea.* Berkeley: University of California Press.

Newman, R. A. 1989. Developmental plasticity of *Scaphiopus couchii* tadpoles in an unpredictable environment. *Ecology* 70:1775–1787.

Ohmart, R. D. 1982. *Past and Present Biotic Communities of the Lower Colorado River Mainstem and Selected Tributaries. Vol. 5, The Gila River, San Pedro River, Santa Cruz River.* Boulder City, Nevada: Bureau of Reclamation.

Ortega, A., A. Gonzáles-Romero, & R. Barbault. 1986. Rythms journaliers d'activité et partage de ressources dans une communauté de lézards du désert de Sonora, Mexique. *Revue d'Ecologie (La Terre et la Vie)* 41:355–360.

Parizek, D. A., P. C. Rosen, & C. R. Schwalbe. 1995. Ecology of the Mexican rosy boa and Ajo Mountain whipsnake in a desert rockpile snake assemblage. Final report to Arizona Heritage Program. Phoenix: Arizona Game and Fish Department.

Platz, J. E., R. W. Clarkson, J. C. Rorabaugh, & D. M. Hillis. 1990. *Rana berlandieri:* Recently introduced populations in Arizona and southeastern California. *Copeia* 1990:324–333.

Rodríguez-Robles, J. A., D. G. Mulcahy, & H. W. Greene. 1999. Feeding ecology of the desert nightsnake, *Hypsiglena torquata* (Colubridae). *Copeia* 1999:93–100.

Rosen, P. C. 2000. A monitoring study of vertebrate community ecology in the northern Sonoran Desert, Arizona. Ph.D. dissertation, University of Arizona.

Rosen, P. C., & C. H. Lowe, Jr. 1996. Ecology of the amphibians and reptiles at Organ Pipe Cactus National Monument, Arizona. Technical Report No. 53. Tucson: Cooperative Park Studies Unit (USGS Sonoran Desert Field Station), University of Arizona.

Rosen, P. C., P. A. Holm, & C. H. Lowe. 1995. Ecology and status of shovelnosed snakes *(Chionactis)* and leafnosed snakes *(Phyllorhynchus)* at and near Organ Pipe Cactus National Monument, Arizona. Final report to Arizona Heritage Program. Phoenix: Arizona Game and Fish Department.

Rosen, P. C., & C. R. Schwalbe. 2002. Widespread effects of introduced species on aquatic reptiles and amphibians in the Sonoran Desert region. In *Exotic Species in the Sonoran Desert,* edited by B. A. Tellman, pp. 220–240. Tucson: University of Arizona Press.

Rowlands, P. G. 1995. Regional bioclimatology of the California desert. In *The California Desert: An Introduction to Natural Resources and Man's Impact,* 2 vols., edited by J. Latting & P. G. Roseland, pp. 95–134. Riverside, California: June Latting Books and University of California, Riverside Press.

Ruthven, A. G. 1907. A collection of reptiles and amphibians from southern New Mexico and Arizona. *Bulletin of the American Museum of Natural History* 23:483–603.

Savage, J. M. 2002. *The Amphibians and Reptiles of Costa Rica: A Herpetofauna Between Two Continents, Between Two Seas.* Chicago: University of Chicago Press.

Schluter, D. 1990. Species-for-species matching. *American Naturalist* 136:560–568.

Schwalbe, C. R., & C. H. Lowe. 2000. Amphibians and reptiles of the Sierra de Alamos. In *The Tropical Deciduous Forest of Alamos: Biodiversity of a Threatened Ecosystem in Mexico,* edited by R. H. Robichaux & D. A. Yetman, pp. 172–199. Tucson: University of Arizona Press.

Secor, S. M. 1994. Natural history of the sidewinder, *Crotalus cerastes.* In *Herpetology of the North American Deserts,* edited by P. R. Brown & J. W. Wright, pp. 281–301. Southwestern Herpetologists Society Special Publication No. 5. Los Angeles.

Shreve, F. 1951. *Vegetation of the Sonoran Desert.* Carnegie Institution of Washington Publication No. 591. Washington, D.C.

Slevin, J. R. 1928. *The Amphibians of Western North America.* Occasional Papers of the California Academy of Sciences XVI:1–152. San Francisco.

Smith, G. E. P. 1910. Groundwater supply and irrigation in the Rillito Valley. University of Arizona Agricultural Experiment Station Bulletin No. 64: 81–244.

Smith, P. W., & M. M. Hensley. 1957. The mud turtle *Kinosternon flavescens stejnegeri* Hartweg, in the United States. *Proceedings of the Biological Society of Washington* 70:201–204.

———. 1958. Notes on a small collection of amphibians and reptiles from the vicinity of the Pinacate lava cap in northwestern Sonora, Mexico. *Transactions of the Kansas Academy of Science* 61:64–76.

Stebbins, R. C. 1966. *A Field Guide to Western Reptiles and Amphibians*. Boston: Houghton Mifflin.

———. 1985. *A Field Guide to Western Reptiles and Amphibians*. 2d ed. Boston: Houghton Mifflin.

———. 2003. *A Field Guide to Western Reptiles and Amphibians*. 3d ed. Boston: Houghton Mifflin.

Stewart, J. N. 1993. *Colorado Desert Wildflowers*. Los Olivos, California: Cachuma Press.

Sullivan, B. K., R. W. Bowker, K. B. Malmos, & E. W. Gergus. 1996. Arizona distribution of three Sonoran Desert anurans: *Bufo retiformis, Gastrophryne olivacea*, and *Pternohyla fodiens. Great Basin Naturalist* 56:38–47.

Tanner, W. W. 1969. New records and distributional notes for reptiles of the Nevada Test Site. *Great Basin Naturalist* 29:31–34.

Tanner, W. W., & C. D. Jorgensen. 1963. Reptiles of the Nevada Test Site. *Brigham Young University Science Bulletin*, Biological Series III:1–35.

Thornber, J. J. 1910. The grazing ranges of Arizona. *University of Arizona Agricultural Experiment Station Bulletin No. 65:[cf1] 245–360.*

Turner, D. S., & C. R. Schwalbe. 1998. Ecology of Cowles fringe-toed lizard. Final report to Arizona Game and Fish Department, Heritage Fund. Phoenix.

Turner, D. S., C. R. Schwalbe, & P. L. Warren. 1997. *Reptile and Plant Inventory of the Mohawk Dunes: Inventory and Monitoring of Unique Sand Dune Ecosystems, Barry M. Goldwater Air Force Range, Arizona.* Legacy Resource Management Program (U.S. Air Force), Project 95–1009. Phoenix.

Turner, F. B., P. A. Medica, K. W. Bridges, & R. I. Jennrich. 1982. A population model of the lizard *Uta stansburiana* in southern Nevada. *Ecological Monographs* 52:243–259.

Turner, R. M. 1994. Mohave Desertscrub. In *Biotic Communities, Southwestern United States and Northwestern Mexico,* 2d ed., edited by D. E. Brown, pp. 157–168. Salt Lake City: University of Utah Press.

Turner, R. M., & D. E. Brown. 1994. Sonoran Desertscrub. In *Biotic Communities, Southwestern United States and Northwestern Mexico,* 2d ed., edited by D. E. Brown, pp. 181–221. Salt Lake City: University of Utah Press.

Turner, R. M., R. H. Webb, J. E. Bowers, & J. R. Hastings. 2003. *The Changing Mile Revisited.* Tucson: University of Arizona Press.

Van Denburgh, J. 1922. *The Reptiles of Western North America.* 2 vols. San Francisco: California Academy of Sciences.

Van Denburgh, J., & J. R. Slevin. 1913. A list of the amphibians and reptiles of Arizona, with notes on the species in the collection of the Academy. *Proceedings of the California Academy of Sciences,* Fourth Series III:391–454.

Van Devender, T. R. 1990. Late quaternary vegetation and climate of the Sonoran Desert, United States and Mexico. In *Packrat Middens: The Last 40,000 Years of Biotic Change,* edited by J. L. Betancourt, T. R. Van Devender, & P. S. Martin, pp. 135–165. Tucson: University of Arizona Press.

Vitt, L. J., & R. D. Ohmart. 1974. Reproduction and ecology of a Colorado River population of *Sceloporus magister* (Sauria: Iguanidae). *Herpetologica* 30: 410–417.

———. 1975. Ecology, reproduction, and reproductive effort of the iguanid lizard *Urosaurus graciosus* on the lower Colorado River. *Herpetologica* 31:56–65.

———. 1978. Herpetofauna of the lower Colorado River: Davis Dam to the Mexican border. *Proceedings of the Western Foundation of Vertebrate Zoology* 2:35–72.

Vitt, L. J., R. C. Van Loben Sels, & R. D. Ohmart. 1981. Ecological relationships among arboreal desert lizards. *Ecology* 62:398–410.

Wirt, E. B., & P. A. Holm. 1997. Climatic effects on survival and reproduction of the desert tortoise (*Gopherus agassizii*) in the Maricopa Mountains, Arizona. Final report to Arizona Game and Fish Department, Heritage Fund I920035. Phoenix.

Zweifel, R. G., & C. H. Lowe. 1966. The ecology of a population of *Xantusia vigilis*, the desert night lizard. *American Museum Novitates* 2247:1–57.

22. Amphibians of Vekol Valley

Bowker, R. W., & B. K. Sullivan. 1991. Anura: *Bufo punctatus* × B. retiformis. Herpetological Review 22:54.

Duellman, W. E., & L. Trueb. 1994. *Biology of Amphibians.* Baltimore: Johns Hopkins University Press.

Enderson, E. F., & R. L. Bezy. 2000. Geographic distribution: *Pternohyla fodiens.* Herpetological Review 31:251–252.

Ferguson, J. H., & C. H. Lowe. 1969. Evolutionary relationships of the *Bufo punctatus* group. *American Midland Naturalist* 81:435–446.

Jones, K. B., L. P. Kepner, & W. G. Kepner. 1983. Anurans of Vekol Valley, central Arizona. *Southwestern Naturalist* 28:469–450.

Ruibal, R., & S. Hillman. 1981. Cocoon structure and function in the burrowing hylid frog, *Pternohyla fodiens. Journal of Herpetology* 15:403–404.

Sullivan, B. K., R. W. Bowker, K. B. Malmos, & E. W. A. Gergus. 1996. Arizona distribution of three Sonoran Desert anurans. *Great Basin Naturalist* 56:38–47.

Sullivan, B. K., K. B. Malmos, E. W. A. Gergus, & R. W. Bowker. 2000. Evolutionary implications

of advertisement call variation in *Bufo debilis,
B. punctatus,* and *B. retiformis. Journal of Herpetology* 34:368–374.

Turner, R. M., R. H. Webb, J. E. Bowers, & James Rodney Hastings. 2003. *The Changing Mile Revisited.* Tucson: University of Arizona Press.

Van Devender, T. R. 1990. Late Quaternary vegetation and climate of the Sonoran Desert, United States and Mexico. In *Packrat Middens: The Last 40,000 Years of Biotic Change,* edited by J. L. Betancourt, T. R. Van Devender, & P. S. Martin, pp. 134–163. Tucson: University of Arizona Press.

23. From the Ground Up: Biological Soil Crusts in the Sonoran Desert

Cameron, R. E. 1958. Fixation of nitrogen by algae and associated organisms in semi-arid soils: Identification and characterization of soil organisms. Master's thesis, University of Arizona.

———. 1960. Communities of soil algae occurring in the Sonoran Desert in Arizona. *Journal of the Arizona Academy of Science* 1:85–88.

———. 1961. Algae of the Sonoran Desert in Arizona. Ph.D. dissertation, University of Arizona.

———. 1962. Species of *Nostoc vaucher* occurring in the Sonoran Desert in Arizona. *Transactions of the American Microscopical Society* 81(4):379–384.

———. 1963. Algae of southern Arizona. Part I. Introduction—blue-green algae. *Revue Algologique* 4: 282–318.

———. 1964. Algae of southern Arizona. Part II. Algal flora (exclusive of blue-green algae). *Revue Algologique* 7:151–177.

———. 1964. Terrestrial algae of southern Arizona. *Transactions of the American Microscopical Society* 83:212–218.

Cameron, R. E., & W. H. Fuller. 1960. Nitrogen fixation by some algae in Arizona soils. *Soil Science Society of America Proceedings* 24(5):353–356.

Faust, W. F. 1970. The effect of algal-mold crusts on the hydrologic processes of infiltration, runoff, and soil erosion under simulated conditions. Master's thesis, University of Arizona.

———. 1971. Blue-green algal effects on some hydrologic processes at the soil surface. Hydrology and Water Resources in Arizona and the Southwest: Proceedings of the 1971 Meetings of the Arizona Section, American Water Resources Association, and Hydrology Section, Tempe, Arizona. Arizona Academy of Science.

Haring, I. M. 1961. A checklist of the mosses of the state of Arizona. *Bryologist* 64:222–240.

Johnsen, A. B. 1978. *Key to the Mosses of Arizona.* Research Paper No. 14. Flagstaff: Museum of Northern Arizona.

Johnson, R. M. 1969. Growth of indigenous bacteria in desert soil. *Journal of the Arizona Academy of Science* 5:240–242.

Johnson, R. M., & R. E. Cameron. 1973. The physiology and distribution of bacteria in hot and cold

deserts. *Journal of the Arizona Academy of Science* 8:84–90.

Kaurivi, J. Z. U. 1996. Radiometric analysis of microphytic soil crusts in the semi-arid lands of Utah and Arizona. Master's thesis, University of Arizona.

Mayland, H. F. 1965. Isotopic nitrogen fixation by desert algal crust organisms. Ph.D. dissertation, University of Arizona.

McCleary, J. A. 1962. Distributional studies of Arizona mosses. *American Midland Naturalist* 67:68–78.

Moberg, R. 1999. The lichen genus *Physcia* in the Sonoran Desert and adjacent areas. *Symbolae Botanicae Upsalienses* 32(1):163–186.

Nash III, T. H., O. L. Lange, & L. Kappen. 1982. Photosynthetic patterns of Sonoran desert lichens. II. A multivariate laboratory analysis. *Flora* 172:419–426.

Nash III, T. H., T. J. Moser et al. 1982. Photosynthetic patterns of Sonoran Desert lichens. I. Environmental considerations and preliminary field measurements. *Flora* 172:335–345.

Ranzoni, F. V. 1968. Fungi isolated in culture from soils of the Sonoran Desert. *Mycologia* 60:356–371.

Sylla, D. 1987. Effect of microphytic crust on emergence of range grasses. Master's thesis, University of Arizona.

25. New Life for the Colorado River Delta

Felger, R. S. 2000. *Flora of the Gran Desierto and Rio Colorado of Northwestern Mexico.* Tucson: University of Arizona Press.

Galindo-Bect, M., E. Glenn, H. Page, K. Fitzsimmons, L. Galindo-Bect, J. Hernandez-Ayon, R. Petty, J. Garcia-Hernandez, & D. Moore. 2000. Penaeid shrimp landings in the upper Gulf of California in relation to Colorado River freshwater discharge. *Fishery Bulletin* 98:222–225.

Glenn, E., D. Radtke, B. Shaw, & A. Huete, editors. 2001. The Lower Colorado River basin and delta. Special issue, *Journal of Arid Environments* 49:1–220.

Glenn, E. P., F. Zamora-Arroyo, P. L. Nagler, M. Briggs, W. Shaw, & K. Flessa. 2001. Ecology and conservation biology of the Colorado River delta, Mexico. *Journal of Arid Environments* 49:5–15.

Hinojosa-Huerta, O., P. L. Nagler, Y. Carrillo-Guerrero, E. Zamora-Hernández, J. García-Hernández, F. Zamora-Arroyo, K. Gillon, & E. Glenn. 2002. Andrade Mesa wetlands of the All-American Canal. *Natural Resources Journal* 42:899–914.

Leopold, A. 1949. The green lagoons. In *A Sand County Almanac,* pp. 150–158. New York: Oxford University Press.

Nagler, P., O. Hinojosa-Huerta, E. Glenn, J. Garcia-Hernandez, & A. Huete. 2005. Regeneration of native trees in the presence of invasive saltcedar in the delta of the Lower Colorado River, Mexico. *Conservation Biology* 19:1842–1852.

Pitt, J., C. Fitzer, & L. Force. 2002. New water for the Colorado River: Economic and environmental considerations for replacing the bypass flow. *University of Denver Water Law Review* 6:68–86.

Sykes, G. 1937. *The Colorado Delta.* Washington, D.C.: Carnegie Institution.

Zamora-Arroyo, F., P. L. Nagler, M. Briggs, D. Radtke, H. Rodriguez, J. Garcia, C. Valdes, A. Huete, & E. P. Glenn. 2001. Regeneration of native trees in response to flood releases from the United States into the delta of the Colorado River, Mexico. *Journal of Arid Environments* 49:49–64.

26. Marine Fishes of the Upper Gulf Biosphere Reserve, Northern Gulf of California

Allard, D. C. 1999. The origins and early history of the steamer *Albatross,* 1880–1887. *Marine Fisheries Review* 61:1–21.

Applegate, S. P., F. Sotelo-Macias, & L. Espinosa-Arrubarrena. 1993. An overview of the Mexican shark fisheries, with suggestions for shark conservation in Mexico. *National Oceanic and Atmospheric Administration, National Marine Fisheries Service Technical Report* 115:31–37.

Arvizu, J., & H. Chávez. 1972. Sinopsis sobre la biología del totoaba, *Cynoscion macdonaldi* Gilbert, 1890. *Food and Agriculture Organization, United Nations, Fisheries Synopsis* 108:1–21.

Baba, J., C. D. Peterson, & H. J. Schrader. 1991. Fine-grained terrigenous sediment supply and dispersal in the Gulf of California during the last century. *American Association of Petroleum Geologists Memoir* 47:589–602.

Bahre, C. J., L. Bourillón, & J. Torre. 2000. The Seri and commercial totoaba fishing (1930–1965). *Journal of the Southwest* 42:559–575.

Barlow, G. W. 1961. Intra- and interspecific differences in rate of oxygen consumption in gobiid fishes of the genus *Gillichthys. Biological Bulletin* 121(2): 209–229.

———. Species structure of the gobiid fish *Gillichthys mirabilis* from coastal sloughs of the eastern Pacific. *Pacific Science* 17:47–72.

Barrera-Guevara, J. C. 1990. The conservation of *Totoaba macdonaldi* (Gilbert), Pisces: Sciaenidae, in the Gulf of California, Mexico. *Journal of Fish Biology* 37 (Supplement A): 201–202.

Berdegué A., J. 1956. *Peces de Importancia Comercial en la Costa Noroccidental de México.* Mexico City: Dirección General de Pesca e Industrias Conexas, Secretaría de Marina.

Bernardi, G., L. Findley, & A. Rocha-Olivares. 2003. Vicariance and dispersal across Baja California in disjunct marine fish populations. *Evolution* 57(7): 1599–1609.

Bowen, T. 2000. *Unknown Island: Seri Indians, Europeans, and San Esteban Island in the Gulf of California.* Albuquerque: University of New Mexico Press.

Bray, N. A., & J. M. Robles. 1991. Physical oceanography of the Gulf of California. *American Association of Petroleum Geologists Memoir* 47:511–553.

Breder, C. M., Jr. 1928a. *Elasmobranchii* from Panama to Lower California. *Bulletin of the Bingham Oceanographic Collection, Yale University* 2(1):1–13.

———. 1928b. *Nematognathii, Apodes, Isospondyli, Synentognathi,* and *Thoracostraci* from Panama to Lower California. *Bulletin of the Bingham Oceanographic Collection, Yale University* 2(2):1–25.

———. 1928c. *Heterosomata* to *Pediculati* from Panama to Lower California. *Bulletin of the Bingham Oceanographic Collection, Yale University* 2(3):1–56.

Brusca, R. C., L. T. Findley, P. A. Hastings, M. E. Hendrickx, J. Torre-Cosio, & A. M. van der Heiden. 2005. Macrofaunal diversity in the Gulf of California. In *Biodiversity, Ecosystems, and Conservation in Northern Mexico,* edited by J.-L. E. Cartron, G. Ceballos, & R. S. Felger, pp. 179–203. New York: Oxford University Press.

Carriquiry, J. D., & A. Sánchez. 1999. Sedimentation in the Colorado River delta and upper Gulf of California after nearly a century of discharge loss. *Marine Geology* 158:125–148.

Castro-Aguirre, J. L., J. Arvizu-Martínez, & J. Paez. 1970. Contribución al conocimiento de los peces del Golfo de California. *Revista de la Sociedad Mexicana de Historia Natural* 31:107–181.

Chute, G. R. 1928. The totuava fishery of the California Gulf. *California Fish and Game Bulletin* 14:275–281.

Cisneros-Mata, M. A., G. Montemayor-López, & M. J. Román-Rodríguez. 1995. Life history and conservation of *Totoaba macdonaldi. Conservation Biology* 9:806–814.

Crabtree, C. B. 1989. A new silverside of the genus *Colpichthys* (Atheriniformes: Atherinidae) from the Gulf of California, Mexico. *Copeia* 1989:558–568.

Cudney-Bueno, R., & P. J. Turk Boyer. 1998. La pesca con chinchorros: Curvina golfina. In *Pescando entre Mareas del Alto Golfo de California: Un Guía sobre la Pesca Artesanal, su Gente y sus Propuestas de Manejo,* pp. 19–25. Serie Técnica 1. Puerto Peñasco, Sonora: Centro Intercultural de Estudios de Desiertos y Océanos.

Diario Oficial. 1993. Decreto por el que se declara area natural protegida con el carácter de Reserva de la Biósfera, la Región conocida como Alto Golfo de California y Delta del Río Colorado, ubicada en aguas del Golfo de California y los municipios de Mexicali, B.C., de Puerto Peñasco y San Luis Río Colorado, Sonora. *Diario Oficial de la Federación,* June 10, pp. 24–28. Mexico City.

Dunn, J. R. 1997. Charles Henry Gilbert (1859–1928): Pioneer ichthyologist of the American West. In *Collection Building in Ichthyology and Herpetology,* edited by T. W. Pietsch & W. D. Anderson, Jr., pp. 265–278. American Society of Ichthyologists and Herpetologists Special Publication No. 3. Lawrence, Kansas.

Engel, J., & R. Kvitek. 1998. Effects of otter trawling on a benthic community in Monterey Bay National Marine Sanctuary. *Conservation Biology* 12:1204–1214.

Findley, L. T., P. A. Hastings, A. M. van der Heiden, R. Güereca, J. Torre, & D. A. Thomson. 1999. Distribución de la ictiofauna endémica del Mar de Cortés. Abstract. In *Libro de Resúmenes: VII Congreso de la Asociación de Investigadores del Mar de Cortés,* May 25–28, p. 51. Hermosillo, Sonora.

Findley, L. T., M. E. Hendrickx, R. C. Brusca, A. M. van der Heiden, P. A. Hastings, & J. Torre. In press. *Macrofauna del Golfo de California (Macrofauna of the Gulf of California).* CD-ROM version 1.0. Macrofauna Golfo Project. Washington, D.C.: Center for Applied Biodiversity Science, Conservation International.

Fish, M. P., & W. H. Mowbray. 1970. *Sounds of Western North Atlantic Fishes.* Baltimore: Johns Hopkins University Press.

Flanagan, C. A., & J. R. Hendrickson. 1976. Observation on the commercial fishery and reproductive biology of the totoaba, *Cynoscion macdonaldi,* in the northern Gulf of California. *Fishery Bulletin* 74:531–554.

Flint, R., & S. Flint. 2005. *Documents of the Coronado Expedition, 1539–1542: They Were Not Familiar with His Majesty, Nor Did They Wish to Be His Subjects.* Dallas: Southern Methodist University Press.

Flores-Skydancer, L., & P. J. Turk Boyer. 2002. *The Vaquita of the Gulf of California.* Educational Series, Intercultural Center of the Study of Deserts and Oceans, Puerto Peñasco, Sonora. [Also published in Spanish as *La Vaquita del Golfo de California.*]

Galindo-Bect, M. S., E. P. Glenn, H. M. Page, K. Fitzsimmons, L. A. Galindo-Bect, J. M. Hernández-Ayon, R. R. Petty, J. García-Hernández, & D. Moore. 2000. Penaeid shrimp landings in the Upper Gulf of California in relation to Colorado River freshwater discharge. *Fishery Bulletin* 98:222–225.

Gallo-Reynoso, J. P. 1998. La vaquita marina y su hábitat crítico en el Alto Golfo de California. *Gaceta Ecológica* 47:29–44. Instituto Nacional de Ecología, SEMARNAP, Mexico City.

García-Caudillo, J. M. & J. V. Gómez-Palafox. In prep. La valoración económica ambiental de la captura incidental en la pesquería de camarón en el Golfo de California. Mexico City: Instituto Nacional de Ecología, Secretaría de Medio Ambiente y Recursos Naturales (SEMARNAT).

Gilbert, C. H. 1890. A preliminary report on the fishes collected by the steamer *Albatross* on the Pacific coast of North America during the year 1889, with descriptions of twelve new genera and ninety-two new species. *Proceedings of the United States National Museum* 13:49–126.

———. 1892. Scientific results of explorations by the U.S. Fish Commission steamer *Albatross.* No. XXII. Descriptions of thirty-four new species of fishes collected in 1888 and 1889, principally among the Santa Barbara Islands and in the Gulf of California. *Proceedings of the United States National Museum* 14:539–566.

Gilbert, C. H., & N. B. Scofield. 1898. Notes on a collection of fishes from the Colorado basin in Arizona. *Proceedings of the United States National Museum* 20:487–499.

Glenn, E. P., R. S. Felger, A. Búrquez, & D. S. Turner. 1992. Ciénega de Santa Clara: Endangered wetland in the Colorado River delta, Sonora, México. *Natural Resources Journal* 32:817–824.

Glenn, E. P., C. Lee, R. Felger, & S. Zengel. 1996. Effects of water management on the wetlands of the Colorado River delta, México. *Conservation Biology* 10:1175–1186.

Glenn, E. P., F. Zamora-Arroyo, P. L. Nagler, M. Briggs, W. Shaw, & K. Flessa. 2001. Ecology and conservation biology of the Colorado River delta, Mexico. *Journal of Arid Environments* 49(1):5–15.

Guevara-Escamilla, S. R. 1974. Ecología de peces del Alto Golfo de California y Delta del Río Colorado. Master's thesis, Universidad Autónoma de Baja California, Ensenada.

Heath, W. G. 1967. Ecological significance of temperature tolerance in Gulf of California shore fishes. *Journal of the Arizona Academy of Sciences* 4:172–178.

Hedgpeth, J. W., & E. F. Ricketts. 1978. *The Outer Shores, Part 2, Breaking Through.* Eureka, California: Mad River Press.

Hendrickson, J. R. 1979. Totoaba: Sacrifice in the Gulf of California, letter to my grandchildren. *Oceans* (September 1979): 14–18.

Hildebrand, S. F. 1943. A review of the American anchovies (family Engraulidae). *Bulletin of the Bingham Oceanographic Collection, Yale University* 8(2):1–165.

Huang, D., & G. Bernardi. 2001. Disjunct Sea of Cortez–Pacific Ocean *Gillichthys mirabilis* populations and the evolutionary origin of their Sea of Cortez endemic relative, *Gillichthys seta. Marine Biology* 138:421–428.

Huey, L. M. 1953. Fisher folk of the Sea of Cortés. *Pacific Discovery* 6:8–13.

INE. 1995. Programa de manejo de la Reserva de la Biosfera del Alto Golfo de California y Delta del Río Colorado. Reprinted February 1997. Mexico City: Instituto de Ecología (INE), Secretaría de Medio Ambiente, Recursos Naturales y Pesca (SEMARNAP).

Jordan, D. S., & C. H. Gilbert. 1882. List of fishes collected by Lieut. Henry E. Nichols, U.S.N., in the Gulf of California and on the west coast of Lower California, with descriptions of four new species. *Proceedings of the United States National Museum* 4:273–279.

Lagomarsino, I. V. 1991. Endangered species status review, *Totoaba macdonaldi.* National Marine Fisheries Service Southwest Region Administrative Report No. SWR-91–01. Terminal Island, California.

Lavín, M. F., V. M. Godínez, & L. G. Alvarez. 1998. Inverse-estuarine features of the upper Gulf of

California. *Estuarine, Coastal, and Shelf Science* 47:769–795.

Lavín, M. F., & S. Sánchez. 1999. On how the Colorado River affected the hydrography of the upper Gulf of California. *Continental Shelf Research* 19:1545–1560.

Lindsey, G. E. 1983. History of scientific exploration in the Sea of Cortéz. In *Island Biogeography in the Sea of Cortéz,* edited by T. J. Case & M. L. Cody, pp. 3–12. Berkeley: University of California Press.

Magallón-Barajas, F. J. 1987. The Pacific shrimp fishery of Mexico. *California Cooperative Fisheries Investigations Report* 28:43–52.

Maluf, L. Y. 1983. Physical oceanography. In *Island Biogeography in the Sea of Cortéz,* edited by T. J. Case & M. L. Cody, pp. 26–45. Berkeley: University of California Press.

Matthews, J. B. 1968. The tides of Puerto Peñasco, Gulf of California. *Journal of the Arizona Academy of Sciences* 5:131–134.

Minckley, C. O., J. R. Campoy-Favela, J. A. Dávila-Paulin, M. S. Thorson, & C. J. Schleusner. 2001. Monitoring and conservation efforts for desert pupfish, *Cyprinodon macularius,* and Quitobaquito pupfish, *Cyprinodon eremus,* in the Upper Gulf of California and Colorado River Delta Biosphere Reserve, the Pinacate and Greater Altar Desert Biosphere Reserve, and in northeastern Baja California. Abstract. In *Proceedings of the Desert Fishes Council, Volume XXXII,* pp. 26–27, 2000 Annual Symposium, November 16–19, Death Valley, California.

Minckley, W. L. 1999. Chamberlain's 1904 survey of Arizona fishes. *Journal of the Southwest* 41:177–237.

———. 2002. Fishes of the lowermost Colorado River, its delta and estuary: A commentary on biotic change. In *Libro Jubilar en Honor al Dr. Salvador Contreras Balderas,* edited by M. L. Lozano-Vilano, pp. 63–78. Monterrey: Ediciones Universidad Autónoma de Nuevo León.

Moffatt, N. A., & D. A. Thomson. 1975. Taxonomic status of the gulf grunion *(Leuresthes sardina)* and its relationship to the California grunion *(L. tenuis). Transactions of the San Diego Society of Natural History* 18:75–84.

Moore, J., & R. Boardman. 1991. List of type specimens in the fish collection at the Yale Peabody Museum, with a brief history of ichthyology at Yale University. *Postilla* 206:1–36.

Morales-Ortiz, C. 1999. Descripción del desarrollo embrionario de totoaba *(Totoaba macdonaldi)* bajo condiciones de laboratorio. Bachelor's thesis, Facultad de Ciencias Marinas, Universidad Autónoma de Baja California, Ensenada.

Moriarty, J. R. 1965. The discovery and earliest explorations of the Gulf of California. *Journal of San Diego History* 11:1–19.

Mueller, G. A., & P. C. Marsh. 2002. *Lost, a Desert River and Its Native Fishes: A Historical Perspective of the Lower Colorado River.* U.S. Geological Survey, Biological Resources Division, Information and Technology Report No. USGS/BRD/ITR–2002–0010:1–69. Fort Collins, Colorado.

Munro-Palacio, G. 1994. Historia del la región de Puerto Peñasco. *CEDO News* 6:22–25.

Musick, J. A., M. M. Harbin, S. A. Berkeley, G. H. Burgess, A. M. Eklund, L. Findley, R. G. Gilmore, J. T. Golden, D. S. Ha, G. R. Huntsman, J. C. McGovern, S. J. Parker, S. G. Poss, E. Sala, T. W. Schmidt, G. R. Sedberry, H. Weeks, & S. G. Wright. 2000. Marine, estuarine, and diadromous fish stocks at risk of extinction in North America (exclusive of Pacific salmonids). *Fisheries* 25:6–30.

Nava-Romo, J. M. 1994. Impactos a corto y largo plazo en la diversidad y otras características ecológicas de la comunidad béntico-demersal capturada por la pesquería de camarón en el norte del Alto Golfo de California, México. Master's thesis, Instituto Tecnológico y de Estudios Superiores de Monterrey, Campus Guaymas.

Nelson, J. S., E. J. Crossman, H. Espinosa-Pérez, L. T. Findley, C. R. Gilbert, R. N. Lea, & J. D. Williams. 2004. *Common and Scientific Names of Fishes from the United States, Canada, and Mexico.* 6th ed. Bethesda, Maryland: American Fisheries Society.

Ness, G. E. 1993. The search for Caláfia's Island, being a loose account of the early Spanish explorations off northwest Mexico and of certain myths pertaining to the region, with supplemental musings by the author. *American Association of Petroleum Geologists Memoir* 47:1–17.

Ortiz de Montellano, G. P. 1987. Impacto de la pesca de arrastre sobre la población juvenil de *Totoaba macdonaldi.* Technical Report No. 7. Hermosillo: Centro de Investigación y Desarrollo de Sonora (CIDESON).

Ortiz-Viveros, D. 1999. Regulación iónica y osmótica de los juveniles de *Totoaba macdonaldi* ante cambios de salinidad. Master's thesis, Facultad de Ciencias Marinas, Universidad Autónoma de Baja California, Ensenada.

Pérez-Mellado, J., & L. T. Findley. 1985. Evaluación de la ictiofauna acompañante del camarón capturada en las costas de Sonora y norte de Sinaloa, México. In *Recursos Potenciales de México: La Pesca Acompañante del Camarón,* edited by A. Yáñez-Arancibia, pp. 201–254. Mexico City: Programa Universitario de Alimentos, Instituto de Ciencias del Mar y Limnología, y el Instituto Nacional de la Pesca. Universidad Nacional Autónoma de México.

Present, T. 1987. Genetic differentiation of disjunct Gulf of California and Pacific outer coast populations of *Hypsoblennius jenkinsi. Copeia* 1987:1010–1024.

Reynolds, W. W., & D. A. Thomson. 1974. Responses of young gulf grunion, *Leuresthes sardina,* to gradients of temperature, light, turbulence, and oxygen. *Copeia* 1974:747–758.

Roden, G. I. 1964. Oceanographic aspects of the Gulf of California. In *Marine Geology of the Gulf of Cali-*

fornia, edited by T. H. van Andel & G. G. Shore, Jr., pp. 30–58. American Association of Petroleum Geologists Memoir No. 3. Tulsa, Oklahoma.

Rodriguez, C. A., K. W. Flessa, & D. L. Dettman. 2001. Effects of upstream diversion of Colorado River water on the estuarine bivalve mollusc *Mulinia coloradoensis*. *Conservation Biology* 15:249–258.

Rodriguez, C. A., K. W. Flessa, M. A. Téllez-Duarte, D. L. Dettman, & G. A. Ávila-Serrano. 2001. Macrofaunal and isotopic estimates of the former extent of the Colorado River estuary, upper Gulf of California, México. *Journal of Arid Environments* 49(1):183–193.

Rojas-Bracho, L., & B. L. Taylor. 1999. Risk factors affecting the vaquita *(Phocoena sinus)*. *Marine Mammal Science* 15(4):974–989.

Román-Rodríguez, M. J. 1990. Alimentación de *Totoaba macdonaldi* (Gilbert) (Pisces: Sciaenidae) en la parte norte del Alto Golfo de California. *Ecológica* 1:1–9. Hermosillo, Sonora.

Román-Rodríguez, M. J., J. C. Barrera-G., & J. Campoy-F. 1998. La curvina golfina: Volvió para quedarse? *Voces del Mar* 1:1–2. CEDO, Puerto Peñasco, Sonora.

Román-Rodríguez, M. J., & M. G. Hammann. 1997. Age and growth of totoaba, *Totoaba macdonaldi* (Sciaenidae), in the upper Gulf of California. *Fishery Bulletin* 95:620–628.

Romero C., J. M. 1978. *Composición y variabilidad de la fauna de acompañamiento del camarón en la zona norte del Golfo de California.* Guaymas, Sonora: Escuela de Ciencias Marítimas y Alimentarias, Instituto Tecnológico y de Estudios Superiores de Monterrey.

Sykes, G. 1937. *The Colorado Delta.* Washington, D.C.: Carnegie Institution of Washington; New York: American Geographical Society.

Tanner, Z. L. 1892. Report upon the investigations of the U.S. Fish Commission steamer *Albatross* for the year ending June 30, 1889. *Report of the Commissioner, United States Commission of Fish and Fisheries* 16:395–512.

Thomson, D. A. 1969. Marine research in the Gulf of California. Final Technical Report to the Office of Naval Research, 1967–1969.

———. 2002. *Tide Calendar for the Northern Gulf of California.* Tucson: Printing and Graphic Services, University of Arizona.

Thomson, D. A., L. T. Findley, & A. N. Kerstitch. 1979. *Reef Fishes of the Sea of Cortez: The Rocky-Shore Fishes of the Gulf of California.* New York: John Wiley and Sons.

———. 2000. *Reef Fishes of the Sea of Cortez: The Rocky-Shore Fishes of the Gulf of California.* Rev. ed. Austin: University of Texas Press.

Thomson, D., & M. Gilligan. 1983. The rocky shore fishes. In *Island Biogeography in the Sea of Cortéz,* edited by T. J.Case & M. L. Cody, pp. 98–129. Berkeley: University of California Press.

Thomson, D. A., & C. E. Lehner. 1979. Resilience of a rocky intertidal fish community in a physically unstable environment. *Journal of Experimental Marine Biology and Ecology* 22:1–29.

Thomson, D. A., & N. McKibbin. 1976. *Gulf of California Fishwatcher's Guide.* Tucson: Golden Puffer Press.

Thomson, D. A., & K. A. Muench. 1976. Influence of tides and waves on the spawning behavior of the Gulf of California grunion, *Leuresthes sardina* (Jenkins and Evermann). *Bulletin of the Southern California Academy of Sciences* 75:198–203.

Thurston, R. C. 1973. Early explorations in the Gulf of California. Master's thesis. United States International University.

Todd, E. S., & A. W. Ebeling. 1966. Aerial respiration in the longjaw mudsucker *Gillichthys mirabilis* (Teleostei: Gobiidae). *Biological Bulletin* 130: 265–288.

Townsend, C. H. 1916. Scientific results of the expedition to the Gulf of California in charge of C. H. Townsend, by the U.S. Fisheries steam-ship "*Albatross*" in 1911, Commander G. H. Burrage, U.S.N., commanding. I. Voyage of the "*Albatross*" to the Gulf of California in 1911. *Bulletin of the American Museum of Natural History* 35:399–476.

Varela-Romero, A., G. Ruiz-Campos, L. M. Yépiz-Velázquez, & J. Alanís-García. 2002. Distribution, habitat, and conservation status of desert pupfish *(Cyprinodon macularius)* in the lower Colorado River basin, Mexico. *Reviews in Fish Biology and Fisheries* 12:157–165.

Vidal, O., R. L. Brownell, & L. T. Findley. 1999. Vaquita, *Phocoena sinus* Norris and McFarland, 1958. In *Handbook of Marine Mammals, Vol. 6: The Second Book of Dolphins and the Porpoises,* edited by S. H. Ridgway & R. Harrison, pp. 357–378. San Diego: Academic Press.

Walker, B. W. 1960. The distribution and affinities of the marine fish fauna of the Gulf of California. *Systematic Zoology* 9:123–133.

Watling, L., & E. A. Norse. 1998. Disturbance of the seabed by mobile fishing gear: A comparison to forest clearcutting. *Conservation Biology* 12:1180–1197.

Whitehead, P. J. P., G. J. Nelson, & T. Wongratana. 1988. FAO species catalogue, vol. 7. Clupeoid fishes of the world (suborder Clupeoidei). An annotated and illustrated catalogue of the herrings, sardines, pilchards, sprats, anchovies and wolf-herrings. Part 2, Engraulididae. *FAO Fisheries Synopsis* No. 125, vol. 7, part 2:305–579. Rome: FAO.

Whitehead, P. J. P., & R. Rodríguez-Sánchez. 1995. Engraulidae: Anchoas, anchovetas. In *Guía FAO para la identificación de especies para los fines de la pesca, Pacífico centro-oriental. Vol. 2, Vertebrados,* part 1:647–1200, edited by W. Fisher, F. Krupp, W. Schneider, C. Sommer, K. E. Carpenter, & V. H. Niem, pp. 1067–1087. Rome: FAO.

Zengel, S. A., & E. P. Glenn. 1996. Presence of the endangered desert pupfish (*Cyprinodon macularius*, Cyprinodontidae) in Cienega de Santa Clara, Mexico, following an extensive marsh dry-down. *Southwestern Naturalist* 41(1):73–78.

27. Hovering Over the Alto Golfo: The Status and Conservation of Birds from the Río Colorado to the Gran Desierto

American Ornithologists' Union. 1998. *Check-list of North American Birds*. 7th ed. Washington, D.C.: American Ornithologists' Union.

Audubon, J. W. 1906. *Audubon's Western Journal, 1849–1850*. Cleveland: A. H. Clark.

Bancroft, G. 1922. Some winter birds of the Colorado delta. *The Condor* 24:98.

———. 1926. The faunal areas of Baja California del Norte. *The Condor* 28:209–215.

———. 1927. Notes on the breeding coastal and insular birds of central lower California. *The Condor* 29:188–195.

———. 1932. *The Flight of the Least Petrel*. New York: G. P. Putnam's Sons.

Banks, R. C., C. Cicero, J. L. Dunn, A. W. Kratter, P. C. Rasmussen, J. V. Remsen Jr., J. D. Rising, & D. F. Stotz. 2004. Forty-fifth supplement to the American Ornithologists' Union Check-list of North American Birds. *The Auk* 121:985–995.

Bates, J. M. 1992. Frugivory on *Bursera microphylla* (Burseraceae) by wintering gray vireos (*Vireo vicinior*, Vireonidae) in the coastal deserts of Sonora, Mexico. *Southwest Naturalist* 37:252–258.

Briggs, M. K., & S. Cornelius. 1998. Opportunities for ecological improvement along the lower Colorado River and delta. *Wetlands* 18:513–529.

California Department of Fish and Game. 1999. Birds in the List of Special Animals, June 1999. http://www.dfg.ca.gov/endangered/birds.html.

Cardiff, E. A. 1961. Two new species of birds for California and notes on species of the Imperial Valley and Salton Sea area of California. *The Condor* 63:183.

Cervantes-Sanchez, J., & E. Mellink. 2001. Nesting of Brandt's Cormorants in the northern Gulf of California. *Western Birds* 32:134–135.

Daniels, B. E., D. R. Willick, & T. E. Wurster. 1993. Observation of a Bendire's thrasher from northeast Baja California. *Euphonia* 1:42–43.

Diario Oficial. 2002. Norma Oficial Mexicana NOM-059-ECOL-2001, Protección ambiental—Especies nativas de México de flora y fauna silvestres—Categorías de riesgo y especificaciones para su inclusión, exclusión o cambio—Lista de especies en riesgo. *Diario Oficial de la Federación*, March 6. Mexico City: Secretaría de Medio Ambiente y Recursos Naturales.

Dimmitt, M. A. 2000. Biomes and communities of the Sonoran Desert region. In *A Natural History of the Sonoran Desert*, edited by S. J. Phillips & P. W.

Comus, pp. 3–18. Tucson: Arizona-Sonora Desert Museum; Berkeley: University of California Press.

Donlan, C. J., B. R. Tershy, B. S. Keitt, J. A. Sanchez, B. Wood, A. Weinstein, D. A. Croll, & M. A. Hermosillo. 2000. Island conservation action in northwest México. In *Proceedings of the Fifth California Islands Symposium*, edited by D. R. Browne, K. L. Mitchell, & H. W. Chaney, pp. 330–338. Santa Barbara: Santa Barbara Museum of Natural History.

Dunning, B. 1988. An unusual concentration of boobies in the northern Gulf of California. *Aves Mexicanas* 1(88–1):1–2.

Eddleman, W. R., & C. J. Conway. 1998. Clapper rail (*Rallus longirostris*). In *The Birds of North America*, edited by A. Poole & F. Gill, no. 340. Philadelphia: Birds of North America.

Escalante, P., A. M. Sada, & J. R. Gil. 1996. *Listado de nombres comunes de las aves de México*. Mexico City: Comisión Nacional para el Conocimiento y Uso de la Biodiversidad.

Evens, J. G., G. W. Page, S. A. Laymon, & R. W. Stallcup. 1991. Distribution, relative abundance, and status of the California black rail in western North America. *The Condor* 93:952–966.

Ezcurra, E., R. S. Felger, A. D. Russell, & M. Equihua. 1988. Freshwater islands in a desert sand sea: The hydrology, flora, and phytogeography of the Gran Desierto oases of northwestern Mexico. *Desert Plants* 9:35–44, 55–63.

Felger, R., B. Broyles, M. Wilson, & G. Nabhan. 1997. The binational Sonoran Desert biosphere network and its plant life. *Journal of the Southwest* 39:411–560.

Flores, R. E., & W. R. Eddleman. 1995. California black rail use of habitat in southwestern Arizona. *Journal of Wildlife Management* 59:357–363.

Fradkin, L. P. 1984. *A River No More*. Tucson: University of Arizona Press.

Gallucci, T. 1981. Summer bird records from Sonora, Mexico. *American Birds* 35:243–247.

García-Hernández, J., O. Hinojosa-Huerta, V. Gerhart, Y. Carrillo-Guerrero, & E. P. Glenn. 2001. Willow flycatcher (*Empidonax traillii*) surveys in the Colorado River delta wetlands: Implications for management. *Journal of Arid Environments* 49:161–169.

Glenn, E., C. Lee, R. Felger, & S. Zengel. 1996. Effects of water management on the wetlands of the Colorado River delta, Mexico. *Conservation Biology* 10:1175–1186.

Glenn, E. P., F. Zamora-Arroyo, P. L. Nagler, M. Briggs, W. Shaw, & K. Flessa. 2001. Ecology and conservation biology of the Colorado River delta, Mexico. *Journal of Arid Environments* 49:5–15.

Grinnell, J. 1906. Stone and Rhoads' "On a collection of birds and mammals from the Colorado delta, Lower California." *The Condor* 8:78.

———. 1926. Occurrence of the roseate spoonbill in the Colorado delta. *The Condor* 28:102.

———. 1928. A distributional summation of the ornithology of Lower California. *University of California Publications of Zoology* 32:1–300.

Groschupf, K., B. T. Brown, & R. R. Johnson. 1988. *An Annotated Checklist of the Birds of Organ Pipe Cactus National Monument, Arizona.* Tucson: Southwest Parks and Monuments Association.

Hinojosa-Huerta, O., S. DeStefano, & W. Shaw. 2001a. Abundance and distribution of the Yuma clapper rail *(Rallus longirostris yumanensis)* in the Colorado River delta, Mexico. *Journal of Arid Environments* 49:171–182.

Hinojosa-Huerta, O., J. García-Hernández, & W. Shaw. 2002. *Report on the Surveys for Willow Flycatchers in the Colorado River Delta, Mexico.* Tucson: School of Renewable Natural Resources, University of Arizona.

Hinojosa-Huerta, O., P. L. Nagler, Y. Carrillo-Guerrero, E. Zamora-Hernández, J. García-Hernández, F. Zamora-Arroyo, K. Gillion, & E. P. Glenn. 2002. Andrade Mesa wetlands of the All-American Canal. *Natural Resources Journal* 42:899–914.

Hinojosa-Huerta, O., W. Shaw, & S. DeStefano. 2001b. Detections of California black rails in the Colorado River delta, Mexico. *Western Birds* 32:228–232.

Hornaday, W. T. 1908. *Camp-Fires on Desert and Lava.* New York: Charles Scribner's Sons.

Huey, L. M. 1927. Birds recorded in spring at San Felipe, northeastern Lower California, Mexico, with the description of a new woodpecker from that locality. *Transactions of the San Diego Society of Natural History* 5:13–40.

Hughes, J. M. 1999. Yellow-billed cuckoo *(Coccyzus americanus).* In *The Birds of North America,* edited by A. Poole & F. Gill, no. 418. Philadelphia: Birds of North America.

Hutto, R. L. 2000. On the importance of *en route* periods to the conservation of migratory landbirds. *Studies in Avian Biology* 20:109–114.

Iturribarría-Rojas, H. 2002. Estimación de abundancia y afinidad de habitat del tecolote llanero *(Athene cunicularia hypugea)* en el Valle de Mexicali, Baja California y Sonora, México. Senior thesis, Facultad de Ciencias Químicas y Biológicas, Universidad Autónoma de Guadalajara, Guadalajara.

Kaufman, K., & J. Witzeman. 1979. A harlequin duck reaches Sonora, Mexico. *Continental Birdlife* 1:16–17.

Kniffen, F. B. 1932. The primitive cultural landscape of the Colorado delta. *University of California Publications in Geography* 5:43–66.

Kramer, G. W., & R. Migoya. 1989. The Pacific coast of Mexico. In *Habitat Management for Migrating and Wintering Waterfowl in North America,* edited by L. M. Smith, R. L. Pederson, & R. M. Kaminski, pp. 507–528. Lubbock: Texas Tech University Press.

Leopold, A. 1949. *A Sand County Almanac.* New York: Oxford University Press.

———. 1953. *Round River.* New York: Oxford University Press.

Lumholtz, C. 1990. *New Trails in Mexico.* Tucson: University of Arizona Press. Originally published 1912.

Mearns, E. A. 1907. *Mammals of the Mexican Boundary of the United States.* Bulletin of the U.S. Natural History Museum No. 56. Washington, D.C.

Mellink, E., J. A. Castillo-Guerrero, & A. de la Cerda. 2002. Noteworthy waterbird records in the delta of the Río Colorado, Mexico, 2002. *Western Birds* 33:249–253.

Mellink, E. & V. Ferreira-Bartrina. 2000. On the wildlife of wetlands of the Mexican portion of the Río Colorado delta. *Bulletin of the Southern California Academy of Sciences* 99:115–127.

Mellink, E., E. Palacios, & S. Gonzalez. 1997. Nonbreeding waterbirds of the delta of the Rio Colorado, Mexico. *Journal of Field Ornithology* 68: 113–123.

Mellink, E., & A. M. Rea. 1994. Taxonomic status of the California gnatcatchers of northwestern Baja California, Mexico. *Western Birds* 25:50–62.

Miller, A. H., H. Friedman, L. Griscom, & R. T. Moore. 1957. Distributional check-list of the birds of Mexico, part 2. *Pacific Coast Avifauna* 33.

Molina, K. C., & K. L. Garrett. 2001. Breeding birds of the Cerro Prieto geothermal ponds. *Monographs of Field Ornithology* 3:23–28.

Mora, M. A. 1997. Feeding flights of cattle egrets nesting in an agricultural ecosystem. *Southwest Naturalist* 42:52–58.

Morrison, R. I. G., R. K. Ross, & M. M. Torres. 1992. *Aerial Surveys of Nearctic Shorebirds Wintering in Mexico: Some Preliminary Results.* Progress Note, Canadian Wildlife Service. Ottawa.

Murphy, R. C. 1917. Natural history observations from the Mexican portion of the Colorado Desert, with a note on the Lower Californian pronghorn and a list of the birds. *Abstract Proceedings of the Linnean Society of New York* 28:43–101.

National Audubon Society. 2002. *The Christmas Bird Count Historical Results (Online).* Available at *http://www.audubon.org/bird/cbc* (February 21, 2002).

Nelson, E. W. 1921. *Lower California and Its Natural Resources.* Memoir No. 16. Washington, D.C.: National Academy of Sciences.

Newcomer, M. W., & G. K. Silber. 1989. Sightings of Laysan albatross in the northern Gulf of California. *Western Birds* 21:139–140.

North, A. W. 1910. *Camp and Camino in Lower California.* New York: Baker & Taylor.

Palacios, E., D. W. Anderson, E. Mellink, & S. Gonzalez-Guzman. 2000. Distribution and abundance of burrowing owls on the peninsula and islands of Baja California. *Western Birds* 31:89–96.

Palacios, E., & E. Mellink. 1992. Breeding bird records from Montague Island, northern Gulf of California. *Western Birds* 23:41–44.

———. 1993. Additional breeding bird records from Montague Island, northern Gulf of California. *Western Birds* 24:259–262.

———. 1996. Status of the least tern in the Gulf of California. *Journal of Field Ornithology* 67:48–58.

Parnell, J. F., R. M. Erwin, & K. C. Molina. 1995. Gull-billed tern. In *The Birds of North America,* edited by A. Poole & F. Gill, no. 140. Philadelphia: Birds of North America.

Patten, M. A., E. Mellink, H. Gómez de Silva, & T. E. Wurster. 2001. Status and taxonomy of the Colorado Desert avifauna of Baja California. *Monographs in Field Ornithology* 3:29–63.

Patten, M. A., K. Radamaker, & T. E. Wurster. 1993. Noteworthy observations from northeastern Baja California. *Western Birds* 24:89–93.

Peresbarbosa, E., & E. Mellink. 1994. More records of breeding birds from Montague Island, northern Gulf of California. *Western Birds* 25:201–202.

———. 2001. Nesting waterbirds of Isla Montague, northern Gulf of California, Mexico: Loss of eggs due to predation and flooding, 1993–1994. *Waterbirds* 24:265–271.

Petit, D. R. 2000. Habitat use by landbirds along Nearctic-Neotropical migration routes: Implications for conservation of stopover habitats. *Studies in Avian Biology* 20:15–33.

Piest, L., & J. Campoy. 1999. *Report of Yuma Clapper Rail Surveys at the Ciénega de Santa Clara, Sonora, 1998.* Yuma: Arizona Game and Fish Department.

Powell, A. N. 1998. Western snowy plovers and California least terns. In *Status and Trends of the Nation's Biological Resources,* 2 vols., edited by M. J. Mac, P. A. Opler, C. E. Puckett-Haecker, & P. D. Doran, 2:629–631. Reston, Virginia: U.S. Department of the Interior, U.S. Geological Survey.

Powell, B. F., & R. J. Steidl. 2000. Nesting habitat and reproductive success of southwestern riparian birds. *The Condor* 102:823–831.

Price, W. 1899. Some winter birds of the lower Colorado Valley. *Bulletin of the Cooper Ornithology Club* 1:89–93.

Pyle, P. 1997. *Identification Guide to North American Birds, Part I.* Bolinas, California: Slate Creek Press.

Ramsar Convention Bureau. 1998. Internet home page (revised 02/98). http://www.iucn.org/themes/ramsar/about_infopack-2e.htm.

Rosenberg, K. V., R. D. Ohmart, W. C. Hunter, & B. W. Anderson. 1991. *Birds of the Lower Colorado River Valley.* Tucson: University of Arizona Press.

Ruiz-Campos, G., & M. Rodríguez-Meraz. 1997. Composición taxonómica y ecológica de la avifauna de los ríos El Mayor y Hardy, y áreas adyacentes, en el Valle de Mexicali, Baja California, México. *Anales del Instituto de Biología, Universidad Nacional Autónoma de México, Serie Zoología* 68:291–315.

Russell, S. M., & D. W. Lamm. 1978. Notes on the distribution of birds in Sonora, Mexico. *Wilson Bulletin* 90:123–131.

Russell, S. M., & G. Monson. 1998. *The Birds of Sonora.* Tucson: University of Arizona Press.

Saunders, G. B., & D. C. Saunders. 1981. *Waterfowl and Their Wintering Grounds in Mexico, 1937–1964.*

Resource Publication No. 138. Washington, D.C.: U.S. Fish and Wildlife Service.

SEMARNAP. 1995. *Programa de Manejo Reserva de la Biosfera del Alto Golfo de California y Delta del Río Colorado.* Special Publication No. 1. Mexico City: Secretaría del Medio Ambiente, Recursos Naturales y Pesca.

Sferra, S. J., T. E. Corman, C. E. Paradzick, J. W. Rourke, J. A. Spencer, & M. W. Summer. 1997. *Arizona Partners in Flight Southwestern Willow Flycatcher Survey: 1993–1996 Summary Report.* Nongame and Endangered Wildlife Program Technical Report No. 113. Phoenix: Arizona Game and Fish Department.

Simon, D., & W. F. Simon. 1974. A yellow-billed loon in Baja California, Mexico. *Western Birds* 5:23.

Sogge, M. K., R. M. Marshall, S. J. Sferra, & T. J. Tibbitts. 1997. *A Southwestern Willow Flycatcher Natural History Summary and Survey Protocol.* NRTR-97/12. Flagstaff: USGS Colorado Plateau Research Station, Northern Arizona University.

Stone, W., & S. N. Rhoads. 1905. On a collection of birds and mammals from the Colorado delta, Lower California. *Proceedings of the Academy of Natural Sciences of Philadelphia* 57:676–690.

Sykes, G. 1937. *The Colorado Delta.* Special Publication No. 19. New York: American Geographical Society; Washington, D.C.: Carnegie Institution.

Unitt, P. 1984. *The Birds of San Diego County.* San Diego Society Natural History Memoir No. 13. San Diego.

———. 1987. *Empidonax traillii extimus:* An endangered subspecies. *Western Birds* 18:137–162.

U.S. Fish and Wildlife Service. 1993–96. *Winter Waterfowl Survey in Mexico.* Portland, Oregon: U.S. Department of the Interior, Fish and Wildlife Service.

———. 2001. Endangered and threatened wildlife and plants: 12-month finding for a petition to list the yellow-billed cuckoo *(Coccyzus americanus)* in the western continental United States. *Federal Register* 66, no. 143 (July 25).

Valdés-Casillas, C., E. P. Glenn, O. Hinojosa-Huerta, Y. Carrillo-Guerrero, J. García-Hernández, F. Zamora-Arroyo, M. Muñoz-Viveros, M. Briggs, C. Lee, E. Chavarría-Correa, J. Riley, D. Baumgartner, & C. Condon. 1998. *Wetland Management and Restoration in the Colorado River Delta: The First Steps.* Special Publication of CECARENA-ITESM Campus Guaymas and NAWCC. Mexico City.

van Riper III, C., J. Hart, C. Olson, C. O'Brien, A. Banks, M. Lomow, & K. Covert. 1999. *Use of the Mexico Colorado River Delta Region by Neotropical Migrant Landbirds: Report to Cooperators.* Flagstaff: USGS Biological Resources Division, Colorado Plateau Research Station, Northern Arizona University.

van Rossem, A. J. 1945. *A Distributional Survey of the Birds of Sonora, Mexico.* Occasional Papers Museum Zoology No. 21. Baton Rouge: Louisiana State University.

van Rossem, A. J., & M. Hachisuka. 1937. A further report on birds from Sonora, Mexico, with description of two new races. *Transactions of the San Diego Society of Natural History* 8:321–336.

Velarde, E., & D. W. Anderson. 1994. Conservation and management of seabird islands in the Gulf of California: Setbacks and successes. In *Seabirds on Islands: Threats, Case Studies, and Action Plans,* edited by D. N. Nettleship, J. Burger, & M. Gochfeld, pp. 229–243. Cambridge: Birdlife International.

Western Hemisphere Shorebird Reserve Network (WHSRN). 1993. *Western Hemisphere Reserve Network Site Profiles.* WA Publication No. 4. Manomet, Massachusetts, and Buenos Aires: Wetlands for the Americas.

Wilbur, S. R. 1987. *Birds of Baja California.* Berkeley: University of California Press.

Williams, A. Alvarez de. 1973. *Primeros Pobladores de la Baja California—Introducción a la Antropología de la Península.* Mexicali: Universidad Autónoma de Baja California.

Wurster, T. E., & K. Radamaker. 1992. Semipalmated sandpiper records for Baja California. *Euphonia* 1:37 38.

Zamora-Arroyo, F., P. L. Nagler, M. Briggs, D. Radtke, H. Rodríguez, J. García, C. Valdés, A. Huete, & E. P Glenn. 2001. Regeneration of native trees in response to flood releases from the United States into the delta of the Colorado River, Mexico. *Journal of Arid Environments* 49:49–64.

Zengel, S., & E. Glenn. 1996. Presence of the endangered desert pupfish (*Cyprinodon macularius,* Cyprinidontidae) in Cienega de Santa Clara, Mexico, following an extensive marsh dry-down. *Southwestern Naturalist* 41:73–78.

Zengel, S., V. Mertetsky, E. Glenn, R. Felger, & D. Ortiz. 1995. Cienega de Santa Clara, a remnant wetland in the Rio Colorado delta (Mexico): Vegetation distribution and the effects of water flow reduction. *Ecological Engineering* 4:19–36.

28. Aquatic Mammals of the Northern Sea of Cortez and Colorado River Delta

Aurioles, D. 1988. Behavioral ecology of California sea lions in the Gulf of California. Ph.D. dissertation, University of California, Santa Cruz.

Brownell, R. L. Jr., L. T. Findley, O. Vidal, A. Robles, & S. Manzanilla-N. 1987. External morphology and pigmentation of the vaquita, *Phocoena sinus* (Cetacea: Mammalia). *Marine Mammal Science* 3(1):22–30.

Carbajal, N., A. Souza, & R. Durazo. 1997. A numerical study of the ex-ROFI of the Colorado River. *Journal of Marine Systems* 12:17–33.

Cisneros, M. A., G. Montemayor-López, & M. J. Román-Rodríguez. 1995. Life history and conservation of *Totoaba macdonaldi. Conservation Biology* 9:806–814.

Cudney-Bueno, R., & P. Turk Boyer. 1998. *Pescando entre mareas del Alto Golfo de California.* Puerto Peñasco, Sonora: Centro Intercultural de Estudios de Desiertos y Océanos.

Findley, L. T., J. M. Nava, & J. Torre. 1996. Hábitos alimenticios de la vaquita, *Phocoena sinus. Proceedings of the XXI International Reunion of the Mexican Society of Marine Mammalogy.* Chetumal, Quintana Roo, Mexico.

Gallo-Reynoso, J. P. 1997. Situación y distribución de las nutrias en México, con énfasis en *Lontra longicaudis annectens* Major, 1897. *Revista Mexicana de Mastozoología* 2:10–32.

———. 1998. La vaquita marina y su hábitat crítico en el Alto Golfo de California. *Gaceta Ecológica* 47:29–44. Instituto Nacional de Ecología, SEMAR-NAP, Mexico City.

Guerrero-Ruíz, M., D. Gendron, & J. Urbán-R. 1998. Distribution, movements, and communities of killer whales (*Orcinus orca*) in the Gulf of California. *Report of the International Whaling Commission* 48:537–543.

Heyning, J. E. 1984. Functional morphology involved in intraspecific fighting of the beaked whale, *Mesoplodon carlhubbsi. Canadian Journal of Zoology* 62:1645–1654.

Heyning, J. E., & W. F. Perrin. 1994. *Evidence for Two Species of Common Dolphins (Genus* Delphinus*) from the Eastern North Pacific.* Los Angeles County Museum Contributions in Science No. 442. Los Angeles.

Hoffmeister, D. F. 1986. *Mammals of Arizona.* Tucson: University of Arizona Press.

Jaramillo-Legorreta, A. M., L. Rojas-Bracho, & T. Gerrodette. 1999. A new abundance estimate for vaquitas: First step for recovery. *Marine Mammal Science* 15:957–973.

Leatherwood, S., & R. R. Reeves. 1983. *The Sierra Club Handbook of Whales and Dolphins.* San Francisco: Sierra Club Books.

Leatherwood, S., R. R. Reeves, W. F. Perrin, & W. E. Evans. 1988. *Whales, Dolphins, and Porpoises of the Eastern North Pacific and Adjacent Arctic Waters: A Guide to Their Identification.* New York: Dover.

Leopold, A. S. 1959. *Wildlife of Mexico: The Game Birds and Mammals.* Berkeley: University of California Press.

Mellink, E. 1995. Status of the muskrat in the Valle de Mexicali and delta del Río Colorado, Mexico. *California Fish and Game* 81(1):33–38.

Mellink, E., & J. Luévano. 1998. Status of beavers (*Castor canadensis*) in Valle de Mexicali, Mexico. *Bulletin of the Southern California Academy of Sciences* 97(3):115–120.

Mellink, E., J. Luévano, & J. Domínguez. 1999. *Mamíferos de la Peninsula de Baja California (Excluyendo Cetáceos).* Ensenada: CICESE.

Mellink, E., & A. Orozco-Meyer. 2002. A group of gray whales (*Eschrichtius robustus*) in the northeastern Gulf of California, México. *Southwestern Naturalist* 47:129–132.

Morrison, J. I., S. L. Postel, & P. H. Gleick. 1996. *The Sustainable Use of Water in the Lower Colorado River Basin.* Pacific Institute/Global Water Policy Project. Oakland, California: United Nations Environment Programme.

Nava-Romo, J. M. 1995. Impactos a corto y largo plazo en la diversidad y otras características ecológicas de la comunidad bentónico-demersal capturada por la pesquería del camarón en el norte del Alto Golfo de California, México. Master's thesis, Instituto Tecnológico y de Estudios Superiores de Monterrey, Campus Guaymas.

Navarro-Serment, C. J., & S. Manzanilla-Naim. 1999. Stranding of Baird's beaked whales, *Berardius bairdii,* in the upper Gulf of California. *Proceedings of the XXIV International Reunion of the Mexican Society of Marine Mammalogy.* Mazatlán, Sinaloa, Mexico.

Norris, K. S., & W. N. McFarland. 1958. A new harbor porpoise of the genus *Phocoena* from the Gulf of California. *Journal of Mammalogy* 39:22–39.

Pérez-Cortés, H. 1996. Contribución al conocimiento de la biología de la vaquita, *Phocoena sinus.* Master's thesis, Instituto de Ciencias del Mar y Limnología, Universidad Nacional Autónoma de México.

Reeves, R. R., B. D. Smith, E. A. Crespo, & G. N. di Sciara, compilers. 2003. *Dolphins, Whales, and Porpoises: 2002–2010 Conservation Action Plan for the World's Cetaceans.* IUCN/SSC Cetacean Specialist Group. Gland, Switzerland, and Cambridge, U.K.: IUCN.

Rojas-Bracho, L., & B. L. Taylor. 1999. Risk factors affecting the vaquita *(Phocoena sinus). Marine Mammal Science* 15:974–989.

Silber, G. K., M. W. Newcomer, & H. Pérez-Cortés-M. 1990. Killer whales *(Orcinus orca)* attack and kill a Bryde's whale *(Balaenoptera edeni). Canadian Journal of Zoology* 68:1603–1606.

Silber, G. K., M. W. Newcomer, H. Pérez-Cortés-M., & G. M. Ellis. 1994. Cetaceans of the northern Gulf of California: Distribution, occurrence, and relative abundance. *Marine Mammal Science* 10:283–298.

Thomson, D. A., L. T. Findley, & A. N. Kerstitch. 2000. *Reef Fishes of the Sea of Cortez.* Rev. ed. Austin: University of Texas Press.

Urbán R., J., L. Rojas-Bracho, M. Guerrero-Ruíz, A. Jaramillo-Legorreto, & L. T. Findley. 2005. Cetacean diversity and conservation in the Gulf of California. In *Biodiversity, Ecosystems, and Conservation in Northern Mexico,* edited by J.-L. E. Cartron, G. Ceballos, & R. S. Felger, pp. 276–297. New York: Oxford University Press.

Vidal, O. 1995. Population biology and incidental mortality of the vaquita, *Phocoena sinus. Report of the International Whaling Commission* 16:247–272.

Vidal, O., L. T. Findley, & S. Leatherwood. 1993. *Annotated Checklist of the Marine Mammals of the Gulf of California.* Proceedings of the San Diego Society of Natural History No. 28. San Diego.

Vidal, O., & J. P. Gallo-Reynoso. 1996. Die-offs of marine mammals and sea birds in the Gulf of California, Mexico. *Marine Mammal Science* 12:627–635.

29. Invertebrate Biodiversity in the Northern Gulf of California

Alvarez-Borrego, S. 1983. Gulf of California. In *Ecosystems of the World, 26: Estuaries and Enclosed Seas,* edited by B. H. Ketchum, pp. 427–449. New York: Elsevier Scientific.

Alvarez-Borrego, S., & J. R. Lara-Lara. 1991. The physical environment and primary productivity of the Gulf of California. In *The Gulf and Peninsular Province of the Californias,* edited by B. R. T. Simoneit & J. P. Drophin, pp. 555–567. Memoir No. 47. Tulsa, Oklahoma: American Association of Petroleum Geologists.

Astro, R., & T. Hayashi, editors. 1971. *Steinbeck: The Man and His Work.* Corvallis: Oregon State University Press.

Beebe, W. 1938. *The Zaca Venture.* New York: Harcourt, Brace.

Beegel, S. F., S. Shillinglaw, & W. N. Tiffney, Jr., editors. 1997. *Steinbeck and the Environment.* Tuscaloosa: University of Alabama Press.

Bowen, Thomas. 2000. *Unknown Island: Seri Indians, Europeans, and San Estaban Island in the Gulf of California.* Albuquerque: University of New Mexico Press & the University of Arizona Southwest Center.

Bray, N. A., & J. M. Robles. 1991. Physical oceanography of the Gulf of California. In *The Gulf and Peninsular Province of the Californias,* edited by J. P. Dauphin & B. R. T. Simoneit, pp. 511–553. Memoir No. 47. Tulsa, Oklahoma: American Association of Petroleum Geologists.

Briggs, J. C. 1974. *Marine Zoogeography.* New York: McGraw-Hill.

Brusca, R. C. 1973. *A Handbook to the Common Intertidal Invertebrates of the Gulf of California.* Tucson: University Arizona Press.

———. 1980a. The Allan Hancock Foundation of the University Southern California. *Association Systematics Collections Newsletter* 8(1):1–7.

———. 1980b. *Common Intertidal Invertebrates of the Gulf of California.* 2d ed. Tucson: University Arizona Press.

———. 1993. The Arizona/Sea of Cortez years of J. Laurens Barnard. *Journal Natural History* 27: 727–730.

———. 2002a. On the Vermilion Sea. *sonorensis* (Winter): 2–9. Arizona-Sonora Desert Museum, Tucson.

———. 2002b. Biodiversity in the Northern Gulf of California (Biodiversidad en el Golfo de California Norte). *CEDO News* 10(1):1–45.

———. 2004a. The Gulf of California—An overview. In *Seashore Guide to the Northern Gulf of California,* by R. C. Brusca, E. Kimrey, & W. Moore, pp. 1–8. Tucson: Arizona-Sonora Desert Museum.

————. 2004b. A history of discovery in the northern Gulf of California. In *Seashore Guide to the Northern Gulf of California,* by R. C. Brusca, E. Kimrey, & W. Moore, pp. 9–24. Tucson: Arizona-Sonora Desert Museum.

Brusca, R. C., & G. C. Bryner. 2004. A case study of two Mexican biosphere reserves: The Upper Gulf of California/Colorado River Delta and Pinacate/Gran Desierto de Altar Biosphere Reserves. In *Science and Politics in the International Environment,* edited by N. E. Harrison & G. C. Bryner, pp. 21–52. New York: Rowman & Littlefield.

Brusca, R. C., J. Campoy Fabela, C. Castillo Sánchez, R. Cudney-Bueno, L. T. Findley, J. García-Hernández, E. Glenn, I. Granillo, M. E. Hendrickx, J. Murrieta, C. Nagel, M. Román, & P. Turk Boyer. 2001. A case study of two Mexican biosphere reserves: The Upper Gulf of California/Colorado River Delta and Pinacate/Gran Desierto de Altar biosphere reserves. 2000 UNESCO Conference on Biodiversity and Society. *Columbia University Earthscape* (an electronic journal), www.earthscape.org/rr1/cbs01.html.

Brusca, R. C., L. T. Findley, P. A. Hastings, M. E. Hendrickx, J. Torre Cosio, & A. M. van der Heiden. 2005. Biodiversity in the Gulf of California (Sea of Cortez). In *Biodiversity, Ecosystems, and Conservation in Northern Mexico,* edited by J.-L. E. Cartron, G. Ceballos, & R. S. Felger, pp. 179–203. New York: Oxford University Press.

Brusca, R. C., E. Kimrey, & W. Moore. 2004. *Seashore Guide to the Northern Gulf of California.* Tucson: Arizona-Sonora Desert Museum.

Brusca, R. C., & D. A. Thomson. 1977. The Pulmo Reefs of Baja California—True coral reef formation in the Gulf of California. *Ciencias Marinas* 1(3):37–53.

Brusca, R. C., & B. R. Wallerstein. 1979. Zoogeographic patterns of idoteid isopods in the northeast Pacific, with a review of shallow-water zoogeography for the region. *Bulletin of the Biological Society of Washington* 3:67–105.

Carpenter, P. P. 1857. Report on the state of our knowledge with regard to the Mollusca of the west coast of North America. *Report, British Association for the Advancement of Science, for 1856:* 159–368.

Carriquiry, J. D., & A. Sánchez. 1999. Sedimentation in the Colorado River delta and upper Gulf of California after nearly a century of discharge loss. *Marine Geology* 158:125–145.

Castro-Aguirre, J. L., & R. Torres-Orozco. 1993. Consideraciones acerca del origen de la ictiofauna de Bahía Magdalena-Almejas, un sistema lagunar de la costa occidental de Baja California Sur, México. *Anales de la Escuela Nacional de Ciencias Biológicas de México* 38:67–73.

Cudney-Bueno, R. 2000. Management and conservation of benthic resources harvested by small-scale hookah divers in the northern Gulf of California,

Mexico: The black murex snail fishery. Master's thesis, University of Arizona.

D'Agrosa, C., O. Vidal, & W. C. Graham. 1995. Mortality of the vaquita *(Phocoena sinus)* in gillnet fisheries during 1993–1994. In *Biology of Phocoenids,* special issue 16, edited by A. Bjorge & G. Donovan, pp. 283–291. Cambridge: IWC.

Dayton, P. K., S. Thrush, & F. C. Coleman. 2002. *Ecological Effects of Fishing in Marine Ecosystems of the United States.* Arlington, Virginia: Pew Oceans Commission.

Diario Oficial. 1993. Decreto por el que se declara area natural protegida con el carácter de Reserva de la Biosfera, la región conocida como Alto Golfo de California y Delta del Río Colorado, ubicada en aguas del Golfo de California y los municipios de Mexicali, B.C., de Puerto Peñasco y San Luis Río Colorado, Sonora. *Diario Oficial de la Federación,* June 10, pp. 24–28. Mexico City.

Duque-Caro, H. 1990. Neogene stratigraphy, palaeoceanography, and palaeobiogeography in northwest South America and the evolution of the Panama Seaway. *Palaeogeography, Palaeoclimatology, Palaeoecology* 77:203–234.

Engel, J., & R. Kvitek. 1998. Effects of otter trawling on a benthic community in Monterey Bay National Marine Sanctuary. *Conservation Biology* 12:1204–1214.

Evermann, B. W., & O. P. Jenkins. 1891. Report upon a collection of fishes made at Guaymas, Sonora, Mexico, with descriptions of new species. *Proceedings U.S. National Museum* 14(846):121–165.

Ezcurra, E., R. S. Felger, A. D. Russell, & M. Equihua. 1988. Freshwater islands in a desert sand sea: The hydrology, flora, and phytogeography of the Gran Desierto oases of northwestern Mexico. *Desert Plants* 9(2):35–44, 55–63.

Felger, R. S. 2000. *Flora of the Gran Desierto and Río Colorado of Northwestern Mexico.* Tucson: University of Arizona Press.

Findley, L. T., M. E. Hendrickx, R. C. Brusca, A. M. van der Heiden, P. A. Hastings, & J. Torre. In press. *Macrofauna del Golfo de California (Macrofauna of the Gulf of California).* CD-ROM version 1.0. Macrofauna Golfo Project. Washington, D.C.: Conservation International. [Spanish and English editions]

Foster, J. W. 1975. Shell middens, paleoecology, and prehistory: The case from Estero Morua, Sonora, Mexico. *Kiva* 41:185–194.

Galindo-Bect, M. S., E. P. Glenn, H. M. Page, K. Fitzsimmons, L. A. Galindo-Bect, J. M. Hernández-Ayon, R. L. Petty, J. García-Hernández, & D. Moore. 2000. Penaeid shrimp landings in the upper Gulf of California in relation to Colorado River freshwater discharge. *Fisheries Bulletin* 98:222–225.

García-Caudillo, J. M. 1999. El uso de los excluidores de peces en la pesca comercial de camarón: Situación actual y perspectivas. *Pesca y Conservación* 3(7):5.

Gifford, E. W. 1946. Archaeology in the Punta Peñasco region, Sonora. *American Antiquity* 11:215–221.

Gilbert, C. H. 1892. Scientific results of explorations by the U.S. Fish Commission steamer *Albatross.* XXII. Descriptions of thirty-four new species of fishes collected in 1888 and 1889, principally among the Santa Barbara Islands and in the Gulf of California. *Proceedings U.S. National Museum* 14[for 1891](880):539–566.

Glenn, E. P., J. García, R. Tanner, C. Congdon, & D. Luecke. 1999. Status of wetlands supported by agricultural drainage water in the Colorado River delta, Mexico. *HortScience* 34:39–45.

Glenn, E. P., C. Lee, R. Felger, & S. Zengel. 1996. Effects of water management on the wetlands of the Colorado River delta, Mexico. *Conservation Biology* 10:1175–1186.

Glenn, E. P., P. L. Nagler, R. C. Brusca, & Osvel Hinojosa-Huerta. 2005. Coastal wetlands of the northern Gulf of California: Inventory and conservation status. *Aquatic Conservation* 16:5–28.

Greenberg, J. B., & C. Vélez-Ibáñez. 1993. Community dynamics in a time of crisis: An ethnographic overview of the upper gulf. In *Maritime Community and Biosphere Reserve: Crisis and Response in the Upper Gulf of California,* edited by T. R. McGuire & J. B. Greenberg, pp. 12–28. Occasional Paper No. 2, Bureau of Applied Research in Anthropology. Tucson: University of Arizona.

Hedgpeth, J. W. 1978. *The Outer Shores. Parts 1 and 2: Ed Ricketts and John Steinbeck Explore the Pacific Coast.* Eureka, California: Mad River Press.

Hendrickx, M. E., R. C. Brusca, & L. T. Findley, editors. 2005. *A Distributional Checklist of the Macrofauna of the Gulf of California, Mexico. Part 1. Invertebrates. [Listado y Distribución de la Macrofauna del Golfo de California, México. Parte 1. Invertebrades.]* Tucson: Arizona-Sonora Desert Museum and Conservation International.

Hendrickx, M. E., & A. Toledano-Granados. 1994. *Catálogo de moluscos pelecípodos, gasterópodos y poliplacoforos: Colección de referencia.* Estación Mazatlán, ICML, UNAM, and CONABIO.

Hornaday, W. T. 1908. *Camp-Fires on Desert and Lava.* New York: Scribner's. Reprint. Tucson: University of Arizona Press, 1983.

Jordan, D. S. 1895. The fishes of Sinaloa. *Proceedings of the California Academy of Sciences* 5:377–514. Reprinted in Contributions to Biology, Hopkins Laboratory of Biology, Stanford University Publications No. 1, pp. 1–71.

Jordan, D. S., & C. H. Gilbert. 1882. Catalogue of the fishes collected by Mr. John Xantus at Cape San Lucas, which are now in the United States National Museum, with descriptions of eight new species. *Proceedings of the U.S. National Museum* 5(290): 353–371.

Kowalewski, M., G. E. Avila Serrano, K. W. Flessa, & G. A. Goodfriend. 2000. Dead delta's former pro-ductivity: Two trillion shells at the mouth of the Colorado River. *Geology* 28:1059–1062.

Lavín, M. F., V. M. Godínez, & L. G. Alvarez. 1998. Inverse-estuarine features of the upper Gulf of California. *Estuarine, Coastal, Shelf Science* 47:769–795.

Lumholtz, C. 1912. *New Trails in Mexico.* New York: Charles Scribner's Sons.

Maluf, L. Y. 1983. Physical oceanography. In *Island Biogeography in the Sea of Cortéz,* edited by T. J. Case & M. L. Cody, pp. 26–45. Berkeley: University of California Press.

Morales-Abril, G. 1994. Reserva de la Biósfera Alto Golfo de California y Delta del Río Colorado. *Ecologica* 3:26–27.

Musick, J. A., M. M. Harbin, S. A. Berkeley, G. H. Burgess, A. M. Eklund, L. Findley, R. G. Gilmore, J. T. Golden, D. S. Ha, G. R. Huntsman, J. C. McGovern, S. J. Parker, S. G. Poss, E. Sala, T. W. Schmidt, G. R. Sedberry, H. Weeks, & S. G. Wright. 2000. Marine, estuarine, and diadromous fish stocks at risk of extinction in North America (exclusive of Pacific salmonids). *Fisheries* 25(11):6–30.

Pérez-Mellado, J., & L. T. Findley. 1985. Evaluación de la ictiofauna acompañante del camarón capturado en las costas de Sonora y norte de Sinaloa, México. In *Recursos Potentiales de México: La Pesca Acompañante del Camarón,* edited by A. Yañéz-Arancibia, pp. 201–254. Programa Universitario de Alimentos, Instituto de Ciencias del Mar y Limnología, Instituto Nacional de la Pesca. Mexico City: Universidad Nacional Autónoma de México.

Ricketts, E., & J. Calvin. 1939. *Between Pacific Tides.* Stanford: Stanford University Press.

Ritter, E. W. 1985. Investigations of archaeological variability in northeastern Baja California Sur, Mexico. *The Archaeology of West and Northwest Mesoamerica,* edited by M. S. Foster & P. C. Weigand, pp. 393–418. Boulder, Colorado: Westview Press.

———. 1998. Investigations of prehistoric behavioral ecology and culture change within the Bahía de Los Angeles region, Baja California. *Pacific Coast Archaeological Society Quarterly* 34(3):9–43.

Rodríguez, C. A., K. W. Flessa, & D. L. Dettman. 2001. Effects of upstream diversion of Colorado River water on the estuarine bivalve mollusc *Mulinia coloradoensis. Conservation Biology* 15:249–258.

Rosenblatt, R. H. 1967. The zoogeographic relationships of the marine shore fishes of tropical America. *Studies in Tropical Oceanography* 5:570–592.

Rosenblatt, R. H., & R. S. Waples. 1986. A genetic comparison of allopatric populations of shore fish species from the eastern and central Pacific Ocean: Dispersal or vicariance? *Copeia* 1986:275–284.

Sala, E., O. Aburto-Oropeza, G. Paredes, I. Parra, J. C. Barrera, & P. K. Dayton. 2002. A general model for designing networks of marine reserves. *Science* 298:1991–1993.

Sala, E., O. Aburto-Oropeza, G. Paredes, & G. Thompson. In press. Spawning aggregations and reproductive behavior of reef fishes in the Gulf of California. *Bulletin of Marine Science.*

Schwartzlose, R. A., D. Alvarez-Millán, & P. Brueggeman. 1992. *Golfo de California: Bibliografía de las Ciencias Marinas.* Ensenada: Instituto de Investigaciones Oceanológicas, Universidad Autónoma de Baja California.

Snyder-Conn, E., & R. C. Brusca. 1977. Shrimp population dynamics and fishery impact in the northern Gulf of California. *Ciencias Marinas* 1(3):54–67.

Steinbeck, J. 1945. *Cannery Row.* New York: Penguin Books.

Steinbeck, J., & E. F. Ricketts. 1941. *Sea of Cortez: A Leisurely Journal of Travel and Research.* New York: Viking Press.

Stuiver, M., and P. J. Reimer. 1993. Extended 14C database and revised CALIB radiocarbon calibration program. *Radiocarbon* 35:215–230.

Thomson, D. A., L. T. Findley, & A. N. Kerstitch. 1979. *Reef Fishes of the Sea of Cortez: The Rocky-Shore Fishes of the Gulf of California.* New York: John Wiley & Sons.

———. 2000. *Reef Fishes of the Sea of Cortez: The Rocky-Shore Fishes of the Gulf of California.* Rev. ed. Austin: University of Texas Press.

University of Southern California. 1985. *Catalog of Allan Hancock Foundation Publications.* Los Angeles: University of Southern California.

Van Syoc, R. J. 1992. Living and fossil populations of a western Atlantic barnacle, *Balanus subalbidus* Henry, 1974, in the Gulf of California region. *Proceedings of the San Diego Society of Natural History* 12:9–27.

Vidal, O. 1995. Population biology and incidental mortality of the vaquita, *Phocoena sinus.* Special issue, *Report of the International Whaling Commission,* No. 16, pp. 247–272.

Walker, B. W. 1960. The distribution and affinities of the marine fish fauna of the Gulf of California. *Systematic Zoology* 9(3–4):123–133.

Watling, L., & E. A. Norse. 1998. Disturbance of the seabed by mobile fishing gear: A comparison to forest clearcutting. *Conservation Biology* 12:1180–1197.

Whitmore, R. C., R. C. Brusca, J. L. León de la Luz, P. González-Zamorano, R. Mendoza-Salgado, E. S. Amador-Silva, G. Holguin, F. Galván-Magaña, P. A. Hastings, J.-L. E. Cartron, R. S. Felger, J. A. Seminoff, & C. C. McIvor. 2005. The ecological importance of mangroves in Baja California Sur: Conservation implications for an endangered ecosystem. In *Biodiversity, Ecosystems, and Conservation in Northern Mexico,* edited by J.-L. E. Cartron, G. Ceballos, & R. S. Felger, pp. 298–333. New York: Oxford University Press.

Zeitzschel, B. 1969. Primary productivity in the Gulf of California. *Marine Biology* 3(3): 201–207.

30. Sea Turtles of the Alto Golfo: A Struggle for Survival

Agler, W. E. 1913. Green turtles in lower California. *U.S. Bureau of Foreign and Domestic Commerce, Daily Consular and Trade Reports* No. 55 (March 6): 1181.

Alvarado, J., & A. Figueroa. 1992. Recapturas post-anidatorias de hembras de tortuga marina negra *(Chelonia agassizi)* marcadas en Michoacán, México. *Biotropica* 24:560–560.

Aschmann, H. 1966. *The Natural and Human History of Baja California.* Los Angeles: Dawson's Book Shop.

Averett, W. E. 1920. Lower California green turtle fishery. *Pacific Fishermen* 18:24–25.

Bjorndal, K. A. 1997. Foraging ecology and nutrition of sea turtles. In *The Biology of Sea Turtles,* edited by P. L. Lutz & J. A. Musick, pp. 199–232. Boca Raton: CRC Press.

Bocourt, M. 1868. Description de quelqes cheloniens nouveaux appartenant à la faune mexicaine. *Annales des Sciences Naturelles Zoologie et Biologie Animale* 10:121–122.

Boyer, R. 1995. Turtle hatching/Nacimiento de caguamas. *CEDO News/Noticias del CEDO* (Centro de Estudios de Desiertos y Océanos) 7:1, 5–6.

Bowen, B. W., F. A. Abreu-Grobois, G. H. Balazs, N. Kamezaki, C. J. Limpus, & R. J. Ferl. 1995. Trans-Pacific migrations of the loggerhead sea turtle demonstrated with mitochondrial DNA markers. *Proceedings of the National Academy of Sciences* 92:3731–3734.

Brusca, R. C. 1980. *Common Intertidal Invertebrates of the Gulf of California.* 2d ed. Tucson: University of Arizona Press.

Caldwell, D. K. 1962. Carapace length–body weight relationship and size and sex ratio of the northeastern Pacific green turtle, *Chelonia mydas carrinegra. Contributions in Science at Los Angeles City Museum* 62:3–10.

———. 1963. The sea turtle fishery of Baja California, México. *California Fish and Game* 49:140–151.

Caldwell, D. K., & M. C. Caldwell. 1962. The black "steer" of the Gulf of California. *Los Angeles County Museum of Science and History Quarterly* 61:1–31.

Carr, A. 1961. Pacific turtle problem. *Natural History* 70:64–71.

———. 1987. New perspectives on the pelagic stage of sea turtle development. *Conservation Biology* 1:103.

Carr, A., & A. B. Meylan. 1980. Evidence of passive migration of green turtle hatchlings in Sargassum. *Copeia* 1980:366–368.

Chaloupka, M. Y., & J. A. Musick. 1997. Age, growth, and population dynamics. In *The Biology of Sea Turtles,* edited by P. L. Lutz & J. A. Musick, pp. 233–274. Boca Raton: CRC Press.

Cliffton, K., D. O. Cornejo, & R. S. Felger. 1982. Sea turtles of the Pacific coast of México. In *Biology and Conservation of Sea Turtles,* edited by K. A. Bjorndal, pp. 199–209. Washington, D.C.: Smithsonian Institution Press.

Cornelius, S. E. 1982. Status of sea turtles along the Pacific coast of Middle America. In *Biology and Conservation of Sea Turtles,* edited by K. A. Bjorndal, pp. 211–219. Washington, D.C.: Smithsonian Institution Press.

Craig, J. A. 1926. A new fishery in México. *California Fish and Game* 12:166–169.

Cudney-Bueno, R. J., & P. J. Turk Boyer. 1998. *Pescando entre Mareas del Alto Golfo de California.* Puerto Peñasco, Sonora: Centro Intercultural de Estudios de Desiertos y Océanos.

Delgado, S., & W. J. Nichols. 2005. Saving sea turtles from the ground up: Awakening sea turtle conservation in northwestern Mexico. *Maritime Studies* 3/4:89–104.

Diario Oficial. 1990. Acuerdo por el que se establece veda para las especies y subespecies de tortuga marina en aguas de jurisdicción federal del Golfo de México y Mar Caribe, así como en las costas del Océano Pacífico, incluyendo el Golfo de California. *Diario Oficial de la Federación,* May 28. Mexico City.

———. 1999. Modificación a la Norma Oficial Mexicana 002-PESC-1993, Para ordenar aprovechameinto de las especies de camarón en aguas de jurisdicción federal de los Estados Unidos Mexicanos, publicada el 31 de diciembre de 1993. *Diario Oficial de la Federación,* December 29. Mexico City.

Dutton, D. L., P. H. Dutton, R. Boulon, W. C. Coles, & M. Y. Chaloupka. 2003. New insights into population biology of leatherbacks from 20 years of research: Profile of a Caribbean nesting population in recovery. In *Proceedings of the Twenty-Second Annual Symposium on Sea Turtle Biology and Conservation,* edited by J. A. Seminoff, pp. 1–2. NOAA Technical Memorandum NMFS-SEFSC-503. Miami.

Eckert, S. A., K. L. Eckert, P. Ponganis, & G. L. Kooyman, 1989. Diving and foraging behavior of leatherback sea turtles *(Dermochelys coriacea). Canadian Journal of Zoology* 67:2834–2840.

Eckert, S. A., & L. Sarti. 1997. Distant fisheries implicated in the loss of the world's largest leatherback nesting population. *Marine Turtle Newsletter* 78:2–7.

Felger, R. S., K. Cliffton, & P. J. Regal. 1976. Winter dormancy in sea turtles: Independent discovery and exploitation in the Gulf of California, México, by two local cultures. *Science* 191:283–285.

Felger, R. A., & M. B. Moser. 1985. *People of the Desert and Sea: Ethnobotany of the Seri Indians.* Tucson: University of Arizona Press.

Felger, R. S., W. J. Nichols, & J. A. Seminoff. 2005. Sea turtles in northwestern Mexico: Conservation, ethnobiology, and desperation. In *Biodiversity, Ecosystems, and Conservation in Northwestern Mexico,* edited by J.-L. E. Cartron, G. Ceballos, & R. S. Felger, pp. 405–424. New York: Oxford University Press.

Figueroa, A., J. Alvarado, F. Hernández, G. Rodríguez, & J. Robles. 1993. *The Ecological Recovery of Sea Turtles of Michoacán, Mexico: Special Attention to the Black Turtle* (Chelonia agassizi). Final report to WWF-USFWS, Albuquerque, New Mexico.

Frazier, J. 2003. Prehistoric and ancient historic interactions between humans and marine turtles. In *The Biology of Sea Turtles,* vol. 2, edited by P. L. Lutz, J. A. Musick, & J. Wyneken, pp. 1–38. Boca Raton: CRC Press.

Fritts, T. H., M. L. Stinson, & R. Marquez M. 1982. Status of sea turtle nesting in southern Baja California, Mexico. *Bulletin of the Southern California Academy of Sciences* 81:51–60.

Gardner, S. C., & W. J. Nichols. 2001. Assessment of sea turtle mortality rates in the Bahía Magdalena region, Baja California Sur, México. *Chelonian Conservation and Biology* 4:197–199.

Groombridge, B., & R. Luxmoore. 1989. *The Green Turtle and Hawksbill (Reptilia: Cheloniidae): World Status, Exploitation, and Trade.* Lausanne, Switzerland: Secretariat of the Convention on International Trade in Endangered Species of Wild Fauna and Flora.

Hilton-Taylor, C., compiler. 2000. *2000 IUCN Red List of Threatened Species.* Gland, Switzerland, and Cambridge, U.K.: IUCN.

Karl, S. A., & B. W. Bowen. 1999. Evolutionary significant units versus geopolitical taxonomy: Molecular systematics of an endangered sea turtle genus. *Conservation Biology* 13:990–999.

Kopitsky, K. L., R. L. Pitman, & P. H. Dutton. 2005. Aspects of olive ridley feeding ecology in the eastern tropical Pacific. In *Proceedings of the Twenty-first Annual Symposium on Sea Turtle Biology and Conservation,* edited by M. Coyne & R. D. Clark, p. 217. NOAA Tech. Memo. NMFS-SEFSC-528.

López-Mendilaharsu, M. 2002. Ecología alimenticia de *Chelonia mydas agassizii* en Bahía Magdalena, Baja California Sur, México. Master's thesis, Centro de Investigaciones Biológicas del Noroeste, S.C., Mexico.

López-Mendilaharsu, M., S. Gardner, & J. A. Seminoff. 2003. Natural history notes: *Chelonia mydas agassizii* (east Pacific green turtle); Diet. *Herpetological Review* 34:139–140.

Márquez, R., M. Jiménez, M. A. Carrasco, & N. A. Villanueva. 1998. Comments on the population trends of sea turtles of the *Lepidochelys* genus, after total ban of 1990. *Oceanides* 13:41–62.

Meylan, A. B., & M. Donnelly. 1999. Status justification for listing the hawksbill turtle *(Eretmochelys imbricata)* as critically endangered on the 1996 IUCN Red List of threatened animals. *Chelonian Conservation and Biology* 3:200–224.

Moser, E. W. 1963. Seri bands. *Kiva* 28:14–27.

Musick, J. A., & C. J. Limpus. 1997. Habitat utilization and migration in juvenile sea turtles. In *The Biology of Sea Turtles,* edited by P. L. Lutz & J. A. Musick, pp. 137–164. Boca Raton: CRC Press.

Nabhan, G. P. 2003. *Singing the Turtles to Sea.* Berkeley: University of California Press.

Navarro, C. 1997. Tide bits: Turtle hatching. *CEDO News* 7(4):29, 32.

Nichols, W. J. 2003. Biology and conservation of the sea turtles of Baja California. Ph.D. dissertation, University of Arizona.

Nichols, W. J., K. E. Bird, & S. García. 2000. Community-based research and its application to sea turtle conservation in Bahía Magdalena, BCS, Mexico. *Marine Turtle Newsletter* 89:4–7.

Nichols, W. J., L. Brooks, M. López, & J. A. Seminoff. 2001. Record of pelagic east Pacific green turtles associated with *Macrocystis* mats near Baja California Sur, Mexico. *Marine Turtle Newsletter* 93:10–11.

Nichols, W. J., A. Resendiz, J. A. Seminoff, & B. Resendiz. 2000. Transpacific migration of a loggerhead turtle monitored by satellite telemetry. *Bulletin of Marine Science* 67:937–947.

Nichols, J. W., and C. Safina. 2004. Lunch with a turtle poacher. *Conservation in Practice* 5:30–36.

Nichols, W. J., J. A. Seminoff, A. Resendiz, P. Dutton, & F. A. Abreu-Grobois. 1999. Using molecular genetics and biotelemetry to study life history and long distance movement: A tale of two turtles. In *Proceedings of the Eighteenth Annual Symposium on Sea Turtle Biology and Conservation,* compiled by F. A. Abreu-Grobois, R. Briseño-Dueñas, R. Márquez-Millan, & L. Sarti-Martínez, pp. 102–103. NOAA Technical Memorandum NMFS-SEFC-436. Miami.

Norris, J. N. 1975. Marine algae of the northern Gulf of California. Ph.D. dissertation, University of California, Santa Barbara.

Olguín-Mena, M. 1990. Las tortugas marinas en la costa oriental de Baja California y costa occidental de Baja California Sur, México. Master's thesis, Universidad Autonoma B.C.S., La Paz, México.

Paladino, F. V., M. P. O'Connor, & J. R. Spotila. 1990. Metabolism of leatherback turtles: Gigantothermy and thermoregulation of dinosaurs. *Nature* 344:858–860.

Parsons, J. J. 1962. *The Green Turtle and Man.* Gainesville: University Presses of Florida.

Pitman, R. L. 1990. Pelagic distribution and biology of sea turtles in the eastern tropical Pacific. Pages 143–148 In *Proceedings of the Tenth Annual Symposium on Sea Turtle Biology and Conservation,* compiled by T. H. Richardson, J. I. Richardson, & M. Donnelly, pp. 143–148. NOAA Technical Memorandum NMFS-SEFC-278. Miami.

Pritchard, P. C. H. 1999. Status of the black turtle. *Conservation Biology* 13:1000–1003.

Pritchard, P. C. H., & P. Trebbau. 1984. *Turtles of Venezuela.* Oxford, Ohio: Society for the Study of Amphibians and Reptiles.

Resendiz, A., B. Resendiz, W. J. Nichols, J. A. Seminoff, & N. Kamezaki. 1998. First confirmation of a trans-Pacific migration of a tagged loggerhead sea turtle (*Caretta caretta),* released in Baja California. *Pacific Science* 52:151–153.

Seminoff, J. A. 1994. Conservation of the marine turtles of Mexico: A survey of nesting beach conservation projects. Master's thesis, University of Arizona.

———. 2000. The biology of the east Pacific green turtle (*Chelonia mydas agassizii*) at a warm temperate foraging area in the Gulf of California, Mexico. Ph.D. dissertation, University of Arizona.

Seminoff, J. A., J. A. Alvarado, C. Delgado, J. L. López, & G. Hoeffer. 2002. First direct evidence of a green sea turtle migration from Michoacán, México, to a foraging area along the Sonoran Coast of the Gulf of California. *Southwestern Naturalist* 47:314–316.

Seminoff, J. A., J. L. Lopez, G. Hoeffer, H. Romero, L. Monti, & G. Nabhan. 2005. Sea turtles and Seris: Benefits of a binational stewardship program in the Infiernillo Channel, Gulf of California, México. In *Proceedings of the Twenty-first Annual Symposium on Sea Turtle Biology and Conservation,* edited by M. Coyne & R. D. Clark, p. 320–321. NOAA Tech. Memo. NMFS-SEFSC-528.

Seminoff, J. A., W. J. Nichols, A. Resendiz, & L. Brooks. 2003. Occurrence of hawksbill turtles, *Eretmochelys imbricata,* near Baja California. *Pacific Science* 57:9–16.

Seminoff, J. A., W. J. Nichols, A. Resendiz, & S. Hidalgo. 2000. *Chelonia mydas agassizii* (east Pacific green turtle): Diet. *Herpetological Review* 31:103.

Seminoff, J. A., A. Resendiz, S. Hidalgo, & W. J. Nichols. 2002. Diet of the east Pacific green turtle, *Chelonia mydas,* in the central Gulf of California, México. *Journal of Herpetology* 36:447–453.

Seminoff, J. A., A. Resendiz, & W. J. Nichols. 2002. Home range of the green turtle (*Chelonia mydas*) at a coastal foraging ground in the Gulf of California, México. *Marine Ecology Progress Series* 242:253–265.

Seminoff, J. A., A. Resendiz, W. J. Nichols, & T. T. Jones. 2002. Growth rates of wild green turtles (*Chelonia mydas*) at a temperate foraging habitat in the Gulf of California, México. *Copeia* 2002:610–617.

Seminoff, J. A., A. Resendiz, B. Resendiz, & W. J. Nichols. 2004. Occurrence of loggerhead sea turtles (*Caretta caretta*) in the Gulf of California, Mexico: Evidence of life-history variation in the Pacific Ocean. *Herpetological Review* 35:24–27.

Shaw, C. E. 1947. First records of the red-brown loggerhead turtle from the eastern Pacific. *Herpetologica* 4:55–56.

Spotila, J. R., R. D. Reina, A. C. Steyermark, P. T. Plotkin, & F. V. Paladino. 2000. Pacific leatherback turtles face extinction. *Nature* 405:529–530.

Townsend, C. H. 1916. Voyage of the *Albatross* to the Gulf of California in 1911. *Bulletin of the American Museum of Natural History* 31; Art. 13:117–130.

Vidal, O. 1993. Aquatic mammal conservation in Latin America: Problems and perspectives. *Conservation Biology* 7:788–795.

Wagner, H. R. 1929. *Spanish Voyages to the Northwest Coast of America in the Sixteenth Century.* San Francisco: California Historical Society.

Witham, R., & C. R. Futch. 1977. Early growth and oceanic survival of pen-reared sea turtles. *Herpetologica* 33:404–409.

Witzell, W. 1983. *Synopsis of Biological Data on the Hawksbill Turtle Eretmochelys imbricata (Linnaeus, 1766)*. FAO Fisheries Synopsis No. 137. Rome: FAO.

31. In Search of *El Burro,* the Tidal Bore of the Río Colorado Delta

Bowden, C. 1987. The last wave. *City Magazine* 2(1): 42–48.

Bureau of Reclamation. 1975. *Final Environmental Statement, Colorado Basin Salinity Control Project, Title I*. Washington, D.C.: Government Printing Office.

Chanson, H. 2001. Flow field in a tidal bore: A physical model. In *Proceedings of the 29th IAHR Congress, Beijing, Theme E,* pp. 365–373. Beijing: Tsinghua University Press.

Clancy, E. P. 1968. *The Tides, Pulse of the Earth*. Garden City, New York: Doubleday.

Daniels, M., & E. Daniels. 1954. Tidal bore. *Arizona Highways* 30(5):24–29.

Derby, G. H. 1852. *Report to the Secretary of War Communicating a Reconnaissance of the Gulf of California and the Colorado River*. Senate Executive Document 81, 32d Congress, 1st session. Washington, D.C.: Government Printing Office.

Fox, W. T. 1983. *At the Sea's Edge: An Introduction to Coastal Oceanography for the Amateur Naturalist*. New York: Prentice Hall.

Freeman, L. R. 1923. *The Colorado River Yesterday, Today, and Tomorrow*. New York: Dodd, Mead.

Gordon, J. H. 1924. Tidal bore at the mouth of the Colorado River. *Monthly Weather Review* 52:98–99.

Hardy, R. W. H. 1977. *Travels in the Interior of Mexico in 1825, 1826, 1827, and 1828*. Glorieta, New Mexico: Rio Grande Press.

Hendricks, W. O. 1990. The forest of the American Nile. *Perspectives: Sherman Library and Gardens* 24:1–5.

Ives, J. C. 1861. *Report upon the Colorado River of the West, Explored in 1857 and 1858 by Lieutenant Joseph C. Ives, Corps of Topographical Engineers, Under the Direction of the Office of Explorations and Surveys, A. A. Humphreys, Captain Topographical Engineers, in Charge*. Washington, D.C.: Government Printing Office.

Kira, G. S. 2000. *The Unforgettable Sea of Cortez: Baja California's Golden Age, 1947–1977; The Life and Writings of Ray Cannon*. Torrance, California: Cortez Publications.

Krygier, J. B. 1997. Envisioning the American West: Maps, the representational barrage of nineteenth-century expedition reports, and the production of scientific knowledge. *Cartography and GIS* 24(1):27–50.

Leavitt, F. H. 1943. Steam navigation on the Colorado River. *California Historical Society Quarterly* 22(1943):1–25, 151–172.

Leigh, R. 1941. *Forgotten Waters*. New York: J. B. Lippincott.

Lingenfelter, R. E. 1978. *Steamboats on the Colorado River*. Tucson: University of Arizona Press.

Luecke, D. F., J. Pitt, C. Congdon, E. Glenn, C. Valdés-Casillas, & M. Briggs. 1999. *A Delta Once More: Restoring Riparian and Wetland Habitat in the Colorado River Delta*. Washington, D.C.: EDF.

Lynch, D. K. 1982. Tidal bores. *Scientific American* 247(4):146–156.

Martin, R. 1989. *A Story That Stands Like a Dam: Glen Canyon and the Struggle for the Soul of the West*. New York: Henry Holt.

Pattie, J. O. [1833] 1930. *The Personal Narrative of James O. Pattie of Kentucky*. Edited by Timothy Flint. Chicago: Lakeside Press.

Rowbotham, F. W. 1983. *The Severn Bore*. London: David & Charles.

Sykes, Godfrey G. 1891–1892. Unpublished diary: "Sch *Hilda,*" in possession of the Sykes family.

———. 1893–1902. Unpublished diary. Microfilm from the Huntington Library, California.

———. 1903. Unpublished daily diary, in possession of the Sykes family.

Sykes, G. 1937. *The Colorado Delta*. Special Publication No. 19. New York: American Geographical Society.

———. 1944. *A Westerly Trend . . . Being a Veracious Chronicle of More Than Sixty Years of Joyous Wanderings, Mainly in Search of Space and Sunshine*. Tucson: Arizona Pioneers Historical Society.

Thompson, R. W. 1968. *Tidal Flat Sedimentation on the Colorado River Delta, Northwestern Gulf of California*. Geological Society of America Memoir No. 107. New York.

Tricker, R. A. R. 1964. *Bores, Breakers, Waves, and Wakes*. New York: American Elsevier.

U.S. Army Corps of Engineers, Los Angeles District. 1982. *Colorado River Basin, Hoover Dam, Review of Flood Control Regulation, Final Report*. Washington, D.C.: Government Printing Office.

Waters, F. 1946. *The Colorado*. New York: Rinehart & Company.

33. Conservation and Landscape Transformation in Northwestern Mexico

Anaya, A. L., J. Arévalo, E. M. Hentshel, J. J. Consejo, & D. Gutiérrez. 1992. Las áreas naturales protegidas como alternativa de conservación: Bosquejo histórico y problemática de México. In *Las Áreas Naturales Protegidas de México,* edited by A. L. Anaya, pp. 15–37. Mexico City: Sociedad Botánica de México.

Archer, S. 1989. Have southern Texas savannas been converted to woodlands in recent history? *American Naturalist* 134:545–561.

———. 1994. Woody plant encroachment into southwestern grasslands and savannas: Rates, patterns, and proximate causes. In *Ecological Implications of Livestock Herbivory in the West,* edited by M. Vavra, W. A. Laycock, & R. D. Pieper. Denver: Society for Range Management.

Arriaga, L., J. M. Espinoza-Rodríguez, C. Aguilar-Zúñiga, E. Martínez-Romero, L. Gómez-Mendoza, & E. Loa. 2000. *Regiones Terrestres Prioritarias de México.* Mexico City: CONABIO.

Bahre, C. J. 1991. *A Legacy of Change: Historic Impact on Vegetation of the Arizona Borderlands.* Tucson: University of Arizona Press.

Barral, H. 1988. El hombre y su impacto en los ecosistemas a través del ganado. In *Estudio Integrado de los Recursos Vegetación, Suelo y Agua en la Reserva de la Biosfera de Mapimí. I. Ambiente Natural y Humano,* edited by C. Montaña, pages 241–268. Mexico City: Instituto de Ecología.

Benítez, H., & E. Loa. 1996. Regiones prioritarias para la conservación en México. *Biodiversitas* 2:7–10.

Bergman, C. 2002. *Red Delta: Fighting for Life at the End of the Colorado Delta.* Golden, Colorado: Defenders of Wildlife, Fulcrum Publishers.

Brown, D. E., editor. 1982. Biotic Communities of the American Southwest United States and Mexico. Special issue, *Desert Plants* 4:1–342.

Brown, D. E., & C. H. Lowe. 1980. *Biotic Communities of the Southwest.* General Technical Report No. RM-78. Fort Collins, Colorado: USDA, Forest Service, Rocky Mountain Forest and Range Experiment Station.

Búrquez, A. 1997. Distributional limits of Euglossine and Meliponine bees (Hymenoptera: Apidae) in northwestern Mexico. *Pan-Pacific Entomologist* 73:137–140.

Búrquez, A., & C. Castillo. 1994. Reserva de la Biosfera El Pinacate y Gran Desierto de Altar: Entorno biológico y social. *Estudios Sociales* V(9):9–64.

Búrquez, A., & A. Martínez-Yrízar. 2000. El desarrollo económico y la conservación de los recursos naturales. In *Sonora 2000: A Debate; Problemas y Soluciones, Riesgos y Oportunidades,* I, edited by Almada Bay. Mexico City: Ed. Cal y Arena.

Búrquez, A., A. Martínez-Yrízar, R. S. Felger, & D. Yetman. 1999. Vegetation and habitat diversity at the southern edge of the Sonoran Desert. In *Ecology of Sonoran Desert Plants and Plant Communities,* edited by R. Robichaux, pp. 36–67. Tucson: University of Arizona Press.

Búrquez, A., A. Martínez, & P. S. Martin. 1992. From the high Sierra to the coast: Changes in vegetation along Highway 16, Maycoba-Hermosillo. In *Geology and Mineral Resources of the Northern Sierra Madre Occidental, México,* edited by K. F. Clark, J. Roldán-Quintana, & R. H. Schmidt. El Paso: El Paso Geological Society.

Búrquez, A., A. Martínez-Yrízar, M. E. Miller, K. Rojas, M. A. Quintana, & D. Yetman. 1998. Mexican grasslands and the changing aridlands of Mexico: An overview and a case study in northwestern Mexico. In *The Future of Arid Grasslands: Identifying Issues, Seeking Solutions,* edited by B. Tellman, D. Finch, C. Edminster, & R. Hamre, pp. 21–32. Proceedings

RMRS-P-3. Fort Collins, Colorado: USDA, Forest Service, Rocky Mountain Research Station.

Búrquez, A., M. Miller, & A. Martínez-Yrízar. 2002. Mexican grasslands, thornscrub, and the transformation of the Sonoran Desert by invasive exotic buffelgrass *(Pennisetum ciliare).* In *Invasive Species in Sonoran Desert Communities,* edited by B. Tellman, pp. 126–146. Tucson: University of Arizona Press.

Búrquez, A., & M. A. Quintana. 1994. Islands of diversity: Ironwood ecology and the richness of perennials in a Sonoran Desert biological reserve. In *Ironwood: An Ecological and Cultural Keystone of the Sonoran Desert,* edited by G. P. Nabhan & J. L. Carr, pp. 9–27. Occasional Papers in Conservation Biology No. 1. Washington, D.C.: Conservation International.

Camou, E., editor. 1991. *Potreros, Vegas y Mahuechis: Sociedad y Ganadería en la Sierra Sonorense.* Hermosillo: Secretaría de Fomento Educativo y Cultura/Instituto Sonorense de Cultura.

Celis, P. 1992. Diagnóstico de la contaminación del agua en el estado de Sonora. In *Ecología, Recursos Naturales y Medio Ambiente en Sonora,* edited by J. L. Moreno, pp. 165–188. Hermosillo: Secretaría de Infraestructura Urbana y Ecología/El Colegio de Sonora.

Challenger, A. 1998. *Utilización y Conservación de los Ecosistemas Terrestres de México: Pasado, Presente y Futuro.* Mexico City: CONABIO/Instituto de Biología/Sierra Madre.

Clifton, K., D. O. Cornejo, & R. S. Felger. 1982. Sea turtles of the Pacific coast of México. In *Biological Conservation of Sea Turtles,* edited by K. Bjorndal, pp. 199–209. Washington, D.C.: Smithsonian Institution Press.

Colosio, L. D. 1993. El espíritu conservacionista. In *Areas Protegidas de México.* Mexico City: SEDESOL.

Cox, J. R., M. H. Martin, F. A. Ibarra, J. H. Fourie, N. F. G. Rethman, & D. G. Wilcox. 1988. The influence of climate and soils on the distribution of four African grasses. *Journal of Range Management* 41:127–139.

Del Castillo, J. M. 1994. Protección y restauración ecológica-ambiental de la presa Abelardo L. Rodríguez Luján en Hermosillo, Sonora. *Estudios Sociales* V(9):65–102.

Denman, C. 1992. Productos tóxicos y potencialmente peligrosos en la industria fronteriza. In *Ecología, Recursos Naturales y Medio Ambiente en Sonora,* edited by J. L. Moreno, pp. 277–298. Hermosillo: Secretaría de Infraestructura Urbana y Ecología/El Colegio de Sonora.

Doode, S., M. A. Cisneros, & G. Montemayor. 1992. Pesca y medio ambiente en Guaymas: Algunos aspectos sobre la problemática ambiental. In *Ecología, Recursos Naturales y Medio Ambiente en Sonora,* edited by J. L. Moreno, pp. 165–188. Hermosillo: Secretaría de Infraestructura Urbana y Ecología/El Colegio de Sonora.

Doode, S., & E. P. Pérez, editors. 1994. *Sociedad, Economía y Cultura Alimentaria.* Hermosillo: Centro de Investigación en Alimentación y Desarrollo/ Centro de Investigaciones y Estudios Superiores en Antropología Social.

Estévez, P. M. 1999. Fundamentos de la sustentabilidad relacionados con la elaboración de la norma, leyes y reglamentos del cielo limpio y protección a observatorios astronómicos ópticos. Bachelor's thesis, Universidad de Sonora, Hermosillo.

Ezcurra, E., & C. Montaña. 1988. La evolución del uso de los recursos naturales renovables en el norte árido de México. In *Estudio Integrado de los Recursos Vegetación, Suelo y Agua en la Reserva de la Biosfera de Mapimí. I. Ambiente Natural y Humano,* edited by C. Montaña, pp. 269–290. Mexico City: Instituto de Ecología.

Felger, R. S. 1999. The flora of Cañón de Nacapule: A desert-bounded tropical canyon near Guaymas, Sonora, Mexico. *Proceedings of the San Diego Society of Natural History,* No. 35.

———. 2000. *Flora of the Gran Desierto and Río Colorado of Northwestern Mexico.* Tucson: University of Arizona Press.

Felger, R. S., K. D. Clifton, & P. Regal. 1976. Winter dormancy in sea turtles: Independent discovery and exploitation in the Gulf of California by two local cultures. *Science* 191:283–285.

Felger, R. S., & M. B. Johnson. 1995. Trees of the northern Sierra Madre Occidental and sky islands of southwestern North America. In *Biodiversity and Management of the Madrean Archipelago: The Sky Islands of Southwestern United States and Northwestern Mexico,* coordinated by L. F. DeBano, P. F. Ffolliott, A. Ortega-Rubio, G. J. Gottfried, R. H. Hamre, & C. B. Edminster. General Technical Report RM-GTR-264. Fort Collins, Colorado: USDA, Forest Service, Rocky Mountain Forest and Range Experiment Station.

Felger, R. S., M. B. Johnson, & M. F. Wilson. 2001. *Trees of Sonora, Mexico.* New York: Oxford University Press.

Felger, R. S., & C. H. Lowe. 1976. The island and coastal vegetation and flora of the Gulf of California, Mexico. *Natural History Museum of Los Angeles County, Contributions in Science* No. 285. Los Angeles.

Felger, R. S., & M. B. Moser. 1985. *People of the Desert and Sea: Ethnobotany of the Seri Indians.* Tucson: University of Arizona Press.

Felger, R. S., W. J. Nichols, & J. A. Seminoff. 2005. Sea turtles in northwestern Mexico: Conservation, ethnobiology, and desperation. In *Biodiversity, Ecosystems, and Conservation in Northern Mexico,* edited by J.-L. E. Cartron, G. Ceballos, & R. S. Felger, pp. 405–425. New York: Oxford University Press.

Felger, R. S., & M. F. Wilson, editors. 1995. Northern Sierra Madre Occidental and its Apachian outliers: A neglected center of biodiversity. In *Biodiversity and Management of the Madrean Archipelago:*

The Sky Islands of Southwestern United States and Northwestern Mexico, coordinated by L. F. DeBano, P. F. Ffolliott, A. Ortega-Rubio, G. J. Gottfried, R. H. Hamre, & C. B. Edminster. General Technical Report RM-GTR-264. Fort Collins, Colorado: USDA, Forest Service, Rocky Mountain Forest and Range Experiment Station.

Flores, O., & P. Geréz. 1988. *Conservación en México: Síntesis sobre Vertebrados Terrestres, Vegetación y Uso del Suelo.* Mexico City: INIREB/Conservation International.

Fradkin, P. L. 1981. *A River No More: The Colorado River and the West.* Tucson: University of Arizona Press.

Friedman, S. L. 1996. Vegetation and flora of the coastal plains of the Río Mayo region, southern Sonora, México. Master's thesis, Arizona State University.

Garza-Salazar, F., S. J. Debrott, & J. M. Haro. 1992. Observaciones recientes de las poblaciones de la codorniz mascarita *(Colinus virginianus ridgwayi)* en Sonora, México. *Ecológica* 2:1–6. Available at IMADES, Hermosillo, Sonora.

Gentry, H. S. 1942. *Rio Mayo Plants: A Study of the Flora and Vegetation of the Valley of the Rio Mayo in Sonora.* Publication No. 527. Washington, D.C.: Carnegie Institution of Washington.

———. 1949. Land plants collected by the *Velero III,* Allan Hancock Pacific expedition, 1937–1941. *Allan Hancock Pacific Expeditions* 13:1–245. Los Angeles: University of Southern California Press.

Glenn, E. P., R. S. Felger, A. Búrquez, & D. S. Turner. 1992. Ciénega de Santa Clara: Endangered wetland in the Colorado River delta, Sonora, México. *Natural Resources Journal* 32:817–824.

Hanselka, C. W., & D. Johnson. 1991. Establecimiento y manejo de praderas de zacate buffel común en el sur de Texas y en México. In *Memoria del Simposium Internacional Aprovechamiento Integral del Zacate Buffel.* Ciudad Victoria: Séptimo Congreso Nacional de la Sociedad Mexicana de Manejo de Pastizales.

Hastings, J. R., & R. M. Turner. 1965. *The Changing Mile: An Ecological Study of Vegetation Change with Time in the Lower Mile of an Arid and Semiarid Region.* Tucson: University of Arizona Press.

INE/CONABIO. 1995. *Reservas de la Biosfera y Otras Áreas Protegidas de México.* Mexico City: Instituto Nacional de Ecología/Comisión Nacional para el Conocimiento y Uso de la Biodiversidad.

INEGI. 1990. *Sonora: Cuaderno de Información para la Planeación.* Mexico City: Instituto Nacional de Estadística, Geografía e Informática.

———. 1993. *Anuario Estadístico del Estado de Sonora.* Hermosillo: Instituto Nacional de Estadística, Geografía e Informática/Gobierno del Estado de Sonora.

Janzen, D. H. 1988. Tropical dry forest: The most endangered major tropical ecosystem. In *Biodiversity,* edited by E. O. Wilson, pp. 130–137. Washington, D.C.: National Academy Press.

Jardel, E. J., R. Gutiérrez, & P. León. 1992. Conservación de la diversidad biológica y problemática agraria en la Reserva de la Biosfera de Manantlán. In *Las Áreas Naturales Protegidas de México*, edited by A. L. Anaya, pp. 129–151. Mexico City: Sociedad Botánica de México.

Johnson, D. A., & A. Navarro. 1992. Zacate buffel y biodiversidad en el Desierto Sonorense. In *Ecología, Recursos Naturales y Medio Ambiente en Sonora*, edited by J. L. Moreno, pp. 117–122. Hermosillo: Secretaría de Infraestructura Urbana y Ecología/El Colegio de Sonora.

Johnston, M. C. 1963. Past and present grasslands of southern Texas and northeastern México. *Ecology* 44:456–466.

Joseph, S. M. 1993. Un nuevo sistema de ciudades: Bases teóricas y su aplicación en el estado de Sonora. *Estudios Sociales* IV(7):55–93.

Lara, F. 1992. Industria, ciudad y medio ambiente en la frontera Sonorense. In *Ecología, Recursos Naturales y Medio Ambiente en Sonora*, edited by J. L. Moreno, pp. 267–276. Hermosillo: Secretaría de Infraestructura Urbana y Ecología/El Colegio de Sonora.

Machado, M. A. 1981. *The North Mexican Cattle Industry, 1910–1975*. College Station: Texas A&M University Press.

Marshall, J. T. 1957. Birds of pine-oak woodland in southern Arizona and adjacent Mexico. *Pacific Coast Avifauna* 32:1–125.

Martínez-Yrízar, A., A. Búrquez, & M. Maass. 2000. Structure and functioning of tropical deciduous forests in western Mexico. In *Tropical Deciduous Forest of Alamos: Biodiversity of a Threatened Ecosystem*, edited by R. Robichaux, pp. 19–35. Tucson: University of Arizona Press.

Medellín, R. A., C. Manterola, M. Valdéz, D. G. Hewitt, D. Doan-Crider, & T. E. Fulbright. 2005. History, ecology, and conservation of the pronghorn antelope, bighorn sheep, and black bear in Mexico. In *Biodiversity, Ecosystems, and Conservation in Northern Mexico*, edited by J.-L. E. Cartron, G. Ceballos, & R. S. Felger, pp. 387–404. New York: Oxford University Press.

Mittermeier, R. A., & C. Goettsch Mittermeier. 1992. La importancia de la diversidad biológica de México. In *México ante los Retos de la Biodiversidad*, edited by J. Sarukhán & R. Dirzo, pp. 63–73. Mexico City: CONABIO.

Moran, R. 1996. *The Flora of Guadalupe Island, Mexico*. Memoirs of the California Academy of Sciences No. 19. San Francisco.

Moreno, J. L. 1994. El uso del agua en un distrito agrícola de riego por bombeo: El caso de la Costa de Hermosillo, Sonora. In *Sociedad, Economía y Cultura Alimentaria*, edited by S. Doode & E. P. Pérez, pp. 239–272. Hermosillo: Centro de Investigación en Alimentación y Desarrollo/Centro de Investigaciones y Estudios Superiores en Antropología Social.

———. 2000. Apropiación y sobreexplotación del agua subterránea en la Costa de Hermosillo, 1945–

2000. Ph.D. dissertation, Centro de Investigaciones y Estudios Superiores en Antropología Social, Universidad de Guadalajara.

———, editor. 1992. *Ecología, Recursos Naturales y Medio Ambiente en Sonora*. Hermosillo: Secretaría de Infraestructura Urbana y Ecología/El Colegio de Sonora.

Moreno-Vázquez, J. L. 1991. El futuro de la problemática ambiental en Cananea y Nacozari. *Estudios Sociales* II(2):105–118.

Nabhan, G. P., & M. J. Plotkin. 1994. Introduction. In *Ironwood: An Ecological and Cultural Keystone of the Sonoran Desert*, edited by G. P. Nabhan & J. L. Carr, pp. 5–7. Occasional Papers in Conservation Biology No. 1. Washington, D.C.: Conservation International.

Nabhan, G. P., & H. Suzán. 1994. Boundary effects on endangered cacti and their nurse plants in and near a Sonoran Desert biosphere reserve. In *Ironwood: An Ecological and Cultural Keystone of the Sonoran Desert*, edited by G. P. Nabhan & J. L. Carr, pp. 55–68. Occasional Papers in Conservation Biology No. 1. Washington, D.C.: Conservation International.

Navarro, A. 1985. Flora y vegetación de la Sierra de Mazatán. Bachelor's thesis, Escuela de Agricultura y Ganadería, Universidad de Sonora.

Ortega, A., & L. Arriaga, editors. 1991. *La Reserva de la Biosfera El Vizcaíno en la Península de Baja California*. Publication No. 4. La Paz: Centro de Investigaciones Biológicas de Baja California Sur.

Otero, A., & J. J. Consejo. 1992. Sian Ka'an ¿un sueño perdido? In *Las Áreas Naturales Protegidas de México*, edited by A. L. Anaya, pp. 153–167. Mexico City: Sociedad Botánica de México.

Ortíz, M. E. 1993. Planeación y desarrollo urbano para Sonora en el sexenio 1992–1997. *Estudios Sociales* IV(7):227–233.

Pimentel, D., J. Houser, E. Preiss, O. White, H. Feng, L. Mesnick, T. Barsky, S. Tariche, J. Schreck, & S. Alpert. 1997. Water resources: Agriculture, the environment, and society. *Bioscience* 47:97–114.

Rzedowski, J. 1978. *La Vegetación de México*. Mexico City: Limusa-Wiley.

———. 1991a. Diversidad y orígenes de la flora fanerogámica de México. *Acta Botánica Mexicana* 14:3–22.

———. 1991b. El endemismo en la flora fanerogámica mexicana: Una apreciación analítica preliminar. *Acta Botánica Mexicana* 15:47–64.

Shreve, F. 1951. *Vegetation of the Sonoran Desert*. Publication No. 591. Washington, D.C.: Carnegie Institution of Washington.

Steinbeck, J., & E. F. Ricketts. 1951. *The Log from the Sea of Cortez*. New York: Viking Penguin.

Stoleson, S. H., R. S. Felger, G. Ceballos, C. Raish, M. F. Wilson, & A. Búrquez. 2005. Recent history of natural resource use and population growth in northern Mexico. In *Biodiversity, Ecosystems, and Conservation in Northern Mexico*, edited by J.-L. E.

Cartron, G. Ceballos, & R. S. Felger, pp. 52–86. New York: Oxford University Press.

Tewksbury, J. J., & C. A. Petrovich. 1994. The influences of ironwood as a habitat modifier species: A case study on the Sonoran Desert coast of the Sea of Cortez. In *Ironwood: An Ecological and Cultural Keystone of the Sonoran Desert,* edited by G. P. Nabhan & J. L. Carr, pp. 29–54. Occasional Papers in Conservation Biology No. 1. Washington, D.C.: Conservation International.

Thompson, R. 1989. *Pioneros de la Costa de Hermosillo (La Hacienda de Costa Rica, 1844).* Hermosillo, Sonora: Ed. Yescas.

Trejo, I., & R. Dirzo. 2000. Deforestation of seasonally dry tropical forest: A national and local analysis in Mexico. *Biological Conservation* 94:133–142.

Turner, R. M., J. E. Bowers, & T. L. Burgess. 1995. *Sonoran Desert Plants: An Ecological Atlas.* Tucson: University of Arizona Press.

Vargas, F., S. Escobar, & R. del Angel. 2000. *Áreas Naturales Protegidas de México con Decretos Federales.* Mexico City: INE/RDS/PNUD.

White, S. S. 1948. The vegetation and flora of the region of the Río de Bavispe in northeastern Sonora, México. *Lloydia* 11:220–302.

Wiggins, I. 1980. *Flora of Baja California.* Stanford, California: Stanford University Press.

Yetman, D. A., & A. Búrquez. 1994. Buffelgrass—Sonoran Desert nightmare. *Arizona Riparian Council Newsletter* 3:1, 8–10.

———. 1996. A tale of two species: Speculation on the introduction of *Pachycereus pringlei* in the Sierra Libre, Sonora, Mexico, by *Homo sapiens. Desert Plants* 12:23–32.

34. Growing a Conservation Community: The CEDO Story

Boyer, Edward Henri. 1987. The natural disappearance of a top carnivore and its impact on an intertidal community: The interplay of temperature and predation on community structure. Ph.D. dissertation, University of Arizona.

Boyer, R. E. 1994. Live vaquita at CEDO. *CEDO News* 6(2):1, 7.

———. 1995. Turtle hatching, fishermen lend a hand. *CEDO EcoUpdate* 7(1):1, 7.

Brownell, R. L., Jr. 1982. Status of the cochito, *Phocoena sinus,* in the Gulf of California. In FAO Advisory Committee on Marine Resources Research, Working Party on Marine Mammals, *Mammals in the Seas,* Vol. 4, *Small Cetaceans, Seals, Sirenians, and Otters.* Food and Agriculture Organization Fisheries Series 4. Rome: FAO.

Brusca, Richard C. 1980. *Common Intertidal Invertebrates of the Gulf of California.* Tucson: University of Arizona Press.

———. 2002. Biodiversity in the northern Gulf of California. *CEDO News* 10(1):1, 30.

Cudney-Bueno, Richard 2000. Management and conservation of benthic resources harvested by small-scale hookah divers in the northern Gulf of California, Mexico: The black murex snail fishery. Master's thesis, University of Arizona.

———. 2001. Co-management of the hookah diving fisheries. *CEDO News* 9(2):12, 42.

Cudney-Bueno, Richard, & Peggy J. Turk Boyer. 1998. *Pescando entre Mareas del Alto Golfo de California—Una Guía sobre la Pesca Artesanal, su Gente y sus Propuestas de Manejo.* CEDO Technical Series No. 1. Puerto Peñasco, Sonora: CEDO.

D'Agrosa, C., O. Vidal, & W. C. Graham. 1995. Mortality of the vaquita *(Phocoena sinus)* in gillnet fisheries during 1993–94. *Report of the International Whaling Commission* (special issue 16): 282–291.

Dawson, E. Y. 1966. *Marine Algae in the Vicinity of Puerto Peñasco, Sonora, Mexico.* Gulf of California Field Guide Series No. 1. Tucson: University of Arizona.

Dungan, M. L., T. E. Miller, & D. A. Thomson. 1982. Catastrophic decline of a top carnivore in the Gulf of California rocky intertidal zone. *Science* 216: 989–991.

Flores-Skydancer, Lourdes, & Peggy J. Turk Boyer. 2002. *The Vaquita of the Gulf of California.* CEDO Bilingual Educational Series. Puerto Peñasco, Sonora: CEDO.

Hoyos, David. 1991. Shortened season for shrimp industry? Drastic drop in catch spurs action. *CEDO News* 3(2):5.

Instituto Nacional de Ecología. 2003, in prep. Programa de conservación y manejo, Reserva de la Biosfera Alto Golfo de California y Delta del Río Colorado.

Jaramillo-Legorreta, A. M., L. Rojas-Bracho, & T. Gerodette. 1999. A new abundance estimate for vaquitas: First step for recovery. *Marine Mammal Science* 15(4):957–973.

Lewin, R. A. 1977. *Prochloron,* type genus of the Prochlorophyta. *Phycologia* 16:217.

Lively, C. M. 1986. Competition, comparative life histories, and maintenance of a shell dimorphism in the acorn barnacle *Chthamalus anisopoma. Evolution* 40:231–242.

Magatagan, M., E. Boyer, & P. Turk. 1983. Registro de *Phocoena sinus* y otros mamíferos marinos de Puerto Peñasco, Sonora, México. Paper presented at VII Reunión Internacional para el Estudio de Mamíferos Marinos, La Paz, Baja California Sur.

Maldonado, F., P. Turk, R. Boyer, L. Findley, & O. Vidal. 1984. Observaciones de ballenas rorcuales en el alto Golfo de California (Marzo 1983–Marzo 1984) y registro de varamiento de un cachalote pigmeo *(Kogia breviceps).* Paper presented at IX Reunión Internacional para el Estudio de Mamíferos Marinos, La Paz, Baja California Sur.

McCourt, R. M., A. F. Michaels, & R. W. Hoshaw. 1984. Seasonality of symbiotic *Prochloron* (Prochlorophyta) and its didemnid host in the northern Gulf of California. *Phycologia* 23(1):95–101.

Michaels, Anthony Francis. 1983. The evolution of marine algae—Invertebrate symbiosis with special reference to the *Procholoron–Didemnum*

candidum symbiosis. Master's thesis, University
of Arizona.

Nava-Romo, J. M. 1994. Impactos a corto y largo plazo
en la diversidad y otras características ecológicas
de la comunidad bénito-demersal capturada por
la pesquería de camarón en el norte del alto Golfo
de California, México. Master's thesis, Instituto
Tecnológico y de Estudios Superiores de Monterrey–Campus Guaymas.

Navarro, Carlos. 1997. Tide bits, turtle hatching.
CEDO News 7(4):32.

Norris, James Newcome IV. 1975. Marine algae of the
northern Gulf of California. Ph.D. dissertation,
University of California, Santa Barbara.

Paine, R. T. 1966. Food web complexity and species
diversity. *American Naturalist* 100:65–75.

Rivera Montijo, A., & Peggy J. Turk Boyer. 1992. Análisis preliminar de la pesca por el sistema de arrastre
en el alto Golfo de California. Paper presented at
IV Congreso de la Asociación de Investigadores
del Mar de Cortés, September 2–4, Universidad
Autónoma de Baja California, Ensenada.

Robles, Alejandro. 1993. The challenge of the biosphere reserve. *CEDO News* 5(2):9.

Rojas-Bracho, L., & A. Jaramillo. 2002. Vaquita. In
Encyclopedia of Marine Mammals, edited by W. F.
Perrin, B. Würsig, & H. Thewwissen, pp. 1277–1280.
New York: Academic Press.

Thomson, Donald A., Lloyd T. Findley, & Alex N. Ker-
stich. 1979. *Reef Fishes of the Sea of Cortez.* New
York: John Wiley & Sons.

Thomson, D. A., & Nonie McKibbin. 1976. *Gulf of California Fishwatcher's Guide.* Tucson: Golden Puffer
Press.

Turk, Peggy J. 1981. Intertidal migration and formation of breeding clusters of labial-spine morphs of
the thaid gastropod *Acanthina angelica.* Master's
thesis, University of Arizona.

Turk, Peggy J., R. Boyer, B. Villa-R., G. Silber, &
M. Corona-C. 1986. Avistamientos de mamíferos
marinos durante dos cruceros simultáneos en la
parte norte del Golfo de California, February
18–21, 1986. Abstract. XI Reunión Internacional
para el Estudio de Mamíferos Marinos, April 2–6,
1986, Guaymas, Sonora.

Turk Boyer, Peggy J. 2001. Vaquita: On the brink of
extinction or salvation? *CEDO News* 9(2):20–26.
www.cedointercultural.org/vaquita_english.pdf.

———, editor. 2001. *Voces del Mar y del Desierto: Una
Publicación sobre las Reservas de la Biosfera Alto
Golfo de California y Delta del Río Colorado, El
Pinacate y Gran Desierto de Altar* 1:1–3.

Turk Boyer, Peggy J., & R. E. Boyer. 1990. Young ecologists. *CEDO News* 3(1):29.

———. 1991. Pelicans in danger. *CEDO News* 3(2):1, 18.

Turk Boyer, Peggy J., & Lourdes Flores-Skydancer.
2002. Setting the stage for conservation of vaquita:
Fishermen and community involvement. Paper
presented at the 54th International Whaling Com-

mission meeting, April 24–May 10, Shimonoseki,
Japan.

Turk Boyer, P., E. L. Johnson III, K. Mangin, & K.
Scully. 2004. Onshore sea surface temperatures
from the northern Gulf of California, Puerto
Peñasco, Sonora, Mexico, 1964–2003. Abstracts,
Gulf of California Conference, June 13–16, Tucson.

Turk Boyer, P. J., P. T. Raimondi, & C. M. Lively. 1986.
Variaciones temporales y anuales del substrato y
temperatura del agua y su afecto en la abundancia
y distribución de los organismos más comunes de
la zona entremareal de la parte norte del Golfo de
California en Puerto Peñasco, Sonora. Paper presented at I Intercambio Académico sobre Investigaciones en el Mar de Cortés, April 9–10,
Hermosillo, Sonora.

Turk Boyer, P., & G. K. Silber. 1994. Estimate of
vaquita, *Phocoena sinus,* mortality in the northern
Gulf of California, Mexico. *Reports of the International Whaling Commission* (special issue 15):
628–629.

Vidal, O. 1995. Population biology and incidental
mortality of the vaquita, *Phocoena sinus.* In *Biology
of the Phocoenids* 16 (special issue), edited by A.
Bjorge & G. P. Donovan, pp. 247–272. Cambridge:
International Whaling Commission.

Vidal, O., A. Aguayo, L. Findley, A. Robles, L. Bouril-
lon, Y. Vomend, P. Turk, K. Garate, L. Marnas, &
J. Rosas. 1987. Avistamientos de mamíferos marinos durante el crucero "Guaymas I" en la región
superior del Golfo de California, primavera de
1984. In *Memoria X Reunión Internacional para el
Estudio de Mamíferos Marinos,* March 24–27, 1985,
La Paz, Baja California Sur, pp. 7–35.

Vidal, O., L. T. Findley, P. J. Turk, & R. E. Boyer. 1987.
Recent records of pygmy sperm whales in the Gulf
of California, México. *Marine Mammal Science*
3(4):354–356.

Yensen, Nicholas Patrick. 1979. The function of the
labial spine and the effect of prey size on "switch-
ing" polymorphs of *Acanthina angelica* (Gastropoda; Thaididae). Ph.D. dissertation, University
of Arizona.

35. Cooperation Across Borders: A Brief History of Sonoran Desert Conservation Beyond Boundaries

Chester, Charles. 2001. The grassroots campaign to
establish an international Sonoran Desert biosphere reserve. In *Ecosystems and Sustainable Development,* edited by Y. Villacampa, C. A. Brebbia, &
J. L. Usó, pp. 419–433. Boston: WIT Press.

Earth Times. 1996. *Efforts to preserve the desert know
no bounds. Earth Times* (December): 1–15.

Murrieta-Saldivar, Joaquin. 2000. Scenic beauty and
human perceptual dimensions of the Pinacate y
Gran Desierto de Altar Biosphere Reserve, Sonora,
Mexico (visitors, community, and managers).
Ph.D. dissertation, University of Arizona.

36. Vertebrates of the Río Colorado: What Can Be Done?

Davis, G. P. 1982. *Man and Wildlife in Arizona: The American Exploration Period, 1824–1865*. Phoenix: Arizona Game and Fish Department; Tucson: University of Arizona Cooperative Wildlife Research Unit.

Dill, W. A. 1944. The fishery of the lower Colorado River. *California Fish and Game* 30:109–211.

Dobyns, H. F. 1978. Who killed the Gila? *Journal of Arizona History* 19:17–30.

———. 1981. *From Fire to Flood: Historic Human Destruction of Sonoran Desert Riverine Oases*. Ballena Press Anthropological Papers No. 20. Socorro, New Mexico: Ballena Press.

Ezcurra, E., R. S. Felger, A. D. Russell, & M. Equihua. 1988. Freshwater islands in a desert sand sea: The hydrology, flora, and phytogeography of the Gran Desierto oases of northwestern Mexico. *Desert Plants* 9:35–44, 55–63.

Felger, R. S. 2000. *Flora of the Gran Desierto and Río Colorado of Northwestern Mexico*. Tucson: University of Arizona Press.

Gilbert, C. H., & N. B. Scofield. 1898. Notes on a collection of fishes from the Colorado basin in Arizona. *Proceedings of the United States National Museum* 20:487–499.

Glenn, E. P., R. S. Felger, A. Búrquez, & D. S. Turner. 1992. Ciénega de Santa Clara: Endangered wetland in the Rio Colorado delta, Sonora, Mexico. *Natural Resources Journal* 32:817–824.

Glenn, E. P., C. Lee, R. Felger, & S. Zengel. 1996. Effects of water management on the wetlands of the Colorado River delta, Mexico. *Conservation Biology* 10:1175–1186.

Gómez Estrada, J. A. 2000. *La Gente del Delta del Río Colorado*. Mexicali: Universidad Autónoma de Baja California.

Grinnell, J. 1914. An account of the mammals and birds of the Lower Colorado Valley, with special reference to the distributional problems presented. *University of California Publications in Zoology* 12:51–294.

———. 1928. A distributional summation of the ornithology of Lower California. *University of California Publications in Zoology* 32:1–300.

Grismer, L. L. 1994. The origin and evolution of the peninsular herpetofauna of Baja California, Mexico. *Herpetological Natural History* 2:51–106.

———. 2002. *Amphibians and Reptiles of Baja California, Including Its Pacific Islands and the Islands in the Sea of Cortés*. Berkeley: University of California Press.

Hendricks, W. O. 1996. *Guillermo Andrade y el Desarrollo del Delta Mexicano del Río Colorado*. Mexicali: Universidad Autónoma de Baja California.

Hinojosa-Huerta, O., S. DeStephano, & W. W. Shaw. 2001. Distribution and abundance of the Yuma clapper rail *(Rallus longirostris yumanensis)* in the Colorado River delta, Mexico. *Journal of Arid Environments* 49:171–182.

Kelly, W. H. 1977. *Cocopa Ethnography*. Anthropological Papers of the University of Arizona No. 29. Tucson: University of Arizona Press.

Kerig, D. P. 2001. *El Valle de Mexicali y la Colorado River Land Company, 1902–1946*. Mexicali: Universidad Autónoma de Baja California.

Leopold, A. 1949. The green lagoons. In *The Sand County Almanac*, pp. 150–158. New York: Oxford University Press.

———. 1953. *Round River: From the Journals of Aldo Leopold*. Edited by L. B. Leopold. New York: Oxford University Press.

———. 1959. *Wildlife of Mexico: The Game Birds and Mammals*. Los Angeles: University of California Press.

Mearns, E. A. 1907. *Mammals of the Mexican Boundary with the United States*. Bulletin of the United States National Museum No. 56. Washington, D.C.: Government Printing Office.

Mellink, E. 1995. Status of the muskrat in the Valle de Mexicali and the delta del Rio Colorado, Mexico. *California Fish and Game* 81:33–38.

———. 2000. Captain Edward William Funcke: Hunting from sea to desert. *Journal of San Diego History* 46:35–51.

Mellink, E., & V. Ferreira-Bartrina. 2000. On the wildlife of wetlands of the Mexican portion of the Rio Colorado delta. *Bulletin of the Southern California Academy of Sciences* 99:115–127.

Mellink, E., & J. Luévano. 1998. Status of beavers *(Castor canadensis)* in Valle de Mexicali, Mexico. *Bulletin of the Southern California Academy of Sciences* 97:115–120.

Minckley, W. L. 1982. Trophic interrelations among introduced fishes in the lower Rio Colorado, southwestern United States. *California Fish and Game* 68:78–89.

Mueller, G. A., & P. C. Marsh. 2002. *Lost, a Desert River and Its Native Fishes: A Historical Perspective of the Lower Colorado River*. U.S. Geological Survey, Biological Resources Division, Information and Technology Report USGS/BRD/ITR-2002-0010:1–69.

Murphy, R. C. 1917. Natural history observations from the Mexican portion of the Colorado Desert, with a note on the Lower California pronghorn and a list of birds. *Proceedings of the Linnean Society of New York* 28:43–101.

Nabhan, G. P., A. M. Rea, K. Reichhardt, E. Mellink, & C. F. Hutchinson. 1982. Papago influences on habitat and biotic diversity: Quitobac oasis ethnoecology. *Journal of Ethnobiology* 2:124–143.

Nelson, E. W. 1921. Lower California and its natural resources. *Memoirs of the National Academy of Sciences* 16:1–194.

Ohmart, R. D., B. W. Anderson, & W. C. Hunter. 1988. *The Ecology of the Lower Rio Colorado from Davis Dam to the Mexico–United States Border: A Community Profile*. Biological Reports No. 85(7.19). Washington, D.C.: U.S. Fish and Wildlife Service.

Patten, M. A., E. Mellink, H. Gómez de Silva, & T. E. Wurster. 2001. Status and taxonomy of the Colorado Desert avifauna of Baja California. *Monographs in Field Ornithology* 3:29–63.

Pattie, J. O. 1831. *The Personal Narrative of James O. Pattie of Kentucky.* Cincinnati: John H. Wood.

Rodriguez, C. A., K. W. Flessa, & D. L. Dettman. 2001. Effects of upstream diversion of Colorado River water on the estuarine bivalve mollusc *Mulinia coloradoensis. Conservation Biology* 15:249–258.

Rosenberg, K. V., R. D. Ohmart, W. C. Hunter, & B. W. Anderson. 1991. *Birds of the Lower Río Colorado Valley.* Tucson: University of Arizona Press.

Sánchez-Ramírez, O. 1990. *Crónica agrícola del Valle de Mexicali.* Mexicali: Universidad Autónoma de Baja California.

Sykes, G. 1937a. Delta, estuary, and lower portion of the channel of the Colorado River, 1933 to 1935. *Carnegie Institution of Washington Publications* 480:1–70.

———. 1937b. *The Colorado Delta.* Publication No. 19. New York: American Geographical Society; Washington, D.C.: Carnegie Institution of Washington.

Varady, R. G., K. B. Hankins, A. Kaus, E. Young, & R. Merideth. 2001. . . . to the Sea of Cortés: Nature, water, culture, and livelihood in the lower Colorado River basin and delta--an overview of issues, policies, and approaches to environmental restoration. *Journal of Arid Environments* 49:195–209.

Weber, D. J. 1970. *The Taos Trappers: The Fur Trade in the Far Southwest, 1540–1846.* Norman: University of Oklahoma Press.

Williams, A. Alvarez de. 1983. Cocopa. In *Southwest,* edited by A. Ortiz, pp. 99–112. Handbook of North American Indians, vol. 10, William C. Sturtevant, general editor. Washington, D.C.: Smithsonian Institution.

Williams, D. F. 1986. *Mammalian Species of Special Concern in California.* Sacramento: California Department of Fish and Game.

Zengel, S. A., V. J. Meretsky, E. P. Glenn, R. S. Felger, & D. Ortiz. 1995. Ciénega de Santa Clara, a remnant wetland in the Rio Colorado delta (Mexico): Vegetation distribution and the effects of water flow reduction. *Ecological Engineering* 4:19–36.

38. Changing Place-Names in El Pinacate

Hornaday, William T. 1909. *Camp-Fires on Desert and Lava.* New York: Charles Scribner's Sons. Reprint. Tucson: University of Arizona Press, 1983.

Lumholtz, Carl. 1912. *New Trails in Mexico.* London: T. Fisher Unwin. Reprint. Tucson: University of Arizona Press, 1990.

39. Our Grand Desert: A Gazetteer

Abbey, Edward. 1973. *Cactus Country.* New York: Time-Life Books.

———. 1984. A walk in the desert hills. In *Beyond the Wall,* pp. 1–49. New York: Holt, Rinehart, and Winston.

Adams, David K., & Andrew C. Comrie. 1997. The North American monsoon. *Bulletin of the American Meteorological Society* 78:2197–2213.

Ahlstrom, Richard V. N., editor. 2000. *Living in the Western Papaguería: An Archaeological Overview of the Barry M. Goldwater Air Force Range in Southwestern Arizona.* SWCA Cultural Resource Report No. 98–186. Tucson: ARCADIS Geraghty and Miller Environmental Services and SWCA Environmental Consultants.

Ahlstrom, Richard V. N., editor, with Mark L. Chenault, Ann Henshaw, Annick Lascaux, Stephen E. Nash, Elizabeth Noll, Lee Terzis, Arthur W. Vokes, and David Wrobleski. 2001. *A Cultural Resources Overview and Assessment for the Cabeza Prieta National Wildlife Refuge.* SWCA Cultural Resource Report No. 01–24. Tucson: SWCA Environmental Consultants.

Ajo Copper News. 2005. Tohono O'odham may form district for Hia Ced. February 25, 1.

Aleshire, Peter. 2004. Historic Butterfield Stage Trail now an easy half-day outing. *Arizona Highways,* January, 42–45.

Allen, Paul. 1996. Indians get fraction of land back. *Tucson Citizen,* October 15, 1A, 5A.

Almada, Francisco R. 1952. *Diccionario de Historia, Geografía y Biografía Sonorenses.* Chihuahua: privately printed.

———. 1990. *Diccionario de Historia, Geografía y Biografía Sonorenses.* 3d ed. Hermosillo: Instituto Sonorense de Cultura.

Alvarez, Albert, & Kenneth Hale. 1970. Toward a manual of Papago grammar. *International Journal of Linguistics* 36(2):83–97.

Annerino, John. 1993. *Canyons of the Southwest.* San Francisco: Sierra Club Books.

———. 1996. *Adventuring in Arizona.* San Francisco: Sierra Club Books. Reprint. Tucson: University of Arizona Press, 2003.

———. 1999. *Dead in Their Tracks: Crossing America's Desert Borderlands.* New York: Four Walls Eight Windows.

Aporta, Claudio. 2003. New ways of mapping: Using GPS software to plot place names and trails in Igloolik (Nunavut). *Arctic: Journal of the Arctic Institute of North America* 56:321–327.

Arizona Daily Star. 1931. Pioneer presents Lockwood Tucson history information. October 27.

———. 1942. Ignacio [*sic*] Bonillas near death after stroke. January 24.

———. 1944. Former envoy dies on border. February 1.

Arizona Highways. 1984. The Gila Trail. November, 16–29.

Arizona State Board on Geographic and Historic Names. 2001. Minutes, July 11 and October 30. Phoenix.

Badamo, Kira Ramakrishna. 1995. The power of I'itoi Mo'o. *Federal Archaeology* 8:39.

Bailey, L. R., editor. 1963. *Survey of a Route on the 32nd Parallel for the Texas Western Railroad, 1854: The A. B. Gray Report and Including the Reminiscences* of Peter R. Brady Who Accompanied the Expedition. Los Angeles: Westernlore Press.

Bancroft, Hubert Howe. 1889. *The Works of Hubert Howe Bancroft, vol. 17: History of Arizona and New Mexico, 1530–1888.* San Francisco: History Company.

Barnes, Will C. 1935. *Arizona Place Names.* Tucson: University of Arizona. Reprint. Tucson: University of Arizona Press, 1988.

Barney, James M. 1943. El Camino del Diablo. *Arizona Highways,* March, 14–19.

Barrios-Matrecito, Valdemar. 1988. *Por las Rutas del Desierto.* Hermosillo: Gobierno del Estado de Sonora.

Bartlett, John Russell. 1965. *Personal Narrative of Explorations and Incidents in Texas, New Mexico, California, Sonora, and Chihuahua.* 2 vols. Chicago: Rio Grande Press. Originally published New York: D. Appleton, 1854.

Beattie, G. W. 1928. Diary of a ferryman and trader at Fort Yuma, 1855–1857. *Annual Report: Historical Society of Southern California* XIV (part 1): 89–128; continued 1929, XIV (part 2): 213–242.

Beatty, Jenny T. 1996. Flying in formation with Sandy Lanham. *Woman Pilot,* November–December, 10–13.

Bee, Robert L. 1983. Quechan. In *Southwest,* edited by Alfonso Ortiz, pp. 86–98. Handbook of North American Indians, vol. 10, William C. Sturtevant, general editor. Washington, D.C.: Smithsonian Institution.

Bell, Fillman, Keith M. Anderson, & Yvonne G. Stewart. 1980. *The Quitobaquito Cemetery and Its History.* Tucson: National Park Service, Western Archeological Center.

———. 1982. Quitobaquito: A Sand Papago cemetery. *Kiva* 47:215–237.

Bennett, Peter S., & Michael R. Kunzmann. 1989. *A History of the Quitobaquito Resource Management Area, Organ Pipe Cactus National Monument, Arizona.* Technical Report No. 26. Tucson: Cooperative National Park Resource Studies Unit, University of Arizona.

Betancourt, Julio L., Thomas R. Van Devender, & Paul S. Martin, editors. 1990. *Packrat Middens: The Last 40,000 Years of Biotic Change.* Tucson: University of Arizona Press.

Bezy, John V., James T. Gutmann, & Gordon B. Haxel. 2000. *A Guide to the Geology of Organ Pipe Cactus National Monument and the Pinacate Biosphere Reserve.* Tucson: Arizona Geological Survey.

Blake, William P. 1855. *Explorations and Surveys for a Railroad Route from the Mississippi River to the Pacific Ocean.* Washington, D.C.: Government Printing Office.

Blount, G., & N. Lancaster. 1990. Development of the Gran Desierto sand sea, northwestern Mexico. *Geology* 18:724–728.

Bolton, Herbert Eugene. 1919. *Kino's Historical Memoir of Pimería Alta.* 2 vols. Los Angeles: Arthur H. Clark.

———. 1936. *Rim of Christendom.* New York: Macmillan. Reprint. Tucson: University of Arizona Press, 1984.

Bonillas, Ygnacio S., Jr. 1910. Estudio químico y óptico de una labradorita del Pinacate, Sonora. *Instituto Geológico de México, Parergones* 3:427–432.

Bowden, Charles. 1984. The Sierra Pinacate. *Arizona Highways,* November, 40–45.

———. 1987. Staying put. *City Magazine,* January, 31–33.

———. 1994. Mohawk Dunes: Our legacy of sand remains a world apart. *Arizona Highways,* January, 38–44.

Bowden, Charles, & Jack W. Dykinga. 1992. *The Sonoran Desert.* New York: Harry N. Abrams.

Bowen, Thomas. 2000. *Unknown Island: Seri Indians, Europeans, and San Esteban Island in the Gulf of California.* Albuquerque: University of New Mexico Press; Tucson: University of Arizona Southwest Center.

Bowers, Janice Emily. 1980. Flora of Organ Pipe Cactus National Monument. *Journal of the Arizona-Nevada Academy of Science* 15(1):1–11, 15(2):33–47.

———. 1982. The plant ecology of inland dunes in western North America. *Journal of Arid Environments* 5:199–220.

———. 1984. Plant geography of southwestern sand dunes. *Desert Plants* 6:31–42, 51–54.

———. 1986. *Seasons of the Wind: A Naturalist's Look at the Plant Life of Southwestern Sand Dunes.* Flagstaff: Northland Press.

———. 1988. *A Sense of Place: The Life and Work of Forrest Shreve.* Tucson: University of Arizona Press.

Boyd, Eva Jolene. 1995. *Noble Brutes: Camels on the American Frontier.* Plano, Texas: Wordware.

Boyer, Peggy J. Turk. 1996. Reserves in action/Reservas en acción. *CEDO News/Noticias del CEDO (Centro Intercultural de Estudios de Desiertos y Océanos)* 7:1, 5–6. Puerto Peñasco, Sonora.

Brazel, Anthony J., & Kenneth E. Evans. 1984. *Major Storms and Floods in Arizona, 1862–1983.* Precipitation Series No. 6. Tempe: Laboratory of Climatology, Arizona State University.

Brickler, Stanley K., Brock Tunnicliff et al. [10 additional names]. 1986. *Natural Resources Management Plan for Luke Air Force Range.* Tucson: School of Renewable Resources, University of Arizona.

Brown, Bryan T., Lupe P. Hendrickson, R. Roy Johnson, & William Werrell. 1983. *An Inventory of Surface Water Resources at Organ Pipe Cactus National Monument, Arizona.* Technical Report No. 10. Tucson: National Park Service and University of Arizona.

Brown, B[ryan] T., & R. R[oy] Johnson. 1983. The distribution of bedrock depressions (tinajas) as surface water in Organ Pipe Cactus National Monument, Arizona. *Journal of the Arizona-Nevada Academy of Science* 18:61–68.

Brown, David E., editor. 1994. *Biotic Communities, Southwestern United States and Northwestern Mexico.*

Salt Lake City: University of Utah Press. Originally published in special issue, *Desert Plants* 4 (1982).

Browne, J. Ross. 1950. *A Tour Through Arizona 1864, or Adventures in the Apache Country.* Tucson: Arizona Silhouettes.

Broyles, Bill. 1982. Desert thirst: The ordeal of Pablo Valencia. *Journal of Arizona History* 23:357–380.

———. 1993. The Devil's Highway. *Arizona Highways,* February, 4–13.

———. 1995. Desert wildlife water developments: Questioning use in the Southwest. *Wildlife Society Bulletin* 23:663–675.

———. 1996a. Surface water resources for prehistoric peoples in western Papaguería of the North American south-west. *Journal of Arid Environments* 33: 483–495.

———. 1996b. *Organ Pipe Cactus National Monument: A Sonoran Desert Sanctuary.* Tucson: Southwest Parks and Monuments.

———. 1997. Wildlife water developments in southwestern Arizona. *Journal of the Arizona-Nevada Academy of Science* 30:30–42.

———. 2003. *Our Sonoran Desert.* Tucson: Rio Nuevo Press.

Broyles, Bill, Richard S. Felger, & Charles Bowden. 2001. The Sonoran corridor. In *The Gulf of California: A World Apart* [Spanish edition: *El Golfo de California: Un Mundo Aparte*], edited by Patricio Robles-Gil, Exequiel Ezcurra, & Eric Mellink, pp. 244–267. Mexico City: Pegaso-Agrupación Sierra Madre.

Broyles, Bill, Richard S. Felger, Gary Paul Nabhan, & Luke Evans. 1997. Our grand desert: A gazetteer for northwestern Sonora, southwestern Arizona, and northeastern Baja California. *Journal of the Southwest* 39(3 & 4):703–856.

Bryan, Kirk. 1925. *The Papago Country, Arizona: A Geographic, Geologic, and Hydrologic Reconnaissance with a Guide to Desert Watering Places.* Water-Supply Paper No. 499. Washington, D.C.: United States Geological Survey.

Búrquez, Alberto, & Carlos Castillo. 1993. *Propuesto de Reserva de la Biosfera: El Pinacate y Gran Desierto de Altar.* 2 vols. Hermosillo: Gobierno del Estado de Sonora y Secretaría de Desarrollo Social.

———. 1994. Reserva de la Biosfera El Pinacate y Gran Desierto de Altar: Entorno biológio y social. *Estudios Sociales* 5(9):9–64.

Búrquez-Montijo, Alberto, & Angelina Martínez-Yrizar. 1992. Las áreas naturales protegidas y el desarrollo ecológico del estado de Sonora. In *Ecología, Recursos Naturales y Medio Ambiente en Sonora,* edited by José Luis Moreno, pp. 39–72. Hermosillo: Secretaría de Infraestructura Urbana y Ecología, and Colegio de Sonora.

Búrquez, A., A. Martínez-Yrízar, R. S. Felger, & D. Yetman. 1999. Vegetation and habitat diversity at the southern edge of the Sonoran Desert. In *Ecology of Sonoran Desert Plants and Plant Communities,* edited by R. H. Robichaux, pp. 36–67. Tucson: University of Arizona Press.

Burrus, Ernest J. 1971. *Kino and Manje: Explorers of Sonora and Arizona.* Rome: Jesuit Historical Institute.

Burt, W. H. 1938. *Faunal Relationships and Geographic Distribution of Mammals in Sonora.* Museum of Zoology Miscellaneous Publication No. 39. Ann Arbor: University of Michigan.

California State Military Museum. 2005. www.militarymuseum.org.

Carhart, Arthur H. 1955. One man can wipe out our wildlife refuges. *Sports Afield,* June, 21–25.

Carr, John N. 1994. *It Was a Rough Road.* Phoenix: Heart Track.

Case, Ted J., Martin L. Cody, & Exequiel Ezcurra, editors. 2002. *A New Island Biogeography of the Sea of Cortés.* New York: Oxford University Press.

Casillas, Arturo González. 1992. Hidrocontaminación salina del Río Colorado. In *Ecología, Recursos Naturales y Medio Ambiente en Sonora,* edited by José Luis Moreno, pp. 223–240. Hermosillo: Secretaría de Infraestructura Urbana y Ecología, and Colegio de Sonora.

Castetter, Edward F., & Willis H. Bell. 1951. *Yuman Indian Agriculture.* Albuquerque: University of New Mexico Press.

Cecil-Stephens, B. A. 1891. The Colorado Desert and its recent flooding. *Journal of the American Geographical Society of New York* 23:367–377.

Childers, Morlin. 1966. Ghosts of Port Isabel. *Desert* 29(11):25–26.

Childs, Thomas, with Henry F. Dobyns. 1954. Sketch of the "Sand Indians." *Kiva* 19(2–4):27–39.

Chittenden, Newton H. 1901. Among the Cocopahs. *Land of Sunshine* 14:196–204.

Chronic, Halka. 1995. *Roadside Geology of Arizona.* Missoula, Montana: Mountain Press.

Clotts, H[erbert] V. 1915. Report on Nomadic Papago surveys. United States Indian Service manuscript, Laguna Nigel, California; copy on file, Arizona State Museum, Tucson.

———. 1917. History of the Papago Indians and the Papago, Gila Bend, Maricopa, Chiu Chiuschu, That Mamili, Cocklebur, and Nomadic Papago reservations. United States Indian Service manuscript, Laguna Nigel, California; copy on file, Arizona State Museum, Tucson.

Clyde, Norman. 1975. *El Picacho del Diablo: The Conquest of Lower California's Highest Peak.* Los Angeles: Dawson's Book Shop.

Comrie, Andrew C., & Bill Broyles. 1998. Precipitation variability at high spatial resolution from a storage gauge network in the southwest desert. Preprint. American Meteorological Society, 10th Symposium on Meteorological Observations and Instrumentations, 11–16 January, Phoenix, 3A.6–7.

———. 2002. Variability and spatial modeling of fine-scale precipitation data for the Sonoran Desert of south-west Arizona. *Journal of Arid Environments* 50:573–592.

Conklin, Enoch. 1878. *Picturesque Arizona: Being the Result of Travels and Observations in Arizona During the Fall and Winter of 1877.* New York: Mining Record Printing Establishment.

Cope, Edward D. 1873. Zoological description. In *Gray's Atlas of the United States, with General Maps of the World, Accompanied by Descriptions Geographical, Historical, Scientific, and Statistical,* edited by O. W. Gray, pp. 32–36. Philadelphia: Steadman, Brown, & Lyon.

Cornelius, Steve. 1998. *Fragmentation of Natural Resource Management in the Sonoran Desert.* Tucson: Sonoran Institute.

Cozzens, Samuel Woodworth. 1988. *Explorations and Adventures in Arizona and New Mexico* Secaucus, New Jersey: Castle.

Crawford, James M. 1989. *Cocopah Dictionary.* Berkeley: University of California Press.

Crosby, Harry W. 1994. *Antigua California.* Albuquerque: University of New Mexico Press.

Davis, Goode P., Jr. 2001. *Man and Wildlife in Arizona.* Edited by Neil B. Carmony & David E. Brown. Phoenix: Arizona Game and Fish Department.

Davis, Owen K., Alan H. Cutler, Keith H. Meldahl, Manuel R. Palacios-Fest, Joseph F. Schreiber, Jr., Brian E. Lock, Lester J. Williams, Nicholas Lancaster, Christopher A. Shaw, & Stephen M. Sinitiere. 1990. Quaternary and environmental geology of the northeastern Gulf of California. In *Geologic Excursions Through the Sonoran Desert Region, Arizona and Sonora,* edited by George E. Gehrels & Jon E. Spencer, pp. 136–153. Special Paper No. 7. Tucson: Arizona Geological Survey.

Davis, W. M. 1930. Physiographic contrasts, East and West. *Scientific Monthly* 30:394–415, 500–519.

DeJong, David H. 2003. A scheme to rob them of their land: Water, allotment, and the economic integration of the Pima Reservation. *Journal of Arizona History* 44:99–132.

Derby, George H. 1969. *Derby's Report on the Opening of the Colorado, 1850–1851.* Edited by Odie B. Faulk. Albuquerque: University of New Mexico Press.

Devine, David. 2004. *Slavery, Scandal, and Steel Rails.* New York: iUniverse.

Dice, Lee R. 1939. The Sonoran Biotic Province. *Ecology* 20:118–129.

———. 1943. *The Biotic Provinces of North America.* Ann Arbor: University of Michigan Press.

Dice, Lee R., & Philip M. Blossom. 1937. *Studies of Mammalian Ecology in Southwestern North America.* Carnegie Institution of Washington Publication No. 485. Washington, D.C.

Dimmitt, Mark. 2000. Biomes and communities of the Sonoran Desert region. In *A Natural History of the Sonoran Desert,* edited by Steven J. Phillips & Patricia Wentworth Comus, pp. 3–18. Tucson: Arizona-Sonora Desert Museum; Berkeley: University of California Press.

Dobyns, Henry F. 1955. The case of paint vs. garlic. *Arizona Quarterly* XI:156–160.

Dollar, Tom. 2000. 5,000 square miles of silence. *Wildlife Conservation* 103 (May–June): 36–43.

Dolley, Frank S. 1957. Wife at Port Isabel. *Westerners Brandbook, Number 7.* Los Angeles: Los Angeles Corral of Westerners International.

Donlon, C. Josh. 2003. Rats ahoy! Rats begone! *CEDO News* 10(2).

Donlon, C. Josh et al. [20 coauthors]. 2002. Black rat *(Rattus rattus)* eradication from the San Jorge Islands, Mexico. Island Conservation and Ecology Group technical report.

Doyel, David E., & Lorraine Marquez Eiler. 2003. *Hia C'ed O'odham Traditional Cultural Places on the Barry M. Goldwater Range Southwestern Arizona.* Estrella Cultural Research Paper No. 7. Prepared for Luke Air Force Base, project no. F02604–98-M-V015. Phoenix.

Duncan, Robert L. [using pseudonym James Hall Roberts]. 1966. *The Burning Sky.* New York: Ballantine Books.

Edmonson, Travis. 2001. *Thoughts That Didn't Pass.* Tucson: self-published.

Emory, William H. 1859. *Report on the United States and Mexican Boundary Survey.* Washington, D.C.: Cornelius Wendell. Reprint. Austin: Texas State Historical Association, 1987.

Erickson, Winston P. 2003. *Sharing the Desert: The Tohono O'odham in History.* Tucson: University of Arizona Press.

Esquer, Gumersindo. 1928. *Campos de Fuego.* Hermosillo, Sonora: El Modelo.

Etter, Patricia A. 1998. *To California on the Southern Route, 1849: A History and Annotated Bibliography.* Spokane, Washington: Arthur H. Clark.

Evans, George W. B. 1945. *Mexican Gold Trail: The Journal of a Forty-Niner* San Marino, California: Huntington Library.

Executive Order 8038 Establishing the Cabeza Prieta Game Range. 1939. Washington, D.C.: *Federal Register,* January 27.

Executive Order 8892 Withdrawing Public Lands for Use of the War Department, Arizona [Goldwater Range]. 1941. Washington, D.C.: *Federal Register,* September 9. Amendments in Public Land Order 56, 1942, *Federal Register,* November 19; Public Land Order 97, 1943, *Federal Register,* March 26.

Ezell, Paul H. 1994. Plants without water: The Pima-Maricopa experience. *Journal of the Southwest* 36: 315–392.

Ezcurra, E[xequiel]. 1984. The vegetation of El Pinacate, Sonora, a quantitative study. Ph.D. dissertation, University College of North Wales.

Ezcurra, Exequiel, Richard S. Felger, Ann D. Russell, & Miguel Equihua. 1988. Freshwater islands in a desert sand sea: The hydrology, flora, and phytogeography of the Gran Desierto oases of northwestern Mexico. *Desert Plants* 9:35–44, 55–63.

Faulk, Odie B. 1973. *Destiny Road: The Gila Trail and the Opening of the Southwest.* New York: Oxford University Press.

Felger, Richard Stephen. 1966. Ecology of the islands and gulf coast of Sonora, Mexico. Ph.D. dissertation, University of Arizona.

———. 1982. Vegetation and flora of the Gran Desierto, Sonora, Mexico. *Desert Plants* 2:87–114.

———. 1993. *Mirabilis tenuiloba* S. Watson (Nyctaginaceae) new for Arizona. *Madroño* 40:178.

———. 2000. *Flora of the Gran Desierto and Río Colorado of Northwestern Mexico.* Tucson: University of Arizona Press.

Felger, Richard S., Matthew B. Johnson, & Michael F. Wilson. 2001. *Trees of Sonora, Mexico.* New York: Oxford University Press.

Felger, R. S., & C. H. Lowe. 1976. *The Island and Coastal Vegetation and Flora of the Gulf of California, Mexico.* Contributions in Science No. 285. Los Angeles: Natural History Museum of Los Angeles County.

Felger, Richard S., & Mary Beck Moser. 1985. *People of the Desert and Sea: Ethnobotany of the Seri Indians.* Tucson: University of Arizona Press.

Felger, R. S., D. S. Turner, & M. F. Wilson. 2003. Flora and vegetation of the Mohawk Dunes, Arizona. *Sida* 20:1153–1185.

Felger, Richard S., Peter L. Warren, L. Susan Anderson, & Gary P. Nabhan. 1992. Vascular plants of a desert oasis: Flora and ethnobotany of Quitobaquito, Organ Pipe Cactus National Monument, Arizona. *Proceedings of the San Diego Society of Natural History* 8:1–39.

Finch, L. Boyd. 1996. *Confederate Pathway to the Pacific: Major Sherod Hunter and Arizona Territory, C.S.A.* Tucson: Arizona Historical Society.

Fletcher, Colin. 1997. *River: One Man's Journey Down the Colorado, Source to Sea.* New York: Alfred A. Knopf.

Flint, Richard, & Shirley Flint. 2005. *Documents of the Coronado Expedition, 1539–1542: They Were Not Familiar with His Majesty, Nor Did They Wish To Be His Subjects.* Dallas: Southern Methodist University Press.

Fontana, Bernard L. 1974. Man in arid lands: The Piman Indians of the Sonoran Desert. In *Desert Biology,* edited by G. W. Brown, 2:489–528. New York: Academic Press.

———. 1983. Pima and Papago: Introduction. In *Southwest,* edited by Alfonzo Ortiz, pp. 125–148. Handbook of North American Indians, vol. 10, William C. Sturtevant, general editor. Washington, D.C.: Smithsonian Institution.

———. 1987. The Vikita: A biblio history. *Journal of the Southwest* 29:259–272.

———. 1989. *Of Earth and Little Rain.* Tucson: University of Arizona Press.

Forbes, Jack D. 1965. *Warriors of the Colorado: The Yumas of the Quechan Nation and Their Neighbors.* Norman: University of Oklahoma Press.

Fourr, William "Uncle Billy." 2004. Reminiscences of Uncle Billy Fourr. *Cochise County Historical Journal* 34(1):25–49.

Fowlie, Jack A. 1965. *The Snakes of Arizona.* Falbrook, California: Azul Quinta.

Fradkin, Philip L. 1995. *A River No More.* Berkeley: University of California Press.

Franzi, Emil, & Terri Solty Luke. 1998. WWI ace Frank Luke: An enigmatic American hero. *Arizona Highways,* February, 14–23.

Fürsich, Franz T., & Karl W. Flessa. 1987. Taphonomy of tidal flat molluscs in the northern Gulf of California: Paleoenvironmental analysis despite the perils of preservation. *Palaios* 2:543–559.

Gaillard, D[avid] D. 1896. The perils and wonders of a true desert. *Cosmopolitan* 21:592–605.

Garate, Donald T. 1999. Who named Arizona? The Basque connection. *Journal of Arizona History* 40: 53–82.

———. 2005. Arizonac: A twentieth-century myth. *Journal of Arizona History* 46(2):161–184.

Gehlbach, Frank R. 1981. *Mountain Islands and Desert Seas.* College Station: Texas A&M Press.

Gentry, Howard Scott. 1965. Letter to Ronald L. Ives, October 24. In possession of Bill Broyles.

Gila Bend Sun. 1999. Tom Farley, interesting character! April 15, 7.

———. 2004a. Looking back: A visit with Tom Farley. May 27, 17.

———. 2004b. Looking back: Tom Farley. June 3, 17.

———. 2004c. Marion Henry Getzwiller, 87. May 27, 5.

———. 2004d. Woodpile gang repairs Farley cabin. May 20, 17.

Glenn, Edward P., Richard S. Felger, Alberto Búrquez, & Dale S. Turner. 1992. Ciénega de Santa Clara: Endangered wetland in the Colorado River delta, Sonora, Mexico. *Natural Resources Journal* 32: 817–824.

Glenn, Edward P., Christopher Lee, Richard Felger, & Scott Zengel. 1996. Effects of water management on the wetlands of the Colorado River delta, Mexico. *Conservation Biology* 10:1175–1186.

Goff, John S. 1981. *King S. Woolsey.* Cave Creek, Arizona: Black Mountain Press.

Gordon, James H. 1924. Tidal bore at mouth of Colorado River, December 8 to 10, 1923. *Monthly Weather Review* 51:98–99.

Granger, Byrd H. 1960. *Arizona Place Names.* Tucson: University of Arizona Press.

———. 1983. *Arizona's Names: "X" Marks the Spot.* Tucson: Treasure Chest.

Greeley, Ronald, Michael B. Womer, Ronald P. Papson, & Paul D. Spudis. 1978. *Aeolian Features of Southern California: A Comparative Planetary Geology Guidebook.* Washington, D.C.: Office of Planetary Geology, National Aeronautics and Space Administration.

Greene, Jerome A. 1977. Historic resource study: Organ Pipe Cactus National Monument, Arizona. Denver: National Park Service. Unpublished manuscript, on file at Organ Pipe Cactus National Monument.

Grey, Zane. 1969. *Desert Gold.* New York: Pocket Books.

Griffith, James S. 1992. *Beliefs and Holy Places: A Spiritual Geography of the Pimería Alta.* Tucson: University of Arizona Press.

Gudde, Erwin G. 1998. *California Place Names.* 4th ed. Revised and enlarged by William Broght. Berkeley: University of California Press.

Gunn, John. 2000. *An Assessment of the Desirability to Change the Future Management of Natural Resources in "Areas 1" and "9" Located in the Sand Tank Mountains and Sentinel Plain, Maricopa County, Arizona.* Mesa, Arizona: Southwest Natural Resource Management Consultants.

Gutmann, James T. 1976. Geology of Crater Elegante, Sonora, Mexico. *Geological Society of America Bulletin* 87:1718–1729.

———. 2002. Strombolian and effusive activity as precursors to phreatomagmatism: Eruptive sequence at maars of the Pinacate volcanic field, Sonora, Mexico. *Journal of Volcanology and Geothermal Research* 113:345–356.

Gutmann, James T., & D. B. Prival. 1996. Strombolian and hydromagmatic volcanism in the Pinacate Volcanic Field. *Geological Society of America Abstracts with Programs* 28:A-503.

Gutmann, James T., Brent D. Turrin, & John C. Dohrenwend. 2000. Basaltic rocks from the Pinacate Volcanic Field yield notably young ^{40}Ar/^{39}Ar ages. *EOS, Transactions, American Geophysical Union* 81:33, 37.

Hackbarth, Mark R. 1995. *Archaeological Survey of the Butterfield Stage Overland Route, Gila Bend to Mobile, Maricopa County, Arizona.* Tempe, Arizona: Northland Research.

Haff, P. K. 1986. Booming dunes. *American Scientist* 74:376–381.

Hafford, William. 1993. When yesterday was new. *Arizona Highways,* November, 4–9.

Haley, J. Evetts. 1948. *Jeff Milton: Good Man with a Gun.* Norman: University of Oklahoma Press.

Hall, John A., Pat Comer, Anne Gondor, Rob Marshall, & Stephanie Weinstein. 2001. *Conservation Elements of and a Biodiversity Management Framework for the Barry M. Goldwater Range, Arizona.* Tucson: Nature Conservancy.

Hall, Norman S. 1928. *The Balloon Buster: Frank Luke of Arizona.* Garden City, New York: Doubleday, Doran & Co.

Hardy, R. W. H. 1829. *Travels in the Interior of Mexico, in 1825, 1826, 1827, and 1828.* London: Henry Colburn & Richard Bentley. Reprint. Glorieta, New Mexico: Rio Grande Press, 1977.

Hargett, Janet Lee. 1967. Louis John Frederick Jaeger: Entrepreneur at Yuma Crossing. Master's thesis, University of Arizona.

Harris, Benjamin Butler. 1960. *The Gila Trail: The Texas Argonauts and the California Gold Rush.* Norman: University of Oklahoma Press.

Harshberger, John W. 1911. Phytogeographic survey of North America. In Engler & Drude, *Vegetation der Erde,* vol. 13.

Hartmann, Gayle Harrison, & Mary Charlotte Thurtle. 2001. The archaeology of Tinajas Altas, a desert water hole in southwestern Arizona. *Kiva* 66: 489–518.

Hartmann, William K. 1989. *Desert Heart.* Tucson: Fisher Books.

Hayden, Julian D. 1966. Communication re: Ives' "Kino's exploration of the Pinacate region." *Journal of Arizona History* 7:196–200.

———. 1972. Hohokam petroglyphs of the Sierra Pinacate, Sonora, and the Hohokam shell expeditions. *Kiva* 37:74–83.

———. 1976. Changing climate in the Sierra Pinacate of Sonora, Mexico. In *Desertification: Process, Problems, and Perspectives,* pp. 70–86. Tucson: Arid/ Semi-arid Natural Resources Program.

———. 1980. Sierra Pinacate. In *Camera, Spade, and Pen: An Inside View of Southwestern Archaeology,* edited by Marc Gaede & Marnie Gaede, pp. 145– 152. Tucson: University of Arizona Press.

———. 1987. The Vikita ceremony of the Papago. *Journal of the Southwest* 29:273–323ff.

———. 1998. *The Sierra Pinacate.* Tucson: Southwest Center and University of Arizona Press.

Hendricks, William O. 1967. Guillermo Andrade and land development on the Mexican Colorado River delta, 1874–1905. Ph.D. dissertation, University of Southern California.

———. 1971. Port Otis. *Brand Book II.* San Diego, California: San Diego Corral of the Westerners.

Hinojosa-Huerta, Osvel, Pamela L. Nagler, Yamilett Carrillo-Guerrero, Enrique Zamora-Hernández, Jaqueline García-Hernández, Francisco Zamora-Arroyo, Kara Gillon, & Edward P. Glenn. 2002. Andrade Mesa wetlands of the All-American Canal. *Natural Resources Journal* 42:899–914.

Hodgson, W. 1999. Vascular plants of Arizona: Agavaceae, Agave family, part one, Agave L. *Journal of the Arizona-Nevada Academy of Science* 32:1–21.

Hogner, Dorothy Childs. 1938. *Westward, High, Low, and Dry.* New York: E. P. Dutton.

Homburg, Jeffery A., Jeffery H. Altschul, & Rein Vanderpot. 1994. *Intermontane Settlement Trends in the Eastern Papaguería.* Technical Series No. 37. Tucson: Statistical Research.

Hornaday, William T. 1908. *Camp-Fires on Desert and Lava.* New York: Charles Scribner's Sons. Reprint. Tucson: University of Arizona Press, 1983.

———. 1931. *Thirty Years War for Wild Life.* Stamford, Connecticut: Permanent Wildlife Protection Fund.

Hoy, Bill. 1990. Sonoyta and Santo Domingo. *Journal of Arizona History* 31:117–140.

———. 1993. *Spanish Terms of the Sonoran Desert Borderlands: A Basic Glossary.* Calexico: San Diego State University, Imperial Valley Campus.

———. 1994. War in Papaguería: Manuel Gándara's 1840–41 Papago expedition. *Journal of Arizona History* 35:141–162.

———. 1995. Hardscrabble days at the Ajo mines: George Kippen's diary, 1855–1858. *Journal of Arizona History* 36:233–250.

———. 1999. Don Tomás and Tomasito: The Childs family legacy in southern Arizona. *Journal of Arizona History* 40:1–28.

Hoy, Wilton E. [Bill]. 1969. A quest for the meaning of Quitobaquito. *Kiva* 34:213–218.

———. 1970. Organ pipe cactus historical research. Ms. on file, Organ Pipe Cactus National Monument.

Humphrey, Robert R. 1987. *Ninety Years and 535 Miles: Vegetation Changes Along the Mexican Border.* Albuquerque: University of New Mexico Press.

Hunt, Henry. 1998. *Hidden Trails in the Sonoran Desert.* Arizona City: Desert Press.

Hutchins, Carleen Maley. 1962. The physics of violins. *Scientific American.* Reprinted in *Science and the Arts,* pp. 76–89. New York: Scientific American, 1995.

International Boundary Commission. 1898. *Report upon the Survey and Re-marking of the Boundary Between the United States and Mexico West of the Rio Grande, 1891–1896.* Senate Document No. 47, 55th Congress, 2d session. Washington, D.C.

Irish, Lynn. 1972. Place names of Organ Pipe Cactus National Monument. Ms. on file, Organ Pipe Cactus National Monument.

Irwin, Catherine. ca. 1970. *El Camino del Diablo.* Yuma: Yuma County Historical Society.

Ives, Joseph Christmas. 1861. *Report upon the Colorado River of the West, explored in 1857 and 1858.* [U.S. House of Representatives] Executive Document No. 90. 36th Congress, 1st session. Washington, D.C.

Ives, Ronald L. 1935. Geologic verification of a Papago legend. *Masterkey* 9:160–161.

———. 1949. The Sonoran Railroad project. *Journal of Geography* 48:197–206.

———. 1950. Puerto Peñasco, Sonora. *Journal of Geography* 49:349–361.

———. 1962. In memoriam—Alberto Celaya. *Explorers Journal* 40:91–92.

———. 1964. *The Pinacate Region, Sonora, Mexico.* Occasional Papers of the California Academy of Sciences No. 47. San Francisco.

———. 1965. Letter to Paul H. Ezell, October 8. In possession of Bill Broyles.

———. 1984. *José Velásquez: Saga of a Borderland Soldier.* Tucson: Southwestern Mission Research Center.

———. 1989. *Land of Lava, Ash, and Sand.* Edited by James W. Byrkit & Karen J. Dahood. Tucson: Arizona Historical Society.

Jaeger, Edmund C. 1958. "Dry lake" filled with water. *Desert Magazine,* June, 24–26.

Jahns, Richard H. 1959. Collapse depressions of the Pinacate volcanic field, Sonora, Mexico. In *Southern Arizona Guidebook 2,* pp. 165–184. Tucson: Arizona Geological Society.

James, George Wharton. 1906. *The Wonders of the Colorado Desert.* Boston: Page. Reprint. Boston: Little, Brown, 1911.

Jewell, Donald R. 1959. Frank Pinkley: "The Boss." *Desert Magazine,* September, 12.

Johnson, William W., Jr. 1997. *Soil Survey of Gila Bend–Ajo Area, Arizona, Parts of Maricopa and Pima Counties.* U.S. Department of Agriculture, Natural Resources Conservation Service. N.p.

Jones, Richard D. 1969. An analysis of Papago communities. Ph.D. dissertation, University of Arizona.

Karns, Harry. 1954. *Luz de Tierra Incógnita.* Tucson: Arizona Silhouettes.

Keith, Stanton B. 1974. *Index of Mining Properties in Pima County, Arizona.* Tucson: Arizona Bureau of Geology and Mineral Technology.

Kelly, William H. 1977. *Cocopa Ethnography.* Anthropological Papers of the University of Arizona No. 29. Tucson: University of Arizona Press.

King, W[illiam] S. 1961. Papago village descriptions. Bureau of Ethnic Research manuscript, archives folder A-781, Arizona State Museum. Tucson.

Kowalewski, Michal, & Karl W. Flessa. 1995. Comparative taphonomy and faunal composition of shelly cheniers from northeastern Baja California, Mexico. *Ciencias Marinas* 21:155–177.

———. 1996. A dead delta's prehistoric productivity. Geological Society of America, convention press release, October 30.

Kroeber, Clifton B., & Bernard L. Fontana. 1986. *Massacre on the Gila: An Account of the Last Major Battle Between American Indians, with Reflections on the Origin of War.* Tucson: University of Arizona Press.

Kupel, Douglas E. 1999. Roadside rest: From stage station to the space age in Gila Bend. *Journal of Arizona History* 40:345–376.

Laird, David. 1998. *Desert Stories: A Reader's Guide to the Sonoran Borderlands/Historias del Desierto: Guía para Lectores de la Zona Fronteriza Sonorense.* Tucson: Arizona-Sonora Desert Museum Press.

L'Amour, Louis. 1957. *Last Stand at Papago Wells.* New York: Fawcett.

———. 1966. *Kid Rodelo.* New York: Bantam Books.

Lancaster, N., R. Greeley, & P. R. Christensen. 1987. Dunes of the Gran Desierto sand-sea, Sonora, Mexico. *Earth Surface Processes and Landforms* 12:277–288.

Lehto, E[lenor]. 1979. "Extinct" wire-lettuce, *Stephanomeria schottii* (Compositae), rediscovered in Arizona after more than one hundred years. *Desert Plants* 1:22.

Lenon, Bob. 1987. The routes of the explorers in Pimería Alta. Paper presented to Arizona Historical Convention, Flagstaff.

Leopold, Aldo. 1966. *A Sand County Almanac.* New York: Ballantine Books.

Lingenfelter, Richard E. 1978. *Steamboats on the Colorado River, 1852–1916.* Tucson: University of Arizona Press.

Lumholtz, Carl. 1912. *New Trails in Mexico.* London: T. Fisher Unwin. Reprint. Glorieta, New Mexico: Rio Grande Press, 1971.

Lynch, Daniel James. 1981. Genesis and geochronology of alkaline volcanism in the Pinacate Volcanic Field, northwestern Sonora, Mexico. Ph.D. dissertation, University of Arizona.

———. 1982. Volcanic processes in Arizona. *Fieldnotes from the Arizona Bureau of Geology* 12:1–9.

———. 1989. Neogene volcanism in Arizona: The recognizable volcanoes. In *Geologic Evolution of Arizona*, edited by J. P. Jenney & S. J. Reynolds, pp. 681–700. Digest No. 17. Tucson: Arizona Geological Society.

Lynch, Daniel J., & James T. Gutmann. 1987. Volcanic structures and alkaline rocks in the Pinacate Volcanic Field of Sonora, Mexico. In *Geologic Diversity of Arizona and Its Margins,* Special Paper No. 5, pp. 309–322. Tucson: Arizona Bureau of Geology and Mineral Technology.

MacDougal, Daniel T. 1904. Delta and desert vegetation. *Botanical Gazette* 38:44–63.

———. 1908a. Across Papaguería. *Bulletin of the American Geographical Society* XL (December): 1–21.

———. 1908b. *Botanical Features of North American Deserts.* Washington, D.C.: Carnegie Institution.

MacPherson, Earl. 1973. *Gillespie's Gold.* Phoenix: Southland Press.

Malusa, Jim. 1993. A river ran through it. *Destination Discovery,* May, 22–29.

Marie, James R., & Kenneth J. Hollett. 1996. *Determination of Hydraulic Characteristics and Yield of Aquifers Underlying Vekol Valley, Arizona, Using Several Classical and Current Methods.* USGS Water Supply Paper No. 2453. Washington, D.C.: U.S. Government Printing Office.

Marshall, Rob, Susan Anderson, Michael Batcher, Pat Comer, Steve Cornelius, Robin Cox, Anne Gondor, Dave Gori, John Humke, Rafaela Paredes Aguilar, Iva E. Parra, & Sabra Schwartz. 2000. *An Ecological Analysis of Conservation Priorities in the Sonoran Desert Ecoregion.* Tucson: Nature Conservancy, IMADES, and Sonoran Institute.

Martin, Douglas C. 1954. *Yuma Crossing.* Albuquerque: University of New Mexico Press.

Martínez del Rio, Carlos, & Bill Broyles. 2000. The Sonoran Desert National Park. *Wild Earth* 10 (Summer): 53–56.

Masich, Andrew E. n.d. San Ysidro Ranch Archaeological Project. Report prepared for Rio Colorado Chapter of the Arizona Historical Society, Yuma.

Mathiot, M. 1963. *A Dictionary of Papago Usage.* Language Science Monographs, vol. 8. Bloomington: Indiana University.

Matson, Daniel S., & Bernard L. Fontana, editors. 1996. *Before Rebellion: Letters and Reports of Jacobo Sedelmayr, S.J.* Tucson: Arizona Historical Society.

Matthiessen, Peter. 1989. *The River Styx and Other Stories.* New York: Random House.

May, Larry A. 1973. Resource reconnaissance of the Gran Desierto region, northwestern Sonora, Mexico. Master's thesis, University of Arizona.

McGee, Emma R. 1915. *Life of W J McGee.* Farley, Iowa: privately printed.

McGee, W. J. 1901. The Old Yuma Trail. *National Geographic Magazine* 12(3):103–107, (4):129–143.

McGinnies, William G. 1981. *Discovering the Desert.* Tucson: University of Arizona Press.

McGivney, Annette. 1998. An eye to the future: The next national parks. *Backpacker* 26 (December): 52–66.

———. 2001. The big empty. *Backpacker* 29 (February): 50–58.

McGuire, Randall, & Linda Mayro. 1978. *Papago Wells Project: Archaeological Surveys Near Kaka and Stoa Pitk, the Papago Reservation, Arizona.* Archaeological Series No. 120. Tucson: Arizona State Museum.

McGuire, Randall H., & Michael B. Schiffer, editors. 1982. *Hohokam and Patayan: Prehistory of Southwestern Arizona.* New York: Academic Press.

McKee, Edwin D. 1979. *A Study of Global Sand Seas.* Professional Paper No. 1052. Washington, D.C.: U.S. Geological Survey.

McLaughlin, Steven P., & Janice E. Bowers. 1982. Effects of wildfire on a Sonoran Desert plant community. *Ecology* 63:246–248.

McVaugh, Rogers. 1956. *Edward Palmer: Plant Explorer of the American West.* Norman: University of Oklahoma Press.

Mearns, Edgar A. 1907. *Mammals of the Mexican Boundary of the United States.* Washington, D.C.: U.S. Government Printing Office. Reprint. New York: Arno Press, 1974.

Medrano, Lourdes. 2005. Place to call home: O'odham help their landless kin carve out a tiny homeland. *Arizona Daily Star,* February 6, 1A, 15A.

Menges, Christopher M., & Philip A. Pearthree. 1989. Late Cenozoic tectonism in Arizona and its impact on regional landscape evolution. In *Geologic Evolution of Arizona,* edited by J. P. Jenney & S. J. Reynolds, pp. 649–680. Digest No. 17. Tucson: Arizona Geological Society.

Miller, G. A. 1979. *Status of Mineral Resource Information for Luke Air Force Range, Arizona.* Phoenix: Arizona Department of Mineral Resources.

Minnich, Richard A., Ernesto Franco-Vizcaíno, Joaquín Sosa-Ramírez, Jack H. Burk, W. James Barry, Michael G. Barbour, & Horacio de la Cueva-Salcido. 1997. A land above: Protecting Baja California's Sierra San Pedro Mártir within a biosphere reserve. *Journal of the Southwest* 39(3–4):613–695.

Moreno, Daniel. 1960. *Los Hombres de la Revolución.* Mexico City: Editores.

Munro, Guillermo. 1992. *Las Voces Vienen del Mar.* Hermosillo: Instituto Sonorense de Cultura.

Nabhan, Gary Paul. 1982. *The Desert Smells Like Rain.* San Francisco: North Point Press.

———. 1985. *Gathering the Desert.* Tucson: University of Arizona Press.

Nabhan, Gary Paul, & John L. Carr, editors. 1994. *Ironwood: An Ecological and Cultural Keystone of the Sonoran Desert.* Occasional Paper No. 1. Washington, D.C.: Conservation International.

Nabhan, G[ary] P[aul], & R[ichard] S. Felger. 1978. Teparies in southwestern North America. *Economic Botany* 32:2–19.

Nabhan, Gary Paul, & Andrew R. Holdsworth. 1998. *State of the Biome: Uniqueness, Biodiversity, Threats, and the Adequacy of Protection in the Sonoran Bioregion.* Tucson: Wildlands Project.

Nabhan, Gary P., A. M. Rea, K. L. Reichhardt, E. Mellink, & C. F. Hutchinson. 1982. Papago influences on habitat and biotic diversity: Quitovac oasis ethnoecology. *Journal of Ethnobiology* 2:124–143.

Nagel, Carlos. 1992. A different view of the border: The white map syndrome. In *Land Use Changes in the Western Sonoran Desert Border Area: A Regional Forum; Abstracts and Supporting Material,* edited by Wendy Laird, unpaginated. Tucson: Sonoran Institute and Lincoln Institute of Land Policy.

Narragansett Map. 1875. *Mouth of the Colorado River.* Washington, D.C.: U.S. Department of the Navy.

National Gazetteer of the United States of America: Arizona, 1986. 1987. U.S. Geological Survey Professional Paper 1200-AZ. Washington, D.C.: U.S. Government Printing Office.

Nelson, Kent. 1984. The man at Quitobaquito. *Southern Review* 20:693–700.

———. 1991. *Language in the Blood.* Salt Lake City: Peregrine Smith.

Nentvig, Juan. 1980. *Rudo Ensayo: A Description of Sonora and Arizona in 1764.* Tucson: University of Arizona Press.

Nichol, A[ndrew] A. 1939. O'Neill's grave in O'Neill's Pass in the O'Neill Mountains. *Random Papers for Southwestern National Monuments,* July, 65–67.

———. 1948. Letter to William R. Supernaugh, May 7. On file, Organ Pipe Cactus National Monument.

Nori, Franco, Paul Sholtz, & Michael Bretz. 1997. Booming sand. *Scientific American,* September, 84–89.

Norris, Robert M. 1995. Geology of the California deserts: A summary. In *The California Desert: An Introduction to Natural Resources and Man's Impact,* edited by June Latting & Peter G. Rowlands, pp. 27–58. Riverside, California: June Latting Books.

North, Arthur W. 1977. *Camp and Camino in Lower California.* Glorieta, New Mexico: Rio Grande Press. Originally published New York: Baker & Taylor, 1910.

O'Bryon, Eleanor Dart. 1989. *Coming Home from Devil Mountain.* Tucson: Harbinger Books.

Ocaña-García, Samuel. 1993. *Propuesta para la Declaración de Reserva de la Biosfera: Alto Golfo de California y Delta del Río Colorado.* Hermosillo, Sonora: Comité para la Preservación de la Vaquita y la Totoaba.

Officer, James E., Mardith Schuetz-Miller, & Bernard L. Fontana. 1996. *The Pimería Alta.* Tucson: Southwestern Mission Research Center.

O'Neal, Bill. 1987. *The Arizona Rangers.* Austin: Eakin Press.

Ortega-Noriega, Sergio, & Ignacio del Río, editors. 1985. *Historia General de Sonora.* 3 vols. Hermosillo: Gobierno del Estado de Sonora.

Orth, Donald J., & Roger L. Payne. 1997. *Principles, Policies, and Procedures: Domestic Geographic Names.* United States Board on Geographic Names. Reston, Virginia: United States Geological Survey, Office of Geographic Names.

Paredes Aguilar, Rafaela, Thomas R. Van Devender, & Richard S. Felger. 2000. *Cactaceas de Sonora, México.* Tucson: Arizona-Sonora Desert Museum Press.

Pattie, James Ohio. 1930. *The Personal Narrative of James O. Pattie of Kentucky.* Chicago: R. R. Donnelley & Sons.

Peacock, Doug. 1986. A lonely desert rendezvous. *American West* 23(4):62–71.

———. *Walking It Off: A Veteran's Chronicle of War and Wilderness.* Spokane: Eastern Washington University Press.

Peaden, Carroll H. 1978. John the Baptist: Early-day longhair. *Arizona Republic Magazine,* November 26, 20–25.

Pumpelly, Raphael. 1918. *My Reminiscences,* vol. 1. New York: Henry Holt.

Ralfe, J. 1828. *The Naval Biography of Great Britain: Consisting of Historical Memoirs of Those Officers of the British Navy Who Distinguished Themselves During the Reign of His Majesty George III,* vol. 2. Charing-Cross, England: Whitmore & Fenn. Reprint. Boston: Gregg Press, 1972.

Rea, Amadeo M. 1997. *At the Desert's Green Edge: An Ethnobotany of the Gila River Pima.* Tucson: University of Arizona Press.

Reid, John C. 1935. *Reid's Tramp, or a Journal of Ten Months Travel Through Texas, New Mexico, Arizona, Sonora, and California* Austin: Steck. Originally published Selma, Alabama: John Hardy, 1858.

Reisner, Marc. 1986. *Cadillac Desert: The American West and Its Disappearing Water.* New York: Penguin Books.

Reynolds, Anna M. 1996. *Ajo: The Desert Speaks.* Cornville, Arizona: mAjo Productions.

Rickard, Forrest R. 1996. *The Development of Ajo, Arizona.* Ajo: Forrest R. Rickard.

Robles-Gil, Patricio, Exequiel Ezcurra, & Eric Mellink, editors. 2001. *The Gulf of California: A World Apart.* Mexico City: Pegaso-Agrupación Sierra Madre. Spanish edition titled *El Golfo de California: Un Mundo Aparte.*

Roca, Paul M. 1967. *Paths of the Padres Through Sonora.* Tucson: Arizona Pioneers' Historical Society.

Rodriguez, Carlie A., Karl W. Flessa, Miguel A. Téllez-Duarte, David L. Dettman, & Guillermo A. Avila-Serrano. 2001. Macrofaunal and isotopic estimates of the former extent of the Colorado River estuary, upper Gulf of California, México. *Journal of Arid Environments* 49:183–193.

Roosevelt, Kermit. 1920. *The Happy Hunting-Grounds.* New York: Charles Scribner's.

Ross, Clyde P. 1923. *The Lower Gila Region: A Geographic, Geologic, and Hydrologic Reconnaissance, with a Guide to Desert Watering Places.* Water-Supply Paper No. 498. Washington, D.C.: United States Geological Survey.

Rube, B. Johnny. 1996. *A Wooden Road Through the Hollow of God's Hand: Taming the American Sahara.* Yuma: Arizona Historical Society.

Rutman, Susan. 1995. An assessment of wildland fire at Organ Pipe Cactus National Monument, Arizona. Ms. on file, Organ Pipe Cactus National Monument.

Sanders, E. M. 1921. The natural regions of Mexico. *Geographical Review* 11:212–226.

Saxton, D., L. Saxton, & L. Enos. 1983. *Papago/Pima-English Dictionary.* Tucson: University of Arizona Press.

Schneider, Joan S. 1993. Antelope Hill: A cultural resources inventory and inquiry into prehistoric milling implement quarrying and production behaviors along the lower Gila River, Yuma County, Arizona. In *Glyphs and Quarries of the Lower Colorado River Valley: The Results of Five Cultural Resource Surveys,* edited by Joseph E. Ezzo & Jeffrey Altschul, pp. i–79. Technical Series No. 44. Tucson: Statistical Research.

Schneider, Joan S., & Jeffrey H. Altschul. 2000. *Of Stones and Spirits: Pursuing the Past of Antelope Hill.* Technical Series No. 76. Tucson: Statistical Research.

Sellers, William D., & Richard H. Hill 1974. *Arizona Climate, 1931–1972.* Tucson: University of Arizona Press.

Serafín, Federico Iglesias. 1992. *Monumento 204: San Luis Río Colorado.* San Luis R. C., Sonora: Artec.

Shackley, M. Steven. 2005. *Obsidian: Geology and Archaeology in the North American Southwest.* Tucson: University of Arizona Press.

Shaffer, Mark. 1999. Yodaville exists for bombing runs; Arizona's newest town inviting target. *Arizona Republic,* August 23.

Shafiqullah, M., P. E. Damon, D. J. Lynch, S. J. Reynolds, W. A. Rehrig, & R. H. Raymond. 1980. K-Ar geochronology and geologic history of southwestern Arizona and adjacent areas. *Arizona Geological Society Digest* 12:201–243.

Sheldon, Charles. 1993. *The Wilderness of the Southwest: Charles Sheldon's Quest for Desert Bighorn Sheep and Adventures with the Havasupai and Seri Indians.* Edited by Neil B. Carmony & David E. Brown. Salt Lake City: University of Utah Press.

Shreve, Forrest. 1951. *Vegetation of the Sonoran Desert.* Carnegie Institution of Washington Publication No. 591. Washington, D.C.

Shreve, Forrest, & Ira L. Wiggins. 1964. *Vegetation and Flora of the Sonoran Desert,* vols. 1 & 2. Stanford, California: Stanford University Press.

Shumaker, Jon M. 2000. *A Class 1 Cultural Resources Overview of the Proposed Sonoran Desert National Monument, Maricopa and Pinal Counties, Arizona.* Report prepared for Sonoran Desert National Park Friends, Tucson.

Simmons, Hilah L. 1965. The geology of the Cabeza Prieta Game Range. Ms. on file, Cabeza Prieta National Wildlife Refuge, Ajo, Arizona.

Simmons, Norman M. 1966. Flora of the Cabeza Prieta Game Range. *Journal of the Arizona Academy of Science* 4:93–104.

Simposio de Investigación sobre la Zona Ecológica de El Pinacate. 1988. Hermosillo, Sonora: Arizona-México Commission.

Smith, C. C. 1935. Camels in the Southwest. *Arizona Historical Review* 1:90–96.

Smith, Hobart M. 1939. *The Mexican and Central American Lizards of the Genus* Sclerporus. Field Museum Publication No. 455, Zoological Series No. 26. Chicago.

Smith, Roger Stanley Uhr. 1970. Migration and wind regime of small barchan dunes within the Algodones Chain, Imperial County, California. Master's thesis, University of Arizona.

Smith, Olga Wright. 1956. *Gold on the Desert.* Albuquerque: University of New Mexico Press.

Smith, Walter. 1986. *The Effects of Eastern North Pacific Tropical Cyclones on the Southwestern United States.* Technical Memorandum NWS [National Weather Service] WR-197. Washington, D.C.: National Oceanic and Atmospheric Administration.

Sobarzo, Horacio. 1991. *Vocabulario Sonorense.* Hermosillo: Gobierno del Estado de Sonora.

Sonoran Desert National Park, Arizona: A Proposal. 1966. National Park Service report. Organ Pipe Cactus National Monument, Arizona.

Sowls, Lyle K. 1997. *Javelinas and Other Peccaries: Their Biology, Management, and Use.* College Station: Texas A&M University Press.

Spicer, Edward H. 1962. *Cycles of Conquest.* Tucson: University of Arizona Press.

Spilken, Aron. 1983. *Escape!* New York: New American Library.

Stanton, Robert Brewster. 1965. *Down the Colorado.* Norman: University of Oklahoma Press.

Stephen, Leslie, & Sidney Lee. 1917. *The Dictionary of National Biography.* 8 vols. London: Oxford University Press.

Stewart, John H., Forrest G. Poole, Keith B. Ketner, Raul J. Madrid, Jaime Roldán-Quintana, & Ricardo Amaya-Martínez. 1990. Tectonics and stratigraphy of the Paleozoic and Triassic southern margin of North America, Sonora, Mexico. In *Geologic Excursions Through the Sonoran Desert Region, Arizona and Sonora,* edited by George E. Gehrels & Jon E. Spencer, pp. 183–202. Tucson: Arizona Geological Survey.

Stewart, Jon Mark. 1993. *Colorado Desert Wildflowers.* Palm Desert, California: Cachuma Press.

Summers, Richard A. 1937. *The Devil's Highway.* New York: Thomas Nelson & Sons.

Supernaugh, William. 1975. Interview, May 3. Conducted by William Werrell. On file, Organ Pipe Cactus National Monument, Arizona.

Swanson, Mark T. 1992. *An Archaeological Investigation of the Historic Black Settlement at Mobile, Arizona.* Technical Series No. 34. Tucson: Statistical Research.

Sykes, Glenton G. 1976. Five walked out. *Journal of Arizona History* 17:127–136.

Sykes, Godfrey. 1915a. The mythical Straits of Anian. *Bulletin of the American Geographical Society* 47: 161–172.

———. 1915b. The isles of California. *Bulletin of the American Geographical Society* 47:745–761.

———. 1915c. How California got its name. *Out West* 41:225–230.

———. 1931. Rainfall investigations in Arizona by means of long-period rain gauges. *Geographical Review* 21:229–233.

———. 1937. *The Colorado Delta.* New York: American Geographical Society. Reprint. Port Washington, New York: Kennikat Press, 1970.

———. 1951. Summer journey on the Devil's Road. *Desert Magazine* 14(6):5–6.

Talbot, Trisha. 1996. Flax, jojoba, sesame . . . some crops fail to find a place in Yuma's rotation. *Agriculture,* July 14. Yuma, Arizona.

Taylor, Issac. 1898. *Names and Their Histories: A Handbook of Historical Geography and Topographical Nomenclature.* London: Rivingtons.

Thomas, Robert K. 1991. Papago land use west of the Papago Indian Reservation, south of the Gila River, and the problem of Sand Papago identity. In *Ethnology of Northwest Mexico: A Sourcebook,* edited by Randall H. McGuire, pp. 357–399. Spanish Borderlands Sourcebook No. 6. New York: Garland.

Thompson, Robert Wayne. 1968. *Tidal Flat Sedimentation on the Colorado River Delta, Northwestern Gulf of California.* Memoir No. 107. Boulder: Geological Society of America.

Thompson-Olais, Laura. 1994. *Sonoran Pronghorn Recovery Plan Revision.* Albuquerque: U.S. Fish and Wildlife Service.

Tinker, Ben. 1978. *Mexican Wilderness and Wildlife.* Austin: University of Texas Press.

Tosdal, R. M., G. B. Haxel, T. H. Anderson, C. D. Connors, D. J. May, & J. E. Wright. 1990. Highlights of Jurassic, Late Cretaceous to Early Tertiary, and Middle Tertiary tectonics, south-central Arizona and north-central Sonora. In *Geologic Excursions Through the Sonoran Desert Region, Arizona and Sonora,* Special Paper No. 7, edited by George E. Gehrels & Jon E. Spencer, pp. 76–89. Tucson: Arizona Geological Survey.

Tosdal, Richard M., Gordon B. Haxel, & James E. Wright. 1989. Jurassic geology of the Sonoran Desert region, southern Arizona, southeastern California, and northernmost Sonora: Construction

of a continental-margin magmatic arc. In *Geologic Evolution of Arizona,* Digest No. 17, edited by J. P. Jenney & S. J. Reynolds, pp. 397–434. Tucson: Arizona Geological Society.

Tucson Citizen. 1954. Bonillas rose from bootblack to national figure in Mexico. September 28.

Turner, Beverly. 2001. Town of Gila Bend, Minutes of Special Council Meeting, July 2. Gila Bend, Arizona.

Turner, Dale S. 1998. Ecology of the fringe-toed lizard, *Uma notata,* in Arizona's Mohawk Dunes. Master's thesis, University of Arizona.

Turner, Dale S., Richard S. Felger, Kathryn Mauz, Carianne S. Funicelli, Tom Van Devender, & Jim Malusa. 2000. *Biological Resources of the Proposed Sonoran Desert National Monument, Arizona.* Tucson: Drylands Institute.

Turner, R[aymond] M. 1990. Long-term vegetation change at a fully protected Sonoran Desert site. *Ecology* 71:464–477.

———. 1994. Mohave desertscrub. In *Biotic Communities, Southwestern United States and Northwestern Mexico,* edited by David E. Brown, pp. 157–168. Salt Lake City: University of Utah Press. Originally published in special issue, *Desert Plants* 4 (1982).

Turner, Raymond M., Janice E. Bowers, & Tony L. Burgess. 1995. *Sonoran Desert Plants: An Ecological Atlas.* Tucson: University of Arizona Press.

Turner, Raymond M., & David E. Brown. 1994. Sonoran desertscrub. In *Biotic Communities: Southwestern United States and Northwestern Mexico,* edited by David E. Brown, pp. 180–221. Salt Lake City: University of Utah Press. Reprint of *Desert Plants* 4 (1982): 1–341.

Turner, Raymond M., Robert H. Webb, Janice E. Bowers, & James Rodney Hastings. 2003. *The Changing Mile Revisited.* Tucson: University of Arizona Press.

United States Geological Survey. 1987. *The National Gazetteer of the United States of America: Arizona 1986.* Professional Paper No. 1200-AZ. Washington, D.C.: U.S. Government Printing Office.

Valentine, Fernando. 1994. Schuk Toak: Pinacate Peak. *Noticias del CEDO* 6(2):22–27.

Van Devender, Thomas R. 1990. Late Quaternary vegetation and climate of the Sonoran Desert, United States and Mexico. In *Packrat Middens: The Last 40,000 Years of Biotic Change,* edited by Julio L. Betancourt, Thomas R. Van Devender, & Paul S. Martin, pp. 134–165. Tucson: University of Arizona Press.

Van Devender, T. R., T. L. Burgess, R. S. Felger, & R. M. Turner. 1990. Holocene vegetation of the Hornaday Mountains of northwestern Sonora, Mexico. *Proceedings of the San Diego Society of Natural History* 2:1–19.

Van Valkenburgh, Richard. 1945. Tom Childs of Ten-Mile Wash. *Desert Magazine* 9(2):3–5.

Vasey, G., & J. N. Rose. 1890. List of plants collected by Dr. Edward Palmer in Lower California in 1889.

Contributions from the United States National Herbarium 1:9–28.

Verdugo-Fimbres, María Isabel. 1985. *Presente y Pasado: Historia del Municipio de Puerto Peñasco.* Hermosillo, Sonora.

Vista. 1996. Workshops. 1:4–8. International Sonoran Desert Alliance Newsletter, Ajo.

Walker, Henry P., & Don Bufkin. 1986. *Historical Atlas of Arizona.* Norman: University of Oklahoma Press.

Ward, Evan R. 1999. Saline solutions: Arizona water politics, Mexican-American relations, and the Wellton-Mohawk Valley. *Journal of Arizona History* 40:276–292.

———. 2003. *Border Oasis: Water and the Political Ecology of the Colorado River Delta, 1940–1975.* Tucson: University of Arizona Press.

Webb, Robert H., & Howard G. Wilshire. 1983. *Environmental Effects of Off-Road Vehicles: Impacts and Management in Arid Regions.* New York: Springer-Verlag.

Weese, A. O. 1941. Letter to director of U.S. National Park Service. U.S. Fish and Wildlife Service, Record Unit 7176, Box 31, Folder 7, Smithsonian Institution Archives.

Westover, William H. 1966. *Yuma Footprints.* Tucson: Arizona Pioneers' Historical Society.

Williams, Anita Alvarez de. 1983. Cocopa. In *Southwest,* edited by Alfonzo Ortiz, pp. 99–112. Handbook of North American Indians, vol. 10, William C. Sturtevant, general editor. Washington, D.C.: Smithsonian Institution.

Williams, Jeanne. 1976. *A Lady Bought with Rifles.* New York: Coward, McCann & Geoghegen.

Wilson, E. D. 1931. New mountains in the Yuma Desert, Arizona. *Geographical Review* 21:221–228.

———. 1933. *Geology and Mineral Deposits of Southern Yuma County, Arizona.* Arizona Bureau of Mines Bulletin 134, vol. 4, No. 2. Tucson.

Winsor, Mulford. 1954. José María Redondo. Ms. on file, Yuma Public Library, Yuma.

Wood, Charles Arthur. 1972. Reconnaissance geology and geophysics of the Pinacate craters, Sonora, Mexico. Master's thesis, University of Arizona.

Woodin, Ann. 1964. *Home Is the Desert.* New York: Macmillan. Reprint. Oracle, Arizona: Oracle Press, 1994.

Yates, Richard, & Mary Marshall. 1974. *The Lower Colorado River: A Bibliography.* Yuma: Arizona Western College.

Yetman, David. 1996. *Sonora: An Intimate Geography.* Albuquerque: University of New Mexico Press.

Zengel, Scott A., & Edward P. Glenn. 1996. Presence of the endangered desert pupfish (*Cyprinodon macularius,* Cyprinidontidae) in Ciénega de Santa Clara, Mexico, following an extensive marsh drydown. *Southwestern Naturalist* 41:73–78.

Zepeda, Ofelia. 1983. *A Papago Grammar.* Tucson: University of Arizona Press.

———. 1985. *The Sand Papago Oral History Project.* Tucson: Division of Archeology, Western Archeological and Conservation Center, National Park Service.

———. 1995. *Ocean Power: Poems from the Desert.* Tucson: University of Arizona Press.

Zwinger, Ann. 1993. White-winged doves and desert bighorns. In *Counting Sheep: Twenty Ways of Seeing Desert Bighorn,* edited by Gary Paul Nabhan, pp. 132–154. Tucson: University of Arizona Press.

Contributors

Jayne Belnap is field station leader for the Canyonlands Research Station, U.S. Geological Survey, Moab, Utah. She has spent most of her adult life studying the biology and ecology of arid land organisms. Most of her focus has been on the ecological role of biological soil crusts in different deserts of the world, including in the western United States, Australia, Mongolia, China, South Africa, Tanzania, and Kenya. She has even ventured into tropical rain forests, following the trail of crusts (they are there, but instead of being on the ground, are on top of the trees).

Although she has tried multiple times to live away from the Utah desert, the silver cord connecting her heart to canyon country keeps pulling her back. It has been over 20 years since she last tried to leave, and now she has given up, having decided to just stay forever. Her nose has been in the dirt most of this time, as she figures that the answer to what holds the desert together lies under our feet, unseen by most eyes.

Photographer **Michael Berman** works in mixed media, painting, and photography. His photojournalism appears in periodicals such as *High Country News* and *New Mexico Magazine*, and his artwork has been reviewed in *Art in America*. He has exhibited throughout the United States, and his work is included in the collections of the Metropolitan Museum of Art (New York), the Amon Carter Museum of Western Art (Fort Worth), and the Museum of New Mexico (Santa Fe). He has received fellowships from both the Wurlitzer Foundation and the Arizona Commission of the Arts. His work is represented by Etherton Gallery (Tucson), Scheinbaum & Russek (Santa Fe), and Joseph Bellows Gallery (La Jolla). Michael majored in biology at Colorado College and earned a M.F.A in photography from Arizona State University. He was born in New York City but now lives in San Lorenzo, New Mexico, with his wife, Jennifer Six. His work appears in books with Bill Broyles (*Sunshot*, 2006) and Charles Bowden (*Inferno*, 2006). He confides, "When you pack a view camera into the desert alone, there are choices between weight and water. What is important to me as an artist is the wandering; what I bring back are these photographs."

Robert L. "Bob" Bezy was born in Phoenix in 1941 and spent his childhood roaming the irrigation ditches, canals, and desert near his home. He became fascinated by insects, lizards, snakes, and toads and kept a collection of live and preserved specimens. During his years at Brophy College Preparatory he decided that he would pursue a career in herpetology.

The 1960s were spent at the University of Arizona, where he received both his undergraduate and doctoral degrees working with Charles H. Lowe. As an assistant in the university's herpetology collection he developed a passion for both field and museum work. In 1970 he left Tucson to join the curatorial staff of the Natural History Museum of Los Angeles County. He was promoted to curator emeritus in 1997 and returned to live in the Sonoran Desert.

Fieldwork has taken him throughout the southwestern United States and northern Mexico and to Central America, Australia, and Africa. The systematics and evolution of night lizards (Xantusiidae) is a major focus of his research. He has always had a deep interest in the amphibians and reptiles of the Sonoran Desert, which he continues to pursue in both the field and museum.

Charles Bowden writes for anyone who pays him or interests him: lately it's been *GQ, Mother Jones, Wild Earth, Aperture, Mountain Gazette* and, of course, the *Arivaca Connection*. He uses the money he loots from magazines to finance books, most recently, *Down by the River: Drugs, Money, Murder and Family*. He lives in the Sonoran Desert because, to date, there is no known cure. He is currently working on a book about geography that is off the map but deep in the human heart.

At one time Bowden seemed headed to be a history professor at a midwestern university. But somewhere between teaching undergraduate classes and completion of his doctoral dissertation, he turned off the highway into a bigger world: journalism. He lusted for tomorrow's history today. He proudly bills himself as a newsman and has tracked stories on four continents. His uncounted articles, editorials, and essays have appeared in newspapers, *Geo, Esquire, Harper's, Arizona Highways, Outside, Orion, Buzzworm,* and *Phoenix*. He was co-founder and editor of and frequent contributor to *City Magazine,* a comet that blazed across Tucson's skies in the 1980s.

Bowden has authored 15 books. His desert books include *Killing the Hidden Waters, Blue Desert, Frog Mountain Blues, The Sonoran Desert* (with Jack Dykinga), *Desierto, Mezcal,* and *Redline.* Others of his southwestern books peel back the skin of victims and perpetrators in a tragic world: *Down by the River, Juarez: The Laboratory of Our Future, Chihuahua: Pictures from the Edge, Blues for Cannibals, Blood Orchid,* and, with Michael Binstein, *Trust Me: Charlie Keating and the Missing Billions.*

He once described the quest for news as an insatiable monster inside himself that had to be fed. The many awards and accolades he has received matter far less to him than the phone call for the next assignment. In following Hohokam shell trails, the route of Carl Lumholtz, and undocumented foreign workers, he has walked the length and breadth of the Dry Borders.

Diane Boyer is at her happiest when wandering in a desert. In deference to her great-grandfather, Godfrey Sykes, she stands on her head on summits (as he did on Pinacate Peak in 1907), although with less panache. She currently supports her demanding *Wanderlust bacillus* treatment regimen by working as a photo archivist and field assistant for the U.S. Geological Survey, making frequent trips to areas throughout the Southwest, including the middle and lower Colorado River. Some of her favorite desert memories include hiking El Camino del Diablo from Quitobaquito to Yuma, sea kayaking in the Colorado delta, sliding down sand dunes in Namibia, conducting oral history interviews with Julian Hayden, and camping in the Pinacate with her grandfather, Glenton Sykes.

Peggy J. Turk Boyer is the founding and acting executive director and program director of CEDO, the Intercultural Center for the Study of Deserts and Oceans, a unique binational organization. She completed a M.S. degree from the University of Arizona in 1983 with studies in marine ecology. Since 1980 she has worked in the northern Gulf of California doing research, education, and conservation. Peggy and CEDO helped involve fishermen in the establishment of one of the first marine protected areas in Mexico, the Reserva de la Biosfera Alto Golfo de California y Delta del Río Colorado, and she helped develop management programs for this reserve and the adjacent Reserva de la Biosfera El Pinacate y Gran Desierto de Altar. Protection of vaquita, an endemic and endangered porpoise of the northern gulf; development of sustainable fisheries; and above all community participation have been the focus of the programs she develops. Peggy has written numerous arti-

cles, produces bilingual educational publications, and edits *CEDO News,* a newsletter journal of the northern Gulf of California. Peggy was given the International Award for Excellence by the Margarita Miranda de Mascareñas Foundation in 1996 and was nominated for a PEW Fellows Program in Conservation and the Environment in 1998.

Bill Broyles is a research associate at the Southwest Center, University of Arizona. He taught in the public high school classroom for 31 years and now studies the Sonoran Desert. He has written four books—*Where Edges Meet: Organ Pipe Cactus National Monument; Our Sonoran Desert; Desert Babies A–Z;* and *Sunshot: Peril and Wonder in the Gran Desierto*—and numerous articles in such periodicals as *Arizona Highways, Journal of Arid Environments, Wildlife Society Bulletin, Journal of the Southwest,* and *Journal of Arizona History.* He is coordinator for the Sonoran Desert National Park Friends. He first met his wife, Joan Scott, at the intersection of El Camino del Diablo and the trail to Buckhorn Tank.

Richard C. "Rick" Brusca is executive program director at the Arizona-Sonora Desert Museum. He is also an adjunct scholar at the University of Arizona and Centro de Investigación en Alimentación y Desarrollo (CIAD), Mexico. Before moving to Arizona, he served as director of the Marine Biology Graduate Program, University of Charleston, South Carolina (1993–1999). Previous appointments include Joshua L. Bailey curator and director of research and collections at the San Diego Natural History Museum (1987–1993), chair of the Invertebrate Zoology Department at the Los Angeles County Natural History Museum (1984–1987), and professor of biology at the University of Southern California, Los Angeles (1975–1986).

Rick is the author of more than 100 research publications and 13 books, including the largest-selling English-language text on invertebrate zoology *(Invertebrates)* and the much-used *Common Intertidal Invertebrates of the Sea of Cortez.* He has received numerous research grants from the National Science Foundation, National Oceanic and Atmospheric Administration, National Geographic Society, National Park Service, Charles Lindberg Fund, and other agencies and foundations. His areas of research include Sonoran Desert natural history, invertebrate zoology, freshwater and marine ecology, conservation biology, arthropod diversification, phylogenetics, and global biodiversity. He has conducted field expeditions throughout the world, on every continent, but has maintained his research programs in the Sonoran Desert and the Sea of Cortez for more than 30 years. He is a Fellow in both the American Association for the Advancement of Science and the Linnean Society of London.

Alberto Búrquez is a senior scientist at the Instituto de Ecología, Universidad Nacional Autónoma de México (UNAM), Hermosillo, Sonora. He has a Ph.D. from Cambridge University and a M.Sc. from Facultad de Ciencias, UNAM. His interests include the population biology of desert plants and their interaction with animals, community ecology, and the effect of exotic plant invaders on the diversity and function of Sonoran Desert ecosystems.

Yamilett Carrillo-Guerrero is an economist turned environmentalist by the touch of the Sonoran Desert and the Gulf of California. Currently, she is coordinator of the Wetlands Program of Pronatura Sonora and a Ph.D. student in the School of Natural Resources at the University of Arizona. Her work is centered on conserving nature by building partnerships with governments and local communities, with a special emphasis on wetland restoration on private and *ejido* lands.

Photographer **Jack Dykinga** won a Pulitzer Prize for his feature photography with the *Chicago Sun-Times.* He moved to Tucson in 1976 and worked as picture editor at the *Arizona Daily Star* and then as a free-lance photographer. In 1981 he learned large-format color photography, and his work has appeared in *National Geographic, Time, Arizona Highways,* and countless other magazines, books, and calendars. He is the author of *Large Format Nature Photography* (2001) and *Jack Dykinga's Arizona* (2004). His photos in *The Secret Forest* (1993) were influential in creation of the Reserva Sierra de Alamos y Arroyo Cuchujaqui in Sonora, and his photo collaboration with Charles Bowden in *Stone Canyons of the Colorado Plateau* (1996) helped clinch the case to establish Escalante–Grand Staircase National Monument and Paria Canyon National Monument. "I'm telling the story of the environment," he says. "Projects I work on are motivated by a passion to preserve the wild land" (Lou Jacobs, "Jack Dykinga: A view camera pageant of nature," *Rangefinder* 52 [June 2003]: 12–15).

Despite his Los Angeles upbringing, **Erik F. Enderson** developed a passion for the natural world at an early age. Egged on by his father's stories of 10-foot rattlesnakes that wandered the nearby mountains of his southern California home, he began to take a particular interest in the region's amphibians and reptiles. By his teens he had become fascinated with the area's rapidly disappearing frog fauna and at 14 made his first of many excursions into the wilds of California's Sierra Nevada in search of the golden trout *(Oncorhynchus aguabonita)* and the now-endangered state frog, *Rana aurora draytonii* (California red-legged frog).

Now in his thirties and a resident of Tucson since 1993, Erik works as a technical writer and semiprofessional photographer. He's traveled throughout the Sonoran Desert of Arizona and Mexico conducting field research and photographing the region's herpetofauna. His greatest interest still lies with the Southwest's native frogs. He has also served as president of the Tucson Herpetological Society and editor of its monthly publication, the *Sonoran Herpetologist.*

Luke Evans grew up in Tucson and spent his formative and subsequent years roaming the deserts and mountains of the Southwest. His obsession with the area covered in this volume can be traced to a newspaper article in the early 1990s describing the exploits of Bill Broyles in the Cabeza Prieta National Wildlife Refuge. The barren wastes described therein sounded appealing, and a call to Broyles resulted in an invitation to join him on his legendary rain-gauge and tinaja surveys. Since then, Evans has had the good fortune to meet many other sun-stricken wanderers who share his affection for snooping the deserts of North America's Empty Quarter, discovering its natural treasures, and learning its history. He is a connoisseur of old maps and has applied this interest to uncovering the ever-changing place-name history of this region. He holds a B.A. in history and a M.S. in natural resource policy from the University of Arizona. He currently resides at the foot of the San Bernardino Mountains in Southern California, where he lives with his wife, Jeanne Wade Evans, who encourages his various interests.

Exequiel Ezcurra is director of the Biodiversity Research Center of the Californias at the San Diego Museum of Natural History. Previously he was president of the Instituto Nacional Ecologica (INE) in the Cabinet of President Vicente Fox. He has produced more than 100 publications in ecology and conservation, most dealing with New World drylands. As director general of natural resources in President Carlos Salinas's administration, he proposed and guided establishment of the Pinacate and Alto Golfo biosphere reserves. He was awarded the 1992 Faustino Miranda Research Medal by the Universidad Nacional Autónoma de México, the 1993 Julian Hayden Award by the Sonoran Desert International Alliance, and Pronatura's 1993 Recognition for Conservation. In 1994 he was honored with the Conservation Biology Award, granted by the International Society for Conservation Biology. He has also received awards from the U.S. National Park Service and the U.S. National Oceanic and Atmospheric Administration for his support of binational protected areas along the United States–Mexico borderlands. He was born in Argentina and earned his advanced degrees at the University College of North Wales, Bangor.

Richard Stephen Felger: Since we lived by the sea in California I was first a marine biologist but had been growing cactus and succulents by age 10. My first field trip to the Dry Borders region was to Organ Pipe Cactus National Monument, even though a guy at the auto club said there's nothing there. We went on to tidepools at Puerto Peñasco and saw more wonders I knew only from books and specimens at the Los Angeles County Museum of Natural History, where I volunteered in the collections. I had worn out my first copy of Ricketts's part of the *Sea of Cortez*. A trip to Alamos, traveling across the Sonoran Desert with my beloved high school biology teacher, Nancy Thomas Neely, and her husband, Peter, further fueled the desert connection. Peter introduced me to renowned professor Raymond Cowles at UCLA, who included me on field trips to the desert with his students. I went to the University of Arizona because it was close to the splendors of the Sonoran Desert and the Gulf of California. My work was greatly facilitated by travels with Alexander "Ike" Russell and Jean Russell, who introduced me to Mary Beck and Edward Moser. That led to our studies of ethnobiology among the Seris.

I returned to the Natural History Museum in Los Angeles as senior curator of botany but was soon back in Tucson, established the Research Department at the Arizona-Sonora Desert Museum, and became associated with the Environmental Research Laboratory, University of Arizona. In the early 1990s I founded Drylands Institute in Tucson. Continuing research provided study opportunities in deserts around the world, but the Sonoran Desert is home, where Silke Schneider and I live in a mesquite bosque with various animals.

Lloyd T. Findley feels that he's quite a lucky fellow, having been able to study what he was interested in and do so in his adopted country of Mexico. He has been fascinated by fishes since his high-school skin-diving days in southern California. He first saw the fishes of the Gulf of California in Bahía Topolobampo as a high school foreign exchange student in Los Mochis, Sinaloa. Further trips to the gulf inspired him to earn his bachelor's degree in zoology at California State College (now University) at Long Beach. That same desire led him to a master's degree in zoology/fisheries at the University of California, Los Angeles, where Boyd W. Walker, probably the person most knowledgeable about gulf fishes, took him on as a student in fish systematics/taxonomy and gave him access to the school's great ichthyological collection from the gulf.

Findley's correspondence with Donald A. Thomson, at the University of Arizona in Tucson, eventually led to enrollment at the U of A to pursue a Ph.D. under "DAT" and to take the part-time assistant curatorship of the Fish Collection at the Department of Biology (now

Ecology and Evolutionary Biology). Eight years of intensive collecting, curating, and studying gulf fishes with Thomson, John Hendrickson, and many of their students led to publication of *The Reef-Fishes of the Sea of Cortez,* by Thomson, Findley, and Alex Kerstitch.

Findley returned to Los Angeles, where he met and married the love of his life, Sandra Hull. He accepted a teaching position at the Guaymas, Sonora, Marine Sciences School of the Instituto Tecnológico y de Estudios Superiores de Monterrey (the "Tec"). Courses included oceanography, ichthyology, and eventually the biology of marine mammals. He and his students saw a great opportunity to study the whales and dolphins of the region and launched a ten-year research program on the cetaceans of the gulf, including gray and fin whales and the endangered vaquita. The research proved so successful that some scientists still consider Findley a marine mammalogist.

Since 1996 he has concentrated on gulf ichthyofauna, working with the Guaymas Unit of the Centro de Investigación en Alimentación y Desarrollo. And through former students at the Tec, he has maintained a close relationship with the Guaymas-based Gulf of California Program of Conservation International (CI). Research projects with both Mexican and American colleagues have been numerous, the most extensive being a compilation of information on the more than six thousand species of macrofauna inhabiting the Gulf of California, soon to be published with five coauthors by CI as a CD-ROM.

Another long-term project involves the systematics, ecology, and conservation of native trouts of the Sierra Madre Occidental. Findley and his colleagues, mainly Héctor Espinosa of the Instituto de Biología, Universidad Nacional Autónoma de México, have incorporated the entire Mexican ichthyofauna into the sixth edition of the American Fisheries Society's *Common and Scientific Names of Fishes from the United States, Canada, and Mexico*, the first edition to include Mexico.

Findley sees much to be done in gulf research and conservation but realizes that his luck continues, having two daughters who are "naturals" at snorkeling and fish watching in the warm waters of the Gulf of California.

Jaqueline García-Hernández has conducted scientific work since 1996 in the Colorado River delta. Specifically, she is interested in the effects of contaminants on the reproductive success of fish and birds and their implications for wetland management. She received a Ph.D. in Soil, Water, and Environmental Sciences at the University of Arizona and is currently working at the Centro de Investigación en Alimentación y Desarrollo (CIAD), a research center based in Guaymas, Sonora. She continues her research in the Colorado River delta but is also exploring environmental education and outreach projects and evaluating the effects of contaminants on the marine life of the Gulf of California.

Edward P. Glenn was born in Tucson in 1947, when most of Arizona's towns were still connected by dirt roads and Phoenix was the only city. He received a B.A., M.S., and Ph.D. in botanical sciences from the University of Hawaii in Honolulu and then returned to Tucson to take a job with the Environmental Research Laboratory of the University of Arizona, where he remains today. He specializes in arid land studies, including new crops, ecophysiology of desert plants, and conservation biology. His interest in the Colorado River delta was sparked during plant-collecting trips with Richard Felger, when they realized that far from being a dead ecosystem, the delta is still alive and well. Currently, he is a professor at U of A's Department of Soil, Water, and Environmental Science.

David J. Griffin was born and raised in the East and Midwest and has spent the last 15 years in the West. After jobs as a sign painter's assistant, a construction worker, and even a U.S. postal carrier, he studied conservation and biology and received his B.S. in wildlife science from Oregon State University. During the early 1990s David worked at Arctic National Wildlife Refuge and Noatak National Park and Preserve in Alaska and traveled to the Taimyr Penninsula, Siberia, to work with researchers studying airborne contaminants. From 1994 to 1999 he worked for the University of Arizona and developed his knowledge of desert birds while conducting wildlife surveys at Cabeza Prieta National Wildlife Refuge and the Barry M. Goldwater Air Force Range, and later at the Marine Corps Air Ground Combat Center in Twentynine Palms, California. During the summer of 1996 David broadened his knowledge of Arizona birds as a member of the Arizona Game and Fish Department's Breeding Bird Atlas Field crew. In 1999 he moved to the San Diego area, where he worked as a wildlife biologist at a nonprofit land trust and for an environmental consulting firm. Most recently he worked for the U.S. Fish and Wildlife Service at San Diego National Wildlife Refuge, where he conducted studies of the California gnatcatcher and other endangered and sensitive animals and plants.

In 1997 David reinitiated the Sierra Pinta–Cabeza Prieta NWR Christmas Bird Count (which was started in 1955) and has organized and conducted it since; and since 1999 he has helped organize and conduct the Ajo–Cabeza Prieta NWR Christmas Bird Count with CPNWR staff. David is an avid photographer, but walking, hiking, and spending time on the Cabeza Prieta NWR and Barry M. Goldwater Air Force Range are two of his greatest passions. Currently living in Las Cruces,

New Mexico, he regularly travels to the Sonoran Desert to explore his favorite places and discover new ones.

He says, "My infatuation with the desert began when I moved to Oregon, a place often thought of as forested, wet, and rainy. To escape the clouds and moisture I took trips to the southeastern corner of the state: a dry place of sagebrush and bunchgrass, high desert, the Great Basin. My haunts were vast, rugged, and stark areas, but full of life. My romance with the desert further developed with my move to Arizona. In the first two years there, I spent about 300 days camped out on the CPNWR and BMGR. As beautiful as it was, my first impressions of the Sonoran Desert were not all 'love at first sight.' My love for the borderlands came on strong only after I spent considerable time pressed against its heart, and listened to and learned the songs that beat from within."

Philip A. Hastings: The wet state of Florida was the setting for both my early life and early career. I grew up near the ocean in Pensacola, where I spent much of my time exploring the area's numerous beaches, bayous, and creeks. I received a bachelor's degree in zoology from the University of South Florida in Tampa and a master's degree in marine biology from the University of West Florida in Pensacola and then worked for four years as a marine biologist at the Harbor Branch Foundation on the state's east coast. My calling to the desert Southwest came in 1980, when, seeking a change of scenery, I entered the Ph.D. program at the University of Arizona under the direction of Donald A. Thomson. "DAT" and my fellow graduate students in the Department of Ecology and Evolutionary Biology introduced me to the Gulf of California and its fishes, as well as to the rich Sonoran Desert. After completing my degree, I remained at the university as a research scientist and later as curator of fishes and invertebrates. It was also in Tucson that I met my wife, Marty Eberhardt, who became director of the Tucson Botanical Gardens, expanding it from a small neighborhood garden to a jewel in the Tucson landscape. Our tranquil life in the Sonoran desert with our two sons was disrupted in 1999 when I was invited to join the faculty at the University of California, San Diego, and to become curator of the marvelous Marine Vertebrate Collection at the Scripps Institution of Oceanography. In many ways the move to SIO has facilitated my research in the Gulf of California.

I am a systematist in the broad sense, with interests in the diversity, evolution, ecology, and behavior of marine fishes. My students and I employ techniques spanning the fields of morphology, ethology, and molecular biology. For the past several years I have focused my studies on the family Chaenopsidae, commonly called tube blennies because of their habit of occupying vacant tests or shells of invertebrates. These curious fishes have been an interest of mine ever since I discovered and described a new species of tube blenny from the northern Gulf of Mexico over 25 years ago (*Chaenopsis roseola,* pink-flecked pikeblenny). My interest in them blossomed after I moved to the University of Arizona and discovered the rich and accessible diversity of chaenopsids in the Gulf of California.

Like most of my colleagues, I am deeply concerned about the growing negative environmental impacts of humans. This concern has led to several projects on the conservation of fishes of the Gulf of California and more recently on those of coastal California.

Julian D. Hayden (1911–1998), owner of Hayden Excavation Company in Tucson, was better known for his seminal archaeological work and publications and for his unique knowledge of the Sierra Pinacate. He proudly called himself a field archaeologist and had conducted pioneering digs in California, Sonora, Arizona, and Nevada. He produced a number of papers, reports, and books, including *The Sierra Pinacate* (1998). His articles appeared in *American Antiquity, American Anthropologist, Kiva,* and *Journal of the Southwest.* He was a blue-collar scholar equally at home with cowboys and ditch diggers or eminent scientists and leaders such as Barry Goldwater. He was a keen observer, voracious reader, and profound thinker who asked penetrating questions and deduced original answers. He traced ideas and theories in the same way he did prehistoric trails: because they might lead someplace closer to understanding ancient people. He encouraged and inspired many students who are now professionals and scholars. When someone once asked him how he managed to find such a wonderful old adobe home to live in, he snorted, "I built it." In 1998 his car was still a 1952 Chevy coupe; someone asked him, "What are you going to do with it after you die?" and for once Julian was stumped for an answer. Hayden stands alongside Malcolm Rogers and Paul Ezell, his close friends and peers, as preeminent pioneers of southwestern desert archaeology.

Robert S. Henry: I first came to southwestern Arizona in 1976 to study white-tailed deer at Organ Pipe Cactus National Monument as part of a graduate program at the University of Arizona. Starting in the lovely month of June, I spent all of three summers and much of the intervening seasons on the monument, making over 200 hikes into the mountains. For the next five years, still working for the U of A, I researched the effect of artificial oases on wildlife along the Central Arizona Project canal, then under construction west of Phoenix. The next move was to Yuma, where I've lived with my family for the past 16 years, working as a biologist for the Arizona Game and Fish Department. My area of re-

sponsibility is all of southwestern Arizona, including the Dry Borders area, but cooperative efforts with Mexico have expanded the fun to neighboring Sonora and Baja California. There've been no reasons to leave.

Osvel Hinojosa-Huerta is director of conservation of Pronatura Sonora and is a member of the Technical Committee of the binational Sonoran Joint Venture. He obtained his M.Sc. and Ph.D. in wildlife ecology from the School of Natural Resources of the University of Arizona and currently is a Ph.D. student in the same program. Osvel has been working on multiple conservation and research projects in northwestern Mexico since 1997, in particular in riparian and wetland areas of the Sonoran Desert. While in the field, he developed a fascination for birds, which lately has evolved into a career focus, hobby, and goal for life. Some of his recent activities include developing bird conservation plans, evaluating the status of endangered species, and implementing community-based monitoring and conservation programs for birds.

Letty Bender Hofstra: After graduating from high school Letty worked at Valley National Bank in Casa Grande. She married and lived in various places before settling in Prescott, Arizona, where the last of her six children was born. She and her current husband, Peter Hofstra, now live in Arkansas on the shore of Beaver Lake, but annually they return to Arizona to spend the winters and revisit the Big Horn, where the family has adopted two miles of Interstate 8 frontage. Each year they faithfully pick up highway litter (about 65 trash bags and 35 man-hours per mile), but they enjoy doing it and know that their parents would be proud.

Kevin C. Horstman works as a registered geologist in Tucson. He grew up in the Sonoran Desert of central Arizona, where he developed an interest in the geology of deserts at a young age. He earned his B.S. and M.S. degrees in geology from Northern Arizona University and his Ph.D. in geosciences from the University of Arizona; his university research focused on structural geology and remote sensing of the central Transition Zone and the Basin and Range of Arizona.

His professional work has encompassed research and exploration projects in deserts around the world, either on the ground or by advanced remote sensing analysis. His research areas include the Sonoran Desert of Arizona, California's Mojave Desert, and the high desert of the Colorado Plateau in northern Arizona. He has worked in other arid regions, including the Arabian Desert, the desert of northern Somalia, and the arid basins of the Chilean Andes. His enthusiasm for deserts extends beyond Earth: in addition to his long career in the southwestern deserts, his professional work includes mapping approximately 2 million square miles of the arid Tharsis Plateau of Mars as part of the geological analysis for Project Viking.

Peter L. Kresan has been exploring the Sonoran Desert for over 30 years. He recently retired as senior lecturer in the Department of Geosciences at the University of Arizona in Tucson, where he taught physical, historical, environmental and field geology. He received numerous awards for teaching. Peter is also a professional photographer with photos published in *Arizona Highways, National Geographic,* Time-Life Books, and numerous other publications and textbooks.

Wendy Laird Benner has a master's degree in public administration and policy with an emphasis in environmental policy. She currently works at Matson & Associates, researching and managing expert witness testimony for toxic torts. Previously, she worked at the U.S. Environmental Protection Agency, Office of International Affairs and Region 9, where she acted as United States–Mexico border coordinator. She was also United States–Mexico border program director for the Sonoran Institute and executive director of the Tucson Aububon Society.

Pilot **Sandy Lanham**'s excellence was recognized in 2001 with a MacArthur Fellowship, or Gal-ship, as she calls it. She was employed as a flight instructor, social worker, belly dancer, and print salesperson before finding her life's work flying researchers to remote places to conduct biological surveys. Her nonprofit organization is Environmental Flying Services.

Her commitment to flying scientific surveys in Mexico and the southwestern United States has been tested with near crashes, a broken engine that had to be hand carried a thousand miles from a remote airstrip to a repair shop, and stresses of the intense job. "I am flying, doing whale sharks and lobsters. Pronghorn too coming up. But this year I'm bringing my own food. Two years ago, we stayed in a cowboy bunker and ate goat stew, peanuts, and oranges for a week. No one bought food and there was no town for over a hundred miles. A sniveling old cowboy with anthrax I think made the stew, starting it at puberty. A snowstorm blew in, dark clouds hung like tits on a sow. We huddled together at night. Flying all day was the only way to get warm.

"When we finally got back to Chihuahua, I was sick. So I ordered tortilla soup from room service. They delivered it two hours late and a dead mouse was floating in it. More important, they forgot to put the Kahlua in my coffee (by then cold). Then, since it was Saturday, Disco Nite began—boom, boom, boom until 3 in the

morning. I nearly quit flying for good, forever, that night. Really. Oh yes, I'm looking forward to the pronghorn in Coahuila again this year."

Her airplane Emily, a 1956 Cessna 182, was possibly the oldest of its model still flying when strenuous flying under harsh conditions forced its retirement in 2004. "I called my airplane Emily because it was a humble name. In a world of flash, an unassuming nature is often scorned, yet I bet my life on her. Because of Emily's steady, droning heart, people lived their dreams." Her "new" plane, a 1958 Cessna 182, will use many of Emily's trusted parts—propeller, engine, seats, wheels, brakes, radios, and instruments. The replacement plane is named Ginny, in honor of Virginia Furrow, the 86-year-old visionary who funded Emily. Lanham has a B.A. degree from Western Michigan University, but she played in the woods as a child and considers that the most important education of all.

Carlos Martínez del Rio is a natural historian who lives in the high plains, teaching and doing research at the University of Wyoming. After growing feral in northern Mexico, he was partially domesticated by a B.S. from the Universidad Nacional Autónoma de México and a Ph.D. from the University of Florida. At an early age he became imprinted with the mixture of expansiveness and intimacy of North America's arid lands. He has studied birds, bats, cacti, and mistletoes in the Sonoran Desert, in the arid lands of Chile, and in Wyoming's Red Desert. His research combines hi-tech physiological measurements, mathematical modeling, and good old direct observations. His eighty-some publications cover topics that range from how hummingbirds cope with their sugary and watery diet to the use of natural ratios of stable isotopes to estimate the flow of water and nutrients from saguaros to the animals that feed on their nectar and fruit.

Angelina Martínez-Yrízar is a research ecologist at the Instituto de Ecología, Universidad Nacional Autónoma de México (UNAM), Hermosillo, Sonora. She has a Ph.D. in ecology from Cambridge University and a M.Sc. from Facultad de Ciencias, UNAM. Her studies focus on the structure and functioning of the Sonoran Desert and tropical deciduous forest ecosystems in Mexico.

Kathryn Mauz obtained her Ph.D. at the University of Arizona, the third installment of a lifetime double major in natural history and the surface of the earth. Since coming to Arizona, she has divided her time between floristic work in small and crusty dry island mountain ranges, staring at dry plants through a microscope, staring at dry parts of the Earth from space, and wittingly or not, contributing to the conservation of large and amazing natural areas in the Sonoran Desert. The first of these floristic endeavors was in the Sawtooth Mountains, later incorporated by the Ironwood Forest National Monument. From the Sawtooths, two big mountains—Comobabi and Table Top—loomed and beckoned to the south and west. To the west was public land, and so began her work in the Table Top Mountains and part of what was to become the Sonoran Desert National Monument. Recently, her research has been devoted to (Earth from space) describing phenology and land-use dynamics in dry forests of west Mexico, (natural wonders) measuring saguaros and spatial variability in their growth rates, and (floristic) documenting historic plant taxonomic changes in the former riparian areas of the Tucson Basin.

Anita Bender McGee (d. 2005): Soon after the end of World War II my family moved from the desert to Casa Grande, Arizona, where I graduated from high school, worked at Mandell & Meyer department store, and married T. C. "Jim" McGee, who had recently served in the war. We farmed alfalfa and cotton near Coolidge and then moved to Yuma to farm. Jim then worked for the Bureau of Reclamation at Imperial Dam, and I worked at Yuma Proving Ground. In 1967 Jim retired, we moved to Phoenix, and I went to work for the U.S. Geological Survey, Water Resources Division, until 1974. Being retired, Jim and I traveled throughout the country in a recreational vehicle. My mother came to live with us, and we found she loved traveling, too! Mother passed away July 1992, and I lost Jim a year later. In January 2002 I moved to four and a half acres of desert land at Congress, Arizona, and built a home on "this little piece of heaven on earth." As they say, "You can take the girl out of the desert, but you can't take the desert out of the girl." My sister, family, and I return annually to the Big Horn and ranch.

Eric Mellink, Departamento de Biología de la Conservación, Centro de Investigación Científica y de Educación Superior de Ensanada, Baja California: I grew up in the Sonoran Desert and have formal training in animal husbandry, arid lands ecology, and wildlife ecology and management. My interests range from traditional and present-day uses of wildlife by humans to ecology and conservation. Most of my research has focused on rodents and waterbirds, but I have worked with other vertebrates as well. I am particularly fascinated by the Sonoran Desert and the Gulf of California's coasts and islands, but I also greatly enjoy working in other areas and habitats. Indeed, I have been collaborating on a research project on vertebrate ecology in *Opuntia* communities in eastern Jalisco for some years and recently conducted fieldwork along the entire western coast of Mexico. I am certainly a field-oriented ecologist and naturalist and try to evade the lab (except at coffee time), as well as administrative meetings (I have a hard time sitting in one place for too long!).

Author **Guillermo Munro Palacio** lives in Puerto Peñasco, Sonora, along the coast he powerfully chronicles in his first novel, *Las Voces Vienen del Mar.* He studied as a graphic designer, is a professional photographer, and has worked in cinema, painting, radio, and television. He also wrote the award-winning novels *Los Sufrimientos de Puerto Esperanza* (1996) and *El Camino del Diablo* (1997), and recently finished his fourth novel, *No Me Da Miedo Morir.* His prolific writings have appeared in newspapers, magazines, and books throughout Mexico. He has served as director of cultural promotion for the city of Puerto Peñasco, where he is town historian and founding editor of *Nuestra Gente,* a history magazine.

Joaquin Murrieta-Saldivar, Ph.D., is associate director of the Sonoran Institute's Sonoran Desert Ecoregion Program. He spearheaded the concept of La Ruta de Sonora Ecotourism Association. A native of the Sonoran Desert, he envisions a new culture of conservation and responsible living.

Gary Paul Nabhan: Among his many accomplishments during his years of studying and living in the Southwest, Gary cofounded the nonprofit conservation group Native Seeds/SEARCH, spearheaded the Ironwood Alliance (responsible for research and public support that led to the 120,000acre Ironwood Forest National Monument), and initiated the Traditional Native American Farmers' Association. For such cross-cultural collaborations, he has been awarded a MacArthur Fellowship and a Lifetime Achievement Award from the Society for Conservation Biology. Gary crosses disciplinary, linguistic, and ethnic boundaries with apparent ease, an essential skill for someone who lives and works among many different communities in the Southwest.

In his position as first director of the Center for Sustainable Environments at Northern Arizona University, Gary is responsible for coordinating an expanding array of environmentally oriented programs and initiatives that bridge the NAU campus with the surrounding region. He is also a tenured professor in applied indigenous studies and the Center for Environmental Sciences and Education, and he helps oversee the graduate certificate program in conservation ecology. Gary's writing is widely anthologized and translated and has won the John Burroughs Medal for Nature Writing, a Western States Book Award, and a Lannan Literary Fellowship. Gary has authored and edited over 15 books, including *The Desert Smells Like Rain: A Naturalist in*

Papago Indian Country, Gathering the Desert, The Forgotten Pollinators (with Stephen Buchmann), *Efrain of the Sonoran Desert: A Lizard's Life in the Sonoran Desert* (with Amalia Astorga and Janet Miller), and *Ironwood: An Ecological and Cultural Keystone of the Sonoran Desert*. One of his latest books is *Singing the Turtles to Sea: The Comcáac (Seri) Art and Science of Reptiles* (2003).

Pam Nagler came to the University of Arizona in 1999 to study with Ed Glenn. For her B.A., M.S., and Ph.D., she specialized in physical geography and the application of remote sensing to different landscapes. Her research focus has shifted from small, agricultural plots to river, delta, and estuary sites in arid lands. The riparian corridor in the Colorado River delta became the most exciting place to study scaling issues related to ground-based studies and image acquisition, as well as habitat conservation along the border. Currently, she is an assistant research scientist at U of A's Department of Soil, Water, and Environmental Science.

Although he was born in Mexico City, **Carlos J. Navarro-Serment** fell in love with the Sea of Cortez and its surrounding lands when he moved to Guaymas, Sonora, to attend college. There he participated in a wide array of research projects from his very first day as a biochemical engineering student, dissecting beached whale carcasses, collecting vaquita specimens, and gathering data on great white sharks. The many days spent in wild fishing camps or traveling along surprisingly lonely dirt roads at night, with the desert floor and the Milky Way as the only boundaries, marked him for life.

Since graduating, Carlos has been involved in an even wider spectrum of research, conservation, and environmental education projects, most of them in northwest Mexico but with occasional escapades in the Yucatan peninsula and Central America. However, he keeps returning again and again to his beloved arid and rough *noroeste*. Also an avid wildlife photographer and author, Carlos tries to share his love for the creatures that call this area of extremes home by contributing photographs and articles to Mexican and international publications.

Steve Nelson is an outdoor recreation planner with the USDA Forest Service, Gifford Pinchot National Forest. From 1979 to 1988 he held a similar position with the Bureau of Land Management, California Desert District, in El Centro, California. A confirmed desert rat despite his current domicile in the Northwest rain forest, Steve returns to Baja California and the Colorado River delta as often as he can. An avid sea kayaker, Steve has paddled extensively in the Gulf of California.

Tad Nichols (1911–2000) studied photography under Ansel Adams and Brett Weston. He traveled widely in search of images, from the deserts of Africa to the volcanoes of Mexico to the wild rivers of America. His photographs appeared in a variety of publications, including the book *Glen Canyon: Images of a Lost World* (1999). Tad, who lived in Tucson most of his life, was especially interested in geology, anthropology, and the American Southwest.

Wallace "J." Nichols has devoted himself to the investigation and conservation of endangered marine species and the protection of coastal wildlands. By working with the fishermen and communities affected by these species' endangered status, J. is leading a successful campaign to ensure that our seas are safer, allowing these animal populations a chance to recover, and that their habitats are protected in perpetuity.

Nichols is director of Conservation Science at ProPenínsula, a San Diego–based organization dedicated to the preservation of the unique natural environment of the Baja California peninsula. He is a research associate at the California Academy of Sciences in San Francisco. He is also cofounder of WiLDCOAST, an international conservation team dedicated to marine protection and education, and co-vice-chair of the IUCN (World Conservation Union) Marine Turtle Specialist Group—Eastern Pacific Region. In 1998 he founded, and now advises, the Grupo Tortuguero, a grassroots conservation network spanning more than 25 coastal communities in northwest Mexico. He holds a Ph.D. in wildlife and fisheries sciences and evolutionary biology from the University of Arizona. J. also has a master's degree in natural resource economics and policy from the Duke University Nicholas School of the Environment and bachelor's degrees in biology and Spanish from DePauw University.

J.'s research and interest in nature have taken him from South America to the Arctic Circle to conduct and observe biological conservation projects. His research as a Fulbright Scholar focused on the "connectedness" of ocean ecosystems, specifically the long-distance migration of loggerhead sea turtles from Japan to Mexico and back—a project that has reached hundreds of thousands of schoolchildren and scientists around the world. By working closely with fishermen and exchanging knowledge with them, Nichols and his team are keeping oceans wild by easing the pressure to exploit endangered species.

Nichols's work has been published in numerous scientific journals, has been featured in television documentaries (PBS, National Geographic Explorer, Outdoor Life Network) and radio programs (NPR's "Living on Earth," BBC, NHK Japan, Canadian Broadcasting Company), and is the topic of numerous magazine and newspaper articles (*National Geographic, National Wildlife, Newsweek, Scientific American, Wall Street Journal, Los Angeles Times, Popular Science, Christian Science Monitor, Sinra-Japan,* and *Vogue-Italy*).

J. hasn't quite given up his childhood fondness for overturning stones and catching turtles, and he recognizes the importance of storytelling to learning about the natural world. He published *Chelonia: Return of the Sea Turtle,* a book for young people that tells the true story of the rescue, rehabilitation, release, and successful migration of a sea turtle. *Chelonia* was published in Spanish in 2002 and has been distributed to schools and libraries throughout the Californias. His next educational project is an animated film, *Adelita's Journey,* the true story of one turtle's historic transoceanic migration.

J. often travels in search of coastal wilderness and in 2003 trekked 1,900 km from Oregon to Mexico to bring attention to coastal and marine issues. When not seeking new adventures or following sea turtles, he can be found working at his office perched on a cliff above the Pacific Ocean. J., his partner Dana, their daughters Julia and Grayce, and their dogs Red and Greta share a home beneath giant redwood trees in Davenport, on the coast of northern California.

Adrianne G. Rankin, currently archaeologist for the Barry M. Goldwater Range–East and Luke Air Force Base, specializes in prehistoric and historic cultures in the western Sonoran Desert, including desert-adapted agricultural strategies and reconstruction of paleo-environments. She works closely with tribal groups to identify and understand sacred sites.

She received her B.A. with honors in anthropology from Lake Forest College and completed coursework for her master's degree at Arizona State University. She has conducted surveys and excavations in California, New Mexico, northern Sonora, and Arizona. Between 1989 and 1996 she supervised surveys of 8,000 acres and recorded 200 prehistoric and historic sites at Organ Pipe Cactus National Monument. One of the most significant sites was a large prehistoric village, with a reservoir, that was part of the shell-trading network and involved other reservoir-based villages in the Cabeza Prieta National Wildlife Refuge and Goldwater Range. In addition, she located an 1880s Hia C'ed O'odham village identified in oral histories and recorded the ceremonial resting place of cremated bighorn sheep remains.

Since 1996 she has worked for the Goldwater East's Range Management Office–Environmental Science Management Section, which manages 1.1 million acres. She has overseen surveys of more than 170,000 acres that have yielded over 1,250 prehistoric and historic sites, traditional cultural places, and sacred sites. She continues to work closely with 26 Native American tribes and groups who claim cultural affiliation with the

area. Understanding how people view and use the landscape is extremely important if we are to ensure that culturally significant sites are identified and protected.

With Lorraine Marquez Eiler (Hia C'ed O'odham) and Joseph Joaquin (Tohono O'odham) she coauthored "Water and the Human Spirit," an essay explaining the cultural values of natural water sources in the Sonoran Desert, and with Jeffrey Altschl she is coeditor of *Fragile Pattern Areas—Cultural Resources of the Western Papaguería* (in press).

Philip C. Rosen, assistant research scientist in the School of Natural Resources at the University of Arizona, though of ichthyological descent, has been a herpetologist since age 12. He was attracted to the Southwest's reptile diversity, arriving in 1983 by way of Michigan and his native New York. Inevitably, his conservation interests drew him into aquatic vertebrate ecology in southern Arizona, which, along with trying to save humanity from humanity, contributed to much-delayed progress toward degrees (M.S. at Arizona State University, 1987, and Ph.D. at the University of Arizona, 2000). His fascination with the dry borderlands originated in a search for relatively intact ecosystems in which to study snake ecology and predator-prey dynamics (his Ph.D. topics). He currently pursues varied interests in herpetology, conservation, natural philosophy, and population-community-restoration ecology.

Sue Rutman is a plant ecologist and ardent conservationist, passions that began in her childhood with a penchant for eating dirt. She arrived in the Sonoran Desert 20 years ago after earning a master's degree from the College of Environmental Science and Forestry at the State University of New York, Syracuse. She's enjoyed learning about desert plants ever since. As botanist for the U.S. Fish and Wildlife Service from 1986 to 1994, she worked to protect rare plants in Arizona. In 1994 she began working at Organ Pipe Cactus National Monument, studying the biology and ecology of desert plants as well as historic and prehistoric human impacts on the environment.

John Shepard is associate director of the Sonoran Institute. Before joining the institute, he worked for the Wilderness Society, a national organization dedicated to the preservation of America's wild public lands.

Jeffrey A. Seminoff has been studying sea turtles in Mexico since 1993, but his interest in the Gulf of California began to blossom when he moved to Tucson in 1985. Soon after his arrival, the cobble beaches of central Sonora and the secluded coasts of Baja California became the primary destinations of his constant field trips. After a 1986 visit to the famous green turtle nesting beach in Tortuguero, Costa Rica, Jeff's interest in sea turtles was piqued, but it wasn't until he witnessed a Baja fisherman's slaughter of two green turtles in 1987 that he realized the need for research and conservation of sea turtles in northwest Mexico.

After receiving a M.S. (1994) and Ph.D. (2000) from the University of Arizona, Jeff was a Postdoctoral Fellow at the Archie Carr Center for Sea Turtle Research at the University of Florida. Since 2002 he has been an ecologist in the Marine Turtle Research Program for the National Marine Fisheries Service in La Jolla, California. Jeff's current studies focus on the foraging ecology and habitat use of sea turtles throughout Latin America, and he works a great deal with Latin American colleagues to build their capacity as sea turtle researchers. Jeff is also a member of the World Conservation Union's (IUCN) Marine Turtle Specialist Group, and he chairs the Task Force for the IUCN Species Survival Commission's Red List Programme.

Hilah Simmons: Born and bred in the briar patch, Los Angeles, I find that California is a great place to be from—away from! After earning my bachelor of arts degree at Pomona in religion, of all things, I followed Norm to Colorado to earn my Ph.T.—"Put hubby through"—by teaching school for three years while he earned his master's degree.

Then I followed him to Ajo, Arizona, where he managed the Cabeza Prieta Game Range while I managed to be wife and mother and camp follower. It wasn't exactly a piece of cake with the office right there in the house. There I had the chance to study and write "The Geology of the Cabeza Prieta Game Range." I loved the desert and could have stayed there forever, but our next move was to the Northwest Territories of Canada, where I continued my W.A.M. (wife and mother) status. The children and I continued to be camp followers in the Mackenzie Mountains.

After 16 years in the "frozen North"—I could have stayed there forever—we came to Gladstone Valley, Alberta, our home base for the last 20 years. The four kids grew up and went north, east, south, and west. I continue to follow Norm around the world and try to keep our base camp operational here on the ranch. I give a few piano lessons, write a "Nature Notes" column for the local weekly, play trombone in the town band, pump organ in the country church, and practice my banjo. I'm so thankful for the idyllic, adventuresome life.

Norman Simmons has enjoyed an international career. He was born in the Philippines. He has studied bighorn sheep in Colorado and on the Cabeza Prieta National Wildlife Refuge, Arizona, as well as Dall's sheep and woodland caribou in Canada's Northwest Territories. He was assistant refuge manager, Cabeza Prieta NWR, from

1961 to 1966. He has worked for the U.S. Fish and Wildlife Service, Canadian Wildlife Service, and Northwest Territories Department of Renewable Resources. He has assisted aboriginal peoples with native rights negotiations and conservation in the Northwest Territories, Bolivia, Panama, and Taiwan. He has consulted on renewable natural resources management in Tibet, Mexico, Ecuador, Bolivia, Peru, and Panama, and he is adjunct professor at two universities in Canada and one in Peru. He served on the United Nations committee that formulated the biosphere reserve concept and served as a biosphere reserve director and a biosphere reserves coordinator for the circumpolar Northern Science Network. He also manages two family trusts and a cattle ranch in Alberta, Canada.

Dale S. Turner has worked for The Nature Conservancy as a conservation planner since 2001, leading the planning teams that prepare site conservation plans that guide Conservancy action on the ground. He had a major role in the Apache Highlands Ecoregional Assessment, determining the sites that are important for future action planning. In addition, he serves the Arizona chapter as a general science support resource.

Dale has a M.S. in wildlife and fisheries sciences from the University of Arizona (1998) and a B.A. in behavioral sciences from Rice University (1982). He studied dune-dwelling lizards and plants for his thesis and conducted a herpetological inventory for the Arizona Game and Fish Department. Most recently, he worked for the National Park Service, studying saguaros in Saguaro National Park and helping direct a biological inventory program. He also has a long history as a volunteer activist for a variety of conservation groups. He maintains his sanity by exploring big wild places in the Sonoran Desert.

A westerner by birth, **Raymond M. Turner** attended Utah State University, the University of Utah (B.S. 1948, botany), and Washington State University (Ph.D. 1954, botany). He taught at the University of Arizona (1954–1962) before joining the U.S. Geological Survey.

Ray's interest in desert vegetation dynamics has resulted in studies of long-term permanent vegetation plots as well as the use of repeat photography for documenting landscape change. His fascination with repeat photography was aroused during preparation, with Rod Hastings, of *The Changing Mile,* a book describing vegetation change in southern Arizona and northern Sonora. Turner is also author or coauthor of publications describing changes in riparian vegetation along the Gila and Colorado rivers and changes in permanent vegetation study plots at the Desert Laboratory, Tucson, and at MacDougal Crater, Pinacate Biosphere Reserve, Sonora; and of the book *Bibliography of Repeat Photography for Evaluating Landscape Change* (1984).

Retired since 1989, he has subsequently coauthored three books, *Sonoran Desert Plants: An Ecological Atlas* (1995, with Janice E. Bowers and Tony L. Burgess), *Kenya's Changing Landscape* (1998, with H. Awala Ochung' and Jeanne B. Turner), and a new edition of *The Changing Mile*, aptly named *The Changing Mile Revisited* (2003, with Robert H. Webb, Janice E. Bowers, and James Rodney Hastings). He still periodically succumbs to his affliction and might be seen using the camera to recapture old landscape scenes in such places as New Mexico's "bootheel" country and Kenya's Rift Valley.

Stewart Udall served as secretary of the interior under U.S. presidents John Kennedy and Lyndon Johnson. He remains a powerful voice for conservation of public lands and natural resources, fair treatment of Native Americans, and reversing environmental pollution. He promoted the "Parks for America" program and oversaw implementation of the Wilderness Act and development of the Endangered Species Act. North Cascades and Redwoods became national parks under his auspice.

Born January 31, 1920, on a farmstead in St. Johns, Arizona, Udall developed a keen appreciation for nature and the out-of-doors at an early age. After serving as an Army Air Force gunner in World War II, he went on to become a lawyer and a member of the U.S. House of Representatives from southern Arizona (1954–1961). His district included the Dry Borders region north of the border. He served as interior secretary from 1960 to 1969.

Udall authored *The Quiet Crisis* (1963) and *The Energy Balloon* (1974), both important contributions to the environmental movement. His other books include *To the Inland Empire: Coronado and Our Spanish Legacy* (1987), *Myths of August* (1994), and *Forgotten Founders* (2002). He lives in Santa Fe, New Mexico, where he continues to write and to practice law, especially on behalf of Native Americans who are victims of uranium mining.

Thomas R. Van Devender, senior research scientist at the Arizona-Sonora Desert Museum since 1983, has conducted research on a broad range of natural history activities. He has authored well over a hundred research publications including journal articles, book chapters, and six books, on packrat middens and the paleoecology of the southwestern deserts, the desert grassland, the cacti of Sonora, and the Sonoran desert tortoise.

His dissertation at the University of Arizona in 1973 reconstructed the ice-age environments of the Sonoran Desert using plant and animal macrofossils preserved in ancient packrat middens. At the museum he has continued his paleoecological research in both the Sonoran and Chihuahuan deserts of the southwestern United States and northern Mexico. He has a special interest in the history and biogeography of the Sonoran

Desert as it developed from dry tropical forests and evolved from tropical ancestors 15–20 million years ago.

Van Devender has a long-term interest in the flora of the Sonoran Desert and has collected over 20,000 herbarium specimens, many of them deposited at the herbaria at the University of Arizona (Tucson), Universidad de Sonora (Hermosillo), and Centro de Investigaciones Biológicas del Noroeste (La Paz). He has surveyed local floras in Sonora, including the tropical deciduous forest of the Río Cuchujaqui near Alamos and the pine-oak forests in the Sierra Madre Occidental near Yécora. He has studied Sonoran Desert floras in the Sierra Bacha on the coast of the Gulf of California (Sonora), near Cataviña (Baja California), and in the Tucson Mountains and Sycamore Canyon (Arizona).

Anita Alvarez Williams: The Mexican desert border city of Mexicali was home to my husband, Charlie, and me for more than fifty years. We were raised there, and so were our three daughters, Ila, Lisa, and Sybil. Charlie and I now live in a cabin in an oak grove on the U.S. side of the border, enjoying a kindly mountain climate.

I'm a citizen of both the United States and Mexico and have a bachelor's degree in art history from Pomona College, class of 1953. My research on the Cucapá/Cocopa/Cocopah Indians began in the early years of the Baja symposiums when Sherman Foundation director Bill Hendricks loaned me two extraordinary albums of photos taken around 1900 of Chandler-Otis fishing and hunting trips on the Hardy River. Among the photos were beautiful pictures of Cucapá Indians. When a family friend, geographer Dave Henderson, saw those photos, he said to me, "These are great! Why don't you write a book to go with them?" So I did. *Travelers Among the Cucapá* appeared in 1975. It drew the attention of the Somerton Cocopah, who asked me to do a book for them, so I did — *The Cocopah People.*

With the encouragement and help of Julian Hayden, I expanded my research to the archaeology and anthropology of the entire Baja California peninsula and wrote *Primeros Pobladores de la Baja California,* in Spanish. This led to the job of founding and directing a center for the Indians of Baja California; working with the Cucapá, Pai Pai, Kiliwa, and Kumeyaay to secure land titles and water rights for them; and trying to improve their health care and education. This in turn led to working with Madeleine and Tupper Ansel Blake and Peter Steinhart on the Two Eagles–Dos Aguilas Smithsonian exhibit on the remaining wilderness of the Mexican American borderlands.

My interest in the Colorado River coincided with my research and growing friendship with the native people of the lower river, the Cucapá. Their two-thousand-year-old presence on the lower river gave them certain rights, I thought, that were being flagrantly denied. I still believe that the Cucapá deserve an uncontaminated, flowing river entering the Sea of Cortez. And the more I learn, the more I am convinced that we *all* need that healthy exchange between the river and the gulf. In defense of the lower Colorado River, I worked with Jim Richardson and Jim Carrier on their *National Geographic* Colorado River article and book, and with Linda Harrar and Sandra Postel on the PBS documentary *Last Oasis,* as well as doing the research for the River exhibit of the University of Baja California Museum. I continue campaigning for the restoration of water to the Colorado River delta.

Before he became research director of Drylands Institute, **Michael F. Wilson** worked in environmental and public health, agriculture, and technical/scientific illustration. His interest in the entomology and botany of the Southwest began long before he relocated to Arizona in 1987. Volunteer work at the Santa Barbara Museum of Natural History starting at the age of nine exposed him to a wide variety of disciplines and many spectacular insects with the cryptic label "SW RES. ST. ARIZ." Because of those specimens from the Southwest

Research Station in the Chiricahua Mountains, he took his first trip to southern Arizona in 1974 and has been studying the biology of the region ever since. Michael received his undergraduate degree from the University of California at Santa Cruz and did his master's work at the University of Arizona.

For the past ten years he has worked for Drylands Institute in Tucson. He is a coauthor of *Trees of Sonora,* with Richard Felger and Matt Johnson, and is writing a series of scientific articles on the moths of Sonora. With Felger he is currently working on *Medicinal Plants of Arizona and Sonora,* a work that will cover about 1,000 plants with ethnopharmacologic uses. His hobbies include raising enormous numbers of plants and insects and painting in oils and gouache.

Enrique Zamora-Hernández is an innate ornithologist from Ensenada, Baja California, with world-class bird identification skills. The observation of birds has been his passion since an early age and has led to jobs in the islands of the Gulf of California, the Pacific islands off Baja California, and the Alto Golfo region. Enrique was field coordinator for Pronatura Sonora but has taken a leave to enjoy the avifauna of the Baja California peninsula.

A. crassipes, 214; *A. fimbriatus,* 150, 214; *A. hypochondriacus,* 151; *A. obcordatus,* 214; *A. palmeri,* 151, *151,* 214, Plate 15.27; *A. ×tucsonensis,* 214; *A. watsonii,* 214

Amargosa culture, 129, *130*

Amaro Domínguez, Joaquín, 616

amberrats, *60*

Ambidexter, 425

Ambrosia, 204; *A. acanthicarpa,* 216; *A. ambrosioides,* 152, 216; *A. confertiflora,* 152, 216; *A. cordifolia,* 216; *A. deltoidea,* 152, 216; *A. dumosa,* 66, 217; *A. ilicifolia,* 61, 66, 217, 662; *A. monogyra* (see *Hymenoclea monogyra*); *A. salsola* (see *Hymenoclea salsola*)

Ambystomatidae, *313,* 330

Ambystoma tigrinum, 313, 330, 569

American Slough, 590

Ammobroma sonorae. See *Pholisma sonorae*

Ammodramus savannarum, 300, 405

Ammospermophilus harrisii, 278

amolillo, 150, 173, 213, 261

ampelis americano, 403

Amphibia (amphibians), 326, 329–30

Amphipoda (amphipods), *426, 488;* common, *489–91;* pelagic/ hyperiid, *491–92*

Amphispiza belli, 300, 405; *A. bilineata,* 286, 300, 405, Plate 19.6

Amsinckia intermedia, 153, 224; *A. tessellata,* 153, 225

Anacardiaceae, 151, 215

Anacystis, 344

Anagallis arvensis, 259

Anas acuta, 293, 392; *A. americana,* 292, 392; *A. clypeata,* 293, 392; *A. crecca,* 293, 392; *A. cyanoptera,* 292, 392; *A. discors,* 292, 392; *A. penelope,* 392; *A. platyrhynchos,* 292, 392, Plate 27.4; *A. strepera,* 292, 392

Anasazi culture, 131

Anatidae, 187, 292, 391–93

anchoa, 377; chicotera, 377; golfina, 377; del golfo, 377; misteriosa, 377; ojitos, 377; persistente, 377; trompuda, 377

Anchoa helleri, 367, 377; *A. ischana,* 377; *A. lucida,* 377; *A. mundeoloides,* 366, 377; *A. nasus,* 377; *A. parri,* 367, 377; *A. walkeri,* 377

anchoveta, 378; bocona, 378; escamuda, 378

Anchovia macrolepidota, 378

Anchoviella parri, 366

anchovy, 365–67, 370, 377; bignose, 377; bigscale, 378; bright, 377; gulf, 367, 377; mystery, 377; northern gulf, 366, 377; persistent, 377; sharpnose, 377

Ancyclopsetta dendritica, 381

Andrade, Guillermo, 607, 635

Andrade Mesa wetlands, 361, *362,* 590

Andrews, J. D., 77

Andropogon barbinodis. See *Bothriochloa barbinodis*

Androsace occidentalis, 260

Anemone tuberosa, 260

Anemopsis californica, 173–74, Plate 15.30

angelfish (ángel), 380; Cortez (de Cortés), 380

angelote, 377; del Pacífico, 377

angels' trumpets, 248

Angiosperms, 150–77

Anguilliformes, 377

Angulo Gallardo, Melquiades, 93, 98

ani, 295

animals: domesticated, 148; fossil records of, 63–65. *See also specific animals*

Anisacanthus thurberi, 213

Anisotremus davidsonii, 379; *A. interruptus,* 379

Annelida, *421, 426,* 470–79

Anoda abutiloides, 246; *A. pentaschista,* 246

Anodonta imbecillus, 569

Anomura, *426,* 479

Another Dawn (movie), 678

Anser albifrons, 391

Anseriformes, 292, 391–93

anteater, giant, 63

Antelope Bridge, 590

Antelope Hill, 590

Antelope Hill quarry, 144

Antelope Hills, 590

Antelope Hill Station, 590

Antelope Peak, 48, 590, *591*

Antelope Tank, 590

Antennariidae, 378

Antennarius avalonis, 378

Anthozoa, *426,* 435

Anthuridea, 492

Anthus rubescens, 299, 403; *A. spragueii,* 299

Antilocapra americana sonoriensis, 14, 189, 274, 278, 590, Plate 18.1

Antilocapridae, 278

Antirrhinum cyathiferum, 261; *A. filipes,* 261; *A. kingii* var. *watsonii* (see *A. watsonii*); *A. nuttallianum,* 261; *A. watsonii,* 261

Antrozous pallidus pallidus, 277

Anura, *313,* 329–30, 338–42, *341*

Apache del desierto, 139

Apaches, 134, 138–39

Apalone spinifera, 314, 331, 569

Aphelocoma californica, 297

Aphrodita mexicana, 425, 471; *A. sonorae,* 425, 471, Plate 29.6

Apiaceae, 215

Apis mellifera, 177, 340, 569

Aplysia californica, 422, 457; *A. vaccaria,* 425, 457

Apocynaceae, 151, 215

Apocynum cannabinum, 151, 215; *A. sibiricum* (see *A. cannabinum*)

Apodanthera undulata, 235

Apodidae, 295, 400

Apodiformes, 295, 400

Apogonidae, 379

Apogon retrosella, 379

Appendicularia (appendicularians), *421, 426*

Aprisa virgata, 397

Aquila chrysaetos, 187, 280, 293, 395, 614

Arabis perennans. See *Boechera perennans*

Araby, 591

Araiza, "El Mocho," 92

Ara macao, 187

Arbacia incisa, 426, 501

arca, 180

Arca pacifica, 179–80, *180*

Archaeogastropoda, 440–42

"An Archaeological Survey of Northwestern Papaguería" (Ezell), 81, 691

archaeology, 131, 142–46. *See also native peoples*

Archaic period, 129–30, *130*

Arch Canyon, 591

Archilochus alexandri, 285, 295, 400

Arctostaphylos peninsularis, 67

Ardea alba, 187, 292, 385, 394, Plate 27.8; *A. herodias,* 187, 292, 394, Plate 27.6

Ardeidae, 292, 394–95

ardillón, 192

area of critical environmental concern (ACEC), 16

Arecaceae, 151, 215

Arenaria interpres, 397; *A. melanocephala,* 397

Areneños. See Hia C'ed O'odham

Argemone gracilenta, 168, 250, 602; *A. ochroleuca,* 250

Argentiformes, 378

Argentina sialis, 378

argentine (argentina), 378; Pacific (del Pacífico), 378

Argentinidae, 378

Argyrochosma limitanea, 212

Argythamnia. See *Ditaxis*

Arida. See *Machaeranthera*

Arid Lands Project, 50

Ariidae, 378

Ariopsis c.f. *guatemalensis,* 378

ariosa, 224

Aristida adscensionis, 251; *A. californica,* 169, 251; *A. c.* var. *californica,* 251; *A. c.* var. *glabrata,* 251; *A. glauca* (see *A. purpurea* var. *nealleyi*); *A. hamulosa* (see *A. ternipes* var. *gentilis*); *A. parishii,* 251; *A. purpurea* var. *nealleyi,* 251; *A. p.* var. *parishii* (see *A. parishii*); *A. ternipes,* 251; *A. t.* var. *gentilis,* 251; *A. t.* var. *ternipes,* 251

Aristolochiaceae, 151, 215

Aristolochia watsonii, 151, 215

Arizona, 591; Highway 84, 591; Highway 85, 591; Highway 86, 591; southwestern, 28–29, Plate 2.2

Arizona Breeding Birds Atlas project, 285

Arizona elegans, 313, 334

Arizona Flora (Kearney and Peebles), 199, 705

Arizona State Board of Geographic and Historic Names, 582

Arizona Uplands vegetation type, 7, 17, 65, 198, 203, 286, 316–17, 329, 338; herpetofauna, 315–18, 324–25

Armando, José, 93

Armenta, Abraham, 140, 591

Armenta Well, 591

arrowhead, 150, 214

arrow-leaf, 222

arrows, fishing, 184

Bates Pass Tinaja, 594

Bates Well, 594

batfish, 378; roundel, 378

Bathygobius ramosus, 381

Batis maritima, 153, 224

Batrachoididae, 378

Batrachoidiformes, 378

baví, 241

baya, 185

Beale, Edward F., 600

bean, 148; desert, 162, 198, 241; Mexican jumping, 594; tepary, 133, 161–62, *162*, 198, 241, 598, 631, 670

Bean, L. J., 147, 699

Bean Pass, 594

beardtongue, Mojave, 262

beargrass, 168, 248; desert, 661; desert tree-, 62, 66–67, 168, 248; tree, 619

Beargrass Family, 168, 248

beaver, 64, 190, 278, 414, 417, 566, 568

Bebbia juncea var. *aspera*, 217

Bechtel, Kenneth, 421

Beck, Benjamin B., 282, 709

bedstraw: desert, 261; starry, 261

Beebe, William, *The Zaca Venture*, 420, 724

Beebee, Emily, 671

Beech Family, 165, 241–42

bee fly, *245*

bee-plant, sticky, 232

Bee Spring, 594

beetle: black stink, 644; pinacatl, 644; spider, 62–63

Bell, Charlie, 594, 596

Bell, W. H., 147

Bellflower Family, 231–32

Bell Mine, 594

Bell Pass, 594

Belnap, Jayne, 343–48

Belonidae, 378

Beloniformes, 378

Beloperone californica. See *Justicia californica*

Beltrán, Dario, 550

Beltrán, Olivia, 550

Beltrones, Manlio Fabio, 560

Belvedere Scientific Fund, 421

bench marks (BM), 596; BM Bat, 596; BM Charley, 596; BM Cholla, 596; BM Monson, 596; BM Simmons, 596

Bender, Anita, 73–74, 73–79, *78*

Bender, Laura, 71–76, *73–74*

Bender, Letty, *73–74, 73–79, 78*

Bender, O. A., 71, 594, 642

Bender, O. L., Jr., *73*

Bender, O. L. "Les," 71–79, *72, 75,* 626, 677

Bender, Thursia, 71

Bender family, 71, 140, 594–95

Bender Ranch, 73–79, *76*

Bender Spring, 594

Bender Wash, 594

Benner, Wendy Laird, 560–65

Benson, L. and R. A. Darrow, *Trees and Shrubs of the Southwest,* 200, 705

Benson, Scott, 509

Bentley, Lee, 658

bequilla, 241

Berardius bairdii, 411, 416

Berberidaceae, 224

Berberis haematocarpa, 62, 224; *B. harrisoniana*, 224

Bermúdez, Enrique, 650

Bermúdez, Juan, 111, 140, 650, 675

Bernardia incana, 236

berrendos, 189

berros, 227

berrugata, 380; aleta amarilla, 380

berrugato: californiano, 380; panameño, 380; real, 380

Betaeus longidactylus, 423–24, 487

Betancourt, Julio, et al., *Packrat Middens*, 59, 689

Bethard, C. T. "Tom," 634, 640

Betty Lee Mine, 594

Betty Lee Tank, 595

Bezy, Robert L., 338–42

bi:bhiag, 234

Bibles, D. Dean, 19

Big Horn Reservoir, 595

Big Horn Road, 595

bighorn sheep, 141, 273, 597; desert, 17–18, 112, 191, 278, 543, 658, *Plate 18.5*

Big Horn Station, 71–73, *72,* 595

Big Horn Station well, *73*

Bignoniaceae (Bignonia Family), 153, 224

Big Pass, 595

big root, 235

Big Tank, 595

Big Wash, 595

billfish, 381

Binational Network of Sonoran Desert Biosphere Reserves (proposed), 564

biological diversity, 537–47

biosphere reserves, 24–25, 560–61, 563–65. *See also* Reserva de la Biosfera Alto Golfo y Delta del Río Colorado (AG); Reserva de la Biosfera El Pinacate y El Gran Desierto de Altar (PI)

birds, 186–88, 280–91; checklist, 291–302, 391–407; conservation areas, *384*

Birthwort Family, 151, 215

bisbita americana, 403

Bisson, Henri, 19

bittern, 292, 394–95; American, 385, 394, *Plate 27.7*; least, 292, 394

bitterweed, 220

Bivalvia, 180–81, *426, 460–68*

biznaga, 230

blackbird, 301, 406; Brewer's, 301, 406; red-winged, 301, 389, 406; rusty, 301, 406; yellow-headed, 301, 406

Black Bottom Tank, 595

black brush, 266

Black Butte, 595

Black Day, Blue Night (movie), 593

Black Gap, 595

Black Gap Well, 595

Black Mountain Catchments, 595

Black Mountain (Pima Co.), 595

Black Mountain (SD), 595

Black Mountain Well, 595

Black Tanks, 595

bladderpod, 227; desert, 227; white, 227

bladderpod bush, 232

bladder sage, 62, 243, 654

bladder stem, 172, 258

Blair, John, 657

Blaisdell, 595

Blaisdell, Hiram W., 595

Blake, William P., 608, 738

Blankenship, Lon, 140, 595, 603

Blankenship Well and Ranch, 595

blanket-flower, Arizona, 219

blanquillo, 379

blazingstar, 167, 245; silver, 245; triangle-seed, 245; white-stem, 245

bledo, 214

Blenniidae, 381

Blennioidei, 380–81

blenny: bay, *370,* 381; browncheek, *372,* 382; combtooth, 381; flap-scale, 381; labrisomid, 380, 382;

largemouth, 380; mussel, 381; phallic, 382; porehead, 382; red-rump, 382; redside, 381; sargassum, 380; signal, elusive, 381; signal, gulf, 381; Sonora, 368, 371, 381; throatspotted, 382; tube, 381–82; warthead, 382; zebraface, 382

Blindman Butte, 596

bluebird: eastern, 298; mountain, 298, 403; western, 298, 403

Bluebird Mine Well, 596

blue dicks, 167, 244

blue-eyed grass, 271

Blue Plateau, 596

Blythe, Thomas H., 607

boa. *See under* snake

bobcat, 190, 278

Bob Curtis Tank, 596

bobo: blue, 380; enmascarado, 394; pata azul, 394; vientre-blanco, 394

bobwhite, masked, 543

Boca la Bolsa, 596

bocón, 379; punteado, 379

Boddie, John R., 609

Bodianus diplotaenia, 382

Boechera perennans, 226

Boerhavia, 168; *B. coccinea*, 248; *B. coulteri* (see *B. spicata*); *B. c.* var. *palmeri* (see *B. spicata*); *B. erecta*, 248; *B. e.* var. *erecta*, 248; *B. e.* var. *intermedia*, 248; *B. intermedia* (see *B. e.* var. *intermedia*); *B. megaptera*, 248; *B. pterocarpa*, 248; *B. spicata*, 168, 248; *B. s.* var. *palmeri* (see *B. spicata*); *B. triqueta* (see *B. e.* var. *intermedia*); *B. watsonii* (see *B. spicata*); *B. wrightii*, 248

Boidae, 334

Bojórquez, Ramón, 667, 669, 671

Bolboschoenus maritimus, 271

Bollmannia ocellata, 366, 381

bolsero: de Baltimore, 406; de Bullock, 406; cuculado, 406; tunero, 406

Bombus sonorus, 177

Bombycilla cedrorum, 299, 403

Bombycillidae, 299, 403

Bombyliidae, 245

Bommeria hispida, 212

bonefish, 377; Cortez, 377

Bonillas, Ygnacio S., Jr., 596, 738

Bonillas Cone, 596

Caridea, *426, 486–88*

Carlowrightia arizonica, 213

Carnegiea gigantea, 7, 21, 59, 65–66, 154–55, 228, 304

Carnegie Desert Laboratory, 85

Carnegie Peak, 602, *645*

Carnivora (carnivores), 274–76, 278, 417

carp, common, 184, 569

carpa: común, 184; elegante, 184; gigante del colorado, 185

Carpenter, Philip, 418, 725

carpenter bee, 177

carpetweed, threadstem, 247

Carpetweed Family, 247–48

carpintero: collarejo, 400; collarejo desértico, 400; de Gila, 400; listado, 400

Carpodacus cassinii, 301, 406; *C. mexicanus,* 301, 406; *C. purpureus,* 301, 406

Carrillo-Guerrero, Yamilett, 383–91; bird checklist, 391–407

carrizo, 256, 598, 602

carrot: false, 215; wild, 215

Carrot Family, 215

cártamo, 218

Carthamus tinctorius, 204, 218

Carthartidae, 292

Caryophyllaceae, 232

cascabel, 186

cascanueces americano, 402

Casmerodius egretta. See *Ardea alba*

Cassia covesii. See *Senna covesii*

Castañedo, José, 93

castañeta, 380, 382; cola de tijera, 382

Castela emoryi, 262, 594, 654, *Plate 17.24*

Castetter, E. F., 147

Castilleja exserta, 261; *C. lanata,* 262

Castle Rock, 602

castor, 64, 190, 417

Castor canadensis, 64, 190, 414, 417, 566, 568; *C. c. frondator,* 278

Castoridae, 278, 417

Castro Padilla, Carlos, 93, 95–96

cat, 274–75, 278

Catapyrenium lachneum, 346; *C. lacinulatum,* 346; *C. squamulosum,* 345, *346*

catbird, gray, 298, 403

catchfly, sleepy, 232

Cathartes aura, 197, 292, 395

Cathartidae, 292, 395

Catharus guttatus, 298, 403; *C. ustulatus,* 298, 403

Catherpes mexicanus, 298, 402

Catostomidae, 372

cattail, 141, 176, 385; southern, 264

Cattail Family, 176, 264

cattle, 188, 278; brands, 73, *74–75;* grazing, 21, 340, 363, 544–45, 671

Caucalis microcarpa. See *Yabea microcarpa*

Caudata, *313,* 330

Caulanthus lasiophyllus, 226

Caulolatilus affinis, 379

cazón, 376; bironche, 185, 376; hilacho, 376; mamón, 376; segador, 185, 376

cebadilla silvestre, 254

cebollín, 235, 244

cedkam, 224–25

ce'ecem vipinoi, 229

Celastraceae, 232

Celaya, Alberto, 80–84, *81, 84,* 577, 603, 650, 671

Celaya Crater, 603

Celtis pallida, 176, 264, 287; *C. reticulata,* 264; *C. tala* (see *C. pallida*)

Cement Tank, 603

Cemetery Wash, 603

ce:mǐ, 231

Cenchrus ciliaris (see *Pennisetum ciliare*): *C. echinatus,* 252; *C. incertus* (see *C. spinifex*); *C. palmeri,* 252; *C. pauciflorus* (see *C. spinifex*); *C. spinifex,* 252

Centaurea melitensis, 218

Centaurium calycosum, 242

centaury, 242

Central Gulf Coast vegetation type, 66

Centro Intercultural de Estudios de Desiertos y Océanos (CEDO), 548–59, *550*

Centrostephanus coronatus, 426, 501

Century Plant Family, 150, 213–14, *Plates 15.25–15.26*

cenzontle norteño, 403

Cephalochordata, *421, 426,* 504

Cephalopholis panamensis, 379

Cephalopoda, *426,* 440

cepuliñ bavĭ, 241

Ceramic period, *130,* 130–31; ceramic groups, *132. See also* pottery

Cerastium texanum, 232

cerceta: aliazul, 392; aliverde, 392; castaña, 392

Cercidium. See *Parkinsonia*

cereus, night-blooming. *See under* cactus

Ceriantipatharia, *435*

cernícalo americano, 395

Cerro el Aguila, 603

Cerro Blanco, 603

Cerro Borrego, 603

Cerro del Borrego, 603

Cerro el Chivo, 603

Cerro Cipriano, 603

Cerro Colorado, 40, 195, 603

Cerro los Cuates, 603

Cerro el Halcón, 603

Cerro el Huérfano, 603

Cerro Kino, 603

Cerro Lágrimas de Apache, 603

Cerro la Lava, 603

Cerro el Mayo, 603

Cerro los Ojos, 604

Cerro Pinto, 604

Cerro Prieto, 604

Cerro Prieto Geothermal Area, 32

Cerro Prieto salt ponds, 359, *360*

Cerro la Silla, 604, *604*

Cerro Sombrero, 604

Cerro Tecolote, 604

Certhia americana, 298, 402

Certhiidae, 298, 402

Cervidae, 278

Cetacea, 416

Cetengraulis mysticetus, 378

Cetorhinidae, 377

Cetorhinus maximus, 377

ce'ul, 261

Chaenactis carphoclinia, 218; *C. stevioides,* 218

Chaenaxis tuba, 63

Chaenopsidae, *372,* 381–82

Chaenopsis alepidota, 382

Chaetodipterus zonatus, 381

Chaetodipus, 287; *C. baileyi baileyi,* 287; *C. intermedius phasma,* 287; *C. penicillatus penicillatus,* 287; *C. p. pricei,* 287

Chaetognatha, *421, 426,* 503

Chaetura vauxi, 295, 400

chalapo, 380

Chamaesaracha coronopus, 262

Chamaesyce. See *Euphorbia*

chambo, 381

chamizo, 217; de agua, 232; cenizo,

232–33; forrajero, 216; grande, 233; volador, 233

chamomile, false, 221

Chamomilla suaveolens. See *Matricaria discoidea*

chano, 415; norteño, 380; sureño, 380

chapacolor, 251

chapaturrín, 401

Chappell, James "Chapo," 604, 646

Chappell Well, 604

Charadriidae, 294, 396

Charadriiformes, 294, 396–99

Charadrius alexandrinus nivosus, 396; *C. melodus,* 396; *C. montanus,* 396; *C. semipalmatus,* 294, 396; *C. vociferus,* 294, 396; *C. wilsonia,* 396

charale, 378

Charina trivirgata, 313, 323, 334, *Plates 21.8–21.9*

Charlie Bell Pass, 604

Charlie Bell Road, 604

Charlie Bell Well, 604, *605*

charlock, 227

charrito ojón, 379

chat, yellow-breasted, 300, 404

checklists: birds, 291–302, 391–407; fishes, 376–82; herpetofauna, 329–37; invertebrates, *434–504;* mammals, 277–79, 416–17; place names, 585–679; plants, 149–92, 211–71

cheeseweed, 167, 247

Cheilanthes deserti (see *Notholaena californica*): *C. lindheimeri,* 212; *C. parryi,* 212; *C. standleyi* (see *Notholaena standleyi*); *C. villosa,* 212; *C. wrightii,* 212; *C. yavapensis,* 212

Chelonia agassizii, 513; *C. mydas,* 186, *314, 331, 507, 508, 509, 510, 513–15, 514, Plate 30.11; C. m. agassizii,* 513

Cheloniidae, *331,* 506–9, 511, 516–18

Chen caerulescens, 292, 391; *C. rossi,* 392

cheniers, 34, 628

Chenopodiaceae, 157–58, 232–34

Chenopodium, 158; *C. murale,* 158, 233, 628; *C. pratericola,* 233; *C. watsonii,* 233

cherioni, 604

Cherioni Wash, *44,* 604

Cherioni Well, 604

Chia Canyon, 605

Colidotea findleyi, 426, *493*

colimbo: ártico, 393; común, 393; gorjirrojo, 393; piquiamarillo, 393

Colinus virginianus ridgwayi, 543

Collema coccophorum, 345, *346*; *C. tenax*, 345, *346*, Plate 23.11

Colonia Díaz, 607

Colonia Lerdo, 92, 607

The Colorado Delta (Sykes), 99, 117, 126, 693

Colorado Desert, 608

Colorado River, 608–9; agriculture, 141–42; bird conservation areas, *384*; flow, *109*; habitat alteration, 414–15, 429–30; Knowland family river cruise, 99, 101–2; remnant vegetation, Plate 28.9; salt pan, Plate 28.10; Sykes' and McLean's voyage, 117–26

Colorado River Buff Ware, 130–31

Colorado River delta, *33*; aerial survey, 355–56, *356*; conservation and management, 357–58, 566–70; ecozones, *358*, 358–63; exhibit, 108–9; fishing, 105–7; flora and vegetation, *102*, *207*; Landsat images, Plate 2.1, Plate 2.4, Plates 2.1–2.2; maps, *35*, *100*, *520*; physical geography, 30, 31–34; salt pan, Plate 28.10; steamboats, *101*; tidal bore, 108, 360, 386, 519–29, *522*, 527–28, 608, 627; tidal range, 408, 422. *See also* Reserva de la Biosfera Alto Golfo y Delta del Río Colorado (AG)

Colorado River Riparian Corridor, 358–59, *358–59*

colorín: azul, 406; lazulita, 406; sietecolores, 406

Colpichthys hubbsi, 369, 378; *C. regis*, 369, 378

Colubridae, 334–35

Colubrina californica, 260

Columba fasciata, 294; *C. livia*, 294, 389, 407

Columbidae, 294, 399

Columbiformes, 294, 399

Columbina inca, 294, 399, 568; *C. passerina*, 294, 399; *C. talpacoti*, 399

Combat Village, 609

comb-bur: arched, 226; broad-wing, 226; mixed-nut, 225

comb jellies, *439*

Comcáac. *See* Seris

Comisión Nacional del Agua, 359

Commelinaceae, 234

Commelina erecta, 234

Commicarpus scandens, 248

Common Intertidal Invertebrates of the Gulf of California (Brusca), 422, 724

community stewardship, 565

compass plant, 220

Compositae. *See* Asteraceae

Compton, John F., 606

conch, smooth, 183

Condalia globosa, 260; *C. lycioides* (see *Ziziphus obtusifolia* var. *canescens*); *C. warnockii*, 172, 260

cone, princely, 181

conejo (animal), 192

conejo (fish), 379

Conepatus mesoleucus venaticus, 278

coney, gulf, 379

confiturilla negra, 265

congrio: espantoso, 377; picudo, 377

congriperla, 378; adornada, 378; cornuda, 378

Conklin, Enoch, 612, 659, 740

Conley, Richard H., 609

Conley, Samuel R., 609

Conley Tank, 609

Conley Well, 609

Conner, Charles, 5, 203

cono, 181

Consag. *See* Rocas Consag

Consag, Ferdinand, Father, 33, 653

conservation, 7–11, 23–26, 357–58, 430, 517–18, 548–61, 563–70; areas, *384*; Mexico, 537–47

Constrictor constrictor, 64

Contopus cooperi, 296, 401; *C. sordidulus*, 296, 401

Contreras Delgadillo, Juan, 92

Conus, 144, 426; *C. angulatus*, 425, *444*; *C. princeps*, 181

Convolvulaceae, 234

Conyza canadensis, 218; *C. coulteri* (see *Laennecia coulteri*)

coot, 293, 396; American, 188, 294, 385, 396

Copepoda, 426

copetón gorjicenizo, 401

Cophosaurus texanus, 332

copper, 44–45

Copper Canyon, 609

copperleaf, 236

Copper Mine Mountain, 609

Copper Mountains, 609

coquillo amarillo, 235

coquito, 235

Coraciiformes, 295, 400

Coragyps atratus, 292, 395

Coralliozetus micropes, 382

corals, 436

Corbicula fluminea, 569

corbina, California, 380

cormorant (cormorán), 292, 394; Brandt's (de brandt), 394, 628; double-crested (bicrestado), 292, 394, 628

corn, 148, 162, 168, 171–72, 198, 607, 631. *See also* maize

Cornejo, Dennis, 200

Cornelia Arroyo, 609

Corner Well, 609

Cornez, Rio, 609

cornuda: cabeza de pala, 376; común, 376; gigante, 376; prieta, 376

corona de cristo, 243, 262

Corrales, Miguel, 95

correcaminos mayor, 399

Corrigan, 609

Cortés, Agustín, 550

Cortés, Hernan, 418

Corvidae, 297, 402

corvina (corvina), 370, 380; bigeye (ojona), 380; gulf (golfina), 185, 368, 374, 380, 415; orangemouth (boquinaranja), 184, 380; shortfin (aleta corta), *371*, 380; striped (rayada), 380

corvina cabaicucho, 185, 380

corvinata negra, 380

corvineta bizca, 380

Corvus brachyrhynchos, 402; *C. corax*, 297, 402; *C. cryptoleucus*, 297

Corydalis aurea, 271

Corynopuntia. *See* Grusonia

Corynorhinus townsendii. *See* Plecotus townsendii pallescens

Coryphaena hippurus, 379

Coryphaenidae, 379

Coryphopterus urospilus, 381

cósahui, 165, 243

Cosmocampus arctus, 378

cosón, 190

Coss, Hal, 65

costurero: piquicorto, 397; piquilargo, 397

Cottea pappophoroides, 253

cotton, 167

Cotton Center, 609

cottontail, desert, 192, 276, 279

cottonwood, 13, 33, *102*, 355, 357–58, 387–88, 608–9; Frémont, 64, 173, 207, 261, 384, 414, 638

Cotula australis, 218

Cougar Canyon, 610

County Line Hill, 610

Coursetia glandulosa, 200, 239, 614; *C. microphylla* (see *C. glandulosa*)

Covillea glutinosa. *See* *Larrea divaricata*

cowbird: bronzed, 301, 406, 568; brown-headed, 282, 301, 389, 406

cowboy's fried eggs, 250

cowpea, 164

coyote, 125–26, 189, 275, 278, Plate 18.8

Coyote Peak, 610

Coyote Peak Tanks, 610

Coyote Tinaja, 610

Coyote Wash, 610

Coyote Water, 610

coypu, 414

crab: blue, 183, 432n1; fiddler, Plate 29.10; hermit, *481*; mole and sand, *480*; porcelain, 479–80; purse, 423; "true," 481–86

Crabb, Henry, A., 618

Crabtree, Ben, 369, 716

Craig, J. A., 516, 728

crane, 294, 396; sandhill, 294, 384, 388, 396

cranesbill, 242

Crassulaceae, 158, 234–35

Crassula connata, 234

Cráter Elena, 610

Crater Range, 610

craters, 38, *40*, 195–96

crayfish, 569

creeper, 298, 402; brown, 298, 402

creosotebush, 55–56, 62, 66, 82, 176–77, 265, 623; dune, 265

Crescentia alata, 304

Cressa truxillensis, 234, 627

crinklemat: fanleaf, 226; Palmer's, *153*, 226; woolly, 226

croaker, 370, 380; black, 380; golden, 380; gulf, 380; rock, 380; squinteyed, 380; yellowfin, 380

Crocker, Fred, 607

crocodile, American, 185

Crocodilichthys gracilis, 382

Crocodylus acutus, 185

Crossidium aberrans, 345, *346*; *C. erosum*, 346

ironwood, 65–67, 161, 200–201, 240, 384, 545; repeat photographs, 54–55, *55*

Isla Gore, *33*, 627

Isla Montague, *33*, 355, 627

Isla Pelícano, 628

Isla Pinta, 628, *628*

Isla Sacatosa, 628

Islas San Jorge, 382, 628, *628*

Isla Vega, 628

Isocoma acradenia, 152, 220

Isomeris arborea, 232

Isopisthus remifer, 380

Isopoda (isopods), 426, *426*, 492–94

Isostichopus fuscus, 426–27, 503

Istiophoridae, 381

Istiophorus platypterus, 381

Isurus oxyrinchus, 377

'isvigĭ, 230

'i:vadhoḍ, 220

Ivalon, 629

Ives, Joseph C., 365, 521, 730

Ives, Ronald L.: ashes of, 611; *Land of Lava, Ash, and Sand*, 80, 692; naming places, 633; *Pinacate Region, Sonora, Mexico*, 80, 692; place descriptions, 647–48, 653; place named for, 629; on place names, 581; stories about, 627; works, 692, 743

Ives Flow, 38, *39*, 629

Ixobrychus exilis, 292, 394

Ixoreus naevius, 298

jabalí, 192

jaboncillo, 173, 261

jabonero doble punteado, 379

jack, 379; green, 379; Pacific cre-valle, 379

Jack in the Pulpit, 629

jackrabbit: Allen's, 276, 338; ante-lope, 190, 279, 338; black-tailed, 190, 276, 279

Jackson, Earl, 629

Jacksons Hole Tinaja, 629

Jacks Well, 629

Jacobinia ovata. See *Justicia candi-cans*

Jacquemontia pringlei, 234

jaeger, 398–99; long-tailed, 398; parasitic, 398; pomarine, 398

Jaeger, Louis J. F., 613, 629

Jaeger Wagon Road, 629

jaguar, 64, 275, 304, 568

jaguarundi, 275

jaiba azul, 183

James, George Wharton, 663; *The Wonders of the Colorado Desert*, 608, 743

Janusia gracilis, 246

jaqueta, 380, 382; de Cortés, 380

jaquetones, 377

jara, 222

Jarava speciosa. See *Stipa speciosa*

jarrito, 262

jasmine, rock, 260

Jatropha cardiophylla, 160, 238; *J. cinerea*, 160, 238; *J. cuneata*, 66, 160, *161*, 238

javelina, 75, 192, 274, 278, *Plate 18.7*

Javelina Mountain, 47, 629, *629*

Javelina Tank, 629

Javelina Tinajas, 629

Javelina Well, 629

jawfish, 379; finespotted, 379

jay, 297, 402; pinyon, 297; Steller's, 297; western scrub-, 297

jécota, 220

Jeffers, Robinson, "The Dead Men's Child," 670

jellyfish, *439*

Jenkins, Jesse D., *51*

jewelflower, Arizona, 228

jiavul, 230

Johnson, Jim, 677

Johnson, Lyndon, 533–35

Johnson Well, *77*, 630

Johnson Well ranch house, *76*

Johnston, Marshall, 200

John the Baptist Mountains, 629

joint fir, *82*, 213

jojoba, 174, 262

Jojoba Family, 174, 262

Jordan, David Starr, 365, 419

Jorgenson, Clive, 58

jorobado papelillo, 379

Jose Juan Hill, 630

Jose Juan Tank, 630, *630*

Joshua tree, 61–62, 65

juancito, 192

Juárez, Benito Pablo, 659

jumete, 215–16

Juncaceae, 165, 243

Junco hyemalis, 301, 405

junco, dark-eyed, 301, 405

Juncus, 165; *J. acutus* subsp. *leopoldii*, 243; *J. arcticus* var. *mexicanus*, 243; *J. balticus*

var. *mexicanus* (see *J. arcticus* var. *mexicanus*); *J. bufonius*, 243; *J. cooperi*, 243

juniper: California, 62, 65–67; Rocky Mountain, 61, 65; rose-berry, 65, 213; Utah, 65

Juniper Tank, 630

Juniperus, 59; *J. californica*, 62, 65–67; *J. coahuilensis*, 65, 213, 629; *J. erythrocarpa* var. *coahui-lensis* (see *J. coahuilensis*); *J. monosperma*, 213; *J. osteo-sperma*, 65; *J. scopulorum*, 65

jurel, 379; bonito, 379; toro, 379

Justicia californica, 150, 213, 626; *J. candicans*, 213; *J. longii*, 213

kacha, 253

Ka:do:di Do'ag 'marble mountain,' 630

Kaka 'cleared fields,' 630

kakaicu 'i:vakĭ, 225

Kaka Valley, 630

Kaka Wash, 630

ka:kowani, 227

Kalil, Syde, 630, 633

Kalilville, 630

kalisp, 240

Kallstroemia californica, 265, *Plate 17.25*; *K. grandiflora*, 265

kasvañ, 214

kaupdam, 233

kawk kuavulĭ, 260

Kearney, T. H., and R. H. Peebles, *Arizona Flora*, 199, 705

Keck, Eric, 105–7

Keckiella antirrhinoides, 262

Keener, Chris, 348

Keith, Stanton B., 643, 743

kek cehedagĭ, 240

Kelland, Ralph, 667

Kelly, William H., 141, 697, 702

Kerrick, James, 658

kestrel, American, 293, 395

Keuper, Ann, 560

Kid Rodelo (L'Amour), 671, 743

Kilham, Walter, 111

Kiliwas, *136*, 138

Killbright, John, 637

killdeer, 294, 396

Kim, 630

kingbird: Cassin's, 296, 401; eastern, 401; thick-billed, 296; tropical, 296, 401; western, 296, 401

kingfish: highfin, 380; Panama, 380

kingfisher, 295, 400; belted, 295, 400; green, 400

kinglet, 298, 403; golden-crowned, 298; ruby-crowned, 298, 403

King of Arizona (Kofa) National Monument, 9

Kino, Eusebio Francisco, Padre: assigning place names, 577, 602, 623, 626, 649, 678; on Baja Cali-fornia as a peninsula, 418, 432n2; climbing Pinacate Peak, 637, 644–45; explorations, 33; fic-tional account of, 601; field notes, xiii; introduction of plants and animals, 149; place descriptions, 645, 647; places named for, 39, 603, 630–31; 1701 map, 593; 1699 route, 601, 619

Kino Crater, 630

Kino Pass, 631

Kino Peak, 631, *631*

Kinosternidae, 330–31

Kinosternon flavescens, 314; *K. f. ari-zonense*, 330; *K. sonoriense*, 64, 186, *314*, 331, 568; *K. s. longifemo-rale*, 331

Kino Tinajas, 631

Kinter, 631

kipukas, 634

Kitanemuk, 140

kite, 293, 395; white-tailed, 283, 293, 395

kittiwake, black-legged, 398

ki:weco vaṣai, 253

knotweed, silversheath, 259

Knowland, Smokey, 99, 101–2

Koanophyllon palmeri, 220

Koeberliniaceae (Koeberlinia Fam-ily), 243

Koeberlinia spinosa, 243

Kofa wildlife refuge, 10, *10*

Kogia breviceps, 412, 416, 551, *552*; *K. sima*, 416

Kohatk Wash, 631

ko:kṣam, 252

komagĭ 'u'us, 222

komagĭ va:s, 238

Konsák, Ferdinand, Father. See Con-sag, Ferdinand, Father

ko'okomaḍk, 240

Ko'okomadk-kam 'place of the blue palo verde,' 631

ko'ovĭ ta:tamĭ, 241

Ligurta, 632

Ligurta Wash, 632

Liliaceae (sensu lato), 166–67, 244

lily: Ajo (desert), 167, 244; mariposa, desert, 166, 244; sand, blue, 167, 244; zephyr, yellow, 244

Lily Family, 166–67, 244

limberbush, 160, 238; ashy, 160, 238

Lime Hill, 632

Limnodromus griseus, 397; *L. scolopaceus*, 294, 397

Limosa fedoa, 397

Linaceae, 244

Linanthus aureus, 257; *L. bigelovii*, 257; *L. demissus*, 257; *L. dichotomus*, 257; *L. jonesii* (see *L. bigelovii*)

Linaria canadensis var. *texana*, 262; *L. texana* (see *L. c.* var. *texana*)

Linckia columbiae, 426, 499

Linepithema humile, 569

Lingenfelter, Richard, 607, 743

Linum lewisii (see *L. perenne* subsp. *lewisii*): *L. perenne* subsp. *lewisii*, 244

Lipotes vexillifer, 409

lisa, 378; blanca, 378; rayada, 184, 378

Litopenaeus stylirostris, 183, 517

Little Ajo Mountains, 632

Little Bruce Tank, 632

Little Pass, 632

Little Rainbow Valley, 632

Little Table Top, 632

Little Tenmile Wash, 632

Little Tule Tank, 632

Little Tule Well, 632

liveforever, Arizona, 158, 235

lizard, *313, 318, 320–21, 326–27, 331–33*; beaded, 331; brush, long-tailed, 333; collared, Basin and Range, 332; collared, Sonoran Desert, 332; collared and leopard, 332; earless, greater, 332; earless, lesser, 332; fringe-toed, Colorado Desert, 186, 333, 638; fringe-toed, Mojave, 319; fringe-toed, Yuman Desert, 333; horned, desert, 332; horned, flat-tailed, 332, 568; horned, regal, 333; horned, round-tailed, 63; iguanas and related lizards, 332–33; leopard, long-nosed, 332; night, 332; night, desert, 332; side-blotched, 333; spiny, Clark, 333; spiny, desert, 333; tree, 333, 568;

zebra-tailed, 63, 332. *See also* iguana, desert

lizardfish, 378; California, 378; lance, 378

lizard tail, 250

Lizard-Tail Family, 173–74, 261

Llano el Chinero, 606

Loasaceae, 167, 244–45

lobo, 417

lobo marino, 192; de California, 417

Lobotes pacificus, 379

Lobotidae, 379

lobster, spiny and slipper, *488*

Lockley, Arthur S., 367

Locomotive Rock, 633

locoweed, sand, 239

locust, hill, 240

Loeflingia squarrosa, 232

Loeseliastrum schottii, 257

loess, 42

Logan, Patti, 105–7

Logfia. See *Filago*

Lomatium nevadense, 215

longspur, 404–5; chestnut-collared, 301, 405; McCown's, 405

Lontra canadensis, 414, 417

Lookout Mountain, 633

Lookout Well, 633

loon, 292, 393; common, 292, 393; Pacific, 393; red-throated, 393; yellow-billed, 393

Looseboom Tank, 633

loosestrife, California, 245

Loosestrife Family, 245

López Collada, Jorge, 93, 95–96, 97, 617

Lophiiformes, 378

Lophocereus. See *Pachycereus*

Lophodytes cucullatus, 293, 393

Lophortyx. See *Callipepla*

Lord Will Mine, 633

loro, 380

Los Diputados, 613

Los Pozitos, 646

Los Pozos de San Miguel, 647

Lost, 633

Lost Cabin Mine, 633

Lost City, 633

Lost Horse Peak, 633

Lost Horse Tank, 633

Los Vidrios, *675, 675*

lotus, hairy, 240

Lotus humistratus, 240; *L. rigidus*, 240; *L. salsuginosus*, 240; *L. strigosus*, 240

Louw, Gideon N., 7, 684

Lowe, Charles, 50, *51*, 91, *91*, 310–11

Lower Colorado River Valley vegetation type, 7, 17, 65–66, 198, 203, *284, 316–17*, 338; herpetofauna, 315–17, 324–25, 329

Lower Well, 633

Luidia columbia, 426, *499*; *L. phragma*, 426, *500*

Luke, Frank, Jr., 633

Luke Air Force Range, 633

Lukeville, 633

Luke-Williams Airfields, 633

Lumholtz, Carl: on Apache trade, 139; assigning place names, 643, 671; explorations of, 147, 385, 419; ironwood tree photograph, 55, *55*; *New Trails in Mexico*, 50, 80–82, 577, 689; place descriptions, 586, 611, 647, 654, 656, 658, 670; on place names, 601, 603–4; tanks named for, 633

Lumholtz Tanks, 633

Luna y Arellano, Tristán de, 662

Lung, Edison, 637

Lung, Elsie, 637

lupine (lupino): Arizona, 240; elegant, 240; Mojave, 240

Lupinus arizonicus, 240; *L. concinnus*, 240; *L. sparsiflorus*, 240

Luticola cohnii, 344; *L. mutica*, 344

Lutjanidae, 379

Lutjanus argentiventris, 379; *L. guttatus*, 379; *L. novemfasciatus*, 379

Lutra canadensis, 568

Lycium, 204; *L. andersonii*, 174, 263; *L. berlandieri*, 174, 263; *L. brevipes*, 174, 263; *L. californicum*, 263, 586; *L. exsertum*, 175, 263; *L. fremontii*, 175, 263, *Plate 15.31*; *L. macrodon*, 263; *L. parishii*, 263

Lycurus setosus, 255

Lydig, Jane, 643

Lynch, Daniel "Dan," 610, 629, 634, 744

Lynchberg, 634

Lyngbya aestuari, 344

Lynx rufus, 190; *L. r. baileyi*, 278

lyre-pod, 227

Lyrocarpa coulteri, 227

Lytechinus pictus, 426, *502*

Lythraceae, 245

Lythrum californicum, 245

Lythrypnus dalli, 381

maaris, 39

macabí de Cortés, 377

macarela, 381; estornino, 381

macaw, scarlet, 187

MacDougal, Daniel Trembly, 50, 85, 385, 419, 634, 676

MacDougal Crater, *39*, 40, 195–96, 634

MacDougal Pass, 634; repeat photographs, 50–52, *51*

Machaeranthera arida (see *M. coulteri*): *M. arizonica* (see *M. coulteri*); *M. asteroides*, 220; *M. carnosa*, 220; *M. coulteri*, 220; *M. gracilis*, 221; *M. pinnatifida* var. *gooddingii*, 221; *M. tagetina*, 221

machete, *371, 377*; del Pacífico, 377

Machita, Pia, 666

Macías Valenzuela, Anselmo, 98

mackerel, 381; frigate, 381; Pacific chub, 381

MacMahon, James A., 282, 286, 710

Macroptilium atropurpureum, 240

Macrotus californicus, 277

Madder Family, 261

Magagnini, Stephen, 109, 693

Maggies Nipple, 634

maize, 133, 169, 171–72, 179, 670. *See also* corn

Majors Tank, 634

Makaira indica, 381

Malacanthidae, 379

Malacoctenus gigas, 368, 371, 381; *M. hubbsi*, 381; *M. tetranemus*, 382

Malacostraca, 479

Malacothrix californica var. *glabrata* (see *M. glabrata*): *M. coulteri*, 221; *M. fendleri*, 221; *M. glabrata*, 221; *M. sonorae*, 221

mala mujer, 264

mal de ojo, 167, 247, 265

Maldonado, Felipe, 550

Maldonado, Francisco, 552

mallard, 292, 392, *Plate 27.4*

Mallory, T. Dwight, 8, 85, 87–90, *88–89*

mallow: alkali, 247; alkali, arrowleaf, 247; bladder, 246; globe, 167; globe, caliche, 247; globe, Coulter's, 247; globe, desert, 247; rose-, desert, 246; velvet-, orange, 247; velvet-, pink, 246

Mallow Family, 167, 246–47

Podiceps auritas, 393; *P. nigricollis*, 292, 393
Podicipedidae, 292, 393
Podicipediformes, 292, 393
Podilymbus podiceps, 292, 393
Poecile gambeli, 297
Poeciliidae, 372
Pogonophora, 426
poinsettia, wild, 237
Point Invincible, 646
Point of the Pintas, 646
Pokeweed Family, 168, 251
Polanisia dodecandra, 232; *P. trachy-sperma* (see *P. dodecandra*)
Polemoniaceae, 257
Polinices recluzianus, 182
Polioptila caerulea, 298, 403; *P. cali-fornica*, 403; *P. melanura*, 298, 385, 403
pollen, 35
polluela: negra, 396; sora, 396
Polychaeta (polychaetes), 423, 425, *426, 470–79*
Polydactylus approximans, 380
Polygalaceae, 257
Polygala macradenia, 257
Polygonaceae, 172, 258–59
Polygonum argyrocoleon, 259
Polynemidae, 380
Polyplacophora, 468–70
Polypogon monspeliensis, 256; *P. viridis*, 256
Polyprionidae, 379
Pomacanthidae, 380
Pomacanthus zonipectus, 380
Pomacentridae, 380, 382
Pomadasys panamensis, 380
pomegranate, 204, 260
Pomegranate Family, 260
pompano: gafftopsail, 379; paloma, 379
pondweed: horned, 265; sago, 259
Pondweed Family, 259
Pooecetes gramineus, 300, 405
poorwill, common, 284, 295, 400
popcorn-flower, Arizona, 226
poppy: gold, desert, 250; gold, little, 250; gold, Mexican, 250; prickly, 168, 250, 602; prickly, Mexican, 250; summer, 265
Poppy Family, 168, 250
Populus fremontii, 64, 173, 261, 384
Porcellanidae, *479–80*
porcupine, 64

porgy, 380; Pacific, 184, 380
Porichthys analis, 378; *P. mimeticus*, 378
Porifera, *421, 426, 434–35*
Porophyllum gracile, 153, 222
Porphyrosiphon fuscus, 344
porpoise, 416; Burmeister's, 552; Gulf of California, 13, 416, 551–54, 568 (*see also* vaquita)
Porter, Eliot, 99
Portillo Laguna, Juan, *106*
Port Otis, 646
Portulacaceae (Portulaca Family), 172, 259
Portulaca halimoides, 259; *P. olera-cea*, 172, 259; *P. parvula* (see *P. halimoides*); *P. retusa*, 259; *P. suffrutescens*, 259; *P. umbrati-cola*, 259
Porzana carolina, 294, 396
Poston, Charles D., 620
Potamogetonaceae, 259
Potamogeton pectinatus. See *Stucke-nia pectinata*
Pottebaum, Henry, 646
Pottebaum Tank, 646
pottery, 130–31, *132*, 143; sherds, *133, 145. See also* Ceramic period
Poverty Flat Tank, 646
poverty weed, 158, 233
Powell, John Wesley, 99
Powers, Fred, 646
Powers Well, 646
Poyner Water, 646
pozo, 12, 384, 418–20, *419, 647, 647*
Pozo Caballo, 647
Pozo la Cholla, 647
Pozo Nuevo, 647
Pozo Redondo, 647
Pozo Redondo Mountains, 647
Pozo Redondo Valley, 647
Pozo Salado (CP), 647
Pozo Salado (OP), 647
Pozo Tres Ojitos, 647
pradero: común, 406; occidental, 406
Prenanthella exigua, 222
Presa Derivadora, 648
preservation of artifacts and sites, 144–46
Price, Bonnie, 662
Price, Lee, 662
Price, William W., 384, 722
prickly pear. *See under* cactus
primrose: desert, white, 250; dune,

168; evening, Arizona, 250; eve-ning, dune, 250; evening, yellow, 250; willow-herb, 249
Primrose Family, 259–60
Primulaceae, 259–60
Prionotus ruscarius, 379; *P. stephano-phrys*, 379
Probopyrus pandalicola, 426, 493
Proboscidea altheifolia, 167, 247; *P. parviflora*, 167, *167*, 247
Procambarus clarki, 569
Procellaridae, 393
Procellariiformes, 393–94
Prochloron didemni, 554
Procyonidae, 274, 278
Procyon lotor, 191, 275; *P. l. pallidus*, 278
Progne subis, 283, 287, 297, 402
Programa Para la Conservación de Murcielagos Migratorios, 305
projectile points: Clovis, 129; fishing arrows, 184
PRONATURA, Friends of, 563
pronghorn, 278; Sonoran, 14, 189, 274, 278, 353–54, 590, *Plate 18.1*
Prosopis, 66, 201, 384, 545; *P. glandu-losa*, 82, 162–64, *163*, 199–200; *P. g.* var. *torreyana*, 199, 241; *P. juliflora*, 199–200; *P. j.* var. *tor-reyana* (see *P. g.* var. *torreyana*); *P. j.* var. *velutina* (see *P. velutina*); *P. pubescens*, 164, *164*, 241, 672, 676; *P. velutina*, 162–64, 198–200, 199, 241, 619
Protemblemaria bicirrus, 382
Protococcus grevillei, 344
Protosiphon cinnamomeus, 344
Psaltriparus minimus, 297
Psathyrotes ramosissima, 222
Pseudognaphalium canescens, 222. See also *Gnaphalium*
Pseudorca crassidens, 410, 416
Pseudorontium cyathiferum. See *Antirrhinum cyathiferum*
Pseudupeneus grandisquamis, 380
Psilostrophe cooperi, 222, 662
Psora cerebriformis, 346; *P. crenata*, 346; *P. decipiens*, 345, 346; *P. icte-rica*, 346; *P. pacifica*, 346; *P. tuck-ermanii*, 346
Psoralea rhombifolia. See *Pediome-lum rhombifolium*
Psorothamnus emoryi, 164, 241;

P. schottii, 241; *P. spinosus*, 198, 241, 251, 662
Ptelea trifoliata, 261
Ptereleotridae, 382
Ptereleotris carinata, 382
Pteridaceae, 212–13, *Plate 17.18*
Pternohyla fodiens, 313, 330, 340–41, *341–42, Plate 22.10*
Pterostegia drymarioides, 259
Pterygoneurum ovatum, 345, 346, *Plate 23.9*
Ptilogonatidae, 299, 403
Ptinus priminidi, 62
Ptychocheilus lucius, 185
Puentes Cuates, 648
Puerto Blanco Drive, 648
Puerto Blanco Mountains, 648
Puerto Blanco Pass, 648
Puerto Blanco Tinaja, 648
Puerto Isabel, *36*, 648
Puerto Peñasco, 92, 98, *427*, 648, *648*; Station Beach reef, 368; tide prediction graph, 525
puffer, 382; bullseye, 382; naked, 382; Peruvian, 382
Puffinus creatopus, 393; *P. griseus*, 393; *P. opisthomelas*, 393
Pulmonata, 460
puma, 191
Puma concolor, 191, 274–75, 610, *Plate 18.4*; *P. c. azteca*, 278; *P. c. browni*, 275, 278
Pumpelly, Raphael, 601, 745
pumpkin, 159
puncture vine, 266
Punicaceae, 260
Punica granatum, 204, 260
Punta Borrascosa, 648, *649*
Punta Gordo, 648
Punta Machorro, 648
Punta el Machorro, 648
Punta Pelícano, 649
Punta Peñasco, 649
pupfish, desert, 13, 372, 626
Pupillidae, 63
purplemat, 242
purslane, 172, 259; dwarf, 259; horse, 214; western sea-, 214
Pycnogonida, 421, 426, 495
pygmy-cedar, 222
Pyramid Peak, 649
Pyrocephalus rubinus, 283, 296; *P. r. flammeus*, 401
pyrrhuloxia, 287, 301, 405